THE WORLD ALMANAC®

2009 WORLD ATLAS

The World Almanac® World Atlas

© COPYRIGHT 2009 BY HAMMOND WORLD ATLAS CORPORATION

Published by HAMMOND WORLD ATLAS CORPORATION, part of the Langenscheidt Publishing
Group, 36-36 33rd Street, Long Island City, NY, 11106

Printed in Canada

Library of Congress
Cataloging-in-Publication Data
Hammond World Atlas Corporation.
The World Almanac World Atlas.
p. cm
Includes Index.
ISBN 978-0843-709971 (softcover : alk. paper)
l. Atlases.
l. Title: World Atlas
ll. Title.
G1021. H5972003
912--dc22   2003056695

HAMMOND

THE WORLD ALMANAC®

2009 WORLD ATLAS

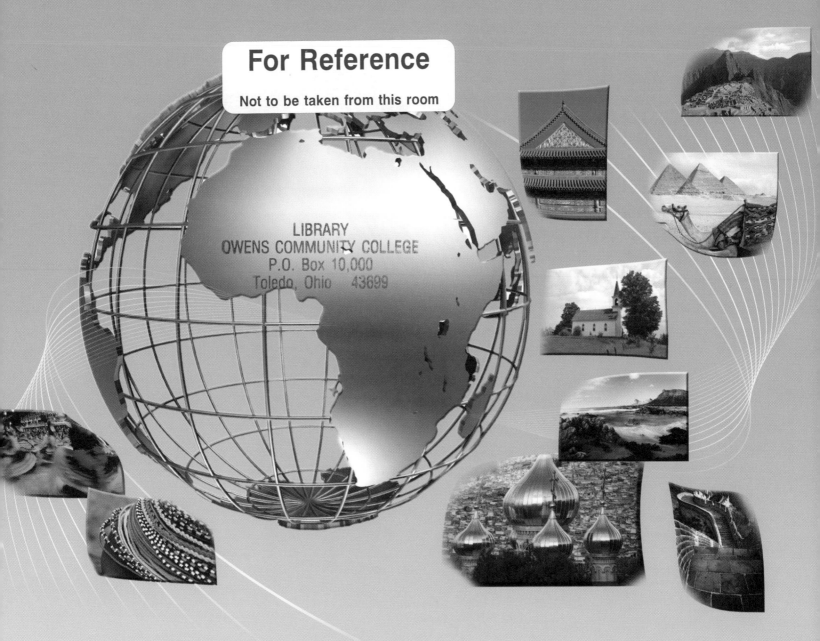

Contents

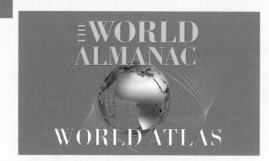

INTERPRETING MAPS

Designed to enhance your knowledge and enjoyment of maps, these pages explain such cartographic principles as scale, projection and symbology. This section also includes a brief explanation of the boundary and name policies followed in this atlas.

Endsheets   Map Locator / World Time Zones
6-7   Using This Atlas
8   Map Projections

FINDING THE FACTS

10-20   **World: Facts and Figures**

For individual subjects in this section, and for Nation Facts and Figues, please see the complete World Almanac Section contents on the opposite page.

Nations: Facts and Figures

22-77   Nations A-Z within each Continent or Region

WORLD/CONTINENTS/REGIONS

This collection of regional maps is completely generated from a computer database structured by latitude and longitude. The realistic topography is achieved by combining the political map data with digital bathymetric and hypsometric relief data, and shaded relief. The maps are arranged by continent, and a stunning satellite image and political map of that continent introduce each section. Continent thematic maps are also included in each section, providing for special geographical comparisons. Over 70 inset maps highlight metropolitan and other areas of special interest.

80-81   World - Political Map 1:80.5M
82-83   World - Physical Map 1:80.5M

Europe and Northern Asia

85   Europe 1:20.7M
86   Geographical Comparisons: Temperature, Climate, Vegetation
87   Geographical Comparisons: Rainfall, Population, Land Use, Minerals
88   Metropolitan London, Metropolitan Paris 1:570K
89   United Kingdom, Ireland 1:3.45M
90-91   Southern England and Wales 1:1.15M
92-93   Northeastern Ireland, Northern England and Wales 1:1.15M
94   Central Scotland 1:1.15M
95   Scandinavia and Finland 1:6.9M Iceland 1:6.9M
96-97   Baltic Region 1:3.45M
98-99   North Central Europe 1:3.45M Berlin 1:1.15M
100-101   West Central Europe 1:3.45M
102-103   Spain, Portugal 1:3.45M Barcelona, Madrid, Lisbon 1:1.15M Azores, Canary Islands, Madeira 1:6.9M
104-105   Southern Italy, Albania, Greece 1:3.45M Athens, Malta 1:1.15M
106-107   Hungary, Northern Balkan States 1:3.45M Vienna, Budapest 1:1.15M
108-109   Netherlands, Northwestern Germany 1:1.15M
110-111   Belgium, Northern France, Western Germany 1:1.15M
112-113   Southern Germany, Czech Republic, Upper Austria 1:1.15M
114-115   Central Alps Region 1:1.15M
116-117   Northern Italy 1:1.15M Monaco 1:115K
118-119   Northeastern Europe 1:6.9M St. Petersburg, Moscow 1:1.15M
120-121   Southeastern Europe 1:6.9M
122-123   Russia and Neighboring Countries 1:20.7M

Asia

125   Asia 1:48.3M
126   Geographical Comparisons: Temperature, Climate, Vegetation
127   Geographical Comparisons: Rainfall, Population, Land Use, Minerals
128-129   Eastern Asia 1:13.8M Hong Kong 1:1.15M
130   Northeastern China 1:6.9M Beijing-Tianjin, Shanghai 1:3.45M
131   Korea 1:3.45M Seoul 1:1.15M
132-133   Central and Southern Japan 1:3.45M Ryukyu Islands 1:6.9M
134   Northern Japan 1:3.45M
135   Tokyo-Yokohama, Osaka-Nagoya 1:1.15M
136   Indochina 1:6.9M
137   Southeastern China, Taiwan, Philippines 1:10.3M
138-139   Indonesia, Malaysia 1:10.3M
140-141   Southern Asia 1:10.3M
142-143   Ganges Plain 1:3.45M
144   Punjab Plain 1:10.3M
145   Central Asia 1:3.45M
146-147   Southwestern Asia 1:10.3M
148   Northern Middle East 1:6.9M
159   Eastern Mediterranean Region 1:3.45M Central Israel 1:1.15M

Africa

151   Africa 1:34.5M Cape Verde 1:6.9M
152   Geographical Comparisons: Temperature, Climate, Vegetation
153   Geographical Comparisons: Rainfall, Population, Land Use, Minerals
154-155   Northern Africa 1:17.2M
156-157   Northern West Africa 1:6.9M
158   Northern Morocco, Algeria, Tunisia 1:3.45M
159   Northeastern Africa 1:6.9M
160-161   Southern West Africa 1:6.9M
162   East Africa 1:6.9M
163   Southern Africa 1:17.2M
164-165   South Africa 1:6.9M Cape Town, Johannesburg, Mauritius and Réunion 1:3.45M Madagascar 1:6.9M

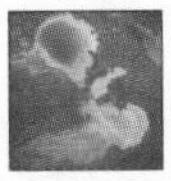

Australia, New Zealand and Pacific

167 Australia, New Zealand 1:19.1M

168 Geographical Comparisons:
Temperature, Climate,
Vegetation

169 Geographical Comparisons:
Rainfall, Population,
Land Use, Minerals

170-171 Western and Central
Australia 1:6.9M
Perth, Adelaide 1:1.15M

172 Northeastern Australia 1:6.9M
Brisbane, Sydney 1:1.15M

173 Southeastern Australia 1:6.9M
Melbourne 1:1.15M

174-175 Central Pacific Ocean 1:31M
New Zealand 1:10.3M

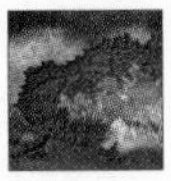

North America

177 North America 1:34.5M

178 Geographical Comparisons:
Temperature, Climate,
Vegetation

179 Geographical Comparisons:
Rainfall, Population,
Land Use, Minerals

180-181 Canada 1:13.8M

182-183 United States 1:13.8M
Hawaii 1:3.45M
Oahu 1:1.15M

184-185 Southweastern Canada
Northwestern
United States 1:6.9M

186-187 Southwestern
United States 1:6.9M

188-189 Southeastern Canada,
Northeastern
United States 1:6.9M
Montreal,
Toronto-Buffalo 1:1.15M

190-191 Southeastern
United States 1:6.9M

192 Alaska 1:10.3M

193 Seattle-Tacoma,
Sacramento-San Francisco-
San Jose, Detroit,
Chicago-Milwaukee 1:1.15M

194 Los Angeles-San Diego 1:1.15M
Metropolitan
Los Angeles 1:570K

195 Denver, Kansas City,
New Orleans, Oklahoma City,
Phoenix, San Antonio,
Salt Lake City,
St. Louis 1:1.15M

196-197 New York-Philadelphia-
Washington 1:1.15M
Metropolitan New York 1:570K

198-199 Middle America 1:10.3M
Puerto Rico,
Lesser Antilles 1:6.9M

200-201 Northern and Central
Mexico 1:6.9M
Distrito Federal-Veracruz 1:3.45M
Distrito Federal 1:1.15M

202-203 Southern Mexico,
Central America,
Western Caribbean 1:6.9M

South America and Polar Regions

205 South America 1:27.6M

206 Geographical Comparisons:
Temperature, Climate,
Vegetation

207 Geographical Comparisons:
Rainfall, Population,
Land Use, Minerals

208-209 Northern South America 1:14.9M

210-211 Colombia, Venezuela,
Ecuador 1:6.9M

212 Northeastern Brazil 1:6.9M

213 Southeastern Brazil 1:6.9M
Rio de Janeiro-São Paulo 1:3.45M

214 Peru 1:6.9M
Galápagos Islands 1:6.9M

215 Southern South America 1:14.9M

216-217 Southern Chile and
Argentina 1:6.9M
Santiago-Valparaíso,
Buenos Aires 1:3.45M

218 Arctic Regions 1:34.5M
Antarctica 1:57.5M

LOOKING IT UP

The Master Index at the end of the map section lists 60,000 places and other features appearing in this atlas, complete with page numbers and easy-to-use alpha-numeric references. Preceding the index is a list of abbreviations used in the index.

220 Using the Index and
Index Abbreviations

221-292 Index

292 Acknowledgements - Photo Credits

FINDING THE FACTS

These 69 pages – a 12-page section of World Facts and Figures, and a 57-page section of Nation Facts and Figures – provide a wide variety of compelling information selected from The World Almanac® and Book of Facts. The world section (pages 10-20) provides information on the world as a whole; the nations section (pages 22-77) on each individual nation. Nations are arranged by continent and in alphabetical order, and are referenced to the map section for quick access to complementary information.

World: Facts and Figures

10-11 About the World Almanac Sections;
Nation Locator Guide

12 Rankings by Population and Area

13 Ocean Areas, Ocean Depths
and Islands

14 Rivers and Waterfalls

15 Continental Altitudes and Lakes

16 Reservoirs and Dams

17 Global Temperatures

18 Precipitation and Deserts

19 Languages, Population,
and Oil and Gas Reserves

20 Energy Charts

Nations: Facts and Figures

22-77 Nations A-Z within
each Continent or Region

22 Africa

36 Asia

51 Australia, New Zealand and
the Pacific

55 Europe

67 North America Including
Central America and the
Islands of the Caribbean

74 South America

Note: Numbers following each entry indicate map scale (M=million, K=thousand).

Using This Atlas

Offering a broad range of features and functions, The World Almanac® World Atlas is more than a geographical reference work of superior quality and a guide for virtual global exploration. It also includes a compendium of compelling facts and figures from The World Almanac® and Book of Facts that will enhance your understanding of the connections in the world around you. The information provided below will help you to get the most enjoyment and benefit from its use.

World Map Section

The detailed maps of all regions of the Earth are arranged by continent. The chapters for each of the continents are introduced with a stunning satellite image and a political continent map, followed by two pages of thematic maps. Eight thematic subjects range from Climate and Land Use to Population Distribution. The detailed regional maps employ a variety of different symbols: Line patterns, surface colors, and textures highlight distinctive features such as mountains, national parks, urban areas, forests, and deserts. These maps also provide a wealth of information on roadways and canals, geographic features, and political divisions. All of the geographic maps and the complex information they contain are the product of modern computer-assisted map development and compilation techniques.

Map Frames

The map frames contain a number of graphic features that make the atlas easy to use. A locator map at the top of the map page shows the position of the individual map section within a larger geographic area. The blue triangles along the four edges of each map refer by page number to the adjacent map sections, and thus make it easy to find neighboring areas quickly in the atlas. The letters and numerals positioned along the outside of the map, in the green map frame, are search coordinates used to locate places and objects listed in the map index. In addition, integrated legends provide basic information about the region covered by each map.

Map Scales

A map's scale describes the relationship of any length on the map to a corresponding length on the Earth's surface. A scale of 1:3,000,000 means that one cm on the map represents 3,000,000 cm (30 km) in nature. Thus a scale of 1:1,000,000 is larger than 1:3,000,000, just as 1/1 is larger than 1/3. The most densely populated areas are shown at a scale of 1:1 M, while selected metropolitan areas are covered at either 1: 500,000 or 1:1 M. Other populous areas are presented at 1:3 M and 1:6 M, allowing you to accurately compare areas and distances of similar regions. Remaining regions, including the continent maps, are presented at 1:9 M and smaller scales.

Boundary and Name Policies

The atlas shows the internationally recognized national boundaries. Boundary disputes, armistice lines, and de facto boundaries are indicated by special symbols where appropriate. Generally, the names of places and geographic objects appear in the language of the respective country. Accepted conventional names are used for certain major foreign places names. Name usage also tends to vary depending upon cultural factors, however, and is subject to change over time, not least of all for political reasons. In several cases where, for example, a new name has not gained universal acceptance or the use of a traditional name persists, a second name has been entered in parentheses. Thus, the selection of names is not entirely systematic and reflects important aspects of common usage.

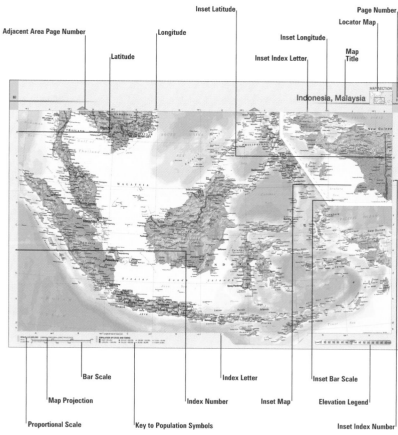

World Locator Map

A simplified world map overlaid with the outlines of all maps in the Map Section is located on the front end sheet. The World Locator Map shows at a glance which maps cover a given area. The page numbers for each map make it easy to locate specific regions quickly.

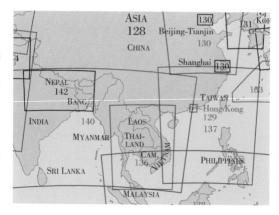

Symbols used on World Maps

FIRST ORDER (NATIONAL) BOUNDARY

▬▬▬	Land Boundary	▬▬▬	Armistice Boundary
─ ─ ─	Water Boundary	─··─··─	De Facto Boundary
▬·▬·▬	Disputed Boundary	··········	Undefined

SECOND ORDER (INTERNAL) BOUNDARY

▬▬▬	Land Boundary	─ ─ ─	Water Boundary

THIRD ORDER (INTERNAL) BOUNDARY

▬▬▬	Land Boundary	─ ─ ─	Water Boundary

CITIES AND TOWNS

Stockholm	First Order (National) Capital	■ ◉ ● ○	Towns
Salt Lake City	Second Order (Internal) Capital	■ ◉ ● ○	
		□	Neighborhood
Manchester	Third Order (Internal) Capital	▭	City and Urban Area Limits

TRANSPORTATION

✈	International Airport	───	Railroads
✛	Other Airport	·········	Ferries
	Highways/Roads	·····	Tunnels (Road, Railroad)

DRAINAGE FEATURES

	Shoreline, River	▭	Intermittent Lake
	Intermittent River	▭	Dry Lake
··········	Canal	▭	Salt Pan
▭	Lake, Reservoir		Swamp/Marsh

OTHER PHYSICAL FEATURES

▲	Elevation
⤬	Pass
●	Falls
✳	Rapids
	Desert/Sand Area
	Lava Flow
	Glacier/Ice Shelf

ELEVATION LEGEND

Height

m.	ft.
6000	19700
4000	13000
2000	6500
1500	5000
1000	3300
500	1600
200	700
0	0
200	700
500	1600
1000	3300
2000	6500
3000	9800
4000	13000
5000	16400
6000	19700

Depth

The color tints in this bar represent both elevation of land areas and depth of the oceans. The changes between colors are labeled in feet and meters.

CULTURAL FEATURES

⁛	Ruins
●	Dam
♣	Park
✗	Wildlife Area
■	Point of Interest
⌣	Well
⊗	Air Base
⊚	Naval Base
	International Date Line
▭▭▭	Ancient Walls
▭	Native Reservation/Reserve
▭	Military/Government Reservation
▭	State Park/Recreation Area
▨	National Park/Forest/ Recreation/Wildlife Area

Abbreviations used on the maps

Abor. Rsv.	Aboriginal Reserve	**Fk.**	Fork	**NB**	National Battlefield	**PN**	Park National
Admin.	Administration	**For.**	Forest	**NBP**	National Battlefield Park	**Prom.**	Promontory
AFB	Air Force Base	**Ft.**	Fort	**NCA**	National Conservation Area	**Prsv.**	Preserve
Amm. Dep.	Ammunition Depot	**G.**	Gulf			**Pt.**	Point
Arch.	Archipelago	**Govt.**	Government	**NHP**	National Historical Park	**R.**	River
Aut.	Autonomous	**Gd.**	Grand	**NHS**	National Historic Site	**Rec.**	Recreation(al)
B.	Bay	**Gt.**	Great	**NL**	National Lakeshore	**Ref.**	Refuge
Bfld.	Battlefield	**Har.**	Harbor	**NM**	National Monument	**Reg.**	Region
Bk.	Brook	**Hist.**	Historic(al)	**NMEM**	National Memorial	**Rep.**	Republic
Br.	Branch	**Hts.**	Heights	**NMILP**	National Military Park	**Res.**	Reservoir, Reservation
C.	Cape	**I., Is.**	Island(s)	**No.**	Northern	**Sa.**	Sierra
Can.	Canal	**Ind. Res.**	Indian Reservation	**NP**	National Park	**Sd.**	Sound
Cap.	Capital	**Int'l**	International	**NPP**	National Park and Preserve	**So.**	Southern
C.G.	Coast Guard	**IR**	Indian Reservation			**SP**	State Park
Chan.	Channel	**Isth.**	Isthmus	**NPRSV**	National Preserve	**Spr., Sprgs.**	Spring, Springs
Co.	County	**Jct.**	Junction	**NRA**	National Recreation Area	**St.**	State
Consv.	Conservation	**L.**	Lake	**NRIV**	National River	**Sta.**	Station
Cord.	Cordillera	**Lag.**	Lagoon	**NRSV**	National Reserve	**Stm.**	Stream
Cr.	Creek	**Mem.**	Memorial	**NS**	National Seashore	**Str.**	Strait
b	Center	**Mil.**	Military	**NWR**	National Wildlife Refuge	**Terr.**	Territory
Dep.	Depot	**Mon.**	Monument	**Obl.**	Oblast	**Tun.**	Tunnel
Depr.	Depression	**Mt.**	Mount	**Occ.**	Occupied	**Twp.**	Township
Des.	Desert	**Mtn.**	Mountain	**Okr.**	Okrug	**UNDOF**	United Nations Disengagement Observer Force
Dist.	District	**Mts.**	Mountains	**Passg.**	Passage		
DMZ	Demilitarized Zone	**Nat.**	Natural	**Pen.**	Peninsula		
Est.	Estuary	**Nat'l**	National	**Pk.**	Peak	**Val.**	Valley
Fed.	Federal	**Nav.**	Naval	**Plat.**	Plateau	**Vill.**	Village

Index to the World Map Section

Aa (riv.), Ger.	50/D5
Aach (riv.), Ger.	57/F2
Aach, Ger.	57/E2
Aachen, Ger.	53/F2
Aalbach (riv.), Ger.	54/C3
Aalborg (int'l arpt.), Den.	38/C3
Aalburg, Neth.	50/C5
Aalen, Ger.	54/D5
Aalsmeer, Neth.	50/B4
Aalst, Belg.	52/D2
Aalten, Neth.	50/D5
Aalter, Belg.	52/C1
Aar (riv.), Ger.	53/H3
Aarau, Swi.	56/E3
Aarberg, Swi.	56/D3

The index facilitates the search for a specific place in the atlas. It contains an alphabetical list of place names and geographic objects shown in the maps. Each index entry gives the page and coodinate grid location of the desired place or object. A list of the abbreviations used in the index is found on the first index page.

Rankings by Populat[ion]

POPULATION AND LAND AREA OF T[HE]

Population Rank as of 2003	Continent or Region	Population (estimated, in thousands)				
		1650	1750	1850	1900	1950
1.	Asia	335,000	476,000	754,000	932,000	1,411,000
2.	Africa	100,000	95,000	95,000	118,000	229,000
3.	Europe	100,000	140,000	265,000	400,000	392,000
4.	North America	5,000	5,000	39,000	106,000	221,000
5.	South America	8,000	7,000	20,000	38,000	111,000
6.	Australia, New Zealand, and the Pacific	2,000	2,000	2,000	6,000	12,000
7.	Antarctic	No indigenous inhabitants				
	WORLD	550,000	725,000	1,175,000	1,600,000	2,556,000

Note: Areas are as defined by the U.S. Bureau of the Census and strictly only to 1950 a[rea]. Bureau area for Europe includes all of Russia (approximately 6,600,000 sq mi [17,100,000 [sq km]) to totals because of rounding.

LARGEST POPULATIONS

Rank	Country	Population	Persons per sq mi	Persons per sq km	Rank
1.	China[1]	1,286,975,000	357	138	1.
2.	India	1,065,462,000	928	358	2.
3.	United States	288,369,000	81	31	3.
4.	Indonesia	219,883,000	312	120	4.
5.	Brazil	178,470,000	55	21	5.
6.	Pakistan	153,578,000	511	197	6.
7.	Bangladesh	146,736,000	2,838	1,096	7.
8.	Russia	143,246,000	22	8	8.
9.	Japan	127,654,000	838	324	9.

Map type faces

The use of different type faces helps the reader distinguish between categories of map content.

Major Political Arenas

LUXEMBOURG

Internal Political Divisions

SAXONY-ANHALT

Historical Regions

Polabská Nížina

Cities and Towns

Norfolk Sumter Smyrna

Neighborhoods

BIGGIN HILL

Points of Interest

MISSION SAN BUENAVENTURA

Water Features

L. Elsinore

Capes, Points, Peaks, Passes

Cape Horn...Pt. La Jolla

Mt. Rainier

Islands, Peninsulas

Cape Breton I.

Mountain Ranges, Plateaus, Hills

Serra do Norte

Deserts, Plains, Valleys

San Fernando Valley

Spelling of names

The spelling of geographic names conforms to the rules of the respective official language of each country. Where the official language is written in Latin characters, local spellings, including diacritical marks and modified letters, have been used. For countries with languages written in non-Latin characters, such as China, Russia or the Arabic-speaking countries, an international standard form is used, which may deviate in some cases from conventional American usage.

The World Almanac Sections – World and Nations

Two sections – one devoted to World Facts and Figures, and one to Nation Facts and Figures – provide a wide variety of information selected from The World Almanac® and Book of Facts. The 12-page world section (pages 9-20) offers data on the world as a whole. The 57-page nations section (pages 22-77) provides data on each individual nation. Nations are arranged in alphabetical order, and are referenced to the map section for quick access to complementary information. A concurrent reading of maps and related almanac data helps shed light on the impact of geography on the economy, culture, and other spheres of human activity.

Map Projections

Simply stated, the mapmaker's challenge is to project the earth's curved surface onto a flat plane. To achieve this elusive goal, cartographers have developed map projections — formulas that govern this conversion of geographic data. Every point on earth can be identified with the aid of a geographic coordinate grid, and this grid can be projected onto a flat surface. This section explores some of the most widely used projections. It also introduces a new projection, the Hammond Optimal Conformal.

General Principles and Terms

The earth rotates around its axis once a day. Its end points are the north and south poles; the imaginary line circling the earth midway between the poles is the equator. The arc from the equator to either pole is divided into 90 degrees of latitude. The equator represents 0° latitude. Circles of equal latitude, called parallels, are traditionally shown at every fifth or tenth degree. Circles of latitude become progressively smaller toward the poles.

The equator is divided into 360 degrees. Lines circling the globe from pole to pole through the degree points on the equator are called meridians, or great circles. All meridians are equal in length. By international agreement the meridian passing through the Greenwich Observatory near London has been chosen as the prime meridian, or 0° longitude. The distance in degrees from the prime meridian to any point east or west is its longitude.

While meridians are all equal in length, parallels become shorter as they approach the poles. Whereas one degree of latitude represents approximately 69 miles (112 km) anywhere on the globe, a degree of longitude varies from 69 miles (112 km) at the equator to zero at the poles. Each degree of latitude and longitude is divided into 60 minutes. One minute of latitude equals one nautical mile (1.15 land miles or 1.85 km).

How to Flatten a Sphere: The Art of Controlling Distortion

There is only one way to represent the earth's sphere with absolute precision: on a globe. All attempts to project our planet's surface onto a plane result in distortion. Depending upon the map projection selected, distortions appear in shapes and area sizes, angles, or distances between points on the earth.

Only the parallels or the meridians (or some other set of lines) can maintain the same length as on a globe of corresponding scale. All other lines must be either too long or too short. Accordingly, the scale on a flat map cannot be true everywhere; there will always be different scales in different parts of a map. On world maps or maps of very large areas, variations in scale may be extreme. On maps of small areas, variations in scale may be relatively insignificant. Most maps seek to preserve either true area relationships (equal area projections) or true angles and shapes (conformal projections); some attempt to achieve overall balance.

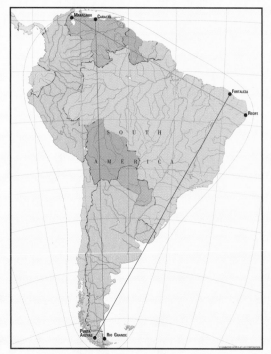

Projections: Selected Examples

Mercator Projection

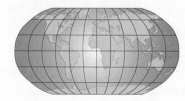

This projection is especially useful because all compass directions appear as straight lines, making it a valuable navigational tool. Moreover, it is a comformal projection – every small region conforms to its shape on a globe. But because its meridians are evenly-spaced vertical lines which never converge (unlike the meridians on a globe), the horizontal parallels must be drawn farther and farther apart at higher latitudes to maintain a correct relationship. Only the equator is true to scale, and the sizes of areas in the higher latitudes are dramatically distorted.

Robinson Projection

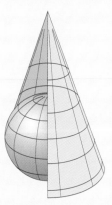

The Robinson is a compromise projection that combines elements of both conformal and equal area projections to show the whole earth with relatively true shapes and reasonably equal areas. The Robinson is used mostly for world maps. To create the World Political and World Physical maps on pages 80-83, this projection has been used.

Conic Projection

The original idea of this projection is to project lines of latitude and longitude from the planet's center onto a cone. The axis length of the cone is variable. To produce working maps, the cone is simply "cut open" and "laid flat." In the conic projection illustrated here, the cone can be made tangent to any desired parallel. One popular conic projection, the Lambert Conformal Conic, uses two standard parallels of conforming lengths near the top and the bottom of the map to further reduce errors of scale. This projection has been used to create most of the national and regional maps in this atlas.

Hammond Optimal Conformal

As its name implies, this new conformal projection presents the optimal view of an area by reducing shifts in scale over an entire region to the minimum degree possible. While conformal maps generally preserve all small shapes, large shapes can become very distorted because of varying scales, causing considerable inaccuracy in distance measurements. The concept underlying the Optimal Conformal is that for any region on the globe, there is an ideal projection for which scale variation can be made as small as possible. Consequently, unlike other projections, the Optimal Conformal does not use one standard formula to construct a map. Each map is a unique projection — the optimal projection for that particular area.

After a cartographer defines the subject area (in the illustration, left, indicated by the red outline around South America), a sophisticated computer program evaluates the size and shape of the region, and projects the most distortion-free conformal map possible. This projection has been used to create the continent maps in this atlas.

◄ *Hammond Optimal Conformal Projection*

World Almanac Section

				1900	1950		1980			Land Area	
North America	100,000	95,000	754,000	932,000	1,411,000		2003	(1,000 sq mi)	(1,000 sq km)	% of Earth Land Area
South America	5,000	140,000	95,000	118,000	229,000	2,601,000	3,817,000	12,000	31,000	21.4
Australia, New Zealand, and the Pacific	8,000	5,000	265,000	400,000	392,000	470,000	856,000	11,500	29,800	20.5
tarctic	2,000	7,000	39,000	106,000	221,000	484,000	729,000	8,800	22,800	15.7
RLD		2,000	20,000	38,000	111,000	372,000	505,000	8,300	21,400	
	550,000	2,000	No indigenous inhabitant	6,000		242,000	364,000	6,800		
efined by the U.S. D	725,000			12,000						

World Facts and Figures from The World Almanac®

WORLD FACTS AND FIGURES

About the World Almanac Sections

The information from *The World Almanac®* is presented in two parts. This first part, preceding the Map Section, contains facts and figures characterizing key aspects of the world and its population. The second part, on pages 22-77, presents detailed information on every nation of the world.

The nations in the second part are arranged in alphabetical order under the heading for the part of the world in which they are located. To find information on a particular nation, turn to the region in which it lies, as indicated by the abbreviation in parentheses below. Note that Russia is covered under Europe, as its capital and the bulk of the population are located in Europe; similarly, Turkey is covered under Asia, since that is where its capital and the majority of its population are found.

Nation Locator Guide—for pages 22-77

(AF) Africa

(AS) Asia

(AU) Australia, New Zealand, and the Pacific

(E) Europe

(NA) North America, including Central America and the islands of the Caribbean

(SA) South America

Afghanistan **(AS)**	Bolivia **(SA)**	Congo, Democratic	Ethiopia **(AF)**
Albania **(E)**	Bosnia and Herzegovina **(E)**	Republic of the **(AF)**	Fiji **(AU)**
Algeria **(AF)**	Botswana **(AF)**	Congo Republic **(AF)**	Finland **(E)**
Andorra **(E)**	Brazil **(SA)**	Costa Rica **(NA)**	France **(E)**
Angola **(AF)**	Brunei **(AS)**	Côte d'Ivoire **(AF)**	Gabon **(AF)**
Antigua and Barbuda **(NA)**	Bulgaria **(E)**	Croatia **(E)**	Gambia **(AF)**
Argentina **(SA)**	Burkina Faso **(AF)**	Cuba **(NA)**	Georgia **(AS)**
Armenia **(AS)**	Burma	Cyprus **(AS)**	Germany **(E)**
Australia **(AU)**	(see Myanmar)	Czech Republic **(E)**	Ghana **(AF)**
Austria **(E)**	Burundi **(AF)**	Denmark **(E)**	Greece **(E)**
Azerbaijan **(AS)**	Cambodia **(AS)**	Djibouti **(AF)**	Grenada **(NA)**
Bahamas **(NA)**	Cameroon **(AF)**	Dominica **(NA)**	Guatemala **(NA)**
Bahrain **(AS)**	Canada **(NA)**	Dominican Republic **(NA)**	Guinea **(AF)**
Bangladesh **(AS)**	Cape Verde **(AF)**	East Timor **(AS)**	Guinea-Bissau **(AF)**
Barbados **(NA)**	Central African Republic **(AF)**	Ecuador **(SA)**	Guyana **(SA)**
Belarus **(E)**	Chad **(AF)**	Egypt **(AF)**	Haiti **(NA)**
Belgium **(E)**	Chile **(SA)**	El Salvador **(NA)**	Honduras **(NA)**
Belize **(NA)**	China **(AS)**	Equatorial Guinea **(AF)**	Hungary **(E)**
Benin **(AF)**	Colombia **(SA)**	Eritrea **(AF)**	Iceland **(E)**
Bhutan **(AS)**	Comoros **(AF)**	Estonia **(E)**	India **(AS)**

Indonesia **(AS)**
Iran **(AS)**
Iraq **(AS)**
Ireland **(E)**
Israel **(AS)**
Italy **(E)**
Jamaica **(NA)**
Japan **(AS)**
Jordan **(AS)**
Kazakhstan **(AS)**
Kenya **(AF)**
Kiribati **(AU)**
Korea, North **(AS)**
Korea, South **(AS)**
Kosovo **(E)**
Kuwait **(AS)**
Kyrgyzstan **(AS)**
Laos **(AS)**
Latvia **(E)**
Lebanon **(AS)**
Lesotho **(AF)**
Liberia **(AF)**
Libya **(AF)**
Liechtenstein **(E)**
Lithuania **(E)**
Luxembourg **(E)**
Macedonia **(E)**
Madagascar **(AF)**
Malawi **(AF)**
Malaysia **(AS)**
Maldives **(AS)**

Mali **(AF)**
Malta **(E)**
Marshall Islands **(AU)**
Mauritania **(AF)**
Mauritius **(AF)**
Mexico **(NA)**
Micronesia **(AU)**
Moldova **(E)**
Monaco **(E)**
Mongolia **(AS)**
Montenegro **(E)**
Morocco **(AF)**
Mozambique **(AF)**
Myanmar **(AS)**
Namibia **(AF)**
Nauru **(AU)**
Nepal **(AS)**
Netherlands **(E)**
New Zealand **(AU)**
Nicaragua **(NA)**
Niger **(AF)**
Nigeria **(AF)**
North Korea
  (see Korea, North)
Norway **(E)**
Oman **(AS)**
Pakistan **(AS)**
Palau **(AU)**
Panama **(NA)**
Papua New Guinea **(AS)**
Paraguay **(SA)**

Peru **(SA)**
Philippines **(AS)**
Poland **(E)**
Portugal **(E)**
Qatar **(AS)**
Romania **(E)**
Russia **(E)**
Rwanda **(AF)**
Saint Kitts and Nevis **(NA)**
Saint Lucia **(NA)**
Saint Vincent and the
  Grenadines **(NA)**
Samoa **(AU)**
San Marino **(E)**
São Tomé and Príncipe **(AF)**
Saudi Arabia **(AS)**
Senegal **(AF)**
Serbia **(E)**
Seychelles **(AF)**
Sierra Leone **(AF)**
Singapore **(AS)**
Slovakia **(E)**
Slovenia **(E)**
Solomon Islands **(AU)**
Somalia **(AF)**
South Africa **(AF)**
South Korea
  (see Korea, South)
Spain **(E)**
Sri Lanka **(AS)**
Sudan **(AF)**

Suriname **(SA)**
Swaziland **(AF)**
Sweden **(E)**
Switzerland **(E)**
Syria **(AS)**
Taiwan **(AS)**
Tajikistan **(AS)**
Tanzania **(AF)**
Thailand **(AS)**
Togo **(AF)**
Tonga **(AU)**
Trinidad and Tobago **(NA)**
Tunisia **(AF)**
Turkey **(AS)**
Turkmenistan **(AS)**
Tuvalu **(AU)**
Uganda **(AF)**
Ukraine **(E)**
United Arab Emirates **(AS)**
United Kingdom **(E)**
United States **(NA)**
Uruguay **(SA)**
Uzbekistan **(AS)**
Vanuatu **(AU)**
Vatican City **(E)**
Venezuela **(SA)**
Vietnam **(AS)**
Yemen **(AS)**
Zambia **(AF)**
Zimbabwe **(AF)**

A WORD ABOUT THE DATA

The facts and figures given here are based on data collected for *The World Almanac®* and represent the latest information available at the time of compilation.

Data on pages 10 through 20 and pages 22 through 77 used under license from *The World Almanac® and Book of Facts.* ©2009 by World Almanac Education Group, Inc. All rights reserved.

The World Almanac® and Book of Facts is a registered trademark of World Almanac Education Group, Inc

LOCATIONS PICTURED IN PHOTOS INTRODUCING THE REGIONS OF THE WORLD

AFRICA
page 22 right bottom, *Camel resting by the pyramids at Giza (Al Jizah), Egypt*

ASIA
page 36 left, *Tea harvesting, China;* page 36 mid bottom, *Festival celebration, Hong Kong;* page 36 mid right: *Market stall lantern, Tokyo, Japan*

AUSTRALIA, NEW ZEALAND, AND THE PACIFIC
page 51 left, *Reef formations, South Pacific;* page 51 right bottom, *Opera House, Sydney, Australia*

EUROPE
page 55 left, *Marienplatz, Munich, Germany*

NORTH AMERICA, INCLUDING CENTRAL AMERICA AND THE ISLANDS OF THE CARIBBEAN
page 67 left, *Buffalo near Grand Teton Mountains, Wyoming, United States;* page 67 right top, *Los Angeles, California, United States*

SOUTH AMERICA
page 74 left, *Machu Picchu, Peru;* page 74 mid bottom, *Rio de Janeiro, Brazil*

Chief abbreviations used in the World Almanac Section

cu	cubic	est.	estimate(d)	ft	foot, feet	in	inch(es)	km	kilometer(s)
m	meter(s)	mi	mile(s)	mm	millimeters(s)	NA	not available	Pres.	President
sq	square	yd	yard(s)						

World Facts and Figures

RANKINGS BY POPULATION AND AREA

POPULATION AND LAND AREA OF THE WORLD, 1650–2009

Population Rank as of 2007	Continent or Region	Population (estimated, in thousands)							Land Area		
		1650	1750	1850	1900	1950	1980	2009	(1,000 sq mi)	(1,000 sq km)	% of Earth Land Area
1.	Asia	335,000	476,000	754,000	932,000	1,411,000	2,601,000	4,044,835	12,000	31,000	21.4
2.	Africa	100,000	95,000	95,000	118,000	229,000	470,000	945,171	11,500	29,800	20.5
3.	Europe	100,000	140,000	265,000	400,000	392,000	484,000	734,500	8,800	22,800	15.7
4.	North America	5,000	5,000	39,000	106,000	221,000	372,000	528,922	8,300	21,400	14.8
5.	South America	8,000	7,000	20,000	38,000	111,000	242,000	383,817	6,800	17,500	12.1
6.	Australia, New Zealand, and the Pacific	2,000	2,000	2,000	6,000	12,000	23,000	33,850	3,200	8,400	5.8
7.	Antarctic	No indigenous inhabitants							14,000		9.7
	WORLD	550,000	725,000	1,175,000	1,600,000	2,556,000	4,458,000	6,671,097	56,000	145,000	100.0

Note: Areas are as defined by the U.S. Bureau of the Census and strictly apply only to 1950 and after; before then, areas may be defined differently. The Census Bureau area for Europe includes all of Russia (approximately 6,600,000 sq mi [17,100,000 sq km]); the area figure for Asia excludes Russia. Figures may not add to totals because of rounding.

LARGEST POPULATIONS

Rank	Country	Population	Persons per sq mi	Persons per sq km
1.	China[1]	1,321,851,888	367	142
2.	India	1,129,866,154	984	380
3.	United States	303,935,000	82	32
4.	Indonesia	245,452,739	348	134
5.	Brazil	190,010,647	58	22
6.	Pakistan	169,270,617	563	217
7.	Bangladesh	150,448,339	2,910	1,124
8.	Russia	141,377,752	22	8
9.	Nigeria	135,031,164	384	148
10.	Japan	127,467,972	881	340

[1]Excluding Hong Kong and Macau.

SMALLEST POPULATIONS

Rank	Country	Population	Persons per sq mi	Persons per sq km
1.	Vatican City	921	*	*
2.	Tuvalu	11,992	1,181	461
3.	Nauru	13,528	1,668	644
4.	Palau	20,842	118	45
5.	San Marino	29,615	1,253	484
6.	Monaco	32,671	43,394	16,754
7.	Liechtenstein	34,247	554	214
8.	Saint Kitts and Nevis	39,349	390	151
9.	Marshall Islands	61,782	883	341
10.	Dominica	68,925	237	91

*Area only 0.17 sq mi (0.4 sq km).

LARGEST LAND AREAS

Rank	Country	Land Area sq mi	Land Area (sq km)
1.	Russia	6,562,112	16,995,800
2.	China	3,600,946	9,326,410
3.	United States	3,537,437	9,161,923
4.	Canada	3,511,021	9,093,507
5.	Brazil	3,265,075	8,456,510
6.	Australia	2,941,298	7,617,930
7.	India	1,147,955	2,973,190
8.	Argentina	1,056,641	2,736,690
9.	Kazakhstan	1,030,815	2,669,800
10.	Algeria	919,595	2,381,740

SMALLEST LAND AREAS

Rank	Country	Land Area sq mi	Land Area (sq km)
1.	Vatican City	0.17	0.44
2.	Monaco	0.75	1.95
3.	Nauru	8	21
4.	Tuvalu	10	26
5.	San Marino	24	61
6.	Liechtenstein	62	160
7.	Marshall Islands	70	181
8.	Saint Kitts and Nevis	101	261
9.	Maldives	116	300
10.	Malta	122	316

OCEANS, OCEAN DEPTHS, AND ISLANDS

AREAS AND AVERAGE DEPTHS OF OCEANS, SEAS, AND GULFS

Geographers and mapmakers recognize four major bodies of water: the Pacific, the Atlantic, the Indian, and the Arctic oceans. The Atlantic and Pacific oceans are considered divided at the equator into the North and South Atlantic and the North and South Pacific. The Arctic Ocean is the name for waters north of the continental landmasses in the region of the Arctic Circle.

	Area (sq mi)	Area (sq km)	Average Depth (ft)	Average Depth (m)
Pacific Ocean	64,186,300	166,241,800	12,925	3,940
Atlantic Ocean	33,420,000	86,557,400	11,730	3,575
Indian Ocean	28,350,500	73,427,500	12,598	3,840
Arctic Ocean	5,105,700	13,223,700	3,407	1,038
South China Sea	1,148,500	2,974,600	4,802	1,464
Caribbean Sea	971,400	2,515,900	8,448	2,575
Mediterranean Sea	969,100	2,510,000	4,926	1,501
Bering Sea	873,000	2,261,000	4,893	1,491
Gulf of Mexico	582,100	1,508,000	5,297	1,615
Sea of Okhotsk	537,500	1,392,000	3,192	973
Sea of Japan	391,100	1,013,000	5,468	1,667
Hudson Bay	281,900	730,100	305	93
East China Sea	256,600	664,600	620	189
Andaman Sea	218,100	564,900	3,667	1,118
Black Sea	196,100	507,900	3,906	1,191
Red Sea	174,900	453,000	1,764	538
North Sea	164,900	427,100	308	94

BIGGEST ISLANDS

Island	Area (sq mi)	Area (sq km)
Greenland (Denmark)	840,000	2,180,000
New Guinea (Indonesia, Papua New Guinea)	306,000	793,000
Borneo (Indonesia, Malaysia, Brunei)	280,100	725,500
Madagascar	226,658	587,040
Baffin (Canada)	195,928	507,450
Sumatra (Indonesia)	165,000	427,350
Honshu (Japan)	87,805	227,410
Great Britain (United Kingdom)	84,200	218,080
Victoria (Canada)	83,897	217,290
Ellesmere (Canada)	75,767	196,240
Celebes (Indonesia)	69,000	178,710
South (New Zealand)	58,384	151,210
Java (Indonesia)	48,900	126,650
North (New Zealand)	44,204	114,490
Cuba	42,804	110,860
Newfoundland (Canada)	42,031	108,860
Luzon (Philippines)	40,680	105,360

PRINCIPAL OCEAN DEPTHS

Name of Area	Location (latitude)	Location (longitude)	Depth (m)	Depth (fathoms)	Depth (ft)
PACIFIC OCEAN					
Marianas Trench	11° 22′ N	142° 36′ E	10,924	5,973	35,840
Tonga Trench	23° 16′ S	174° 44′ W	10,800	5,906	35,433
Philippine Trench	10° 38′ N	126° 36′ E	10,057	5,499	32,995
Kermadec Trench	31° 53′ S	177° 21′ W	10,047	5,494	32,963
Bonin Trench	24° 30′ N	143° 24′ E	9,994	5,464	32,788
Kuril Trench	44° 15′ N	150° 34′ E	9,750	5,331	31,988
Izu Trench	31°05′ N	142°10′ E	9,695	5,301	31,808
New Britain Trench	06°19′ S	153°45′ E	8,940	4,888	29,331
Yap Trench	08°33′ N	138°02′ E	8,527	4,663	27,976
Japan Trench	36°08′ N	142°43′ E	8,412	4,600	27,599
Peru-Chile Trench	23°18′ S	71°14′ W	8,064	4,409	26,457
Palau Trench	07°52′ N	134°56′ E	8,054	4,404	26,424
Aleutian Trench	50°51′ N	177°11′ E	7,679	4,199	25,194
ATLANTIC OCEAN					
Puerto Rico Trench	19° 55′ N	65°27′ W	8,605	4,705	28,232
South Sandwich Trench	55°42′ S	25°56′ W	8,325	4,552	27,313
Romanche Gap	0°13′ S	18°26′ W	7,728	4,226	25,354

World Facts and Figures

RIVERS AND WATERFALLS

LONGEST RIVERS

River	Outflow	Length (mi)	Length (km)
AFRICA			
Congo	Atlantic Ocean	2,900	4,670
Niger	Gulf of Guinea	2,590	4,170
Nile	Mediterranean	4,160	6,690
Zambezi	Indian Ocean	1,700	2,740
ASIA			
Amur	Tatar Strait	1,780	2,860
Brahmaputra	Bay of Bengal	1,800	2,900
Chang	East China Sea	3,964	6,380
Euphrates	Shatt al-Arab	1,700	2,740
Huang	Yellow Sea	3,395	5,460
Indus	Arabian Sea	1,800	2,900
Lena	Laptev Sea	2,734	4,400
Mekong	South China Sea	2,700	4,350
Ob	Gulf of Ob	2,268	3,650
Ob-Irtysh	Gulf of Ob	3,362	5,410
Yenisey	Kara Seav	2,543	4,090
AUSTRALIA			
Murray-Darling	Indian Ocean	2,310	3,720
EUROPE			
Danube	Black Sea	1,776	2,860
Volga	Caspian Sea	2,290	3,690
NORTH AMERICA			
Mississippi	Gulf of Mexico	2,340	3,770
Mississippi-Missouri-Red Rock	Gulf of Mexico	3,710	5,970
Missouri	Mississippi River	2,315	3,730
Missouri-Red Rock	Mississippi River	2,540	4,090
Rio Grande	Gulf of Mexico	1,900	3,060
Yukon	Bering Sea	1,979	3,180
SOUTH AMERICA			
Amazon	Atlantic Ocean	4,000	6,440
Japura	Amazon River	1,750	2,820
Madeira	Amazon River	2,013	3,240
Parana	Rio de la Plata	2,485	4,000
Purus	Amazon River	2,100	3,380
Sao Francisco	Atlantic Ocean	1,988	3,200

NOTABLE WATERFALLS

Name (Location)	Height (ft)	Height (m)
AFRICA		
Tugela# (South Africa)	2,014	614
Victoria, Zambezi River* (Zimbabwe-Zambia)	343	105
AUSTRALIA, NEW ZEALAND		
Wallaman, Stony Creek# (Australia)	1,137	347
Wollomombi (Australia)	1,100	335
Sutherland, Arthur River# (New Zealand)	1,904	580
EUROPE		
Krimml# (Austria)	1,312	400
Gavarnie* (France)	1,385	422
Mardalsfossen (Northern) (Norway)	1,535	468
Mardalsfossen (Southern)# (Norway)	2,149	655
Skjeggedal, Nybuai River#** (Norway)	1,378	420
Trummelbach# (Switzerland)	1,312	400
NORTH AMERICA		
Della# (Canada)	1,443	440
Niagara: Horseshoe (Canada)	173	53
Takakkaw, Daly Glacier# (Canada)	1,200	366
Niagara: American (U.S.)	182	55
Ribbon** (U.S.)	1,612	491
Silver Strand, Meadow Brook** (U.S.)	1,170	357
Yosemite#*** (U.S.)	2,425	739
SOUTH AMERICA		
Iguazu (Argentina-Brazil)	230	70
Glass (Brazil)	1,325	404
Patos-Maribondo, Grande River (Brazil)	115	35
Paulo Afonso, Sao Francisco River (Brazil)	275	84
Urubupunga, Parana River (Brazil)	39	12
Great, Kamarang River (Guyana)	1,600	488
Kaieteur, Potaro River (Guyana)	741	226
Angel#*(Venezuela)	3,212	979
Cuquenan (Venezuela)	2,000	610

Note: If the river name is not shown, it is the same as that of the falls. "Height" is the total drop in one or more leaps.

#Falls of more than one leap; *falls that diminish greatly seasonally; **falls that reduce to a trickle or are dry for part of each year.

The estimated mean annual flow, in cubic feet per second (cubic meters in parentheses), of major waterfalls is as follows: Niagara, 212,200 (6,000); Paulo Afonso, 100,000 (2,800); Urubupunga, 97,000 (2,700); Iguazu, 61,000 (1,700); Patos-Maribondo, 53,000 (1,500); Victoria, 35,400 (1,000); and Kaieteur, 23,400 (660).

CONTINENTAL ALTITUDES AND LAKES

HIGHEST CONTINENTAL ALTITUDES

Continent	Highest Point	Elevation (ft)	Elevation (m)
Asia	Mount Everest, Nepal-Tibet	29,035	8,850
South America	Mount Aconcagua, Argentina	22,834	6,960
North America	Mount McKinley, Alaska, U.S.	20,320	6,194
Africa	Kilimanjaro, Tanzania	19,340	5,895
Europe	Mount Elbrus, Russia	18,510	5,642
Antarctica	Vinson Massif	16,864	5,140
Australia	Mount Kosciusko, New South Wales	7,310	2,228

LOWEST CONTINENTAL ALTITUDES

Continent	Lowest Point	Feet Below Sea Level	Meters Below Sea Level
Asia	Dead Sea, Israel-Jordan	1,348	411
South America	Valdes Peninsula, Argentina	131	40
North America	Death Valley, California, U.S.	282	86
Africa	Lake Assal, Djibouti	512	156
Europe	Caspian Sea, Russia, Azerbaijan	92	28
Antarctica	Bentley Subglacial Trench	8,327[1]	2,538[1]
Australia	Lake Eyre, South Australia	52	16

[1]Estimated level of the continental floor. Lower points that have yet to be discovered may exist further beneath the ice.

MAJOR NATURAL LAKES OF THE WORLD

Name	Continent	Area (sq mi)	Area (sq km)	Maximum Depth (ft)	Maximum Depth (m)
Caspian Sea[1]	Asia-Europe	143,244	371,000	3,363	1,025
Superior	North America	31,700	82,100	1,330	405
Victoria	Africa	26,828	69,484	270	82
Huron	North America	23,000	59,600	750	229
Michigan	North America	22,300	57,800	923	281
Aral Sea[1]	Asia	13,000[2]	33,700[2]	220	67
Tanganyika	Africa	12,700	32,900	4,823	1,470
Baykal	Asia	12,162	31,500	5,315	1,620
Great Bear	North America	12,096	31,330	1,463	446
Nyasa (Malawi)	Africa	11,150	28,880	2,280	695
Great Slave	North America	11,031	28,570	2,015	614
Erie	North America	9,910	25,670	210	64
Winnipeg	North America	9,417	24,390	60	18
Ontario	North America	7,340	19,010	802	244
Balkhash[1]	Asia	7,115	18,430	85	26
Ladoga	Europe	6,835	17,700	738	225

Note: A lake is generally defined as a body of water surrounded by land.

[1]Salt lake.

[2]Approximate figure, could be less. The diversion of feeder rivers since the 1960s has devastated the Aral—once the world's fourth-largest lake (26,000 sq mi [67,000 sq km]). By 2000, the Aral had effectively become three lakes, with the total area shown.

World Facts and Figures

RESERVOIRS AND DAMS

WORLD'S LARGEST-CAPACITY RESERVOIRS

Rank	Name	Country	Capacity (1,000 acre-ft)	Capacity (1,000,000 cu m)
1.	Kariba	Zimbabwe/Zambia	146,400	180,600
2.	Bratsk	Russia	137,000	169,000
3.	High Aswan	Egypt	131,300	162,000
4.	Akosombo	Ghana	119,950	147,960
5.	Daniel Johnson	Canada	115,000	141,851
6.	Xinfeng	China	112,660	138,960
7.	Guri	Venezuela	109,400	135,000
8.	W. A. C. Bennett	Canada	60,235	74,300
9.	Krasnoyarsk	Russia	59,425	73,300
10.	Zeya	Russia	55,450	68,400

WORLD'S HIGHEST DAMS

Rank	Name	Country	Height Above Lowest Formation (ft)	Height Above Lowest Formation (m)
1.	Nurek	Tajikistan	984	300
2.	Grand Dixence	Switzerland	935	285
3.	Inguri	Georgia	892	272
4.	Vajont	Italy	860	262
5.	Manuel M. Torres	Mexico	856	261
6.	Alvaro Obregon	Mexico	853	260
7.	Mauvoisin	Switzerland	820	250
8.	Mica	Canada	797	243
9.	Alberto Lleras C	Colombia	797	243
10.	Sayano-Shushensk	Russia	794	242

WORLD'S LARGEST-VOLUME EMBANKMENT DAMS

Rank	Name	Country	Volume (1,000 cu yd)	Volume (1,000 cu m)
1.	Tarbela	Pakistan	194,230	148,500
2.	Fort Peck	U.S.	125,630	96,050
3.	Tucurui	Brazil	111,400	85,200
4.	Ataturk	Turkey	111,200	85,000
5.	Yacireta*	Argentina	105,900	81,000
6.	Rogun*	Tajikistan	98,750	75,500
7.	Oahe	U.S.	92,000	70,339
8.	Guri	Venezuela	91,560	70,000
9.	Parambikulam	India	90,460	69,165
10.	High Island West	China	87,600	67,000

*Under construction.

Photos (from left to right): Tarbela Dam, Indus River, Pakistan; Grande Dixence Dam, Lac des Dix, Switzerland; Fort Peck Dam, Missouri River, Montana, U.S.; Lake Kariba Dam, Zambezi River, Zambia/Zimbabwe; Vajont Dam, Vajont Valley, Italy

GLOBAL TEMPERATURES

HIGHEST MOUNTAINS

Rank	Peak	Place	Height (ft)	Height (m)
1.	Everest	Nepal-Tibet	29,035	8,850
2.	K2 (Godwin Austen)	Kashmir	28,250	8,611
3.	Kanchenjunga	India-Nepal	28,208	8,598
4.	Lhotse I (Everest)	Nepal-Tibet	27,923	8,511
5.	Makalu I	Nepal-Tibet	27,824	8,481
6.	Lhotse II (Everest)	Nepal-Tibet	27,560	8,400
7.	Dhaulagiri	Nepal	26,810	8,172
8.	Manaslu I	Nepal	26,760	8,156
9.	Cho Oyu	Nepal-Tibet	26,750	8,153
10.	Nanga Parbat	Kashmir	26,660	8,126

AVERAGE GLOBAL TEMPERATURES, 1900–2000

Decade	Degrees Fahrenheit	Degrees Celsius
1900-09	56.52	13.62
1910-19	56.57	13.65
1920-29	56.74	13.74
1930-39	57.00	13.89
1940-49	57.13	13.96
1950-59	57.06	13.92
1960-69	57.05	13.92
1970-79	57.04	13.91
1980-89	57.36	14.09
1990-99	57.64	14.24
2000	57.60	14.22

HIGHEST MEASURED TEMPERATURE

Continent or Region	Temperature (degrees Fahrenheit)	Temperature (degrees Celsius)	Place	Elevation (ft)	Elevation (m)	Date
Africa	136	58	El Azizia, Libya	367	112	Sept. 13, 1922
North America	134	57	Death Valley, California (Greenland Ranch)	−178	−54	July 10, 1913
Asia	129	54	Tirat Tsvi, Israel	−722	−220	June 21, 1942
Australia	128	53	Cloncurry, Queensland	622	190	Jan. 16, 1889
Europe	122	50	Seville, Spain	26	8	Aug. 4, 1881
South America	120	49	Rivadavia, Argentina	676	206	Dec. 11, 1905
Antarctica	59	15	Vanda Station, Scott Coast	49	15	Jan. 5, 1974

LOWEST MEASURED TEMPERATURE

Continent or Region	Temperature (degrees Fahrenheit)	Temperature (degrees Celsius)	Place	Elevation (ft)	Elevation (m)	Date
Antarctica	−129.0	−89	Vostok	11,220	3,420	July 21, 1983
Asia	−90.0	−68	Oimekon, Russia	2,625	800	Feb. 6, 1933
Asia	−90.0	−68	Verkhoyansk, Russia	350	107	Feb. 7, 1892
Greenland	−87.0	−66	Northice	7,687	2,343	Jan. 9, 1954
North America	−81.4	−63	Snag, Yukon, Canada	2,120	646	Feb. 3, 1947
Europe	−67.0	−55	Ust'-Shchugor, Russia	279	85	Jan.*
South America	−27.0	−33	Sarmiento, Argentina	879	268	June 1, 1907
Africa	−11.0	−24	Ifrane, Morocco	5,364	1,635	Feb. 11, 1935
Australia	−9.4	−23	Charlotte Pass, New South Wales	5,758	1,755	June 29, 1994
Oceania	14.0	−10	Haleakala Summit, Maui, Hawaii	9,750	2,972	Jan. 2, 1961

* Exact day and year unknown.

World Facts and Figures

PRECIPITATION AND DESERTS

HIGHEST AVERAGE ANNUAL PRECIPITATION

Continent or Region	Precipitation (in)	Precipitation (mm)	Place	Elevation (ft)	Elevation (m)	Years of Data
South America	523.6[1,2]	13,300[1,2]	Lloro, Colombia	520[3]	158[3]	29
Asia	467.4[1]	11,870[1]	Mawsynram, India	4,597	1,401	38
Oceania	460.0[1]	11,680[1]	Mt. Waialeale, Kauai, Hawaii	5,148	1,569	30
Africa	405.0	10,290	Debundscha, Cameroon	30	9	32
South America	354.0[2]	8,992[2]	Quibdo, Colombia	120	37	16
Australia	340.0	8,636	Bellenden Ker, Queensland	5,102	1,555	9
North America	256.0	6,502	Henderson Lake, British Columbia	12	4	14
Europe	183.0	4,648	Crkvica, Bosnia-Herzegovina	3,337	1,017	22

[1]The value given is continent's highest and possibly the world's depending on measurement practices, procedures, and period of record variations.

[2]The official greatest average annual precipitation for South America is 354 in (8,992 mm) at Quibdo, Colombia. The 523.6 in (13,300 mm) average at Lloro, Colombia (14 mi [23 km] SE and at a higher elevation than Quibdo) is an estimated amount.

[3]Approximate elevation.

LOWEST AVERAGE ANNUAL PRECIPITATION

Continent or Region	Precipitation (in)	Precipitation (mm)	Place	Elevation (ft)	Elevation (m)	Years of Data
South America	0.03	0.8	Arica, Chile	95	29	59
Africa	< 0.1	< 3	Wadi Halfa, Sudan	410	125	39
Antarctica	0.8[1]	20[1]	Amundsen-Scott South Pole Station	9,186	2,800	10
North America	1.2	30	Batagues, Mexico	16	5	14
Asia	1.8	46	Aden, Yemen	22	7	50
Australia	4.05	103	Mulka (Troudaninna), South Australia	160[2]	49[2]	42
Europe	6.4	163	Astrakhan, Russia	45	14	25
Oceania	8.93	227	Puako, Hawaii	5	2	13

[1]The value given is the average amount of solid snow accumulating in one year as indicated by snow markers. The liquid content of the snow is undetermined.

[2]Approximate elevation.

NOTABLE DESERTS OF THE WORLD

Arabian (Eastern), 70,000 sq mi (181,000 sq km) in Egypt between the Nile River and Red Sea, extending southward into Sudan

Chihuahuan, 140,000 sq mi (363,000 sq km) in Texas, New Mexico, Arizona, and Mexico

Gibson, 120,000 sq mi (311,000 sq km) in the interior of Western Australia

Gobi, 500,000 sq mi (1,295,000 sq km) in Mongolia and China

Great Sandy, 150,000 sq mi (388,000 sq km) in Western Australia

Great Victoria, 150,000 sq mi (388,000 sq km) in South and Western Australia

Kalahari, 225,000 sq mi (583,000 sq km) in southern Africa

Kara Kum, 120,000 sq mi (311,000 sq km) in Turkmenistan

Kyzyl Kum, 100,000 sq mi (259,000 sq km) in Kazakhstan and Uzbekistan

Libyan, 450,000 sq mi (1,165,000 sq km) in the Sahara, extending from Libya through southwestern Egypt into Sudan

Nubian, 100,000 sq mi (259,000 sq km) in the Sahara in northeastern Sudan

Patagonia, 300,000 sq mi (777,000 sq km) in southern Argentina

Rub al-Khali (Empty Quarter), 250,000 sq mi (648,000 sq km) in the southern Arabian Peninsula

Sahara, 3,500,000 sq mi (9,065,000 sq km) in northern Africa, extending westward to the Atlantic; largest desert in the world

Sonoran, 70,000 sq mi (181,000 sq km) in southwestern Arizona and southeastern California extending into northwestern Mexico

Syrian, 100,000 sq mi (259,000 sq km) arid wasteland extending over much of northern Saudi Arabia, eastern Jordan, southern Syria, and western Iraq

Taklimakan, 140,000 sq mi (363,000 sq km) in Xinjiang Province, China

Thar (Great Indian), 100,000 sq mi (259,000 sq km) arid area extending 400 mi (640 km) along the India-Pakistan border

LANGUAGES, POPULATION GROWTH, AND OIL AND GAS RESERVES

TOP TEN LANGUAGES

Language	Major Countries Where Spoken	Native Speakers
Mandarin	China, Taiwan	874,000,000
Hindi	India	366,000,000
English	U.S., Canada, Britain	341,000,000
Spanish	Spain, Latin America	322,000,000
Arabic	Arabian Peninsula	207,000,000
Bengali	India, Bangladesh	207,000,000
Portuguese	Portugal, Brazil	176,000,000
Russian	Russia	167,000,000
Japanese	Japan	125,000,000
German	Germany, Austria	100,000,000

WORLD POPULATION THROUGH HISTORY

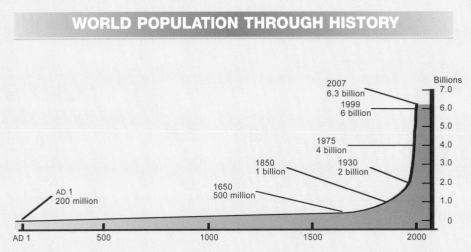

PRINCIPAL KNOWN CRUDE OIL AND NATURAL GAS RESERVES, JANUARY, 2007

	Crude Oil (billion barrels)		Natural Gas (trillion cubic feet)			Crude Oil (billion barrels)		Natural Gas (trillion cubic feet)	
	OGJ	WO	OGJ	WO		OGJ	WO	OGJ	WO
NORTH AMERICA					Iraq	115.0	115.0	112.0	84.0
Canada	179.2	12.0	57.9	53.7	Kuwait	101.5	100.9	55.0	57.0
Mexico	12.4	12.4	14.6	20.0	Oman	5.5	4.8	30.0	27.1
United States	21.8	21.8	204.4	204.4	Qatar	15.2	20.3	910.5	906.0
SOUTH AMERICA					Saudi Arabia	262.3	262.2	240.4	243.5
Argentina	2.5	2.4	16.1	21.4	United Arab Emirates	97.8	70.3	214.4	205.6
Trinidad and Tobago	0.7	0.6	18.8	18.8	**AFRICA**				
Venezuela	80.0	52.6	152.4	150.9	Algeria	12.3	11.4	161.7	160.7
WESTERN EUROPE					Egypt	3.7	3.7	58.5	66.8
Netherlands	0.1	0.2	50.0	50.5	Libya	41.5	34.1	52.7	51.5
Norway	7.8	8.0	82.3	83.3	Nigeria	36.2	37.2	181.9	182.0
United Kingdom	3.9	3.8	17.0	17.8	**ASIA AND OCEANIA**				
EASTERN EUROPE AND FORMER USSR					Australia	1.6	4.0	30.4	119.5
Kazakhstan	30.0	NA	100.0	NA	China	16.0	16.2	80.0	55.6
Russia	74.4	60.0	1,680.0	1,688.7	India	5.6	4.0	38.0	27.3
Turkmenistan	0.6	NA	100.0	NA	Indonesia	4.3	5.0	97.8	91.5
Ukraine	0.4	NA	39.0	NA	Malaysia	3.0	2.9	75.0	58.0
Uzbekistan	0.6	NA	65.0	NA	Pakistan	0.3	0.3	28.0	30.1
MIDDLE EAST					**WORLD**				
Iran	136.3	131.5	974.0	965.0	TOTAL	1,317.4	1,119.6	6,182.6	6,226.6

OGJ = *Oil and Gas Journal*, January 2007

WO = *World Oil*, Year-End 2005

NOTE: Data for Kuwait and Saudi Arabia include one-half of the reserves in the Neutral Zone between Kuwait and Saudi Arabia. All reserve figures except those for the former USSR and natural gas reserves in Canada are *proved reserves* recoverable with present technology and prices at the time of estimation. Former USSR and Canadian natural gas figures include *proved* and some *probable reserves.*

CARBON DIOXIDE EMISSION, AND MAJOR ENERGY USERS AND PRODUCERS

WORLD CARBON DIOXIDE EMISSIONS FROM THE USE OF FOSSIL FUELS, 2005

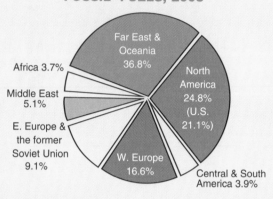

- Far East & Oceania 36.8%
- North America 24.8% (U.S. 21.1%)
- Central & South America 3.9%
- W. Europe 16.6%
- E. Europe & the former Soviet Union 9.1%
- Middle East 5.1%
- Africa 3.7%

NATIONS MOST RELIANT ON NUCLEAR ENERGY, 2006
(nuclear energy generation as % of total electricity generated)

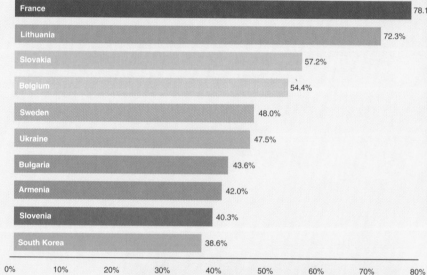

Nation	%
France	78.1%
Lithuania	72.3%
Slovakia	57.2%
Belgium	54.4%
Sweden	48.0%
Ukraine	47.5%
Bulgaria	43.6%
Armenia	42.0%
Slovenia	40.3%
South Korea	38.6%

0%   10%   20%   30%   40%   50%   60%   70%   80%

WORLD'S MAJOR PRODUCERS OF PRIMARY ENERGY, 2005
(quadrillion Btu)

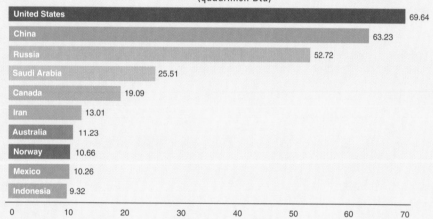

Country	quadrillion Btu
United States	69.64
China	63.23
Russia	52.72
Saudi Arabia	25.51
Canada	19.09
Iran	13.01
Australia	11.23
Norway	10.66
Mexico	10.26
Indonesia	9.32

0   10   20   30   40   50   60   70

WORLD'S MAJOR CONSUMERS OF PRIMARY ENERGY, 2005
(quadrillion Btu)

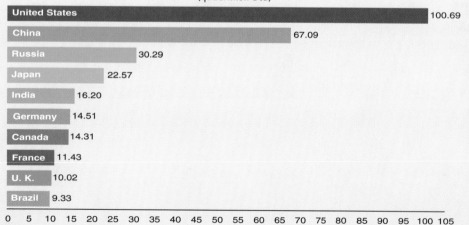

Country	quadrillion Btu
United States	100.69
China	67.09
Russia	30.29
Japan	22.57
India	16.20
Germany	14.51
Canada	14.31
France	11.43
U. K.	10.02
Brazil	9.33

0 5 10 15 20 25 30 35 40 45 50 55 60 65 70 75 80 85 90 95 100 105

THE WORLD ALMANAC

WORLD ATLAS

World Almanac Section

Nation Facts and Figures from The World Almanac®

Nigeria	246,000	2,838	197	5.	Palau	11,000	*	
Hong Kong and Macau.	127,654,000	22	1,096	6.	San Marino	13,000	1,100	
	124,009,000	838	8	7.	Monaco	20,000	1,625	
		353	324	8.	Liechtenstein	28,000	113	62
			136	9.	Saint Kitts and Nevis	32,000	1,217	44
				10.	Marshall Islands	33,000	41,608	470
					Antigua and Barbuda	39,000	550	16,065

LARGEST LAND AREAS

*Area only 0.17 sq mi (0,4 sq km).

Country	Land Area sq mi		Land Area)				56,000	386	212
Russia							68,000	800	149
China								400	309
nada	6,59								154

AFRICA

Among African nations, Sudan occupies the largest total area, but Nigeria has the largest population, ranking ninth in the world.

ALGERIA

FOR MAP, SEE PAGE 154

Population: 33,739,635

Ethnic groups: Arab-Berber 99%

Principal languages: Arabic (official), French, Berber dialects

Chief religion: Sunni Muslim (official) 99%

Area: 919,600 sq mi (2,381,741 sq km)

Topography: The Tell, located on the coast, comprises fertile plains 50-100 mi (80-160 km) wide. Two major chains of the Atlas Mountains, running roughly east to west and reaching 7,000 ft (2,100 m), enclose a dry plateau region. Below lies the Sahara, mostly desert with major mineral resources.

Capital: Algiers (pop., 3,060,000)

Independence date: July 5, 1962   **Government type:** republic

Head of state: Pres. Abdelaziz Bouteflika

Head of government: Prime Min. Abdelaziz Belkhadem

Monetary unit: dinar

GDP: $268.9 billion (2007 est.)   **Per capita GDP:** $8,100

Industries: petroleum, natural gas, light industries, mining, electrical, petrochemical, food processing

Chief crops: wheat, barley, oats, grapes, olives, citrus, fruits

Minerals: petroleum, natural gas, iron ore, phosphates, uranium, lead, zinc

Life expectancy at birth (years): male, 69.1; female, 72.0

Literacy rate: 61.6%

Website: www.algeria-us.org

ANGOLA

FOR MAP, SEE PAGE 163

Population: 12,531,357

Ethnic groups: Ovimbundu 37%, Kimbundu 25%, Bakongo 13%

Principal languages: Portuguese (official), Bantu and other African languages

Chief religions: indigenous beliefs 47%, Roman Catholic 38%, Protestant 15%

Area: 481,400 sq mi (1,246,700 sq km)`

Topography: Most of Angola consists of a plateau elevated 3,000 to 5,000 ft (900 to 1,500 m) above sea level, rising from a narrow coastal strip. There is also a temperate highland area in the west-central region, a desert in the south, and a tropical rain forest covering Cabinda.

Capital: Luanda (pop., 2,623,000)

Independence date: November 11, 1975   **Government type:** republic

Head of state: Pres. José Eduardo dos Santos

Head of government: Prime Min. Fernando da Piedade Dias dos Santos

Monetary unit: kwanza

GDP: $80.95 billion (2007 est.)   **Per capita GDP:** $6,500

Industries: petroleum, mining, cement, basic metal products, fish processing, food processing

Chief crops: bananas, sugarcane, coffee, sisal, corn, cotton, manioc, tobacco, vegetables, plantains

Minerals: petroleum, diamonds, iron ore, phosphates, copper, feldspar, gold, bauxite, uranium

Life expectancy at birth (years): male, 36.1; female, 37.6

Literacy rate: 42%

Website: www.angola.org

ABOUT THE WORLD ALMANAC DATA: Population figures for cities generally pertain to the entire metropolitan area. GDP (gross domestic product) estimates are based on so-called purchasing power parity calculations, which make use of weighted prices in order to take into account differences in price levels between countries. Please note that the addresses and content of websites are subject to change.

CHIEF ABBREVIATIONS USED IN THE WORLD ALMANAC SECTION

est.	estimate(d)	ft	foot, feet	Gov.-Gen.	Governor-General	in	inch(es)	km	kilometer(s)	m	meter(s)
mi	mile(s)	NA	not available	pop.	population	Pres.	President	Prime Min.	Prime Minister	sq	square

BENIN

FOR MAP, SEE PAGE 161

Population: 8,294,943

Ethnic groups: 42 groups, including Fon, Adja, Yoruba, and Bariba

Principal languages: French (official), Fon, Yoruba, various tribal languages

Chief religions: indigenous beliefs 50%, Christian 30%, Muslim 20%

Area: 43,480 sq mi (112,620 sq km)

Capital: Porto-Novo (pop., 238,000)

Topography: Most of Benin is flat and covered with dense vegetation. The coast is hot, humid, and rainy.

Independence date: August 1, 1960

Government type: republic

Head of state and government: Pres. Thomas Yayi Boni

Monetary unit: CFA franc

GDP: $12.18 billion (2007 est.)

Per capita GDP: $1,500

Industries: textiles, food processing, chemical production, construction materials

West African fruit seller

Chief crops: cotton, corn, cassava, yams, beans, palm oil, peanuts

Minerals: offshore oil, limestone, marble

Life expectancy at birth (years): male, 50.3; female, 51.4

Literacy rate: 37.5%

Website: www.beninembassyus.org

BOTSWANA

FOR MAP, SEE PAGE 163

Population: 1,842,323

Ethnic groups: Tswana 79%, Kalanga 11%, Basarwa 3%

Principal languages: English (official), Setswana

Chief religions: indigenous beliefs 85%, Christian 15%

Area: 231,800 sq mi (600,370 sq km)

Topography: The Kalahari Desert, supporting nomadic Bushmen and wildlife, spreads over the southwest; there are swamplands and farming areas in the north, and rolling plains in the east where livestock are grazed.

Capital: Gaborone (pop., 199,000)

Independence date: September 30, 1966

Government type: parliamentary republic

Head of state and government: Pres. Festus Mogae

Monetary unit: pula

GDP: $24.1 billion (2007 est.)

Per capita GDP: $14,700

Industries: mining, livestock processing, textiles

Chief crops: sorghum, maize, millet, beans, sunflowers, groundnuts

Minerals: diamonds, copper, nickel, salt, soda ash, potash, coal, iron ore, silver

Life expectancy at birth (years): male, 31.0; female, 30.5

Literacy rate: 69.8%

Website: www.gov.bw

BURKINA FASO

FOR MAP, SEE PAGE 161

Population: 14,761,339

Ethnic groups: Mossi (approximately 40%), Gurunsi, Senufo, Lobi, Bobo, Mande, Fulani

Principal languages: French (official), Sudanic languages

Chief religions: Muslim 50%, indigenous beliefs 40%, Christian (mainly Roman Catholic) 10%

Area: 105,900 sq mi (274,200 sq km)

Topography: Landlocked Burkina Faso is in the savanna region of West Africa. The north is arid, hot, and thinly populated.

Capital: Ouagadougou (pop., 821,000)

Independence date: August 5, 1960   **Government type:** republic

Head of state: Pres. Blaise Compaoré

Head of government: Prime Min. Paramanga Ernest Yonli

Monetary unit: CFA franc

GDP: $17.5 billion (2007 est.)   **Per capita GDP:** $1,200

Industries: cotton lint, beverages, agricultural processing, soap, cigarettes, textiles, gold

Chief crops: peanuts, shea nuts, sesame, cotton, sorghum, millet, corn, rice

Minerals: manganese, limestone, marble, gold, antimony, copper, nickel, bauxite, lead, phosphates, zinc, silver

Life expectancy at birth (years): male, 42.6; female, 45.8

Literacy rate: 36%

Website: www.burkinaembassy–usa.org

BURUNDI

FOR MAP, SEE PAGE 162

Population: 8,691,005

Ethnic groups: Hutu 85%, Tutsi 14%, Twa (Pygmy) 1%

Principal languages: Kirundi, French (both official); Swahili

Chief religions: Roman Catholic 62%, indigenous beliefs 23%, Muslim 10%, Protestant 5%

Area: 10,750 sq mi (27,830 sq km)

Topography: Much of the country is grassy highland, with mountains reaching 8,900 ft (2,700 m). The southernmost source of the White Nile is located in Burundi. Lake Tanganyika is the second deepest lake in the world.

Capital: Bujumbura (pop., 346,000)

Independence date: July 1, 1962

Government type: in transition

Head of state and government: Pres. Pierre Nkurunziza

Monetary unit: franc

GDP: $6.4 billion (2007 est.)

Per capita GDP: $800

Industries: light consumer goods, assembly of imported components, public works construction, food processing

Chief crops: coffee, cotton, tea, corn, sorghum, sweet potatoes, bananas, manioc

Minerals: nickel, uranium, rare earth oxides, peat, cobalt, copper, platinum (not yet exploited), vanadium

Life expectancy at birth (years): male, 42.7; female, 44.0

Literacy rate: 35.3%

Website: www.burundiembassy-usa.org

CAMEROON

FOR MAP, SEE PAGE 154

Population: 18,467,692

Ethnic groups: Highlanders 31%, Equatorial Bantu 19%, Kirdi 11%, Fulani 10%, northwest Bantu 8%, east Nigritic 7%

Principal languages: English, French (both official); 24 African language groups

Chief religions: indigenous beliefs 40%, Christian 40%, Muslim 20%

Nation Facts and Figures

Cameroon (*continued*)

Area: 183,570 sq mi (475,440 sq km)

Topography: A low coastal plain with rain forests is in the south; plateaus in the center lead to forested mountains in the west, including Mt. Cameroon, 13,350 ft (4,070 m); grasslands in the north lead to marshes around Lake Chad.

Capital: Yaoundé (pop., 1,616,000)

Independence date: January 1, 1960   **Government type:** republic

Head of state: Pres. Paul Biya

Head of government: Prime Min. Ephraim Inoni

Monetary unit: CFA franc

GDP: $40 billion (2007 est.)   **Per capita GDP:** $2,300

Industries: petroleum production and refining, food processing, light consumer goods, textiles, lumber

Chief crops: coffee, cocoa, cotton, rubber, bananas, oilseed, grains, root starches

Minerals: petroleum, bauxite, iron ore

Life expectancy at birth (years): male, 47.1; female, 48.8

Literacy rate: 63.4%

Website: www.spm.gov.cm

CAPE VERDE

For map, see page 151

Population: 426,113

Ethnic groups: Creole 71%, African 28%, European 1%

Principal languages: Portuguese (official), Crioulo

Chief religions: Roman Catholic (infused with indigenous beliefs), Protestant (mostly Church of the Nazarene)

Area: 1,560 sq mi (4,030 sq km)

Topography: Cape Verde Islands are 15 in number, volcanic in origin (active crater on Fogo). The landscape is eroded and stark, with vegetation mostly in interior valleys.

Capital: Praia (pop., 82,000)

Independence date: July 5, 1975

Government type: republic

Head of state: Pres. Pedro Pires

Head of government:
Prime Min. José Maria Neves

Monetary unit: escudo

Ripe papayas

GDP: $3.7 billion (2007 est.)   **Per capita GDP:** $7,000

Industries: food and beverages, fish processing, shoes and garments, salt mining, ship repair

Chief crops: bananas, corn, beans, sweet potatoes, sugarcane, coffee, peanuts

Minerals: salt, basalt rock, limestone, kaolin

Life expectancy at birth (years): male, 66.8; female, 73.5

Literacy rate: 71.6%

Website: www.virtualcapeverde.net

CENTRAL AFRICAN REPUBLIC

For map, see page 155

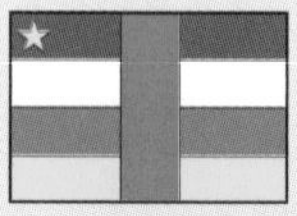

Population: 4,434,873

Ethnic groups: Baya 33%, Banda 27%, Mandjia 13%, Sara 10%, Mboum 7%, M'Baka 4%, Yakoma 4%

Principal languages: French (official), Sangho (national), tribal languages

Chief religions: indigenous beliefs 35%, Protestant 25%, Roman Catholic 25%, Muslim 15%

Area: 240,530 sq mi (622,984 sq km)

Topography: Mostly rolling plateau, average altitude 2,000 ft (600 m), with rivers draining south to the Congo and north to Lake Chad. Open, well-watered savanna covers most of the area, with an arid area in the northeast and tropical rain forest in the southwest.

Capital: Bangui (pop., 689,000)

Independence date: August 13, 1960

Government type: in transition

Head of state: Pres. François Bozizé

Head of government: Prime Élie Doté

Monetary unit: CFA franc

GDP: $3.1 billion (2007 est.)   **Per capita GDP:** $700

Industries: diamond mining, sawmills, breweries, textiles, footwear, assembly of bicycles and motorcycles

Chief crops: cotton, coffee, tobacco, manioc, yams, millet, corn, bananas

Minerals: diamonds, uranium, gold, oil

Life expectancy at birth (years): male, 39.7; female, 43.1

Literacy rate: 60%   **Website:** www.state.gov/r/pa/ei/bgn/4007.htm

CHAD

For map, see page 155

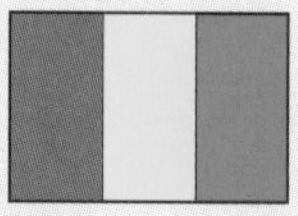

Population: 10,111,337

Ethnic groups: about 200 groups; largest are Arabs in north and Sara in south

Principal languages: French, Arabic (both official); Sara; more than 120 different languages and dialects

Chief religions: Muslim 51%, Christian 35%, animist 7%, other 7%

Area: 496,000 sq mi (1,284,000 sq km)

Topography: Wooded savanna, steppe, and desert in the south; part of the Sahara in the north. Southern rivers flow north to Lake Chad, surrounded by marshland.

Capital: N'Djamena (pop., 797,000)

Independence date: August 11, 1960

Government type: republic

Head of state: Pres. Idriss Déby

Head of government: Prime Min. Youssof Saleh Abbas

Monetary unit: CFA franc

GDP: $16 billion (2007 est.)   **Per capita GDP:** $1,600

Industries: cotton textiles, meatpacking, beer brewing, natron, soap, cigarettes, construction materials

Chief crops: cotton, sorghum, millet, peanuts, rice, potatoes, manioc

Minerals: petroleum (unexploited but exploration under way), uranium, natron, kaolin

Life expectancy at birth (years): male, 47.0; female, 50.1

Literacy rate: 40%

Website: www.chadembassy.org

COMOROS

For map, see page 165

Population: 731,775

Ethnic groups: Antalote, Cafre, Makoa, Oimatsaha, Sakalava (all are mostly an African-Arab mix)

Principal languages: Arabic, French (both official); Shikomoro (a blend of Swahili and Arabic)

Chief religion: Muslim (official) 98%

Area: 840 sq mi (2,170 sq km)

Topography: The islands are of volcanic origin, with an active volcano on Grande Comore.

Capital: Moroni (pop., 53,000)

Independence date: July 6, 1975

Government type: in transition

Head of state and government: Pres. Ahmed Abdallah Mohamed Sambi

Monetary unit: franc

GDP: $1.262 billion (2007 est.)   **Per capita GDP:** $600

Industries: tourism, perfume distillation

Chief crops: vanilla, cloves, perfume essences, copra, coconuts, bananas, cassava

Life expectancy at birth (years): male, 59.3; female, 63.9

Literacy rate: 57.3%

Website: www.state.gov/r/pa/ei/bgn/5236.htm

CONGO, DEMOCRATIC REPUBLIC OF THE

Population: 68,008,922   <small>FOR MAP, SEE PAGE 151</small>

Ethnic groups: Over 200 groups; the four largest, the Mongo, Luba, Kongo (all Bantu), and Mangbetu-Azande (Hamitic), make up 45% of the population

Principal languages: French (official), Lingala, Kingwana (a Swahili dialect), Kikongo, Tshiluba

Chief religions: Roman Catholic 50%, Protestant 20%, Kimbanguist 10%, Muslim 10%

Area: 905,570 sq mi (2,345,410 sq km)

Topography: Congo includes the bulk of the Congo River basin. The vast central region is a low-lying plateau covered by rain forest. Mountainous terraces in the west, savannas in the south and southeast, grasslands toward the north, and the high Ruwenzori Mountains in the east surround the central region. A short strip of territory borders the Atlantic Ocean. The Congo River is 2,718 mi (4,374 km) long.

Capital: Kinshasa (pop., 5,277,000)

Independence date: June 30, 1960

Government type: republic with strong presidential authority (in transition)

Head of state and government: Pres. Joseph Kabila

Monetary unit: Congolese franc

GDP: $19.07 billion (2007 est.)   **Per capita GDP:** $300

Industries: mining, mineral processing, consumer products, cement

Chief crops: coffee, sugar, palm oil, rubber, tea, quinine, cassava, palm oil, bananas, root crops, corn, fruits

Minerals: cobalt, copper, cadmium, petroleum, industrial and gem diamonds, gold, silver, zinc, manganese, tin, germanium, uranium, radium, bauxite, iron ore, coal

Life expectancy at birth (years): male, 47.1; female, 51.3

Literacy rate: 77.3%

Website: www.state.gov/r/pa/ei/bgn/2823.htm

CONGO REPUBLIC

<small>FOR MAP, SEE PAGE 151</small>

Population: 3,903,318

Ethnic groups: Kongo 48%, Sangha 20%, M'Bochi 12%, Teke 17%

Principal languages: French (official), Lingala, Monokutuba, Kikongo, many local languages and dialects

Chief religions: Christian 50%, animist 48%, Muslim 2%

Area: 132,000 sq mi (342,000 sq km)

Topography: Much of the Congo is covered by thick forests. A coastal plain leads to the fertile Niari Valley. The center is a plateau; the Congo River basin consists of flood plains in the lower portion and savanna in the upper.

Capital: Brazzaville (pop., 1,080,000)

Independence date: August 15, 1960   **Government type:** republic

Head of state and government: Pres. Denis Sassou-Nguesso

Monetary unit: CFA franc

GDP: $14 billion (2007 est.)   **Per capita GDP:** $3,700

Industries: petroleum extraction, cement, lumber, brewing, sugar, palm oil, soap, flour, cigarettes

Chief crops: cassava, sugar, rice, corn, peanuts, vegetables, coffee, cocoa

Minerals: petroleum, potash, lead, zinc, uranium, copper, phosphates, natural gas

Life expectancy at birth (years): male, 48.5; female, 56.6

Literacy rate: 74.9%   **Website:** www.state.gov/r/pa/ei/bgn/2825.htm

CÔTE D'IVOIRE (IVORY COAST)

<small>FOR MAP, SEE PAGE 160</small>

Population: 18,373,060

Ethnic groups: Akan 42%, Voltaiques (Gur) 18%, north Mandes 17%, Krous 11%, south Mandes 10%

Principal languages: French (official), Dioula, many native dialects

Chief religions: Muslim 35-40%, Christian 20-30%, indigenous beliefs 25-40%

Area: 124,500 sq mi (322,460 sq km)

Familiar wildlife of sub-Saharan Africa: zebras (right) rank among the favorite prey of lions (left)

Nation Facts and Figures

Côte d'Ivoire (Ivory Coast) *(continued)*

Topography: Forests cover the western half of the country, and range from a coastal strip to halfway to the north in the east. A sparse inland plain leads to low mountains in the northwest.

Official capital: Yamoussoukro (pop., 416,000); de facto capital, Abidjan (pop., 3,337,000)

Independence date: August 7, 1960   **Government type:** in transition

Head of state: Pres. Laurent Gbagbo

Head of government: Prime Min. Charles Konan Banny

Monetary unit: CFA franc

GDP: $32.9 billion (2007 est.)   **Per capita GDP:** $1,800

Industries: foodstuffs, beverages, wood products, oil refining, truck and bus assembly, textiles, fertilizer, building materials, electricity

Chief crops: coffee, cocoa beans, bananas, palm kernels, corn, rice, manioc, sweet potatoes, sugar, cotton, rubber

Minerals: petroleum, natural gas, diamonds, manganese, iron ore, cobalt, bauxite, copper

Life expectancy at birth (years): male, 40.3; female, 44.8

Literacy rate: 48.5%

Website: www.state.gov/r/pa/ei/bgn/2846.htm

DJIBOUTI

FOR MAP, SEE PAGE 155

Population: 506,221

Ethnic groups: Somali 60%, Afar 35%

Principal languages: French, Arabic (both official); Afar, Somali

Chief religions: Muslim 94%, Christian 6%

Area: 8,500 sq mi (22,000 sq km)

Topography: The territory—divided into a low coastal plain, mountains behind, and an interior plateau—is arid, sandy, and desolate.

Capital: Djibouti (pop., 502,000)

Independence date: June 27, 1977   **Government type:** republic

Head of state: Pres. Ismail Omar Guelleh

Head of government: Prime Min. Dileita Mohamed Dileita

Monetary unit: Djibouti franc

GDP: $1.9 billion (2006 est.)   **Per capita GDP:** $1,000

Industries: construction, agricultural processing

Chief crops: fruits, vegetables

Life expectancy at birth (years): male, 41.8; female, 44.4

Literacy rate: 46.2%

Website: www.state.gov/r/pa/ei/bgn/5482.htm

EGYPT

FOR MAP, SEE PAGE 155

Population: 81,713,517

Ethnic groups: Egyptian Arab 99%

Principal languages: Arabic (official), English, French

Chief religions: Muslim (official; mostly Sunni) 94%, Coptic Christian and other 6%

Area: 386,660 sq mi (1,001,450 sq km)

Topography: Almost entirely desolate and barren, with hills and mountains in the east and along the Nile. The Nile Valley, where most of the people live, stretches 550 mi (885 km).

Capital: Cairo (pop., 10,834,000)

Independence date: February 28, 1922   **Government type:** republic

Head of state: Pres. Hosni Mubarak

The Great Sphinx and pyramids at Giza (Al Jizah), Egypt

Head of government: Prime Min. Ahmed Nazif

Monetary unit: pound

GDP: $431.9 billion (2007 est.)   **Per capita GDP:** $5,400

Industries: textiles, food processing, tourism, chemicals, hydrocarbons, construction, cement, metals

Chief crops: cotton, rice, corn, wheat, beans, fruits, vegetables

Minerals: petroleum, natural gas, iron ore, phosphates, manganese, limestone, gypsum, talc, asbestos, lead, zinc

Life expectancy at birth (years): male, 68.2; female, 73.3

Literacy rate: 51.4%

Website: www.sis.gov.eg

EQUATORIAL GUINEA

FOR MAP, SEE PAGE 154

Population: 562,339

Ethnic groups: Fang 83%, Bubi 10%

Principal languages: Spanish, French (both official); Fang, Bubi, pidgin English, Portuguese Creole, Ibo

Chief religions: nominally Christian and predominantly Roman Catholic, traditional practices

Area: 10,831 sq mi (95,000 sq km)

Topography: Bioko Island consists of two volcanic mountains and a connecting valley. Rio Muni, with over 90% of the area, has a coastal plain and low hills beyond.

Capital: Malabo (pop., 33,000)

Independence date: October 12, 1968   **Government type:** republic

Head of state: Pres. Teodoro Obiang Nguema Mbasogo

Head of government: Prime Min. Miguel Abia Bieto Borico

Monetary unit: CFA franc

GDP: $25.7 billion (2005 est.)   **Per capita GDP:** $44,100

Industries: petroleum, fishing, sawmilling, natural gas

Chief crops: coffee, cocoa, rice, yams, cassava, bananas, palm oil, nuts

Minerals: oil, petroleum, gold, manganese, uranium

Life expectancy at birth (years): male, 53; female, 57.4

Literacy rate: 78.5%

Website: www.state.gov/r/pa/ei/bgn/7221.htm

ERITREA

FOR MAP, SEE PAGE 155

Population: 5,028,475

Ethnic groups: Tigrinya 50%, Tigre and Kunama 40%, Afar 4%, Saho 3%

Principal languages: Arabic, Tigrinya (both official); Afar, Amharic, Tigre, Kunama, other Cushitic languages

Chief religions: Muslim, Coptic Christian, Roman Catholic, Protestant

Area: 46,840 sq mi (121,320 sq km)

Topography: Eritrea includes many islands of the Dahlak Archipelago. It has low coastal plains in the south and a mountain range with peaks to 9,000 ft (2,700 m) in the north.

Capital: Asmara (pop., 556,000)   Independence date: May 24, 1993

Government type: in transition

Head of state and government: Pres. Isaias Afwerki

Monetary unit: nakfa

GDP: $4.8 billion (2006 est.)   Per capita GDP: $1,000

Industries: food processing, beverages, clothing and textiles

Chief crops: sorghum, lentils, vegetables, corn, cotton, tobacco, coffee, sisal

Minerals: gold, potash, zinc, copper, salt, possibly oil and natural gas

Life expectancy at birth (years): male, 51.3; female, 54.1

Literacy rate: 25%

Website: www.state.gov/r/pa/ei/bgn/2854.htm

ETHIOPIA

For map, see page 155

Population: 78,254,090

Ethnic groups: Oromo 40%, Amhara and Tigre 32%, Sidamo 9%, Shankella 6%, Somali 6%, Afar 4%, Gurage 2%

Principal languages: Amharic, Tigrinya, Oromigna, Guaragigna, Somali, Arabic, over 200 other languages

Chief religions: Muslim 45-50%, Ethiopian Orthodox 35-40%, animist 12%

Area: 435,190 sq mi (1,127,130 sq km)

Topography: A high central plateau, between 6,000 and 10,000 ft (1,800 and 3,000 m) high, rises to higher mountains near the Great Rift Valley, cutting in from the southwest. The Blue Nile and other rivers cross the plateau, which descends to plains on both the west and southeast.

Capital: Addis Ababa (pop., 2,723,000)

Independence date: more than 2,000 years ago (ancient kingdom of Aksum)

Government type: federal republic

Head of state: Pres. Girma Wolde Giorgis

Head of government: Prime Min. Meles Zenawi

Monetary unit: birr

GDP: $55 billion (2007 est.)   Per capita GDP: $700

Industries: food processing, beverages, textiles, chemicals, metals processing, cement

Chief crops: cereals, pulses, coffee, oilseed, sugarcane, potatoes, qat

Minerals: small reserves of gold, platinum, copper, potash, natural gas

Life expectancy at birth (years): male, 40.0; female, 41.8

Literacy rate: 35.5%

Website: www.ethiopianembassy.org

GABON

For map, see page 154

Population: 1,484,149

Ethnic groups: Fang, Bapounou, Nzebi, Obamba, European

Principal languages: French (official), Fang, Myene, Nzebi, Bapounou/Eschira, Bandjabi

Chief religion: Christian 55-75%

Area: 103,350 sq mi (267,670 sq km)

Topography: Heavily forested, the country consists of coastal lowlands; plateaus in the north, east, and south; and mountains in the north, southeast, and center. The Ogooue River system covers most of Gabon.

Capital: Libreville (pop., 611,000)

Independence date: August 17, 1960   Government type: republic

Head of state: Pres. Omar Bongo Ondimba

Head of government: Prime Min. Jean Eyeghe Ndong

Monetary unit: CFA franc

GDP: $20.1 billion (2007 est.)   Per capita GDP: $13,800

Industries: food and beverages, textile, lumber, cement, petroleum extraction and refining, mining, chemicals, ship repair

Chief crops: cocoa, coffee, sugar, palm oil, rubber

Minerals: petroleum, manganese, uranium, gold, iron ore

Life expectancy at birth (years): male, 54.9; female, 58.1

Literacy rate: 63.2%

Website: www.state.gov/r/pa/ei/bgn/2826.htm

THE GAMBIA

For map, see page 160

Population: 1,735,464

Ethnic groups: Mandinka 42%, Fula 18%, Wolof 16%, Jola 10%, Serahuli 9%

Principal languages: English (official), Mandinka, Wolof, Fula, other native dialects

Chief religions: Muslim 90%, Christian 9%

Area: 4,400 sq mi (11,300 sq km)

Topography: The country consists of a narrow strip of land on each side of the lower Gambia River.

Capital: Banjul (pop., 372,000)

Independence date: February 18, 1965

Government type: republic

Head of state and government: Pres. Yahya Jammeh

Monetary unit: dalasi

GDP: $1.4 billion (2007 est.)   Per capita GDP: $800

Industries: processing of peanuts, fish, and hides; tourism; beverages; agricultural machinery assembly; woodworking; metalworking; clothing

Chief crops: peanuts, millet, sorghum, rice, corn, sesame, cassava, palm kernels

Life expectancy at birth (years): male, 52.8; female, 56.9

Literacy rate: 47.5%

Website: www.visitthegambia.gm

West African craftswoman

GHANA

FOR MAP, SEE PAGE 161

Population: 23,382,848

Ethnic groups: Akan 44%, Moshi-Dagomba 16%, Ewe 13%, Ga 8%, Gurma 3%, Yoruba 1%

Principal languages: English (official); about 75 African languages, including Akan, Moshi-Dagomba, Ewe, and Ga

Chief religions: Christian 63%, indigenous beliefs 21%, Muslim 16%

Area: 92,100 sq mi (238,540 sq km)

Topography: Most of Ghana consists of low fertile plains and scrubland, cut by rivers and by the artificial Lake Volta.

Capital: Accra (pop., 1,847,000)

Independence date: March 6, 1957   Government type: republic

Head of state and government: Pres. John Agyekum Kufuor

Monetary unit: cedi

GDP: $31.2 billion (2007 est.)   Per capita GDP: $1,400

Industries: mining, lumbering, light manufacturing, aluminum smelting, food processing

Chief crops: cocoa, rice, coffee, cassava, peanuts, corn, shea nuts, bananas

Minerals: gold, diamonds, bauxite, manganese

Life expectancy at birth (years): male, 55.4; female, 57.2

Literacy rate: 64.5%

Website: www.ghana.gov.gh

GUINEA

FOR MAP, SEE PAGE 160

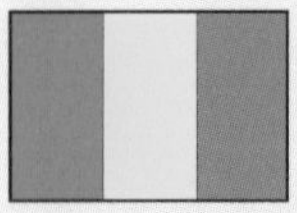

Population: 10,211,437

Ethnic groups: Peuhl 40%, Malinke 30%, Soussou 20%

Principal languages: French (official), many African languages

Chief religions: Muslim 85%, Christian 8%, indigenous beliefs 7%

Area: 94,930 sq mi (245,860 sq km)

Topography: A narrow coastal belt leads to the mountainous middle region, the source of the Gambia, Senegal, and Niger rivers. Upper Guinea, farther inland, is a cooler upland. The southeast is forested.

Capital: Conakry (pop., 1,366,000)

Independence date: October 2, 1958   Government type: republic

Head of state: Pres. Gen. Lansana Conté

Head of government: Prime Min. Cellou Dalein Diallo

Monetary unit: franc

GDP: $9.7 billion (2007 est.)   Per capita GDP: $1,000

Industries: mining, alumina refining, light manufacturing, agricultural processing

Chief crops: rice, coffee, pineapples, palm kernels, cassava, bananas, sweet potatoes

Minerals: bauxite, iron ore, diamonds, gold, uranium

Life expectancy at birth (years): male, 48.5; female, 51.0

Literacy rate: 35.9%

Website: www.state.gov/r/pa/ei/bgn/2824.htm

GUINEA-BISSAU

FOR MAP, SEE PAGE 160

Population: 1,503,182

Ethnic groups: Balanta 30%, Fula 20%, Manjaca 14%, Mandinga 13%, Papel 7%

Principal languages: Portuguese (official), Crioulo, tribal languages

Chief religions: indigenous beliefs 50%, Muslim 45%, Christian 5%

Area: 13,950 sq mi (36,120 sq km)

Topography: A swampy coastal plain covers most of the country; to the east is a low savanna region.

Capital: Bissau (pop., 336,000)   Independence date: September 24, 1973

Head of state: Pres. Joao Bernardo Vieira

Head of government: Prime Min. Aristide Gomes

Monetary unit: CFA franc

GDP: $901.2 million (2007 est.)   Per capita GDP: $600

Industries: agricultural processing, beer, soft drinks

Chief crops: rice, corn, beans, cassava, cashew nuts, peanuts, palm kernels, cotton

Minerals: phosphates, bauxite, petroleum

Life expectancy at birth (years): male, 45.1; female, 48.9

Literacy rate: 34%

Website: www.state.gov/r/p/ei/bgn/2824.htm

KENYA

FOR MAP, SEE PAGE 162

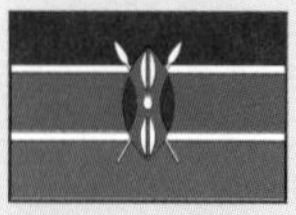

Population: 37,953,838

Ethnic groups: Kikuyu 22%, Luhya 14%, Luo 13%, Kalenjin 12%, Kamba 11%, Kisii 6%, Meru 6%

Principal languages: English, Swahili (both official); numerous indigenous languages

Chief religions: Protestant 45%, Roman Catholic 33%, indigenous beliefs 10%, Muslim 10%

Area: 224,960 sq mi (582,650 sq km)

Topography: The northern three-fifths of Kenya is arid. To the south, there are a low coastal area and a plateau varying from 3,000 to 10,000 ft (900 to 3,000 m). The Great Rift Valley enters the country north to south, flanked by high mountains.

Typical door of a residence on the island of Lamu, Kenya

Capital: Nairobi (pop., 2,575,000)

Independence date: December 12, 1963   Government type: republic

Head of state: Pres. Mwai Kibaki

Head of government: Prime Min. Raila Amolo Odinga

Monetary unit: shilling

GDP: $57.6 billion (2007 est.)   Per capita GDP: $1,600

Industries: small-scale consumer goods, agricultural processing, oil refining, cement, tourism

Chief crops: coffee, tea, corn, wheat, sugarcane, fruit, vegetables

Minerals: gold, limestone, soda ash, salt barites, rubies, fluorspar, garnets

Life expectancy at birth (years): male, 44.8; female, 45.1

Literacy rate: 78.1%

Website: www.kenyaembassy.com

LESOTHO

FOR MAP, SEE PAGE 164

Population: 2,128,180

Ethnic groups: Sotho 99%

Principal languages: Sesotho, English (both official); Zulu, Xhosa

Chief religions: Christian 80%, indigenous beliefs 20%

Area: 11,720 sq mi (30,350 sq km)

Topography: Lesotho is landlocked and mountainous, with altitudes from 5,000 to 11,000 ft (1,500 to 3,300 m).

Capital: Maseru (pop., 170,000)   Independence date: October 4, 1966

Government type: modified constitutional monarchy

Head of state: King Letsie III

Head of government: Prime Min. Pakalitha Mosisili

Monetary unit: loti

GDP: $3.1 billion (2007 est.)   Per capita GDP: $1,500

Industries: food, beverages, textiles, apparel assembly, handicrafts, construction, tourism

Chief crops: corn, wheat, pulses, sorghum, barley

Minerals: diamonds

Life expectancy at birth (years): male, 36.8; female, 36.8

Literacy rate: 83%

Website: www.lesotho.gov.ls

LIBERIA

For map, see page 160

Population: 3,334,587

Ethnic groups: Kpelle, Bassa, Dey, and other tribes 95%; Americo-Liberians 2.5%, Caribbean 2.5%

Principal languages: English (official), Mande, West Atlantic, and Kwa languages

Chief religions: indigenous beliefs 40%, Christian 40%, Muslim 20%

Area: 43,000 sq mi (111,370 sq km)

Topography: Marshy Atlantic coastline rises to low mountains and plateaus in the forested interior; six major rivers flow in parallel courses to the ocean.

Capital: Monrovia (pop., 572,000)

Independence date: July 26, 1847   Government type: republic

Head of state and government: Pres. Ellen Johnson-Sirleaf

Monetary unit: Liberian dollar (LDR)

GDP: $1.5 billion (2007 est.)   Per capita GDP: $500

Industries: rubber processing, palm oil processing, timber, diamonds

Chief crops: rubber, coffee, cocoa, rice, cassava, palm oil, sugarcane, bananas

Minerals: iron ore, diamonds, gold

Life expectancy at birth (years): male, 46.9; female, 49.0

Literacy rate: 38.3%

Website: www.state.gov/r/pa/ei/bgn/6628.htm

LIBYA

For map, see page 155

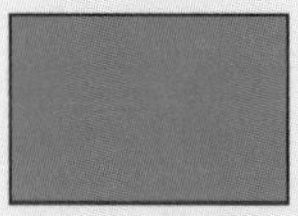

Population: 6,173,579

Ethnic groups: Arab-Berber 97%

Principal languages: Arabic (official), Italian, English

Chief religion: Muslim (official; mostly Sunni) 97%

Area: 679,360 sq mi (1,759,540 sq km)

Topography: Desert and semidesert regions cover 92% of the land, with low mountains in the north, higher mountains in the south, and a narrow coastal zone.

Capital: Tripoli (pop., 2,006,000)

Independence date: December 24, 1951

Government type: Islamic Arabic Socialist "Mass-State"

Head of state and government: Col. Muammar al-Qaddafi

Monetary unit: dinar

GDP: $78.8 billion (2007 est.)   Per capita GDP: $13,100

Industries: petroleum, food processing, textiles, handicrafts, cement

Chief crops: wheat, barley, olives, dates, citrus, vegetables, peanuts, soybeans

Minerals: petroleum, natural gas, gypsum

Life expectancy at birth (years): male, 74.1; female, 78.6

Literacy rate: 76.2%

Website: www.libya–un.org

MADAGASCAR

For map, see page 165

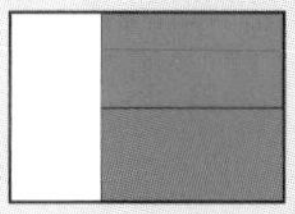

Population: 20,042,551

Ethnic groups: Mainly Malagasy (Indonesian-African); also Cotiers, French, Indian, Chinese

Principal languages: Malagasy, French (both official)

Chief religions: indigenous beliefs 52%, Christian 41%, Muslim 7%

Area: 226,660 sq mi (587,040 sq km)

Topography: Madagascar has a humid coastal strip in the east, fertile valleys in the mountainous center plateau region, and a wider coastal strip in the west.

Capital: Antananarivo (pop., 1,678,000)

Independence date: June 26, 1960   Government type: republic

Head of state: Pres. Marc Ravalomanana

Head of government: Prime Min. Jacques Sylla

Monetary unit: Malagasy franc

GDP: $20 billion (2007 est.)   Per capita GDP: $1,000

Industries: meat processing, soap, breweries, tanneries, sugar, textiles, glassware, cement, automobile assembly, paper, petroleum, tourism

Chief crops: coffee, vanilla, sugarcane, cloves, cocoa, rice, cassava, beans, bananas, peanuts

Minerals: graphite, chromite, coal, bauxite, salt, quartz, tar sands, semiprecious stones, mica

Life expectancy at birth (years): male, 54.2; female, 59.0

Literacy rate: 80%

Website: www.state.gov/r/pa/ei/bgn/5460.htm

MALAWI

For map, see page 163

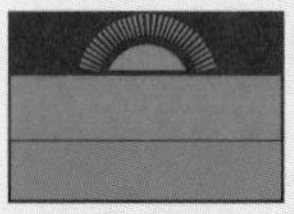

Population: 13,931,831

Ethnic groups: Chewa, Nyanja, Tumbuka, Yao, Lomwe, Sena, Tonga, Ngoni, Ngonde

Principal languages: Chichewa, English (both official); several African languages

Chief religions: Protestant 55%, Roman Catholic 20%, Muslim 20%

Area: 45,750 sq mi (118,480 sq km)

Topography: Malawi stretches 560 mi (900 m) north to south along Lake Malawi (Lake Nyasa), most of which belongs to Malawi. High plateaus and mountains line the Rift Valley the length of the nation.

Capital: Lilongwe (pop., 587,000)   Independence date: July 6, 1964

Government type: republic

Head of state and government: Pres. Bingu wa Mutharikai

Monetary unit: kwacha

GDP: $10.5 billion (2007 est.)   Per capita GDP: $800

Industries: tobacco, tea, sugar, sawmill products, cement, consumer goods

Chief crops: tobacco, sugarcane, cotton, tea, corn, potatoes, cassava, sorghum, pulses

Minerals: limestone, uranium, coal, and bauxite

Life expectancy at birth (years): male, 37.1; female, 37.9

Literacy rate: 58%

Website: www.malawi.gov.mw

MALI

For map, see page 154

Population: 12,324,029

Ethnic groups: Mande 50% (Bambara, Malinke, Soninke), Peul 17%, Voltaic 12%, Tuareg and Moor 10%, Songhai 6%

Principal languages: French (official), Bambara and other African languages

Chief religions: Muslim 90%, indigenous beliefs 9%

Area: 480,000 sq mi (1,240,000 sq km)

Topography: A landlocked grassy plain in the upper basins of the Senegal and Niger rivers, extending north into the Sahara.

Capital: Bamako (pop., 1,240,000)

Independence date: September 22, 1960   **Government type:** republic

Head of state: Pres. Amadou Toumani Touré

Head of government: Prime Min. Oumane Issoufi Maiga

Monetary unit: CFA franc

GDP: $14.2 billion (2007 est.)   **Per capita GDP:** $1,200

Industries: food processing, construction, gold mining

Chief crops: cotton, millet, rice, corn, vegetables, peanuts

Minerals: gold, phosphates, kaolin, salt, limestone, uranium

Life expectancy at birth (years): male, 44.7; female, 45.9

Literacy rate: 38%

Website: www.maliembassy.us

MAURITANIA

For map, see page 154

Population: 3,364,940

Ethnic groups: mixed Maur/black 40%, Maur 30%, black 30%

Principal languages: Hassaniya Arabic, Wolof (both official); Fulani, Pulaar, Soninke (all national); French

Chief religion: predominantly Muslim (official)

Area: 398,000 sq mi (1,030,700 sq km)

Topography: The fertile Senegal River valley in the south gives way to a wide central region of sandy plains and scrub trees. The north is arid and extends into the Sahara.

Capital: Nouakchott (pop., 600,000)

Independence date: November 28, 1960 **Government type:** Islamic republic

Head of state: Pres. Sidi Ould Cheikh Abdallahi

Head of government: Prime Min. Zeine Ould Zeidane

Monetary unit: ouguiya

GDP: $5.8 billion (2007 est.)   **Per capita GDP:** $1,800

Industries: fish processing, mining

Chief crops: dates, millet, sorghum, rice, corn, dates

Minerals: iron ore, gypsum, copper, phosphate, diamonds, gold, oil

Life expectancy at birth (years): male, 50.2; female, 54.6

Literacy rate: 41.2%

Website: www.ambarim-dc.org

MAURITIUS

For map, see page 165

Population: 1,260,781

Ethnic groups: Indo-Mauritian 68%, Creole 27%, Sino-Mauritian 3%, Franco-Mauritian 2%

Principal languages: English (official), Creole, French, Hindi, Urdu, Hakka, Bhojpuri

Chief religions: Hindu 52%, Christian 28%, Muslim 17%

Area: 720 sq mi (1,860 sq km)

Topography: Mauritius is a volcanic island nearly surrounded by coral reefs. A central plateau is encircled by mountain peaks.

Capital: Port Louis (pop., 143,000)

Independence date: March 12, 1968   **Government type:** republic

Head of state: Pres. Anerood Jugnauth

Head of government: Prime Min. Navin Ramgoolan

Monetary unit: Mauritian rupee

GDP: $14.9 billion (2007 est.)   **Per capita GDP:** $11,900

Industries: food processing, textiles, clothing, chemicals, metal products, transport equipment, nonelectrical machinery, tourism

Chief crops: sugarcane, tea, corn, potatoes, bananas, pulses

Life expectancy at birth (years): male, 68.1; female, 76.1

Literacy rate: 82.9%

Website: www.gov.mut

MOROCCO

For map, see page 156

Population: 34,272,968

Ethnic groups: Arab-Berber 99%

Principal languages: Arabic (official), Berber dialects, French, Spanish, English

Chief religion: Muslim (official) 99%

Area: 172,410 sq mi (446,550 sq km)

Topography: Morocco consists of five natural regions: mountain ranges (Riff in the north, Middle Atlas, Upper Atlas, and Anti-Atlas); rich plains in the west; alluvial plains in the southwest; well-cultivated plateaus in the center; and a pre-Sahara arid zone extending from the southeast.

Capital: Rabat (pop., 1,759,000)   **Independence date:** March 2, 1956

Government type: constitutional monarchy

Head of state: King Mohammed VI

Head of government: Prime Min. Driss Jettou

Monetary unit: dirham

GDP: $127 billion (2007 est.)   **Per capita GDP:** $3,800

Industries: mining, food processing, leather goods, textiles, construction, tourism

Chief crops: barley, wheat, citrus, wine, vegetables, olives

Minerals: phosphates, iron ore, manganese, lead, zinc

Life expectancy at birth (years): male, 68.1; female, 72.7

Literacy rate: 43.7%

Website: www.mincom.gov.ma

Casbah, Ait Ben Haddou, Morocco

MOZAMBIQUE

FOR MAP, SEE PAGE 163

Population: 21,284,701

Ethnic groups: Shangaan, Chokwe, Manyika, Sena, Makua

Principal languages: Portuguese (official) and dialects, English

Chief religions: indigenous beliefs 50%, Christian 30%, Muslim 20%

Area: 309,500 sq mi (801,590 sq km)

Topography: Coastal lowlands make up nearly half the country, with plateaus rising in steps to the mountains along the western border.

Capital: Maputo (pop., 1,221,000)

Independence date: June 25, 1975   **Government type:** republic

Head of state: Pres. Armando Guebuza

Head of government: Prime Min. Luisa Diogo

Monetary unit: metical

GDP: $17.8 billion (2007 est.)   **Per capita GDP:** $900

Industries: food, beverages, chemicals, petroleum products, textiles, cement, glass, asbestos, tobacco

Chief crops: cotton, cashew nuts, sugarcane, tea, cassava, corn, coconuts, sisal, citrus and tropical fruits

Minerals: coal, titanium, natural gas, tantalum, graphite

Life expectancy at birth (years): male, 37.8; female, 36.3

Literacy rate: 42.3%

Website: www.embamoc-usa.org

NAMIBIA

FOR MAP, SEE PAGE 163

Population: 2,063,927

Ethnic groups: Ovambo 50%, Kavangos 9%, Herero 7%, Damara 7%, white 6%, mixed 7%

Principal languages: English (official), Afrikaans, German, Oshivambo, Herero, Nama

Chief religions: Lutheran 50%, other Christian 30%, indigenous beliefs 10-20%

Area: 318,700 sq mi (825,420 sq km)

Topography: Three distinct regions include the Namib Desert along the Atlantic coast, a mountainous central plateau with woodland savanna, and the Kalahari Desert in the east. True forests are found in the northeast. There are four rivers, but little other surface water.

Capital: Windhoek (pop., 237,000)

Independence date: March 21, 1990

Government type: republic

Head of state: Pres. Hifikepunye Pohamba

Head of government: Prime Min. Nahas Angula

Monetary unit: Namibia dollar

GDP: $10.7 billion (2007 est.)

Per capita GDP: $5,200

Elephants on the savanna at dawn

Industries: meatpacking, fish processing, dairy products, mining

Chief crops: millet, sorghum, peanuts

Minerals: diamonds, copper, uranium, gold, lead, tin, lithium, cadmium, zinc, salt, vanadium, natural gas

Life expectancy at birth (years): male, 42.4; female, 38.6

Literacy rate: 38%

Website: www.namibianembassyusa.org

NIGER

FOR MAP, SEE PAGE 154

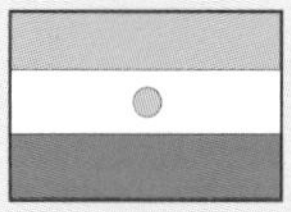

Population: 13,272,679

Ethnic groups: Hausa 56%, Djerma 22%, Fula 9%, Tuareg 8%, Beri Beri (Kanouri) 4%

Principal languages: French (official); Hausa, Djerma, Fulani (all national)

Chief religion: Muslim 80%

Area: 489,000 sq mi (1,267,000 sq km)

Topography: Mostly arid desert and mountains. A narrow savanna in the south and the Niger River basin in the southwest contain most of the population.

Capital: Niamey (pop., 890,000)

Independence date: August 3, 1960   **Government type:** republic

Head of state: Pres. Tandja Mamadou

Head of government: Prime Min. Hama Amadou

Monetary unit: CFA franc

GDP: $9 billion (2007 est.)   **Per capita GDP:** $700

Industries: mining, cement, brick, textiles, food processing, chemicals

Chief crops: cowpeas, cotton, peanuts, millet, sorghum, cassava, rice

Minerals: uranium, coal, iron ore, tin, phosphates, gold, petroleum

Life expectancy at birth (years): male, 42.4; female, 42.0

Literacy rate: 15.3%

Website: www.nigerembassyusa.org

NIGERIA

FOR MAP, SEE PAGE 154

Population: 138,283,240

Ethnic groups: more than 250; Hausa and Fulani 29%, Yoruba 21%, Igbo (Ibo) 18%, Ijaw 10%

Principal languages: English (official), Hausa, Yoruba, Igbo (Ibo), Fulani

Chief religions: Muslim 50%, Christian 40%, indigenous beliefs 10%

Area: 356,670 sq mi (923,770 sq km)

Topography: Four east-to-west regions divide Nigeria: a coastal mangrove swamp 10 to 60 mi (16 to 100 km) wide, a tropical rain forest 50 to 100 mi (80 to 160 km) wide, a plateau of savanna and open woodland, and semidesert in the north.

Capital: Abuja (pop., 452,000)

Independence date: October 1, 1960   **Government type:** republic

Head of state and government: Pres. Umaru Musa Yar'Adua

Monetary unit: naira

GDP: $294.8 billion (2007 est.)   **Per capita GDP:** $2,200

Industries: petroleum extraction, mining, agricultural processing, cotton, rubber, wood, hides and skins, textiles, cement and other construction materials, footwear, chemicals, fertilizer, printing, ceramics, steel

Chief crops: cocoa, peanuts, palm oil, corn, rice, sorghum, millet, cassava, yams

Minerals: natural gas, petroleum, tin, columbite, iron ore, coal, limestone, lead, zinc

Life expectancy at birth (years): male, 50.9; female, 51.1

Literacy rate: 57.1%

Website: www.nigeriaembassyusa.org

Nation Facts and Figures

RWANDA

FOR MAP, SEE PAGE 162

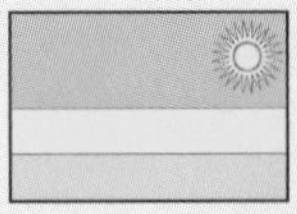

Population: 10,186,063

Ethnic groups: Hutu 84%, Tutsi 15%, Twa (Pygmy) 1%

Principal languages: Kinyarwanda, French, English (all official); Swahili

Chief religions: Roman Catholic 57%, Protestant 26%, Adventist 11%, Muslim 5%

Area: 10,170 sq mi (26,340 sq km)

Topography: Grassy uplands and hills cover most of the country, with a chain of volcanoes in the northwest. The source of the Nile River has been located in the headwaters of the Kagera (Akagera) River, southwest of Kigali.

Capital: Kigali (pop., 656,000)

Independence date: July 1, 1962   Government type: republic

Head of state: Pres. Paul Kagame

Head of government: Prime Min. Bernard Makuza

Monetary unit: franc

GDP: $8.6 billion (2007 est.)   Per capita GDP: $1,000

Industries: cement, agricultural products, small-scale beverages, soap, furniture, shoes, plastic goods, textiles, cigarettes

Chief crops: coffee, tea, pyrethrum, bananas, beans, sorghum, potatoes

Minerals: gold, tin ore, tungsten ore, methane

Life expectancy at birth (years): male, 38.4; female, 40.0

Literacy rate: 48%

Website: www.gov.rw

SÃO TOMÉ AND PRÍNCIPE

FOR MAP, SEE PAGE 154

Population: 205,901

Ethnic groups: mestizo, black, Portuguese

Principal languages: Portuguese (official), Creole, Fang

Chief religions: predominantly Roman Catholic

Area: 390 sq mi (1,000 sq km)

Topography: São Tomé and Príncipe islands, part of an extinct volcano chain, are both covered by lush forests and croplands.

Capital: São Tomé (pop., 54,000)   Independence date: July 12, 1975

Government type: republic

Head of state: Pres. Fradique Melo de Menezes

Head of government: Prime Min. Tomé Vera Cruz

Monetary unit: dobra

GDP: $278 million (2006 est.)   Per capita GDP: $1,200

Industries: light construction, textiles, soap, beer, fish processing, timber

Chief crops: cocoa, coconuts, palm kernels, copra, cinnamon, pepper, coffee, bananas, papayas, beans

Life expectancy at birth (years): male, 65.1; female, 68.2

Literacy rate: 79.3%

Website: www.saotome.st

SENEGAL

FOR MAP, SEE PAGE 160

Population: 12,853,259

Ethnic groups: Wolof 43%, Pular 24%, Serer 15%, Jola 4%, Mandinka 3%, Soninke 1%

Principal languages: French (official), Wolof, Pulaar, Jola, Mandinka

Chief religions: Muslim 94%, Christian 5%

Area: 75,750 sq mi (196,190 sq km)

Water-loving hippopotamuses

Topography: Low rolling plains cover most of Senegal, rising somewhat in the southeast. Swamp and jungles are in the southwest.

Capital: Dakar (pop., 2,167,000)

Independence date: April 4, 1960   Government type: republic

Head of state: Pres. Abdoulaye Wade

Head of government: Prime Min. Macky Sall

Monetary unit: CFA franc

GDP: $20.6 billion (2007 est.)   Per capita GDP: $1,700

Industries: agricultural and fish processing, mining, fertilizer production, petroleum refining, construction materials

Chief crops: peanuts, millet, corn, sorghum, rice, cotton, tomatoes, green vegetables

Minerals: phosphates, iron ore

Life expectancy at birth (years): male, 54.9; female, 58.2

Literacy rate: 39.1%

Website: www.senegalembassy.uk

SEYCHELLES

FOR MAP, SEE PAGE 81

Population: 82,247

Ethnic groups: mainly Seychellois (mix of French, African, and Asian)

Principal languages: English, French, Creole (all official)

Chief religions: Roman Catholic 87%, Anglican 7%

Area: 180 sq mi (460 sq km)

Topography: A group of 86 islands, about half of them composed of coral, the other half granite, the latter predominantly mountainous.

Capital: Victoria (pop., 25,000)

Independence date: June 29, 1976

Government type: republic

Head of state and government: Pres. James Michel

Monetary unit: rupee

GDP: $1.7 billion (2007 est.)

Per capita GDP: $18,400

A Seychelles beach

Industries: fishing, tourism, coconut and vanilla processing, rope, boat building, printing, furniture, beverages

Chief crops: coconuts, cinnamon, vanilla, sweet potatoes, cassava, bananas

Life expectancy at birth (years): male, 66.1; female, 77.1

Literacy rate: 58%

Website: www.seychelles.com

SIERRA LEONE

FOR MAP, SEE PAGE 160

Population: 6,286,617

Ethnic groups: Temne 30%, Mende 30%, other tribes 30%; Creole 10%

Principal languages: English (official), Mende in the south, Temne in the north, Krio (English Creole)

Chief religions: Muslim 60%, indigenous beliefs 30%, Christian 10%

Area: 27,700 sq mi (71,740 sq km)

Topography: The heavily indented, 210-mi (340-km) coastline has mangrove swamps. Behind are wooded hills, rising to a plateau and mountains in the east.

Capital: Freetown (pop., 921,000)

Independence date: April 27, 1961　**Government type:** republic

Head of state and government: Pres. Ernest Bai Koroma

Monetary unit: leone

GDP: $4.9 billion (2007 est.)　**Per capita GDP:** $800

Industries: mining, small-scale manufacturing, petroleum refining

Chief crops: rice, coffee, cocoa, palm kernels, palm oil, peanuts

Minerals: diamonds, titanium ore, bauxite, iron ore, gold, chromite

Life expectancy at birth (years): male, 40.2; female, 45.2

Literacy rate: 31.4%

Website: www.embassyofsierraleone.org

Rural life in Sierra Leone

SOMALIA

FOR MAP, SEE PAGE 155

Population: 9,379,907

Ethnic groups: Somali 85%, Bantu and other 15%

Principal languages: Somali, Arabic (both official); Italian, English

Chief religion: Sunni Muslim (official)

Area: 246,200 sq mi (637,660 sq km)

Topography: The coastline extends for 1,700 mi (2,700 km). Hills cover the north; the center and south are flat.

Capital: Mogadishu (pop., 1,175,000)

Independence date: July 1, 1960　**Government type:** in transition

Head of state: Pres. Abdullahi Yusuf Ahmed

Head of government: Prime Min. Nur Hassan Hussein

Monetary unit: shilling

GDP: $5.6 billion (2007 est.)　**Per capita GDP:** $600

Industries: sugar refining, textiles, wireless communication

Chief crops: bananas, sorghum, corn, coconuts, rice, sugarcane, mangoes, sesame seeds, beans

Minerals: uranium and largely unexploited reserves of iron ore, tin, gypsum, bauxite, copper, salt, natural gas, likely oil reserves

Life expectancy at birth (years): male, 46.0; female, 49.5

Literacy rate: 37.8%　**Website:** www.state.gov/r/pa/ei/bgn/2863.htm

SOUTH AFRICA

FOR MAP, SEE PAGE 163

Population: 43,786,115

Ethnic groups: black 75%, white 14%, mixed 8%, Indian 3%

Principal languages: Afrikaans, English, Ndebele, Pedi, Sotho, Swazi, Tsonga, Tswana, Venda, Xhosa, Zulu (all official)

Chief religions: Christian 68%, indigenous beliefs and animist 29%

Area: 471,010 sq mi (1,219,910 sq km)

Topography: The large interior plateau reaches close to the country's 2,700-mi (4,300-km) coastline. There are few major rivers or lakes; rainfall is sparse in the west, more plentiful in the east.

Capitals: Pretoria (administrative) (pop., 1,590,000), Cape Town (legislative) (pop., 2,993,000), Bloemfontein (judicial) (pop., 1,590,000)

Independence date: May 31, 1910

Government type: republic

Head of state and government: Pres. Thabo Mvuyelwa Mbeki

Monetary unit: rand

GDP: $467.6 billion (2007 est.)　**Per capita GDP:** $10,600

Industries: mining, automobile assembly, metalworking, machinery, textile, iron and steel, chemicals, fertilizer, foodstuffs

Chief crops: corn, wheat, sugarcane, fruits, vegetables

Minerals: gold, chromium, antimony, coal, iron ore, manganese, nickel, phosphates, tin, uranium, gem diamonds, platinum, copper, vanadium, salt, natural gas

Diamond mining—a key source of South Africa's wealth

Life expectancy at birth (years): male, 44.0; female, 44.0

Literacy rate: 85%

Website: www.gov.za

Cape Town, South Africa

SUDAN

FOR MAP, SEE PAGE 155

Population: 40,218,455

Ethnic groups: black 52%, Arab 39%, Beja 6%

Principal languages: Arabic (official), Nubian, Ta Bedawie; Nilotic, Sudanic dialects; English

Chief religions: Sunni Muslim 70%, indigenous beliefs 25%, Christian 5%

Area: 967,500 sq mi (2,505,810 sq km)

Topography: The north consists of the Libyan Desert in the west and the mountainous Nubia Desert in the east, with the narrow Nile valley between. The center contains large, fertile, rainy areas with fields, pasture, and forest. The south has rich soil and heavy rain.

Capital: Khartoum (pop., 4,286,000)

Independence date: January 1, 1956

Government type: republic with strong military influence

Head of state and government: Pres. Gen. Omar Hassan Ahmad Al-Bashir

Monetary unit: dinar (SDD)

GDP: $107.8 billion (2007 est.)

Per capita GDP: $2,500

Industries: oil, cotton ginning, textiles, cement, edible oils, sugar, soap distilling, shoes, petroleum refining, pharmaceuticals, armaments, automobile/light truck assembly

Chief crops: cotton, groundnuts, sorghum, millet, wheat, gum arabic, sugarcane, cassava, mangos, papaya, bananas, sweet potatoes, sesame

Minerals: petroleum, iron ore, copper, chromium ore, zinc, tungsten, mica, silver, gold

Life expectancy at birth (years): male, 57.0; female, 59.4

Literacy rate: 46.1%

Website: www.sudanembassy.org

SWAZILAND

FOR MAP, SEE PAGE 165

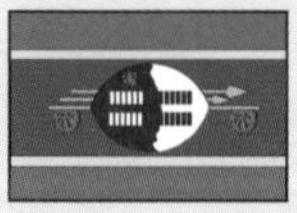

Population: 1,128,814

Ethnic groups: African 97%, European 3%

Principal languages: English, siSwati (both official)

Chief religions: Christian 60%, Muslim 10%, indigenous and other 30%

Area: 6,700 sq mi (17,360 sq km)

Topography: The country descends from W to E in broad belts, becoming more arid in the low veld region, then rising to a plateau in the E.

Capitals: Mbabane (administrative) (pop., 70,000)

Independence date: September 6, 1968

Government type: constitutional monarchy

Head of state: King Mswati III

Head of government: Prime Min. Absalom Themba Dlamini

Monetary unit: lilangeni

GDP: $5.4 billion (2007 est.)

Per capita GDP: $4,800

Industries: mining, wood pulp, sugar, soft drink concentrates, textile and apparel

Chief crops: sugarcane, cotton, corn, tobacco, rice, citrus, pineapples, sorghum, peanuts

Minerals: asbestos, coal, clay, cassiterite, gold, diamonds, quarry stone, talc

Life expectancy at birth (years): male, 39.1; female, 35.9

Literacy rate: 78.3%

Website: www.gov.sz

TANZANIA

FOR MAP, SEE PAGE 162

Population: 40,213,162

Ethnic groups: mainland: Bantu 95%; Zanzibar: Arab, African, mixed

Principal languages: Swahili, English (both official); Arabic, many local languages

Chief religions: Christian 30%, Muslim 35%, indigenous beliefs 35%; Zanzibar is 99% Muslim

Area: 364,900 sq mi (945,090 sq km)

Topography: Hot, arid central plateau, surrounded by the lake region in the west, temperate highlands in the north and south, and the coastal plains. Mt. Kilimanjaro, 19,340 ft (5,895 m), is the highest peak in Africa.

Capital: Dodoma (pop., 155,000)

Independence date: April 26, 1964   **Government type:** republic

Head of state: Pres. Jakaya Mrisho Kikwete

Head of government: Prime Min. Edward Lowassa

Monetary unit: shilling

GDP: $43.5 billion (2007 est.)   **Per capita GDP:** $1,100

Industries: agricultural processing, mining, oil refining, shoes, cement, textiles, wood products, fertilizer, salt

Chief crops: coffee, sisal, tea, cotton, pyrethrum, cashew nuts, tobacco, cloves, corn, wheat, cassava, bananas, fruits, vegetables

Minerals: tin, phosphates, iron ore, coal, diamonds, gemstones, gold, natural gas, nickel

Life expectancy at birth (years): male, 43.2; female, 45.6

Literacy rate: 67.8%

Website: www.tanzania.go.tz/index2E.html

Masai giraffe calf, Serengeti National Park, Tanzania

TOGO

FOR MAP, SEE PAGE 161

Population: 5,858,673

Ethnic groups: 37 African tribes; largest are Ewe, Mina, and Kabre

Principal languages: French (official), Ewe, Mina in the south; Kabye, Dagomba in the north

Chief religions: indigenous beliefs 51%, Christian 29%, Muslim 20%

Area: 21,930 sq mi (56,790 sq km)

Topography: A range of hills running southwest to northeast splits Togo into two savanna plains regions.

Capital: Lomé (pop., 799,000)   **Independence date:** April 27, 1960

Government type: republic

Head of state: Pres. Faure Gnassingbé

Head of government: Prime Min. Edem Kodjo

Monetary unit: CFA franc

GDP: $5.1 billion (2007 est.)   Per capita GDP: $1,600

Industries: mining, agricultural processing, cement, handicrafts, textiles, beverages

Chief crops: coffee, cocoa, cotton, yams, cassava, corn, beans, rice, millet, sorghum

Minerals: phosphates, limestone, marble

Life expectancy at birth (years): male, 51.1; female, 55.1

Literacy rate: 51.7%

Website: www.state.gov/r/pa/ei/bgn/5430.htm

TUNISIA

For map, see page 157

Population: 10,378,140

Ethnic groups: Arab 98%, European 1%, Jewish and other 1%

Principal languages: Arabic (official), French prevalent

Chief religion: Muslim (official; mostly Sunni) 98%

Area: 63,170 sq mi (163,610 sq km)

Topography: The north is wooded and fertile. The central coastal plains are given to grazing and orchards. The south is arid, merging into the Sahara Desert.

Capital: Tunis (pop., 1,996,000)

Independence date: March 20, 1956   Government type: republic

Head of state: Pres. Gen. Zine al-Abidine Ben Ali

Head of government: Prime Min. Mohamed Ghannouchi

Monetary unit: dinar

GDP: $77.2 billion (2007 est.)   Per capita GDP: $7,500

Industries: petroleum, mining, tourism, textiles, footwear, agribusiness, beverages

Chief crops: olives, olive oil, grain, tomatoes, citrus fruit, sugar beets, dates, almonds

Minerals: petroleum, phosphates, iron ore, lead, zinc, salt

Life expectancy at birth (years): male, 73.0; female, 76.4

Literacy rate: 67.8%

Website: www.state.gov/r/pa/ei/bgn/5439.html

UGANDA

For map, see page 162

Population: 31,367,972

Ethnic groups: Baganda 17%, Ankole 8%, Basoga 8%, Iteso 8%, Bakiga 7%; many other groups

Principal languages: English (official), Swahili, Ganda, many Bantu and Nilotic languages, Arabic

Chief religions: Protestant 33%, Roman Catholic 33%, indigenous beliefs 18%, Muslim 16%

Area: 91,140 sq mi (236,040 sq km)

Topography: Most of Uganda is a high plateau 3,000 to 6,000 ft (900 to 1,800 m) high, with the high Ruwenzori range in the west (Mt. Margherita 16,750 ft [5,105 m]) and volcanoes in the southwest; the northeast is arid, and the west and southwest rainy. Lakes Victoria, Edward, and Albert form much of the borders.

Capital: Kampala (pop., 1,246,000)   Independence date: October 9, 1962

Government type: republic   Head of state: Pres. Yoweri Kaguta Museveni

Head of government: Prime Min. Apollo Nsibambi

Monetary unit: shilling

GDP: $31.5 billion (2007 est.)   Per capita GDP: $1,100

Industries: sugar, brewing, tobacco, cotton textiles, cement

Chief crops: coffee, tea, cotton, tobacco, cassava, potatoes, corn, millet, pulses

Minerals: copper, cobalt, limestone, salt

Life expectancy at birth (years): male, 43.8; female, 46.8

Literacy rate: 62.7%   Website: www.ugandaembassy.com

ZAMBIA

For map, see page 163

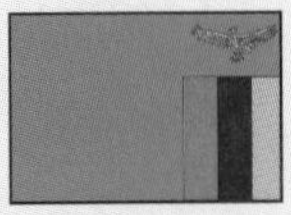

Population: 11,669,534

Ethnic groups: more than 70 groups; largest are Bemba, Tonga, Ngoni, and Lozi

Principal languages: English (official), Bemba, Kaonda, Lozi, Lunda, Luvale, Nyanja, Tonga, 70 others

Chief religions: Christian 50-75%, Hindu and Muslim 24-49%

Area: 290,580 sq mi (752,610 sq km)

Topography: Zambia is mostly high plateau country covered with thick forests and drained by several important rivers, including the Zambezi.

Capital: Lusaka (pop., 1,394,000)

Independence date: October 24, 1964   Government type: republic

Head of state and government: Pres. Levy Patrick Mwanawasa

Monetary unit: kwacha

GDP: $15.9 billion (2007 est.)   Per capita GDP: $1,400

Industries: mining, construction, foodstuffs, beverages, chemicals, textiles, fertilizer

Chief crops: corn, sorghum, rice, peanuts, sunflower seed, vegetables, flowers, tobacco, cotton, sugarcane, cassava

Minerals: copper, cobalt, zinc, lead, coal, emeralds, gold, silver, uranium

Life expectancy at birth (years): male, 35.2; female, 35.2

Literacy rate: 78.9%   Website: www.zana.gov.zm

ZIMBABWE

For map, see page 163

Population: 12,382,920

Ethnic groups: Shona 82%, Ndebele 14%

Principal languages: English (official), Shona, Sindebele, numerous dialects

Chief religions: syncretic (Christian-indigenous mix) 50%, Christian 25%, indigenous beliefs 24%

Area: 150,800 sq mi (390,580 sq km)

Topography: Zimbabwe is high plateau country, rising to mountains on the eastern border, sloping down on the other borders.

Capital: Harare (pop., 1,469,000)

Independence date: April 18, 1980

Government type: republic

Head of state and government: Pres. Robert Mugabe (in dispute)

Monetary unit: Zimbabwe dollar

GDP: $6.2 billion (2007 est.)

Per capita GDP: $500

Industries: mining, steel, wood products, cement, chemicals, fertilizer, clothing and footwear, foodstuffs, beverages

Chief crops: corn, cotton, tobacco, wheat, coffee, sugarcane, peanuts

Minerals: coal, chromium ore, asbestos, gold, nickel, copper, iron ore, vanadium, lithium, tin, platinum group metals

Life expectancy at birth (years): male, 40.1; female, 37.9

Literacy rate: 85%

Website: www.state.gov/r/pa/ei/bgn/5479.htm

Devil's Cataract, Victoria Falls, on the Zambesi River between Zambia and Zimbabwe

ASIA

Asia has three of the five most populous countries in the world. China and India, each with more than 1 billion people, rank number 1 and number 2, respectively. Indonesia, with well over 200 million, is number 4.

AFGHANISTAN

FOR MAP, SEE PAGE 147

Population: 32,738,376

Ethnic groups: Pashtun 44%, Tajik 25%, Hazara 10%, Uzbek 8%

Principal languages: Dari (Afghan Persian), Pashtu (both official); Turkic (including Uzbek, Turkmen); Balochi, Pashai, many others

Chief religions: Muslim (official; Sunni 85%, Shi'a 15%)

Area: 250,000 sq mi (647,500 sq km)

Topography: The country is landlocked and mountainous, much of it over 4,000 ft (1,200 m) above sea level. The Hindu Kush Mountains tower 16,000 ft (4,800 m) above Kabul and reach a height of 25,000 ft (7,600 m) to the east. Trade with Pakistan flows through the 35-mi (56-km) Khyber Pass. There are large desert regions, though mountain rivers produce intermittent fertile valleys.

Capital: Kabul (pop., 2,956,000)

Independence date: August 19, 1919

Government type: transitional administration

Head of state and government: Pres. Hamid Karzai

Monetary unit: afghani

GDP: $35 billion (2007 est.)   **Per capita GDP:** $1,000

Industries: textiles, soap, furniture, shoes, fertilizer, cement, handwoven carpets

Chief crops: wheat, fruits, nuts

Minerals: natural gas, petroleum, coal, copper, chromite, talc, barites, sulfur, lead, zinc, iron ore, salt, precious and semiprecious stones

Life expectancy at birth (years): male, 42.3; female, 42.7

Literacy rate: 36%

Website: www.afghanistanembassy.org

ARMENIA

FOR MAP, SEE PAGE 121

Population: 2,968,586

Ethnic groups: Armenian 93%, Russian 2%

Principal languages: Armenian (official), Russian

Chief religions: Armenian Apostolic 94%, other Christian 4%, Yezidi 2%

Area: 11,500 sq mi (29,800 sq km)

Topography: Mountainous, with many peaks above 10,000 ft (3,000 m).

Capital: Yerevan (pop., 1,079,000)

Independence date: September 21, 1991

Government type: republic

Head of state: Pres. Serzh Sargsyan

Head of government: Prime Min. Tigran Sargsyan

Monetary unit: dram

GDP: $16.8 billion (2007 est.)

Per capita GDP: $5,700

Industries: machine tools, forging-pressing machines, electric motors, tires, knitted wear, footwear, silk fabric, chemicals, trucks, instruments, microelectronics, jewelry, software development, food processing

Chief crops: grapes, vegetables

Minerals: gold, copper, molybdenum, zinc, alumina

Life expectancy at birth (years): male, 67.7; female, 75.4

Literacy rate: 99%

Website: www.gov.am/en

AZERBAIJAN

For map, see page 121

Population: 8,177,717

Ethnic groups: Azeri 90%, Dagestani 3%, Russian 3%, Armenian 2%

Principal languages: Azeri (official), Russian, Armenian

Chief religions: Muslim 93%, Russian Orthodox 3%, Armenian Orthodox 2%

Area: 33,440 sq mi (86,600 sq km)

Topography: The Great Caucasus Mountains in the north and the Karabakh Upland in the west border the Kur-Abas Lowland; climate is arid except in the subtropical southeast.

Capital: Baku (pop., 1,816,000)

Independence date: August 30, 1991   **Government type:** republic

Head of state: Pres. Ilham Aliyev

Head of government: Prime Min. Artur Rasizade

Monetary unit: manat

GDP: $72.2 billion (2007 est.)   **Per capita GDP:** $9,000

Industries: petroleum products, oilfield equipment, steel, iron ore, cement, chemicals, textiles

Chief crops: cotton, grain, rice, grapes, fruit, vegetables, tea, tobacco

Minerals: petroleum, natural gas, iron ore, nonferrous metals, alumina

Life expectancy at birth (years): male, 59.1; female, 67.6

Literacy rate: 97%

Website: www.president.az

BAHRAIN

For map, see page 146

Population: 718,306

Ethnic groups: Arab 73%, Asian 19%, Iranian 8%

Principal languages: Arabic (official), English, Farsi, Urdu

Chief religions: Muslim (official; Shi'a 70%, Sunni 30%)

Area: 240 sq mi (620 sq km)

Topography: Bahrain Island, and several adjacent, smaller islands, are flat, hot, and humid, with little rain.

Capital: Manama (pop., 139,000)   **Independence date:** August 15, 1971

Government type: constitutional monarchy

Head of state: King Hamad bin Isa al-Khalifa

Head of government: Prime Min. Khalifa bin Sulman al-Khalifa

Monetary unit: dinar

GDP: $24.61 billion (2007 est.)   **Per capita GDP:** $34,700

Industries: petroleum processing and refining, aluminum smelting, offshore banking, ship repairing, tourism

Chief crops: fruit, vegetables

Minerals: oil, natural gas

Life expectancy at birth (years): male, 71.5; female, 76.5

Literacy rate: 88.5%

Website: www.bahrain.gov.bh/english/index.asp

BANGLADESH

For map, see page 140

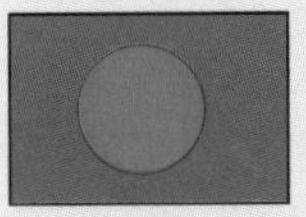

Population: 153,546,901

Ethnic groups: Bengali 98%

Principal languages: Bangla (official, also known as Bengali), English

Chief religions: Muslim (official) 83%, Hindu 16%

Area: 56,000 sq mi (144,000 sq km)

Topography: The country is mostly a low plain cut by the Ganges and Brahmaputra rivers and their delta. The land is alluvial and marshy along the coast, with hills only in the extreme southeast and northeast.

Capital: Dhaka (pop., 11,560,000)

Independence date: December 16, 1971

Government type: parliamentary democracy

Head of state: Pres. Iajuddin Ahmed

Head of government: Prime Min. Khaleda Zia

Monetary unit: taka

GDP: $209.2 billion (2007 est.)   **Per capita GDP:** $1,400

Industries: cotton textiles, jute, garments, tea processing, paper newsprint, cement, chemical fertilizer, light engineering

Chief crops: rice, jute, tea, wheat, sugarcane, potatoes, tobacco, pulses, oilseeds, spices, fruit

Minerals: natural gas, coal

Life expectancy at birth (years): male, 61.8; female, 61.6

Literacy rate: 56%

Website: www.bangladeshgov.com

BHUTAN

For map, see page 143

Population: 2,376,680

Ethnic groups: Bhote 50%, Nepalese 35%, indigenous tribes 15%

Principal languages: Dzongkha (official), Tibetan, Nepalese dialects

Chief religions: Lamaistic Buddhist (official) 75%, Hindu 25%

Area: 18,000 sq mi (47,000 sq km)

Topography: Bhutan is comprised of very high mountains in the north, fertile valleys in the center, and thick forests in the Duar Plain in the south.

Capital: Thimphu (pop., 35,000)

Independence date: August 8, 1949

Government type: monarchy

Head of state and government: King Jigme Singye Wangchuk

Head of government: Prime Min. Lyonpo Sangay Ngedup

Monetary unit: ngultrum

GDP: $3.5 billion (2006 est.)   **Per capita GDP:** $1,400

Industries: cement, wood products, processed fruits, alcoholic beverages

Chief crops: rice, corn, root crops, citrus, foodgrains

Minerals: gypsum, calcium carbide

Life expectancy at birth (years): male, 54.3; female, 53.7

Literacy rate: 42.2%

Website: www.kingdomofbhutan.com

BRUNEI

For map, see page 138

Population: 381,371

Ethnic groups: Malay 67%, Chinese 15%, indigenous 6%

Principal languages: Malay (official), English, Chinese

Chief religions: Muslim (official) 67%; Buddhist 13%; Christian 10%; indigenous beliefs, other 10%

Area: 2,230 sq mi (5,770 sq km)

Topography: Brunei has a narrow coastal plain, with mountains in the east, hilly lowlands in the west. There are swamps in the west and northeast.

Brunei *(continued)*

Capital: Bandar Seri Begawan (pop., 61,000)

Independence date: January 1, 1984

Government type: independent sultanate

Head of state and government: Sultan Sir Muda Hassanal Bolkiah Mu'izzadin Waddaulah

Monetary unit: Brunei dollar

GDP: $9.6 billion (2006 est.)   **Per capita GDP:** $33,600

Industries: petroleum, petroleum refining, liquefied natural gas, construction

Chief crops: rice, vegetables, fruits

Minerals: petroleum, natural gas

Life expectancy at birth (years): male, 71.9; female, 76.8

Literacy rate: 88.2%   **Website:** www.gov.bn

Li River and "pinnacles," China

CAMBODIA

FOR MAP, SEE PAGE 136

Population: 14,241,640

Ethnic groups: Khmer 90%, Vietnamese 5%, Chinese 1%

Principal languages: Khmer (official), French, English

Chief religion: Theravada Buddhist (official) 95%

Area: 69,900 sq mi (181,040 sq km)

Topography: The central area, formed by the Mekong River basin and Tonle Sap lake, is level. Hills and mountains are in the southeast, a long escarpment separates the country from Thailand in the northwest. 76% of the area is forested.

Capital: Phnom Penh (pop., 1,157,000)

Independence date: November 9, 1953

Government type: constitutional monarchy

Head of state: King Norodom Sihanouk

Head of government: Prime Min. Hun Sen

Monetary unit: riel

GDP: $25.8 billion (2007 est.)   **Per capita GDP:** $1,800

Industries: tourism, garments, rice milling, fishing, wood and wood products, rubber, cement, gem mining, textiles

Chief crops: rice, rubber, corn, vegetables

Minerals: gemstones, iron ore, manganese, phosphates

Life expectancy at birth (years): male, 55.7; female, 61.2

Literacy rate: 35%

Website: www.cambodia.gov.kh

Angkor Wat ruins, Cambodia

CHINA

FOR MAP, SEE PAGE 128

(Statistical data do not include Hong Kong or Macau.)

Population: 1,330,044,605

Ethnic groups: 56 groups; Han 92%; also Zhuang, Manchu, Hui, Miao, Uygur, Yi, Tujia, Tong, Tibetan, Mongol, et al.

Principal languages: Mandarin (official), Yue (Cantonese), Wu (Shanghaiese), Minbei (Fuzhou), Minnan (Hokkien-Taiwanese), Xiang, Gan, Hakka, minority languages

Chief religions: officially atheist; Buddhism, Taoism; some Muslims, Christians

Area: 3,705,410 sq mi (9,596,960 sq km)

The Forbidden City (former imperial residence), Beijing, China

Topography: Two-thirds of China's vast territory is mountainous or desert; only one-tenth is cultivated. Rolling topography rises to high elevations in the Daxinganlingshanmai separating Manchuria and Mongolia in the north; the Tien Shan in Xinjiang; and the Himalayan range and Kunlunshanmai in the southwest and in Tibet. Length is 1,860 mi (3,000 km) from north to south, width east to west is more than 2,000 mi (3,200 km). The eastern half of China is one of the world's best-watered lands. Three great river systems, the Chang (Yangtze), Huang (Yellow), and Xi, provide water for vast farmlands.

Capital: Beijing (pop., 10,848,000)

Independence date: 221 BC

Government type: Communist Party-led state

Head of state: Pres. Hu Jintao

Head of government: Premier Wen Jiabao   **Monetary unit:** yuan (renminbi)

GDP: $7,043 billion (2007 est.)   **Per capita GDP:** $5,300

Industries: iron and steel, coal, machine building, armaments, textiles and apparel, petroleum, cement, chemical fertilizers, footwear, toys, food processing, automobiles, consumer electronics, telecommunications

Chief crops: rice, wheat, potatoes, sorghum, peanuts, tea, millet, barley, cotton, oilseed

Minerals: coal, iron ore, petroleum, natural gas, mercury, tin, tungsten, antimony, manganese, molybdenum, vanadium, magnetite, aluminum, lead, zinc, uranium

Life expectancy at birth (years): male, 70.4; female, 73.7

Literacy rate: 81.5%

Website: www.china-embassy.org

HONG KONG, formerly a British dependency, in 1997 became a special administrative region of China, which agreed to allow the territory to keep its capitalist system for 50 years. Hong Kong is a major center for trade and banking and has a per capita GDP of $42,000 (2007 est.), among the highest in the world. Population, 7,018,636 including fewer than 20,000 British; area, 422 sq mi (1,090 sq km); chief executive, Donald Tsang.

MACAU, formerly under Portuguese control, reverted to China in 1999, again with a guarantee of noninterference in its way of life and capitalist system for 50 years. The per capita GDP is $28,400 (2006). Population, 460,823; area, 6 sq mi; chief executive, Ho Hau-wah (Edmund).

CYPRUS

FOR MAP, SEE PAGE 149

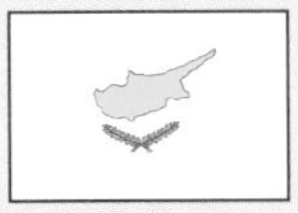

Population: 792,604

Ethnic groups: Greek 85%, Turkish 12%

Principal languages: Greek, Turkish (both official); English

Chief religions: Greek Orthodox 78%, Muslim 18%

Area: 3,570 sq mi (9,250 sq km)

Topography: Two mountain ranges run east to west, separated by a wide, fertile plain.

Capital: Nicosia (pop., 205,000)

Independence date: August 16, 1960

Government type: republic

Head of state and government: Pres. Demetris Christofias

Monetary unit: euro

GDP: Greek Cypriot area, $21.4 billion (2007 est.); Turkish Cypriot area, $4.5 billion (2007 est.)

Per capita GDP: Greek Cypriot area, $27,100; Turkish Cypriot area, $7,100

Industries: food, beverages, textiles, chemicals, metal products, tourism, wood products

Chief crops: potatoes, citrus, vegetables, barley, grapes, olives, vegetables

Minerals: copper, pyrites, asbestos, gypsum, salt, marble, clay earth pigment

Life expectancy at birth (years): male, 75.1; female, 79.9

Literacy rate: 97%

Website: www.cyprusembassy.net

The TURKISH REPUBLIC OF NORTHERN CYPRUS declared independence in 1983 but failed to gain international recognition. Area, 1,295 sq mi (3,354 sq km); population, 87,800; capital, Lefkosa (Nicosia); president, Mehmet Ali Talat.

EAST TIMOR

FOR MAP, SEE PAGE 139

Population: 1,107,432

Ethnic groups: Austronesian; Papuan

Principal languages: Tetum, Portuguese (both official); Indonesian, English, other native languages

Chief religions: Roman Catholic 90%, Muslim 4%, Protestant 3%

Area: 5,740 sq mi (14,880 sq km)

Topography: Terrain is rugged, rising to 9,721 ft (2,963 m) at Mt. Ramelau.

Capital: Dili (pop., 49,000)

Independence date: May 20, 2002

Government type: republic

Head of state: Pres. José Ramos-Horta

Head of government: Prime Min. Kay Rala Xanana Gusmao

Monetary unit: U.S. dollar and Indonesian rupiah

GDP: $2.2 billion (2007 est.)   Per capita GDP: $2,000

Industries: printing, soap manufacturing, handicrafts, woven cloth

Chief crops: coffee, rice, maize, cassava, sweet potatoes, soybeans, cabbage, mangoes, bananas, vanilla

Minerals: gold, petroleum, natural gas, manganese, marble

Life expectancy at birth (years): male, 63.3; female, 67.9

Literacy rate: 48%

Website: www.timor-leste.gov.tl

GEORGIA

FOR MAP, SEE PAGE 121

Population: 4,630,841

Ethnic groups: Georgian 70%, Armenian 8%, Russian 6%, Azeri 6%

Principal languages: Georgian (official), Russian, Armenian, Azeri, Abkhaz (official in Abkhazia)

Chief religions: Georgian Orthodox 65%, Muslim 11%, Russian Orthodox 10%, Armenian Apostolic 8%

Area: 26,900 sq mi (69,700 sq km)

Topography: Georgia is separated from Russia in the northeast by the main range of the Caucasus Mountains.

Capital: Tbilisi (pop., 1,064,000)

Independence date: April 9, 1991   Government type: republic

Head of state: Pres. Mikhail Saakashvili

Head of government: Prime Min. Lado Gurgenidze

Monetary unit: lari

GDP: $19.7 billion (2007 est.)   Per capita GDP: $4,200

Industries: steel, aircraft, machine tools, electrical appliances, mining, chemicals, wood products, wine

Chief crops: citrus, grapes, tea, vegetables

Minerals: manganese, iron ore, copper, coal, oil

Life expectancy at birth (years): male, 72.4; female, 79.4

Literacy rate: 99%

Website: www.parliament.ge

INDIA

FOR MAP, SEE PAGE 125

Population: 1,147,995,898

Ethnic groups: Indo-Aryan 72%, Dravidian 25%

Principal languages: Hindi, English, Bengali, Telugu, Marathi, Tamil, Urdu, Gujarati, Malayalam, Kannada, Oriya, Punjabi, Assamese, Kashmiri, Sindhi, and Sanskrit (all official); Hindustani, a mix of Hindi and Urdu spoken in the north, is popular but not official

Columned architectural treasures of India: Agra Fort (left); the Qutb Minar complex, near Delhi (right)

Nation Facts and Figures

India *(continued)*

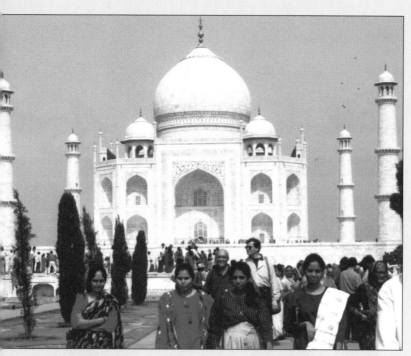

Taj Mahal, Agra, India

Chief religions: Hindu 82%, Muslim 12%, Christian 2%, Sikh 2%

Area: 1,269,350 sq mi (3,287,590 sq km)

Topography: The Himalaya Mountains, highest in world, stretch across India's northern borders. Below, the Ganges Plain is wide, fertile, and among the most densely populated regions of the world. The area below includes the Deccan Peninsula. Close to one-quarter of the area is forested.

Capital: New Delhi (pop. of city proper, 300,000)

Independence date: August 15, 1947

Government type: federal republic

Head of state: Pres. Pratibha Patil

Head of government: Prime Min. Manmohan Singh

Monetary unit: rupee

GDP: $2,965 billion (2007 est.)   **Per capita GDP:** $2,700

Industries: textiles, chemicals, food processing, steel, transport equipment, cement, mining, petroleum, machinery, software

Chief crops: rice, wheat, oilseed, cotton, jute, tea, sugarcane, potatoes

Minerals: coal, iron ore, manganese, mica, bauxite, titanium ore, chromite, natural gas, diamonds, petroleum, limestone

Life expectancy at birth (years): male, 63.3; female, 64.8

Literacy rate: 52%   **Website:** www.indianembassy.org

INDONESIA

FOR MAP, SEE PAGE 138

Population: 237,512,359

Ethnic groups: Javanese 45%, Sundanese 14%, Madurese 8%, Malay 8%

Principal languages: Bahasa Indonesia (official, modified form of Malay), English, Dutch, Javanese, other dialects

Chief religions: Muslim 88%, Protestant 5%, Roman Catholic 3%, Hindu 2%, Buddhist 1%

Area: 705,190 sq mi (1,826,440 sq km)

Topography: Indonesia comprises over 13,500 islands (6,000 inhabited), including Java (one of the most densely populated areas in the world with over 2,000 persons per sq mi [770 per sq km]), Sumatra, Kalimantan (most of Borneo), Sulawesi (Celebes), and West Irian (Irian Jaya, the western half of New Guinea). Also: Bangka, Billiton, Madura, Bali, Timor. The mountains and plateaus on the major islands have a cooler climate than the tropical lowlands.

Capital: Jakarta (pop., 12,296,000)   **Independence date:** August 17, 1945

Government type: republic

Head of state and government: Pres. Susilo Bambang Yudhoyono

Monetary unit: rupiah

GDP: $845.6 billion (2007 est.)   **Per capita GDP:** $3,400

Industries: petroleum and natural gas, textiles, apparel, footwear, mining, cement, chemical fertilizers, plywood, rubber, food, tourism

Chief crops: rice, cassava, peanuts, rubber, cocoa, coffee, palm oil, copra

Minerals: petroleum, tin, natural gas, nickel, bauxite, copper, coal, gold, silver

Life expectancy at birth (years): male, 66.8; female, 71.8

Literacy rate: 83.8%

Website: www.embassyofindonesia.org

IRAN

FOR MAP, SEE PAGE 125

Population: 65,875,223

Ethnic groups: Persian 51%, Azeri 24%, Gilaki/Mazandarani 8%, Kurd 7%, Arab 3%, Lur 2%, Balochi 2%, Turkmen 2%

Principal languages: Farsi (Persian; official), Kurdish, Pashto, Luri, Balochi, Gilaki, Mazandarami, Turkic languages (including Azeri and Turkish), Arabic

Chief religions: Muslim (official; Shi'a 89%, Sunni 10%)

Area: 636,000 sq mi (1,648,000 sq km)

Topography: Interior highlands and plains surrounded by high mountains, up to 18,000 ft (5,500 m). Large salt deserts cover much of area, but there are many oases and forest areas. Most of the population inhabits the north and northwest.

Capital: Tehran (pop., 7,190,000)   **Independence date:** April 1, 1979

Rice terraces, Bali, Indonesia

Temple Mount, with the Dome of the Rock shrine, Jerusalem, Israel

Government type: Islamic republic

Religious head: Ayatollah Sayyed Ali Khamenei

Head of state and government: Pres. Mahmoud Ahmadinejad

Monetary unit: rial

GDP: $852.6 billion (2007 est.)   **Per capita GDP:** $12,300

Industries: petroleum, petrochemicals, textiles, construction materials, food processing, metal fabricating, armaments

Chief crops: wheat, rice, other grains, sugar beets, fruits, nuts, cotton

Minerals: petroleum, natural gas, coal, chromium, copper, iron ore, lead, manganese, zinc, sulfur

Life expectancy at birth (years): male, 68.3; female, 71.1

Literacy rate: 72.1%

Websites: www.daftar.org
www.iran-un.org

IRAQ

For map, see page 146

Population: 28,221,181

Ethnic groups: Arab 75%-80%, Kurdish 15%-20%

Principal languages: Arabic (official), Kurdish (official in Kurdish regions), Assyrian, Armenian

Chief religions: Muslim (official; Shi'a 60-65%, Sunni 32-37%)

Area: 168,750 sq mi (437,070 sq km)

Topography: Mostly an alluvial plain, including the Tigris and Euphrates rivers, descending from mountains in the north to desert in the southwest. The Persian Gulf region is marshland.

Capital: Baghdad (pop., 5,620,000)

Independence date: October 3, 1932   **Government type:** in transition

Head of state: Pres. Jalal Talabani

Head of government: Prime Min. Nouri Kamel al-Maliki

Monetary unit: dinar

GDP: $100 billion (2007 est.)   **Per capita GDP:** $3,600

Industries: petroleum, chemicals, textiles, construction materials, food processing

Chief crops: wheat, barley, rice, vegetables, dates, cotton

Minerals: petroleum, natural gas, phosphates, sulfur

Life expectancy at birth (years): male, 67.1; female, 69.5

Literacy rate: 58%

Website: www.state.gov/r/pa/ei/bgn/6804.htm

ISRAEL

For map, see page 149

Population: 6,500,389

Ethnic groups: Jewish 80%, Arab and other 20%

Principal languages: Hebrew, Arabic (both official); English

Chief religions: Jewish 80%, Muslim (mostly Sunni) 15%, Christian 2%

Area: 8,020 sq mi (20,770 sq km)

Topography: The Mediterranean coastal plain is fertile and well-watered. In the center is the Judean Plateau. A triangular-shaped semidesert region, the Negev, extends from south of Beersheba to an apex at the head of the Gulf of Aqaba. The eastern border drops sharply into the Jordan Rift Valley, including Lake Tiberias (Sea of Galilee) and the Dead Sea, which is 1,312 ft (400 m) below sea level, the lowest point on the earth's surface.

Capital: Jerusalem (pop., 686,000)

Independence date: May 14, 1948   **Government type:** republic

Head of state: Pres. Shimon Peres

Head of government: Prime Min. Ehud Olmert

Monetary unit: new shekel

GDP: $184.9 billion (2007 est.)   **Per capita GDP:** $28,800

Industries: high-tech design and manufactures, wood and paper products, food, beverages, tobacco, caustic soda, cement, diamond cutting

Chief crops: citrus, vegetables, cotton

Minerals: potash, copper ore, natural gas, phosphate rock, magnesium bromide, clays, sand

Life expectancy at birth (years): male, 77.1; female, 81.4

Literacy rate: 95%

Website: www.israelemb.org

The PALESTINIAN AUTHORITY is responsible for civil government in the Gaza Strip and portions of the West Bank. Gaza: population, 1,537,269; area, 139 sq mi (360 sq km). West Bank: total population, 2,611,904; area, 2,263 sq mi (5,860 sq km).

JAPAN

For map, see page 129

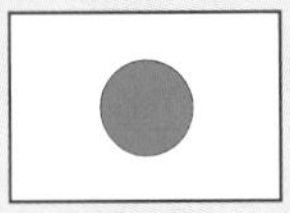

Population: 127,288,419

Ethnic groups: Japanese 99%; Korean, Chinese, and other 1%

Principal languages: Japanese (official), Ainu, Korean

Chief religions: Shinto and Buddhist observed together by 84%

Area: 145,883 sq mi (377,835 sq km)

Topography: Japan consists of four main islands: Honshu ("mainland"), 87,805 sq mi; Hokkaido, 30,144 sq mi (227,415 sq km); Kyushu, 14,114 sq mi (36,555 sq km); and Shikoku, 7,049 sq mi (18,257 sq km). The coast, deeply indented, measures 16,654 mi (26,802 km). The northern islands are a continuation of the Sakhalin Mountains. The Kunlun range of China continues into the southern islands, the ranges meeting in the Japanese Alps. In a vast transverse fissure crossing Honshu east to west rises a group of volcanoes, mostly extinct or inactive, including 12,388-ft (3,776-m) Mt. Fuji (Fujiyama) near Tokyo.

Capital: Tokyo (pop., 34,997,000)   **Independence date:** 660 BC

Government type: parliamentary democracy

Head of state: Emperor Akihito

Head of government: Prime Min. Yasuo Fukuda

Monetary unit: yen

GDP: $4,346 billion (2007 est.)

Per capita GDP: $33,800

Industries: motor vehicles, electronic equipment, machine tools, steel and nonferrous metals, ships, chemicals, textiles, processed foods

Chief crops: rice, sugar beets, vegetables, fruit

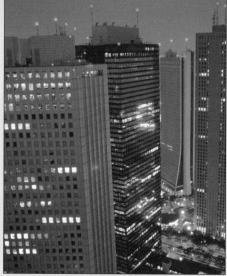

Three aspects of Japan: Mt. Fuji (top), a lake temple (above left), and Tokyo (above right)

Japan *(continued)*

Life expectancy at birth (years): male, 77.7; female, 84.5

Literacy rate: 99%

Websites: www.us.emb-japan.go.jp
www.jnto.go.jp

JORDAN

FOR MAP, SEE PAGE 146

Population: 6,198,677

Ethnic groups: Arab 98%, Armenian 1%, Circassian 1%

Principal languages: Arabic (official), English

Chief religions: Muslim (official; mostly Sunni) 92%, Christian 6%

Area: 35,300 sq mi (91,540 sq km)

Topography: About 88% of Jordan is arid. Fertile areas are in the west. The only port is on the short Aqaba Gulf coast. The country shares the Dead Sea (1,312 ft [400 m] below sea level) with Israel.

Capital: Amman (pop., 1,237,000)

Independence date: May 25, 1946

Government type: constitutional monarchy

Head of state: King Abdullah II

Head of government: Prime Min. Marouf al-Bakhit

Monetary unit: dinar

GDP: $28.2 billion (2007 est.)

Per capita GDP: $4,700

Industries: mining, petroleum refining, cement, light manufacturing, tourism

Chief crops: wheat, barley, citrus, tomatoes, melons, olives

Minerals: phosphates, potash, shale oil

Life expectancy at birth (years): male, 75.6; female, 80.7

Literacy rate: 86.6%

Websites: www.nic.gov.jo
www.jordanembassyus.org

KAZAKHSTAN

FOR MAP, SEE PAGE 122

Population: 15,340,533

Ethnic groups: Kazakh 53%, Russian 30%, Ukrainian 4%, Uzbek 3%, German 2%, Uighur 1%

Principal languages: Kazakh, Russian (both official); Ukranian, German, Uzbek

Chief religions: Muslim 47%, Russian Orthodox 44%

Area: 1,049,200 sq mi (2,717,300 sq km)

Topography: Kazakhstan extends from the lower reaches of the Volga River in Europe to the Altay Mountains on the Chinese border.

Capital: Astana (pop., 332,000)

Independence date: December 16, 1991

Government type: republic

Head of state: Pres. Nursultan A. Nazarbayev

Head of government: Prime Min. Daniyal Akhmetov

Monetary unit: tenge

GDP: $161.5 billion (2007)   **Per capita GDP:** $10,400

Industries: oil, mining, iron and steel, tractors and other agricultural machinery, electric motors, construction materials

Chief crops: spring wheat, cotton

Minerals: petroleum, natural gas, coal, iron ore, manganese, chrome ore, nickel, cobalt, copper, molybdenum, lead, zinc, bauxite, gold, uranium

Life expectancy at birth (years): male, 60.7; female, 71.7

Literacy rate: 98.4%

Website: www.kazakhembus.com

KOREA, NORTH

FOR MAP, SEE PAGE 131

Population: 23,479,089

Ethnic group: Korean

Principal language: Korean (official)

Chief religions: activities almost nonexistent; traditionally Buddhist, Confucianist, Chondogyo

Area: 46,540 sq mi (120,540 sq km)

Topography: Mountains and hills cover nearly all the country, with narrow valleys and small plains in between. The northern and the eastern coasts are the most rugged areas.

Capital: Pyongyang (pop., 3,228,000)

Independence date: September 9, 1948

Government type: Communist state

Leader: Kim Jong Il

Monetary unit: won

GDP: $40.0 billion (2007 est.)   **Per capita GDP:** $1,900

Industries: military products, machine building, electric power, chemicals, mining, metallurgy, textiles, food processing

Chief crops: rice, corn, potatoes, soybeans, pulses

Minerals: coal, lead, tungsten, zinc, graphite, magnesite, iron ore, copper, gold, pyrites, salt, fluorspar

Life expectancy at birth (years): male, 68.4; female, 73.9

Literacy rate: 99%

Website: www.korea-dpr.com

KOREA, SOUTH

FOR MAP, SEE PAGE 131

Population: 49,232,844

Ethnic group: Korean

Principal language: Korean (official)

Chief religions: Christian 49%, Buddhist 47%, Confucianist 3%

Area: 38,020 sq mi (98,480 sq km)

Topography: The country is mountainous, with a rugged eastern coast. The western and southern coasts are deeply indented, with many islands and harbors.

Capital: Seoul (pop., 9,714,000)

Independence date: August 15, 1948

Government type: republic

Head of state: Pres. Lee Myung-bak

Head of government: Prime Min. Han Seung-soo

Monetary unit: won

GDP: $1,206 billion (2007 est.)

Per capita GDP: $24,600

Industries: electronics, automobile production, chemicals, shipbuilding, steel, textiles, clothing, footwear, food processing

A painting from a Seoul museum

Chief crops: rice, root crops, barley, vegetables, fruit

Minerals: coal, tungsten, graphite, molybdenum, lead

Life expectancy at birth (years): male, 72.0; female, 79.5

Literacy rate: 98%

Website: www.korea.net

Seoul, South Korea

KUWAIT

FOR MAP, SEE PAGE 146

Population: 2,596,799

Ethnic groups: Arab 80%, South Asian 9%, Iranian 4%

Principal languages: Arabic (official), English

Chief religion: Muslim 85% (official; Sunni 70%, Shi'a 30%)

Area: 6,880 sq mi (17,820 sq km)

Topography: The country is flat, very dry, and extremely hot.

Capital: Kuwait City (pop., 1,222,000)

Independence date: June 19, 1961

Government type: constitutional monarchy

Head of state: Emir Sheikh Sabah al-Ahmad al-Jabir al-Sabah

Head of government: Prime Min. Sheikh Nasir Muhammad al-Ahmad al-Sabah

Monetary unit: dinar

GDP: $138.6 billion (2007 est.)   Per capita GDP: $55,300

Industries: petroleum, petrochemicals, desalination, food processing, construction materials

Minerals: petroleum, natural gas

Life expectancy at birth (years): male, 75.9; female, 77.9

Literacy rate: 78.6%   Website: www.kuwait-info.org.uk

KYRGYZSTAN

FOR MAP, SEE PAGE 145

Population: 5,356,869

Ethnic groups: Kyrgyz 52%, Russian 18%, Uzbek 13%, Ukrainian 3%, German 2%

Principal languages: Kyrgyz, Russian (both official); Uzbek

Chief religions: Muslim 75%, Russian Orthodox 20%

Area: 76,600 sq mi (198,500 sq km)

Topography: Kyrgystan is a landlocked country nearly covered by the Tien Shan and Pamir Mountains; the average elevation is 9,020 ft (2,750 m). A large lake, Issyk-Kul, in the northeast is 1 mi (1.6 km) above sea level.

Capital: Bishkek (pop., 806,000)   Independence date: August 31, 1991

Government type: republic

Head of state: Pres. Kurmanbek Bakiyev

Head of government: Prime Min. Feliks Kulov

Monetary unit: som

GDP: $10.4 billion (2007 est.)   Per capita GDP: $2,000

Industries: small machinery, textiles, food processing, cement, shoes, sawn logs, refrigerators, furniture, electric motors

Chief crops: tobacco, cotton, potatoes, vegetables, grapes, fruits and berries

Minerals: gold and rare earth metals, coal, oil, natural gas, nepheline, mercury, bismuth, lead, zinc

Life expectancy at birth (years): male, 63.8; female, 72.1

Literacy rate: 97%

Website: www.kyrgyzstan.org

LAOS

FOR MAP, SEE PAGE 136

Population: 6,677,534

Ethnic groups: Lao Loum 68%, Lao Theung 22%, Lao Soung (includes Hmong and Yao) 9%

Principal languages: Lao (official), French, English, and various ethnic languages

Laos *(continued)*

Chief religions: Buddhism 60%, animist and other 40%

Area: 91,400 sq mi (236,800 sq km)

Topography: Laos is landlocked, dominated by jungle. High mountains along the eastern border are the source of the east to west rivers slicing across the country to the Mekong River, which defines most of the western border.

Capital: Vientiane (pop., 716,000)   **Independence date:** July 19, 1949

Government type: Communist

Head of state: Pres. Khamtai Siphandon

Head of government: Prime Min. Boungnang Vorachith

Monetary unit: kip

GDP: $12.61 billion (2007 est.)   **Per capita GDP:** $1,900

Industries: mining, timber, electric power, agricultural processing, construction, garments, tourism

Chief crops: sweet potatoes, vegetables, corn, coffee, sugarcane, tobacco, cotton, tea, peanuts, rice

Minerals: gypsum, tin, gold, gemstones

Life expectancy at birth (years): male, 52.7; female, 56.8

Literacy rate: 57%

Website: www.laoembassy.com/discover/index.htm

Thean Hou Temple, Kuala Lumpur, Malaysia

LEBANON

FOR MAP, SEE PAGE 149

Population: 3,971,941

Ethnic groups: Arab 95%, Armenian 4%

Principal languages: Arabic (official), French, English, Armenian

Chief religions: Muslim 70%, Christian 30%

Topography: There is a narrow coastal strip, and two mountain ranges running north to south enclosing the fertile Beqaa Valley. The Litani River runs south through the valley, turning west to empty into the Mediterranean.

Area: 4,000 sq mi (10,400 sq km)

Capital: Beirut (pop., 1,792,000)

Independence date: November 22, 1943   **Government type:** republic

Head of state: Pres. Emile Lahoud

Head of government: Prime Min. Fouad Siniora

Monetary unit: pound

GDP: $40.7 billion (2007 est.)   **Per capita GDP:** $10,400

Industries: banking, food processing, jewelry, cement, textiles, mineral and chemical products, wood and furniture products, oil refining, metal fabricating

Chief crops: citrus, grapes, tomatoes, apples, vegetables, potatoes, olives, tobacco

Minerals: limestone, iron ore, salt

Life expectancy at birth (years): male, 69.6; female, 74.9

Literacy rate: 86.4%

Website: www.lebanonembassyus.org

MALAYSIA

FOR MAP, SEE PAGE 138

Population: 25,259,428

Ethnic groups: Malay and other indigenous 58%, Chinese 24%, Indian 8%

Principal languages: Malay (official), English, Chinese dialects, Tamil, Telugu, Malayalam, Panjabi, Thai; Iban and Kadazan in the east

Chief religions: Muslim (official) 60%, Buddhist 19%, Christian 9%, Hindu 6%, Confucianist/Taoist 3%

Area: 127,320 sq mi (329,750 sq km)

Topography: Most of western Malaysia is covered by tropical jungle, including the central mountain range that runs north to soth through the peninsula. The western coast is marshy, the eastern coast, sandy. Eastern Malaysia has a wide, swampy coastal plain, with interior jungles and mountains.

Capital: Kuala Lumpur (pop., 1,352,000)

Independence date: August 31, 1957

Government type: federal parliamentary democracy with a constitutional monarch

Head of state: Paramount Ruler Syed Sirajuddin Syed Putra Jamalullail

Head of government: Prime Min. Datuk Seri Abdullah Ahmad Badawi

Monetary unit: ringgit

GDP: $357.9 billion (2007 est.)   **Per capita GDP:** $14,400

Industries: rubber/oil-palm goods, light manufacturing, electronics, mining, logging

Chief crops: rubber, palm oil, cocoa, rice, coconuts, pepper

Minerals: tin, petroleum, copper, iron ore, natural gas, bauxite

Life expectancy at birth (years): male, 69.3; female, 74.8

Literacy rate: 83.5%

Websites: www.tourism.gov.my

   www.gov.my

MALDIVES

FOR MAP, SEE PAGE 125

Population: 379,174

Ethnic groups: Dravidian, Sinhalese, Arab

Principal languages: Divehi (Sinhala dialect, Arabic script; official), English

Chief religion: Muslim (official; mostly Sunni)

Area: 116 sq mi (300 sq km)

Topography: The Maldives consists of 19 atolls with 1,190 islands, 198 inhabited. None of the islands are over 5 sq mi (13 sq km) in area, and all are nearly flat.

Capital: Male (pop., 83,000)   **Independence date:** July 26, 1965

Government type: republic

Head of state and government: Pres. Maumoon Abdul Gayoom

Monetary unit: rufiyaa

GDP: $2.8 billion (2006 est.)   Per capita GDP: $3,900

Industries: fish processing, tourism, shipping, boatbuilding, coconut processing, garments, woven mats, rope, handicrafts, coral and sand mining

Chief crops: coconuts, corn, sweet potatoes

Life expectancy at birth (years): male, 62.4; female, 65.0

Literacy rate: 93.2%   Website: www.themaldives.com

MONGOLIA

For map, see page 128

Population: 2,996,081

Ethnic groups: Mongol 85%, Turkic 7%, Tungusic 5%

Principal languages: Khalkha Mongol, Turkic, Russian

Chief religion: Tibetan Buddhist Lamaism 96%

Area: 604,000 sq mi (1,565,000 sq km)

Topography: Mongolia is mostly a high plateau with mountains, salt lakes, and vast grasslands. Arid lands in the southern are part of the Gobi Desert.

Capital: Ulaanbaatar (pop., 812,000)

Independence date: July 11, 1921

Government type: republic

Head of state: Pres. Nambaryn Enkhbayar

Head of government: Prime Min. Miyeegombo Enkhbold

Monetary unit: tugrik

GDP: $8.5 billion (2007 est.)   Per capita GDP: $2,900

Industries: construction materials, mining, food and beverages, processing of animal products

Chief crops: wheat, barley, potatoes, forage crops

Minerals: oil, coal, copper, molybdenum, tungsten, phosphates, tin, nickel, zinc, wolfram, fluorspar, gold, silver, iron, phosphate

Life expectancy at birth (years): male, 62.0; female, 66.5

Literacy rate: 97.8%

Website: www.mongolianembassy.us

MYANMAR (FORMERLY BURMA)

For map, see page 141

Population: 47,758,181

Ethnic groups: Burman 68%, Shan 9%, Karen 7%, Rakhine 4%, Chinese 3%, Indian 2%, Mon 2%

Principal languages: Burmese (official); many ethnic minority languages

Chief religions: Buddhist 89%, Christian 4%, Muslim 4%, animist 1%

Area: 262,000 sq mi (678,500 sq km)

Topography: Mountains surround Myanmar on the west, north, and east, and dense forests cover much of the nation. North to south rivers provide habitable valleys and communications, especially the Irrawaddy, navigable for 900 mi (1,400 km).

Capital: Yangon (Rangoon) (pop., 3,874,000); Nay Pyi Taw (admin. capital)

Independence date: January 4, 1948

Hsinbyume Pagoda, Mingun, Myanmar

Government type: military

Head of state: Gen. Than Shwe

Head of government: Lt. Gen. Soe Win

Monetary unit: kyat

GDP: $91.1 billion (2007 est.)   Per capita GDP: $1,900

Industries: agricultural processing, knit and woven apparel, wood and wood products, mining, construction materials, pharmaceuticals, fertilizer

Chief crops: rice, pulses, beans, sesame, groundnuts, sugarcane

Minerals: petroleum, tin, antimony, zinc, copper, tungsten, lead, coal, marble, limestone, precious stones, natural gas

Life expectancy at birth (years): male, 54.2; female, 57.9

Literacy rate: 83.1%   Website: www.state.gov/r/pa/ei/bgn/35910.htm

---

NEPAL

For map, see page 142

Population: 29,519,114

Ethnic groups: Newar, Indian, Gurung, Magar, Tamang, Rai, Limbu, Sherpa, Tharu

Principal languages: Nepali (official); about 30 dialects and 12 other languages

Chief religions: Hindu (official) 86%, Buddhist 8%, Muslim 4%

Area: 54,400 sq mi (140,800 sq km)

Topography: The Himalayas stretch across the north, the hill country with its fertile valleys extends across the center, while the southern border region is part of the flat, subtropical Ganges Plain.

Capital: Kathmandu (pop., 741,000)   Independence date: 1768

Government type: constitutional monarchy

Head of state: King Gyanendra Bir Bikram Shah Dev

Head of government: Prime Min. Girija Prasad Koirala

Monetary unit: rupee

GDP: $30.7 billion (2007 est.)   Per capita GDP: $1,100

Industries: tourism, carpet, textile, rice, jute, sugar, oilseed mills, cigarette, cement and brick production

Chief crops: rice, corn, wheat, sugarcane, root crops

Minerals: quartz, lignite, copper, cobalt, iron ore

Life expectancy at birth (years): male, 59.7; female, 59.1

Literacy rate: 27.5%   Website: www.nepalembassy/usa.org

Machapuchare peak, Nepal

OMAN

FOR MAP, SEE PAGE 147

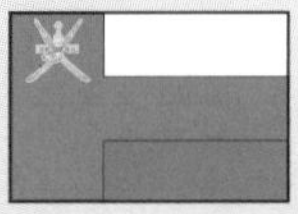

Population: 3,309,440

Ethnic groups: Arab, Baluchi, South Asian, African

Principal languages: Arabic (official), English, Baluchi, Urdu, Indian dialects

Chief religion: Muslim 75% (official; mostly Ibadhi)

Area: 82,030 sq mi (212,460 sq km)

Topography: Oman has a narrow coastal plain up to 10 mi (16 km) wide, a range of barren mountains reaching 9,900 ft (3,000 m), and a wide, stony, mostly waterless plateau, with an average altitude of 1,000 ft (300 m). Also, an exclave at the tip of the Musandam peninsula controls access to the Persian Gulf.

Capital: Muscat (pop., 638,000)

Independence date: 1650   Government type: absolute monarchy

Head of state and government: Sultan Qabus bin Said

Monetary unit: rial Omani

GDP: $61.2 billion (2007 est.)   Per capita GDP: $19,100

Industries: oil and gas, construction, cement, copper

Chief crops: dates, limes, bananas, alfalfa, vegetables

Minerals: petroleum, copper, asbestos, marble, limestone, chromium, gypsum, natural gas

Life expectancy at birth (years): male, 70.7; female, 75.2

Literacy rate: approaching 80%

Website: www.state.gov/r/pa/ei/bgn/35834.htm

PAKISTAN

FOR MAP, SEE PAGE 147

Population: 167,762,040

Ethnic groups: Punjabi, Sindhi, Pashtun, Balochi

Principal languages: English, Urdu (both official); Punjabi, Sindhi, Siraiki, Pashtu, Balochi, Hindko, Brahui, Burushaski

Chief religions: Muslim 97% (official; Sunni 77%, Shi'a 20%)

Area: 310,400 sq mi (803,940 sq km)

Topography: The Indus River rises in the Hindu Kush and Himalaya mountains in the north (highest is K2, or Godwin Austen, 28,250 ft [8,610 m], second highest in the world), then flows over 1,000 mi (1,600 km) through fertile valley and empties into Arabian Sea. The Thar Desert and Eastern Plains flank the Indus Valley.

Capital: Islamabad (pop., 698,000)

Independence date: August 14, 1947

Government type: republic with strong military influence

Head of state: Pres. Pervez Musharraf

Head of government: Prime Min. Syed Yousaf Raza Gillani

Monetary unit: rupee

GDP: $446.1 billion (2007 est.)   Per capita GDP: $2,600

Industries: textiles, food processing, beverages, construction materials, clothing, paper products

Chief crops: cotton, wheat, rice, sugarcane, fruits, vegetables

Minerals: natural gas, limited petroleum, poor quality coal, iron ore, copper, salt, limestone

Life expectancy at birth (years): male, 61.7; female, 63.6

Literacy rate: 42.7%   Website: www.pakistan.gov.pk

PAPUA NEW GUINEA

FOR MAP, SEE PAGE 174

Population: 5,921,144

Ethnic groups: Melanesian, Papuan, Negrito, Micronesian, Polynesian

Principal languages: English (official), pidgin English, Motu; 715 indigenous languages

Chief religions: indigenous beliefs 34%, Roman Catholic 22%, Protestant 44%

Area: 178,700 sq mi (462,840 sq km)

Topography: Thickly forested mountains cover much of the center of the country, with lowlands along the coasts. Included are some islands of the Bismarck and Solomon groups, such as the Admiralty Islands, New Ireland, New Britain, and Bougainville.

Capital: Port Moresby (pop., 275,000)

Independence date: September 16, 1975

Government type: parliamentary democracy

Head of state: Queen Elizabeth II, represented by Gov-Gen. Sir Paulias Matane

Head of government: Prime Min. Sir Michael Somare

Monetary unit: kina

GDP: $16.6 billion (2007 est.)   Per capita GDP: $2,900

Industries: copra and palm oil processing, wood products, mining, construction, tourism

Chief crops: coffee, cocoa, coconuts, palm kernels, tea, rubber, sweet potatoes, fruit, vegetables

Minerals: gold, copper, silver, natural gas, oil

Life expectancy at birth (years): male, 62.4; female, 66.8

Literacy rate: 64.5%

Website: www.pngtourism.org.pg

PHILIPPINES

FOR MAP, SEE PAGE 137

Population: 92,681,453

Ethnic groups: Christian Malay 91.5%, Muslim Malay 4%, Chinese 1.5%

Principal languages: Filipino, English (both official); many dialects

Chief religions: Roman Catholic 83%, Protestant 9%, Muslim 5%

Area: 115,830 sq mi (300,000 sq km)

Topography: The country consists of some 7,100 islands stretching 1,100 mi (1,770 km) north to south. About 95% of the area and population are on the 11 largest islands, which are mountainous, except for the heavily indented coastlines and the central plain on Luzon.

Capital: Manila (pop., 10,352,000)

Independence date: July 4, 1946   Government type: republic

Head of state and government: Pres. Gloria Macapagal Arroyo

Monetary unit: peso

GDP: $298.9 billion (2007 est.)   Per capita GDP: $3,300

Fishing boat, Boracay, Philippines

Industries: textiles, pharmaceuticals, chemicals, wood products, food processing, electronics assembly

Chief crops: rice, coconuts, corn, sugarcane, bananas, pineapples, mangoes

Minerals: petroleum, nickel, cobalt, silver, gold, salt, copper

Life expectancy at birth (years): male, 66.7; female, 72.6

Literacy rate: 94.6%

Websites: www.philippineembassy-usa.org
www.gov.ph

QATAR
For map, see page 146

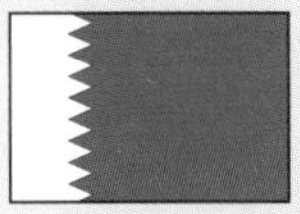

Population: 928,635

Ethnic groups: Arab 40%, Pakistani 18%, Indian 18%, Iranian 10%

Principal languages: Arabic (official), English

Chief religion: Muslim (official) 95%

Area: 4,420 sq mi (11,440 sq km)

Topography: Qatar is mostly a flat desert, with some limestone ridges; vegetation of any kind is scarce.

Capital: Doha (pop., 286,000)

Independence date: September 3, 1971

Government type: traditional monarchy

Head of state: Emir Hamad bin Khalifa ath-Thani

Head of government: Prime Min. Abdullah bin Khalifa ath-Thani

Monetary unit: riyal

GDP: $57.69 billion (2007)   Per capita GDP: $75,900

Industries: oil production and refining, fertilizers, petrochemicals, steel reinforcing bars, cement

Chief crops: fruits, vegetables

Minerals: petroleum, natural gas

Life expectancy at birth (years): male, 70.9; female, 76.0

Literacy rate: 79%

Website: english.mofa.gov.qa

SAUDI ARABIA
For map, see page 146

Population: 28,161,417

Ethnic groups: Arab 90%, Afro-Asian 10%

Principal language: Arabic (official)

Chief religion: Muslim (official)

Area: 756,990 sq mi (1,960,580 sq km)

Topography: Saudi Arabia is bordered by the Red Sea on the west. The highlands on the west, up to 9,000 ft (2,700 m), slope as an arid, barren desert to the Persian Gulf on the east.

Capital: Riyadh (pop., 5,126,000)

Independence date: September 23, 1932

Government type: constitutional monarchy with strong Islamic influence

Head of state and government: King Abdallah bin Abd al-Aziz Al Saud

Monetary unit: riyal

GDP: $572.2 billion (2007 est.)   Per capita GDP: $20,700

Industries: oil production and refining, basic petrochemicals, cement, construction, fertilizer, plastics

Chief crops: wheat, barley, tomatoes, melons, dates, citrus

Minerals: petroleum, natural gas, iron ore, gold, copper

Life expectancy at birth (years): male, 73.3; female, 77.3

Literacy rate: 78%

Website: www.saudiebassy.net

SINGAPORE
For map, see page 138

Population: 4,608,167

Ethnic groups: Chinese 77%, Malay 14%, Indian 8%

Principal languages: Chinese, Malay, Tamil, English (all official)

Chief religions: Buddhist, Muslim, Christian, Taoist, Hindu

Area: 250 sq mi (650 sq km)

Topography: Singapore is a flat, formerly swampy island. The nation includes 40 nearby islets.

Capital: Singapore (pop., 4,253,000)

Independence date: August 9, 1965

Government type: republic   Head of state: Pres. S. R. Nathan

Head of government: Prime Min. Lee Hsien Loong

Monetary unit: Singapore dollar

GDP: $222.7 billion (2007 est.)   Per capita GDP: $48,900

Industries: electronics, chemicals, financial services, oil-drilling equipment, petroleum refining, rubber products, processed food and beverages, ship repair, entrepot trade, biotechnology

Chief crops: rubber, copra, fruit, orchids, vegetables

Life expectancy at birth (years): male, 79.0; female, 84.3

Literacy rate: 93.5%

Website: www.gov.sg

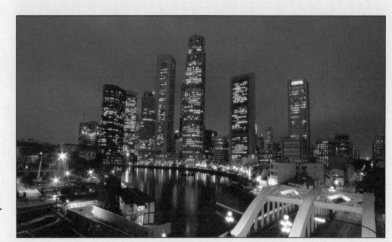

Singapore

SRI LANKA
For map, see page 140

Population: 21,128,773

Ethnic groups: Sinhalese 74%, Tamil 18%, Moor 7%

Principal languages: Sinhala, Tamil (both official); English

Chief religions: Buddhist 70%, Hindu 15%, Christian 8%, Muslim 7%

Area: 25,330 sq mi (65,610 sq km)

Topography: The coastal area and the northern half are flat; the south-central area is hilly and mountainous.

Capitals: Colombo (administrative) (pop., 648,000), Sri Jayawardenepura Kotte (legislative) (pop., 117,000)

Buddha statue, Polonnaruwa, Sri Lanka

Independence date: February 4, 1948

Government type: republic

Head of state: Pres. Mahinda Rajapaksa

Sri Lanka (continued)

Tea plantation, Sri Lanka

Head of government: Prime Min. Ratnasiri Wickremanayake

Monetary unit: rupee

GDP: $83.2 billion (2007 est.)   **Per capita GDP:** $4,100

Industries: rubber processing, agricultural commodities, clothing, cement, petroleum refining, textiles, tobacco

Chief crops: rice, sugarcane, grains, pulses, oilseed, spices, tea, rubber, coconuts

Minerals: limestone, graphite, mineral sands, gems, phosphates, clay

Life expectancy at birth (years): male, 70.3; female, 75.6

Literacy rate: 90.2%   **Website:** www.slembassyusa.org

SYRIA

FOR MAP, SEE PAGE 148

Population: 19,747,586

Ethnic groups: Arab 90%, Kurds, Armenians, and other 10%

Principal languages: Arabic (official), Kurdish, Armenian

Chief religions: Sunni Muslim 74%, other Muslims 16%, Christian 10%

Area: 71,500 sq mi (185,180 sq km)

Topography: Syria has a short Mediterranean coastline, then stretches east and south with fertile lowlands and plains, alternating with mountains and large desert areas.

Capital: Damascus (pop., 2,228,000)

Independence date: April 17, 1946

Government type: republic (under military regime)

Head of state: Pres. Bashar al-Assad

Head of government: Prime Min. Muhammad Naji al-Otari

Monetary unit: pound

GDP: $83 billion (2007 est.)

Per capita GDP: $4,300

Industries: petroleum, textiles, food processing, beverages, tobacco

Chief crops: wheat, barley, cotton, lentils, chickpeas, olives, sugar beets

Minerals: petroleum, phosphates, chrome and manganese ores, asphalt, iron ore, rock salt, marble, gypsum

Life expectancy at birth (years): male, 68.5; female, 71.0

Literacy rate: 70.8%   **Website:** www.syrianembassy.us

TAIWAN

FOR MAP, SEE PAGE 137

Population: 22,920,946

Ethnic groups: Taiwanese 84%, mainland Chinese 14%, aborigine 2%

Principal languages: Mandarin Chinese (official), Taiwanese (Min), Hakka dialects

Chief religions: Buddhist, Confucian, and Taoist 93%; Christian 5%

Area: 13,890 sq mi (35,980 sq km)

Topography: A mountain range forms the backbone of the island; the eastern half is very steep and craggy, and the western slope is flat, fertile, and well cultivated.

Capital: Taipei (pop., 2,624,00)

Independence date: 1949

Government type: democracy

Head of state: Pres. Ma Ying-jeou

Head of government: Premier Liu Chao-shiuan

Monetary unit: Taiwan dollar (TWD)

GDP: $690.1 billion (2007 est.)

Per capita GDP: $29,800

Industries: electronics, petroleum refining, chemicals, textiles, iron and steel, machinery, cement, food processing

Lungshan Temple, Taipei, Taiwan

Chief crops: rice, corn, vegetables, fruit, tea

Minerals: coal, natural gas, limestone, marble, asbestos

Life expectancy at birth (years): male, 74.3; female, 80.1

Literacy rate: 86%

Website: www.gio.gov.tw

TAJIKISTAN

FOR MAP, SEE PAGE 145

Population: 7,211,884

Ethnic groups: Tajik 65%, Uzbek 25%, Russian 4%

Principal languages: Tajik (official), Russian

Chief religion: Muslim (Sunni 85%, Shi'a 5%)

Area: 55,300 sq mi (143,100 sq km)

Topography: Mountainous region that contains the Pamirs and the Trans-Alai mountain system.

Capital: Dushanbe (pop., 554,000)

Independence date: September 9, 1991

Government type: republic   Head of state: Pres. Imomali Rakhmonov

Head of government: Prime Min. Akil Akilov

Monetary unit: somoni

GDP: $11.9 billion (2007 est.)   Per capita GDP: $1,600

Industries: aluminum, zinc, lead, chemicals and fertilizers, cement, vegetable oil, metal-cutting machine tools, refrigerators and freezers

Chief crops: cotton, grain, fruits, grapes, vegetables

Minerals: petroleum, uranium, mercury, brown coal, lead, zinc, antimony, tungsten, silver, gold

Life expectancy at birth (years): male, 61.5; female, 67.6

Literacy rate: 98%   Website: www.state.gov/r/pa/ei/bgn/5775.htm

THAILAND

FOR MAP, SEE PAGE 136

Population: 65,493,298

Ethnic groups: Thai 75%, Chinese 14%

Principal languages: Thai, Chinese, Malay, Khmer

Chief religions: Buddhism (official) 95%, Muslim 4%

Area: 198,000 sq mi (514,000 sq km)

Topography: A plateau dominates the northeast third of Thailand, dropping to the fertile alluvial valley of the Chao Phraya River in the center. Forested mountains are in the north, with narrow fertile valleys. The southern peninsula region is covered by rain forests.

Capital: Bangkok (pop., 6,486,000)   Independence date: 1238

Government type: constitutional monarchy

Head of state: King Bhumibol Adulyadej

Head of government: Prime Min. Thaksin Shinawatra

Monetary unit: baht

GDP: $519.9 billion (2007 est.)   Per capita GDP: $8,000

Industries: tourism, textiles and garments, agricultural processing, beverages, tobacco, cement, light manufacturing, electric appliances and components, computers and parts, integrated circuits, furniture, plastics

Chief crops: rice, cassava, rubber, corn, sugarcane, coconuts, soybeans

Minerals: tin, rubber, natural gas, tungsten, tantalum, lead, gypsum, lignite, fluorite

Life expectancy at birth (years): male, 69.2; female, 73.7

Literacy rate: 93.8%

Website: www.thaiembdc.org

River market, Thailand

Hagia Sophia, Istanbul, Turkey

TURKEY

FOR MAP, SEE PAGE 148

Population: 71,892,807

Ethnic groups: Turk 80%, Kurd 20%

Principal languages: Turkish (official), Kurdish, Arabic, Armenian, Greek

Chief religion: Muslim 99.8% (mostly Sunni)

Area: 301,380 sq mi (780,580 sq km)

Topography: Central Turkey has wide plateaus, with hot, dry summers and cold winters. High mountains ring the interior on all but the west, with more than 20 peaks over 10,000 ft (3,000 m). Rolling plains are in the west; mild, fertile coastal plains are in the south and west.

Capital: Ankara (pop., 3,428,000)

Independence date: October 29, 1923

Government type: republic

Head of state: Pres. Abdullah Gül

Head of government: Prime Min. Recep Tayyip Erdogan

Monetary unit: Turkish lira

GDP: $667.7 billion (2007 est.)   Per capita GDP: $9,400

Industries: textiles, food processing, autos, mining, steel, petroleum, construction, lumber, paper

Chief crops: tobacco, cotton, grain, olives, sugar beets, pulse, citrus

Minerals: antimony, coal, chromium, mercury, copper, borate, sulfur, iron ore

Life expectancy at birth (years): male, 69.7; female, 74.6

Literacy rate: 85%   Website: www.turkey.org

TURKMENISTAN

FOR MAP, SEE PAGE 145

Population: 5,179,571

Ethnic groups: Turkmen 77%, Uzbek 9%, Russian 7%, Kazakh 2%

Principal languages: Turkmen, Russian, Uzbek

Chief religions: Muslim 89%, Eastern Orthodox 9%

Area: 188,500 sq mi (488,100 sq km)

Topography: The Kara Kum Desert occupies 80% of the area. The country is bordered on the west by the Caspian Sea.

Capital: Ashgabat (pop., 574,000)

Nation Facts and Figures

Turkmenistan *(continued)*

Independence date: October 27, 1991

Government type: republic with authoritarian rule

Head of state and government: Pres. Gurbanguly Berdimuhamedov

Monetary unit: manat

GDP: $47.4 billion (2007 est.)   Per capita GDP: $9,200

Industries: petroleum products, textiles, food processing

Chief crops: cotton, grain

Minerals: petroleum, natural gas, coal, sulfur, salt

Life expectancy at birth (years): male, 57.9; female, 64.9

Literacy rate: 98%

Website: www.turkmenistanembassy.org

UNITED ARAB EMIRATES

FOR MAP, SEE PAGE 146

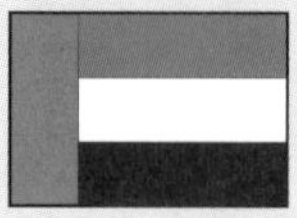

Population: 4,621,399

Ethnic groups: Arab and Iranian 42%, Indian 50%

Principal languages: Arabic (official), Persian, English, Hindi, Urdu

Chief religion: Muslim 96% (official; Shi'a 16%)

Area: 32,000 sq mi (82,880 sq km)

Topography: A barren, flat coastal plain gives way to uninhabited sand dunes on the south. The Hajar Mountains are on the east.

Capital: Abu Dhabi (pop., 475,000)

Independence date: December 2, 1971

Government type: federation of emirates

Head of state: Pres. Khalifa bin Zayid al-Nuhayyan

Head of government: Prime Min. Sheik Muhammad bin Rashid al-Maktum

Monetary unit: dirham

GDP: $145.8 billion (2007 est.)   Per capita GDP: $55,200

Industries: petroleum, fishing, petrochemicals, construction materials, boatbuilding, handicrafts, pearling

Chief crops: dates, vegetables, watermelons

Minerals: petroleum, natural gas

Life expectancy at birth (years): male, 72.5; female, 77.6

Literacy rate: 79.2%

Websites: www.government.ae/gov/en/index.jsp
        www.uaeinteract.com

UZBEKISTAN

FOR MAP, SEE PAGE 145

Population: 28,268,440

Ethnic groups: Uzbek 80%, Russian 6%, Tajik 5%, Kazakh 3%, Karakalpak 3%, Tatar 2%

Principal languages: Uzbek (official), Russian, Tajik

Chief religions: Muslim 88% (mostly Sunni), Eastern Orthodox 9%

Area: 172,740 sq mi (447,400 sq km)

Topography: Uzbekistan consists mostly of plains and desert.

Capital: Tashkent (pop., 2,155,000)

Independence date: August 31, 1991

Government type: republic with authoritarian rule

Head of state: Pres. Islam A. Karimov

Head of government: Prime Min. Shavkat Mirziyaev

Monetary unit: som

GDP: $62.3 billion (2007 est.)   Per capita GDP: $2,200

Industries: textiles, food processing, machine building, metallurgy, natural gas, chemicals

Chief crops: cotton, vegetables, fruits, grain

Minerals: natural gas, petroleum, coal, gold, uranium, silver, copper, lead and zinc, tungsten, molybdenum

Life expectancy at birth (years): male, 60.7; female, 67.7

Literacy rate: 97.3%   Website: www.gov.uz

VIETNAM

FOR MAP, SEE PAGE 136

Population: 86,116,559

Ethnic groups: Vietnamese 85%-90%, Chinese, Hmong, Thai, Khmer, Cham

Principal languages: Vietnamese (official), English, French, Chinese, Khmer

Chief religions: Buddhist, Roman Catholic

Area: 127,240 sq mi (329,560 sq km)

Topography: Vietnam is long and narrow, with a 1,400-mi (2,300-km) coast. About 22% of the country is readily arable, including the densely settled Red River valley in the north, narrow coastal plains in the center, and the wide, often marshy Mekong River Delta in the south. The rest consists of semiarid plateaus and barren mountains, with some stretches of tropical rain forest.

Capital: Hanoi (pop., 3,977,000)   Independence date: September 2, 1945

Government type: Communist

Head of state: Pres. Tran Duc Luong

Head of government: Prime Min. Phan Van Khai

Monetary unit: dong

GDP: $222.5 billion (2007 est.)   Per capita GDP: $2,600

Industries: food processing, garments, shoes, machine building, mining, cement, chemical fertilizer, glass, tires, oil, coal, steel, paper

Chief crops: paddy rice, corn, potatoes, rubber, soybeans, coffee, tea, bananas

Minerals: phosphates, coal, manganese, bauxite, chromate, offshore oil and gas

Life expectancy at birth (years): male, 67.9; female, 73.0

Literacy rate: 93.7%

Website: www.vietnamembassy-usa.org

YEMEN

FOR MAP, SEE PAGE 146

Population: 23,013,376

Ethnic groups: Mainly Arab; Afro-Arab, South Asian, European

Principal language: Arabic (official)

Chief religions: Muslim (official; Sunni 60%, Shi'a 40%)

Area: 203,850 sq mi (527,970 sq km)

Topography: A sandy coastal strip leads to well-watered fertile mountains in the interior.

Capital: Sanaa (pop., 1,469,000)   Independence date: May 22, 1990

Government type: republic

Head of state: Pres. Ali Abdullah Saleh

Head of government: Prime Min. Abd-al-Qadir Bajamal

Monetary unit: rial

GDP: $52.61 billion (2007 est.)   Per capita GDP: $2,400

Industries: oil, cotton textiles, leather goods, food processing, handicrafts, aluminum products, cement

Chief crops: grain, fruits, vegetables, pulses, qat, coffee, cotton

Minerals: petroleum, rock salt, marble, coal, gold, lead, nickel, copper

Life expectancy at birth (years): male, 59.5; female, 63.3

Literacy rate: 38%   Website: www.nic.gov.ye

The nation of Australia, which spans the entire continent of Australia, has the sixth biggest land area among the countries of the world. The Pacific island nations of Nauru and Tuvalu fall among the world's five smallest countries in terms of land area. Tuvalu and Nauru, along with Palau, rank among the five smallest countries in terms of population.

AUSTRALIA, NEW ZEALAND, AND THE PACIFIC

AUSTRALIA

FOR MAP, SEE PAGE 167

Population: 20,600,856
Ethnic groups: white 92%, Asian 7%, Aborigine and other 1%
Principal languages: English (official), aboriginal languages
Chief religions: Anglican 26%, Roman Catholic 26%, other Christian 24%
Area: 2,967,910 sq mi (7,686,850 sq km)
Topography: An island continent. The Great Dividing Range along the eastern coast has Mt. Kosciusko, 7,310 ft (2,230 m). The western plateau rises to 2,000 ft (600 m), with arid areas in the Great Sandy and Great Victoria deserts. The northwestern part of Western Australia and the Northern Territory are arid and hot. The northeast has heavy rainfall, and Cape York Peninsula has jungles.
Capital: Canberra (pop., 373,000)

Independence date: January 1, 1901
Government type: democratic, federal state system
Head of state: Queen Elizabeth II, represented by Gov.-Gen. Michael Jeffery
Head of government: Prime Min. John Howard
Monetary unit: Australian dollar
GDP: $766.8 billion (2007 est.)　**Per capita GDP:** $37,500
Industries: mining, industrial and transport equipment, food processing, chemicals, steel
Chief crops: wheat, barley, sugarcane, fruits
Minerals: bauxite, coal, iron ore, copper, tin, silver, uranium, nickel, tungsten, mineral sands, lead, zinc, diamonds, natural gas, petroleum
Life expectancy at birth (years): male, 77.4; female, 83.3
Literacy rate: 100%　**Website:** www.australia.com

Ayers Rock (Uluru), Northern Territory, Australia

Perth, Australia

Nation Facts and Figures

FIJI – NAURU

FIJI

For map, see page 174

Population: 931,545

Ethnic groups: Fijian 51%, Indian 44%

Principal languages: English (official), Fijian, Hindustani

Chief religions: Christian 52%, Hindu 38%, Muslim 8%

Area: 7,050 sq mi (18,270 sq km)

Topography: Fiji consists of 322 islands (106 inhabited), many mountainous, with tropical forests and large fertile areas. Viti Levu, the largest island, has over half the total land area.

Capital: Suva (pop., 210,000)

Independence date: October 19, 1970

Government type: republic

Head of state: Pres. Ratu Josefa Iloilo

Head of government: Prime Min. Laisenia Qarase

Monetary unit: Fiji dollar

GDP $5.1 billion (2007 est.)   **Per capita GDP:** $5,500

Industries: tourism, sugar, clothing, copra, small cottage industries

Chief crops: sugarcane, coconuts, cassava, rice, sweet potatoes, bananas

Minerals: gold, copper, offshore oil potential

Life expectancy at birth (years): male, male, 66.7; female, 71.8

Literacy rate: 92.5%

Websites: www.embassy.org/embassies/fj.html
www.fiji.org.fj

Traditional hut, Lifou Island, New Caledonia (French overseas territory)

Head of state and government: Pres. Kessai Note

Monetary unit: U.S. dollar

GDP: $115 million (2001 est.)   **Per capita GDP:** $1,600

Industries: copra, fish, tourism, craft items from shell, wood, and pearls

Chief crops: coconuts, tomatoes, melons, taro, breadfruit, fruits

Minerals: deep seabed minerals

Life expectancy at birth (years): male, 67.8; female, 71.7

Literacy rate: 93.7%   **Website:** www.miembassyus.org

KIRIBATI

For map, see page 174

Population: 110,252

Ethnic groups: Micronesian

Principal languages: English (official), I-Kiribati

Chief religions: Roman Catholic 52%, Protestant 40%

Area: 280 sq mi (720 sq km)

Topography: Kiribati comprises 33 coral islands, all of which, except Banaba (Ocean) Island, are low-lying, with soil of coral sand and rock fragments, subject to erratic rainfall.

Capital: South Tarawa (pop., 42,000)

Independence date: July 12, 1979

Government type: republic

Head of state and government: Pres. Anote Tong

Monetary unit: Australian dollar

GDP: $240 million (2006 est.)   **Per capita GDP:** $1,000

Industries: fishing, handicrafts

Chief crops: copra, taro, breadfruit, sweet potatoes, vegetables

Life expectancy at birth (years): male, 58.3; female, 64.4

Literacy rate: NA   **Website:** www.state.gov/r/pa/ei/bgn/1836.htm

MARSHALL ISLANDS

For map, see page 174

Population: 63,174

Ethnic groups: Micronesian

Principal languages: English, Marshallese (both official); Malay-Polynesian dialects, Japanese

Chief religion: mostly Protestant

Area: 70 sq mi (181 sq km)

Topography: The Marshalls are low coral limestone and sand islands.

Capital: Majuro (pop., 25,000)

Independence date: October 21, 1986   **Government type:** republic

MICRONESIA

For map, see page 174

Population: 107,673

Ethnic groups: 9 distinct Micronesian and Polynesian groups

Principal languages: English (official), Trukese, Pohnpeian, Yapese, Kosrean, Ulithian, Woleaian, Nukuoro, Kapingamarangi

Chief religions: Roman Catholic 50%, Protestant 47%

Area: 270 sq mi (700 sq km)

Topography: The country includes both high mountainous islands and low coral atolls; volcanic outcroppings on Pohnpei, Kosrae, and Truk.

Capital: Palikir, on Pohnpei (pop., 7,000)

Independence date: November 3, 1986

Government type: republic

Head of state and government: Pres. Joseph J. Urusemal

Monetary unit: U.S. dollar

GDP: $277 million (2004 est.)   **Per capita GDP:** $2,300

Industries: tourism, construction, fish processing, craft items from shell, wood, and pearls

Chief crops: black pepper, tropical fruits and vegetables, coconuts, cassava, sweet potatoes

Minerals: deep-seabed minerals

Life expectancy at birth (years): male, 66.7; female, 71.3

Literacy rate: 89%   **Website:** www.fsmgov.org

NAURU

For map, see page 174

Population: 13,770

Ethnic groups: Nauruan 58%, other Pacific Islander 26%, Chinese 8%, European 8%

Principal languages: Nauruan (official), English

Chief religions: Protestant 66%, Roman Catholic 33%

Area: 8 sq mi (21 sq km)

Topography: Mostly a plateau bearing high-grade phosphate deposits, surrounded by a sandy shore and coral reef in concentric rings.

Capital: offices in Yaren District

Independence date: January 31, 1968

Government type: republic

Head of state and government: Pres. Marcus Stephens

Monetary unit: Australian dollar

GDP: $60 million (2005 est.)   Per capita GDP: $5,000

Industries: mining, offshore banking, coconut products

Chief crops: rice, corn, wheat, sugarcane, root crops

Minerals: phosphates

Life expectancy at birth (years): male, 58.4; female, 65.7

Literacy rate: NA   Website: www.un.int/nauru

A New Zealand shepherd with his sheep

NEW ZEALAND

FOR MAP, SEE PAGE 175

Population: 4,154,311

Ethnic groups: New Zealand European 75%, Maori 10%, other European 5%, Pacific Islander 4%

Principal languages: English, Maori (both official)

Chief religions: Protestant 52%, Roman Catholic 15%

Area: 103,740 sq mi (268,680 sq km)

Topography: Each of the two main islands (North and South Islands) is mainly hilly and mountainous. The eastern coasts consist of fertile plains, especially the broad Canterbury Plains on South Island. A volcanic plateau is in the center of North Island. South Island has glaciers and 15 peaks over 10,000 ft (3,000 m).

Capital: Wellington (pop., 343,000)

Independence date: September 26, 1907

Government type: parliamentary democracy

Head of state: Queen Elizabeth II, represented by Gov.-Gen. Dame Anand Satyanand

Head of government: Prime Min. Helen Clark

Monetary unit: New Zealand dollar

GDP: $112.6 billion (2007 est.)

Per capita GDP: $27,300

Industries: food processing, wood and paper products, textiles, machinery, transport equipment, banking and insurance, tourism, mining

Chief crops: wheat, barley, potatoes, pulses, fruits, vegetables

Minerals: natural gas, iron ore, sand, coal, gold, limestone

Life expectancy at birth (years): male, 75.5; female, 81.6

Literacy rate: 99%

Websites: www.govt.nz www.nzembassy.com

Shotover River, New Zealand

PALAU

FOR MAP, SEE PAGE 174

Population: 21,093

Ethnic groups: Palauan (Micronesian/Malayan/Melanesian mix) 70%, Asian 28%, white 2%

Principal languages: English (official); Palauan, Sonsorolese, Tobi, Angaur, Japanese (all official in certain states)

Chief religions: Roman Catholic 49%, Modekngei 30%

Area: 180 sq mi (460 sq km)

Topography: Palau is made up of a mountainous main island and low coral atolls, usually fringed with large barrier reefs.

Capital: Melekeok (pop. 300)

Independence date: October 1, 1994

Government type: republic

Head of state and government: Pres. Tommy Esang Remengesau, Jr.

Monetary unit: U.S. dollar

GDP: $124.5 million (2004 est.)   Per capita GDP: $7,600

Industries: tourism, craft items, construction, garment making

Chief crops: coconuts, copra, cassava, sweet potatoes

Minerals: gold, deep-seabed minerals

Life expectancy at birth (years): male, 66.7; female, 73.2

Literacy rate: 92%   Website: www.visit-palau.com

SAMOA

FOR MAP, SEE PAGE 175

Population: 217,083

Ethnic groups: Samoan 92.5%, Euronesians 7%

Principal languages: Samoan, English (both official)

Chief religion: Christian 99.7%

Area: 1,100 sq mi (2,860 sq km)

Topography: Samoa consists of two main islands, Savaii (659 sq mi [1,710 sq km]) and Upolu (432 sq mi [1,120 sq km]), both ruggedly mountainous, and several small islands, of which Manono and Apolima are inhabited.

Capital: Apia (pop., 40,000)   Independence date: January 1, 1962

Government type: constitutional monarchy

Head of state: Malietoa Tanumafili II

Head of government: Prime Min. Tuilaepa Sailele Malielegaoi

Nation Facts and Figures

Samoa *(continued)*

Monetary unit: tala

GDP: $1.2 billion (2006 est.)   Per capita GDP: $2,100

Industries: food processing, building materials, auto parts

Chief crops: coconuts, bananas, taro, yams

Life expectancy at birth (years): male, 67.6; female, 73.3

Literacy rate: 80%

Website: www.govt.ws

SOLOMON ISLANDS

FOR MAP, SEE PAGE 174

Population: 581,208

Ethnic groups: Melanesian 93%, Polynesian 4%, Micronesian, European, and others 3%

Principal languages: English (official), Melanesian pidgin, and 120 indigenous languages

Chief religions: Anglican 45%, Roman Catholic 18%, other Christian 35%

Area: 10,980 sq mi (28,450 sq km)

Topography: 10 large volcanic and rugged islands and 4 groups of smaller ones.

Capital: Honiara (pop., 56,000)

Independence date: July 7, 1978

Government type: parliamentary democracy

Head of state: Queen Elizabeth II, represented by Gov.-Gen. Sir Nathaniel Waena

Head of government: Prime Min. Derek Sikua

Monetary unit: Solomon Islands dollar (SBD)

GDP: $800 million (2002 est.)   Per capita GDP: $600

Industries: fish, mining, timber

Chief crops: cocoa, beans, coconuts, palm kernels, rice, potatoes, vegetables, fruit

Minerals: gold, bauxite, phosphates, lead, zinc, nickel

Life expectancy at birth (years): male, 69.9; female, 75.0

Literacy rate: NA   Website: www.commerce.gov.sb

TONGA

FOR MAP, SEE PAGE 175

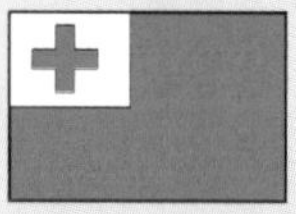

Population: 118,993

Ethnic groups: Polynesian

Principal languages: Tongan, English (both official)

Chief religions: Wesleyan 41%, Roman Catholic 16%, Mormon 14%

Area: 290 sq mi (750 sq km)

Topography: Tonga comprises 170 volcanic and coral islands, 36 inhabited.

Capital: Nuku'alofa (pop., 35,000)

Independence date: June 4, 1970

Government type: constitutional monarchy

Head of state: King Taufa'ahau Tupou IV

Head of government: Prime Min. Feleti Seveli

Monetary unit: pa'anga

GDP: $877 million (2006 est.)

Per capita GDP: $2,200

Industries: tourism, fishing

Chief crops: squash, coconuts, copra, bananas, vanilla beans, cocoa, coffee, ginger, black pepper

Life expectancy at birth (years): male, 66.7; female, 71.8

Literacy rate: 98.5%

Website: www.pmo.gov.to

TUVALU

FOR MAP, SEE PAGE 174

Population: 12,181

Ethnic group: Polynesian 96%, Micronesian 4%

Principal languages: Tuvaluan, English, Samoan, Kiribati (on the island of Nui)

Chief religion: Church of Tuvalu (Congregationalist) 97%

Area: 10 sq mi (26 sq km)

Topography: Tuvalu's nine islands are all low-lying coral atolls, nowhere rising more than 15 ft (4.6 m) above sea level.

Capital: Funafuti (pop., 6,000)   Independence date: October 1, 1978

Government type: parliamentary democracy

Head of state: Queen Elizabeth II, represented by Gov.-Gen. Filoimea Telito

Head of government: Prime Min. Maatia Toafa

Monetary unit: Australian dollar

GDP: $14.9 million (2002 est.)   Per capita GDP: $1,600

Industries: fishing, tourism, copra

Chief crops: coconuts

Life expectancy at birth (years): male, 65.5; female, 70.0

Literacy rate: 55%   Website: www.timelesstuvalu.com

VANUATU

FOR MAP, SEE PAGE 174

Population: 215,053

Ethnic groups: Melanesian 98%, French, Vietnamese, Chinese, other Pacific Islanders

Principal languages: Bislama, English, French (all official); more than 100 local languages

Chief religions: Presbyterian 37%, Anglican 15%, Roman Catholic 15%, other Christian 10%, indigenous beliefs 8%

Area: 5,700 sq mi (14,760 sq km)

Topography: Dense forest with narrow coastal strips of cultivated land.

Capital: Port-Vila (pop., 34,000)   Independence date: July 30, 1980

Government type: republic

Head of state: Pres. Kalkot Mataskelekele

Head of government: Prime Min. Ham Lini

Monetary unit: vatu

GDP: $739 million (2006 est.)   Per capita GDP: $2,900

Industries: food and fish freezing, wood processing, meat canning

Chief crops: copra, coconuts, cocoa, coffee, taro, yams, coconuts, fruits, vegetables

Minerals: manganese

Life expectancy at birth (years): male, 60.6; female, 63.6

Literacy rate: 53%

Website: www.vanuatugovernment.gov.vu

EUROPE

Twenty-seven nations are members of the European Union: Austria, Belgium, Bulgaria, Cyprus, Czech Republic, Denmark, Estonia, Finland, France, Germany, Greece, Hungary, Ireland, Italy, Latvia, Lithuania, Luxembourg, Malta, the Netherlands, Poland, Portugal, Romania, Slovakia, Slovenia, Spain, Sweden, and the United Kingdom.

ALBANIA

FOR MAP, SEE PAGE 105

Population: 3,619,778
Ethnic groups: Albanian 95%, Greek 3%
Principal languages: Albanian (Tosk is the official dialect), Greek
Chief religions: Muslim 70%, Albanian Orthodox 20%, Roman Catholic 10%
Area: 11,100 sq mi (28,750 sq km)
Topography: Apart from a narrow coastal plain, Albania consists of hills and mountains covered with scrub forest, cut by small east to west rivers.
Capital: Tiranë (pop., 367,000)
Independence date: November 28, 1912   **Government type:** republic
Head of state: Pres. Alfred Moisiu
Head of government: Prime Min. Sali Berisha   **Monetary unit:** lek
GDP: $19.76 billion (2007 est.)   **Per capita GDP:** $5,500
Industries: food processing, textiles and clothing, lumber, oil, cement, chemicals, mining, basic metals, hydropower
Chief crops: wheat, corn, potatoes, vegetables, fruits, sugar beets, grapes
Minerals: petroleum, natural gas, coal, chromium, copper, timber, nickel
Life expectancy at birth (years): male, 74.4; female, 80.0
Literacy rate: 93%
Website: www.albaniantourism.com

ANDORRA

FOR MAP, SEE PAGE 103

Population: 72,413
Ethnic groups: Spanish 43%, Andorran 33%, Portuguese 11%, French 7%
Principal languages: Catalan (official), Castilian Spanish, French
Chief religion: predominantly Roman Catholic
Area: 174 sq mi (450 sq km)
Topography: High mountains and narrow valleys cover the country.
Capital: Andorra la Vella (pop., 21,000)
Independence date: 1278
Government type: parliamentary co-principality
Heads of state: president of France & bishop of Urgel (Spain), as co-princes
Head of government: Pres. Albert Pintat Santolèria
Monetary unit: euro
GDP: $2.77 billion (2005)   **Per capita GDP:** $38,800
Industries: tourism, cattle raising, timber, tobacco, banking
Chief crops: tobacco, rye, wheat, barley, oats, vegetables
Minerals: iron ore, lead
Life expectancy at birth (years): male, 80.6; female, 86.6
Literacy rate: 100%
Website: www.andorra.ad/ang/home/index.tm

AUSTRIA*

FOR MAP, SEE PAGE 101

Population: 8,205,533
Ethnic groups: German 88%
Principal languages: German (official), Serbo-Croatian, Slovenian
Chief religions: Roman Catholic 78%, Protestant 5%

*Member of the European Union

Nation Facts and Figures

Austria *(continued)*

Area: 32,380 sq mi (83,860 sq km)

Topography: Austria is primarily mountainous, with the Alps and foothills covering the western and southern provinces. The eastern provinces and Vienna are located in the Danube River Basin.

Capital: Vienna (pop., 2,179,000)

Independence date: 1156

Government type: federal republic

Head of state: Pres. Heinz Fischer

Head of government: Chancellor Wolfgang Schüssel

Monetary unit: euro

GDP: $319.7 billion (2007 est.)   **Per capita GDP:** $39,000

Industries: construction, machinery, vehicles and parts, food, chemicals, lumber and wood processing, paper and paperboard, commercial equipment, tourism

Chief crops: grains, potatoes, sugar beets, fruit

Minerals: iron ore, oil, timber, magnesite, lead, coal, copper

Life expectancy at birth (years): male, 75.0; female, 81.5

Literacy rate: 98%   **Website:** www.austria.org

Innsbruck, Austria

BELARUS

FOR MAP, SEE PAGE 85

Population: 9,685,768

Ethnic groups: Belarusian 81%, Russian 11%

Principal languages: Belarusian, Russian

Chief religions: Eastern Orthodox 80%, other 20%

Area: 80,200 sq mi (207,600 sq km)

Topography: Belarus is a landlocked country consisting mostly of hilly lowland with significant marsh areas in the south.

Capital: Minsk (pop., 1,705,000)   **Independence date:** August 25, 1991

Government type: republic

Head of state: Pres. Aleksandr Lukashenko

Head of government: Prime Min. Sergey Sidorsky

Monetary unit: ruble

GDP: $104.7 billion (2007 est.)   **Per capita GDP:** $10,200

Industries: machine tools, tractors, trucks, earthmovers, motorcycles, domestic appliances, chemical fibers, fertilizer, textiles

Chief crops: grain, potatoes, vegetables, sugar beets, flax

Minerals: oil and natural gas, granite, dolomitic limestone, marl, chalk, sand, gravel, clay

Life expectancy at birth (years): male, 62.8; female, 74.7

Literacy rate: 98%

Website: www.belarusembassy.org

BELGIUM*

FOR MAP, SEE PAGE 98

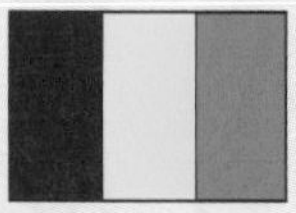

Population: 10,403,951

Ethnic groups: Fleming 58%, Walloon 31%

Principal languages: Dutch, French, German (all official); Flemish, Luxembourgish

_____

*Member of the European Union

Chief religions: Roman Catholic 75%; Protestant, other 25%

Area: 11,780 sq mi (30,510 sq km)

Topography: Mostly flat, the country is trisected by the Scheldt and Meuse, major commercial rivers. The land becomes hilly and forested in the southeast (Ardennes) region.

Capital: Brussels (pop., 998,000)

Independence date: October 4, 1830

Government type: parliamentary democracy under a constitutional monarch

Head of state: King Albert II

Head of government: Premier Guy Verhofstadt

Monetary unit: euro

GDP: $378.9 billion (2007 est.)   **Per capita GDP:** $36,500

Industries: engineering and metal products, motor vehicle assembly, processed food and beverages, chemicals, basic metals, textiles, glass, petroleum, coal

Chief crops: sugar beets, fresh vegetables, fruits, grain, tobacco

Minerals: coal, natural gas

Life expectancy at birth (years): male, 75.3; female, 81.8

Literacy rate: 98%

Website: www.diplobel.us

BOSNIA AND HERZEGOVINA

FOR MAP, SEE PAGE 106

Population: 4,590,310

Ethnic groups: Bosniak 48%, Serbian 37%, Croatian 14%

Principal languages: Bosnian (official), Croatian, Serbian

Chief religions: Muslim 40%, Orthodox 31%, Roman Catholic 15%, Protestant 4%

Area: 19,740 sq mi (51,130 sq km)

Topography: Hilly with some mountains. About 36% of the land is forested.

Capital: Sarajevo (pop., 579,000)

Independence date: March 1, 1992

Government type: federal republic

Heads of state: collective presidency with rotating leadership

Head of government: Prime Min. Adnan Terzic

Monetary unit: converted marka (BAM)

GDP: $29.9 billion (2007 est.)   **Per capita GDP:** $6,600

Industries: steel, mining, vehicle assembly, textiles, tobacco products, wooden furniture, tank and aircraft assembly, domestic appliances, oil refining

Chief crops: wheat, corn, fruits, vegetables

Minerals: coal, iron, bauxite, manganese, copper, chromium, lead, zinc

Life expectancy at birth (years): male, 69.8; female, 75.5

Literacy rate: NA

Website: www.bhembassy.org

BULGARIA*

FOR MAP, SEE PAGE 107

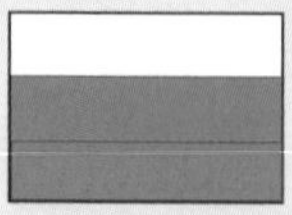

Population: 7,262,675

Ethnic groups: Bulgarian 84%, Turk 10%, Roma 5%

Principal languages: Bulgarian (official), Turkish

Chief religions: Bulgarian Orthodox 84%, Muslim 12%

Area: 42,820 sq mi (110,910 sq km)

Topography: The Stara Planina (Balkan) Mountains stretch east to west across the center of the country, with the Danubian plain on the north, the Rhodope Mountains on the southwest, and the Thracian Plain on the southeast.

Capital: Sofia (pop., 1,076,000)

Independence date: March 3, 1878

Government type: republic

Head of state: Pres. Georgi Parvanov

Head of government: Prime Min. Sergei Stanishev

Monetary unit: lev

GDP: $86.73 billion (2007 est.)

Per capita GDP: $11,800

Industries: electricity, gas and water, food, beverages and tobacco, machinery and equipment, base metals, chemical products, coke, refined petroleum, nuclear fuel

A Bulgarian cathedral

Chief crops: vegetables, fruits, tobacco, wheat, barley, sunflowers, sugar beets

Minerals: bauxite, copper, lead, zinc, coal

Life expectancy at birth (years): male, 68.1; female, 75.6

Literacy rate: 98%

Website: www.government.bg/English

CROATIA

For map, see page 106

Population: 4,491,543

Ethnic groups: Croat 78%, Serb 12%, Bosniak 1%

Principal languages Croatian (official), Serbian

Chief religions: Roman Catholic 88%, Orthodox 5%

Area: 21,830 sq mi (56,540 sq km)

Topography: Flat plains in the northeast; highlands, low mountains along the Adriatic coast.

Capital: Zagreb (pop., 688,000)   Independence date: June 25, 1991

Government type: parliamentary democracy

Head of state: Pres. Stipe Mesic

Head of government: Prime Min. Ivo Sanader

Monetary unit: kuna

GDP: $69.44 billion (2007 est.)   Per capita GDP: $15,500

Industries: chemicals and plastics, machine tools, fabricated metal, electronics, pig iron and rolled steel products, aluminum, paper, wood products, construction materials, textiles, shipbuilding, tourism

Chief crops: wheat, corn, sugar beets, sunflower seed, barley, alfalfa, clover, olives, citrus, grapes, soybeans, potatoes

Minerals: oil, coal, bauxite, iron ore, calcium, natural asphalt, silica, mica, clays, salt

Life expectancy at birth (years): male, 70.2; female, 78.3

Literacy rate: 97%

Website: www.vlada.hr/default.asp?ru=2

CZECH REPUBLIC*

For map, see page 99

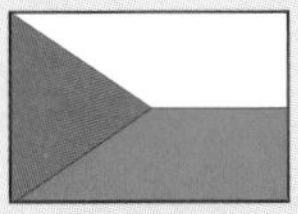

Population: 10,220,911

Ethnic groups: Czech 81%, Moravian 13%, Slovak 3%

Principal languages: Czech (official), German, Polish, Romani

Chief religions: atheist 40%, Roman Catholic 39%, Protestant 5%, Orthodox 3%

Area: 30,350 sq mi (78,870 sq km)

Topography: Bohemia, in the west, is a plateau surrounded by mountains; Moravia is hilly.

Capital: Prague (pop., 1,170,000)

Independence date: January 1, 1993   Government type: republic

Head of state: Pres. Václav Klaus

Head of government: Prime Min. Jiri Paroubek

Monetary unit: koruna

GDP: $249.1 billion (2007 est.)   Per capita GDP: $24,400

Industries: metallurgy, machinery and equipment, motor vehicles, glass, armaments

Chief crops: wheat, potatoes, sugar beets, hops, fruit

Minerals: coal, kaolin, clay, graphite

Life expectancy at birth (years): male, 72.5; female, 79.2

Literacy rate: 99.9%   Website: www.czech.cz

Prague, Czech Republic

DENMARK*

For map, see page 96

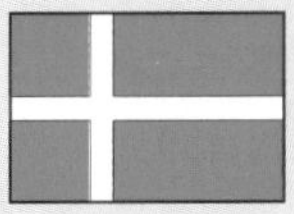

Population: 5,484,723

Ethnic groups: Mainly Danish; German minority in south

Principal languages: Danish (official), Faroese, Greenlandic (an Inuit dialect), German

Chief religions: Evangelical Lutheran (official) 95%, other Christian 3%, Muslim 2%

Area: 16,640 sq mi (43,090 sq km)

Topography: Denmark consists of the Jutland Peninsula and about 500 islands, 100 inhabited. The land is flat or gently rolling and is almost all in productive use.

Capital: Copenhagen (pop., 1,066,000)

Independence date: 10th century

Government type: constitutional monarchy

Head of state: Queen Margrethe II

Head of government: Prime Min. Anders Fogh Rasmussen

Monetary unit: krone

GDP: $204.6 billion (2007 est.)   Per capita GDP: $37,400

Industries: food processing, machinery and equipment, textiles and clothing, chemical products, electronics, construction, furniture, shipbuilding

Chief crops: barley, wheat, potatoes, sugar beets

Minerals: petroleum, natural gas, salt, limestone, stone, gravel and sand

Life expectancy at birth (years): male, 75.2; female, 79.8

Literacy rate: 100%

Website: www.ambwashington.um.dk/en

GREENLAND (Kalaallit Nunaat), a huge island situated between the North Atlantic and the Polar Sea and separated from the North American continent by the Davis Strait and Baffin Bay, is part of the Danish realm but possesses home rule. Population, 56,326; area, 836,660 sq mi (2,166,086 sq km), 81% of which is ice-capped; capital, Nuuk (Godthab).

*Member of the European Union

Nation Facts and Figures

ESTONIA – GERMANY

ESTONIA*

FOR MAP, SEE PAGE 97

Population: 1,307,605

Ethnic groups: Estonian 65%, Russian 28%

Principal languages: Estonian (official), Russian, Ukrainian, Finnish

Chief religions: Evangelical Lutheran, Russian Orthodox, Estonian Orthodox

Area: 17,460 sq mi (45,230 sq km)

Topography: Estonia is a marshy lowland with numerous lakes and swamps; about 40% forested. Elongated hills show evidence of former glaciation. There are more than 800 islands on the Baltic coast.

Capital: Tallinn (pop., 391,000)

Independence date: August 20, 1991   **Government type:** republic

Head of state: Pres. Arnold Rüütel

Head of government: Prime Min. Andrus Ansip

Monetary unit: kroon

GDP: $29.4 billion (2007 est.)   **Per capita GDP:** $21,800

Industries: engineering, electronics, wood and wood products, textile, information technology, telecommunications

Chief crops: potatoes, vegetables

Minerals: oil shale, peat, phosphorite, clay, limestone, sand, dolomite, sea mud

Life expectancy at birth (years): male, 65.8; female, 77.3

Literacy rate: 100%   **Website:** www.riik.ee/en/

FINLAND*

FOR MAP, SEE PAGE 95

Population: 5,244,749

Ethnic groups: Finnish 93%, Swedish 6%

Principal languages: Finnish, Swedish (both official); Russian, Sami

Chief religion: Evangelical Lutheran 89%

Area: 130,130 sq mi (337,030 sq km)

Topography: South and central Finland are generally flat areas with low hills and many lakes. The north has mountainous areas, 3,000 to 4,000 ft (900 to 1,200 m) above sea level.

Capital: Helsinki (pop., 1,075,000)

Independence date: December 6, 1917

Government type: republic   **Head of state:** Pres. Tarja Halonen

Head of government: Prime Min. Matti Vanhanen

Monetary unit: euro

GDP: $185.9 billion (2007 est.)   **Per capita GDP:** $35,500

Industries: metal products, electronics, shipbuilding, pulp and paper, copper refining, foodstuffs, chemicals, textiles, clothing

Chief crops: barley, wheat, sugar beets, potatoes

Minerals: copper, zinc, iron ore, silver

Life expectancy at birth (years): male, 74.7; female, 81.9

Literacy rate: 100%

Website: www.finland.org/en/

The ÅLAND ISLANDS (Ahvenanmaa), constituting an autonomous province, are a group of small islands in the Gulf of Bothnia. Population 26,008; area, 590 sq mi (1,500 sq km); capital, Mariehamn.

FRANCE*

FOR MAP, SEE PAGE 100

Population: 60,094,658

Ethnic groups: French, with Slavic, North African, Indochinese, Basque minorities

Parisian landmarks: Arc de Triomphe (left), Eiffel Tower (right)

Principal languages: French (official), Italian, Breton, Alsatian (German), Corsican, Gascon, Portuguese, Provençal, Dutch, Flemish, Catalan, Basque, Romani

Chief religions: Roman Catholic 83–88%, Muslim 5–10%

Area: 211,210 sq mi (547,030 sq km)

Topography: A wide plain covers more than half of the country, in the north and west, drained to the west by the Seine, Loire, and Garonne rivers. The Massif Central is a mountainous plateau in the center. In the east are the Alps (Mt. Blanc is the tallest peak in Western Europe, 15,771 ft [4,807 m]), the lower Jura range, and the forested Vosges. The Rhone flows from Lake Geneva to the Mediterranean. The Pyrenees are in the southwest, on the border with Spain.

Capital: Paris (pop., 9,794,000)   **Independence date:** 486

Government type: republic

Head of state: Pres. Nicholas Sarkosy

Head of government: Prime Min. François Fillon

Monetary unit: euro

GDP: $2,067 billion (2007 est.)   **Per capita GDP:** $33,800

Industries: machinery, chemicals, automobiles, metallurgy, aircraft, electronics, textiles, food processing, tourism

Chief crops: wheat, cereals, sugar beets, potatoes, wine grapes

Minerals: coal, iron ore, bauxite, zinc, potash

Life expectancy at birth (years): male, 75.8; female, 83.3

Literacy rate: 99%   **Website:** www.info-france-usa.org

GERMANY*

FOR MAP, SEE PAGE 98

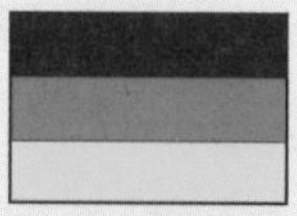

Population: 82,369,548

Ethnic groups: German 92%, Turkish 2%

Principal languages: German (official), Turkish, Italian, Greek, English, Danish, Dutch, Slavic languages

Chief religions: Protestant 34%, Roman Catholic 34%, Muslim 4%

Area: 137,890 sq mi (357,070 sq km)

Topography: Germany is flat in the north, hilly in the center and west, and mountainous in Bavaria in the south. The chief rivers are the Elbe, Weser, Ems, Rhine, and Main, all flowing toward the North Sea, and the Danube, flowing toward the Black Sea.

Capital: Berlin (pop., 3,327,000)

Independence date: January 18, 1871

Government type: federal republic

Head of state: Pres. Horst Köhler

Head of government: Chancellor Angela Merkel

Monetary unit: euro

*Member of the European Union

Looking down a German street

GDP: $2,833 billion (2007 est.)
Per capita GDP: $34,400

Industries: mining, steel, cement, chemicals, machinery, vehicles, machine tools, electronics, food and beverages, shipbuilding, textiles

Chief crops: potatoes, wheat, barley, sugar beets, fruit, cabbages

Minerals: iron ore, coal, potash, lignite, uranium, copper, natural gas, salt, nickel

Life expectancy at birth (years): male, 75.6; female, 81.7

Literacy rate: 99%

Website: www.germany–info.org

Bavarian village church, Germany

GREECE*

FOR MAP, SEE PAGE 105

Population: 10,722,816

Ethnic groups: Greek 98%

Principal languages: Greek (official), English, French

Chief religions: Greek Orthodox (official) 98%, Muslim 1%

Area: 50,940 sq mi (131,940 sq km)

Topography: About three-quarters of Greece is nonarable, with mountains in all areas. Pindus Mountains run through the country north to south. The heavily indented coastline is 9,385 mi (15,100 km) long. Of over 2,000 islands, only 169 are inhabited, among them Crete, Rhodes, Milos, Kerkira (Corfu), Chios, Lesbos, Samos, Euboea, Delos, and Mykonos.

Capital: Athens (pop., 3,215,000)   Independence date: 1829

Government type: parliamentary republic

Head of state: Pres. Karolos Papoulias

Head of government: Prime Min. Konstantinos (Kostas) Karamanlis

Monetary unit: euro

Parthenon, Athens, Greece

―――――――
*Member of the European Union

GDP: $326.4 billion (2007 est.)   Per capita GDP: $30,500

Industries: tourism, food and tobacco processing, textiles, chemicals, metal products, mining, petroleum

Chief crops: wheat, corn, barley, sugar beets, olives, tomatoes, tobacco, potatoes

Minerals: bauxite, lignite, magnesite, petroleum, marble

Life expectancy at birth (years): male, 76.4; female, 81.6

Literacy rate: 97%   Website: www.greekembassy.org

HUNGARY

FOR MAP, SEE PAGE 106

Population: 9,930,915

Ethnic groups: Hungarian 90%, Roma 4%, German 3%, Serb 2%

Principal languages: Hungarian (official), Romani, German, Slavic languages, Romanian

Chief religions: Roman Catholic 68%, Protestant 25%

Area: 35,920 sq mi (93,030 sq km)

Topography: The Danube River forms the Slovak border in the northwest, then swings south to bisect the country. The eastern half of Hungary is mainly a great fertile plain, the Alfold; the west and north are hilly.

Capital: Budapest (pop., 1,708,000)

Independence date: 1001   Government type: parliamentary democracy

Head of state: Pres. László Sólyom

Head of government: Prime Min. Ferenc Gyurcsány

Monetary unit: forint

GDP: $194.2 billion (2007 est.)   Per capita GDP: $19,500

Industries: mining, metallurgy, construction materials, processed foods, textiles, pharmaceuticals, motor vehicles

Chief crops: wheat, corn, sunflower seed, potatoes, sugar beets

Minerals: bauxite, coal, natural gas

Life expectancy at birth (years): male, 68.1; female, 76.7

Literacy rate: 99%   Website: www.hungary.hu

ICELAND

FOR MAP, SEE PAGE 95

Population: 304,367

Ethnic groups: Icelandic 94%

Principal language: Icelandic (official)

Chief religion: Evangelical Lutheran 93%

Area: 40,000 sq mi (103,000 sq km)

Topography: Iceland is of recent volcanic origin. Three-quarters of the surface is wasteland: glaciers, lakes, a lava desert. There are geysers and hot springs.

Capital: Reykjavík (pop., 184,000)

Independence date: June 17, 1944

Government type: constitutional republic

Head of state: Pres. Olafur Ragnar Grímsson

Head of government: Prime Min. Halldór Ásgrímsson

Monetary unit: krona

GDP: $11.9 billion (2007 est.)   Per capita GDP: $39,400

Industries: fish processing, aluminum smelting, ferrosilicon production, geothermal power, tourism

Chief crops: potatoes, turnips   Minerals: diatomite

Life expectancy at birth (years): male, 78.2; female, 82.3

Literacy rate: 99.9%

Website: www.iceland.is

Nation Facts and Figures

IRELAND – LATVIA

IRELAND*

FOR MAP, SEE PAGE 89

Population: 4,156,119

Ethnic groups: Celtic; English minority

Principal languages: English, Irish Gaelic (both official); Irish Gaelic spoken by small number in western areas

Chief religions: Roman Catholic 92%, Anglican 3%

Area: 27,140 sq mi (70,280 sq km)

Topography: Ireland consists of a central plateau surrounded by isolated groups of hills and mountains. The coastline is heavily indented by the Atlantic Ocean.

Capital: Dublin (pop., 1,015,000)   **Independence date:** December 6, 1921

Government type: parliamentary republic

Head of state: Pres. Mary McAleese

Head of government: Prime Min. Bertie Ahern

Monetary unit: euro

GDP: $187.5 billion (2007 est.)   **Per capita GDP:** $45,600

Industries: food products, brewing, textiles, clothing, chemicals, pharmaceuticals, machinery, transport equipment, glass and crystal, software

Chief crops: turnips, barley, potatoes, sugar beets, wheat

Minerals: zinc, lead, natural gas, barite, copper, gypsum, limestone, dolomite, peat, silver

Life expectancy at birth (years): male, 74.7; female, 80.2

Literacy rate: 98%

Websites: www.irlgov.ie   www.irelandemb.org

ITALY*

FOR MAP, SEE PAGE 85

Population: 58,145,321

Ethnic groups: mostly Italian; small minorities of German, Slovene, Albanian

Principal languages: Italian (official), German, French, Slovenian, Albanian

Chief religion: predominantly Roman Catholic

Area: 116,310 sq mi (301,230 sq km)

Topography: Italy occupies a long boot-shaped peninsula, extending southeast from the Alps into the Mediterranean, with the islands of Sicily and Sardinia offshore. The alluvial Po Valley drains most of the north. The rest of the country is rugged and mountainous, except for intermittent coastal plains, like the Campania, south of Rome. The Apennine Mountains run down through the center of the peninsula.

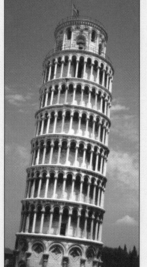

Leaning Tower of Pisa, Italy

Capital: Rome (pop., 2,665,000)

Independence date: March 17, 1861

Government type: republic

Head of state: Pres. Giorgio Napolitano

Head of government: Prime Min. Silvio Berlusconi

Monetary unit: euro

GDP: $1,800 billion (2007 est.)

Per capita GDP: $31,000

Industries: tourism, machinery, iron and steel, chemicals, food processing, textiles, motor vehicles, clothing, footwear, ceramics

Chief crops: fruits, vegetables, grapes, potatoes, sugar beets, soybeans, grain, olives

---

*Member of the European Union

Colosseum, Rome, Italy

Minerals: mercury, potash, marble, sulfur, natural gas, oil, coal

Life expectancy at birth (years): male, 76.5; female, 82.5

Literacy rate: 98%

Websites: www.italyemb.org   www.travel.it

KOSOVO

FOR MAP, SEE PAGE 106

Population: 2,126,708

Ethnic groups: Albanian 88%, Serbian 7%, Bosniak 2%

Principal languages: Albanian, Serbian

Chief religions: Muslim 90%, Serbian Orthodox 10%

Area: 4,203 sq mi (10,887 sq km)

Topography: Kosovo is mostly highland with canyons and wide valleys. The principal river, the Beli Drim, bisects the southwest region. Arable land is found in the west and northwest.

Capital: Priština (pop., 250,000)

Independence date: February 17, 2008

Government type: UN protectorate   **Head of state:** Pres. Fatmir Sejdiu

Head of government: Prime Min. Hashim Thaçi

Monetary unit: euro

GDP: $4 billion (2007 est.)   **Per capita GDP:** $1,800

Industries: Mining and smelting, leather products, machinery, appliances

Chief crops: grains, fruit, nuts, tobacco, potatoes

Minerals: lead, zinc, lignite, chromite, magnesite, halloysite, nickel

Life expectancy at birth (years): male, 71.0; female, 77.2

Literacy rate: 94.1%

Websites: www.state.gov/r/pa/ei/bgn/100931.htm

LATVIA*

FOR MAP, SEE PAGE 97

Population: 2,245,423

Ethnic groups: Latvian 58%, Russian 30%, Belarusian 4%, Ukrainian 3%, Polish 2%, Lithuanian 1%

Principal languages: Latvian (official), Russian, Belarusian, Ukrainian, Polish

Chief religions: Lutheran, Roman Catholic, Russian Orthodox

Area: 24,900 sq mi (64,590 sq km)

Topography: Latvia is a lowland with numerous lakes, marshes and peat bogs. The principal river, the Western Dvina (Daugava), rises in Russia. There are glacial hills in the east.

Capital: Riga (pop., 733,000)

Independence date: August 21, 1991

Government type: republic   **Head of state:** Pres. Vaira Vike-Freiberga

Head of government: Prime Min. Aigars Kalvitis

Monetary unit: lat

GDP: $40 billion (2007 est.)   Per capita GDP: $17,700

Industries: motor vehicles, railroad cars, synthetic fibers, agricultural machinery, fertilizers, household appliances, pharmaceuticals, processed foods, textiles

Chief crops: grain, sugar beets, potatoes, vegetables

Minerals: peat, limestone, dolomite, amber

Life expectancy at birth (years): male, 65.9; female, 76.1

Literacy rate: 99.8%

Websites: www.latvia-usa.org

LIECHTENSTEIN

For map, see page 115

Population: 34,498

Ethnic groups: Alemannic 86%; Italian, Turkish, and other 14%

Principal languages: German (official), Alemannic dialect

Chief religions: Roman Catholic 80%, Protestant 7%

Area: 62 sq mi (161 sq km)

Topography: The Rhine Valley occupies one-third of the country; the Alps cover the rest.

Capital: Vaduz (pop., 5,000)   Independence date: January 23, 1719

Government type: hereditary constitutional monarchy

Head of state: Prince Hans-Adam II   Head of government: Otmar Hasler

Monetary unit: Swiss franc

GDP: $1.786 billion (2001 est.)   Per capita GDP: $25,000

Industries: electronics, metal manufacturing, textiles, ceramics, pharmaceuticals, food products, precision instruments, tourism

Chief crops: wheat, barley, corn, potatoes

Life expectancy at birth (years): male, 75.8; female, 83

Literacy rate: 100%

Website: www.liechtenstein.li/en

LITHUANIA*

For map, see page 97

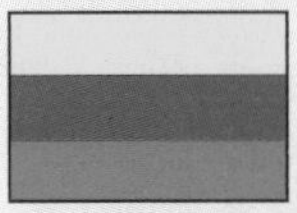

Population: 3,565,205

Ethnic groups: Lithuanian 81%, Russian 9%, Polish 7%, Belarusian 2%

Principal languages: Lithuanian (official), Belarusian, Russian, Polish

Chief religion: predominantly Roman Catholic

Area: 25,200 sq mi (65,200 sq km)

Topography: Lithuania is a lowland with hills in the west and south; fertile soil; many small lakes and rivers, with marshes especially in the north and west.

Capital: Vilnius (pop., 549,000)   Independence date: March 11, 1990

Government type: republic   Head of state: Pres. Valdas Adamkus

Head of government: Prime Min. Algirdas Brazauskas

Monetary unit: litas

GDP: $59.6 billion (2007 est.)   Per capita GDP: $16,700

Industries: machine tools, electric motors, household appliances, petroleum refining, shipbuilding, furniture making, textiles, food processing, fertilizers, agricultural machinery, optical equipment, electronic components, computers, amber

Chief crops: grain, potatoes, sugar beets, flax, vegetables

Minerals: peat

Life expectancy at birth (years): male, 68.2; female, 79.0

Literacy rate: 98%

Websites: www.president.lt/en   www.ltembassyus.org

LUXEMBOURG*

For map, see page 111

Population: 486,006

Ethnic groups: Mixture of French and German

Principal languages: Luxembourgish (national), German, French (official)

Chief religion: majority is Roman Catholic; 1979 law forbids collection of such statistics

Area: 1,000 sq mi (2,590 sq km)

Topography: Heavy forests (Ardennes) cover the north; the south is a low, open plateau.

Capital: Luxembourg (pop., 77,000)   Independence date: 1839

Government type: constitutional monarchy

Head of state: Grand Duke Henri

Head of government: Prime Min. Jean-Claude Juncker

Monetary unit: euro

GDP: $38.8 billion (2007 est.)   Per capita GDP: $80,800

Industries: banking, iron and steel, food processing, chemicals, metal products, tires, glass, aluminum

Chief crops: barley, oats, potatoes, wheat, fruits, wine grapes

Life expectancy at birth (years): male, 75.3; female, 82.1

Literacy rate: 100%   Website: www.luxembourg-usa.org

MACEDONIA (FORMER YUGOSLAV REPUBLIC OF MACEDONIA)

For map, see page 105

Population: 2,061,315

Ethnic groups: Macedonian 67%, Albanian 23%, Turkish 4%, Roma 2%, Serb 2%

Principal languages: Macedonian (official), Albanian, Turkish, Romani, Serbo-Croatian

Chief religions: Macedonian Orthodox 67%, Muslim 30%

Area: 9,780 sq mi (25,330 sq km)

Topography: Macedonia is a landlocked, mostly mountainous country, with deep river valleys and three large lakes; the country is bisected by the Vardar River.

Capital: Skopje (pop., 447,000)   Independence date: September 17, 1991

Government type: republic   Head of state: Pres. Branko Crvenkovski

Head of government: Prime Min. Vlado Buckovski

Monetary unit: euro

GDP: $17.3 billion (2007 est.)   Per capita GDP: $8,400

Industries: mining, textiles, wood products, tobacco, food processing, buses

Chief crops: rice, tobacco, wheat, corn, millet, cotton, sesame, mulberry leaves, citrus, vegetables

Minerals: chromium, lead, zinc, manganese, tungsten, nickel, iron ore, asbestos, sulfur

Life expectancy at birth (years): male, 72.5; female, 77.2

Literacy rate: NA   Website: www.macedonia.co/uk/mcic

MALTA*

For map, see page 104

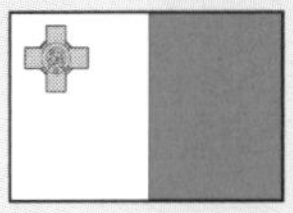

Population: 403,532

Ethnic group: Maltese, other Mediterranean

Principal languages: Maltese (a Semitic dialect), English (both official)

---

*Member of the European Union

Malta *(continued)*

Chief religion: Roman Catholic (official) 91%

Area: 124 sq mi (321 sq km)

Topography: The island of Malta is 95 sq mi (246 sq km); other islands in the group: Gozo, 26 sq mi (67 sq km); Comino, 1 sq mi (2.6 sq km). The coastline is heavily indented. Low hills cover the interior.

Capital: Valletta (pop., 83,000)

Independence date: September 21, 1964

Government type: parliamentary democracy

Head of state: Pres. Edward (Eddie) Fenech-Adami

Head of government: Prime Min. Lawrence Gonzi

Monetary unit: euro

GDP: $9.3 billion (2007 est.)   **Per capita GDP:** $23,200

Industries: tourism, electronics, shipbuilding, construction, food and beverages, textiles, footwear, clothing, tobacco

Chief crops: potatoes, cauliflower, grapes, wheat, barley, tomatoes, citrus, cut flowers, green peppers

Minerals: limestone, salt

Life expectancy at birth (years): male, 76.5; female, 81.0

Literacy rate: 88.76%   **Website:** www.gov.mt/index.asp?l=2

MOLDOVA

FOR MAP, SEE PAGE 107

Population: 4,324,450

Ethnic groups: Moldovan/Romanian 65%, Ukrainian 14%, Russian 13%

Principal languages: Moldovan (official), Russian, Gagauz (a Turkish dialect)

Chief religion: Eastern Orthodox 99%

Area: 13,000 sq mi (33,700 sq km)

Topography: The country is landlocked; mainly hilly plains, with steppelands in the south near the Black Sea.

Capital: Chisinau (pop., 662,000)   **Independence date:** August 27, 1991

Government type: republic

Head of state: Pres. Vladimir Voronin

Head of government: Prime Min. Vasile Tarlev

Monetary unit: leu

GDP: $10 billion (2007 est.)   **Per capita GDP:** $2,200

Industries: food processing, agricultural machinery, foundry equipment, household appliances, hosiery, sugar, vegetable oil, shoes, textiles

Chief crops: vegetables, fruits, wine, grain, sugar beets, sunflower seed, tobacco

Minerals: lignite, phosphorites, gypsum, limestone

Life expectancy at birth (years): male, 60.9; female, 69.4

Literacy rate: 96%   **Website:** www.tourism.md/eng

MONACO

FOR MAP, SEE PAGE 116

Population: 32,796

Ethnic groups: French 47%, Monegasque 16%, Italian 16%

Principal languages: French (official), English, Italian, Monegasque

Chief religion: Roman Catholic (official) 90%

Area: 0.75 sq mi (1.9 sq km)

Topography: Monaco-Ville sits atop a high promontory; the rest of the principality rises from the port up the hillside.

Capital: Monaco (pop., 32,000)   **Independence date:** 1419

Government type: constitutional monarchy

Head of state: Prince Rainier III

Head of government: Min. of State Patrick Leclercq

Monetary unit: euro

GDP: $976.3 million (2006 est.)   **Per capita GDP:** $30,000

Industries: tourism, construction, small-scale industrial and consumer products

Life expectancy at birth (years): male, 75.5; female, 83.5

Literacy rate: 99%   **Website:** www.monaco-consulate.com

MONTENEGRO

FOR MAP, SEE PAGE 106

Population: 678,177

Ethnic groups: Montenegrins 43%, Serbs 32%, Bosniaks 8%, Albanians 5%

Principal languages: Serbian of the Ijekavian dialect (official), Albanian

Chief religions: Orthodox 74%, Muslim 18%, Roman Catholic 2%

Area: 5,333 sq mi (13,812 sq km)

Topography: From high peaks along the borders with Kosovo and Albania, to a narrow coastal plain only one to four miles wide, Montenegro contains some of Europe's most diverse and rugged terrain.

Capital: Prodgorica (pop., 179,500)

Independence date: June 3, 2006   **Government type:** republic

Head of state: Pres. Filip Vujanovic

Head of government: Prime Min. Milo Dukanovic

Monetary unit: euro

GDP: $26.4 billion (2006 est.)   **Per capita GDP:** $3,800

Industries: Mining, manufacturing, chemicals, clothing, textiles, forestry

Chief crops: olives, wine, potatoes, corn, citrus fruit, vegetables

Minerals: coal, bauxite, aluminum

Life expectancy at birth (years): male, 71.0; female, 76.0

Literacy rate: 93%   **Website:** www.gom.cg.yu/eng.com

NETHERLANDS*

FOR MAP, SEE PAGE 108

Population: 16,645,313

Ethnic groups: Dutch 83%

Principal languages: Dutch (official), Frisian, Flemish

Chief religions: Roman Catholic 31%, Protestant 21%, Muslim 4%

Area: 16,030 sq mi (41,530 sq km)

Topography: The land is flat, with an average altitude of 37 ft (11 m) above sea level. Much land is below sea level, reclaimed and protected by some 1,500 mi (2,400 km) of dikes. Since 1920 the government has been draining the IJsselmeer, formerly the Zuider Zee.

Capital: Amsterdam (pop., 1,145,00); seat of government, The Hague (pop., 705,00)

Independence date: 1579

Government type: parliamentary democracy under a constitutional monarch

Head of state: Queen Beatrix

Head of government: Prime Min. Jan Peter Balkenende

Monetary unit: euro

GDP: $638.9 billion (2007 est.)

Per capita GDP: $38,600

Traditional attributes of the Netherlands: tulips (top, with windmill in background) and wooden shoes (bottom)

*Member of the European Union

Industries: agroindustries, metal and engineering products, electrical machinery and equipment, chemicals, petroleum,construction, micro-electronics, fishing

Chief crops: grains, potatoes, sugar beets, fruits, vegetables

Minerals: natural gas, petroleum

Life expectancy at birth (years): male, 76.2; female, 81.3

Literacy rate: 99%   Website: www.netherlands-embassy.org

NETHERLANDS DEPENDENCIES, constitutionally on a level of equality with the Netherlands homeland within the kingdom, are Aruba and the Netherlands Antilles. ARUBA: population, 101,541; area, 75 sq mi (193 sq km); capital, Oranjestad. NETHERLANDS ANTILLES (CURAÇAO, BONAIRE, SAINT EUSTATIUS, SABA, southern part of SAINT MAARTEN): population, 225,369; area, 371 sq mi (960 sq km), capital, Willemstad, on Curaçao.

NORWAY

FOR MAP, SEE PAGE 95

Population: 4,644,457

Ethnic groups: Norwegian, Sami

Principal languages: Norwegian (official), Sami, Finnish

Chief religion: Evangelical Lutheran (official) 86%

Area: 125,180 sq mi (324,220 sq km)

Norwegian coast

Topography: A highly indented coast is lined with tens of thousands of islands. Mountains and plateaus cover most of the country, which is only 25% forested.

Capital: Oslo (pop., 795,000)

Independence date: June 7, 1905

Government type: hereditary constitutional monarchy

Head of state: King Harald V

Head of government: Prime Min. Jens Stoltenberg

Monetary unit: krone

GDP: $257.4 billion (2007 est.)   Per capita GDP: $55,600

Industries: petroleum and gas, food processing, shipbuilding, pulp and paper products, metals, chemicals, timber, mining, textiles, fishing

Chief crops: barley, wheat, potatoes

Minerals: petroleum, copper, natural gas, pyrites, nickel, iron ore, zinc, lead

Life expectancy at birth (years): male, 76.6; female, 82.2

Literacy rate: 100%   Website: www.norway.no

POLAND*

FOR MAP, SEE PAGE 99

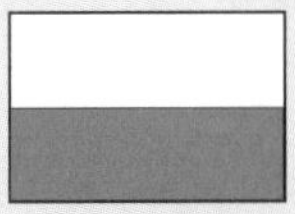

Population: 38,500,696

Ethnic groups: Polish 98%, German 1%

Principal languages: Polish (official), Ukrainian, German

Chief religion: Roman Catholic 95%

Area: 120,730 sq mi (312,680 sq km)

Topography: Poland consists mostly of lowlands forming part of the Northern European Plain. The Carpathian Mountains along the southern border rise to 8,200 ft (2,500 m).

Capital: Warsaw (pop., 2,200,000)

Independence date: November 11, 1918   Government type: republic

Head of state: Pres. Lech Kaczynski

Head of government: Prime Min. Donald Tusk

Monetary unit: zloty

GDP: $624.6 billion (2007 est.)   Per capita GDP: $16,200

Industries: machine building, iron and steel, mining, chemicals, ship-building, food processing, glass, beverages, textiles

Chief crops: potatoes, fruits, vegetables, wheat

Minerals: coal, sulfur, copper, natural gas, silver, lead, salt

Life expectancy at birth (years): male, 70.0; female, 78.5

Literacy rate: 99%

Websites: www.polandembassy.org;   www.poland.pl

PORTUGAL*

FOR MAP, SEE PAGE 102

Population: 10,676,910

Ethnic groups: mainly Portuguese

Principal language: Portuguese (official)

Chief religion: Roman Catholic 94%

Area: 35,670 sq mi (92,390 sq km)

Topography: Portugal north of the Tajus River, which bisects the country northeast to southwest, is mountainous, cool, and rainy. To the south there are drier, rolling plains and a warm climate.

Capital: Lisbon (pop., 1,962,000)

Independence date: 1143   Government type: republic

Head of state: Pres. Aníbal Cavaco Silva

Head of government: Prime Min. José Sócrates Carvalho Pinto de Sousa

Monetary unit: euro

GDP: $232 billion (2007 est.)   Per capita GDP: $21,800

Industries: textiles, footwear, pulp and paper, cork, metalworking, oil refining, chemicals, fish canning, wine, tourism

Chief crops: grain, potatoes, olives, grapes

Minerals: tungsten, iron ore, uranium ore, marble

Life expectancy at birth (years): male, 74.9; female, 80.9

Literacy rate: 87.4%

Website: www.presidenciarepublica.pt/en/main.html

ROMANIA*

FOR MAP, SEE PAGE 107

Population: 22,246,862

Ethnic groups: Romanian 90%, Hungarian, Roma, and others 10%

Principal languages: Romanian (official), Hungarian, German, Romani

Chief religions: Romanian Orthodox 70%, Roman Catholic 6%, Protestant 6%

Area: 91,700 sq mi (237,500 sq km)

Topography: The Carpathian Mountains encase the north-central Transylvanian plateau. There are wide plains south and east of the mountains, through which flow the lower reaches of the rivers of the Danube system.

Capital: Bucharest (pop., 1,853,000)

Independence date: May 9, 1877   Government type: republic

Head of state: Pres. Traian Basescu

Head of government: Prime Min. Calin Constantin Anton Popescu-Tariceanu

Monetary unit: lei

GDP: $246.7 billion (2007 est.)   Per capita GDP: $11,100

Industries: textiles, footwear, light machinery, auto assembly, mining, timber, construction materials, metallurgy, chemicals, food processing, petroleum refining

Chief crops: wheat, corn, sugar beets, sunflower seed, potatoes, grapes

Minerals: petroleum, natural gas, coal, iron ore, salt

Life expectancy at birth (years): male, 67.6; female, 74.8

Romania *(continued)*

Literacy rate: 97%

Websites: www.gov.ro/engleza/index.html;   www.roembus.org

RUSSIA

FOR MAP, SEE PAGE 122

Population: 140,702,094

Ethnic groups: Russian 82%, Tatar 4%, Ukrainian 3%, Chuvash 1%, Bashkir 1%, Belarusian 1%, Moldavian 1%

Principal languages: Russian (official), many others

Chief religions: Russian Orthodox, Muslim

Area: 6,592,800 sq mi (17,075,400 sq km)

Topography: Russia contains every type of climate except the distinctly tropical and has a varied topography. The European portion is a low plain, grassy in the south, wooded in the north, with the Ural Mountains on the east and the Caucasus Mountains on the south. The Urals stretch north to south for 2,500 mi (4,000 km). The Asiatic portion is also a vast plain, with mountains on the south and in the east; tundra covers the extreme north, with forest belt below; plains, marshes are in the west, desert in the southwest.

Capital: Moscow (pop., 10,469,000)

Independence date: August 24, 1991

Government type: federal republic

Head of state: Pres. Dmitry Medvedev

Head of government: Prime Min. Vladimir Putin

Monetary unit: ruble

GDP: $2,076 billion (2007 est.)

Per capita GDP: $14,600

Industries: mining, extractive industries, machine building, shipbuilding, vehicles, commercial equipment, agricultural machinery, construction equipment, instruments, consumer durables, textiles, foodstuffs, handicrafts

St. Basil's Cathedral, Moscow, Russia

Chief crops: grain, sugar beets, sunflower seed, vegetables, fruits

Minerals: large variety, including oil, natural gas, coal, strategic minerals

Life expectancy at birth (years): male, 59.9; female, 73.3

Literacy rate: 98%   Website: www.russiaembassy.org

SAN MARINO

FOR MAP, SEE PAGE 117

Population: 29,973

Ethnic groups: Sammarinese, Italian

Principal language: Italian (official)

Chief religion: predominantly Roman Catholic

Area: 23 sq mi (60 sq km)

Topography: The country lies on the slopes of Mt. Titano.

Capital: San Marino (pop., 5,000)

Independence date: September 3, 301   Government type: republic

Heads of state and government: two co-regents appointed every 6 months

Monetary unit: euro

GDP: $850 million (2004 est.)   Per capita GDP: $34,100

Industries: tourism, banking, textiles, electronics, ceramics, wine

Chief crops: wheat, grapes, corn, olives

Minerals: building stone

Life expectancy at birth (years): male, 78.0; female, 85.3

Literacy rate: 96%   Website: www.visitsanmarino.com

SERBIA

FOR MAP, SEE PAGE 106

Population: 10,159,046

Ethnic groups: Serb 63%, Albanian 14%

Principal languages: Serbian (official), Albanian, Hungarian

Chief religions: Orthodox 65%, Muslim 19%, Roman Catholic 4%

Area: 34,185 sq mi (88,538 sq km)

Topography: The terrain of this landlocked country varies widely, with fertile plains drained by the Danube and other rivers in the north, limestone basins in the east ancient mountains and hills in the southeast.

Capital: Belgrade (pop., 1,118,000)

Independence date: February 4, 2003   Government type: federal republic

Head of state and government: Pres. Svetozar Marović

Monetary unit: new dinar

GDP: $56.9 billion (2007 est.)   Per capita GDP: $7,700

Industries: machine building, metallurgy, mining, consumer goods, electronics, petroleum products, chemicals, pharmaceuticals

Chief crops: cereals, fruits, vegetables, tobacco, olives

Minerals: oil, gas, coal, antimony, copper, lead, zinc, nickel, gold, pyrite, chrome

Life expectancy at birth (years): male, 71.0; female, 77.2

Literacy rate: 93%   Website: www.gov.yu

SLOVAKIA

FOR MAP, SEE PAGE 99

Population: 5,455,407

Ethnic groups: Slovak 86%, Hungarian 11%, Roma 2%

Principal languages: Slovak (official), Hungarian

Chief religions: Roman Catholic 60%, Protestant 8%, Orthodox 4%

Area: 18,860 sq mi (48,850 sq km)

Topography: Mountains (Carpathians) in the north, and the fertile Danube plane in the south.

Capital: Bratislava (pop., 425,000)

Independence date: January 1, 1993   Government type: republic

Head of state: Pres. Ivan Gašparovič

Head of government: Prime Min. Mikulás Dzurinda

Monetary unit: koruna

GDP: $107.6 billion (2007 est.)   Per capita GDP: $19,800

Industries: metal and metal products, food and beverages, electricity, chemicals and manmade fibers, machinery, paper and printing, earthenware and ceramics, transport vehicles, textiles, electrical and optical apparatus, rubber products

Chief crops: grains, potatoes, sugar beets, hops, fruit

Minerals: coal, iron ore, copper, manganese, salt

Life expectancy at birth (years): male, 70.2; female, 78.4

Literacy rate: NA

Websites: www.government.gov.sk/english/
www.slovakembassy-us.org

SLOVENIA*

For map, see page 106

Population: 2,007,711

Ethnic groups: Slovene 88%, Croat 3%, Serb 2%, Bosniak 1%

Principal languages: Slovenian (official), Serbo-Croatian

Chief religion: Roman Catholic 71%

Area: 7,820 sq mi (20,250 sq km)

Topography: Mostly hilly; 42% of the land is forested.

Capital: Ljubljana (pop., 256,000)

Independence date: June 25, 1991 **Government type:** republic

Head of state: Pres. Danilo Türk

Head of government: Prime Min. Janez Jansa

Monetary unit: euro

GDP: $54.8 billion (2007 est.) **Per capita GDP:** $27,300

Industries: metallurgy and metal products, electronics, trucks, electric power equipment, wood products, textiles, chemicals, machine tools

Chief crops: potatoes, hops, wheat, sugar beets, corn, grapes

Minerals: coal, lead, zinc, mercury, uranium, silver

Life expectancy at birth (years): male, 72.2; female, 79.9

Literacy rate: 99% **Website:** www.sigov.si

SPAIN*

For map, see page 102

Population: 40,491,051

Ethnic groups: Castilian, Catalan, Basque, Galician

Principal languages: Castilian Spanish (official), Catalan, Galician, Basque

Chief religion: Roman Catholic 94%

Area: 194,890 sq mi (504,780 sq km)

Topography: The interior is a high, arid plateau broken by mountain ranges and river valleys. The northwest is heavily watered; the south has lowlands and a Mediterranean climate.

Capital: Madrid (pop., 5,103,000) **Independence date:** 1492

Government type: constitutional monarchy

Head of state: King Juan Carlos I de Borbon y Borbon

Head of government: Prime Min. José Luis Rodriguez Zapatero

Monetary unit: euro

GDP: $1.362 trillion (2007 est.) **Per capita GDP:** $33,700

Industries: textiles and apparel, food and beverages, metals and metal manufacture, chemicals, shipbuilding, automobiles, machine tools, tourism

Chief crops: grain, vegetables, olives, wine grapes, sugar beets, citrus

Spanish olive groves

*Member of the European Union

Minerals: coal, iron ore, uranium, mercury, pyrites, fluorspar, gypsum, zinc, lead, tungsten, copper, kaolin, potash

Life expectancy at birth (years): male, 76.0; female, 82.9

Literacy rate: 97% **Website:** www.embaspain.ca

SWEDEN*

For map, see page 95

Population: 9,045,389

Ethnic groups: Swedish 89%, Finnish 2%; Sami and others 9%

Principal languages: Swedish (official), Sami, Finnish

Chief religion: Lutheran 87%

Area: 173,730 sq mi (449,960 sq km)

Topography: Mountains along the northwestern border cover 25% of Sweden; flat or rolling terrain covers the central and southern areas, which include several large lakes.

Capital: Stockholm (pop., 1,697,000)

Independence date: June 6, 1523

Government type: constitutional monarchy

Head of state: King Carl XVI Gustaf

Head of government: Prime Min. Goran Persson

Monetary unit: krona

GDP: $333.1 billion (2007 est.) **Per capita GDP:** $36,900

Industries: iron and steel, precision equipment, pulp and paper products, processed foods, motor vehicles

Chief crops: barley, wheat, sugar beets

Minerals: zinc, iron ore, lead, copper, silver, uranium

Life expectancy at birth (years): male, 78.1; female, 82.6

Literacy rate: 99% **Website:** www.sweden.se

SWITZERLAND

For map, see page 114

Population: 7,581,520

Ethnic groups: German 65%, French 18%, Italian 10%, Romansch 1%

Principal languages: German, French, Italian (all official); Romansch (semi-official)

Chief religions: Roman Catholic 46%, Protestant 40%

Area: 15,940 sq mi (41,290 sq km)

Topography: The Alps cover 60% of the land area; the Jura, near France, 10%. Running between, from northeast to southwest, are midlands, 30%.

Capitals: Bern (administrative) (pop., 320,000), Lausanne (judicial) (pop., 285,000)

Matterhorn, Switzerland

Nation Facts and Figures

Switzerland *(continued)*

Independence date: August 1, 1291

Government type: federal republic

Head of state and government: the president is elected by the Federal Assembly to a nonrenewable one-year term

Monetary unit: franc

GDP: $300.9 billion (2007 est.)   **Per capita GDP:** $39,800

Industries: machinery, chemicals, watches, textiles, precision instruments

Chief crops: grains, fruits, vegetables   **Minerals:** salt

Life expectancy at birth (years): male, 77.5; female, 83.3

Literacy rate: 99%   **Website:** www.swissemb.orgl

Stonehenge, England

Arundel Castle, England

UKRAINE

FOR MAP, SEE PAGE 120

Population: 45,994,287

Ethnic groups: Ukrainian 78%, Russian 17%

Principal languages: Ukrainian (official), Russian, Romanian, Polish, Hungarian

Chief religions: Ukrainian Orthodox (Kiev patriarchate and Russian patriarchate), Autocephalous Orthodox, Ukrainian Greek Catholic

Area: 233,100 sq mi (603,700 sq km)

Topography: Ukraine is part of the East European plain. Mountainous areas include the Carpathians in the southwest and the Crimean chain in the south. Arable black soil constitutes a large part of the country.

Capital: Kiev (pop., 2,618,000)   **Independence date:** August 24, 1991

Government type: constitutional republic

Head of state: Pres. Viktor Yushchenko

Head of government: Prime Min. Yuriy Yekhanurov

Monetary unit: hryvnia

GDP: $321.3 billion (2007 est.)   **Per capita GDP:** $6,900

Industries: mining, electric power, ferrous and nonferrous metals, machinery and transport equipment, chemicals, food processing

Chief crops: grain, sugar beets, sunflower seeds, vegetables

Minerals: iron ore, coal, manganese, natural gas, oil, salt, sulfur, graphite, titanium, magnesium, kaolin, nickel, mercury

Life expectancy at birth (years): male, 61.4; female, 72.3

Literacy rate: 98%

Websites: www.ukraineinfo.us;   www.kmu.gov.ua/control/en

UNITED KINGDOM*

FOR MAP, SEE PAGE 89

Population: 60,943,912

Ethnic groups: English 81.5%, Scottish 9.6%, Irish 2.4%, Welsh 1.9%, Ulster 1.9%; West Indian, Indo-Pakistani, and other 2.8%

Principal languages: English (official), Welsh and Scottish Gaelic

Chief religions: Christian 72%, Muslim 3%, many others

Area: 94,530 sq mi (244,820 sq km)

Topography: England is mostly rolling land, rising to the Uplands of southern Scotland; the Lowlands are in the center of Scotland, and the granite Highlands are in the north. The coast is

Houses of Parliament with Big Ben, London, United Kingdom

*Member of the European Union

heavily indented, especially on the west. The Severn, 220 mi (354 km), and the Thames, 215 mi (346 km), are the longest rivers.

Capital: London (pop., 7,619,000)

Independence date: 1801   **Government type:** constitutional monarchy

Head of state: Queen Elizabeth II

Head of government: Prime Min. Gordon Brown

Monetary unit: pound

GDP: $1,782 billion (2004 est.)   **Per capita GDP:** $29,600

Industries: machine tools, electric power and automation equipment, rail, shipbuilding, aircraft, motor vehicles and parts, electronics and communication equipment, mining, chemicals, paper and paper products, food processing, textiles, clothing and other consumer goods

Chief crops: cereals, oilseed, potatoes, vegetables

Minerals: coal, petroleum, natural gas, tin, limestone, iron ore, salt, clay, chalk, gypsum, lead, silica

Life expectancy at birth (years): male, 75.8; female, 80.8

Literacy rate: 99%   **Website:** www.britainusa.com

The CHANNEL ISLANDS—Jersey, Guernsey, and the dependencies of Guernsey (Alderney, Brechou, Great Sark, Little Sark, Herm, Jethou, and Lihou)—are situated off the northwest coast of France. Jersey and Guernsey have separate legal existences and lieutenant governors named by the Crown. Population, 156,493; area, 75 sq mi (194 sq km).

The ISLE OF MAN, in the Irish Sea, has its own laws and a lieutenant governor appointed by the Crown. Population, 75,441; area 221 sq mi (572 sq km).

VATICAN CITY (THE HOLY SEE)

FOR MAP, SEE PAGE 104

Population: 921

Ethnic groups: Italian, Swiss, other

Principal languages: Latin (official), Italian, French, Monastic Sign Language, various others

Chief religion: Roman Catholic

Area: 0.17 sq mi (0.4 sq km)

Independence date: February 11, 1929

Government type: ecclesiastical state   **Sovereign:** Pope Benedict XVI

Monetary unit: euro   **Website:** www.vatican.va/phome_en.htm

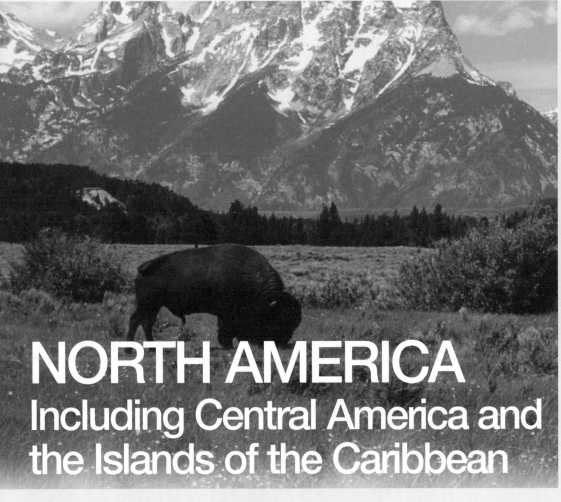

NORTH AMERICA
Including Central America and the Islands of the Caribbean

Two of the world's five biggest countries, in terms of land area, are in North America: Canada, which ranks Number 3, and the United States, Number 4. The United States, has the third largest population in the world, while Canada is the world's ninth most sparsely populated country.

ANTIGUA AND BARBUDA
For map, see page 199

Population: 69,842

Ethnic groups: black, British, Portuguese, Lebanese, Syrian

Principal languages: English (official), local dialects

Chief religions: predominantly Protestant, some Roman Catholic

Area: 174 sq mi (440 sq km)

Topography: These are mostly low-lying and limestone coral islands. Antigua is mostly hilly with an indented coast; Barbuda is a flat island with a large lagoon on the west.

Capital: Saint John's (pop., 28,000)

Independence date: November 1, 1981

Government type: constitutional monarchy with British-style parliament

Head of state: Queen Elizabeth II, represented by Gov.-Gen. James Carlisle

Head of government: Prime Min. Baldwin Spencer

Monetary unit: East Caribbean dollar

GDP: $1.189 billion (2007 est.)   **Per capita GDP:** $10,900

Industries: tourism, construction, light manufacturing

Chief crops: cotton, fruits, vegetables, bananas, coconuts, cucumbers, mangoes, sugarcane

Life expectancy at birth (years): male, 69.3; female, 74.1

Literacy rate: 89%   **Website:** www.antigua-barbuda.com

Chief religions: Baptist 32%, Anglican 20%, Roman Catholic 19%, other Christian 24%

Area: 5,380 sq mi (13,940 sq km)

Topography: Nearly 700 islands (29 inhabited) and over 2,000 islets in the western Atlantic Ocean extend 760 mi (1,220 km) northwest to southeast.

Capital: Nassau (pop.,222,000)

Independence date: July 10, 1973

Government type: independent commonwealth

Head of state: Queen Elizabeth II, represented by Gov.-Gen. Arthur D. Hanna

Head of government: Prime Min. Perry Christie

Monetary unit: Bahamas dollar

GDP: $5.3 billion (2004 est.)

Per capita GDP: $17,700

Industries: tourism, banking, cement, oil refining and transshipment, pharmaceuticals, steel pipe

Chief crops: citrus, vegetables

Minerals: salt, aragonite

Life expectancy at birth (years): male, 62.3; female, 69.1

Literacy rate: 98.2%

Website: www.bahamas.gov.bs

Nassau, the Bahamas

THE BAHAMAS
For map, see page 199

Population: 307,451

Ethnic groups: black 85%, white 12%

Principal languages: English, Creole (among Haitian immigrants)

BARBADOS
For map, see page 199

Population: 281,968

Ethnic groups: black 90%, white 4%

Principal language: English

Barbados *(continued)*

Chief religions: Protestant 67%, Roman Catholic 4%

Area: 165 sq mi (430 sq km)

Topography: The island lies alone in the Atlantic almost completely surrounded by coral reefs. The highest point is Mt. Hillaby, 1,115 ft (340 m).

Capital: Bridgetown (pop., 140,000)

Independence date: November 30, 1966

Government type: parliamentary democracy

Head of state: Queen Elizabeth II, represented by Gov.-Gen. Sir Clifford Husbands

Head of government: Prime Min. Owen Arthur

Monetary unit: Barbados dollar

GDP: $5.5 billion (2007 est.)   **Per capita GDP:** $19,700

Industries: tourism, sugar, light manufacturing, component assembly for export

Chief crops: sugarcane, vegetables, cotton

Minerals: petroleum, natural gas

Life expectancy at birth (years): 69.5; female, 73.8

Literacy rate: 97.4%

Website: www.barbados.gov.bb

BELIZE

FOR MAP, SEE PAGE 202

Population: 301,022

Ethnic groups: mestizo 49%, Creole 25%, Maya 11%, Garifuna 6%

Principal languages: English (official), Spanish, Mayan, Creole, Garifuna (Carib)

Chief religions: Roman Catholic 50%, Protestant 27%

Area: 8,860 sq mi (22,960 sq km)

Topography: Belize has swampy lowlands in the north, Maya Mountains in the south, coral reefs and cays near the coast.

Capital: Belmopan (pop., 9,000)

Independence date: September 21, 1981

Government type: parliamentary democracy

Head of state: Queen Elizabeth II, represented by Gov.-Gen. Sir Colville Young

Head of government: Prime Min. Said Musa

Monetary unit: Belize dollar

GDP: $2.3 billion (2007 est.)   **Per capita GDP:** $7,800

Industries: garment production, food processing, tourism, construction

Chief crops: bananas, coca, citrus, sugarcane

Life expectancy at birth (years): male, 65.1; female, 69.9

Literacy rate: 70.3%   **Website:** www.belize.gov.bz

CANADA

FOR MAP, SEE PAGE 180

Population: 33,679,263

Ethnic groups: British 28%, French 23%, other European 15%, Amerindian 2%

Principal languages: English, French (both official)

Chief religions: Roman Catholic 46%, Protestant 36%, other 18%

Area: 3,851,810 sq mi (9,976,140 sq km)

Topography: Canada stretches 3,426 mi (5,514 km) from east to west and extends south from the North Pole to the U.S. border. Its seacoast includes 36,356 mi (58,509 km) of mainland and 115,133 mi (185,289 km) of islands, including the Arctic islands almost from Greenland to near the Alaskan border.

Images of Canada: Vancouver, British Columbia (top); Manitoba farmland (middle); lobster traps in Nova Scotia (above left); Welland Canal, Ontario (above right)

Capital: Ottawa (pop., 1,093,000)

Independence date: July 1, 1867

Government type: confederation with parliamentary democracy

Head of state: Queen Elizabeth II, represented by Gov.-Gen. Michaelle Jean

Head of government: Prime Min. Stephen Harper

Monetary unit: Canadian dollar

GDP: $1,274 billion (2007 est.)   **Per capita GDP:** $38,200

Industries: transport equipment, chemicals, mining, food products, wood and paper products, fish products, petroleum and natural gas

Chief crops: wheat, barley, oilseed, tobacco, fruits, vegetables

Minerals: iron ore, nickel, zinc, copper, gold, lead, molybdenum, potash, silver, coal, petroleum, natural gas

Life expectancy at birth (years): male, 76.6; female, 83.5

Literacy rate: 97%

Websites: www.statcan.ca   www.canada.gc.ca

COSTA RICA

FOR MAP, SEE PAGE 203

Population: 4,191,948

Ethnic groups: European and mestizo 94%, black 3%, Amerindian 1%, Chinese 1%

Principal languages Spanish (official), English spoken around Puerto Limon

Chief religions: Roman Catholic (official) 76%, Protestant 14%

Area: 19,700 sq mi (51,100 sq km)

Topography: Lowlands by the Caribbean are tropical. The interior plateau, with an altitude of about 4,000 ft (1,200 m), is temperate.

Capital: San José (pop., 1,085,000)

Independence date: September 15, 1821   Government type: republic

Head of state and government: Pres. Óscar Arias Sánchez

Monetary unit: colon

GDP: $56 billion (2007 est.)

Per capita GDP: $13,500

Industries: microprocessors, food processing, textiles and clothing, construction materials, fertilizer, plastic products

Chief crops: coffee, pineapples, bananas, sugar, corn, rice, beans, potatoes

Life expectancy at birth (years): male, 74.1; female, 79.3

Literacy rate: 95.5%

Website: www.costarica-embassy.com

CUBA

For map, see page 203

Population: 11,423,952

Ethnic groups: Creole 51%, white 37%, black 11%, Chinese 1%

Principal language: Spanish (official)

Chief religions: Roman Catholic, Santeria

Area: 42,800 sq mi (110,860 sq km)

Topography: The coastline is about 2,500 mi (4,000 km). The northern coast is steep and rocky, and the southern coast low and marshy. Low hills and fertile valleys cover more than half the country. The Sierra Maestra, in the east, is the highest of three mountain ranges.

Capital: Havana (pop., 2,189,000)

Independence date: May 20, 1902   Government type: Communist state

Head of state and government: Pres. Raúl Castro Ruz

Monetary unit: peso

GDP: $51.1 billion (2007 est.)

Per capita GDP: $4,500

Industries: sugar, petroleum, tobacco, chemicals, construction, mining, cement, agricultural machinery, biotechnology

Chief crops: sugar, tobacco, citrus, coffee, rice, potatoes, beans

Minerals: cobalt, nickel, iron ore, copper, manganese, salt, silica, petroleum

Life expectancy at birth (years): male, 74.8; female, 79.4

Literacy rate: 95.7%

Website: www.cubagob.cu/ingles/default.htm

Scuba diving in the Caribbean

DOMINICA

For map, see page 199

Population: 72,514

Ethnic groups: black, Carib Amerindian

Principal languages: English (official), French patois

Chief religions: Roman Catholic 77%, Protestant 15%

Area: 290 sq mi (750 sq km)

Topography: Mountainous, with a central ridge running from north to south, terminating in cliffs. Dominica is volcanic in origin, with numerous thermal springs; there is rich deep topsoil on the leeward side, red tropical clay on the windward coast.

Capital: Roseau (pop., 27,000)

Independence date: November 3, 1978

Government type: parliamentary democracy

Head of state: Pres. Nicholas Liverpool

Head of government: Prime Min. Roosevelt Skerrit

Monetary unit: East Caribbean dollar

GDP: $485 million (2006 est.)   Per capita GDP: $3,800

Industries: soap, coconut oil, tourism, copra, furniture, cement blocks, shoes

Chief crops: bananas, citrus, mangoes, root crops, coconuts, cocoa

Life expectancy at birth (years): male, 71.5; female, 77.4

Literacy rate: 94%

Website: www.ndcdominica.dm

DOMINICAN REPUBLIC

For map, see page 199

Population: 9,507,133

Ethnic groups: Creole 73%, white 16%, black 11%

Principal language: Spanish (official)

Chief religion: Roman Catholic 95%

Area: 18,810 sq mi (48,730 sq km)

Topography: The Cordillera Central range crosses the center of the country, rising to over 10,000 ft (3,000 m), the highest mountains in the Caribbean. The Cibao Valley to the north is a major agricultural area.

Capital: Santo Domingo (pop., 1,865,000)

Independence date: February 27, 1844

Government type: republic

Head of state and government: Pres. Leonel Fernández Reyna

Monetary unit: peso

GDP: $85.4 billion (2007 est.)

Per capita GDP: $9,200

Industries: tourism, sugar processing, mining, textiles, cement, tobacco

Chief crops: sugarcane, coffee, cotton, cocoa, tobacco, rice, beans, potatoes, corn, bananas

Minerals: nickel, bauxite, gold, silver

Life expectancy at birth (years): male, 66.0; female, 69.4

Literacy rate: 82.1%

Website: www.domrep.org

EL SALVADOR

For map, see page 202

Population: 7,066,403

Ethnic groups: mestizo 90%, white 9%, Amerindian 1%

Principal languages: Spanish (official), Nahua

Chief religions: Roman Catholic 83%, many Protestant groups

Area: 8,120 sq mi (21,040 sq km)

El Salvador (continued)

Topography: A hot Pacific coastal plain in the south rises to a cooler plateau and valley region, densely populated. The north is mountainous, including many volcanoes.

Capital: San Salvador (pop., 1,424,000)

Independence date: September 15, 1821   **Government type:** republic

Head of state and government: Pres. Antonio Elías Saca González

Monetary unit: colon

GDP: $36 billion (2007 est.)   **Per capita GDP:** $5,200

Industries: food processing, beverages, petroleum, chemicals, fertilizer, textiles, furniture, light metals

Chief crops: coffee, sugar, corn, rice, beans, oilseed, cotton, sorghum

Minerals: petroleum

Life expectancy at birth (years): male, 67.3; female, 74.7

Literacy rate: 71.5%

Website: www.elsalvador.org

GRENADA

FOR MAP, SEE PAGE 199

Population: 90,303

Ethnic groups: black 82%, Creole 13%

Principal languages: English (official), French patois

Chief religions: Roman Catholic 53%, Anglican 14%, other Protestant 33%

Area: 131 sq mi (339 sq km)

Topography: The main island is mountainous; the country includes Carriacou and Petit Martinique islands.

Capital: Saint George's (pop., 33,000)

Independence date: February 7, 1974

Government type: parliamentary democracy

Head of state: Queen Elizabeth II, represented by Gov.-Gen. Daniel Williams

Head of government: Prime Min. Keith Mitchell

Monetary unit: East Caribbean dollar

GDP: $982 million (2006 est.)
Per capita GDP: $3,900

Nutmeg factory, Grenada

Industries: food and beverages, textiles, light assembly operations, tourism, construction

Chief crops: bananas, cocoa, nutmeg, mace, citrus, avocados, root crops, sugarcane, corn, vegetables

Life expectancy at birth (years): male, 62.7; female, 66.3

Literacy rate: 98%

Website: www.grenadagrenadines.com

GUATEMALA

FOR MAP, SEE PAGE 202

Population: 13,002,206

Ethnic groups: mestizo 55%, Amerindian 43%

Principal languages: Spanish (official); more than 20 Amerindian languages, including Quiche, Cakchiquel, Kekchi, Mam, Garifuna, and Xinca

Chief religions: mostly Roman Catholic; some Protestant, indigenous Mayan beliefs

Area: 42,040 sq mi (108,890 sq km)

Topography: The central highland and mountain areas are bordered by the narrow Pacific coast and the lowlands and fertile river valleys on the Caribbean. There are numerous volcanoes in the south, more than half a dozen over 11,000 ft (3,350 m).

Capital: Guatemala City (pop., 951,000)

Independence date: September 15, 1821

Government type: republic

Head of state and government: Pres. Álvaro Colom

Monetary unit: quetzal

GDP: $67.45 billion (2007 est.)

Per capita GDP: $5,400

Industries: sugar, textiles and clothing, furniture, chemicals, petroleum, metals, rubber, tourism

Chief crops: sugarcane, corn, bananas, coffee, beans, cardamom

Minerals: petroleum, nickel

Life expectancy at birth (years): male, 64.3; female, 66.1

Literacy rate: 63.6%

Website: www.guatemala-embassy.org

HAITI

FOR MAP, SEE PAGE 203

Population: 8,924,553

Ethnic groups: black 95%, Creole and other 5%

Principal languages: French, Creole (both official)

Chief religions: Roman Catholic 80%, Protestant 16%; voodoo widely practiced

Area: 10,710 sq mi (27,750 sq km)

Topography: About two-thirds of Haiti is mountainous. Much of the rest is semiarid. Coastal areas are warm and moist.

Capital: Port-au-Prince (pop., 1,961,000)

Independence date: January 1, 1804   **Government type:** republic

Head of state: Pres. René Préval

Head of government: Prime Min. Jacques Édouard Alexis

Monetary unit: gourde

GDP: $15.8 billion (2007 est.)   **Per capita GDP:** $1,900

Industries: sugar refining, flour milling, textiles, cement, light assembly industries

Chief crops: coffee, mangoes, sugarcane, rice, corn, sorghum

Minerals: bauxite, copper, calcium carbonate, gold, marble

Life expectancy at birth (years): male, 50.5; female, 53.1

Literacy rate: 45%

Website: www.haiti.org

HONDURAS

FOR MAP, SEE PAGE 202

Population: 7,639,327

Ethnic groups: mestizo 90%, Amerindian 7%, black 2%, white 1%

Principal languages: Spanish (official), Garífuna, Amerindian dialects

Chief religion: Roman Catholic 97%

Area: 43,280 sq mi (112,090 sq km)

Topography: The Caribbean coast is 500 mi (800 km) long. The Pacific coast, on the Gulf of Fonseca, is 40 mi (65 km) long. Honduras is mountainous, with wide fertile valleys and rich forests.

Capital: Tegucigalpa (pop., 1,007,000)

Independence date: September 15, 1821

Government type: republic

Head of state and government: Pres. José Manuel Zelaya Rosales

Monetary unit: lempira

GDP: $24.7 billion (2007 est.)

Per capita GDP: $3,300

Industries: sugar, coffee, textiles, clothing, wood products

Chief crops: bananas, coffee, citrus

Minerals: gold, silver, copper, lead, zinc, iron ore, antimony, coal

Life expectancy at birth (years): male, 65.0; female, 67.4

Literacy rate: 74%

Website: www.hondurasemb.org

JAMAICA

FOR MAP, SEE PAGE 203

Population: 2,801,544

Ethnic groups: black 91%, mixed 7%, East Indian and other 2%

Principal languages: English, patois English

Chief religions: Protestant 61%, Roman Catholic 4%, spiritual cults and other 35%

Area: 4,240 sq mi (10,990 sq km)

Topography: Four-fifths of Jamaica is covered by mountains.

Capital: Kingston (pop., 575,000)   Independence date: August 6, 1962

Government type: parliamentary democracy

Head of state: Queen Elizabeth II, represented by Gov.-Gen. Sir Kenneth Hall

Head of government: Prime Min. Portia Simpson Miller

Monetary unit: Jamaican dollar

GDP: $13.5 billion (2007 est.)   Per capita GDP: $4,800

Industries: tourism, bauxite, textiles, food processing, light manufactures, rum, cement, metal, paper, chemical products

Chief crops: sugarcane, bananas, coffee, citrus, potatoes, vegetables

Minerals: bauxite, gypsum, limestone

Life expectancy at birth (years): male, 74.0; female, 78.2

Literacy rate: 85%

Websites: www.cabinet.gov.jm
        www.jis.gov.jm

MEXICO

FOR MAP, SEE PAGE 177

Population: 109,955,400

Ethnic groups: mestizo 60%, Amerindian 30%, white 9%

Principal languages: Spanish (official), Náhuatl, Maya, Zaptec, Otomi, Miztec, other indigenous

Mayan ruins, Chichen Itza, Mexico

Cathedral on the Zocalo (main square), Mexico City, Mexico

Chief religions: Roman Catholic 89%, Protestant 6%

Area: 761,610 sq mi (1,972,550 sq km)

Topography: The Sierra Madre Occidental Mountains run northwest to southeast near the west coast; the Sierra Madre Oriental Mountains run near the Gulf of Mexico. They join south of Mexico City. Between the two ranges lies the dry central plateau, 5,000 to 8,000 ft (1,500 to 2,400 m) in altitude, rising toward the south, with temperate vegetation. Coastal lowlands are tropical. About 45% of the land is arid.

Capital: Mexico City (pop., 18,660,000)

Independence date: September 16, 1810

Government type: federal republic

Head of state and government: Pres. Felipe de Jesús Calderón Hinojosa

Monetary unit: new peso

GDP: $1,353 billion (2007 est.)   Per capita GDP: $12,500

Industries: food and beverages, tobacco, chemicals, iron and steel, petroleum, mining, textiles, clothing, motor vehicles, consumer durables, tourism

Chief crops: corn, wheat, soybeans, rice, beans, cotton, coffee, fruit, tomatoes

Minerals: petroleum, silver, copper, gold, lead, zinc, natural gas

Life expectancy at birth (years): male, 72.2; female, 77.8

Literacy rate: 89.6%

Website: www.presidencia.gob.mx/?NLang=en

NICARAGUA

FOR MAP, SEE PAGE 203

Population: 5,780,586

Ethnic groups: mestizo 69%, white 17%, black 9%, Amerindian 5%

Principal languages: Spanish (official), indigenous languages, English on Atlantic coast

Chief religion: Roman Catholic 85%

Area: 50,000 sq mi (129,490 sq km)

Topography: Both the Caribbean and the Pacific coasts are over 200 mi (320 m) long. The Cordillera Mountains, with many volcanic peaks, run northwest to southeast through the middle of the country. Between this and a volcanic range to the east lie Lakes Managua and Nicaragua.

Capital: Managua (pop., 1,098,000)

Independence date: September 15, 1821

Nicaragua (continued)

Government type: republic

Head of state and government: Pres. José Daniel Ortega Saavedra

Monetary unit: gold cordoba

GDP: $18.2 billion (2007 est.) **Per capita GDP:** $3,200

Industries: food processing, chemicals, machinery and metal products, textiles, clothing, petroleum refining and distribution, beverages, footwear, wood

Chief crops: coffee, bananas, sugarcane, cotton, rice, corn, tobacco, sesame, soya, beans

Minerals: gold, silver, copper, tungsten, lead, zinc

Life expectancy at birth (years): male, 68.0; female, 72.2

Literacy rate: 68.2% **Website:** www.consuladodenicaragua.com

PANAMA

FOR MAP, SEE PAGE 203

Population: 3,292,693

Ethnic groups: mestizo 70%, Amerindian-West Indian 14%, white 10%, Amerindian 6%

Principal languages: Spanish (official), English

Chief religions: Roman Catholic 85%, Protestant 15%

Area: 30,200 sq mi (78,200 sq km)

Topography: 2 mountain ranges run the length of the isthmus. Tropical rain forests cover the Caribbean coast and E Panama.

Capital: Panamá (pop., 930,000)

Independence date: November 3, 1903 **Government type:** republic

Head of state and government: Pres. Martín Torrijos Espino

Monetary unit: balboa

GDP: $29.1 billion (2007 est.) **Per capita GDP:** $9,000

Industries: construction, petroleum refining, brewing, cement, sugar milling

Chief crops: bananas, rice, corn, coffee, sugarcane, vegetables

Minerals: copper

Life expectancy at birth (years): male, 69.8; female, 74.6

Literacy rate: 90.8% **Website:** www.embassyofpanama.org

Panama Canal

SAINT KITTS AND NEVIS

FOR MAP, SEE PAGE 199

Population: 39,619

Ethnic group: black, British, Portuguese, Lebanese

Principal language: English (official)

Chief religions: Anglican, other Protestant, Roman Catholic

Area: 101 sq mi (261 sq km)

Topography: Saint Kitts has forested volcanic slopes; Nevis rises from beaches to a central peak.

Capital: Basseterre (pop., 13,000)

Independence date: September 19, 1983

Government type: constitutional monarchy

Head of state: Queen Elizabeth II, represented by Gov.-Gen. Sir Cuthbert Montraville Sebastian

Head of government: Prime Min. Denzil Llewellyn Douglas

Monetary unit: East Caribbean dollar

GDP: $726 million (2006 est.) **Per capita GDP:** $8,200

Industries: sugar processing, tourism, cotton, salt, copra, clothing, footwear, beverages

Chief crops: sugarcane, rice, yams, vegetables, bananas

Life expectancy at birth (years): male, 69.0; female, 74.9

Literacy rate: 97%

Website: www.stkittsnevis.net

SAINT LUCIA

FOR MAP, SEE PAGE 199

Population: 172,884

Ethnic groups: black 90%, mixed 6%, East Indian 3%, white 1%

Principal languages: English (official), French patois

Chief religions: Roman Catholic 90%, Protestant 10%

Area: 240 sq mi (620 sq km)

Topography: Saint Lucia is mountainous, volcanic in origin; Soufriere, a volcanic crater, is in the south. Wooded mountains run north to south to Mt. Gimie, 3,145 ft (960 m), with streams through fertile valleys.

Capital: Castries (pop., 14,000)

Independence date: February 22, 1979

Government type: parliamentary democracy

Head of state: Queen Elizabeth II, represented by Gov.-Gen. Calliopa Pearlette Louisy

Head of government: Prime Min. Kenny Anthony

Monetary unit: East Caribbean dollar

GDP: $1.2 billion (2006 est.) **Per capita GDP:** $4,800

Industries: clothing, assembly of electronic components, beverages, corrugated cardboard boxes, tourism

Chief crops: bananas, coconuts, vegetables, citrus, root crops, cocoa

Minerals: pumice

Life expectancy at birth (years): male, 69.5; female, 76.9

Literacy rate: 67%

Website: www.stlucia.gov.lc

SAINT VINCENT AND THE GRENADINES

FOR MAP, SEE PAGE 199

Population: 118,432

Ethnic groups: black 66%, mixed 19%, East Indian 6%, Carib Amerindian 2%

Principal languages: English (official), French patois

Chief religions: Anglican 47%, Methodist 28%, Roman Catholic 13%

Area: 131 sq mi (339 sq km)

Topography: St. Vincent is volcanic, with a ridge of thickly wooded mountains running its length.

Capital: Kingstown (pop., 29,000)

Independence date: October 27, 1979

Government type: constitutional monarchy

Head of state: Queen Elizabeth II, represented by Gov.-Gen. Sir Frederick Nathaniel Ballantyne

Head of government: Prime Min. Ralph Gonsalves

Monetary unit: East Caribbean dollar

GDP: $902 million (2007 est.)   Per capita GDP: $3,600

Industries: food processing, cement, furniture, clothing

Chief crops: bananas, coconuts, sweet potatoes, spices

Life expectancy at birth (years): male, 71.3; female, 74.9

Literacy rate: 96%   Website: www.svgtourism.com

TRINIDAD AND TOBAGO

For map, see page 199

Population: 1,047,366

Ethnic groups: black 40%, East Indian 40%, mixed 18%

Principal languages: English (official), Hindi, French, Spanish, Chinese

Chief religions: Roman Catholic 29%, Hindu 24%, Protestant 14%, Muslim 6%

Area: 1,980 sq mi (5,130 sq km)

Topography: Three low mountain ranges cross Trinidad east to west, with a well-watered plain between the north and central ranges. Parts of the east and west coasts are swamps. Tobago, 116 sq mi (300 sq km), lies 20 mi (30 km) northeast.

Capital: Port-of-Spain (pop., 55,000)

Independence date: August 31, 1962

Government type: parliamentary democracy

Head of state: Pres. George Maxwell Richards

Head of government: Prime Min. Patrick Augustus Mervyn Manning

Monetary unit: Trinidad and Tobago dollar

GDP: $22.9 billion (2007 est.)   Per capita GDP: $21,700

Industries: petroleum products, chemicals, tourism, food processing, cement, beverage, cotton textiles

Chief crops: cocoa, sugarcane, rice, citrus, coffee, vegetables

Minerals: petroleum, natural gas, asphalt

Life expectancy at birth (years): male, 65.9; female, 71.8

Literacy rate: 94%   Website: www.gov.tt

UNITED STATES

For map, see page 182

Population: 303,934,117 (50 states and District of Columbia)

Ethnic groups: white 75.1%, black 12.3%, Asian 3.6%, Amerindian and Alaska native 0.9% (Hispanics of any race or group 12.5%)

Principal languages: English, Spanish

Chief religions: Protestant 56%, Roman Catholic 28%, Jewish 2%

Area: 3,794,085 sq mi (9,826,635 sq km)

Topography: The area comprising the contiguous 48 states has a vast central plain, mountains in the west, and hills and low mountains in the east. Rugged mountains and broad river valleys are found in Alaska, and rugged, volcanic topography in Hawaii.

Capital: Washington, D.C. (pop., 4,098,000)

Independence date: July 4, 1776

Government type: federal republic

Head of state and government: Pres. George W. Bush

Monetary unit: U.S. dollar

GDP: $13,860 billion (2007 est.)   Per capita GDP: $46,000

Industries: petroleum, steel, motor vehicles, aerospace, telecommunications, chemicals, electronics, food processing, consumer goods, lumber, mining

Chief crops: wheat, other grains, corn, fruits, vegetables, cotton

Minerals: coal, copper, lead, molybdenum, phosphates, uranium, bauxite, gold, iron, mercury, nickel, potash, silver, tungsten, zinc, petroleum, natural gas

Life expectancy at birth (years): male, 74.6; female, 80.4

Literacy rate: 97%

Websites: www.census.gov
www.whitehouse.gov
www.firstgov.gov

MAJOR OUTLYING U.S. AREAS include two commonwealths—the Northern Mariana Islands in the Pacific Ocean and Puerto Rico in the West Indies—as well as the unincorporated territories American Samoa and Guam in the Pacific and the Virgin Islands in the West Indies.

AMERICAN SAMOA: population, 57,496; area, 77 sq mi; capital, Pago Pago on island of Tutuila

GUAM: population, 175,877; area, 212 sq mi; capital, Hagatña

NORTHERN MARIANA ISLANDS: population, 86,616; area, 184 sq mi; seat of government, Saipan

PUERTO RICO: population, 3,959,450; area, 3,515 sq mi; capital: San Juan

VIRGIN ISLANDS (ST. JOHN, ST. CROIX, ST. THOMAS): population, 108,210; area, 136 sq mi; capital: Charlotte Amalie on St. Thomas

Three U.S. hallmarks: Statue of Liberty, New York (left); cable car, San Francisco (middle); New England church, New Hampshire (right)

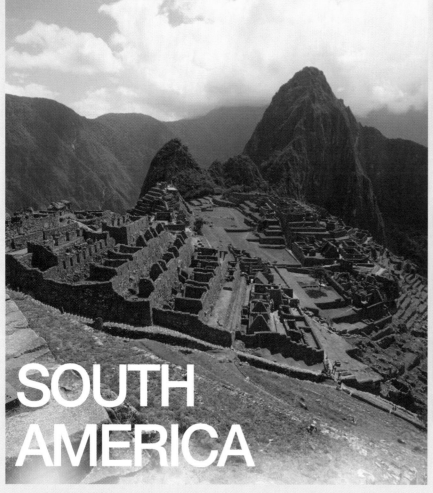

SOUTH AMERICA

Brazil is the biggest nation in South America, and the fifth biggest in the world, in terms of both land area and population. It also has the continent's largest economy.

ARGENTINA

FOR MAP, SEE PAGE 215

Population: 40,677,348

Ethnic groups: European 97%, Amerindian 3%

Principal languages: Spanish (official), English, Italian, German, French

Chief religion: Roman Catholic 92% (official)

Area: 1,068,300 sq mi (2,766,890 sq km)

Topography: Mountains in the west are the Andean, Central, Misiones, and Southern ranges. Aconcagua is the highest peak in the western hemisphere, altitude 22,834 ft (6,060 m). East of the Andes are heavily wooded plains, called the Gran Chaco in the north, and the fertile, treeless Pampas in the central region. Patagonia, in the south, is bleak and arid. Rio de la Plata, an estuary in the northeast, 170 by 140 mi (270 by 225 km), is mostly fresh water, from the 2,485-mi (4,000-km) Parana and 1,000-mi (1,600-km) Uruguay rivers.

Capital: Buenos Aires (pop., 13,047,000)

Iguaçú Falls, Argentine-Brazilian border

Independence date: July 9, 1816 **Government type:** republic

Head of state and government: Pres. Cristina Fernández de Kirchner

Monetary unit: peso

GDP: $523.7 billion (2007 est.) **Per capita GDP:** $13,000

Industries: food processing, motor vehicles, consumer durables, textiles, chemicals and petrochemicals, printing, metallurgy, steel

Chief crops: sunflower seeds, lemons, soybeans, grapes, corn, tobacco, peanuts, tea, wheat

Minerals: lead, zinc, tin, copper, iron ore, manganese, petroleum, uranium

Life expectancy at birth (years): male, 72.0; female, 79.7

Literacy rate: 96.2%

Websites: www.turismo.gov.ar/eng/menu.htm

BOLIVIA

FOR MAP, SEE PAGE 208

Population: 9,247,816

Ethnic groups: Quechua 30%, mestizo 30%, Aymara 25%, white 15%

Principal languages: Spanish, Quechua, Aymara (all official)

Chief religion: Roman Catholic (official) 95%

Area: 424,160 sq mi (1,098,580 sq km)

Topography: The great central plateau, at an altitude of 12,000 ft (3,600 m), over 500 mi (800 km) long, lies between two great cordilleras having three of the highest peaks in South America. Lake Titicaca, on the Peruvian border, is the highest lake in the world on which steamboats ply (12,506 ft [3,812 m]). The east-central region has semitropical forests; the llanos, or Amazon-Chaco lowlands, are in the east.

Capitals: La Paz (adminstrative) (pop., 1,477,000), Sucre (judicial) (pop., 212,000)

Independence date: August 6, 1825

Government type: republic

Head of state and government: Pres. Juan Evo Morales Aima

Monetary unit: boliviano

GDP: $39.78 billion (2007 est.)   Per capita GDP: $4,400

Industries: mining, smelting, petroleum, food and beverages, tobacco, handicrafts, clothing

Chief crops: soybeans, coffee, coca, cotton, corn, sugarcane, rice, potatoes

Minerals: tin, natural gas, petroleum, zinc, tungsten, antimony, silver, iron, lead, gold

Life expectancy at birth (years): male, 62.5; female, 67.9

Literacy rate: 83.1%

Website: www.state.gov/r/pa/ei/bgn/35751.htm

BRAZIL

For map, see page 205

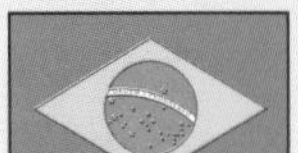

Population: 191,908,598

Ethnic groups: European 55%, Creole 38%, African 6%

Principal languages: Portuguese (official), Spanish, English, French

Chief religion: Roman Catholic (nominal) 80%

Area: 3,286,490 sq mi (8,511,970 sq km)

Topography: Brazil's Atlantic coastline stretches 4,603 mi (7,408 km). In the north is the heavily wooded Amazon basin covering half the country. Its network of rivers is navigable for 15,814 mi (25,450 km). The Amazon itself flows 2,093 mi (3,368 km) in Brazil, all navigable. The northeast region is semiarid scrubland, heavily settled and poor. The south-central region, favored by climate and resources, has almost half of the population and produces 75% of farm goods and 80% of industrial output. The narrow coastal belt includes most of the major cities.

Capital: Brasília (pop., 3,099,000)

Independence date: September 7, 1822

Government type: federal republic

Head of state and government: Pres. Luis Inacio Lula da Silva

Monetary unit: real

GDP: $1,838 billion (2007 est.)

Per capita GDP: $9,700

Ipanema Beach and Rio de Janeiro, Brazil

Industries: textiles, shoes, chemicals, cement, lumber, aircraft, motor vehicles and parts, other machinery and equipment

Chief crops: coffee, soybeans, wheat, rice, corn, sugarcane, cocoa, citrus

Minerals: bauxite, gold, iron ore, manganese, nickel, phosphates, platinum, tin, uranium, petroleum

Life expectancy at birth (years): male, 67.5; female, 75.6

Literacy rate: 83.3%

Website: www.brasilemb.org

CHILE

For map, see page 215

Population: 16,432,536

Ethnic groups: European and mestizo 95%, Amerindian 3%

Principal languages: Spanish (official), Araucanian

Chief religions: Roman Catholic 89%, Protestant 11%

Area: 292,260 sq mi (756,950 sq km)

Topography: The Andes Mountains on the eastern border include some of the world's highest peaks; on the west is the 2,650 mi (4,265 km) Pacific coast. The country's width varies between 100 and 250 mi (160 and 400 km). In the north is the Atacama Desert, in the center are agricultural regions, in the south, forests and grazing lands.

Capital: Santiago (pop., 5,478,000)

Independence date: September 18, 1810

Government type: republic

Head of state and government: Pres. Verónica Michelle Bachelet Jeria

Monetary unit: peso

GDP: $234.4 billion (2007 est.)

Per capita GDP: $14,400

Industries: mining, food-stuffs, fish processing, iron and steel, wood and wood products, transport equipment, cement, textiles

Chief crops: wheat, corn, grapes, beans, sugar beets, potatoes, fruit

Minerals: copper, timber, iron ore, nitrates, precious metals, molybdenum

Life expectancy at birth (years): male, 73.1; female, 79.8

Literacy rate: 95.2%

Website: www.chileangovernment.cl

Torres del Paine National Park, Chile

TIERRA DEL FUEGO is the largest (18,800 sq mi [48,700 sq km]) island in the archipelago of the same name at the southern tip of South America, an area of majestic mountains, tortuous channels, and high winds. Part of the island is in Chile, part in Argentina. Punta Arenas, on a mainland peninsula, is the world's southernmost city (population about 70,000); Puerto Williams is the southern-most settlement.

COLOMBIA

For map, see page 210

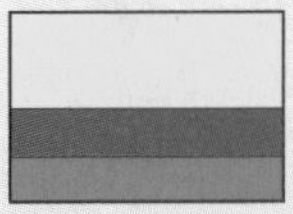

Population: 45,013,674

Ethnic groups: mestizo 58%, European 20%, Creole 14%, black 4%, black-Amerindian 1%, Amerindian 3%

Principal language: Spanish (official)

Chief religion: Roman Catholic 90%

Nation Facts and Figures

Colombia *(continued)*

Area: 439,740 sq mi (1,138,910 sq km)

Topography: Three ranges of Andes—Western, Central, and Eastern Cordilleras—run through the country from north to south. The eastern range consists mostly of high tablelands, densely populated. The Magdalena River rises in the Andes and flows north to the Caribbean through a rich alluvial plain. Sparsely settled plains in the east are drained by the Orinoco and Amazon systems.

Capital: Bogotá (pop., 7,290,000)

Independence date: July 20, 1810

Government type: republic

Head of state and government: Pres. Álvaro Uribe Vélez

Monetary unit: peso

GDP: $320.4 billion (2007 est.)   **Per capita GDP:** $7,200

Industries: textiles, food processing, oil, clothing and footwear, beverages, chemicals, cement, gold, coal, emeralds

Chief crops: coffee, cut flowers, bananas, rice, tobacco, corn, sugarcane, cocoa beans, oilseed, vegetables

Minerals: petroleum, natural gas, coal, iron ore, nickel, gold, copper, emeralds

Life expectancy at birth (years): male, 67.6; female, 75.4

Literacy rate: 91.3%

Website: www.colombiaembassy.org

ECUADOR

FOR MAP, SEE PAGE 208

Population: 13,927,650

Ethnic groups: mestizo 65%, Amerindian 25%, black 3%

Principal languages: Spanish (official), Amerindian languages (especially Quechua)

Chief religion: Roman Catholic 95%

Area: 109,480 sq mi (283,560 sq km)

Topography: Two ranges of Andes run north and south, splitting the country into three zones: hot, humid lowlands on the coast; temperate highlands between the ranges; and rainy, tropical lowlands to the east.

Capital: Quito (pop., 1,451,000)

Independence date: May 24, 1822

Government type: republic

Head of state and government: Pres. Rafael Correa

Monetary unit: U.S. dollar

GDP: $98.3 billion (2007 est.)

Per capita GDP: $7,100

Industries: petroleum, food processing, textiles, metal work, paper and wood products, chemicals, plastics, fishing, lumber

Chief crops: bananas, coffee, cocoa, rice, potatoes, manioc (tapioca), plantains, sugarcane

Minerals: petroleum

Life expectancy at birth (years): male, 73.2; female, 79.0

Literacy rate: 90.1%

Website: www.ecuador.org

An Ecuadoran market

GUYANA

FOR MAP, SEE PAGE 211

Population: 770,794

Ethnic groups: East Indian 50%, black 36%, Amerindian 7%

Principal languages: English (official), Amerindian dialects, Creole, Hindi, Urdu

Chief religions: Christian 50%, Hindu 35%, Muslim 10%

Area: 83,000 sq mi (214,970 sq km)

Topography: Dense tropical forests cover much of the land, although a flat coastal area up to 40 mi (65 km) wide, where 90% of the population lives, provides rich alluvial soil for agriculture. A grassy savanna divides the two zones.

Guyanese rain forest

Capital: Georgetown (pop., 231,000)

Independence date: May 26, 1966   **Government type:** republic

Head of state: Pres. Bharrat Jagdeo

Head of government: Prime Min. Samuel Hinds

Monetary unit: Guyana dollar

GDP: $4.1 billion (2007 est.)   **Per capita GDP:** $5,300

Industries: sugar, rice milling, timber, textiles, mining

Chief crops: sugar, rice, wheat, vegetable oils

Minerals: bauxite, gold, diamonds

Life expectancy at birth (years): male, 60.1; female, 64.8

Literacy rate: 98.1%

Website: www.guyana.org

PARAGUAY

FOR MAP, SEE PAGE 205

Population: 6,831,306

Ethnic groups: mestizo 95%

Principal languages: Spanish, Guaraní (both official)

Chief religion: Roman Catholic 90%

Area: 157,050 sq mi (406,750 sq km)

Topography: The Paraguay River bisects the country. To the east are fertile plains, wooded slopes, and grasslands. To the west is the Gran Chaco plain, with marshes and scrub trees. The extreme west is arid.

Capital: Asunción (pop., 1,639,000)

Independence date: May 14, 1811

Government type: republic

Head of state and government: Pres. Fernando Lugo

Monetary unit: guarani

GDP: $26.5 billion (2007 est.)   **Per capita GDP:** $4,000

Industries: sugar, cement, textiles, beverages, wood products

Chief crops: cotton, sugarcane, soybeans, corn, wheat, tobacco, cassava, fruits, vegetables

Minerals: iron ore, manganese, limestone

Life expectancy at birth (years): male, 72.1; female, 77.3

Literacy rate: 92.1%

Website: www.paraguay.com

PERU

FOR MAP, SEE PAGE 214

Population: 29,041,593

Ethnic groups: Amerindian 45%, mestizo 37%, white 15%

Principal languages: Spanish, Quechua (both official); Aymara

Chief religion: Roman Catholic (official) 90%

Area: 496,230 sq mi (1,285,220 sq km)

Topography: An arid coastal strip, 10 to 100 mi (16 to 160 km) wide, supports much of the population thanks to widespread irrigation. The Andes cover 27% of the land area. The uplands are well-watered, as are the eastern slopes reaching to the Amazon basin, which covers half the country with its forests and jungles.

Capital: Lima (pop., 7,899,000)

Independence date: July 28, 1821   **Government type:** republic

Head of state: Pres. Alan García Pérez

Head of government: Prime Min. Jorge Alfonso Alejandro Del Castillo Gálvez

Monetary unit: new sol

GDP: $217.5 billion (2007 est.)   **Per capita GDP:** $7,600

Industries: mining, petroleum, fishing, textiles, clothing, food processing, cement, auto assembly, steel, shipbuilding, metal fabrication

Chief crops: coffee, cotton, sugarcane, rice, wheat, potatoes, corn, plantains, coca

Minerals: copper, silver, gold, petroleum, iron ore, coal, phosphate, potash

Life expectancy at birth (years): male, 67.5; female, 71.0

Literacy rate: 88.3%

Website: www.peru.info/perueng.asp

SURINAME

FOR MAP, SEE PAGE 211

Population: 475,996

Ethnic groups: East Indians 37%, Creole 31%, Javanese 15%, Maroons 10%, Amerindian 2%, Chinese 2%, white 1%

Principal languages: Dutch (official), English, Sranang Tongo (an English Creole), Hindustani, Javanese

Chief religions: Hindu 27%, Protestant 25%, Roman Catholic 23%, Muslim 20%

Area: 63,040 sq mi (163,270 sq km)

Topography: A flat Atlantic coast, where dikes permit agriculture. Inland is a forest belt; to the south, largely unexplored hills cover 75% of the country.

Capital: Paramaribo (pop., 253,000)

Independence date: November 25, 1975   **Government type:** republic

Head of state and government: Pres. Runaldo Ronald Venetiaan

Monetary unit: guilder

GDP: $3.4 billion (2007 est.)   **Per capita GDP:** $7,800

Industries: mining, alumina production, oil, lumbering, food processing, fishing

Chief crops: paddy rice, bananas, palm kernels, coconuts, plantains, peanuts

Minerals: kaolin, bauxite, gold, nickel, copper, platinum, iron ore

Life expectancy at birth (years): male, 66.8; female, 71.6

Literacy rate: 93%   **Website:** www.surinameembassy.org

URUGUAY

FOR MAP, SEE PAGE 215

Population: 3,477,778

Ethnic groups: white 88%, mestizo 8%, black 4%

Principal languages: Spanish (official), Portunol/Brazilero (Portuguese-Spanish)

Chief religion: Roman Catholic 66%

Area: 68,040 sq mi (176,220 sq km)

Topography: Uruguay is composed of rolling, grassy plains and hills, well watered by rivers flowing west to the Uruguay River.

Capital: Montevideo (pop., 1,341,000)

Independence date: August 25, 1825   **Government type:** republic

Head of state and government: Pres. Tabaré Ramón Vázquez Rosas

Monetary unit: peso

GDP: $37 billion (2007 est.)   **Per capita GDP:** $10,700

Industries: food processing, electrical machinery, transport equipment, petroleum products, textiles, chemicals, beverages

Chief crops: rice, wheat, corn, barley

Life expectancy at birth (years): male, 72.7; female, 79.2

Literacy rate: 97.3%

Website: www.uruwashi.org

VENEZUELA

FOR MAP, SEE PAGE 210

Population: 26,414,815

Ethnic groups: Spanish, Italian, Portuguese, Arab, German, black, indigenous

Principal languages: Spanish (official), numerous indigenous dialects

Chief religion: Roman Catholic 96%

Area: 352,140 sq mi (912,050 sq km)

Topography: The flat coastal plain and Orinoco Delta are bordered by the Andes Mountains and hills. Plains, called llanos, extend between the mountains and the Orinoco. The Guiana Highlands and plains are south of the Orinoco, which stretches 1,600 mi (2,600 km) and drains 80% of Venezuela.

Capital: Caracas (pop., 3,226,000)

Independence date: July 5, 1811

Caracas, Venezuela

Government type: federal republic

Head of state and government: Pres. Hugo Rafael Chávez Frías

Monetary unit: bolivar

GDP: $335 billion (2007 est.)

Per capita GDP: $12,800

Industries: petroleum, mining, construction materials, food processing, textiles, steel, aluminum, motor vehicle assembly

Chief crops: corn, sorghum, sugarcane, rice, bananas, vegetables, coffee

Minerals: petroleum, natural gas, iron ore, gold, bauxite

Life expectancy at birth (years): male, 71.0; female, 77.3

Literacy rate: 91.1%

Website: www.embavenez-us.org

World
Map Section

World

Continents

Regions / Nations

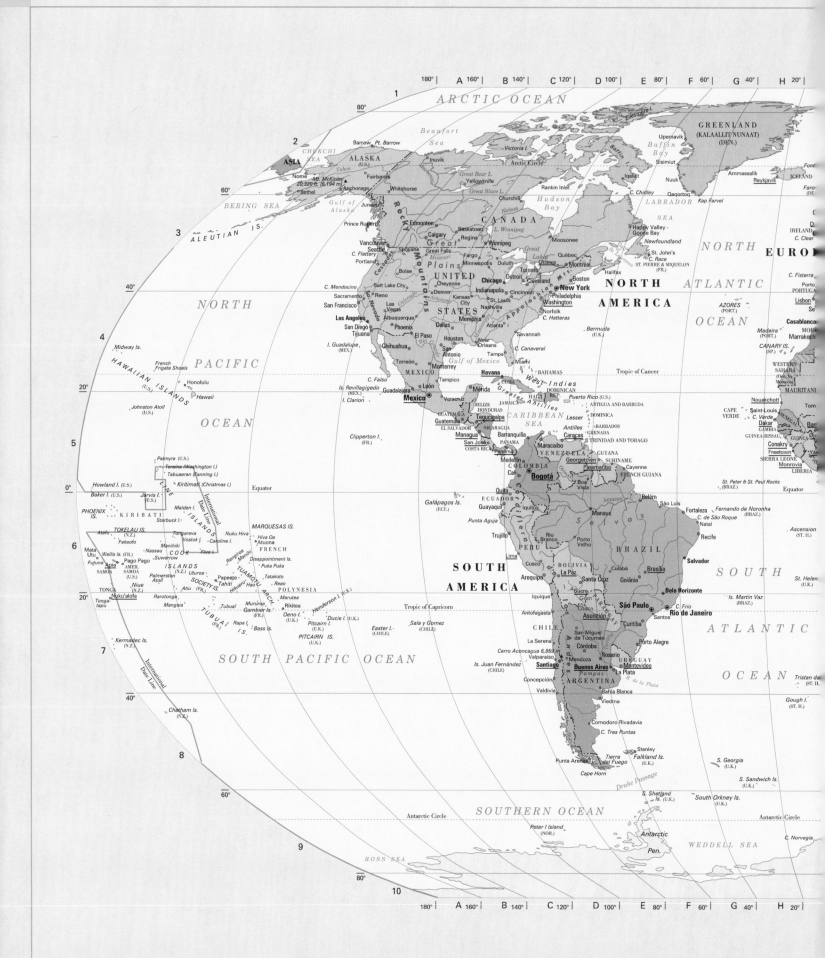

ARCTIC OCEAN

1

A 160° B 140° C 120° D 100° E 80° F 60° G 40° H 20°

180°

80°

2

Beaufort
Sea

GREENLAND
(KALAALLIT NUNAAT)
(DEN.)

CHUKCHI
SEA

ASIA

Barrow Pt. Barrow

ALASKA
(U.S.)

Nome

Victoria I.

Upernavik

Baffin
Bay

Sisimiut

Font

ICELAND

Inuvik

Arctic Circle

Ammassalik

Reykjavík

60°

Mt. McKinley
20,320 ft. (6,194 m)

Anchorage

Fairbanks

Yellowknife

Iqaluit

Nuuk

Faro
(DE.)

BERING SEA

Bethel

Yukon

Great Bear L.

Rankin Inlet

C. Chidley

Qaqortoq

Kap Farvel

3

ALEUTIAN IS.

Juneau

Whitehorse

Great Slave L.

Churchill

Hudson
Bay

LABRADOR

SEA

Happy Valley -
Goose Bay

IRELAND

C. Clear

NORTH EURO

Prince Rupert

Edmonton

CANADA

Saskatoon

L. Winnipeg

Nelson

Moosonee

Newfoundland

St. John's

Vancouver
Seattle
Spokane

Calgary
Regina

Winnipeg

Great

Québec

C. Race
ST. PIERRE & MIQUELON
(FR.)

NORTH

C. Fisterra

Portland

Great Falls

Fargo

Minneapolis

Duluth

Toronto

Ottawa

Montréal

Halifax

Boston

ATLANTIC

Porto
PORTUGAL

C. Flattery

Boise

Missouri

Great
Lakes

Detroit

Cleveland

New York

Lisbon

40°

C. Mendocino

Salt Lake City

Cheyenne

Chicago

Indianapolis

Philadelphia
Washington

NORTH

AZORES
(PORT.)

OCEAN

Madeira
(PORT.)

Casablanca

NORTH

Sacramento
Reno

Denver

Kansas
City

St. Louis

Cincinnati

Nashville

Norfolk

AMERICA

MOR

Marrakech

San Francisco

Las
Vegas

UNITED

Memphis

Atlanta

C. Hatteras

Bermuda
(U.K.)

CANARY IS.
(SP.)

Los Angeles

Albuquerque

Arkansas

STATES

Dallas

Savannah

20°

PACIFIC

San Diego
Tijuana

Phoenix

El Paso

Houston

New
Orleans

C. Canaveral

Tampa

Tropic of Cancer

WESTERN
SAHARA
(Occ. by
Morocco)

MAURITANI

4

Midway Is.

Chihuahua

Rio

San
Antonio

Miami

BAHAMAS

Nouakchott

French
Frigate Shoals

Torreón

Gulf of Mexico

West Indies

CAPE
VERDE

Saint-Louis
C. Verde

HAWAIIAN ISLANDS
(U.S.)

Honolulu

MEXICO

Monterrey

CUBA

Havana

Greater Antilles

DOMINICAN
REP.

Dakar

GAMBIA

Johnston Atoll
(U.S.)

Hawaii

C. Falso

León

Tampico

Mérida

Puerto Rico (U.S.)

HAITI

GUINEA-BISSAU

GUINEA

Is. Revillagigedo
(MEX.)

Guadalajara

Veracruz

BELIZE

JAMAICA

ANTIGUA AND BARBUDA

Conakry

OCEAN

I. Clarion

Mexico

GUATEMALA

HONDURAS

DOMINICA

Lesser

Freetown

SIERRA LEONE

5

Clipperton I.
(FR.)

Guatemala
EL SALVADOR

Tegucigalpa

CARIBBEAN

BARBADOS

Monrovia

LIBERIA

Managua

NICARAGUA

SEA

Antilles

GRENADA

Barranquilla

Caracas

TRINIDAD AND TOBAGO

Palmyra (U.S.)

San José
COSTA RICA

PANAMA
Panama

Maracaibo

VENEZUELA

GUYANA

St. Peter & St. Paul Rocks
(BRAZ.)

Teraina (Washington I.)

Medellín

Georgetown

SURINAME

Tabuaeran (Fanning I.)

COLOMBIA

Cali

Paramaribo

Cayenne

0°

Howland I. (U.S.)

Kiritimati (Christmas I.)

Equator

Bogotá

Boa
Vista

FRENCH GUIANA

Equator

Baker I. (U.S.)

Jarvis I.
(U.S.)

ECUADOR

Belém

São Luís

PHOENIX
IS.

KIRIBATI

Galápagos Is.
(ECU.)

Quito

Iquitos

Manaus

Fortaleza

Fernando de Noronha
(BRAZ.)

Ascension
(ST. H.)

Starbuck I.

Guayaquil

Amazon

C. de São Roque

Natal

Atafu

MARQUESAS IS.

Nuku Hiva

Punta Aguja

Branco

Porto
Velho

Recife

6

Mata
Utu

TOKELAU IS.
(N.Z.)

Fakaofo

Tongareva

Vostok I.

Caroline I.

Hiva Oa
Atuona

FRENCH

Trujillo

Rio

BRAZIL

Salvador

ST. HELENA

Wallis Is. (FR.)

Nassau

Manihiki

Flint I.

Rangiroa

Disappointment Is.

PERU

BOLIVIA

Brasília

SOUTH

Futuna

Pago Pago

Suwarrow

Puka Puka

Lima

Goiânia

St. Helena
(U.K.)

SAMOA

AMER.
SAMOA

COOK

Palmerston
Atoll

Uturoa

Tatakoto

SOUTH

La Paz

Santa Cruz

Apia

ISLANDS
(N.Z.)

Papeete
Tahiti

Reao

AMERICA

Cuiabá

Belo Horizonte

Niue
(N.Z.)

SOCIETY IS.
(FR.)

Atiu

Hikueru

Sucre

20°

Tonga-
tapu

Nuku'alofa

Rarotonga

Marutea

Iquique

POLYNESIA

TONGA

Tubuai

Mururoa

Henderson I. (U.K.)

Tropic of Capricorn

Antofagasta

Asunción

Gran

São Paulo

Is. Martín Vaz
(BRAZ.)

Rikitea

Mangaia

Gambier Is.
(FR.)

Oeno I.
(U.K.)

Ducie I. (U.K.)

Chaco

São Paulo

Rio de Janeiro

ATLANTIC

TUBUAI IS.
(FR.)

Rapa I.

Bass Is.

Pitcairn I.
(U.K.)

Sala y Gomez
(CHILE)

Easter I.
(CHILE)

CHILE

San Miguel
de Tucumán

Santos

C. Frio

PITCAIRN IS.
(U.K.)

Curitiba

7

Kermadec Is.
(N.Z.)

Cerro Aconcagua 6,959 m

La Serena

Córdoba

Rosario

Pôrto Alegre

SOUTH

Valparaíso

Mendoza

URUGUAY

St. Helena
(U.K.)

OCEAN

SOUTH PACIFIC OCEAN

Is. Juan Fernández
(CHILE)

Santiago

Buenos Aires

Montevideo
La Plata

Tristan da
(ST. H.)

Concepción

Pampas

R. de la Plata

40°

Chatham Is.
(N.Z.)

ARGENTINA

Bahía Blanca

Gough I.
(ST. H.)

Valdivia

Viedma

8

Comodoro Rivadavia

C. Tres Puntas

Stanley

Falkland Is.
(U.K.)

S. Georgia
(U.K.)

60°

Punta Arenas

Tierra
del Fuego

Cape Horn

Drake Passage

S. Sandwich Is.
(U.K.)

S. Shetland
Is. (U.K.)

South Orkney Is.
(U.K.)

Antarctic Circle

SOUTHERN OCEAN

Antarctic Circle

C. Norvegia

9

Peter I Island
(NOR.)

Antarctic
Pen.

WEDDELL SEA

ROSS SEA

80°

10

180°

A 160° B 140° C 120° D 100° E 80° F 60° G 40° H 20°

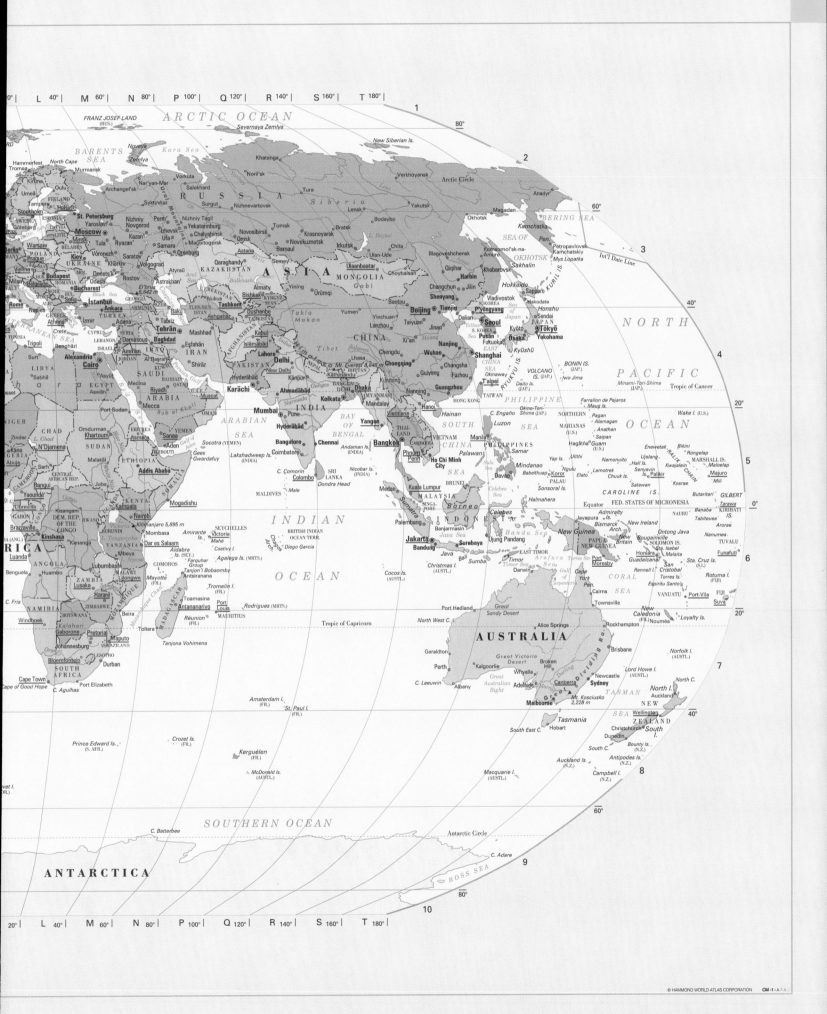

POPULATION OF CITIES AND TOWNS

◉ OVER 5,000,000	◎ 500,000 - 1,999,999
● 2,000,000 - 4,999,999	○ UNDER 500,000

SCALE 1:80,500,000 ROBINSON PROJECTION STANDARD PARALLELS 38° N and 38° S

MILES   0   1000   2000   3000   4000

KILOMETERS   0   1000   2000   3000   4000

ARCTIC OCEAN

Queen Elizabeth Is.   Ellesmere I.

Beaufort   Greenland
Sea   Baffin
Bay

Pt. Barrow   Victoria I.
Wrangel I.   Devon I.
CHUKCHI   Arctic Circle
SEA   Denmark Str.
Yukon   Great Bear L.   Iceland
Mt. McKinley   LABRADOR   Kap Farvel   ICELAND BASIN
6,194 m   Great Slave L.   Hudson   SEA
BERING SEA   Bay   Ungava   Irel.
Gulf of   Pen.
Alaska   Churchill   NORTH
Aleutian Is.   L. Winnipeg   Newfoundland
ALEUTIAN TRENCH   Great   St.   C. Race   ATLANTIC
Vancouver   NORTH   Lakes   Montreal
Seattle   AMERICA   RIDGE   OCEAN
MENDOCINO FRACTURE ZONE   Rocky Mountains   Chicago   Appalachian Mts   New York   Azores
NORTH   Denver   Ohio   MID-ATLANTIC
San Francisco   Great   Arkansas   C. Hatteras   Madeira
MURRAY FRACTURE ZONE   Basin   Dallas   Tropic of Cancer   Cap Blanc
PACIFIC   Baja   Mississippi   Miami   Canary Is.
California   Gulf of Mexico   Bahamas   West   Cape Verde Is.   Cape
Hawaiian Is.   MOLOKAI FRACTURE ZONE   Cuba   Milwaukee Deep   Indies   Verde
Honolulu   Yucatan   Greater Antilles   -8,605 m
CLARION FRACTURE ZONE   Mexico   Pen.   Hispaniola
OCEAN   CARIBBEAN   Lesser   Trinidad
CENTRAL   Clipperton I.   SEA   Antilles
PACIFIC   GUATEMALA   Maracaibo
BASIN   MIDDLE-AMERICAN TRENCH   BASIN   Guiana Highlands   ROMANCHE FRACTURE ZONE
CLIPPERTON FRACTURE ZONE   Bogota   Llanos   BRASIL   Ascension
Equator   Galapagos Is.   Cordillera   Amazon   Marajo   BASIN   MID-ATLANTIC
Phoenix   Selvas   Belem
Is.   PERU   SOUTH   Brazilian   S O U T H
Northern   Marquesas   Madeira   AMERICA   Highlands
Cook Is.   Is.   BASIN   PERU-CHILE   RIO GRANDE   SOUTH
Samoan   PACIFIC RISE   Gran   Rio de Janeiro   ATLANTIC
Is.   Tahiti   TRENCH   NAZCA RIDGE   Choco   PLATEAU
Southern   Society   Tuamotu Arch.   los Andes   ATLANTIC
Cook Is.   Is.   Tropic of Capricorn   Sala y Gomez   CHILE   Cerro Aconcagua   R. de la Plata   OCEAN   Tristan
TONGA TRENCH   Tubuai Is.   Pitcairn I.   Easter I.   TRENCH   6,959 m   Pampas
KERMADEC TRENCH   SOUTH PACIFIC OCEAN   Is. Juan Fernandez   Santiago   ARGENTINE
LOUISVILLE RIDGE   CHILE   RISE   BASIN   BASIN
EAST   Pen.
SOUTHWEST   Valdes
PACIFIC   CHILE RISE   C. Tres Puntas
Chatham Is.   BASIN   Falkland Is.
Str. of Magellan   Tierra   S. Georgia   Meteor Deep
del Fuego   -8,325 m
PACIFIC-ANTARCTIC RIDGE   Cape Horn   SCOTIA   SEA   S. Sandwich Is.
Drake Passage   S. Shetland   WEDDELL
AMUNDSEN ABYSSAL PLAIN   Is.   ABYSSAL
Antarctic   PLAIN   C. Norvegia
ROSS SEA   Pen.   WEDDELL SEA

POPULATION OF CITIES AND TOWNS

- ◉ OVER 5,000,000
- ⊕ 2,000,000 - 4,999,999
- ⊙ 500,000 - 1,999,999
- ○ UNDER 500,000

SCALE 1:80,500,000   ROBINSON PROJECTION   STANDARD PARALLELS 38° N and 38° S

MILES   0   1000   2000   3000   4000

KILOMETERS   0   1000   2000   3000   4000

THE WORLD ALMANAC
WORLD ATLAS

Europe

The terrain in this high-oblique, northwest-looking image, is indicative of the rugged, mountainous landscape characterizing most of Greece. Two major landform regions are captured in this image: the northwest to southeast-trending Mountains of Pindus in central Greece (north of the Gulf of Corinth), and the Peloponnisos Peninsula (south of the Gulf of Corinth). The Pindus, a massive continuation of the Dinaric Alps of Albania and the former Yugoslavia, make the land inhospitable and travel difficult. This rugged terrain caused the Greeks to become a seafaring people.

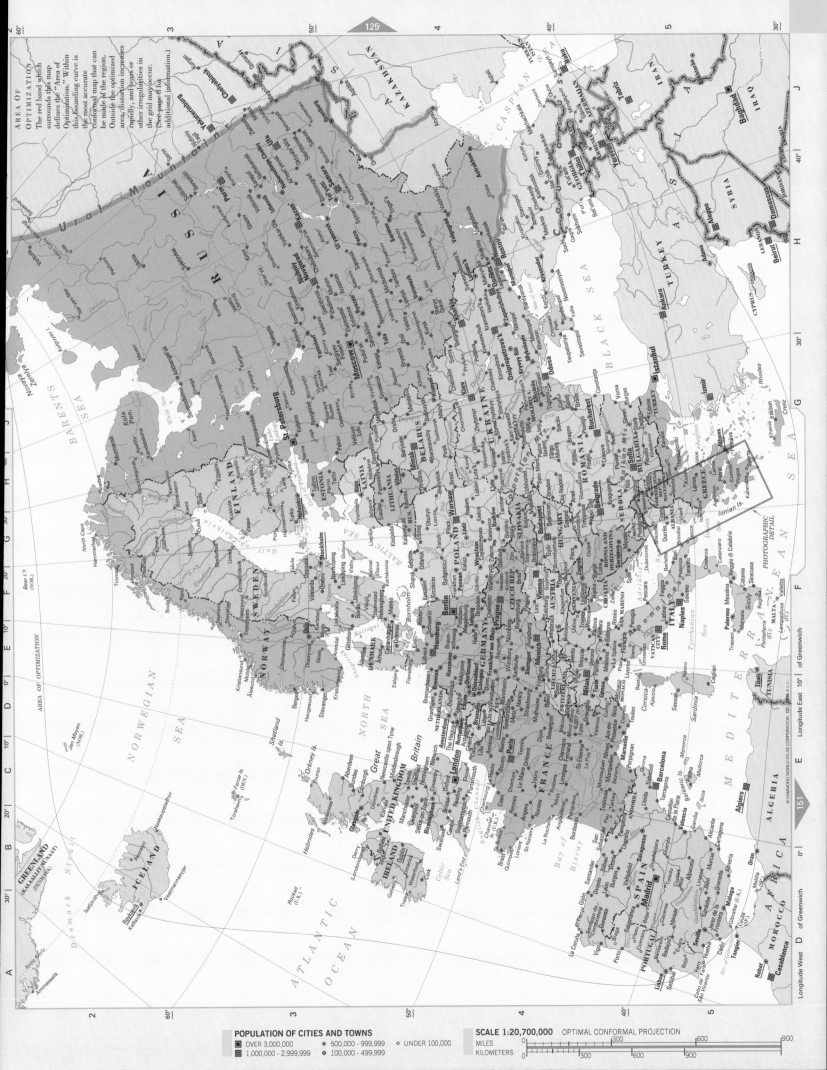

POPULATION OF CITIES AND TOWNS

- ■ OVER 3,000,000
- ▣ 1,000,000 - 2,999,999
- ● 500,000 - 999,999
- ◉ 100,000 - 499,999
- ○ UNDER 100,000

SCALE 1:20,700,000   OPTIMAL CONFORMAL PROJECTION

MILES

KILOMETERS

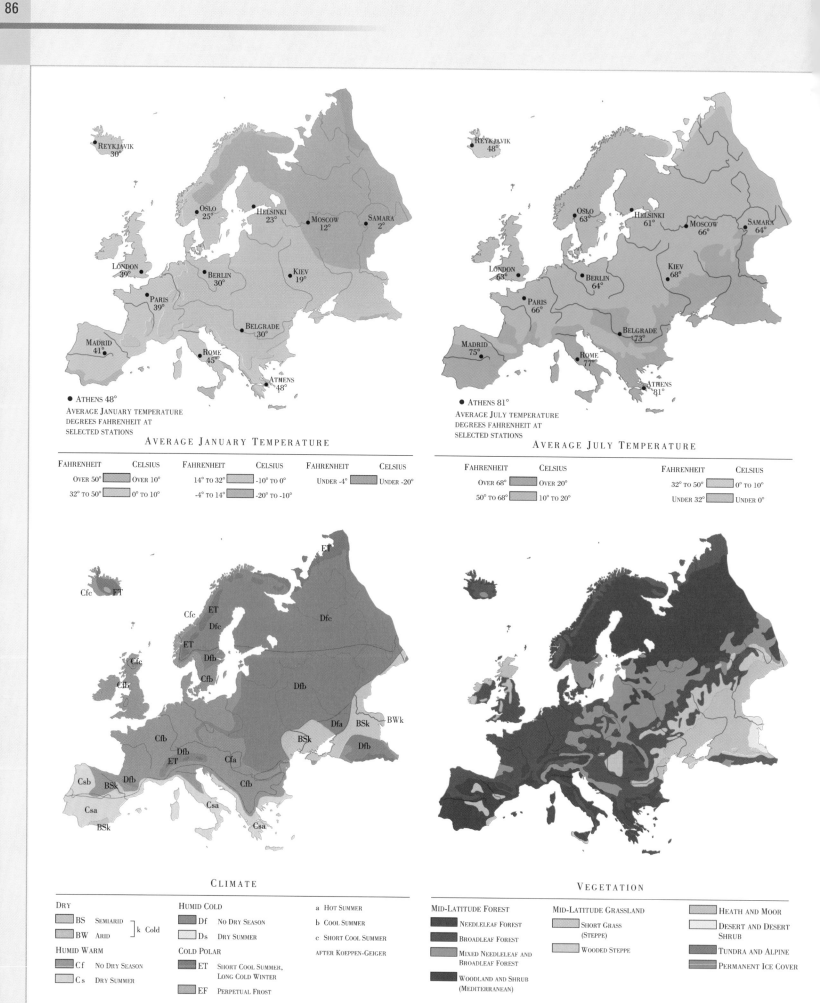

AVERAGE JANUARY TEMPERATURE

REYKJAVIK 30°
OSLO 25°
HELSINKI 23°
MOSCOW 12°
SAMARA 2°
LONDON 39°
BERLIN 30°
KIEV 19°
PARIS 39°
BELGRADE 30°
MADRID 41°
ROME 45°
ATHENS 48°

● Athens 48°
AVERAGE JANUARY TEMPERATURE
DEGREES FAHRENHEIT AT
SELECTED STATIONS

FAHRENHEIT	CELSIUS	FAHRENHEIT	CELSIUS	FAHRENHEIT	CELSIUS
OVER 50°	OVER 10°	14° TO 32°	-10° TO 0°	UNDER -4°	UNDER -20°
32° TO 50°	0° TO 10°	-4° TO 14°	-20° TO -10°		

AVERAGE JULY TEMPERATURE

REYKJAVIK 48°
OSLO 63°
HELSINKI 61°
MOSCOW 66°
SAMARA 64°
LONDON 63°
BERLIN 64°
KIEV 68°
PARIS 66°
BELGRADE 73°
MADRID 75°
ROME 77°
ATHENS 81°

● Athens 81°
AVERAGE JULY TEMPERATURE
DEGREES FAHRENHEIT AT
SELECTED STATIONS

FAHRENHEIT	CELSIUS	FAHRENHEIT	CELSIUS
OVER 68°	OVER 20°	32° TO 50°	0° TO 10°
50° TO 68°	10° TO 20°	UNDER 32°	UNDER 0°

CLIMATE

DRY
BS SEMIARID
BW ARID] k Cold

HUMID WARM
Cf NO DRY SEASON
Cs DRY SUMMER

HUMID COLD
Df NO DRY SEASON
Ds DRY SUMMER

COLD POLAR
ET SHORT COOL SUMMER, LONG COLD WINTER
EF PERPETUAL FROST

a HOT SUMMER
b COOL SUMMER
c SHORT COOL SUMMER

AFTER KOEPPEN-GEIGER

VEGETATION

MID-LATITUDE FOREST
NEEDLELEAF FOREST
BROADLEAF FOREST
MIXED NEEDLELEAF AND BROADLEAF FOREST
WOODLAND AND SHRUB (MEDITERRANEAN)

MID-LATITUDE GRASSLAND
SHORT GRASS (STEPPE)
WOODED STEPPE

HEATH AND MOOR
DESERT AND DESERT SHRUB
TUNDRA AND ALPINE
PERMANENT ICE COVER

● BERLIN 23

AVERAGE ANNUAL RAINFALL
IN INCHES AT SELECTED STATIONS

AVERAGE ANNUAL RAINFALL

INCHES	CM	INCHES	CM	INCHES	CM
OVER 80	OVER 200	40 TO 60	100 TO 150	10 TO 20	25 TO 50
60 TO 80	150 TO 200	20 TO 40	50 TO 100	UNDER 10	UNDER 25

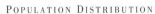

● CITIES WITH OVER 2,000,000
INHABITANTS

POPULATION DISTRIBUTION

DENSITY PER		SQ. MI.	SQ. KM.	SQ. MI.	SQ. KM.
SQ. MI.	SQ. KM.	130 TO 260	50 TO 100	3 TO 25	1 TO 10
OVER 260	OVER 100	25 TO 130	10 TO 50	UNDER 3	UNDER 1

LAND USE

- CEREALS, LIVESTOCK
- DAIRY, LIVESTOCK
- LIVESTOCK HERDING
- SPECIAL CROPS
- FRUIT AND TRUCK FARMING
- PASTURE LIVESTOCK
- DAIRY, CEREALS
- GENERAL FARMING, LIVESTOCK
- FORESTS
- NONPRODUCTIVE

MINERAL RESOURCES

ENERGY & FUELS
- ◆ COAL
- ⬡ LIGNITE
- ▲ NATURAL GAS
- ● PETROLEUM
- ▪ URANIUM

IRON & FERROALLOYS
- 1 CHROMIUM
- 2 COBALT
- 3 IRON ORE
- 4 MANGANESE
- 5 MOLYBDENUM
- 6 NICKEL
- 7 TUNGSTEN
- 8 VANADIUM

OTHER MAJOR RESOURCES
- 1 ANTIMONY
- 2 ASBESTOS
- 3 BAUXITE
- 4 COPPER
- 5 FLORSPAR
- 6 GRAPHITE
- 7 LEAD
- 8 MAGNESITE
- 9 MERCURY
- 10 PHOSPHATES
- 11 PLATINUM
- 12 POTASH
- 13 SILVER
- 14 SULFER
- 15 TITANIUM
- 16 ZINC

London, Paris

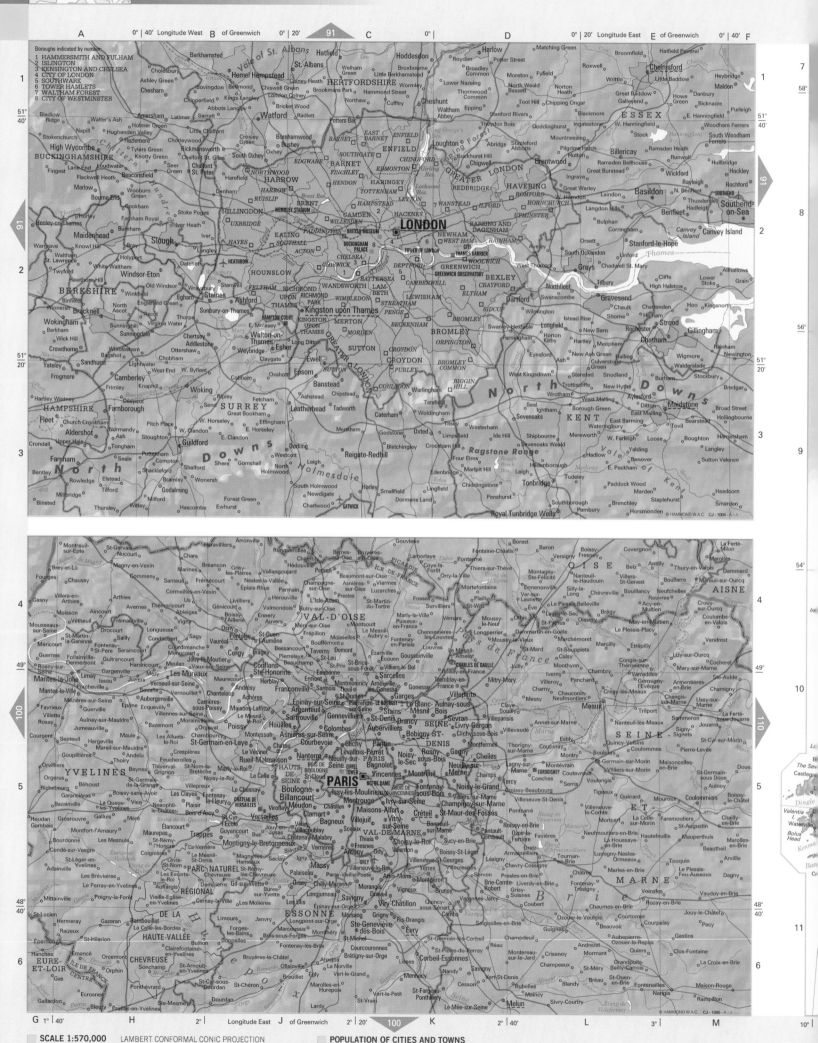

Southern England and Wales

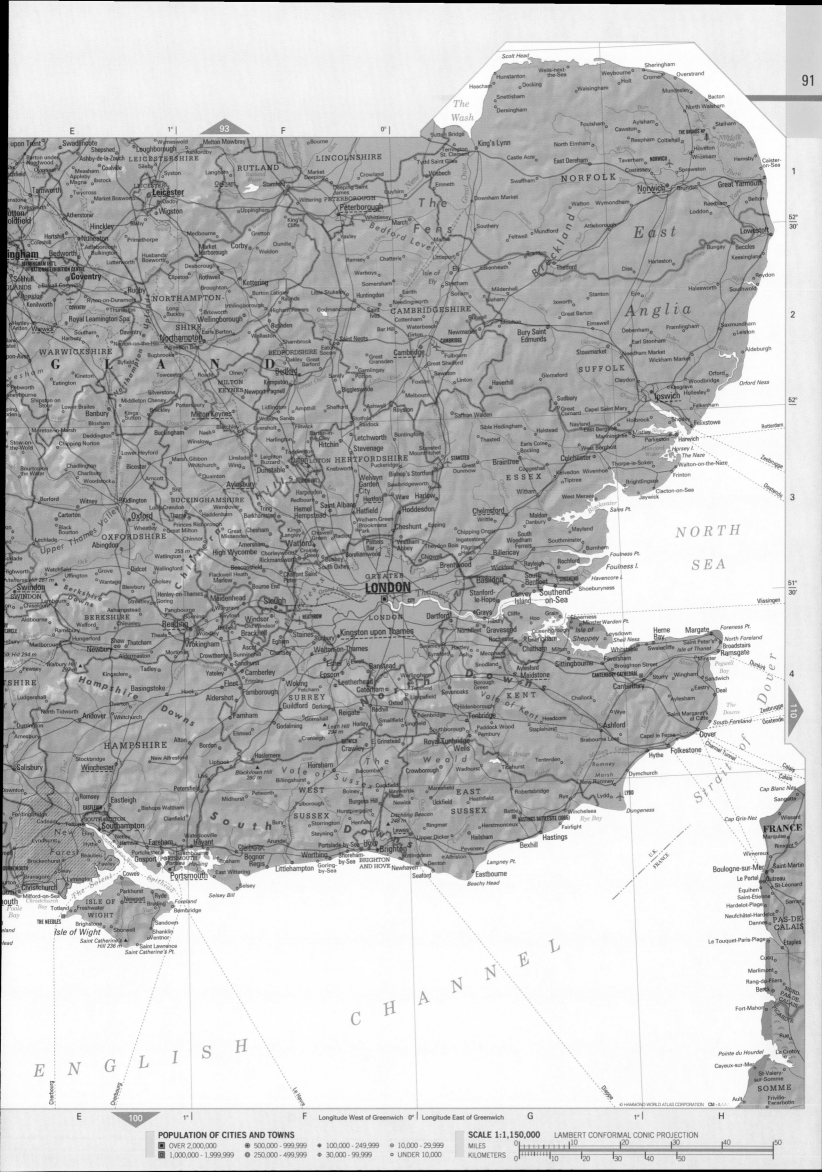

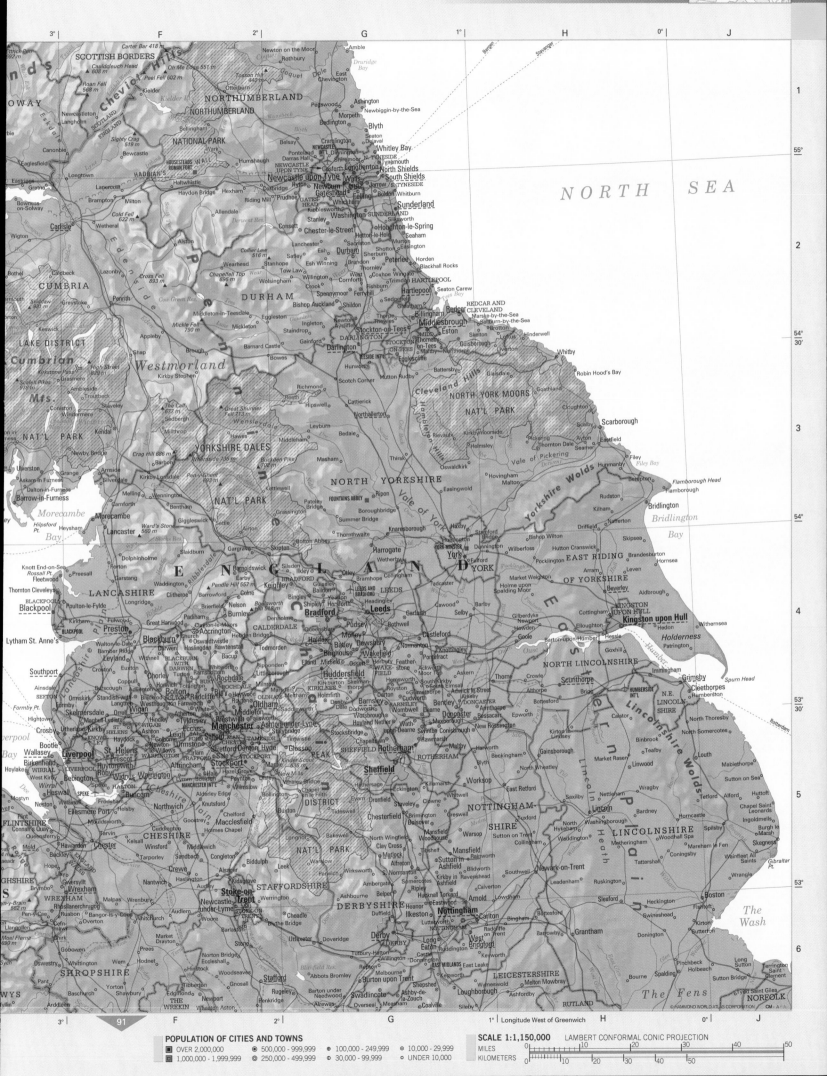

POPULATION OF CITIES AND TOWNS

- ■ OVER 2,000,000
- ■ 1,000,000 - 1,999,999
- ● 500,000 - 999,999
- ◉ 250,000 - 499,999
- ● 100,000 - 249,999
- ◌ 30,000 - 99,999
- ● 10,000 - 29,999
- ○ UNDER 10,000

SCALE 1:1,150,000 LAMBERT CONFORMAL CONIC PROJECTION

MILES 0 10 20 30 40 50

KILOMETERS 0 10 20 30 40 50

Central Scotland

NORTH SEA

NORTH

SEA

West Highlands

North Highland

Grampian Mountains

Monadhliath Mountains

Cairngorm Mts.

Mountains

ABERDEENSHIRE

Braemar

Strathmore

ANGUS

PERTH AND KINROSS

Sidlaw Hills

Ochil Hills

FIFE

STIRLING

ARGYLL AND BUTE

Cowal

Campsie Fells

Pentland Hills

Lammermuir Hills

EAST LOTHIAN

WEST LOTHIAN

MIDLOTHIAN

Glasgow

Edinburgh

EDINBURGH

Moorfoot Hills

SCOTTISH BORDERS

SOUTH LANARKSHIRE

NORTH AYRSHIRE

Island of Arran

Island of Bute

SOUTH AYRSHIRE

EAST AYRSHIRE

Kyle

Carrick

Southern Uplands

Lowther Hills

Cheviot Hills

NORTHUMBERLAND NATIONAL PARK

NORTHUMBERLAND

DUMFRIES AND GALLOWAY

Firth of Clyde

Sound of Bute

MILES

KILOMETERS

POPULATION OF CITIES AND TOWNS
- ■ OVER 2,000,000
- ▣ 1,000,000 - 1,999,999
- ● 500,000 - 999,999
- ◉ 250,000 - 499,999
- ● 100,000 - 249,999
- ◎ 30,000 - 99,999
- ● 10,000 - 29,999
- ○ UNDER 10,000

© HAMMOND WORLD ATLAS CORPORATION

CM - A-A

20° J 22° K 24° 95 26° M 28° N 30° P 32° Q

FINLAND

Mäntyluoto Noormarkku **PORI** Pirkkala Ylöjärvi **Tampere** Kangasala Orivesi Sysmä Mäntyharju Ruokolahti **RESPUBLIKA KARELIYA**

Pori Ulvila Nakkila **TAMPERE-PIRKKALA** Lempäälä Valkeakoski Heinola Anjalankoski Lappeenranta Imatra Priozersk

Rauma Eura Huittinen Hattula **Hämeenlinna** Hollola **Lahti** Orimattila Kouvola Salpausselkä Svetogorsk Kamennogorsk **Lake Ladoga**

LÄNSI SUOMEN LÄÄNI Forssa Janakkala Hausjärvi Riihimäki Mäntsälä **ETELÄ-SUOMEN LÄÄNI** Elimäki Karhula Hamina Kotka Primorsk **LENINGRADSKAYA OBLAST'**

Uusikaupunki Mynämäki **TURKU** Lieto Kaarina Paimio Halikko Salo Lohja Nurmijärvi Kerava **HELSINKI-VANTAA** Porvoo (Borgå) Kotka

ST. PETERSBURG Kronshtadt Lomonosov Petrodvorets Pushkin Kolpino

Gulf of Finland **Tallinn** **ESTONIA** Narva **RUSSIA**

Saaremaa **Gulf of Riga** **LATVIA** **Riga**

LITHUANIA **Vilnius** **BELARUS** **Minsk**

Kaliningrad **RUSSIA** **KALININGRADSKAYA OBLAST'**

20° 99 22° 24° 95 26° M 120 28° N 30° P

POPULATION OF CITIES AND TOWNS

- ■ OVER 2,000,000
- ● 500,000 - 999,999
- ● 100,000 - 249,999
- ○ 10,000 - 29,999
- ■ 1,000,000 - 1,999,999
- ◎ 250,000 - 499,999
- ● 30,000 - 99,999
- ○ UNDER 10,000

SCALE 1:3,450,000 LAMBERT CONFORMAL CONIC PROJECTION

POPULATION OF CITIES AND TOWNS
- ■ OVER 2,000,000
- ◉ 500,000 - 999,999
- • 100,000 - 249,999
- ○ 10,000 - 29,999
- ▣ 1,000,000 - 1,999,999
- ◎ 250,000 - 499,999
- • 30,000 - 99,999
- ○ UNDER 10,000

SCALE 1:3,450,000 LAMBERT CONFORMAL CONIC PROJECTION

MILES   50   100   150

KILOMETERS   50   100   150

Height 6000 19700 · 4000 13000 · 3000 9900 · 2000 6600 · 1500 5000 · 1000 3300 · 500 1600 · 200 700 · m. ft. · 200 700 · 500 1600 · 1000 3300 · 2000 6600 · 3000 9900 · 4000 13000 · 5000 16400 · 6000 19700 · Depth

POPULATION OF CITIES AND TOWNS

- ■ OVER 2,000,000
- ■ 1,000,000 - 1,999,999
- ◉ 500,000 - 999,999
- ◉ 250,000 - 499,999
- ● 100,000 - 249,999
- ● 30,000 - 99,999
- ○ 10,000 - 29,999
- ○ UNDER 10,000

SCALE 1:3,450,000   LAMBERT CONFORMAL CONIC PROJECTION

MILES

KILOMETERS

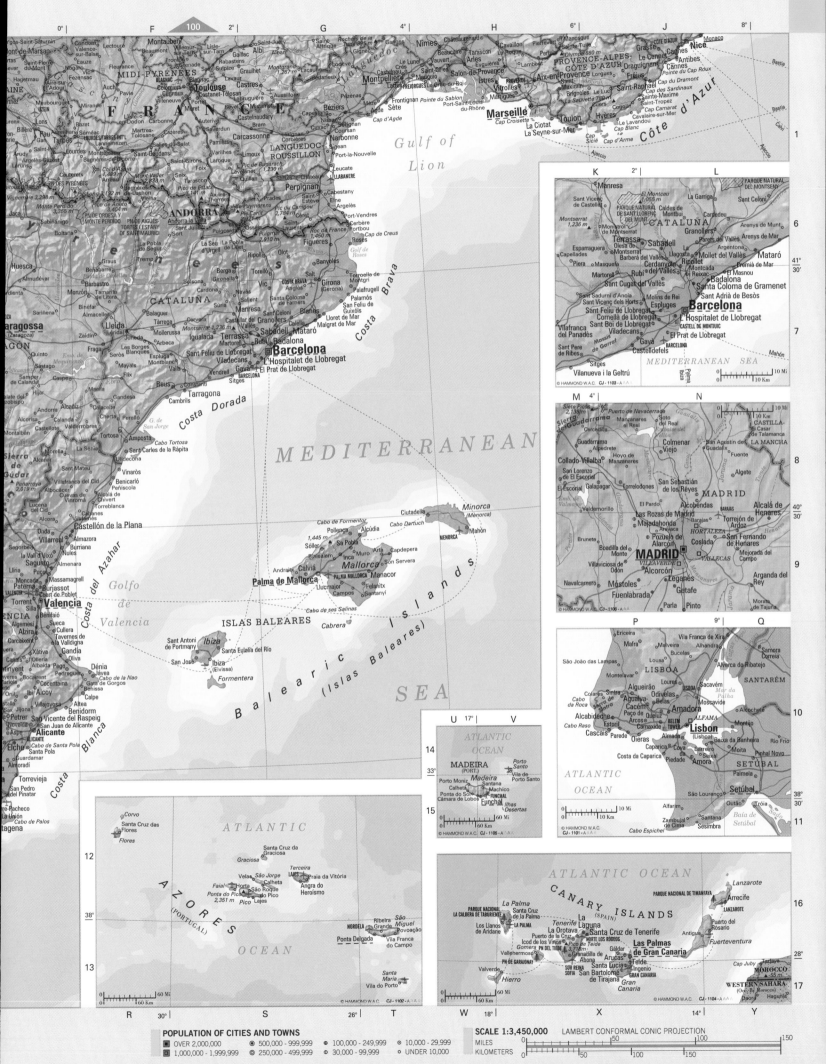

POPULATION OF CITIES AND TOWNS
- OVER 2,000,000
- 1,000,000 - 1,999,999
- 500,000 - 999,999
- 250,000 - 499,999
- 100,000 - 249,999
- 30,000 - 99,999
- 10,000 - 29,999
- UNDER 10,000

SCALE 1:3,450,000   LAMBERT CONFORMAL CONIC PROJECTION

SCALE 1:3,450,000   LAMBERT CONFORMAL CONIC PROJECTION

MILES
0   50   100   150

KILOMETERS
0   50   100   150

POPULATION OF CITIES AND TOWNS

■ OVER 2,000,000	● 500,000 - 999,999	● 100,000 - 249,999	○ 10,000 - 29,999
▣ 1,000,000 - 1,999,999	● 250,000 - 499,999	○ 30,000 - 99,999	○ UNDER 10,000

POPULATION OF CITIES AND TOWNS

■ OVER 2,000,000	● 500,000 - 999,999
▣ 1,000,000 - 1,999,999	● 250,000 - 499,999
● 100,000 - 249,999	○ 10,000 - 29,999
● 30,000 - 99,999	○ UNDER 10,000

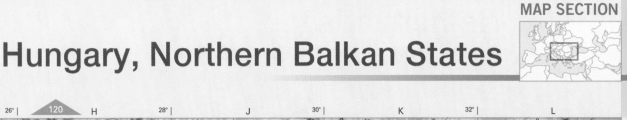

Height 6000 4000 2000 1500 1000 500 200 m. 0 200 700 1600 3300 6600 9900 16400 19700 Depth
19700 13000 6500 5000 3300 1600 700

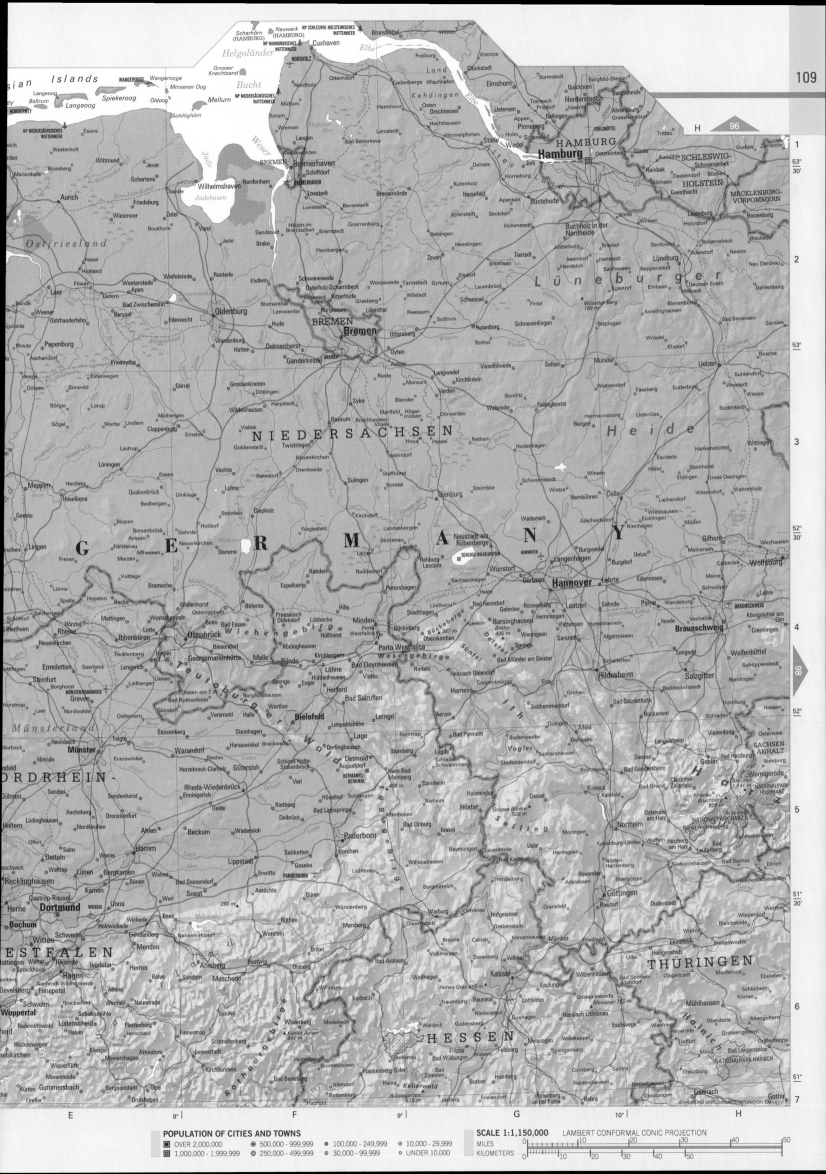

UNITED KINGDOM

NETHERLANDS

BELGIË / BELGIE

Strait of Dover

Antwerp (Antwerpen)
Brussels (Bruxelles)
Ghent (Gent)

WEST-VLAANDEREN
OOST-VLAANDEREN
HAINAUT
NORD

Collines de l'Artois
Artois
PAS-DE-CALAIS
NORD-PAS-DE-CALAIS
PICARDIE
Ponthieu
Vimeu

SOMME
PICARDY
OISE
AISNE
SEINE-MARITIME
EURE
YVELINES
VAL-D'OISE
SEINE-ET-MARNE
MARNE
Brie

PARIS
Boulogne-Billancourt

FRANCE
CHAMPAGNE

Longitude East of Greenwich

Height Depth

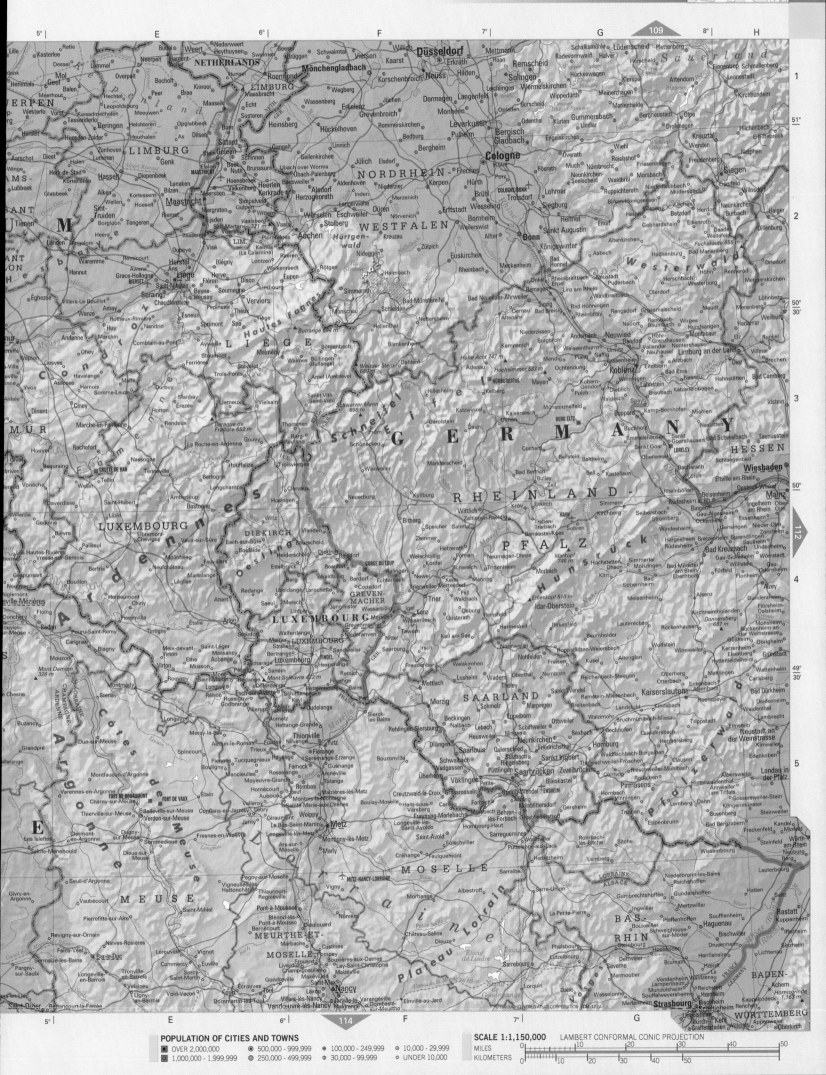

POPULATION OF CITIES AND TOWNS
- ■ OVER 2,000,000
- ▣ 1,000,000 - 1,999,999
- ◉ 500,000 - 999,999
- ◎ 250,000 - 499,999
- ● 100,000 - 249,999
- ⊙ 30,000 - 99,999
- ○ 10,000 - 29,999
- ○ UNDER 10,000

SCALE 1:1,150,000   LAMBERT CONFORMAL CONIC PROJECTION

MILES

KILOMETERS

SCALE 1:1,150,000   LAMBERT CONFORMAL CONIC PROJECTION

MILES   0   10   20   30   40   50

KILOMETERS   0   10   20   30   40   50

POPULATION OF CITIES AND TOWNS

■ OVER 2,000,000	◉ 500,000 - 999,999	● 100,000 - 249,999	○ 10,000 - 29,999
▣ 1,000,000 - 1,999,999	◉ 250,000 - 499,999	● 30,000 - 99,999	○ UNDER 10,000

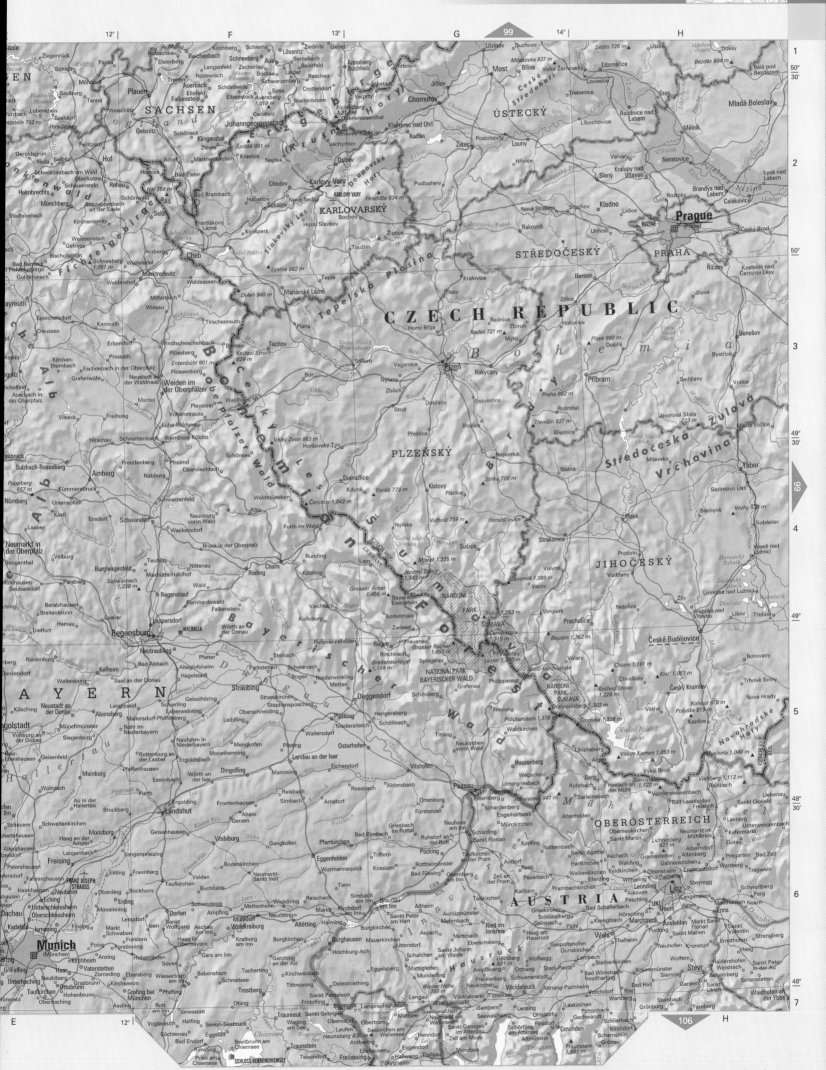

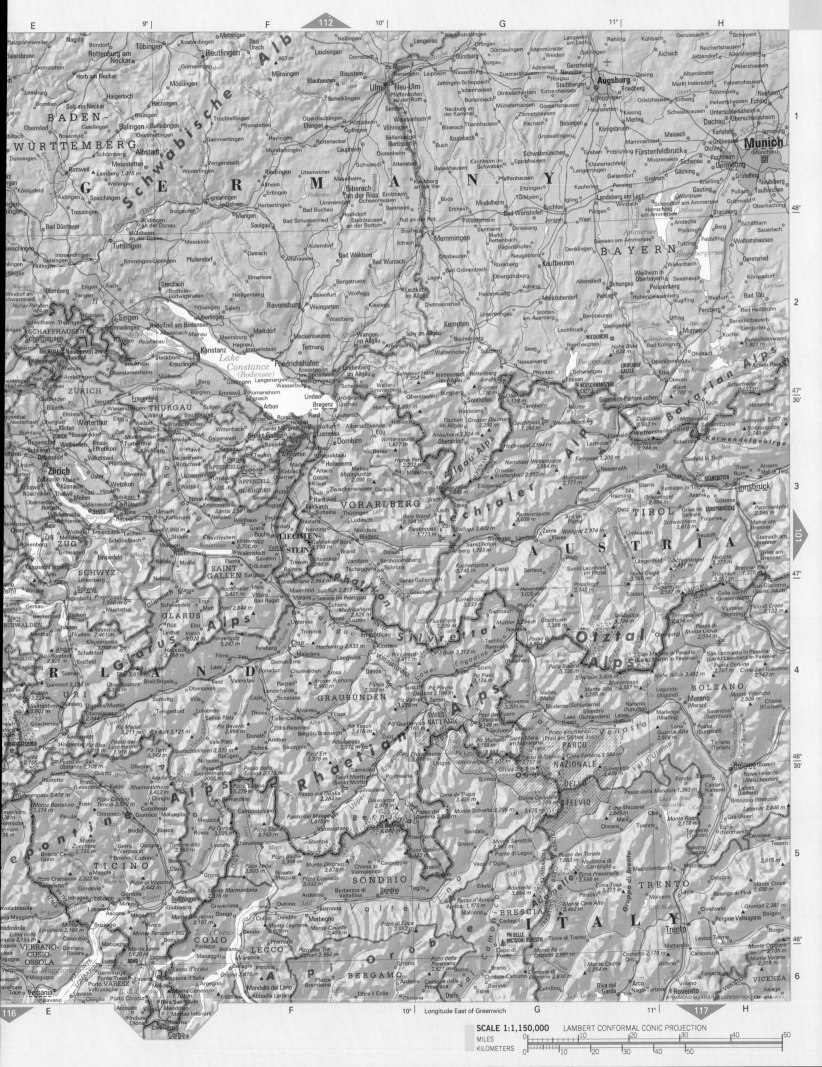

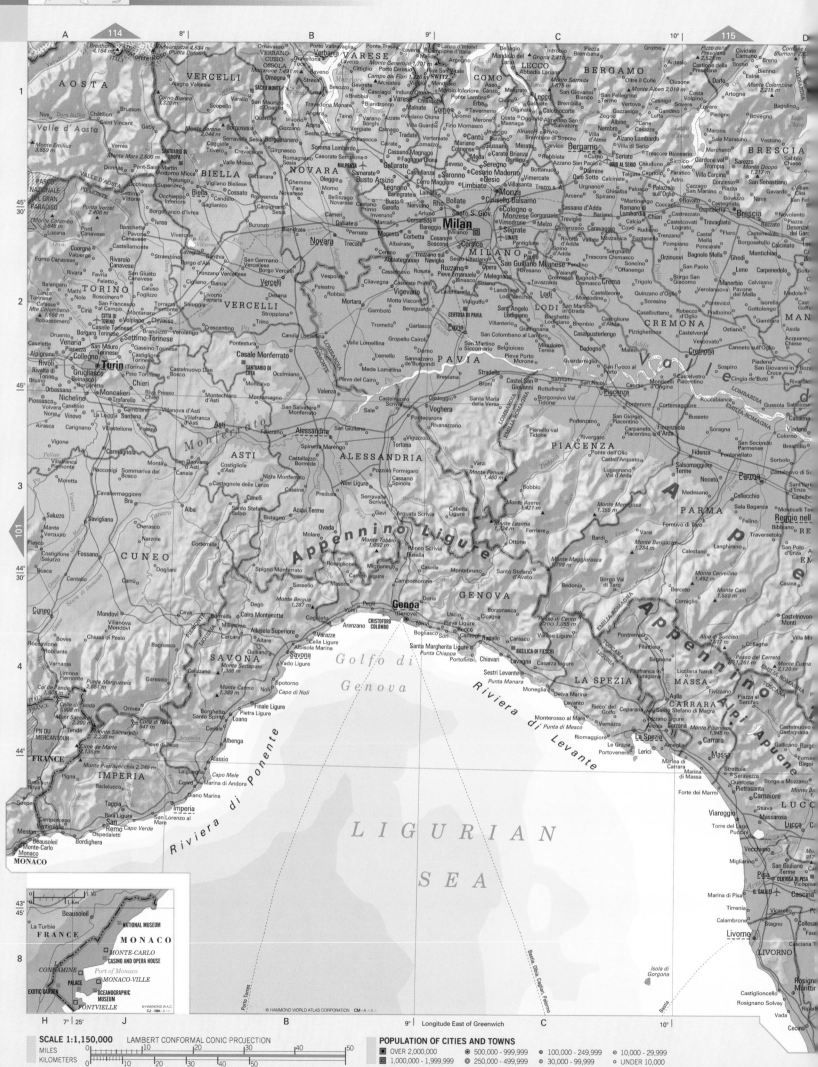

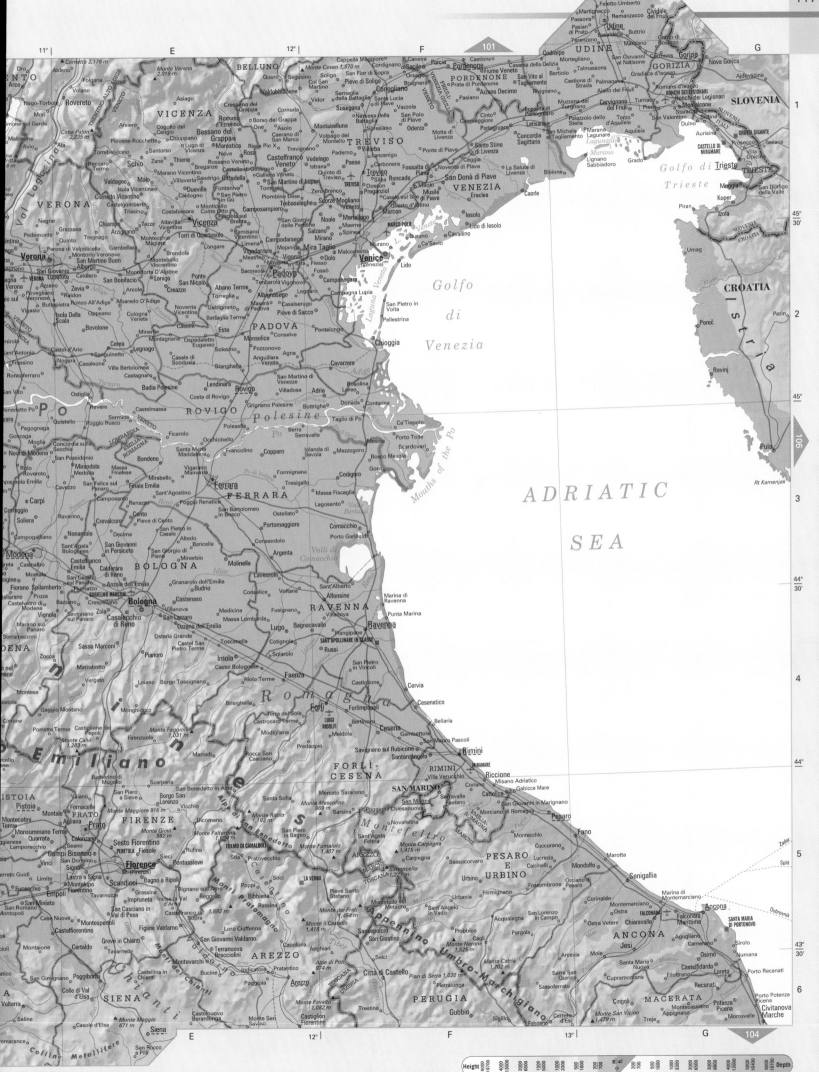

ADRIATIC

SEA

Golfo
di
Venezia

Golfo di Trieste

CROATIA

SLOVENIA

UDINE

GORIZIA

TRIESTE

PORDENONE

BELLUNO

TREVISO

VENEZIA

Venice
(Venezia)

VICENZA

VERONA

PADOVA

ROVIGO

Polesine

Po

FERRARA

BOLOGNA

RAVENNA

Romagna

Ravenna

Rimini

FORLÌ-
CESENA

RIMINI

SAN MARINO

Montefeltro

PESARO
E
URBINO

Pesaro

Fano

Senigallia

ANCONA

Ancona

MACERATA

PERUGIA

AREZZO

FIRENZE

Florence
(Firenze)

Prato

SIENA

Chianti

Appennino Tosco-Emiliano

Appennino Umbro-Marchigiano

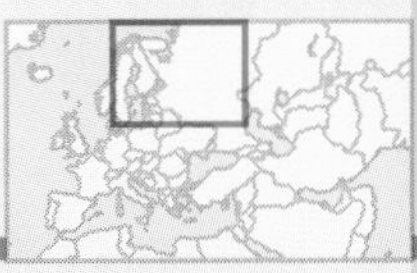

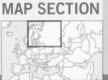

Northeastern Europe

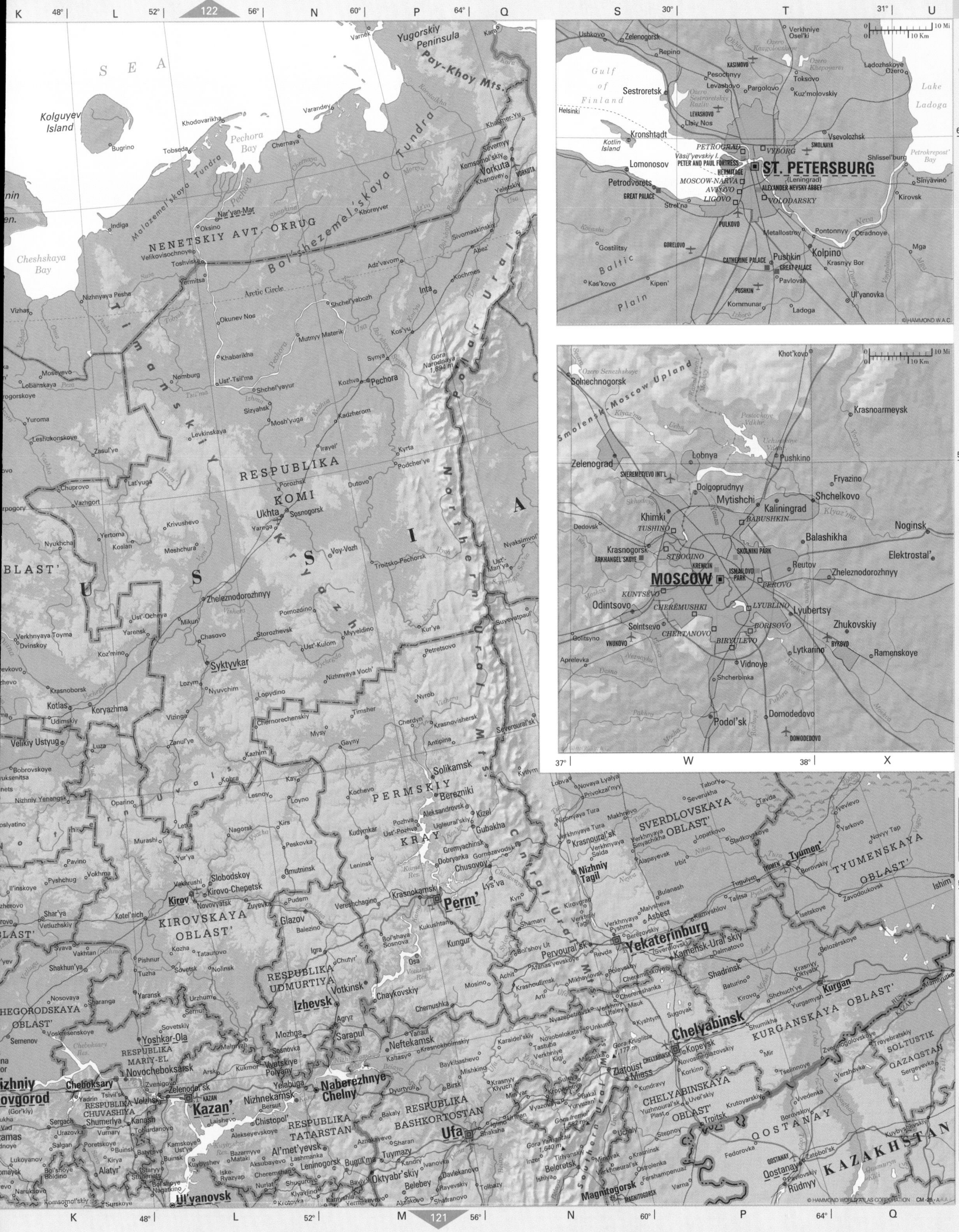
K
L
N
P
Q
122
121
145
SEA
Kolguyev Island
Pechora Bay
Cheshskaya Bay
Yugorskiy Peninsula
Pay-Khoy Mts.
NENETSKIY AVT. OKRUG
Nar'yan-Mar
Malozemel'skaya Tundra
Bol'shezemel'skaya Tundra
Vorkuta
Arctic Circle
Polar Urals
Northern Urals
Central Urals
Southern Urals
Gora Narodnaya 1,894 m
Timanskiy Kryazh
RESPUBLIKA KOMI
Ukhta
Pechora
Inta
Syktyvkar
R U S S I A
Kotlas
Velikiy Ustyug
Kirov
KIROVSKAYA OBLAST'
Perm'
PERMSKIY KRAY
Solikamsk
Berezniki
Nizhniy Tagil
SVERDLOVSKAYA OBLAST'
Yekaterinburg
Tyumen'
TYUMENSKAYA OBLAST'
Chelyabinsk
CHELYABINSKAYA OBLAST'
KURGANSKAYA OBLAST'
Kurgan
Magnitogorsk
Izhevsk
RESPUBLIKA UDMURTIYA
Yoshkar-Ola
RESPUBLIKA MARIY-EL
Cheboksary
RESPUBLIKA CHUVASHIYA
Kazan'
RESPUBLIKA TATARSTAN
Naberezhnye Chelny
Ufa
RESPUBLIKA BASHKORTOSTAN
Ul'yanovsk
Nizhniy Novgorod
KAZAKHSTAN
QOSTANAY
Qostanay
Rudnyy
S
T
U
Gulf of Finland
Lake Ladoga
Kotlin Island
Kronshtadt
Sestroretsk
ST. PETERSBURG
(Leningrad)
Lomonosov
Petrodvorets
Pushkin
Kolpino
Baltic Plain
W
X
Moscow Upland
Zelenograd
Lobnya
Mytishchi
Kaliningrad
Khimki
Krasnogorsk
MOSCOW
Odintsovo
Lyubertsy
Balashikha
Noginsk
Elektrostal'
Zhukovskiy
Podol'sk
Domodedovo
Vidnoye
Ramenskoye
© HAMMOND W.A.C.
© HAMMOND WORLD ATLAS CORPORATION

POPULATION OF CITIES AND TOWNS

- ■ OVER 2,000,000
- ▣ 1,000,000 - 1,999,999
- ◉ 500,000 - 999,999
- ◎ 250,000 - 499,999
- ⊕ 100,000 - 249,999
- ⊙ 30,000 - 99,999
- ⊙ 10,000 - 29,999
- ○ UNDER 10,000

SCALE 1:6,900,000 LAMBERT CONFORMAL CONIC PROJECTION

MILES 0 100 200 300

KILOMETERS 0 100 200 300

POPULATION OF CITIES AND TOWNS

■ OVER 2,000,000   ● 500,000 - 999,999   • 100,000 - 249,999   ○ 10,000 - 29,999

▣ 1,000,000 - 1,999,999   ◉ 250,000 - 499,999   • 30,000 - 99,999   ○ UNDER 10,000

Russia and Neighboring Countries

RUSSIA
(Administrative divisions are named only when they differ from their respective capitals.)

1. RESPUBLIKA ADYGEYA
2. RESPUBLIKA KARACHAYEVO-CHERKESIYA
3. RESPUBLIKA KABARDINO-BALKARIYA
4. RESPUBLIKA SEVERNAYA OSETIYA-ALANIYA
5. RESPUBLIKA INGUSHETIYA
6. RESPUBLIKA CHECHNYA
7. RESPUBLIKA DAGESTAN
8. RESPUBLIKA MORDOVIYA
9. RESPUBLIKA CHUVASHIYA
10. RESPUBLIKA MARIY-EL
11. RESPUBLIKA TATARSTAN
12. RESPUBLIKA BASHKORTOSTAN
13. RESPUBLIKA UDMURTIYA
14. RESPUBLIKA KHAKASIYA
15. YEVREYSKAYA AVTONOMNAYA OBLAST'

POPULATION OF CITIES AND TOWNS

■ OVER 2,000,000	⬤ 500,000 - 999,999	○ 50,000 - 99,999
■ 1,000,000 - 1,999,999	⬤ 100,000 - 499,999	○ UNDER 50,000

SCALE 1:20,700,000 LAMBERT CONFORMAL CONIC PROJECTION

MILES 0 — 300 — 600 — 900
KILOMETERS 0 — 300 — 600 — 900

© HAMMOND WORLD ATLAS CORPORATION

Asia

The delta of the Indus River, the longest river in southwest Asia, is the highlight of this southeast-looking, low-oblique image. Fed by snowmelt and glacial meltwater from the mountains of the Tibet Plateau, the Indus River flows nearly 1800 miles (2897 km.) before emptying into the Arabian Sea. After leaving the Tibet Plateau, the river flows onto the Punjab Plains of western Pakistan and through a vast alluvial lowland where it receives its major tributary, the Panjnad (five streams). In this severely arid landscape the rivers form precarious strips of fertile land.

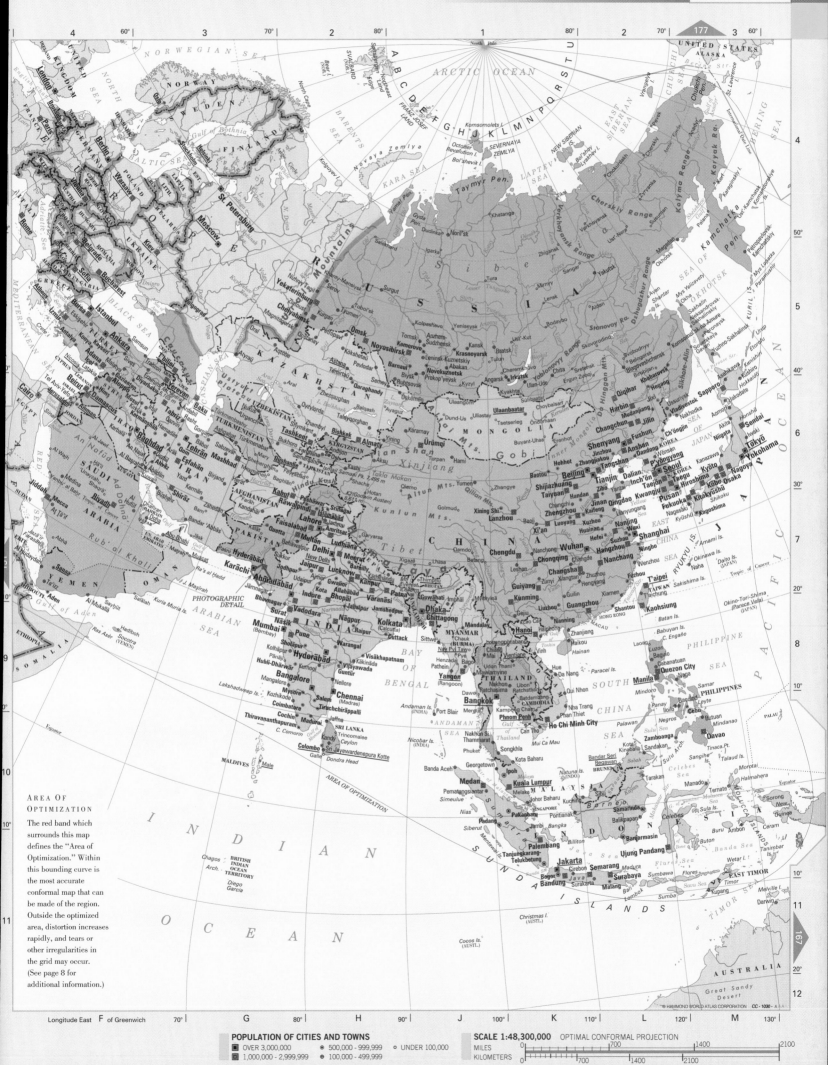

POPULATION OF CITIES AND TOWNS

■ OVER 3,000,000   ● 500,000 - 999,999   ○ UNDER 100,000
▣ 1,000,000 - 2,999,999   ● 100,000 - 499,999

SCALE 1:48,300,000   OPTIMAL CONFORMAL PROJECTION

MILES
KILOMETERS

© HAMMOND WORLD ATLAS CORPORATION   CC-1030 · A · A

AREA OF OPTIMIZATION

The red band which surrounds this map defines the "Area of Optimization." Within this bounding curve is the most accurate conformal map that can be made of the region. Outside the optimized area, distortion increases rapidly, and tears or other irregularities in the grid may occur. (See page 8 for additional information.)

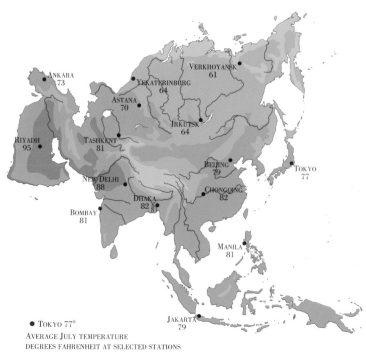

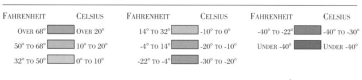

AVERAGE JANUARY TEMPERATURE

FAHRENHEIT	CELSIUS	FAHRENHEIT	CELSIUS	FAHRENHEIT	CELSIUS
OVER 68°	OVER 20°	14° TO 32°	-10° TO 0°	-40° TO -22°	-40° TO -30°
50° TO 68°	10° TO 20°	-4° TO 14°	-20° TO -10°	UNDER -40°	UNDER -40°
32° TO 50°	0° TO 10°	-22° TO -4°	-30° TO -20°		

AVERAGE JULY TEMPERATURE

FAHRENHEIT	CELSIUS	FAHRENHEIT	CELSIUS	FAHRENHEIT	CELSIUS
OVER 86°	OVER 30°	50° TO 68°	10° TO 20°	UNDER 32°	UNDER 0°
68° TO 86°	20° TO 30°	32° TO 50°	0° TO 10°		

CLIMATE

HUMID TROPICAL
- Af NO DRY SEASON
- Am SHORT DRY SEASON
- Aw DRY WINTER

DRY
- BS SEMIARID } h HOT
- BW ARID } k COLD

AFTER KOEPPEN-GEIGER

HUMID WARM
- Cf NO DRY SEASON
- Cw DRY WINTER
- Cs DRY SUMMER

HUMID COLD
- Df NO DRY SEASON
- Dw DRY WINTER
- Ds DRY SUMMER

COLD POLAR
- ET SHORT COOL SUMMER, LONG COLD WINTER
- E COLD AND UNCLASSIFIED HIGHLANDS

a HOT SUMMER
b COOL SUMMER
c SHORT COOL SUMMER
d VERY COLD WINTER

VEGETATION

TROPICAL FOREST
- TROPICAL RAINFOREST
- LIGHT TROPICAL FOREST
- WOODLAND AND SHRUB

TROPICAL GRASSLAND
- GRASS AND SHRUB (SAVANNA)
- WOODED SAVANNA

MID-LATITUDE FOREST
- NEEDLELEAF FOREST
- BROADLEAF FOREST
- MIXED NEEDLELEAF AND BROADLEAF FOREST
- WOODLAND AND SHRUB (MEDITERRANEAN)

MID-LATITUDE GRASSLAND
- SHORT GRASS (STEPPE)
- WOODED STEPPE
- DESERT AND DESERT SHRUB
- TUNDRA AND ALPINE
- UNCLASSIFIED HIGHLANDS

Asia – Geographical Comparisons

● Tokyo 61

Average annual rainfall
In Inches at selected stations

AVERAGE ANNUAL RAINFALL

INCHES	CM	INCHES	CM	INCHES	CM
Over 80	Over 200	40 to 60	100 to 150	10 to 20	25 to 50
60 to 80	150 to 200	20 to 40	50 to 100	Under 10	Under 25

Cities on rainfall map: Ankara 13, Verkhoyansk 6, Astana 12, Riyadh 4, Tehran 9, Tashkent 17, Ulaanbaatr 7, Beijing 25, Tokyo 61, New Delhi 28, Chongqing 43, Bombay 82, Cherrapunji 449, Manila 82, Padang 151

● Cities with over 3,000,000
Inhabitants

POPULATION DISTRIBUTION

DENSITY PER		SQ. MI.	SQ. KM.	SQ. MI.	SQ. KM.
SQ. MI.	SQ. KM.	130 to 260	50 to 100	3 to 25	1 to 10
Over 260	Over 100	25 to 130	10 to 50	Under 3	Under 1

LAND USE

Cereals, Livestock	Diversified Tropical & Subtropical Crops	Special Crops
Cash Crops, Mixed Farming	Livestock Ranching & Herding	Forests
Dairy, Livestock		Nonproductive

MINERAL RESOURCES

ENERGY & FUELS
- ◆ Coal
- ⬡ Lignite
- ▲ Natural Gas
- ● Petroleum
- ▪ Uranium

IRON & FERROALLOYS
- 1 Chromium
- 2 Cobalt
- 3 Iron Ore
- 4 Manganese
- 5 Molybdenum
- 6 Nickel
- 7 Tungsten

OTHER MAJOR RESOURCES
- 1 Antimony
- 2 Asbestos
- 3 Bauxite
- 4 Borax
- 5 Copper
- 6 Diamonds
- 7 Gold
- 8 Graphite
- 9 Lead
- 10 Magnesite
- 11 Mercury
- 12 Mica
- 13 Phosphates
- 14 Platinum
- 15 Potash
- 16 Silver
- 17 Sulfer
- 18 Tin
- 19 Titanium
- 20 Zinc

Height 6000 4000 3000 2000 1500 1000 500 200 0 m. 200 500 1000 2000 3000 4000 5000 6000 Depth
19700 13000 9500 6500 5000 3300 1600 700 700 1600 3300 6500 9800 13000 16400 19700

POPULATION OF CITIES AND TOWNS

■ OVER 2,000,000   ● 500,000 - 999,999   ◉ 50,000 - 99,999
□ 1,000,000 - 1,999,999   ● 100,000 - 499,999   ○ UNDER 50,000

SCALE 1:13,800,000   LAMBERT CONFORMAL CONIC PROJECTION

MILES 0   200   400   600
KILOMETERS 0   200   400   600

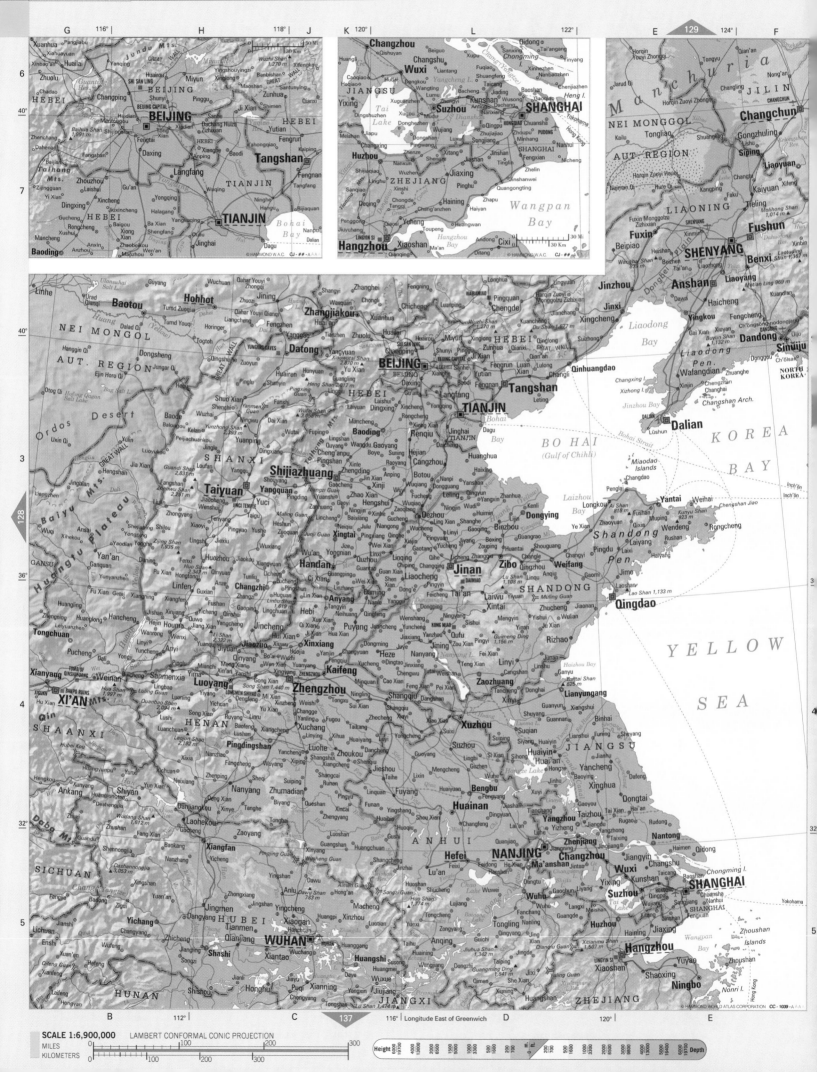

POPULATION OF CITIES AND TOWNS

- ◼ OVER 2,000,000
- ◼ 1,000,000 - 1,999,999
- ⊙ 500,000 - 999,999
- ⊙ 250,000 - 499,999
- ⊛ 100,000 - 249,999
- ⊛ 30,000 - 99,999
- ⊙ 10,000 - 29,999
- ○ UNDER 10,000

SCALE 1:3,450,000   LAMBERT CONFORMAL CONIC PROJECTION

MILES

KILOMETERS

Longitude East of Greenwich

SEA OF JAPAN

SOUTH KOREA

KANGWŎN-DO

CH'UNGCH'ŎNG-BUKTO

KYŎNGSANG-BUKTO

TAEGU

KYŎNGSANG-NAMDO

PUSAN

KOREA STRAIT

Western Channel

Eastern Channel

KOREA STRAIT

SOUTH KOREA
JAPAN

Tsushima

GOTO ISLANDS

SAIKAI NAT'L PARK

NAGASAKI

Nagasaki

Fukue-jima

Amakusa Sea

EAST CHINA SEA

Kami-Koshiki I.

Shimo-Koshiki I.

Kagoshima

KAGOSHIMA

ŌSUMI ISLANDS

KIRISHIMA-YAKU NAT'L PARK

Kuro-shima

Iō-shima

Mage-shima

Nishino'omote

Tanega-shima

Kuchinoerabu

Kamiyaku

Yaku-shima

Shanghai

Ullŭng I.
(S. KOREA)

Liancourt Rocks
(Sovereignty disputed)

OKI ISLANDS

Dōgo

DAISEN-OKI NAT'L PARK

Dōzen

DAISEN-OKI NAT'L PARK

SAN'IN KAIGIN NATIONAL-PARK

Wakasa Bay

SHIMANE

Matsue

TOTTORI

TOTTORI

CHŪGOKU

OKAYAMA

HIROSHIMA

Hiroshima

YAMAGUCHI

Yamaguchi

Shimonoseki

Kitakyūshū

Fukuoka

FUKUOKA

SAGA

KUMAMOTO

Kumamoto

ŌITA

Ōita

Beppu

ASO NAT'L PARK

Kyūshū Highlands

MIYAZAKI

Miyazaki

Kyūshū

CHŪGOKU-KYŪSHŪ NAT'L PARK

Sea of Suo

Sea of Iyo

SETO-NAIKAI NAT'L PARK

EHIME

Matsuyama

KAGAWA

Takamatsu

TOKUSHIMA

Tokushima

KŌCHI

Kōchi

Shikoku

SHIKOKU-KYŪSHŪ

Tosa Bay

KYŌTO

Kyōto

HYŌGO

Kōbe

ŌSAKA

Ōsaka

NARA

WAKAYAMA

Wakayama

Kii Channel

PACIFIC OCEAN

Height Depth

Central and Southern Japan

Honshū

Izu Islands

FUJI-HAKONE-IZU NAT'L PARK
(JAPAN)

Hachijō-jima
Hachijō
HACHIJŌJIMA

Aoga-shima

Beyoneisu-retsugan

PACIFIC

OCEAN

EAST
CHINA
SEA

Ryukyu Islands
(Nansei - Shotō)

OKINAWA

Shanghai

Kagoshima
Kyūshū

KAGOSHIMA

Naze

Amami-ōshima
Kikai

Setouchi

Tokuno

Amami Islands

Tokunoshima

Okinoerabu

Yoron

Hedo-misaki

Okinawa Is.
Iheya
Ie
Motobu
Yonaha-dake
498 m
Nago
Okinawa
Ginowan
Gushikawa
Kumé
Naha
Urasoe
Itoman
Kyan-zaki

Keelung
Senkaku-Shotō

Sakishima Islands
Hirara
Yonaguni
Ishigaki
Tamara
Miyako
Miyako Is.
Iriomote
Ishigaki
Yaeyama Is.

Kitadaitō

Minamidaitō

PACIFIC
OCEAN

Okidaitō

© HAMMOND W.A.C.   CJ-1116-A

POPULATION OF CITIES AND TOWNS

■ OVER 2,000,000	◉ 500,000 - 999,999	⊕ 100,000 - 249,999	○ 10,000 - 29,999
▣ 1,000,000 - 1,999,999	◉ 250,000 - 499,999	⊕ 30,000 - 99,999	○ UNDER 10,000

SCALE 1:3,450,000   LAMBERT CONFORMAL CONIC PROJECTION

MILES

KILOMETERS

© HAMMOND WORLD ATLAS CORPORATION   CM-1038-A

Northern Japan

SCALE 1:3,450,000   LAMBERT CONFORMAL CONIC PROJECTION

© HAMMOND WORLD ATLAS CORPORATION

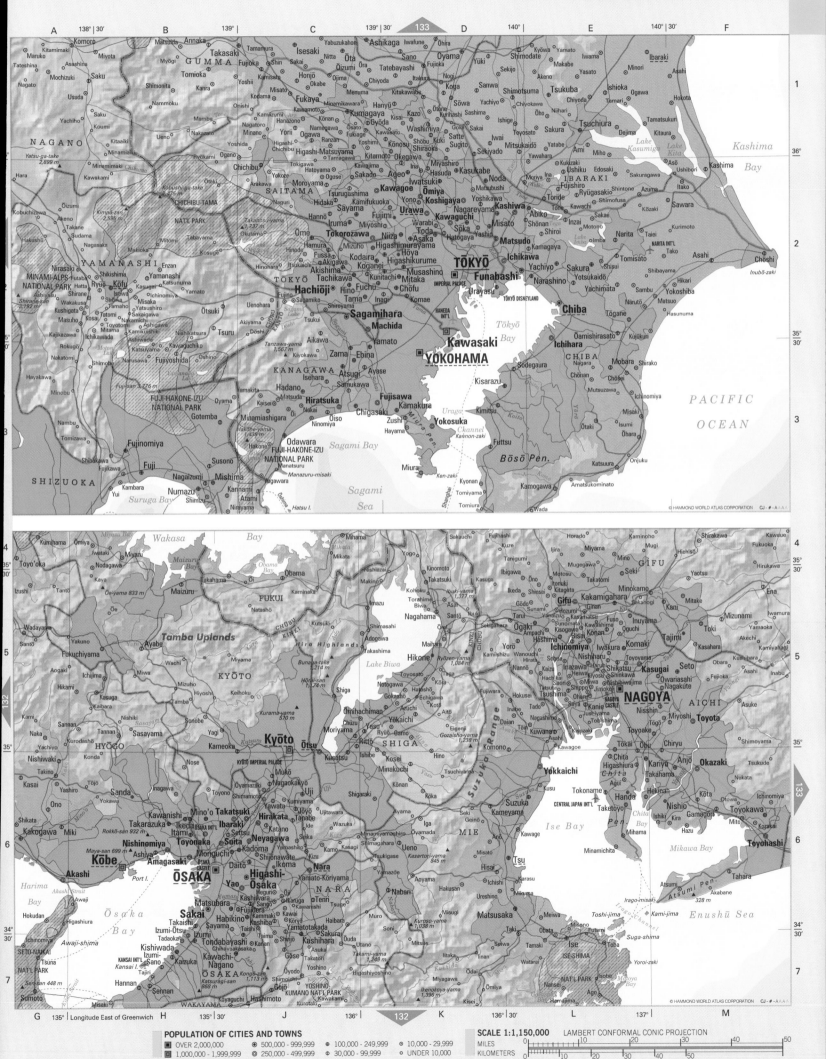

Indochina

SCALE 1:6,900,000   LAMBERT CONFORMAL CONIC PROJECTION

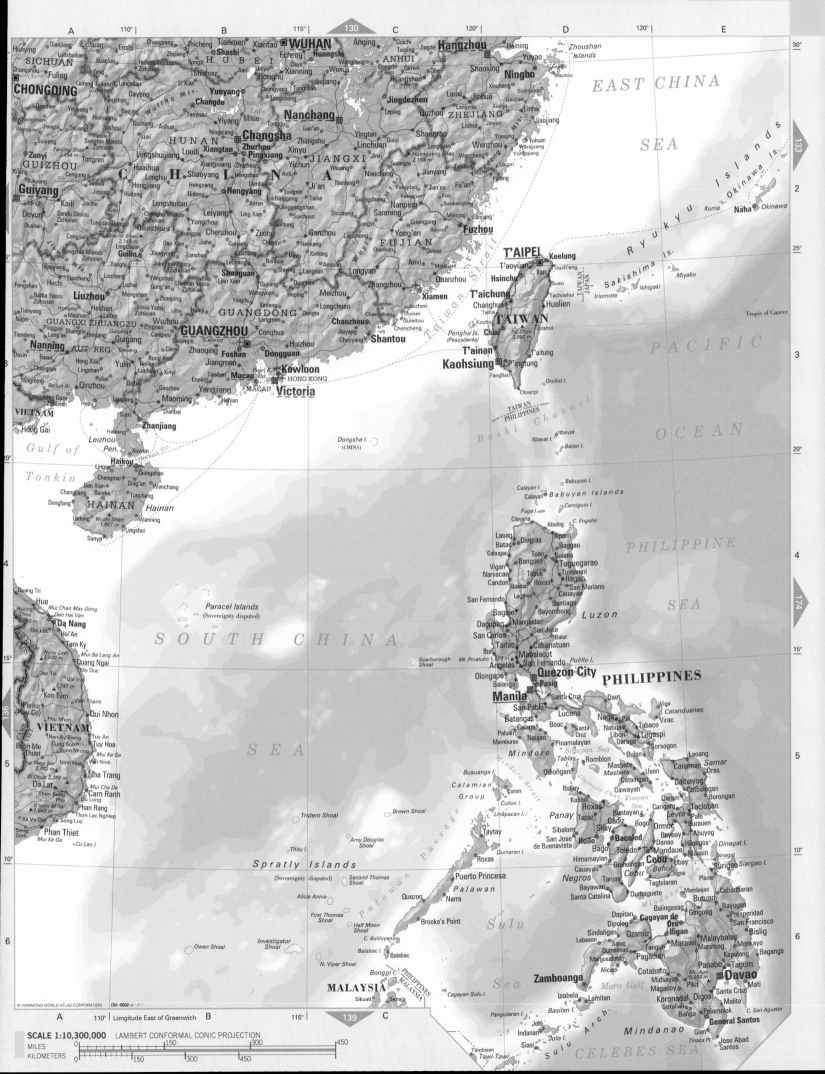

SCALE 1:10,300,000 LAMBERT CONFORMAL CONIC PROJECTION

MILES
0   150   300   450

KILOMETERS
0   150   300   450

POPULATION OF CITIES AND TOWNS

| ■ OVER 2,000,000 | ◉ 500,000 - 999,999 | ⊙ 100,000 - 249,999 | ○ 10,000 - 29,999 |
| ■ 1,000,000 - 1,999,999 | ◉ 250,000 - 499,999 | ⊙ 30,000 - 99,999 | ○ UNDER 10,000 |

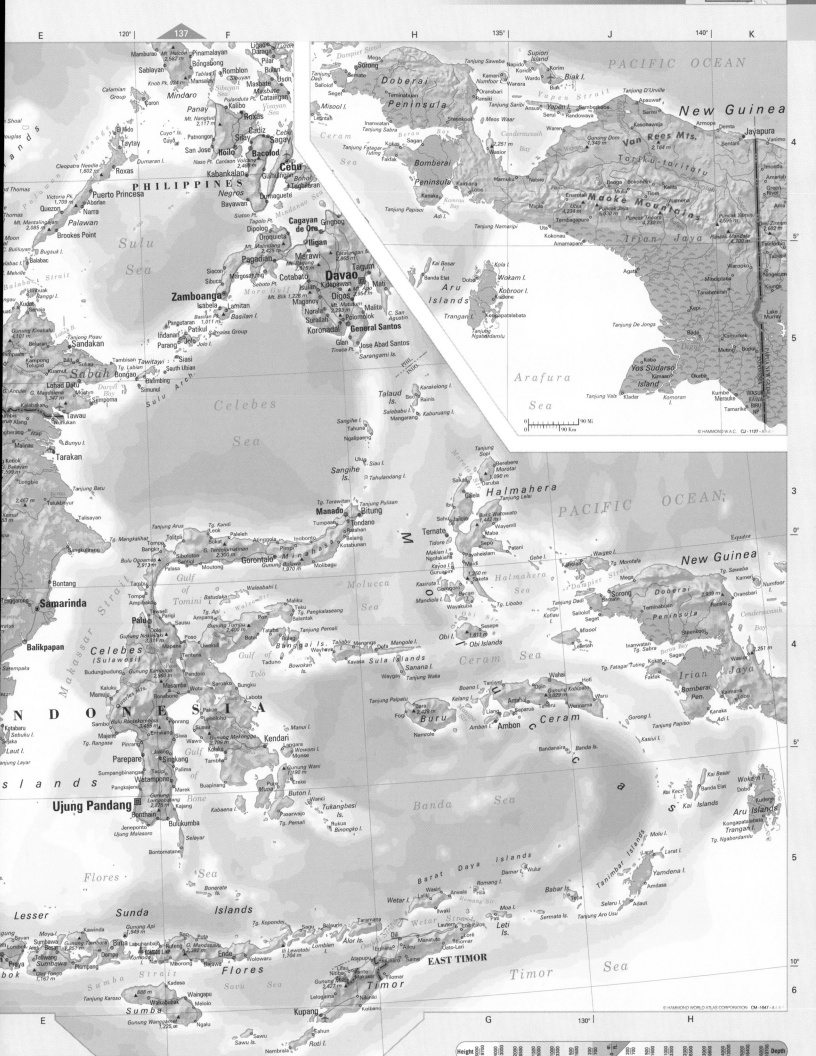

© HAMMOND W.A.C.   CJ - 1127 - A A A

© HAMMOND WORLD ATLAS CORPORATION   CM -1047 - A A A

| Height | 6000 | 4700 | 13000 | 2000 | 6600 | 1000 | 3300 | 500 | 1600 | 200 | 700 | | | 200 | 700 | 500 | 1600 | 2000 | 6600 | 4000 | 13400 | 6000 | 20000 | Depth |

POPULATION OF CITIES AND TOWNS

■ OVER 2,000,000	◉ 500,000 - 999,999	● 100,000 - 249,999	○ 10,000 - 29,999
■ 1,000,000 - 1,999,999	◉ 250,000 - 499,999	● 30,000 - 99,999	○ UNDER 10,000

SCALE 1:10,300,000   LAMBERT CONFORMAL CONIC PROJECTION

MILES   0   150   300   450

KILOMETERS   0   150   300   450

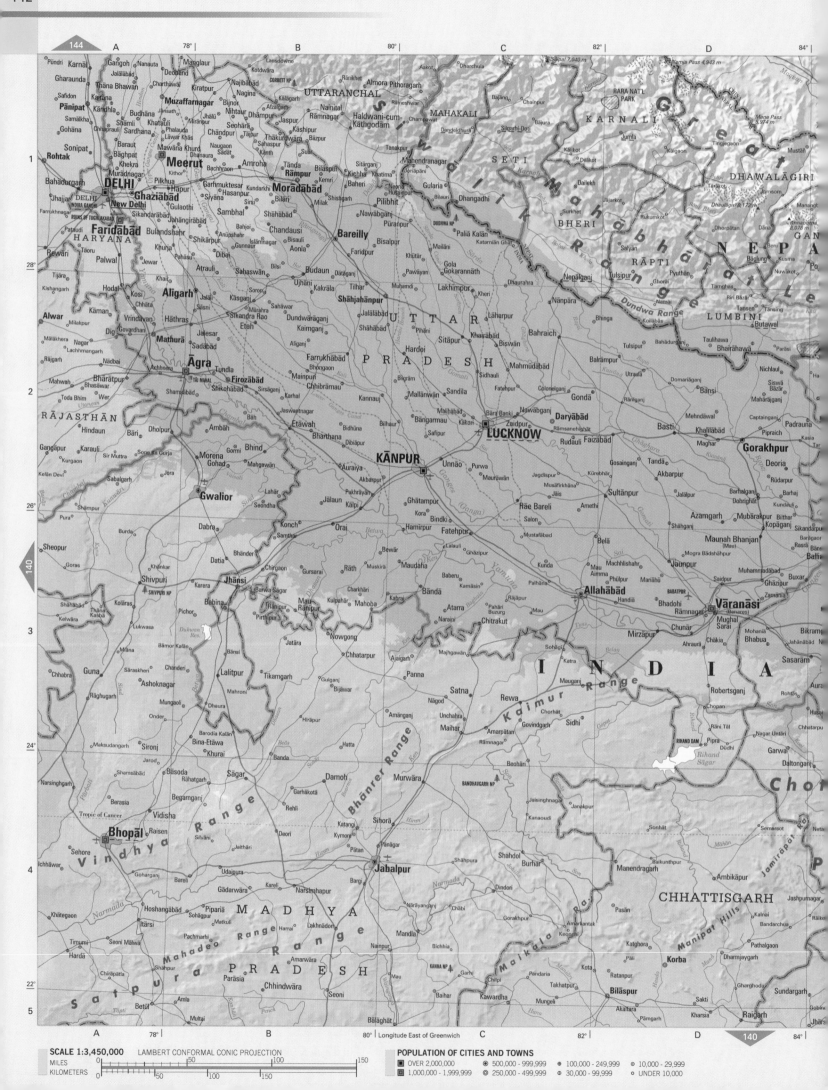

SCALE 1:3,450,000
LAMBERT CONFORMAL CONIC PROJECTION

MILES
0   50   100   150

KILOMETERS
0   50   100   150

POPULATION OF CITIES AND TOWNS

▪ OVER 2,000,000
▪ 1,000,000 - 1,999,999
● 500,000 - 999,999
● 250,000 - 499,999
● 100,000 - 249,999
● 30,000 - 99,999
○ 10,000 - 29,999
○ UNDER 10,000

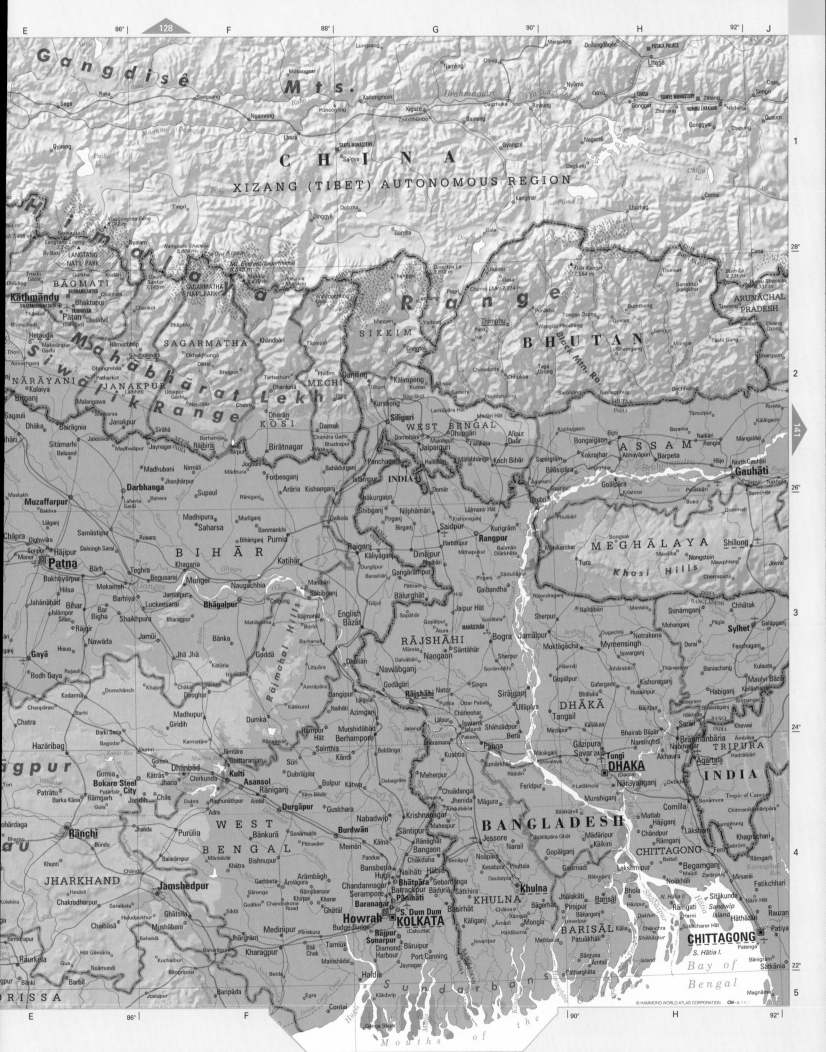

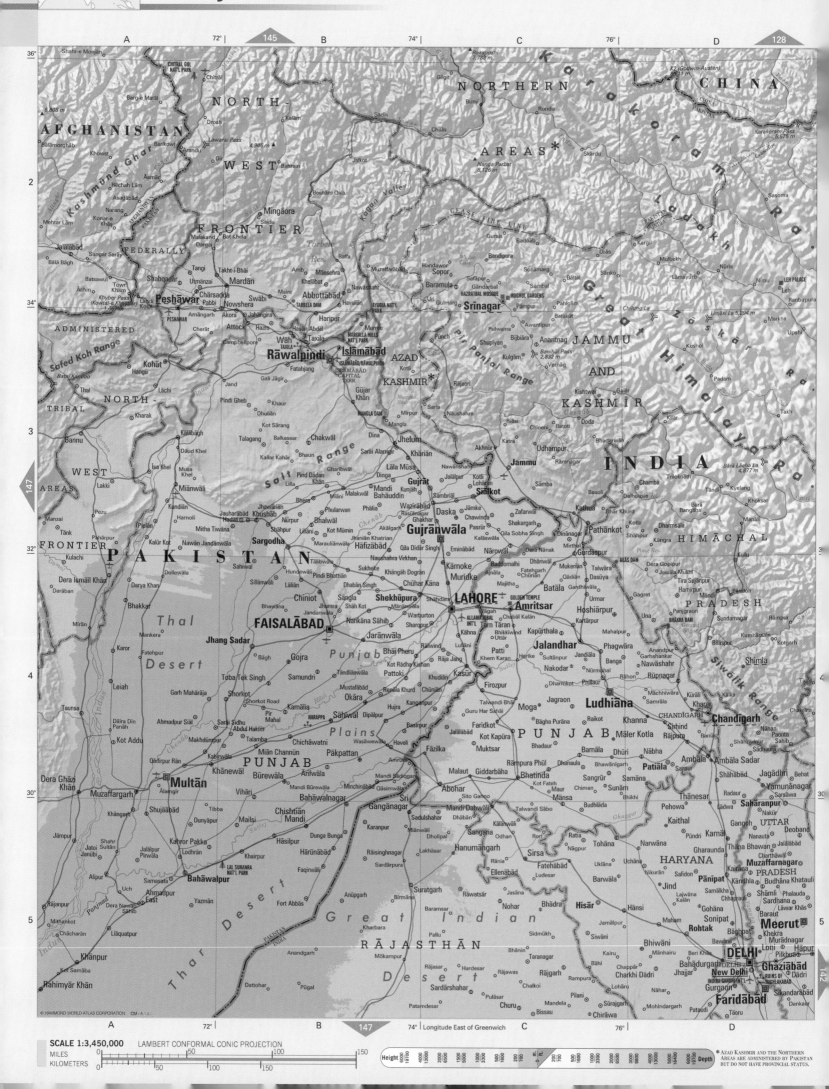

POPULATION OF CITIES AND TOWNS

- OVER 2,000,000
- 1,000,000 - 1,999,999
- 500,000 - 999,999
- 250,000 - 499,999
- 100,000 - 249,999
- 30,000 - 99,999
- 10,000 - 29,999
- UNDER 10,000

SCALE 1:10,300,000   LAMBERT CONFORMAL CONIC PROJECTION

MILES   0   150   300   450
KILOMETERS   0   150   300   450

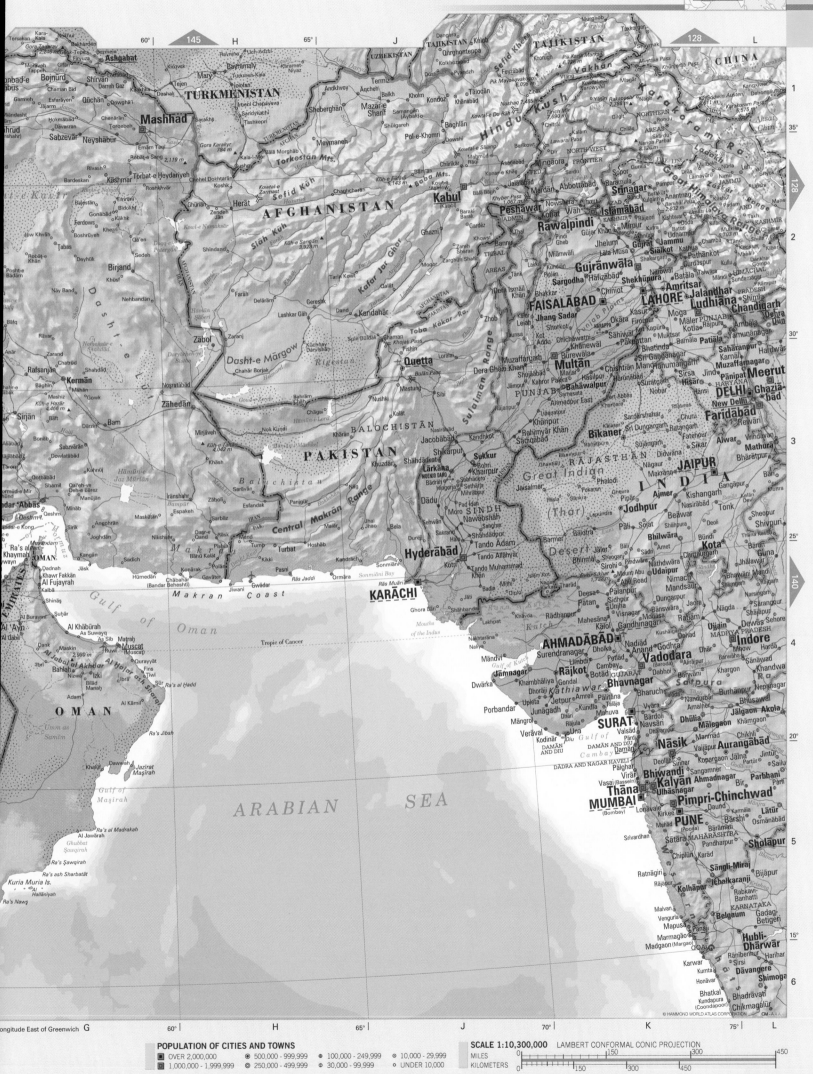

POPULATION OF CITIES AND TOWNS

■ OVER 2,000,000	● 500,000 - 999,999
■ 1,000,000 - 1,999,999	● 250,000 - 499,999

● 100,000 - 249,999   ○ 10,000 - 29,999
● 30,000 - 99,999   ○ UNDER 10,000

SCALE 1:10,300,000   LAMBERT CONFORMAL CONIC PROJECTION

MILES

KILOMETERS

© HAMMOND WORLD ATLAS CORPORATION

Northern Middle East

SCALE 1:6,900,000   LAMBERT CONFORMAL CONIC PROJECTION

MILES 0   100   200   300
KILOMETERS 0   100   200   300

Eastern Mediterranean Region

POPULATION OF CITIES AND TOWNS

■ OVER 2,000,000	◉ 500,000 - 999,999	● 100,000 - 249,999	◦ 10,000 - 29,999
▣ 1,000,000 - 1,999,999	◎ 250,000 - 499,999	◌ 30,000 - 99,999	· UNDER 10,000

SCALE 1:3,450,000   LAMBERT CONFORMAL CONIC PROJECTION

MILES

KILOMETERS

EGYPT
① AL GHARBIYAH
② AL QALYUBIYAH
③ BŪR SA'ID

Africa

Several physiographic features are captured in this southeast-looking, high-oblique image. The Nile River Delta, the large, dark area at the bottom of the image, extends from the capital city of Cairo at the apex of the delta to the Suez Canal. The entire region is classified as desert (less than 10 inches [25 cm.] of rainfall per year). Desert-like areas are visible southwest of the delta and in the northwestern Sinai. Major rock outcrops (darker areas) are seen encircling the Red Sea. The two bodies of water flanking the southern end of the Sinai Peninsula are the Gulf of Suez and the Gulf of Aqaba.

AREA OF OPTIMIZATION

The red band which surrounds this map defines the "Area of Optimization." Within this bounding curve is the most accurate conformal map that can be made of the region. Outside the optimized area, distortion increases rapidly, and tears or other irregularities in the grid may occur. (See page 8 for additional information.)

POPULATION OF CITIES AND TOWNS

■ OVER 3,000,000	● 500,000 - 999,999
■ 1,000,000 - 2,999,999	● 100,000 - 499,999
	○ UNDER 100,000

SCALE 1:34,500,000   OPTIMAL CONFORMAL PROJECTION

© HAMMOND W.A.C.   CJ - 1136 - A-A-A   LAMBERT CONFORMAL CONIC PROJECTION   © HAMMOND WORLD ATLAS CORPORATION   CC - A-A-A

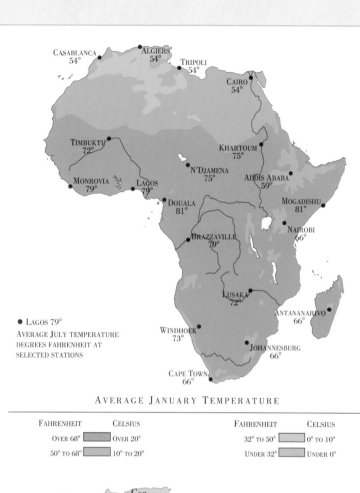

AVERAGE JANUARY TEMPERATURE

CASABLANCA 54°
ALGIERS 54°
TRIPOLI 54°
CAIRO 54°
TIMBUKTU 72°
KHARTOUM 75°
MONROVIA 79°
LAGOS 79°
N'DJAMENA 75°
ADDIS ABABA 59°
DOUALA 81°
MOGADISHU 81°
BRAZZAVILLE 79°
NAIROBI 66°
LUSAKA 72°
ANTANANARIVO 66°
WINDHOEK 73°
JOHANNESBURG 66°
CAPE TOWN 66°

● LAGOS 79°
AVERAGE JULY TEMPERATURE
DEGREES FAHRENHEIT AT
SELECTED STATIONS

FAHRENHEIT	CELSIUS	FAHRENHEIT	CELSIUS
OVER 68°	OVER 20°	32° TO 50°	0° TO 10°
50° TO 68°	10° TO 20°	UNDER 32°	UNDER 0°

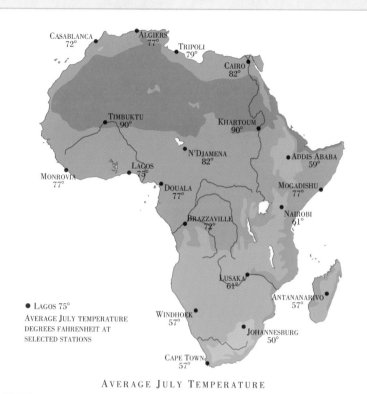

AVERAGE JULY TEMPERATURE

CASABLANCA 72°
ALGIERS 77°
TRIPOLI 79°
CAIRO 82°
TIMBUKTU 90°
KHARTOUM 90°
MONROVIA 77°
LAGOS 75°
N'DJAMENA 82°
ADDIS ABABA 59°
DOUALA 77°
MOGADISHU 77°
BRAZZAVILLE 72°
NAIROBI 61°
LUSAKA 61°
ANTANANARIVO 57°
WINDHOEK 57°
JOHANNESBURG 50°
CAPE TOWN 57°

● LAGOS 75°
AVERAGE JULY TEMPERATURE
DEGREES FAHRENHEIT AT
SELECTED STATIONS

FAHRENHEIT	CELSIUS	FAHRENHEIT	CELSIUS
OVER 86°	OVER 30°	50° TO 68°	10° TO 20°
68° TO 86°	20° TO 30°	UNDER 50°	UNDER 10°

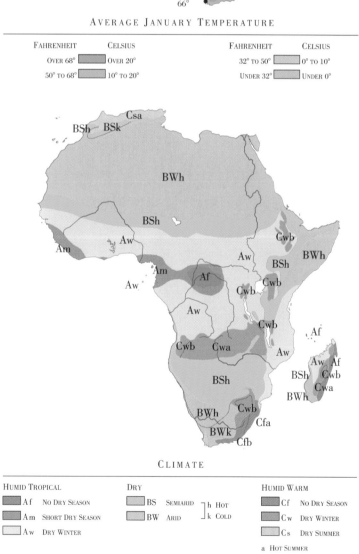

Csa
BSh BSk
BWh
BSh
Am Aw
Aw
Am
Af
Aw Aw
BSh
Cwb
Cwb
BWh
Cwb
Cwb
Cwa
Af
Aw
Aw Af
BSh Cwb
BSh Cwa
BWh
Cwb
BWh
Cfa
BWk Cfb

CLIMATE

HUMID TROPICAL		DRY		HUMID WARM	
Af	NO DRY SEASON	BS	SEMIARID]h HOT	Cf	NO DRY SEASON
Am	SHORT DRY SEASON	BW	ARID k COLD	Cw	DRY WINTER
Aw	DRY WINTER			Cs	DRY SUMMER

a HOT SUMMER
b COOL SUMMER

AFTER KOEPPEN-GEIGER

VEGETATION

TROPICAL FOREST
TROPICAL RAINFOREST
LIGHT TROPICAL FOREST
WOODLAND AND SHRUB

TROPICAL GRASSLAND
GRASS AND SHRUB (SAVANNA)
WOODED SAVANNA

MID-LATITUDE FOREST
MIXED NEEDLELEAF AND BROADLEAF FOREST
WOODLAND AND SHRUB (MEDITERRANEAN)

MID-LATITUDE GRASSLAND
SHORT GRASS (STEPPE)

DESERT AND DESERT SHRUB
RIVER VALLEY AND OASIS
UNCLASSIFIED HIGHLANDS

Africa – Geographical Comparisons

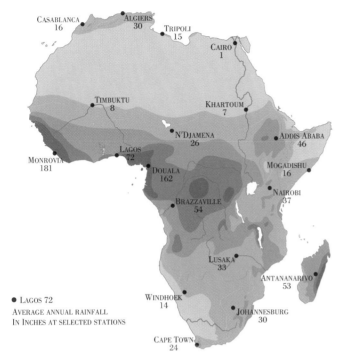

CASABLANCA 16

ALGIERS 30

TRIPOLI 15

CAIRO 1

TIMBUKTU 8

KHARTOUM 7

N'DJAMENA 26

ADDIS ABABA 46

LAGOS 72

MONROVIA 181

DOUALA 162

MOGADISHU 16

BRAZZAVILLE 54

NAIROBI 37

LUSAKA 33

ANTANANARIVO 53

WINDHOEK 14

● LAGOS 72
AVERAGE ANNUAL RAINFALL
IN INCHES AT SELECTED STATIONS

JOHANNESBURG 30

CAPE TOWN 24

AVERAGE ANNUAL RAINFALL

INCHES	CM	INCHES	CM	INCHES	CM
OVER 80	OVER 200	40 TO 60	100 TO 150	10 TO 20	25 TO 50
60 TO 80	150 TO 200	20 TO 40	50 TO 100	UNDER 10	UNDER 25

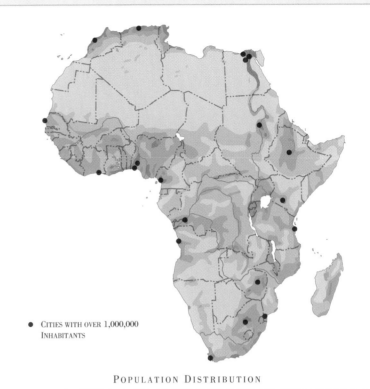

● CITIES WITH OVER 1,000,000
INHABITANTS

POPULATION DISTRIBUTION

DENSITY PER		SQ. MI.	SQ. KM.	SQ. MI.	SQ. KM.
SQ. MI.	SQ. KM.	130 TO 260	50 TO 100	3 TO 25	1 TO 10
OVER 260	OVER 100	25 TO 130	10 TO 50	UNDER 3	UNDER 1

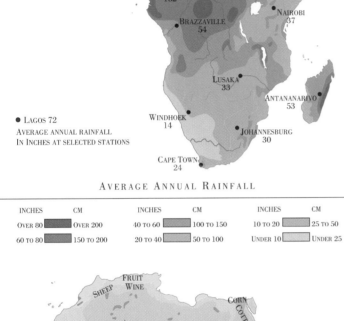

SHEEP

FRUIT WINE

CORN

COTTON

DATES

PEANUTS

CATTLE

CATTLE

COTTON

CATTLE

PEANUTS

HOGS

COFFEE

COFFEE

COCOA COCOA

PALM OIL

SHEEP

SHEEP

COCOA

BANANAS

COFFEE

CATTLE

SISAL

PALM OIL

COFFEE

CORN
TOBACCO COPRA

SHEEP

CORN
CATTLE

SHEEP SHEEP

LAND USE

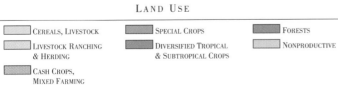

CEREALS, LIVESTOCK	SPECIAL CROPS	FORESTS	
LIVESTOCK RANCHING & HERDING	DIVERSIFIED TROPICAL & SUBTROPICAL CROPS	NONPRODUCTIVE	
CASH CROPS, MIXED FARMING			

MINERAL RESOURCES

ENERGY & FUELS
◆ COAL
▲ NATURAL GAS
● PETROLEUM
■ URANIUM

IRON & FERROALLOYS
1 CHROMIUM
2 COBALT
3 IRON ORE
4 MANGANESE
5 NICKEL
6 VANADIUM

OTHER MAJOR RESOURCES
1 ANTIMONY
2 ASBESTOS
3 BAUXITE
4 COPPER
5 DIAMONDS
6 GOLD
7 LEAD
8 MICA
9 PHOSPHATES
10 PLATINUM
11 TIN
12 ZINC

A 20° B 15° C 10°

SPAIN

Granada · Cartagena
Jerez · Málaga · Cerro de Mulhacén 3.478 m
Cádiz · Marbella · Gibraltar (U.K.) · Almería
Tangier · Ceuta (SP.) · Melilla (SP.)
Larache · Tétouan · Al Hoceima · Nador · Tlemcen
Ksar el Kebir · Taza · Taourirt · Oujda
Kenitra · Fès · Taza
Casablanca · Rabat · Meknès
El Jadida · Khouribga

MOROCCO

Safi · Essaouira · Beni Mellal
Marrakech · Jebel Toubkal 4,165 m
Agadir · Inezgane · Taroudant
Sidi Ifni · Tiznit
Tan-Tan

Mediterranean Sea

Algiers (El Djezair) · Béjaïa · Jijel · Annaba · **Tunis**
Cherchell · Skikda · Ariana · MALTA
Mostaganem · Constantine · Souk Ahras · Sousse
Oran · El Asnam · Khemis Miliana · Sétif · Batna · Kairouan
Sidi Bel Abbès · Relizane · Bou Saâda · Tébessa · Sfax
Saïda · Djelfa · Biskra · Gafsa · **Tripoli** (Tarabulus)
El Bayadh · Messaad · Laghouat · El Oued · **TUNISIA**
Ghardaïa · Touggourt · Nalut · Tripolitania

ALGERIA

Grand Erg Occidental · Grand Erg Oriental
El Golea · Ghadamès

Plateau du Tademaït · Hamada du Tinrhert · Hamadat Tinghert
Adrar · In Salah · Ohanet · Fezzan
Reggane · Tidikelt · Illizi

SAHARA

Tanezrouft · Ahaggar · Tahat 2,918 m

Plateau du Djado

MALI

Tombouctou (Timbuktu) · Gao
Gourma-Rharous · Ansongo

NIGER

Agadez

MAURITANIA

Nouakchott

WESTERN SAHARA
(Occupied by Morocco)

SENEGAL
Dakar
THE GAMBIA
Banjul
GUINEA-BISSAU
Bissau
GUINEA
Conakry
SIERRA LEONE
Freetown
LIBERIA
Monrovia

BURKINA FASO
Ouagadougou
Bamako

CÔTE D'IVOIRE
Yamoussoukro
Abidjan

GHANA
Accra

TOGO
Lomé

BENIN
Porto-Novo
Cotonou

Lagos

NIGERIA
Abuja
Kano

CAMEROON
Yaoundé
Douala

EQUATORIAL GUINEA

SÃO TOMÉ AND PRÍNCIPE

GABON
Libreville

ATLANTIC OCEAN

Gulf of Guinea

Equator

B 15° C 10° Longitude West D of Greenwich 5° E 0° Longitude East F of Greenwich 5° G 10° H 15°

Height 6000 19700 4000 13000 2000 6600 1500 5000 1000 3300 500 1600 200 700 Sea level 0 200 700 500 1600 1000 3300 2000 6600 4000 13000 6000 19700 Depth

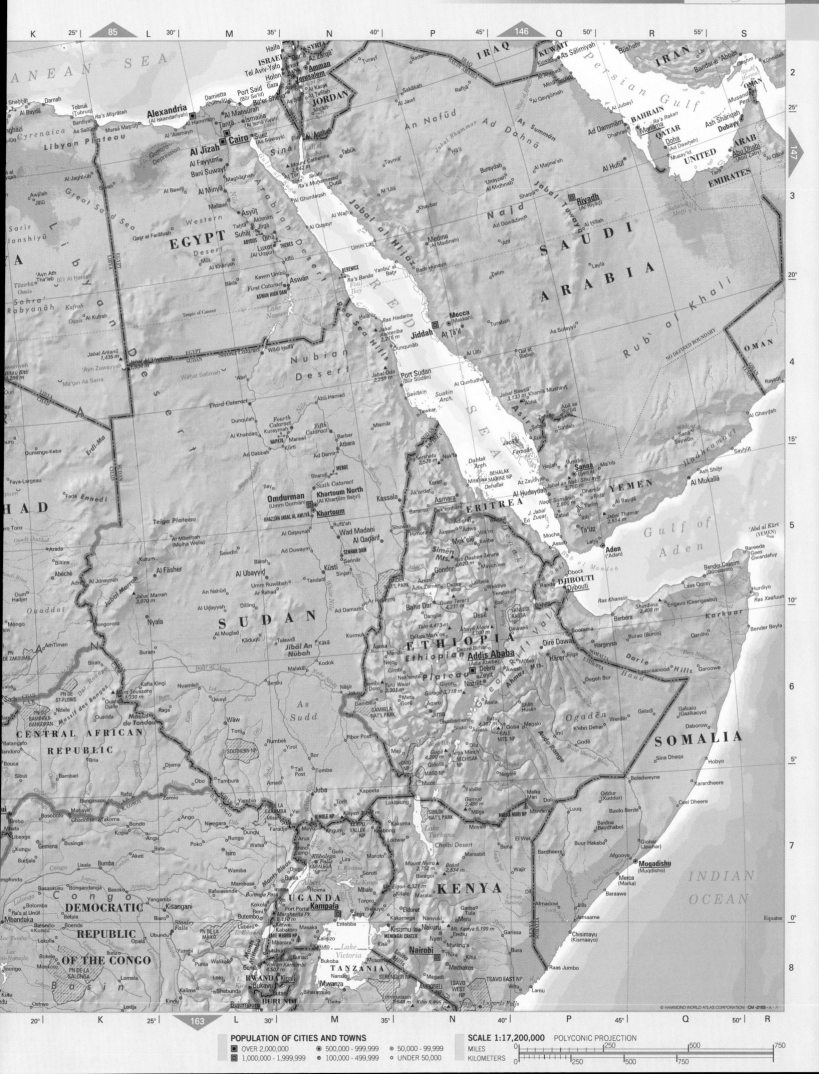

MEDITERRANEAN SEA

POPULATION OF CITIES AND TOWNS
- ■ OVER 2,000,000
- ◉ 500,000 - 999,999
- ◎ 50,000 - 99,999
- ▣ 1,000,000 - 1,999,999
- ◉ 100,000 - 499,999
- ○ UNDER 50,000

SCALE 1:17,200,000 POLYCONIC PROJECTION

MILES

KILOMETERS

Northern West Africa

MOROCCO is divided into 7 non-administrative regions shown here. Scale does not permit showing the boundaries and names of Morocco's provinces and prefectures.

ATLANTIC OCEAN

SPAIN

Cádiz
Chiclana de la Frontera
Barbate de Franco
Algeciras
Gibraltar (U.K.)
La Línea de la Concepción
Punta Almina
Ceuta (SP.)
Cap Spartel
TANGIER (IBN BATOUTA)
Tangier
Asilah (Tanger)
Tétouan
Al Hoceima
Mijas
Marbella
Str. of Gibraltar
AL HOCEIMA (CHERIF AL IDRISSI)
Jebel Bouhalla 2,170 m

Larache
Chefchaouene
Ksar el Kebir
Souk el Arba du Rharb
Ouezzane
Er Rif

Kenitra
Salé
Rabat
RABAT (SALE)
Sidi Kacem
NORD-OUEST
Ain el Aouda
VOLUBILIS
Moulay Idriss
Meknes
Fes
CENTRE-NORD

Mohammedia
CASABLANCA
(Dar-el-Beida)
CASABLANCA (MOHAMMED V)
Berrechid
El Jadida
Azemmour
Settat
Boulaouane
Oualidia
Cap Safi
El Hrad Harrara
Khouribga
Oued Zem
Khenifra
El Kbab
Moyen Atlas

Safi
Sidi Bennour
Jemaa Sahim
El Boroug
Benguerir
Kasba Tadla
Beni Mellal
Midelt
CENTRE

Essaouira
Chemaia
El Kelaa des Srarhna
MOROCCO
Er Rachidia
CENTRE-SUD
Goulmima

Cap Sim
Chichaoua
Marrakech
Aït Ourir
MARRAKECH (MENARA)
Jebel Azourki 3,690 m
Jebel Rhat 3,825 m
Jbel M'Goun 4,071 m
GORGES DU ZIZ
Erfoud

Tamanar
Imi n'Tanout
TENSIFT
Tahannout
Jebel Toubkal 4,165 m
Iadet 3,615m
PARC NAT DU TOUBKAL
Jebel Anhrmer 3,609 m
OUARZAZATE
Jebel Siroua 3,304 m
Ouarzazate
Jebel Saghro
Boumalne
Tinerhir
Jebel Rhart 1,650 m

AGADIR (AL MASSIRA)
Cap Rhir
Djebel Aoulkil 3,348 m
Taroudannt
Oulad Teima
Taliouine
Agdz
Tazenakht
Zagora

Agadir
Inezgane
Biougra
Irherm
Irherm n'Ougdal
Haut Atlas
1,730 m
Foum Zguid
Tagounit

Tiznit
Anti-Atlas
Jebel Lkst 2,359 m
Jebel Bani
SUD
2,531 m

Tafraout
Sidi Ifni
Tata
Oued Draa

Bou Izakarn
Foum el Hassane
Akka
Hamada du Drâa

Guelmim
Assa

Cap Drâa
Tan-Tan
Oued Drâa
Jebel Ouarkziz
TINDOUF

Tarfaya
Cap Juby
55 m
Tindouf
BORDJ FLYE

Daora
Hagunia
Hasi el Farsia
MECERIA MAURITANIA

EL AAIUN (HASSAN)
El Aaiún
Saguia el Hamra

Edchera
Semara

Lemsid
Bu Craa
Tifariti
El Eglab
Chenachane

Cabo Bojador
Sebjet Arudd
Sebkha Azefal
Aïn Ben Tili
Yetti

WESTERN SAHARA
(Occupied by Morocco)
Aaglet Yeraifia
Bir Aidiat
Bir Moghrein

Guelta Zemmur
Bir Bel Guerdâne
Sebkhet Iguetat

Sebkhet Oumm ed Droûs Telli
TIRIS ZEMMOUR
El Mzereb
El Mzereb

Ad Dakhla
Tropic of Cancer
Punta Durnford
El Aatf
Buir Taiaret
El Aargub
Fuch
Aaglet Tennuaca
Sebkhet Oumm ed Drous Guebli

Aïoun 'Abd el Mâlek
Karêt
Erg el Ahmor
'Erg

366 m
Tiris
Sebjet Tiznit
Rhâllamane
Kreb en Nâga

Cabo Barbas
Edferik
Kediet Idjill 915 m
Zouérat
Hamami
Agleïgat
Hamada Safia

Adrar Soutuf
Bir Anzârane
Galb Azefal
El Khatt
Zemlet Taftat 330 m
Erg Ijoubbane
Tsoudenni

Guerguerat
Aguent
Touâjil
Guelb er Rîchat 519 m
El Khi
MALI

NOUÂDHIBOU
Cansado
El Djouf
TOMBOUCTOU

Nouâdhibou
Güera
Cabo Blanco
B. de Levrier
Tichla
Zug
Ouarane
MAURITANIA
HODH ECH CHARGUI
Erg Atouili

Cap d'Arguin
DAKHLET NOUÂDHIBOU
Agüeni
Chûm
Ouadane
ADRAR
INCHIRI

PARC NATIONAL DU BANC D'ARGUIN
Atar
Chinguitti

Madeira Is.
(PORT.)
Porto Moniz
Porto Santo
Vila de Porto Santo
Madeira
Santana
Machico
FUNCHAL
Calheta
Funchal
Ribeira Brava
Ilhas Desertas

Ilhas Selvagens
(PORT.)

Canary Islands
(SPAIN)

PN LA CALDERA DE TABURIENTE
La Palma
Santa Cruz de la Palma
Los Llanos de Aridane
PN DE TIMANFAYA
Lanzarote
Arrecife
LANZAROTE

Tenerife
Santa Cruz de Tenerife
La Laguna
La Orotava
NORTE LOS RODEOS
Icod de los Vinos
Puerto de la Cruz
Gáldar
Arucas
Fuerteventura
Puerto del Rosario

Vallehermoso
PN DEL TEIDE
Pico de Teide 3,718 m
Las Palmas de Gran Canaria
Antigua

PN BE GARAJONAY
Granadilla de Abona
Santa Lucía
SUR REINA SOFIA
Telde
Ingenio
Tarfaya

Gomera
San Bartolomé de Tirajana
GRAN CANARIA
Gran Canaria

Valverde
Hierro

Height 6000 19700 4000 13000 2000 6500 1000 3300 500 1500 200 700 100 300 0 m 0 200 700 500 1600 1000 3300 2000 6600 3000 9800 4000 13100 5070 16700 Depth

A 16° B 12° 160 C 8° D
Longitude West of Greenwich 4°

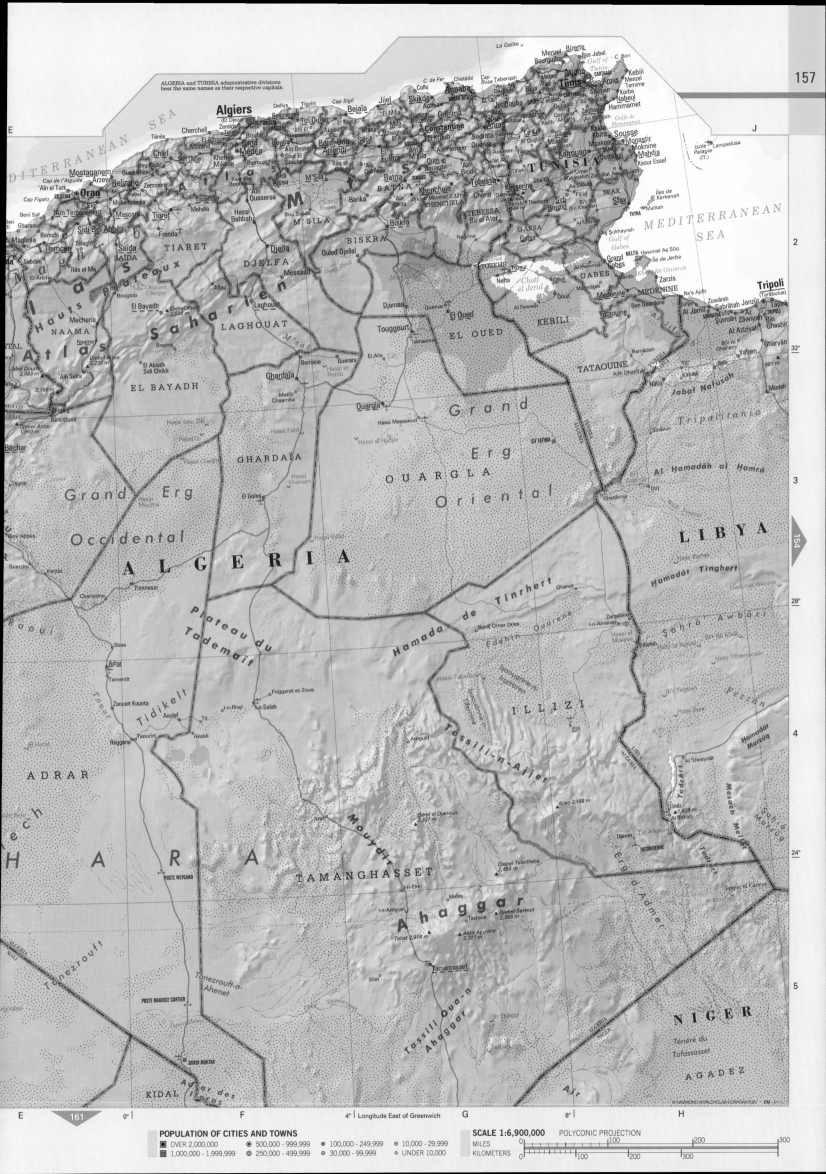

Northern Morocco, Algeria, Tunisia

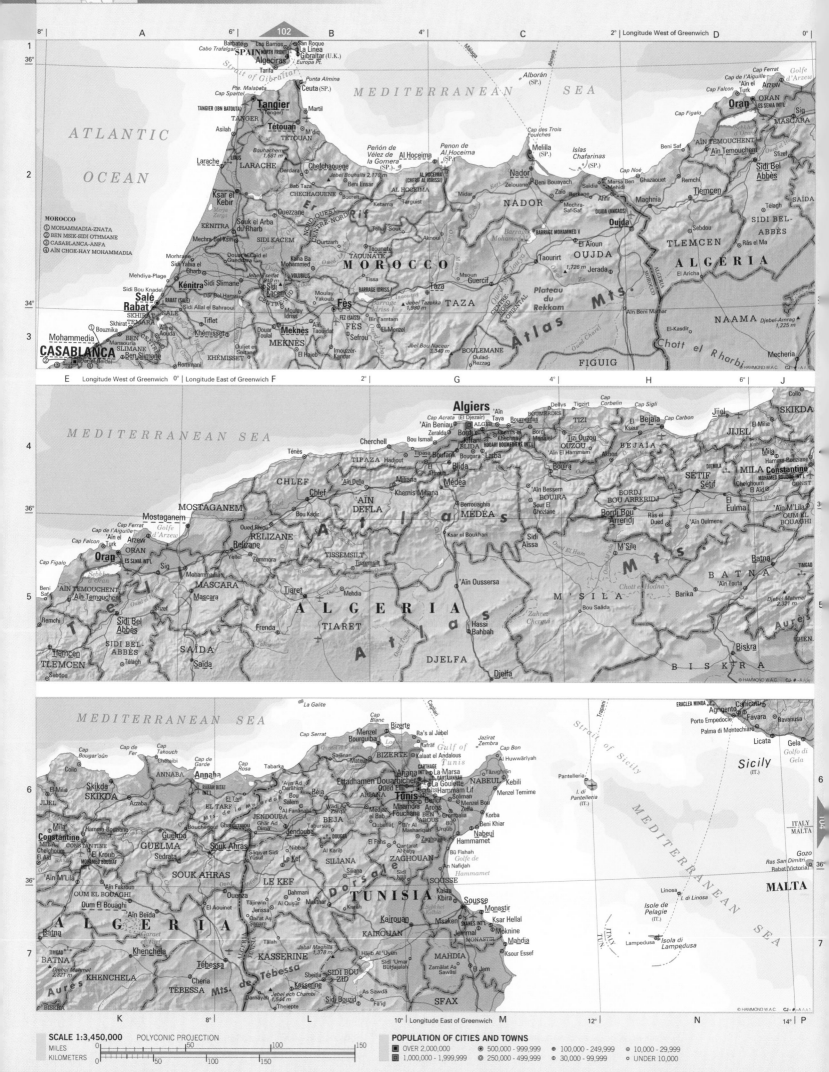

SCALE 1:3,450,000   POLYCONIC PROJECTION

MILES 0   50   100   150

KILOMETERS 0   50   100   150

POPULATION OF CITIES AND TOWNS

■ OVER 2,000,000	◉ 500,000 - 999,999	● 100,000 - 249,999	○ 10,000 - 29,999
▣ 1,000,000 - 1,999,999	◎ 250,000 - 499,999	◦ 30,000 - 99,999	○ UNDER 10,000

MOROCCO
① MOHAMMADIA-ZNATA
② BEN MSIK-SIDI OTHMANE
③ CASABLANCA-ANFA
④ AÏN CHOK-HAY MOHAMMADIA

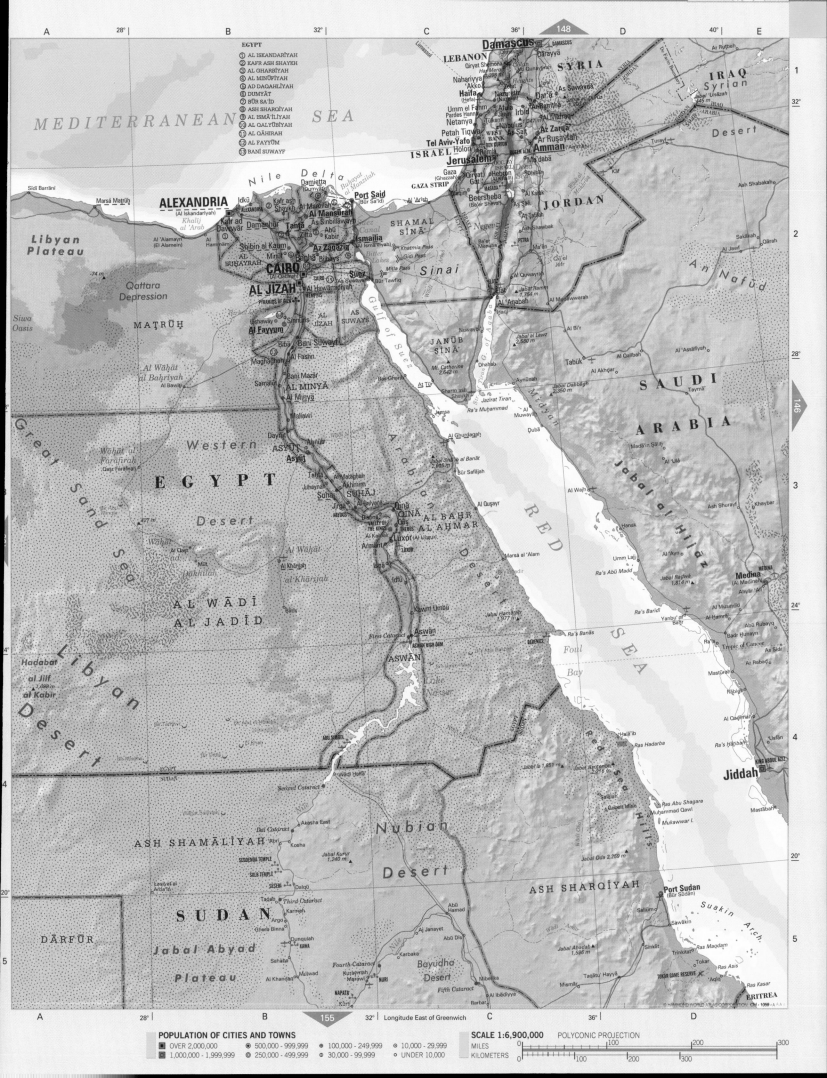

154

SCALE 1:6,900,000   POLYCONIC PROJECTION

MILES
KILOMETERS

© Hammond World Atlas Corporation   CM-A

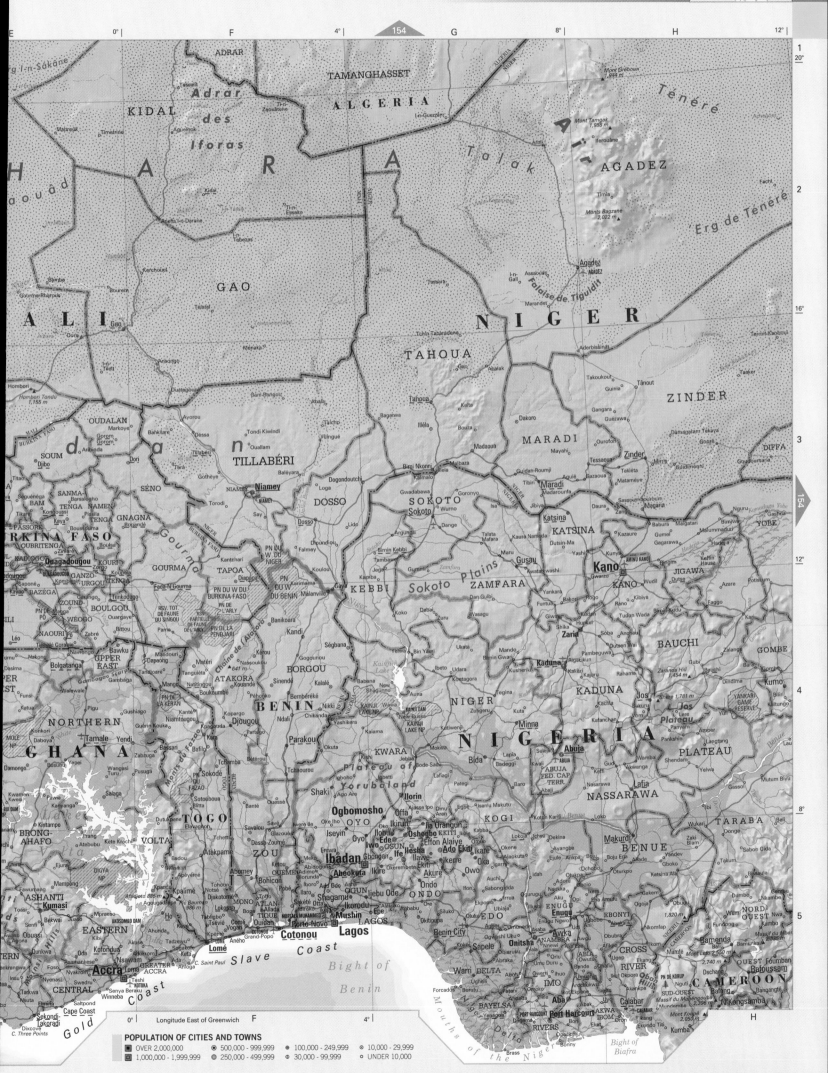

POPULATION OF CITIES AND TOWNS

■ OVER 2,000,000	● 500,000 - 999,999	● 100,000 - 249,999	○ 10,000 - 29,999
▣ 1,000,000 - 1,999,999	◉ 250,000 - 499,999	● 30,000 - 99,999	○ UNDER 10,000

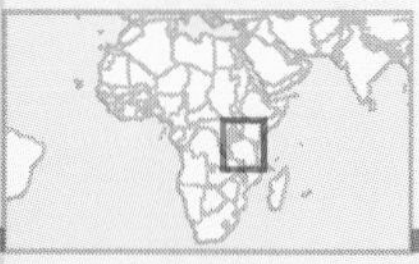

155   32°   A   B   C   40°   D

DEM. REP. OF THE CONGO

ORIENTALE

UGANDA

SUDAN / KENYA

ETHIOPIA

Lake Turkana (L. Rudolf)

Chalbi Desert

EASTERN

NORTH EASTERN

SOMALIA

RIFT VALLEY

WESTERN

Kampala

Entebbe

KENYA

Lake Victoria

Mt Kenya (Batian) 5,199 m

CENTRAL

Nairobi

NYANZA

MARA

RWANDA

Kigali

KAGERA

BURUNDI

Bujumbura

KIGOMA

Lake Victoria

Mt Kilimanjaro 5,892 m

Moshi

Arusha

Mombasa

TSAVO EAST NAT'L PARK

COAST

Pemba I.

Tanga

TANGA

ZANZIBAR

Zanzibar I.

SHINYANGA

Mwanza

MWANZA

SERENGETI NATIONAL PARK

NGORONGORO

SINGIDA

DODOMA

Dodoma

TABORA

Tabora

TANZANIA

Masai Steppe

MOROGORO

PWANI

Dar es Salaam

DEM. REP. OF THE CONGO

KATANGA

RUKWA

Lake Rukwa

Lake Tanganyika

Monts Mitumba

Lake Nyasa

IRINGA

Mbeya

MBEYA

RUAHA NATIONAL PARK

SELOUS GAME RESERVE

Mafia I.

INDIAN OCEAN

ZAMBIA

NORTHERN

LUAPULA

MALAWI

NORTHERN

EASTERN

RUVUMA

LINDI

Mtwara

MTWARA

NIASSA

CABO DELGADO

MOZAMBIQUE

Arquipélago das Querimbas

32° Longitude East of Greenwich   36°   163   40°

A   B   C   D

POPULATION OF CITIES AND TOWNS
■ OVER 2,000,000
▣ 1,000,000 - 1,999,999
● 500,000 - 999,999
◉ 250,000 - 499,999
● 100,000 - 249,999
◎ 30,000 - 99,999
○ 10,000 - 29,999
○ UNDER 10,000

© HAMMOND WORLD ATLAS CORPORATION   CC - 2102 - A - A

POPULATION OF CITIES AND TOWNS

■ OVER 2,000,000	● 500,000 - 999,999	● 50,000 - 99,999
■ 1,000,000 - 1,999,999	● 100,000 - 499,999	○ UNDER 50,000

SCALE 1:17,200,000   POLYCONIC PROJECTION

MILES

KILOMETERS

SAME SCALE AS MAIN MAP

Australia, New Zealand and the Pacific

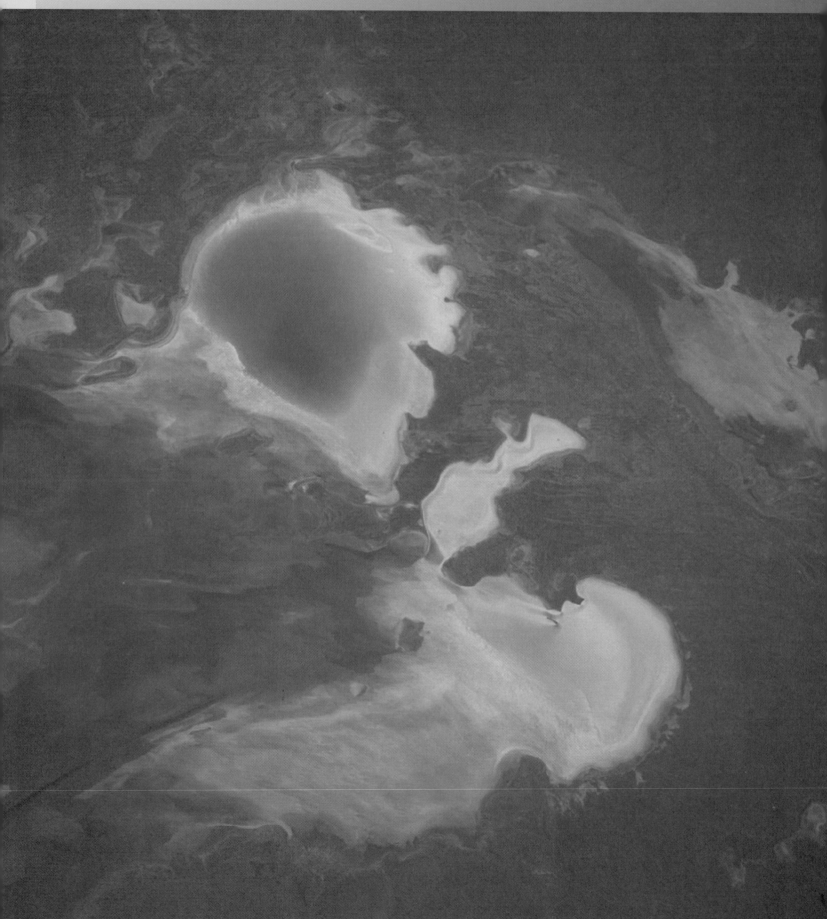

The Lake Eyre Basin is located in the arid interior of south central Australia. This basin is one of the largest areas of internal drainage in the world. It consists of two distinct, but interrelated basins: the north basin and the south basin. The much larger north basin shown here (the highly reflective areas) consists of two very large, normally dry lakebeds. The western lobe (bottom of the image) is Belt Bay, and the eastern lobe is Madigan Bay. The color change, especially in the Madigan Bay lobe, indicates that there was some water in this lobe at the time the image was taken.

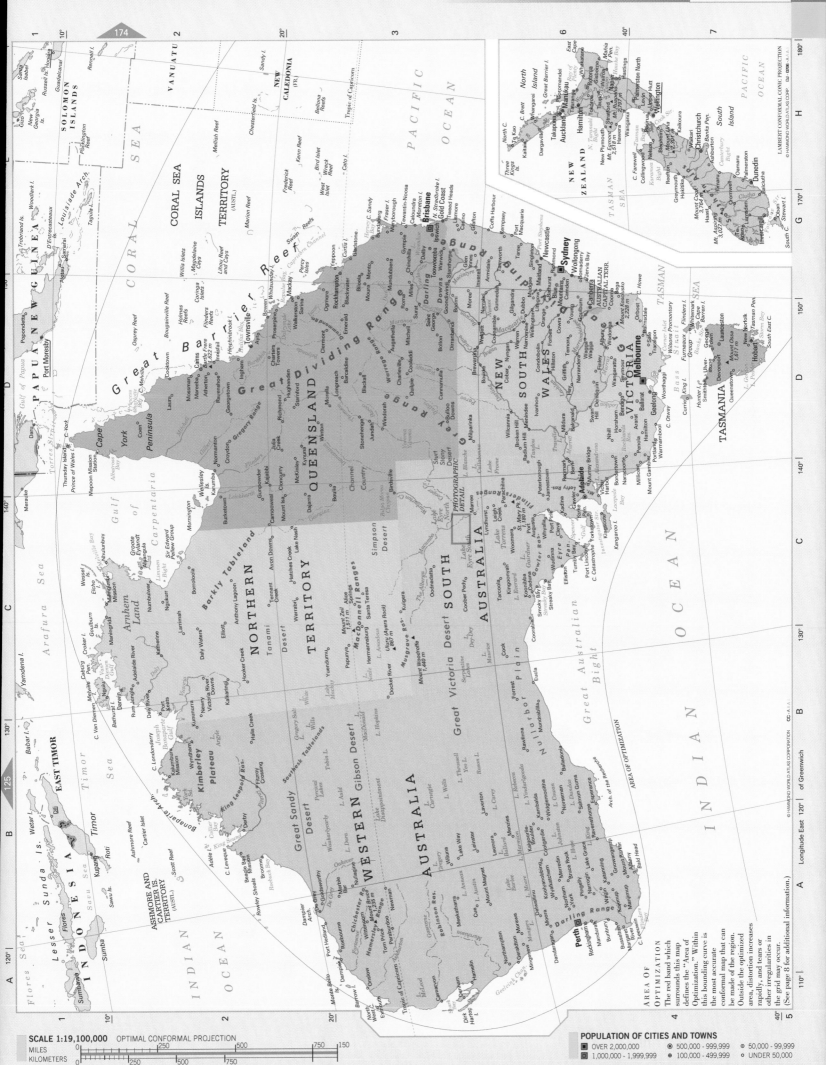

SCALE 1:19,100,000   OPTIMAL CONFORMAL PROJECTION

MILES

KILOMETERS

POPULATION OF CITIES AND TOWNS

■ OVER 2,000,000	◉ 500,000 - 999,999	◦ 50,000 - 99,999
▣ 1,000,000 - 1,999,999	● 100,000 - 499,999	∘ UNDER 50,000

AREA OF OPTIMIZATION
The red band which surrounds this map defines the "Area of Optimization." Within this bounding curve is the most accurate conformal map that can be made of the region. Outside the optimized area, distortion increases rapidly, and tears or other irregularities in the grid may occur.
(See page 8 for additional information.)

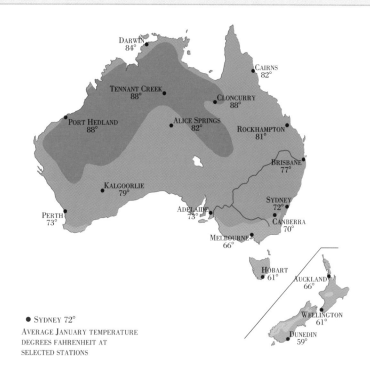

DARWIN
84°

CAIRNS
82°

TENNANT CREEK
88°

CLONCURRY
88°

PORT HEDLAND
88°

ALICE SPRINGS
82°

ROCKHAMPTON
81°

BRISBANE
77°

KALGOORLIE
79°

SYDNEY
72°

ADELAIDE
73°

CANBERRA
70°

PERTH
73°

MELBOURNE
66°

HOBART
61°

AUCKLAND
66°

WELLINGTON
61°

DUNEDIN
59°

● SYDNEY 72°
AVERAGE JANUARY TEMPERATURE
DEGREES FAHRENHEIT AT
SELECTED STATIONS

AVERAGE JANUARY TEMPERATURE

FAHRENHEIT	CELSIUS	FAHRENHEIT	CELSIUS	FAHRENHEIT	CELSIUS
OVER 86°	OVER 30°	50° TO 68°	10° TO 20°	UNDER 32°	UNDER 0°
68° TO 86°	20° TO 30°	32° TO 50°	0° TO 10°		

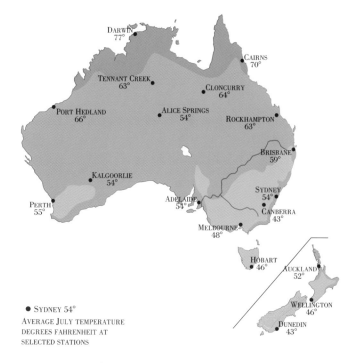

DARWIN
77°

CAIRNS
70°

TENNANT CREEK
63°

CLONCURRY
64°

PORT HEDLAND
66°

ALICE SPRINGS
54°

ROCKHAMPTON
63°

BRISBANE
59°

KALGOORLIE
54°

SYDNEY
54°

ADELAIDE
54°

CANBERRA
43°

PERTH
55°

MELBOURNE
48°

HOBART
46°

AUCKLAND
52°

WELLINGTON
46°

DUNEDIN
43°

● SYDNEY 54°
AVERAGE JULY TEMPERATURE
DEGREES FAHRENHEIT AT
SELECTED STATIONS

AVERAGE JULY TEMPERATURE

FAHRENHEIT	CELSIUS	FAHRENHEIT	CELSIUS
OVER 68°	OVER 20°	32° TO 50°	0° TO 10°
50° TO 68°	10° TO 20°	UNDER 32°	UNDER 0°

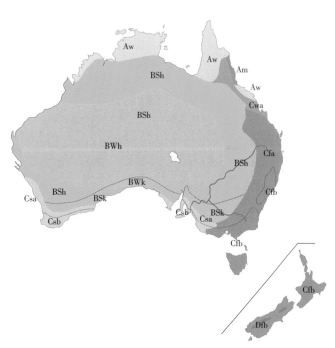

Aw

Aw

Am

BSh

Aw

Cwa

BSh

BWh

Cfa

BSh

BWk

Cfb

Csa

BSh

BSk

Csb

Csb

BSk

Csa

Cfb

Cfb

Dfb

CLIMATE

HUMID TROPICAL

Am SHORT DRY SEASON

Aw DRY WINTER

DRY

BS SEMIARID ⎫ h HOT

BW ARID ⎭ k COLD

HUMID WARM

Cf NO DRY SEASON

Cw DRY WINTER

Cs DRY SUMMER

HUMID COLD

Df NO DRY SEASON

a HOT SUMMER

b COOL SUMMER

AFTER KOEPPEN-GEIGER

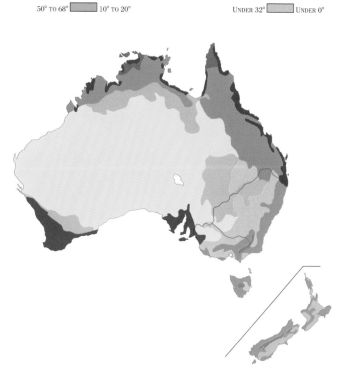

VEGETATION

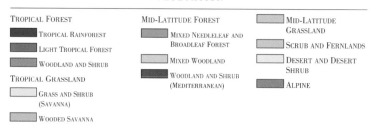

TROPICAL FOREST

TROPICAL RAINFOREST

LIGHT TROPICAL FOREST

WOODLAND AND SHRUB

TROPICAL GRASSLAND

GRASS AND SHRUB
(SAVANNA)

WOODED SAVANNA

MID-LATITUDE FOREST

MIXED NEEDLELEAF AND
BROADLEAF FOREST

MIXED WOODLAND

WOODLAND AND SHRUB
(MEDITERRANEAN)

MID-LATITUDE
GRASSLAND

SCRUB AND FERNLANDS

DESERT AND DESERT
SHRUB

ALPINE

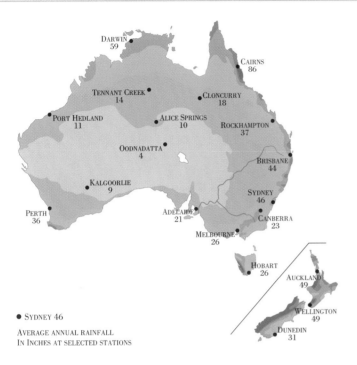

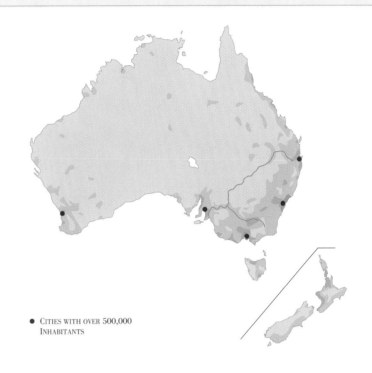

- SYDNEY 46

AVERAGE ANNUAL RAINFALL
IN INCHES AT SELECTED STATIONS

- CITIES WITH OVER 500,000
  INHABITANTS

AVERAGE ANNUAL RAINFALL

INCHES	CM	INCHES	CM	INCHES	CM
OVER 80	OVER 200	40 TO 60	100 TO 150	10 TO 20	25 TO 50
60 TO 80	150 TO 200	20 TO 40	50 TO 100	UNDER 10	UNDER 25

POPULATION DISTRIBUTION

DENSITY PER		SQ. MI.	SQ. KM.	SQ. MI.	SQ. KM.
SQ. MI.	SQ. KM.	25 TO 130	10 TO 50	UNDER 3	UNDER 1
OVER 130	OVER 50	3 TO 25	1 TO 10		

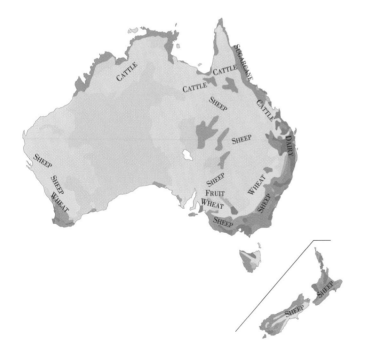

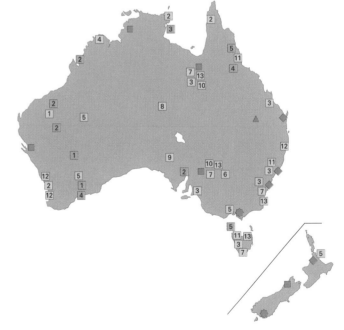

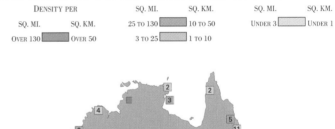

LAND USE

CEREALS, LIVESTOCK	PASTURE LIVESTOCK	FORESTS
LIVESTOCK RANCHING & HERDING	CASH CROPS, MIXED FARMING	NONPRODUCTIVE
DAIRY, LIVESTOCK		

MINERAL RESOURCES

ENERGY & FUELS	IRON & FERROALLOYS	OTHER MAJOR RESOURCES		
◆ COAL	1 COBALT	1 ASBESTOS	6 GYPSUM	11 TIN
⬟ LIGNITE	2 IRON ORE	2 BAUXITE	7 LEAD	12 TITANIUM
▲ NATURAL GAS	3 MANGANESE	3 COPPER	8 MICA	13 ZINC
■ URANIUM	4 NICKEL	4 DIAMONDS	9 OPALS	
	5 TUNGSTEN	5 GOLD	10 SILVER	

Height 6000 4000 2000 1500 1000 500 200 0 200 700 1500 3000 6000 9000 19700 Depth

© HAMMOND WORLD ATLAS CORPORATION   CM -A

Western and Central Australia

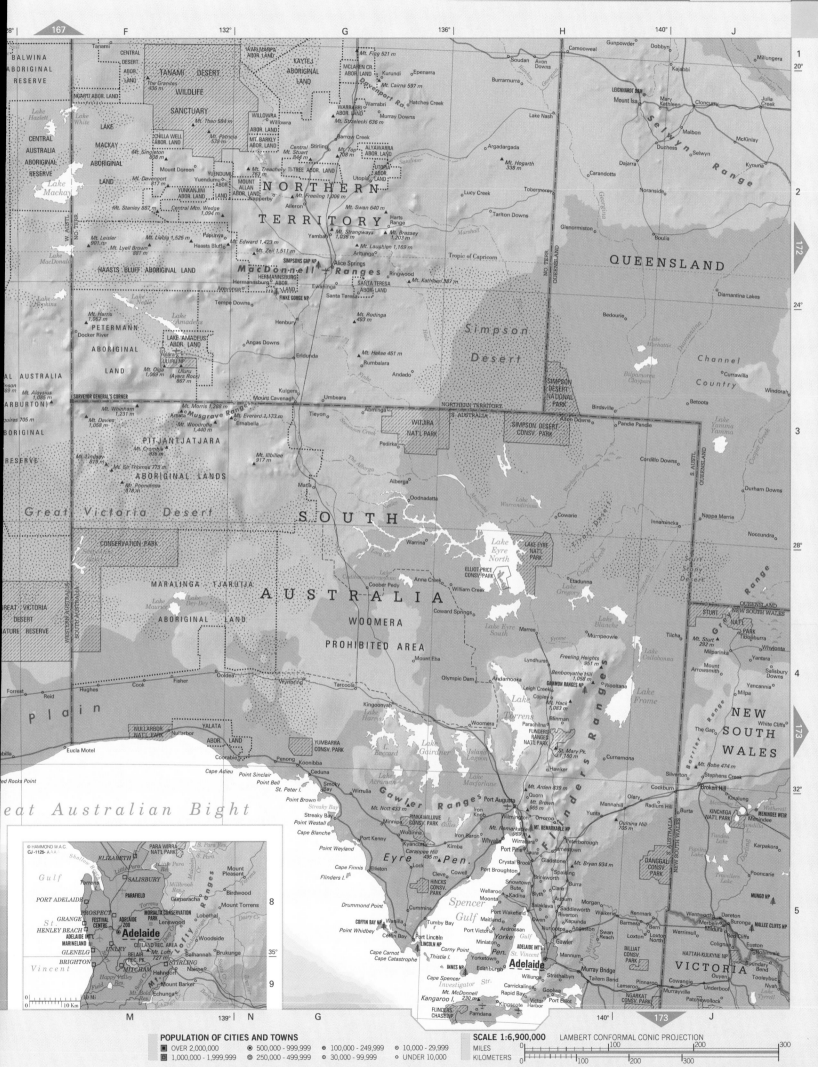

Northeastern Australia

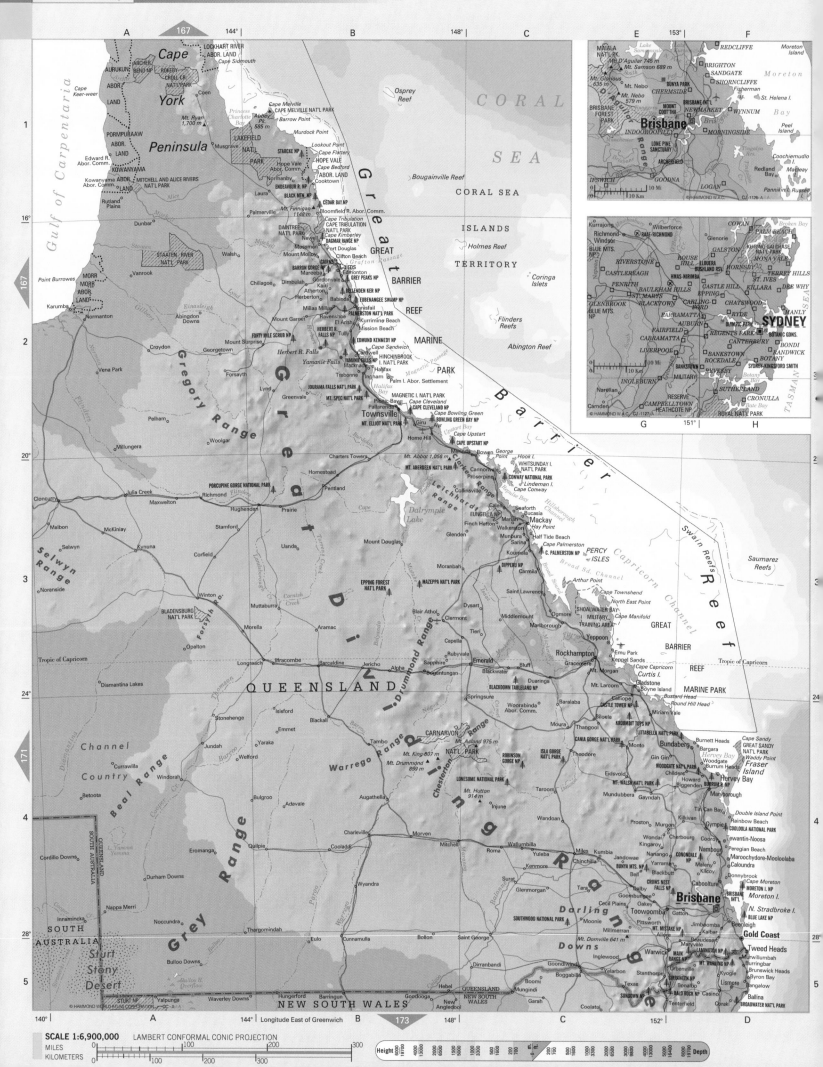

SCALE 1:6,900,000   LAMBERT CONFORMAL CONIC PROJECTION

MILES

KILOMETERS

Longitude East of Greenwich

Height   Depth

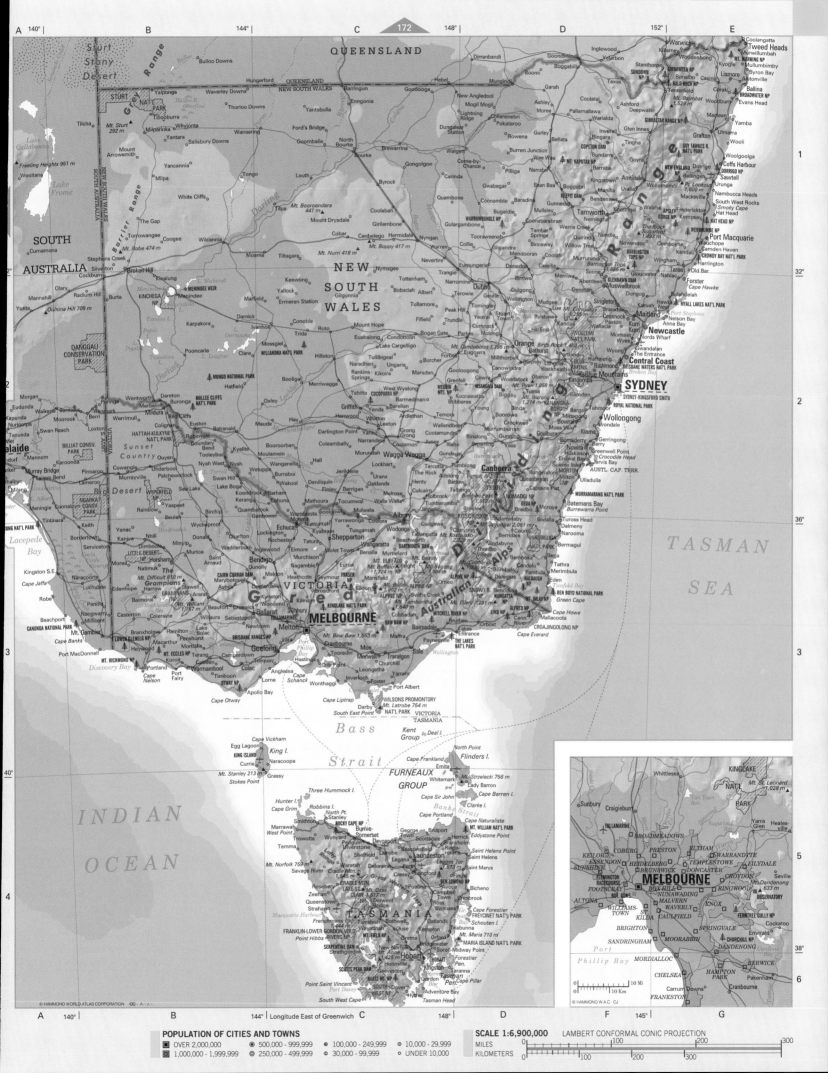

125

CHINA

Xiangtan • Changsha ■ Nanchang
Hengyang • Zhuzhou Jingdezhen
Huangyang Shan 2,158 m • Ningbo Kucang Shan 1,875 m
Tonggu Zhang 1,826 m • Wenzhou
Ganzhou
Xiamen • Fuzhou
Guangzhou
Chaozhou Shantou
Macau ■ **Shantou**
MACAU HONG KONG Kaohsiung

EAST CHINA SEA

Tokara Is. • Kyūshū • Ōsumi Is.
Naze • Amami Is.
Okinawa Is. Naha
Ishigaki Sakishima Is. Daito Is.

JAPAN

Tori-Shima (JAPAN)

Mukoshima Is.
Ogasawara • Chichishima Is.
BONIN IS. (JAPAN) Hahashima Is.
Ritaiō

VOLCANO IS. • Iwo Jima (JAPAN)
Minamiiō

Minami-Tori-Shima (JAPAN)

Tropic of Cancer

Taipei
Taichung
Tainan
TAIWAN

RYUKYU IS.

Bashi Channel

20°

Luzon Strait

SOUTH
CHINA
SEA

Laoag
Vigan • Babuyan Is.
Baguio • Luzon
Dagupan
Cabanatuan
Mt. Pinatubo 1,759 m
Manila ■ **Quezon City**
Batangas • Lucena
Mindoro Naujan
Legaspi

Calayan I.
Babuyan Is.

Okino-Tori-Shima (JAPAN)

Farallon de Pajaros
Maug Is.
Asuncion
• Agrihan
• Pagan
Alamagan
Guguan
Sarigan
Anatahan • Farallon de Medinilla
Saipan (Capitol Hill)
Aguijan • Tinian
Rota

Hagåtña • **Guam**
(U.S.)

NORTHERN
MARIANA
ISLANDS
(U.S.)

3°

PHILIPPINES

Itbayat I.
Batan Is.

Catanduanes I.

PHILIPPINE
SEA

M
i
c

NORTH

Wake I. (U.S.)

Enewetak • Bikini • Rongelap Rongerik • Bikar
Ujelang Utirik
Wotho Ailuk
Ujae Kwajalein Erikub Wotje
Lae Namu Maloelap
Ailinglapalap Aur
Namorik Jaluit Majuro
Ebon Mili

MARSHALL
ISLANDS

RATAK CHAIN
RALIK CHAIN

Itbayat I.
Masbate Samar
Iloilo Bacolod Tacloban
Panay • Leyte
Palawan Negros Cebu Bohol
• Butuan
Quezon Cagayan de Oro
Zamboanga **Davao**
Basilan General Santos

10°

MALAYSIA
Sabah
Tawau

Sulu Archipelago
Tarakan

Borneo

Sulu Sea
Balabac Str.

Celebes
Sea

Sangihe Is.
Talaud Is.

Ulithi
Yap Is.
Colonia
Ngulu
Babelthuap
Koror
Sonsorol Is.

PALAU

Kayangel Is.

Gaferut
Faraulep West Fayu
Sorol Woleai Olimarao Pikelot
Ifalik Elato Lamotrek
Eauripik Satawan
Puluwat

Namonuito
Hall Is.
Pulap Moen
Chuuk Is.
Oroluk Senyavin Is.
Ant Palikir
Pohnpei Mokil
Pingelap
Ngatik

Nukuoro

Kapingamarangi

Makin
Butaritari
Abaiang • Bikenibeu
Tarawa Maiana
Kuria Abemama
Aranuka

GILBERT

Banaba Nonouti
Tabiang Utiroa Nikunau
Onotoa Tamana
Arorae

ISLANDS

NAURU

o
n
e
s
i
a

FEDERATED STATES OF MICRONESIA

CAROLINE ISLANDS Etal Lukunor
Lelu Kosrae

Samarinda
Palu
Ujung Pandang

Gulf of Tomini
Gorontalo
Manado
Ternate
Halmahera
Morotai
Waigeo
Sorong
Misool
Obi Is.
Sula Is.
Ceram Sea
Ceram
Fakfak
Buru
Ambon
Banda Sea

0° Equator

M
e
l
a
n
e
s
i
a

Mussau
Ninigo Atolls St. Matthias Group
Admiralty
Islands
Manus Lorengau Lyra Reef
Kavieng
Lavongai **New Ireland**
Namatanai
BISMARCK ARCHIPELAGO
Bismarck
Karkar I. *Sea*
Madang Rabaul
Umboi **New**
Britain

Nuguria Is.
Nissan I.
Tauu Is.
Nukumanu Atoll
Buka Tulin Is.
Bougainville
Arawa Kieta
Choiseul
Ontong Java

Lolua • Nanumea
Niutao
Nanumanga

Nui
Nukufetau • Vaitupu
Funafuti

TUVALU

Niulakita

INDONESIA

Kendari
Buton
Kolaka
Selayar

Gulf of Bone
Kai Is.
Aru Is.

New Guinea

Jayapura
Vanimo
Aitape Wewak
Mt. Wilhelm
4,509 m
Mt. Hagen
Goroka
PAPUA
NEW GUINEA

Puncak Jaya 5,030 m
Maoke Mts.

Kimbe
Kundiawa
Lae
Bulolo
Wau
Bulolo

Solomon Sea

Santa Isabel
Buala
Auki Malaita
Gizo **New**
Georgia
Is. **Honiara**
Guadalcanal

Kirakira
San
Cristobal
Reef Is.
Lata Nendö
Utupua
Vanikolo

Duff Is.

SANTA CRUZ IS.

Ahau
Rotuma I.

WALLIS
FUTU

5°

Flores Sea
Sumbawa
Flores
Ruteng
Sumba
Savu Sea
Kupang Timor
EAST TIMOR

Selayar
Wetar
Alor Is.
Leti
Babar
Is. Tanimbar Is. Yos Sudarso
Merauke

Daru
Gulf of
Papua
Port Moresby

Trobriand Is.
D'Entrecasteaux
Woodlark I.
Popondetta Normanby I.
Esa'ala Milne Bay
Samarai Tagula I.
Louisiade Arch.
Rossel I.

Pocklington
Reef

Rennell I.

SOLOMON
ISLANDS

VANUATU

Torres Is.
Banks Is.

FIJI

Vanua
Levu

Lolua

INDIAN
OCEAN

Arafura Sea

Torres Strait
C. York

Espiritu Santo
Tabwemasana 1,879 m
Luganville
Norsup Ambrym
Malakula Epi
Port-Vila Éfaté
NEW HEBRIDES

Maewo
Pentecost
Shepherd

Yasawa
Group
Lautoka Nadi
Viti Levu **Suva**
Vunisea Kandavu

Lambasa Savusavu
Moala
Group

10°

Timor
Sea

Melville
Darwin

Pine Creek
Katherine

Cape
York
Coen
Peninsula

Cooktown

CORAL

SEA

NEW
CALEDONIA
(FR.)

Torres Is.
Chesterfield
Koumac Hienghène
Mont Panié 1,628 m
Bellona **New** Koné
Reefs Bourail
Caledonia Nouméa
Humboldt 1,618 m
Île des Pins

Anatom
Thio
LOYALTY IS.
Isangel Tanna

C
o
r
a
l

S
e
a

SOUTH

AUSTRALIA

Wyndham
Kimberley
Broome
Plateau
Halls Creek

Great Sandy
Desert

Port Hedland
Roebourne
Marble Bar
Onslow

Daly Waters

Tennant Creek

Camooweal
Normanton

Cloncurry Hughenden

Townsville
Bowen
Mackay

Great

Barrier

Rockhampton

Reef

Kingston Norfolk I. (AUSTL.)

Macau
Curti
KERMADE
(N.Z.)

20°

Exmouth
Carnarvon

Mt. Bruce
1,235 m
Tropic of Capricorn
Gibson Desert
Uluru (Ayers Rock)
867 m
Musgrave Ranges

Alice Springs

Birdsville

Clermont
Emerald
Bundaberg

Gympie
Roma
Toowoomba
Brisbane
Gold Coast

Lord Howe I.
(AUSTL.)

SOUTH

Geraldton
Northampton
Meekatharra
Wiluna
Leonora

L. Carnegie

Lake
Eyre

Great Victoria Desert

Coober Pedy

Oodnadatta

Marree

Charleville

Cunnamulla
Saint
George

Bourke
Cobar
Dubbo

Moree
Armidale
Tamworth
Gunnedah

Three
Kings
Is.
North Cape

NEW
ZEALA

30°

Kalgoorlie-Boulder

Nullarbor Plain

Norseman
Merredin
Northam
Perth

Great Australian
Bight

Streaky Bay
Port Lincoln

Woomera
Port Augusta
Whyalla Port Pirie
Adelaide
Murray Bridge

Broken Hill
Wagga Wagga
Mildura
Murray
Mt. Kosciusko
2,228 m
Orange
Canberra
Lithgow Wollongong
Newcastle
Sydney
Port Macquarie
Grafton

Whangarei
Auckland
Manukau
Hamilton Tauranga
Rotorua
North

TASMAN SEA

Height 6000 19700 4000 13100 3000 9800 2000 6500 1500 5000 1000 3300 500 1600 200 700 m ft. 0 200 700 1000 3300 2000 6500 3000 9800 4000 13100 6000 19700 Depth

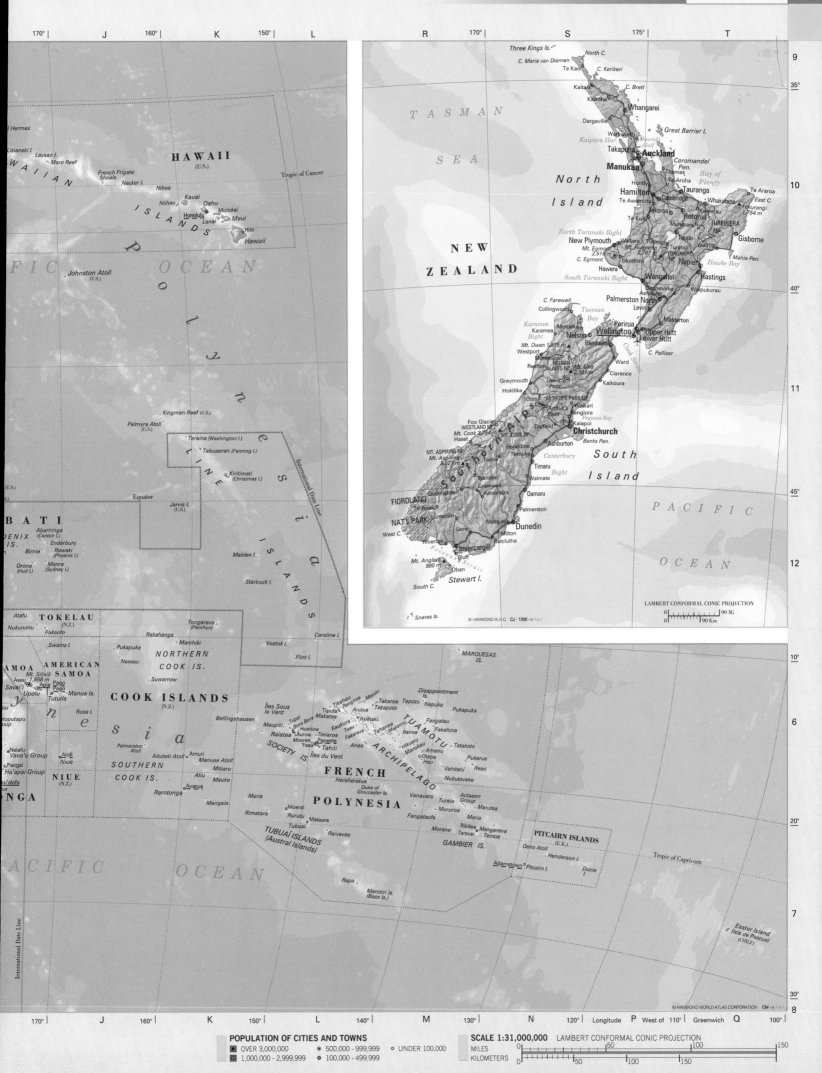

THE WORLD ALMANAC
WORLD ATLAS

North America

The Grand Canyon, one of the deepest canyons in the world, with a depth of 1 mile (1.6 km.), can be seen in this spectacular, west-looking, low-oblique image. The Colorado River cut through rocks billions of years old to create this canyon. The Grand Canyon is 277 miles (466 km.) long and averages nearly 10 miles (16 km.) in width. The snow-covered, forested Kaibab Plateau (north of the canyon) and the Coconino Plateau (south of the canyon) are visible. Western portions of the Painted Desert can be seen east of the canyon where the Little Colorado joins the Colorado River.

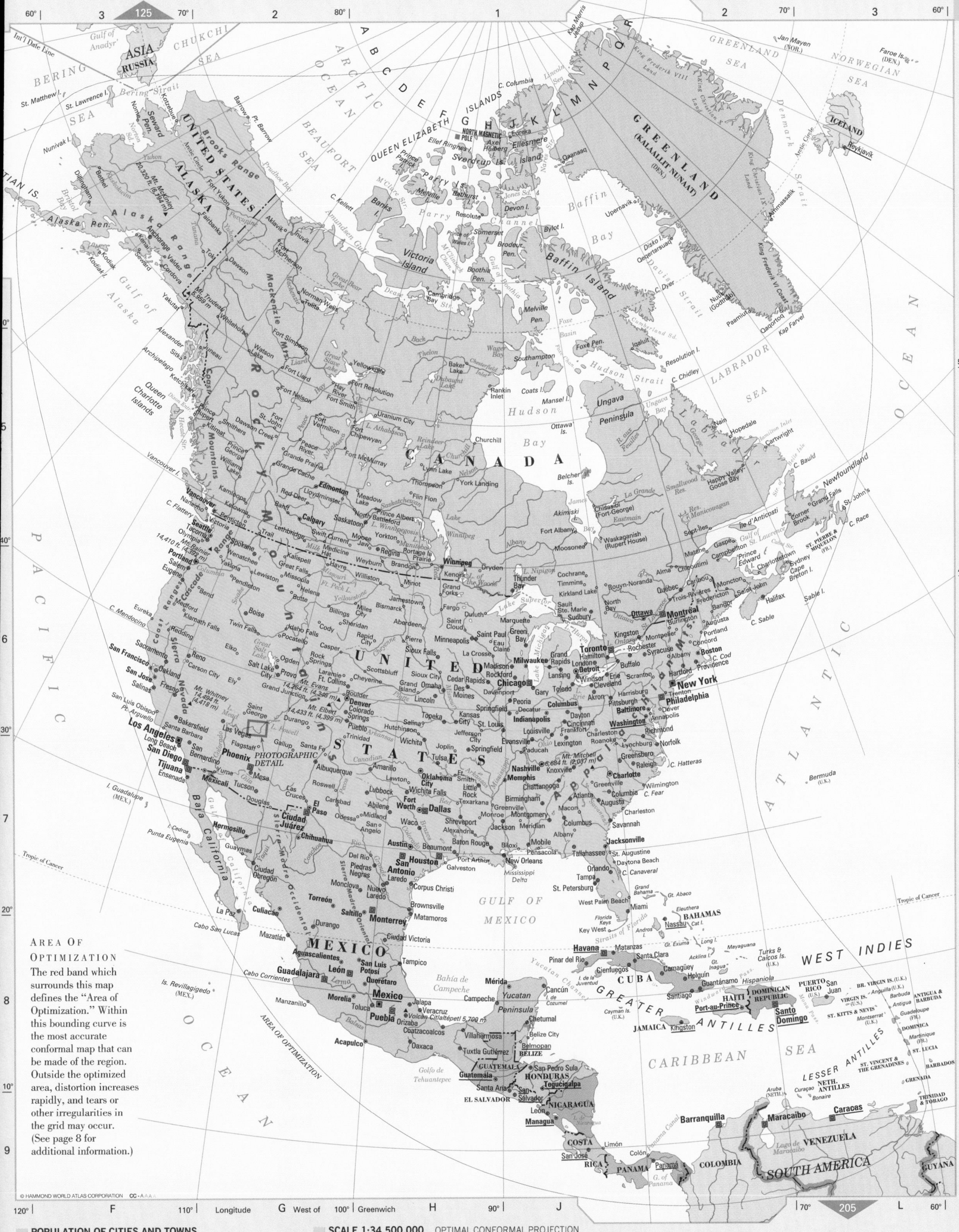

AREA OF OPTIMIZATION

The red band which surrounds this map defines the "Area of Optimization." Within this bounding curve is the most accurate conformal map that can be made of the region. Outside the optimized area, distortion increases rapidly, and tears or other irregularities in the grid may occur. (See page 8 for additional information.)

POPULATION OF CITIES AND TOWNS

◘ OVER 3,000,000	● 500,000 - 999,999
☐ 1,000,000 - 2,999,999	● 100,000 - 499,999
	○ UNDER 100,000

SCALE 1:34,500,000 OPTIMAL CONFORMAL PROJECTION

MILES 0 ... 500 ... 1000 ... 1500
KILOMETERS 0 ... 500 ... 1000 ... 1500

Longitude   West of 100° Greenwich

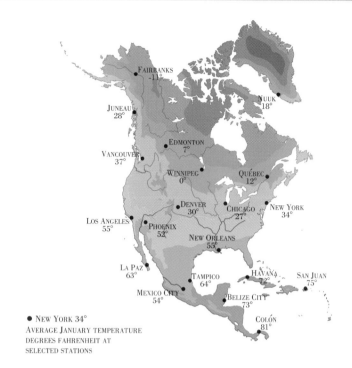

● NEW YORK 34°
AVERAGE JANUARY TEMPERATURE
DEGREES FAHRENHEIT AT
SELECTED STATIONS

● NEW YORK 73°
AVERAGE JULY TEMPERATURE
DEGREES FAHRENHEIT AT
SELECTED STATIONS

AVERAGE JANUARY TEMPERATURE

FAHRENHEIT	CELSIUS	FAHRENHEIT	CELSIUS	FAHRENHEIT	CELSIUS
OVER 68°	OVER 20°	14° TO 32°	-10° TO 0°	-40° TO -22°	-40° TO -30°
50° TO 68°	10° TO 20°	-4° TO 14°	-20° TO -10°	UNDER -40°	UNDER -40°
32° TO 50°	0° TO 10°	-22° TO -4°	-30° TO -20°		

AVERAGE JULY TEMPERATURE

FAHRENHEIT	CELSIUS	FAHRENHEIT	CELSIUS	FAHRENHEIT	CELSIUS
OVER 86°	OVER 30°	50° TO 68°	10° TO 20°	14° TO 32°	-10° TO 0°
68° TO 86°	20° TO 30°	32° TO 50°	0° TO 10°	UNDER 14°	UNDER -10°

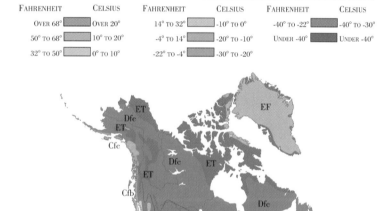

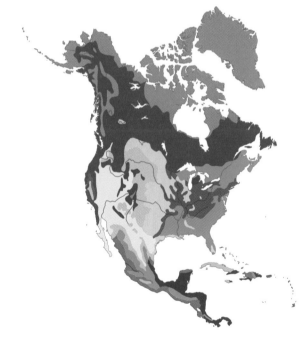

CLIMATE

HUMID TROPICAL
Af NO DRY SEASON
Am SHORT DRY SEASON
Aw DRY WINTER

DRY
BS SEMIARID ⎤ h HOT
BW ARID ⎦ k COLD

HUMID WARM
Cf NO DRY SEASON
Cw DRY WINTER
Cs DRY SUMMER

HUMID COLD
Df NO DRY SEASON
Ds DRY SUMMER

COLD POLAR
ET SHORT COOL SUMMER, LONG COLD WINTER
EF PERPETUAL FROST
a HOT SUMMER
b COOL SUMMER
c SHORT COOL SUMMER

AFTER KOEPPEN-GEIGER

VEGETATION

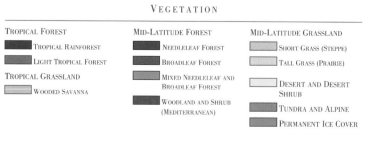

TROPICAL FOREST
TROPICAL RAINFOREST
LIGHT TROPICAL FOREST

TROPICAL GRASSLAND
WOODED SAVANNA

MID-LATITUDE FOREST
NEEDLELEAF FOREST
BROADLEAF FOREST
MIXED NEEDLELEAF AND BROADLEAF FOREST
WOODLAND AND SHRUB (MEDITERRANEAN)

MID-LATITUDE GRASSLAND
SHORT GRASS (STEPPE)
TALL GRASS (PRAIRIE)
DESERT AND DESERT SHRUB
TUNDRA AND ALPINE
PERMANENT ICE COVER

● NEW YORK 42

AVERAGE ANNUAL RAINFALL
IN INCHES AT SELECTED STATIONS

AVERAGE ANNUAL RAINFALL

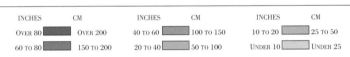

INCHES	CM	INCHES	CM	INCHES	CM
OVER 80	OVER 200	40 TO 60	100 TO 150	10 TO 20	25 TO 50
60 TO 80	150 TO 200	20 TO 40	50 TO 100	UNDER 10	UNDER 25

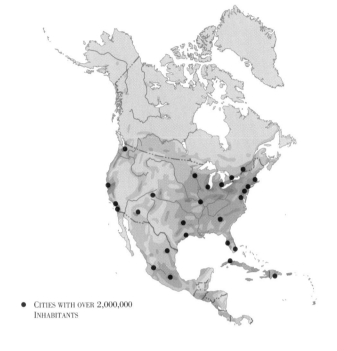

● CITIES WITH OVER 2,000,000
INHABITANTS

POPULATION DISTRIBUTION

DENSITY PER		SQ. MI.	SQ. KM.	SQ. MI.	SQ. KM.
SQ. MI.	SQ. KM.	130 TO 260	50 TO 100	3 TO 25	1 TO 10
OVER 260	OVER 100	25 TO 130	10 TO 50	UNDER 3	UNDER 1

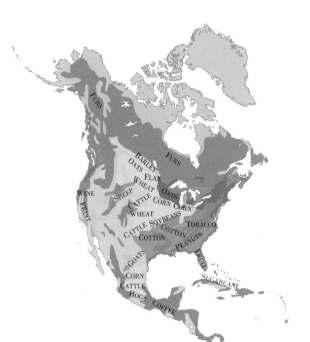

LAND USE

CEREALS, LIVESTOCK	COTTON & SPECIAL CROPS	DAIRY
LIVESTOCK RANCHING & LIMITED AGRICULTURE	DIVERSIFIED TROPICAL CROPS	FORESTS
FRUIT, TRUCK & MIXED FARMING	GENERAL FARMING	UNPRODUCTIVE

MINERAL RESOURCES

ENERGY & FUELS
◆ COAL
▲ NATURAL GAS
● PETROLEUM
■ URANIUM

IRON & FERROALLOYS
1 COBALT
2 IRON ORE
3 MANGANESE
4 MOLYBDENUM
5 NICKEL
6 TUNGSTEN
7 VANADIUM

OTHER MAJOR RESOURCES
1 ANTIMONY
2 ASBESTOS
3 BAUXITE
4 BORAX
5 COPPER
6 FLUORSPAR
7 GOLD
8 GRAPHITE
9 LEAD
10 MERCURY
11 MICA
12 PHOSPHATES
13 PLATINUM
14 POTASH
15 SILVER
16 SULFUR
17 TITANIUM
18 ZINC

Height 6000 19700 4000 13000 2000 6500 1500 5000 1000 3300 500 1600 300 1000 200 700 el. 0 200 700 1000 3300 2000 6500 3000 9900 4000 13000 5000 16400 6000 19700 Depth

Map continued at right

Map continued at left

Map continued at left

POPULATION OF CITIES AND TOWNS

■ OVER 2,000,000	● 500,000 - 999,999	⊚ 50,000 - 99,999
▣ 1,000,000 - 1,999,999	● 100,000 - 499,999	○ UNDER 50,000

SCALE 1:13,800,000   LAMBERT CONFORMAL CONIC PROJECTION

MILES

KILOMETERS

© HAMMOND WORLD ATLAS CORPORATION   CM · A · I

© HAMMOND W.A.C.   CJ · 156 · A · A · A

PACIFIC OCEAN

BRITISH COLUMBIA

Vancouver Island

Vancouver

ALBERTA

SASKATCHEWAN

WASHINGTON

Seattle

Spokane

MONTANA

OREGON

Portland

Salem

Eugene

IDAHO

Boise

WYOMING

SOUTH DAK

NEBR

PACIFIC OCEAN

Sacramento

San Francisco

Oakland

San Jose

NEVADA

Las Vegas

UTAH

Salt Lake City

Provo

COLORADO

Denver

Colorado Springs

Pueblo

CALIFORNIA

Los Angeles

Long Beach

San Diego

Tijuana

Mexicali

ARIZONA

Phoenix

Scottsdale

Mesa

Tucson

NEW MEXICO

Albuquerque

BAJA CALIFORNIA

SONORA

CHIHUAHUA

El Paso

Ciudad Juárez

COAHUILA DE ZARAGOZA

Nuevo Laredo

Torreón

Saltillo

MEXICO

ZACATECAS

SAN LUIS POTOSÍ

Aguascalientes

JALISCO

Guadalajara

León

GUANAJUATO

Querétaro

HAWAII

Kauai

Niihau

Oahu

Honolulu

Molokai

Lanai

Kahoolawe

Maui

HALEAKALA

Hawaii

Mauna Kea

Hilo

PACIFIC OCEAN

Kauai Channel

Kaiwi Channel

Alenuihaha Channel

Oahu (inset)

Kauai Channel

PACIFIC OCEAN

Kaena Pt.

HONOLULU

Pearl City

Oahu

Honolulu

Diamond Head Crater

Koko Head

© HAMMOND W.A.C. CJ - 1158 - A

© HAMMOND W.A.C. CJ - 1157 - A

Height 6000 19700 4000 13000 2000 6500 1500 5000 900 3300 600 2000 300 1000 200 700 0 El. 0 200 700 600 1600 900 3300 2000 6500 4000 13000 6000 19700 Depth

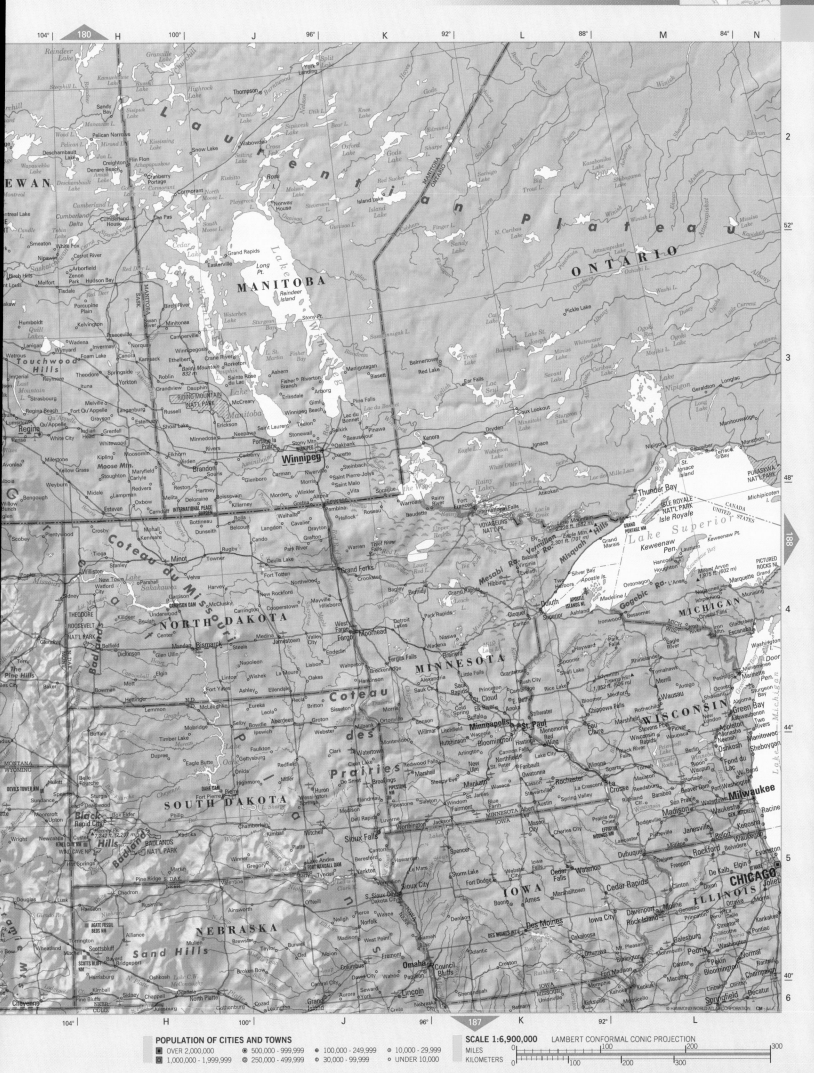

POPULATION OF CITIES AND TOWNS

◼ OVER 2,000,000	◉ 500,000 - 999,999
▣ 1,000,000 - 1,999,999	◎ 250,000 - 499,999

● 100,000 - 249,999	◦ 10,000 - 29,999
◦ 30,000 - 99,999	◦ UNDER 10,000

SCALE 1:6,900,000   LAMBERT CONFORMAL CONIC PROJECTION

MILES   0   100   200   300
KILOMETERS   0   100   200   300

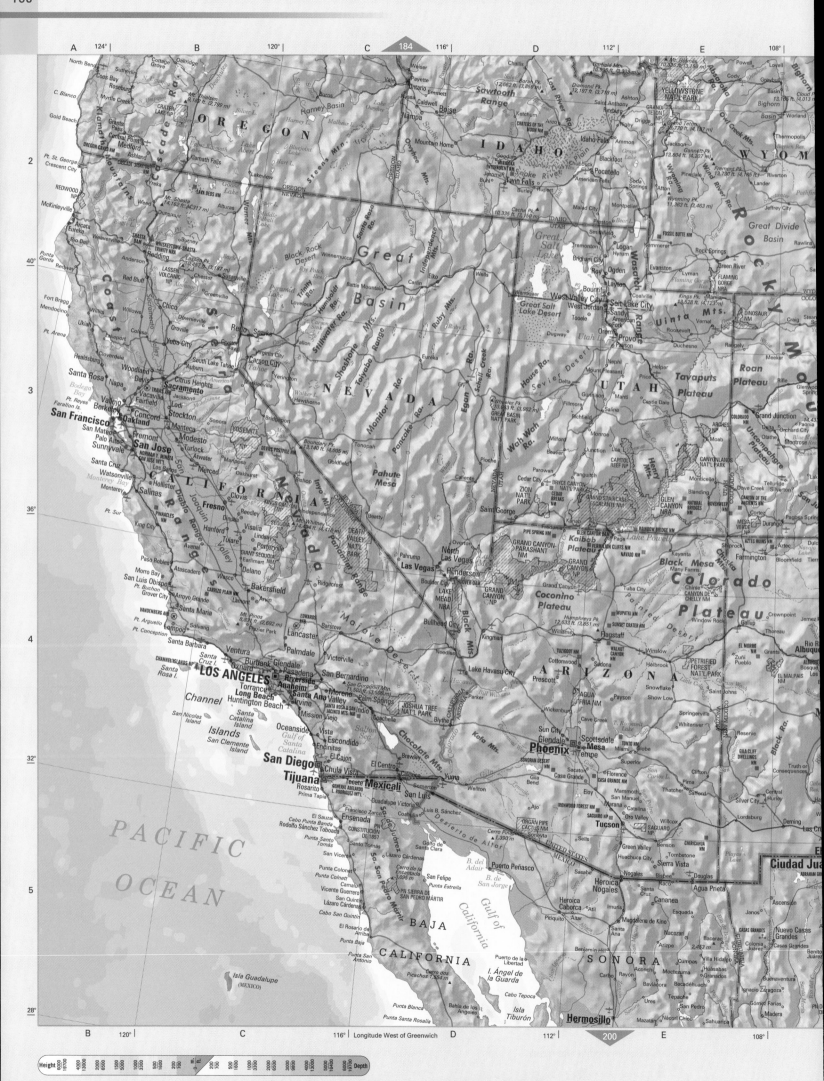

A 124° B 120° C 116° D 112° E 108°

OREGON

IDAHO

WYOM

2

REDWOOD

40°

Great

Basin

NEVADA

3

San Francisco
Oakland

San Jose

36°

CALIFORNIA

UTAH

Tavaputs
Plateau

Roan
Plateau

ROCKY MOU

NEVADA

SIERRA

Las Vegas

Colorado

Plateau

Coconino
Plateau

4

LOS ANGELES

Mojave Desert

ARIZONA

32°

San Diego
Tijuana

Mexicali

Phoenix
Tempe

Mesa

Tucson

Ciudad Jua

PACIFIC

OCEAN

5

BAJA

Gulf of
California

SONORA

CALIFORNIA

Hermosillo

28°

B 120° C 116° Longitude West of Greenwich D 112° E 108°

Height 6000 19700 4000 13000 2000 6500 1500 5000 1000 3300 500 1600 200 700 100 330 0 0 200 700 1000 3300 2000 6500 3000 9900 4000 13000 5000 16400 6000 19700 Depth

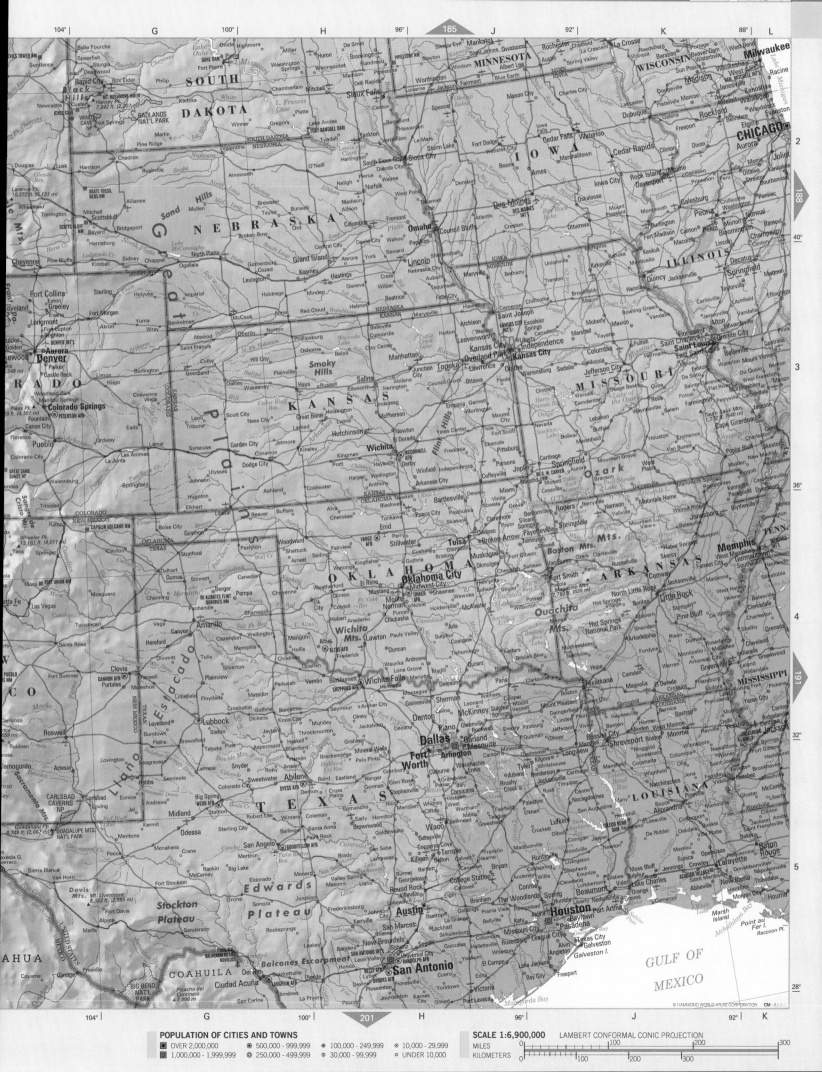

POPULATION OF CITIES AND TOWNS

■ OVER 2,000,000   ◉ 500,000 - 999,999   ◉ 100,000 - 249,999   ◦ 10,000 - 29,999
▣ 1,000,000 - 1,999,999   ◉ 250,000 - 499,999   ◦ 30,000 - 99,999   ◦ UNDER 10,000

SCALE 1:6,900,000   LAMBERT CONFORMAL CONIC PROJECTION

MILES 0   50   100   200   300
KILOMETERS 0   100   200   300

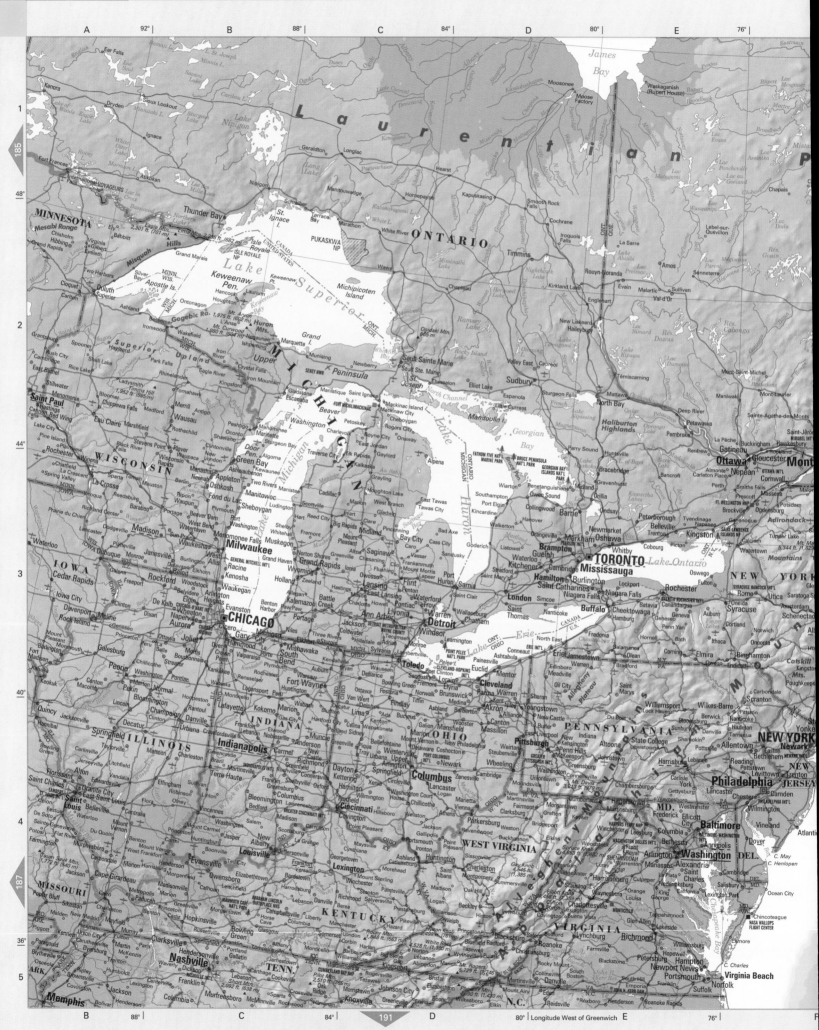

POPULATION OF CITIES AND TOWNS

■ OVER 2,000,000
□ 1,000,000 - 1,999,999
◉ 500,000 - 999,999
◎ 250,000 - 499,999
● 100,000 - 249,999
◉ 30,000 - 99,999
◦ 10,000 - 29,999
○ UNDER 10,000

SCALE 1:6,900,000   LAMBERT CONFORMAL CONIC PROJECTION

MILES
KILOMETERS

© HAMMOND WORLD ATLAS CORPORATION   CM - A·A·A·A

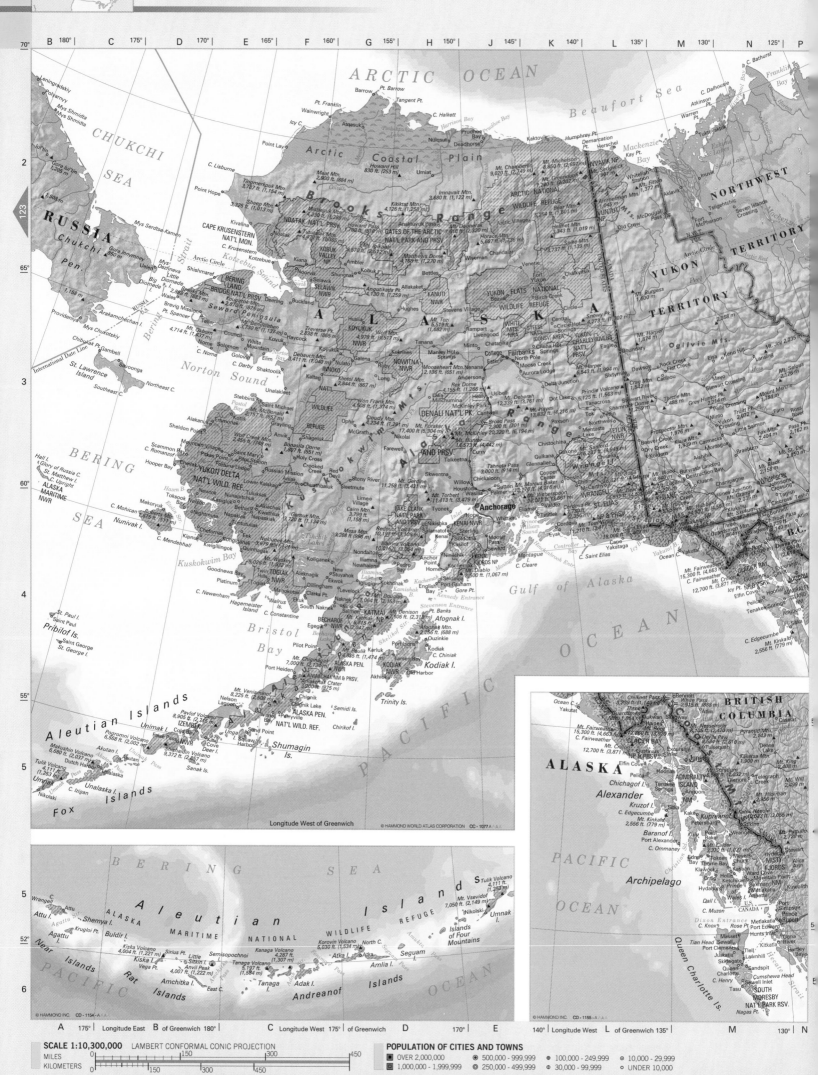

SCALE 1:10,300,000 LAMBERT CONFORMAL CONIC PROJECTION

MILES 0 150 300 450

KILOMETERS 0 150 300 450

POPULATION OF CITIES AND TOWNS

■ OVER 2,000,000	● 500,000-999,999	● 100,000-249,999	◦ 10,000-29,999
▣ 1,000,000-1,999,999	● 250,000-499,999	● 30,000-99,999	◦ UNDER 10,000

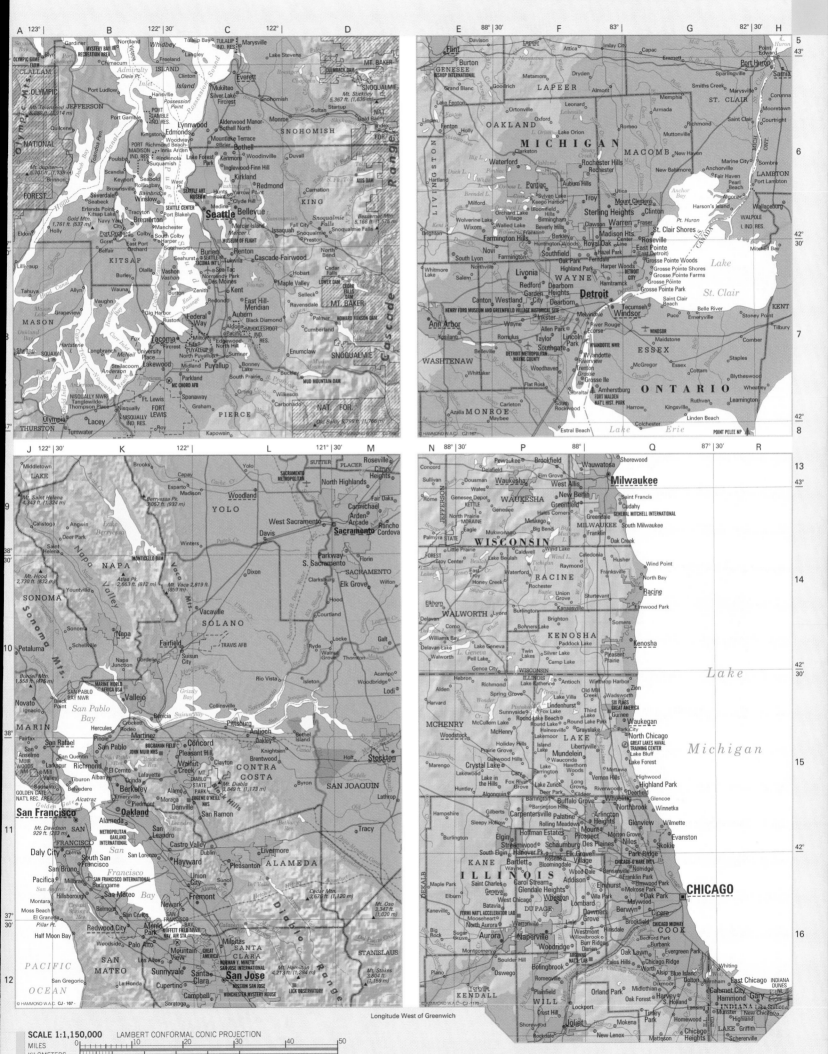

Los Angeles – San Diego

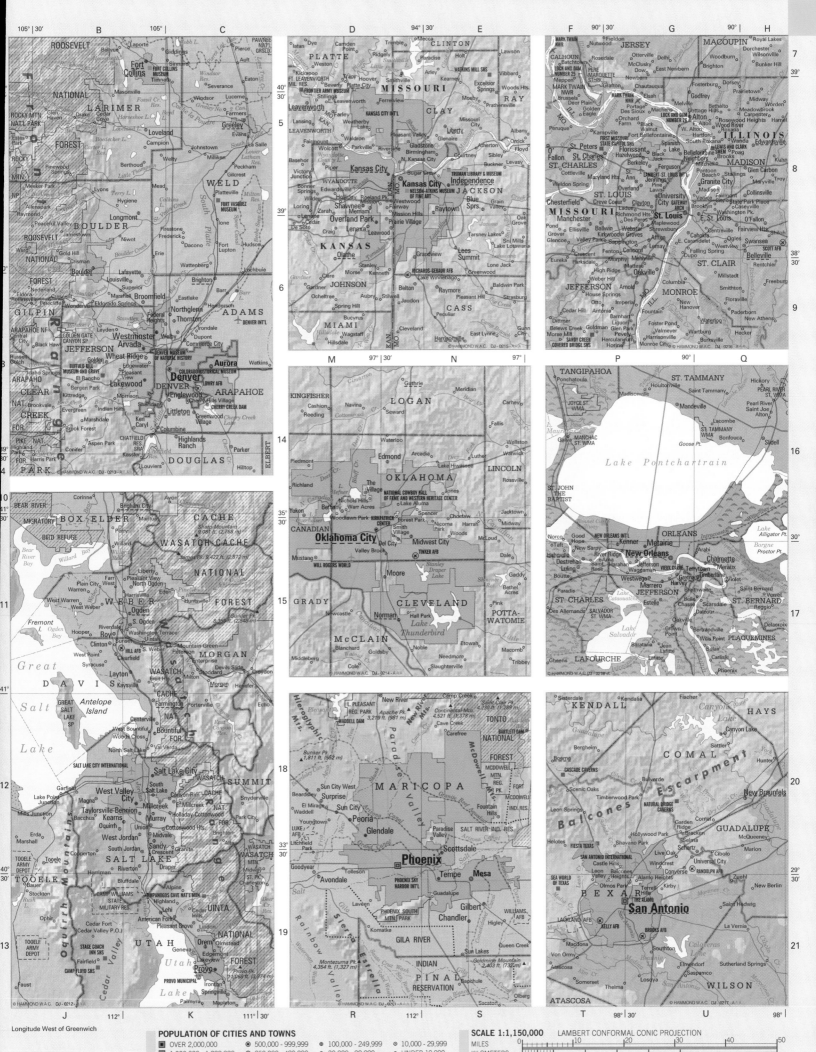

POPULATION OF CITIES AND TOWNS

■ OVER 2,000,000	● 500,000 - 999,999	● 100,000 - 249,999	● 10,000 - 29,999
■ 1,000,000 - 1,999,999	● 250,000 - 499,999	● 30,000 - 99,999	○ UNDER 10,000

SCALE 1:1,150,000   LAMBERT CONFORMAL CONIC PROJECTION

MILES

KILOMETERS

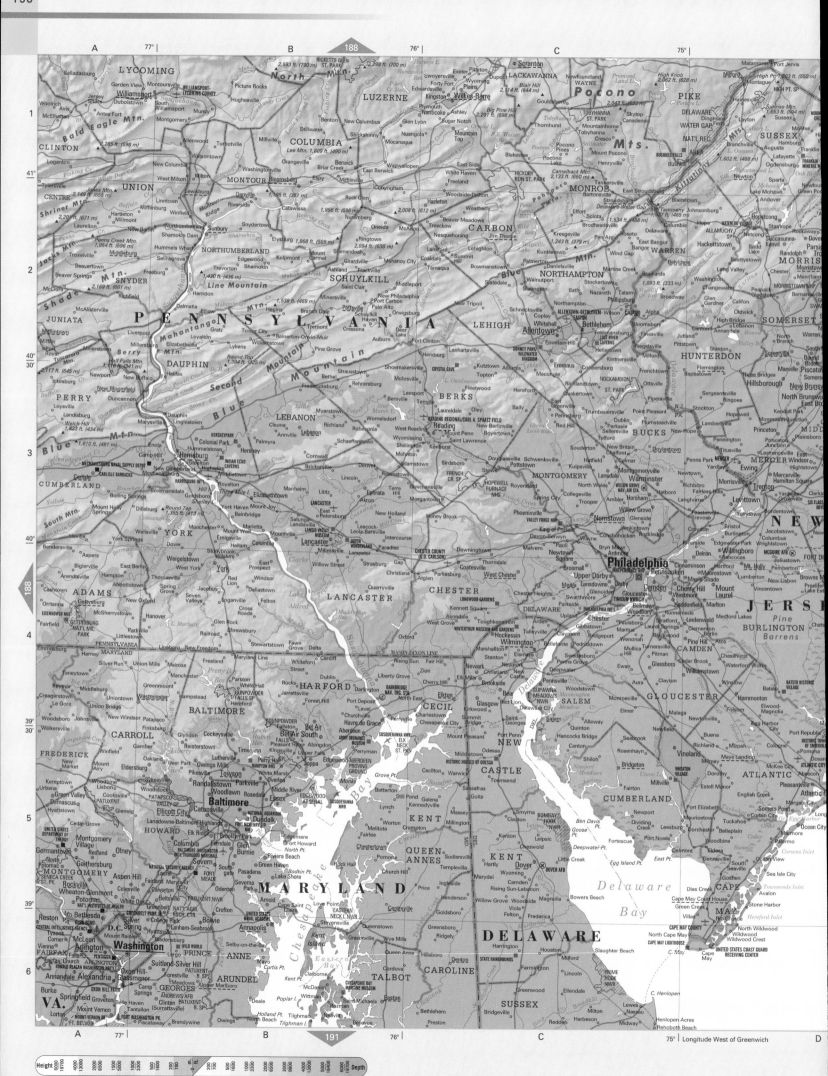

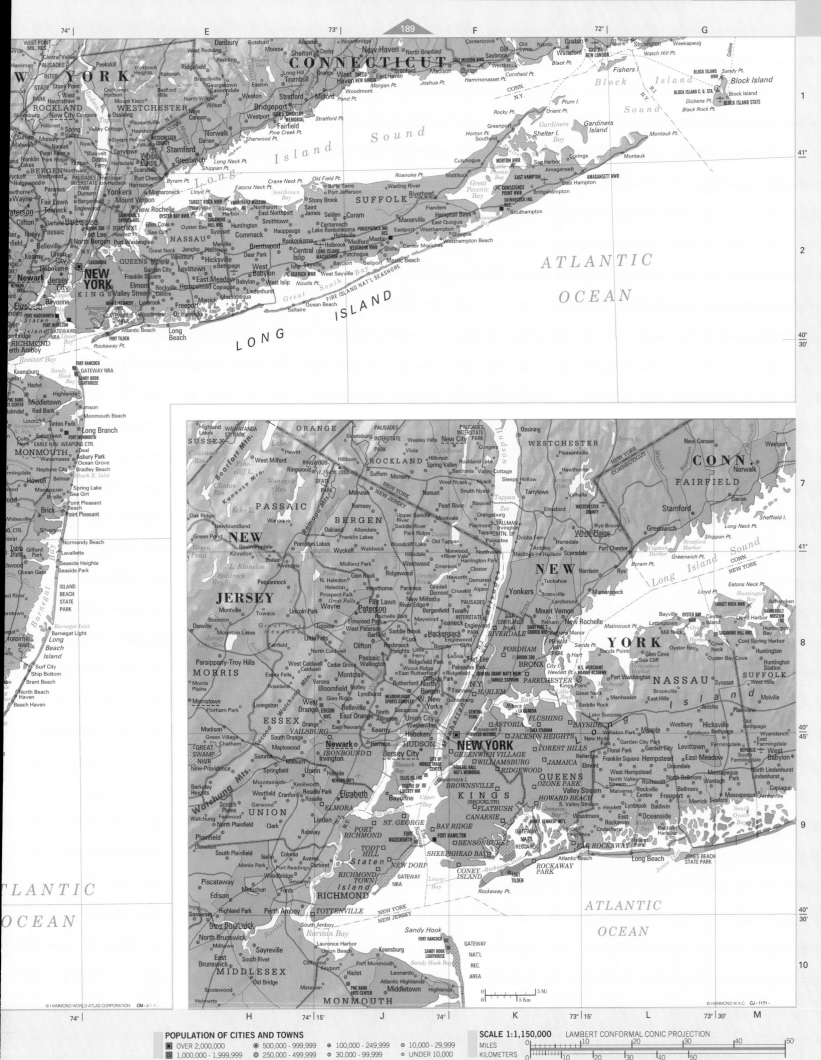

POPULATION OF CITIES AND TOWNS

- OVER 2,000,000
- 1,000,000 - 1,999,999
- 500,000 - 999,999
- 250,000 - 499,999
- 100,000 - 249,999
- 30,000 - 99,999
- 10,000 - 29,999
- UNDER 10,000

SCALE 1:1,150,000   LAMBERT CONFORMAL CONIC PROJECTION

MILES

KILOMETERS

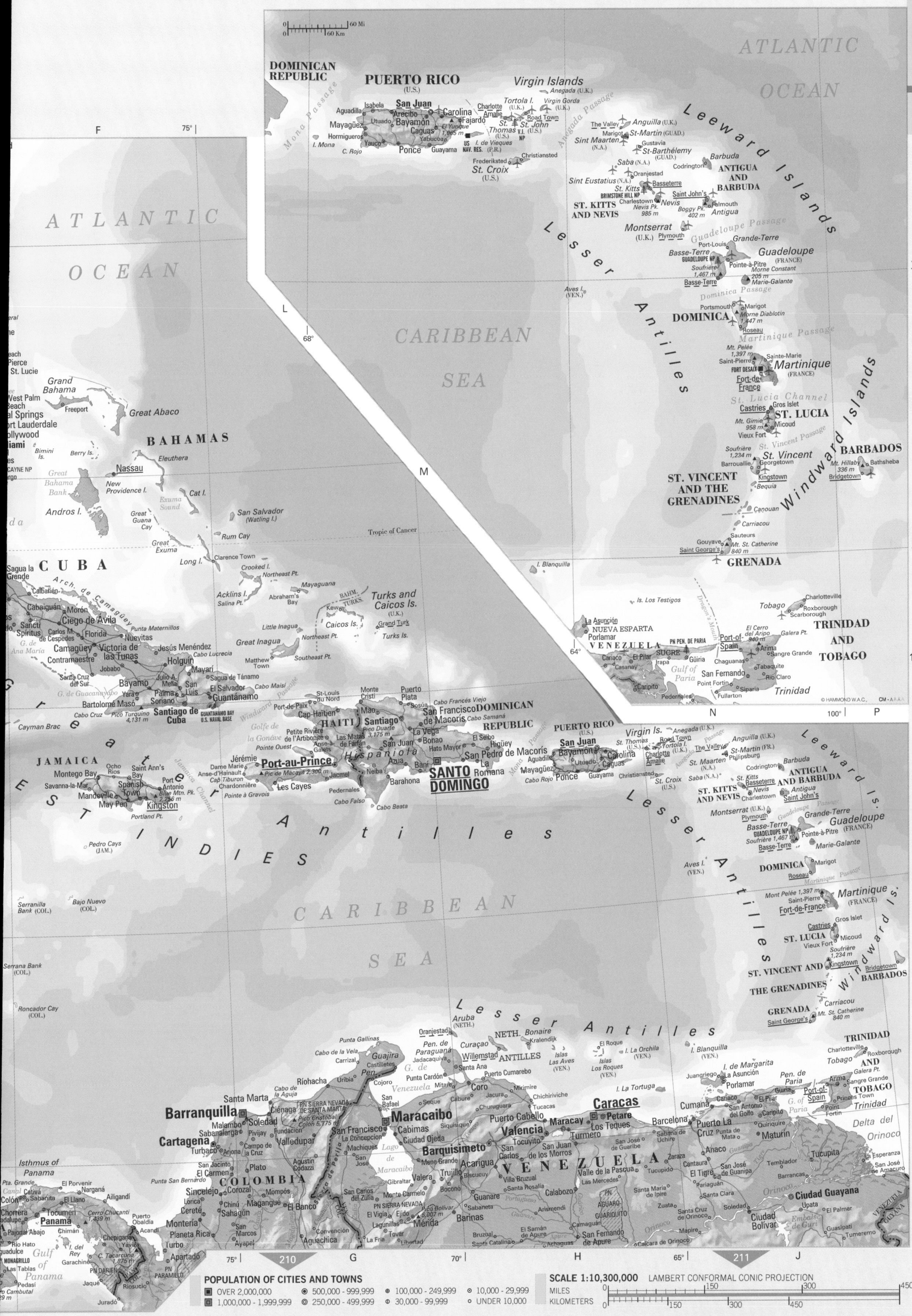

ATLANTIC OCEAN

DOMINICAN REPUBLIC

PUERTO RICO (U.S.)

Virgin Islands

Leeward Islands

Aguadilla · Isabela · Arecibo · San Juan · Carolina · Charlotte Amalie · St. Thomas · St. John · Road Town · Tortola I. · Virgin Gorda · Anegada (U.K.)

Mayagüez · Bayamón · Caguas · Fajardo

The Valley · Anguilla (U.K.)

Yauco · Ponce · Guayama · Yabucoa

Sint Maarten (N.A.) · St-Martin (GUAD.) · Gustavia · St-Barthélemy (GUAD.)

I. Mona · C. Rojo · US I. de Vieques NAV. RES. (P.R.)

Saba (N.A.) · Oranjestad · Codrington · Barbuda

Christiansted · St. Croix (U.S.) · Frederiksted

Sint Eustatius (N.A.) · St. Kitts · BRIMSTONE HILL NP · Nevis · Saint John's · ANTIGUA AND BARBUDA

ST. KITTS AND NEVIS · Charlestown · Nevis Pk. 985 m · Boggy Pk. 402 m · Falmouth · Antigua

Montserrat (U.K.) · Plymouth

Port-Louis · Grande-Terre · Guadeloupe (FRANCE)

Basse-Terre · GUADELOUPE NP · Pointe-à-Pitre · Morne Constant 205 m

Soufrière 1,467 m · Basse-Terre · Marie-Galante

Aves I. (VEN.)

Portsmouth · Marigot · Morne Diablotin 1,447 m · DOMINICA · Roseau

Dominica Passage

Martinique Passage

Mt. Pelée 1,397 m · Sainte-Marie · Saint-Pierre · FORT DÉSAIX · Martinique (FRANCE) · Fort-de-France

St. Lucia Channel

Castries · Gros Islet · Mt. Gimie 958 m · Micoud · ST. LUCIA · Vieux Fort

Soufrière 1,234 m · St. Vincent · Georgetown · BARBADOS · Mt. Hillaby 336 m · Bathsheba

Barrouallie · Kingstown · Bridgetown

ST. VINCENT AND THE GRENADINES · Bequia · Canouan · Carriacou · Sauteurs

Gouyave · Mt. St. Catherine 840 m · Saint George's · GRENADA

I. Blanquilla (VEN.)

CARIBBEAN SEA

Lesser Antilles · Windward Islands

ATLANTIC OCEAN

Vero Beach · Ft. Pierce · St. Lucie · West Palm Beach · Ft. Lauderdale · Hollywood · Miami · Bimini Is. · BISCAYNE NP · Largo

Grand Bahama · Freeport · Great Abaco · Eleuthera

BAHAMAS · Nassau · New Providence I. · Berry Is. · Cat I.

Great Bahama Bank · Andros I. · Exuma Sound · Great Guana Cay · Great Exuma · Long I. · San Salvador (Watling I.) · Rum Cay

Tropic of Cancer

Clarence Town · Crooked I. · Northeast Pt. · Mayaguana

Acklins I. · Salina Pt. · BAHM. TURKS. · Kew · Turks and Caicos Is. (U.K.) · Abraham's Bay · Caicos Is. · Grand Turk · Turks Is.

Great Inagua · Little Inagua · Matthew Town · Southeast Pt.

Is. Los Testigos · Tobago · Charlotteville · Roxborough · Scarborough

Sagua la Grande · Caibarién · Calbañen · Sancti Spíritus · Carlos M. de Céspedes · Ciego de Ávila · Morón · Punta Maternillos

CUBA · Camagüey · Victoria de las Tunas · Jesús Menéndez · Nuevitas · Holguín · Mayarí · Sagua de Tánamo · Cabo Maisí

Contramaestre · Jobabo · Julio A. Mella · San Luis · El Salvador · Guantánamo · GUANTÁNAMO BAY U.S. NAVAL BASE

Santa Cruz del Sur · G. de Guacanayabo · Yara · Bayamo · Palma Soriano · Santiago de Cuba

Bartolomé Masó · Cabo Cruz · Pico Turquino 4,131 m

Cayman Brac

La Asunción · NUEVA ESPARTA · Porlamar · El Cerro del Aripo 940 m · Galera Pt. · TRINIDAD AND TOBAGO

VENEZUELA · SUCRE · Port-of-Spain · Arima · Sangre Grande

Cariaco · El Pilar · Irapa · Güiria · Chaguanas · Tabaquite · Rio Claro

Casanay · Gulf of Paria · Point Fortin · Siparia · Fullarton · Trinidad · Caripito · Pedernales

© HAMMOND W.A.C. · CM-AAAA

JAMAICA · Montego Bay · Ocho Rios · Saint Ann's Bay · Port Antonio · Blue Mtn. Pk. 2,256 m · Spanish Town · Kingston · Portland Pt.

Savanna-la-Mar · Mandeville · May Pen · Pedro Cays (JAM.)

Serranilla Bank (COL.) · Bajo Nuevo (COL.) · Serrana Bank (COL.) · Roncador Cay (COL.)

West Indies

St-Louis du Nord · Monte Cristi · Puerto Plata · Cabo Francés Viejo · Cabo Samaná

Cap-Haïtien · Mao · Santiago · Pico Duarte 3,175 m · San Francisco de Macorís · DOMINICAN REPUBLIC

HAITI · Golfe de la Gonâve · Petite Rivière de l'Artibonite · La Vega · Bonao · El Seibo · Higüey

Pointe Ouest · Jérémie · Anse-à-Galets · San Juan · Hato Mayor · La Romana

Dame Marie · Port-au-Prince · Las Matas de Farfán · Azua · Bani · San Pedro de Macorís

Anse-d'Hainault · Cap Tiburon · Jacmel · Neiba · Barahona · SANTO DOMINGO

Chardonnière · Les Cayes · Pedernales · Cabo Falso · Cabo Beata

Hispaniola

Windward Passage · Great Antilles

CARIBBEAN SEA

Lesser Antilles

VENEZUELA · COLOMBIA

Aruba (NETH.) · Oranjestad · Curaçao · NETH. Bonaire · Willemstad · ANTILLES · Kralendijk · El Roque · I. La Orchila (VEN.) · I. Blanquilla (VEN.)

Punta Gallinas · Pen. de Paraguaná · Islas Las Aves (VEN.) · Islas Los Roques (VEN.) · I. La Tortuga (VEN.) · TRINIDAD AND TOBAGO

Barranquilla · Cartagena · Santa Marta · Ciénaga · PN SIERRA NEVADA DE SANTA MARTA · Pico Cristóbal Colón 5,775 m · Riohacha · Maracaibo · Cabimas · CARACAS · Petare · Maracay · Cumaná · Porlamar

Valledupar · Lago de Maracaibo · Barquisimeto · Valencia · Los Teques · Barcelona · Puerto La Cruz · Maturín · Ciudad Guayana

VENEZUELA · Barinas · Orinoco · Ciudad Bolívar · Ciudad Guayana

Panama · Gulf of Panama · Isthmus of Panama

POPULATION OF CITIES AND TOWNS

OVER 2,000,000 · 1,000,000 - 1,999,999 · 500,000 - 999,999 · 250,000 - 499,999 · 100,000 - 249,999 · 30,000 - 99,999 · 10,000 - 29,999 · UNDER 10,000

SCALE 1:10,300,000 · LAMBERT CONFORMAL CONIC PROJECTION

MILES · KILOMETERS · 0 · 150 · 300 · 450

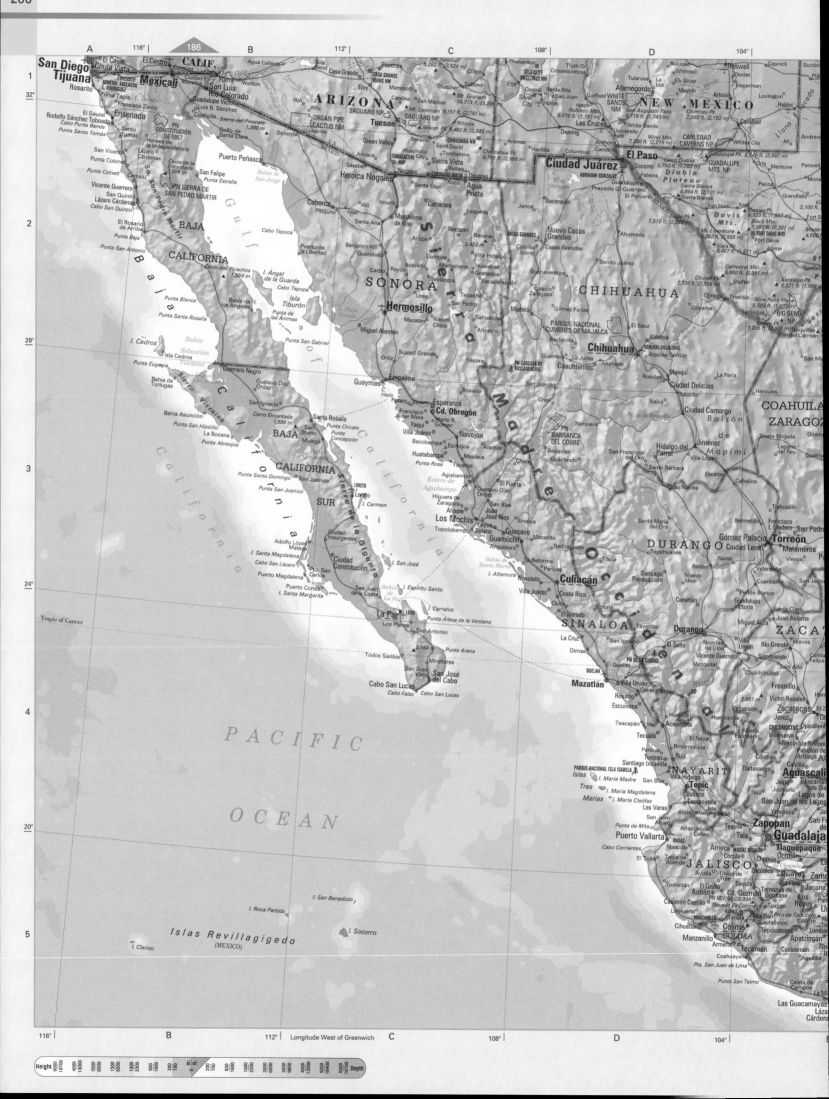

A   116°   B   112°   C   108°   D   104°

PACIFIC

OCEAN

San Diego
Tijuana

Mexicali

ARIZONA

Tucson

NEW MEXICO

El Paso

Ciudad Juárez

CALIF.

BAJA

CALIFORNIA

SONORA

Hermosillo

CHIHUAHUA

Chihuahua

Guaymas

Cd. Obregón

BAJA

CALIFORNIA

SUR

Navojoa

Los Mochis

COAHUILA
ZARAGOZA

DURANGO

Gómez Palacio
Torreón
Ciudad Lerdo

Culiacán

SINALOA

Durango

ZACAT

Tropic of Cancer

La Paz

Cabo San Lucas
San José
del Cabo

Mazatlán

Zacatecas

Aguascali

NAYARIT

Tepic

Zapopan
Guadalaja
Tlaquepaque
JALISCO

Puerto Vallarta

Colima
COLIMA
Manzanillo

P A C I F I C

O C E A N

I. San Benedicto

Roca Partida

Islas Revillagigedo
(MEXICO)

I. Socorro

I. Clarion

116°   B   112°   Longitude West of Greenwich   C   108°   D   104°

Height   Depth

POPULATION OF CITIES AND TOWNS

■ OVER 2,000,000	● 500,000 - 999,999 ○ 100,000 - 249,999 ○ 10,000 - 29,999
■ 1,000,000 - 1,999,999	● 250,000 - 499,999 ○ 30,000 - 99,999 ○ UNDER 10,000

SCALE 1:6,900,000   LAMBERT CONFORMAL CONIC PROJECTION

MILES

KILOMETERS

GULF OF MEXICO

Bahía de Campeche

Golfo de Tehuantepec

PACIFIC OCEAN

MEXICO

GUATEMALA

BELIZE

HONDURAS

EL SALVADOR

Yucatan Peninsula

QUINTANA ROO

CAMPECHE

YUCATÁN

CHIAPAS

© HAMMOND WORLD ATLAS CORPORATION   CM -1067 - A

SCALE 1:6,900,000   LAMBERT CONFORMAL CONIC PROJECTION

MILES

KILOMETERS

0   100   200   300

Longitude West of Greenwich

POPULATION OF CITIES AND TOWNS

■ OVER 2,000,000
◉ 500,000 - 999,999
◉ 100,000 - 249,999
○ 10,000 - 29,999
▣ 1,000,000 - 1,999,999
◉ 250,000 - 499,999
◦ 30,000 - 99,999
○ UNDER 10,000

South America

The highest mountain peak in the Americas, Mount Aconcagua, at 22,831 feet (6959 m.) above sea level, is visible in this northeast-looking, low-oblique image. Several major snow-covered peaks with summits exceeding 20,000 feet (6100 m.) rise along the north-south axis of the cohesive and massive structure of the Andes Mountains through this area of Argentina and Chile. The narrow east-west valley immediately south of Mount Aconcagua contains a section of the American Highway that connects Mendoza, Argentina, with Santiago, Chile.

AREA OF OPTIMIZATION
The red band which surrounds this map defines the "Area of Optimization." Within this bounding curve is the most accurate conformal map that can be made of the region. Outside the optimized area, distortion increases rapidly, and tears or other irregularities in the grid may occur. (See page 8 for additional information.)

POPULATION OF CITIES AND TOWNS
■ OVER 3,000,000
■ 1,000,000 - 2,999,999
● 500,000 - 999,999
● 100,000 - 499,999
○ UNDER 100,000

SCALE 1:27,600,000   OPTIMAL CONFORMAL PROJECTION
MILES 0 400 800 1200
KILOMETERS 0 400 800 1200

Longitude West G of Greenwich

© HAMMOND WORLD ATLAS CORPORATION   CM·A·A·A

AVERAGE JANUARY TEMPERATURE

FAHRENHEIT	CELSIUS	FAHRENHEIT	CELSIUS	FAHRENHEIT	CELSIUS
OVER 86°	OVER 30°	50° TO 68°	10° TO 20°	UNDER 32°	UNDER 0°
68° TO 86°	20° TO 30°	32° TO 50°	0° TO 10°		

AVERAGE JULY TEMPERATURE

FAHRENHEIT	CELSIUS	FAHRENHEIT	CELSIUS	FAHRENHEIT	CELSIUS
OVER 86°	OVER 30°	50° TO 68°	10° TO 20°	UNDER 32°	UNDER 0°
68° TO 86°	20° TO 30°	32° TO 50°	0° TO 10°		

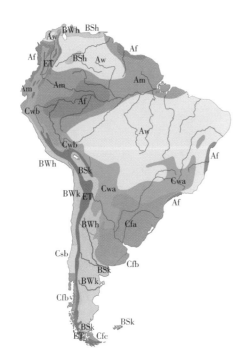

CLIMATE

HUMID TROPICAL
- Af NO DRY SEASON
- Am SHORT DRY SEASON
- Aw DRY WINTER

DRY
- BS SEMIARID
- BW ARID
  - h HOT
  - k COLD

HUMID WARM
- Cf NO DRY SEASON
- Cw DRY WINTER
- Cs DRY SUMMER

COLD POLAR
- ET SHORT COOL SUMMER, LONG COLD WINTER

- a HOT SUMMER
- b COOL SUMMER
- c SHORT COOL SUMMER
- AFTER KOEPPEN-GEIGER

VEGETATION

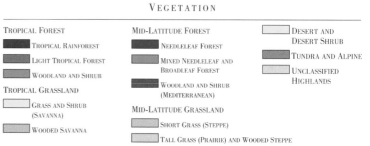

TROPICAL FOREST
- TROPICAL RAINFOREST
- LIGHT TROPICAL FOREST
- WOODLAND AND SHRUB

TROPICAL GRASSLAND
- GRASS AND SHRUB (SAVANNA)
- WOODED SAVANNA

MID-LATITUDE FOREST
- NEEDLELEAF FOREST
- MIXED NEEDLELEAF AND BROADLEAF FOREST
- WOODLAND AND SHRUB (MEDITERRANEAN)

MID-LATITUDE GRASSLAND
- SHORT GRASS (STEPPE)
- TALL GRASS (PRAIRIE) AND WOODED STEPPE

- DESERT AND DESERT SHRUB
- TUNDRA AND ALPINE
- UNCLASSIFIED HIGHLANDS

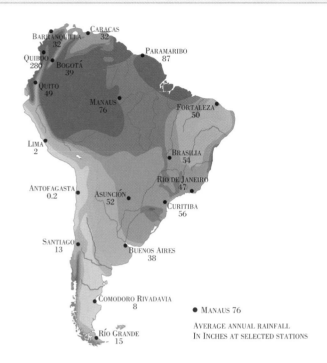

● MANAUS 76

AVERAGE ANNUAL RAINFALL
IN INCHES AT SELECTED STATIONS

AVERAGE ANNUAL RAINFALL

INCHES	CM	INCHES	CM	INCHES	CM
OVER 80	OVER 200	40 TO 60	100 TO 150	10 TO 20	25 TO 50
60 TO 80	150 TO 200	20 TO 40	50 TO 100	UNDER 10	UNDER 25

● CITIES WITH OVER 1,000,000
INHABITANTS

POPULATION DISTRIBUTION

DENSITY PER		SQ. MI.	SQ. KM.	SQ. MI.	SQ. KM.
SQ. MI.	SQ. KM.	130 TO 260	50 TO 100	3 TO 25	1 TO 10
OVER 260	OVER 100	25 TO 130	10 TO 50	UNDER 3	UNDER 1

LAND USE

▭ CEREALS, LIVESTOCK	▭ DIVERSIFIED TROPICAL CROPS	▭ FORESTS
▭ LIVESTOCK & MIXED FARMING	▭ LIVESTOCK GRAZING & RANCHING	▭ NONPRODUCTIVE
▭ TRUCK FARMING, SPECIAL CROPS		

MINERAL RESOURCES

ENERGY & FUELS
◆ COAL
▲ NATURAL GAS
● PETROLEUM
▪ URANIUM

IRON & FERROALLOYS
1 CHROMIUM
2 IRON ORE
3 MANGANESE
4 MOLYBDENUM
5 NICKEL
6 TUNGSTEN

OTHER MAJOR RESOURCES
1 ANTIMONY
2 ASBESTOS
3 BAUXITE
4 COPPER
5 DIAMONDS
6 GOLD
7 IODINE
8 LEAD
9 MICA
10 NITRATES
11 PHOSPHATES
12 SILVER
13 TIN
14 TITANIUM
15 ZINC

POPULATION OF CITIES AND TOWNS

- ☐ OVER 2,000,000
- ◉ 500,000 - 999,999
- ○ 50,000 - 99,999
- ☐ 1,000,000 - 1,999,999
- ● 100,000 - 499,999
- ○ UNDER 50,000

SCALE 1:14,900,000   LAMBERT CONFORMAL CONIC PROJECTION

MILES   200   400   600
KILOMETERS   200   400   600

© HAMMOND WORLD ATLAS CORPORATION   CM-2107-A-AA

Colombia, Venezuela, Ecuador

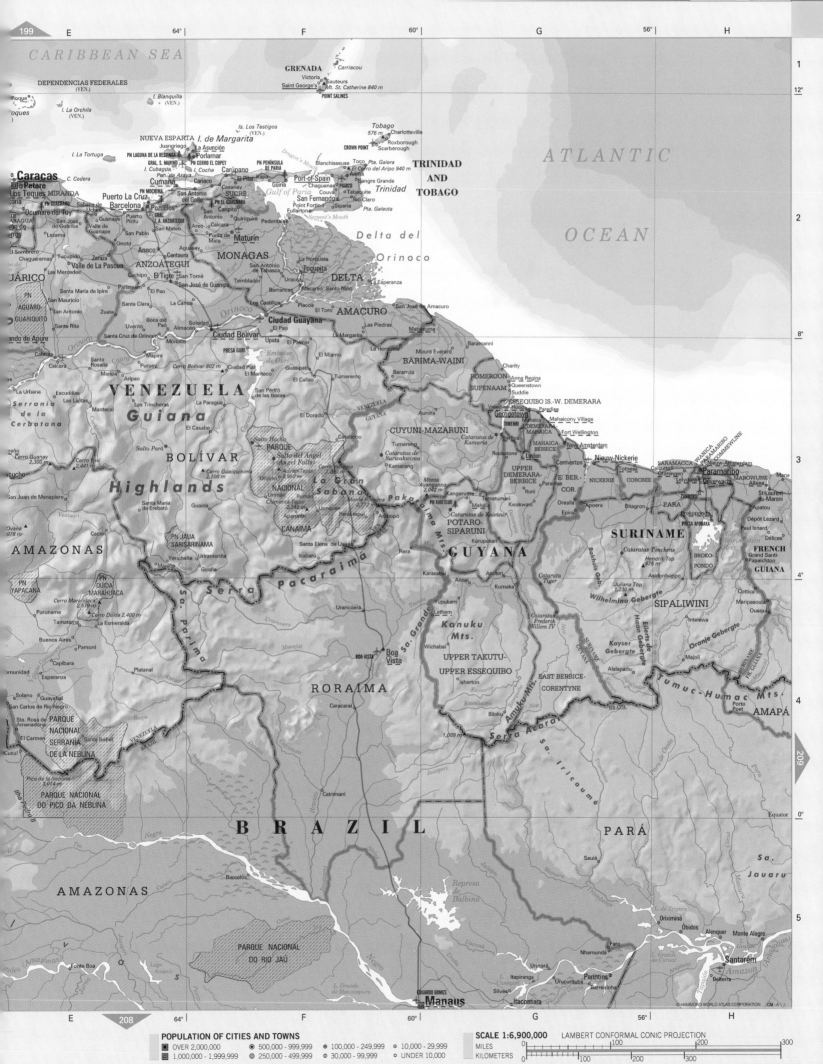

Northeastern Brazil

Southeastern Brazil

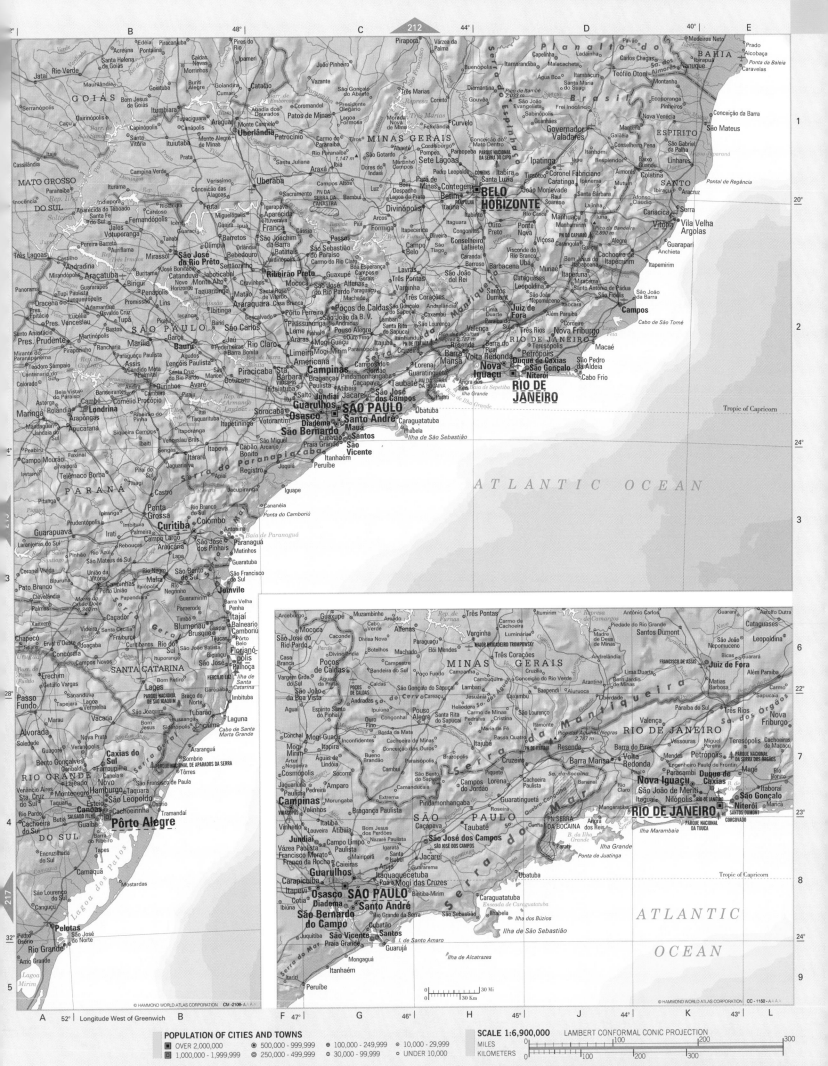

Longitude West of Greenwich

POPULATION OF CITIES AND TOWNS

■ OVER 2,000,000	● 500,000 - 999,999	● 100,000 - 249,999	◉ 10,000 - 29,999
▣ 1,000,000 - 1,999,999	● 250,000 - 499,999	◉ 30,000 - 99,999	○ UNDER 10,000

SCALE 1:6,900,000   LAMBERT CONFORMAL CONIC PROJECTION

MILES

KILOMETERS

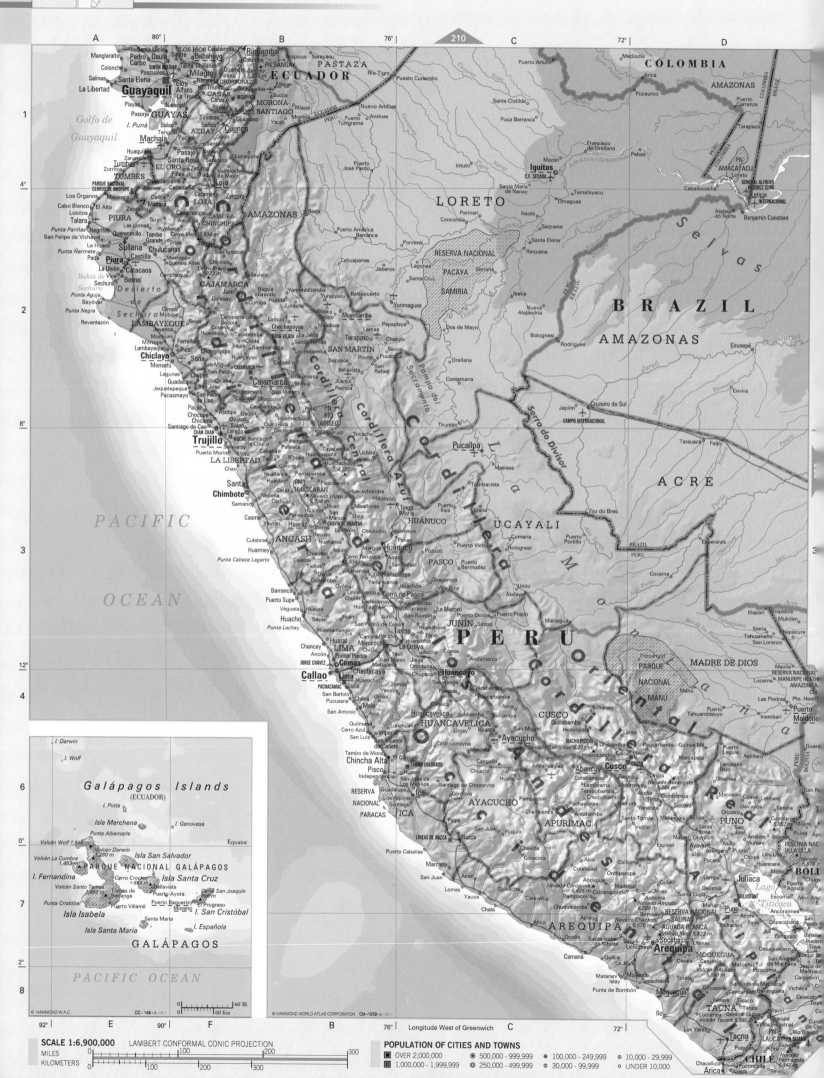

SCALE 1:6,900,000   LAMBERT CONFORMAL CONIC PROJECTION

MILES   0   100   200   300

KILOMETERS   0   100   200   300

POPULATION OF CITIES AND TOWNS

■ OVER 2,000,000	◉ 500,000 - 999,999	● 100,000 - 249,999	• 10,000 - 29,999
▣ 1,000,000 - 1,999,999	◉ 250,000 - 499,999	● 30,000 - 99,999	∘ UNDER 10,000

Longitude West of Greenwich

Southern South America

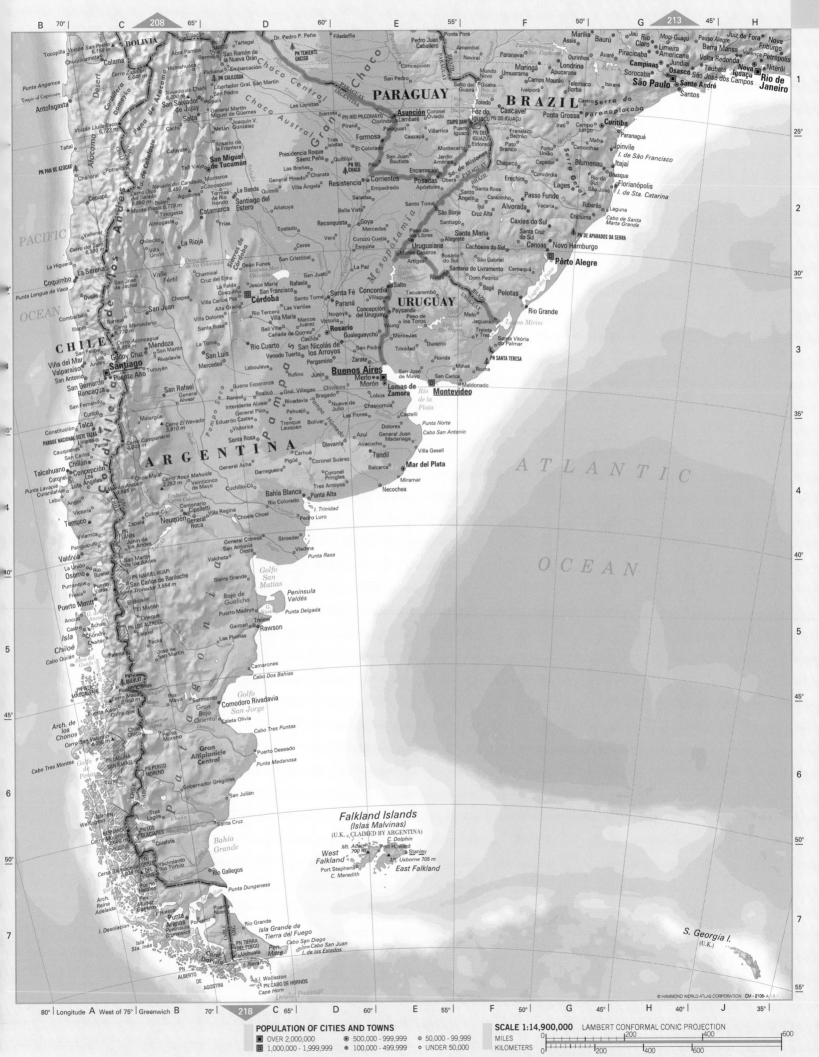

POPULATION OF CITIES AND TOWNS
- ■ OVER 2,000,000
- ■ 1,000,000 - 1,999,999
- ● 500,000 - 999,999
- ● 100,000 - 499,999
- ● 50,000 - 99,999
- ○ UNDER 50,000

SCALE 1:14,900,000   LAMBERT CONFORMAL CONIC PROJECTION

MILES 0   200   400   600

KILOMETERS 0   200   400   600

CHILE
① REGIÓN METROPOLITANA
② LIBERTADOR GENERAL
   BERNARDO O'HIGGINS

PACIFIC OCEAN

SANTIAGO

Viña del Mar
Valparaíso

CHILE

Cordillera de los Andes

MENDOZA

SAN JUAN

SAN LUIS

LA PAMPA

ARGENTINA

BUENOS AIRES

NEUQUÉN

LA ARAUCANÍA

BÍO-BÍO

RÍO NEGRO

Patagonia

CHUBUT

LOS LAGOS

Isla Chiloé

Archipiélago de los Chonos

Península de Taitao

AISÉN DEL GENERAL CARLOS IBÁÑEZ DEL CAMPO

SANTA CRUZ

Golfo San Jorge

Comodoro Rivadavia

Golfo San Matías

Península Valdés

© HAMMOND WORLD ATLAS CORPORATION   CM-A

Longitude West of Greenwich

SANTIAGO (ARTURO MERINO BENÍTEZ)
Viña del Mar
Valparaíso
CHILE
Maipú
San Antonio
REGIÓN METROPOLITANA
Puente Alto
PACIFIC OCEAN

Height

Southern Chile and Argentina

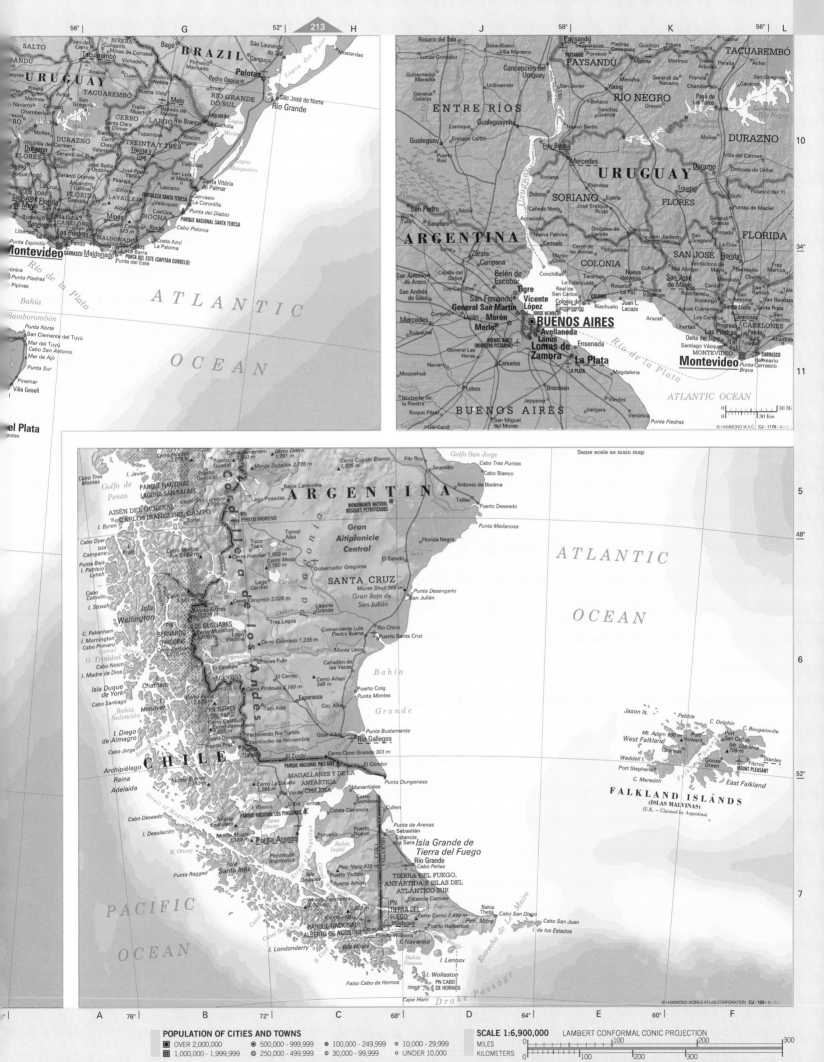

Arctic Regions, Antarctica

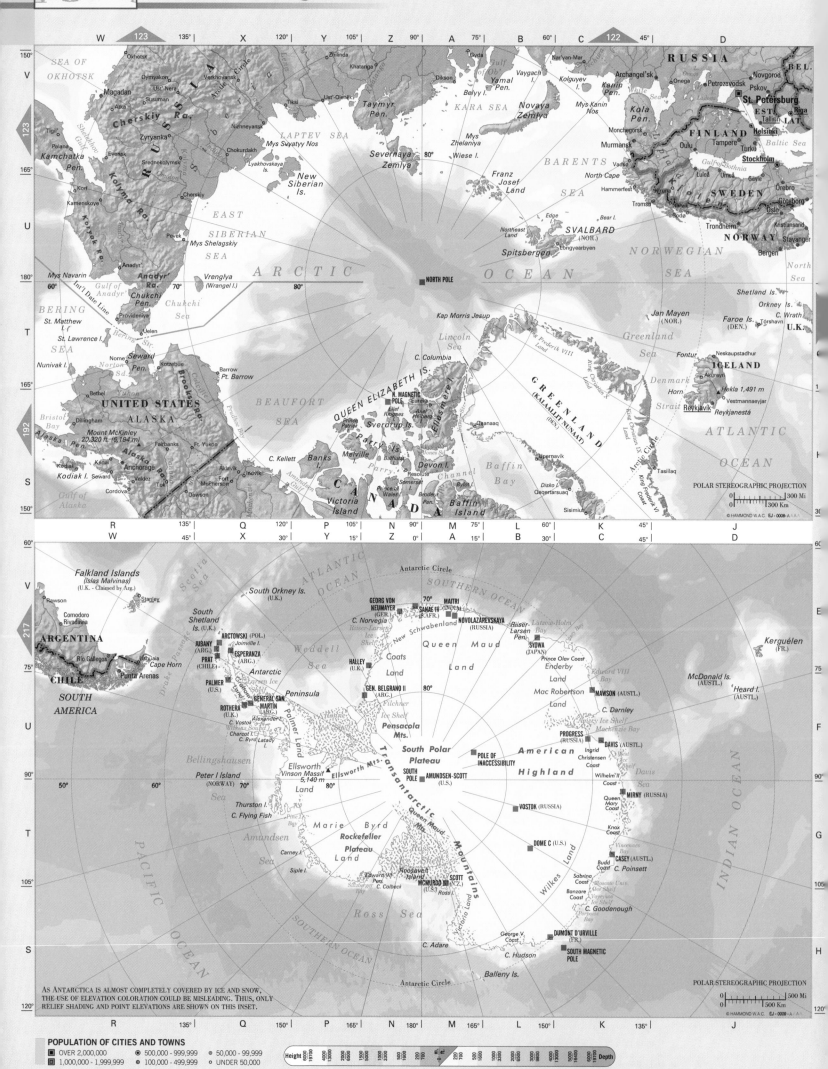

POLAR STEREOGRAPHIC PROJECTION

As Antarctica is almost completely covered by ice and snow, the use of elevation coloration could be misleading. Thus, only relief shading and point elevations are shown on this inset.

POLAR STEREOGRAPHIC PROJECTION

POPULATION OF CITIES AND TOWNS

■ OVER 2,000,000
◉ 500,000 - 999,999
◦ 50,000 - 99,999
▣ 1,000,000 - 1,999,999
● 100,000 - 499,999
○ UNDER 50,000

Index to the World Map Section

Using the Index

This index is a comprehensive listing of the places and geographic features found in the atlas. Names are arranged in strict alphabetical order, without regard to hyphens or spaces. Every name is followed by the country or area to which it belongs. Except for cities, towns, countries and cultural areas, all entries include a reference to feature type, such as province, river, island, peak, and so on. The page number and alpha-numeric code appear in blue to the right of each listing. The page number directs you to the largest scale map on which the name can be found, or in the case of a nation, on which the nation is depicted in its entirety. The code refers to the grid squares formed by the horizontal and vertical lines of latitude and longitude on each map. Following the letters from left to right and the numbers from top to bottom helps you to locate quickly the square containing the place or feature. Inset maps have their own alpha-numeric codes. Names that are accompanied by a point symbol are indexed to the symbol's location on the map. Other names are indexed to the initial letter of the name. When a map name contains a subordinate or alternate name, both names are listed in the index. To conserve space and provide room for more entries, many abbreviations are used in this index. The primary abbreviations are listed below.

Abbreviations

A

Ab,Can	Alberta
Abor.	Aboriginal
Acad.	Academy
ACT	Australian Capital Territory
A.F.B.	Air Force Base
Afld.	Airfield
Afg.	Afghanistan
Afr.	Africa
Ak,US	Alaska
Al,US	Alabama
Alb.	Albania
Alg.	Algeria
Amm. Dep.	Ammunition Depot
And.	Andorra
Ang.	Angola
Angu.	Anguilla
Ant.	Antarctica
Anti.	Antigua and Barbuda
Ar,US	Arkansas
Arch.	Archipelago
Arg.	Argentina
Arm.	Armenia
Arpt.	Airport
Aru.	Aruba
ASam.	American Samoa
Ash.	Ashmore and Cartier Islands
Aus.	Austria
Austl.	Australia
Aut.	Autonomous
Az,US	Arizona
Azer.	Azerbaijan
Azor.	Azores

B

Bahm.	Bahamas, The
Bahr.	Bahrain
Bang.	Bangladesh
Bar.	Barbados
BC,Can	British Columbia
Bela.	Belarus
Belg.	Belgium
Belz.	Belize
Ben.	Benin
Berm.	Bermuda
Bfld.	Battlefield
Bhu.	Bhutan
Bol.	Bolivia
Bor.	Borough
Bosn.	Bosnia and Herzegovina
Bots.	Botswana
Braz.	Brazil
BrIn.	British Indian Ocean Territory
Bru.	Brunei
Bul.	Bulgaria
Burk.	Burkina Faso
Buru.	Burundi
BVI	British Virgin Islands

C

Ca,US	California
CAfr.	Central African Republic
Camb.	Cambodia
Camr.	Cameroon
Can.	Canada
Can.	Canal
Canl.	Canary Islands
Cap.	Capital
Cap. Dist.	Capital District
Cap. Terr.	Capital Territory
Cay.	Cayman Islands
C.d'Iv.	Côte d'Ivoire
C.G.	Coast Guard
Chan.	Channel
Chl.	Channel Islands
Co.	County
Co,US	Colorado
Col.	Colombia
Com.	Comoros
Cont.	Continent
CpV.	Cape Verde Islands
CR	Costa Rica
Cr.	Creek
Cro.	Croatia
CSea.	Coral Sea Islands Territory
Ct,US	Connecticut
Ctr.	Center
Ctry.	Country
Cyp.	Cyprus
Czh.	Czech Republic

D

DC,US	District of Columbia
De,US	Delaware
Den.	Denmark
Depr.	Depression
Dept.	Department
Des.	Desert
DF	Distrito Federal
Dist.	District
Djib.	Djibouti
Dom.	Dominica
Dpcy.	Dependency
D.R.Congo	Democratic Republic of the Congo
DRep.	Dominican Republic

E

Ecu.	Ecuador
Emb.	Embankment
Eng.	Engineering
Eng,UK	England
EqG.	Equatorial Guinea
Erit.	Eritrea
ESal.	El Salvador
Est.	Estonia
Eth.	Ethiopia
ETim.	East Timor
Eur.	Europe

F

Falk.	Falkland Islands
Far.	Faroe Islands
Fed. Dist.	Federal District
Fin.	Finland
Fl,US	Florida
For.	Forest
Fr.	France
FrAnt.	French Southern and Antarctic Lands
FrG.	French Guiana
FrPol.	French Polynesia
FYROM	Former Yugoslav Rep. of Macedonia

G

Ga,US	Georgia
Galp.	Galapagos Islands
Gam.	Gambia, The
Gaza	Gaza Strip
GBis.	Guinea-Bissau
Geo.	Georgia
Ger.	Germany
Gha.	Ghana
Gib.	Gibraltar
Glac.	Glacier
Gov.	Governorate
Govt.	Government
Gre.	Greece
Grld.	Greenland
Gren.	Grenada
Grsld.	Grassland
Guad.	Guadeloupe
Guat.	Guatemala
Gui.	Guinea
Guy.	Guyana

H

Har.	Harbor
Hi,US	Hawaii
Hist.	Historic(al)
Hon.	Honduras
Hts.	Heights
Hun.	Hungary

I

Ia,US	Iowa
Ice.	Iceland
Id,US	Idaho
Il,US	Illinois
IM	Isle of Man
In,US	Indiana
Ind. Res.	Indian Reservation
Indo.	Indonesia
Int'l	International
Ire.	Ireland
Isl., Isls.	Island, Islands
Isr.	Israel
Isth.	Isthmus
It.	Italy

J

Jam.	Jamaica
Jor.	Jordan

K

Kaz.	Kazakhstan
Kiri.	Kiribati
Kos.	Kosovo
Ks,US	Kansas
Kuw.	Kuwait
Ky,US	Kentucky
Kyr.	Kyrgyzstan

L

La,US	Louisiana
Lab.	Laboratory
Lag.	Lagoon
Lakesh.	Lakeshore
Lat.	Latvia
Lcht.	Liechtenstein
Ldg.	Landing
Leb.	Lebanon
Les.	Lesotho
Libr.	Liberia
Lith.	Lithuania
Lux.	Luxembourg

M

Ma,US	Massachusetts
Madg.	Madagascar
Madr.	Madeira
Malay.	Malaysia
Mald.	Maldives
Malw.	Malawi
Mart.	Martinique
May.	Mayotte
Mb,Can	Manitoba
Md,US	Maryland
Me,US	Maine
Mem.	Memorial
Mex.	Mexico
Mi,US	Michigan
Micr.	Micronesia, Federated States of
Mil.	Military
Mn,US	Minnesota
Mo,US	Missouri
Mol.	Moldova
Mon.	Monument
Mona.	Monaco
Mong.	Mongolia
Mont.	Montenegro
Monts.	Montserrat
Mor.	Morocco
Moz.	Mozambique
Mrsh.	Marshall Islands
Mrta.	Mauritania
Mrts.	Mauritius
Ms,US	Mississippi
Mt.	Mount
Mt,US	Montana
Mtn., Mts.	Mountain, Mountains
Mun. Arpt.	Municipal Airport
Myan.	Myanmar

N

NAm.	North America
Namb.	Namibia
NAnt.	Netherlands Antilles
Nat'l	National
Nav.	Naval
NB,Can	New Brunswick
Nbrhd.	Neighborhood
NC,US	North Carolina
NCal.	New Caledonia
ND,US	North Dakota
Ne,US	Nebraska
Neth.	Netherlands
Nf,Can	Newfoundland
Nga.	Nigeria
NH,US	New Hampshire
NI,UK	Northern Ireland
Nic.	Nicaragua
NJ,US	New Jersey
NKor.	North Korea
NM,US	New Mexico
NMar.	Northern Mariana Islands
Nor.	Norway
NS,Can	Nova Scotia
Nv,US	Nevada
Nun.,Can	Nunavut
NW,Can	Northwest Territories
NY,US	New York
NZ	New Zealand

O

Obl.	Oblast
Oh,US	Ohio
Ok,US	Oklahoma
On,Can	Ontario
Or,US	Oregon

P

Pa,US	Pennsylvania
PacUS	Pacific Islands, U.S.
Pak.	Pakistan
Pan.	Panama
Par.	Paraguay
Par.	Parish
PE,Can	Prince Edward Island
Pen.	Peninsula
Phil.	Philippines
Phys. Reg.	Physical Region
Pitc.	Pitcairn Islands
Plat.	Plateau
PNG	Papua New Guinea
Pol.	Poland
Port.	Portugal
Poss.	Possession
Pkwy.	Parkway
PR	Puerto Rico
Pref.	Prefecture
Prov.	Province
Prsv.	Preserve
Pt.	Point

Q

Qu,Can	Quebec

R

Rec.	Recreation(al)
Ref.	Refuge
Reg.	Region
Rep.	Republic
Res.	Reservoir, Reservation
Reun.	Réunion
RI,US	Rhode Island
Riv.	River
Rom.	Romania
Rsv.	Reserve
Rus.	Russia
Rvwy.	Riverway
Rwa.	Rwanda

S

SAfr.	South Africa
Sam.	Samoa
SAm.	South America
SaoT.	São Tomé and Príncipe
SAr.	Saudi Arabia
Sc,UK	Scotland
SC,US	South Carolina
SD,US	South Dakota
Seash.	Seashore
Sen.	Senegal
Serb.	Serbia
Sey.	Seychelles
SGeo.	South Georgia and Sandwich Islands
Sing.	Singapore
Sk,Can	Saskatchewan
SKor.	South Korea
SLeo.	Sierra Leone
Slov.	Slovenia
Slvk.	Slovakia
SMar.	San Marino
Sol.	Solomon Islands
Som.	Somalia
Sp.	Spain
Spr., Sprs.	Spring, Springs
SrL.	Sri Lanka
Sta.	Station
StH.	Saint Helena
Str.	Strait
StK.	Saint Kitts and Nevis
StL.	Saint Lucia
StP.	Saint Pierre and Miquelon
StV.	Saint Vincent and the Grenadines

T

Tah.	Tahiti
Tai.	Taiwan
Taj.	Tajikistan
Tanz.	Tanzania
Ter.	Terrace
Terr.	Territory
Thai.	Thailand
Tn,US	Tennessee
Tok.	Tokelau
Trg.	Training
Trin.	Trinidad and Tobago
Trkm.	Turkmenistan
Trks.	Turks and Caicos Islands
Tun.	Tunisia
Tun.	Tunnel
Turk.	Turkey
Tuv.	Tuvalu
Twp.	Township
Tx,US	Texas

U

UAE	United Arab Emirates
Ugan.	Uganda
UK	United Kingdom
Ukr.	Ukraine
Uru.	Uruguay
US	United States
USVI	U.S. Virgin Islands
Ut,US	Utah
Uzb.	Uzbekistan

V

Va,US	Virginia
Val.	Valley
Van.	Vanuatu
VatC.	Vatican City
Ven.	Venezuela
Viet.	Vietnam
Vill.	Village
Vol.	Volcano
Vt,US	Vermont

W

Wa,US	Washington
Wal,UK	Wales
Wall.	Wallis and Futuna
WBnk.	West Bank
Wi,US	Wisconsin
Wild.	Wildlife, Wilderness
WSah.	Western Sahara
WV,US	West Virginia
Wy,US	Wyoming

Y

Yem.	Yemen
Yk,Can	Yukon Territory

Z

Zam.	Zambia
Zim.	Zimbabwe

A

100 Mile House,
BC, Can. 184/C3
Aa (riv.), Ger. 108/D5
Aach (riv.), Ger. 115/F2
Aach, Ger. 115/E2
Aachen, Ger. 111/F2
Aalbach (riv.), Ger. 112/C3
Aalborg
(int'l arpt.), Den. 96/C3
Aalburg, Neth. 108/C5
Aalen, Ger. 112/D5
Aalsmeer, Neth. 108/B4
Aalst, Belg. 110/D2
Aalten, Neth. 108/D5
Aalter, Belg. 110/C1
Aar (riv.), Ger. 111/H3
Aarau, Swi. 114/E3
Aarberg, Swi. 114/D3
Aarburg, Swi. 114/D3
Aardenburg, Neth. 110/C1
Aare (riv.), Swi. 101/H3
Aargau (canton), Swi. 114/E3
Aarred (lake), WSah. 156/B4
Aarschot, Belg. 111/D2
Aartselaar, Belg. 111/D1
Aarwangen, Swi. 114/D3
Aba, China 128/H5
Aba, D.R. Congo 162/A2
Aba, Nga. 161/G5
Abã as Su'ūd, SAr. 146/D5
Abacaxis (riv.), Braz. 208/G5
Abadab (peak),
Sudan 159/C5
Ābādān, Iran 146/E2
Ābādeh, Iran 146/F2
Abadia dos Dourados,
Braz. 213/C1
Abadla, Alg. 157/E3
Abádszalók, Hun. 106/E2
Abaeté, Braz. 213/C1
Abaetetuba, Braz. 209/J4
Abaiang (isl.), Kiri. 174/G4
Abakan, Rus. 122/K4
Abancay, Peru 214/C4
Abano Terme, It. 117/E2
Abar Kūh, Iran 146/F2
Abarán, Sp. 102/E3
Abashiri (lake),
Japan 134/C2
Abashiri, Japan 134/D1
Abasolo, Mex. 201/F4
Abasolo, Mex. 201/F3
Abay, Kaz. 145/F3
Abaya Hayk (lake),
Eth. 155/N6
Abbadia Lariana, It. 115/F6
Abbadia San Salvatore,
It. 101/J5
Abbeville, La, US 187/J5
Abbeville, SC, US 191/H3
Abbeville, Fr. 110/A3
Abbey (peak),
Austl. 171/B1
Abbeyfeale, Ire. 89/P10
Abbeyleix, Ire. 89/Q10
Abbiategrasso, It. 116/B2
Abbot (mt.), Austl. 171/B3
Abbotsinch (int'l arpt.),
Sc, UK 94/B5
Abbottābād, Pak. 144/B2
Abbottstown,
Pa, US 196/B4
Abcoude, Neth. 108/B4
Abdul Hakīm, Pak. 144/B4
Abdulino, Rus. 121/K1
Abéché, Chad 155/K5
Abemama (isl.), Kiri. 174/G4
Abenberg, Ger. 112/D4
Abengourou, C.d'Iv. 160/E5
Abenrå, Den. 96/C4
Abens (riv.), Ger. 98/F4
Abensberg, Ger. 113/E6
Abeokuta, Nga. 161/F5
Abercarn, Wal, UK 90/C3
Aberchirder,
Sc, UK 94/D1
Aberdare, Wal, UK 90/C3
Aberdare NP, Kenya 162/C3
Aberdeen, Austl. 173/D2
Aberdeen (lake),
Nun., Can. 180/F2
Aberdeen, SAfr. 164/C4
Aberdeen, Sc, UK 94/D2
Aberdeen (pol. reg.),
Sc, UK 94/D2
Aberdeen, SD, US 185/J4
Aberdeen, Ms, US 191/F3
Aberdeen, Md, US 196/B5
Aberdeen, Wa, US 184/C4
Aberdeen Proving Ground,
Md, US 196/B5
Aberdeenshire,
Sc, UK 94/D2
Aberdeenshire (pol. reg.),
Sc, UK 94/D2
Aberdour, Sc, UK 94/C4
Aberdour (bay),
Sc, UK 94/D1
Aberfeldy, Sc, UK 94/C3
Aberfoyle, Sc, UK 94/B4
Abergavenny,
Wal, UK 90/C3
Abergele, Wal, UK 92/E5
Aberlour, Sc, UK 94/C2
Abernethy, Sc, UK 94/C4
Abert (lake), Or, US 184/C5
Abertillery, Wal, UK 90/C3
Aberystwyth, Wal, UK 90/B2
Abhá, SAr. 146/D5
Abhar, Iran 146/E1
Abhayāpuri, India 143/H2

Abhe Bad (lake),
Djib.,Eth. 155/P5
Abia (prov.), Nga. 161/G5
Abiko, Japan 135/E2
Abilene, Tx, US 187/H4
Abilene, Ks, US 187/H3
Abingdon (reef),
Austl. 171/C2
Abingdon, Sc, UK 94/C6
Abino (pt.), On, Can. 189/R10
Abiquiu, NM, US 190/B2
Abitibi (lake),
On,Qu, Can. 181/H4
Abitibi (riv.),
On, Can. 181/H4
Abkhazia Aut. Rep.,
Geo. 121/G4
Ableiges, Fr. 88/H4
Abnūb, Egypt 159/B3
Abohar, India 144/C1
Aboisso, C.d'Iv. 160/E5
Abomey, Ben. 161/F5
Abondance, Fr. 114/C5
Abony, Hun. 106/D2
Aboyne, Sc, UK 94/D2
Abra (riv.), Phil. 137/D4
Abra Pampa, Arg. 215/C1
Abraham Gonzalez
(int'l arpt.), Mex. 190/D5
Abrantes, Port. 102/A3
Abreojos (pt.), Mex. 184/B3
Abrud, Rom. 107/F2
Abruzzi (prov.), It. 101/K5
Abruzzo, PN de, It. 104/C2
Absam, Aus. 115/H3
Absaroka (range),
Mt,Wy, US 184/F4
Absecon, NJ, US 196/D5
Acton, Ca, US 194/B2
Abtsgmünd, Ger. 112/D5
Abu Dhabi (Abū Ẓaby)
(cap.), UAE 147/F4
Abu el-Husein (well),
Egypt 159/B4
Abū Ḥammād,
Egypt 149/B4
Abu Hashim (well),
Egypt 159/C4
Abū Ḥummuṣ, Egypt 149/B4
Abū Kabīr, Egypt 149/B4
Abū Kamāl, Syria 148/E3
Abū Qashsh,
WBnk. 149/G8
Abu Shagara (cape),
Sudan 159/D4
Abu Simbel (ruin),
Egypt 159/B4
Ad Dilinjāt, Egypt 149/B4
Abuja (cap.), Nga. 161/G4
Abuja (int'l arpt.),
Nga. 161/G4
Abuja Capital Territory,
Nga. 161/G4
Abukuma (riv.), Japan 133/G2
Abukuma (plat.),
Japan 133/G2
Abulog, Phil. 137/D4
Abunã (riv.), Braz. 208/E6
Abuta, Japan 134/D5
Abuyē Mēda (peak),
Eth. 155/N5
Abuyog, Phil. 137/E5
Åby, Swe. 96/G2
Åbybro, Den. 96/C3
Abydos (ruin), Egypt 159/B3
Acacias, Col. 210/C4
Acacoyagua, Mex. 202/C3
Acadia NP,
Me, US 189/G2
Acadian Village,
La, US 187/J5
Acajutiba, Braz. 212/C3
Acámbaro, Mex. 201/E4
Acampo, Ca, US 193/M10
Acandí, Col. 210/B2
Acaponeta (riv.),
Mex. 184/D4
Acaponeta, Mex. 184/D4
Acapulco de Juárez,
Mex. 198/B4
Acaraí (mts.),
Braz.,Guy. 211/G4
Acaraí, Serra (mts.),
Braz. 208/G3
Acaraú (riv.), Braz. 212/B1
Acaraú, Braz. 212/B1
Acari, Braz. 212/C2
Acari (riv.), Braz. 208/G5
Acari, Peru 214/C4
Acatlán de Osorio,
Mex. 202/B2
Acatlán de Pérez Figueroa,
Mex. 201/N8
Acatzingo, Mex. 201/M7
Acayucan, Mex. 202/C2
Accha, Peru 214/C4
Acciaroli, It. 104/D2
Accra (cap.), Gha. 161/E5
Accrington,
Eng, UK 93/F4
Aceuchal, Sp. 102/B3
Ach (riv.), Aus. 113/G6
Achacachi, Bol. 208/D7
Achaguas, Ven. 210/D2
Achao, Chile 216/B4
Achar, Uru. 217/K10
Achéguor (well),
Niger 154/H4
Achen (pass), Ger. 115/H2
Acheng, China 129/D2
Achères, Fr. 88/J5
Achhnera, India 142/A2

Achicourt, Fr. 110/B3
Achill (isl.), Ire. 88/N10
Achill Head (pt.), Ire. 88/N9
Achiltibuie, Sc, UK 89/R7
Achim (well), Mrta. 160/D2
Achinsk, Rus. 122/K4
Achnasheen, Sc, UK 94/A1
A'chralaig (peak),
Sc, UK 94/A1
Achuapa, Nic. 202/E3
Achupallas, Ecu. 214/B1
Acireale, It. 104/D4
Acklins (isl.), Bahm. 199/G3
Acland (mt.),
Austl. 171/C4
Acobamba, Peru 214/C3
Acolla, Peru 214/C3
Acolman, Mex. 201/R9
Acomayo, Peru 214/D4
Acomayo, Peru 214/B3
Aconcagua (peak),
Arg. 216/C2
Aconchi, Mex. 184/C2
Acopiara, Braz. 212/C2
Acora, Peru 214/D4
Acqualagna, It. 117/E3
Acquanegra sul Chiese,
It. 116/D2
Acquapendente, It. 104/B1
Acqui Terme, It. 116/B3
Acraman (lake),
Austl. 171/G5
Acrata (pt.), Alg. 158/G4
Acre (riv.), Braz. 208/E6
Acre (state), Braz. 214/C3
Acreúna, Braz. 213/B1
Acri, It. 104/E3
Acropolis, Gre. 105/N9
Actaeon Group (isls.),
FrPol. 175/M7
Acton, Ca, US 194/B2
Actopan, Mex. 201/N7
Actopan, Mex. 201/N7
Acu, China 128/J5
Açu (riv.), Braz. 212/C2
Açú, Braz. 212/B2
Açude Aratas (res.),
Braz. 212/B2
Açude Banabuiu (res.),
Braz. 212/C2
Acula, Mex. 201/P8
Aculeo (lag.), Chile 216/N8
Acy-en-Multien, Fr. 88/L4
Ad Dahnā' (des.), SAr. 146/D3
Ad-Dakhla, WSah. 156/B5
Ad Damazin, Sudan 155/M5
Ad Damir, Sudan 155/M4
Ad Dammām, SAr. 146/F3
Ad Daqahliyah (gov.),
Egypt 159/B1
Ad Dilinjāt, Egypt 149/B4
Adria, It. 117/F2
Ad Dujayl, Iraq 148/F3
Ad Duwaym, Sudan 155/M5
Ada, Gha. 161/F5
Ada, Serb. 106/E3
Ada, Ok, US 188/D3
Adainville, Fr. 88/G5
Adair (cape),
Nun., Can. 181/J1
Adair, Bahia del (bay),
Mex. 184/D5
Adaja (riv.), Sp. 102/C2
Adak (isl.), Ak, US 192/C6
Adak (str.), Ak, US 192/C6
Adam (mt.), Falk., UK 217/E6
Adamantina, Braz. 213/B2
Adamaoua (plat.),
Camr.,Nga. 151/D4
Adamello (peak), It. 115/G5
Adaminaby, Austl. 173/D3
Adams (lake),
BC, Can. 184/D3
Adams (co.), Co, US 195/C3
Adams (co.), Pa, US 196/A4
Adams (mt.), Wa, US 184/C4
Adamstown (cap.),
Pitc. 175/M7
Adamstown, Pa, US 196/B3
Adanwa (plat.),
Nga. 161/H5
'Adan, Yem. 146/D6
Adana, Turk. 149/D1
Adana (prov.), Turk. 148/C2
Adapazari, Turk. 107/K5
Adare, Ire. 89/P10
Adare (cape), Ant. 218/M
Adarza (peak), Fr. 102/E1
Add (riv.), Sc, UK 94/A4
Addington, It. 101/H4
Addison, Il, US 193/P16
Addison, Eng, UK 88/B2
Addo Elephant NP,
SAfr. 164/D4
Addokeieh (Adī K'eyih),
Erit. 146/C6
Adelaide, SAfr. 164/D4
Adelaide (pen.),
Nun., Can. 180/G2
Adelaide (int'l arpt.),
Austl. 171/M8
Adelaide, Austl. 171/M8
Adelaide Zoo,
Austl. 171/M8
Adelanto, Ca, US 194/C1
Adelboden, Swi. 114/D4
Adelheidsdorf, Ger. 109/H3
Adelmannsfelden,
Ger. 112/D5
Adelong, Austl. 173/D2
Adelschlag, Ger. 112/D5
Adelsheim, Ger. 112/C4
Adelsried, Ger. 112/D6

Aden (gulf), Afr.,Asia 125/D8
Adenau, Ger. 111/F3
Adendorf, Ger. 109/H2
Adi (isl.), Indo. 139/H4
Adī Ugrī, Erit. 146/C6
Adieu (cape), Austl. 171/G5
Adige (riv.), It. 101/J4
Adige (Etsch) (riv.), It. 115/G4
Adigrat, Eth. 146/C6
Adilābād, India 140/C4
Adilcevaz, Turk. 148/E2
Adiora (well), Mali 156/E1
Adirondack (mts.),
NY, US 183/L3
Aḍīs Ābeba (Addis Ababa)
(cap.), Eth. 155/N6
Adiyaman, Turk. 148/D2
Adiyaman (prov.),
Turk. 148/D2
Adjud, Rom. 107/H2
Adjuntas, Presa de la
(res.), Mex. 201/F4
Adler/Sochi (int'l arpt.),
Rus. 120/F4
Adliswil, Swi. 115/E3
Admiralty (inlet),
Nun., Can. 181/H1
Admiralty (isl.),
Ak, US 180/C4
Admiralty Island Nat'l Mon.,
Ak, US 192/M4
Admiralty (isls.),
PNG 174/D5
Admiralty (inlet),
Wa, US 193/B2
Adnan Menderes
(int'l arpt.), Turk. 148/A2
Ado (riv.), Japan 135/J5
Ado Ekiti, Nga. 161/G5
Ado Odo, Nga. 161/F5
Adogawa, Japan 135/K5
Adolfo López Mateos,
Mex. 184/B3
Adoni, India 140/C4
Adour (riv.), Fr. 100/C5
Adra, India 143/F4
Adra, Sp. 102/D4
Adrano, It. 104/D4
Adrar (phys. reg.),
Mrta. 154/C3
Adrar, Alg. 157/E4
Adrar (pol. reg.),
Mrta. 160/C1
Adrar (prov.), Alg. 157/E4
Adrar (reg.), Mrta. 156/C5
Adrar bou Nasser (peak),
Mor. 156/E2
Adrar Sotuf (mts.),
WSah. 156/B5
Adria, It. 117/F2
Adrian, Mi, US 188/C3
Adriatic (sea), Eur. 85/F4
Adro, It. 116/C1
Adulis (ruin), Erit. 146/C6
Adur (riv.), Eng, UK 91/F5
Adwa, Eth. 146/C6
Adwick le Street,
Eng, UK 93/G4
Adycha (riv.), Rus. 123/P3
Adygeya, Resp., Rus. 120/F3
Adz'va (riv.), Rus. 119/P2
Aegean (sea),
Gre.,Turk. 105/J3
Aerø (isl.), Den. 96/D4
Aeron (riv.), Wal, UK 90/B2
Aesch bei Spiez, Swi. 114/D4
Aetsä, Fin. 97/K1
Afadjoto (peak), Gha. 161/F5
'Afak, Iraq 146/E2
Afándou, Gre. 105/K4
Aff (riv.), Fr. 100/B3
Affoltern im Emmental,
Swi. 114/D3
Affric (lake), Sc, UK 94/A2
Affton, Mo, US 195/G8
Afghanistan (ctry.) 147/H2
Afmadow, Som. 155/P7
Afogados da Ingázeira,
Braz. 212/C2
Afognak (mtn.),
Ak, US 192/H4
Afognak (isl.), Ak, US 192/H4
Afollé, Massif de
(phys. reg.), Mrta. 160/C2
Afonso Bezerra,
Braz. 212/C2
Afonso Cláudio,
Braz. 213/D2
Afrânio, Braz. 212/B2
Africa (cont.) 109
'Afrin, Turk. 149/E1
'Afrin, Syria 149/E1
Afrique (peak), Fr. 114/A3
Afsluitdijk (dam),
Neth. 108/C3
Afton, Wy, US 184/F5
Afton, Mo, US 195/G8
Afuá, Braz. 209/J4
Afula, Isr. 149/G6
Afyon, Turk. 148/B2
Afyon (prov.), Turk. 148/B2
Agadez, Niger 161/G2
Agadez (dept.), Niger 154/H5
Agadir, Mor. 156/D2
Agago (riv.), Ugan. 162/B2
Agamor (well), Mali 156/E2
Agano (riv.), Japan 133/F2

Agassiz Ice Cap (ice field),
Nun., Can. 181/T6
Agattu (isl.), Ak, US 192/A5
Agattu (str.), Ak, US 192/A5
Agbabu, Nga. 161/G5
Agboville, C.d'Iv. 160/E5
Aĝdam, Azer. 121/H5
Agde, Fr. 100/E5
Ageo, Japan 135/D2
Ager (riv.), Aus. 113/G2
Agerisee (lake), Swi. 115/E3
Agger (riv.), Ger. 111/G1
Agghā Jārī, Iran 146/E2
Aghagallon, NI, UK 92/B3
Aghagower (riv.), Ire. 89/P10
Agiabampo, Mex. 184/C3
Agiasos, Gre. 105/J3
Agigea, Rom. 107/H3
Agigea (riv.), It. 101/H4
Agina, It. 117/E2
Aginskiy Buryatskiy
Aut. Okrug, Rus. 123/Q7
Aginskoye, Rus. 129/K1
Agliana, It. 117/D5
Aĝliköy, Turk. 148/C1
Agly (riv.), Fr. 100/E5
Agna, It. 117/E2
Agnanderón, Gre. 105/G3
Agnita, Rom. 107/G3
Agno, It. 104/D2
Agno (int'l arpt.), Swi. 115/E6
Agnone, It. 104/D2
Ago, Japan 135/L7
Agogna (riv.), It. 101/H4
Agogo, It. 101/K3
Agordo, It. 101/K3
Agout (riv.), Fr. 100/D5
Agra, India 142/A2
Agraciada, Uru. 217/J10
Agrado, Col. 210/C4
Agreda, Sp. 102/E2
Aĝri (riv.), Turk. 148/E2
Aĝri, Turk. 148/E2
Agrią, Gre. 105/H3
Agrigento, It. 104/C4
Agrihan (isl.), NMar. 174/D3
Agrinion, Gre. 105/G3
Agrio (riv.), Arg. 216/C3
Agropoli, It. 104/D2
Agra, India 143/F4
Agryz, Rus. 119/M4
Agsumal (dry lake),
WSah. 156/B4
Agigoual (peak), Fr. 100/E4
Aguá, Uru. 217/G2
Aiguá, Uru. 217/G2
Agua Boa, Braz. 212/B5
Agua Branca, Braz. 212/B2
Agua Dulce,
Ca, US 194/B2
Agua Dulce, Mex. 202/C2
Agua Fria (riv.),
Az, US 195/R19
Agua Fria NM,
Az, US 186/E4
Agua Hedionda (lake),
Ca, US 194/C4
Agua Larga, Ven. 210/D2
Agua Prieta, Mex. 184/C2
Aguachica, Col. 210/C2
Aguadilla, PR 199/M8
Aguadulce, Pan. 210/A2
Aguaí, Braz. 213/G7
Agualva-Cacém,
Port. 103/P10
Aguan (riv.), Hon. 198/D4
Aguanus (riv.),
Qu, Can. 189/J1
Aguapeí (riv.), Braz. 213/B2
Aguarico (riv.),
Peru 210/B5
Aguas Belas, Braz. 212/C3
Aguas Corrientes,
Uru. 217/K11
Aguas da Prata,
Braz. 213/G6
Aguas de Lindóia,
Braz. 213/G7
Aguas Formosas,
Braz. 212/B5
Aguas, Serra das (hills),
Braz. 213/H7
Aguasay, Ven. 211/F2
Aguascalientes,
Mex. 184/E4
Aguascalientes (state),
Mex. 198/A3
Aguavermelha, Reprêsa
(res.), Braz. 213/B1
Agudos, Braz. 213/B2
Agueda (riv.), Sp. 102/B2
Agueda, Port. 102/A2
Agüeraktem (well),
Mali 156/D5
Aggliano, It. 116/B3
Aguijan (isl.), NMar. 174/D3
Aguilar, Sp. 102/C4
Aguilar de Campóo,
Sp. 102/D1
Aguilares, Arg. 215/C2
Aguilas, Sp. 102/E4
Aguililla, Mex. 184/E5
Aguja (pt.), Peru 214/A2
Agulhas (cape),
SAfr. 164/M11
Agulhas Negras, Pico das
(peak), Braz. 213/J7
Agung (vol.), Indo. 138/E5
Agusan (riv.), Phil. 137/F6
Agustín Codazzi,
Col. 210/C2
Ahaggar (plat.), Alg. 154/F3
Ahaggar (mts.), Alg. 157/G5
Ahaggar (dept.), Niger 157/H5
Aham, Ger. 113/F5
Ahar, Iran 121/H5
Ahaus, Ger. 108/E4
Ahfir, Mor. 158/C2
Ahirli, Turk. 148/C2

Ahlat, Turk. 148/E2
Ahlen, Ger. 109/E5
Aïssa (peak), Alg. 157/E2
Ahlerstedt, Ger. 109/G2
Aist (riv.), Aus. 113/H6
Ahmadābād, India 147/K4
Aitape, PNG 174/D5
Ahmadpur East, Pak. 144/A4
Aith, Japan 135/K5
Ahmadpur Siāl, Pak. 144/A4
Aitkin, Mn, US 185/K4
Ahmar (mts.), Eth. 155/P6
Aitolikón, Gre. 105/G3
Ahmed (well), WSah. 156/B5
Aitrach, Ger. 115/G2
Ahmeyine (well),
Mrta. 156/B5
Aitrang, Ger. 115/G2
Ageræk, Den. 96/C4
Aitutaki Atoll (isl.),
CookIs. 175/J6
Ahoghill, NI, UK 92/B2
Aiud, Rom. 107/F2
Ahome, Mex. 184/C3
Aiuruoca, Braz. 213/J6
Ahr (riv.), Ger. 101/G1
Aiuruoca (riv.),
Braz. 213/J7
Ahraurā, India 142/D3
Aix-en-Provence, Fr. 100/F5
Ahrensburg, Ger. 109/H1
Aiyina, Gre. 105/H4
Ahse (riv.), Ger. 109/E5
Aiyinion, Gre. 105/H2
Ahuacatlán, Mex. 201/K8
Aiyion, Gre. 105/H3
Ahuacatlán, Mex. 184/D4
Aizawl, India 141/F3
Ahuachapán, ESal. 202/D3
Aizu-Wakamatsu,
Japan 133/F2
Ahualulco, Mex. 201/E4
Ahuimanu, Hi, US 182/W13
Ajaccio, Fr. 104/A2
Ahumada, Mex. 184/D2
Ajaccio, Golfe d' (gulf),
Fr. 104/A2
Ahun, Fr. 100/E3
Akwa Ibom (state),
Nga. 161/G5
Ahus, Swe. 96/F4
Ajaigarh, India 142/C3
Ahvāz, Iran 146/E2
Ajalpan, Mex. 201/M8
Ahvenanmaa (prov.),
Fin. 95/F4
Ajaria Aut. Rep.,
Geo. 121/G4
Ahwar, Yem. 146/E6
Ajo, It. 96/C1
Ai (riv.), China 131/C2
Ajax, On, Can. 189/R8
Ai 'āl, Jor. 149/D4
Ai-Ais Hot Springs,
Namb. 164/B2
Ajbābiya, Libya 155/K1
Ajdābiyā (riv.), It. 101/H4
Ajdovšćina, Slov. 101/K4
Ahshima (isl.), Japan 132/B3
Ajigasawa, Japan 134/B3
Aibag Gol (riv.),
China 130/B2
Ajka, Hun. 106/C2
Aichach, Ger. 112/E6
Ajigawa, Japan 135/E3
Aïn Beïda, Alg. 158/K7
Akharnai, Gre. 105/N8
Aïn Beniau, Alg. 158/K6
Akheloós (riv.), Gre. 105/G3
Aïn Bessem, Alg. 158/H5
Akhisar, Turk. 148/A2
Aïn Chok-Hay Mohammadia
(prov.), Mor. 156/D2
Akhmīm, India 144/C3
Aïn Defla, Alg. 158/F4
Akhtopol, Bul. 107/H4
Aïn Defla (prov.),
Alg. 158/F4
Akhtuba (riv.), Rus. 121/H3
Aïn el Aouda, Mor. 158/A3
Aki, Japan 132/C4
Aïn el Bey (int'l arpt.),
Alg. 158/K6
Akiachak, Ak, US 192/F3
Aïn el Hammam,
Alg. 158/H5
Akigawa, Japan 135/C2
Aïn el Turk, Alg. 158/D2
Akimiski (isl.),
On, Can. 181/H3
Aïn Fakroun, Alg. 158/K6
Akıncı (pt.), Turk. 149/D1
Aïn M'lila, Alg. 158/K6
Akıncılar, Turk. 148/D1
Aïn Oulmene, Alg. 158/H5
Akirkeby, Den. 96/F4
Aïn Oussera, Alg. 158/G5
Akishima, Japan 135/C2
Aïn Sefra, Alg. 157/E2
Akita (pref.), Japan 134/B4
Aïn Taoujdat, Mor. 158/B3
Akiyama, Japan 135/C2
Aïn Temouchent,
Alg. 158/D2
Akjoujt, Mrta. 160/B2
Aïn Touta, Alg. 158/H5
Akkeshi, Japan 134/D2
Aïna Haina, Hi, US 182/W13
Akko, Isr. 149/G6
Aincourt, Fr. 88/H4
Akkeshi, Japan 134/D2
Aínos (peak), Gre. 105/G3
Akköy, Turk. 148/A2
Aínos NP, Gre. 105/G3
Akora, Pak. 144/B2
Aipe, Col. 210/C4
Ak'ordat, Erit. 146/C5
Air (plat.), Niger 154/G4
Air Force (isl.),
Nun., Can. 181/J2
Airaires, Sp. 103/M2
Airdrie, Ab, Can. 184/E3
Airdrie, Sc, UK 94/C5
Aire (riv.), Eng, UK 91/G2
Aire, Canal d' (canal),
Fr. 110/B2
Aire-sur-la-Lys, Fr. 110/B2
Aire-sur-l'Adour, Fr. 100/C5
Airolo, Swi. 115/E4
Airvault, Fr. 100/C3
Aisch (riv.), Ger. 112/D4
Aiseau-Presles,
Belg. 111/D3
Aisén del General Carlos
Ibáñez del Campo
(pol. reg.), Chile 216/B5

Aksay Kazakzu Zizhixian,
China 128/F4
Akşehir, Turk. 148/B2
Akşehir Lake (lake),
Turk. 148/B2
Akseki, Turk. 149/B1
Aksoran (peak), Kaz. 145/G3
Aksu, China 128/D3
Aksu, Turk. 149/B1
Aksum, Eth. 146/C6
Aktepe, Turk. 149/E1
Akti (pen.), Gre. 105/J2
Akto, China 145/G5
Akune, Japan 132/B4
Akure, Nga. 161/G5
Akureyri, Ice. 95/N6
Akuse, Gha. 161/F5
Akutan (isl.),
Ak, US 192/E5
Akutan, Ak, US 192/E5
Akutan Pass (chan.),
Ak, US 192/E5
Akwa Ibom (state),
Nga. 161/G5
Akyab (Sittwe),
Myan. 141/F3
Akyazı, Turk. 107/K5
Āl, Nor. 96/C1
Al 'āl, Jor. 149/D4
Al Anbār (gov.), Iraq 148/E3
Al 'Aqabah, Jor. 149/D5
Al 'Arīsh, Egypt 149/C4
Al 'Ayn, UAE 147/G4
Al Azizīyah, Libya 154/H1
Al 'Azīzīyah, Iraq 148/F3
Al Badrashayn,
Egypt 149/B5
Al Baḥr Al Aḥmar (gov.),
Egypt 159/C3
Al Bājūr, Egypt 149/B4
Al Balqā' (gov.), Jor. 149/D4
Al Balyanā, Egypt 159/B3
Al Baṣrah, Iraq 146/E2
Al Baṭrūn, Leb. 149/D3
Al Baydā, Libya 155/K1
Al Biqā' (gov.), Leb. 149/D3
Al Biqā' (valley), Leb. 149/D3
Al Bīrah, WBnk. 149/G8
Al Buḥayrah (gov.),
Egypt 159/B1
Al Fāsher, Sudan 155/L5
Al Fatḥah, Iraq 148/E3
Al Ḥaffah, Syria 149/E2
Al Fāw, Iraq 146/E2
Al Fayyūm, Egypt 149/B5
Al Fayyūm (gov.),
Egypt 159/B1
Al Ghurdaqah,
Egypt 159/C3
Al Hadīthah, Iraq 148/E3
Al Ḥaḍr, Iraq 148/E3
Al Ḥaffah, Syria 149/E2
Al Ḥajar ash Sahrqī
(mts.), Oman 147/G4
Al Hamādah al Hamrā
(upland), Libya 154/H2
Al Ḥammāmāt, Tun. 104/B4
Al Ḥasakah, Syria 148/E2
Al Ḥasakah (prov.),
Syria 148/E2
Al Ḥawāmidīyah,
Egypt 149/B5
Al Ḥayy, Iraq 146/E2
Al Ḥillah, Iraq 148/F3
Al Hindīyah, Iraq 146/E2
Al Hirmil, Leb. 149/E3
Al Hoceima (prov.),
Mor. 158/B2
Al Hoceima, Mor. 158/B2
Al Ḥudaydah, Yem. 146/D6
Al Iskandarīyah, Iraq 148/F3
Al Iskandarīyah
(Alexandria), Egypt 149/A4
Al Iskandarīyah (gov.),
Egypt 159/B1
Al Ismā'īlīyah,
Egypt 149/C4
Al Ismā'īlīyah (gov.),
Egypt 159/C4
Al Jabal Akaur (mts.),
Oman 147/G4
Al Jaghbūb, Libya 155/K2
Al Janub (gov.), Leb. 149/D3
Al Jifārah (plain),
Libya 157/H2
Al Jizah, Egypt 149/B5
Al Junaynah, Sudan 155/K5
Al Karak (gov.), Jor. 149/D4
Al Karak, Jor. 149/D4
Al Khāburah, Oman 147/G4
Al Khalīl (Hebron),
WBnk. 149/D4
Al Khāliṣ, Iraq 148/F3
Al Khānkah, Egypt 149/B5
Al Kharṭūm Baḥri
(Khartoum North),
Sudan 155/M4
Al Khubar, SAr. 146/F3
Al Khums, Libya 154/H1
Al Kiswah, Syria 149/E3
Al Kūfah, Iraq 148/F3
Al Kufrah, Libya 155/K3
Al Lādhiqīyah (prov.),
Syria 148/C3
Al Lādhiqīyah (Latakia),
Syria 149/D2
Al Madīnah, SAr. 146/C4
Al Madīnah al Fikrīyah,
Egypt 159/B3

Al Mafraq (gov.), Jor. 149/E3
Al Mafraq, Jor. 149/E3
Al Maghrib (reg.), Mor. 154/E1
Al Maḥallah al Kubrá, Egypt 149/B4
Al Maḥmūdīyah, Egypt 149/B4
Al Mālikīyah, Syria 148/E2
Al Mansûrah, Egypt 149/B4
Al Manzilah, Egypt 149/B4
Al Marāghah, Egypt 159/B3
Al Marj, Libya 155/K1
Al Maṭarīyah, Egypt 149/C4
Al Mawṣil (Mosul), Iraq 148/E2
Al Mayyâdin, Syria 148/E3
Al Mazra'ah, Jor. 149/D4
Al Minyâ (gov.), Egypt 159/B2
Al Mubarraz, SAr. 146/E4
Al Mudawwarah, Jor. 149/D5
Al Mukallā, Yem. 146/E6
Al Munastīr (prov.), Alg. 158/M7
Al Musayyib, Iraq 148/F3
Al Muthanná (gov.), Iraq 148/F4
Al Qâbil, Oman 147/G4
Al Qaḍārif, Sudan 146/C6
Al Qâdisīyah (gov.), Iraq 148/F4
Al Qâhirah (gov.), Egypt 159/B1
Al Qâhirah (Cairo) (cap.), Egypt 159/B2
Al Qâ'im, Iraq 148/E3
Al Qâmishlī, Syria 148/E2
Al Qanâṭir al Khayrīyah, Egypt 149/B4
Al Qantarah, Egypt 149/C4
Al Qasr, Jor. 149/D4
Al Qunayṭirah (prov.), Syria 149/D3
Al Qunayṭirah, Syria 149/D3
Al Qurnah, Iraq 146/F2
Al Quṣayr, Syria 149/E2
Al Quṭayfah, Syria 149/E3
Al Quwayrah, Jor. 149/D5
Al Ubayyiḍ, Sudan 155/M5
Al 'Uwaynāt (peak), Sudan 155/L3
Al Wādī Al Jadīd (gov.), Egypt 159/B3
Al Wāḥāt al Baḥrīyah (oasis), Egypt 159/B2
Al Wāḥāt al Khārijah (oasis), Egypt 159/B3
Al Wāsiṭah, Egypt 149/B5
Al Yâmūn, WBnk. 149/G7
Ala (pt.), It. 104/B1
Ala, It. 117/E1
Alabama (riv.), Al,Ga, US 191/G4
Alabama (state), US 191/G3
Alabaster, Al, US 191/G3
Alaca, Turk. 148/C1
Alacalı, Turk. 107/J5
Alaçam, Turk. 148/C1
Alaçatı, Turk. 105/K3
Alachua, Fl, US 191/H4
Alacrán (reef), Mex. 202/D1
Alacranes (isls.), Cuba 203/F1
Aladağ, Turk. 149/C1
Alaejos, Sp. 102/C2
Alagir, Rus. 121/H4
Alagna Valsesia, It. 116/A1
Alagnon (riv.), Fr. 100/E4
Alagoa Grande, Braz. 212/D2
Alagoas (state), Braz. 212/C4
Alagoinhas, Braz. 212/C4
Alagón (riv.), Sp. 102/C2
Alagón, Sp. 103/E2
Alajärvi, Fin. 118/D3
Alajuela, CR 203/E4
Alakanuk, Ak, US 192/F3
Alakol' (lake), Kaz. 128/D2
Alakol (lake), Kaz. 122/J5
Alalaú (riv.), Braz. 211/F5
Alamagan (isl.), NMar. 174/D3
'Alāmarvdasht (riv.), Iran 146/F3
Alameda, Ca, US 193/K11
Alaminos, Phil. 137/C4
Alamo (lake), Az, US 186/D4
Alamo, Mex. 202/B1
Alamo, Ca, US 193/K11
Alamo Heights, Tx, US 195/U21
Alamogordo, NM, US 187/F4
Alamor, Ecu. 214/A2
Alamos, Mex. 184/C3
Åland (isl.), Fin. 95/G3
Aland (riv.), Ger. 98/F2
Alanya, Turk. 149/C1
Alaotra (lake), Madg. 165/J7
Alapaha (riv.), Fl,Ga, US 191/H4
Alaplı, Turk. 107/K5
Alarcón, Embalse de (res.), Sp. 102/D3
Alaşehir, Phil. 148/B2
Alaska (state), US 192/G2
Alaska (range), Ak, US 192/H3
Alaska (pen.), Ak, US 192/G4

Alaska, Gulf of (gulf), Ak, US 192/J4
Alassio, It. 116/B5
Alatyr', Rus. 119/K5
Alaverdi, Arm. 121/H4
Alavus, Fin. 118/D3
Alaw (riv.), Wal, UK 92/D5
Alaw, Llyn (lake), Wal, UK 92/D5
Alayor, Sp. 103/G3
Alayskiy (mts.), Kyr. 145/F5
Alazeya (riv.), Rus. 123/R3
Alb (riv.), Ger. 112/B5
Alba, It. 101/H4
Alba (prov.), Rom. 107/F2
Alba de Tormes, Sp. 102/C2
Alba Fucens (ruin), It. 104/C1
Alba Iulia, Rom. 107/F2
Albacete, Sp. 102/E3
Albacete (prov.), Sp. 102/E3
Albaida, Sp. 103/E3
Albairate, It. 116/B2
Âlbæk, Den. 96/D3
Albanel (lake), Qu, Can. 188/F1
Albania (ctry.) 105/F2
Albany, Austl. 170/C5
Albany (riv.), On, Can. 180/H3
Albany, Ca, US 193/K11
Albany, Ga, US 191/G4
Albany, Ky, US 188/C4
Albany, Mo, US 195/E5
Albany (cap.), NY, US 188/F3
Albany, Or, US 184/C4
Albany County (int'l arpt.), NY, US 188/F3
Albaredo d'Adige, It. 117/E2
Albarine (riv.), Fr. 114/B5
Albarracín, Sp. 102/E2
Albatross (bay), Austl. 167/D2
Albatross Rock (pt.), Namb. 164/A2
Albbruck, Ger. 114/E2
Albemarle (sound), NC, US 191/J2
Albemarle, NC, US 191/H3
Albemarle (pt.), Ecu. 214/E6
Alben (peak), It. 101/H4
Alberche (riv.), Sp. 102/C2
Alberhill, Ca, US 194/C3
Alberndorf in der Riedmark, Aus. 113/H6
Alberschwende, Aus. 115/F3
Albersdorf, Ger. 96/C4
Albersweiler, Ger. 112/B4
Albert (lake), Austl. 173/A2
Albert (lake), D.R.Congo,Ugan. 155/M7
Albert, Fr. 110/B3
Albert Kanaal (riv.), Belg. 111/E2
Albert Nile (riv.), Ugan. 155/M7
Alberta (prov.), Can. 180/E3
Alberti, Arg. 216/E3
Albertinia, SAfr. 164/C4
Albertirsa, Hun. 106/D2
Alberto de Agostini, PN, Chile 215/B7
Alberton, SAfr. 164/Q13
Albertshofen, Ger. 112/D3
Albertville, Al, US 191/G3
Albertville, Fr. 114/C6
Albestroff, Fr. 111/F6
Albeuve, Swi. 114/D4
Albi, Fr. 100/E5
Albignasego, It. 117/E2
Albina, Sur. 209/H2
Albinea, It. 116/D3
Albino, It. 116/C1
Albion, Mi, US 188/C3
Albisola Marina, It. 116/B4
Albisola Superiore, It. 116/B4
Alblasserdam, Neth. 108/B5
Albocácer, Sp. 103/F2
Alborán (isl.), Mor. 156/C2
Ålborg (bay), Den. 96/D3
Ålborg, Den. 96/C3
Albox, Sp. 102/D4
Albright-Knox Art Gallery, NY, US 189/S10
Albristhorn (peak), Swi. 114/D5
Albufeira, Port. 102/A4
Albula (riv.), Swi. 101/H3
Albuñol, Sp. 102/D4
Albuquerque (int'l arpt.), NM, US 186/F4
Albuquerque, NM, US 186/F4
Albuquerque, Cayos de (isls.), Col. 203/F3
Alburquerque, Sp. 102/B3
Alburtis, Pa, US 196/C3
Albury, Aust. 173/C3
Alby-sur-Chéran, Fr. 114/C6
Alca, Peru 214/C4
Alcabideche, Port. 103/P10
Alcácer do Sal, Port. 102/A3
Alcalá de Chivert, Sp. 103/F2
Alcalá de Guadaira, Sp. 102/C4
Alcalá de Henares, Sp. 103/N9
Alcalá de los Gazules, Sp. 102/C4
Alcalá la Real, Sp. 102/D4

Alcanadre (riv.), Sp. 103/E2
Alcanar, Sp. 103/E2
Alcanices, Sp. 102/B2
Alcañiz, Sp. 103/E2
Alcântara, Braz. 212/A1
Alcántara, Sp. 102/B3
Alcântara, Embalse de (res.), Sp. 102/B3
Alcantarilla, Sp. 102/E4
Alcaraz, Sp. 102/D3
Alcaraz, Sierra de (range), Sp. 102/D3
Alcatraz (isl.), Ca, US 193/K11
Alcaudete, Sp. 102/C4
Alcázar de San Juan, Sp. 102/D3
Alcira, Sp. 103/E3
Alcira, Arg. 216/D2
Alçıtepe, Turk. 105/K2
Alcoa, Tn, US 191/H3
Alcobaça, Braz. 212/C5
Alcobaça, Port. 102/A3
Alcobendas, Sp. 103/N8
Alcochete, Port. 103/Q10
Alcora, Sp. 103/E2
Alcorcón, Sp. 103/N9
Alcorisa, Sp. 103/E2
Alcoutim, Port. 102/B4
Alcoy, Sp. 103/E3
Alcúdia, Sp. 103/G3
Aldabra (isls.), Sey. 151/E6
Aldama, Mex. 184/D2
Aldama, Mex. 201/F4
Aldan (plat.), Rus. 123/N4
Aldan (riv.), Rus. 123/N4
Aldan, Rus. 125/N3
Alde (riv.), Eng, UK 91/H2
Aldeburgh, Eng, UK 91/H2
Aldeia Nova de São Bento, Port. 102/B4
Alden, Il, US 193/N15
Aldenhoven, Ger. 111/F2
Aldeno, It. 115/H6
Aldergrove (int'l arpt.), BC, Can. 184/C2
Aldergrove, NI, UK 92/B2
Alderley Edge, Eng, UK 93/F5
Alderney (isl.) 100/C2
Aldershot, Eng, UK 91/F4
Alderwood Manor-Bothell North, Wa, US 193/C2
Aldine, Tx, US 187/J5
Aldingen, Ger. 115/E1
Aldred (lake), Pa, US 196/B4
Aldridge, Eng, UK 91/E1
Ale Water (riv.), Sc, UK 94/D6
Aleg, Mrta. 160/B2
Alegre, Braz. 213/D2
Alegrete, Braz. 215/E2
Alejandro Gallinal, Uru. 217/K10
Alejandro Roca, Arg. 216/E2
Alejandro Selkirk (isl.), Chile 205/A6
Alejo Ledesma, Arg. 216/E2
Aleknagik, Ak, US 192/G4
Aleksandrovac, Serb. 106/E3
Aleksandrovsk, Rus. 119/N4
Aleksandrów Kujawski, Pol. 99/K2
Aleksandrów Lódzki, Pol. 99/K3
Alekseyevka, Kaz. 145/F2
Alekseyevka, Kaz. 145/F2
Alekseyevka, Rus. 120/F2
Aleksin, Rus. 118/H5
Aleksinac, Serb. 106/E4
Além Paraíba, Braz. 213/L6
Alençon, Fr. 100/D2
Alenquer, Braz. 209/H4
Alenuihaha (chan.), Hi, US 182/T10
Alerce Andino, PN, Chile 216/B4
Aléria, Fr. 104/A1
Alert (pt.), Nun., Can. 181/S6
Aleşd, Rom. 106/F2
Alessandria (prov.), It. 116/B3
Alessandria, It. 116/B3
Alestrup, Den. 96/C3
Ålesund, Nor. 95/C3
Aletschhorn (peak), Swi. 114/D5
Aleutian (range), Ak, US 192/G4
Aleutian (isls.), Ak, US 192/G4
Alexander (mt.), Austl. 170/B2
Alexander (arch.), Ak, US 192/L4
Alexander (isl.), Ant. 218/V
Alexander Bay, SAfr. 164/B3
Alexander City, Al, US 191/G3
Alexander Nevsky Abbey, Rus. 119/T7
Alexandria, Braz. 212/C2
Alexandria (Al Iskandarīyah), Egypt 149/A4
Alexandria (int'l arpt.), Egypt 149/A4
Alexándria, Gre. 105/H2
Alexandra, NZ 175/R12
Alexandria, Rom. 107/G4
Alexandria, SAfr. 164/D4
Alexandria, La, US 187/J5

Alexandria, Mn, US 185/K4
Alexandria, Sc, UK 94/B5
Alexandria, Va, US 196/A6
Alexandrina (lake), Austl. 99/H4
Alexandroúpolis, Gre. 105/J2
Alexis Creek, BC, Can. 184/C2
Alfaro, Sp. 102/E1
Alfatar, Bul. 107/H4
Alfed (riv.), Ger. 109/H3
Alfenas, Braz. 213/H6
Alfhausen, Ger. 109/E2
Alfiós (riv.), Gre. 105/G4
Alfonsine, It. 117/F3
Alfonso Bonilla Aragón (int'l arpt.), Col. 210/B4
Alfred NP, Austl. 173/D3
Alfreton, Eng, UK 93/G5
Alfter, Ger. 111/G2
Alga, Kaz. 121/L2
Algarrobo, Chile 216/N8
Algarve (reg.), Port. 102/A4
Algeciras, Sp. 102/C4
Algeciras, Col. 210/C4
Algemesi, Sp. 103/E3
Alger (prov.), Alg. 158/G4
Algeria (ctry.) 154/E2
Algermissen, Ger. 109/G4
Algete, Sp. 103/N8
Alghero, It. 104/A2
Algiers (El Djezair) (cap.), Alg. 158/G4
Algoa (bay), SAfr. 164/D4
Algodón (riv.), Peru 208/D4
Algodonales, Sp. 102/C4
Algoma, Wi, US 185/M4
Algoma, Sp. 193/C3
Algonac, Mi, US 193/G6
Algonquin, Il, US 193/P14
Algorta, Uru. 217/K10
Algueirão, Port. 103/P10
Algund (Lagundo), It. 115/H4
Alhama de Granada, Sp. 102/D4
Alhama de Murcia, Sp. 102/E4
Alhambra, Ca, US 194/F7
Alhambra, Braz. 212/D2
Alhandra, Port. 103/P10
Alhaurín el Grande, Sp. 102/C4
'Alī al Gharbī, Iraq 146/E2
'Alī ash Sharqī, Iraq 146/E2
Ali Bayramlı, Azer. 121/J5
Alia, It. 104/C4
Alia, Sp. 102/C3
Aliağa, Turk. 148/A2
Aliákmon (riv.), Gre. 105/G2
Aliákmonos (lake), Gre. 105/G2
Aliartos, Gre. 105/H3
Alibates Flint Quarries Nat'l Mon., Tx, US 187/G4
Alibey (lake), Ukr. 107/J5
Alibeyköy, Turk. 107/J5
Alicante, Sp. 103/E3
Alicante (int'l arpt.), Sp. 103/E3
Alice, Tx, US 190/D5
Alice (pt.), It. 105/E3
Alice Arm, BC, Can. 192/N4
Alice Springs, Austl. 171/G2
Aliceville, Al, US 191/G3
Alicia, Phil. 137/D6
Alicudi (isl.), It. 104/D3
Alicurá (res.), Arg. 216/C4
Alife, It. 104/D2
Afiganj, India 142/B2
Aligarh, India 144/D2
Alijó, Port. 102/B2
Alima (riv.), Congo 154/J8
Alingar (riv.), Afg. 144/A2
Alingsås, Swe. 96/E3
Alínpur, India 143/G2
Alipur Duār, India 143/G3
Alisos (riv.), Mex. 186/E5
Alistráti, Gre. 105/H2
Alivérion, Gre. 105/J3
Aliwal North, SAfr. 164/D3
Aljezur, Port. 102/A4
Aljustrel, Port. 102/A4
Alken, Belg. 111/E2
Alkmaar, Neth. 108/B3
Alkmaan (well), Alg. 157/H4
Alkoven, Aus. 113/H6
Allada, Ben. 161/F5
Allahābād, India 142/C3
Allakaket, Ak, US 192/H2
Allaman, Swi. 114/C5
Allan (hills), Sk, Can. 185/G3
Allan, Aus. 107/N7
Allanmyo, Myan. 141/G4
Allanridge, SAfr. 164/D2
Allanson, Austl. 170/C5
Allariz, Sp. 102/B1
Alle, Swi. 114/D3
Allegan, Mi, US 188/C3
Allegheny (mts.), US 183/H4
Allegheny (plat.), US 188/E3
Allegheny (riv.), US 188/D3
Allen (riv.), Eng, UK 90/C2
Allen Park, Mi, US 193/F7
Allendale, SC, US 191/H3
Allendale, NJ, US 197/J7
Allende, Mex. 201/E3
Allende, Mex. 201/E3
Allendorf, Ger. 109/H4

Allensbach, Ger. 115/F2
Allenspark, Co, US 195/A2
Allentown, Pa, US 196/C2
Allentsteig, Aus. 99/H4
Allenwood, Pa, US 196/B1
Alleppey, India 140/C6
Aller (riv.), Ger. 109/H3
Allerkanal (canal), Ger. 109/H4
Allersberg, Ger. 112/E4
Allershausen, Ger. 113/E6
Allgäuer Alps (range), Aus.,Ger. 98/F5
Alliance, Ne, US 185/H5
Alliance, Oh, US 188/D3
Allier (riv.), Fr. 100/E3
Alligator (pt.), La, US 195/Q16
Alloa, Sc, UK 94/C4
Allonnes, Fr. 114/C5
Allora, Austl. 171/C5
Allos, Fr. 101/G4
Alloway, NJ, US 196/C4
Allschwil, Swi. 114/D2
Alm (riv.), Aus. 113/G7
Alma, Mi, US 188/C3
Alma, Qu, Can. 189/G1
Almacelles, Sp. 103/F2
Almada, Port. 103/P10
Almadén, Sp. 102/C3
Almafuerte, Arg. 216/D2
Almagro, Sp. 102/D3
Almanor (lake), Ca, US 186/B2
Almansa, Sp. 103/E3
Almanza, Sp. 102/C1
Almanzor, Pico de (peak), Sp. 102/C2
Almanzora (riv.), Sp. 102/D4
Almas (riv.), Braz. 209/J6
Almas, Braz. 212/A3
Almas, Pico das (peak), Braz. 212/B4
Almaty (int'l arpt.), Kaz. 145/G4
Almaty, Kaz. 145/G4
Almaty (prov.), Kaz. 145/G4
Almazora, Sp. 103/E3
Almeida, Port. 102/B2
Almeirim, Braz. 209/H4
Almeirim, Port. 102/A3
Almelo, Neth. 108/D4
Almenara, Braz. 212/B5
Almenara (peak), Sp. 102/D3
Almenara, Sp. 103/E3
Almendra, Embalse de (res.), Sp. 102/B2
Almendralejo, Sp. 102/B3
Almenno San Salvatore, It. 116/C1
Almería, Neth. 108/C4
Almería, Sp. 102/D4
Almería, Golfo de (gulf), Sp. 102/D4
Al'met'yevsk, Rus. 119/M5
Almhult, Swe. 96/F3
Almina (pt.), Sp. 158/B2
Almirós, Gre. 105/H3
Almirou (gulf), Gre. 105/J5
Almodôvar, Port. 102/A4
Almodóvar del Campo, Sp. 102/C3
Almodóvar del Río, Sp. 102/C4
Almoharín, Sp. 102/C3
Almond (riv.), Sc, UK 94/C4
Almont (riv.), Fr. 88/L6
Almonte, On, Can. 196/D1
Almonte, Sp. 102/C4
Almora, India 142/B1
Almoradi, Sp. 103/E3
Almorox, Sp. 102/C3
Almte. Montt (gulf), Chile 217/B7
Almudévar, Sp. 103/E1
Almuñécar, Sp. 102/D4
Almus, Turk. 148/D1
Alness, Sc, UK 94/B1
Alness (riv.), Sc, UK 94/B1
Alnwick, Eng, UK 94/E6
Alofi (isl.), Wall., Fr. 174/H6
Alofi, NZ 175/J6
Along, India 141/G2
Alónnisos (isl.), Gre. 105/H3
Alor (isl.), Indo. 139/F5
Alor Setar, Malay. 141/H6
Alora, Sp. 102/C4
Alotau, PNG 174/E2
Aloysius (mt.), Austl. 171/F3
Alpachiri, Arg. 216/D3
Alpe di Poti (peak), It. 117/E6
Alpedrete, Sp. 103/M8
Alpen, Ger. 108/D5
Alpena, Mi, US 188/D2
Alpercatas, Braz. 212/A2
Alpercatas, Serra das (mts.), Braz. 209/J5
Alperschällihorn (peak), Swi. 115/F4
Alpes de Provence (range), Fr. 101/G5
Alpha, Austl. 171/B3
Alpha, NJ, US 196/C2
Alphen aan de Rijn, Neth. 108/B4
Alpi Apuane (range), It. 101/J4
Alpi Dolomitiche (range), It. 115/H4
Alpi Orobie (range) It. 101/J3

Alpiarça, Port. 102/A3
Alpine, NJ, US 197/K8
Alpine, Ut, US 195/K13
Alpine, Wy, US 184/F5
Alpirsbach, Ger. 115/E1
Alpnach, Swi. 115/E4
Alps (mts.), Eur. 85/E4
Alqôsh, Iraq 148/E2
Als (isl.), Den. 98/F1
Alsace (pol. reg.), Fr. 98/D4
Alsager, Eng, UK 93/F5
Alsask, Sk, Can. 184/F3
Alsasua, Sp. 102/D1
Alsdorf, Ger. 111/F2
Alsenz (riv.), Ger. 111/G4
Alsenz, Ger. 111/G4
Alsfeld, Ger. 101/H1
Alsheim, Ger. 112/B3
Alsip, Il, US 193/Q16
Alstahaug, Nor. 95/C2
Alster (riv.), Ger. 109/H1
Alsting, Fr. 111/F5
Alt (riv.), Eng, UK 93/E4
Alta, Nor. 95/D2
Alta, Ut, US 195/K12
Alta, Ia, US 185/K5
Alta Floresta, Braz. 209/G5
Alta Gracia, Arg. 216/D2
Altach, Aus. 115/F3
Altadena, Ca, US 194/F7
Altagracia, Nic. 202/E4
Altai (mts.), Asia 128/E2
Altaï, China 128/F2
Altamaha (riv.), Ga, US 191/H4
Altamira, Braz. 209/H4
Altamira, Mex. 202/B1
Altamira do Maranhão, Braz. 212/A2
Altamonte Springs, Fl, US 191/H4
Altamura, It. 104/E2
Altar, Mex. 184/C2
Altar (vol.), Ecu. 210/B5
Altar de los Sacrificios (ruin), Guat. 202/D2
Altar, Desierto de (des.), Mex. 186/D4
Altare, It. 116/B4
Altavilla Vicentina, It. 117/E1
Altay, China 128/F2
Altay, Mong. 128/G2
Altay, Mong. 128/G2
Altay, Resp., Rus. 122/J4
Altayskiy Kray, Rus. 145/G2
Altdorf, Swi. 115/E4
Altdorf bei Nürnberg, Ger. 113/E4
Altea, Sp. 103/E3
Altedo, It. 117/E3
Altena, Ger. 109/E6
Altenahr, Ger. 111/G2
Altenau, Ger. 109/H5
Altenau (riv.), Ger. 109/F5
Altenbeken, Ger. 109/F5
Altenberg bei Linz, Aus. 113/H6
Altenburg, Ger. 98/G3
Altenfelden, Aus. 113/G6
Altenglan, Ger. 111/G4
Altengottern, Ger. 109/H6
Altenkirchen, Ger. 111/G2
Altenmünster, Ger. 112/D6
Altenstadt, Ger. 115/F2
Altenstadt, Ger. 112/B2
Altensteig, Ger. 112/B5
Altentreptow, Ger. 98/G2
Altepexi, Mex. 201/M8
Alter Rhein (riv.), Ger. 108/D5
Altes Land (phys. reg.), Ger. 109/G3
Altheim, Aus. 113/G6
Althengstett, Ger. 112/B5
Althofen, Aus. 101/L3
Althütte, Ger. 112/C5
Altimir, Bul. 107/G4
Altınözü, Turk. 149/E1
Altınoluk, Turk. 148/A1
Altınova, Turk. 149/A1
Altıntaş, Turk. 148/B2
Altınyayla, Turk. 149/A1
Altiplano (plat.), Bol.,Peru 205/C4
Altkirch, Fr. 114/D2
Altlandsberg, Ger. 98/Q6
Altmark (phys. reg.), Ger. 98/F2
Altmühl (riv.), Ger. 101/J2
Altmünster, Aus. 113/G7
Altnaharra, Sc, UK 89/H7
Alto (peak), Braz. 212/A4
Alto (peak), It. 115/G4
Alto Araguaia, Braz. 209/H7
Alto de Tamar (peak), Col. 210/C3
Alto Garças, Braz. 212/A4
Alto Lucero, Mex. 201/N7
Alto Parnaíba, Braz. 212/A3
Alto Purús (riv.), Peru 208/D6
Alto Santo, Braz. 212/C2
Alto Yuruá (riv.), Peru 214/C3
Altomünster, Ger. 112/E6
Alton, La, US 195/Q16
Alton, Il, US 195/F4
Altona, Mb, Can. 185/J3
Altona, Pa, US 188/E3
Altoona, Pa, US 188/E3
Altopascio, It. 117/D5
Altotonga, Mex. 201/M7
Altötting, Ger. 113/F6
Altrincham, Eng, UK 93/F5

Altrip, Ger. 112/B4
Altun (mts.), China 125/H6
Altun Ha (ruin), Belz. 202/D2
Aluminé, Arg. 216/C3
Alunda, Swe. 96/H1
Alupka, Ukr. 120/E3
Alushta, Ukr. 120/E3
Alva, Ok, US 187/H3
Alva, Sc, UK 94/C4
Alvalade, Port. 102/A4
Álvares, Mex. 201/P8
Alvarez, Arg. 216/E2
Alvarado, Mex. 201/N8
Alvaro Obregón, Presa (dam), Mex. 184/C2
Alvdal, Nor. 95/D3
Alveringem, Belg. 110/B1
Alvesta, Swe. 96/F3
Alverca, Port. 103/P10
Alvik, Nor. 96/B1
Alvin, Tx, US 187/J5
Alvito, Port. 102/B3
Alvorada, Braz. 213/A4
Alvorada do Norte, Braz. 212/A4
Alvsborg (co.), Swe. 95/E4
Alvsbyn, Swe. 96/H1
Alwen (riv.), Wal, UK 92/E5
Alxa Youqi, China 128/H4
Alxa Zuoqi, China 128/J4
Alyawarra Abor. Land, Austl. 171/G2
Alyth, Sc, UK 94/C3
Alytus, Lith. 97/L4
Alz (riv.), Ger. 101/K2
Alzano Lombardo, It. 116/C1
Alzenau in Unterfranken, Ger. 112/C2
Alzette (riv.), Lux. 111/F4
Alzey, Ger. 112/B3
Ama, La, US 195/P17
Amacayacú, PN, Col. 208/D4
Amacuro (riv.), Ven. 211/F2
Amacuro (delta), Ven. 211/F2
Amacuzac (riv.), Mex. 201/K8
Amadeus (lake), Austl. 167/C3
Amadjuak (lake), Nun., Can. 181/J2
Amadora, Port. 103/P10
Amagansett, NY, US 197/F2
Amagansett NWR, NY, US 197/F2
Amagasaki, Japan 135/H6
Amagi-san (peak), Japan 133/F3
Amagi, Japan 132/B4
Amaguaña, Ecu. 210/B5
Amajac (riv.), Mex. 201/N7
Amál, Swe. 96/E2
Amala (riv.), Kenya 162/B3
Amalfi, Col. 210/C3
Amalia, SAfr. 164/D2
Amaliás, Gre. 105/G4
Amaluza, Ecu. 214/B2
Amambaí, Braz. 215/E1
Amambai (riv.), Braz. 209/H8
Amami (isls.), Japan 125/M7
Amami-O-Shima (isl.), Japan 125/M7
Amaná (lake), Braz. 208/F4
Amance, Fr. 114/C2
Amánganj, India 142/C3
Amangarh, Pak. 144/A2
Amantea, It. 104/E3
Amanu (isl.), FrPol. 175/U6
Amanzimtoti, SAfr. 165/E3
Amapá, Braz. 209/H3
Amapá (state), Braz. 211/H4
Amarante, Port. 102/B2
Amarante, Braz. 212/B2
Amarante do Maranhão, Braz. 212/A2
Amarapura, Myan. 141/G3
Amareleja, Port. 102/B3
Amargosa, Braz. 212/C4
Amargosa (riv.), Ca, US 186/D3
Amaro (peak), It. 104/D1
Amaro, India 142/C3
Amarume, Japan 134/A4
Amarwāra, India 142/B4
Amasra, Turk. 107/L5
Amasya, Turk. 148/C1
Amasya (prov.), Turk. 148/C1
Amata, Austl. 171/F3
Amatlán de Cañas, Mex. 184/D4
Amatsukominato, Japan 135/K2
Amawalk (res.), NY, US 197/K5
Amay, Belg. 111/E2
Amazcala, Mex. 201/N7
Amazon (Amazonas) (riv.), Braz.,Peru 214/C1

Amazônia, PN da (Tapajós), Braz. 209/G4
Ambāh, India 142/B2
Ambahikily, Madg. 165/G8
Ambajogai, India 147/L5
Ambala Sadar, India 144/D4
Ambalangoda, SrL. 140/D6
Ambalavao, Madg. 165/H8
Ambam, Camr. 154/H7
Ambanja, Madg. 165/J6
Ambaro (bay), Madg. 165/J6
Ambato, Ecu. 210/B5
Ambato Boeny, Madg. 165/H7
Ambatofinandrahana, Madg. 165/H8
Ambatolampy, Madg. 165/H7
Ambatomaidy, Madg. 165/H7
Ambatomanoina, Madg. 165/H7
Ambatondrazaka, Madg. 165/J7
Ambazac, Fr. 100/D4
Ambelos (cape), Gre. 105/H3
Amberg, Ger. 113/E4
Ambergris Cay (isl.), Belz. 202/D2
Ambérieu-en-Bugey, Fr. 114/B6
Amberloup, Belg. 111/E3
Ambikāpur, India 142/D4
Ambilobe, Madg. 165/J6
Ambinanindrano, Madg. 165/J8
Ambinanitelo, Madg. 165/J6
Ambler, Ak, US 192/G2
Amblève (riv.), Belg. 98/D3
Amblève, Belg. 111/F3
Ambo, Peru 214/B3
Amboasary, Madg. 165/H9
Amboavory, Madg. 165/J7
Ambodifototra, Madg. 165/J7
Ambodiharina, Madg. 165/J8
Ambohidratrimo, Madg. 165/H7
Ambohijanahary, Madg. 165/J7
Ambohimahasoa, Madg. 165/H8
Ambohimandroso, Madg. 165/H8
Ambohinihaonana, Madg. 165/H7
Ambohitsilaozana, Madg. 165/H7
Ambolomoty, Madg. 165/H7
Ambon (isl.), Indo. 139/G4
Ambon, Indo. 139/G4
Ambondro, Madg. 165/H9
Amboni Caves, Tanz. 162/C4
Amborompotsy, Madg. 165/H8
Amboseli NP, Kenya 162/C3
Ambositra, Madg. 165/H8
Ambovombe, Madg. 165/H9
Ambrym (isl.), Van. 174/F6
Amchitka (isl.), Ak, US 192/B6
Amchitka Pass (chan.), Ak, US 192/B6
Amealco, Mex. 201/K6
Ameca, Mex. 184/D4
Amecameca de Juárez, Mex. 201/R10
Ameghino, Arg. 216/E2
Ameglia, It. 116/C4
Ameisberg (peak), Aus. 113/G5
Ameland (isl.), Neth. 108/C2
Amelia, It. 104/C1
Amelinghausen, Ger. 109/H2
Amer (chan.), Neth. 108/B5
American (lake), Wa, US 193/B3
American (riv.), Ca, US 193/M9
American Falls (mts.), Id, US 186/D2
American Fork, Ut, US 195/K13
American, North Fork (riv.), Ca, US 186/B3
American Samoa (dpcy.), US 175/W6
American, South Fork (riv.), Ca, US 186/B3
Americana, Braz. 213/G3
Americus, Ga, US 191/G3
Ameringkogel (peak), Aus. 101/L3
Amersfoort, SAfr. 165/E2
Amersfoort, Neth. 108/C4
Amersham, Eng, UK 91/F3
Amery Ice Shelf, Ant. 218/E
Amesbury, Eng, UK 91/E4
Amet, India 147/K3
Amethi, India 142/C2
Amfíklia, Gre. 105/H3
Amfilokhía, Gre. 105/G3
Amfissa, Gre. 105/H3
Amga (riv.), Rus. 123/N3
Amga, Rus. 123/N3
Amguema (riv.), Rus. 123/T3
Amgun' (riv.), Rus. 123/P4
Amherst, NS, Can. 189/H2
Amherst, NY, US 189/S10
Amherstburg, On, Can. 193/F7
Ami, Japan 135/E1
Amiata (peak), It. 101/J4

Amiens, Fr. 110/B4
Amik (lake), Turk. 148/D2
Amila (isl.), Ak, US 192/D6
Amilcar Cabral (int'l arpt.), CpV. 151/K10
Amillis, Fr. 88/M5
Amindaion, Gre. 105/G2
Aminu Kano (int'l arpt.), Nga. 161/H3
Amisk (lake), Sk, Can. 185/H2
Amistad (res.), Mex.,US 190/C4
Amistad Nat'l Rec. Area, Tx, US 187/G5
Amite, La, US 187/K5
Amityville, NY, US 197/M9
Amla, India 142/B5
Amlagora, India 143/F4
Amli, Nor. 96/C2
'Amman (gov.), Jor. 149/E4
Amman (riv.), Wal, UK 90/C3
Amman ('Ammān) (cap.), Jor. 149/D4
Ammanford, Wal, UK 90/C3
Ammarfjället (peak), Swe. 95/E2
Ammassalik, Grld 218/J
Ammer (riv.), Ger. 112/B5
Ammerman (mtn.), Yk, Can. 192/K2
Ammersee (lake), Ger. 101/J3
Amnéville, Fr. 111/F5
Amol, Iran 146/F1
Amora, Port. 103/P10
Amorbach, Ger. 112/C3
Amorgós, Gre. 105/J4
Amorgós (isl.), Gre. 105/J4
Amory, Ms, US 191/F3
Amos, Qu, Can. 188/E1
Amot, Nor. 96/B2
Amotfors, Swe. 96/E2
Amozoc, Mex. 201/L7
Ampachi, Japan 135/L5
Ampanefena, Madg. 165/J6
Ampangalana (canal), Madg. 165/J8
Ampanihy, Madg. 165/H9
Amparafaravola, Madg. 165/J6
Amparai, SrL. 140/D6
Amparo, Braz. 213/G7
Ampasindava (bay), Madg. 165/H6
Ampato (peak), Peru 214/D4
Ampefy, Madg. 165/H7
Amper (riv.), Ger. 113/E6
Ampfing, Ger. 113/F6
Ampflwang im Hausruckwald, Aus. 113/G6
Ampitatafika, Madg. 165/H6
Amposta, Sp. 103/F2
Amqui, Qu, Can. 189/H1
Amravati, India 140/C3
Amreli, India 147/K4
'Amrit (ruin), Syria 149/D2
Amritsar, India 144/C4
Amroha, India 142/B1
Amrum (isl.), Ger. 98/E1
Amstel (riv.), Neth. 108/B4
Amstelveen, Neth. 108/B4
Amsterdam, NY, US 188/F3
Amsterdam, SAfr. 165/E2
Amsterdam (cap.), Neth. 108/B4
Amsterdam (isl.), Fr. 81/N7
Amsterdam Rijnkanaal (riv.), Neth. 108/C4
Amsterdam (Schipol) (int'l arpt.), Neth. 108/B4
Amstetten, Aus. 101/L2
Amu Darya (riv.), Asia 125/F8
Amudat, Ugan. 162/B2
Amukta Pass (chan.), Ak, US 192/D5
Amuku (mts.), Guy. 211/G4
Amund Ringnes (isl.), Nun., Can. 181/S7
Amundsen (gulf), NW, Can. 180/D1
Amundsen (bay), Ant. 218/D
Amundsen (sea), Ant. 218/S
Amundsen-Scott, US, Ant. 218/A
Amunge (lake), Swe. 96/F1
Amur (riv.), Rus. 129/P2
Amurrio, Sp. 102/D1
Amurskaya Oblast, Rus. 123/N4
Amyun, Leb. 149/D2
An Nabk, Syria 149/E2
An Nahud, Sudan 155/L5
An Najaf, Iraq 148/E4
An Najaf (gov.),Iraq 148/E4
An Nāşirīyah,Iraq 146/E2
An Nu'maniyah,Iraq 148/E3
An Teallach (peak), Sc, UK 94/A1
An Uaimh, Ire. 89/Q10
Ana María (gulf), Cuba 199/F3
Anaa (isl.), FrPol. 175/L6
Anabar (riv.), Rus. 123/L3
'Anabtā, WBnk. 149/G7
Anachucuna (mtn.), Pan. 210/B2
Anaco, Ven. 211/E2
Anaconda-Deer Lodge County, Mt, US 184/E4
Anadarko, Ok, US 187/H4
Anadyr' (gulf), Rus. 125/T3

Anadyr' (range), Rus. 218/U
Anadyr' (riv.), Rus. 125/S3
Anadyr', Rus. 123/T3
Anáfi (isl.), Gre. 105/J4
Anaheim, Ca, US 194/G8
Anaheim Lake, BC, Can. 184/B2
Anáhuac, Mex. 190/C5
Anahuac, Tx, US 190/E4
Anahuac, Mex. 184/D2
Anak, NKor. 131/C3
Anakāpalle, India 140/D4
Anaktuvuk Pass, Ak, US 192/H2
Analalava, Madg. 165/H6
Analamaitso (plat.), Madg. 165/J7
Analavory, Madg. 165/H7
Anambas (isls.), Indo. 138/C3
Anambra (state), Nga. 161/G5
Anamur, Turk. 149/C1
Anamur (pt.), Turk. 149/C1
Anan, Japan 132/D4
Anand, India 147/K4
Ananea, Peru 214/D4
Ananea, Bol. 214/D4
Anantapur, India 140/C5
Anantnag, India 144/C3
Anapa, Rus. 120/F3
Anápolis, Braz. 209/J7
Anapu (riv.), Braz. 209/H4
Anār, Iran 147/G2
Anārak, Iran 146/F2
'Anātā, WBnk. 149/G8
Anathan (isl.), NMar. 174/D3
Anatolia (reg.), Turk. 148/B2
Añatuya, Arg. 215/D2
Anauá (riv.), Braz. 208/F3
Ancash (dept.), Peru 214/B3
Anchieta, Braz. 213/D2
Anchor (bay), Mi, US 193/G6
Anchor Point, Ak, US 192/H4
Anchorage, Ak, US 192/J3
Anchorville, Mi, US 193/G6
Anchovy, Jam. 203/G2
Ancient City of Oc-Eo, Viet. 136/D4
Ancoeur (riv.), Fr. 88/L6
Ancohuma (peak), Bol. 214/D4
Ancón, Peru 214/B3
Ancón de Sardinas (bay), Col. 210/B4
Ancona (prov.), It. 117/G5
Ancona, It. 117/G5
Ancoraimes, Bol. 214/D4
Ancre (riv.), Fr. 110/B3
Ancrum, Sc, UK 94/D5
Ancud, Chile 216/B4
Ancud, Golfo de (gulf), Chile 215/B5
Anda, China 129/N2
Andacollo, Arg. 216/C3
Andagua, Peru 214/C4
Andahuaylas, Peru 214/C4
Andäl, India 143/F4
Andalgala, Arg. 215/C2
Andalsnes, Nor. 95/C3
Andalucia (aut. comm.), Sp. 102/C4
Andalusia, Al, US 191/G4
Andalusia (reg.), Sp. 102/C4
Andaman (sea), Asia 141/F5
Andaman (isls.), India 141/F5
Andaman and Nicobar (isls.), India 141/F5
Andamarca, Peru 214/C3
Andamooka, Austl. 171/H5
Andaraí, Braz. 212/B4
Andau, Aus. 101/M3
Andebu, Nor. 96/C3
Andechs, Ger. 115/H2
Andeer, Swi. 115/F4
Andelfingen, Swi. 115/E3
Andelle (riv.), Fr. 110/A5
Andelot-Blancheville, Fr. 114/B1
Andelsbach (riv.), Ger. 115/F2
Andelu, Fr. 88/H5
Andemaka, Madg. 165/H8
Anderlues, Belg. 111/E3
Andermatt, Swi. 115/E4
Andernach, Ger. 111/G3
Anderson (res.), Mex. 198/C4
Anderson, Ak, US 192/H3
Anderson, NW, Can. 180/D2
Anderson, In, US 188/C3
Anderson, Ca, US 186/B2
Anderson, SC, US 191/H3
Anderson, Tx, US 187/J5
Andes (mts.), SAm. 205/C5
Andes, Cordillera de los (mts.), SAm. 215/B4
Andfjorden (chan.), Nor. 95/F1
Andhra Pradesh (state), India 140/C4
Andijk, Neth. 108/C3
Andijon (pol. reg.), Uzb. 145/F4
Andijon, Uzb. 145/F4
Andikíthira (isl.), Gre. 105/H5
Andilamena, Madg. 165/J7

Andilanatoby, Madg. 165/J7
Andimeshk, Iran 146/E2
Andíparos (isl.), Gre. 105/J4
Andira, Braz. 213/B2
Andissa, Gre. 105/J3
Andoas, Peru 214/B2
Andohajango, Madg. 165/J6
Andong, SKor. 131/E4
Andorf, Aus. 113/G6
Andorno Micca, It. 116/B1
Andorra (ctry.) 103/F1
Andorra, Sp. 103/E2
Andorra la Vella (cap.), And. 100/D5
Andover, Eng, UK 91/E4
Andover, NJ, US 196/D2
Andøy, Nor. 95/F1
Andøya (isl.), Nor. 95/E1
Andradas, Braz. 213/G7
Andradina, Braz. 213/B2
Andraitx, Sp. 103/G3
Andramasina, Madg. 165/H7
Andranolava, Madg. 165/H8
Andranomavo (riv.), Madg. 165/H7
Andranopasy, Madg. 165/G8
Andreanof (isls.), Ak, US 192/C6
Andrelândia, Braz. 213/D6
Andrespol, Pol. 99/K3
Andrésy, Fr. 88/J5
Andrezel, Fr. 88/L6
Andria, It. 104/E2
Andriba, Madg. 165/H7
Andringitra (mts.), Madg. 165/H8
Andritsaina, Gre. 105/G4
Androka, Madg. 165/H9
Androntany (cape), Madg. 165/J6
Andros (isl.), Bahm. 199/F3
Andros, Gre. 105/J4
Andros (isl.), Gre. 105/J4
Androscoggin (riv.), Me,NH, US 189/G2
Andújar, Sp. 102/C3
Aneby, Swe. 96/F3
Anecón Grande (peak), Arg. 216/C4
Anegada (bay), Arg. 216/E4
Anegada (isl.), UK 199/J4
Anegada Passage (chan.), NAm. 199/J4
Aného, Togo 161/F5
Aneityum (isl.), Van. 174/F7
Añelo, Arg. 216/C3
Aneto, Pico de (peak), Sp. 103/F1
Anfu, China 141/K2
Ang Nam Ngum (res.), Laos 141/H4
Ang Thong, Thai. 136/C3
Angamos (pt.), Chile 215/B1
Angara (riv.), Rus. 125/J4
Angaston, Austl. 171/H5
Angel (riv.), Ger. 109/E5
Angel (falls), Ven. 211/F3
Angeles, Phil. 137/D4
Angeles National Forest, Ca, US 194/B1
Angelholm, Swe. 96/E3
Angelholm (int'l arpt.), Swe. 96/E3
Angelina (riv.), Tx, US 187/J5
Angeln (reg.), Ger. 98/E1
Angelus (lake), Mi, US 193/F6
Angera, It. 116/B1
Angermanalven (riv.), Swe. 95/G2
Angermünde, Ger. 99/G2
Angers, Fr. 100/C3
Angical do Piauí, Braz. 212/B2
Angicos, Braz. 212/C2
Angkor (temple), Camb. 136/C3
Anglem (mt.), NZ 175/R12
Anglès, Sp. 103/G2
Anglesey (isl.), Wal, UK 92/D5
Angleton, Tx, US 187/J5
Anglin (riv.), Fr. 100/D3
Annonay, Fr. 100/F4
Angol, Chile 216/B3
Angola (ctry.) 163/C4
Angola, In, US 188/C3
Angoon, Ak, US 192/M4
Angostura (res.), Mex. 198/C4
Angostura, Mex. 184/C3
Angoulême, Fr. 100/D4
Angra do Heroísmo, Azor., Port. 103/S12
Angra dos Reis, Braz. 213/J7
Angren, Uzb. 145/F4
Anguilla (isl.), UK 199/J3
Anguillara Veneta, It. 117/E2
Angus (pol. reg.), Sc,UK 94/C3
Angtikada (peak), NAm. 192/G4
Anhée, Belg. 111/D3
Anholt (isl.), Den. 96/D3
Anhui (prov.), China 129/L5
Anhua, China 141/J2
Ani, Japan 134/B4
Aniak, Ak, US 192/G3
Aniakchak (crater), Ak, US 192/G4

Aniakchak Nat'l Mon. and Prsv., Ak, US 192/F4
Aniche, Fr. 110/C3
Animas (riv.), Co,NM, US 186/F3
Animas, Punta De Las (pt.), Mex. 184/B2
'Anīn, Isr. 149/G6
Anina, Rom. 106/E3
Aniva (cape), Rus. 129/R2
Aniva (bay), Rus. 134/C1
Anivorano, Madg. 165/J7
Anizy-le-Château, Fr. 110/C4
Antarctic (pen.), Ant. 218/W
Anjär, India 147/K4
Anjo, Japan 135/M6
Anjou (reg.), Fr. 100/C3
Anjou, Qu, Can. 189/N6
Anjouan (isl.), Com. 165/H6
Anjozorobe, Madg. 165/H7
Anju, NKor. 131/C3
Ankang, China 128/J5
Ankara (cap.), Turk. 148/C2
Ankara (prov.), Turk. 148/C1
Ankaramena, Madg. 165/H8
Ankaratra (mass.), Madg. 165/H7
Ankarsrum, Swe. 96/G3
Ankavandra, Madg. 165/H7
Ankazoabo, Madg. 165/H8
Ankazobe, Madg. 165/H7
Ankazomborona, Madg. 165/H7
Ankazomiriotra, Madg. 165/H7
Ankerika, Madg. 165/H7
Ankililioka, Madg. 165/H8
Ankilizato, Madg. 165/H8
Anklam, Ger. 96/C
Ankum, Ger. 109/E3
Anlong, China 141/J2
Anloo, Neth. 108/D2
Anlu, China 130/C5
Anma (isl.), SKor. 131/D5
Ann (cape), Ma, US 189/G3
Ann Arbor, Mi, US 188/D3
Anna (lake), Va, US 188/E4
Anna Bay, Austl. 173/E2
Anna Pavlowna, Neth. 108/B3
Anna Pink (bay), Chile 216/B5
Anna Regina, Guy. 211/G3
Annaba, Alg. 158/K6
Annaberg-Buchholz, Ger. 113/G1
Annaclone, NI, UK 92/B3
Annai, Guy. 211/G4
Annaka, Japan 135/M1
Annalong, NI, UK 92/C3
Annan, Sc, UK 93/E2
Annan (riv.), Sc, UK 94/C6
Annandale, Va, US 196/A6
Annandale, NJ, US 196/D2
Annapolis (cap.), Md, US 196/B6
Annapurna (peak), Nepal 142/D1
Annbank Station, Sc, UK 94/B6
Annecy, Fr. 114/C5
Annecy (lake), Fr. 114/C5
Annecy-le-Vieux, Fr. 114/C6
Annemasse, Fr. 114/C5
Annet-sur-Marne, Fr. 88/L5
Annette, Ak, US 192/M4
Annezin, Fr. 110/B2
Anniston, Al, US 191/G3
Annonay, Fr. 100/F4
Annville, Pa, US 196/B3
Annweiler, Ger. 111/G5
Anø, Japan 135/K6
Ano Viánnos, Gre. 105/J5
Anoia (riv.), Sp. 103/K7
Anoka, Mn, US 185/K4
Anosibe An' Ala, Madg. 165/J7
Anou-Zeggarene (riv.), Niger 161/G2
Anould, Fr. 114/C1
Anóyia, Gre. 105/J5
Anping, China 130/C3
Anqing, China 130/D3
Anren, China 141/K2
Anrhomer (peak), Mor. 156/D3
Anröchte, Ger. 109/F5
Ans, Belg. 111/E2
Ansai, China 130/B3
Ansan, SKor. 131/F7
Ansbach, Ger. 112/D4
'Anzah, WBnk. 149/G7
Anse-à-Galets, Haiti 203/H2
Anse-d'Hainault, Haiti 203/H2
Anse Rouge, Haiti 203/H2
Ansfelden, Aus. 113/G6
Anshan, China 131/B2
Anshun, China 141/J2
Anson, Tx, US 187/H4
Ansong, SKor. 131/D4
Ansongo, Mali 161/F2
Ant (isl.), Anti. 174/E4
Antakya, Turk. 149/E1
Antalaha, Madg. 165/J6
Antalya (prov.), Turk. 148/B2
Antalya (int'l arpt.), Turk. 149/B1
Antalya, Turk. 149/B1

Antalya, Gulf of (gulf), Turk. 149/B1
Antanambao Manampotsy, Madg. 165/J7
Antananarivo (prov.), Madg. 165/H7
Antananarivo (cap.), Madg. 165/H7
Antanifotsy, Madg. 165/H7
Antanimieva, Madg. 165/G8
Antanimora, Madg. 165/H9
Antar (peak), Alg. 157/E3
Antarctic (pen.), Ant. 218/W
Antarctic Circle 218/Z
Antarctica (cont.) 176
Antequera, Sp. 102/C4
Antes Fort, Pa, US 196/A1
Anthering, Aus. 113/G7
Anthony, NM, US 186/F4
Anti-Atlas (mts.), Mor. 154/C2
Anti-Lebanon (mts.), Leb. 149/D3
Antibes, Fr. 101/G5
Anticosti, Ile d' (isl.), Qu, Can. 181/K4
Antiesen (riv.), Aus. 113/G6
Antifer, Cap d' (cape), Fr. 100/D2
Antigo, Wi, US 185/L4
Antigonish, NS, Can. 189/J2
Antigua, Canl., Sp. 156/B3
Antigua (isl.), Anti. 199/N8
Antigua and Barbuda (ctry.) 199/N8
Antigua Guatemala, Guat. 202/D3
Antiguo Morelos, Mex. 201/F4
Antilly, Fr. 88/L4
Antioquia, Col. 210/C3
Antioquia (dept.), Col. 210/C3
Antipodes (isls.), NZ 81/T8
Antisana (vol.), Ecu. 210/B5
Antlers, Ok, US 187/J4
Antofagasta, Chile 215/B1
Antoing, Belg. 110/C2
Antokonosy Manambondro, Madg. 165/H8
Antón, Pan. 210/A2
Antón Lizardo, Mex. 201/P7
Antón Lizardo (pt.), Mex. 201/P7
Antongil (bay), Madg. 165/J6
Antonia, Mo, US 195/G9
Antonibe, Madg. 165/H6
Antoniesberg (peak), SAfr. 164/C4
Antonina do Norte, Braz. 212/C2
Antônio Carlos, Braz. 213/K6
Antônio Carlos, Braz. 213/D6
Antonito, Co, US 190/B2
Antonovo, Bul. 107/H4
Antony, Fr. 88/J5
Antrim, NI, UK 92/B2
Antrim (dist.), NI, UK 92/B2
Antrim (mts.), NI, UK 92/B1
Antronapiana, It. 114/E5
Antsalova, Madg. 165/H7
Antsambalahy, Madg. 165/J6
Antsenavolo, Madg. 165/H7
Antsirabe, Madg. 165/H7
Antsirañana, Madg. 165/J6
Antsiranana (prov.), Madg. 165/J6
Antsohihy, Madg. 165/H6
Antuco (vol.), Chile 216/C3
Antulai (mt.), Malay. 139/E3
Antwerp, NY, US 189/S9
Antwerp (Deurne) (int'l arpt.), Belg. 108/B6
Antwerpen, Belg. 108/B6
Aprica, Passo dell' (pass), It. 115/G5
Aprilia, It. 104/C2
Apriltsi, Bul. 107/G4
Apsheronsk, Rus. 120/F3
Apsley Gorge NP, Austl. 173/E1
'Ar'ara, Isr. 149/G7
Apua (pt.), Hi, US 182/U11
Apucarana, Braz. 213/B2
Apuiarés, Braz. 212/C2
Apure (riv.), Ven. 208/E2
Apure (prov.), Ven. 210/D3
Apurímac (dept.), Peru 214/C4
Apurímac (riv.), Peru 214/C3
Aqaba (gulf), Asia 125/B7
Aqmola (obl.), Kaz. 145/H2
'Aqrabah, WBnk. 149/G8
'Aqrah, Iraq 148/E2
Aqsay, Kaz. 121/K5
Aqsū, Kaz. 121/K4
Aqtaū, Kaz. 121/J5
Aqtöbe, Kaz. 121/K5
Aqtöbe (int'l arpt.), Kaz. 145/C2
Aqtöbe (obl.), Kaz. 145/C2
Aquanaval (riv.), Mex. 201/E3
Aquaro-Guariquito, PN, Ven. 211/E2
Aquia, Peru 208/E2
Aquidauana, Braz. 209/G8
Aquidauana (riv.), Braz. 209/G8
Aquila, Swi. 117/G3
Aquileia, It. 117/G2
Aquiles Serdán, Mex. 184/D2
Aquin, Haiti 203/H2
Aquiraz, Braz. 212/C1

Aomori (pref.), Japan 134/B3
Aomori, Japan 134/B3
Aonla, India 142/B1
Aoral (peak), Camb. 136/D3
Aos, Gre. 105/J4
Aosta, It. 101/G4
Aosta, Valle d' (valley), It. 116/A1
Aouderas (ruin), Mrta. 160/C2
Aouk, Bahr (riv.), Chad 155/K6
Aoukar (pol. reg.), Mrta. 154/D4
Aoulef, Alg. 157/F4
Aoyama, Japan 135/K6
Apache (mts.), Tx, US 190/B4
Apache (peak), Braz. 213/B4
Apache, Rio das (riv.), Braz. 213/B4
Apache (peak), Az, US 195/R18
'Arab, Baḩr al (riv.), Sudan 155/L6
Apalachicola, Fl, US 191/G4
Apan, Mex. 201/L7
Apaporis (riv.), Col. 208/D3
Aparados da Serra, PN de, Braz. 213/B4
Aparecida, Braz. 213/J7
Aparecida do Taboado, Braz. 213/B2
Aparición, Ven. 210/D2
Aparri, Phil. 137/D4
Araca, Bol. 208/E7
Apatadó, Col. 210/B3
Apatfalva, Hun. 106/E2
Apatin, Serb. 106/D3
Apatity, Rus. 118/G2
Apatzingán de la Constitución, Mex. 184/E5
Apaxco, Mex. 201/K7
Apaxtla de Castrejon, Mex. 201/F5
Apeldoorn, Neth. 108/C4
Apelern, Ger. 109/G4
Apen, Ger. 109/E2
Apennines (mts.), It. 85/F4
Apensen, Ger. 109/G2
Aphrodisias (ruin), Turk. 148/B2
Api (peak), Indo. 139/E5
Api (cape), Indo. 139/F4
Api (cape), Indo. 138/C3
Apiacás, Serra dos (mts.), Braz. 209/G6
Apiaí, Braz. 213/B3
Apizaco, Mex. 201/L7
Aplao, Peru 214/C4
Apo (mt.), Phil. 137/E6
Apodi, Braz. 212/C2
Apodi, PN do, Braz. 212/C2
Apollo Bay, Austl. 173/B3
Apollonia, Gre. 105/J4
Apolo, Bol. 214/D4
Aporé, Braz. 213/B1
Aporé (riv.), Braz. 209/H7
Apostle (isls.), Wi, US 185/L4
Apostle Islands Nat'l Lakeshore, Wi, US 185/L4
Apóstoles, Arg. 215/E2
Apóstoles Andreas (cape), Cyp. 149/D2
Apoteri, Guy. 211/G3
Appalachian (mts.), US 183/K4
Appen, Ger. 109/G1
Appennino Ligure (mts.), It. 101/H4
Appennino Tosco-Emiliano, It. 101/J4
Appennino Umbro-Marchigiano (mts.), It. 101/K5
Appenweier, Ger. 114/D1
Appenzell, Swi. 115/F3
Appenzell (canton), Swi. 115/F3
Appignano, It. 117/G4
Appingedam, Neth. 108/D2
Apple Valley, Ca, US 194/C1
Appleton, NY, US 189/S9
Appleton, Wi, US 115/G5

Aquitaine (pol. reg.), Fr. 100/C4
Ar-Asgat, Mong. 128/J2
Ar Horqin Qi, China 130/E2
Ar Ramādī, Iraq 148/E3
Ar Ramthā, Jor. 149/D3
Ar Raqqah, Syria 148/D3
Ar Raqqah (prov.), Syria 148/D2
Ar Rastan, Syria 149/E2
Ar Rayyān, Qatar 146/F3
Ar Riyāḍ (Riyadh) (cap.), SAr. 146/E4
Ar Rumaythah, Iraq 148/F4
Ar Ruşayfah, Jor. 149/E3
Ar Ruţbah, Iraq 148/E3
Ara (riv.), Japan 133/F2
Arab, Al, US 191/G3
'Arab, Baḩr al (riv.), Sudan 155/L6
Araban, Turk. 148/D2
Arabi, La, US 195/Q17
Arabian (sea), Asia 125/F8
Arabian (des.), Egypt 155/M2
Arabian (pen.), SAr. 146/D3
Araç, Turk. 120/D4
Araç (riv.), Turk. 120/E4
Araca, Bol. 208/E7
Araça (riv.), Braz. 211/F4
Aracaju, Braz. 212/C3
Aracataca, Col. 210/C2
Aracati, Braz. 212/C2
Araçatuba, Braz. 213/B2
Aracena, Sp. 102/B4
Araci, Braz. 212/B3
Aracruz, Braz. 213/D1
Araçuaí, Braz. 212/B5
Araçuaí (riv.), Braz. 212/B5
Arad, Rom. 106/E2
Arad (prov.), Rom. 106/E2
'Arad, Isr. 149/D4
Arag (prov.), Rom. 106/E2
Aragarças, Braz. 209/H7
Aragats (peak), Arm. 121/H4
Aragón (aut. comm.), Sp. 103/E2
Aragón (riv.), Sp. 103/E1
Aragua (state), Ven. 211/E2
Araguaia (riv.), Braz. 205/D3
Araguaia, PN do, Braz. 209/H6
Araguaiana, Braz. 209/H7
Araguaína, Braz. 209/H6
Araguari, Braz. 213/B1
Araguari (riv.), Braz. 209/H3
Araguatins, Braz. 209/J5
Arai, Japan 133/F2
Araioses, Braz. 212/B1
Arāk, Iran 146/E2
Arakamchechan (isl.), Rus. 192/D3
Arakan (mts.), Myan. 141/F3
Arakawa, Japan 135/C2
Arakhthos (riv.), Gre. 105/G3
Araklı, Turk. 148/D1
Aral (sea), Asia 145/C3
Aral, Kaz. 145/D3
Aral Mangy Qaraqumy (des.), Kaz. 145/D3
Aralık, Turk. 148/F2
Aralsor (lake), Kaz. 121/H2
Aramac, Austl. 171/H3
Aran (isls.), Ire. 89/P10
Aran Fawddwy (peak), Wal, UK 92/E6
Aranda de Duero, Sp. 102/D2
Arandelovac, Serb. 106/E3
Arani, India 140/C5
Aranjuez, Sp. 102/D2
Aransas Pass, Tx, US 190/D5
Arantina, Braz. 213/J6
Aranuka (isl.), Kiri. 174/G5
Arao, Japan 135/A2
Arapaca, Braz. 213/B3
Arapiraca, Braz. 212/C2
Arapiuns (riv.), Braz. 211/H5
Arapongas, Braz. 213/B2
'Ar'ara, Isr. 149/G7
Araranguá, Braz. 213/B4
Araraquara, Braz. 213/B2
Araras, Braz. 213/G6
Ararat, Austl. 173/B3
Ararat, Braz. 212/A1
Araria, India 143/F2
Araripe, Chapada do (uplands), Braz. 212/C2
Araripina, Braz. 212/B2
Aras (riv.), Asia 146/E1
Aratane (well), Mrta. 160/C2
Aratoca, Col. 210/C3
Arauá (riv.), Braz. 212/B5
Arauca, Col. 210/D3
Arauca (riv.), Col.,Ven. 211/E3
Arauca (dept.), Col. 210/D3
Araucária, Braz. 209/G6
Arauco, Chile 216/B3
Arauquita, Col. 210/D3
Araure, Ven. 210/D2
Aravis, Col des (pass), Fr. 114/C5
Arawa, PNG 174/E5
Arawale Nat'l Rsv., Kenya 162/D3
Araxá, Braz. 213/C1
Araya (pen.), Ven. 211/E2
Araya, Punta (pt.), Ven. 211/E2
Arba Minch', Eth. 155/N6
Arbeca, Sp. 103/F2
Arbīl (gov.), Iraq 148/E3
Arboga, Swe. 96/F2

Arbois, Fr. 114/B4
Arbois, Mont d' (peak), Fr. 114/C6
Arboletas, Col. 210/C3
Arbon, Swi. 115/F2
Arborfield, Sk, Can. 185/H2
Arborg, Mb, Can. 185/J3
Arbrå, Swe. 96/G1
Arbroath, Sc, UK 94/D3
Arc (riv.), Fr. 100/F5
Arc-en-Barrois, Fr. 114/B3
Arc-et-Senans, Fr. 114/B3
Arc-lès-Gray, Fr. 114/B3
Arc-sur-Tille, Fr. 114/B3
Arcachon, Fr. 100/C4
Arcachon, Bassin d' (lag.), Fr. 100/C4
Arcachon, Pointe d' (pt.), Fr. 100/C4
Arcadia, Ca, US 194/F7
Arcadia, Fl, US 191/H5
Arcadia, Ok, US 195/N14
Arcas, Cayos (isl.), Mex. 202/D1
Arcata, Ca, US 184/B5
Arceburgo, Braz. 213/G6
Arcene, It. 116/C1
Arceto, It. 117/D3
Archena, Sp. 102/E3
Archer City, Tx, US 187/H4
Arches, Fr. 114/C1
Arches NP, Ut, US 186/B3
Archidona, Sp. 102/C4
Archman, Trkm. 121/L5
Arcipelago Toscano (isl.), It. 101/H5
Arcisate, It. 115/E6
Arco, It. 115/G6
Arco, Paso del (pass), Arg. 216/C3
Arcola, It. 116/C4
Arcola, It. 117/E2
Arcole, It. 117/E2
Arcos, Braz. 213/C2
Arcos de Jalón, Sp. 102/D2
Arcos de la Frontera, Sp. 102/C4
Arcos de Valdevez, Port. 102/A2
Arcoverde, Braz. 212/C3
Arctic (ocean) 218/D
Arctic (plain), Ak, US 192/F2
Arctic Bay, Nun., Can. 181/H1
Arctic Circle 218/J
Arctic Red (riv.), NW, Can. 192/M2
Arctic Village, Ak, US 192/J2
Arctowski, Pol., Ant. 218/W
Arda (riv.), Bul. 107/H5
Ardabīl, Iran 121/J5
Ardahan, Turk. 148/E1
Ardal, Iran 146/F2
Ardalstangen, Nor. 96/B1
Ardanuç, Turk. 148/E1
Ardèche (riv.), Fr. 100/F4
Ardee, Ire. 92/B4
Arden (mt.), Austl. 171/H5
Arden, De, US 196/C4
Arden, Den. 96/C3
Arden-Arcade, Ca, US 193/M9
Ardennes (for.), Belg. 100/F1
Ardennes (dept.), Fr. 111/D4
Ardennes, Canal des (canal), Fr. 111/D4
Ardersier, Sc, UK 94/B1
Ardeşen, Turk. 148/E1
Ardesio, It. 115/F6
Ardestan, Iran 146/F2
Ardez, Swi. 115/G4
Ardila (riv.), Sp. 102/B3
Ardino, Bul. 107/G5
Ardivachar (pt.), Sc, UK 89/Q8
Ardle (riv.), Sc, UK 94/C3
Ardlethan, Austl. 173/C2
Ardmore, Ok, US 187/H4
Ardmore, Pa, US 196/C4
Ardnamurchan (pt.), Sc, UK 89/Q8
Ardon, Swi. 114/D5
Ardooie, Belg. 110/C2
Ardres, Fr. 110/A2
Ardrossan, Austl. 171/H5
Ardrossan, Sc, UK 94/B5
Ards (pen.), Sc, UK 92/C3
Ards (dist.), NI, UK 92/C2
Ardsley, NY, US 197/K7
Are, Swe. 95/E3
Areado, Braz. 213/G6
Arecibo, PR 199/M8
Areia Branca, Braz. 212/C2
Arena, Punta de la (pt.), Mex. 184/C3
Arena de la Ventana Punta (pt.), Mex. 184/C3
Arenal (vol.), CR 203/E4
Arenápolis, Braz. 209/G6
Arenas de San Pedro, Sp. 102/C2
Arenas, Punta de (pt.), Arg. 217/C7
Arendal, Nor. 96/C3
Arendonk, Belg. 108/C6
Arendtsville, Pa, US 196/A4
Arenig Fawr (peak), Wal, UK 92/E6
Arenzano, It. 116/B4
Areo, Ven. 211/E2
Areópolis, Gre. 105/H4
Arequipa (dept.), Peru 214/C5

Arequipa, Peru 214/D5
Arequito, Arg. 216/E2
Aresing, Ger. 112/E5
Arévalo, Sp. 102/C2
Arezzo, It. 117/E6
Arezzo (prov.), It. 117/E5
Arga (riv.), Sp. 102/E1
Argalasti, Gre. 105/H3
Argamasilla de Alba, Sp. 102/D3
Argamasilla de Calatrava, Sp. 102/C3
Arganda, Sp. 103/N9
Argegno, It. 115/F6
Argelès-Gazost, Fr. 100/C5
Argelès-sur-Mer, Fr. 100/E5
Argen (riv.), Ger. 115/F2
Argenbühl, Ger. 115/F2
Argens (riv.), Fr. 101/G5
Argenta, It. 117/E3
Argentan, Fr. 100/C2
Argentat, Fr. 100/D4
Argentera (peak), It. 101/G4
Argenteuil, Fr. 88/J5
Argentière, Aiguille d' (peak), Swi. 114/D6
Argentina (ctry.) 215/C4
Argentina (riv.), It. 116/A5
Argentino (lake), Arg. 217/B6
Argenton-sur-Creuse, Fr. 100/D3
Argentona, Sp. 103/L6
Argeş (prov.), Rom. 107/G3
Argeş (riv.), Rom. 107/G3
Arghandab (riv.), Afg. 147/J2
Argıthanı, Turk. 148/B2
Argolís (gulf), Gre. 105/H4
Argonne (for.), Fr. 98/C4
Argonne National Laboratory, Il, US 193/P16
Árgos, Gre. 105/H4
Árgos Orestikón, Gre. 105/G2
Argostólion, Gre. 105/G3
Arguello (pt.), Ca, US 186/B4
Arguin, Cap d' (cape), Mrta. 156/A5
Argun' (riv.), Rus. 123/M4
Arguut, Mong. 128/H2
Argyle (lake), Austl. 167/B2
Argyll and Bute (pol. reg.), Sc, UK 94/A4
Arhangay (prov.), Mong. 128/G2
Arhreijît (well), Mrta. 156/B5
Århus, Den. 96/D3
Århus (co.), Den. 96/D3
Ariana, Tun. 158/M6
Ariano Irpino, It. 104/D2
Ariari (riv.), Col. 210/C4
Arias, Arg. 216/E2
Arica, Chile 214/D5
Arıcak, Turk. 148/E2
Arid (cape), Austl. 170/D5
Arida, Japan 132/D3
Aridhaía, Gre. 105/H2
Arido (peak), Ca, US 194/A1
Aridol (lake), WSah. 156/B4
Ariège (riv.), Fr. 100/D5
Arifiye, Turk. 107/K5
Ārifwāla, Pak. 144/B4
Arīḩā, Syria 149/E2
Arikaree (riv.), Co, US 187/G3
Arilje, Serb. 106/E4
Arima, Trin. 211/F2
Arinos (riv.), Braz. 209/G6
Arinos, Braz. 212/A4
Arinthod, Fr. 114/B5
Ario de Rosales, Mex. 201/E5
Aripao, Ven. 211/E3
Aripuanã, Braz. 208/G6
Aripuanã (riv.), Braz. 205/C3
Ariquemes, Braz. 208/F5
Arish, Austl. 171/B2
Arismendi, Ven. 210/D2
Arivechi, Mex. 184/D2
Arivonimamo, Madg. 165/H7
Ariza, Sp. 102/D2
Arizona, Arg. 216/D2
Arizona (canal), Az, US 195/R18
Arizona (state), US 186/D4
Arizpe, Mex. 184/C2
Årjäng, Swe. 96/E2
Arjeplog, Swe. 95/F2
Arjona, Sp. 102/C4
Arjona, Col. 210/C2
Arkadelphia, Ar, US 187/J4
Arkaig (lake), Sc, UK 94/A3
Arkalokhórion, Gre. 105/J5
Arkansas (riv.), US 190/E3
Arkansas (state), US 190/E3
Arkansas City, Ar, US 187/K4
Arkansas City, Ks, US 187/H3
Arkanū (peak), Libya 155/K3
Arkhángelos, Gre. 148/B2
Arkhangel'sk (int'l arpt.), Rus. 118/J2
Arkhangel'sk (Archangel), Rus. 118/J2
Arkhangel'skaya Oblast, Rus. 118/H3
Arkhangel'skoye, Rus. 119/W9
Arklow, Ire. 92/B6
Arkona (cape), Ger. 96/E4
Arkonam, India 140/C5
Arkticheskiy Institut (isls.), Rus. 122/H2
Arla, Swe. 96/G2
Arlan (peak), Trkm. 145/B5
Arlanda (int'l arpt.), Swe. 96/G2
Arlanza (riv.), Sp. 102/C1
Arlazón (riv.), Sp. 102/D1
Arlbergpass (pass), Aus. 115/G3
Arles, Fr. 100/F5
Arlesheim, Swi. 114/D3
Arley, Mo, US 195/E5
Arlington, Mn, US 185/K4
Arlington, Ga, US 191/G4
Arlington, Va, US 196/A6
Arlington Heights, Il, US 188/C3
Arló, Hun. 99/L4
Arlon, Belg. 111/E4
Arluno, It. 116/B1
Arly (riv.), Fr. 114/C6
Arly, PN de l', Burk. 161/F4
Arly, Réserve Totale de Faune de l', Burk. 161/F4
Armada, Mi, US 193/G6
Armadale, Sc, UK 94/C5
Armagh (dist.), NI, UK 92/B3
Armagh, NI, UK 92/B3
Armançon (riv.), Fr. 100/F3
Armando Laydner, Represa de (res.), Braz. 213/B2
Armant, Egypt 159/C3
Armavir, Rus. 121/G3
Arme, Cap d' (cape), Fr. 101/G5
Armenia, Col. 208/C3
Armenia (ctry.) 121/H5
Armentières, Fr. 110/B2
Armentières-en-Brie, Fr. 88/M5
Armería, Mex. 184/E5
Armidale, Austl. 173/D1
Armilla, Sp. 102/D4
Armstrong, Arg. 216/E2
Armstrong, BC, Can. 184/D3
Armthorpe, Eng, UK 93/G4
Armūr, India 140/C4
Armutlu, Turk. 107/J5
Army Ordnance Museum, Md, US 196/B5
Arnage, Fr. 100/D3
Arnager (int'l arpt.), Den. 96/F4
Arnaía, Gre. 105/H2
Arnaud (riv.), Qu, Can. 181/J3
Arnauti (cape), Cyp. 149/C2
Arnedo, Sp. 102/D1
Arnett, Ok, US 187/H3
Arnhem, Neth. 108/C5
Arnhem Land (reg.), Austl. 167/C2
Arno (riv.), It. 101/J5
Arno (isl.), Mrsh. 174/G4
Arnold, Eng, UK 93/G6
Arnold, Md, US 196/B5
Arnold, Mo, US 195/G9
Arnoldstein, Aus. 101/K3
Arnon (riv.), Fr. 100/E3
Arnouville-lès-Gonesse, Fr. 88/K5
Arnprior, On, Can. 188/E2
Arnsberg, Ger. 109/F6
Arnstadt, Ger. 101/J1
Arnstein, Ger. 112/C3
Arnstorf, Ger. 113/F5
Aro Usu (cape), Indo. 139/H5
Aroab, Namb. 164/B2
Aroche, Sp. 102/B4
Arolsen, Ger. 109/G6
Aron (riv.), Fr. 100/E3
Arona, Canl. 103/X16
Arona, It. 116/B1
Aronde (riv.), Fr. 110/B5
Arorae (isl.), Kiri. 174/G5
Arosa, Swi. 115/F4
Arosser Rothern (peak), Swi. 115/F4
Ærøskøbing, Den. 96/D4
Arpaçay, Turk. 148/E1
Arpajon, Fr. 88/J6
Arpajon-sur-Cère, Fr. 100/E4
Arqalyq, Kaz. 145/E2
Arquata Scrivia, It. 116/B3
Arques, Fr. 110/B2
'Arrābah, WBnk. 149/G7
Arrah, India 143/E3
Arraias (riv.), Braz. 209/H6
Arraias, Braz. 212/A4
Arraiján, Pan. 210/B2
Arran (isl.), Sc, UK 89/R8
Arrancabarba (peak), Nic. 203/E4
Arras, Fr. 110/B3
Arreau, Fr. 100/D5
Arrecife, Canl., Sp. 156/B3
Arrecifes, Arg. 216/E2
Arrée, Monts d' (mts.), Fr. 100/B2
Arriaga, Mex. 202/C2
Arriondas, Sp. 102/C1
Arrochar, Sc, UK 94/B4
Arroio Grande, Braz. 213/A5
Arronville, Fr. 88/J4
Arroscia (riv.), It. 116/B4
Arroux (riv.), Fr. 100/F3
Arrow (riv.), Eng, UK 90/C2
Arrowbear Lake, Ca, US 194/C2
Arroyo de la Luz, Sp. 102/B3
Arroyo Grande, Ca, US 186/B4
Arroyo Hondo (riv.), Ca, US 193/L12
Arroyo Trabuco (riv.), Ca, US 194/C3
Ars, Den. 96/C3
Ars-sur-Moselle, Fr. 111/F5
Arsen'yev, Rus. 129/P3
Arsiero, It. 117/E1
Arslanköy, Turk. 149/D1
Arta (gulf), Gre. 105/G3
Árta, Gre. 105/G3
Artá, Sp. 103/G3
Arteaga, Mex. 184/E5
Arteixo, Sp. 102/A1
Artem, Rus. 129/P3
Artemisa, Cuba 203/F1
Artesia, NM, US 187/F4
Artesia, Ca, US 194/F8
Arth, Swi. 115/E3
Arthies, Fr. 88/H4
Arthur (pt.), Austl. 171/C3
Arthur (riv.), Austl. 170/C5
Arthur Kill (riv.), NJ,NY, US 197/J9
Arthur's (pass), NZ 175/S11
Arthur's Pass NP, NZ 175/S11
Artigas, Uru. 215/E3
Artogne, It. 116/D1
Artois (reg.), Fr. 98/A3
Artova, Turk. 148/D1
Artur Nogueira, Braz. 213/F7
Arturo Merino Benitez (Santiago) (int'l arpt.), Chile 216/N8
Artux, China 145/G5
Artvin, Turk. 148/E1
Artvin (prov.), Turk. 148/E1
Aru (isls.), Indo. 139/H5
Arua, Ugan. 162/A2
Aruba (isl.), Aru., Neth. 199/H5
Arucas, Canl., Sp. 156/B3
Arudy, Fr. 100/C5
Arujá, Braz. 213/G8
Arun (riv.), China 143/F2
Arunāchal Pradesh (state), India 141/F2
Arundel, Eng, UK 91/F5
Aruppukkottai, India 140/C6
'Arūrah, WBnk. 149/G7
Arus (cape), Indo. 139/F3
Arusha, Tanz. 162/C3
Arusha (pol. reg.), Tanz. 162/C4
Arusha NP, Tanz. 162/C3
Arutua (isl.), FrPol. 175/L6
Aruwimi (riv.), D.R. Congo 155/K7
Arvada, Co, US 195/B3
Arvayheer, Mong. 128/H2
Arve (riv.), Fr. 114/C6
Arviat, Nun., Can. 180/G2
Arvidsjaur, Swe. 95/F2
Arvika, Swe. 96/E2
Arvin, Ca, US 186/C4
Arvon (mt.), Mi, US 185/L4
Arys', Kaz. 145/E4
Arz (riv.), Fr. 100/B3
Arzachena, It. 104/A2
Arzamas, Rus. 119/K5
Arzbach, Ger. 111/G3
Arzberg, Ger. 113/F2
Arzen, Ger. 109/G4
Arzew, Alg. 158/E5
Arzignano, It. 117/E1
Arzl im Pitztal, Aus. 115/G3
Arzúa, Sp. 102/A1
Ås, Nor. 96/D2
As, Belg. 111/E1
Aš, Czh. 113/F2
As Sabkhah, Syria 148/D3
Aş Şaff, Egypt 149/B5
Aş Şāfī, Jor. 149/D4
As Sālimīyah, Kuw. 146/E3
As Sallūm, Egypt 155/L1
As Salmān, Iraq 148/F4
As Salţ, Jor. 149/D3
As Sanţah, Egypt 149/B4
Aş Şarīḩ, Jor. 149/D3
As Sinbillāwayn, Egypt 149/B4
As Sudd (reg.), Sudan 155/M6
As Sulaymānīyah (gov.), Iraq 148/F3
As Sulaymānīyah, Iraq 148/F3
As Suwaydā' (prov.), Syria 148/D3
As Suwaydā', Syria 149/E3
Aş Şuwayrah, Iraq 148/F3
As Suways, Egypt 159/C2
As Suways (gov.), Egypt 159/C2
Asaba, Nga. 161/G5
Asadābād, Afg. 144/A2
Asadābād, Iran 146/E2
Asagny, PN d', C.d'Iv. 160/D5
Asahan (riv.), Indo. 138/A3
Asahi, Japan 133/G3
Asahi (riv.), Japan 132/C3
Asahi, Japan 135/F1
Asahi, Japan 135/L5
Asahi, Japan 135/M5
Asahi-dake (peak), Japan 134/C2
Asahikawa, Japan 134/C2
Asai, Japan 135/K5
Asaka, Japan 135/D2
Asake (riv.), Japan 135/K5
Asama-yama (peak), Japan 133/F2
Asan (bay), SKor. 131/D4
Asansol, India 143/F4
Asashi-dake (peak), Japan 133/F1
Asashina, Japan 135/A1
Asawanwah (well), Libya 155/J3
Asbach, Ger. 111/G2
Asbach-Bäumenheim, Ger. 112/D5
Asbest, Rus. 119/P4
Asbestos (mts.), SAfr. 164/C3
Asbury Park, NJ, US 196/D3
Ascención, Bol. 208/F7
Ascención (bay), Mex. 198/D4
Ascensión, Mex. 184/D2
Ascensión, Arg. 216/E2
Aschach (riv.), Aus. 113/G6
Aschach an der Donau, Aus. 113/H6
Aschaffenburg, Ger. 112/C3
Aschau am Inn, Ger. 113/F6
Ascheberg, Ger. 109/E5
Aschendorf, Ger. 109/E2
Aschersleben, Ger. 98/F3
Ascoli Piceno, It. 101/K5
Ascoli Satriano, It. 104/D2
Ascona, Swi. 115/E5
Ascope, Peru 214/B2
Åseda, Swe. 96/F3
Asela, Eth. 155/N6
Åsele, Swe. 95/F2
Asendorf, Ger. 109/G2
Asendorf, Ger. 109/F3
Asenovgrad, Bul. 105/J1
Åseral, Nor. 96/B2
Aserei (peak), It. 116/C3
Asfeld, Fr. 111/D5
Ash, Eng, UK 88/D3
Ash, Eng, UK 88/A3
Ash Shabakah, Iraq 148/E4
Ash Shamal (gov.), Leb. 149/E2
Ash Shāmīyah, Iraq 148/F4
Ash Shāriqah, UAE 147/G3
Ash Sharqāt, Iraq 148/E3
Ash Sharqīyah (state), Sudan 159/C5
Ash Shawbak, Jor. 149/D4
Asha, Nga. 161/F5
Ashanti (uplands), C.d'Iv. 154/E6
Ashanti (pol. reg.), Gha. 161/E5
Asharoken, NY, US 197/M8
Ashbourne, Ire. 92/B4
Ashbourne, Eng, UK 93/G5
Ashburton (riv.), Austl. 167/A3
Ashburton, NZ 175/S11
Ashby (canal), Eng, UK 91/E1
Ashby-de-la-Zouch, Eng, UK 91/E1
Ashcroft, BC, Can. 184/C3
Ashdod, Isr. 149/F8
Asheboro, NC, US 191/J3
Ashern, Mb, Can. 185/J3
Asheville, NC, US 191/H3
Asheweig (riv.), On, Can. 185/M2
Ashford, Austl. 173/D1
Ashford, Eng, UK 91/G4
Ashford, Eng, UK 88/B2
Ashford, Ire. 92/B5
Ashgabat (cap.), Trkm. 145/C5
Ashhurst, NZ 175/T11
Ashibetsu, Japan 134/C2
Ashigawa, Japan 135/B2
Ashikaga, Japan 135/C1
Ashington, Eng, UK 93/G1
Ashino (lake), Japan 135/C3
Ashiwada, Japan 135/B3
Ashiya, Japan 135/H6
Ashiyasu, Japan 135/A2
Ashizuri-misaki (cape), Japan 132/C4
Ashland, Ks, US 187/H3
Ashland, Ky, US 188/D4
Ashland, Oh, US 188/D3
Ashland, Or, US 184/C5
Ashland, Pa, US 196/B2
Ashley, ND, US 185/J4
Ashley, Pa, US 196/C1
Ashmore (reef), Austl. 167/B2
Ashmore and Cartier Islands Territory (dpcy.), Austl. 167/B2
Ashmūn, Egypt 149/B4
Ashoknagar, India 142/A3
Ashoro, Japan 134/C2
Ashqelon, Isr. 149/F8
Ashta, India 140/C3
Ashtabula, Oh, US 188/D3
Ashton, Id, US 184/F4
Ashton, SAfr. 164/M10
Ashton-in-Makerfield, Eng, UK 93/F5
Ashton-under-Lyne, Eng, UK 93/F5
Asia (cont.) 83
Asia, Peru 214/B4
Asiago, It. 115/H6
Asikkala, Fin. 97/L1
Asilah, Mor. 158/A2
Asillo, Peru 214/D4
Asinara (isl.), It. 104/A2
Asinara, Golfo dell' (gulf), It. 104/A2
Asino, Rus. 122/J4
Asipovichy, Bela. 120/D1
'Asīr (mts.), SAr. 146/D5
Asis (cape), Sudan 159/D5
Aşkale, Turk. 148/E2
Askeaton, Ire. 89/P10
Asker, Nor. 96/D2
Askersund, Swe. 96/F2
Askim, Nor. 96/D2
Askim, Swe. 96/D3
Askion (peak), Gre. 105/G2
Askja (crater), Ice. 95/P6
Askov, Den. 96/C4
Askvoll, Nor. 95/C3
Asmara (cap.), Erit. 146/C5
Asnen (lake), Swe. 96/F3
Asnières-sur-Oise, Fr. 88/K4
Asnières-sur-Seine, Fr. 88/J5
Asō, Japan 135/E2
Aso NP, Japan 132/B4
Aso-san (peak), Japan 132/B4
Asola, It. 116/D2
Asolo, It. 117/E1
Āsosa, Eth. 155/M5
Asoteriba (peak), Sudan 159/D4
Aspach, Aus. 113/G6
Aspe, Sp. 103/E3
Aspen, Co, US 186/F3
Aspen Hill, Md, US 196/A5
Aspen Park, Co, US 195/B3
Aspendos (ruin), Turk. 149/B1
Asperg, Ger. 112/C5
Aspermont, Tx, US 187/G4
Aspers, Pa, US 196/A4
Aspetuck (riv.), Ct, US 197/E1
Aspiring (mt.), NZ 175/R11
Asprópirgos, Gre. 105/H3
Asquith, Sk, Can. 184/G2
Assa, Mor. 156/C3
Assa Aguiene (peak), Alg. 157/G5
Assab, Erit. 146/D6
Assaba (pol. reg.), Mrta. 160/C2
Assam (state), India 141/F2
Assaré, Braz. 212/C2
Asse, Belg. 111/D2
Assemini, It. 104/A3
Assen, Neth. 108/D3
Assenede, Belg. 110/C1
Assens, Den. 96/C4
Assens, Den. 96/D3
Assentoft, Den. 96/D3
Assesse, Belg. 111/E3
Assiniboia, Sk, Can. 185/G3
Assiniboine (mt.), BC, Can. 184/E3
Assiniboine (riv.), Mb,Sk, Can. 185/H3
Assinika (lake), Qu, Can. 188/F1
Assis, Braz. 213/B2
Assling, Ger. 113/F6
Asso, It. 116/C1
Assomada, CpV. 151/K10
Astakós, Gre. 105/G3
Astana (cap.), Kaz. 145/F2
Asten, Neth. 108/C6
Asten, Aus. 113/H6
Asti (prov.), It. 116/B3
Asti, It. 101/H4
Astico (riv.), It. 117/E1
Astipálaia, Gre. 148/A2
Astolfo Dutra, Braz. 213/L6
Astorga, Braz. 213/B2
Astoria, Or, US 184/C4
Åstorp, Swe. 96/E3
Astrakhan', Rus. 121/J3
Astrakhanskaya Oblast, Rus. 121/H3
Astros, Gre. 105/H4
Astudillo, Sp. 102/C1
Asturias (aut. comm.), Sp. 102/B1
Asuka, Japan 135/J7
Asuke, Japan 135/M5
Asunción (cap.), Par. 215/E2
Asuncion (isl.), NMar. 174/D3
Asunción Ixtaltepec, Mex. 198/B4
Asunden (lake), Swe. 96/F3
Aswa (riv.), Ugan. 155/M7
Aswān (gov.), Egypt 159/C4
Aswān, Egypt 159/C3
Aswan High (dam), Egypt 159/C4
Asyūţ (gov.), Egypt 159/B3
Asyūţ, Egypt 159/B3
Aszód, Hun. 107/R9
Aţ Ţafīlah, Jor. 149/D4
Aţ Ţafīlah (gov.), Jor. 149/D4
Aţ Ţā'if, SAr. 146/D4
At Tall, Syria 149/E3
At Tall al Kabīr, Egypt 149/B4
At Ta'mīn (gov.), Iraq 148/E3
Aţ Ţūr, WBnk. 149/G8
Atabapo (riv.), Ven. 211/E4
Atacama (des.), Chile 205/B4
Atacames, Ecu. 210/B4
Atafu (isl.), Tok. 175/H5
Atakpamé, Togo 161/F5
Atalaia, Braz. 212/C3
Atalaia do Norte, Braz. 214/D2
Atalándi, Gre. 105/H3
Atalaya, Peru 214/C3
Atami, Japan 133/F3
Atar, Mrta. 154/C3
Atarfe, Sp. 102/D4
Atarra, India 142/C3
Atas Bogd (peak), Mong. 128/G3
Atascadero, Ca, US 186/B4
Atascosa (co.), Tx, US 195/T21
Atascosa, Tx, US 195/T21
Atatürk (dam), Turk. 148/D2
Atatürk (res.), Turk. 148/D2
Ataturk (int'l arpt.), Turk. 107/J5
Atbara (riv.), Eth. 155/N5
Atbara, Sudan 155/M4
Atbasar, Kaz. 145/E2
Atchafalaya (riv.), La, US 187/K5
Atchafalaya (bay), La, US 187/K5
Atchison, Ks, US 187/J3
Atco, NJ, US 196/D4
Atebubu, Gha. 161/E5
Ateca, Sp. 102/E2
Ateelva (riv.), Nor. 95/G1
Atén, Bol. 214/D4
Atencingo, Mex. 201/L8
Atenco, Mex. 201/Q10
Atenco, Mex. 201/R9
Atengo (riv.), Mex. 184/D4
Atessa, It. 104/D1
Atglen, Pa, US 196/C4
Ath, Belg. 110/C2
Athabasca, Ab, Can. 184/E2
Athabasca (riv.), Ab, Can. 180/E3
Athabasca (lake), Ab,Sk, Can. 180/E3
Athapapuskow (lake), Mb, Can. 185/H2
Athār Ţulmaythah (Ptolemaïs) (ruin), Libya 155/K1
Athboy, Ire. 89/Q10
Athenry, Ire. 89/P10
Athens (Athínai) (cap.), Gre. 105/N9
Athens, Al, US 191/G3
Athens, Ga, US 191/H3
Athens, Tn, US 191/G3
Athens, Tx, US 187/J4
Atherstone, Eng, UK 91/E1
Atherton, Austl. 171/B2
Atherton, Eng, UK 93/F4
Atherton, Mo, US 195/E5
Athgarh, India 140/E3
Athi (riv.), Kenya 162/C3
Athínai (Athens) (cap.), Gre. 105/N9
Athis-Mons, Fr. 88/K5
Athlone, Ire. 89/Q10
Atholl (for.), Sc, UK 94/B3
Áthos (peak), Gre. 105/J2
Athy, Ire. 89/Q10
Ati, Chad 155/J5
Atibaia, Braz. 213/G8
Atibaia (riv.), Braz. 213/G7
Atico, Peru 214/C5
Atienza, Sp. 102/D2
Atikokan, On, Can. 185/L3
Atil, Mex. 184/C2
Atitlán (lake), Guat. 202/D3
Atiu (isl.), Cookls. 175/K7
Atizapan, Mex. 201/Q10
Atka, Ak, US 192/D5
Atka (isl.), Ak, US 192/C5
Atkarsk, Rus. 121/H2
Atkinson (pt.), NW, Can. 192/M2
Atlacomulco de Fabela, Mex. 201/K7
Atlanta (cap.), Ga, US 191/G3
Atlantic (ocean) 80/G3
Atlantic (co.), NJ, US 196/D4
Atlantic Beach, NY, US 197/L9
Atlantic City, NJ, US 196/D5
Atlantic Highlands, NJ, US 197/J10
Atlantico (dept.), Col. 210/C2
Atlántida, Uru. 217/L11
Atlantique (prov.), Ben. 161/F5
Atlas (mts.), Mor. 154/E1
Atlas (peak), Ca, US 193/K10
Atlas Saharien (mts.), Alg. 154/E1
Atlatlahuaca, Mex. 201/Q10
Atlin, BC, Can. 192/M3
'Atlit, Isr. 149/F6
Atlixco, Mex. 201/L8
Atmore, Al, US 191/G4
Atocha, Bol. 208/E8
Atomium, The, Belg. 111/D2
Atotonilco, Mex. 201/L6
Atouila, 'Erg (des.), Mali 156/D5
Atoyac, Mex. 201/E5
Atoyac (riv.), Mex. 202/B2
Atqasuk, Ak, US 192/G1
Atrai (riv.), Bang. 143/G3
Atrak (riv.), Iran 147/G1
Atran (riv.), Swe. 96/E3
Atrato (riv.), Col. 208/C2
Atrauli, India 142/B1
Atsugi, Japan 135/C3
Atsumi, Japan 133/F3
Atsumi (pen.), Japan 135/M6
Attalens, Swi. 114/C4
Attalla, Al, US 191/G3
Attapu, Laos 136/D3
Attawapiskat (lake), On, Can. 185/L2
Attawapiskat (riv.), On, Can. 181/H3
Attel (riv.), Ger. 113/F7
Attendorn, Ger. 109/E6
Atteridgeville, SAfr. 164/Q12
Attersee (lake), Aus. 113/G7
Attert, Belg. 111/E4
Attica, Mi, US 193/F5
Attigny, Fr. 111/D5
'Attīl, WBnk. 149/G7
Attock, Pak. 144/B3
Attu, Ak, US 192/A5
Attu (isl.), Ak, US 192/A5
Atuel (riv.), Arg. 215/C4
Atuntaqui, Ecu. 210/B4
Åtvidaberg, Swe. 96/G2
Atwater, Ca, US 186/B3
Atyraū (obl.), Kaz. 145/B3
Atyraū, Kaz. 121/J3
Atyraū (int'l arpt.), Kaz. 121/J3
Au, Swi. 115/F3
Au, Aus. 115/F3
Au in der Hallertau, Ger. 113/E5
Au Sable (riv.), Mi, US 188/C2
Auari (riv.), Braz. 211/E3
Aubange, Belg. 111/E4
Aube (dept.), Fr. 111/D6
Aube (riv.), Fr. 98/C4
Aubenas, Fr. 100/F4
Aubepierre-Ozouer-le-Repos, Fr. 88/L6
Aubergenville, Fr. 88/H5
Aubert (peak), Swi. 114/C4
Aubervilliers, Fr. 88/K5
Aubetin (riv.), Fr. 110/C6
Aubette (riv.), Fr. 110/A5
Aubette de Magny (riv.), Fr. 88/H4
Aubigny-en-Artois, Fr. 110/B3
Aubigny-sur-Nère, Fr. 100/E3
Aubin, Fr. 100/E4
Aubonne, Swi. 114/C5
Auboué, Fr. 111/E5
Aubrac, Monts du (mts.), Fr. 100/E4
Aubrives, Fr. 111/D3
Auburn, Ky, US 195/D6
Auburn, Austl. 171/H5
Auburn, Al, US 191/G3
Auburn, Ca, US 186/B3
Auburn, In, US 188/C3
Auburn, Me, US 189/G2
Auburn, Ne, US 187/J2
Auburn, NY, US 188/E3
Auburn, Pa, US 196/B2
Auburn, Wa, US 184/C4
Auburn Hills, Mi, US 193/F6
Aubusson, Fr. 100/E4
Aucá Mahuida (peak), Arg. 216/C3
Auch, Fr. 100/D5
Auchel, Fr. 110/B3
Auchinleck, Sc, UK 94/B6
Auchterarder, Sc, UK 94/C4
Auchtermuchty, Sc, UK 94/C4
Auchy-lès-Hesdin, Fr. 110/B3
Auckland, NZ 175/S10
Auckland (int'l arpt.), NZ 175/S10
Auckland (isls.), NZ 81/T8
Aude (riv.), Fr. 100/E5
Auderghem, Belg. 111/D2
Audeux (riv.), Fr. 114/C3
Audierne (bay), Fr. 100/A3
Audincourt, Fr. 114/C3
Audo (range), Eth. 155/P6
Audruicq, Fr. 110/B2
Audun-le-Roman, Fr. 111/E5
Audun-le-Tiche, Fr. 111/E5
Aue (riv.), Ger. 109/E2
Aue, Ger. 113/F1
Auer (Ora), It. 115/H5
Auerbach, Ger. 113/F1
Auerbach in der Oberpfalz, Ger. 113/E3
Auersberg (peak), Ger. 113/F2
Aufess (riv.), Ger. 112/E3
Auffargis, Fr. 88/H5
Augathella, Austl. 171/B4
Augher, NI, UK 92/A3
Aughnacloy, NI, UK 92/B3
Aughrim, Ire. 92/B6
Augrabies Falls NP, SAfr. 164/C3
Augrabiesvalle (falls), SAfr. 164/C3
Augsburg, Ger. 112/D6
Augub (peak), Namb. 164/A2
Augusta, Ga, US 191/H3
Augusta (cap.), Me, US 189/G2
Augusta, It. 104/D4
Augusta, Austl. 170/B5
Augusta, NJ, US 196/D1
Augusta, Golfo di (gulf), It. 104/D4
Augustdorf, Ger. 109/F5
Augustenborg, Den. 96/C4
Augusto César Sandino (int'l arpt.), Nic. 202/E3
Augustów, Pol. 97/K5
Augustus (mt.), Austl. 170/C3
Auk Bok (isl.), Myan. 136/B3
Auki, Sol. 174/F5
Aukstaitija NP, Lith. 97/M4
Auld (lake), Austl. 167/B3
Aulencia (riv.), Sp. 103/M9
Aulendorf, Ger. 115/F2
Aulla, It. 116/C4
Aulnay-sous-Bois, Fr. 88/K5
Aulnay-sur-Mauldre, Fr. 88/H5
Aulne (riv.), Fr. 100/A2
Aulnoy, Fr. 88/M5
Aulnoye-Aymeries, Fr. 110/C3
Aulnut (int'l arpt.), Fr. 100/E4
Ault, Co, US 195/C1
Ault (peak), Swi. 115/F4
Ault, Fr. 110/A3
Aumale, Fr. 110/A4
Aumetz, Fr. 111/E5
Aumühle, Ger. 109/H1
Aunay-sur-Odon, Fr. 100/C2
Aunette (riv.), Fr. 110/B5
Auneuil, Fr. 110/B5
Auning, Den. 96/D3
Aur (isl.), Mrsh. 174/G4
Aura, NJ, US 196/C4
Aurach, Ger. 112/D4
Aurach (riv.), Ger. 112/D3
Auraiya, India 142/B2
Aurangābād, India 143/E3
Aurangābād, India 147/L5
Auray, Fr. 100/B3
Aureilhan, Fr. 100/D5
Aurich, Ger. 109/E2
Auriflama, Braz. 213/B2
Aurillac, Fr. 100/E4
Aurisina, It. 117/G1
Aurland, Nor. 96/B1
Aurolzmünster, Aus. 113/G6
Aurora, Braz. 212/C2
Aurora, Guy. 211/G3
Aurora, Co, US 195/C3
Aurora, Il, US 187/K2
Aurora, Mo, US 187/J3
Aurora Lodge, Ak, US 192/J3
Aus, Namb. 164/B2
Ausa (riv.), It. 117/G1
Aussillon, Fr. 100/E5
Aust-Agder (co.), Nor. 95/C4
Austin, Nv, US 186/C3
Austin (lake), Austl. 167/A3
Austin (isl.), Nun., Can. 180/G2
Austral (Tubuaï Islands) (isls.), FrPol. 175/K7
Australia (cont.) 125
Australia (ctry.) 125
Australian Alps (range), Austl. 173/C3
Australian Capital Territory (cap. terr.), Austl. 173/D2
Australind, Austl. 170/B5
Austria (ctry.) 101/L3
Austurhorn (pt.), Ice. 95/P7
Auterive, Fr. 100/D5
Authie (riv.), Fr. 100/D1
Autlán de Navarro, Mex. 184/D5
Automne (riv.), Fr. 110/B5
Autreppe, Belg. 110/C3
Autun, Fr. 100/F3
Auvergne (pol. reg.), Fr. 100/E4
Auvers-sur-Oise, Fr. 88/J4
Auvézère (riv.), Fr. 100/D4
Aux Sables (riv.), On, Can. 188/D2
Auxerre, Fr. 100/E3
Auxi-le-Château, Fr. 110/B3
Auxonne, Fr. 114/B3
Auyán-Tepuí (peak), Ven. 211/F3
Auyuittuq NP, Nun., Can. 181/K2
Auzangate (peak), Peru 214/D4
Āvaj, Iran 146/E1
Avallon, Fr. 100/E3
Avalon (pen.), Nf, Can. 181/L4
Avalon, Ca, US 194/B4
Avalon, NJ, US 196/D5
Avanne-Aveney, Fr. 114/B3
Avaré, Braz. 213/B2
Avarua, NZ 175/K7
Avdat (ruin), Isr. 149/D4
Avebury Stone Circle, Eng, UK 91/E4
Aveiro, Port. 102/A2
Aveiro (dist.), Port. 102/A2
Aveley, Eng, UK 88/D2
Avelgem, Belg. 110/C2
Avellaneda, Arg. 217/J11
Avellino, It. 104/D2
Avelon (riv.), Fr. 110/A5
Avenal, Ca, US 186/B3
Avenches, Swi. 114/D4
Avenel, NJ, US 197/H9
Avernes, Fr. 88/H4
Aversa, It. 104/D2
Aves (isl.), Ven. 199/J4
Avesnes-le-Comte, Fr. 110/B3
Avesnes-sur-Helpe, Fr. 110/C3
Avesta, Swe. 96/G1
Aveyron (riv.), Fr. 100/D4
Avezzano, It. 104/C1
Avich (lake), Sc, UK 94/A4
Aviemore, Sc, UK 94/C2
Avignon, Fr. 100/F5
Aviḩayil, Isr. 149/F7
Ávila de los Caballeros, Sp. 102/C2
Avilés, Sp. 102/C1
Avio, It. 117/D1
Avion, Fr. 110/B3
Avis, Pa, US 196/A1
Avisio (riv.), It. 115/H5
Avize, Fr. 110/D6
Avlum, Den. 96/C3
Avoca, Austl. 173/C4
Avoca, Austl. 173/B3
Avoca (riv.), Ire. 92/B6
Avoch, Sc, UK 94/B1
Avola, It. 104/D4
Avon (riv.), Eng, UK 90/C6
Avon (riv.), Sc, UK 94/C1
Avon, Fr. 100/E2
Avon (riv.), Fr. 88/L6
Avon Valley NP, Austl. 170/C4
Avon Water (riv.), Sc, UK 94/B5
Avonbeg (riv.), Ire. 92/B6
Avondale, Austl. 173/D2
Avondale, Az, US 195/R19
Avondale, Pa, US 196/C4
Avonlea, Sk, Can. 185/G3
Avonmore (riv.), Ire. 92/B5
Avranches, Fr. 100/C2
Avre (riv.), Fr. 98/B4
Avrillé, Fr. 100/C3
Awa-shima (isl.), Japan 134/A4
A'waj (riv.), Syria 149/E3
Awaji, Japan 135/H6

Awans, Belg. 111/E2
Awasa, Eth. 155/N6
Awash, Eth. 155/P6
Awash Wenz (riv.), Eth. 155/P5
Awaso, Gha. 161/E5
Awat, China 128/D3
Awbārī, Libya 154/H2
Awbārī (des.), Libya 157/H4
Awe (lake), Sc, UK 94/A4
Awjilah, Libya 155/K2
Awka, Nga. 161/G5
Awsīm, Egypt 149/B4
Ax-les-Thermes, Fr. 100/D5
Axamo (int'l arpt.), Swe. 96/F3
Axams, Aus. 115/H3
Axarfjördhur (inlet), Ice. 95/N6
Axel, Neth. 108/A6
Axel Heiberg (isl.), Nun., Can. 181/S7
Axim, Gha. 161/E5
Axios (riv.), Gre. 105/H2
Axis (dam), Wa, US 193/D2
Axminster, Eng, UK 90/D5
Axochiapan, Mex. 201/L8
Ay (riv.), Rus. 119/N5
Ay, Fr. 110/C5
Ayabaca, Peru 214/B2
Ayabe, Japan 135/H5
Ayacucho, Peru 214/C4
Ayacucho (dept.), Peru 214/C4
Ayacucho, Arg. 216/F3
Ayagöz, Kaz. 128/D2
Ayaguz (riv.), Kaz. 128/C2
Ayama, Japan 135/K6
Ayamé I, Barrage d' (dam), C.d'Iv. 160/E5
Ayamé II, Barrage d' (dam), C.d'Iv. 160/E5
Ayamonte, Sp. 102/B4
Ayancık, Turk. 148/C1
Ayanganna (mtn.), Guy. 211/G3
Ayapel, Col. 210/C2
Ayaş, Turk. 148/C1
Ayase, Japan 135/C3
Ayaviri, Peru 214/D4
Aybak, Afg. 145/E5
'Aybāl, Jabal (peak), WBnk. 149/G7
Aybastı, Turk. 148/D1
Aydar Köli (lake), Trkm. 145/E4
Aydın, Turk. 148/A2
Aydın (prov.), Turk. 148/B2
Aydıncık, Turk. 148/C1
Aydıncık, Turk. 149/C1
Aydınkent, Turk. 149/B1
Ayer, Swi. 114/D5
Ayers Rock (Uluru) (peak), Austl. 171/F3
Ayeyarwady (div.), Myan. 141/F4
Ayeyarwady (Irrawaddy) (riv.) Myan. 141/G4
Ayiá, Gre. 105/H3
Ayía Paraskeví, Gre. 105/K3
Ayiásos, Gre. 105/K3
Áyios Ioánnis (cape), Gre. 105/J5
Áyios Kírikos, Gre. 105/K4
Áyios Konstandínos, Gre. 105/H3
Áyios Matthaíos, Gre. 105/F3
Áyios Nikólaos, Gre. 105/J5
Aylesbury, Eng, UK 91/F3
Aylesford, Eng, UK 91/G4
Ayllón, Sp. 102/D2
Aylmer (lake), NW, Can. 180/F2
'Ayn al 'Arab, Syria 148/D2
'Ayn Zuwayyah (well), Libya 155/K3
Ayna, Peru 214/C4
Ayon (isl.), Rus. 123/S3
Ayora, Sp. 103/E3
Ayotzintepec, Mex. 202/B2
'Ayoûn 'Abd el Mâlek (well), Mrta. 156/D4
'Ayoûn el 'Atroûs, Mrta. 160/C2
Ayr, Austl. 171/B2
Ayr, Sc, UK 94/B6
Ayr (riv.), Sc, UK 94/B5
Aytré, Fr. 100/C3
Ayubia NP, Pak. 144/B3
Ayutla, Mex. 184/D4
Ayutla de los Libres, Mex. 198/B4
Ayutthaya (ruin), Thai. 136/C3
Ayvacık, Turk. 105/K3
Ayvalık, Turk. 148/A2
Aywaille, Belg. 111/E3
Az Zabadānī, Syria 149/E3
Az Zāhirīyah, WBnk. 149/D4
Az Zaqāzīq, Egypt 149/B4
Az Zarqā' (gov.), Jor. 149/E3
Az Zarqā', Jor. 149/E3
Az Zāwiyah, Libya 154/H1
Az Zaydīyah, Yem. 146/D5
Azad Kashmir (terr.), Pak. 144/B3
Azahar (coast), Sp. 103/F3
Azalea, Or, US 184/C5
Azalia, Mi, US 193/E7
Azamgarh, India 142/D2
Azángaro (riv.), Peru 214/D4
Azángaro, Peru 214/D4
Azao (peak), Alg. 157/H4
Azaouâd (phys. reg.), Mali 154/E4
Āzarān, Iran 146/E1
Āzarbāyjān-e Gharbī (prov.), Iran 148/F2
A'zāz, Syria 149/E1
Azemmour, Mor. 156/C2
Azerbaijan (ctry.) 121/H4
Azilal, Mor. 156/D3
Azīmganj, India 143/G3
Azogues, Ecu. 210/B5
Azores (dpcy.), Port. 103/R12
Azourki (peak), Mor. 156/D3
Azov, Rus. 120/F3
Azov (sea), Rus.,Ukr. 120/E3
Azoyú, Mex. 202/B2
Azpeitia, Sp. 102/D1
Azrou, Mor. 156/D2
Aztec, NM, US 186/F3
Aztec Ruins Nat'l Mon., NM, US 186/E3
Azua de Compostela, DRep. 199/G4
Azuaga, Sp. 102/C3
Azuara, Sp. 103/E2
Azuay (dept.), Ecu. 210/B5
Azuchi, Japan 135/K5
Azuero, Peninsula de (pen.), Pan. 208/B2
Azuga, Rom. 107/G3
Azul (mtn.), CR 203/E4
Azul (riv.), Guat. 202/D2
Azul, Arg. 216/F3
Azul, Cordillera (mts.), Peru 214/B2
Azuma, Japan 135/E2
Azuma-san (peak), Japan 133/G2
Azumaya-san (peak), Japan 133/F2
Azur, Côte d' (coast), Fr. 101/G5
Azusa, Ca, US 194/C2
Azzaba, Alg. 158/K6
Azzano Decimo, It. 117/F1
Azzano San Paolo, It. 116/C1
Azzate, It. 116/B1
'Azzūn, WBnk. 149/G7

B

Ba (riv.), Viet. 136/E3
Ba Lang An (cape), Viet. 136/E3
Ba Quan (cape), Viet. 136/D4
Baar, Swi. 115/E3
Baarle-Hertog, Belg. 108/B6
Baarle-Nassau, Neth. 108/B6
Baarn, Neth. 108/C4
Bab el Mandeb (str.), Asia 146/D6
Baba (mts.), Afg. 147/J2
Baba (peak), Bul. 105/H1
Baba (pt.), Turk. 107/K5
Baba Burnu (pt.), Turk. 105/K3
Babadag, Rom. 107/J3
Babaeski, Turk. 107/H5
Babahoyo, Ecu. 210/B5
Babai Khola (riv.), Nepal 142/C1
Babakale, Turk. 105/K3
Babar (isls.), Indo. 139/G5
Babatorun, Turk. 149/E1
Babatpur (int'l arpt.), India 142/D3
Babbacombe (bay), Eng, UK 90/C6
Babbitt, Mn, US 185/L4
B'abdā, Leb. 149/D3
Babelthuap (isl.), Palau 174/C4
Babenhausen, Ger. 115/G1
Babenhausen, Ger. 112/B3
Babensham, Ger. 113/F6
Baberu, India 142/C3
Babia (peak), Pol. 120/A2
Babian (riv.), China 141/H3
Bābil (gov.), Iraq 148/F3
Bābil (Babylon) (ruin), Iraq 148/F3
Babīna, India 142/B3
Babinda, Austl. 171/B2
Babine (riv.), BC, Can. 180/D3
Bābol, Iran 146/F1
Babruysk, Bela. 120/D1
Babuyan (isl.), Phil. 137/D4
Babylon, NY, US 197/E2
Bac Giang, Viet. 136/D1
Bac Lieu, Viet. 136/D4
Bac Ninh, Viet. 141/J3
Bacabal, Braz. 212/A2
Bacadéhuachi, Mex. 184/C2
Bacajá (riv.), Braz. 209/H4
Bacalar, Mex. 202/D2
Bacalar (lag.), Mex. 202/D2
Bacan (isl.), Indo. 139/G4
Bacău, Rom. 107/H2
Bacău (prov.), Rom. 107/H2
Baccarat, Fr. 114/C1
Bacchiglione (riv.), It. 117/E2
Bacchus, Ut, US 195/J12
Bacerac, Mex. 184/E5
Bacharach, Ger. 111/G3
Bachhraon, India 142/B1
Bachíniva, Mex. 184/D2
Back (riv.), Md, US 196/B5
Back (riv.), Nun., Can. 180/F2
Bačka (reg.), Serb. 106/D3
Bačka Palanka, Serb. 106/D3
Bačka Topola, Serb. 106/D3
Bäckefors, Swe. 96/E2
Backnang, Ger. 112/C5
Bacobampa, Mex. 184/C3
Bacolod, Phil. 139/F1
Bács-Kiskun (prov.), Hun. 106/D2
Bácsalmás, Hun. 106/D2
Bacup, Eng, UK 93/F4
Bad (riv.), SD, US 185/H5
Bad Abbach, Ger. 113/F5
Bad Axe, Mi, US 188/D3
Bad Bellingen, Ger. 114/D2
Bad Bergzabern, Ger. 112/A4
Bad Berneck, Ger. 113/E2
Bad Bocklet, Ger. 112/D2
Bad Brambach, Ger. 113/F2
Bad Breisig, Ger. 111/G3
Bad Brückenau, Ger. 112/C2
Bad Buchau, Ger. 115/F1
Bad Camberg, Ger. 112/B2
Bad Doberan, Ger. 96/D4
Bad Driburg, Ger. 109/G5
Bad Dürkheim, Ger. 112/B4
Bad Dürrheim, Ger. 115/E1
Bad Ems, Ger. 111/G3
Bad Endorf, Ger. 113/F7
Bad Essen, Ger. 109/F4
Bad Freienwalde, Ger. 99/H2
Bad Gandersheim, Ger. 109/H5
Bad Goisern, Aus. 101/K3
Bad Grund, Ger. 109/H5
Bad Hall, Aus. 113/H6
Bad Harzburg, Ger. 109/H5
Bad Heilbrunn, Ger. 115/H2
Bad Herrenalb, Ger. 112/B5
Bad Hersfeld, Ger. 101/H1
Bad Hofgastein, Aus. 101/K3
Bad Homburg vor der Höhe, Ger. 112/B2
Bad Honnef, Ger. 111/G2
Bad Hönningen, Ger. 111/G2
Bad Ischl, Aus. 101/K3
Bad Karlshafen, Ger. 109/G5
Bad Kissingen, Ger. 112/D2
Bad Kohlgrub, Ger. 115/H2
Bad König, Ger. 112/C3
Bad Königshofen, Ger. 112/D2
Bad Kreuznach, Ger. 111/G4
Bad Krozingen, Ger. 114/D2
Bad Langensalza, Ger. 109/H6
Bad Lauterberg, Ger. 109/H5
Bad Leonfelden, Aus. 113/H5
Bad Liebenzell, Ger. 112/B5
Bad Lippspringe, Ger. 109/F3
Bad Marienberg, Ger. 111/G2
Bad Mergentheim, Ger. 112/C4
Bad Munder am Deister, Ger. 109/G4
Bad Nauheim, Ger. 112/B2
Bad Nenndorf, Ger. 109/G4
Bad Neuenahr-Ahrweiler, Ger. 111/G2
Bad Neustadt an der Saale, Ger. 112/D2
Bad Oeynhausen, Ger. 109/F4
Bad Orb, Ger. 112/C2
Bad Peterstal-Griesbach, Ger. 114/E1
Bad Plaas, SAfr. 165/E2
Bad Pyrmont, Ger. 109/G5
Bad Ragaz, Swi. 115/F4
Bad Rappenau, Ger. 112/C4
Bad Reichenhall, Ger. 101/K3
Bad Rothenfelde, Ger. 109/F4
Bad Sachsa, Ger. 109/H5
Bad Salzdetfurth, Ger. 109/G4
Bad Salzschlirf, Ger. 112/C1
Bad Salzuflen, Ger. 109/F4
Bad Salzungen, Ger. 98/F3
Bad Sankt-Leonhard im Lavanttal, Aus. 101/L3
Bad Sassendorf, Ger. 109/F5
Bad Schallerbach, Aus. 113/G6
Bad Schwalbach, Ger. 111/H3
Bad Schwartau, Ger. 96/D5
Bad Segeberg, Ger. 96/D5
Bad Soden-Salmünster, Ger. 112/C2
Bad Sooden-Allendorf, Ger. 109/G6
Bad Tölz, Ger. 115/H2
Bad Vilbel, Ger. 112/B2
Bad Vöslau, Aus. 101/M3
Bad Waldsee, Ger. 115/F2
Bad Wildungen, Ger. 109/G6
Bad Wimpfen, Ger. 112/C4
Bad Wimsbach-Neydharting, Aus. 113/G6
Bad Windsheim, Ger. 112/D4
Bad Wörishofen, Ger. 115/G1
Bad Wurzach, Ger. 115/F2
Bad Zell, Aus. 113/H6
Bad Zwischenahn, Ger. 109/F2
Badagara, India 140/C5
Badain Jaran (des.), China 128/H3
Badajoz, Sp. 102/B3
Badalona, Sp. 103/L7
Badalucco, It. 116/A5
Badbergen, Ger. 109/E3
Baddeckenstedt, Ger. 109/H4
Baddomalhi, Pak. 144/C4
Baden, Aus. 101/M2
Baden, Swi. 115/E3
Baden-Baden, Ger. 112/B5
Baden-Württemberg (state), Ger. 101/H2
Badener (peak), Ger. 112/B5
Badenoch (reg.), Sc, UK 94/B3
Badenweiler, Ger. 114/D2
Badgastein, Aus. 101/K3
Badgingarra NP, Austl. 170/B4
Badia Polesine, It. 117/E2
Badiar, PN du, Gui. 160/B3
Badile (peak), It. 115/F5
Badīn, Pak. 147/J4
Badiraguato, Mex. 184/D3
Badlands (plat.), SD, US 185/H5
Badlands NP, SD, US 185/H5
Badonviller, Fr. 114/C1
Badou, Togo 161/F5
Badovinci, Serb. 106/D3
Badrāh, Pak. 147/J3
Badrah, Iraq 146/E2
Badulla (riv.), India 143/F3
Badulla, SrL. 140/D6
Bāduriā, India 143/G4
Baena, Sp. 102/C4
Baependi, Braz. 213/J6
Baerenkopf (peak), Fr. 114/C2
Baesweiler, Ger. 111/F2
Baeza, Sp. 102/D4
Baffa, Pak. 144/B2
Baffin (bay), Can.,Grld. 177/K2
Baffin (isl.), Nun., Can. 181/H1
Baffin (bay), Tx, US 190/D5
Bafia, Camr. 154/H7
Bafilo, Togo 161/F4
Bafing (riv.), Gui. 154/C5
Bafoulabé, Mali 160/C3
Bafoussam, Camr. 154/H6
Bāfq, Iran 147/G2
Bafra, Turk. 148/C1
Bafra (cape), Turk. 148/C1
Bāft, Iran 147/G3
Bag Salt (lake), China 130/B3
Bagaces, CR 203/E4
Bagadó, Col. 210/B3
Bagaha, India 143/E2
Bagamoyo, Tanz. 162/C4
Baganga, Phil. 137/E6
Bagda (mts.), China 128/E3
Bagé, Braz. 215/F3
Bagenkop, Den. 96/D4
Baggao, Phil. 137/D4
Baggy (pt.), Eng, UK 90/B4
Bāgh, Pak. 144/B4
Baghain (riv.), India 142/C3
Baghdād (Baghdad) (cap.), Iraq 148/F3
Bagheria, It. 104/C3
Baghlān, Afg. 147/J1
Bāghpat, India 144/D5
Bağırpaşa (peak), Turk. 148/E2
Bagley, Mn, US 185/K4
Bāglung, Nepal 142/D1
Bāgmati (riv.), India 143/E2
Bāgmati (zone), Nepal 143/E2
Bagn, Nor. 96/C1
Bagnacavallo, It. 117/F4
Bagnasco, It. 116/B4
Bagnères-de-Bigorre, Fr. 100/D5
Bagnères-de-Luchon, Fr. 100/D5
Bagneux, Fr. 88/J5
Bagni di Lucca, It. 116/D4
Bagno a Ripoli, It. 117/E5
Bagnolet, Fr. 88/K5
Bagnoli Irpino, It. 104/D2
Bagnolo Cremasco, It. 116/C2
Bagnolo in Piano, It. 117/D3
Bagnolo Mella, It. 116/D2
Bagnolo San Vito, It. 117/D2
Bagnols-sur-Cèze, Fr. 100/F4
Bagnone, It. 116/C4
Bago, Phil. 137/D5
Bago (Pegu), Myan. 141/G4
Bago (div.), Myan. 141/G4
Bagoe (riv.), Mali 154/D5
Bagolino, It. 116/D1
Bagshot, Eng, UK 88/A3
Bagua Grande, Peru 214/B2
Baguio, Phil. 137/D4
Baguirmi (reg.), Chad 154/J5
Bagzane (peak), Niger 161/H2
Bāh, India 142/B2
Bahādurganj, India 143/F2
Bahādurgarh, India 144/D5
Bahamas, The (ctry.) 199/F2
Bahāwalnagar, Pak. 144/B5
Bahāwalpur, Pak. 144/A5
Bahçe, Turk. 148/D2
Bahçesaray, Turk. 148/E2
Baheri, India 142/B1
Bahi (swamp), Tanz. 162/B4
Bahia (state), Braz. 212/B4
Bahía Asunción, Mex. 184/B3
Bahía Blanca, Arg. 216/E3
Bahía de Caráquez, Ecu. 210/A5
Bahía de los Angeles, Mex. 184/B2
Bahía de Tortugas, Mex. 184/B3
Bahía, Islas de la (isls.), Hon. 198/D4
Bahía Solano, Col. 210/B3
Bahir Dar, Eth. 155/N5
Bahjoi, India 142/B1
Bahlah, Oman 147/G4
Baḩr al 'Arab (riv.), Sudan 155/L6
Baḩr al Milḩ (lake), Iraq 148/E3
Bahraich, India 142/C2
Bahrain (ctry.) 146/F3
Bahrain, Gulf of (gulf), Asia 146/F3
Baia de Aramă, Rom. 107/F3
Baia Mare, Rom. 107/F2
Baia Sprie, Rom. 107/F2
Baïbokoum, Chad 154/J6
Baicheng, China 128/D3
Baicheng, China 129/M2
Băicoi, Rom. 107/G3
Baidong (lake), China 130/D5
Baie-Comeau, Qu, Can. 189/G1
Baie-Saint-Paul, Qu, Can. 189/G2
Baienfurt, Ger. 115/F2
Baiersbronn, Ger. 112/B5
Baiersdorf, Ger. 112/E3
Baigorrita, Arg. 216/E2
Baigou (riv.), China 130/G7
Baihar, India 142/C4
Baihua (mtn.), China 130/G7
Ba'ījī, Iraq 148/E3
Baikunthpur, India 142/D4
Bailadores, Ven. 210/D2
Baildon, Eng, UK 93/G4
Băile Govora, Rom. 107/G3
Băile Herculane, Rom. 106/F3
Băile Olănești, Rom. 107/G3
Băile Tușnad, Rom. 107/G2
Bailén, Sp. 102/D3
Băilești, Rom. 107/F3
Bailieborough, Ire. 89/Q10
Bailleul, Fr. 110/B2
Bailong (riv.), China 128/H5
Bailu (riv.), China 130/C4
Baima, China 128/H5
Bain (riv.), Eng, UK 93/H5
Bainang, China 143/G1
Bainbridge, Ga, US 191/G4
Bainbridge, Pa, US 196/B3
Bainbridge (isl.), Wa, US 193/B2
Bainbridge Naval Training Sta., Md, US 196/B4
Baingoin, China 128/E5
Bains-les-Bains, Fr. 114/C2
Bairāgnia, India 143/E2
Baird (inlet), Ak, US 192/F3
Baird, Tx, US 187/H4
Bairin Youqi, China 129/L3
Bairnsdale, Austl. 173/C3
Baïse (riv.), Fr. 100/D5
Baixa da Banheira, Port. 103/P10
Baixa Grande, Braz. 212/B4
Baixiang, China 130/C3
Baixo Guandu, Braz. 213/D1
Baiyin, China 128/H4
Baiyu (mts.), China 130/B3
Baiyun (int'l arpt.), China 137/B3
Baja (pt.), Mex. 184/B2
Baja, Hun. 106/D2
Baja (pt.), Chile 217/B6
Baja California (state), Mex. 184/B2
Baja California (pen.), Mex. 184/B2
Baja California Sur (state), Mex. 184/B3
Bajánsenye, Hun. 101/M3
Bajestān, Iran 147/G2
Bājil, Yem. 146/D5
Bajina Bašta, Serb. 106/D4
Bajmbat (mt.), Austl. 173/E1
Bajmok, Serb. 106/D3
Bajo Boquete, Pan. 203/F4
Bajo de Gualicho (plain), Arg. 215/C5
Bajram Curri, Alb. 105/G1
Bakanas (riv.), Kaz. 145/G3
Bakau, Gam. 160/A3
Bakayan (peak), Indo. 139/E3
Bakel, Sen. 160/B3
Baker (lake), Nun., Can. 180/G2
Baker (riv.), Chile 217/B5
Baker (isl.), Pac., US 175/H4
Baker, La, US 187/K5
Baker, Mt, US 185/G4
Baker (mt.), Wa, US 184/C3
Baker City, Or, US 184/D4
Baker Lake, Nun., Can. 180/G2
Bakersfield, Ca, US 186/C4
Bakhchysaray, Ukr. 120/E3
Bakhmach, Ukr. 120/E2
Bākhtarān, Iran 146/E2
Bakhtiyārpur, India 143/E3
Bakhuis (mts.), Sur. 211/G4
Bakkaflói (bay), Ice. 95/P6
Baklan, Turk. 148/B2
Bakonyszombathely, Hun. 106/C2
Bakora Corridor Game Rsv., Ugan. 162/B2
Bakovský Potok (riv.), Czh. 113/G2
Bakoye (riv.), Gui. 160/C4
Baku (cap.), Azer. 121/J4
Baku (int'l arpt.), Azer. 121/J4
Balâ, Turk. 148/C2
Bala, Wal, UK 92/E6
Balabac, Phil. 139/E2
Balabac (str.), Malay.,Phil. 139/E2
Balabac (isl.), Phil. 139/E2
Ba'labakk, Leb. 149/E2
Bālāghāt, India 142/C5
Balaguer, Sp. 103/F2
Balaïtous (peak), Fr. 100/C5
Balaka, Malw. 163/F3
Balakhna, Rus. 119/J4
Balaklava, Austl. 171/H5
Balakovo, Rus. 121/H1
Bal'amā, Jor. 149/E3
Bālān, Rom. 107/G2
Balancán, Mex. 202/D2
Balanga, Phil. 137/D5
Bālāngir, India 140/D3
Balao, Ecu. 214/B1
Balarāmpur, India 143/F4
Balashikha, Rus. 119/W9
Balashov, Rus. 121/G2
Balasore (Baleshwar), India 140/E3
Balassagyarmat, Hun. 99/K4
Balaton (lake), Cro. 106/C2
Balatonföldvár, Hun. 106/C2
Balatonfüred, Hun. 106/C2
Balatonszabadi, Hun. 106/D2
Balatonszentgyörgy, Hun. 106/C2
Balbina (res.), Braz. 205/D3
Balbriggan, Ire. 92/B4
Balcarce, Arg. 216/F3
Balcary (pt.), Sc, UK 92/E2
Balchik, Bul. 107/J4
Balclutha, NZ 175/R12
Balcones Escarpment (plat.), Tx, US 195/T20
Balcones Heights, Tx, US 195/T21
Bald (pt.), Austl. 170/C5
Bald Eagle Mtn. (mtn.), Pa, US 196/A1
Bald Rock NP, Austl. 173/E1
Baldock, Eng, UK 91/F3
Baldwin, NY, US 197/L9
Baldwin Harbour, NY, US 197/L9
Baldwin Park, Mo, US 195/E6
Baldwin Park, Ca, US 194/G7
Baldy (mtn.), Mb, Can. 185/H3
Baldy Beacon (peak), Belz. 202/D2
Bale Mountains NP, Eth. 155/N6
Baleares (Balearic) (isls.), Sp. 103/G3
Baleia, Ponta da (pt.), Braz. 212/C5
Baleine, Grand Rivière de la (riv.), Qu, Can. 181/J3
Baleine, Petite Rivière de la (riv.), Qu, Can. 181/J3
Baleine, Rivière à la (riv.), Qu, Can. 181/K3
Balen, Belg. 111/E1
Baler, Phil. 137/D4
Balerna, Swi. 115/F6
Balesa (riv.), Kenya 162/C2
Baleshwar (Balasore), India 140/E3
Balfour, SAfr. 164/E2
Balfron, Sc, UK 94/B4
Balgatay, Mong. 128/G2
Balhannah, Austl. 171/M8
Bali (sea), Indo. 138/D5
Bali (isl.), Indo. 138/D5
Bāli Chak, India 143/F4
Balice (int'l arpt.), Pol. 99/K3
Baliem (riv.), Indo. 139/J4
Balıkesir, Turk. 148/A2
Balıkesir (prov.), Turk. 148/A2
Balikpapan, Indo. 139/E4
Balimbing, Phil. 139/E2
Baling, Malay. 141/H6
Balingasag, Phil. 137/D6
Bālinge, Swe. 96/G2
Balingen, Ger. 115/E1
Balk, Neth. 108/C3
Balkan (pol. reg.), Trkm. 145/B4
Balkan (mts.), Bul.,Serb. 85/F3
Balkhash (lake), Kaz. 125/G5
Ballagan (pt.), Ire. 92/B4
Ballaghaderreen, Ire. 89/P10
Ballangen, Nor. 95/F1
Ballantrae, Sc, UK 92/C1
Ballarat, Austl. 173/B3
Ballard (lake), Austl. 167/B3
Ballarpur, India 140/C4
Ballater, Sc, UK 94/C2
Ballaugh, IM, UK 92/D3
Ballens, Swi. 114/C4
Balleny (isls.), Ant. 218/L
Ballia, India 143/E3
Ballina, Austl. 173/E1
Ballinamallard, NI, UK 89/Q9
Ballinasloe, Ire. 89/P10
Ballinderry (riv.), NI, UK 92/B2
Ballinger, Tx, US 187/H5
Ballingry, Sc, UK 94/C4
Ballinrobe, Ire. 89/P10
Balloch, Sc, UK 94/B2
Ballon, Col du (pass), Fr. 114/C2
Ballon d'Alsace (peak), Fr. 114/C2
Ballon de Servance (peak), Fr. 114/C2
Ballwin, Mo, US 195/F8
Bally, Pa, US 196/C3
Ballycarry, NI, UK 92/C2
Ballycastle, NI, UK 92/B1
Ballycastle, Ire. 89/P9
Ballyclare, NI, UK 92/B2
Ballyeaston, NI, UK 92/B2
Ballygawley, NI, UK 92/A3
Ballygeary, Ire. 89/Q10
Ballygowan, NI, UK 92/C3
Ballyhaunis, Ire. 89/P10
Ballyheigue, Ire. 88/P10
Ballyliffin, Ire. 92/A1
Ballymena (dist.), NI, UK 92/B2
Ballymena, NI, UK 92/B2
Ballymoney (dist.), NI, UK 92/B1
Ballymoney, NI, UK 92/B1
Ballynahinch, NI, UK 92/C3
Ballynure, NI, UK 92/C2
Ballyquintin (pt.), NI, UK 92/C3
Ballyshannon, Ire. 89/P9
Balmaceda (peak), Chile 217/B6
Balmazújváros, Hun. 99/L5
Balmhorn (peak), Swi. 114/D5
Balmoral, Austl. 173/B3
Balmoral Castle, Sc, UK 94/C2
Balneário Camboriú, Braz. 213/B3
Balneario Claromecó, Arg. 216/E3
Balneario de los Novillos, PN, Mex. 187/G5
Balochistān (reg.), Pak. 147/J3
Balonne (riv.), Austl. 167/D3
Bālotra, India 147/K3
Balqash, Kaz. 145/G3
Balrāmpur, India 142/D2
Balranald, Austl. 173/B2
Balş, Rom. 107/G3
Bálsamo (pt.), Ecu. 210/A5
Balsapuerto, Peru 214/B2
Balsas, Braz. 212/A2
Balsas (riv.), Mex. 201/F5
Balsthal, Swi. 114/D3
Baltanás, Sp. 102/C2
Bălţi, Mol. 107/H2
Baltic (sea), Swe. 95/F5
Baltic (plain), Rus. 119/S7
Baltic Spit (bar), Pol.,Rus. 97/H4
Balţīm, Egypt 149/B4
Baltimore, Md, US 196/B5
Baltimore (co.), Md, US 196/B4
Baltimore-Washington (int'l arpt.), Md, US 196/B5
Baltiysk, Rus. 97/H4
Baltray, Ire. 92/B4
Baltrum (isl.), Ger. 109/E1
Bælum, Den. 96/D3
Bālurghāt, India 143/G3
Balve, Ger. 109/E6
Balya, Turk. 120/C5
Balykshi, Kaz. 121/J3
Balzar, Ecu. 210/B5
Balzers, Lcht. 115/F3
Bam (prov.), Burk. 161/E3
Bam, Iran 147/G3
Bama Yaozu Zizhixian, China 141/J3
Bamaji (lake), On, Can. 185/K3
Bamako (cap.), Mali 160/D3
Bamako (Senou) (int'l arpt.), Mali 160/D3
Bambamarca, Peru 214/B2
Bambana (riv.), Nic. 203/E3
Bambari, CAfr. 155/K6
Bamberg, Ger. 112/D3
Bamberg, SC, US 191/H3
Bamble, Nor. 96/C2
Bambuí, Braz. 213/C2
Bamenda, Camr. 161/H5
Bāmīān, Afg. 145/E6
Bamingui-Bangoran, PN du, CAfr. 155/J6
Bammental, Ger. 112/B4
Bampūr (riv.), Iran 147/H3
Ban Boun Tai, Laos 141/H3
Ban Chiang (ruin), Thai. 136/C2
Ban Houayxay, Laos 141/H3
Ban Kantang, Thai. 136/B5
Ban Kengkok, Laos 141/J4
Ban Pak Phanang, Thai. 136/C4
Banaba (isl.), Kiri. 174/F5
Banagher, Ire. 89/Q10
Banamba, Mali 160/D3
Banana (isls.), SLeo. 160/B4
Bananal, Braz. 213/J7
Bananal, Ilha do (isl.), Braz. 209/H6
Banar (riv.), Bang. 143/H3
Banarlı, Turk. 107/H5
Banās (pt.), Egypt 159/C4
Banās (riv.), India 147/L3
Banat (reg.), Serb. 106/E3
Banatsko Novo Selo, Serb. 106/E3
Banaz, Turk. 148/B2
Banbar, China 128/G5
Banbridge, NI, UK 92/B3
Banbridge (dist.), NI, UK 92/B3
Banbury, Eng, UK 91/E2
Banc d'Arguin, Mrta. 156/A5
Banc d'Arguin, PN du, Mrta. 154/B3
Banc d'Arguin, PN du, Mrta. 160/A2
Banchette, It. 116/A2
Banchory, Sc, UK 94/D2
Banco Chinchorro (isls.), Mex. 198/D4
Bancroft, On, Can. 188/E2
Banda (isls.), Indo. 139/H4
Bāndā, India 142/C3
Banda, India 142/B3
Banda (sea), Indo. 139/G5
Banda Aceh, Indo. 138/A2
Bandai-san (peak), Japan 133/G2
Bandama (riv.), C.d'Iv. 154/D6
Bandama Blanc (riv.), C.d'Iv. 160/D4
Bandama Rouge (riv.), C.d'Iv. 160/D4
Bandar Beheshtī, Iran 147/H3
Bandar-e 'Abbās, Iran 147/G3
Bandar-e Anzalī, Iran 146/E1
Bandar-e Deylam, Iran 146/F2
Bandar-e Lengeh, Iran 147/F3
Bandar-e Māhshahr, Iran 146/E2
Bandar-e Torkeman, Iran 146/F1
Bandar Seri Begawan (cap.),Bru. 138/D3
Bande, Sp. 102/B1
Bandeira do Sul, Braz. 213/G6
Bandeira, Pico da (peak), Braz. 213/D2
Bandeirantes, Braz. 213/B2
Bandelier Nat'l Mon., NM, US 187/F4
Bandera, Tx, US 187/H5
Banderilla, Mex. 201/N7
Bandhavgarh NP, India 142/C4
Bandholm, Den. 96/D4
Bandiagara, Mali 160/E3
Bandipura, India 144/C2
Bandırma (gulf), Turk. 107/H5
Bandırma, Turk. 107/H5
Bandon, Ire. 89/P11
Bandon (riv.), Ire. 89/P11
Bandundu, D.R. Congo 163/C1
Bandung, Indo. 138/C5
Bañeres, Sp. 103/E3
Banes, Cuba 203/H1
Banff, Ab, Can. 184/E3
Banff, Sc, UK 94/D1
Banff NP, Ab, Can. 184/E3
Banfora, Burk. 160/D4
Bang Lang (res.), Thai. 136/C5
Banga, Phil. 137/D6
Banga, India 144/C4
Bangalore, India 140/C5
Bangalow, Austl. 171/D5
Bangaon, India 143/G4
Bāngarmau, India 142/C2
Bangassou, CAfr. 155/K7
Bangau (cape), Malay. 139/E2
Banggai (isls.), Indo. 139/F4
Banghiang (riv.), Laos 136/D2
Bangka (str.), Indo. 138/B4
Bangka (isl.), Indo. 138/C4
Bangkok (Krung Thep) (cap.),Thai. 136/C3
Bangkok (int'l arpt.), Thai. 136/C3
Bangkok, Bight of (bay), Thai. 141/H5
Bangladesh (ctry.) 140/E3
Bangor, NI, UK 92/C2
Bangor (int'l arpt.), Me, US 189/G2
Bangor, Me, US 189/G2
Bangor, Pa, US 196/C2
Bangor, Wal, UK 92/D5
Bangued, Phil. 137/D4
Bangui (cap.), CAfr. 155/J7
Bangweulu (swamp), Zam. 162/A5
Bangweulu (lake), Zam. 163/E3
Banhā, Egypt 149/B4
Banhine, PN de, Moz. 163/F5
Bani (riv.), Mali 154/D5
Baní, DRep. 199/G4
Banī Mazār, Egypt 159/B2
Banī Suhaylah, Gaza 149/D4
Banī Suwayf (gov.), Egypt 159/B1
Banī Suwayf, Egypt 159/B2
Bánica, DRep. 203/J2
Banifing (riv.), Mali 160/D3
Banihāl (pass), India 144/C3
Banikoara, Ben. 161/F4
Banister (riv.), Va, US 191/J2
Bāniyās, Syria 149/D2
Banja Koviljača, Serb. 106/D3
Banja Luka, Bosn. 106/C3
Banjarmasin, Indo. 138/D4
Banjul (cap.), Gam. 160/A3
Bānka, India 143/F3
Bankas, Mali 160/E3
Bankeryd, Swe. 96/F3
Bankfoot, Sc, UK 94/C3
Bankhead, Sc, UK 94/D2
Bānki, India 143/E4

Banks (cape), Austl. 173/B3
Banks (str.), Austl. 173/C4
Banks (isl.), NW, Can. 180/D2
Banks (pen.), NZ 175/S11
Banks (pt.), Ak, US 192/H4
Banks (lake), Wa, US 184/D4
Banks (isls.), Van. 174/F6
Bānkurā, India 143/F4
Bankya, Bul. 105/H1
Banmankhi, India 143/F3
Bann (riv.), Ire. 89/Q10
Bann (riv.), NI, UK 92/B3
Banna (riv.), It. 116/A3
Bannockburn, Sc, UK 94/C4
Bannockburn Battlesite, Sc, UK 94/C4
Bannu, Pak. 144/A3
Baños, Ecu. 214/B1
Banpo Ruins, China 130/B4
Bansberia, India 143/G4
Bānsdīh, India 143/E3
Bānsi, India 142/D2
Bansin, Ger. 96/F5
Banská Bystrica, Slvk. 99/K4
Banská Štiavnica, Slvk. 106/D1
Bansko, Bul. 105/H2
Banskobystrický (pol. reg.), Slvk. 99/K4
Banstead, Eng, UK 88/C3
Bānswāra, India 147/K4
Bantayan, Phil. 137/D5
Banté, Ben. 161/F4
Bantenan (cape), Indo. 138/D5
Bantong Group (isls.), Thai. 136/B5
Bantry, Ire. 89/P11
Bañuelo (peak), Sp. 102/C3
Banyak (isls.), Indo. 138/A3
Banyoles, Sp. 103/G1
Banyuwangi, Indo. 138/D5
Banzare (coast), Ant. 218/J
Baode, China 130/B3
Baodi, China 130/H7
Baoding, China 130/G7
Baofeng, China 130/C4
Baoji, China 128/J5
Baojing, China 141/J2
Baokang, China 130/B5
Baoruco (mts.), DRep. 203/J2
Baoshan, China 141/G2
Baoshan, China 130/L8
Baotou, China 130/B2
Baoulé (riv.), Mali 154/D5
Baoying, China 130/D4
Bapaume, Fr. 110/B3
Bapchule, Az, US 195/S19
Baptistown, NJ, US 196/C2
Bāqa el Gharbiyya, Isr. 149/G7
Baqên, China 128/F5
Ba'qūbah, Iraq 148/F3
Bar, Mont. 106/D4
Bar (riv.), Fr. 98/C4
Bar Bigha, India 143/E3
Bar el Ksaïb (well), Mali 156/D5
Bar Harbor, Me, US 189/G2
Bar-le-Duc, Fr. 111/E6
Bar-sur-Aube, Fr. 100/F2
Bar-sur-Seine, Fr. 100/F2
Bara, Swe. 96/E4
Bāra Banki, India 142/C2
Bārā Lācha La (pass), India 144/D3
Barabai, Indo. 138/E4
Barabinsk, Rus. 145/G1
Baraboo, Wi, US 185/L5
Baracaldo, Sp. 102/D1
Baracoa, Cuba 203/H1
Barada (riv.), Syria 149/E3
Baradero, Arg. 217/J10
Baradine, Austl. 173/D1
Baragoi, Kenya 162/C2
Baraguá, Cuba 203/G1
Baragua, Ven. 210/D2
Barajas (int'l arpt.), Sp. 103/N9
Barajevo, Serb. 106/E3
Barākar (riv.), India 143/F3
Barakī Barak, Afg. 147/J2
Baralaba, Austl. 171/C4
Baram (cape), Malay. 138/D3
Baram (riv.), Malay. 138/D3
Barama (riv.), Guy. 208/F2
Baramanni, Guy. 211/G3
Baramula, India 144/C2
Bāran, India 147/L3
Baranagar, India 143/G4
Baranavichy, Bela. 120/C1
Barani (well), Alg. 156/E4
Baranoa, Col. 210/C2
Baranof (isl.), Ak, US 192/L4
Baranya (prov.), Hun. 106/C3
Barão de Cocais, Braz. 213/D1
Barão de Grajaú, Braz. 212/B2
Baraolt, Rom. 107/G2
Baraque de Fraiture (hill), Belg. 111/E3
Barat Daya (isls.), Indo. 139/G5
Barataria, La, US 195/P17
Barauli, India 143/E2
Baraut, India 144/D5
Baraya, Col. 210/C4
Barbacena, Braz. 213/D2
Barbacoas, Col. 210/B4
Barbados (ctry.) 199/P9
Barbalha, Braz. 212/C2
Barbaros, Turk. 107/H5
Barbas (cape), Mor. 156/A5
Barbastro, Sp. 103/F1
Barbate de Franco, Sp. 102/C4
Barbeau (peak), Nun., Can. 181/T6
Barberà del Vallès, Sp. 103/L6
Barberino di Mugello, It. 117/E5
Barbers (pt.), Hi, US 182/V13
Barberton, Oh, US 188/D3
Barberton, SAfr. 165/E2
Barbona (peak), It. 116/D5
Barbosa, Col. 210/C3
Barbourville, Ky, US 188/D4
Barbuda (isl.), Anti. 199/N8
Barcaldine, Austl. 171/B3
Barcarrota, Sp. 102/B3
Barcău (riv.), Rom. 106/F2
Barcellona Pozzo di Gotto, It. 104/D3
Barcelona, Ven. 211/E2
Barcelona, Sp. 103/L7
Barcelona (int'l arpt.), Sp. 103/L7
Barcelos, Port. 102/A2
Barcelos, Braz. 211/F5
Barcin, Pol. 99/J2
Barcoo (riv.), Austl. 167/D3
Barcs, Hun. 106/C3
Barczewo, Pol. 97/J5
Bardejov, Slvk. 99/L4
Bardi, It. 116/C3
Bardīyah, Libya 155/L1
Bārdoli, India 147/K4
Bardolino, It. 117/D1
Bardonia, NY, US 197/K7
Bardsdale, Ca, US 194/B2
Bardsey (isl.), Wal, UK 92/D6
Bardstown, Ky, US 188/C4
Bareggio, It. 116/B2
Bareilly, India 142/B4
Barellan, Austl. 173/C2
Barendrecht, Neth. 108/B5
Barentin, Fr. 100/D2
Barents (sea), Eur. 122/D2
Barentu, Erit. 146/C5
Bäretswil, Swi. 115/E3
Barfleur, Pointe de (pt.), Fr. 100/C2
Barga, It. 116/D4
Bargara, Austl. 171/D4
Bargarh, India 140/D3
Bargfeld-Stegen, Ger. 109/H1
Bargi, India 142/B4
Bargo, Austl. 173/D2
Bargteheide, Ger. 109/H1
Bārh, India 143/E3
Barhaj, India 142/D2
Barhalganj, India 142/D2
Barham, Austl. 173/C2
Barhiya, India 143/F3
Bāri, India 142/A2
Bari, It. 104/E2
Bari Sardo, It. 104/A3
Bariano, It. 116/C1
Baricella, It. 117/E3
Barichara, Col. 210/C3
Barīdī (pt.), SAr. 146/C4
Barigazzo (peak), It. 116/C3
Barika, Alg. 158/H5
Barillas, Guat. 202/D3
Barima (riv.), Guy. 211/G2
Barima-Waini (pol. reg.), Guy. 211/F3
Barinas (state), Ven. 210/D2
Barinas, Ven. 210/D2
Barinitas, Ven. 210/D2
Bariri, Braz. 213/B2
Barisāl (pol. reg.), Bang. 143/H4
Barisan Mountains (mts.), Indo. 138/B4
Barito (riv.), Indo. 138/D4
Baritu, PN, Arg. 215/D1
Bark (lake), On, Can. 188/E2
Bark (riv.), Wi, US 193/N13
Barka Kāna, India 143/E4
Barker, NY, US 189/S9
Barki Saria, India 143/E3
Barking and Dagenham (bor.), Eng, UK 88/D2
Barkley (sound), BC, Can. 184/B3
Barkley (lake), Ky,Tn, US 191/G2
Barkly East, SAfr. 164/D3
Barkly Tableland (plat.), Austl. 167/C2
Barkly West, SAfr. 164/D3
Barkol Kazak Zizhixian, China 128/F3
Barlee (lake), Austl. 167/A3
Barlee (range), Austl. 170/B2
Barlee Range Nature Rsv., Austl. 170/B2
Barletta, It. 104/E2
Barlin, Fr. 110/B3
Barlinek, Pol. 99/H2
Barmedman, Austl. 173/C2
Barmera, Austl. 171/J5
Barmstedt, Ger. 109/G1
Barnāla, India 144/C4
Bärnbach, Aus. 101/L3
Barnegat (inlet), NJ, US 196/D4
Barnegat (bay), NJ, US 196/D4
Barnegat, NJ, US 196/D4
Barnegat Light, NJ, US 196/D4
Barneveld, Neth. 108/C4
Barnhart, Mo, US 195/G9
Barnoldswick, Eng, UK 93/F4
Barnsley, Eng, UK 93/G4
Barnsley (co.), Eng, UK 93/G5
Barnstaple, Eng, UK 90/B4
Barnstaple (Bideford) (bay), Eng, UK 90/B4
Barnstorf, Ger. 109/F3
Barntrup, Ger. 109/G5
Barnwell, SC, US 191/H3
Baroghil (pass), Pak. 145/F5
Baron, Fr. 88/L4
Barone (peak), It. 116/B1
Barow (riv.), Ire. 92/A5
Barowghil (pass), Afg. 147/K1
Barquisimeto, Ven. 210/D2
Barquisimeto (int'l arpt.), Ven. 210/D2
Barr (lake), Co, US 195/C3
Barr, Co, US 195/C3
Barr, Fr. 114/D1
Barra, Braz. 212/B3
Barra (isl.), Sc, UK 89/Q8
Barra Bonita, Braz. 213/B2
Barra Bonita, Represa de (res.), Braz. 213/B2
Barra da Choça, Braz. 212/B4
Barra del Colorado, PN, CR 198/E5
Barra do Bugres, Braz. 209/G7
Barra do Corda, Braz. 212/A2
Barra do Garças, Braz. 209/H7
Barra do Mendes, Braz. 212/B3
Barra do Piraí, Braz. 213/K7
Barra do Ribeiro, Braz. 213/B4
Barra Head (pt.), Sc, UK 89/Q8
Barra Mansa, Braz. 213/J7
Barra Velha, Braz. 213/B3
Barraba, Austl. 173/D1
Barrackpur, India 143/G4
Barrage de Lagdo (dam), Camr. 154/H6
Barranca, Peru 214/B3
Barranca, Peru 214/B2
Barranca de Upía, Col. 210/C3
Barranca del Cobre PN, Mex. 184/D3
Barrancabermeja, Col. 210/C3
Barrancas, Ven. 211/F2
Barrancas, Col. 210/C2
Barrancas, Chile 216/N8
Barranco de Loba, Col. 210/C2
Barrancos, Port. 102/B3
Barranquilla, Col. 210/C2
Barras, Braz. 212/B2
Barreal, Arg. 215/C3
Barreiras, Braz. 212/A4
Barreirinhas, Braz. 212/B1
Barreiro, Port. 103/P10
Barreiros, Braz. 212/D3
Barren (isl.), Madg. 165/G7
Barren, Nosy (Barren Islands) (isls.), Madg. 165/G7
Barretal, Mex. 201/F3
Barretos, Braz. 213/B2
Barrhead, Ab, Can. 184/E2
Barrhead, Sc, UK 94/B5
Barrie, On, Can. 188/E2
Barrier (range), Austl. 171/J4
Barrington, Il, US 193/P15
Barrington Hills, Il, US 193/P15
Barrington Tops (peak), Austl. 173/D1
Barrington Tops NP, Austl. 173/D1
Barro Duro, Braz. 212/B2
Barron Gorge NP, Austl. 171/B2
Barroso, Braz. 213/D2
Barrouallie, StV. 199/N9
Barrow, Ak, US 192/G1
Barrow (pt.), Ak, US 192/G1
Barrow (isl.), Austl. 167/A3
Barrow (riv.), Ire. 89/Q10
Barrow (pt.), Austl. 171/B1
Barrow (str.), Nun., Can. 180/G1
Barrow-in-Furness, Eng, UK 93/E3
Barrow Island, Austl. 170/B2
Barrowford, Eng, UK 93/F4
Barruelo de Santullán, Sp. 102/C1
Barry, Wal, UK 90/C4
Barsakel'mes (lake), Uzb. 145/C4
Barsinghausen, Ger. 109/G4
Barssel, Ger. 109/E2
Barstow, Ca, US 186/C4
Bartang (riv.), Taj. 145/F5
Bartenheim, Fr. 114/D2
Barth, Ger. 96/E4
Bartholomä, Ger. 112/C5
Bartholomäberg, Aus. 115/F3
Bartica, Guy. 211/G3
Bartın, Turk. 107/L5
Bartle Frere (peak), Austl. 167/D2
Bartlesville, Ok, US 187/J3
Bartlett, Tx, US 187/H5
Bartlett (dam), Az, US 195/S18
Bartlett (res.), Az, US 195/S18
Bartlett, Il, US 193/P16
Bartolomé Masó, Cuba 203/G1
Bartolomeu Dias, Moz. 163/G5
Bartonsville, Pa, US 196/C2
Bartoszyce, Pol. 97/J4
Bartow, Fl, US 191/H5
Bartow, Ger. 96/E5
Barú (vol.), Pan. 203/F4
Bāruipur, India 143/G4
Barumun (riv.), Indo. 138/B3
Barus, Indo. 138/A3
Baruun-Urt, Mong. 129/K2
Barwa Sāgar, India 142/B3
Barwāha, India 147/L4
Barwāla, India 144/C5
Barwon (riv.), Austl. 167/D3
Barycz (riv.), Pol. 99/J3
Barysaw, Bela. 97/N4
Barysh, Rus. 121/H1
Barzanò, It. 116/C1
Bas-Rhin (dept.), Fr. 114/D1
Basaldella, It. 117/G1
Basauri, Sp. 102/D1
Basavilbaso, Arg. 217/J10
Bascharage, Lux. 111/E4
Basehor, Ks, US 195/D5
Basel, Swi. 114/D2
Basel/Mulhouse (int'l arpt.), Fr. 114/D2
Baselga di Pinè, It. 115/H5
Baselland (canton), Swi. 114/D3
Bashee (riv.), SAfr. 164/E3
Bashi (chan.), Phil.,Tai. 137/C3
Bashkortostan, Resp., Rus. 122/G6
Bāsht, Iran 146/F2
Basilan (isl.), Phil. 139/F2
Basilan (peak), Phil. 139/F2
Basildon, Eng, UK 91/G3
Basilica di Fieschi, It. 116/C4
Basilicata (reg.), It. 104/D2
Basingstoke, Eng, UK 91/E4
Basingstoke (canal), Eng, UK 88/A3
Basīrhāt, India 143/G4
Basīrpur, Pak. 144/B4
Başkale, Turk. 148/F2
Baskatong (res.), Qu, Can. 188/F2
Baskil, Turk. 148/D2
Başkomutan NP, Turk. 148/B2
Bāsoda, India 142/A4
Basodino (peak), It. 115/E5
Basoko, D.R. Congo 155/K7
Basoli, India 144/C3
Bass (str.), Austl. 167/D4
Bass Rock (isl.), Sc, UK 94/D4
Bassae (Vassés) (ruin), Gre. 105/G4
Bassano, Ab, Can. 184/E3
Bassano del Grappa, It. 117/E1
Bassari, Togo 161/F4
Bassas da India (isl.), Reun., Fr. 163/G5
Basse-Normandie (pol. reg.), Fr. 100/C2
Basse Santa Su, Gam. 160/B3
Basse-Terre, Guad., Fr. 199/N8
Basse-Terre (isl.), Guad., Fr. 199/J4
Bassecourt, Swi. 114/D3
Bassein (riv.), Myan. 141/F4
Bassein (Vasai), India 147/K5
Bassenge, Belg. 111/E2
Bassenheim, Ger. 111/G3
Bassenthwaite (lake), Eng, UK 93/E2
Basseterre (cap.), StK. 199/N8
Bassum, Ger. 109/F3
Basswood (lake), Can.,US 188/B1
Båstad, Swe. 96/E3
Bastak, Iran 147/F3
Bastām, Iran 147/G1
Bastelicaccia, Fr. 104/A2
Bastheim, Ger. 112/D2
Bastī, India 142/D2
Bastia, Fr. 104/A1
Bastia, It. 101/K5
Bastogne, Belg. 111/E4
Bastos, Braz. 213/B2
Bastrop, Tx, US 187/H5
Basyūn, Egypt 149/B4
Bat Shelomo, Isr. 149/F6
Bat Yam, Isr. 149/F7
Bata, EqG. 154/G7
Batabanó (gulf), Cuba 198/E3
Batac, Phil. 137/D4
Batagay, Rus. 123/P3
Batal (pass), Pak. 144/A3
Batalha, Braz. 212/B2
Batalha, Port. 102/A3
Batan (isls.), Phil. 137/D3
Batang, China 128/G6
Batangafo, CAfr. 155/J6
Batangas, Phil. 137/D5
Batarasa, Phil. 137/C6
Batatais, Braz. 213/C2
Batavia, NY, US 188/E3
Batavia, Il, US 193/P16
Bataysk, Rus. 120/F3
Batchtown, Il, US 195/F7
Batdâmbâng, Camb. 136/C3
Bate (bay), Austl. 171/H9
Batéké (plat.), Congo 154/H8
Batemans Bay, Austl. 173/D2
Batesburg-Leesville, SC, US 191/H3
Batesville, Ms, US 187/K4
Bath, Me, US 189/G3
Bath, NY, US 188/E3
Bath, Eng, UK 90/D4
Bath, Pa, US 196/C2
Bath and Northeast Somerset (co.), Eng, UK 90/D4
Bathgate, Sc, UK 94/C5
Bathmen, Neth. 108/D4
Bathurst, Austl. 173/D2
Bathurst (cape), NW, Can. 192/N1
Bathurst, NB, Can. 189/H2
Bathurst (isl.), Nun., Can. 181/R7
Bathurst (inlet), Nun., Can. 180/F2
Bathurst Inlet, Nun., Can. 180/F2
Batian (Mt. Kenya) (peak), Kenya 162/C3
Batiquitos (lag.), Ca, US 194/C4
Batiscan (riv.), Qu, Can. 189/F2
Batley, Eng, UK 93/G4
Batlow, Austl. 173/D2
Batman, Turk. 148/E2
Batman (dam), Turk. 148/E2
Batna (prov.), Alg. 157/G2
Batna, Alg. 158/J5
Baton Rouge (cap.), La, US 187/K5
Batopilas, Mex. 184/D3
Batoti, India 144/C3
Batouri, Camr. 154/H7
Baṭrā' (Petra) (ruin), Jor. 149/D4
Båtsfjord, Nor. 95/J1
Batsto (riv.), NJ, US 196/D4
Batsto, NJ, US 196/D4
Batsto Historic Village, NJ, US 196/D4
Battaglia Terme, It. 117/E2
Battenberg, Ger. 109/F6
Bätterkinden, Swi. 114/D3
Batticaloa, SrL. 140/D6
Battipaglia, It. 104/D2
Battle, Eng, UK 91/G5
Battle (riv.), Ab,Sk, Can. 180/E3
Battle Creek, Mi, US 188/C3
Battle Mountain, Nv, US 184/D5
Battleford, Sk, Can. 184/F2
Battock (mt.), Sc, UK 94/D3
Batu (peak), Eth. 155/N6
Batu (cape), Indo. 139/E3
Batu (isls.), Indo. 138/A4
Batu (bay), Malay. 138/D3
Batu (peak), Malay. 138/D3
Batu Gajah, Malay. 138/B3
Batu Pahat, Malay. 138/B3
Batu Puteh (peak), Malay. 138/B3
Batudaka (isl.), Indo. 139/F4
Batuensambang (peak), Indo. 138/D3
Bat'umi, Geo. 121/G4
Bat'umi (int'l arpt.), Geo. 121/G4
Baturaja, Indo. 138/B4
Baturité, Braz. 212/C2
Batys Qazaqstan, Kaz. 122/E5
Bauchi (state), Nga. 161/H4
Bauchi, Nga. 161/H4
Baudette, Mn, US 185/K3
Baudó (mts.), Col. 210/B3
Baudó (riv.), Col. 210/B3
Bauer, Ut, US 195/J13
Bauld (cape), Nf, Can. 189/L1
Baulmes, Swi. 114/C4
Bauman (peak), Togo 161/F5
Baume-les-Dames, Fr. 114/C3
Baumholder, Ger. 111/G4
Baunach, Ger. 112/D3
Baunach (riv.), Ger. 112/D2
Baunatal, Ger. 109/G6
Baunei, It. 104/A2
Bauru, Braz. 213/B2
Bautzen, Ger. 99/H3
Bavans, Fr. 114/C3
Bavarian Alps (mts.), Aus.,Ger. 115/G3
Bavay, Fr. 110/C3
Båven (lake), Swe. 96/G2
Baveno, It. 115/E6
Baviácora, Mex. 184/C2
Bavilliers, Fr. 114/C2
Bavispe, Río de (riv.), Mex. 184/C2
Baw Baw (mt.), Austl. 173/C3
Baw Baw NP, Austl. 173/C3
Bawāna, India 144/D5
Bawang (cape), Indo. 138/C4
Bawean (isl.), Indo. 138/D5
Bawku, Gha. 161/E4
Baxoi, China 141/G2
Bay City, Mi, US 188/D3
Bay City, Tx, US 187/J5
Bay Minette, Al, US 191/G4
Bay Roberts, Nf, Can. 189/L2
Bay Saint Louis, Ms, US 191/F4
Bayamo, Cuba 203/G1
Bayamón, PR 199/M8
Bayan, Mong. 128/G2
Bayan Har (mts.), China 128/G5
Bayan-Hongor (prov.), Mong. 128/G2
Bayan-Ölgiy (prov.), Mong. 128/E2
Bayan-Ulaan, Mong. 128/H2
Bayanaul'skiy NP, Kaz. 145/G2
Bayanhongor, Mong. 128/H2
Bayanhushuu, Mong. 128/F2
Bayannuur, Mong. 128/F2
Bayano (lake), Pan. 203/G4
Bayanterem, Mong. 129/K2
Bayantsagaan, Mong. 128/H2
Bayard, Ne, US 185/H5
Bayat, Turk. 148/C1
Bayawan, Phil. 139/F2
Baybach (riv.), Ger. 111/G3
Baybay, Phil. 137/D5
Bayburt, Turk. 148/E1
Bayburt (prov.), Turk. 148/E1
Baydaratskaya (bay), Rus. 122/G2
Baydhabo (Baidoa), Som. 155/P7
Bayel, Fr. 114/A1
Bayerischer Wald (mts.), Ger. 113/F4
Bayerischer Wald NP, Ger. 113/G5
Bayern (state), Ger. 98/F4
Bayeux, Braz. 212/D2
Bayeux, Fr. 100/C2
Baygorria (res.), Uru. 217/K10
Baykal (mts.), Rus. 123/L4
Baykal (lake), Rus. 125/L4
Baykan, Turk. 148/E2
Bayombong, Phil. 137/D4
Bayon, Fr. 114/C1
Bayona, Sp. 102/A1
Bayonet Point, Fl, US 191/H4
Bayonne, Fr. 100/C5
Bayonne, NJ, US 197/J9
Bayport, NY, US 197/E2
Bayramaly, Trkm. 147/H1
Bayramiç, Turk. 105/K3
Bayreuth, Ger. 113/E3
Bayrūt (Beirut) (cap.), Leb. 149/D3
Bays, Lake of (lake), On, Can. 188/E2
Bayşehir (lake), Turk. 148/B2
Bayt Ḩanīnā, WBnk. 149/G8
Bayt Ḩānūn, Gaza 149/D4
Bayt Laḩm (Bethlehem), WBnk. 149/G8
Bayt Sāḩūr, WBnk. 149/G8
Baytik Shan (mts.), China,Mong. 128/E2
Baytown, Tx, US 187/J5
Bayudha (des.), Sudan 159/C5
Bayugan, Phil. 137/E6
Bayville, NY, US 197/L8
Baza, Sp. 102/D4
Bazainville, Fr. 88/G5
Bazardüzü (peak), Azer. 121/H4
Bazaruto, Ilha do (isl.), Moz. 163/G5
Bazèga (prov.), Burk. 161/E4
Bazemont, Fr. 88/H5
Bazet, Fr. 100/D5
Bazhong, China 128/J5
Bazin (riv.), Qu, Can. 188/F2
Bāzpur, India 142/B1
Bazzano, It. 117/E3
Be, Nosy (isl.), Madg. 165/H6
Beach Haven, NJ, US 196/D4
Beachport, Austl. 173/B3
Beachwood, NJ, US 196/D4
Beachy Head (pt.), Eng, UK 91/G5
Beacon (peak), Wal, UK 90/C2
Beaconsfield, Austl. 173/C4
Beaconsfield, Eng, UK 91/F3
Beaconsfield, Qu, Can. 189/N7
Beal (range), Austl. 171/A4
Bealanana, Madg. 165/J6
Beale (cape), BC, Can. 184/B3
Beampingaratra (ridge), Madg. 165/H9
Bear (isl.), Nor. 218/E
Bear (riv.), US 186/E2
Bear (mt.), Ak, US 192/K3
Bear (mtn.), Ak, US 192/K2
Bear, De, US 196/C4
Bear (lake), Ut, US 186/E2
Bear Creek (lake), Co, US 195/B3
Bear River (bay), Ut, US 195/J11
Bear River Migratory Bird Refuge (nat'l wild. ref.), Ut, US 195/J10
Beardsley, Az, US 195/R18
Beardsley (canal), Az, US 195/R18
Bearfort (mtn.), NJ, US 197/H7
Bearma (riv.), India 142/B4
Bearpaw (mts.), Mt, US 184/F3
Bearsden, Sc, UK 94/B5
Beartooth (mts.), Mt,Wy, US 184/F4
Beās (riv.), India 142/B3
Beas de Segura, Sp. 102/D3
Beasain, Sp. 102/D1
Beata (isl.), DRep. 203/J2
Beata (cape), DRep. 203/J2
Beatenberg, Swi. 114/D4
Beatty, Nv, US 186/C3
Beattystown, NJ, US 196/D2
Beau Bassin-Rose Hill, Mrts. 165/T15
Beaucaire, Fr. 100/F5
Beaucamps-le-Vieux, Fr. 110/A4
Beauchamp, Fr. 88/J4
Beaucourt, Fr. 114/C3
Beaudesert, Austl. 171/D4
Beaufort, Austl. 173/B3
Beaufort (sea), Can.,US 177/C2
Beaufort, Fr. 114/B4
Beaufort, Lux. 111/F4
Beaufort, SC, US 191/H3
Beaufort West, SAfr. 164/C4
Beaugency, Fr. 100/D3
Beaujolais, Monts du (mts.), Fr. 100/F4
Beauly (riv.), Sc, UK 94/B2
Beauly, Sc, UK 94/B2
Beauly Firth (lake), Sc, UK 94/B2
Beaumaris, Wal, UK 92/D5
Beaume, Fr. 100/F3
Beaumont, Tx, US 187/J5
Beaumont, Ca, US 194/D3
Beaumont, Fr. 100/E4
Beaumont, Belg. 111/D3
Beaumont-de-Lomagne, Fr. 100/D5
Beaumont-sur-Oise, Fr. 88/J4
Beaupréau, Fr. 100/C3
Beauquesne, Fr. 110/B3
Beauraing, Belg. 111/D3
Beaurainville, Fr. 110/A3
Beaurevoir, Fr. 110/C4
Beausejour, Mb, Can. 185/J3
Beautheil, Fr. 88/M5
Beautor, Fr. 110/C4
Beauvais, Fr. 110/B5
Beauval, Sk, Can. 184/G2
Beauval, Fr. 110/B3
Beauvoir, Fr. 88/L6
Beaver (lake), Ar, US 190/E2
Beaver (riv.), Yk, Can. 180/E2
Beaver, Ak, US 192/J2
Beaver (isl.), Mi, US 188/C2
Beaver (riv.), Ok, US 186/G3
Beaver (riv.), On, Can. 185/L2
Beaver, Ut, US 186/D3
Beaver Creek, Yk, Can. 192/K3
Beaver Meadows, Pa, US 196/C2
Beaver Springs, Pa, US 196/A2
Beaverhead (riv.), Mt, US 184/E4
Beaverlodge, Ab, Can. 184/D2
Beavertown, Pa, US 196/A2
Bebedouro, Braz. 213/B2
Beberibe, Braz. 212/C2
Bebington, Eng, UK 93/E5
Bebra, Ger. 109/G7
Becal, Mex. 202/D1
Beccles, Eng, UK 91/H2
Bečej, Serb. 106/E3
Becerreá, Sp. 102/B1
Bechar (prov.), Alg. 156/E3
Bechar, Alg. 157/E3
Becharof (lake), Ak, US 192/G4
Bechhofen, Ger. 111/G5
Bechtheim, Ger. 112/B3
Bechyně, Czh. 113/H4
Beckdorf, Ger. 109/G2
Beckenried, Swi. 115/E4
Beckingen, Ger. 111/F5
Beckley, WV, US 188/D4
Beckum, Ger. 109/F5
Beclean, Rom. 107/G2
Becs de Bosson (peak), Swi. 114/D5
Bédarieux, Fr. 100/E5
Bedburg, Ger. 111/F2
Bedburg-Hau, Ger. 108/D5
Beder, Den. 96/D3
Bedford (cape), Austl. 171/B1
Bedford, Qu, Can. 188/F2
Bedford, Eng, UK 91/F2
Bedford, In, US 188/C4
Bedford, SAfr. 164/D4
Bedford, Va, US 188/E4
Bedford Hills, NY, US 197/E1
Bedford Level (phys. reg.), Eng, UK 91/F2
Bedford Park, Il, US 193/Q16
Bedfordshire (co.), Eng, UK 91/F2
Bedlington, Eng, UK 93/G1
Bedonia, It. 116/C3
Bedouaram (well), Niger 154/H4
Bedretto, Swi. 115/E5
Bedsted, Den. 96/C3
Bedum, Neth. 108/D2
Bedworth, Eng, UK 91/E2
Beebe Seep (canal), Co, US 195/C2
Beechworth, Austl. 173/C3
Beek, Neth. 111/E2
Beelen, Ger. 109/F5
Beelitz, Ger. 98/P7
Beenleigh, Austl. 171/D4
Beer (pt.), Eng, UK 90/C5
Be'er Sheva', Isr. 149/D4
Beerfelden, Ger. 112/B3
Beernem, Belg. 110/C1
Beerzel, Belg. 111/D1
Beesel, Neth. 108/D6
Beeville, Tx, US 190/D4
Befandriana, Madg. 165/J6
Befandriana, Madg. 165/G8
Beforona, Madg. 165/J7
Befotaka, Madg. 165/J6
Beg (lake), NI, UK 92/B2
Bega, Austl. 173/D3
Bega (riv.), Ger. 109/F5
Bega Veche (riv.), Cro. 106/E3
Begamganj, Bang. 143/H4
Begamganj, India 142/B4
Bégard, Fr. 100/B2
Begarslan (peak), Trkm. 121/K4
Begejci, Serb. 106/E3
Begichev (isl.), Rus. 123/M2
Begna (riv.), Nor. 95/D3
Begusarai, India 143/F3
Béhague (pt.), FrG. 209/H3
Behala (str.), Indo. 138/B4
Behāla, India 140/E3
Behamberg, Aus. 113/H6
Behat, India 144/D4
Behbahān, Iran 146/F2
Behenjy-Afovany, Madg. 165/H7
Béhoust, Fr. 88/H5
Behren-lès-Forbach, Fr. 111/F5
Behri (riv.), Nepal 142/C1
Behshahr, Iran 146/F1
Bei (riv.), China 137/A2
Bei (mts.), China 128/F3
Bei'an, China 129/N2
Beierfeld, Ger. 113/F1
Beigua (peak), It. 116/B4
Beijing (mun.), China 129/L3
Beijing (cap.), China 130/H7
Beijing Capital (int'l arpt.), China 130/H6
Beilen, Neth. 108/D3
Beiliu, China 141/K3
Beilngries, Ger. 113/E4
Beilstein, Ger. 112/C4
Beilun (pass), China 137/A3
Bein Tharsuinn (peak), Sc, UK 94/B1
Beindersheim, Ger. 112/B3
Beinn a' Chuallaich (peak), Sc, UK 94/B3
Beinn a' Ghlò (peak), Sc, UK 94/C3
Beinn a' Mheadhoin (lake), Sc, UK 94/B2
Beinn Bhàn (peak), Sc, UK 94/A3
Beinn Bheula (peak), Sc, UK 94/B4
Beinn Bhrotain (peak), Sc, UK 94/C2
Beinn Bhuidhe (peak), Sc, UK 94/B4
Beinn Bhuidhe Mhór (peak),Sc, UK 94/B2
Beinn Dearg (peak), Sc, UK 94/B1
Beinn Dearg (peak), Sc, UK 94/C3
Beinn Dòrain (peak), Sc, UK 94/B4
Beinn Eighe (peak), Sc, UK 94/A1
Beinn Heasgarnich (peak), Sc, UK 94/B3
Beinn Mholach (peak), Sc, UK 94/B3
Beinn Mhór (peak), Sc, UK 94/A4
Beinwil am See, Swi. 114/E3
Beipiao, China 130/E2
Beira, Moz. 163/F4
Beiru (riv.), China 130/C4
Beirut (Bayrūt), (cap.), Leb. 149/D3
Beirut (int'l arpt.), Leb. 149/D3
Beitbridge, Zim. 163/E5
Beith, Sc, UK 94/B5
Beiuş, Rom. 106/F2
Beizhen, China 131/A2
Beja, Port. 102/B3
Beja (dist.), Port. 102/A4
Béja, Tun. 158/L6
Béja (gov.), Tun. 158/L6
Bejaïa (prov.), Alg. 158/H4
Bejaïa, Alg. 158/H4
Béjar, Sp. 102/C2
Bejhi (riv.), Pak. 147/J3
Bekabad, Uzb. 145/E4
Bekasi, Indo. 138/C5
Békés, Hun. 106/E2
Békés (prov.), Hun. 106/E2
Békéscsaba, Hun. 106/E2
Bekilli, Turk. 148/B2
Bekily, Madg. 165/H9
Bekitro, Madg. 165/H9
Bekwai, Gha. 161/E5
Bel Air, Md, US 196/B4
Bel Air South, Md, US 196/B5
Belā, India 140/D2
Bela, Pak. 147/J3
Belá, Slvk. 99/K4
Bela Crkva, Serb. 106/E3
Bela Cruz, Braz. 212/B1
Bela Palanka, Serb. 106/F4
Bělá pod Bezdězem, Czh. 113/H1
Belā Pratāpgarh, India 142/C3
Bela Vista, Braz. 209/G8
Bela Vista, Moz. 165/F2
Bela Vista do Paraíso, Braz. 213/B2
Belair, La, US 195/Q17
Belair Rec. Pk., Austl. 171/M9
Belan (riv.), India 142/D3

Belarus (ctry.) 85/G3
Belas, Port. 103/P10
Belaya (riv.), Rus. 122/F4
Belbo (riv.), It. 116/B3
Bełchatów, Pol. 99/K3
Belchen (peak), Ger. 114/D2
Belcher (chan.), Nun., Can. 181/S7
Belcher (isls.), On, Can. 181/H3
Belchite, Sp. 103/E2
Belcourt, ND, US 185/J3
Beldānga, India 143/G4
Belebey, Rus. 119/M5
Beled Weyne, Som. 155/Q7
Belém, Braz. 209/J4
Belém, Braz. 212/D2
Belém de São Francisco, Braz. 212/C3
Belem Tower, Port. 103/P10
Belén, Arg. 215/C2
Belen, NM, US 186/F4
Belén, Chile 214/D5
Belén, Nic. 198/D5
Belen, Turk. 149/E1
Belen, Turk. 149/C1
Belén de Escobar, Arg. 217/J11
Belene, Bul. 107/G4
Beles Wenz (riv.), Eth. 155/N5
Belesar, Embalse de (res.), Sp. 102/B1
Belev, Rus. 120/F1
Belews Creek, Mo, US 195/F9
Belfair, Wa, US 193/B3
Belfast (cap.), NI, UK 92/C2
Belfast (dist.), NI, UK 92/B2
Belfast, SAfr. 165/E2
Belfast, Me, US 189/G2
Belfast Lough (bay), NI, UK 92/C2
Belfaux, Swi. 114/D4
Belfield, ND, US 185/H4
Belfort (dept.), Fr. 114/C2
Belfort, Fr. 114/C2
Belgioioso, It. 116/C2
Belgium (ctry.) 98/C3
Belgorod, Rus. 120/F2
Belgorodskaya Oblast, Rus. 120/F2
Belgrade, Mt, US 184/F4
Belgrade (Beograd) (cap.),Serb. 106/E3
Beli Drim (riv.), Kos. 106/E4
Beli Manastir, Cro. 106/D3
Beli Timok (riv.), Serb. 106/F4
Belitsa, Bul. 105/H2
Belitung (isl.), Indo. 138/C4
Belize (riv.), Belz. 202/D2
Belize (ctry.) 202/D2
Belize City, Belz. 202/D2
Beljanica (peak), Serb. 106/E3
Bel'kovskiy (isl.), Rus. 123/N2
Bell, Austl. 171/C4
Bell (pt.), Austl. 171/G5
Bell (pen.), Nun., Can. 181/H2
Bell (riv.), Qu, Can. 181/J4
Bell, Ca, US 194/F8
Bell, Ger. 111/G3
Bell Gardens, Ca, US 194/F8
Bell Rock (Inchcape) (isl.), Sc, UK 94/D4
Bell Ville, Arg. 215/D3
Bella Coola, BC, Can. 184/B2
Bella Vista, Arg. 215/E2
Bellac, Fr. 100/D3
Bellaghy, NI, UK 92/B2
Bellagio, It. 115/F6
Bellano, It. 115/F5
Bellary, India 140/C4
Bellavista, Peru 214/B2
Bellavista, Peru 214/B2
Bellavista (cape), It. 104/A3
Bellavista, Ecu. 214/E7
Belle (riv.), On, Can. 193/G7
Belle-Anse, Haiti 203/H2
Belle Chasse, La, US 195/Q17
Belle Fourche (riv.), Wy, US 185/G5
Belle Glade, Fl, US 191/H5
Belle Haven, Va, US 196/A6
Belle-Ile (isl.), Fr. 100/B3
Belle Isle (str.), NF, Can. 189/K1
Belle Terre, NY, US 197/E2
Belleek, NI, UK 92/B3
Bellefontaine, Oh, US 188/D3
Bellefonte, De, US 196/C4
Bellegarde-sur-Valserine, Fr. 114/B5
Bellenberg, Ger. 115/G1
Bellenden Ker NP, Austl. 171/B2
Belleplain, NJ, US 196/D5
Bellerive-sur-Allier, Fr. 100/E3
Bellerose, NY, US 197/L9
Belleu, Fr. 110/C5
Belleville, On, Can. 188/E2
Belleville, Fr. 114/A5
Belleville, Il, US 195/H8
Belleville, Mi, US 193/E7
Belleville, NJ, US 197/J8
Belleville-sur-Meuse, Fr. 111/E5
Bellevue, Md, US 196/B6
Belley, Fr. 114/B6
Bellflower, Ca, US 194/F8
Bellheim, Ger. 112/B4
Bellignat, Fr. 114/B5
Bellinge, Den. 96/D4
Bellingen, Austl. 173/E1
Bellingham, Wa, US 184/C3
Bellingshausen (isl.), FrPol. 175/K6
Bellingshausen (sea), Ant. 218/U
Bellingwolde, Neth. 109/E2
Bellinzago Novarese, It. 116/B1
Bellinzona, Swi. 115/F5
Bellmawr, NJ, US 196/C4
Bellmead, Tx, US 187/H5
Bellmore, NY, US 197/L9
Bello, Col. 208/C2
Bellona Reefs (reef), NCal., Fr. 174/E7
Bellot (str.), Nun., Can. 180/G1
Bellport, NY, US 197/F2
Bellshill, Sc, UK 94/B5
Belluno (prov.), It. 117/E1
Belluno, It. 101/K3
Bellville, Tx, US 187/H5
Bellville, SAfr. 164/L10
Bellvue, Co, US 195/B1
Bellwald, Swi. 114/E5
Belm, Ger. 109/F4
Belmar, NJ, US 196/D3
Bélmez, Sp. 102/C3
Belmont, Ca, US 193/K11
Belmonte, Braz. 212/C4
Belmonte, Sp. 102/D3
Belmonte, Port. 102/B2
Belmopan (cap.), Belz. 202/D2
Belmullet, Ire. 89/P9
Belo Campo, Braz. 212/B4
Belo Horizonte, Braz. 213/D1
Belo Jardim, Braz. 212/C3
Belo-Tsiribihina, Madg. 165/H7
Beloeil, Qu, Can. 189/P6
Beloeil, Belg. 110/C2
Belogorsk, Rus. 129/N1
Beloha, Madg. 165/H9
Beloit, Wi, US 185/L5
Beloit, Ks, US 187/H3
Belomorsk, Rus. 118/G2
Belorado, Sp. 102/D1
Belorechensk, Rus. 120/F3
Belören, Turk. 148/C2
Beloretsk, Rus. 119/N5
Beloslav, Bul. 107/H4
Belovo, Bul. 105/J1
Belovo, Rus. 122/J4
Beloye (lake), Rus. 122/D3
Belper, Eng, UK 93/G5
Belsand, India 143/E2
Belt, Mt, US 184/F4
Belterwijde (lake), Neth. 108/D3
Beltheim, Ger. 111/G3
Belton, Tx, US 187/H5
Belton, Mo, US 195/D6
Beltsville, Md, US 196/B5
Beltzville (lake), Pa, US 196/C2
Belukha (peak), Rus. 128/E2
Belvedere, Ca, US 193/K11
Belvidere, NJ, US 196/C2
Belyando (riv.), Austl. 167/D3
Belyy (isl.), Rus. 218/A
Belzig, Ger. 98/G2
Bełżyce, Pol. 99/M3
Bemaraha (plat.), Madg. 165/H7
Bemarivo (riv.), Madg. 165/H7
Bembéréké, Ben. 161/F4
Bembibre, Sp. 102/B1
Bemboka, Austl. 173/D3
Bemetāra, India 140/D3
Bemidji, Mn, US 185/K4
Bemmel, Neth. 108/C5
Ben Aigan (hill), Sc, UK 94/C1
Ben Alder (peak), Sc, UK 94/B3
Ben Améra (well), Mrta. 156/B5
Ben Avon (peak), Sc, UK 94/C2
Ben Boyd NP, Austl. 173/D3
Ben Chonzie (peak), Sc, UK 94/C4
Ben Cleuch (peak), Sc, UK 94/C4
Ben Cruachan (peak), Sc, UK 94/A4
Ben Davis (pt.), NJ, US 196/C5
Ben Gurion (int'l arpt.), Isr. 149/F7
Ben Hope (peak), Sc, UK 89/R7
Ben Ime (peak), Sc, UK 94/B4
Ben Lawers (peak), Sc, UK 94/B3
Ben Ledi (peak), Sc, UK 94/B4
Ben Lomond (peak), Sc, UK 94/B4
Ben Lomond NP, Austl. 173/C4
Ben Lui (peak), Sc, UK 94/B4
Ben Macdui (peak), Sc, UK 94/C2
Ben More (peak), Sc, UK 89/Q8
Ben More (peak), Sc, UK 94/B4
Ben More Assynt (peak), Sc, UK 89/R7
Ben Msik-Sidi Othmane (prov.), Mor. 158/A2
Ben Nevis (peak), Sc, UK 94/B3
Ben Rinnes (peak), Sc, UK 94/C2
Ben Slimane, Mor. 156/D2
Ben Slimane (prov.), Mor. 158/A3
Ben Starav (peak), Sc, UK 94/A3
Ben Tee (peak), Sc, UK 94/B2
Ben Tirran (peak), Sc, UK 94/C3
Ben Tre, Viet. 136/D4
Ben Vane (peak), Sc, UK 94/B4
Ben Vorlich (peak), Sc, UK 94/B4
Ben Vrackie (peak), Sc, UK 94/C3
Ben Wyvis (peak), Sc, UK 94/B1
Ben Zohra (well), Alg. 156/E3
Benabarre, Sp. 103/F1
Benahmed, Mor. 156/D2
Benalla, Austl. 173/C3
Benalmádena, Sp. 102/C4
Ben Arous, Tun. 158/M6
Ben Arous (gov.), Tun. 158/M6
Benavente, Sp. 102/C1
Benavides, Tx, US 190/D5
Benbane (pt.), NI, UK 92/B1
Benbecula (isl.), Sc, UK 89/Q8
Benbonyathe (peak), Austl. 171/H4
Benburb, NI, UK 92/B3
Bend, Or, US 184/C4
Bendeleben (mt.), Ak, US 192/F2
Bendemeer, Austl. 173/D1
Bendersville, Pa, US 196/A4
Bendigo, Austl. 173/C3
Bendorf, Ger. 96/C4
Bene Beraq, Isr. 149/F7
Benedict (mt.), Nf, Can. 181/L3
Benediktbeuern, Ger. 115/H2
Benediktenwand (peak), Ger. 115/H2
Beneditinos, Braz. 212/B2
Benenitra, Madg. 165/H8
Benešov, Czh. 113/H3
Benevento, It. 104/D2
Benfeld, Fr. 114/D1
Bengal, Bay of (gulf), Asia 140/E4
Bengbu, China 130/D4
Benghāzī, Libya 154/K1
Bengkalis, Indo. 138/B3
Bengkalis (isl.), Indo. 138/B3
Bengkayang, Indo. 138/C3
Bengkulu, Indo. 138/B4
Bengough, Sk, Can. 185/G3
Bengtsfors, Swe. 96/E2
Benguela, Ang. 163/B3
Benguerir, Mor. 156/D2
Beni, D.R. Congo 162/A2
Beni (riv.), Bol. 205/C4
Beni Abbes, Alg. 157/E3
Beni Bouayach, Mor. 158/C2
Beni Ensar, Mor. 158/B2
Beni Khiar, Tun. 158/M6
Beni Mellal, Mor. 156/D2
Beni Ounif, Alg. 157/E2
Benicarló, Sp. 103/F2
Benicia, Ca, US 193/K10
Benidorm, Sp. 103/E3
Benifayó, Sp. 103/E3
Benin (ctry.) 161/F4
Benin, Bight of (bay), Afr. 151/C4
Benin City, Nga. 161/G5
Benisa, Sp. 103/F3
Benito Juárez, Mex. 184/D2
Benjamin, Tx, US 187/H4
Benjamin Constant, Braz. 214/D2
Benjamin Hill, Mex. 184/C2
Benjamín, Isla (isl.), Chile 216/B5
Benkei-misaki (cape), Japan 134/B2
Benkelman, Ne, US 187/G2
Bennachie (hill), Sc, UK 94/D2
Bennan (pt.), Sc, UK 94/A6
Bennett (isl.), Rus. 123/Q2
Bennettsville, SC, US 191/J3
Bennington, Vt, US 188/F3
Bénoue, PN de la, Camr. 154/H6
Bensenville, Il, US 193/Q16
Bensheim, Ger. 112/B3
Benson, Mn, US 185/K4
Benson, Az, US 186/E5
Benta (riv.), Hun. 107/Q10
Bentheim, Ger. 109/E4
Bentley, Eng, UK 93/G4
Bento Gonçalves, Braz. 213/B4
Benton, Ar, US 187/J4
Benton, La, US 187/J4
Benton, Pa, US 196/B1
Benton Harbor, Mi, US 188/C3
Bentong, Malay. 138/B3
Benue (state), Nga. 161/H5
Benue (riv.), Nga. 154/G6
Benxi, China 131/B2
Benxi, China 131/C2
Beočin, Serb. 106/D3
Beograd (int'l arpt.), Serb. 106/E3
Beohāri, India 142/C3
Beppu (bay), Japan 132/B4
Beppu, Japan 132/B4
Bequia (isl.), StV. 199/N9
Bequimão, Braz. 212/A1
Beraber (well), Alg. 154/E1
Beragh, NI, UK 92/A2
Beraketa, Madg. 165/H8
Berane, Serb. 106/D4
Berasia, India 142/A4
Berat, Alb. 105/F2
Beratus (peak), Indo. 139/E4
Beratzhausen, Ger. 113/E4
Berau (riv.), Indo. 139/E3
Berau (bay), Indo. 139/H4
Berbenno di Valtellina, It. 115/F5
Berbera, Som. 155/Q5
Berbérati, CAfr. 154/J7
Berbice (riv.), Guy. 208/G2
Berceto, It. 116/C3
Berchem, Belg. 108/B6
Bercher, Swi. 114/C4
Berching, Ger. 113/E4
Berchtesgaden, Ger. 101/K3
Berchtesgaden, NP, Ger. 101/K3
Berck, Fr. 110/A3
Berdorf, Lux. 111/F4
Berdsk, Rus. 145/H2
Berdyans'k, Ukr. 120/F3
Berdychiv, Ukr. 120/D2
Berea, Ky, US 188/C4
Bereguardo, It. 116/C2
Berehove, Ukr. 99/M4
Berekum, Gha. 161/E5
Berenguela, Bol. 214/D5
Berenice (ruin), Egypt 159/C4
Beresford, SD, US 185/J5
Beresford, NB, Can. 189/H2
Bereşti, Rom. 107/H2
Berettyóújfalu, Hun. 106/E2
Berevo, Madg. 165/H7
Berezina (riv.), Bela. 120/D1
Berezniki, Rus. 119/N4
Berezovo, Rus. 122/G3
Berg (riv.), SAfr. 164/B4
Berg, Swi. 115/F2
Berg, Lux. 111/F4
Berg, Ger. 112/B5
Berg bei Rohrbach, Aus. 113/G5
Berga, Sp. 103/F1
Bergama, Turk. 148/A2
Bergamo, It. 116/C1
Bergamo (prov.), It. 115/F6
Bergara, Sp. 102/D1
Bergatruete, Ger. 115/F2
Bergen, Ger. 109/G3
Bergen, Ger. 96/E4
Bergen, Neth. 108/B3
Bergen, Nor. 96/A1
Bergen (co.), NJ, US 196/D2
Bergen op Zoom, Neth. 108/B5
Bergen Park, Co, US 195/B3
Bergenfield, NJ, US 197/K8
Bergerac, Fr. 100/D4
Bergheim, Tx, US 195/T20
Bergheim, Aus. 113/G7
Bergheim, Ger. 111/F2
Bergisch Gladbach, Ger. 111/G2
Bergkamen, Ger. 109/E5
Bergnäset, Swe. 118/D2
Bergneustadt, Ger. 111/G1
Bergrheinfeld, Ger. 98/F4
Bergse Maas (riv.), Neth. 108/B5
Bergshamra, Swe. 96/H2
Bergsviken, Swe. 95/G2
Bergtheim, Ger. 112/D3
Berguent, Mor. 158/C2
Bergues, Fr. 110/B2
Bergum, Neth. 108/D2
Bergumermeer (lake), Neth. 108/D2
Bergün-Bravuogn, Swi. 115/F4
Bergviken (lake), Swe. 96/G1
Berh, Mong. 129/K2
Berikat (cape), Indo. 138/C4
Bering (isl.), Rus. 123/S4
Bering (sea), Asia,NAm. 123/U4
Bering (str.), Rus.,US 125/U3
Bering Land Bridge Nat'l Prsv., Ak, US 192/E2
Beringen, Belg. 111/E1
Beritarikap (cape), Indo. 138/B4
Berja, Sp. 102/D4
Berkel, Neth. 108/B5
Berkel (riv.), Ger. 98/D2
Berkeley, Ca, US 186/B3
Berkeley, Mo, US 195/G8
Berkeley Heights, NJ, US 197/H9
Berkhamsted, Eng, UK 88/B1
Berkheim, Ger. 115/G1
Berkhout, Neth. 108/B3
Berkley, Mi, US 193/F6
Berkovitsa, Bul. 105/H1
Berks (co.), Pa, US 196/C3
Berkshire (co.), Eng, UK 91/E3
Berkshire Downs (hills), Eng, UK 91/E3
Berlaimont, Fr. 110/C3
Berlanga de Duero, Sp. 102/D2
Berlare, Belg. 110/D1
Berleburg, Ger. 109/F6
Berlicum, Neth. 108/C5
Berlin (cap.), Ger. 98/Q6
Berlin (state), Ger. 98/Q6
Berlin, NH, US 189/G2
Berlin, NJ, US 196/D4
Berlin, Wi, US 185/L5
Bermagui, Austl. 173/D3
Bermejo, Bol. 215/D1
Bermejo (riv.), Arg. 205/D5
Bermeo, Sp. 102/D1
Bermillo de Sayago, Sp. 102/B2
Bermuda (isl.), UK 177/L6
Bern (canton), Swi. 114/D4
Bern (cap.), Swi. 114/D4
Bern-Belp (int'l arpt.), Swi. 114/D4
Bernal, Peru 214/A2
Bernalda, It. 104/E2
Bernalillo, NM, US 186/F4
Bernard (riv.), NW, Can. 180/D1
Bernardo O'Higgins, PN, Chile 215/B6
Bernardsville, NJ, US 196/D2
Bernau, Ger. 114/E2
Bernau, Ger. 98/Q6
Bernay, Fr. 100/D2
Bernbeuren, Ger. 115/G2
Bernburg, Ger. 98/F3
Berne (riv.), Ger. 109/F2
Bernes-sur-Oise, Fr. 88/J4
Bernese Alps (mtn.), Swi. 101/G3
Bernhardswald, Ger. 113/F4
Bernice, La, US 187/J4
Bernier (isl.), Austl. 170/B3
Bernier (bay), Nun., Can. 180/G1
Bernina (peak), Swi. 115/F5
Bernina (mtn.), Swi. 115/F5
Bernina, Passo del (pass), Swi. 115/G5
Bernissart, Belg. 110/C3
Bernkastel-Kues, Ger. 111/G4
Bernsbach, Ger. 113/F1
Bernville, Pa, US 196/B3
Beromünster, Swi. 114/E3
Beroroha, Madg. 165/H8
Beroun, Czh. 113/H3
Berounka (riv.), Czh. 99/G4
Berovo, FYROM 105/H2
Berra, It. 117/E3
Berre, Étang de (lake), Fr. 100/F5
Berrechid, Mor. 156/D2
Berri, Austl. 171/J5
Berriane, Alg. 157/F2
Berridale, Austl. 173/D3
Berriedale, Sc, UK 89/S7
Berrigan, Austl. 173/C2
Berriozábal, Mex. 202/C2
Berrotarán, Arg. 216/D2
Berrouaghia, Alg. 158/G4
Berry, Austl. 173/D2
Berry (isls.), Bahm. 199/F2
Berry, Fr. 100/D3
Berry (pt.), Eng, UK 90/C6
Berry (mtn.), Pa, US 196/A2
Berryessa (peak), Ca, US 193/K9
Bersenbrück, Ger. 109/E3
Berthoud, Co, US 195/B2
Bertinoro, It. 117/F4
Bertiolo, It. 117/G1
Bertogne, Belg. 111/E3
Bertolinia, Braz. 212/B2
Bertoua, Camr. 154/H7
Bertrand (peak), Arg. 217/B6
Bertrandville, La, US 195/Q17
Bertrix, Belg. 111/E4
Bertry, Fr. 110/C3
Beru (isl.), Kiri. 174/G5
Beruit (isl.), Malay. 138/D3
Bervie Water (riv.), Sc, UK 94/D3
Berwick, NS, Can. 189/H2
Berwick, Pa, US 196/B1
Berwick-upon-Tweed, Eng, UK 94/D5
Berwyn, Il, US 193/Q16
Berwyn (mts.), Wal, UK 92/E6
Berzence, Hun. 106/C2
Bès (riv.), Fr. 100/E2
Besalampy, Madg. 165/H7
Besançon, Fr. 114/C3
Besar (peak), Indo. 139/E4
Besbre (riv.), Fr. 100/E3
Beşiri, Turk. 148/E2
Beška, Serb. 106/E3
Beskids (mts.), Pol. 99/L4
Beşkonak, Turk. 149/B1
Beslan, Rus. 121/H4
Besna Kobila (peak), Serb. 106/F4
Besozzo, It. 116/B1
Bessacarr, Eng, UK 93/G4
Bessancourt, Fr. 88/J4
Bessarabia (reg.), Mol. 107/J2
Bessbrook, NI, UK 92/B3
Bessemer, Al, US 191/G3
Bessemer (mtn.), Wa, US 193/D2
Bessines-sur-Gartempe, Fr. 100/D3
Best, Neth. 108/C5
Bestensee, Ger. 98/Q7
Bestwig, Ger. 109/F6
Bet She'an, Isr. 149/D3
Bet Shemesh, Isr. 149/F8
Betanantanana, Madg. 165/H7
Betanzos, Sp. 102/A1
Beth She'arim (ruin), Isr. 149/G6
Bethal, SAfr. 164/E2
Bethalto, Il, US 195/G8
Bethanie, Namb. 164/B2
Bethany (res.), Ca, US 193/L11
Bethany, Mo, US 185/K5
Bethany, Ok, US 195/M14
Bethel, Ak, US 192/F3
Bethel, Pa, US 196/B3
Bethel Acres, Ok, US 195/N15
Bethel Island, Ca, US 193/L10
Bétheniville, Fr. 111/D5
Béthény, Fr. 110/D5
Bethesda, Md, US 196/A6
Bethesda, Wal, UK 92/D5
Béthisy-Sainte-Pierre, Fr. 110/B5
Bethlehem, SAfr. 164/E3
Bethlehem, Pa, US 196/C2
Bethlehem, Md, US 196/B6
Bethoncourt, Fr. 114/C2
Bethpage, NY, US 197/M9
Bethulie, SAfr. 164/D3
Bethune, Sk, Can. 185/G3
Béthune (riv.), Fr. 100/D2
Béthune, Fr. 110/B2
Betim, Braz. 213/C1
Betioky, Madg. 165/H8
Betpaqala (plain), Kaz. 128/A2
Betroka, Madg. 165/H8
Betschdorf, Fr. 112/A5
Betsiamites (riv.), Qu, Can. 189/G1
Betsiboka (riv.), Madg. 165/H7
Bettancourt-la-Ferrée, Fr. 111/D6
Bette (peak), Libya 155/J3
Bettembourg, Lux. 111/F4
Betterton, Md, US 196/B5
Bettiah, India 143/E2
Bettlach, Swi. 114/D3
Bettles, Ak, US 192/H2
Betuwe (phys. reg.), Neth. 108/C5
Betwa (riv.), India 142/B3
Betz, Fr. 88/L4
Betzdorf, Ger. 111/G2
Betzenstein, Ger. 113/E3
Beulah, Austl. 173/B2
Beulah, ND, US 185/H4
Beulah (lake), Wi, US 193/P14
Beulakerwijde (lake), Neth. 108/C3
Beuningen, Neth. 108/C5
Beure, Fr. 114/C3
Beuvray (peak), Fr. 100/F3
Beuvron (riv.), Fr. 100/D3
Beuvronne (riv.), Fr. 88/L5
Beuvry, Fr. 110/B3
Bevensen, Ger. 109/H2
Bever (riv.), Ger. 109/E4
Beveren, Belg. 108/B6
Beverin (peak), Swi. 115/F4
Beverley, Austl. 170/C5
Beverley, Eng, UK 93/H4
Beverly, Mo, US 195/D5
Beverly Hills, Ca, US 194/F7
Beverly Hills, Mi, US 193/F6
Beverstedt, Ger. 109/F2
Beverungen, Ger. 109/G5
Beverwijk, Neth. 108/B4
Bewār, India 142/B3
Bewl Bridge (res.), Eng, UK 91/G4
Bex, Swi. 114/D5
Bexar (co.), Tx, US 195/T21
Bexbach, Ger. 111/G5
Bexhill, Eng, UK 91/G5
Bexley (bor.), Eng, UK 88/D2
Beyçayırı, Turk. 107/H5
Beycuma, Turk. 107/K5
Beyne-Heusay, Belg. 111/E2
Beynes, Fr. 88/H5
Beyoneisu-Retsugan (isl.), Japan 133/F5
Beypazarı, Turk. 107/K5
Beyşehir, Turk. 148/B2
Bezaha, Madg. 165/H8
Bezau, Aus. 115/F3
Bezdan, Serb. 106/D3
Bezděz (peak), Czh. 113/H1
Bezdrev (lake), Czh. 113/H4
Bezhetsk, Rus. 118/H4
Béziers, Fr. 100/E5
Bhabua, India 142/D3
Bhadarwāh, India 144/C3
Bhadaur, India 144/C4
Bhadohi, India 142/D3
Bhādra, India 144/C5
Bhadreswar, India 140/A3
Bhāgalpur, India 143/F3
Bhāi Pheru, Pak. 144/B4
Bhairab (riv.), Bang. 143/G4
Bhairab Bāzār, Bang. 143/H3
Bhakkar, Pak. 144/A4
Bhākra (dam), India 144/D4
Bhaktapur, Nepal 143/E2
Bhalwāl, Pak. 144/B3
Bhamo, Myan. 141/G3
Bhānder, India 142/B3
Bhānrer (range), India 142/B4
Bhānwad, India 140/A3
Bharatpur, Nepal 143/E2
Bhārātpur, India 142/A2
Bharthana, India 142/B2
Bharuch, India 147/K4
Bhasāwar, India 142/A2
Bhātāpāra, India 140/D3
Bhatinda, India 144/C4
Bhatkal, India 147/K6
Bhātpāra, India 143/G4
Bhavāni, India 140/C5
Bhavnagar, India 147/K4
Bhawāna, Pak. 144/B4
Bhawāni Mandi, India 147/L4
Bhera, Pak. 144/B3
Bheri (zone), Nepal 142/C1
Bhilai, India 140/D3
Bhīlwāra, India 147/K3
Bhīma (riv.), India 147/L5
Bhima (riv.), India 140/C4
Bhīmavaram, India 140/D4
Bhimunipatnam, India 140/D4
Bhinga, India 142/C2
Bhiwandi, India 147/K5
Bhiwāni, India 144/D5
Bhojpur, Nepal 143/F2
Bhokardan, India 140/C3
Bhola, Bang. 143/H4
Bhongaon, India 142/B2
Bhopāl, India 140/C3
Bhor, India 147/K5
Bhraoin (lake), Sc, UK 94/A1
Bhuban, India 140/E3
Bhumibol (dam), Thai. 136/B2
Bhusawal, India 147/L4
Bhutan (ctry.) 140/E2
Bi Doup (peak), Viet. 136/E3
Biá (riv.), Braz. 208/E4
Bia (riv.), C.d'Iv. 160/E5
Biafra, Bight of (bay), Camr. 154/G7
Biak (isl.), Indo. 139/J4
Biak (int'l arpt.), Indo. 139/J4
Biała Podlaska, Pol. 99/M2
Białobrzegi, Pol. 99/L3
Białogard, Pol. 96/G4
Białowieski NP, Pol. 99/K4
Białowieski NP, Pol. 99/M2
Białystok, Pol. 99/M2
Bianca (peak), It. 115/G4
Biancavilla, It. 104/D4
Biandrate, It. 116/B2
Biandronno, It. 116/B1
Bianze, It. 116/B2
Biarritz, Fr. 100/C5
Biasca, Swi. 115/E5
Bibā, Egypt 159/B2
Bibai, Japan 134/B2
Bibbiano, It. 116/D3
Bibbiena, It. 117/E5
Biberach, Ger. 114/E1
Biberach, Ger. 115/G1
Biberach an der Riss, Ger. 115/F1
Biberist, Swi. 114/D3
Bibione, It. 117/G1
Biblián, Ecu. 210/B5
Biblis, Ger. 112/B3
Bicas, Braz. 213/K6
Bicaz, Rom. 107/H2
Bicester, Eng, UK 91/E3
Bicheno, Austl. 173/D4
Bicknacre, Eng, UK 88/E1
Bicske, Hun. 106/D2
Bida, Nga. 161/G4
Bīdar, India 140/C4
Biddeford, Me, US 189/G3
Biddiyā, WBnk. 149/G7
Biddū, WBnk. 149/G8
Biddulph, Eng, UK 93/F5
Bidean nam Bian (peak), Sc, UK 94/A3
Bideford, Eng, UK 90/B4
Bidente (riv.), It. 117/F4
Bidhūna, India 142/B2
Bīdokht, Iran 147/G2
Biebesheim am Rhein, Ger. 112/B3
Biebrza (riv.), Pol. 99/M2
Biel, Swi. 114/D3
Bielawa, Pol. 99/J3
Bieldside, Sc, UK 94/D2
Bielefeld, Ger. 109/F4
Bieler (lake), Nun., Can. 181/J1
Bieler (lake), Swi. 114/D3
Biella, It. 116/B1
Biella (prov.), It. 116/B1
Bielsk Podlaski, Pol. 99/M2
Bielsko-Biała, Pol. 99/K4
Bien Hoa, Viet. 136/D4
Bienenbüttel, Ger. 109/H2
Bienne (riv.), Fr. 114/B5
Bienno, It. 115/G6
Bientina, It. 116/D5
Bienville (lake), Qu, Can. 181/J3
Bière, Swi. 114/C4
Bierset (int'l arpt.), Belg. 111/E2
Bierum, Neth. 108/D2
Bieruń, Pol. 99/J3
Biesbosch (reg.), Neth. 108/B5
Biesenthal, Ger. 98/Q6
Biesles, Fr. 114/B1
Biesme (riv.), Fr. 111/D5
Bieszczadzki NP, Pol. 99/M4
Bietigheim, Ger. 112/C5
Bietschhorn (peak), Swi. 114/D5
Bièvre (riv.), Fr. 88/J5
Bièvre, Belg. 111/E4
Big (des.), Austl. 173/B2
Big (isl.), Nun., Can. 180/D1
Big (isl.), On, Can. 180/G4
Big (lake), Mi, US 193/E6
Big (riv.), Mo, US 195/F9
Big Belt (mts.), Mt, US 184/F4
Big Bend, Swaz. 165/E2
Big Bend, Wi, US 193/P14
Big Bend NP, Tx, US 187/G5
Big Blue (riv.), Ks,Ne, US 187/H2
Big Diomede (isl.), Rus. 192/E2
Big Fork (riv.), Mn, US 185/K4
Big Hole (riv.), Mt, US 184/E4
Big Hole, SAfr. 164/D3
Big Lake, Tx, US 187/G5
Big Lost (riv.), Id, US 186/D2
Big Muskego (lake), Wi, US 193/P14
Big Pine (hill), Pa, US 196/C1
Big Pines, Ca, US 194/C2
Big Rapids, Mi, US 188/C3
Big River, Sk, Can. 184/G2
Big Rock, Il, US 193/N16
Big Sandy (riv.), Wy, US 186/E2
Big Sioux (riv.), Ia,SD, US 185/J5
Big Spring, Tx, US 187/G4
Big Stone (lake), Mn,SD, US 185/J4
Big Thompson (riv.), Co, US 195/B2
Big Thompson, North Fork (riv.), Co, US 195/A2
Big Timber, Mt, US 184/F4
Big Trout (lake), On, Can. 180/H3
Big Tujunga Canyon (canyon), Ca, US 194/B2
Big Wood (riv.), Id, US 186/D2
Biga, Turk. 107/H5
Bigadiç, Turk. 148/B2
Bigbury (bay), Eng, UK 90/C6
Biggar, Sk, Can. 184/G2
Biggar, Sc, UK 94/C5
Bigge (riv.), Ger. 111/G1
Biggenden, Austl. 171/D4
Biggleswade, Eng, UK 91/F2
Bighorn (basin), Wy, US 186/E1
Bighorn (lake), Mt,Wy, US 184/F4
Bighorn (mts.), Wy, US 182/E3
Bighorn (riv.), Wy, US 184/G4
Biglerville, Pa, US 196/A4
Bignona, Sen. 160/A3
Biguaçu, Braz. 213/B3
Bihać, Bosn. 101/L4
Bihar, India 143/E3
Biharamulo, Tanz. 162/A3
Biharamulo Game Rsv., Tanz. 162/A3
Bihārīganj, India 143/F3
Biharkeresztes, Hun. 106/E2
Bihor (co.), Rom. 99/M5
Bihorel, Fr. 100/D2
Bihoro, Japan 134/D2
Bijagós (arch.), GBis. 151/A3
Bijagós, Arquipélago do (isl.) GBis. 154/B5
Bījār, Iran 146/E1
Bījāwar, India 142/B3
Bijbiāra, India 144/C3
Bijeljina, Bosn. 106/D3
Bijelo Polje, Mont. 106/D4
Bijiang, China 141/G2
Bijie, China 141/J2
Bijni, India 143/H2
Bijnor, India 142/B1
Bīkaner, India 147/K3
Bikar (isl.), Mrsh. 174/G3
Bikin, Rus. 129/P2
Bikin (riv.), Rus. 129/Q2
Bikini (isl.), Mrsh. 174/F3
Bikramganj, India 143/E3
Bikuar, PN do, Ang. 163/C4
Bila Tserkva, Ukr. 120/D2
Bilāra, India 140/B2
Bilāri, India 142/B1
Bilāsipāra, India 143/H2
Bilāspur, India 142/D4
Bilāspur, India 142/B1
Bilāspur, India 144/D4
Bilaukraung (range), Myan. 141/G5
Bilauktaung (range), Myan.,Thai. 136/B3
Bilba Morea Claypan (lake), Austl. 167/C3
Bilbao, Sp. 102/D1
Bilbays, Egypt 149/B4
Bileća, Bosn. 105/F1
Bilecik, Turk. 148/B1
Bilecik (prov.), Turk. 148/B1
Biłgoraj, Pol. 99/M3
Bilgrām, India 142/C2
Bilhaur, India 142/C2
Bilhorod-Dnistrovs'kyy, Ukr. 107/K2
Bilibino, Rus. 123/S3
Bilin, Myan. 141/G4
Bilin (riv.), Myan. 136/B2
Bílina (riv.), Czh. 113/G2
Bílina, Czh. 113/G1
Biliu (riv.), China 131/B3
Bill of Portland (pt.), Eng, UK 90/D5
Bill Williams (riv.), Az, US 186/D4
Bille (riv.), Ger. 109/H1
Billerbeck, Ger. 109/E5
Billère, Fr. 100/C5
Billericay, Eng, UK 88/E2
Billiat Conservation Park, Austl. 173/B2

Billiat Consv. Park, Austl. 171/J5
Billigheim, Ger. 112/C4
Billinge, Eng, UK 93/F4
Billingham, Eng, UK 93/G2
Billings, Mt, US 184/F4
Billingsfors, Swe. 96/E2
Billund (int'l arpt.), Den. 96/C4
Billund, Den. 96/C4
Bilma, Niger 154/H4
Biloela, Austl. 171/C4
Biloku, Guy. 211/G4
Biloxi, Ms, US 191/F4
Bilpa Morea Claypan (lake), Austl. 171/H3
Bilqas Qism Awwal, Egypt 149/B4
Bilsi, India 142/B1
Bilthar, India 142/D2
Biltine, Chad 155/K5
Bilzen, Belg. 111/E2
Bima, Indo. 139/E5
Bimberi (peak), Austl. 173/D2
Bimbo, CAfr. 155/J7
Bimini (isls.), Bahm. 199/F2
Bina (riv.), Ger. 113/F6
Bina-Etāwa, India 142/B3
Binalong, Austl. 173/D2
Binasco, It. 116/C2
Binbrook, On, Can. 189/Q9
Binche, Belg. 111/D3
Binchuan, China 141/H2
Bindki, India 142/C2
Bindura, Zim. 163/F4
Binéfar, Sp. 103/F2
Binga (mtn.), Moz. 163/F4
Bingara, Austl. 173/D1
Bingen, Ger. 111/G4
Bingerville, C.d'Iv. 160/E5
Binghamton, NY, US 188/F3
Bingley, Eng, UK 93/G4
Bıngöl, Turk. 148/E2
Bıngöl (prov.), Turk. 148/E2
Binh Son, Viet. 136/E3
Binhai, China 130/D4
Binhon (peak), Myan. 141/G4
Binisalem, Sp. 103/G3
Binjai, Indo. 138/A3
Binkılıç, Turk. 107/J5
Binnaway, Austl. 173/D1
Binningen, Swi. 114/D2
Binongko (isl.), Indo. 139/F5
Bintang (peak), Malay. 138/B2
Binyamina, Isr. 149/F6
Bío-Bío (riv.), Chile 215/B4
Bío-Bío (pol. reg.), Chile 216/B3
Biograd, Cro. 106/B4
Biogradska NP, Mont. 106/D4
Bioko (isl.), EqG. 151/C4
Biougra, Mor. 156/C3
Bipoint (Bissau) (int'l arpt.), GBis. 160/B4
Bippen, Ger. 109/E3
Bīr, India 147/L5
Bi'r Abu Minqâr (well), Egypt 159/A3
Bîr Aïdiat (well), Mrta. 156/C4
Bir Bel Guerdâne (well), Mrta. 156/C4
Bi'r Ghadir (well), Egypt 159/C3
Bîr Ounâne (well), Mali 156/E5
Bi'r Zayt, WBnk. 149/G8
Birāk, Libya 154/H2
Birao, CAfr. 155/K5
Birātnagar, Nepal 143/F2
Biratori, Japan 134/C2
Birch (mts.), Ab, Can. 180/E3
Birch Creek, Ak, US 192/J2
Birch Hills, Sk, Can. 185/G2
Birch River, Mb, Can. 185/H2
Birchip, Austl. 173/B2
Bird Islet (isl.), Austl. 167/E3
Birds Rock (peak), Austl. 173/D2
Birdsboro, Pa, US 196/C3
Birdwood, Austl. 171/M8
Birecik, Turk. 148/D2
Bīrganj, Nepal 143/E2
Biritiba-Mirim, Braz. 213/G8
Bīrjand, Iran 147/G2
Birkat Qārūn (lake), Egypt 148/B4
Birken-Honigsessen, Ger. 111/G2
Birkenau, Ger. 112/B3
Birkenfeld, Ger. 111/G4
Birkenhead, Eng, UK 93/E5
Birkenheide, Ger. 112/B4
Birkenwerder, Ger. 98/Q6
Birkirkara, Malta 104/L7
Birkkarspitze (peak), Aus. 115/H3
Bîrlad, Rom. 107/H2
Birmingham, Eng, UK 91/E2
Birmingham (co.), Eng, UK 91/E2
Birmingham (int'l arpt.), Eng, UK 91/E2
Birmingham, Al, US 191/G3
Birmingham, Mi, US 193/F6
Birmingham, Mo, US 195/E5
Birmitrapur, India 143/E4
Birnam, Sc, UK 94/C3
Birnhorn (peak), Aus. 101/K3
Birni Nkonni, Niger 161/G3
Birnie (isl.), Kiri. 175/H5
Birnin Kebbi, Nga. 161/G3
Birobijan, Rus. 129/P2
Bīrpur, India 143/F2
Birr, Ire. 89/Q10
Birs (riv.), Swi. 101/G3
Birsk, Rus. 119/M5
Birstein, Ger. 112/C2
Biruaca, Ven. 211/E3
Biržai, Lith. 97/L3
Birżebbuġa, Malta 104/M7
Bis (lake), Rom. 107/F4
Bisa-Nadi Nat'l Rsv., Kenya 162/C2
Bisai, Japan 135/L5
Bīsalpur, India 142/B1
Bisamberg, Aus. 107/N7
Bisauli, India 142/B1
Biscarrosse, Fr. 100/C4
Biscarrosse,Etang de (lake), Fr. 100/C4
Biscay (bay), Fr.,Sp. 100/B4
Biscayne NP, Fl, US 191/H5
Bisceglie, It. 104/E2
Bischberg, Ger. 112/D3
Bischheim, Fr. 111/G6
Bischofsgrün, Ger. 113/E2
Bischofsheim, Ger. 112/B3
Bischofsheim an der Rhön, Ger. 112/D2
Bischofshofen, Aus. 101/K3
Bischofszell, Swi. 115/F3
Bischwiller, Fr. 114/D2
Biscubio (riv.), It. 117/F5
Biscucuy, Ven. 210/D2
Bīshah (riv.), SAr. 146/D4
Bishkek (cap.), Kyr. 145/F4
Bishnupur, India 143/F4
Bishop, Ca, US 186/C3
Bishop Auckland, Eng, UK 93/G2
Bishopbriggs, Sc, UK 94/B5
Bishop's Falls, Nf, Can. 189/L1
Bishop's Stortford, Eng, UK 91/G3
Bishopton, Sc, UK 94/B5
Bisingen, Ger. 112/B6
Biskra, Alg. 158/H5
Biskupiec, Pol. 97/J5
Bislig, Phil. 137/E6
Bismarck (cap.), ND, US 185/H4
Bismarck, On, Can. 189/Q9
Bismarck (arch.), PNG 174/D5
Bismarck (sea), PNG 174/D5
Bismil, Turk. 148/E2
Bismuna (lag.), Nic. 203/F3
Bispgarden, Swe. 95/F3
Bispingen, Ger. 109/G2
Bissau (cap.), GBis. 160/B4
Bissau, India 144/C5
Bissendorf, Ger. 109/F4
Bissett, Mb, Can. 185/K3
Bissingen, Ger. 112/D5
Bistagno, It. 116/B3
Bistrita (riv.), Rom. 107/G2
Bistrita, Rom. 107/G2
Bistrita-Năsăud (prov.), Rom. 107/G2
Biswān, India 142/C2
Bita (riv.), Col. 208/E2
Bitam, Gabon 154/H7
Bitburg, Ger. 111/F4
Bitche, Fr. 111/G5
Bitkin, Chad 155/J5
Bitlis (prov.), Turk. 148/E2
Bitlis, Turk. 148/E2
Bitola, FYROM 105/G2
Bitonto, It. 104/E2
Bitter (lakes), Egypt 159/C2
Bitterfontein, SAfr. 164/B3
Bitterroot (range), Id,Mt, US 184/E4
Bitti, It. 104/A2
Bitung, Indo. 139/G3
Bituruna, Braz. 213/B3
Biwa, Japan 135/K5
Bixby, Ok, US 190/E3
Biyalā, Egypt 149/B4
Biyang, China 130/C4
Bizard (isl.), Qu, Can. 189/M7
Bizerte, Tun. 158/L6
Bizerte (gov.), Tun. 158/L6
Bizerte (lake), Tun. 158/L6
Bjärred, Swe. 96/E4
Bjelovar, Cro. 106/C3
Bjerkvik, Nor. 95/F1
Bjerringbro, Den. 96/C3
Bjørkelangen, Nor. 96/D2
Björklinge, Swe. 96/G1
Bjørnafjorden (estu.), Nor. 96/A1
Bjorne (pen.), Nun., Can. 181/S7
Bjugn, Nor. 95/D3
Bjuv, Swe. 96/E3
Blå Jungfrun NP, Swe. 96/G3
Blace, Serb. 106/E4
Blachownia, Pol. 99/K3
Black (sea), Asia,Eur. 125/C5
Black (bay), On, Can. 185/L3
Black (riv.), On, Can. 185/L2
Black (mt.), Yk, Can. 192/M3
Black (riv.), China,Viet. 128/H7
Black (for.), Ger. 98/D5
Black (pt.), Eng, UK 90/A6
Black (pt.), NI, UK 92/C2
Black (isl.), Sc, UK 94/B1
Black (mts.), Wal, UK 90/C3
Black (mts.), Wal, UK 90/C3
Black (mesa), Az, US 186/E3
Black (mts.), Az, US 187/D4
Black (pt.), Ct, US 197/F1
Black (range), NM, US 186/F4
Black (riv.), NY, US 188/F3
Black (hills), SD, US 182/F3
Black (riv.), Wi, US 185/L4
Black Canyon of the Gunnison Nat'l Park, Co, US 186/F3
Black Diamond, Ab, Can. 184/E3
Black Diamond, Wa, US 193/C3
Black Eagle, Mt, US 184/F4
Black Forest (Schwarzwald) (for.), Ger. 112/B6
Black Hawk, Co, US 195/B3
Black Jack, Mo, US 195/G8
Black Mountain NP, Austl. 171/B1
Black Mtn. (mtn.), Wal, UK 90/C3
Black Point, Ca, US 193/K10
Black River, Jam. 203/G2
Black River Falls, Wi, US 185/L4
Black Rock (des.), Nv, US 186/C2
Black Rock (pt.), RI, US 197/G1
Black Sea Lowland (reg.), Mol.,Ukr. 107/J3
Black Sugarloaf (peak), Austl. 173/D1
Black Volta (riv.), Burk. 154/E5
Black Walnut, Mo, US 195/G8
Black Warrior (riv.), Al, US 191/G3
Blackadder Water (riv.), Sc, UK 94/D5
Blackall, Austl. 171/B4
Blackburn, Eng, UK 93/F4
Blackburn, Sc, UK 94/C5
Blackburn with Darwen, (co.), Eng, UK 93/F4
Blackbutt, Austl. 171/D4
Blackcraig (peak), Sc, UK 94/B6
Blackdown (hills), Eng, UK 90/C5
Blackdown (hill), Eng, UK 91/F4
Blackdown Tableland NP, Austl. 171/C3
Blackfoot (res.), Id, US 184/F5
Blackheath, Austl. 173/D2
Blackmoor (upland), Eng, UK 90/B5
Blackpool, Eng, UK 93/E4
Blackpool (co.), Eng, UK 93/F4
Blackrod, Eng, UK 93/F4
Blackshear (lake), Ga, US 191/H3
Blackstone, Va, US 188/E4
Blackville, NB, Can. 189/H2
Blackwater, Austl. 171/C3
Blackwater (riv.), Ire. 89/P10
Blackwater (riv.), Eng, UK 88/A2
Blackwater (res.), Sc, UK 94/B3
Blackwater (riv.), Mo, US 187/J3
Blackwell, Ok, US 187/H3
Blackwood (riv.), Austl. 170/B5
Blackwood, NJ, US 196/C4
Bladensburg, Md, US 196/B6
Bladensburg NP, Austl. 171/A3
Bladnoch (riv.), Sc, UK 92/D2
Blaenau Gwent (co.), Wal, UK 90/C3
Blagnac, Fr. 100/D5
Blagnac (int'l arpt.), Fr. 100/D5
Blagny, Fr. 111/E4
Blagoevgrad, Bul. 105/H1
Blagoveshchensk, Rus. 129/N1
Blaine Lake, Sk, Can. 185/G2
Blainville, Qu, Can. 189/N6
Blair, Ne, US 185/J5
Blair (hill), Pa, US 196/C1
Blair Atholl, Sc, UK 94/C3
Blairstown, NJ, US 196/D2
Blaise (riv.), Fr. 100/F2
Blaj, Rom. 107/F2
Blakely, Ga, US 191/G4
Blakeslee, Pa, US 196/C1
Blamont, Fr. 114/C3
Blanc (cape), Fr. 101/G5
Blanc (peak), Fr. 114/C6
Blanc (cape), Mrta. 154/B3
Blanc, Cap (cape), Tun. 158/L6
Blanc Nez (cape), Fr. 110/A2
Blanca (peak), NM, US 187/F4
Blanca (pt.), Mex. 184/B2
Blanca (bay), Arg. 205/C6
Blanca, Cordillera (mts.), Peru 208/C5
Blanca, Costa (coast), Sp. 103/E4
Blanchard, Ok, US 195/M15
Blanche (lake), Austl. 167/D3
Blanche (peak), Swi. 114/D5
Blanche (cape), Austl. 171/G5
Blanco (cape), CR 203/E4
Blanco (cape), Mor. 156/A5
Blanco (cape), Peru 208/B4
Blanco (lake), Chile 217/C7
Blanco (riv.), Bol. 208/F6
Blanco (riv.), Tx, US 187/H5
Blanding, Ut, US 186/E3
Blandy, Fr. 88/L6
Blanes, Sp. 103/G2
Blangy-sur-Bresle, Fr. 110/A4
Blankenberge, Belg. 110/C1
Blankenfelde, Ger. 98/Q7
Blankenheim, Ger. 111/F3
Blanquilla (isl.), Ven. 208/F1
Blanquillo, Uru. 217/G2
Blansko, Czh. 99/J4
Blantyre, Malw. 163/G4
Blantyre, Sc, UK 94/B5
Blanzy, Fr. 100/F3
Blaricum, Neth. 108/C4
Blas (peak), Swi. 115/E4
Blatná, Czh. 113/G4
Blato, Cro. 104/E1
Blatten, Swi. 114/D5
Blau (riv.), Ger. 112/C6
Blaubeuren, Ger. 112/C6
Blauen (peak), Ger. 114/D2
Blaustein, Ger. 112/C6
Blauvelt, NY, US 197/K7
Blåvands (pt.), Den. 96/C4
Blavet (riv.), Fr. 100/B3
Blaye, Fr. 100/C4
Blayney, Austl. 173/D2
Bleckede, Ger. 109/H2
Bled, Slov. 101/L3
Blefjell (peak), Nor. 96/C2
Blégny, Belg. 111/E2
Bléharies, Belg. 110/C2
Bleiburg, Aus. 106/B2
Bleicherode, Ger. 109/H6
Bleik (peak), Ger. 115/G2
Bleiswijk, Neth. 108/B4
Blekinge (co.), Swe. 95/E4
Blendecques, Fr. 110/B2
Blender, Ger. 109/G3
Blenheim, NZ 175/S11
Blénod-lès-Pont-à-Mousson, Fr. 111/F6
Bléone (riv.), Fr. 101/G4
Blesberg (peak), SAfr. 164/C4
Blessington, Ire. 92/B5
Bletterans, Fr. 114/B4
Bleury, Fr. 88/H6
Bleus (mts.), D.R. Congo 155/L7
Bleus, Monts (mts.), D.R. Congo 162/A2
Blida (prov.), Alg. 158/G4
Blida, Alg. 158/G4
Blies (riv.), Ger. 111/G5
Blieskastel, Ger. 111/G5
Blik (mt.), Phil. 139/F2
Blinnenhorn (peak), Swi. 115/E5
Blithe (riv.), Eng, UK 93/F6
Blithfield (res.), Eng, UK 93/G6
Block (isl.), RI, US 189/G3
Block Island C. G. Sta., RI, US 197/G1
Block Island (New Shoreham), RI, US 197/G1
Block Island NWR, RI, US 197/G1
Blodelsheim, Fr. 114/D2
Bloemendaal, Neth. 108/B4
Bloemfontein, (cap.), SAfr. 164/D3
Bloemhof, SAfr. 164/D2
Bloemhofdam (res.), SAfr. 164/D2
Blois, Fr. 100/D3
Blomberg, Ger. 109/E1
Blomberg, Ger. 109/G5
Blomstermåla, Swe. 96/G3
Blonay, Swi. 114/C5
Blönduós, Ice. 95/N6
Blondvein (riv.), Mb,On, Can. 180/G3
Bloody Foreland (pt.), Ire. 89/P9
Bloomfield, NJ, US 197/J8
Bloomfield, NM, US 186/F3
Bloomfield Hills, Mi, US 193/F6
Bloomingdale, NJ, US 197/H7
Bloomingdale, Il, US 193/P16
Bloomington, Mn, US 185/K4
Bloomington, Il, US 185/L5
Bloomington, Ca, US 194/C2
Bloomsburg, Pa, US 196/B2
Bloomsbury, NJ, US 196/C2
Blora, Indo. 138/D5
Blotzheim, Fr. 114/D2
Blountstown, Fl, US 191/G4
Blovice, Czh. 113/G3
Blšanka (riv.), Czh. 101/K1
Bludenz, Aus. 115/F3
Blue (mtn.), India 141/F3
Blue (riv.), Ok, US 190/D3
Blue (mts.), Or,Wa, US 182/C2
Blue Head (pt.), Sc, UK 94/C1
Blue Island, Il, US 193/Q16
Blue Lake NP, Austl. 171/D4
Blue Marsh Lake (res.), Pa, US 196/B3
Blue Mesa (res.), Co, US 186/F3
Blue Mountain (peak), Jam. 203/G2
Blue Mountain (ridge), Pa, US 196/A3
Blue Mountains, Austl. 173/D2
Blue Mountains NP, Austl. 173/D2
Blue Nile (riv.), Sudan, Eth. 155/M5
Blue Ridge (mts.), US 191/H3
Blue Ridge Parkway, US 188/D4
Blue Springs, Mo, US 195/E5
Bluefield, WV, US 188/D4
Bluefields, Nic. 203/F4
Bluefields (bay), Nic. 203/F4
Bluejoint (lake), Or, US 186/C2
Bluenose (lake), Nun., Can. 180/E2
Bluff, NZ 175/R12
Bluff (pt.), Austl. 170/B3
Bluff, Austl. 171/C3
Bluff (peak), Austl. 170/C5
Bluffdale, Ut, US 195/K13
Bluffton, In, US 188/C3
Blumberg, Ger. 115/E2
Blümlisalp (peak), Swi. 114/D5
Blyn, Wa, US 193/B1
Blyth, Austl. 171/H5
Blyth, Eng, UK 93/G1
Blythe, Ca, US 186/D4
Blytheville, Ar, US 187/K4
Bnom Mhai (peak), Viet. 136/D4
Bo, SLeo. 160/C5
Bø, Nor. 96/C2
Bo Hai (Chihli) (gulf), China 130/D3
Boa Esperança, Braz. 213/C2
Boa Esperança, Represa (res.), Braz. 209/J5
Boa Viagem, Braz. 212/C2
Boa Vista, Braz. 211/F4
Boa Vista (int'l arpt.), Braz. 211/F4
Boa Vista (isl.), CpV. 151/K10
Boac, Phil. 137/D5
Boaco, Nic. 202/E3
Boadilla del Monte, Sp. 103/N9
Bo'ai, China 130/C4
Boano (isl.), Indo. 139/G4
Boas (riv.), Nun., Can. 181/H2
Boavita, Col. 210/C3
Boaz, Al, US 191/G3
Boba, Hun. 106/C2
Bobai, China 141/J3
Bobaomby (cape), Madg. 165/J5
Bobbili, India 140/D4
Bobbio, It. 116/C3
Bobenheim-Roxheim, Ger. 112/B3
Bobigny, Fr. 88/K5
Bobingen, Ger. 115/G1
Böblingen, Ger. 112/C5
Bobo Dioulasso, Burk. 160/D4
Boboshevo, Bul. 105/H1
Bobotov Kuk (peak), Mont. 106/D4
Bobovdol, Bul. 105/H1
Bóbr (riv.), Pol. 99/H3
Bobrov, Rus. 120/G2
Bobures, Ven. 210/D2
Boby (peak), Madg. 165/H8
Boca de Aroa, Ven. 210/D2
Boca del Guafo (chan.), Chile 216/B4
Boca del Pao, Ven. 211/E2
Boca del Río, Mex. 201/N7
Bôca do Acre, Braz. 208/E5
Boca Raton, Fl, US 191/H5
Bocaina, Serra da (mts.), Braz. 213/J7
Bocairente, Sp. 103/E3
Bocas del Toro, Pan. 203/F4
Bocay (riv.), Nic. 203/E3
Bochil, Mex. 202/C2
Bochnia, Pol. 99/L4
Bocholt, Ger. 108/D5
Bocholt, Belg. 111/E1
Bochum, Ger. 109/E6
Bockau, Ger. 113/F1
Bockenem, Ger. 109/H4
Bockenheim an der Weinstrasse, Ger. 111/H4
Bockhorn, Ger. 109/F2
Bockhorn, Ger. 113/E6
Boconó, Ven. 210/D2
Bocq (riv.), Belg. 111/D3
Boda, CAfr. 155/J7
Bodafors, Swe. 96/F3
Bodalla, Austl. 173/D3
Bodaybo, Rus. 123/M4
Boddam, Sc, UK 94/E2
Boddington, Austl. 170/C5
Bode (riv.), Ger. 98/F3
Bodega (bay), Ca, US 186/B3
Bodegraven, Neth. 108/B4
Bodélé (reg.), Chad 154/J4
Bodenheim, Ger. 112/B3
Bodenkirchen, Ger. 113/F6
Bodenmais, Ger. 113/G4
Bodensee (Constance) (lake), Swi 101/H3
Bodenteich, Ger. 109/H3
Bodh Gaya, India 143/E3
Bodhan, India 140/C4
Bodināyakkanūr, India 140/C5
Bodio, Swi. 115/E5
Bodkin (pt.), Md, US 196/B5
Bodmin, Eng, UK 90/B6
Bodmin Moor (upland), Eng, UK 90/B6
Bodø, Nor. 95/E2
Bodocó, Braz. 212/C2
Bodrog (riv.), Hun.,Slvk. 99/L4
Bodrum, Turk. 148/A2
Bódvaszilas, Hun. 99/L4
Boedecker (lake), Co, US 195/B2
Boëge, Fr. 114/C5
Boegoeberg (peak), Namb. 164/A2
Boekel, Neth. 108/C5
Boende, D.R. Congo 155/K8
Boerne, Tx, US 195/T20
Boeuf (riv.), La, US 187/K4
Bog of Allen (swamp), Ire. 92/A5
Bogalusa, La, US 191/F4
Bogan (riv.), Austl. 167/D4
Bogan Gate, Austl. 173/C2
Bogandé, Burk. 161/E3
Bogatić, Serb. 106/D3
Bogatynia, Pol. 99/H3
Boğazkale-Alacahöyük NP, Turk. 148/C1
Boğazlıyan, Turk. 148/C2
Bogdanci, FYROM 105/H2
Bogen, Nor. 95/F1
Bogen, Ger. 113/F5
Bogense, Den. 96/D4
Boggabilla, Austl. 171/C5
Boggabri, Austl. 173/D1
Boggy (peak), Anti. 199/N8
Boglárlelle, Hun. 106/C2
Bogliasco, It. 116/C4
Bognor Regis, Eng, UK 91/F5
Bogny-sur-Meuse, Fr. 111/D4
Bogo, Phil. 137/D5
Bogong (mt.), Austl. 173/C3
Bogong NP, Austl. 173/C3
Bogor, Indo. 138/C5
Bogotá (cap.), Col. 208/D3
Bogota, NJ, US 197/J8
Bogovino, FYROM 105/G2
Bogra (pol. reg.), Bang. 143/G3
Bogra, Bang. 143/G3
Bogué, Mrta. 160/B2
Bohain-en-Vermandois, Fr. 110/C4
Bohemia (reg.), Czh. 99/G4
Bohemian (for.), Czh.,Ger. 98/G4
Bohicon, Ben. 161/F5
Böhl-Iggelheim, Ger. 112/B4
Böhme (riv.), Ger. 109/G3
Böhmenkirch, Ger. 112/C5
Bohmte, Ger. 109/F4
Bohners Lake, Wi, US 193/P14
Bohol (isl.), Phil. 137/D6
Böhönye, Hun. 106/C2
Bohu, China 128/E3
Boiling Springs, Pa, US 196/A3
Boipeda, Ilha de (isl.), Braz. 212/C4
Boiro, Sp. 102/A1
Bois-d'Amont, Fr. 114/C4
Bois-d'Arcy, Fr. 88/J5
Bois de Boulogne (dept.), Fr. 88/J5
Bois de Vincennes (dept.), Fr. 88/K5
Bois-des-Filion, Qu, Can. 189/N6
Bois, Rio dos (riv.), Braz. 213/B1
Boisbriand, Qu, Can. 189/N6
Boise (riv.), Id, US 184/E5
Boise City, Ok, US 187/G3
Boissevain, Mb, Can. 185/H3
Boissy-Fresnoy, Fr. 88/L4
Boissy-L'Aillerie, Fr. 88/J4
Boissy-le-Châtel, Fr. 88/M5
Boissy-Saint-Léger, Fr. 88/K5
Boissy-Sans-Avoir, Fr. 88/H5
Boizenburg, Ger. 109/H2
Bojador (cape), Mor. 154/C2
Bojano, It. 106/B5
Boji (plain), Kenya 162/C2
Bojkovice, Czh. 99/J4
Bojnūrd, Iran 147/G1
Bokaro Steel City, India 143/F4
Boké (pol. reg.), Gui. 160/B4
Boké, Gui. 160/B4
Bokhol (plain), Kenya 162/C2
Boknafjorden (estu.), Nor. 95/C4
Bokol (peak), Kenya 162/C2
Bokoro, Chad 154/J5
Bokpyin, Myan. 136/B4
Boksburg, SAfr. 164/Q13
Bokspits, Bots. 164/C2
Bol, Chad 154/H5
Bolama, GBis. 160/B4
Bolān (pass), Pak. 147/J3
Bolaños de Calatrava, Sp. 102/D3
Bolayır, Turk. 105/K2
Bolbec, Fr. 100/D2
Boldeşti-Scăeni, Rom. 107/H3
Boldon, Eng, UK 93/G2
Bole, China 128/D3
Bole, Gha. 161/E4
Bolesławiec, Pol. 99/H3
Bolgatanga, Gha. 161/E4
Boli, China 129/P2
Boliden, Swe. 95/G2
Bolinao, Phil. 137/C4
Bolívar, Arg. 216/E3
Bolívar, Col. 210/B3
Bolívar (dept.), Col. 210/C2
Bolívar, Ecu. 210/A4
Bolívar, Peru 214/B2
Bolivar, Mo, US 187/J3
Bolívar (peak), Ven. 210/D2
Bolívar (peak), Ven. 211/F3
Bolívar (state), Ven. 211/E3
Bolivia (ctry.), Bol. 208/F7
Bollate, It. 116/C1
Bollène, Fr. 100/F4
Bolligen, Swi. 114/D4
Bollin (riv.), Eng, UK 93/F5
Bollnäs, Swe. 96/G1
Bollullos Par del Condado, Sp. 102/B4
Bolmen (lake), Swe. 96/E3
Bolobo, D.R. Congo 154/J8
Bologna, It. 117/E4
Bologna (prov.), It. 117/E3
Bologne, Fr. 114/B1
Bolognesi, Peru 214/C3
Bologoye, Rus. 118/G4
Bolomba, D.R. Congo 155/J7
Bolonchén de Rejón, Mex. 202/D2
Bolovens (plat.), Laos 136/D3
Bolpur, India 143/F4
Bolsena, It. 104/B1
Bolsena (lake), It. 104/B1
Bol'shaya Kinel' (riv.), Rus. 121/K1
Bol'shaya Rogovaya (riv.), Rus. 119/P2
Bol'shaya Synya (riv.), Rus. 119/N2
Bol'shevik (isl.), Rus. 125/H2
Bol'shezemel'skaya (tundra), Rus. 119/M2
Bol'shoy Bolvanskiy Nos (pt.), Rus. 122/F2
Bol'shoy Irgiz (riv.), Rus. 121/J1
Bol'shoy Lyakhov (isl.), Rus. 125/P2
Bol'shoy Lyakhovskiy (isl.), Rus. 123/Q2
Bol'shoy Uzen' (riv.), Rus. 121/J2
Bolsover, Eng, UK 93/G5
Bolsward, Neth. 108/C2
Bolt (pt.), Eng, UK 90/C6
Boltaña, Sp. 103/F1
Boltigen, Swi. 114/D4
Bolton, Eng, UK 93/F4
Bolton (co.), Eng, UK 93/F4
Bolu, Turk. 107/K5
Bolu (prov.), Turk. 107/K5
Bolungavik, Ice. 95/M6
Bolus Head (pt.), Ire. 88/N11
Bolvadin, Turk. 148/B2
Bóly, Hun. 106/D3
Bolzano, It. 115/H5
Bolzano-Bozen (prov.), It. 115/H4
Bom Conselho, Braz. 212/C3
Bom Despacho, Braz. 213/C1
Bom Jardim, Braz. 212/A1
Bom Jardim de Minas, Braz. 213/J6
Bom Jesus, Braz. 213/B4
Bom Jesus, Braz. 212/A3
Bom Jesus da Gurguéia, Serra (mts.), Braz. 209/K5
Bom Jesus de Goiás, Braz. 213/B1
Bom Jesus do Itabapoana, Braz. 213/D2
Bom Jesus dos Perdões, Braz. 213/G8
Bom Retiro, Braz. 213/B3
Boma, D.R. Congo 163/B2
Bomaderry, Austl. 173/D2
Bombala, Austl. 173/D3
Bombay Hook NWR, De, US 196/C5
Bombay (Mumbai), India 147/K5
Bomberai (pen.), Indo. 139/H4
Bombo, Ugan. 162/B2
Bomi, China 141/G2
Bomlitz, Ger. 109/G3
Bømlo (isl.), Nor. 96/A2
Bomu (riv.), D.R. Congo 155/L6
Bon-Encontre, Fr. 100/D4
Bona (mt.), Ak, US 192/K3
Bonaduz, Swi. 115/F4
Bonaire (isl.), NAnt. 199/H5
Bonalbo, Austl. 173/E1
Bonampak (ruin), Mex. 202/D2
Bonao, DRep. 199/G4
Bonaparte (arch.), Austl. 167/B2
Bonaparte (isls.), Austl. 167/B2
Bonasila (mtn.), Ak, US 192/F3
Bonaventure, Qu, Can. 189/H1
Bonaventure (riv.), Qu, Can. 189/H1
Bonavista (bay) Nf, Can. 189/L1
Bonavista, Nf, Can. 189/L1
Bonavista (cape) Nf, Can. 189/L1
Boncourt, Swi. 114/D3
Bondeno, It. 117/E3
Bondo, D.R. Congo 155/K7
Bondoukou, C.d'Iv. 160/E4
Bondowoso, Indo. 138/D5
Bone (gulf), Indo. 139/F4
Bönen, Ger. 109/E5
Bonerate (isls.), Indo. 139/F5
Bonfol, Swi. 114/D3
Bonfouca, La, US 195/Q16
Bong (co.), Libr. 160/C5
Bong (range), Libr. 160/C5
Bongabong, Phil. 139/F1
Bongaigaon, India 143/H2
Bongandanga, D.R. Congo 155/K7
Bongao, Phil. 139/E3
Bonggi (isl.), Malay. 139/E2
Bongka (riv.), Indo. 139/F4
Bongo, Massif des (plat.), CAfr. 155/K6
Bongolava (uplands), Madg. 165/H7
Bongor, Chad 154/J5
Bonham, Tx, US 187/H4
Bonheiden, Belg. 111/D1
Bonhill, Sc, UK 94/B5
Bonhomme, Col du (pass), Fr. 114/D1
Boni Nat'l Rsv., Kenya 162/D3
Bonifacio, Fr. 104/A2
Bonifacio (str.), It. 104/A2
Bonifay, Fl, US 191/G4
Bönigen, Swi. 114/D4
Bonin (isls.), Japan 174/C2
Bonita, Ca, US 194/C5
Bonita Springs, Fl, US 191/H5
Bonito (peak), Hon. 202/E3
Bonn, Ger. 111/G2
Bonndorf im Schwarzwald, Ger. 115/E2
Bonne, Fr. 114/C5
Bonnelles, Fr. 88/J6
Bonner Springs, Ks, US 195/D5
Bonner-West Riverside, Mt, US 184/E4
Bonners Ferry, Id, US 184/D3
Bonnet Carré Spillway, La, US 195/P16
Bonnet, Lac du (lake), Mb, Can. 185/K3
Bonneuil-sur-Marne, Fr. 88/K5
Bonneval, Fr. 100/D2
Bonneville (dam), Wa,Or, US 184/C4
Bonneville, Fr. 114/C5
Bonney Lake, Wa, US 193/C3
Bönnigheim, Ger. 112/C4
Bonnybridge, Sc, UK 94/C5
Bonorva, It. 104/A2
Bons-en-Chablais, Fr. 114/C5
Bonsall, Ca, US 194/C4
Bontberg (peak), SAfr. 164/C4
Bontebok NP, SAfr. 164/C4
Bonthain, Indo. 139/E5
Bonthe, SLeo. 160/B5
Bontoc, Phil. 137/D4
Bonyhád, Hun. 106/D2
Booker T. Washington Nat'l Mon., Va, US 191/J2
Boom, Belg. 111/D1
Boone, Ia, US 185/K5
Boone, NC, US 188/D4
Booneville, Ms, US 191/F3
Boonton, NJ, US 197/H8
Boorabbin NP, Austl. 170/D4
Boorama, Som. 155/P6
Booroondara (mt.), Austl. 173/C1
Boorowa, Austl. 173/D2
Boos (int'l arpt.), Fr. 100/D2
Boos, Ger. 115/G1
Boosaaso (Bender Cassim), Som. 155/Q5
Boostedt, Ger. 96/D4
Boothbay Harbor, Me, US 189/G3
Boothia (pen.), Nun., Can. 180/G1
Boothia (gulf), Nun., Can. 180/G1
Bootle, Eng, UK 93/E5
Booué, Gabon 154/H8
Bopa, Ben. 161/F5
Bopfingen, Ger. 112/D5
Boppard, Ger. 111/G3
Boppy (mt.), Austl. 173/C1
Boqueirão, Braz. 212/C2
Boqueirão, Serra do (mts.), Braz. 212/B3
Boquete (peak), Arg. 216/C4
Boquilla (res.), Mex. 184/D3
Boquillas del Carmen, Mex. 190/C4
Boquira, Braz. 212/B4
Bor, Czh. 113/F3
Bor, Rus. 119/K4
Bor, Serb. 106/F3
Bor, Turk. 148/C2
Bor Ul (mts.), China 128/G3
Bora Bora (isl.), FrPol. 175/K6
Borah (peak), Id, US 184/E4
Borås, Swe. 96/E3
Borāzjān, Iran 146/F3
Borba, Braz. 208/G4
Borba, Port. 102/B3
Borbera (riv.), It. 116/B3
Borbore (riv.), It. 116/B3
Borborema, Planalto da (plat.), Braz. 209/L5
Borča, Serb. 106/E3
Borcea Branch (riv.), Rom. 107/H3
Borchen, Ger. 109/F5
Borçka, Turk. 121/G4
Borculo, Neth. 108/D4
Borda da Mata, Braz. 213/G7

Bordeaux, Fr. 100/C4
Borden (isl.), NW,Nun., Can. 181/R7
Borden (pen.), Nun., Can. 181/H1
Bordentown, NJ, US 196/D3
Bordertown, Austl. 173/B3
Bordj Bou Arreridj, Alg. 158/H4
Bordj Bou Arreridj (prov.), Alg. 158/H4
Bordj el Kiffan, Alg. 158/G4
Bordj Manaïel, Alg. 158/G4
Bordj Moktar, Alg. 157/F5
Bordj Omar Driss, Alg. 157/G3
Bordj Sainte-Marie, Alg. 156/E4
Borehamwood, Eng, UK 88/C2
Borest, Fr. 88/L4
Boretto, It. 116/D3
Borgå (Porvoo), Fin. 97/L1
Borgaretto, It. 116/A2
Borgarnes, Ice. 95/N7
Borgaro Torinese, It. 116/A2
Børgefjell NP, Nor. 95/E2
Borgentreich, Ger. 109/G5
Borger, Tx, US 187/G4
Börger, Ger. 109/E3
Borger, Neth. 108/D3
Borgerhout, Belg. 108/B6
Borges Blanques, Sp. 103/F2
Borghetto Lodigiano, It. 116/C2
Borghetto Santo Spirito, It. 116/B4
Borgholm, Swe. 96/G3
Borgholzhausen, Ger. 109/F4
Borghorst, Ger. 109/E4
Borgloon, Belg. 111/E2
Borgne (lake), La, US 195/Q17
Borgne (riv.), Swi. 114/D5
Borgo (int'l arpt.), Burk. 160/D4
Borgo, Fr. 104/A1
Borgo, It. 115/H5
Borgo a Mozzano, It. 116/D5
Borgo San Dalmazzo, It. 101/G4
Borgo San Giacomo, It. 116/C2
Borgo San Lorenzo, It. 117/E5
Borgo Tossignano, It. 117/E4
Borgo Val di Taro, It. 116/C4
Borgo Vercelli, It. 116/B2
Borgofranco d'Ivrea, It. 116/A1
Borgomanero, It. 116/B1
Borgonovo Val Tidone, It. 116/C2
Borgosatollo, It. 116/D2
Borgosesia, It. 116/B1
Borgou (prov.), Ben. 161/F4
Borgund, Nor. 96/B1
Borio, India 143/F3
Borisoglebsk, Rus. 121/G2
Borispol (int'l arpt.), Ukr. 120/D2
Borja, Peru 214/B2
Borja, Sp. 102/E2
Borken, Ger. 108/D5
Borken, Ger. 109/G6
Børkop, Den. 96/C4
Borkum, Ger. 108/D1
Borkum (isl.), Ger. 108/D1
Borlänge, Swe. 96/F1
Bormida (riv.), It. 101/H4
Bormida, It. 116/B4
Bormida di Millesimo (riv.), It. 116/B4
Bormio, It. 115/G5
Born, Neth. 111/E1
Borna, Ger. 98/G3
Borndiep (chan.), Neth. 108/C2
Borne, Neth. 108/D4
Borne (riv.), Fr. 114/C6
Bornel, Fr. 110/B5
Bornem, Belg. 111/D1
Bornemouth, Eng, UK 91/E5
Bornemouth (co.), Eng, UK 91/E5
Borneo (isl.), Indo.,Malay. 138/D3
Bornheim, Ger. 111/G2
Bornholm (co.), Den. 96/F4
Bornholm (isl.), Den. 96/F4
Bornholmsgat (chan.), Den.,Swi. 99/H1
Borno, It. 115/G6
Bornos, Sp. 102/C4
Börnsen, Ger. 109/H2
Bornu (plain), Nga. 154/H5
Boro (riv.), Sudan 155/L6
Borohoro (mts.), China 128/D3
Borongan, Phil. 137/E5
Borough Green, Eng, UK 88/D3
Borovany, Czh. 113/H5
Borovichi, Rus. 118/G4
Borovo, Bul. 107/G4
Borovo, Cro. 106/D3
Borre, Nor. 96/D2
Borrisokane, Ire. 89/P10
Borrnida (riv.), It. 116/B3
Borşa, Rom. 107/F2
Borsec, Rom. 107/G2
Borso del Grappa, It. 117/E1
Borsod-Abaúj-Zemplén (co.), Hun. 106/E1
Borssele, Neth. 108/A6
Borstel, Ger. 109/F3
Bort-les-Orgues, Fr. 100/E4
Boruca, CR 203/F4
Borūjerd, Iran 146/E2
Boryslav, Ukr. 99/M4
Borzonasca, It. 116/C4
Borzya, Rus. 129/L1
Bosa, It. 104/A2
Bosanska Dubica, Bosn. 106/C3
Bosanska Gradiška, Bosn. 106/C3
Bosanska Kostajnica, Bosn. 106/C3
Bosanska Krupa, Bosn. 106/C3
Bosanski Brod, Bosn. 106/D3
Bosanski Petrovac, Bosn. 106/C3
Bosanski Šamac, Bosn. 106/D3
Bosco Mesola, It. 117/F3
Bosconero, It. 116/A2
Bose, China 141/J3
Boshof, SAfr. 164/D3
Boskoop, Neth. 108/B4
Boskovice, Czh. 99/J4
Bosna (riv.), Bosn. 106/D3
Bosnia and Herzegovina (ctry.) 106/C3
Bošnjaci, Cro. 106/D3
Bōsō (pen.), Japan 133/G3
Bosobolo, D.R. Congo 155/J7
Bosporus (str.), Turk. 107/J5
Bosque Farms, NM, US 186/F4
Bosques Petrificados, Mon. Natural, Arg. 217/C5
Bossangoa, CAfr. 155/J6
Bossier City, La, US 187/J4
Bostān, Iran 146/E2
Bostānābād-e Bālā, Iran 146/E1
Boston (mts.), Ar, US 187/J4
Boston (cap.), Ma, US 189/G3
Boston, Eng, UK 93/H6
Bosut (riv.), Cro. 106/D3
Boswil, Swi. 115/E3
Botād, India 147/K4
Boteler (peak), NC, US 191/H3
Botelerpunt (pt.), SAfr. 165/F2
Botelhos, Braz. 213/G6
Botev (peak), Bul. 105/J1
Botevgrad, Bul. 105/H1
Bothaspas (pass), SAfr. 165/E2
Bothaville, SAfr. 164/D2
Bothel, Ger. 109/G2
Bothell, Wa, US 193/C2
Bothnia (gulf), Fin.,Swe. 218/E
Bothwell, Austl. 173/C4
Botoşani (prov.), Rom. 107/H2
Botoşani, Rom. 107/H2
Botou, China 130/D3
Botrange (peak), Belg. 111/F3
Botrivier, SAfr. 164/L11
Botsford, Ct, US 197/E1
Botswana (ctry.) 163/D5
Bottanuco, It. 116/C1
Botte Donato (peak), It. 104/E3
Botticino, It. 116/D1
Bottineau, ND, US 185/H3
Bottrighe, It. 117/F2
Bottrop, Ger. 108/D5
Botucatu, Braz. 213/B2
Botwood, Nf, Can. 189/L1
Bou (riv.), C.d'Iv. 160/D4
Bou Arfa, Mor. 157/E2
Boû Djébéha (well), Mali 160/E2
Bou Hamdane, Oued (riv.), Alg. 158/K6
Bou Ismaïl, Alg. 158/G4
Bou Izakarn, Mor. 156/C3
Bou Kadir, Alg. 158/F4
Bou Laber (well), Alg. 156/D4
Bou Naceur (peak), Mor. 158/C3
Bou Regreg (riv.), Mor. 158/A3
Bou Salem, Tun. 158/L6
Bou Sellam, Oued (riv.), Alg. 158/H4
Bouaflé, C.d'Iv. 160/D5
Bouafle, Fr. 88/H5
Bouaké, C.d'Iv. 160/D5
Bouar, CAfr. 154/J6
Boubín (peak), Czh. 113/G5
Bouca, CAfr. 155/J6
Bouchain, Fr. 110/C3
Bouchegouf, Alg. 158/K6
Boucherville, Qu, Can. 189/P6
Boucle du Baoulé, PN de la, Mali 154/D5
Boucle Du Baoulé, PN de la, Mali 160/C3
Boudry, Swi. 114/C4
Boufarik, Alg. 158/G4
Bouffémont, Fr. 88/J4
Bougainville (reef), Austl. 167/D2
Bougainville (isl.), PNG 174/E5
Bougainville (cape), Falk., UK 217/F6
Bougara, Alg. 158/G4
Bougar'oûn (cape), Alg. 158/K6
Bough Beech (res.), Eng, UK 88/D3
Bougouni, Mali 160/D4
Bougouriba (prov.), Burk. 160/E4
Bouguenais, Fr. 100/C3
Bouhachem (peak), Mor. 158/B2
Bouhalla (peak), Mor. 158/B2
Bouillancy, Fr. 88/L4
Bouillon, Belg. 111/E4
Bouira (prov.), Alg. 158/G4
Bouira, Alg. 158/G4
Boujad, Mor. 156/D2
Boukhalf (Tangier) (int'l arpt.), Mor. 158/B2
Boukoumbé, Ben. 161/F4
Boulaide, Lux. 111/E4
Boulaouane, Mor. 156/C2
Boulay-Moselle, Fr. 111/F5
Boulazac, Fr. 100/D4
Boulder, Co, US 195/B2
Boulder (co.), Co, US 195/B2
Boulder, Mt, US 184/E4
Boulder City, Nv, US 186/D4
Boulder Hill, Il, US 193/P16
Boulemane, Mor. 156/D2
Boulemane (prov.), Mor. 158/C3
Bouleurs, Fr. 88/L5
Boulgou (prov.), Burk. 161/E4
Boulia, Austl. 171/H2
Bouligny, Fr. 111/E5
Boulkiemde (prov.), Burk. 161/E3
Boullarre, Fr. 88/M4
Boulogne (riv.), Fr. 100/C3
Boulogne-Billancourt, Fr. 88/J5
Boulogne-sur-Mer, Fr. 110/A2
Boulsworth (hill), Eng, UK 93/F4
Boumalne, Mor. 156/D3
Boumerdas (prov.), Alg. 158/G4
Boumerdas, Alg. 158/G4
Boun Nua, Laos 141/H3
Bouna, C.d'Iv. 160/E4
Bound Brook, NJ, US 196/D2
Boundary (peak), Nv, US 186/C3
Boundiali, C.d'Iv. 160/D4
Bountiful, Ut, US 195/K12
Bouquet (res.), Ca, US 194/B1
Bouquet (canyon), Ca, US 194/B2
Bourbon l'Archambault, Fr. 100/E3
Bourbonnais (reg.), Fr. 100/D3
Bourbonne-les-Bains, Fr. 114/B2
Bourbourg, Fr. 110/B2
Bourdonné, Fr. 88/G5
Bourem, Mali 161/E2
Bouressa (riv.), Mali 161/F2
Bourg-en-Bresse, Fr. 114/B5
Bourg-lès-Valence, Fr. 100/F4
Bourg-Saint-Andéol, Fr. 100/F4
Bourg-Saint-Maurice, Fr. 101/G4
Bourg-Saint-Pierre, Swi. 114/D6
Bourganeuf, Fr. 100/D4
Bourges, Fr. 100/E3
Bourget (lake), Fr. 114/B6
Bourgneuf (bay), Fr. 100/B3
Bourgogne (pol. reg.), Fr. 100/F3
Bourgogne (canal), Fr. 114/B3
Bourgoin-Jallieu, Fr. 100/F4
Bourke, Austl. 173/C1
Bourmont, Fr. 114/B1
Bourne (riv.), Eng, UK 91/E4
Bourne End, Eng, UK 91/F4
Bourne, The (riv.), Eng, UK 88/B3
Bournemouth, Eng, UK 91/E5
Bourscheid, Lux. 111/F4
Bourtanger Moor (reg.), Ger. 109/E3
Bousbecque, Fr. 110/C2
Bousso, Chad 154/J5
Boussois, Fr. 110/D3
Boutilimit, Mrta. 160/B2
Boutte, La, US 195/P17
Bouvard (cape), Austl. 170/B5
Bouvet (isl.), Nor. 81/K8
Bouxières-aux-Dames, Fr. 111/F6
Bouxwiller, Fr. 111/G6
Bouznika, Mor. 158/A3
Bouzonville, Fr. 111/F5
Bovalino, It. 104/E3
Bovegno, It. 116/D1
Boven Tapanahoni (riv.), Sur. 211/H4
Bovenden, Ger. 109/G5
Bovenwijde (lake), Neth. 108/D3
Boves, Fr. 110/B4
Bovezzo, It. 116/D1
Bovingdon, Eng, UK 88/B1
Bovino, It. 106/B5
Bovolone, It. 117/E2
Bow (riv.), Ab, Can. 180/E3
Bow Island, Ab, Can. 184/F3
Bowdle, SD, US 185/J4
Bowdon, Eng, UK 93/F5
Bowen, Arg. 216/D2
Bowen, Austl. 171/C3
Bowers Beach, De, US 196/C5
Bowie, Az, US 186/E4
Bowie, Md, US 196/B6
Bowling Green (cape), Austl. 171/B2
Bowling Green, Ky, US 188/C4
Bowling Green, Mo, US 187/K3
Bowling Green, Oh, US 188/D3
Bowling Green Bay NP, Austl. 171/B2
Bowman, ND, US 185/H4
Bowman (bay), Nun., Can. 181/J2
Bowmansdale, Pa, US 196/B3
Bowmanstown, Pa, US 196/C2
Bowmansville, Pa, US 196/B3
Bowmore, Sc, UK 89/Q9
Bowokan (isls.), Indo. 139/F4
Bowral, Austl. 173/D2
Bowron (riv.), BC, Can. 184/C2
Box Elder (co.), Ut, US 195/J11
Boxberg, Ger. 112/C4
Boxholm, Swe. 96/F2
Boxing, China 130/D3
Boxmeer, Neth. 108/C5
Boxtel, Neth. 108/C5
Boyabat, Turk. 148/C1
Boyaca (dept.), Col. 210/C3
Boyagin, Austl. 170/B5
Boychinovtsi, Bul. 107/F4
Boyd (lake), Co, US 195/B2
Boye, China 130/C3
Boyer (riv.), Ia, US 185/K5
Boyertown, Pa, US 196/C3
Boyle, Ab, Can. 184/E2
Boyle, Ire. 89/P10
Boyne (riv.), Ire. 89/Q10
Boyne City, Mi, US 188/C2
Boyne Island, Austl. 171/C3
Boynton Beach, Fl, US 191/H5
Boysen (res.), Wy, US 184/F5
Boyup Brook, Austl. 170/C5
Boz (pt.), Turk. 107/J5
Bozashchy Tübegi (pen.), Kaz. 121/J3
Bozcaada (isl.), Gre. 105/J3
Bozcaada, Turk. 105/K3
Bozdoğan, Turk. 148/B2
Bozeman, Mt, US 184/F4
Bozkir, Turk. 148/C2
Bozkurt, Turk. 120/E4
Bozman, Md, US 196/B6
Bozoum, CAfr. 154/J6
Bozova, Turk. 148/D2
Bozüyük, Turk. 148/B2
Bozyazı, Turk. 149/C1
Bozzolo, It. 116/D2
Bra, It. 116/A3
Braan (riv.), Sc, UK 94/C3
Brač (isl.), Cro. 104/E1
Bracciano (lake), It. 104/B1
Bracebridge, On, Can. 188/E2
Brackel, Ger. 109/H2
Bracken, Tx, US 195/U20
Brackenheim, Ger. 112/C4
Brackettville, Tx, US 187/G5
Bracknell, Eng, UK 91/F4
Bracknell Forest (co.), Eng, UK 91/F4
Braço do Norte, Braz. 213/B4
Brad, Rom. 107/F2
Bradano (riv.), It. 106/B5
Bradda (pt.), IM, UK 92/D3
Bradenton, Fl, US 191/H5
Bradford, Eng, UK 93/G4
Bradford (co.), Eng, UK 93/G4
Bradford, Pa, US 188/E3
Bradley (int'l arpt.), Ct, US 189/F3
Bradley Beach, NJ, US 196/D3
Brady, Tx, US 187/H5
Braemar (reg.), Sc, UK 94/C2
Braeriach (peak), Sc, UK 94/C2
Braga (dist.), Port. 102/A2
Braga, Port. 102/A2
Bragado, Arg. 216/E2
Bragança, Braz. 209/J4
Bragança (dist.), Port. 102/B2
Bragança, Port. 102/B2
Brahmanbāria, Bang. 143/H4
Brahmaputra (riv.), Asia 141/F2
Braich-y-Pwll (pt.), Wal, UK 92/D6
Braid (riv.), NI, UK 92/B2
Brăila (prov.), Rom. 107/H3
Brăila, Rom. 107/H3
Brainards, NJ, US 196/C2
Braine, Fr. 110/C5
Braine-l'Alleud, Belg. 111/D2
Braine-le-Comte, Belg. 111/D2
Brainerd, Mn, US 185/K4
Braintree, Eng, UK 91/G3
Braithwaite, La, US 195/Q17
Brak (riv.), SAfr. 164/C3
Brake, Ger. 109/F2
Brakel, Belg. 110/C2
Brakel, Ger. 109/G5
Brakel, Neth. 108/C5
Brakna (pol. reg.), Mrta. 160/B2
Brålanda, Swe. 96/E2
Bram, Fr. 100/E5
Bramdrupdam, Den. 96/C4
Bramley, Eng, UK 88/B3
Brampton, On, Can. 189/Q8
Bramsche, Ger. 109/E4
Bramstedt, Ger. 109/F2
Bran (riv.), Sc, UK 94/A1
Brancaleone-Marina, It. 104/E4
Branch Dale, Pa, US 196/B2
Branchville, NJ, US 196/D1
Branchville, Ct, US 197/E1
Branco (riv.), Braz. 205/C2
Brand, Aus. 115/F3
Brandberg (peak), Namb. 163/B5
Brandbu, Nor. 96/D1
Brande, Den. 96/C4
Brandenburg (state), Ger. 98/P6
Brandenburg, Ger. 98/G2
Brander, Pass of (pass), Sc, UK 94/A4
Brandfort, SAfr. 164/D3
Brandizzo, It. 116/A2
Brandon, Mb, Can. 185/J3
Brandon, Fl, US 191/H5
Brandon, Ms, US 191/F3
Brandsen, Arg. 217/J11
Brandvlei, SAfr. 164/C3
Brandýs nad Labem, Czh. 113/H2
Brandywine, Md, US 196/B6
Brandywine (riv.), Pa, US 196/C4
Branford, Ct, US 197/F1
Branges, Fr. 114/B4
Braniewo, Pol. 97/H4
Brannenburg, Ger. 101/K3
Brant Beach, NJ, US 196/D4
Branxholm, Austl. 173/C4
Branzoll (Bronzolo), It. 115/H4
Bras d'Or (lake), NS, Can. 189/J2
Brasiléia, Braz. 208/E6
Brasília de Minas, Braz. 212/A5
Brasília, PN de, Braz. 209/J7
Braşov, Rom. 107/G3
Braşov (prov.), Rom. 107/G3
Brasschaat, Belg. 108/B6
Brassey (mt.), Austl. 171/G2
Brasstown Bald (peak), Ga, US 191/H3
Brastad, Swe. 96/D2
Bratislava (cap.), Slvk. 101/M2
Bratislava (Ivanka) (int'l arpt.), Slvk. 106/C1
Bratislavský (pol. reg.), Slvk. 99/J4
Bratsk, Rus. 123/L4
Brattleboro, Vt, US 189/F3
Bratunac, Bosn. 106/D3
Braubach, Ger. 111/G3
Braulio Carrillo, PN, CR 198/E5
Braunau am Inn, Aus. 113/G6
Braunfels, Ger. 112/B1
Braunig (lake), Tx, US 195/U21
Braunlage, Ger. 109/H5
Bräunlingen, Ger. 115/E2
Braunschweig, Ger. 109/H4
Brava (isl.), CpV. 151/J11
Brava (pt.), Chile 217/C7
Brava (pt.), Uru. 217/K11
Brava, Costa (coast), Sp. 103/G2
Bråviken (inlet), Swe. 96/G2
Bravo (peak), Bol. 208/F7
Bravo (peak), Peru 214/B2
Bravo del Norte (riv.), Mex. 198/A2
Brawley, Ca, US 186/D4
Bray (isl.), Nun., Can. 181/J2
Bray, Ire. 92/B5
Bray (pt.), Ire. 92/B5
Bray-Dunes, Fr. 110/B1
Braye (riv.), Fr. 100/D3
Brazey-en-Plaine, Fr. 114/B3
Brazil (ctry.) 205/D3
Brazilian Highlands (uplands), Braz. 205/E4
Brazo Casiquiare (riv.), Ven. 211/E4
Brazo Sur (riv.), Arg. 217/C6
Brazópolis, Braz. 213/H7
Brazos (riv.), Tx, US 190/D3
Brazos, Salt Fork (riv.), Tx, US 190/C3
Brazzaville (cap.), Congo 163/C1
Brčko, Bosn. 106/D3
Brda (riv.), Pol. 96/G5
Brdy (mts.), Czh. 99/G4
Brea, Ca, US 194/G8
Breadalbane (dist.), Sc, UK 94/B4
Breamish (riv.), Eng, UK 94/D6
Bréançon, Fr. 88/J4
Bréau, Fr. 88/L6
Breaza, Rom. 107/G3
Brebbia, It. 116/B1
Brêche (riv.), Fr. 110/B5
Brechen, Ger. 112/B2
Brechin, Sc, UK 94/D3
Brecht, Belg. 108/B6
Breckenridge, Mn, US 185/J4
Breckenridge, Tx, US 187/H4
Breckerfeld, Ger. 109/E6
Breckland (phys. reg.), Eng, UK 91/G2
Brecknock (pen.), Chile 217/C7
Břeclav, Czh. 101/M2
Brecon, Wal, UK 90/C3
Brecon Beacons (mts.), Wal, UK 90/C3
Breda, Neth. 108/B5
Bredaryd, Swe. 96/E3
Bredasdorp, SAfr. 164/M11
Bredebro, Den. 96/C4
Bredene, Belg. 110/B1
Bredstedt, Ger. 96/C4
Breë (riv.), SAfr. 164/B4
Bree, Belg. 111/E1
Breg (riv.), Ger. 98/E5
Bregagno (peak), It. 115/F5
Bregalnica (riv.), FYROM 105/H2
Breganze, It. 117/E1
Bregenz, Aus. 115/F3
Bregenzer Ache (riv.), Aus. 115/F3
Bregovo, Bul. 106/F3
Brégy, Fr. 88/L4
Breidhafjördhur (bay), Ice. 95/M6
Breil-Brigels, Swi. 115/F4
Breisach, Ger. 114/D1
Breitbrunn am Chiemsee, Ger. 113/F7
Breitenauriegel (peak), Ger. 113/G5
Breitenbach, Swi. 114/D3
Breitenbrunn, Ger. 113/E4
Breitenfurt bei Wien, Aus. 107/N7
Breitenworbis, Ger. 109/H6
Breithorn (peak), Swi. 114/D5
Breithorn (peak), Swi. 114/D6
Brejo, Braz. 212/B1
Brejo Santo, Braz. 212/C2
Brejões, Braz. 212/B3
Brembate di Sopra, It. 116/C1
Brembilla, It. 116/C1
Brembio, It. 116/C2
Brembo (riv.), It. 115/F6
Bremen (int'l arpt.), Ger. 109/F2
Bremen, Ger. 109/F2
Bremen (state), Ger. 96/C5
Bremer (riv.), Austl. 171/E7
Bremerhaven, Ger. 109/F1
Bremerton, Wa, US 184/C4
Bremervörde, Ger. 109/G2
Bremgarten, Swi. 115/E3
Bremgarten bei Bern, Swi. 114/D4
Bremnes, Nor. 96/A2
Brend (riv.), Ger. 112/D2
Brendel (lake), Mi, US 193/E7
Brendola, It. 117/E2
Brendon (hills), Eng, UK 90/C4
Brenig, Llyn (lake), Wal, UK 92/E5
Brenne (riv.), Fr. 98/C5
Brenner (pass), Aus. 115/H4
Brenner (riv.), Austl. 171/N9
Brenno (riv.), Swi. 115/E5
Breno, It. 115/G6
Brent (bor.), Eng, UK 88/C2
Brent (res.), Eng, UK 88/C2
Brent (riv.), Eng, UK 88/B2
Brenta (riv.), It. 101/J4
Brenta (peak), It. 115/G5
Brentwood, NY, US 197/E2
Brentwood, Ca, US 193/L11
Brentwood, Eng, UK 88/D2
Brenz (riv.), Ger. 112/D5
Brescello, It. 116/D3
Brescia, It. 116/D1
Brescia (prov.), It. 115/G6
Bresle (riv.), Fr. 100/D1
Bresles, Fr. 110/B5
Bressana, It. 116/C2
Bressanone, It. 101/J3
Bressay (isl.), Sc, UK 89/W13
Bressuire, Fr. 100/C3
Brest, Fr. 100/A2
Brest, Bela. 99/M2
Brest (int'l arpt.), Bela. 99/M2
Brestskaya Voblasts, Bela. 120/C1
Bretagne (pol. reg.), Fr. 100/B2
Bretagne, Monts de (mts.), Fr. 100/B2
Bretagne, Pointe de (pt.), Reun., Fr. 165/S15
Bretaña, Peru 214/C2
Breteuil, Fr. 110/B4
Brétigny-sur-Orge, Fr. 88/J6
Breton, Ab, Can. 184/E2
Breton (cape), NS, Can. 189/K2
Brett (cape), NZ 175/S10
Brett (riv.), Eng, UK 91/G2
Brettach (riv.), Ger. 112/C4
Bretten, Ger. 112/B4
Bretzenheim, Ger. 111/G4
Breuberg, Ger. 112/C3
Breuillet, Fr. 88/J6
Breukelen, Neth. 108/B4
Breuna, Ger. 109/G6
Breuvannes-en-Bassigny, Fr. 114/B1
Breves, Braz. 209/H4
Brevig Mission, Ak, US 192/E2
Brevik, Nor. 96/C2
Brevoort (isl.), Nun., Can. 181/K2
Brewarrina, Austl. 173/C1
Brewer, Me, US 189/G2
Brewster, Ne, US 185/J5
Brewton, Al, US 191/G4
Brey-et-Lû, Fr. 88/G4
Breyten, SAfr. 165/E2
Brežice, Slov. 101/L4
Brezina, Alg. 157/F2
Březnice, Czh. 113/G3
Breznik, Bul. 105/H1
Brezoi, Rom. 107/G3
Brezovo, Bul. 105/J1
Bria, CAfr. 155/K6
Briançon, Fr. 101/G4
Brianne, Llyn (res.), Wal, UK 90/C2
Briar Creek, Pa, US 196/B1
Briare, Fr. 100/E3
Brickerville, Pa, US 196/B3
Bricktown, NJ, US 196/D3
Bride (riv.), Ire. 89/P10
Bride, IM, UK 92/D3
Bridge City, Tx, US 190/E4
Bridge of Allan, Sc, UK 94/C4
Bridge of Don, Sc, UK 94/D2
Bridge of Weir, Sc, UK 94/B5
Bridgehampton, NY, US 197/F2
Bridgend, Wal, UK 90/C3
Bridgeport, Ca, US 186/C3
Bridgeport, Ct, US 197/E1
Bridgeport, Ne, US 185/H5
Bridgeport, NJ, US 196/C4
Bridger, Mt, US 184/F4
Bridgeton, NJ, US 196/C5
Bridgetown, Austl. 170/C5
Bridgetown (cap.), Bar. 199/P9
Bridgeville, De, US 196/C6
Bridgewater, Austl. 173/C4
Bridgewater, NS, Can. 189/H2
Bridgnorth, Eng, UK 90/D1
Bridgton, Me, US 189/G2
Bridgwater, Eng, UK 90/D4
Bridgwater (bay), Eng, UK 90/C4
Bridlington, Eng, UK 93/H3
Bridlington (bay), Eng, UK 93/H3
Bridport, Austl. 173/C4
Bridport, Eng, UK 90/D5
Brie (reg.), Fr. 88/M6
Brie-Comte-Robert, Fr. 88/K5
Brieg Brzeg, Pol. 99/J3
Brielle, Neth. 108/B5
Brielle, NJ, US 196/D3
Brienz, Swi. 114/E4
Brier, Wa, US 193/C2
Brierfield, Eng, UK 93/F4
Brieselang, Ger. 98/Q6
Brig, Swi. 114/D5
Brigach (riv.), Ger. 112/B7
Brigantine, NJ, US 196/D5
Brigend (pol. reg.), Wal, UK 90/C3
Brigham City, Ut, US 195/J10
Brighouse, Eng, UK 93/G4
Bright, Austl. 173/C3
Brightlingsea, Eng, UK 91/H3
Brighton, Eng, UK 91/F5
Brighton and Hove (co.), Eng, UK 91/F5
Brighton, Co, US 195/C3
Brighton, Il, US 195/G7
Brighton, Ut, US 195/K12
Brighton, Wi, US 193/P14
Brignais, Fr. 100/F4
Brignoles, Fr. 100/G5
Brihuega, Sp. 102/D2
Briis-sous-Forges, Fr. 88/J6
Brikama, Gam. 160/A3
Brilhante (riv.), Braz. 209/G8
Brilon, Ger. 109/F6
Brimstone Hill NP, StK. 199/N8
Brindisi, It. 105/E2
Brinkworth, Austl. 171/H5
Brinnon, Wa, US 193/B2
Brión, Sp. 102/A1
Brione, Swi. 115/E5
Briones (res.), Ca, US 193/K11
Brisbane, Austl. 171/F6
Brisbane (int'l arpt.), Austl. 171/F6
Brisbane (riv.), Austl. 171/E7
Brisbane Forest Park, Austl. 171/E6
Brisbane Ranges NP, Austl. 173/C3
Brisbane Water NP, Austl. 173/D2
Brisighella, It. 117/E4
Brissago, Swi. 115/E5
Bristol, Eng, UK 90/D4
Bristol (chan.), Eng,Wal, UK 90/B4
Bristol (co.), Eng, UK 90/D4
Bristol (bay), Ak, US 192/F4
Bristol, Pa, US 196/D3
Bristol, Tn, US 188/D4
Bristow, Ok, US 187/H4
British (mts.), Ak, US 192/K2
British Columbia (prov.), Can. 180/D3
British Empire (range), Nun., Can. 181/S6
British Indian Ocean Territory (dpcy.), UK 125/G10
British Museum, Eng, UK 88/C2
Britstown, SAfr. 164/C3
Brittany (reg.), Fr. 100/B3
Britton, SD, US 185/J4
Brive-la-Gaillarde, Fr. 100/D4
Brives-Charensac, Fr. 100/E4
Briviesca, Sp. 102/D1
Brivio, It. 116/C1
Brněnský (pol. reg.), Slvk. 99/J4
Brnik (int'l arpt.), Slov. 101/L3
Brno, Czh. 99/J4
Broa (bay), Cuba 203/F1
Broad (pass), Ak, US 192/J3
Broad (riv.), NC,SC, US 191/H3
Broad Law (peak), Sc, UK 94/C6
Broad Sound (isls.), Austl. 171/C2
Broadback (riv.), Qu, Can. 188/E1
Broadford, Austl. 173/C3
Broadkill (riv.), De, US 196/C6
Broads NP, The, Eng, UK 91/H1
Broadstairs, Eng, UK 91/H4
Broadus, Mt, US 185/G4
Broadwater NP, Austl. 173/E1
Broadway (hill), Eng, UK 91/E3
Broadway, NJ, US 196/C2
Broc, Swi. 114/D4
Brochet, Mb, Can. 180/F3
Brock (isl.), NW, Can. 181/R7
Brocken (peak), Ger. 109/H5
Brockman (mt.), Austl. 170/C2
Brockton, Ma, US 189/G3
Brockville, On, Can. 188/F2
Brodeur (pen.), Nun., Can. 180/G1
Brodheadsville, Pa, US 196/C2
Brodnica, Pol. 99/K2
Broek in Waterland, Neth. 108/B4
Broek Op Langedijk, Neth. 108/B3
Bröhn (peak), Ger. 109/G4
Broken (bay), Austl. 173/D2
Broken Arrow, Ok, US 187/J3
Broken Bow, Ne, US 185/J5
Broken Bow (lake), Ok, US 187/J4
Broken Bow, Ok, US 187/J4
Broken Hill, Austl. 173/B1
Brokeoff (mts.), NM, US 190/B3
Brokopondo, Sur. 211/H3
Brokopondo (dist.), Sur. 211/H3
Brome, Ger. 98/F2
Bromölla, Swe. 96/F3
Bromsgrove, Eng, UK 90/D2
Bromskirchen, Ger. 109/F6
Bron, Fr. 114/A6
Brønderslev, Den. 96/C3
Brong-Ahafo (pol. reg.), Gha. 161/E5
Broni, It. 116/C2
Bronkhorstspruit, SAfr. 164/E2

Brønnøy, Nor. 95/E2
Brøns, Den. 96/C4
Bronschhofen, Swi. 115/F3
Bronte, It. 104/D4
Bronx (bor.), NY, US 197/E2
Bronx Zoo, NY, US 197/K8
Bronxville, NY, US 197/K8
Brook Forest, Co, US 195/B3
Brooke's Point, Phil. 139/E2
Brookfield, Il, US 193/Q16
Brookhaven, Ms, US 187/K5
Brooklyn (bor.), NY, US 196/D2
Brooklyn, Il, US 195/G8
Brooklyn Park, Md, US 196/B5
Brookmans Park, Eng, UK 88/C1
Brooks (mtn.), Ak, US 192/E2
Brooks, Ab, Can. 184/F3
Brooks, Il, US 195/G8
Brooks (range), Ak, US 192/F2
Brookside, De, US 196/C4
Brooksville, Fl, US 191/H4
Brookton, Austl. 170/C5
Brookvale, Co, US 195/B3
Brookville, NY, US 197/L8
Broomall, Pa, US 196/C4
Broomfield, Co, US 195/B3
Brørup, Den. 96/C4
Brösarp, Swe. 96/F4
Brossard, Qu, Can. 189/P7
Brough (pt.), Sc, UK 89/V14
Broughshane, NI, UK 92/B2
Brousseval, Fr. 114/A1
Brouwersdam (dam), Neth. 108/A5
Brouwershaven, Neth. 108/A5
Brovst, Den. 96/C3
Brown (mt.), Austl. 171/H5
Brown (pt.), Austl. 171/G5
Brown Clee (hill), Eng, UK 90/D2
Brown Shoal (bar), Asia 137/C5
Brownfield, Tx, US 187/G4
Brownhills, Eng, UK 91/E1
Browning, Mt, US 184/E3
Browns Mills, NJ, US 196/D4
Brownsea (isl.), Eng, UK 91/E5
Brownsville, Tn, US 188/B5
Brownsville, Tx, US 190/D5
Brownsville, Wa, US 193/B2
Broxburn, Sc, UK 94/C5
Broye (riv.), Swi. 114/C4
Brozas, Sp. 102/B3
Bruay-la-Buissière, Fr. 110/B3
Bruay-sur-L'Escaut, Fr. 110/C3
Bruce (pen.), On, Can. 188/D2
Bruce (mt.), Austl. 170/C2
Bruce Rock, Austl. 170/C4
Bruchberg (peak), Ger. 109/H5
Bruche (riv.), Fr. 101/G2
Bruchhausen-Vilsen, Ger. 109/G3
Bruchköbel, Ger. 112/B2
Bruchmühlbach-Miesau, Ger. 111/G5
Bruchsal, Ger. 112/B4
Brucht (riv.), Ger. 109/G5
Bruck, Aus. 107/P7
Bruck an der Grossglocknerstrasse, Aus. 101/K3
Bruck an der Mur, Aus. 101/L3
Bruckberg, Ger. 113/F5
Bruckmühl, Ger. 101/J3
Brue (riv.), Eng, UK 90/D4
Bruflat, Nor. 96/C1
Brügg, Swi. 114/D3
Brugg, Swi. 114/E3
Brugge, Belg. 110/C1
Brüggen, Ger. 108/D6
Brugnera, It. 117/F1
Brühl, Ger. 111/F2
Bruinisse, Neth. 108/B5
Brukkaros (peak), Namb. 164/B2
Brukunga, Austl. 171/M8
Brumado, Braz. 212/B4
Brumath, Fr. 111/G6
Brummen, Neth. 108/D4
Brumunddal, Nor. 96/D1
Brune (riv.), Fr. 110/C4
Bruneau (riv.), Id,Nv, US 184/E5
Brunei (ctry.) 138/D2
Brunete, Sp. 103/M9
Brunflo, Swe. 95/E3
Brunico, It. 101/J3
Brünigpass (pass), Swi. 114/E4
Brunn am Gebirge, Aus. 107/N7
Brunoy, Fr. 88/K5
Brunsbüttel, Ger. 109/G1
Brunssum, Neth. 111/E2
Brunstatt, Fr. 114/D2
Brunswick, Ga, US 191/H4
Brunswick, Me, US 189/G3
Brunswick, Oh, US 188/D3
Brunswick Heads, Austl. 171/D5
Brunswick Junction, Austl. 170/B5
Brunswick, Península de (pen.), Chile 215/B7
Brus (lake), Hon. 203/E3
Brusartsi, Bul. 106/F4
Brushy Creek, Tx, US 187/J5
Brusio, Swi. 115/G5
Brussels, Il, US 195/F8
Brussels (int'l arpt.), Belg. 111/D2
Brussels (Bruxelles) (cap.), Belg. 111/D2
Brusson, It. 116/A1
Bruthen, Austl. 173/C3
Bruyères, Fr. 114/C1
Bruyères-le-Châtel, Fr. 88/J6
Bruyères-sur-Oise, Fr. 88/J4
Bruz, Fr. 100/C2
Bruzual, Ven. 210/D2
Bryan, Tx, US 187/H5
Bryan, Oh, US 188/C3
Bryan (mt.), Austl. 171/H5
Bryansk, Rus. 120/E1
Bryanskaya Oblast, Rus. 120/E1
Bryce Canyon NP, Ut, US 186/D3
Bryn Brawd (peak), Wal, UK 90/C2
Bryn Mawr, Pa, US 196/C3
Bryne, Nor. 96/A2
Brzeg Dolny, Pol. 99/J3
Brzesko, Pol. 99/L4
Brzozów, Pol. 99/M4
Bua, Swe. 96/E3
Buala, Sol. 174/E5
Buba, GBis. 160/B4
Bubaque, GBis. 160/B4
Bubendorf, Swi. 114/D3
Bubikon, Swi. 115/E3
Bubu (riv.), Tanz. 162/B4
Buc, Fr. 88/J5
Bucak, Turk. 148/B2
Bucakkişla, Turk. 149/C1
Bucaramanga, Col. 210/C3
Bucasia, Austl. 171/C3
Bucelas, Port. 103/P10
Buch, Ger. 115/G1
Buchan (gulf), Nun., Can. 181/J1
Buchan (reg.), Sc, UK 94/D1
Buchan Ness (pt.), Sc, UK 94/E2
Buchanan (lake), Tx, US 187/H5
Buchanan, Libr. 160/C5
Buchans, Nf, Can. 189/K1
Bucharest (Bucureşti) (cap.), Rom. 107/H4
Buchbach, Ger. 113/F6
Büchen, Ger. 109/H2
Buchen, Ger. 112/C3
Buchenberg, Ger. 115/G2
Buchholz, Ger. 111/G3
Buchholz in der Nordheide, Ger. 109/G2
Buchloe, Ger. 115/G1
Buchon (pt.), Ca, US 186/B4
Buchs, Swi. 115/F3
Bucine, It. 117/E6
Buck, The (peak), Sc, UK 94/D2
Buckden Pike (peak), Eng, UK 93/F3
Bückeburg, Ger. 109/G4
Buckie, Sc, UK 94/D1
Buckingham, Qu, Can. 188/F2
Buckingham, Eng, UK 91/F3
Buckingham Palace, Eng, UK 88/C2
Buckland, Ak, US 192/F2
Buckley, Wal, UK 93/E5
Buckley, Wa, US 193/C3
Buckner, Mo, US 195/E5
Bucks (co.), Pa, US 196/C3
Bucksburn, Sc, UK 94/D2
Bucquoy, Fr. 110/B3
Buctouche, NB, Can. 189/H2
Bucureşti (co.), Rom. 107/G3
Bucy-le-Long, Fr. 110/C5
Bucyrus, Oh, US 188/D3
Bucyrus, Ks, US 195/D6
Budai hegy (hill), Hun. 107/Q9
Budakeszi, Hun. 107/Q9
Budaörs, Hun. 107/R10
Budapest (cap.), Hun. 107/R9
Budapest (co.), Hun. 107/R9
Budaun, India 142/B1
Budd (coast), Ant. 218/H
Budd (inlet), Wa, US 193/B3
Budd Lake, NJ, US 196/D2
Buddon Ness (pt.), Sc, UK 94/D4
Buddusò, It. 104/A2
Bude, Eng, UK 90/B5
Bude (bay), Eng, UK 90/B5
Budějovický (pol. reg.), Slvk. 99/H4
Budel, Neth. 108/C6
Büdelsdorf, Ger. 96/C4
Budge-Budge, India 143/G4
Budhāna, India 144/D5
Budhanilantha, Nepal 143/E2
Budhlāda, India 144/C5
Budia, Sp. 102/D2
Büdingen, Ger. 112/C2
Budrio, It. 117/E3
Budva, Mont. 106/D4
Budzhak (reg.), Mol. 107/J2
Buea, Camr. 154/G7
Buelna (int'l arpt.), Mex. 184/D4
Buena, NJ, US 196/D4
Buena Esperanza, Arg. 216/D2
Buena Fe, Ecu. 210/B5
Buena Park, Ca, US 194/G8
Buena Vista, Co, US 187/F3
Buenaventura, Mex. 184/D2
Buenaventura, Col. 210/B4
Buenavista, Mex. 201/Q9
Buenavista, Phil. 137/E6
Bueno (riv.), Chile 216/B4
Bueno Brandão, Braz. 213/G7
Buenópolis, Braz. 212/A5
Buenos Aires (cap.), Arg. 217/J11
Buenos Aires (lake), Arg.,Chile 205/B7
Buenos Aires (prov.), Arg. 216/E3
Buenos Aires, Col. 210/B4
Buenos Aires, Peru 214/B2
Buenos Aires (Jorge Newbery) (int'l arpt.), Arg. 217/J11
Buenos Aires (Ministro Pistarini) (int'l arpt.), Arg. 217/J11
Buerarema, Braz. 212/C4
Buesaco, Col. 210/B4
Buet (peak), Fr. 114/C5
Bueu, Sp. 102/A1
Buffalo (mt.), Austl. 173/C3
Buffalo (lake), Ab, Can. 184/E2
Buffalo (riv.), SAfr. 165/E2
Buffalo (riv.), Ar, US 190/E3
Buffalo, Mn, US 185/K4
Buffalo, NY, US 189/S10
Buffalo, Ok, US 187/H3
Buffalo, SD, US 185/H4
Buffalo, Wy, US 184/G4
Buffalo Bill Museum and Grave, Co, US 195/B3
Buffalo Narrows, Sk, Can. 184/F2
Buffalo Springs Nat'l Rsv., Kenya 162/C2
Buffelsrivier (riv.), SAfr. 164/B3
Buford, Ga, US 191/G3
Buftea, Rom. 107/G3
Bug (riv.), Pol. 99/M2
Buga, Col. 210/B4
Bugaba, Pan. 203/F4
Bugac, Hun. 106/D2
Bugala (isl.), Ugan. 162/B3
Bugalagrande, Col. 210/B3
Bugat, Mong. 128/F2
Buğdaylı, Turk. 107/H5
Bugel (pt.), Indo. 138/D5
Buggenhout, Belg. 111/D1
Bugojno, Bosn. 106/C3
Bugosa (prov.), Ugan. 162/B2
Bugsuk (isl.), Phil. 139/E2
Bugul'ma, Rus. 119/M5
Buguruslan, Rus. 121/K1
Buh (riv.), Ukr. 99/M3
Buhayrat al Asad (lake), Syria 148/D2
Buḩayrat ath Tharthār (res.), Iraq 148/E3
Buhi, Phil. 137/D5
Buhl, Fr. 114/D2
Bühl, Ger. 115/E2
Bühler (riv.), Ger. 112/C4
Bühlerzell, Ger. 112/C5
Buhuşi, Rom. 107/H2
Bui (dam), Gha. 161/E4
Bui Gorge (res.), Gha. 161/E4
Bui NP, Gha. 161/E4
Buin (peak), Swi. 115/G4
Buin, Chile 216/N8
Buíque, Braz. 212/C3
Bujalance, Sp. 102/C4
Bujanovac, Serb. 106/E4
Bujumbura (cap.), Buru. 162/A3
Bujumbura (int'l arpt.), Buru. 162/A3
Buk, Pol. 99/J2
Buka (isl.), PNG 174/E5
Bukadaban (peak), China 128/F4
Būkān, Iran 146/E1
Bukasa (isl.), Ugan. 162/B3
Bukavu, D.R. Congo 162/A3
Bukene, Tanz. 162/B4
Buket Bubat (peak), Malay. 141/H6
Bukhoro (pol. reg.), Uzb. 145/D4
Bukhoro, Uzb. 145/D5
Bukhovo, Bul. 105/H1
Bukittinggi, Indo. 138/B4
Bükki NP, Hun. 99/L4
Bukoba, Tanz. 162/A3
Buku (cape), Indo. 138/B4
Bülach, Swi. 115/E2
Bulahdelah, Austl. 173/E2
Bulan, Phil. 139/F1
Bulancak, Turk. 148/D1
Bulandshahr, India 142/A1
Bulanık, Turk. 148/E2
Bulawa (peak), Indo. 139/F3
Bulawayo, Zim. 163/E5
Buldan, Turk. 148/B2
Buldibuyo, Peru 214/B3
Bulgan, Mong. 128/H1
Bulgan (prov.), Mong. 128/H2
Bulgan, Mong. 128/H2
Bulgan, Mong. 128/H3
Bulgaria (ctry.) 107/G4
Bŭlgarovo, Bul. 107/H4
Bulgheria (peak), It. 104/D2
Buliluyan (cape), Phil. 139/E2
Bulkley (riv.), BC, Can. 184/B2
Bull (pt.), NI, UK 92/B1
Bull Shoals (lake), Ar,Mo, US 187/J3
Bullange, Belg. 111/F3
Bullas, Sp. 102/E3
Bulle, Swi. 114/D4
Buller (isl.), NZ 175/S11
Bullerup, Den. 96/D4
Bullhead City, Az, US 186/D4
Bullion, Fr. 88/H6
Bulloo (riv.), Austl. 167/D3
Bulloo River Overflow (swamp), Austl. 171/A5
Bully-les-Mines, Fr. 110/B3
Bulnayn (mts.), Mong. 128/G2
Bulnes, Chile 216/B3
Bultfontein, SAfr. 164/D3
Bulukumba, Indo. 139/F5
Bulverde, Tx, US 195/U20
Bumba, D.R. Congo 155/K7
Bumtang (riv.), Bhu. 143/H2
Bumthang, Bhu. 143/H2
Bunaga-take (peak), Japan 135/J5
Bunbury, Austl. 170/B5
Bundaberg, Austl. 171/D4
Bundarra, Austl. 173/D1
Bünde, Ger. 109/F4
Bunde, Ger. 109/E2
Bundoran, Ire. 89/P9
Būndu, India 143/E4
Bungendore, Austl. 173/D2
Bunguran (isl.), Indo. 138/C3
Bunia, D.R. Congo 162/A2
Bunker (peak), Az, US 195/R18
Bunker Hill, Il, US 195/H7
Bunkie, La, US 187/J5
Bunnell, Fl, US 191/H4
Bunnik, Neth. 108/C4
Buñol, Sp. 103/E3
Bunschoten, Neth. 108/C4
Bunya, Austl. 171/E6
Bunya Mountains NP, Austl. 171/C4
Bünyan, Turk. 148/C2
Bunyu (isl.), Indo. 139/E3
Buochs, Swi. 115/E4
Buon Me Thuot, Viet. 136/E3
Buonconvento, It. 101/J5
Buquim, Braz. 212/C3
Būr Sa'īd (gov.), Egypt 149/C4
Būr Sa'īd (Port Said), Egypt 149/C4
Būr Sūdān (Port Sudan), Sudan 159/D5
Burang, China 128/D5
Buranga (pass), Ugan. 155/M7
Burano (riv.), It. 117/F5
Burano, It. 117/F2
Buras-Triumph, La, US 191/F4
Burauen, Phil. 137/D5
Buraydah, SAr. 146/D3
Burbach, Ger. 111/H2
Burbank, Ca, US 194/F7
Burbure, Fr. 110/B2
Burco (Burao), Som. 155/Q6
Burdekin (riv.), Austl. 167/D2
Burdell (mtn.), Ca, US 193/J10
Burdur (lake), Turk. 148/B2
Burdur (prov.), Turk. 148/B2
Burdur, Turk. 148/B2
Burdwān, India 143/F4
Bure (riv.), Eng, UK 91/H1
Büren, Ger. 109/F5
Buren, Neth. 108/C5
Büren an der Aare, Swi. 114/D3
Bürengiyn (mts.), Mong. 128/H2
Bures-sur-Yvette, Fr. 88/J5
Būrewāla, Pak. 144/B4
Bureya (riv.), Rus. 123/P4
Burg, Ger. 96/C4
Burg, Ger. 98/F2
Burg, Ger. 96/D4
Burgas (prov.), Bul. 105/K1
Burgas (bay), Bul. 107/H4
Burgas (int'l arpt.), Bul. 107/H4
Burgau, Ger. 112/D6
Burgaw, NC, US 191/J3
Burgberg im Allgäu, Ger. 115/G2
Burgbernheim, Ger. 112/D4
Burgbrohl, Ger. 111/G3
Burgdorf, Ger. 109/H4
Burgdorf, Swi. 114/D3
Burgebrach, Ger. 112/D3
Burgenland (prov.), Aus. 99/J5
Burgeo, Nf, Can. 189/K2
Burgersdorp, SAfr. 164/D3
Burges (mt.), Austl. 170/D4
Burgess (mt.), Yk, Can. 192/L2
Burgess Hill, Eng, UK 91/F5
Burgfjället (peak), Swe. 95/E2
Burghaslach, Ger. 112/D3
Burghausen, Ger. 113/F6
Burghead, Sc, UK 94/C1
Burghead (bay), Sc, UK 94/C1
Burgheim, Ger. 112/E5
Burgkirchen, Aus. 113/G6
Burgkirchen an der Alz, Ger. 113/F6
Burgkunstadt, Ger. 112/E2
Bürglen, Swi. 115/F2
Burglengenfeld, Ger. 113/F4
Burgos, Mex. 201/F3
Burgos, Sp. 102/D1
Burgsinn, Ger. 112/C2
Burgstall (Postal), It. 115/H4
Burgsteinfurt, Ger. 109/E4
Burgsvik, Swe. 96/H3
Burgundy (reg.), Fr. 100/F3
Burgwedel, Ger. 109/G3
Burhābalang (riv.), India 143/F4
Burhan Budai (mts.), China 128/G4
Burhaniye, Turk. 148/A2
Burhānpur, India 147/L4
Burhar-Dhanpuri, India 142/C4
Burhi Gandok (riv.), India 143/E2
Burica (pen.), Pan. 203/F4
Burica (pt.), Pan. 203/F4
Burin, Nf, Can. 189/L2
Burin (pen.), Nf, Can. 181/L4
Buriram, Thai. 136/C3
Buritama, Braz. 213/B2
Buriti, Braz. 212/B1
Buriti Alegre, Braz. 213/B1
Buriti Bravo, Braz. 212/B2
Buriti dos Lopes, Braz. 212/B1
Buritis, Braz. 212/A4
Buritizeiro, Braz. 212/A5
Burjasot, Sp. 103/E3
Burkardroth, Ger. 112/C2
Burke (chan.), BC, Can. 184/B2
Bürkelkopf (peak), Aus. 115/G4
Burkina Faso (ctry.) 161/E3
Burksville, Il, US 195/G9
Burladingen, Ger. 115/F1
Burley, Wa, US 193/B3
Burlingame, Ca, US 193/K11
Burlington, On, Can. 189/Q9
Burlington, Co, US 187/G3
Burlington, Ia, US 185/L5
Burlington, Il, US 193/N15
Burlington, Ks, US 187/J3
Burlington, NC, US 191/J2
Burlington, NJ, US 196/D3
Burlington (co.), NJ, US 196/D4
Burlington, Vt, US 188/F2
Burlington, Wi, US 188/B3
Burma (Myanmar) (ctry.) 141/G3
Bürmoos, Aus. 113/F7
Burnas (lake), Ukr. 107/K3
Burnet, Tx, US 187/H5
Burnett Heads, Austl. 171/D4
Burney, Ca, US 186/B2
Burney (peak), Chile 217/B7
Burnham, Il, US 193/Q16
Burnham-on-Sea, Eng, UK 90/D4
Burnie-Somerset, Austl. 173/C4
Burnley, Eng, UK 93/F4
Burns, Or, US 184/D5
Burns Lake, BC, Can. 184/B2
Burnside (riv.), Nun., Can. 180/E2
Burntisland, Sc, UK 94/C4
Burntwood, Eng, UK 91/E1
Burntwood (riv.), Mb, Can. 180/G3
Buronga, Austl. 173/B2
Buronzo, It. 116/B2
Burqā, WBnk. 149/G7
Burqīn, WBnk. 149/G7
Burr Ridge, Il, US 193/Q16
Burra, Austl. 171/H5
Burrel, Alb. 105/G2
Burrendong (res.), Austl. 173/D2
Burrewarra (pt.), Austl. 173/D2
Burriana, Sp. 103/E3
Burringbar, Austl. 171/D5
Burrinjuck (res.), Austl. 173/D2
Burrow (pt.), Sc, UK 92/D2
Burrowes (pt.), Austl. 171/A2
Burrum Heads, Austl. 171/D4
Burrum River NP, Austl. 171/D4
Burry (inlet), Wal, UK 90/B3
Bursa, Turk. 148/B1
Bursa (prov.), Turk. 148/B2
Burscheid, Ger. 111/G1
Bürstadt, Ger. 112/B3
Burt, NY, US 189/S9
Burtenbach, Ger. 112/D6
Burton, Wa, US 193/C3
Burton Latimer, Eng, UK 91/F2
Burton upon Trent, Eng, UK 91/E1
Buru (isl.), Indo. 139/G4
Burullus, Buḩayrat al (lake), Egypt 149/B4
Burundi (ctry.) 162/A3
Bururi, Buru. 162/A3
Buruticupu (riv.), Braz. 212/A2
Burwash Landing, Yk, Can. 192/L3
Bury, Eng, UK 93/F4
Bury (co.), Eng, UK 93/F4
Bury, Fr. 110/B5
Buryatiya, Resp., Rus. 123/M4
Bury Saint Edmunds, Eng, UK 91/G2
Burynshyk (pt.), Kaz. 121/J3
Busalla, It. 116/B3
Busembatia, Ugan. 162/B2
Busenberg, Ger. 111/G5
Buseno, Swi. 115/F5
Bush (riv.), Md, US 196/B5
Bush Kill (riv.), Pa, US 196/C1
Bushey, Eng, UK 88/B2
Bushkill, Pa, US 196/C1
Bushkill Falls, Pa, US 196/C1
Bushmanland (reg.), SAfr. 164/B3
Bushmills, NI, UK 92/B1
Busigny, Fr. 110/C3
Businga, D.R. Congo 155/K7
Buskerud (co.), Nor. 95/D3
Busko-Zdrój, Pol. 99/L3
Buss Craig (pt.), Sc, UK 94/D5
Busselton, Austl. 170/B5
Busseri (riv.), Sudan 155/L6
Busseto, It. 116/D3
Bussolengo, It. 117/D2
Bussum, Neth. 108/C4
Bustamante, Mex. 201/E3
Bustamante, Mex. 201/F4
Bustamante (pt.), Arg. 217/C6
Bustard (pt.), Austl. 171/C4
Buşteni, Rom. 107/G3
Busto Arsizio, It. 116/B1
Busto Garolfo, It. 116/B1
Busuanga (isl.), Phil. 137/C5
Büsum, Ger. 96/C4
Buta, D.R. Congo 155/K7
Buta Ranquil, Arg. 216/C3
Butare, Rwa. 162/A3
Butaritari (isl.), Kiri. 174/G4
Butawal, Nepal 142/D2
Bute (inlet), BC, Can. 184/B3
Bute, Austl. 171/H5
Bute (isl.), Sc, UK 94/A5
Bute, Sound of (sound), Sc, UK 94/A5
Büteeliyn (mts.), Mong. 128/H2
Butembo, D.R. Congo 162/A2
Bütgenbach, Belg. 111/F3
Buti, It. 116/D5
Butiá, Braz. 213/B4
Butiaba, Ugan. 162/A2
Butler, NJ, US 197/H8
Butler, Pa, US 188/E3
Butmir (int'l arpt.), Bosn. 106/D4
Buton (isl.), Indo. 139/F5
Butry-sur-Oise, Fr. 88/J4
Bütschelegg (peak), Swi. 114/D4
Bütschwil, Swi. 115/F3
Butt of Lewis (pt.), Sc, UK 89/Q7
Buttapietra, It. 117/D2
Butte-Silver Bow County, Mt, US 184/E4
Büttelborn, Ger. 112/B3
Butterworth, Malay. 138/B2
Buttes, Swi. 114/C4
Buttevant, Ire. 89/P10
Buttrio, It. 117/G1
Butuan, Phil. 137/E6
Buturlinovka, Rus. 121/G2
Butzbach, Ger. 112/B2
Bützow, Ger. 96/D5
Buëch (riv.), Fr. 100/F4
Buulo Berde, Som. 155/Q7
Buvuma (isl.), Ugan. 162/B2
Buxar, India 142/D3
Buxheim, Ger. 115/G2
Buxtehude, Ger. 109/G2
Buxton, Eng, UK 93/G5
Buy, Rus. 118/J4
Buyant-Uhaa, Mong. 129/K3
Buynaksk, Rus. 121/H4
Buyo, Barrage de (dam), C.d'Iv. 160/D5
Büyük Anafarta, Turk. 105/K2
Büyükarmutlu, Turk. 148/D2
Büyükçekmece, Turk. 107/J5
Büyükeceli, Turk. 149/C1
Büyükkarıştıran, Turk. 107/H5
Büyükyurt, Turk. 148/D2
Buyun Shan (peak), China 131/B2
Buyuni (pt.), Tanz. 162/C4
Buzançais, Fr. 100/D3
Buzancy, Fr. 111/D5
Buzău, Rom. 107/H3
Buzău (prov.), Rom. 107/H3
Buzău (riv.), Rom. 107/H3
Buziaş, Rom. 106/E3
Búzios, Ilha dos (isl.), Braz. 213/H8
Buz'kyy Lyman (estu.), Ukr. 107/K2
Buzsák, Hun. 106/C2
Buzuluk, Rus. 121/K1
Byala, Bul. 107/G4
Byala, Bul. 107/H4
Byala Slatina, Bul. 107/F4
Byam Martin (chan.), Nun., Can. 181/R7
Byam Martin (isl.), Nun., Can. 181/R7
Byarezina (riv.), Bela. 118/E5
Bydgoszcz, Pol. 99/J2
Byfleet, Eng, UK 88/B3
Byford, Austl. 170/L7
Bygland, Nor. 96/B2
Bykhov, Bela. 97/P5
Bykle, Nor. 96/B2
Bykovo (int'l arpt.), Rus. 119/X9
Bylot (isl.), Nun., Can. 181/J1
Bynum Run (riv.), Md, US 196/B4
Byram (riv.), Ct, US 197/E1
Byram (pt.), Ct, US 197/L8
Byram (lake), NY, US 197/L7
Byrd, US, Ant. 218/S
Byrd (cape), Ant. 218/U
Byremo, Nor. 96/B2
Byron, Ca, US 193/L11
Byron (isl.), Chile 217/B5
Byron Bay, Austl. 171/D5
Byrranga (mts.), Rus. 122/K2
Byrum, Den. 96/D3
Bystice (riv.), Czh. 113/F2
Bystrá (peak), Slvk. 99/K4
Bystřice, Czh. 113/H3
Bytantay (riv.), Rus. 123/N3
Bytom, Pol. 99/K3
Bytów, Pol. 96/G4

C

C.F. Secada (int'l arpt.), Peru 214/C1
Ca (riv.), Viet. 141/J4
Ca Mau, Viet. 136/D4
Ca Mau (cape), Viet. 136/D4
Caála, Ang. 163/C3
Caatingas (phys. reg.), Braz. 205/E3
Caazapá, Par. 215/E2
Cabadbaran, Phil. 137/E6
Cabaiguán, Cuba 203/G1
Caballo (res.), NM, US 186/F4
Caban-Coch (res.), Wal, UK 90/C2
Cabana, Peru 214/B3
Cabanaconde, Peru 214/D4
Cabañaquinta, Sp. 102/C1
Cabanatuan, Phil. 137/D4
Cabanes, Sp. 103/F2
Cabano, Qu, Can. 189/G2
Cabella Ligure, It. 116/C3
Cabestany, Fr. 100/E5
Cabeza del Buey, Sp. 102/C3
Cabeza Lagarto (pt.), Peru 214/B3
Cabezón de la Sal, Sp. 102/C1
Cabildo, Arg. 216/E3
Cabimas, Ven. 210/D2
Cabinda, Ang. 163/B2
Cabo, Braz. 212/D3
Cabo Corrientes, Cabo (cape), Mex. 184/D4
Cabo de Hornos, PN, Chile 215/C8
Cabo Delgado (prov.), Moz. 162/C5
Cabo Frio, Braz. 213/D2
Cabo Gracias a Dios, Nic. 203/F3
Cabo Orange, PN do, Braz. 209/H3
Cabo San Lucas, Mex. 184/C4
Cabo Verde, Braz. 213/G6
Cabonga (res.), Qu, Can. 181/J4
Caboolture, Austl. 172/D4
Cabora Bassa (lake), Moz. 163/F4
Cabora Bassa, Barragem de (dam), Moz. 163/F4
Cabot (str.), NS,NF, Can. 181/K4
Cabra, Sp. 102/C4
Cabra de Santo Cristo, Sp. 102/D4
Cabral, Serra do (range), Braz. 212/A5
Cabras, It. 104/A3
Cabrera, Isla de (isl.), Sp. 103/G3
Cabri, Sk, Can. 184/F3
Cabriel (riv.), Sp. 102/E3
Cabrillo Nat'l Mon., Ca, US 194/C5
Cabrobó, Braz. 212/C3
Cabruta, Ven. 211/E3
Cabudare, Ven. 210/D2
Cabugao, Phil. 137/D4
Cabure, Ven. 210/D2
Caçador, Braz. 213/B3
Čačak, Serb. 106/E4
Cacalotán, Mex. 200/D4
Caccia (cape), It. 104/A2
Cáceres, Braz. 208/G7
Cáceres, Sp. 102/B3
Cáceres, Col. 210/C3
Cachapoal (riv.), Chile 216/N9
Cacharí, Arg. 217/J12
Cache (peak), Id, US 184/E5
Cache (co.), Ut, US 195/K11
Cache Creek, BC, Can. 184/C3
Cache la Poudre (riv.), Co, US 195/C2
Cache Slough (riv.), Ca, US 193/L10
Cacheu, GBis. 160/A3
Cachí, Arg. 215/C2
Cachicadán, Peru 214/B3
Cachimbo, Serra do (mts.), Braz. 209/G5
Cachipo, Ven. 211/E2
Cachoeira de Minas, Braz. 213/H7
Cachoeira do Sul, Braz. 213/A4
Cachoeira Paulista, Braz. 213/H7
Cachoeiras de Macacu, Braz. 213/L7
Cachoeirinha, Braz. 213/B4
Caconde, Braz. 213/G6
Caçu, Braz. 213/B1
Caculé, Braz. 212/B4
Čadca, Slvk. 99/K4
Caddo (mts.), Ar, US 190/E3
Cadelbosco di Sopra, It. 116/D3
Cadelle (peak), It. 115/F5
Cadenberge, Ger. 109/G1
Cader Idris (peak), Wal, UK 90/C1
Cadibarrawirracanna (lake), Austl. 171/G4
Cadillac, Mi, US 188/C2
Cadiz, Phil. 139/F1
Cadiz, Ky, US 188/C4
Cádiz, Sp. 102/B4
Cádiz, Golfo de (gulf), Port.,Sp. 102/B4
Cadolzburg, Ger. 112/D4
Cadria (peak), It. 115/G6
Caen, Fr. 100/C2
Caerano di San Marco, It. 117/F1
Caernarfon (bay), Wal, UK 92/D5
Caernarfon, Wal, UK 92/D5
Caernarfon Castle, Wal, UK 92/D5
Caerphilly, Wal, UK 90/C3
Caerphilly (co.), Wal, UK 90/C3
Caesarea (ruin), Isr. 149/G6
Caesarea (ruin), Isr. 149/D3
Caetité, Braz. 212/B4
Cafarnaum, Braz. 212/B3
Cafayate, Arg. 215/C2
Cagayan Sulu (isl.), Phil. 137/C6
Cagli, It. 117/F5
Cagliari, It. 104/A3
Cagliari, Golfo di (gulf), It. 104/A3
Cagnes-sur-Mer, Fr. 101/G5
Caguán (riv.), Col. 208/D3
Caguas, PR 199/M8
Caher, Ire. 89/Q10
Cahirsiveen, Ire. 88/N11
Cahokia, Il, US 195/G8
Cahore (pt.), Ire. 89/Q10
Cahors, Fr. 100/D4
Cahuacan, Mex. 201/Q9
Cahuapanas, Peru 214/B2
Cahuinari (riv.), Col. 210/D5
Cahuita, PN, CR 203/F4
Cahul, Mol. 107/J3
Cai (riv.), Braz. 213/B4
Caia, Moz. 163/G4
Caiapó (riv.), Braz. 209/H7
Caiapó, Serra (mts.), Braz. 209/H7
Caibarién, Cuba 203/G1
Caicara, Ven. 211/F2
Caicara, Ven. 211/E3
Caicó, Braz. 212/C2
Caicos (isls.), UK 199/G3
Caicos Passage (chan.), Bahm. 203/H1
Caieiras, Braz. 213/G8
Cailloma, Peru 214/D4
Cailly (riv.), Fr. 110/A4
Caio (peak), It. 116/D4
Cairate, It. 116/B1
Cairn (mtn.), Ak, US 192/G3
Cairn Curran (dam), Austl. 173/B3
Cairn Gorm (peak), Sc, UK 94/C2
Cairn Table (peak), Sc, UK 94/B6
Cairn Toul (peak), Sc, UK 94/C2
Cairndow, Sc, UK 94/B4
Cairngorm (mts.), Sc, UK 94/B2
Cairns (int'l arpt.), Austl. 172/B2
Cairns (mt.), Austl. 171/G2
Cairns, Austl. 172/B2
Cairnsmore of Carsphairn (peak), Sc, UK 94/B6
Cairo, Ga, US 191/G4
Cairo (peak), It. 104/C2
Cairo (Al Qāhirah) (cap.), Egypt 159/B2
Cairo (int'l arpt.), Egypt 159/B2
Cairo Montenotte, It. 116/B4
Cairns (int'l arpt.), Austl. 172/B2
Cairns (mt.), Austl. 171/G2
Cairns, Austl. 172/B2
Cairnsmore of Carsphairn (peak), Sc, UK 94/B6
Cairo, Ga, US 191/G4

Cairo (peak), It. 104/C2
Cairo (Al Qāhirah) (cap.), Egypt 159/B2
Cairo (int'l arpt.), Egypt 159/B2
Cairo Montenotte, It. 116/B4
Caistor Centre, On, Can. 189/Q9
Caistorville, On, Can. 189/Q9
Caizi (lake), China 130/D5
Cajabamba, Peru 214/B2
Cajabamba, Ecu. 210/B5
Cajacay, Peru 214/B3
Cajamarca (ruin), Peru 214/B2
Cajamarca, Peru 214/B2
Cajamarca (dept.), Peru 214/B2
Cajari, Braz. 212/A1
Cajatambo, Peru 214/B3
Cajazeiras, Braz. 212/C2
Cajibío, Col. 210/B4
Cajon Junction, Ca, US 194/C2
Cajones, Cayos (isl.), Hon. 198/E4
Caju (isl.), Braz. 212/B1
Çal, Turk. 148/B2
Cala d'Oliva, It. 104/A2
Calabar, Nga. 161/H5
Calabar (int'l arpt.), Nga. 161/H5
Calabasas, Ca, US 194/B2
Calabozo, Ven. 211/E2
Calabria, PN della, It. 104/D3
Calaburras (pt.), Sp. 102/C4
Calaceite, Sp. 103/F2
Calacoto, Bol. 214/D5
Calafat, Rom. 106/F4
Calahorra, Sp. 102/E1
Calais, Me, US 189/H2
Calais, Fr. 110/A2
Calais, Canal de (canal), Fr. 110/A2
Calalaste, Sierra de (mts.), Arg. 215/C2
Calama, Chile 215/C1
Calamar, Col. 210/C2
Calamian Group (isls.), Phil. 139/E1
Calamocha, Sp. 102/E2
Calamonte, Sp. 102/B3
Calañas, Sp. 102/B4
Calanda, Sp. 103/E2
Calangianus, It. 104/A2
Calapan, Phil. 137/D5
Călăraşı (prov.), Rom. 107/H3
Călăraşi, Rom. 107/H3
Calasparra, Sp. 102/E3
Calatayud, Sp. 102/E2
Calatorao, Sp. 102/E2
Calauag, Phil. 137/D5
Calaveras (lake), Tx, US 195/U21
Calaveras (res.), Ca, US 193/L12
Calayan, Phil. 137/D4
Calayan (isl.), Phil. 137/D4
Calbayog, Phil. 137/D5
Calberlah, Ger. 109/H4
Calbuco, Chile 216/B4
Calca, Peru 214/D4
Calcanhar, Ponta do (pt.), Braz. 212/D2
Calcasieu (riv.), La, US 187/J5
Calceta, Ecu. 210/A5
Calci, It. 116/D5
Calcinate, It. 116/C1
Calcinato, It. 116/D2
Calcinelli, It. 117/F5
Calcio, It. 116/C2
Calcium, NY, US 188/F2
Calçoene, Braz. 209/H3
Calcutta (Kolkata), India 143/G4
Calcutta (Kolkata) (int'l arpt.), India 143/G4
Calcutta, Sur. 211/H3
Caldaro (Kaltern), It. 101/J3
Caldas, Braz. 213/G6
Caldas (dept.), Col. 210/C3
Caldas da Rainha, Port. 102/A3
Caldas Novas, Braz. 213/B1
Calden, Ger. 109/G6
Calder (mt.), Ak, US 192/M4
Calder (riv.), Eng, UK 93/F4
Caldera de Taburiente, PN de la, Canl., Sp. 156/A3
Calderara di Reno, It. 117/E3
Calderas, Ven. 210/D2
Caldercruix, Sc, UK 94/C5
Calderdale (co.), Eng, UK 93/F4
Caldes de Montbui, Sp. 103/L6
Caldew (riv.), Eng, UK 93/F2
Caldicot, Wal, UK 90/D3
Caldiero, It. 117/E2
Çaldıran, Turk. 148/E2
Caldonazzo, It. 115/H6
Caldono, Col. 210/B4
Caldwell, NJ, US 197/H8
Caldwell, Tx, US 187/H5
Caldwell, Wi, US 193/P14
Caldy (isl.), Eng, UK 90/B3
Caledon, NI, UK 92/B3
Caledon (riv.), SAfr. 164/D3
Caledon, SAfr. 164/L11
Caledonia (hills), NB, Can. 189/H2
Caledonia, Wi, US 193/P14
Caledonian (canal), Sc, UK 94/B2
Calella, Sp. 103/G2
Calen, Austl. 172/C3
Calenzana, Fr. 104/A1
Calenzano, It. 117/E5
Calera de Tango, Chile 216/N8
Calestano, It. 116/D3
Caleta de Campos, Mex. 200/E5
Caleta Olivia, Arg. 216/D5
Calexico, Ca, US 186/D4
Calf of Man (isl.), IM, UK 92/C3
Calf, The (peak), Eng, UK 93/F3
Calgary (int'l arpt.), Ab, Can. 184/E3
Calgary, Ab, Can. 184/E3
Calheta, Azor., Port. 103/S12
Calhoun, Ga, US 191/G3
Calhoun (co.), Il, US 195/F7
Calhoun, Ky, US 188/C4
Cali, Col. 210/B4
Calicut (Kozhikode), India 140/C5
Calida, Costa (coast), Sp. 102/E4
Caliente, Nv, US 186/D3
Califon, NJ, US 196/D2
California (gulf), Mex. 200/B2
California (state), US 186/B3
California, Md, US 188/E4
California, Mo, US 187/J3
Calilegua, PN, Arg. 215/D1
Călimăneşti, Rom. 107/G3
Calimaya, Mex. 201/Q10
Calimere (pt.), India 140/C5
Calimesa, Ca, US 194/C2
Calitri, It. 104/D2
Calixa-Lavallée, Qu, Can. 189/P6
Calizzano, It. 116/B4
Calkiní, Mex. 202/D1
Calkins (lake), Co, US 195/B2
Çalköy, Turk. 148/B2
Callabonna (lake), Austl. 173/A1
Callahonna (lake), Austl. 167/D3
Callalli, Peru 214/D4
Callan, Ire. 89/Q10
Callander, Sc, UK 94/B4
Callantsoog, Neth. 108/B3
Callao, Peru 214/B4
Callapa, Bol. 214/D5
Callaway, Fl, US 191/G4
Calle Larga, Chile 216/N8
Calliope, Austl. 172/C4
Callosa de Segura, Sp. 103/E3
Calne, Eng, UK 90/E4
Calolziocorte, It. 116/C1
Calonne-Ricouart, Fr. 110/B3
Calore (riv.), It. 104/D2
Caloundra, Austl. 172/D4
Calpe, Sp. 103/F3
Calpulálpan, Mex. 201/L7
Caltagirone, It. 104/D4
Caltanissetta, It. 104/D4
Caltavuturo, It. 104/C4
Caluire-et-Cuire, Fr. 100/F4
Calumet (riv.), Il, US 193/Q16
Calumet Sag (chan.), Il, US 193/Q16
Caluso, It. 116/A2
Calvello, It. 104/D2
Calvenzano, It. 116/C2
Calvert (isl.), BC, Can. 184/A3
Calvert, Tx, US 187/H5
Calverton, Md, US 196/B5
Calvi (peak), It. 117/E4
Calvi, Fr. 104/A1
Calviá, Sp. 103/G3
Calvillo, Mex. 200/E4
Calvinia, SAfr. 164/B3
Calvisano, It. 116/D2
Calvitero (peak), Sp. 102/C2
Calw, Ger. 112/B5
Calzada de Calatrava, Sp. 102/D3
Cam or Rhee (riv.), Eng, UK 91/F2
Cam Pha, Viet. 136/D1
Cam Ranh, Viet. 136/E4
Camaçari, Braz. 212/C4
Camacho, Mex. 200/E3
Camacupa, Ang. 163/C3
Camaguán, Ven. 211/E2
Camagüey (arch.), Cuba 199/F3
Camagüey, Cuba 203/G1
Camaiore, It. 116/D5
Camajuaní, Cuba 203/G1
Camalu, Mex. 200/A2
Camamu, Braz. 212/C4
Camamu, Baía de (bay), Braz. 212/C4
Camaná, Peru 214/C5
Camanducaia, Braz. 213/G7
Camaquã, Braz. 213/B4
Camaquã (riv.), Braz. 213/A4
Camargo, Sp. 102/D1
Camarillo, Ca, US 194/A2
Camariñas, Sp. 102/A1
Camarón (cape), Hon. 203/E3
Camarones (bay), Arg. 216/D5
Camarones, Arg. 216/D5
Camas, Sp. 102/B4
Cambados, Sp. 102/A1
Cambará, Braz. 213/B2
Cambay, Gulf of (gulf), India 140/B3
Cambé, Braz. 213/B2
Camberley, Eng, UK 88/A3
Cambiano, It. 116/A3
Cambodia (ctry.) 141/H5
Camboriú, Ponta do (pt.), Braz. 213/C3
Cambrai, Fr. 110/C3
Cambrian (mts.), Wal, UK 92/E5
Cambridge, Eng, UK 91/G2
Cambridge (int'l arpt.), Eng, UK 91/G2
Cambridge, NZ 175/T10
Cambridge, Ma, US 189/G3
Cambridge, Md, US 188/E4
Cambridge, Oh, US 188/D3
Cambridge, On, Can. 188/D3
Cambridge Bay, Nun., Can. 180/F2
Cambridgeshire (co.), Eng, UK 91/F2
Cambrils, Sp. 103/F2
Cambuí, Braz. 213/G7
Cambuquira, Braz. 213/H6
Cambuslang, Sc, UK 94/B5
Cambutal (mtn.), Pan. 210/A3
Camden, Austl. 172/G9
Camden (co.), Eng, UK 88/C2
Camden, Al, US 191/G4
Camden, De, US 196/C5
Camden, Me, US 189/G2
Camden, NJ, US 196/C4
Camden (co.), NJ, US 196/C4
Camden, SC, US 191/H3
Camden Haven, Austl. 173/E1
Camden Point, Mo, US 195/D5
Cameia, PN da, Ang. 163/D3
Camel (riv.), Eng, UK 90/B6
Camelback (mtn.), Pa, US 196/C1
Camerano, It. 117/G5
Cameri, It. 116/B2
Cameron (isl.), Nun., Can. 181/R7
Cameron, Mo, US 187/J3
Cameron, Tx, US 187/H5
Cameroon (ctry.) 154/H7
Cametá, Braz. 209/J4
Camicia (peak), It. 104/C1
Camiguin (isl.), Phil. 137/D4
Camilla, Ga, US 191/G4
Camilo Aldao, Arg. 216/E2
Caminha, Port. 102/A2
Camiri, Bol. 208/F8
Camisano Vicentino, It. 117/E1
Çamlıdere, Turk. 148/C1
Çamlık NP, Turk. 148/C2
Çamlıyayla, Turk. 149/D1
Camoapa, Nic. 203/E3
Camogli, It. 116/C4
Camon, Fr. 110/B4
Camorta (isl.), India 141/F6
Camp Angelus (Angelus Oaks), Ca, US 194/D2
Camp Creek, Az, US 195/S18
Camp Hill, Pa, US 196/B3
Camp Lake, Wi, US 193/P14
Camp Springs, Md, US 196/B6
Campagna Lupia, It. 117/F2
Campagnola Emilia, It. 117/D3
Campana, Arg. 217/J11
Campana (isl.), Chile 217/B6
Campana, PN de la, Chile 216/N8
Campanario, Sp. 102/C3
Campanario (peak), Arg. 216/C2
Campanella (cape), It. 104/D2
Campanha, Braz. 213/H6
Campania (prov.), It. 104/D2
Campbell, Ca, US 193/L12
Campbell (isl.), NZ 81/T8
Campbell River, BC, Can. 184/B3
Campbell Town, Austl. 173/C4
Campbellsville, Ky, US 188/C4
Campbellton, NB, Can. 189/H1
Campbeltown, Sc, UK 89/R9
Campden, On, Can. 189/R9
Campeche (state), Mex. 198/C4
Campeche, Mex. 202/D2
Campeche (bay), Mex. 201/G5
Camperdown, Austl. 173/B3
Camperville, Mb, Can. 185/H3
Campestre, Braz. 213/G6
Campi Bisenzio, It. 117/E5
Campidano (range), It. 104/A3
Campillo de Altobuey, Sp. 102/E3
Campillos, Sp. 102/C4
Campina Verde, Braz. 213/B1
Campinas, Braz. 213/F7
Campion, Co, US 195/B2
Campione d'Italia, It. 115/E6
Campo (int'l arpt.), Braz. 214/C2
Campo Belo, Braz. 213/C2
Campo de Criptana, Sp. 102/D3
Campo de la Cruz, Col. 210/C2
Campo dei Fiori (peak), It. 116/B1
Campo Grande, Braz. 209/H8
Campo Ligure, It. 116/B3
Campo Limpo Paulista, Braz. 213/G8
Campo Maior, Port. 102/B3
Campo Mourão, Braz. 213/A3
Campo Tencia (peak), Swi. 115/E5
Campo Tizzoro, It. 117/D4
Campoalegre, Col. 210/C4
Campobasso, It. 104/D2
Campodarsego, It. 117/E2
Campodolcino, It. 115/F5
Campogalliano, It. 117/D3
Campomorone, It. 116/B3
Camponogara, It. 117/F2
Camporosso, It. 116/A5
Camporredondo, Peru 214/B2
Camporredondo, Embalse de (res.), Sp. 102/C1
Campos (phys. reg.), Braz. 205/D5
Campos Altos, Braz. 213/C1
Campos Belos, Braz. 212/A4
Campos de Hielo Norte (glacier), Chile 217/B5
Campos de Hielo Sur (glacier), Chile 217/B6
Campos del Puerto, Sp. 103/G3
Campos do Jordão, Braz. 213/H7
Campos Gerais, Braz. 213/C2
Campos Novos, Braz. 213/B3
Campos Sales, Braz. 212/B2
Camposampiero, It. 117/E1
Camposanto, It. 117/E3
Campsie Fells (hills), Sc, UK 94/B4
Campti, La, US 190/E4
Camrose, Ab, Can. 184/E2
Çan, Turk. 107/H5
Can (riv.), Eng, UK 88/E1
Can Tho, Viet. 136/D4
Canaçari (lake), Braz. 211/G5
Canada (ctry.) 180
Cañada de Gómez, Arg. 216/E2
Cañada Nieto, Uru. 217/J10
Cañada Rosquín, Arg. 216/E2
Canadensis, Pa, US 196/C1
Canadian (riv.), US 187/F3
Canadian (co.), Ok, US 195/M15
Canadian, Tx, US 187/G4
Canadian, North (riv.), Ok, US 187/H3
Cañadon Grande (mts.), Arg. 216/C5
Cañadón Seco, Arg. 216/D5
Canaima, PN, Ven. 208/F2
Çanakkale, Turk. 105/K2
Çanakkale (prov.), Turk. 148/A2
Canal de Moraleda (chan.), Chile 215/B6
Canalbianco (riv.), It. 117/E2
Canale, It. 116/A3
Canale Cavour (canal), It. 116/B2
Canals, Sp. 103/E3
Canals, Arg. 216/E2
Canandaigua, NY, US 188/E3
Cananea, Mex. 200/C2
Cananéia, Braz. 213/C3
Canápolis, Braz. 213/B1
Cañar, Ecu. 214/B1
Cañar (dept.), Ecu. 210/B5
Canard (riv.), On, Can. 193/G7
Canary (isls.), Canl., Sp. 156/A3
Cañas, CR 203/E4
Cañasgordas, Col. 210/B3
Canatlán de las Manzanas, Mex. 200/D3
Canaveral (cape), Fl, US 191/H4
Canberra, Austl. 173/D2
Canchaque, Peru 214/B2
Canche (riv.), Fr. 100/E1
Cancún, Mex. 202/E1
Cancun (int'l arpt.), Mex. 202/E1
Candado, Nevado del (peak), Arg. 215/C2
Candarave, Peru 214/D5
Çandarli (gulf), Gre.,Turk. 148/A2
Candás, Sp. 102/C1
Candeias, Braz. 212/C4
Candelaria, Mex. 202/D2
Candelaria (riv.), Mex. 202/D2
Candelaria, Arg. 216/D2
Candeleda, Sp. 102/C2
Candelo, Austl. 173/D3
Candelo, It. 116/B1
Candia Lomellina, It. 116/B2
Candiac, Qu, Can. 189/N7
Candiba, Braz. 212/B4
Cândido Mota, Braz. 213/B2
Canding (cape), Indo. 138/D5
Çandır, Turk. 148/C2
Candlewood, NJ, US 196/D3
Cando, ND, US 185/J3
Candon, Phil. 137/D4
Canegrate, It. 116/B1
Canela, Braz. 213/B4
Canelli, It. 116/B3
Canelones (dept.), Uru. 217/F2
Canelones, Uru. 217/K11
Cañete, Sp. 102/E2
Canete, Río de (riv.), Peru 214/B4
Cangallo, Peru 214/C4
Cangas, Sp. 102/A1
Cangas de Narcea, Sp. 102/B1
Cangas de Onís, Sp. 102/C1
Cangkuang (cape), Indo. 138/C5
Cango Caves, SAfr. 164/C4
Cangrejo (peak), Arg. 217/B6
Cangshan, China 130/D4
Canguaretama, Braz. 212/D2
Canguçu, Braz. 213/A4
Cangwu, China 141/K3
Cangyuan (Cangyuan Vazu Zizhixian), China 141/G3
Cangzhou, China 130/D3
Canh Cuoc (isl.), Viet. 136/D1
Cania Gorge NP, Austl. 172/C4
Caniapiscau (lake), Qu, Can. 181/K3
Caniapiskau (riv.), Qu, Can. 181/J3
Canicatti, It. 104/C4
Canik (mts.), Turk. 148/C1
Caniles, Sp. 102/D4
Canindé (riv.), Braz. 209/K5
Canino, It. 104/B1
Canistear (res.), NJ, US 197/H7
Cañitas de Felipe Pescador, Mex. 200/E4
Canjáyar, Sp. 102/D4
Çankırı, Turk. 148/C1
Çankırı (prov.), Turk. 148/C1
Canlaon (vol.), Phil. 139/F1
Canmore, Ab, Can. 184/E3
Cann River, Austl. 173/D3
Canna (isl.), Sc, UK 89/Q8
Cannanore, India 140/C5
Canne (ruin), It. 104/E2
Canner (riv.), Fr. 111/F5
Cannero Riviera, It. 115/E5
Cannes, Fr. 101/G5
Canneto sull'Oglio, It. 116/D2
Canning (peak), Austl. 170/C4
Canning (dam), Austl. 170/L7
Canning (riv.), Austl. 170/K7
Cannobio, It. 115/E5
Cannock, Eng, UK 90/D1
Cannon Falls, Mn, US 185/K4
Cannonball (riv.), ND, US 185/H4
Cannondale, Ct, US 197/E1
Cannonvale, Austl. 172/C3
Caño Guaritico (riv.), Ven. 210/D3
Caño Negro NWF, CR 203/E4
Canoas, Braz. 213/B4
Canoas (riv.), Braz. 213/B3
Canobolas (mt.), Austl. 173/D2
Canoinhas, Braz. 213/B3
Cañón de Río Blanco, PN, Mex. 201/M8
Cañón del Sumidero, PN, Mex. 202/C2
Canora, Sk, Can. 185/H3
Canosa di Puglia, It. 104/E2
Canouan (isl.), StV. 199/N9
Canowindra, Austl. 173/D2
Cansanção, Braz. 212/C3
Canso (cape), NS, Can. 189/J2
Canta, Peru 214/B3
Cantabria (aut. comm.), Sp. 102/C1
Cantabria, Cordillera (mts.), Sp. 102/B1
Cantal, Massif du (mass.), Fr. 100/E4
Cantalejo, Sp. 102/D2
Cantanhede, Braz. 212/A1
Cantanhede, Port. 102/A2
Cantaura, Ven. 211/E2
Canterbury, Eng, UK 91/H4
Canterbury Bight (bay), NZ 175/S11
Canterbury Cathedral, Eng, UK 91/H4
Cantillana, Sp. 102/C4
Canto do Buriti, Braz. 212/B3
Canton, Mi, US 193/E7
Canton, Ms, US 187/K4
Canton, NJ, US 196/C5
Canton, NY, US 188/F2
Canton, Oh, US 188/D3
Canton, Ok, US 190/D2
Canton (Abariringa) (isl.), Kiri. 175/H5
Cantoria, Sp. 102/D4
Cantù, It. 116/C1
Cantwell, Ak, US 192/J3
Cañuelas, Arg. 217/J11
Canunda NP, Austl. 173/B3
Canvey (isl.), Eng, UK 88/E2
Canvey Island, Eng, UK 91/G3
Canwood, Sk, Can. 184/G2
Canyon, Tx, US 187/G4
Canyon (lake), Tx, US 195/U20
Canyon de Chelly Nat'l Mon., Az, US 186/E3
Canyon Lake, Tx, US 195/U20
Canyonlands Nat'l Park, Ut, US 186/E3
Canyon of the Ancients Nat'l Mon., Co, US 186/E3
Canzo, It. 116/C1
Cao (riv.), China 131/C2
Cao Bang, Viet. 141/J3
Cao Lanh, Viet. 136/D4
Cao Xian, China 130/C4
Caodu (riv.), China 137/A2
Caorle, It. 117/F1
Caorso, It. 116/C2
Cap-Chat, Qu, Can. 189/H1
Cap d'Agde (cape), Fr. 100/E5
Cap-de-la-Madeleine, Qu, Can. 189/F2
Cap-Haïtien, Haiti 203/H2
Cap Rock Escarpment (cliff), Tx, US 190/C3
Cap-Rouge, Qu, Can. 189/G2
Cap Roux, Pointe du (pt.), Fr. 101/G5
Capac, Mi, US 193/G5
Capanaparo (riv.), Ven. 208/E2
Capanema, Braz. 209/J4
Capanne (peak), It. 104/B1
Capannoli, It. 117/D5
Capannori, It. 116/D5
Capão Bonito, Braz. 213/B3
Capão Doce, Morro do (hill), Braz. 213/B3
Caparaó, PN do, Braz. 213/D2
Caparica, Port. 103/P10
Caparo (riv.), Ven. 210/D3
Capay, Ca, US 193/K9
Capbreton, Fr. 100/C5
Capdenac-Gare, Fr. 100/E4
Capdepera, Sp. 103/G3
Cape Arid NP, Austl. 170/D5
Cape Barren (isl.), Austl. 167/D5
Cape Breton (isl.), NS, Can. 189/J2
Cape Breton Highlands (uplands), NS, Can. 189/J2
Cape Breton Highlands NP, NS, Can. 189/J2
Cape Cleveland NP, Austl. 172/B2
Cape Coast, Gha. 161/E5
Cape Cod Nat'l Seashore, Ma, US 189/G3
Cape Coral, Fl, US 191/H5
Cape Dorset, Nun., Can. 181/J2
Cape Fear (riv.), NC, US 191/J3
Cape Hatteras Nat'l Seashore, NC, US 191/K3
Cape Krusenstern Nat'l Mon., Ak, US 192/E2
Cape Le Grand NP, Austl. 170/D5
Cape Lookout Nat'l Seashore, NC, US 191/J3
Cape May, NJ, US 196/D6
Cape May (co.), NJ, US 196/D5
Cape May Court House, NJ, US 196/D5
Cape May Lighthouse, NJ, US 196/D6
Cape Melville NP, Austl. 172/B1
Cape Palmerston NP, Austl. 172/C3
Cape Range NP, Austl. 170/B2
Cape Saint Claire, Md, US 196/B5
Cape Town (cap.), SAfr. 164/L10
Cape Town (D.F. Malan) (int'l arpt.), SAfr. 164/L10
Cape Tribulation NP, Austl. 172/B2
Cape Upstart NP, Austl. 172/B2
Cape Verde (ctry.) 151/J9
Cape Yakataga, Ak, US 192/K3
Cape York (pen.), Austl. 167/D2
Capel, Austl. 170/B5
Capela, Braz. 212/C3
Capelinha, Braz. 212/B5
Capella, Austl. 172/C3
Capellades, Sp. 103/K6
Capestang, Fr. 100/E5
Capicciola (pt.), Fr. 104/A2
Capilla del Señor, Arg. 217/J11
Capim (riv.), Braz. 209/J4
Capinópolis, Braz. 213/B1
Capirara (res.), Braz. 215/F1
Capistrano, Braz. 212/C2
Capistrello, It. 104/C2
Capitan (mts.), NM, US 190/B3
Capitão de Campos, Braz. 212/B2
Capitão Poço, Braz. 209/J4
Capitol Reef NP, Ut, US 186/E3
Capivara, Represa (res.), Braz. 209/H8
Capivara, Serra de (range), Braz. 212/A4
Capivari (riv.), Braz. 213/J6
Capljina, Bosn. 105/E1
Caplone (peak), It. 116/D1
Capo di Ponte, It. 115/G5
Capo d'Orlando, It. 104/D3
Capodichino (int'l arpt.), It. 104/D2
Capolona, It. 117/E5
Capoterra, It. 104/A3
Cappella Maggiore, It. 117/F1
Cappoquin, Ire. 89/Q10
Capraia (isl.), It. 104/A1
Caprarola, It. 104/C1
Capreol, On, Can. 188/D2
Capricorn (chan.), Austl. 167/E3
Capricorn (cape), Austl. 172/C3
Caprino Veronese, It. 117/D1
Capriolo, It. 116/C1
Caprivi Strip (reg.), Namb. 163/D4
Captain (har.), Ct, US 197/L7
Captain Cook, Hi, US 182/U11
Captainganj, India 142/D2
Captains Flat, Austl. 173/D2
Capua, It. 106/B5
Capulhuac, Mex. 201/Q10
Capulhuac, Mex. 201/Q10
Caputh, Ger. 98/Q7
Caquetá (riv.), Col. 210/D5
Caquetá (dept.), Col. 210/C4
Caquiaviri, Bol. 214/D5
Car Nicobar (isl.), India 141/F6
Carabobo (state), Ven. 210/D2
Caracal, Rom. 107/G3
Caracaraí, Braz. 211/F4
Caracas (cap.), Ven. 208/E1
Carache, Ven. 210/D2
Caracol, Braz. 212/B3
Caracolí, Col. 210/C3
Carácuaro de Morelos, Mex. 201/E5
Caradon (hill), Eng, UK 90/B5
Caraguatatuba, Braz. 213/H8
Caraguatatuba, Enseada de (bay), Braz. 213/H8
Carahue, Chile 216/B3
Carajás, Serra dos (mts.), Braz. 209/H5
Caranavi, Bol. 208/E7
Carandaí, Braz. 213/D2
Carangola, Braz. 213/D2
Caransebeş, Rom. 106/F3
Carapicuíba, Braz. 213/G8
Carappee Hill (peak), Austl. 171/H5
Caraquet, NB, Can. 189/H2
Caraş-Severin (prov.), Rom. 106/E3
Carasco, It. 116/C4
Caratasca (lag.), Hon. 198/E4
Carate Brianza, It. 116/C1
Caratinga, Braz. 213/D1
Carauari, Braz. 208/E4
Caraúbas, Braz. 212/C2
Caravaca de la Cruz, Sp. 102/E3
Caravaggio, It. 116/C2
Caravela, Ilha (isl.), GBis. 160/A4
Caravelas, Braz. 212/C5
Caravelí, Peru 214/C4
Caraz, Peru 214/B3
Carazinho, Braz. 215/F2
Carballino, Sp. 102/A1
Carballo, Sp. 102/A1
Carberry, Mb, Can. 185/J3
Carbo, Mex. 200/C2
Carbon (cape), Alg. 158/H4
Carbon (co.), Pa, US 196/C2
Carbon (riv.), Wa, US 193/C3
Carbonara (cape), It. 104/A3
Carbonara (peak), It. 104/D4
Carbondale, Pa, US 188/F3
Carbonear, Nf, Can. 189/L2
Carbonera, It. 117/F1
Carboneras, Mex. 201/F3
Carbonia, It. 104/A3
Carbonne, Fr. 100/D5
Carbost, Sc, UK 89/Q8
Carcagente, Sp. 103/E3
Carcarañá, Arg. 216/E2
Carcare, It. 116/B4
Carcassonne, Fr. 100/E5
Carche (peak), Sp. 102/E3
Carchi (dept.), Ecu. 210/B4
Carcross, Yk, Can. 192/M3
Çardak, Turk. 107/H5
Cardal, Uru. 217/K11
Cardedeu, Sp. 103/L6
Cárdenas, Mex. 201/F4
Cárdenas, Cuba 203/F1
Cárdenas, Mex. 202/C2
Cardenden, Sc, UK 94/C4
Cardiel (lake), Arg. 217/C6
Cardiff (cap.), Wal, UK 90/C4
Cardiff (co.), Wal, UK 90/C4
Cardiff, Md, US 196/B4
Cardiff by the Sea, Ca, US 194/C4
Cardigan, Wal, UK 90/B2
Cardona, Sp. 103/F2
Cardona, Uru. 217/K10
Cardoso, Braz. 213/B2
Cardozo, Uru. 217/K10
Cardston, Ab, Can. 184/E3
Cardwell, Austl. 172/B2
Care Alto (peak), It. 115/G5
Careaçu, Braz. 213/H7
Carefree, Az, US 195/S18
Carei, Rom. 99/M5
Carentan, Fr. 100/C2
Carev vrh (peak), FYROM 105/H1
Carey (lake), Austl. 167/B3
Carhaix-Plouguer, Fr. 100/B2
Carhuamayo, Peru 214/B3
Carhuaz, Peru 214/B3
Carhué, Arg. 216/E3
Cariacica, Braz. 213/D2
Cariaco, Ven. 211/F2
Cariamanga, Ecu. 214/B2
Cariati, It. 104/E3
Caribbean (sea), NAm,SAm. 177/L8
Cariboo (mts.), BC, Can. 184/C2
Caribou, Me, US 189/G2
Caribou (range), Id, US 184/F5
Caribou (mts.), Ab, Can. 180/E3
Caridade, Braz. 212/C2
Carigara, Phil. 137/D5
Carignan, Qu, Can. 189/P7
Carignan, Fr. 111/E4
Carignano, It. 116/A3
Cariñena, Sp. 102/E2
Carinhanha, Braz. 212/B4
Carinhanha (riv.), Braz. 212/A4
Carini, It. 104/C3
Caripito, Ven. 211/F2
Caririaçu, Braz. 212/C2
Cariris Novos, Serra dos (mts.), Braz. 212/B2
Carleton (mt.), NB, Can. 189/H2
Carleton (riv.), NS, Can. 189/H2
Carleton, Qu, Can. 189/H1
Carleton, Mi, US 193/F7
Carleton Place, On, Can. 188/E2
Carletonville, SAfr. 164/D2
Carlin, Nv, US 184/D5
Carlindie Abor. Land, Austl. 170/C2
Carling, Fr. 111/F5
Carlingford, Ire. 92/B3
Carlingford (lake), Ire. 92/B3
Carlingford (mtn.), Ire. 92/B3
Carlinville, Il, US 187/K3
Carlisle, Pa, US 188/E3
Carlisle, La, US 195/Q17
Carlisle, Eng, UK 93/F2
Carlisle Barracks Mil. Res., Pa, US 196/A3
Carlit (peak), Fr. 100/D5
Carlos Casares, Arg. 216/E2
Carlos Chagas, Braz. 212/B5
Carlos M. de Cespedes, Cuba 203/G1
Carlow, Ire. 89/Q10
Carlow (co.), Ire. 92/B6
Carloway, Sc, UK 89/Q7
Carlsbad, Ca, US 194/C4
Carlsbad, NM, US 187/F4
Carlsbad Caverns NP, NM, US 187/F4
Carlsberg, Ger. 112/B3
Carlsfeld, Ger. 113/F2
Carlton, Eng, UK 93/G6
Carluke, Sc, UK 94/C5
Carlyle (lake), Il, US 187/K3
Carlyle, Sk, Can. 185/H3
Carmacks, Yk, Can. 192/L3
Carmagnola, It. 116/A3
Carman, Mb, Can. 185/J3
Carmarthen, Wal, UK 90/B3
Carmarthen (bay), Wal, UK 90/B3
Carmarthenshire (co.) Wal, UK 90/B3
Carmaux, Fr. 100/E4
Carmel (pt.), Wal, UK 92/D5
Carmelo, Uru. 217/J11
Carmen (isl.), Mex. 202/C2
Carmen (riv.), Mex. 190/B4
Carmen de Patagones, Arg. 216/E4
Carmensa, Arg. 216/D2
Carmo, Braz. 213/L6
Carmo (peak), It. 116/B4
Carmo da Cachoeira, Braz. 213/H6
Carmo de Minas, Braz. 213/H7
Carmo do Paranaíba, Braz. 213/C1
Carmo do Rio Claro, Braz. 213/C2
Carmona, Sp. 102/C4
Carn Ban (peak), Sc, UK 94/B2
Carn Easgann Bàna (peak), Sc, UK 94/B2
Càrn Eige (peak), Sc, UK 94/A2
Carn Glas-choire (peak), Sc, UK 94/C2
Carn Kitty (hill), Sc, UK 94/C2
Carn Mairg (peak), Sc, UK 94/B3
Carn Mór (peak), Sc, UK 94/C2
Carn na Cailliche (hill), Sc, UK 94/C1
Carn na Saobhaidhe (peak), Sc, UK 94/B2
Carnago, It. 116/B1
Carnamah, Austl. 170/B4
Carnarvon, Austl. 167/A3
Carnarvon NP, Austl. 172/B4
Carnarvon, SAfr. 164/C3
Carnarvonleegte (riv.), SAfr. 164/C3
Carnation, Wa, US 193/D2
Carnaubal, Braz. 212/B2
Carnaxide, Port. 103/P10
Carncastle, NI, UK 92/C2
Carndonagh, Ire. 92/A1

Carnduff, Sk, Can. 185/H3
Carnedd Llewelyn (peak), Wal, UK 92/E5
Carnegie (lake), Austl. 167/B3
Carney, Ok, US 195/N14
Carney (isl.), Ant. 218/S
Carnforth, Eng, UK 93/F3
Carnlough, NI, UK 92/B2
Carnot (cape), Austl. 171/G5
Carnot, CAfr. 154/J7
Carnota, Sp. 102/A1
Carnsore (pt.), Ire. 89/Q10
Carnwath (riv.), NW, Can. 180/D2
Carnwath, Sc, UK 94/C5
Caro, Mi, US 188/D3
Carol Stream, Il, US 193/P16
Carolina, Braz. 212/A2
Carolina, PR 199/M8
Carolina, SAfr. 165/E2
Carolina Beach, NC, US 191/J3
Caroline (isl.), Kiri. 175/K5
Caroline (isls), Micr. 174/D4
Caroní (riv.), Ven. 205/C2
Carora, Ven. 210/D2
Carouge, Swi. 114/C5
Carpaneto Piacentino, It. 116/C3
Carpathian (mts.), Eur. 85/G4
Carpegna (peak), It. 117/F5
Carpegna, It. 117/F5
Carpenedolo, It. 116/D2
Carpentaria, Gulf of (gulf), Austl. 167/C2
Carpenter, Il, US 195/H8
Carpentersville, Il, US 193/P15
Carpentras, Fr. 100/F4
Carpi, It. 117/D3
Carpignano Sesia, It. 116/B1
Carpina, Braz. 212/D2
Carpinteria, Ca, US 194/A2
Carpiquet (int'l arpt.), Fr. 100/C2
Carr (inlet), Wa, US 193/B3
Carrabelle, Fl, US 191/G4
Carrantuohill (peak), Ire. 89/P10
Carrara, It. 116/D4
Carrasco (int'l arpt.), Uru. 217/K11
Carrasquero, Ven. 210/D2
Carreg Ddu (pt.), Wal, UK 92/D6
Carriacou (isl.), Gren. 208/F1
Carrick (reg.), Sc, UK 94/B6
Carrick on Shannon, Ire. 89/P10
Carrick on Suir, Ire. 89/Q10
Carrickalinga, Austl. 171/H5
Carrickfergus, NI, UK 92/C2
Carrickfergus (dist.), NI, UK 92/C2
Carrickmacross, Ire. 89/Q10
Carrickmore, NI, UK 92/A2
Carrières-sous-Poissy, Fr. 88/J5
Carrigaholt, Ire. 89/P10
Carrigaline, Ire. 89/P11
Carrington, ND, US 185/J4
Carrión (riv.), Sp. 102/C1
Carrión de los Condes, Sp. 102/C1
Carrizo (mts.), Az, US 182/D4
Carrizo Plain Nat'l Mon. Ca, US 186/C4
Carrizo Springs, Tx, US 190/D4
Carrizo Wash (riv.), Az,NM, US 186/E4
Carrizozo, NM, US 187/F4
Carroll (co.), Md, US 196/A5
Carrollton, Ky, US 188/C4
Carrollton, Ga, US 191/G3
Carron (lake), Sc, UK 94/A2
Carron (riv.), Sc, UK 94/A2
Carrot (riv.), Sk, Can. 185/H2
Carrot River, Sk, Can. 185/H2
Carrowdore, NI, UK 92/C2
Carrowkeel, Ire. 92/A1
Carrù, It. 116/A4
Carrum Downs, Austl. 173/G6
Carryduff, NI, UK 92/C2
Çarşamba, Turk. 148/D1
Carse of Forth (plain), Sc, UK 94/B4
Carse of Gowrie (plain), Sc, UK 94/C4
Carson (riv.), Nv, US 186/C3
Carson, Ca, US 194/F8
Carson City (cap.), Nv, US 186/C3
Carson Sink (dry lake), Nv, US 186/C3
Carstairs, Ab, Can. 184/E3
Cartagena, Chile 216/N8
Cartagena, Col. 210/C2
Cartagena, Sp. 103/E4
Cartago, Col. 208/C3
Cartago, CR 203/F4
Cártama, Sp. 102/C4
Cartaya, Sp. 102/B4
Carter Bar (hill), Eng, UK 94/D6
Carter Lake (res.), Co, US 195/B2
Carteret, NJ, US 197/J9
Cartersville, Ga, US 191/G3
Carterton, Eng, UK 91/E3
Carthage (int'l arpt.), Tun. 158/M6
Carthage, Mo, US 187/J3
Carthage, Ms, US 191/F3
Carthage, Tn, US 188/C4
Carthage, Tx, US 187/J4
Carthage (Qarṭājannah) (ruin), Tun. 158/M6
Cartí (mtn.), Pan. 210/B2
Cartier Islet (isl.), Austl. 167/B2
Cartwright, Nf, Can. 181/L3
Caruaru, Braz. 212/D3
Carumás, Peru 214/D5
Carúpano, Ven. 211/F2
Caruthersville, Mo, US 187/K3
Carvico, It. 116/C1
Carvin, Fr. 110/B3
Carvoeiro (cape), Port. 102/A3
Cary, NC, US 191/J3
Cary, Il, US 193/P15
Casa Blanca (canal), Az, US 195/S19
Casa Branca, Braz. 213/F6
Casa de Piedra (res.), Arg. 216/D3
Casa Grande, Az, US 186/E4
Casa Grande Nat'l Mon., Az, US 186/E4
Casa Nova, Braz. 212/B3
Casablanca, Chile 216/N8
Casablanca-Anfa (prov.), Mor. 158/A2
Casal di Principe, It. 104/D2
Casalbordino, It. 104/D1
Casalbuttano, It. 116/C2
Casale di Scodosia, It. 117/E2
Casale Monferrato, It. 116/B2
Casale sul Sile, It. 117/F1
Casalecchio di Reno, It. 117/E4
Casaleone, It. 117/E2
Casalmaggiore, It. 116/D3
Casalpusterlengo, It. 116/C2
Casalserugo, It. 117/E2
Casamance (riv.), Sen. 160/A3
Casanare (riv.), Col. 208/D2
Casanare (dept.), Col. 210/D3
Casanay, Ven. 211/F2
Casar de Cáceres, Sp. 102/B3
Casarano, It. 105/F2
Casarsa della Delizia, It. 117/F1
Casarza Ligure, It. 116/C4
Casas Grande (riv.), Mex. 186/E5
Casas Grandes, Mex. 200/D2
Casas Grandes (ruin), Mex. 200/C2
Casas-Ibáñez, Sp. 102/E3
Ca'Savio, It. 117/F2
Casazza, It. 116/C1
Cascada de Bassaseachic, PN, Mex. 200/C2
Cascade (res.), Id, US 184/D4
Cascade (range), Or,Wa, US 184/C5
Cascade Caverns, Tx, US 195/T20
Cascade-Fairwood, Or, US 193/C3
Cascade-Siskiyou Nat'l Mon., Or, US 184/C5
Cascades (pt.), Reun., Fr. 165/S15
Cascais, Port. 103/P10
Cascapédia (riv.), Qu, Can. 189/H1
Cascas, Peru 214/B2
Cascavel, Braz. 215/F1
Cascavel, Braz. 212/C2
Casciago, It. 116/B1
Casciana Terme, It. 116/D5
Cascina, It. 116/D5
Case (inlet), Wa, US 193/B3
Casella, It. 116/B3
Caselle, It. 117/E2
Casentino (valley), It. 117/E5
Caserta, It. 104/D2
Casey (bay), Ant. 218/D
Casey, Austl., Ant. 218/H
Caseyr (cape), Som. 155/R5
Caseyville, Il, US 195/G8
Cashel, Ire. 89/Q10
Cashion, Ok, US 195/M14
Cashmere, Wa, US 184/C4
Cashtown, Pa, US 196/A4
Casigua, Ven. 210/C2
Casilda (pt.), Cuba 203/F1
Casilda, Arg. 216/E2
Casimiro Castillo, Mex. 200/D5
Casina, It. 116/D3
Casinalbo, It. 117/D3
Casino, Austl. 173/E1
Casino and Opera House, Mona. 116/J8
Casitas (lake), Ca, US 194/A2
Casitas Springs, Ca, US 194/A2
Casma, Peru 214/B3
Casnigo, It. 116/C1
Casole d'Elsa, It. 117/E6
Casorate Primo, It. 116/C2
Casorate Sempione, It. 116/B1
Caspe, Sp. 103/E2
Casper, Wy, US 185/G5
Caspian (sea), Asia 125/E5
Caspoggio, It. 115/F5
Cass (co.), Mo, US 195/E6
Cass (lake), Mi, US 193/F6
Cass City, Mi, US 188/D3
Cassai (riv.), Ang. 163/D3
Cassano allo Ionio, It. 104/E3
Cassano d'Adda, It. 116/C1
Cassano Magnago, It. 116/B1
Cassano Spinola, It. 116/B3
Cassel, Fr. 110/B2
Cássia, Braz. 213/C2
Cassiar, BC, Can. 192/N3
Cassiar (mts.), BC, Can. 180/C3
Cassilândia, Braz. 213/B1
Cassine, It. 116/B3
Cassino, It. 104/C2
Cassolnovo, It. 116/B2
Castagnaro, It. 117/E2
Castagneto Carducci, It. 101/J5
Castagnole delle Lanze, It. 116/B3
Castaic, Ca, US 194/B2
Castalla, Sp. 103/E3
Castanet-Tolosan, Fr. 100/D5
Castanhal, Braz. 209/J4
Castaños, Mex. 201/E3
Casteggio, It. 116/C2
Castegnato, It. 116/D1
Castel, Isr. 149/G8
Castel Bolognese, It. 117/E4
Castel d'Ario, It. 117/D2
Castel di Sangro, It. 104/D2
Castel Goffredo, It. 116/D2
Castel Mella, It. 116/D2
Castel San Giovanni, It. 116/C2
Castel San Lorenzo, It. 104/D2
Castel San Pietro Terme, It. 117/E4
Castelbuono, It. 104/D4
Castelcovati, It. 116/C2
Castelfidardo, It. 117/G6
Castelfiorentino, It. 117/D5
Castelfranco di Sopra, It. 117/E5
Castelfranco Emilia, It. 117/E3
Castelfranco Veneto, It. 117/E1
Castelgomberto, It. 117/E1
Casteljaloux, Fr. 100/D4
Castell de Montjuïc, Sp. 103/L7
Castellammare di Stabia, It. 104/D2
Castellammare, Golfo di (gulf), It. 104/C3
Castellamonte, It. 116/A2
Castellanza, It. 116/B1
Castellar del Vallès, Sp. 103/G2
Castellarano, It. 117/D3
Castell'Arquato, It. 116/C3
Castellazzo Bormida, It. 116/B3
Castelldefels, Sp. 103/K7
Castelleone, It. 116/C2
Castelli, Arg. 217/K12
Castellina in Chianti, It. 117/E6
Castello di Godego, It. 117/E1
Castello di Miramare, It. 117/G1
Castello Eurialo (ruin), It. 104/D4
Castello, Monte il (peak), It. 117/E5
Castellón de la Plana, Sp. 103/E3
Castellote, Sp. 103/E2
Castellucchio, It. 116/D2
Castelmassa, It. 117/E2
Castelnau-le-Lez, Fr. 100/E5
Castelnaudary, Fr. 100/D5
Castelnovo di Sotto, It. 116/D3
Castelnovo ne'Monti, It. 116/D4
Castelnuovo Berardenga, It. 117/E6
Castelnuovo di Garfagnana, It. 116/D4
Castelnuovo Don Bosco, It. 116/A2
Castelnuovo Scrivia, It. 116/B3
Castelo Branco, Port. 102/B3
Castelo Branco (dist.), Port. 102/B2
Castelo de Vide, Port. 102/B3
Castelo do Piauí, Braz. 212/B2
Castelsardo, It. 104/A2
Castelsarrasin, Fr. 100/D4
Castelverde, It. 116/C2
Castelvetrano, It. 104/C4
Castelvetro di Modena, It. 117/D3
Castelvetro Piacentino, It. 116/C2
Castenaso, It. 117/E3
Castenedolo, It. 116/D2
Casterton, Austl. 173/B3
Castiglion Fiorentino, It. 101/J5
Castiglione, It. 117/F4
Castiglione d'Adda, It. 116/C2
Castiglione dei Pepoli, It. 117/E4
Castiglione delle Stiviere, It. 116/D2
Castiglione Torinese, It. 116/A2
Castilho, Braz. 213/B2
Castilla, Peru 214/A2
Castilla-La Mancha (aut. comm.), Sp. 102/C3
Castilla y León (aut. comm.), Sp. 102/D2
Castilla y Léon Treviño, Sp. 102/D1
Castillo (peak), Arg. 216/C4
Castillo de San Marcos Nat'l Mon., Fl, US 191/H4
Castillos, Uru. 217/G2
Castione della Presolana, It. 115/G6
Castions, It. 117/F1
Castions di Strada, It. 117/G1
Castle Dale, Ut, US 186/E3
Castle Douglas, Sc, UK 92/E2
Castle Hills, Tx, US 195/T20
Castle Rock, Co, US 187/F3
Castle Rock, Wa, US 184/C4
Castle Rock (lake), Wi, US 185/L5
Castle Tower NP, Austl. 172/C4
Castlebar, Ire. 89/P10
Castlebay, Sc, UK 89/Q8
Castlebellingham, Ire. 92/B4
Castlebridge, Ire. 89/Q10
Castlecaufield, NI, UK 92/B3
Castlecomer, Ire. 89/Q10
Castledawson, NI, UK 92/B2
Castleford, Eng, UK 93/G4
Castlegar, BC, Can. 184/D3
Castlegregory, Ire. 88/N10
Castleisland, Ire. 89/P10
Castlemaine, Austl. 173/C3
Castlereagh, Ire. 89/P10
Castletown, IM, UK 92/D3
Castlewellan, NI, UK 92/C3
Castor, Ab, Can. 184/F2
Castos (riv.), Libr. 154/D6
Castres, Fr. 100/E5
Castrezzato, It. 116/C1
Castricum, Neth. 108/B3
Castries (cap.), StL. 199/N9
Castro, Braz. 213/B3
Castro, Chile 216/B4
Castro Alves, Braz. 212/C4
Castro Daire, Port. 102/B2
Castro de Rey, Sp. 102/B1
Castro del Río, Sp. 102/C4
Castro-Urdiales, Sp. 102/D1
Castro Verde, Port. 102/A4
Castrojeriz, Sp. 102/C1
Castrop-Rauxel, Ger. 109/E5
Castropol, Sp. 102/B1
Castrovillari, It. 104/E3
Castrovirreyna, Peru 214/C4
Castuera, Sp. 102/C3
Casupá, Uru. 217/G2
Cat (isl.), Bahm. 199/F3
Cat (lake), On, Can. 185/K3
Cat Law (peak), Sc, UK 94/C3
Catacamas, Hon. 202/E3
Catacaos, Peru 214/A2
Catacocha, Ecu. 214/B2
Cataduanes (isl.), Phil. 137/D5
Cataguases, Braz. 213/L6
Çatak, Turk. 148/E2
Çatalağzı, Turk. 107/K5
Çatalca, Turk. 107/J5
Çatalçam, Turk. 148/D2
Catalina, Az, US 186/E4
Catalonia (reg.), Sp. 103/E2
Cataluña (aut. comm.), Sp. 103/F2
Catamarca, Arg. 215/C2
Catamayo, Ecu. 214/B1
Catanduanes (isl.), Phil. 137/D5
Catanduva, Braz. 213/B2
Catania, It. 104/D4
Catania, Golfo di (gulf), It. 104/D4
Catanzaro, It. 104/E3
Cataouatche (lake), La, US 195/P17
Catarina, Braz. 212/C2
Catarman, Phil. 137/D5
Catastrophe (cape), Austl. 171/G5
Catatumbo (riv.), Col. 199/G6
Catatungan (mtn.), Phil. 139/F2
Catawba (riv.), NC,SC, US 191/H3
Catawissa, Pa, US 196/B2
Catbalogan, Phil. 137/D5
Catedral (peak), Uru. 217/G2
Catemaco (lake), Mex. 202/C2
Catemaco, Mex. 202/C2
Catende, Braz. 212/D3
Caterham (hill), Eng, UK 94/E5
Caterham, Eng, UK 88/C3
Caterham and Warlingham, Eng, UK 91/F4
Cathcart, SAfr. 164/D4
Cathédrale de Reims, Fr. 110/D5
Catherine (Kātrīnā) (peak), Egypt 159/C2
Catherine Palace, Rus. 119/T7
Ca'Tiepolo, It. 117/F3
Cativá, Pan. 203/G4
Çatköyü, Turk. 148/E2
Catlettsburg, Ky, US 188/D4
Cato (isl.), Austl. 167/E3
Catoche, Cabo (cape), Mex. 202/E1
Catolé do Rocha, Braz. 212/C2
Catonsville, Md, US 196/B5
Catria (peak), It. 117/F6
Catriló, Arg. 216/E3
Catrimani (riv.), Braz. 208/F3
Catrine, Sc, UK 94/B6
Catskill (mts.), NY, US 188/F3
Cattolica, It. 117/F5
Catu, Braz. 212/C4
Cauayan, Phil. 137/D4
Cauayan, Phil. 137/D6
Cauca (dept.), Col. 210/B4
Cauca (riv.), Col. 210/C3
Caucaia, Braz. 212/C1
Caucasia, Col. 210/C3
Caucasus (mts.), Geo. 121/G4
Caudete, Sp. 103/E3
Caudry, Fr. 110/C3
Cauldcleuch Head (peak), Sc, UK 94/D6
Cauquenes, Chile 216/B2
Caura (riv.), Ven. 208/F2
Caussade, Fr. 100/D4
Cauterets, Fr. 100/C5
Cauto (riv.), Cuba 203/G1
Cauvery (riv.), India 140/C5
Cava d'Ispica (ruin), It. 104/D4
Cávado (riv.), Port. 102/A2
Cavaglià, It. 116/B2
Cavaillon, Fr. 100/F5
Cavalaire-sur-Mer, Fr. 101/G5
Cavalcante, Braz. 212/A4
Cavalese, It. 115/H5
Cavalier, ND, US 185/J3
Cavalla (riv.), Libr. 154/D6
Cavallermaggiore, It. 116/A3
Cavallino, It. 117/F2
Cavallo, Capo al (cape), Fr. 104/A1
Cavally (riv.), C.d'Iv. 160/C5
Cavan, Ire. 89/Q10
Cavarzere, It. 117/F2
Cave Creek, Az, US 195/S18
Cave of Ten Thousand Buddhas, Myan. 136/B2
Cavezzo, It. 117/E3
Caviana (isl.), Braz. 209/J3
Cavite, Phil. 137/D5
Cavriana, It. 116/D2
Cawayan, Phil. 137/D5
Cawdor, Sc, UK 94/C1
Cawndilla (lake), Austl. 173/B2
Caxias do Sul, Braz. 213/B4
Caxinas (pt.), Hon. 202/E2
Caxito, Ang. 163/B2
Çay, Turk. 148/B2
Çayağzı, Turk. 107/J5
Cayambe, Ecu. 210/B4
Cayambe (vol.), Ecu. 210/B4
Cayce, SC, US 191/H3
Çaycuma, Turk. 107/L5
Çayeli, Turk. 148/E1
Cayenne (cap.), FrG. 209/H3
Cayeux-sur-Mer, Fr. 110/A3
Çayırhan, Turk. 107/K5
Çaylar, Turk. 148/E2
Cayman (isls.), UK 198/E4
Cayman Brac (isl.), UK 199/F4
Cazalla de la Sierra, Sp. 102/C4
Cazères, Fr. 100/D5
Cazin, Bosn. 101/L4
Cazis, Swi. 115/F4
Cazones (riv.), Mex. 202/B1
Cazorla, Sp. 102/D4
Cazzago San Martino, It. 116/D1
Cea (riv.), Sp. 102/C1
Ceanannus Mór (Kells), Ire. 89/Q10
Ceará (state), Braz. 212/B2
Cébaco (isl.), Pan. 203/F5
Ceballos, Mex. 200/D3
Cebollati (riv.), Uru. 217/G2
Cebollatí, Uru. 217/G2
Cebreros, Sp. 102/C2
Cebu, Phil. 137/D5
Cebu (int'l arpt.), Phil. 137/D5
Cebu (isl.), Phil. 137/D6
Ceccano, It. 104/C2
Cecil (co.), Md, US 196/C4
Cecil Macks (pass), Swaz. 165/E2
Cecil Plains, Austl. 172/C4
Cecil Rhodes (mt.), Austl. 170/D3
Cecilton, Md, US 196/C5
Cecina, It. 101/J5
Cecina (riv.), It. 117/D6
Cecita (lake), It. 104/E3
Ceclavín, Sp. 102/B3
Cedar (riv.), Ia, US 185/L5
Cedar, Ks, US 195/D6
Cedar (valley), Ut, US 195/J13
Cedar (lake), Mb,Sk, Can. 180/F3
Cedar (mtn.), Ca, US 193/L11
Cedar Bay NP, Austl. 172/B1
Cedar Bluff (res.), Ks, US 187/G3
Cedar Breaks Nat'l Mon., Ut, US 186/D3
Cedar Brook, NJ, US 196/D4
Cedar City, Ut, US 186/D3
Cedar Cove, Co, US 195/B2
Cedar Creek (res.), Tx, US 191/D3
Cedar Falls (dam), Wa, US 193/D3
Cedar Falls, Wa, US 193/D3
Cedar Fort (Cedar Valley), Ut, US 195/J13
Cedar Glen, Ca, US 194/C2
Cedar Grove, Md, US 196/A5
Cedar Grove, NJ, US 197/J8
Cedar Hill, Mo, US 195/F9
Cedar Hills, Ut, US 195/K13
Cedar Key, Fl, US 191/H4
Cedarhurst, NY, US 197/L9
Cedartown, Ga, US 191/G3
Cedarville, Ca, US 184/C5
Cedegolo, It. 115/G5
Cedeira, Sp. 102/A1
Cedral, Mex. 201/E4
Cedro, Braz. 212/C2
Cedros (isl.), Mex. 200/B2
Ceduna, Austl. 171/G5
Cee, Sp. 102/A1
Cefalù, It. 104/D3
Cefni (riv.), Wal, UK 92/D5
Cega (riv.), Sp. 102/C2
Ceggia, It. 117/F1
Cegléd, Hun. 106/D2
Čegrane, FYROM 105/G2
Cehegín, Sp. 102/E3
Ceheng Bouyeizu Zizhixian, China 141/J3
Cehu Silvaniei, Rom. 107/F2
Ceiriog (riv.), Wal, UK 93/E6
Çekerek (riv.), Turk. 120/F4
Čelákovice, Czh. 113/H2
Celanova, Sp. 102/B1
Celaya, Mex. 201/E4
Celebes (isl.), Indo. 139/E4
Celebes (sea), Asia 139/F3
Celendín, Peru 214/B2
Celestún, Mex. 202/D1
Celica, Ecu. 214/B2
Céligny, Swi. 114/C5
Celina, Tx, US 187/H4
Celina, Oh, US 188/C3
Celje, Slov. 101/L3
Cella, Sp. 102/E2
Celldömölk, Hun. 106/C2
Celle, Ger. 109/H3
Celle (riv.), Fr. 98/B4
Celle Ligure, It. 116/B4
Celles, Belg. 110/C2
Čelopek, FYROM 106/E5
Celorico da Beira, Port. 102/B2
Celtic (sea), Eur. 89/P11
Cemaes (pt.), Wal, UK 90/B2
Cemaru (peak), Indo. 138/D3
Cembra, It. 115/H5
Cenajo, Embalse del (res.), Sp. 102/E3
Cenderawasih (bay), Indo. 139/H4
Cene, It. 116/C1
Cenepa (riv.), Peru 214/B1
Cengong, China 141/J2
Cenia, Sp. 103/F2
Ceno (riv.), It. 116/C3
Centenario, Arg. 215/C4
Centenario do Sul, Braz. 213/B2
Centennial (mts.), Id, US 184/E4
Center, ND, US 185/H4
Center Moriches, NY, US 197/F2
Center Point, Al, US 191/G3
Centerbrook, Ct, US 197/F1
Centereach, NY, US 197/E2
Centerville, Tn, US 188/C5
Centerville, Tx, US 190/E4
Centerville, Ut, US 195/K12
Cento, It. 117/E3
Cento Croci, Passo di (pass), It. 116/C4
Central (peak), Arg. 216/C4
Central, Braz. 212/B3
Central (pol. reg.), Gha. 161/E5
Central (prov.), Kenya 162/C3
Central (int'l arpt.), Ukr. 107/K2
Central, Ak, US 192/K2
Central, NM, US 186/E4
Central African Republic (ctry.) 155/J6
Central Australia Abor. Land, Austl. 171/F2
Central Australia (Warburton) Abor. Rsv., Austl. 171/E3
Central Butte, Sk, Can. 184/G3
Central City, Ne, US 185/J5
Central City, Co, US 195/A3
Central, Cordillera (mts.), SAm. 208/C5
Central Desert Abor. Rsv., Austl. 171/F2
Central Intelligence Agency Fed. Govt. Res., Va, US 196/A6
Central Island NP, Kenya 162/C2
Central Islip, NY, US 197/E2
Central Makrān (range), Pak. 147/H3
Central, Massif (mass.), Fr. 100/E4
Central Mount Stuart (peak), Austl. 171/G2
Central Mount Wedge (peak), Austl. 171/F2
Central Park, NY, US 197/K8
Central, Planalto (plat.), Braz. 209/J7
Central Point, Or, US 184/C5
Central Siberian (plat.), Rus. 123/L3
Central Ural (mts.), Rus. 119/N4
Central Valley, NY, US 196/D1
Centralia, Wa, US 184/C4
Centralia, Il, US 187/K3
Centre (pol. reg.), Fr. 100/D3
Centre (pol. reg.), Mor. 156/D2
Centre (co.), Pa, US 196/A2
Centre Island, NY, US 197/L8
Centre-Nord (pol. reg.), Mor. 158/B2
Centre-Sud (pol. reg.), Mor. 158/B2
Centreville, Al, US 191/G3
Centreville, Il, US 195/G8
Centreville, Md, US 196/B5
Cenxi, China 141/K3
Čepin, Cro. 106/D3
Ceram (isl.), Indo. 139/G4
Ceram (sea), Indo. 139/G4
Cerano, It. 116/B2
Ceraso (cape), It. 104/A2
Cerbère, Fr. 100/E5
Cercal, Port. 102/A4
Cercedilla, Sp. 103/M8
Čerchov (peak), Czh. 113/F4
Cerdanyola del Vallès, Sp. 103/L7
Cère (riv.), Fr. 100/E4
Cerea, It. 117/E2
Ceredigion (co.), Wal, UK 90/B2
Ceres, Arg. 215/D2
Ceres, Braz. 209/J7
Ceres, SAfr. 164/L10
Cerese, It. 117/D2
Céret, Fr. 100/E5
Cereté, Col. 210/C2
Cerfone (riv.), It. 117/E6
Cerfontaine, Belg. 111/D3
Cergy, Fr. 88/J4
Ceriale, It. 116/B4
Cerignola, It. 104/D2
Çerkeş, Turk. 120/E4
Çerkezköy, Turk. 107/J5
Çermik, Turk. 148/D2
Černá (riv.), Czh. 113/H5
Černá (peak), Czh. 113/G5
Cernavodă, Rom. 107/J3
Cernay, Fr. 114/D2
Cernay-la-Ville, Fr. 88/H5
Cernier, Swi. 114/C3
Cérou (riv.), Fr. 100/D4
Cerralvo, Mex. 190/D5
Cerralvo (isl.), Mex. 200/C3
Cerreto Guidi, It. 117/D5
Cerreto, Passo del (pass), It. 116/D4
Cërrik, Alb. 105/F2
Cerritos, Mex. 201/E4
Cerritos, Ca, US 194/F8
Cerro Azul, Peru 214/B4
Cerro Azul, Mex. 202/B1
Cerro Castillo, Chile 217/B6
Cerro Chato, Uru. 217/G2
Cerro Corá, Braz. 212/C2
Cerro de la Estrella, PN, Mex. 201/Q10
Cerro de las Campanas, PN, Mex. 201/E4
Cerro de Pasco, Peru 214/B3
Cerro de San Antonio, Col. 210/C2
Cerro El Copey, PN, Ven. 211/F2
Cerro Maggiore, It. 116/B1
Cerro Nanchital, Mex. 202/C2
Cerro del Pinacate (peak), Mex. 200/B2
Cerros Colorados (res.), Arg. 215/C4
Cerros de Amotape, PN, Peru 214/A2
Certaldo, It. 117/E5
Certosa di Pavia, It. 116/C2
Certosa di Pisa, It. 116/D5
Cervantes, Austl. 170/B4
Cervaro (riv.), It. 104/D2
Cervati (peak), It. 104/D2
Cervellino (peak), It. 116/D3
Cervera, Sp. 103/F2
Cervera de Pisuerga, Sp. 102/C1
Cervera del Río Alhama, Sp. 102/E1
Cervia, It. 117/F4
Cervialto (peak), It. 104/D2
Cervignano del Friuli, It. 117/G1
Cervina (peak), It. 115/H4
Cervione, Fr. 104/A1
Cervo (riv.), It. 116/B1
Cervo, Sp. 102/B1
Cervo, It. 116/B5
Cervo, Serra do (hills), Braz. 213/G7
Cesano (riv.), It. 117/F6
Cesano Boscone, It. 116/C2
Cesano Maderno, It. 116/C1
César (dept.), Col. 210/C2
César (riv.), Col. 210/C2
Cesen (peak), It. 117/F1
Cesena, It. 117/F4
Cesenatico, It. 117/F4
Cēsis, Lat. 97/L3
České Budějovice, Czh. 113/H5
České Středohoří (mts.), Czh. 113/G2
Českomoravská Vysočina (mts.), Czh. 99/H4
Český Brod, Czh. 113/H2
Český Krumlov, Czh. 113/H5
Český Les Sumava (mts.), Czh. 113/F3
Česma (riv.), Cro. 106/C3
Çeşme, Turk. 105/K3
Cesson, Fr. 88/K6
Cesson-Sévigné, Fr. 100/C2
Cestos (riv.), Libr. 160/C5
Cetinje, Mont. 106/D4
Çetinkaya, Turk. 148/D2
Ceurda del Pozo, Embalse de la (res.), Sp. 102/D2
Ceuta, Sp. 158/B2
Ceva, It. 116/B4
Cevedale (peak), It. 115/G5
Cévennes (mts.), Fr. 100/E4
Cevio, Swi. 115/E5
Ceyhan, Turk. 149/D1
Ceylânpınar, Turk. 148/E2
Ceylon (isl.), SrL. 140/D6
Ceyzériat, Fr. 114/B5
Cèze (riv.), Fr. 100/F4
Cha Da (cape), Viet. 136/E4
Chabás, Arg. 216/E2
Chabjuwardoo (bay), Austl. 170/B2
Chablé, Mex. 202/D2
Chacabuco, Arg. 216/E2
Chachani (peak), Peru 214/D5
Chachapoyas, Peru 214/B2
Chachoengsao, Thai. 136/C3
Chaclacayo, Peru 214/B3
Chaco (riv.), NM, US 186/F3
Chaco (mesa), NM, US 190/B3
Chaco Austral (plain), Arg. 215/D1
Chaco Boreal (plain), Par. 208/F8
Chaco Central (plain), Arg. 215/D1
Chaco, PN, Arg. 215/E2
Chacujal (ruin), Guat. 202/D3
Chad (lake), Niger 154/H5
Chad (ctry.) 155/J4
Chafarinas (isl.), Sp. 158/C2
Chagang-do (prov.), NKor. 131/D2
Chagda, Rus. 123/P4
Chaghcharān, Afg. 145/E6
Chagny, Fr. 100/F3
Chagos (arch.), Brln, UK 125/G10
Chaguanas, Trin. 211/F2
Chaguarpamba, Ecu. 214/B1
Chahuites, Mex. 202/C2
Chaibāsā, India 143/E4
Chailly-en-Brie, Fr. 88/M5
Chain, SKor. 131/E5
Chainat, Thai. 136/C3
Chaîne Annamitique (mts.), Laos 141/H4
Chaîne de la Selle (peak), Haiti 203/J2
Chaîne de l'Atacora (mts.), Ben. 161/F4
Chaitén, Chile 215/B5
Chaiyaphum, Thai. 136/C3
Chākdaha, India 143/G4
Chake Chake, Tanz. 162/C4
Chākia, India 142/D3
Chakradharpur, India 143/E4
Chakrāta, India 144/D4
Chakwāl, Pak. 144/B3
Chala, Peru 214/C4
Chalain (lake), Fr. 114/B4
Chalais, Swi. 114/D5
Chālakudi, India 140/C5
Chalaronne (riv.), Fr. 114/A5
Chalatenango, ESal. 202/D3
Chalbi (des.), Kenya 155/N7
Chalchihuites, Mex. 200/E4
Chalco, Mex. 201/R10
Chale (pt.), Kenya 162/C4
Chaleur (bay), NB,Qu, Can. 189/H2
Chalfont, Pa, US 196/C3
Chalfont Saint Giles, Eng, UK 88/B2
Chalfont Saint Peter, Eng, UK 88/B2
Chalhuanca, Peru 214/C4
Chalifert (canal), Fr. 88/L5
Chalindrey, Fr. 114/B2
Chalk (mts.), Tx, US 190/C4
Chalkyitsik, Ak, US 192/K2
Challans, Fr. 100/C3
Challapata, Bol. 208/E7
Challenger (mts.), Nun., Can. 181/T6
Chalmette, La, US 195/Q17
Chālna Port, Bang. 143/G4
Chalon-sur-Saône, Fr. 114/A4
Châlons-sur-Marne, Fr. 111/D6
Châlonvillars, Fr. 114/C2
Chālūs, Iran 146/F1
Cham, Ger. 113/F4
Cham (riv.), Ger. 113/F4
Cham, Swi. 115/E3
Chama, Zam. 162/B5
Chama (riv.), NM, US 186/F3
Chamah (peak), Malay. 138/B2
Chaman, Pak. 147/J2
Chamba, India 144/D3
Chambal (riv.), India 147/L3
Chambaran, Plateau de (plat.), Fr. 100/F4
Chambas, Cuba 203/G1
Chamberlain (lake), Me, US 189/G2
Chamberlin (mt.), Ak, US 192/K2
Chambersburg, Pa, US 188/E4

Chambéry, Fr. 100/F4
Chambeshi (riv.), Zam. 163/F3
Chambly, Qu, Can. 189/P7
Chambly, Fr. 88/J4
Chambourcy, Fr. 88/J5
Chambry, Fr. 88/L5
Chamchamāl, Iraq 146/D1
Chamechaude (peak), Fr. 100/F4
Chamical, Arg. 215/C3
Chamigny, Fr. 88/M5
Chamizal Nat'l Mem., Tx, US 190/B4
Chamizo, Uru. 217/L11
Chamonix-Mont-Blanc, Fr. 114/C6
Champagne, Yk, Can. 192/L3
Champagne (reg.), Fr. 98/C4
Champagne-Ardenne (pol. reg), Fr. 100/F2
Champagne-sur-Oise, Fr. 88/J4
Champagney, Fr. 114/C2
Champagnole, Fr. 114/B4
Champasak, Laos 136/D3
Champawat, India 142/C1
Champdeuil, Fr. 88/L6
Champeaux, Fr. 88/L6
Champéry, Swi. 114/C5
Champigneulles, Fr. 111/F6
Champigny-sur-Marne, Fr. 88/K5
Champlain (lake), NY,Vt, US 186/F2
Champlitte, Fr. 114/B2
Champotón, Mex. 202/D2
Champotón (riv.), Mex. 202/D2
Champs-sur-Marne, Fr. 88/K5
Champsevraine, Fr. 114/B2
Champvans, Fr. 114/B3
Chamusca, Port. 102/A3
Chan Chan (ruin), Peru 214/B3
Chan May Dong (cape), Viet. 136/E2
Chañaral, Chile 215/B2
Chança (riv.), Port. 102/B4
Chancay, Peru 214/B3
Chanco, Chile 216/B2
Chancy, Swi. 114/B5
Chandalar, Ak, US 192/J2
Chandalar (riv.), Ak, US 192/J2
Chandalar, East Fork (riv.), Ak, US 192/J2
Chandannagar, India 143/G4
Chandausi, India 142/B1
Chanderi, India 142/B3
Chandīgarh, India 144/D4
Chandīgarh (state), India 144/D4
Chandlees (riv.), Braz. 208/D6
Chandler (riv.), Ak, US 192/H2
Chandler, Ok, US 190/D3
Chandler, Qu, Can. 189/H1
Chandler, Az, US 195/S19
Chandolin, Swi. 114/D5
Chāndpur, Bang. 143/H4
Chāndpur, India 142/B1
Chandrapur, India 140/C4
Chanduy, Ecu. 210/A5
Chang (lake), China 130/C5
Chang (riv.), China 130/B5
Changan, SKor. 131/E5
Changbai (peak), China 131/E2
Changbai Chaoxianzu Zizhixian, China 131/E2
Changchun, China 129/N3
Changdang (lake), China 130/D5
Changdao, China 130/E3
Changde, China 137/B2
Changé, Fr. 100/D3
Changewater, NJ, US 196/D2
Changfeng, China 130/D4
Changge, China 130/C4
Changgi-ap (cape), SKor. 132/A2
Changhai, China 131/B3
Changhang, SKor. 131/D4
Changhowŏn, SKor. 131/D4
Changhua, Tai. 137/D3
Changhŭng, SKor. 131/D5
Changis-sur-Marne, Fr. 88/M5
Changji, China 128/E3
Changjiang, China 141/J4
Changjin (res.), NKor. 131/D2
Changjin (lake), NKor. 131/D2
Changle, China 130/D3
Changli, China 130/D3
Changling, China 130/E1
Changning, China 141/H2
Changning, China 141/G3
Ch'angnyŏng, SKor. 131/E5
Changping, China 130/H6
Changqing, China 130/D3
Changsan-got (cape), NKor. 131/C3
Changsha, China 141/K2
Changshou, China 137/A2
Changshu, China 130/L8
Changshun, China 141/J2
Changsŏng, SKor. 131/D5
Changsu, SKor. 131/D5
Changsŭngp'o, SKor. 131/E5
Changtai, China 137/C3
Changtu, China 130/F2
Changuinola, Pan. 203/F4
Ch'angwŏn, SKor. 131/E5
Changxing, China 130/K8
Changyang, China 137/B1
Changyi, China 130/D3
Changyŏn, NKor. 131/C3
Changyuan, China 130/C4
Changzhi, China 130/C3
Changzhou, China 130/K8
Chañi, Nevado de (peak), Arg. 215/C1
Chanlers (falls), Kenya 162/C2
Channel (isls.), UK 100/B2
Channel Country (phys. reg.), Austl. 167/C3
Channel Islands NP, Ca, US 186/C4
Channel-Port aux Basques, Nf, Can. 189/K2
Channel Tunnel, Eng, Fr.,UK 91/H5
Channing, Tx, US 187/G4
Chantada, Sp. 102/B1
Chanteloup-les-Vignes, Fr. 88/J5
Chanthaburi, Thai. 136/C3
Chantilly, Fr. 110/B5
Chantraine, Fr. 114/C1
Chantrey (inlet), Nun., Can. 180/G2
Chao (lake), China 130/D5
Chao Phraya (riv.), Thai. 136/C3
Chaoyang, China 137/C3
Chaoyang, China 130/E2
Chapacura, Bol. 214/D3
Chapada Diamantina, PN, Braz. 209/K6
Chapada dos Veadeiros, PN da, Braz. 209/J6
Chapadinha, Braz. 212/B1
Chapais, Qu, Can. 188/F1
Chapala (lake), Mex. 200/E4
Chapala, Mex. 200/E4
Chaparral, Col. 210/C4
Chaparrosa, Mex. 200/E4
Chapayevsk, Rus. 121/J1
Chapel Hill, NC, US 191/J3
Chapel Ness (pt.), Sc, UK 94/D4
Chapelfell Top (peak), Eng, UK 93/F2
Chapelle-lez-Herlaimont, Belg. 111/D3
Chapeltown, Eng, UK 93/G5
Chaplain (lake), Wa, US 193/D2
Chapleau, On, Can. 188/D2
Chaplin, Sk, Can. 184/G3
Chāpra, India 143/E3
Char (well), Mrta. 156/B5
Chara (riv.), Rus. 123/M4
Charambirá (pt.), Col. 210/B3
Charaña, Bol. 214/D5
Charandra (riv.), Gre. 105/N8
Charata, Arg. 215/D2
Charcas, Mex. 201/E4
Charcot (isl.), Ant. 218/U
Chardonnière, Haiti 203/H2
Charente (riv.), Fr. 100/C4
Chari (riv.), Chad 154/J5
Chārīkār, Afg. 147/J1
Chariton (riv.), Ia,Mo, US 187/J2
Charity, Guy. 211/G3
Chärjew, Trkm. 145/D5
Charkhāri, India 142/B3
Charkhi Dādri, India 144/D5
Charlemagne, Qu, Can. 189/P6
Charlemont, NI, UK 92/B3
Charleroi, Belg. 111/D3
Charleroi à Bruxelles, Canal de (canal), Belg. 111/D2
Charles (peak), Austl. 170/D5
Charles (mt.), Austl. 170/C3
Charles (isl.), Qu, Can. 181/J2
Charles City, Ia, US 185/K5
Charles de Gaulle (int'l arpt.), Fr. 88/K4
Charleston, Ms, US 187/K4
Charleston, Nv, US 184/E5
Charleston, SC, US 191/J3
Charleston, Ut, US 195/L13
Charleston (cap.), WV, US 188/D4
Charlestown, StK. 199/N8
Charlestown, Md, US 196/C4
Charleville, Austl. 172/B4
Charleville-Mézières, Fr. 111/D4
Charlevoix, Mi, US 188/C2
Charlotte (lake), BC, Can. 184/B2
Charlotte, Mi, US 188/C3
Charlotte, NC, US 191/H3
Charlotte Amalie, USVI 199/M8
Charlotte/Douglas (int'l arpt.), NC, US 191/H3
Charlottenberg, Swe. 96/E2
Charlottenburg, Ger. 98/Q6
Charlottetown (cap.), PE, Can. 189/J2
Charlton, Austl. 173/B3
Charlton (isl.), On, Can. 181/H3
Charlton Kings, Eng, UK 90/D3
Charly, Fr. 110/C6
Charmes (res.), Fr. 114/B2
Charmes, Fr. 114/C1
Charmey, Swi. 114/D4
Charnay-lès-Mâcon, Fr. 100/F3
Charny, Fr. 88/L5
Charny-sur-Meuse, Fr. 111/E5
Charolais, Monts du (mts.), Fr. 100/F3
Charouine, Alg. 157/E3
Charquemont, Fr. 114/C3
Chars, Fr. 88/H4
Chārsadda, Pak. 144/A2
Charters Towers, Austl. 172/B3
Charthāwāl, India 144/D5
Chartres, Fr. 100/D2
Chās, India 143/F4
Chaschauna (peak), Swi. 115/G4
Chascomús, Arg. 216/F2
Chase, BC, Can. 184/D3
Chasŏng, NKor. 131/D2
Chassezac (riv.), Fr. 100/F4
Chastre-Villeroux-Blanmont, Belg. 111/D2
Chatanika, Ak, US 192/J2
Château Bougon (int'l arpt.), Fr. 100/C3
Chateau de Versailles, Fr. 88/J5
Château-d'Olonne, Fr. 100/C3
Château-du-Loir, Fr. 100/D3
Château-Porcien, Fr. 111/D4
Château-Renault, Fr. 100/D3
Château-Salins, Fr. 111/F6
Château-Thierry, Fr. 110/C5
Châteaubriant, Fr. 100/C3
Châteaudun, Fr. 100/D2
Châteauguay, Qu, Can. 189/N7
Châteauneuf-sur-Charente, Fr. 100/C4
Châteaurenard, Fr. 100/F5
Châteauroux, Fr. 100/D3
Châteauvillain, Fr. 114/A1
Châtel-Saint-Denis, Swi. 114/C4
Châtelaillon-Page, Fr. 100/C3
Châtelet, Belg. 111/D3
Châtellerault, Fr. 100/D3
Châtenay-Malabry, Fr. 88/J5
Châtenois, Fr. 114/B1
Châtenois-les-Forges, Fr. 114/C2
Chatfield (res.), Co, US 195/B3
Chatham (isls.), Chile 217/B6
Chatham, On, Can. 188/D3
Chatham, Eng, UK 91/G4
Chatham, NJ, US 197/H9
Châtillon, It. 101/G4
Châtillon, Fr. 88/J5
Châtillon-sur-Chalaronne, Fr. 114/A5
Châtillon-sur-Marne, Fr. 110/C5
Châtillon-sur-Seine, Fr. 100/F3
Chatkal (riv.), Kyr. 145/F4
Chatou, Fr. 88/J5
Chatra, India 143/E3
Chatrapur, India 140/E4
Châtres, Fr. 88/L5
Chatsworth (res.), Ca, US 194/B2
Chatsworth, NJ, US 196/D4
Chattahoochee (riv.),US 191/G4
Chattahoochee, Fl, US 191/G4
Chattanooga, Tn, US 191/G3
Chatteris, Eng, UK 91/G2
Chau Doc, Viet. 136/D4
Chaucey, Îles (isls.), Fr. 100/C2
Chauconin-Neufmontiers, Fr. 88/L5
Chaudfontaine, Belg. 111/E2
Chaudière (riv.), Qu, Can. 189/G2
Chauk, Myan. 141/F3
Chaukan (pass), India 141/G2
Chaumes-en-Brie, Fr. 88/L5
Chaumont, Fr. 114/B1
Chaumont-en-Vexin, Fr. 110/A5
Chaunskaya (bay), Rus. 123/T3
Chauny, Fr. 110/C4
Chaussin, Fr. 114/B4
Chaussy, Fr. 88/H4
Chautauqua (lake), NY, US 188/E3
Chautauqua, Il, US 195/G8
Chauvigny, Fr. 100/D3
Chaval, Braz. 212/B1
Chavanoz, Fr. 114/B6
Chaves, Port. 102/B2
Chavín de Huantar (ruin), Peru 214/B3
Chaviña, Peru 214/C4
Chavinillo, Peru 214/B3
Chavornay, Swi. 114/C4
Chawinda, Pak. 144/C3
Chay (riv.), Viet. 136/D1
Chayana (riv.), Bol. 208/E7
Chaykovskiy, Rus. 119/M4
Chazuta, Peru 214/B2
Cheadle, Eng, UK 93/G6
Cheaha (mtn.), Al, US 191/G3
Cheb, Czh. 113/F2
Cheboksary, Rus. 119/K4
Cheboksary (res.), Rus. 119/K4
Cheboygan, Mi, US 188/C2
Chechaouene, Mor. 158/B2
Chechaouene (prov.), Mor. 158/B2
Chechen' (isl.), Rus. 121/H3
Chechnya, Resp., Rus. 122/Q6
Chech'ŏn, SKor. 131/E4
Checotah, Ok, US 187/J4
Chedabucto (bay), NS, Can. 189/J2
Cheduba (isl.), Myan. 141/F4
Cheektowaga, NY, US 189/S10
Cheepash (riv.), On, Can. 188/D1
Cheepay (riv.), On, Can. 188/D1
Chefornak, Ak, US 192/F3
Chegutu, Zim. 163/F4
Chehalis, Wa, US 184/C4
Cheïkh (well), Alg. 157/F3
Cheju, SKor. 129/N5
Cheju (isl.), SKor. 129/N5
Cheju (str.), SKor. 129/N5
Cheka (peak), Rus. 145/C2
Chelan, Wa, US 184/C4
Chelan (lake), Wa, US 184/C4
Chelghoum El Aïd, Alg. 158/J4
Chelles, Fr. 88/K5
Chełm, Pol. 99/M3
Chełmno, Pol. 99/K2
Chelmsford, Eng, UK 91/G3
Chełmża, Pol. 99/K2
Cheltenham, Eng, UK 90/D3
Chelva, Sp. 103/E3
Chelyabinsk (int'l arpt.), Rus. 119/P5
Chelyabinsk, Rus. 119/P5
Chelyabinskaya Oblast, Rus. 145/D2
Chelyuskina (cape), Rus. 123/L2
Chemaïa, Mor. 156/C2
Chemax, Mex. 202/E1
Chemnitz, Ger. 98/G3
Chen (riv.), China 137/A2
Chena Hot Springs, Ak, US 192/J2
Chenāb (riv.), Pak. 147/K2
Chenachane (well), Alg. 156/D4
Cheney, Wa, US 184/D4
Cheng'anpu, China 130/C3
Chengbu Miaozu Zizhixian, China 141/K2
Chengde, China 130/D2
Chengdu, China 128/H5
Chengkou, China 128/J5
Chengmai, China 141/J4
Chengshan Jiao (cape), China 131/B4
Chengwu, China 130/C4
Cheniménil, Fr. 114/C1
Chennai (Madras), India 140/D5
Chennevières-lès-Louvres, Fr. 88/K4
Chenòve, Fr. 114/A3
Chenxi, China 141/K2
Chenzhou, China 141/K2
Chep Lak Kok (int'l arpt.), China 129/T10
Chepelare, Bul. 105/J2
Chepén, Peru 214/B2
Chepes, Arg. 215/C3
Chépica, Chile 216/C2
Chepigana, Pan. 210/B2
Chepo, Pan. 210/B2
Chepstow, Wal, UK 90/D3
Cheptsa (riv.), Rus. 119/M4
Cher (riv.), Fr. 100/E3
Chéran (riv.), Fr. 114/C6
Cherasco, It. 116/A3
Cherāt, Pak. 144/A3
Cheraw, SC, US 191/J3
Cherbourg, Fr. 100/C2
Cherbourg, Austl. 172/C4
Cherchell, Alg. 158/G4
Cherepovets, Rus. 118/H4
Cherf, Oued (riv.), Alg. 158/K6
Cheria, Alg. 158/K7
Cherkas'ka Oblasti, Ukr. 120/D2
Cherkasy, Ukr. 120/E2
Cherkessk, Rus. 121/G3
Chermignon, Swi. 114/D5
Chernaya (riv.), Rus. 119/N1
Cherni Lom (riv.), Bul. 107/H4
Cherni Vrŭkh (peak), Bul. 105/H1
Chernihiv, Ukr. 120/D2
Chernihivs'ka Oblasti, Ukr. 120/D2
Chernivets'ka Oblasti, Ukr. 120/C2
Chernivtsi, Ukr. 107/G1
Chernushka, Rus. 119/N4
Cherokee, Ok, US 187/H3
Cherry Creek (dam), Co, US 195/C3
Cherry Creek (lake), Co, US 195/C3
Cherry Hill, Md, US 196/C4
Cherry Hill, NJ, US 196/C4
Cherry Valley, Ca, US 194/D3
Cherski (range), Rus. 125/P3
Chertsey, Eng, UK 88/B2
Cherven Bryag, Bul. 107/G4
Chervonohrad, Ukr. 120/C2
Cherwell (riv.), Eng, UK 91/E3
Chesaning, Mi, US 188/C3
Chesapeake (bay), US 188/E4
Chesapeake and Delaware (canal), De,Md, US 196/C4
Chesapeake Bay Maritime Museum, Md, US 196/B6
Chesapeake City, Md, US 196/C4
Chesham, Eng, UK 91/F3
Cheshire (co.), Eng, UK 93/F5
Cheshire (plain), Eng, UK 93/F5
Cheshskaya (bay), Rus. 122/E3
Cheshunt, Eng, UK 88/C1
Chesilhurst, NJ, US 196/D4
Chester, Eng, UK 93/F5
Chester, Ca, US 184/C5
Chester (riv.), Md, US 196/B5
Chester, Mt, US 184/F3
Chester, NJ, US 196/D2
Chester, Pa, US 196/C4
Chester (co.), Pa, US 196/C4
Chester, SC, US 191/H3
Chester Heights, Pa, US 196/C4
Chester-le-Street, Eng, UK 93/G2
Chester Morse (lake), Wa, US 193/D3
Chesterfield (inlet), Nun., Can. 180/G2
Chesterfield, Eng, UK 93/G5
Chesterfield, Mo, US 195/F8
Chesterfield (isls.), NCal., Fr. 174/E6
Chesterfield Inlet, Nun., Can. 180/G2
Chesterfield, Nosy (isl.), Madg. 165/G7
Chesterton (range), Austl. 172/B4
Chestertown, Md, US 196/B5
Chesuncook (lake), Me, US 189/G2
Cheswold, De, US 196/C5
Chetumal (bay), Mex. 198/D4
Chetumal, Mex. 202/D2
Chetwynd, BC, Can. 184/C2
Cheung Chau (isl.), China 129/T11
Chevak, Ak, US 192/E3
Cheval Blanc (pt.), Haiti 203/H2
Chevigny-Saint-Sauveur, Fr. 114/B3
Cheviot (hills), Sc, UK 94/D6
Cheviot, The (peak), Eng, UK 94/D6
Chevreuse, Fr. 88/J5
Chevry-Cossigny, Fr. 88/K5
Chew (riv.), Eng, UK 90/D4
Chew Valley (lake), Eng, UK 90/D4
Chewelah, Wa, US 184/D3
Chexbres, Swi. 114/C5
Cheyenne (riv.), SD,Wy, US 185/H5
Cheyenne (cap.), Wy, US 185/G5
Cheyenne, Ok, US 187/H4
Cheyenne Wells, Co, US 187/G3
Cheyres, Swi. 114/C4
Chhabra, India 142/A3
Chhaprauli, India 144/D5
Chhāta, India 142/A2
Chhatarpur, India 142/B3
Chhattisgarh (state), India 140/D3
Chhibrāmau, India 142/B2
Chhindwāra, India 142/B4
Chi (riv.), Thai. 141/H4
Chiai, Tai. 137/D3
Ch'iak-san NP, SKor. 131/E4
Chiampo, It. 117/E1
Chianciano Terme, It. 101/J5
Chiang Kai Shek (int'l arpt.), Tai. 137/D2
Chiang Mai, Thai. 141/G4
Chiang Rai, Thai. 141/G4
Chianti (reg.), It. 117/E5
Chianti, Monti del (mts.), It. 117/E5
Chiapa de Corzo, Mex. 202/C2
Chiapas (state), Mex. 198/C4
Chiappa (pt.), It. 116/C4
Chiaravalle, It. 117/G5
Chiari, It. 116/C1
Chiasso, Swi. 115/F6
Chiat'ura, Geo. 121/G4
Chiautempan, Mex. 201/L7
Chiautla, Mex. 201/R9
Chiautla de Tapia, Mex. 202/B2
Chiavari, It. 116/C4
Chiavenna, It. 115/F5
Chiba, Japan 133/G3
Chibougamau, Qu, Can. 188/F1
Chibougamau (riv.), Qu, Can. 188/F1
Chibougamau (lake), Qu, Can. 188/F1
Chibukak (pt.), Ak, US 192/D3
Chibuto, Moz. 163/F5
Chicago, Il, US 185/M5
Chicago Heights, Il, US 193/Q16
Chicago Midway (int'l arpt.), Il, US 187/L2
Chicago, North Branch (riv.), Il, US 193/Q15
Chicago-O'Hare (int'l arpt.), Il, US 185/M5
Chicago Ridge, Il, US 193/Q16
Chicago Sanitary and Ship Canal, Il, US 193/P16
Chicama, Peru 214/B2
Chichagof (isl.), Ak, US 180/C3
Chichaoua, Mor. 156/C3
Chīchāwatni, Pak. 144/B4
Chichén Itzá (ruin), Mex. 202/D1
Chicheng, China 129/L3
Chichester (range), Austl. 167/A3
Chichester, Eng, UK 91/F5
Chichibu, Japan 133/F3
Chichicastenango, Guat. 202/D3
Chichigalpa, Nic. 202/E3
Chichihualco, Mex. 201/F5
Chichiriviche, Ven. 210/D2
Chichishima (isls.), Japan 174/D2
Chickaloon, Ak, US 192/J3
Chickamauga (lake), Tn, US 191/G3
Chickasaw Nat'l Rec. Area, Ok, US 187/H4
Chickasha, Ok, US 187/H4
Chicla, Peru 214/B3
Chiclana de la Frontera, Sp. 102/B4
Chiclayo, Peru 214/B2
Chico, Ca, US 186/B3
Chico (riv.), Arg. 205/B7
Chicoloapan, Mex. 201/R10
Chicomostoc (ruin), Mex. 200/E4
Chicomuselo, Mex. 202/C3
Chiconcuac, Mex. 201/R9
Chicontepec de Tejeda, Mex. 202/B1
Chicopee, Ma, US 189/F3
Chicoutimi, Qu, Can. 189/G1
Chicualacuala, Moz. 163/F5
Chidley (cape), Nf, Can. 181/K2
Chido, SKor. 131/D5
Chiefland, Fl, US 191/H4
Chiemsee (lake), Ger. 101/K3
Chieo Lan (res.), Thai. 141/G6
Chieri, It. 116/A2
Chierry, Fr. 110/C5
Chiers (riv.), Fr. 111/E5
Chiesa in Valmalenco, It. 115/F5
Chiese (riv.), It. 101/J3
Chieti, It. 104/D1
Chietla, Mex. 201/L8
Chièvres, Belg. 110/C2
Chifeng, China 129/L3
Chifre, Serra do (mts.), Braz. 209/K7
Chigasaki, Japan 133/F3
Chiginagak (mt.), Ak, US 192/G4
Chignahuapan, Mex. 201/L7
Chignecto (bay), NB,NS, Can. 189/H2
Chignik, Ak, US 192/G4
Chignik Lake, Ak, US 192/G4
Chigorodó, Col. 210/B3
Chigu (lake), China 143/H1
Chigwell, Eng, UK 88/D2
Chihayaakasaka, Japan 135/J7
Chihli (Bo Hai) (gulf), China 130/D3
Chihuahua, Mex. 200/D2
Chihuahua (state), Mex. 200/D2
Chikaskia (riv.), Ks,Ok, US 187/H3
Chikballāpur, India 140/C5
Chikhli, India 147/L4
Chikmagalūr, India 147/L6
Chikoy (riv.), Rus. 123/L5
Chikugo (riv.), Japan 132/B4
Chikuma (riv.), Japan 133/F2
Chilac, Mex. 201/M8
Chilaw, SrL. 140/C6
Chilbo-san (peak), NKor. 131/E2
Chilca, Peru 214/B4
Chilcotin (riv.), BC, Can. 180/D3
Childers, Austl. 172/D4
Childersburg, Al, US 191/G3
Childress, Tx, US 187/G4
Chile (ctry.) 215/B3
Chile Chico, Chile 216/C5
Chile, Monte el (peak), Hon. 202/E3
Chilecito, Arg. 215/C2
Chilete, Peru 214/B2
Ch'ilgap-san NP, SKor. 131/D4
Chililabombwe, Zam. 163/E3
Chilka (lake), India 140/E4
Chilko (lake), BC, Can. 180/D3
Chilkoot (pass), Can.,US 192/L4
Chilkoot (pass), Ak, US 192/L3
Chilla Well Abor. Land, Austl. 171/F2
Chillán, Chile 216/B3
Chillanes, Ecu. 214/B1
Chillicothe, Il, US 185/L5
Chilliwack, BC, Can. 184/C3
Chillon, Swi. 114/C5
Chilly-Mazarin, Fr. 88/J5
Chiloé (isl.), Chile 216/B4
Chiloé, PN, Chile 216/B4
Chiloquin, Or, US 184/C5
Chilpancingo de los Bravos, Mex. 201/F5
Chiltern (hills), Eng, UK 91/E3
Chiltern Hundreds (reg.), Eng, UK 88/A2
Chilung La (pass), India 144/D3
Chilwa (lake), Malw. 163/G4
Chimacum, Wa, US 193/B1
Chimalhuacán, Mex. 201/R10
Chimaliro (hill), Malw. 162/B5
Chimaltenango, Guat. 202/D3
Chimán, Pan. 210/B2
Chimanimani, Zim. 163/F4
Chimantá-Tepuí (peak), Ven. 211/F3
Chimay, Belg. 111/D3
Chimbay, Uzb. 145/C4
Chimborazo (dept.), Ecu. 210/B5
Chimborazo (vol.), Ecu. 210/B5
Chimbote, Peru 214/B3
Chimichaqua, Col. 210/C2
Chimoio, Moz. 163/F4
Chimtarga (peak), Taj. 145/E5
Chin (state), Myan. 141/F3
China (ctry.) 128/G4
China, Mex. 201/F3
China, Mex. 202/D2
Chinácota, Col. 210/C3
Chinan, SKor. 131/D5
Chinandega, Nic. 202/E3
Chinati (mts.), Tx, US 190/B4
Chincha Alta, Peru 214/B4
Chinchaga (riv.), Ab,BC, Can. 180/E3
Chinchilla, Sp. 102/E3
Chinchilla, Austl. 172/C4
Chinch'ŏn, SKor. 131/D4
Chinchón, Sp. 102/D2
Chincoteague, Va, US 188/F4
Chinde, Moz. 163/G4
Chindo, SKor. 131/D5
Chindrieux, Fr. 114/B6
Chindu, China 128/G4
Chindwin (riv.), Myan. 141/F3
Chingaza, PN, Col. 210/C3
Chingleput, India 140/C5
Chingola, Zam. 163/E3
Chinguetti, Dhar de (cliff), Mrta. 156/B5
Chinhae, SKor. 131/E5
Chinhoyi, Zim. 163/F4
Chiniak (cape), Ak, US 192/H4
Chiniot, Pak. 144/B4
Chinit (riv.), Camb. 136/D3
Chinju, SKor. 131/E5
Chinko (riv.), CAfr. 155/K6
Chinle, Az, US 186/E3
Chinnor, Eng, UK 91/F3
Chino, Japan 133/F3
Chino, Ca, US 194/C2
Chino (hills), Ca, US 194/G8
Chinook, Mt, US 184/F3
Chinsali, Zam. 162/B5
Chinú, Col. 210/C2
Chiny, Belg. 111/E4
Chinyŏng, SKor. 131/E5
Chioggia, It. 117/F2
Chipatá, Col. 210/C3
Chipata, Zam. 163/F3
Chiping, China 130/D3
Chipiona, Sp. 102/B4
Chipley, Fl, US 191/G4
Chiplūn, India 147/K5
Chippenham, Eng, UK 90/D4
Chippewa (co.), Wi, US 185/L4
Chippewa (riv.), Wi, US 185/L4
Chipping Ongar, Eng, UK 88/D1
Chiprovtsi, Bul. 106/F4
Chiputneticook (lakes), US,Can. 189/H2
Chiquián, Peru 214/B3
Chiquimula, Guat. 202/D3
Chiquimulilla, Guat. 202/D3
Chiquinquirá, Col. 208/D2
Chiquita (sea), Arg. 205/C6
Chīrāla, India 140/D4
Chirāwa, India 144/C5
Chirchiq, Uzb. 145/E4
Chīrgaon, India 142/B3
Chiri-san (peak), SKor. 131/D5
Chiri-san NP, SKor. 131/D5
Chiricahua Nat'l Mon., Az, US 186/E4
Chiriguaná, Col. 210/C2
Chirikof (isl.), Ak, US 192/G4
Chirinos, Peru 214/B2
Chirip (peak), Rus. 134/E1
Chiripa (peak), Nic. 203/E4
Chiriquí (lag.), Pan. 203/F4
Chiriquí, Golfo de (gulf), Pan. 208/B2
Chirkunda, India 143/F4
Chirnside, Sc, UK 94/D5
Chironico, Swi. 115/E5
Chirpan, Bul. 105/J1
Chirripó (mtn.), CR 203/F4
Chirripó, PN, CR 198/E6
Chiryu, Japan 135/M6
Chisana, Ak, US 192/K3
Chisasibi (Fort-George), Qu, Can. 181/J3
Chisholm, Mn, US 188/A2
Chishtiān Mandi, Pak. 144/B5
Chisimba (falls), Zam. 162/A5
Chişinău (cap.), Mol. 107/J2
Chişinău (int'l arpt.), Mol. 107/J2
Chişineu Criş, Rom. 106/E2
Chistochina, Ak, US 192/K3
Chistopol', Rus. 119/L5
Chita, Col. 210/C3
Chita, Japan 135/L6
Chita (bay), Japan 135/L6
Chita (pen.), Japan 135/L6
Chitina, Ak, US 192/K3
Chitinskaya Oblast, Rus. 123/M4
Chitipa, Malw. 162/B5
Chitose, Japan 134/B2
Chitose (int'l arpt.), Japan 134/B2
Chitradurga, India 140/C5
Chitrakut, India 142/C3
Chitral Gol NP, Pak. 144/A2
Chitré, Pan. 210/A3
Chittagong (pol. div.), Bang. 143/H4
Chittagong, Bang. 141/F3
Chittaranjan, India 143/F4
Chittoor, India 140/C5
Chitungwiza, Zim. 163/F4
Chiuduno, It. 116/C1
Chiuppano, It. 117/E1
Chiusa di Pesio, It. 116/A4
Chiusella (riv.), It. 116/A1
Chiusi, It. 101/J5
Chivacoa, Ven. 210/D2
Chivasso, It. 116/A2
Chivato (pt.), Mex. 200/C3
Chivay, Peru 214/D4
Chivé, Bol. 214/D4
Chivhu, Zim. 163/F4
Chivilcoy, Arg. 216/E2
Chixoy (riv.), Guat. 202/D3
Chiyoda, Japan 135/C1
Chiyoda, Japan 135/E1
Chiyokawa, Japan 135/D1
Chizela, Zam. 163/E3
Chlef (riv.), Alg. 158/F4
Chlef (prov.), Alg. 158/F4
Chlef, Alg. 158/F4
Chlum (peak), Czh. 113/H5
Chno Dearg (peak), Sc, UK 94/B3
Ch'o (isl.), NKor. 131/C3
Cho Oyu (peak), Nepal 143/F1
Chobe NP, Bots. 163/D4
Chobham, Eng, UK 88/B3
Choceň, Czh. 99/J4
Choch'iwŏn, SKor. 131/D4
Chocianów, Pol. 99/H3
Chocó (dept.), Col. 203/G5
Chocolate (mts.), Ca, US 186/D4
Chocontá, Col. 210/C3
Chocope, Peru 214/B2
Choctaw, Ok, US 195/N15
Chodavaram, India 140/D4
Chodov, Czh. 113/F2
Chodzież, Pol. 99/J2
Choele Choel, Arg. 216/D3
Chōfu, Japan 133/F3
Choiseul (isl.), Sol. 174/E5
Choisy-au-Bac, Fr. 110/B5
Choisy-le-Roi, Fr. 88/K5
Choix, Mex. 200/C3
Chojna, Pol. 99/H2
Chojnice, Pol. 96/G5
Chojnów, Pol. 99/H3
Chokai-san (peak), Japan 134/B4
Choke Canyon (res.), Tx, US 190/D4
Chola (mts.), China 128/G5
Cholet, Fr. 100/C3
Cholila, Arg. 216/C4
Chŏlla-bukto (prov.), SKor. 131/D5
Ch'ŏlla-namdo (prov.), SKor. 131/D5
Cholula de Rivadabia, Mex. 201/L7
Choluteca, Hon. 202/E3
Choluteca (riv.), Hon. 202/E3
Choma, Zam. 163/E4
Chŏmch'on, SKor. 131/E4
Chomo Lhāri (peak), Bhu. 143/G2
Chomutov, Czh. 113/G2
Chomutovka (riv.), Czh. 113/G2
Chon Buri, Thai. 136/C3
Ch'ŏnan, SKor. 131/D4
Chōnan, Japan 135/E3
Chonchi, Chile 216/B4
Ch'ŏnch'ŏn, NKor. 131/D2
Chone, Ecu. 210/A5

Ch'ŏng – Comit

Ch'ŏng-yang, SKor. 131/D4
Chong'an, China 137/C2
Ch'ŏngch'ŏn (riv.), NKor. 131/D2
Ch'ŏngdo, SKor. 131/E5
Ch'ŏngjin, NKor. 131/E2
Ch'ŏngjin -si (prov.), NKor. 131/E2
Chŏngju, SKor. 131/D5
Ch'ŏngju, SKor. 131/D4
Chŏngju, NKor. 131/C3
Chongli, China 130/C2
Chongmyo Shrine, SKor. 131/G6
Chongoyape, Peru 214/B2
Chŏngsŏn, SKor. 131/E4
Ch'ŏngsong, SKor. 131/E4
Chongyi, China 141/K2
Chongzuo, China 141/J3
Chŏnju, SKor. 131/D5
Ch'ŏnma-san (peak), SKor. 131/G6
Chonos, Archipiélago de los (arch.), Chile 216/B5
Chopan, India 142/D3
Chorcha (mtn.), Pan. 203/F4
Chorley, Eng, UK 93/F4
Chorleywood, Eng, UK 88/B2
Choroszcz, Pol. 99/M2
Chortkiv, Ukr. 120/C2
Ch'ŏrwŏn, SKor. 131/D3
Chorzele, Pol. 99/L2
Chorzów, Pol. 99/K3
Chos-Malal, Arg. 216/C3
Ch'osan, NKor. 131/C2
Chōsei, Japan 135/E3
Chōshi, Japan 133/G3
Choszczno, Pol. 99/H2
Chota, Peru 214/B2
Chota Nāgpur (plat.), India 140/D3
Choteau, Mt, US 184/E4
Chott el Rharbi (depr.), Alg. 158/D3
Chotýšanka (riv.), Czh. 113/H3
Chowagasberg (peak), Namb. 163/C6
Chowan (riv.), NC, US 191/J2
Choybalsan, Mong. 129/K2
Choyr, Mong. 128/J2
Chreïrik (well), Mrta. 156/B5
Christchurch, NZ 175/S11
Christchurch (int'l arpt.), NZ 175/S11
Christchurch, Eng, UK 91/E5
Christchurch (bay), Eng, UK 91/E5
Christian (sound), Ak, US 192/M4
Christiana, Jam. 203/G2
Christiana, SAfr. 164/D2
Christiana, De, US 196/C4
Christiana, Pa, US 196/C4
Christiansfeld, Den. 96/C4
Christiansted, USVI 199/M8
Christina (riv.), De, US 196/C5
Christmas (isl.), Austl. 125/K11
Chrudim, Czh. 99/H4
Chryston, Sc, UK 94/B5
Chrzanów, Pol. 99/K3
Chu Yang Sin (peak), Viet. 136/E3
Chuādānga, Bang. 143/G4
Chuansha, China 130/L8
Chuathbaluk, Ak, US 192/G3
Chubut (riv.), Arg. 216/C4
Chubut (prov.), Arg. 216/C4
Chucanti (peak), Pan. 210/B2
Chūgoku (mts.), Japan 132/C3
Chūgoku (prov.), Japan 132/B4
Chūhar Kāna, Pak. 144/B4
Chukai, Malay. 138/B3
Chukchi (sea), Rus. 125/T3
Chukchi (pen.), Rus. 125/T3
Chukotskiy Aut. Okrug, Rus. 123/S3
Chukotskiy (cape), Rus. 192/D3
Chula Vista, Ca, US 194/C5
Ch'ulp'o, SKor. 131/D5
Chulucanas, Peru 214/A2
Chulym (riv.), Rus. 122/J4
Chuma, Bol. 214/D4
Chumerna (peak), Bul. 105/J1
Chumphon, Thai. 136/B4
Chuna (riv.), Rus. 122/K4
Chunār, India 142/D3
Ch'unch'ŏn, SKor. 131/D4
Ch'ungch'ŏng-bukto (prov.), SKor. 131/D4
Ch'ungch'ŏng-namdo (prov.), SKor. 131/D4
Ch'ungju (lake), SKor. 131/D4
Ch'ungju, SKor. 131/D4
Ch'ungman (riv.), NKor. 131/C2
Ch'ungmu, SKor. 131/E5
Chŭngsan, NKor. 131/C3
Chunhuhub, Mex. 202/D2
Chūniān, Pak. 144/B4
Chunya, Tanz. 162/B5
Chunya (riv.), Rus. 123/L3
Ch'unyang, SKor. 131/E4
Chupa, Peru 214/D4
Chupaca, Peru 214/C4
Chuquibamba, Peru 214/C4
Chuquibambilla, Peru 214/C4
Chuquicamata, Chile 215/C1
Chur, Swi. 115/F4
Churachandpur, India 141/F3
Churcampa, Peru 214/C4
Church, Eng, UK 93/F4
Church Hill, Md, US 196/C5
Churchill, Austl. 173/C3
Churchill (peak), BC, Can. 180/D3
Churchill, Mb, Can. 180/G3
Churchill (cape), Mb, Can. 180/G3
Churchill (riv.), Mb,Sk, Can. 180/F3
Churchill (lake), Sk, Can. 180/F3
Churchill Falls, Nf, Can. 181/K3
Churchill NP, Austl. 173/G5
Churchville, Md, US 196/B4
Churia Ghats (mts.), Nepal 143/E2
Churín, Peru 214/B3
Churnet (riv.), Eng, UK 93/G5
Churu, India 144/C5
Churuguara, Ven. 210/D2
Churumuco de Morelos, Mex. 201/E5
Churwalden, Swi. 115/F4
Chuschi, Peru 214/C4
Chuska (mts.), Az,NM, US 186/E3
Chusovaya (riv.), Rus. 119/N4
Chusovoy, Rus. 119/N4
Chutung, Tai. 137/D3
Chuvashiya, Resp., Rus. 122/Q6
Chuwang-san NP, SKor. 131/E4
Chuxiong, China 141/H2
Chüy (obl.), Kyr. 145/F4
Chuzhou, China 129/L5
Chūzu, Japan 135/K5
Ci Xian, China 130/C3
Ciadîr-Lunga, Mol. 107/J2
Ciamis, Indo. 138/C5
Ciampino (int'l arpt.), It. 104/C2
Ciampino, It. 104/C2
Cianjur, Indo. 138/C5
Cibolo, Tx, US 195/U20
Cicagna, It. 116/C4
Cicero, Il, US 188/C3
Cícero Dantas, Braz. 212/C3
Čičevac, Serb. 106/E4
Cide, Turk. 148/C1
Ciechanów, Pol. 99/L2
Ciechocinek, Pol. 99/K2
Ciego de Ávila, Cuba 203/G1
Ciénaga, Col. 210/C2
Ciénaga de Oro, Col. 210/C2
Cienfuegos, Cuba 203/F1
Cieplice Śląskie Zdrój, Pol. 99/H3
Cieszyn, Pol. 99/K4
Cieza, Sp. 102/E3
Çifteler, Turk. 148/B2
Cifuentes, Sp. 102/D2
Cifuentes, Cuba 203/F1
Cigánd, Hun. 99/L4
Cigliano, It. 116/B2
Cigüela (riv.), Sp. 102/D3
Cihanbeyli, Turk. 148/C2
Cihuatlán, Mex. 200/D5
Cijara, Embalse de (res.), Sp. 102/C3
Cijulang, Indo. 138/C5
Cilacap, Indo. 138/C5
Cilavegna, It. 116/B2
Çıldır (lake), Turk. 148/E1
Cilfaesty (peak), Wal, UK 90/C2
Cili, China 137/B2
Cilleros, Sp. 102/B2
Cima della Laurasca (peak), It. 115/E5
Cima de'Piazzi (peak), It. 115/G5
Cima la Casina (peak), It. 115/G4
Cimarron (range), NM, US 190/B2
Cimarron (riv.), Ks,Ok, US 182/G4
Cime du Cheiron (peak), Fr. 101/G5
Cime du Diable (peak), Fr. 101/G4
Cimone (peak), It. 117/D4
Cimpeni, Rom. 107/F2
Cîmpia Turzii, Rom. 107/F2
Cîmpina, Rom. 107/G3
Cîmpulung, Rom. 107/G3
Cîmpulung Moldovenesc, Rom. 107/G2
Çınar, Turk. 148/E2
Çınarcık, Turk. 107/J5
Cinaruco (riv.), Ven. 210/D3
Cinca (riv.), Sp. 103/F1
Cincar (peak), Bosn. 106/C4
Cincinnati, Oh, US 188/C4
Cinco Saltos, Arg. 216/C3
Cîndrelu (peak), Rom. 107/F3
Çine, Turk. 148/B2
Ciney, Belg. 111/E3
Cingia de'Botti, It. 116/D2
Cingoli, It. 117/G6
Cinisello Balsamo, It. 116/C1
Cinnaminson, NJ, US 196/D4
Cintalapa de Figueroa, Mex. 202/C2
Cinto (peak), Fr. 104/A1
Cinto Caomaggiore, It. 117/F1
Cintruénigo, Sp. 102/E1
Čiovo (isl.), Cro. 106/C4
Cipó, Braz. 212/C3
Cipolletti, Arg. 216/D3
Circeo, PN del, It. 104/C2
Circle, Ak, US 192/K2
Circle, Mt, US 185/G4
Circle Hot Springs, Ak, US 192/K2
Cirebon, Indo. 138/C5
Cirencester, Eng, UK 90/E3
Cires-lès-Mello, Fr. 110/B5
Cirò Marina, It. 105/E3
Ciron (riv.), Fr. 100/C4
Ciserano, It. 116/C1
Cisnădie, Rom. 107/G3
Cisneros, Col. 210/C3
Cisnes (riv.), Chile 216/B5
Cisse (riv.), Fr. 100/D3
Cisterna di Latina, It. 104/C2
Cistierna, Sp. 102/C1
Citlaltépetl (vol.), Mex. 201/M7
Citrus Heights, Ca, US 186/B3
Citrusdal, SAfr. 164/L10
Città del Vaticano (Vatican City) (cap.), VatC. 104/C2
Città di Castello, It. 117/F6
Citta di Torino (int'l arpt.), It. 101/G4
Cittadella, It. 117/E1
Cittanova, It. 104/E3
Cittiglio, It. 115/E6
City (isl.), NY, US 197/K8
City (int'l arpt.), NI, UK 92/C2
Ciudad Acuña, Mex. 201/E2
Ciudad Altamirano, Mex. 201/E5
Ciudad Bolívar, Ven. 211/F2
Ciudad Bolivia, Ven. 210/D2
Ciudad Camargo, Mex. 200/D3
Ciudad Constitución, Mex. 200/C3
Ciudad Cortés, CR 203/F4
Ciudad Cuauhtémoc, Mex. 202/B1
Ciudad de Dolores Hidalgo, Mex. 201/E4
Ciudad de México (Mexico) (cap.), Mex. 201/Q10
Ciudad de Nutrias, Ven. 210/D2
Ciudad de Río Grande, Mex. 200/E4
Ciudad del Carmen, Mex. 202/D2
Ciudad del Maíz, Mex. 201/F4
Ciudad Delicias, Mex. 200/D2
Ciudad Fernández, Mex. 201/E4
Ciudad Frontera, Mex. 201/E3
Ciudad Guayana, Ven. 211/F2
Ciudad Guzmán, Mex. 200/E5
Ciudad Hidalgo, Mex. 201/E5
Ciudad Hidalgo, Mex. 202/C3
Ciudad Insurgentes, Mex. 200/C3
Ciudad Ixtepec, Mex. 202/C2
Ciudad Juárez, Mex. 200/D2
Ciudad Lerdo, Mex. 200/E3
Ciudad Madero, Mex. 202/B1
Ciudad Mante, Mex. 201/F4
Ciudad Mendoza, Mex. 201/M8
Ciudad Miguel Alemán, Mex. 201/F3
Ciudad Obregón, Mex. 200/C3
Ciudad Ojeda, Ven. 210/D2
Ciudad Pemex, Mex. 202/C2
Ciudad Piar, Ven. 211/F3
Ciudad, PN de la, Mex. 200/D4
Ciudad Real, Sp. 102/D3
Ciudad Rodrigo, Sp. 102/B2
Ciudad Serdán, Mex. 201/M8
Ciudad Valles, Mex. 202/B1
Ciudad Victoria, Mex. 201/F4
Ciutadella de Menorca, Sp. 103/G3
Civa Burnu (pt.), Turk. 148/D1
Civate, It. 116/C1
Civezzano, It. 115/H5
Cividale del Friuli, It. 101/K3
Cividate Camuno, It. 115/G6
Civita Castellana, It. 104/C1
Civitavecchia, It. 104/B1
Civray, Fr. 100/D3
Çivril, Turk. 148/B2
Cixi, China 130/L9
Cize, Fr. 114/B4
Cizre, Turk. 148/E2
Cizre (dam), Turk. 148/E2
Cizur, Sp. 102/E1
Clackmannan, Sc, UK 94/C4
Clackmannanshire (pol. reg.), Sc, UK 94/C4
Claerwen (res.), Wal, UK 90/C2
Claiborne, Md, US 196/B6
Clain (riv.), Fr. 100/D3
Clair Engle (lake), Ca, US 186/B2
Claire (lake), Ab, Can. 180/E3
Clairefontaine-en-Yvelines, Fr. 88/H6
Clairvaux-les-Lacs, Fr. 114/B4
Claise (riv.), Fr. 100/D3
Clallam (co.), Wa, US 193/A2
Clamart, Fr. 88/J5
Clamecy, Fr. 100/E3
Clane, Ire. 89/Q10
Clanton, Al, US 191/G3
Clanwilliam, SAfr. 164/B4
Clara (pt.), Arg. 216/D4
Clara, Ire. 89/Q10
Clare, Austl. 171/H5
Clare (isl.), Ire. 88/N10
Clare (riv.), Ire. 89/P10
Clare, Ks, US 195/D6
Clare, Mi, US 188/C3
Claremont, NH, US 189/F3
Claremont, Ca, US 194/C2
Claremore, Ok, US 187/J3
Claremorris, Ire. 89/P10
Clarence (pt.), Nun., Can. 181/T7
Clarence, NZ 175/S11
Clarence (riv.), NZ 175/S11
Clarence, NY, US 189/S9
Clarence Town, Bahm. 199/G3
Clarendon, Tx, US 187/G4
Clarenville, Nf, Can. 189/L1
Claresholm, Ab, Can. 184/E3
Clarion (isl.), Mex. 200/B5
Clark, SD, US 185/J4
Clark, NJ, US 197/H9
Clark Fork (riv.), Id,Mt, US 184/E3
Clarke (isl.), Austl. 173/D4
Clarke (lake), Pa, US 196/B4
Clarks Point, Ak, US 192/G4
Clarksburg, WV, US 188/D4
Clarksburg, NJ, US 196/D3
Clarksburg, Ca, US 193/L10
Clarksdale, Ms, US 187/K4
Clarkston, Wa, US 184/D4
Clarkston, Mi, US 193/F6
Clarksville, Ar, US 187/J4
Clarksville, Tn, US 188/C4
Clarksville, Tx, US 187/J4
Claro (riv.), Braz. 209/H7
Claro, Swi. 115/F5
Clatteringshaws Loch (lake), Sc, UK 92/D1
Claudy, NI, UK 92/A2
Clausen, Ger. 111/G5
Clausthal-Zellerfeld, Ger. 109/H5
Claveria, Phil. 137/D4
Clawson, Mi, US 193/F6
Clay (pt.), IM, UK 92/D3
Clay (co.), Mo, US 195/E5
Clay Center, Ks, US 187/H3
Clay Cross-North Wingfield, Eng, UK 93/G5
Claye-Souilly, Fr. 88/L5
Claymont, De, US 196/C4
Clayton, Ca, US 193/L11
Clayton, De, US 196/C5
Clayton, Ga, US 191/H3
Clayton, Mo, US 195/G8
Clayton, NJ, US 196/C4
Clayton, NM, US 187/G3
Clayton, Ok, US 190/E3
Clayton-le-Moors, Eng, UK 93/F4
Clear (lake), Ca, US 186/B3
Clear (hills), Ab, Can. 180/E3
Clear (cape), Ire. 89/P11
Clear Fork Brazos (riv.), Tx, US 187/H4
Clear Lake, SD, US 185/J4
Cleare (cape), Ak, US 192/J4
Clearfield, Ut, US 195/J11
Clearwater, BC, Can. 184/C3
Clearwater, Fl, US 191/H5
Clearwater (mts.), Id, US 184/D4
Clearwater (riv.), Mn, US 185/K4
Cleburne, Tx, US 187/H4
Cleethorpes, Eng, UK 93/H4
Cleeve (hill), Eng, UK 90/D3
Cleland Rec. Area, Austl. 171/M8
Clementon, NJ, US 196/D4
Clemson, SC, US 191/H3
Cleona, Pa, US 196/B3
Cleopatra Needle (peak), Phil. 139/E1
Clermont, Austl. 172/B3
Clermont, Fr. 110/B5
Clermont-en-Argonne, Fr. 111/E5
Clermont-Ferrand, Fr. 100/E4
Clerval, Fr. 114/C3
Clervaux, Lux. 111/F3
Cles, It. 115/H5
Cleve, Austl. 171/H5
Clevedon, Eng, UK 90/D4
Cleveland (cape), Austl. 172/B2
Cleveland (hills), Eng, UK 93/G3
Cleveland, Mo, US 195/D6
Cleveland, Ms, US 187/K4
Cleveland (mt.), Mt, US 184/E3
Cleveland, Oh, US 188/D3
Cleveland (co.), Ok, US 195/N15
Cleveland, Tn, US 191/G3
Cleveland, Tx, US 187/J5
Cleveland-Hopkins (int'l arpt.), Oh, US 188/D3
Cleveland National Forest, Ca, US 194/C3
Clevelândia, Braz. 213/A3
Clew (bay), Ire. 89/P10
Clewiston, Fl, US 191/H5
Clichy, Fr. 88/J5
Clichy-sous-Bois, Fr. 88/K5
Clifden, Ire. 88/F10
Cliffside Park, NJ, US 197/K8
Cliffwood, NJ, US 197/J10
Clifton, Az, US 186/E4
Clifton, NJ, US 197/J8
Clifton Beach, Austl. 172/B2
Clifton Forge, Va, US 191/J2
Clignon (riv.), Fr. 110/C5
Clingmans (peak), NC,Tn, US 191/H3
Clinton, BC, Can. 184/C3
Clinton, Ct, US 197/F1
Clinton, Ia, US 185/L5
Clinton, La, US 187/K5
Clinton, Mi, US 193/G6
Clinton (riv.), Mi, US 193/F6
Clinton, Mo, US 187/J3
Clinton (co.), Mo, US 195/E5
Clinton, Ms, US 187/K4
Clinton, NC, US 191/J3
Clinton, NJ, US 196/D2
Clinton (res.), NJ, US 196/D1
Clinton, Ok, US 187/H4
Clinton (co.), Pa, US 196/A1
Clinton, SC, US 191/H3
Clinton, Ut, US 195/J11
Clinton, Wa, US 193/C2
Clinton-Colden (lake), NW, Can. 180/F2
Clinton, Middle Branch (riv.), Mi, US 193/G6
Clinton, North Branch (riv.), Mi, US 193/G6
Clintonville, Wi, US 188/B2
Clints Dod (hill), Sc, UK 94/D5
Clio, Mi, US 188/D3
Clitheroe, Eng, UK 93/F4
Cloates (pt.), Austl. 170/B2
Clocolan, SAfr. 164/D3
Clogherhead, Ire. 92/B4
Clonakilty, Ire. 89/P11
Cloncurry, Austl. 172/A3
Clondalkin, Ire. 92/B5
Clonmany, Ire. 92/A1
Clonmel, Ire. 89/Q10
Cloppenburg, Ger. 109/F3
Clorinda, Arg. 215/E2
Clos-Fontaine, Fr. 88/M6
Closter, NJ, US 197/K8
Cloudcroft, NM, US 190/B3
Cloudy (mtn.), Ak, US 192/G3
Cloughmills, NI, UK 92/B2
Cloverdale, Ca, US 186/B3
Clovis, Ca, US 186/C3
Clovis, NM, US 187/G4
Cluanie (lake), Sc, UK 94/A2
Cluj (co.), Rom. 107/F2
Cluj-Napoca, Rom. 107/F2
Cluses, Fr. 114/C5
Clusone, It. 115/F6
Clutha (riv.), NZ 175/R12
Clwyd (co.), Wal, UK 93/E5
Clwyd (riv.), Wal, UK 93/E5
Clwydian (range), Wal, UK 93/E5
Clyde (riv.), NS, Can. 189/H2
Clyde (riv.), Sc, UK 94/B5
Clyde, Firth of (inlet), Sc, UK 89/R8
Clyde Hill, Wa, US 193/C2
Clydesdale (valley), Sc, UK 94/C5
Clywedog (riv.), Wal, UK 90/C2
CN Tower, On, Can. 189/R8
Co Loa Citadel, Viet. 136/D1
Côa (riv.), Port. 102/B2
Coacalco, Mex. 201/Q9
Coachella, Ca, US 186/C4
Coagh, NI, UK 92/B2
Coahuayana de Hidalgo, Mex. 200/E5
Coahuila de Zaragoza (state), Mex. 200/E3
Coahuila, Mex. 200/B1
Coalburn, Sc, UK 94/C5
Coalcomán de Matamoros, Mex. 200/E5
Coaldale, Ab, Can. 184/E3
Coaldale, Pa, US 196/C2
Coalgate, Ok, US 187/H4
Coalhurst, Ab, Can. 184/E3
Coalisland, NI, UK 92/B2
Coalville, Ut, US 186/E2
Coalville, Eng, UK 91/E1
Coaraci, Braz. 212/C4
Coari, Braz. 208/F4
Coari (riv.), Braz. 208/F5
Coasa, Peru 214/D4
Coast (mts.), Can.,US 180/C2
Coast (prov.), Kenya 162/C3
Coast (ranges), Ca, US 184/C5
Coatbridge, Sc, UK 94/B5
Coatepec, Mex. 201/N7
Coatepec Harinas, Mex. 201/K8
Coatesville, Pa, US 196/C4
Coatetelco, Mex. 201/K8
Coaticook, Qu, Can. 189/G2
Coats (isl.), Nun., Can. 181/H2
Coats Land (pol. reg.), Ant. 218/Y
Coatzacoalcos, Mex. 202/C2
Coatzingo, Mex. 201/L8
Coba (ruin), Mex. 202/E1
Coba de Serpe, Sierra de (peak), Sp. 102/B1
Cobán, Guat. 202/D3
Cobar, Austl. 173/C1
Cobb (lake), Co, US 195/C1
Cobberas (mt.), Austl. 173/D3
Cobblestone (mtn.), Ca, US 194/B1
Cobden, Austl. 173/B3
Cóbh, Ire. 89/P11
Cobham (riv.), Mb,On, Can. 185/K2
Cobija, Bol. 208/E6
Cobourg, On, Can. 188/E3
Cobquecura, Chile 216/B3
Coburg (pen.), Austl. 167/C2
Coburg (isl.), Nun., Can. 181/T7
Coburg, Ger. 112/D2
Coca, Ecu. 210/B5
Coca (riv.), Ecu. 210/B5
Cocachacra, Peru 214/D5
Cocal, Braz. 212/B1
Coccaglio, It. 116/C1
Cocentaina, Sp. 103/E3
Cochabamba, Bol. 208/E7
Coche (isl.), Ven. 211/F2
Cochem, Ger. 111/G3
Cocherel, Fr. 88/M4
Cochin, India 140/C6
Cochran, Ga, US 191/H3
Cochrane, Ab, Can. 184/E3
Cochrane, On, Can. 188/D1
Cock Cairn (peak), Sc, UK 94/D3
Cockatoo, Austl. 173/G5
Cockburn (sound), Austl. 170/K7
Cockburn (chan.), Chile 217/B7
Cockeysville, Md, US 196/B5
Cockscomb (peak), SAfr. 164/D4
Coclé del Norte, Pan. 203/F4
Coco (riv.), Hon. 198/E5
Coco, Cayo (isl.), Cuba 203/G1
Coco, Isla del (isl.), CR 208/A2
Cocoa, Fl, US 191/H4
Coconino (plat.), Az, US 186/D4
Cocoparra NP, Austl. 173/C2
Cocorocuma, Cayo (isl.), Hon. 203/F3
Cocos (isls.), Austl. 125/J11
Côcos, Braz. 212/A4
Cocotitlán, Mex. 201/R10
Cocula, Mex. 200/E4
Cod (isl.), Nf, Can. 181/K3
Codajás, Braz. 208/F4
Codegua, Chile 216/N9
Codigoro, It. 117/F3
Codlea, Rom. 107/G3
Codogno, It. 116/C2
Codsall, Eng, UK 90/D1
Coelemu, Chile 216/B3
Coelho Neto, Braz. 212/B2
Coesfeld, Ger. 109/E5
Coeur d'Alene (lake), Id, US 184/D4
Coeur d'Alene, Id, US 184/D4
Coevorden, Neth. 108/D3
Coffin Bay, Austl. 171/G5
Coffin Bay NP, Austl. 171/G5
Coffs Harbour, Austl. 173/E1
Cofre de Perote, PN, Mex. 201/M7
Coggiola, It. 116/B1
Coghinas (lake), It. 104/A2
Cognac, Fr. 100/C4
Cogoleto, It. 116/B4
Cogolin, Fr. 101/G5
Cogollo del Cengio, It. 117/E1
Cogolludo, Sp. 102/D2
Cohansey (riv.), NJ, US 196/C5
Cohuna, Austl. 173/C2
Cohunu NP, Austl. 170/L7
Coiba, Isla de (isl.), Pan. 208/B2
Coig (riv.), Arg. 215/C7
Coignières, Fr. 88/H5
Coihaique, Chile 216/B5
Coihueco, Chile 216/B3
Coimbatore, India 140/C5
Coimbra (dist.), Port. 102/A2
Coimbra, Port. 102/A2
Coín, Sp. 102/C4
Coina (riv.), Port. 103/P10
Coise (riv.), Fr. 100/F4
Cojedes (riv.), Ven. 208/E2
Cojedes (state), Ven. 210/D2
Cojimíes, Ecu. 210/A4
Cojudo Blanco (peak), Arg. 217/C5
Cojutepeque, ESal. 202/D3
Čoka, Serb. 106/E3
Cokeville, Wy, US 184/F5
Col d'Ispéguy (pass), Fr. 100/C5
Col San Martino, It. 117/F1
Colac, Austl. 173/B3
Colares, Port. 103/P10
Colasay, Peru 214/B2
Colatina, Braz. 213/D1
Colbeck (cape), Ant. 218/P
Colbún, Chile 216/C2
Colby, Wa, US 193/B2
Colca (riv.), Peru 214/D4
Colcabamba, Peru 214/C4
Colchester, Eng, UK 91/G3
Cold Bay, Ak, US 192/F4
Cold Fell (peak), Eng, UK 93/F2
Cold Lake, Ab, Can. 184/F2
Cold Spring, Mn, US 185/K4
Cold Spring Harbor, NY, US 197/M8
Coldstream, Sc, UK 94/D5
Coldwater, Ks, US 187/H3
Coldwater, Mi, US 188/C3
Cole, Ok, US 195/M15
Cole (riv.), Eng, UK 91/E3
Coleambally, Austl. 173/C2
Coleman, Tx, US 187/H5
Çölemerik, Turk. 148/E2
Colenso, SAfr. 165/E3
Coleraine, Austl. 173/B3
Coleraine (dist.), NI, UK 92/B1
Coleraine, NI, UK 92/B1
Colesberg, SAfr. 164/D3
Colesville, Md, US 196/A5
Colfax, Wa, US 184/D4
Colgate (cape), Nun., Can. 181/S6
Colgong, India 143/F3
Colhué Huapí (lake), Arg. 216/C5
Colico, It. 115/F5
Coligny, SAfr. 164/D2
Coligny, Fr. 114/B5
Colima, Mex. 200/E5
Colima (state), Mex. 200/D5
Colima, Nevado de (peak), Mex. 200/E5
Colina, Chile 216/N8
Coliseum, Ca, US 194/F8
Coll (isl.), Sc, UK 89/Q8
Collado-Villalba, Sp. 103/N8
Collagna, It. 116/D4
Collarenebri, Austl. 173/D1
Colle di Val d'Elsa, It. 117/E6
Collecchio, It. 116/D3
College, Ak, US 192/J3
College Park, Md, US 196/B6
College Station, Tx, US 187/H5
Collegeville, Pa, US 196/C3
Collegno, It. 101/G4
Collesalvetti, It. 116/D5
Colletorto, It. 104/D2
Collie, Austl. 170/C5
Collier (bay), Austl. 167/B2
Collier (range), Austl. 170/C3
Collier Range NP, Austl. 170/C3
Collierville, Tn, US 187/K4
Collifford (res.), Eng, UK 90/B5
Collingwood, On, Can. 188/D2
Collins, Ms, US 191/F4
Collinstown (int'l arpt.), Ire. 92/B5
Collinsville, Austl. 172/B3
Collinsville, Ca, US 193/L10
Collinsville, Il, US 195/H8
Collinsville, Ok, US 190/E2
Collo, Alg. 158/K6
Collombey, Swi. 114/C5
Collon, Ire. 92/B4
Collonges, Fr. 114/B5
Colma, Ca, US 193/K11
Colmar, Fr. 114/D1
Colmar, Pa, US 196/C3
Colmberg, Ger. 112/D4
Colmenar, Sp. 102/C4
Colmenar de Oreja, Sp. 103/N9
Colmenar Viejo, Sp. 103/N8
Colmillo (cape), Chile 217/B6
Colne (riv.), Eng, UK 93/G4
Colne, Eng, UK 93/F4
Cologna Veneta, It. 117/E2
Cologne, It. 116/C1
Cologne, NJ, US 196/D5
Cologne/Bonn (int'l arpt.), Ger. 111/G2
Cologno Monzese, It. 116/C1
Colombes, Fr. 88/J5
Colombey-les-Belles, Fr. 114/B1
Colombia (ctry.) 208/D3
Colombia, Col. 210/C4
Colombier, Swi. 114/C4
Colombine (peak), It. 116/D1
Colombo, Braz. 213/B3
Colombo (cap.), SrL. 140/C6
Colomiers, Fr. 100/D5
Colomoncagua, Hon. 202/D3
Colón, Arg. 216/E2
Colón, Cuba 203/F1
Colón (mts.), Hon. 203/E3
Colón, Pan. 203/G4
Colón, Uru. 217/G2
Colonche, Ecu. 214/A1
Colonelganj, India 142/C2
Colonia, Micr. 174/C4
Colonia (dept.), Uru. 216/F2
Colonia, NJ, US 197/H9
Colonia Barón, Arg. 216/E3
Colonia del Sacramento, Uru. 217/K11
Colonia Juárez, Mex. 200/C2
Colonia Las Heras, Arg. 216/C5
Colonial Park, Pa, US 196/B3
Colonsay (isl.), Sc, UK 89/Q8
Colorado (peak), Arg. 217/C6
Colorado (riv.), Arg. 215/C4
Colorado, Braz. 213/B2
Colorado (plat.), US 186/E3
Colorado (riv.), US 186/D4
Colorado (state), US 186/F3
Colorado City, Tx, US 187/G4
Colorado Historical Museum, Co, US 195/C3
Colorado Springs, Co, US 187/F3
Colorno, It. 116/D3
Colotlán, Mex. 200/E4
Colquiri, Bol. 208/E7
Colson (pt.), Belz. 202/D2
Colstrip, Mt, US 184/G4
Colt (hill), Sc, UK 94/B6
Coltauco, Chile 216/N9
Colton, Ca, US 194/C2
Colts Neck, NJ, US 196/D3
Coluene (riv.), Braz. 205/D4
Columbe, Ecu. 214/B1
Columbia (riv.), Can.,US 184/C4
Columbia (plat.), US 184/C4
Columbia, Il, US 195/G9
Columbia, Ky, US 188/C4
Columbia, La, US 187/J4
Columbia, Md, US 196/B5
Columbia, Ms, US 191/F4
Columbia, NJ, US 196/C2
Columbia, Pa, US 196/B3
Columbia (co.), Pa, US 196/B1
Columbia (cap.), SC, US 191/H3
Columbia, Tn, US 188/C5
Columbia Falls, Mt, US 184/E3
Columbine (cape), SAfr. 164/K10
Columbus, Ga, US 191/G3
Columbus, In, US 188/C4
Columbus, Ms, US 191/F3
Columbus, Mt, US 184/F4
Columbus, Ne, US 185/J5
Columbus, NJ, US 196/D3
Columbus, NM, US 190/B4
Columbus (cap.), Oh, US 188/D4
Columbus, Tx, US 187/H5
Colunga, Sp. 102/C1
Colusa, Ca, US 186/B3
Colville (riv.), Ak, US 192/G2
Colville, Wa, US 184/D3
Colville (lake), NW, Can. 180/D2
Colvos (passg.), Wa, US 193/B3
Colwyn Bay, Wal, UK 92/E5
Comacchio, It. 117/F3
Comacchio, Valli di (lag.), It. 101/K4
Comai, China 143/H1
Comal, Tx, US 195/U20
Comal (co.), Tx, US 195/U20
Comala, Mex. 200/E5
Comalcalco, Mex. 202/C2
Comanche, Tx, US 187/H5
Comandante Luis Piedra Buena, Arg. 217/C6
Comandante Nicanor Otamendi, Arg. 216/F3
Comănești, Rom. 107/H2
Comarnic, Rom. 107/G3
Comas, Peru 214/C3
Comas, Peru 214/B3
Comayagua, Hon. 202/E3
Comayagua (mts.), Hon. 202/D3
Combapata, Peru 214/D4
Combarbalá, Chile 215/B3
Combeaufontaine, Fr. 114/B2
Comber, On, Can. 193/G7
Comber, NI, UK 92/C2
Comblain-au-Pont, Belg. 111/E3
Combloux, Fr. 114/C6
Combs-la-Ville, Fr. 88/K6
Comé, Ben. 161/F5
Comendador, DRep. 203/J2
Comilla (pol. reg.), Bang. 143/H4
Comines, Fr. 110/C2
Comines, Belg. 110/B2
Comino (isl.), Malta 104/L6
Comitán de Domínguez, Mex. 202/C2

Commack, NY, US 197/E2
Commentry, Fr. 100/E3
Commeny, Fr. 88/H4
Commerce, Ca, US 194/F7
Commerce City,
Co, US 195/C3
Commercy, Fr. 111/E6
Commewijne (dist.),
Sur. 211/H3
Committee (bay),
Nun., Can. 181/H2
Como (lake), It. 101/H3
Como, It. 115/F6
Como, Wi, US 193/P14
Comodoro Rivadavia,
Arg. 216/C5
Comoé (prov.), Burk. 160/D4
Comoe, PN de la,
C.d'Iv. 154/E6
Comoé, PN de la,
C.d'Iv. 160/D4
Comorin (cape),
India 140/C6
Comoros (ctry.) 165/G5
Comox, BC, Can. 184/B3
Compiègne, Fr. 110/B5
Compostela, Phil. 139/G3
Compostela, Mex. 200/D4
Compton, Ca, US 194/F8
Comrat, Mol. 107/J2
Comrie, Sc, UK 94/C4
Comstock, Tx, US 190/C4
Con Son (isl.), Viet. 141/J6
Cona, China 141/F2
Conaica, Peru 214/C4
Conakry (pol. reg.),
Gui. 160/B4
Conakry (cap.), Gui. 160/B4
Conakry (int'l arpt.),
Gui. 160/B4
Conambo (riv.),
Ecu. 210/B5
Conca (riv.), It. 117/F5
Concarneau, Fr. 100/B3
Conceição da Barra,
Braz. 213/E1
Conceição das Alagoas,
Braz. 213/B1
Conceição do Araguaia,
Braz. 209/J5
Conceição do Coité,
Braz. 212/C3
Conceição do Mato Dentro,
Braz. 213/D1
Conceição do Rio Verde,
Braz. 213/H6
Conceição dos Ouros,
Braz. 213/H7
Concepción (lake),
Bol. 208/F7
Concepción, Arg. 215/C2
Concepción, Bol. 208/E6
Concepción, Chile 216/B3
Concepción (pt.),
Mex. 200/C3
Concepción, Par. 215/E1
Concepción, Peru 208/C6
Concepción (bay),
Mex. 200/B3
Concepción de La Vega,
DRep. 199/G4
Concepción del Oro,
Mex. 201/E3
Concepción del Uruguay,
Arg. 217/J10
Conception (pt.),
Ca, US 186/B4
Concesio, It. 116/D1
Conchal, Braz. 213/F7
Conchas (lake),
NM, US 187/F4
Conches, Fr. 88/L5
Conchillas, Uru. 217/J11
Concho (riv.), Tx, US 187/G5
Conchos (riv.), Mex. 200/D2
Concord, Ca, US 186/C3
Concord, NC, US 191/H3
Concord (cap.),
NH, US 189/G3
Concord, Wi, US 193/N13
Concordia, Arg. 215/E3
Concórdia, Braz. 213/A3
Concordia, Mex. 200/D4
Concordia, Peru 214/C2
Concordia Sagittaria,
It. 117/F1
Concordia sulla Secchia,
It. 117/D3
Concrete, Wa, US 184/C3
Condado, Cuba 203/G1
Condamine (riv.),
Austl. 167/E3
Condamine, Austl. 172/C3
Conde, Braz. 212/C3
Condé-sur-L'Escaut, Fr. 110/C3
Condé-sur-Noireau, Fr. 100/C2
Condé-sur-Vesgre, Fr. 88/G5
Condé-sur-Vire, Fr. 100/C2
Condécourt, Fr. 88/H4
Condeúba, Braz. 212/B4
Condino, It. 115/G6
Condobolin, Austl. 173/C2
Condom, Fr. 100/D5
Condon, Or, US 184/C4
Condroz (plat.), Belg. 98/C3
Conecuh (riv.), Al, US 191/G4
Conegliano, It. 117/F1
Conejos, Co, US 187/F3
Conesa, Arg. 216/E2
Conestoga (riv.),
Pa, US 196/A3
Conewago (lake),
Pa, US 196/A3
Confins (int'l arpt.),
Braz. 213/D1

Conflans-en-Jarnisy,
Fr. 111/E5
Conflans-Sainte-Honorine,
Fr. 88/J5
Congaree Swamp
Nat'l Mon., SC, US 191/H3
Congers, NY, US 197/K7
Congis-sur-Thérouanne,
Fr. 88/L4
Congjiang, China 141/J2
Congleton, Eng, UK 93/F5
Conway (cape),
Austl. 172/C3
Conway NP, Austl. 172/C3
Conwy (bay), Wal, UK 92/D5
Conwy (co.), Wal, UK 92/E5
Conwy (riv.), Wal, UK 92/E5
Conwy, Vale of (valley),
Wal, UK 92/E5
Conyngham, Pa, US 196/B2
Coober Pedy,
Austl. 171/G4
Cooch Behar, India 143/G2
Coochiemudlo (isl.),
Austl. 172/F7
Cook (bay), Chile 217/C7
Cook (mt.), NZ 175/S11
Cook (str.), NZ 175/S11
Cook (inlet), Ak, US 180/A3
Cook (co.), Il, US 193/Q16
Cook Islands
(dpcy.), NZ 175/J6
Cooke (mt.), Austl. 170/C5
Cookeville, Tn, US 188/C4
Cookham, Eng, UK 88/A2
Cookhouse, SAfr. 164/D4
Cookstown, NI, UK 92/B2
Cookstown (dist.),
NI, UK 92/B2
Cooksville, Md, US 196/A5
Cooktown, Austl. 172/B1
Coola Coola (swamp),
Austl. 173/B3
Coolah, Austl. 173/D1
Coolamon, Austl. 173/C2
Coolangatta,
Austl. 173/E1
Cooley (pt.), Ire. 92/B4
Coolgardie, Austl. 170/D4
Cooloola NP,
Austl. 172/D4
Cooloongup (lake),
Austl. 170/K7
Cooma, Austl. 173/D2
Coonabarabran,
Austl. 173/D1
Coonalpyn, Austl. 173/A2
Coonamble, Austl. 173/D1
Coonana Abor. Land,
Austl. 170/D4
Coondapoor (Kundapura),
India 147/K6
Coongan Abor. Land,
Austl. 170/C2
Coonoor, India 140/C5
Cooper, Tx, US 187/J4
Coopersburg,
Pa, US 196/C2
Cooperstown,
ND, US 185/J4
Coorow, Austl. 170/C4
Coorong NP, Austl. 173/A3
Coorow, Austl. 170/C4
Cooroy, Austl. 172/D4
Coosa (riv.), Al, US 191/G3
Cootamundra, Austl. 173/D2
Coot'tha (mt.),
Austl. 172/E6
Copacabana, Bol. 214/D5
Copahué (vol.),
Chile 216/C3
Copainalá, Mex. 202/C2
Copala, Mex. 198/B4
Copán (ruin), Hon. 202/D3
Cope (cape), Sp. 102/E4
Copeland (isl.),
NI, UK 92/C2
Copenhagen (København)
(cap.), Den. 96/E4
Copertino, It. 105/F2
Copeton (dam),
Austl. 173/D1
Copiague, NY, US 197/M9
Copiapó, Chile 215/B2
Coplay, Pa, US 196/C2
Copparo, It. 117/E3
Coppename (riv.),
Sur. 211/H3
Copper (riv.), Ak, US 180/B2
Copper Center,
Ak, US 180/B2
Copper Harbor,
Mi, US 189/K1
Copperas Cove,
Tx, US 187/H5
Coppermine (riv.),
NW,Nun., Can. 180/E2
Copperton, Ut, US 195/J12
Coppet, Swi. 114/C5
Copsa Mica, Rom. 107/G2
Coqên, China 128/E5
Coquet (riv.), Eng, UK 94/D6
Coquet Dale (valley),
Eng, UK 93/G1
Coquimbo, Chile 215/B2
Coquitlam,
BC, Can. 184/C3
Corabia, Rom. 107/G4
Coração de Jesus,
Braz. 212/A5
Coracora, Peru 214/C4
Coral, Haiti 203/H2
Coral (sea) 174/E6
Coral Gables, Fl, US 191/H5

Contwig, Ger. 111/G5
Contwoyto (lake),
Nun., Can. 181/H2
Conty, Fr. 110/B4
Convención, Col. 210/C2
Conversano, It. 105/E2
Converse, Tx, US 195/U20
Conway, Ar, US 187/J4
Conway, SC, US 191/J3
Conway, NH, US 189/G3
Corato, It. 104/E2
Corbeil-Essonnes, Fr. 88/K6
Corbelin (cape), Alg. 158/H4
Corbenay, Fr. 114/C2
Corbett NP, India 142/B1
Corbetta, It. 116/B2
Corbie, Fr. 110/B4
Corbières (mts.), Fr. 100/E5
Corbin City,
NJ, US 196/D5
Corby, Eng, UK 91/F2
Corcovado, Braz. 213/K7
Corcovado (vol.), Chile 216/B4
Corcovado (gulf),
Chile 205/B7
Corcovado, PN, CR 203/E4
Cordeiro, Braz. 213/D2
Cordele, Ga, US 191/H4
Cordelia, Ca, US 193/K10
Cordell, Ok, US 187/H4
Cordenons, It. 101/K4
Cordignano, It. 117/F1
Cordillera de Los
Picachos, PN, Col. 208/D3
Cordillera Oriental
(mts.), SAm. 210/B5
Cordisburgo, Braz. 213/C1
Córdoba, Arg. 215/D3
Córdoba (dept.), Col. 203/H4
Córdoba, Mex. 201/N8
Córdoba (plain), SAm. 216/E2
Córdoba, Sp. 102/C4
Córdoba, Sierra de
(mts.), Arg. 215/D3
Cordova, Ak, US 192/J3
Cordova (peak),
Ak, US 192/J3
Cordova, Md, US 196/C6
Coreaú, Braz. 212/C2
Corella, Sp. 102/E1
Coremas, Braz. 212/C2
Corentyne (riv.),
Guy. 208/G3
Corfu (Kérika) (isl.),
Gre. 105/F3
Corgémont, Swi. 114/D3
Corgo, Sp. 102/B1
Coria, Sp. 102/B3
Coria del Río, Sp. 102/B4
Coriano, It. 117/F5
Coribe, Braz. 212/A4
Coricudgy (mt.),
Austl. 173/D2
Corigliano Calabro, It. 104/E3
Corinaldo, It. 117/G5
Coringa Islets (isls.),
Austl. 172/C2
Corinne, Ut, US 195/J10
Corinth, Ms, US 191/F3
Corinth (gulf), Gre. 105/H3
Corinth (Kórinthos)
(ruin), Gre. 105/H4
Corinto, Nic. 202/E3
Cork, Ire. 89/P11
Corleone, It. 104/C4
Corleto Perticara, It. 104/E2
Corlu, Turk. 107/H5
Cormeilles-en-Vexin,
Fr. 88/J4
Cormons, It. 117/G1
Cormontreuil, Fr. 110/D5
Cormorant, Mb, Can. 185/H2
Cormorant (lake),
Mb, Can. 185/H2
Cornacchia (peak), It. 104/D2
Cornaredo, It. 116/C2
Cornberg, Ger. 109/G6
Corndon (peak),
Wal, UK 90/C1
Cornedo Vicentino, It. 117/E1
Cornélio Procópio,
Braz. 213/B2
Cornelius Grinnell
(bay), Nun., Can. 181/K2
Cornell, Ca, US 194/B2
Cornella, Sp. 103/L7
Corner (inlet), Austl. 167/D4
Corner Brook,
Nf, Can. 189/K1
Cornfield (pt.), Ct, US 197/F1
Corniglio, It. 116/D4
Cornimont, Fr. 114/C2
Corning, NY, US 188/E3
Corno alle Scale
(peak), It. 101/J4
Corno di Rosazzo, It. 117/G1
Corno di Blumone
(peak), It. 115/G6
Cornú (peak), Arg. 217/D7
Cornuda, It. 117/F1
Cornwall (isl.),
Nun., Can. 181/S7
Cornwall, On, Can. 188/F2
Cornwall, PE, Can. 189/J2
Cornwall (cape),
Eng, UK 90/A6
Cornwall (co.),
Eng, UK 90/A6
Cornwall, Pa, US 196/B3
Cornwallis (isl.),
Nun., Can. 181/S7
Corny (pt.), Austl. 171/H5
Coro, Ven. 210/D2

Coral Harbour,
Nun., Can. 181/H2
Coral Sea Islands Territory
(dpcy.), Austl. 167/E2
Coral Springs,
Fl, US 191/H5
Corales del Rosario, PN,
Col. 210/C2
Coram, NY, US 197/E2
Corona, Ca, US 194/C3
Coronado (bay), CR 198/E6
Coronado, Ca, US 194/C5
Coronation,
Ab, Can. 184/F2
Coronation (gulf),
Nun., Can. 180/E2
Coronel, Chile 216/B3
Coronel Dorrego,
Arg. 216/E3
Coronel Fabriciano,
Braz. 213/D1
Coronel Moldes,
Arg. 216/E3
Coronel Murta,
Braz. 212/B5
Coronel Oviedo,
Par. 215/E2
Coronel Pringles,
Arg. 216/E3
Coronel Suárez, Arg. 216/E3
Coronel Vidal, Arg. 216/F3
Coronel Vivida,
Braz. 213/A3
Corongo, Peru 214/B3
Coronie (dist.), Sur. 211/G3
Coropuna (peak),
Peru 214/C4
Corovodë, Alb. 105/G2
Corozal, It. 210/C2
Corozal, Belz. 202/D2
Corpach, Sc, UK 94/A3
Corpus Christi, Tx, US 190/D5
Corral, Chile 216/B3
Corral de Almaguer,
Sp. 102/D3
Corral de Bustos, Arg. 216/E2
Corrales, Col. 210/C3
Corralillo, Cuba 203/F1
Corre, Fr. 114/C2
Correa, Arg. 216/E2
Corredor, CR 203/F4
Correggio, It. 117/D3
Corrente (riv.),
Braz. 212/A4
Corrente, Braz. 212/A3
Correntina, Braz. 212/A4
Corrib (lake), Ire. 89/P10
Corrientes (riv.),
Peru 208/C4
Corrientes, Arg. 215/E2
Corrientes (cape),
Ecu. 210/B5
Corrientes (pt.),
Col. 210/B3
Corrigan, Tx, US 187/J5
Corrigin, Austl. 170/C5
Corriverton, Guy. 211/G3
Corryhabbie (peak),
Sc, UK 94/C2
Corryong, Austl. 173/C3
Corse (hill), Sc, UK 94/B5
Corse (cape), Fr. 101/H5
Corse (dept.), Fr. 101/H5
Corserine (peak),
Sc, UK 92/D1
Corsewall (pt.),
Sc, UK 92/D1
Corsica (isl.), Fr. 104/A1
Corsicana, Tx, US 187/H4
Corsico, It. 116/C2
Corsons (inlet),
NJ, US 196/D5
Cortaillod, Swi. 114/C4
Cortegana, Sp. 102/B4
Cortemaggiore, It. 116/C3
Cortemilia, It. 116/B3
Cortez, Co, US 186/E3
Cortina d'Ampezzo, It. 101/K3
Cortines, Arg. 217/J11
Cortland, NY, US 188/E3
Coulogne, Fr. 110/A2
Corumbá, Braz. 208/G7
Corumbá (riv.), Braz. 209/J7
Corumbaú (pt.),
Braz. 212/C5
Coruripe, Braz. 212/C3
Corvallis, Or, US 184/C4
Corve (riv.),
Eng, UK 90/D1
Corvo (peak), It. 104/C1
Corvo (isl.),
Azor., Port. 103/R12
Corzoneso, Swi. 115/E5
Cosalá, Mex. 200/D3
Cosamaloapan,
Mex. 201/P8
Cosautlán, Mex. 201/N7
Coscomatepec,
Mex. 201/M7
Cosenza, It. 104/E3
Coshocton, Oh, US 188/D3
Cosigüina (pt.), Nic. 202/E3
Cosladá, Sp. 103/N9
Cosmo Newberry
Abor. Rsv., Austl. 170/D3
Cosmópolis, Braz. 213/F7
Cosne-Cours-sur-Loire,
Nun., Can. 181/S7
Cosne d'Allier, Fr. 100/E3
Coro, Ven. 210/D2

Coroatá, Braz. 212/A2
Corocoro, Bol. 214/D5
Coromandel, Braz. 213/C1
Coromandel, Braz. 213/C1
Coromandel
(pen.), NZ 175/T10
Coromandel (coast),
India 140/D5
Coron, Phil. 139/F1
Corona, Ca, US 194/C3
Coronado (bay), CR 198/E6
Coronado, Ca, US 194/C5
Coronation,
Ab, Can. 184/F2
Coronation (gulf),
Nun., Can. 180/E2
Coronel, Chile 216/B3
Coronel Dorrego,
Arg. 216/E3
Coronel Fabriciano,
Braz. 213/D1
Coronel Moldes,
Arg. 216/E3
Coronel Murta,
Braz. 212/B5
Coronel Oviedo,
Par. 215/E2
Coronel Pringles,
Arg. 216/E3
Coronel Suárez, Arg. 216/E3
Coronel Vidal, Arg. 216/F3
Coronel Vivida,
Braz. 213/A3
Corongo, Peru 214/B3
Coronie (dist.), Sur. 211/G3
Coropuna (peak),
Peru 214/C4
Corovodë, Alb. 105/G2
Corozal, It. 210/C2
Corozal, Belz. 202/D2
Corpach, Sc, UK 94/A3
Corpus Christi, Tx, US 190/D5
Corral, Chile 216/B3
Corral de Almaguer,
Sp. 102/D3

Cospeito, Sp. 102/B1
Cosquín, Arg. 215/D3
Cossato, It. 116/B1
Cosson (riv.), Fr. 100/D3
Cossonay, Swi. 114/C4
Costa Azul, US 217/G2
Costa Brava (int'l arpt.),
Sp. 103/G2
Costa da Caparica,
Port. 103/P10
Costa de Mosquitos
(phys. reg.), Nic. 203/E4
Costa di Rovigo, It. 117/E2
Costa Masnaga, It. 116/C1
Costa Mesa,
Ca, US 194/G8
Costa Rica (ctry.) 203/F4
Costa Smeralda
(int'l arpt.), It. 104/A2
Costa Volpino, It. 116/D1
Costabissara, It. 117/E1
Costesti, Rom. 107/G3
Cotabambas, Peru 214/C4
Cotabato, Phil. 139/F2
Cotacachi (peak),
Ecu. 210/B4
Cotahuasi, Peru 214/C4
Cotatumbo (riv.),
Col. 203/H4
Cote d'Azur
(int'l arpt.), It. 101/G5
Côte de Hautmont
(hill), Fr. 114/B1
Côte d'Ivoire (ctry.) 160/D5
Côte d'Or (uplands), Fr. 100/F3
Côte du Rif (Al Hoceima)
(mts.), Mor. 158/C2
Côte-Saint-Luc,
Qu, Can. 189/N7
Coteau des Prairies
(plat.), SD, US 185/J4
Coteau-du-Lac,
Qu, Can. 189/M7
Coteau du Missouri
(plat.), ND, US 185/H3
Coteau-Landing,
Qu, Can. 189/M7
Côtes de Meuse
(uplands), Fr. 100/F2
Cothi (riv.), Wal, UK 90/B3
Cotia, Braz. 213/G8
Cotignola, It. 117/E4
Cotonou, Ben. 161/F5
Cotonou (int'l arpt.),
Ben. 161/F5
Cotopaxi (dept.),
Ecu. 210/B5
Cotopaxi (vol.),
Ecu. 210/B5
Cotopaxi, PN,
Ecu. 210/B5
Cotswolds (hills),
Eng, UK 90/D3
Cottage Grove,
Or, US 184/C5
Cottage Hills,
Il, US 195/G8
Cottam, On, Can. 193/G7
Cottbus, Ger. 99/H3
Cottian Alps (mts.), Fr. 101/G4
Cottleville, Mo, US 195/F8
Cottonport, La, US 187/J5
Cottonwood,
Az, US 186/D4
Cottonwood (riv.),
Tx, US 187/G5
Cotulla, Tx, US 190/D4
Coubert, Fr. 88/L6
Coubre, Pointe de la
(pt.), Fr. 100/C4
Couchey, Fr. 114/A3
Coudekerque-Branche,
Fr. 110/B1
Coudersport,
Pa, US 196/B1
Coulee City,
Wa, US 184/D4
Coulee Dam Nat'l Rec. Area,
Wa, US 184/D3
Coulogne, Fr. 110/A2
Coulombs-en-Valois,
Fr. 88/M4
Coulommes, Fr. 88/L5
Coulommiers, Fr. 110/C6
Coulonge (riv.),
Qu, Can. 188/E2
Coulounieix-Chamiers,
Fr. 100/D4
Council, Ak, US 192/F3
Council, Id, US 184/D4
Council Grove,
Ks, US 187/H3
Coupar Angus,
Sc, UK 94/C3
Coupvray, Fr. 88/L5
Couquebevoie, Fr. 88/J5
Coura, It. 105/F5
Courbevoie, Fr. 88/J5
Courcelles, Belg. 111/D3
Courcouronnes, Fr. 88/J6
Courdimanche, Fr. 88/H4
Courgenay, Swi. 114/D3
Courgent, Fr. 88/H5
Courmayeur, It. 114/C6
Cournon-d'Auvergne,
Fr. 100/E4
Couronne (pt.),
Fr. 88/L6
Courquedalin, Swi. 114/D3
Courroux, Swi. 114/D3
Coursan, Fr. 100/E5
Courtelary, Swi. 114/D3
Courtepin, Swi. 114/D4
Courtice, On, Can. 189/S8
Courtisols, Fr. 111/D6

Courtland, Ca, US 193/L10
Courtmacsherry, Ire. 89/P11
Courtney, Mo, US 195/E5
Courtomer, Fr. 88/L6
Cousance, Fr. 114/B4
Coushatta, La, US 187/J4
Cousolre, Fr. 111/D3
Coutances, Fr. 100/C2
Coutevroult, Fr. 88/L5
Coutras, Fr. 100/C4
Coutts, Ab, Can. 184/F3
Couva, Trin. 211/F2
Couvet, Swi. 114/C4
Couvin, Belg. 111/D3
Couzeix, Fr. 100/D4
Covadonga NP, Sp. 102/C1
Covasna, Rom. 107/H3
Covasna (prov.),
Rom. 107/G3
Cove Bay, Sc, UK 94/D2
Cove Neck, NY, US 197/L8
Cres (isl.), Cro. 106/B3
Coventry, Eng, UK 91/E2
Coventry (canal),
Eng, UK 91/E1
Coventry, Ut, US 195/K12
Coventry (co.),
Eng, UK 91/E2
Crescent, Mo, US 195/F8
Crescent, Co, US 195/B3
Crescent, Ut, US 195/K12
Crescent City,
Ca, US 184/B5
Crescentino, It. 116/B2
Cresco, Pa, US 196/C1
Crespano del
Grappa, It. 117/E1
Crespellano, It. 117/E4
Crespières, Fr. 88/H5
Crespin, Fr. 110/C3
Cresskill, NJ, US 197/K8
Cressona, Pa, US 196/B2
Cressy, Austl. 173/C4
Crest, Fr. 100/F4
Crest Hill, Il, US 193/P16
Crestline, Ca, US 194/C2
Creston, Ia, US 185/K5
Creston, BC, Can. 184/D3
Crestview, Fl, US 191/G4
Crestwood Village,
NJ, US 196/D4
Creswick, Austl. 173/B3
Crete (sea), Gre. 105/J4
Crete (isl.), Gre. 105/J4
Créteil, Fr. 88/K5
Creuch (hill),
Sc, UK 94/B5
Creus (cape), Sp. 103/G1
Creuse (riv.), Fr. 100/D3
Creussen, Ger. 113/E3
Creussen (riv.),
Ger. 113/E3
Creutzwald-la-Croix,
Fr. 111/F5
Creuzburg, Ger. 109/H6
Crevacuore, It. 116/B1
Crevalcore, It. 117/E3
Creve Coeur,
Mo, US 195/G8
Crèvecœur-le-Grand,
Fr. 110/B4
Crevillente, Sp. 102/E3
Crevoladossola, It. 115/E5
Crewe, Eng, UK 93/F5
Crib Point, Austl. 173/C3
Criciúma, Braz. 213/B4
Crieff, Sc, UK 94/C4
Criffell (hill), Sc, UK 92/E2
Crikvenica, Cro. 106/B3
Crillon (mt.), Ak, US 192/L4
Crimean (pen.), Ukr. 107/L3
Crimmitschau, Ger. 112/D4
Crimean (pen.) 120/E3
Crimond, Sc, UK 94/E1
Crisenoy, Fr. 88/L6
Crisman, Co, US 195/B2
Crissier, Swi. 114/C4
Cristal, Monts de
(mts.), Gabon 163/B1
Cristalina, Braz. 212/A5
Cristina, Braz. 213/H7
Cristóbal (pt.),
Ecu. 214/E7
Cristóbal Colón (peak),
Col. 210/C2
Cristoforo Colombo
(int'l arpt.), It. 116/B4
Cristuru Secuiesc,
Rom. 107/G2
Crişul Alb (riv.),
Rom. 106/F2
Crişul Negru (riv.),
Rom. 106/E2
Crixás-Açu (riv.),
Braz. 209/H6
Crna Reka (riv.),
FYROM 105/G2
Črnomelj, Slov. 101/L4
Croajingolong NP,
Austl. 173/D3
Croatia (ctry.) 106/B3
Croce (peak), It. 115/H5
Croce, Pico di
(peak), It. 115/H4
Croche (peak), Fr. 114/C6
Croche (mt.), Qu, Can. 189/F2
Crocker (range),
Malay. 139/E3
Crocker (peak),
Ecu. 214/E7
Crockett, Tx, US 187/J5
Crockett, Ca, US 193/K10
Crocodile Head (pt.),
Austl. 173/D2
Crodo, It. 115/E5
Croghan (mtn.),
Ire. 92/B6
Crofton, Md, US 196/B6
Croisette (cape), Fr. 100/F5
Croisilles, Fr. 110/B3
Croissy-Beaubourg, Fr. 88/K5
Croker (isl.), Austl. 167/C2

Cromarty Firth (bay), Sc, UK 94/B1
Crombie (mt.), Austl. 171/F3
Cromdale (hills), Sc, UK 94/C2
Cromwell, NZ 175/R12
Crong A Na (riv.), Viet. 136/D3
Crooked (isl.), Bahm. 199/G3
Crooked Creek, Ak, US 192/G3
Crooked Island Passage (chan.), Bahm. 203/H1
Crookston, Mn, US 185/J4
Crookwell, Austl. 173/D2
Croom, Ire. 89/P10
Crosby, ND, US 185/H3
Crosby, Eng, UK 93/E5
Crosbyton, Tx, US 187/G4
Cross (lake), Mb, Can. 185/J2
Cross City, Fl, US 191/H4
Cross Fell (peak), Eng, UK 93/F2
Cross Plains, Tx, US 187/H4
Cross River (state), Nga. 161/H5
Cross River (res.), NY, US 197/E1
Cross Roads, Pa, US 196/B4
Crossfield, Ab, Can. 184/E3
Crossford, Sc, UK 94/C4
Crosshouse, Sc, UK 94/B5
Crossroads, Ire. 89/P9
Crossville, Tn, US 191/G3
Crostolo (riv.), It. 116/D3
Croton-on-Hudson (Croton-Harmon), NY, US 197/E1
Crotone, It. 105/E3
Crottendorf, Ger. 113/F1
Croult (riv.), Fr. 88/K5
Crouy, Fr. 110/C5
Crouy-sur-Ourcq, Fr. 88/M4
Crow Agency, Mt, US 184/G4
Crowborough, Eng, UK 91/G4
Crowdy Bay NP, Austl. 173/E1
Crowe (riv.), On, Can. 188/E2
Crowley, La, US 187/J5
Crowley's (ridge), Ar, US 191/F3
Crown Point, In, US 188/C3
Crown Point, La, US 195/P17
Crown Point (int'l arpt.), Trin. 211/F2
Crown Prince Frederik (isl.), Nun., Can. 181/H1
Crownpoint, NM, US 186/E4
Crows Nest Falls NP, Austl. 172/D4
Crowthorne, Eng, UK 91/F4
Croydon, Austl. 172/A2
Croydon (bor.), Eng, UK 88/C2
Croydon, Pa, US 196/D3
Croydon, Ut, US 195/K11
Crozet (isls.), Fr. 81/M8
Crozon, Fr. 100/A2
Cruach Mhór (peak), Sc, UK 94/A4
Cruach nan Capull (peak), Sc, UK 94/A5
Crucero, Peru 214/D4
Cruden Bay, Sc, UK 94/E2
Cruick Water (riv.), Sc, UK 94/D3
Crumlin, NI, UK 92/B2
Crummock Water (lake), Eng, UK 93/E2
Crumpton, Md, US 196/C5
Cruseilles, Fr. 114/C5
Crusnes (riv.), Fr. 111/E5
Cruz (cape), Cuba 203/G2
Cruz Alta, Braz. 215/F2
Cruz Alta, Arg. 216/E2
Cruz Alta (peak), Port. 103/P10
Cruz das Almas, Braz. 212/C4
Cruz del Eje, Arg. 215/D3
Cruz Grande, Mex. 202/B2
Cruzeiro, Braz. 213/J7
Cruzeiro do Sul, Braz. 214/C2
Cruzeta, Braz. 212/C2
Cruzília, Braz. 213/J6
Crvenka, Serb. 106/D3
Cryn-y-Brain (peak), Wal, UK 93/E5
Crystal (lake), Pa, US 196/C1
Crystal Bay, Nv, US 186/C3
Crystal Brook, Austl. 171/H5
Crystal Cave, Pa, US 196/C2
Crystal City, Tx, US 190/D4
Crystal Springs, Ms, US 187/K5
Crystal Springs (res.), Ca, US 193/K11
Csenger, Hun. 99/M5
Csepreg, Hun. 101/M3
Csongrád, Hun. 106/E2
Csorna, Hun. 106/C2
Csorvás, Hun. 106/E2
Csóványos (peak), Hun. 106/D2
Csurgó, Hun. 106/C2
Cu Lao (isl.), Viet. 136/E4
Cuajinicuilapa, Mex. 202/B2
Cualedro, Sp. 102/B2
Cuamba, Moz. 163/G3
Cuando (riv.), Ang. 163/D4
Cuango (riv.), Ang. 163/C2
Cuanza (riv.), Ang. 163/B2
Cuart de Poblet, Sp. 103/E3
Cuarto (riv.), Arg. 216/D2
Cuatrociénagas de Carranza, Mex. 190/C5
Cuauhtémoc, Mex. 200/E5
Cuauhtémoc, Mex. 200/D2
Cuautepec, Mex. 201/L6
Cuautitlán, Mex. 201/Q9
Cuautitlán Izcalli, Mex. 201/Q9
Cuautla, Mex. 201/L8
Cuba, Mo, US 187/K3
Cuba, Port. 102/B3
Cuba (ctry.) 203/F1
Cubagua (isl.), Ven. 211/E2
Cuballing, Austl. 170/C5
Cubango (riv.), Ang. 163/C4
Çubuk, Turk. 148/C1
Cucamonga (Rancho Cucamonga), Ca, US 194/C2
Cuccurano, It. 117/F5
Cuchivero (riv.), Ven. 208/E2
Cuchumatanes (mts.), Guat. 202/D3
Cuckmere (riv.), Eng, UK 91/G5
Cucq, Fr. 100/D1
Cúcuta, Col. 210/C3
Cucuyagua, Hon. 202/D3
Cudahy, Ca, US 194/F8
Cudapah, India 140/C5
Cudgewa, Austl. 173/C3
Cudillero, Sp. 102/B1
Cudrefin, Swi. 114/D4
Cudworth, Eng, UK 93/G4
Cue, Austl. 170/C3
Cuéllar, Sp. 102/C2
Cuéllar-Baza, Sp. 102/D4
Cuenca, Sp. 102/D2
Cuenca, Ecu. 210/B5
Cuenca, Sierra de (range), Sp. 102/E2
Cuencamé de Ceniceros, Mex. 200/E3
Cuernavaca, Mex. 201/K8
Cuero, Tx, US 187/H5
Cuers, Fr. 100/G5
Cueto, Cuba 203/H1
Cuetzalán, Mex. 201/M6
Cueva de los Guácharos, PN, Col. 208/C3
Cuevas de Vinromá, Sp. 103/F2
Cuevas del Almanzora, Sp. 102/E4
Cuffley, Eng, UK 88/C1
Cufré, Uru. 217/K11
Cugir, Rom. 107/F3
Cuglieri, It. 104/A2
Cugnaux, Fr. 100/D5
Cuiabá, Braz. 209/G7
Cuiabá (riv.), Braz. 209/G7
Cuicas, Ven. 210/D2
Cuijk, Neth. 108/C5
Cuilapa, Guat. 202/D3
Cuilco (riv.), Guat. 202/C3
Cuillin (sound), Sc, UK 89/Q8
Cuilo (riv.), Ang. 163/C2
Cuisance (riv.), Fr. 114/B4
Cuise-la-Motte, Fr. 110/C5
Cuiseaux, Fr. 114/B5
Cuisery, Fr. 114/A4
Cuisy, Fr. 88/L4
Cuité, Braz. 212/C2
Cuitláhuac, Mex. 201/N8
Cuito (riv.), Ang. 163/C4
Cuiuni (riv.), Braz. 208/F4
Culcairn, Austl. 173/C2
Culdaff (riv.), Ire. 92/A1
Culemborg, Neth. 108/C5
Culgoa (riv.), Austl. 167/D3
Culiacán Rosales, Mex. 200/D3
Culion (isl.), Phil. 137/D5
Cullen, Sc, UK 94/D1
Cullera, Sp. 103/E3
Culleredo, Sp. 102/A1
Cullman, Al, US 191/G3
Culloden Battlesite, Sc, UK 94/B2
Cully, Swi. 114/C5
Cullybackey, NI, UK 92/B2
Culmback (dam), Wa, US 193/D2
Culmore, NI, UK 92/A1
Culoz, Fr. 114/B6
Culpeper, Va, US 188/E4
Culross, Sc, UK 94/C4
Cults, Sc, UK 94/D2
Culver (pt.), Austl. 170/E5
Culver City, Ca, US 194/F7
Culvers (lake), NJ, US 196/D1
Cumaná, Ven. 211/E2
Cumari, Braz. 213/B1
Cumba, Peru 214/B2
Cumbal, Col. 210/B4
Cumbal, Nevado de (peak), Col. 210/B4
Cumberland (pen.), Nun., Can. 181/K2
Cumberland (sound), Nun., Can. 181/K2
Cumberland (lake), Sk, Can. 185/H2
Cumberland (plat.), US 191/G3
Cumberland (isl.), Ga, US 191/H4
Cumberland (falls), Ky, US 191/G2
Cumberland (lake), Ky, US 188/C4
Cumberland (riv.), Ky,Tn, US 183/J4
Cumberland, Md, US 188/E4
Cumberland (co.), NJ, US 196/A3
Cumberland, Wa, US 193/D3
Cumberland House, Sk, Can. 185/H2
Cumbernauld, Sc, UK 94/C5
Cumbres Bastonal, Cerro (peak), Mex. 202/C2
Cumbres de Majalca, PN, Mex. 200/D2
Cumbres de Monterrey, PN de, Mex. 201/E3
Cumbria (co.), Eng, UK 93/E2
Cumbrian (mts.), Eng, UK 93/E2
Cumbum, India 140/C4
Cummins, Austl. 171/G5
Cumnock, Austl. 173/D2
Cumpas, Mex. 200/C2
Çumra, Turk. 148/C2
Cumshewa (pt.), BC, Can. 192/M5
Cunaviche, Ven. 211/E3
Cunco, Chile 216/B3
Cundeelee Abor. Rsv., Austl. 170/D4
Cunderdin, Austl. 170/C4
Cundinamarca (dept.), Col. 210/C3
Cunduacán, Mex. 202/C2
Cunene (riv.), Ang. 163/B4
Cuneo (prov.), It. 116/A3
Cuneo, It. 101/G4
Cunha, Braz. 213/J8
Cunnamulla, Austl. 172/B5
Cunninghame (reg.), Sc, UK 94/B5
Čuokkarašša (peak), Nor. 95/H1
Cuorgnè, It. 101/G4
Cupar, Sc, UK 94/C4
Cupertino, Ca, US 193/K12
Cupra Marittima, It. 101/K5
Cupramontana, It. 117/G6
Ćuprija, Serb. 106/E4
Ćuprija, Serb. 106/E4
Cuquenán (riv.), Ven. 211/F3
Curaçá, Braz. 212/C3
Curaçao (isl.), NAnt. 208/E1
Curacautín, Chile 216/C3
Curacaví, Chile 216/N8
Curahuara de Carangas, Bol. 214/D5
Curanilahue, Chile 216/B3
Curaray (riv.), Ecu. 208/C4
Curaray (riv.), Ecu.,Peru 210/C5
Curarén, Hon. 202/E3
Curaumilla (pt.), Chile 216/N8
Curcubăta (peak), Rom. 107/F2
Cure (riv.), Fr. 98/B5
Curecanti Nat'l Rec. Area, Co, US 195/C2
Curepipe, Mrts. 165/T15
Curepto, Chile 216/B2
Curicó, Chile 216/C2
Curimatá, Braz. 212/A3
Curitibanos, Braz. 213/B3
Curno, It. 116/C1
Curone (riv.), It. 116/C3
Curral Velho, CpV. 151/K10
Current (riv.), Ar,Mo, US 187/K3
Currie, Austl. 173/B3
Currie, Sc, UK 94/C5
Curry, Ak, US 192/H3
Curtea de Argeş, Rom. 107/G3
Curtici, Rom. 106/E2
Curtis (riv.), Austl. 172/C4
Curtis (isl.), NZ 174/G8
Curtis, Sp. 102/A1
Curtis (pt.), Md, US 196/B6
Curú NWR, CR 203/E4
Curuá (riv.), Braz. 209/G4
Curuá Una (riv.), Braz. 211/H5
Curuçá (riv.), Braz. 208/D5
Curup, Indo. 138/B4
Cururupu, Braz. 209/K4
Curuzú Cuatiá, Arg. 215/E2
Curvelo, Braz. 213/C1
Cusco (dept.), Peru 214/C4
Cusco, Peru 214/D4
Cusher (riv.), NI, UK 92/B3
Cushet Law (peak), Eng, UK 94/D6
Cushing, Ok, US 187/H4
Cusna (peak), It. 116/D4
Cusset, Fr. 100/E3
Cusseta, Ga, US 191/G3
Custer, Mt, US 184/G4
Custer, SD, US 185/H5
Custines, Fr. 111/F6
Custódia, Braz. 212/C3
Cut (hill), Eng, UK 90/C5
Cut Bank, Mt, US 184/E3
Cut Knife, Sk, Can. 184/F2
Cutchogue, NY, US 197/F2
Cutervo, Peru 214/B2
Cuthbert, Ga, US 191/G4
Cutral-Có, Arg. 216/C3
Cutro, It. 105/E3
Cuttack, India 140/E3
Cuvergnon, Fr. 88/L4
Cuvier (cape), Austl. 170/B3
Cuxhaven, Ger. 109/F1
Cuyabeno, Ecu. 210/C5
Cuyama (riv.), Ca, US 186/C4
Cuyo, Phil. 139/F1
Cuyo (isls.), Phil. 139/F1
Cuyocuyo, Peru 214/D4
Cuyuni (riv.), Ven. 208/F2
Cuyuni (riv.), Guy., Ven. 211/G3
Cuyuni-Mazaruni (pol. reg.), Guy. 211/F3
Cuzco (ruin), Peru 214/D4
Cwmbran, Wal, UK 90/C3
Cyangugu, Rwa. 162/A3
Cyclades (isls.), Gre. 105/J4
Cypress (hills), Ab,Sk, Can. 184/F3
Cypress, Ca, US 194/F8
Cyprus (ctry.) 149/C2
Cyrenaica (reg.), Libya 155/K1
Cysoing, Fr. 110/C2
Cywyn (riv.), Wal, UK 90/B3
Czaplinek, Pol. 99/J2
Czarna Białostocka, Pol. 99/M2
Czarnków, Pol. 99/J2
Czech Republic (ctry.) 99/H4
Częstochowa, Pol. 99/K3
Człuchów, Pol. 96/G5

D

Da (riv.), China 137/D2
Da Hinggan (mts.), China 129/M2
Da Lat, Viet. 136/E4
Da Nang (cape), Viet. 136/E2
Da Nang, Viet. 136/E2
Da Xian, China 128/J5
Daaden, Ger. 111/G2
Da'an, China 129/M2
Daanbantayan, Phil. 137/D5
Daba (mts.), China 128/J5
Dabajuro, Ven. 210/D2
Dabakala, C.d'Iv. 160/D4
Dabas, Hun. 106/D2
Dabbāgh, Jabal (peak), SAr. 146/C3
Dabeiba, Col. 210/B3
Dabo, Fr. 111/G6
Dabob (bay), Wa, US 193/B2
Dabou, C.d'Iv. 160/D5
Daboya, Gha. 161/E4
Dabra, India 142/B3
Dąbrowa Białostocka, Pol. 97/K5
Dąbrowa Górnicza, Pol. 99/K3
Dabu, China 137/C3
Dachang Huizu Zizhixian, China 130/H7
Dachau, Ger. 113/E6
Dacono, Co, US 195/C2
Dade City, Fl, US 191/H4
Dades, Oued (riv.), Mor. 156/D3
Dadi (cape), Indo. 139/H4
Dādra and Nagar Haveli (state), India 140/B4
Dādri, India 144/D5
Dādu, Pak. 147/J3
Daduru (riv.), SrL. 140/C6
Daen Noi (peak), Thai. 136/B4
Daet, Phil. 137/D5
Dafang, China 141/J2
Dafeng, China 130/E4
Dagana, Sen. 160/B2
Dağardı, Turk. 148/B2
Dağbaşı, Turk. 148/D2
Dagestan, Resp., Rus. 121/H4
Daggaboersnek (pass), SAfr. 164/D4
Dagmar Range NP, Austl. 172/B2
Dagneux, Fr. 114/B6
Dagny, Fr. 88/M5
Dagu, China 130/H7
Daguan, China 141/H2
D'Aguilar (range), Austl. 172/E6
D'Aguilar (mt.), Austl. 172/E6
Dagupan, Phil. 137/D4
Dahana (des.), SAr. 146/D3
Daharki, Pak. 147/J3
Dahei (riv.), China 130/B2
Dahlak (arch.), Erit. 155/N4
Dahlem, Ger. 111/F3
Dahlenburg, Ger. 109/H2
Dahlonega, Ga, US 191/H3
Dahmani, Tun. 158/L7
Dahme (riv.), Ger. 99/G3
Dahn, Ger. 111/G5
Dahūk, Iraq 148/E2
Dahūk (gov.), Iraq 148/E2
Dahuofang (res.), China 130/D2
Dai (lake), China 130/C2
Dai-Segen-dake (peak), Japan 134/B3
Dai-sen (peak), Japan 132/C3
Dai Xian, China 130/C3
Daian, Japan 135/L5
Daicheng, China 130/D3
Daigo, Japan 133/G2
Dailekh, Nepal 142/C1
Dailly, Sc, UK 94/B6
Daimiao, China 130/D3
Daimiel, Sp. 102/D3
Daingerfield, Tx, US 187/J4
Daiō-zaki (pt.), Japan 133/E3
Dāira Dīn Panāh, Pak. 144/A4
Daireaux, Arg. 216/E3
Daisen-Oki NP, Japan 132/C3
Daisetsuzan NP, Japan 134/C2
Daishan, China 137/D1
Daito (isl.), Japan 125/N7
Daitō, Japan 135/J6
Daiyun (peak), China 129/L6
Dajabón, DRep. 203/J2
Dakar (cap.), Sen. 160/A3
Dakar (pol. reg.), Sen. 160/A3
Dākhilah, Wāḥāt ad (oasis), Egypt 159/B3
Dakhin Shābāzpur (isl.), Bang. 143/H4
Dakhlet Nouadhibou (pol. reg.), Mrta. 156/A5
Dakoro, Niger 161/G3
Dakota City, Ne, US 185/J5
Dakovica, Kos. 106/E4
Dakovo, Cro. 106/D3
Dal (falls), Sudan 159/B4
Dala-Järna, Swe. 96/F1
Dalälven (riv.), Swe. 122/B3
Dalaas, Aus. 115/F3
Dalad Qi, China 130/B2
Dalaman, Turk. 148/B2
Dalaman (int'l arpt.), Turk. 148/B2
Dalandzadgad, Mong. 128/H3
Dalarna (reg.), Swe. 95/E3
Dalatangi (pt.), Ice. 95/Q6
Dalbeattie, Sc, UK 92/E2
Dalby, Austl. 172/C4
Dalby, Swe. 96/E4
Dalcour, La, US 195/Q17
Dalcross (int'l arpt.), Sc, UK 94/B1
Dale, Ok, US 195/N15
Dale, Nor. 96/A1
Dalen, Neth. 108/D3
Dalen, Nor. 96/C2
Dalfsen, Neth. 108/D3
Dalgaranger (mt.), Austl. 170/C3
Dalhart, Tx, US 187/G3
Dalhousie (cape), NW, Can. 192/N1
Dalhousie, NB, Can. 189/H1
Dalhousie, India 144/C3
Dali, China 141/H2
Dali, China 130/B4
Dalian (bay), China 131/A3
Dalian, China 131/A3
Dalian (int'l arpt.), China 130/E3
Dalías, Sp. 102/D4
Dalidag (peak), Azer. 121/H5
Dāliyat el Karmil, Isr. 149/G6
Dalj, Cro. 106/D3
Dalkeith, Sc, UK 94/C5
Dalkola, India 143/F3
Dall (lake), Ak, US 192/F3
Dall (isl.), Ak, US 180/C3
Dallas, Tx, US 187/H4
Dallas-Fort Worth (int'l arpt.), Tx, US 187/H4
Dallastown, Pa, US 196/B4
Dallgow, Ger. 98/Q6
Dallol Bosso (riv.), Niger,Mali 161/F3
Dalmatia (reg.), Cro. 106/B3
Dalmatia, Pa, US 196/B2
Dalmellington, Sc, UK 94/B6
Dalmeny, Austl. 173/D3
Dalmine, It. 116/C1
Dal'negorsk, Rus. 129/Q3
Dal'nerechensk, Rus. 129/P2
Daloa, C.d'Iv. 160/D5
Dalry, Sc, UK 94/B5
Dalrymple (lake), Austl. 167/D3
Dalrymple, Sc, UK 94/B6
Dals Långed, Swe. 96/E2
Dalsingh Sarai, India 143/E3
Dalsjöfors, Swe. 96/E3
Dalton, Ga, US 191/G3
Daltonganj, India 143/E3
Dalvík, Ice. 95/N6
Dalwallinu, Austl. 170/C4
Daly (riv.), Austl. 167/C2
Daly (bay), Nun., Can. 180/G2
Damak, Nepal 143/F2
Damān, India 140/B3
Damān and Diu (state), India 140/B3
Damanhūr, Egypt 149/B4
Damar (isl.), Indo. 139/G5
Damascus (int'l arpt.), Syria 149/E3
Damascus, Md, US 196/A5
Damascus (Dimashq) (cap.), Syria 149/E3
Damaturu, Nga. 154/H5
Damāvand (mtn.), Iran 146/F1
Dambach-la-Ville, Fr. 114/D1
Dambaslar, Turk. 107/H5
Dame Marie (cape), Haiti 203/H2
Dame Marie, Haiti 203/H2
Dāmghān, Iran 147/F1
Damietta (riv.), Egypt 149/B4
Damietta (Dumyāṭ), Egypt 149/B4
Daming, China 130/C3
Damion (peak), Fr. 111/D4
Dammard, Fr. 88/M4
Dammartin-en-Goële, Fr. 88/L4
Dammastock (peak), Swi. 115/E4
Damme, Ger. 109/F3
Damme, Belg. 110/C1
Dāmodar (riv.), India 140/E3
Damoh, India 142/B4
Damongo, Gha. 161/E4
Damparis, Fr. 114/B3
Dampier (str.), Indo. 139/H4
Dampier (arch.), Austl. 167/A2
Dampier, Austl. 170/C2
Dampierre, Fr. 88/H5
Dampierre-sur-Salon, Fr. 114/B2
Damprichard, Fr. 114/C3
Damrei (mts.), Camb. 136/C4
Damsterdiep (riv.), Neth. 108/D2
Damvant, Swi. 114/C3
Damxung, China 128/F5
Dan (riv.), NC,Va, US 191/H2
Dan Xian, China 141/J4
Ḍānā, Jor. 149/D4
Dana Point, Ca, US 194/C4
Danané, C.d'Iv. 160/C5
Danao, Phil. 137/D5
Danba, China 128/H5
Danbury, Eng, UK 91/G3
Dancheng, China 130/C4
Dandaragan, Austl. 170/B4
Dandeldhurā, Nepal 142/C1
Dandenong (mt.), Austl. 173/G5
Danderhall, Sc, UK 94/C5
Dandong, China 131/C2
Dane (riv.), Eng, UK 93/F5
Danger (pt.), SAfr. 164/L11
Danggali Conservation Park, Austl. 173/B2
Dangriga, Belz. 202/D2
Dangshan, China 130/D4
Dangtu, China 130/D5
Dangyang, China 129/K5
Danielskuil, SAfr. 164/C3
Danielsville, Pa, US 196/C2
Danilov, Rus. 118/J4
Daning, China 130/B3
Danjoutin, Fr. 114/C2
Dankaur, India 144/D5
Dankov, Rus. 120/F1
Dankova (peak), Kyr. 145/G4
Danlí, Hon. 202/E3
Dannelly (res.), Al, US 191/G3
Dannemora, Swe. 96/G1
Dannenberg, Ger. 98/F2
Dannes, Fr. 110/A2
Dannevirke, NZ 175/T11
Dannhauser, SAfr. 165/E3
Danube (riv.), Eur. 85/F4
Danube, Delta of the (delta), Rom. 107/J3
Danube (Donau) (riv.), Ger. 101/H2
Danube, Mouths of the (delta), Rom.,Ukr. 107/J3
Danville, Il, US 188/C3
Danville, Ky, US 188/C4
Danville, Pa, US 196/B2
Dao Xian, China 141/K2
Daoura, Oued ed (riv.), Alg. 156/D3
Daozhen, China 141/J2
Dapaong, Togo 161/F4
Daphne, Al, US 191/G4
Dapitan, Phil. 137/D6
Daqing, China 129/N2
Daqing (riv.), China 130/H7
Dar-el-Beida (Casablanca), Mor. 156/D2
Dar es Salaam (int'l arpt.), Tanz. 162/C4
Dar es Salaam (pol. reg.), Tanz. 162/C4
Dar es Salaam (cap.), Tanz. 162/C4
Dar Rounga (reg.), CAfr. 155/K6
Dar'ā (prov.), Syria 148/C3
Dar'ā (prov.), Syria 149/E3
Dar'ā, Syria 149/E3
Dārāb, Iran 147/F3
Darabani, Rom. 107/H1
Daraga, Phil. 137/D5
Daram, Phil. 137/D5
Dārān, Iran 146/F2
Daravica (peak), Kos. 105/G1
Dārayyā, Syria 149/E3
Darbhanga, India 143/E2
Darby (cape), Ak, US 192/F3
Darby, Pa, US 196/C4
Darda, Cro. 106/D3
Dardanelle (lake), Ar, US 187/J4
Dardanelles (str.), Turk. 148/A2
Darent (riv.), Eng, UK 88/D3
Dareton, Austl. 173/B2
Darfield, NZ 175/S11
Darfo, It. 115/G6
Dārfūr (state), Sudan 159/A5
Dargaville, NZ 175/S10
Dargle (riv.), Ire. 92/B5
D'Arguin (bay), Mrta. 160/A1
Darhan, Mong. 128/J2
Darie (hills), Som. 155/Q6
Darien, Ga, US 191/H4
Darien, Ct, US 197/M7
Darien, Il, US 193/P16
Darién, PN, Pan. 208/C2
Darién, Serranía del (mts.), Pan. 208/C2
Darkan, Austl. 170/C5
Darlag, China 128/G5
Darling (range), Austl. 167/A4
Darling (riv.), Austl. 167/D4
Darling, SAfr. 164/L10
Darling Downs (reg.), Austl. 167/D3
Darling Downs (range), Austl. 172/C3
Darlington, Eng, UK 93/G2
Darlington (co.), Eng, UK 93/G2
Darlington, Md, US 196/B4
Darlington, SC, US 191/J3
Darlington Point, Austl. 173/C2
Darłowo, Pol. 96/G4
Darmstadt, Ger. 112/B3
Darnah, Libya 155/K1
Darney, Fr. 114/C1
Darnley (bay), NW, Can. 180/D2
Darnley (cape), Ant. 218/E
Daroca, Sp. 102/E2
Darregueira, Arg. 216/E3
Darsser (cape), Ger. 96/E4
Dart (riv.), Eng, UK 90/C6
Dart, West (riv.), Eng, UK 90/C6
Dartford, Eng, UK 88/D2
Dartmoor (upland), Eng, UK 90/B5
Dartmoor NP, Eng, UK 90/C5
Dartmouth (dam), Austl. 173/C3
Dartmouth (res.), Austl. 173/C3
Dartmouth, NS, Can. 189/J2
Dartmouth, Eng, UK 90/C6
Darton, Eng, UK 93/G4
Dartuch (cape), Sp. 103/G3
Daruvar, Cro. 106/C3
Darvel (bay), Malay. 139/E3
Darvel, Sc, UK 94/B5
Darwen, Eng, UK 93/F4
Darwin (bay), Chile 216/B5
Darwin (isl.), Ecu. 214/E6
Darwin (vol.), Ecu. 214/E7
Darwin, Cordillera (mts.), Chile 215/B7
Darya Khan, Pak. 144/A4
Daryābād, India 142/C2
Dashennongjia (peak), China 130/B5
Dashhowuz, Trkm. 145/C4
Dashhowuz (pol. reg.), Trkm. 145/C4
Dashhowuz (int'l arpt.), Trkm. 145/C4
Dasht-e Kavīr (des.), Iran 147/F2
Dasht-e Lūt (des.), Iran 147/G2
Dasht-e Mārgow (des.), Afg. 147/H2
Dasht Kaur (riv.), Pak. 147/H3
Dasing, Ger. 112/E6
Daska, Pak. 144/C3
Dassa-Zoumé, Ben. 161/F5
Dassel, Ger. 109/G5
Dassendorf, Ger. 109/H1
Dasseneiland (isl.), SAfr. 164/B4
Dasūya, India 144/C4
Dātāganj, India 142/B1
Datchet, Eng, UK 88/B2
Date, Japan 134/B2
Datia, India 142/B3
Datian, China 137/C2
Datil, NM, US 190/B3
Datong (mts.), China 128/G4
Datong, China 128/H4
Datong, China 130/C2
Datteln, Ger. 109/E5
Datu (cape), Indo. 138/C3
Datuk (cape), Indo. 138/B3
Daugava (riv.), Lat. 97/L4
Daugavpils, Lat. 97/M4
Daule, Ecu. 210/B5
Daule (riv.), Ecu. 210/B5
Daun, Ger. 111/F3
Daund, India 147/K5
Daung (isl.), Myan. 136/B3
Dauphin, Mb, Can. 185/H3
Dauphin (lake), Mb, Can. 185/J3
Dauphin, Pa, US 196/B3
Dauphin (co.), Pa, US 196/B3
Dauphiné (reg.), Fr. 100/F4
Dauphiné, Alpes du (range), Fr. 100/F4
Dāvangere, India 147/L6
Davao, Phil. 137/E6
Davel, SAfr. 165/E2
Davenport, Wa, US 184/D4
Davenport, Ia, US 185/L5
Davenport (mt.), Austl. 171/F2
Daventry, Eng, UK 91/E2
Daverdisse, Belg. 111/E3
Daveyton, SAfr. 164/E2
Davgaard-Jensen Land (phys. reg.), Grld. 181/T6
David, Pan. 203/F4
David City, Ne, US 185/J5
Davidson, Sk, Can. 185/G3
Davidson (mt.), Ca, US 193/J11
Davies (mt.), Austl. 171/F3
Davis (sea), Ant. 218/F
Davis, Austl., Ant. 218/F
Davis, Ca, US 186/B3
Davis (mt.), Pa, US 188/E4
Davis (mts.), Tx, US 190/B4
Davis (str.), Can.,Grld. 181/L2
Davlekanovo, Rus. 119/M5
Davo (riv.), C.d'Iv. 160/D5
Davos, Swi. 115/F4
Dawa, China 131/B2
Dawa Wenz (riv.), Eth. 155/N7
Dawangja (isl.), China 131/B3
Dawson, Yk, Can. 192/L3
Dawson, Ga, US 191/G4
Dawson (riv.), Austl. 167/D3
Dawson (isl.), Chile 217/C7
Dawson Creek, BC, Can. 184/C2
Dawu, China 128/H5
Dawu (mtn.), China 130/C5
Dawu, China 130/C5
Dax, Fr. 100/C5
Daxing, China 130/H7
Daxue (mts.), China 128/H5
Dayang (riv.), China 131/B2
Dayao, China 141/H2
Daye, China 137/B1
Daying (riv.), China 141/G3
Daylesford, Austl. 173/C3
Dayong, China 137/B2
Dayr al Balaḥ, Gaza 149/D4
Dayr al Ghuṣūn, WBnk. 149/G7
Dayr Az Zawr (prov.), Syria 148/E3
Dayr Ballūṭ, WBnk. 149/G7
Dayr Sharaf, WBnk. 149/G7
Dayrūṭ, Egypt 159/B3
Daysland, Ab, Can. 184/E2
Dayton, Wa, US 184/D4
Dayton, Tn, US 191/G3
Dayton, NJ, US 196/D3
Daytona Beach, Fl, US 191/H4
Dayu, China 141/K2
Dazhizhu Dau (isl.), China 129/T11
D.C. (fed. dist.), US 196/A6
De Aar, SAfr. 164/D3
De Bilt, Neth. 108/C4
De Doorns, SAfr. 164/L10
De Funiak Springs, Fl, US 191/G4
De Grey (riv.), Austl. 167/A3
De Haan, Belg. 110/C1
De Hart (res.), Pa, US 196/B3
De Hoge Veluwe, NP, Neth. 108/C4
De Kalb (co.), Il, US 193/N16
De Land, Fl, US 191/H4
De Leijen (lake), Neth. 108/D2
De Lier, Neth. 108/B5
De Luz, Ca, US 194/C4
De Panne, Belg. 110/B1
De Peel (phys. reg.), Neth. 108/C6
De Pinte, Belg. 110/C2
De Ridder, La, US 187/J5
De Soto, Ks, US 195/D6
De Soto, Mo, US 187/K3
De Wijk, Neth. 108/D3
Dead Sea (sea), Isr.,Jor. 148/C4
Deadhorse, Ak, US 192/J1
Deadman (peak), Austl. 170/C2
Deadwood, SD, US 185/H4
Deal (isl.), Austl. 173/C3
Deal, NJ, US 196/D3
Deale, Md, US 196/B6
Dean (riv.), BC, Can. 184/B2
Dean (chan.), BC, Can. 184/B2
De'an, China 137/C2
Dean (for.), Eng, UK 90/D3
Deán Funes, Arg. 215/D3
Deanmill, Austl. 170/C5
Dearborn Heights, Mi, US 193/F7
Dearne, Eng, UK 93/G4
Dease (str.), Nun., Can. 180/F2
Dease (riv.), BC, Can. 180/D3
Dease Lake, BC, Can. 192/M4
Death Valley NP, Ca, US 186/C3
Debar, FYROM 105/G2
Debauch (mtn.), Ak, US 192/G3
Debe Habe, Nga. 154/H5

Debelets, Bul. 105/J1
Deben (riv.), Eng, UK 91/H2
Dębica, Pol. 99/L3
Dęblin, Pol. 99/L3
Dębno, Pol. 99/H2
Débo (lake), Mali 160/E3
Deborah (mt.), Ak, US 192/J3
Debre Birhan, Eth. 155/N6
Debre Mark'os, Eth. 155/N5
Debre Tabor, Eth. 155/N5
Debre Zeyit, Eth. 155/N6
Debrecen, Hun. 99/L5
Decatur, Al, US 191/G3
Decatur, Il, US 185/L6
Decatur, In, US 188/C3
Decatur, Ga, US 191/G3
Decatur, Tx, US 187/H4
Decazeville, Fr. 100/E4
Deccan (plat.), India 140/C5
Decima, It. 117/E3
Děčín, Czh. 99/H3
Décines-Charpieu, Fr. 114/A6
Decize, Fr. 100/E3
Dedemsvaart, Neth. 108/D3
Dedo (peak), Arg. 216/C5
Dédougou, Burk. 160/E3
Dedza, Malw. 163/F3
Dee (riv.), Sc, UK 94/C3
Deel (riv.), Ire. 92/A4
Deep Fork (riv.), Ok, US 195/N14
Deep River, On, Can. 188/E2
Deepcut, Eng, UK 88/F3
Deepwater, Austl. 173/D1
Deepwater, NJ, US 196/C4
Deepwater (pt.), De, US 196/C5
Deer (isl.), Ak, US 192/F5
Deer Creek (res.), Ut, US 195/L13
Deer Lake, Nf, Can. 189/K1
Deer Lake, Pa, US 196/B2
Deer Lodge, Mt, US 184/E4
Deer Park, Il, US 193/P15
Deer Park, Md, US 196/B5
Deer Park, NY, US 197/E2
Deer Park, Wa, US 184/D4
Deer Plain, Il, US 195/F8
Deerfield, Il, US 193/P15
Deering, Ak, US 192/F2
Deerlijk, Belg. 110/C2
Deeside (valley), Sc, UK 94/D2
Deex Nugaaleed (riv.), Som. 155/Q6
Defensores del Chaco, PN, Par. 208/F8
Defiance, Oh, US 188/C3
Dégelis, Qu, Can. 189/G2
Degerfors, Swe. 96/F2
Degersheim, Swi. 115/F3
Deggendorf, Ger. 113/F5
Deggingen, Ger. 112/C5
Dego, It. 116/B4
DeGrey (riv.), Austl. 170/C2
Deh Bīd, Iran 146/F2
Dehalak (isl.), Erit. 155/P4
Dehalak Marine NP, Erit. 155/P4
Deheq, Iran 146/F2
Dehra Dūn, India 147/L2
Dehri, India 143/E3
Dehua, China 137/C2
Deidesheim, Ger. 112/B4
Deinste, Ger. 109/G1
Deinze, Belg. 110/C2
Deister (mts.), Ger. 109/G4
Deiva Marina, It. 116/C4
Dej, Rom. 107/F2
Deje, Swe. 96/E2
Dejiang, China 141/J2
Dejima, Japan 135/E1
Dekemhare (Dek'emhāre), Erit. 146/C5
Del Campillo, Arg. 216/D2
Del Carril, Arg. 217/J11
Del City, Ok, US 195/N15
Del Dios, Ca, US 194/C4
Del Gran Paradiso, It. 116/A2
Del Mar, Ca, US 194/C5
Del Norte, Co, US 187/F3
Del Rio, Tx, US 187/G5
Del Valle, Arg. 216/E2
Del Valle (lake), Ca, US 193/L11
Delacroix, La, US 195/Q17
Delafield, Wi, US 193/P13
Delano, Ca, US 186/C4
Delareyville, SAfr. 164/D2
Delarode (lake), Sk, Can. 184/G2
Delavan, Wi, US 187/K2
Delavan (lake), Wi, US 193/P14
Delavan Lake, Wi, US 193/N14
Delaware (riv.), US 188/F3
Delaware (state), US 188/F4
Delaware, NJ, US 196/C2
Delaware (bay), NJ, US 188/F4
Delaware, Oh, US 188/D3
Delaware (co.), Pa, US 196/C4
Delaware (pass), Pa, US 196/C2
Delaware City, De, US 196/C4
Delaware Water Gap Nat'l Rec. Area, Pa, US 188/F3
Delbrück, Ger. 109/F5
Delčevo, FYROM 105/H2
Delden, Neth. 108/D4
Delebio, It. 115/F5
Delegate, Austl. 173/D3
Delémont, Swi. 114/D3
Delft, Neth. 108/B4
Delfzijl, Neth. 108/D2
Delgada (pt.), Arg. 216/E4
Delgado (cape), Moz. 162/D5
Delhi, India 144/D5
Delhi (state), India 140/C2
Delhi, Il, US 195/G7
Delhi, La, US 187/K4
Delice, Turk. 148/C2
Delice (riv.), Turk. 120/E5
Delījān, Iran 146/F2
Déljne, NW, Can. 180/D2
Delisle, Sk, Can. 184/G3
Dell Rapids, SD, US 185/J5
Delligsen, Ger. 109/G5
Delmas, SAfr. 164/Q13
Delme (riv.), Ger. 109/F3
Delmenhorst, Ger. 109/F2
Delmiro Gouveia, Braz. 212/C3
Delmont, NJ, US 196/D5
Delnice, Cro. 106/B3
Deloraine, Austl. 173/C4
Deloraine, Mb, Can. 185/H3
Delphi (Dhelfoí) (ruin), Gre. 105/H3
Delphos, Oh, US 188/C3
Delportshoop, SAfr. 164/D3
Delran, NJ, US 196/D4
Delray Beach, Fl, US 191/H5
Delson, Qu, Can. 189/N7
Delta, Ut, US 186/D3
Delta (state), Nga. 161/G5
Delta, Pa, US 196/B4
Delta del Tigre, Uru. 217/K11
Delta du Saloum, PN du, Sen. 160/A3
Delta Junction, Ak, US 192/J3
Delta-Mendota (canal), Ca, US 193/M11
Deltona, Fl, US 191/H4
Delvinë, Alb. 105/G3
Dëma (riv.), Rus. 145/C2
Demanda, Sierra de la (range), Sp. 102/D1
Demarcation (pt.), Ak, US 192/K2
Demarest, NJ, US 197/K8
Demba, D.R. Congo 163/D2
Dembī Dolo, Eth. 155/M6
Demer (riv.), Belg. 98/C3
Demerara (riv.), Guy. 211/G3
Demerara-Mahaica (pol. reg.), Guy. 211/G3
Demerval Lobão, Braz. 212/B2
Deming, NM, US 190/B3
Demini (riv.), Braz. 208/F3
Demirci, Turk. 148/B2
Demirkent, Turk. 148/C2
Demirköprü (dam), Turk. 148/B2
Demirköy, Turk. 107/H5
Demirtaş, Turk. 107/J5
Demmin, Ger. 96/E5
Democratic Republic of the Congo (ctry.) 151/E5
Demone (valley), It. 104/D4
Demopolis, Al, US 191/G3
Dempo (peak), Indo. 138/B4
Dempster (pt.), Austl. 170/D5
Den Burg, Neth. 108/B2
Den Ham, Neth. 108/D4
Den Helder, Neth. 108/B3
Den Oever, Neth. 108/C3
Denain, Fr. 110/C3
Denakil (reg.), Djib.,Eth. 155/P5
Denali NP and Prsv., Ak, US 192/H3
Denare Beach, Sk, Can. 185/H2
Denbigh, Wal, UK 93/E5
Denbighshire (co.), Wal, UK 93/E5
Dender (riv.), Belg. 98/B3
Denderleeuw, Belg. 111/D2
Dendermonde, Belg. 111/D1
Denekamp, Neth. 108/E4
Deng Xian, China 130/C4
Dengfeng, China 130/C4
Dengkou, China 128/J3
Dengta, China 137/B3
Denham (sound), Austl. 170/B3
Denham, Austl. 170/B3
Denholme, Eng, UK 93/G4
Denia, Sp. 103/F3
Deniliquin, Austl. 173/C2
Denio, Nv, US 184/D5
Denison (mt.), Ak, US 192/H4
Denison, Ia, US 185/K5
Denison, Tx, US 187/H4
Denizli, Turk. 148/B2
Denizli (prov.), Turk. 148/B2
Denkendorf, Ger. 113/E5
Denklingen, Ger. 115/G2
Denman, Austl. 173/D2
Denmark, Austl. 170/C5
Denmark (str.), Grld.,Ice. 177/R3
Denmark (ctry.) 96/C4
Dennisville, NJ, US 196/D5
Denpasar, Indo. 138/E5
Dent de Lys (peak), Swi. 114/C4
Dent d'Hérens (peak), It. 114/D6
Dentergem, Belg. 110/C2
Dentlein am Forst, Ger. 112/D4
Denton, Eng, UK 93/F5
Denton, Md, US 196/C6
Denton, Tx, US 190/D3
Denton, Tx, US 187/H4
D'Entrecasteaux (isls.), PNG 174/D5
D'Entrecasteaux (pt.), Austl. 170/B5
Dents du Midi (peak), Swi. 114/C5
Denver (cap.), Co, US 195/C3
Denver (co.), Co, US 195/B3
Denver, Pa, US 196/B3
Denver International (int'l arpt.), Co, US 195/C3
Denver Museum of Natural History, Co, US 195/C3
Denville, NJ, US 196/D2
Denzlingen, Ger. 114/D1
Deoband, India 144/D5
Deogarh, India 140/D3
Deoghar, India 143/F3
Deohā (riv.), India 142/B1
Deolāli, India 147/K5
Deoli, India 140/C3
Déols, Fr. 100/D3
Deorī, India 142/B4
Deoria, India 142/D2
Dependencias Federales (state), Ven. 211/E1
Depew, NY, US 189/S10
Depok, Indo. 138/C5
Deqing, China 137/B3
Deqing, China 130/L9
Dera Ghāzi Khān, Pak. 144/A4
Dera Gopipur, India 144/D4
Dera Ismāīl Khān, Pak. 144/A4
Derbent, Rus. 121/J4
Derby, Eng, UK 93/G6
Derby (co.), Eng, UK 93/G6
Derby, Ct, US 197/E1
Derbyshire (co.), Eng, UK 93/G5
Derdap NP, Serb. 106/F3
Derecske, Hun. 106/E2
Dereköy, Turk. 107/H5
Derendingen, Swi. 114/D3
Derg, Lough (lake), Ire. 89/P10
Derik, Turk. 148/E2
Derinkuyu, Turk. 148/C2
Dernau, Ger. 111/G2
Déroute, Passage de la (chan.), Fr. 100/B2
Derrevaragh (lake), Ire. 92/A4
Derry, NH, US 189/G3
Derryboy, NI, UK 92/C3
Dervaig, Sc, UK 89/Q8
Derventa, Bosn. 106/C3
Dervio, It. 115/F5
Derwent (riv.), Austl. 173/C4
Derwent (riv.), Eng, UK 93/E2
Derwent (res.), Eng, UK 93/F2
Derwent Water (lake), Eng, UK 93/E2
Des Allemands, La, US 195/P17
Des Moines (cap.), Ia, US 185/K5
Des Moines (riv.), Ia,Mn, US 185/J2
Des Peres, Mo, US 195/G8
Desaguadero (riv.), Bol. 208/E7
Desaguadero, Peru 214/D5
Desagües de los Colorados (dry lake), Arg. 215/C2
Desana, It. 116/B2
Descabezado Grande (vol.), Chile 216/C2
Descalvado, Braz. 213/C2
Descartes, Fr. 100/D3
Deschambault (lake), Sk, Can. 185/H2
Deschambault Lake, Sk, Can. 185/H2
Deschutes (riv.), Or, US 184/C4
Desdunes, Haiti 203/H2
Desē, Eth. 155/N5
Dese (riv.), It. 117/F2
Deseado (riv.), Arg. 205/C7
Deseado (cape), Chile 217/B7
Desengaño (pt.), Arg. 217/D6
Desenzano del Garda, It. 116/D2
Désertines, Fr. 100/E3
Desio, It. 116/C1
Desna (riv.), Ukr. 120/D2
Desolación (isl.), Chile 215/A7
Desordem, Serra da (range), Braz. 212/A2
Despatch, SAfr. 164/D4
Dessau, Ger. 98/G3
Dessel, Belg. 108/C6
Dessoubre (riv.), Fr. 114/C3
Destelbergen, Belg. 110/C1
Destrehan, La, US 195/P17
Destruction Bay, Yk, Can. 192/L3
Desulo, It. 104/A2
Desvres, Fr. 110/A2
Deta, Rom. 106/E3
Detern, Ger. 109/E2
Detmold, Ger. 109/F5
Detroit (riv.), Can.,US 193/F7
Detroit Lakes, Mn, US 185/K4
Detroit Metropolitan Wayne County (int'l arpt.), Mi, US 188/D3
Dettelbach, Ger. 112/D3
Dettifoss (falls), Ice. 95/P6
Dettwiller, Fr. 111/G6
Deua NP, Austl. 173/D2
Deuil-la-Barre, Fr. 88/J5
Deûle (riv.), Fr. 110/B2
Deurne, Belg. 108/B6
Deurne, Neth. 108/C6
Deustua, Peru 214/D4
Deutsch Evern, Ger. 109/H2
Deutsch Wagram, Aus. 107/P7
Deutschkreutz, Aus. 101/M3
Deutschlandsberg, Aus. 101/L3
Deux-Montagnes, Qu, Can. 189/N6
Deux-Montagnes (co.), Qu, Can. 189/M6
Deux-Montagnes, Lac des (lake), Qu, Can. 189/M7
Deva, Rom. 106/F3
Dévaványa, Hun. 106/E2
Develi, Turk. 148/C2
Deventer, Neth. 108/D4
Deveron (riv.), Sc, UK 94/D2
Deville, Fr. 111/D4
Devil's (isl.), FrG. 209/H2
Devils (riv.), Mex. 201/E2
Devil's Elbow (pass), Sc, UK 94/C3
Devils Lake, ND, US 185/J3
Devils Paw (peak), Ak, US 192/M4
Devils Postpile Nat'l Mon., Ca, US 186/C3
Devils Slide, Ut, US 195/K11
Devine, Tx, US 187/H5
Devizes, Eng, UK 90/E4
Devnya, Bul. 107/H4
Devoll (riv.), Alb.,Gre. 106/E5
Devon, Ab, Can. 184/E2
Devon (isl.), Nun., Can. 181/S7
Devon (co.), Eng, UK 90/C5
Devon (riv.), Sc, UK 94/C4
Devon-Berwyn, Pa, US 196/C3
Devonport, Austl. 173/C4
Devore, Ca, US 194/C2
Devrek, Turk. 107/K5
Devrek (riv.), Turk. 107/K5
Devrez (riv.), Turk. 120/E4
Dewa (pt.), Indo. 138/A3
Dewa (mts.), Japan 134/B4
Dewās, India 147/L4
Dewetsdorp, SAfr. 164/D3
Dewsbury, Eng, UK 93/G4
Dexter, Me, US 189/G2
Dey-Dey (lake), Austl. 167/C3
Deyang, China 128/H5
Dez (riv.), Iran 122/E6
Dezfūl, Iran 146/E2
Dezhneva (cape), Rus. 192/E2
Dezhou, China 130/D3
Dhabān Singh, Pak. 144/B4
Dhākā (div.), Bang. 143/H4
Dhāka, India 143/E2
Dhaleswari (riv.), Bang. 143/H4
Dhali, Cyp. 149/C2
Dhāmpur, India 142/B1
Dhamtari, India 140/D3
Dhanaula, India 144/C4
Dhanaura, India 142/B1
Dhānbād, India 143/F4
Dhangadhī, Nepal 142/C1
Dhankutā, Nepal 143/F2
Dhār, India 147/L4
Dharampur, India 147/K4
Dharān, Nepal 143/F2
Dhāri, India 147/K4
Dhārīwāl, India 144/C4
Dharmapuri, India 140/C5
Dharmavaram, India 140/C5
Dharmjaygarh, India 142/D4
Dharmsāla, India 144/D3
Dhasan (riv.), India 142/B3
Dhaulāgiri (peak), Nepal 142/D1
Dhaulāgiri (zone), Nepal 142/D1
Dhaurahra, India 142/C1
Dhelfoí, Gre. 105/H3
Dhelvinákion, Gre. 105/G3
Dheskáti, Gre. 105/G3
Dheune (riv.), Fr. 114/A4
Dhībān, Jor. 149/D4
Dhidhimótikhon, Gre. 105/K2
Dhikaia, Gre. 105/K2
Dhilos (ruin), Gre. 105/J4
Dhimitsána, Gre. 105/H4
Dhirfis (peak), Gre. 105/H3
Dhístomon, Gre. 105/H3
Dhofar (reg.), Oman 146/F5
Dhokímion, Gre. 105/G3
Dholka, India 147/K4
Dhomokós, Gre. 105/H3
Dhonoúsa (isl.), Gre. 105/J4
Dhorāji, India 147/K4
Dhronbach (riv.), Ger. 111/F4
Dhūlia, India 147/K4
Dhuliān, India 143/F3
Dhulikhel, Nepal 143/E2
Dhupgāri, India 143/G2
Dhūri, India 144/C4
Di Linh, Viet. 136/E4
Dia (isl.), Gre. 105/J5
Diablo (mt.), Ak, US 192/H4
Diablo (range), Ca, US 186/B3
Diablo (plat.), Tx, US 190/B4
Diablo, Punta del (pt.), Uru. 217/G2
Diablotin (peak), Dom. 199/N9
Diadema, Braz. 213/G8
Diadema Argentina, Arg. 216/D5
Diamante (riv.), Arg. 216/D2
Diamantina, Braz. 212/B5
Diamantina (riv.), Austl. 167/D3
Diamantina, Chapada (hills), Braz. 209/K6
Diamantino, Braz. 209/G6
Diamond Bar, Ca, US 194/G8
Diamond Harbour, India 143/G4
Diamond Head (pt.), Hi, US 182/W13
Dianalund, Den. 96/D4
Dianbai, China 141/K3
Dianjiang, China 137/A1
Diano Marina, It. 116/B5
Dianshan (lake), China 130/L8
Diapaga, Burk. 161/F3
Dias Creek, NJ, US 196/D5
Diavolezza (peak), Swi. 115/F5
Dibai, India 142/B1
Dibeng, SAfr. 164/C2
Dibiāpur, India 142/B2
Dibis (well), Egypt 159/B4
Dibs, Iraq 148/F3
Dickens, Tx, US 187/G4
Dickens (pt.), RI, US 197/G1
Dickinson, ND, US 185/H4
Dickson, Tn, US 188/C4
Dicle (dam), Turk. 148/E2
Dicomano, It. 117/E5
Didam, Neth. 108/D5
Didcot, Eng, UK 91/E3
Didsbury, Ab, Can. 184/E3
Dīdwāna, India 147/K3
Didyma (ruin), Turk. 148/A2
Die Berg (peak), SAfr. 163/F6
Dieblich, Ger. 111/G3
Diébougou, Burk. 160/E4
Dieburg, Ger. 112/B3
Diedersdorf, Ger. 98/Q7
Diefenbaker (lake), Sk, Can. 184/G3
Diego de Almagro (isl.), Chile 217/B6
Diego Garcia (isl.), UK 125/G10
Diekirch (dist.), Lux. 111/F4
Diekirch, Lux. 111/F4
Diemen, Neth. 108/B4
Diemtigen, Swi. 114/D4
Diepenbeek, Belg. 111/E2
Diepenveen, Neth. 108/D4
Diepholz, Ger. 109/F3
Diepoldsau, Swi. 115/F3
Dieppe, Fr. 100/D2
Dierdorf, Ger. 111/G2
Diespeck, Ger. 112/D3
Diessen am Ammersee, Ger. 115/H2
Diest, Belg. 111/E2
Dietenheim, Ger. 115/G1
Dietenhofen, Ger. 112/D4
Dietersheim, Ger. 112/D3
Dietfurt an der Altmühl, Ger. 113/E4
Dietikon, Swi. 115/E3
Dietmannsried, Ger. 115/G2
Dietzenbach, Ger. 112/B2
Dieue-sur-Meuse, Fr. 111/E5
Dieulouard, Fr. 111/F6
Dieuze, Fr. 111/F6
Diever, Neth. 108/D3
Diez, Ger. 112/B2
Diffa, Niger 154/H5
Diffa (dept.), Niger 161/H3
Differdange, Lux. 111/E4
Difficult (mt.), Austl. 173/B3
Dīg, India 142/A2
Digboi, India 141/G2
Digby, NS, Can. 189/H2
Dighwāra, India 143/E3
Digne-les-Bains, Fr. 101/G4
Digoin, Fr. 100/E3
Digor, Turk. 148/E1
Digul (riv.), Indo. 139/K4
Digya NP, Gha. 161/E5
Dijon, Fr. 114/A3
Dikirnis, Egypt 149/B4
Diklosmta (peak), Geo. 121/H4
Diksmuide, Belg. 110/B1
Dīla, Eth. 155/N6
Dilbeek, Belg. 111/D2
Dilek Yarımadası NP, Turk. 148/A2
Dili (cap.), ETim. 139/G5
Dillenburg, Ger. 111/H2
Dillingen, Ger. 111/F5
Dillingen an der Donau, Ger. 112/D5
Dillingham, Ak, US 192/G4
Dillon, Mt, US 184/E4
Dillon, SC, US 191/J3
Dillsburg, Pa, US 196/A3
Dilolo, D.R. Congo 163/D3
Dilsen, Belg. 111/E1
Dimāpur, India 141/F2
Dimaro, It. 115/G5
Dimas, Mex. 200/D4
Dimashq (prov.), Syria 148/D3
Dimbokro, C.d'Iv. 160/D5
Dimboola, Austl. 173/B3
Dîmboviţa (prov.), Rom. 107/G3
Dimbulah, Austl. 172/B2
Dimitriya Lapteva (str.), Rus. 123/P2
Dimitrovgrad, Bul. 105/J1
Dimitrovgrad, Rus. 121/J1
Dimitrovgrad, Serb. 106/F4
Dimlang (peak), Nga. 154/H6
Dimmitt, Tx, US 187/G4
Dimona, Isr. 149/D4
Dimovo, Bul. 107/F4
Dina, Pak. 144/B3
Dinagat (isl.), Phil. 137/E5
Dinagat, Phil. 137/E6
Dinājpur (pol. reg.), Bang. 143/G3
Dinan, Fr. 100/B2
Dīnānagar, India 144/C3
Dinant, Belg. 111/D3
Dinar, Turk. 148/B2
Dinard, Fr. 100/B2
Dinaric Alps (mts.), Cro. 106/C3
Dinas (pt.), Wal, UK 90/B2
Dinder NP, Sudan 155/N5
Dindigul, India 140/C5
Dindori, India 142/C4
Dinga, Pak. 144/B3
Ding'an, China 141/K4
Dingbian, China 128/J4
Dingelstädt, Ger. 109/H6
Dinggyê, China 143/F1
Dingle, Ire. 88/F10
Dingle (bay), Ire. 88/N10
Dingmans Ferry, Pa, US 196/D1
Dingnan, China 137/C3
Dingolfing, Ger. 113/F5
Dingras, Phil. 137/D4
Dingtao, China 130/C4
Dingwall, Sc, UK 94/B1
Dingxi, China 128/H4
Dingxiang, China 130/C3
Dingxing, China 130/G7
Dingyuan, China 130/D4
Dinkel (riv.), Ger. 109/E4
Dinkelsbühl, Ger. 112/D4
Dinkelscherben, Ger. 112/D6
Dinklage, Ger. 109/F3
Dinosaur Nat'l Mon., US 186/E2
Dinslaken, Ger. 108/D5
Dinsmore, Sk, Can. 184/G3
Dintel Mark (riv.), Neth. 108/B5
Dinuba, Ca, US 186/C3
Dinxperlo, Neth. 108/D5
Dioïla, Mali 160/D3
Dion (riv.), Gui. 160/C4
Diósd, Hun. 107/Q10
Diourbel (pol. reg.), Sen. 160/A3
Diourbel, Sen. 160/A3
Dīpālpur, Pak. 144/B4
Diphu, India 141/F2
Diplo, Pak. 147/J4
Dipni (dam), Turk. 148/E2
Dipperu NP, Austl. 172/C3
Dipperz, Ger. 112/C1
Dique (canal), Col. 203/H4
Diré, Mali 160/E2
Dirē Dawa, Eth. 155/P6
Diriamba, Nic. 202/E4
Dirj, Libya 157/H3
Dirk Hartog (isl.), Austl. 167/A3
Dirksland, Neth. 108/B5
Dirlewang, Ger. 115/G2
Dirranbandi, Austl. 172/C5
Dirrington Great Law (hill), Sc, UK 94/D5
Dirty Devil (riv.), Ut, US 186/E3
Disappointment (lake), Austl. 167/B3
Disappointment (isls.), FrPol. 175/L6
Discovery (bay), Austl. 173/B3
Discovery Bay, Jam. 203/G2
Disentis-Mustér, Swi. 115/E4
Disgrazi (peak), It. 115/F5
Disko (isl.), Grld. 177/M3
Disko (Qeqertarsuaq) (isl.), Grld. 181/L2
Disneyland, Ca, US 194/G8
Dison, Belg. 111/E2
Dispur, India 141/F2
Disraëli, Qu, Can. 189/G2
Dissen am Teutoburger Wald, Ger. 109/F4
District of Columbia (fed. dist.), US 196/A6
Distrito Féderal (fed. dist.), Braz. 212/A4
Distrito Federal (fed. dist.), Col. 210/C3
Distrito Federal (fed. dist.), Mex. 201/Q10
Distrito Federal (fed. dist.), Ven. 211/E2
Disūq, Egypt 149/B4
Ditchling Beacon (hill), Eng, UK 91/F5
Dittaino (riv.), It. 104/D4
Dittelbrunn, Ger. 112/D2
Dittmer, Mo, US 195/F9
Ditzingen, Ger. 112/C5
Diu, India 140/B3
Dive (riv.), Fr. 100/D3
Dividing Creek, NJ, US 196/C5
Divinolândia, Braz. 213/G6
Divinópolis, Braz. 213/C2
Divisa Nova, Braz. 213/G6
Divisor, Serra do (mts.), Braz. 208/D5
Divo, C.d'Iv. 160/D5
Divonne-les-Bains, Fr. 114/C5
Divriği, Turk. 148/D2
Dix (lake), Swi. 114/D5
Dixmoor, Il, US 193/Q16
Dixon, Il, US 185/L5
Dixon Entrance (chan.), Can.,US 192/M4
Diyadin, Turk. 148/E2
Diyāla (gov.), Iraq 148/F3
Diyarb Najm, Egypt 149/B4
Diyarbakir (prov.), Turk. 148/E2
Diyarbakır, Turk. 148/E2
Djado (plat.), Niger 151/D2
Djakotomé, Ben. 161/F5
Djamaa, Alg. 157/G2
Djambala, Congo 154/H8
Djanet, Alg. 157/H4
Djebel-Amrag (mtn.), Alg. 158/D3
Djebel Tichka (peak), Mor. 156/C3
Djedi, Oued (riv.), Alg. 157/G2
Djelfa, Alg. 154/F1
Djema, CAfr. 155/L6
Djemila (ruin), Alg. 158/H4
Djénné, Mali 160/D3
Djibo, Burk. 161/E3
Djibouti (ctry.) 155/P5
Djibouti (cap.), Djib. 155/P5
Djougou, Ben. 161/F4
Djúpivogur, Ice. 95/P7
Dnepr (riv.), Rus. 120/D1
Dnipro (riv.), Ukr. 85/H3
Dniprodzerzhyns'k, Ukr. 120/E2
Dnipropetrovs'k, Ukr. 120/E2
Dnipropetrovs'ka Oblasti, Ukr. 120/E2
Dniprovs'kyy Lyman (estu.), Ukr. 107/K2
Dnister (riv.), Ukr. 98/M4
Dnistrovs'kyy Lyman (estu.), Ukr. 107/K2
Dnyapro (riv.), Bela. 97/P4
Do (lake), Mali 161/E3
Do Rāh (pass), Afg. 147/K1
Do Son, Viet. 136/D1
Doany, Madg. 165/J6
Doba, Chad 154/J6
Dobbs Ferry, NY, US 197/K7
Dobele, Lat. 97/K3
Döbeln, Ger. 98/G3
Doberai (pen.), Indo. 139/H4
Dobiegniew, Pol. 99/H2
Dobogó-kő (peak), Hun. 107/Q9
Doboj, Bosn. 106/D3
Dobřany, Czh. 113/G3
Dobre Miasto, Pol. 97/J5
Dobrich, Bul. 107/H4
Dobříš, Czh. 113/H3
Dobruja (reg.), Bul. 107/H4
Dobrush, Bela. 120/D1
Dobryanka, Rus. 119/N4
Doce (riv.), Braz. 209/K7
Dochart (riv.), Sc, UK 94/B4
Dock Junction, Ga, US 191/H4
Docker River, Austl. 171/F3
Doctor Arroyo, Mex. 201/E4
Doctor Pedro P. Peña, Par. 215/D1
Doctor Petru Groza, Rom. 106/F2
Doda (lake), Qu, Can. 188/F1
Doda, India 144/C3
Doda (riv.), India 144/D3
Dodder (riv.), Ire. 92/B5
Doddinghurst, Eng, UK 88/D2
Dodecanese (isl.), Gre. 148/A2
Dodge City, Ks, US 187/G3
Dodger Stadium, Ca, US 194/F7
Dodgeville, Wi, US 185/L5
Dodman (pt.), Eng, UK 90/B6
Dodoma, Tanz. 162/B4
Dodoma (pol. reg.), Tanz. 162/B4
Dodori Nat'l Rsv., Kenya 162/D3
Dodsland, Sk, Can. 184/F3
Dodworth, Eng, UK 93/G4
Doesburg, Neth. 108/D4
Doetinchem, Neth. 108/D5
Doğanhisar, Turk. 148/B2
Doğankent (riv.), Turk. 148/D1
Doğanşar, Turk. 148/D1
Doğanşehir, Turk. 148/D2
Doğanyurt, Turk. 148/C1
Döğer, Turk. 148/B2
Dogliani, It. 116/A3
Dogondoutchi, Niger 161/G3
Doğubayazıt, Turk. 148/F2
Doğukaradeniz (mts.), Turk. 148/D1
Dohad, India 147/K4
Dohrighāt, India 142/D2
Doi Khun Tan NP, Thai. 136/B2
Doilungdêqên, China 140/F2
Doiras, Embalse de (res.), Sp. 102/B1
Dois de Julho (int'l arpt.), Braz. 212/C4
Dois Irmãos, Serra (mts.), Braz. 209/K5
Doische, Belg. 111/D3
Dokka, Nor. 96/D1
Dokkum, Neth. 108/D2
Dokkumer Ee (riv.), Neth. 108/C2
Doksy, Czh. 113/H1
Dolbeau, Qu, Can. 189/F1
Dolcedorme (peak), It. 104/E3
Dole, Fr. 114/B3
Dolent (peak), Swi. 114/D6
Dolgellau, Wal, UK 90/C1
Dolgoprudnyy, Rus. 119/W9
Dolianova, It. 104/A3
Dolinsk, Rus. 129/R2
Dolj (prov.), Rom. 107/F3
Dollar, Sc, UK 94/C4
Dollar Law (peak), Sc, UK 94/C5
Dollard-des-Ormeaux, Qu, Can. 189/N7
Dollard (Dollart) (bay), Ger.,Neth. 109/E2
Doller (riv.), Fr. 98/D5
Dollnstein, Ger. 112/E5
Dolmar (peak), Ger. 112/D1
Dolmen (ruin), It. 104/E2
Dolna Banya, Bul. 105/H1
Dolni Dŭbnik, Bul. 107/G4
Dolnośląskie (prov.), Pol. 99/J3
Dolo, Eth. 155/P7
Dolo, It. 117/F2
Dolo (riv.), It. 116/D4
Doloon, Mong. 128/J3
Dolores, Arg. 216/F3
Dolores, Guat. 202/D2
Dolores (riv.), Co, US 186/E3
Dolores, Co, US 190/A2
Dolores, Uru. 217/J10
Dolores, Ven. 210/D2
Dolphin (cape), UK 217/F6
Dolphin and Union (str.), Nun., Can. 180/E2
Dölsach, Aus. 101/K3
Dolton, Il, US 193/Q16
Dom (peak), Swi. 114/D5
Dom (peak), Indo. 139/J4
Dom Noi (res.), Thai. 136/D3
Dom Pedrito, Braz. 215/F3
Dom Pedro, Braz. 212/A2
Domat-Ems, Swi. 115/F4
Domažlice, Czh. 113/F4
Dombasle-sur-Meurthe, Fr. 111/F6
Dombay-Ul'gen (peak), Geo. 121/G4
Dombes (lake), Fr. 114/B5
Dombóvár, Hun. 106/D2
Dombrád, Hun. 106/E1
Domburg, Neth. 108/A5
Dome C, US, Ant. 218/J
Domérat, Fr. 100/E3
Domeyko, Cordillera (mts.), Chile 215/C1
Dominica (ctry.) 199/N9
Dominica Passage (chan.), Dom.,Guad. 199/N9
Dominican Republic (ctry.) 199/H4
Dommartin-lès-Remiremont, Fr. 114/C2
Dommartin-lès-Toul, Fr. 111/E6
Dommel (riv.), Belg. 111/E1
Domodedovo (int'l arpt.), Rus. 119/W9
Domodossola, It. 115/E5
Domohāni, India 143/G2
Domont, Fr. 88/J4
Dompu, Indo. 139/E5
Domrémy-la-Pucelle, Fr. 114/B1
Dömsöd, Hun. 106/D2
Domusnovas, It. 104/A3
Domuyo (vol.), Arg. 216/C3
Domvilk (mt.), Austl. 172/C5
Domžale, Slov. 101/L3
Don (riv.), Eng, UK 93/G5
Don (ridge), Rus. 122/E5
Don (riv.), Rus. 85/J4
Don Benito, Sp. 102/C3
Donabate, Ire. 92/B5
Donada, It. 117/F2
Donaghadee, NI, UK 92/C2

Donag – Eché F

Donaghmore, NI, UK 92/B2
Donald, Austl. 173/B3
Donaldsonville, La, US 187/K5
Doñana NP, Sp. 102/B4
Donath, Swi. 115/F4
Donau (Danube) (riv.), Ger. 101/H2
Donaueschingen, Ger. 115/E2
Donauwörth, Ger. 112/D5
Doncaster, Eng, UK 93/G4
Doncaster (co.), Eng, UK 93/G4
Donchery, Fr. 111/D4
Dondra Head (pt.), SrL. 140/D6
Donegal, Ire. 89/P9
Donegal (dist.), Ire. 92/A1
Donegal (bay), Ire. 89/P9
Donets (riv.), Rus., Ukr. 121/G2
Donets'k, Ukr. 120/F2
Donets'k (int'l arpt.), Ukr. 120/F2
Donets'ka Oblasti, Ukr. 120/F3
Dong (riv.), Viet. 141/J5
Dong Ha, Viet. 136/D2
Dong Hoi, Viet. 136/D2
Dong Noi (riv.), Viet. 136/D4
Donga (riv.), Nga. 161/H4
Dongar Parāsia, India 142/B4
Dongara, Austl. 170/B4
Dongbei (plain), China 130/E2
Dongchuan, China 141/H2
Dong'e, China 130/D3
Dongen, Neth. 108/B5
Dongfang, China 141/J4
Donggou, China 131/C3
Dongguan, China 141/K3
Dongguang, China 130/D3
Donghai, China 130/D4
Dongio, Swi. 115/E5
Dongkya (pass), China 143/G2
Donglan, China 137/A3
Dongliao (riv.), China 130/F2
Dongming, China 130/C4
Dongo, It. 115/F5
Dongping, China 130/D4
Dongsha (isl.), China 137/C3
Dongshan, China 137/C3
Dongtai, China 130/E4
Dongtiao (riv.), China 130/L9
Dongting (lake), China 137/B2
Dongzhi, China 137/C1
Donihue, Chile 216/N9
Donjek (riv.), Yk, Can. 180/C2
Donji Komren, Serb. 106/E4
Donji Vakuf, Bosn. 106/C3
Donnas, It. 116/A1
Donnersberg (peak), Ger. 111/G4
Donnybrook, Austl. 172/D4
Donnybrook, Austl. 170/B5
Donon (peak), Fr. 114/D1
Donoratico, It. 101/J5
Donzdorf, Ger. 112/C5
Donzy, Fr. 100/E3
Dooleena (peak), Austl. 170/C2
Doon (riv.), Sc, UK 94/B6
Doon (lake), Sc, UK 94/B6
Doonbeg, Ire. 89/P10
Doonerak (mt.), Ak, US 192/H2
Door (pen.), Wi, US 185/M4
Doorn (riv.), SAfr. 164/B3
Doorn, Neth. 108/C4
Doppo (peak), It. 116/D1
Doqên (lake), China 143/G1
Dora (lake), Austl. 167/B3
Dora Riparia (riv.), It. 101/G4
Dorada (coast), Sp. 103/F2
Dorchester, NB, Can. 189/H2
Dorchester, Il, US 195/H7
Dorchester, Eng, UK 90/D5
Dorchester (cape), Nun., Can. 181/J2
Dorchester, NJ, US 196/D5
Dordogne (riv.), Fr. 100/D4
Dordrecht, SAfr. 164/D3
Dordrecht, Neth. 108/B5
Dore (lake), Sk, Can. 184/G2
Dore, Monts (mts.), Fr. 100/E4
Dores do Indaiá, Braz. 213/C1
Dorfen, Ger. 113/F6
Dorfen (riv.), Ger. 113/E6
Dorgali, It. 104/A2
Dori, Burk. 161/E3
Dorion, Qu, Can. 189/M7
Dorking, Eng, UK 88/C3
Dorlisheim, Fr. 114/D1
Dormagen, Ger. 111/F1
Dormans, Fr. 110/C5
Dornach, Swi. 114/D3
Dornbirn, Aus. 115/F3
Dorney Park/ Wildwater Kingdom, Pa, US 196/C2
Dornhan, Ger. 115/E1
Dorno, It. 116/B2
Dornoch Firth (inlet), Sc, UK 94/B1
Dornod (prov.), Mong. 129/K2
Dornogovĭ (prov.), Mong. 129/J3
Dornstadt, Ger. 112/C6
Dornstetten, Ger. 112/B6
Dorog, Hun. 107/Q9
Dorothy, NJ, US 196/D5
Dörpen, Ger. 109/E3
Dorre (isl.), Austl. 170/B3
Dorrigo, Austl. 173/E1
Dorrigo NP, Austl. 173/E1
Dorsale (mts.), Tun. 158/L7
Dorsbach (riv.), Ger. 112/B2
Dorset (co.), Eng, UK 90/D5
Dorsey, Il, US 195/G8
Dorsten, Ger. 108/D5
Dortan, Fr. 114/B5
Dortmund, Ger. 109/E5
Dortmund-Ems (canal), Ger. 109/E4
Dortmund (Wickede) (int'l arpt.), Ger. 109/E5
Dörtyol, Turk. 149/E1
Dorum, Ger. 109/F1
Dorval, Qu, Can. 189/N7
Dörverden, Ger. 109/G3
Dos Bahias (cape), Arg. 216/D5
Dos de Mayo, Peru 214/C2
Dos Hermanas, Sp. 102/C4
Döşemealtı, Turk. 149/B1
Dosewallips (riv.), Wa, US 193/A2
Dōshi, Japan 135/C2
Dōshi (riv.), Japan 135/C2
Dosse (riv.), Ger. 98/G2
Dosso, Niger 161/F3
Dosso (dept.), Niger 161/F3
Dosson, It. 117/F1
Dossor, Kaz. 121/K3
Dot Lake, Ak, US 192/K3
Dothan, Al, US 191/G4
Dötlingen, Ger. 109/F3
Döttingen, Swi. 115/E2
Douai, Fr. 110/C3
Douala, Camr. 154/G7
Douar el Càïd el Gueddara, Mor. 158/A2
Douar Toulal, Mor. 158/B3
Douarnenez, Fr. 100/A2
Douarnenez, Baie de (bay), Fr. 100/A2
Double Island (pt.), Austl. 172/D4
Double Mountain Fork Brazos (riv.), Tx, US 187/G4
Doubs (riv.), Fr. 100/F3
Doubs (dept.), Fr. 114/C3
Doubs, Fr. 114/C4
Doubtful Island (bay), Austl. 170/C5
Douchy-les-Mines, Fr. 110/C3
Doue, Fr. 88/M5
Doué-la-Fontaine, Fr. 100/C3
Douentza, Mali 160/E3
Dougga (ruin), Tun. 158/L6
Douglas, SAfr. 164/C3
Douglas (cap.), IM, UK 92/D3
Douglas, Sc, UK 94/C5
Douglas (mt.), Ak, US 192/H4
Douglas (co.), Co, US 195/C4
Douglas, Ga, US 191/H4
Douglas, Wy, US 185/G5
Douglassville, Pa, US 196/C3
Doulaincourt-Saucourt, Fr. 114/B1
Doullens, Fr. 110/B3
Doune, Sc, UK 94/B4
Doune (peak), Sc, UK 94/B4
Doupovské Hory (mts.), Czh. 101/K1
Dour, Belg. 110/C3
Dourados, Braz. 209/H8
Dourdan, Fr. 88/J6
Dourdou (riv.), Fr. 100/E4
Dourh (peak), Mor. 157/E2
Douro (riv.), Port. 102/B2
Dousman, Wi, US 193/P13
Doussard, Fr. 114/C6
Douvaine, Fr. 114/C5
Douvrin, Fr. 110/B2
Doux (riv.), Fr. 100/F4
Douze (riv.), Fr. 100/C4
Dove Creek, Co, US 186/E3
Dover, Austl. 173/C4
Dover (pt.), Austl. 170/E5
Dover, Eng, UK 91/H4
Dover (cap.), De, US 196/C5
Dover, NJ, US 196/D2
Dover, Pa, US 196/B4
Dover-Foxcroft, Me, US 189/G2
Dover, Strait of (str.), Fr.,UK 91/H5
Dovrefjell NP, Nor. 95/D3
Dow, Il, US 195/G7
Dowerin, Austl. 170/C4
Dowlatābād, Iran 147/G3
Down (dist.), NI, UK 92/C3
Downers Grove, Il, US 193/P16
Downey, Ca, US 194/F8
Downieville, Ca, US 186/B3
Downingtown, Pa, US 196/C4
Downpatrick, NI, UK 92/C3
Doylestown, Pa, US 196/C3
Dōzen (isl.), Japan 132/C3
Dozois (res.), Qu, Can. 188/E2
Drâa (cape), Mor. 156/C3
Drâa, Oued (riv.), Mor. 156/C3
Drac (riv.), Fr. 100/F4
Dracena, Braz. 213/B2
Drachten, Neth. 108/D2
Drăgăneşti-Olt, Rom. 107/G3
Dragoman, Bul. 105/H1
Dragon's Mouth (str.), Trin.,Ven. 211/F2
Draguignan, Fr. 101/G5
Drake (passg.) 215/C8
Drake, Co, US 195/B2
Drake (passg.), SAm. 217/D8
Drakensberg (mts.), SAfr. 164/D3
Dráma, Gre. 105/J2
Drammen, Nor. 96/D2
Drance (riv.), Swi. 114/D5
Drancy, Fr. 88/K5
Drangedal, Nor. 96/C2
Dranse (riv.), Fr. 114/C5
Dransfeld, Ger. 109/G5
Draper, Ut, US 195/K12
Drau (riv.), Aus. 101/K3
Dráva (riv.), Aus. 106/C3
Drava (riv.), Slov. 101/L3
Draveil, Fr. 88/K5
Drawa (riv.), Pol. 99/H2
Drawienski NP, Pol. 99/H2
Drawsko Pomorskie, Pol. 99/H2
Drayton, ND, US 185/J3
Drayton Valley, Ab, Can. 184/E2
Dreghorn, Sc, UK 94/B5
Drei Zinnen (peak), PNG 139/K4
Dreiesselberg (peak), Ger. 113/G5
Dreisam (riv.), Ger. 114/D2
Drensteinfurt, Ger. 109/E5
Drenthe (prov.), Neth. 108/D3
Drentse Hoofdvaart (riv.), Neth. 108/D3
Drentwede, Ger. 109/F3
Dresano, It. 116/C2
Dresden, Ger. 99/G3
Drezdenko, Pol. 99/H2
Driebergen, Neth. 108/C4
Driedorf, Ger. 111/H2
Drigh Road, Pak. 147/J4
Drimoleague, Ire. 89/P11
Drina (riv.), Bosn., Serb. 106/D4
Drinit (gulf), Alb. 105/F2
Drinit (riv.), Alb. 105/F1
Drniš, Cro. 106/C4
Dro, It. 115/G6
Drøbak, Nor. 96/D2
Drobeta-Turnu Severin, Rom. 106/F3
Drochtersen, Ger. 109/G1
Drocourt, Fr. 88/H4
Drogheda, Ire. 92/B4
Drohobych, Ukr. 120/B2
Droitwich, Eng, UK 90/D2
Drolshagen, Ger. 111/G1
Dromiskin, Ire. 92/B4
Dromore (riv.), Ire. 92/A3
Dromore, NI, UK 92/B3
Dronero, It. 101/G4
Dronfield, Eng, UK 93/G5
Drongan, Sc, UK 94/B6
Dronne (riv.), Fr. 100/D4
Dronten, Neth. 108/C3
Dropt (riv.), Fr. 100/D4
Drouette (riv.), Fr. 110/A6
Drowning (riv.), On, Can. 188/C1
Drumbeg, NI, UK 92/C2
Drumcar, Ire. 92/B4
Drumheller, Ab, Can. 184/E3
Drumleck (pt.), Ire. 92/B5
Drummond (range), Austl. 167/D3
Drummond (pt.), Austl. 171/G5
Drummond (mt.), Austl. 172/B4
Drummondville, Qu, Can. 189/F2
Drumochter, Pass of (pass), Sc, UK 94/B3
Drunen, Neth. 108/C5
Druridge (bay), Eng, UK 93/G1
Drusenheim, Fr. 111/G6
Druskininkai, Lith. 97/K4
Druten, Neth. 108/C5
Drvar, Bosn. 106/C3
Drwęca (riv.), Pol. 99/K2
Dry Fork Cheyenne (riv.), Wy, US 187/F2
Dry Tortugas (isl.), Fl, US 191/H5
Dry Tortugas NP, Fl, US 191/H5
Dryanovo, Bul. 105/J1
Dryden, On, Can. 185/K3
Dryden, Tx, US 190/C4
Dryden, Mi, US 193/F6
Drygarn Fawr (peak), Wal, UK 90/C2
Du Bois, Pa, US 188/E3
Du Page (co.), Il, US 193/P16
Du Page (riv.), Il, US 193/P16
Du Page, East Br. (riv.), Il, US 193/P16
Du Quoin, Il, US 187/K3
Duaringa, Austl. 172/C3
Duarte (peak), DRep. 199/G4
Duarte, Ca, US 194/G7
Dubawnt (riv.), NW, Can. 180/F2
Dubawnt (lake), Nun., Can. 180/F2
Dubayy, UAE 147/G3
Dubbo, Austl. 173/D2
Dübendorf, Swi. 115/E3
Dübener Heide (phys. reg.), Ger. 98/G3
Dubino, It. 115/F5
Dublin (cap.), Ire. 92/B5
Dublin (co.), Ire. 92/B5
Dublin, Ca, US 193/L11
Dublin, Ga, US 191/H3
Dublin, Md, US 196/B4
Dublin, Pa, US 196/C3
Dubna, Rus. 118/H4
Dubnica nad Váhom, Slvk. 99/K4
Dubno, Ukr. 120/C2
Dubois, Wy, US 184/F5
Duboistown, Pa, US 196/A1
Dubossary (res.), Mol. 107/J2
Dubrājpur, India 143/F4
Dubrovnik, Cro. 105/F1
Dubrovnik (int'l arpt.), Cro. 105/F1
Dubuque, Ia, US 185/L5
Duchang, China 137/C2
Duchcov, Czh. 113/G1
Duchesne (riv.), Ut, US 186/E2
Duchesne, Ut, US 186/E2
Ducie (isl.), Pitc. 175/N7
Duck (riv.), Tn, US 188/C5
Duck (lake), Mi, US 193/E7
Duckabush (riv.), Wa, US 193/A2
Duda (riv.), Col. 210/C4
Duddon (riv.), Eng, UK 93/E3
Dudelange, Lux. 111/F5
Dudenhofen, Ger. 112/B4
Duderstadt, Ger. 109/H5
Dudh Kosi (riv.), Nepal 143/F2
Dūdhi, India 142/D3
Dudhwa NP, India 142/C1
Dudignac, Arg. 216/E2
Düdingen, Swi. 114/D4
Dudinka, Rus. 122/J3
Dudley, Eng, UK 90/D1
Dudley (co.), Eng, UK 90/D2
Dueñas, Sp. 102/C2
Duero (riv.), Sp. 102/C2
Dueville, It. 117/E1
Dufaja (riv.), Kenya 162/C3
Duff (isls.), Sol. 174/F5
Duffel, Belg. 111/D1
Dufftown, Sc, UK 94/C2
Dufour (Dufourspitze) (peak), Swi. 116/A1
Dufourspitze (peak), Swi. 101/G4
Dugi Otok (isl.), Cro. 106/B3
Dugny-sur-Meuse, Fr. 111/E5
Dugo Selo, Cro. 106/C3
Dugway, Ut, US 186/D2
Duich (lake), Sc, UK 94/A2
Duida (peak), Ven. 211/E4
Duida Marahuaca, PN, Ven. 208/E3
Duingen, Ger. 109/G4
Duisburg, Ger. 108/D6
Duitama, Col. 210/C3
Duiven, Neth. 108/D5
Duke of Gloucester (isls.), FrPol. 175/L7
Duke's (pass), Sc, UK 94/B4
Dukielska (Dukla Pass) (pass), Pol. 99/L4
Dulan, China 128/G4
Dulce (riv.), Arg. 215/D2
Dulce, NM, US 186/F3
Dulce (gulf), Pan. 203/F4
Dulce Nombre de Culmí, Hon. 203/E3
Duleek, Ire. 92/B4
Dŭlgopol, Bul. 107/H4
Duliu (riv.), China 141/J2
Dullewāla, Pak. 144/A4
Dülmen, Ger. 109/E5
Dulnain (riv.), Sc, UK 94/C2
Dulovo, Bul. 107/H4
Dumalinao, Phil. 137/D6
Dumaran (isl.), Phil. 139/E1
Dumaresq (riv.), Austl. 173/D1
Dumas, Ar, US 187/K4
Dumas, Tx, US 187/G4
Dumbarton, Sc, UK 94/B5
Ďumbier (peak), Slvk. 99/K4
Dumbleyung, Austl. 170/C5
Dumbrăveni, Rom. 107/G2
Dume (pt.), Ca, US 194/B2
Dumfries, Sc, UK 92/E1
Dumfries and Galloway (pol. reg.), Sc, UK 94/C6
Dumka, India 143/F3
Dumlu, Turk. 121/G4
Dümmer (lake), Ger. 109/F3
Dumoine (riv.), Qu, Can. 188/E2
Dumoine (lake), Qu, Can. 181/J4
Dumont, NJ, US 197/K8
Dumont d'Urville, Fr., Ant. 218/K
Dumraon, India 143/E3
Dumyāt (gov.), Egypt 159/B1
Dún Laoghaire, Ire. 92/B5
Dun Rig (peak), Sc, UK 94/C5
Dunaföldvár, Hun. 106/D2
Dunaharaszti, Hun. 107/R10
Dunajec (riv.), Pol. 99/L4
Dunakeszi, Hun. 107/R9
Dunany (pt.), Ire. 92/B4
Dunaszekcso, Hun. 106/D2
Dunaújváros, Hun. 106/D2
Dunavecse, Hun. 106/D2
Dunavtsi, Bul. 106/F4
Dunbar, Sc, UK 94/D5
Dunblane, Sc, UK 94/C4
Dunboyne, Ire. 92/B5
Duncan, BC, Can. 184/C3
Duncan, Ok, US 187/H4
Duncannon, Pa, US 196/A3
Duncansby Head (pt.), Sc, UK 89/V14
Duncanville, Tx, US 190/D3
Dund-Us, Mong. 128/F2
Dundalk (bay), Ire. 89/Q10
Dundalk, Md, US 196/B5
Dundalk, Ire. 92/B4
Dundas (lake), Austl. 167/B4
Dundas, On, Can. 189/Q9
Dundas (pen.), NW, Can. 181/R7
Dundee, SAfr. 165/E3
Dundee, Sc, UK 94/D4
Dundee (pol. reg.), Sc, UK 94/D4
Dundgovĭ (prov.), Mong. 128/J2
Dundonald, Sc, UK 94/B5
Dundrum, NI, UK 92/C3
Dundrum (bay), NI, UK 92/C3
Dundurn, Sk, Can. 184/G3
Dundwa (range), Nepal 142/D2
Dundwārāganj, India 142/B2
Dunedin, Fl, US 191/H4
Dunedin, NZ 175/S12
Dunedoo, Austl. 173/D2
Dunellen, NJ, US 197/H9
Dunfanaghy, Ire. 89/Q9
Dunfermline, Sc, UK 94/C4
Dunga Bunga, Pak. 144/B5
Dungannon, NI, UK 92/B3
Dungannon (co.), NI, UK 92/B3
Dungarpur, India 147/K4
Dungarvan, Ire. 89/Q10
Dungau (reg.), Ger. 113/F5
Dungeness (pt.), Eng, UK 91/G5
Dungeness (pt.), Arg. 217/C7
Dungiven, NI, UK 92/B2
Dunglow, Ire. 89/P9
Dungog, Austl. 173/D2
Dungu, D.R. Congo 162/A2
Dungu (riv.), D.R. Congo 162/A2
Dunhua, China 129/N3
Dunhuang, China 128/F3
Dunkeld, Sc, UK 94/C3
Dunkerque (Dunkirk), Fr. 100/E1
Dunkery (hill), Eng, UK 90/C4
Dunkirk (Dunkerque), Fr. 100/E1
Dunkwa, Gha. 161/E5
Dunleer, Ire. 92/B4
Dunloy, NI, UK 92/B2
Dunmanway, Ire. 89/P11
Dunmurry, NI, UK 92/B2
Dunn, NC, US 191/J3
Dunnamanagh, NI, UK 92/A2
Dünnern (riv.), Swi. 114/D3
Dunnet Head (pt.), Sc, UK 89/V14
Dunningen, Ger. 115/E1
Dunnville, On, Can. 189/Q10
Dunolly, Austl. 173/B3
Dunoon, Sc, UK 94/B5
Dunqulah, Sudan 159/B5
Duns, Sc, UK 94/D5
Dunsborough, Austl. 170/B5
Dunseith, ND, US 185/H3
Dunshaughlin, Ire. 92/B4
Dunsmuir, Ca, US 186/B2
Dunstable, Eng, UK 91/F3
Dunyāpur, Pak. 144/A5
Duolun, China 129/L3
Dupo, Il, US 195/G8
Dupont, Pa, US 196/C1
Dupree, SD, US 185/H4
Dupuy (cape), Austl. 170/B2
Duque de Caxias, Braz. 213/K7
Duque de York (isl.), Chile 217/A6
Dūrā, WBnk. 149/D4
Durağan, Turk. 148/C1
Durak, Turk. 149/D1
Durance (riv.), Fr. 100/F5
Durango (state), Mex. 198/A3
Durango, Sp. 102/D1
Durango de Victoria, Mex. 200/D3
Durant, Ok, US 187/H4
Durazno (dept.), Uru. 217/F2
Durazno, Uru. 217/K10
Durban, SAfr. 165/E3
Durbanville, SAfr. 164/L10
Durbion (riv.), Fr. 114/C1
Durbuy, Belg. 111/E3
Dúrcal, Sp. 102/D4
Durdevac, Cro. 106/C2
Durdevo, Serb. 106/E3
Düren, Ger. 111/F2
Durg, India 140/D3
Durgāpur, India 143/F4
Durham, NH, US 189/G3
Durham, NC, US 191/J3
Durham, Eng, UK 93/G2
Durham (co.), Eng, UK 93/F2
Durlston (pt.), Eng, UK 90/E5
Durmitor NP, Mont. 106/D4
Durnford (pt.), WSah. 156/B5
Dürrenroth, Swi. 114/D3
Durrës, Alb. 105/F2
Dürrlauingen, Ger. 112/D6
Dürrwangen, Ger. 112/D4
Dursunbey, Turk. 148/B2
Durūz (peak), Syria 149/E3
D'Urville (cape), Indo. 139/J4
Dusanovac, Kos. 106/E4
Dusey (riv.), On, Can. 185/M3
Dushan, China 141/J2
Dushanbe (cap.), Taj. 145/E5
Dushanbe (int'l arpt.), Taj. 145/E5
Düsseldorf (int'l arpt.), Ger. 108/D6
Düsseldorf, Ger. 108/D6
Duszniki-Zdrój, Pol. 99/J3
Dutch (riv.), Eng, UK 93/H4
Dutch Harbor, Ak, US 192/E5
Dutch Wonderland, Pa, US 196/B3
Dutoitspiek (peak), SAfr. 164/L10
Dutse, Nga. 161/H4
Duvall, Wa, US 193/D2
Duvno, Bosn. 106/C4
Duyun, China 141/J2
Düzce, Turk. 107/K5
Düzici, Turk. 149/E1
Dve Mogili, Bul. 107/G4
Dvina (bay), Rus. 118/H2
Dvořiště (lake), Czh. 113/H4
Dwārka, India 147/J4
Dwārkeswar (riv.), India 143/F4
Dworshak (res.), Id, US 184/D4
Dwyfor (riv.), Wal, UK 92/D6
Dwyka (riv.), SAfr. 164/C4
Dyat'kovo, Rus. 120/E1
Dybvad, Den. 96/D3
Dyce (int'l arpt.), Sc, UK 94/D2
Dyce, Sc, UK 94/D2
Dye, Mo, US 195/D5
Dyer (cape), Nun., Can. 181/K2
Dyer (cape), Chile 217/B6
Dyer, In, US 188/C3
Dyfi (riv.), Wal, UK 90/C1
Dyje (riv.), Czh. 99/J4
Dykh-tau (peak), Rus. 121/G4
Dyle (riv.), Belg. 98/C3
Dyleň (peak), Czh. 113/F3
Dylewska (peak), Pol. 99/K2
Dysart, Austl. 172/C3
Dysselsdorp, SAfr. 164/C4
Dyul'tydag (peak), Rus. 121/H4
Dzaoudzi (cap.), May. 165/H6
Dzaoudzi (int'l arpt.), May. 165/H6
Dzavhan (prov.), Mong. 128/G2
Dzavhan (riv.), Mong. 128/F2
Dzenzik (pt.), Ukr. 120/F3
Dzerzhinsk, Rus. 118/J4
Dzhankoy, Ukr. 120/E3
Dzharylgach (gulf), Ukr. 107/L2
Dzhebel, Bul. 105/J2
Dzhugdzhur (range), Rus. 125/N4
Działdowo, Pol. 99/L2
Dzibalchén, Mex. 202/D2
Dzibilchaltún (ruin), Mex. 202/D1
Dzidzantún, Mex. 202/D1
Dzierżoniów, Pol. 99/J3
Dzitbalché, Mex. 202/D1
Dziuché, Mex. 202/D2
Dzukija NP, Lith. 97/L4
Dzungarian (basin), China 128/E3
Dzur, Mong. 128/G2
Dzüünbayan, Mong. 129/K3
Dzüünbulag, Mong. 129/K2
Dzüünharaa, Mong. 128/J2
Dzuunmod, Mong. 128/J2

E

Eads, Co, US 187/G3
Eagle (riv.), Nf, Can. 181/L3
Eagle (lake), On, Can. 188/A1
Eagle, Ak, US 192/K3
Eagle (lake), Ca, US 184/C5
Eagle, Co, US 186/F3
Eagle (mtn.), Mn, US 185/L4
Eagle, Wi, US 193/P14
Eagle (lake), Wi, US 185/K3
Eagle Butte, SD, US 185/H4
Eagle Pass, Tx, US 190/C4
Eagle River, Wi, US 185/L4
Eaglesham, Sc, UK 94/B5
Ealing (bor.), Eng, UK 88/B2
Ear Falls, On, Can. 185/K3
Earle Naval Weapons Center, NJ, US 196/D3
Earlimart, Ca, US 186/C4
Earl's Seat (peak), Sc, UK 94/B4
Earlston, Sc, UK 94/D5
Earn (riv.), Sc, UK 94/C4
Earn (lake), Sc, UK 94/B4
Easley, SC, US 191/H3
East (mt.), Austl. 170/D4
East (cape), NZ 175/T10
East (cape), Ak, US 192/B6
East (pt.), NJ, US 196/C5
East (riv.), NY, US 197/K8
East (passg.), Wa, US 193/C3
East Alton, Il, US 195/G8
East Anglia (reg.), Eng, UK 91/H2
East Angus, Qu, Can. 189/G2
East Ayrshire (pol. reg.), Sc, UK 94/B6
East Bangor, Pa, US 196/C2
East Berbice-Corentyne (pol. reg.), Guy. 211/G3
East Berlin, Pa, US 196/B4
East Berwick, Pa, US 196/B1
East Brunswick, NJ, US 197/H10
East Caicos (isl.), UK 203/J1
East Canyon (res.), Ut, US 195/K12
East Carondelet, Il, US 195/G8
East China (sea), Asia 125/M6
East Dart (riv.), Eng, UK 90/C5
East Dereham, Eng, UK 91/G1
East Dunbartonshire (pol. reg.), Sc, UK 94/B5
East Falkland (isl.), UK 217/F7
East Farmingdale, NY, US 197/M9
East Frisian (isls.), Ger. 98/D2
East Glen (riv.), Eng, UK 93/H6
East Greenville, Pa, US 196/C3
East Grinstead, Eng, UK 91/F4
East Hampton, NY, US 197/F2
East Haven, Ct, US 197/F1
East Helena, Mt, US 184/F4
East Hill-Meridian, Wa, US 193/C3
East Hills, NY, US 197/L8
East Jordan, Mi, US 188/C2
East Kilbride, Sc, UK 94/B5
East Lamma (chan.), China 129/U11
East Lansing, Mi, US 188/C3
East Leavenworth, Mo, US 195/D5
East Linton, Sc, UK 94/D5
East Liverpool, Oh, US 188/D3
East London, SAfr. 164/D4
East Los Angeles, Ca, US 194/F7
East Lothian (pol. reg.), Sc, UK 94/D5
East Lynne, Mo, US 195/E6
East Meadow, NY, US 197/L9
East Midlands (int'l arpt.), Eng, UK 93/G6
East Millcreek, Ut, US 195/K12
East Millinocket, Me, US 189/G2
East Newark, NJ, US 197/J9
East Newbern, Il, US 195/G7
East Nishnabotna (riv.), Ia, US 187/J2
East Northport, NY, US 197/E2
East Orange, NJ, US 197/J8
East Peckham, Eng, UK 88/E3
East Petersburg, Pa, US 196/B3
East Point, Ga, US 191/G3
East Pointe (East Detroit), Mi, US 193/G7
East Port Orchard, Wa, US 193/B2
East Prospect, Pa, US 196/B4
East Quogue, NY, US 197/F2
East Renfrewshire (pol. reg.), Sc, UK 94/B5
East Retford, Eng, UK 93/H5
East Riding of Yorkshire (co.), Eng, UK 93/H4
East Rockaway, NY, US 197/L9
East Rutherford, NJ, US 197/J8
East Saint Louis, Il, US 195/G8
East Siberian (sea), Rus. 123/S2
East Side, Pa, US 196/C1
East Stroudsburg, Pa, US 196/C2
East Sussex (co.), Eng, UK 91/G5
East Tawas, Mi, US 188/D2
East Timor (ctry.) 139/G5
East Troy, Wi, US 193/P14
East Wemyss, Sc, UK 94/C4
East Wenatchee, Wa, US 184/C4
East Windsor, NJ, US 196/D3
East York, Can. 189/R8
Eastbourne, Eng, UK 91/G5
Eastern (plain), Eng, UK 93/H4
Eastern (pol. reg.), Gha. 161/E5
Eastern (chan.), Japan 132/A4
Eastern (prov.), SLeo. 160/C4
Eastern (bay), Md, US 196/B6
Eastern (prov.), Zam. 162/B5
Eastern Ghats (mts.), India 140/C5
Eastern Neck Island NWR, Md, US 196/B5
Eastern Sayans (mts.), Rus. 122/K4
Easterville, Mb, Can. 185/J2
Eastlake, Co, US 195/C3
Eastleigh (int'l arpt.), Eng, UK 91/E5
Eastleigh, Eng, UK 91/E5
Eastmain (riv.), Qu, Can. 181/J3
Eastman, Ga, US 191/H3
Easton, Ct, US 197/E1
Easton (res.), Ct, US 197/E1
Easton, Pa, US 196/C2
Eastport, Me, US 189/H2
Eastport, NY, US 197/F2
Eastriggs, Sc, UK 93/E2
Eastwood, Eng, UK 93/G6
Eaton, Co, US 195/C1
Eatonia, Sk, Can. 184/F3
Eatons Neck (pt.), NY, US 197/M8
Eatontown, NJ, US 196/D3
Eau (riv.), Eng, UK 93/H5
Eau Claire (lake), Qu, Can. 181/J3
Eau d'Heure (riv.), Belg. 111/D3
Eau d'Heure, Barrage de l' (dam), Belg. 111/D3
Eaubonne, Fr. 88/J5
Eaulne (riv.), Fr. 110/A4
Eauripik (isl.), Micr. 174/D4
Eauze, Fr. 100/D5
Ebano, Mex. 202/B1
Ebble (riv.), Eng, UK 91/E4
Ebbw Vale, Wal, UK 90/C3
Ebebiyín, EqG. 154/H7
Ebeggi (well), Alg. 157/G5
Ebeleben, Ger. 109/H6
Ebeltoft, Den. 96/D3
Ebensee, Aus. 101/K3
Eberbach, Ger. 112/B4
Ebergassing, Aus. 107/P7
Ebergötzen, Ger. 109/H5
Ebermannstadt, Ger. 112/E3
Ebern, Ger. 112/D2
Ebersbach an der Fils, Ger. 112/C5
Ebersberg, Ger. 113/E6
Eberschwang, Aus. 113/G6
Ebersheim, Fr. 114/D1
Eberswalde-Finow, Ger. 99/G2
Ebetsu, Japan 134/B2
Ebian, China 141/H2
Ebina, Japan 135/C3
Ebnat-Kappel, Swi. 115/F3
Eboli, It. 104/D2
Ebolowa, Camr. 154/H7
Ebon (isl.), Mrsh. 174/F4
Ebonyi (state), Nga. 161/H5
Ebrach, Ger. 112/D3
Ebreichsdorf, Aus. 107/N8
Ebro (riv.), Sp. 103/F2
Ebstorf, Ger. 109/H2
Ecatepec, Mex. 201/Q9
Ecclefechan, Sc, UK 93/E1
Eccles, Eng, UK 93/F5
Eceabat, Turk. 107/H5
Echallens, Swi. 114/C4
Echarate, Peru 214/C4
Echaz (riv.), Ger. 112/C6
Èché Fadadinga (riv.), Niger 161/H3

Echigawa, Japan 135/K5
Eching, Ger. 113/E6
Echirolles, Fr. 100/F4
Echo (lake), NJ, US 196/D1
Echo, Ut, US 195/L12
Echoing (riv.),
Mb,On, Can. 185/L2
Echt, Neth. 111/E1
Echterdingen (int'l arpt.),
Ger. 112/C5
Echternach, Lux. 111/F4
Echuca, Austl. 173/C3
Echunga, Austl. 171/M9
Echzell, Ger. 112/B2
Écija, Sp. 102/C4
Ečka, Serb. 106/E3
Eckernförde, Ger. 96/C4
Eckerö (isl.), Fin. 97/H1
Eckerö, Fin. 97/H1
Eclipse Sound (bay),
Nun., Can. 181/H1
Écommoy, Fr. 100/D3
Ecoporanga, Braz. 212/B5
Écorse (riv.), Mi, US 193/F7
Écorse, Mi, US 193/F7
Écouen, Fr. 88/K4
Ecquevilly, Fr. 88/H5
Écrins, PN des, Fr. 101/G4
Écrosnes, Fr. 88/H6
Écrouves, Fr. 111/E6
Ecuador (ctry.) 208/C4
Ecublens, Swi. 114/C4
Ed, Swe. 96/D2
Eday (isl.), Sc, UK 89/V14
Eddystone (pt.),
Austl. 173/D4
Eddystone Rocks (isls.),
Eng, UK 90/B6
Ede, Nga. 161/G5
Ede, Neth. 108/C4
Edéa, Camr. 154/H7
Edegem, Belg. 111/D1
Edehin Ouarene (des.),
Alg. 157/G4
Edéia, Braz. 213/B1
Edelény, Hun. 99/L4
Edemissen, Ger. 109/H4
Eden, Austl. 173/D3
Eden (riv.), Sc, UK 94/D4
Eden, NC, US 188/E4
Eden, Ut, US 195/K11
Edenbridge, Eng, UK 88/D3
Edenburg, SAfr. 164/D3
Edendale, SAfr. 165/E3
Edenhope, Austl. 173/B3
Edenkoben, Ger. 112/B4
Edenside (valley),
Eng, UK 93/F2
Edenton, NC, US 191/J2
Eder (riv.), Ger. 98/E3
Eder-Stausee (lake),
Ger. 109/F6
Edewecht, Ger. 109/E2
Edgar (mt.), Austl. 170/D2
Edge (isl.), Sval. 218/E
Edgecumbe (cape),
Ak, US 192/L4
Edgell (isl.),
Nun., Can. 181/K2
Edgemere, Md, US 196/C5
Edgerton, Ut, US 195/K13
Edgerton, Wy, US 185/G5
Edgewater, Co, US 195/B3
Edgewater Park,
NJ, US 196/D3
Edgewood, Pa, US 196/D2
Edgewood, ND, US 196/B5
Edgewood Arsenal,
Md, US 196/B5
Edgewood-North Hill,
Wa, US 193/C3
Édhessa, Gre. 105/H2
Edinburg, Tx, US 190/D5
Edinburgh (cap.),
Sc, UK 94/C5
Edinburgh (pol. reg.),
Sc, UK 94/C5
Edirne (prov.), Turk. 107/H5
Edirne, Turk. 107/H5
Edison, NJ, US 197/H9
Edison International Field,
Ca, US 194/G8
Edison Nat'l Hist. Site,
NJ, US 197/J8
Edisto Island,
SC, US 191/H3
Edisto, South Fork (riv.),
SC, US 191/H3
Edithburgh, Austl. 171/H5
Édjérir (riv.), Mali 161/F2
Edmond, Ok, US 195/N14
Edmonds, Wa, US 184/C4
Edmonton (int'l arpt.),
Ab, Can. 184/E2
Edmonton (cap.),
Ab, Can. 184/E2
Edmund Kennedy NP,
Austl. 172/B2
Edmundston,
NB, Can. 189/G2
Edna, Tx, US 187/H5
Edna Bay, Ak, US 192/M4
Edo (state), Nga. 161/G5
Edo (riv.), Japan 135/D2
Edolo, It. 115/G5
Edremit, Turk. 148/A2
Edremit (gulf),
Gre.,Turk. 148/A2
Edsbyn, Swe. 96/F1
Edson, Ab, Can. 184/D2
Eduardo Castex,
Arg. 216/D2
Edward (mt.), Austl. 171/F2

Edward (lake),
D.R.Congo 162/A3
Edward River Aboriginal
Community, Austl. 172/A1
Edward VII (pen.),
Ant. 218/P
Edward VIII (bay),
Ant. 218/U
Edwards (riv.), Il, US 187/K2
Edwards (plat.),
Tx, US 187/G5
Edwardsville,
Il, US 195/H8
Edwardsville,
Ks, US 195/D5
Edwardsville,
Pa, US 196/C1
Edzell, Sc, UK 94/D3
Edzná (ruin), Mex. 202/D2
Eek, Ak, US 192/F3
Eeklo, Belg. 110/C1
Eel (riv.), Ca, US 186/B3
Eelde-Paterswolde,
Neth. 108/D2
Eem (riv.), Neth. 108/C4
Eemenes, Neth. 108/C4
Eems (Ems) (riv.),
Ger., Neth 108/D2
Eemshaven (har.),
Neth. 108/D2
Eemskanaal (riv.),
Neth. 108/D2
Eersel, Neth. 108/C2
Efate (isl.), Van. 174/F6
Eferding, Aus. 113/H6
Effigy Mounds Nat'l Mon.,
Ia, US 185/L5
Effingham, Il, US 185/L5
Effingham, On, Can. 189/R9
Effon Alaiye, Nga. 161/G5
Effort, Pa, US 196/C2
Eforie, Rom. 107/J3
Efringen-Kirchen,
Ger. 114/D2
Efyrnwy, Llyn (lake),
Wal, UK 92/E6
Egadi (isls.), It. 104/B3
Egan (range), Nv, US 186/D3
Egan (riv.), Ger. 112/E5
Egaña, Uru. 217/K10
Egedik, Ak, US 192/G4
Eger, Hun. 99/L5
Egeskov, Den. 96/D4
Egestorf, Ger. 109/H2
Egg, Aus. 115/F3
Egg, Swi. 115/E3
Egg Harbor City,
NJ, US 196/D4
Egg Island (pt.),
NJ, US 196/C5
Eggebek, Ger. 96/C4
Eggegebirge (ridge),
Ger. 109/F5
Eggelsberg, Aus. 113/H6
Eggenburg, Aus. 101/L2
Eggenfelden, Ger. 113/F6
Eggenstein-Leopoldshafen,
Ger. 112/B4
Eggesin, Ger. 96/F5
Eggiwil, Swi. 114/D4
Egglescliffe,
Eng, UK 93/G3
Eggstätt, Ger. 113/F7
Egham, Eng, UK 88/B2
Eghezée, Belg. 111/D2
Egilsstadhir, Ice. 95/P6
Egletons, Fr. 100/E4
Eglinton (isl.),
NW, Can. 181/R7
Eglinton, NI, UK 92/A1
Eglisau, Swi. 115/E2
Egly, Fr. 88/J6
Egmond aan Zee,
Neth. 108/B3
Egmont (cape), NZ 175/S10
Egmont (mt.), NZ 175/S10
Egna (Neumarkt), It. 115/H5
Egnach, Swi. 115/F2
Eğridir, Turk. 148/B2
Eğridir (lake), Turk. 148/B2
Eguas, Rio das (riv.),
Braz. 212/A4
Egypt (ctry.) 155/L2
Ehebach (riv.), Ger. 112/D3
Ehekirchen, Ger. 112/D5
Ehime (pref.), Japan 132/C4
Ehingen, Ger. 115/F1
Ehingen, Ger. 112/D4
Ehringshausen, Ger. 112/B1
Ehrwald, Aus. 115/G3
Eibar, Sp. 102/D1
Eibelstadt, Ger. 112/C3
Eibenstock, Ger. 113/F1
Eibergen, Neth. 108/D4
Eich, Ger. 112/B3
Eichel (riv.), Fr. 111/G6
Eichenau, Ger. 112/E6
Eichenbühl, Ger. 112/C3
Eichendorf, Ger. 113/F5
Eichenzell, Ger. 112/C2
Eichstätt, Ger. 112/E5
Eichwalde, Ger. 98/Q7
Eicklingen, Ger. 109/H3
Eid, Nor. 95/C3
Eidfjord, Nor. 96/C1
Eidsvold, Austl. 172/C4
Eidsvold, Nor. 96/D1
Eifel (plat.), Ger. 98/D3
Eiffel Tower, Fr. 88/J5
Eigenji, Japan 135/K5
Eiger (peak), Swi. 114/D4
Eigersund, Nor. 96/A2
Eigg (isl.), Sc, UK 89/Q8

Eight Degree (chan.),
India,Mald. 140/B6
Eijerlandse Gat (chan.),
Neth. 108/B2
Eijsden, Neth. 111/E2
Eikelandsosen, Nor. 96/A1
Eil, Loch (inlet),
Sc, UK 94/A3
Eildon (lake), Austl. 173/C3
Eildon, Austl. 173/C3
Eilerts de Haan (mts.),
Sur. 211/G4
Einbeck, Ger. 109/G5
Eindhoven (int'l arpt.),
Neth. 108/C6
Eindhoven, Neth. 108/C6
Einsiedeln, Swi. 115/E3
Einville-au-Jard, Fr. 111/F6
Eirunepé, Braz. 214/D2
Eisch (riv.), Lux. 111/E4
Eisenach, Ger. 109/H7
Eisenberg, Ger. 112/B3
Eisenhower Nat'l Hist. Site,
Pa, US 196/A4
Eisenhüttenstadt,
Ger. 99/H2
Eiserfeld, Ger. 111/G2
Eisfeld, Ger. 112/D2
Eisingen, Ger. 112/C3
Eislingen, Ger. 112/C5
Eitelborn, Ger. 111/G3
Eiter (riv.), Ger. 109/F3
Eitorf, Ger. 111/G2
Eitting, Ger. 113/E6
Ejea de los Caballeros,
Sp. 103/E1
Ejeda, Madg. 165/H9
Ejido, Ven. 211/F3
Ejin Horo Qi, China 130/B3
Ejin Qi, China 128/H3
Ejutla de Crespo,
Mex. 202/B2
Ekeby, Swe. 96/E3
Ekenäs (Tammisaari),
Fin. 97/K2
Ekeren, Belg. 108/B6
Ekhínos, Gre. 105/J2
Ekibastuz, Kaz. 145/G2
Eksjö, Swe. 96/F3
Ekuk, Ak, US 192/G4
Ekwan (riv.),
Mali 181/H3
Ekwok, Ak, US 192/G4
El Aaiún, WSah. 156/B4
El Aatf (reg.), WSah. 156/B5
El Abiodh Sidi Chrikh,
Alg. 157/F2
El 'Açâba (mass.),
Mrta. 160/C2
El Affroun, Alg. 158/G4
El Águila, Mex. 190/B5
El Aïoun, Mor. 158/C2
El Alto, Peru 214/A2
El Amparo de Apure,
Ven. 210/D3
El Anegado, Ecu. 210/A5
El Aouinet, Alg. 158/K7
El Arhlaf (well),
Mrta. 160/D2
El Astillero, Sp. 102/D1
El Bagre, Col. 210/C2
El Banco, Col. 210/C2
El Barco, Sp. 102/B1
El Barco de Ávila,
Sp. 102/C2
El Baúl, Ven. 210/D2
El Bayadh (prov.),
Alg. 157/F2
El Bayadh, Alg. 157/F2
El Bolsón, Arg. 216/C4
El Bonillo, Sp. 102/D3
El Borouj, Mor. 156/D2
El Burgo de Osma, Sp. 102/D2
El Cajón, Ca, US 194/D5
El Cajón (res.), Hon. 202/D4
El Calafate, Arg. 217/B6
El Callao, Ven. 211/F3
El Capitan (peak),
Mt, US 184/E4
El Carmen, Chile 216/B3
El Carmen, Col. 210/B3
El Carmen de Bolívar,
Col. 210/C2
El Casar de Talamanca,
Sp. 103/N8
El Centro, Ca, US 186/D4
El Cerrito, Col. 210/B4
El Cerrito, Ca, US 193/K11
El Cerro del Aripo
(peak), Trin. 211/F2
El Cerrón (peak),
Ven. 210/D3
El Chico, PN, Mex. 201/L6
El Cocuy, Col. 210/C3
El Colorado, Arg. 215/E2
El Difícil, Col. 210/C2
El Djouf (des.),
Mrta. 154/D3
El Dorado, Mex. 200/D3
El Dorado, Ar, US 187/J4
El Dorado, Ks, US 187/J3
El Dorado, Ven. 211/F3
El Eglab (plat.), Alg. 156/D3
El Empedrado, (Ven.) 210/D2
El Escorial, Sp. 103/M8
El Espinar, Sp. 102/C2
El Eulma, Alg. 158/H4
El Fahs, Tun. 158/L6
El Ferrol, Sp. 102/A1
El Fuerte, Mex. 200/C3
El Fureidîs, Isr. 149/F6

El Gogorrón, PN,
Mex. 198/A3
El Golea, Alg. 157/F3
El Golfete (lake),
Guat. 202/D3
El Granada, Ca, US 193/K11
El Grullo, Mex. 200/D5
El Guachara, PN,
Ven. 211/F2
El Hajeb, Mor. 158/B3
El Hank (cliff), Mali 156/D4
El Harino, Pan. 210/A2
El Harta (well), Alg. 157/E4
El Higo, Mex. 202/B1
El Indio, Tx, US 190/C4
El Jadida, Mor. 156/C2
El Jem, Tun. 158/M7
El Kelaâ des Srarhna,
Mor. 156/D2
El Khatt (cliff), Mrta. 154/C3
El Khatt (depr.),
Mrta. 160/C2
El Khnâchîch (cliff),
Mali 156/E5
El Kroub, Alg. 158/K6
El Kseur, Alg. 158/H4
El Libertador General
Bernardo O'Higgins
(pol. reg.), Chile 216/N8
El Limón, Mex. 201/F4
El Mahia (phys. reg.),
Mali 157/E5
El Maitén, Arg. 216/C4
El Malpais Nat'l Mon.,
NM, US 186/F4
El Manteco, Ven. 211/F3
El-Menzel, Mor. 158/B3
El Miamo, Ven. 211/F3
El Milia, Alg. 158/J4
El Mirage, Az, US 195/H18
El Mirage, Ca, US 194/C1
El Montcau (peak),
Sp. 103/K6
El Monte, Ca, US 194/F7
El Morrito (pt.),
Chile 216/C1
El Mrâyer (well),
Mrta. 156/C5
El Mreyyé (phys. reg.),
Mrta. 160/C2
El Mzereb (well),
Mali 156/D4
El Naranjo de Carlos
Sarabia,
Mex. 201/F4
El Nayar, Mex. 200/D4
El Nevado (peak),
Arg. 216/C2
El Nido, Phil. 139/E1
El Olivar Alto, Chile 216/N9
El Oro (prov.), Ecu. 214/A1
El Oued (prov.), Alg. 157/G2
El Oued, Alg. 157/G2
El Palmar, Ven. 211/F3
El Pao, Ven. 211/F2
El Pao, Ven. 211/E2
El Paraíso, Mex. 201/E5
El Paraíso, Hon. 202/E3
El Paso, Tx, US 186/F5
El Paso International
(int'l arpt.), Tx, US 187/F5
El Pilar, Ven. 211/F2
El Porvenir, Mex. 200/D2
El Porvenir, Mex. 210/B2
El Potosí, Mex. 201/E3
El Potosí, PN, Mex. 198/B3
El Prat de Llobregat,
Sp. 103/L7
El Progreso, Ecu. 214/F7
El Progreso, Guat. 202/D3
El Progreso, Hon. 202/E3
El Progreso Industrial,
Mex. 201/Q9
El Puerto de Santa María,
Sp. 102/B4
El Quelite, Mex. 200/D4
El Quisco, Chile 216/N8
El Rama, Nic. 203/E3
El Rancho, Co, US 195/B3
El Reno, Ok, US 187/H4
El Río, Ca, US 194/A2
El Roble, Pan. 210/A2
El Rosario de Arriba,
Mex. 200/B2
El Sacromonte, PN,
Mex. 201/L7
El Salto, Mex. 200/D4
El Salvador (ctry.) 202/D3
El Salvador, Mex. 201/E3
El Salvador, Cuba 203/H1
El Salvador (int'l arpt.),
ESal. 202/D3
El Samán de Apure,
Ven. 210/D3
El Sauz, Mex. 200/D2
El Sauzal, Mex. 200/A2
El Segundo, Ca, US 194/F8
El Shab (well), Egypt 159/B4
El Tabo, Chile 216/N8
El Tajín (ruin), Mex. 201/M6
El Tama, PN, Ven. 210/C3
El Tambo, Ecu. 210/B5
El Tarf (prov.), Alg. 158/K6
El Tarf, Alg. 158/K6
El Teleno (peak), Sp. 102/B1
El Tepozteco, PN,
Mex. 201/R10
El Tiemblo, Sp. 102/C2
El Tigre, Ven. 211/F2
El Tocuyo, Ven. 210/D2
El Toro, Ca, US 194/C3
El Triunfo, Ecu. 210/B5
El Triunfo, Mex. 202/D2
El Tucuche (peak),
Trin. 211/F2

El Tuito, Mex. 200/D4
El Tuparro, PN, Col. 208/E3
El Valle, Pan. 210/A2
El Venado (isl.),
Nic. 203/F4
El Viejo (peak), Col. 210/C3
El Viejo, Nic. 202/E3
El Vigía, Ven. 210/D2
El Yagual, Ven. 210/D3
El Yunque (peak),
PR 199/M8
El Zacatón, Mex. 200/E4
Elan (riv.), Wal, UK 90/C2
Élancourt, Fr. 88/H5
Elandsrivier (riv.),
SAfr. 164/Q12
Elassón, Gre. 105/H3
Elat (int'l arpt.), Isr. 149/D5
Elat, Isr. 149/D5
Elátia (isl.), Micr. 174/D4
Elazığ (prov.), Turk. 148/D2
Elazig, Turk. 148/D2
Elba, Al, US 191/G4
Elba (isl.), It. 101/H5
Elbasan, Alb. 105/G2
Elbbach (riv.), Ger. 111/G2
Elbe (riv.), Ger. 98/F2
Elbe (Labe) (riv.),
Czh.,Ger. 99/H2
Elbe-Seitenkanaal (canal),
Ger. 109/H2
Elbert (co.), Co, US 195/C4
Elberton, Ga, US 191/H3
Elbeuf, Fr. 100/D2
Elbigenalp, Aus. 115/G3
Elblag, Pol. 97/H4
Elbow, Sk, Can. 184/G3
El'brus (peak), Rus. 121/G4
Elburg, Neth. 108/C4
Elburn, Il, US 193/N16
Elburz (mts.), Iran 146/E1
Elche, Sp. 103/E3
Elche de la Sierra,
Sp. 102/D3
Elchingen, Ger. 112/D6
Elcho (isl.), Austl. 167/C2
Eld (inlet), Wa, US 193/A3
Elda, Sp. 103/E3
Elde (riv.), Ger. 98/G2
Eldersburg, Md, US 196/B5
Eldivan, Turk. 148/C1
Eldon, Wa, US 193/A2
Eldora, Co, US 195/A3
Eldora, NJ, US 196/D5
Eldorado, Arg. 215/F2
Eldorado, Tx, US 187/G5
Eldorado Springs,
Co, US 195/B3
Eldoret, Kenya 162/B2
Eleao (peak), Hi, US 182/W13
Elefsís, Gre. 105/H3
Elek, Hun. 106/E2
Elektrostal', Rus. 119/X9
Elena, Arg. 216/D2
Elesbão Veloso,
Braz. 212/B2
Eleşkirt, Turk. 148/E2
Eleuthera (isl.),
Bahm. 199/F2
Eleven Point (riv.),
Mo, US 187/K3
Elevsís (ruin), Gre. 105/N8
Elevtheroúpolis, Gre. 105/J2
Elfershausen, Ger. 112/C2
Elgg, Swi. 115/E3
Elgin (riv.), Fr. 100/A2
Elgin, Il, US 185/L5
Elgin, Tx, US 187/H5
Elgin, Sc, UK 94/C1
Elgóibar, Sp. 102/D1
Elgon (Wagagai) (peak),
Ugan. 162/B2
Elida, NM, US 192/F3
Elim, Ak, US 192/F3
Elimäki, Fin. 97/M1
Elista, Rus. 121/H3
Elixhausen, Aus. 113/G7
Elizabeth (bay),
Namb. 164/A2
Elizabeth, NJ, US 197/J9
Elizabeth City,
NC, US 191/J2
Elizabethan Village Hist.
Site, Austl. 170/L7
Elizabethton,
Tn, US 188/D4
Elizabethtown,
Pa, US 196/B3
Elizabethville,
Pa, US 196/B2
Elk (mts.), Co, US 190/B3
Elk (riv.), WV, US 191/H2
Elk, Pol. 97/K5
Elk City, Ok, US 187/H4
Elk Grove,
Ca, US 193/M10
Elk Grove Village,
Il, US 193/P16
Elk Island NP,
Ab, Can. 184/E2
Elk Mills, Md, US 196/C4
Elk Point, Ab, Can. 184/F2
Elk Rapids, Mi, US 188/C2
Elk Ridge, Md, US 196/B5
Elk River, Mn, US 185/K4
Elk Slough (riv.),
Ca, US 193/M10
Elkenroth, Ger. 111/G2
Elkhart, In, US 188/C3
Elkhart, Ks, US 187/G3
Elkhart, Tx, US 187/J5
Elkhorn, Mb, Can. 185/H3
Elkhorn, Wi, US 188/B3
Elkhorn (riv.), Ne, US 185/H2

Elkhovo, Bul. 105/K1
Ca, US 194/F7
Elko, Nv, US 184/E5
Elkton, Md, US 196/C4
Ellamar, Ak, US 192/J3
Elland, Eng, UK 93/G4
Elle (riv.), Ger. 111/F2
Ellef Ringnes (isl.),
Nun., Can. 181/R7
Ellefeld, Ger. 113/F2
Ellen (riv.), Eng, UK 93/E2
Ellenberg, Ger. 112/D4
Ellendale, ND, US 185/J4
Ellendale, De, US 196/C6
Ellensburg,
Wa, US 184/C4
Eller (riv.), Ger. 109/H5
Ellerbach (riv.),
Ger. 111/G4
Ellero (riv.), It. 116/A4
Ellery (mt.), Austl. 173/D3
Ellesmere (isl.),
Nun., Can. 181/S6
Ilesmere Port,
Eng, UK 93/F5
Ellezelles, Belg. 110/C2
Ellice (riv.),
Nun., Can. 180/F2
Ellicott City, Md, US 196/B5
Ellinikón (int'l arpt.),
Gre. 105/N9
Elliniká, Austl. 172/C3
Elliot, SAfr. 164/D3
Elliot Lake, On, Can. 188/D2
Elliot Price Consv. Park,
Austl. 171/H4
Elliott (peak), Va, US 191/J2
Emigsville, Pa, US 196/B3
Emilia-Romagna
On, Can. 185/K3
English (riv.),
Fr.,UK 100/B2
English Bay, Ak, US 192/H4
English Bāzār,
India 143/G3

[Additional entries in final column:]
Elysian Park,
Ca, US 194/F7
Elz (riv.), Ger. 112/B6
Elz (riv.), Ger. 112/B2
Elzach, Ger. 114/E1
Elzbach (riv.), Ger. 111/G3
Elze, Ger. 109/G4
Emämshahr (Shāhrūd),
Iran 147/F1
Emán (riv.), Swe. 96/F3
Emancé, Fr. 88/H6
Emas, PN das,
Braz. 209/H7
Emba (riv.), Kaz. 120/K3
Embarcación, Arg. 215/D1
Embarras (riv.),
Il, US 191/F2
Embi, Kaz. 121/L2
Embi (riv.), Kaz. 122/F5
Embira (riv.), Braz. 208/D5
Emborcação, Barragem de
(res.), Braz. 213/C1
Embrach, Swi. 115/E3
Embrun, Fr. 101/G4
Embsen, Ger. 109/H2
Embu, Kenya 162/C3
Emden, Ger. 109/E2
Emeishan, China 141/H2
Emerald, Austl. 172/C3
Emerald, Austl. 173/G5
Emerson, Mb, Can. 185/J3
Emerson, NJ, US 197/K8
Emeryville, Ca, US 193/K11
Emet, Turk. 148/B2
Emilia-Romagna
(prov.), It. 116/C3
Emiliano Zapata,
Mex. 202/D2
Emin, China 128/D2
Emináābād, Pak. 144/C3
Eminence, Mo, US 187/K3
Emir Pasha (gulf),
Tanz. 162/A3
Emirdağ, Turk. 148/B2
Emirgazi, Turk. 148/C2
Emlembe (peak),
Swaz. 165/E2
Emlichheim, Ger. 108/D3
Emma (riv.), Sur. 211/H4
Emmaboda, Swe. 96/F3
Emmanuel Head (pt.),
Eng, UK 94/E5
Emmaus, Pa, US 196/C2
Emmeloord, Neth. 108/C3
Emmen, Neth. 108/D2
Emmendingen, Ger. 114/D1
Emmental (valley),
Swi. 114/D3
Emmer (riv.), Ger. 109/G4
Emmerbach (riv.),
Ger. 115/E2
Emmerich, Ger. 108/D5
Emmett, Mi, US 193/G6
Emmingen-Liptingen,
Ger. 115/E2
Emmitsburg,
Md, US 196/A4
Emmonak, Ak, US 192/F3
Emneth, Eng, UK 91/G1
Emöd, Hun. 106/E2
Emory, Tx, US 187/J4
Emosson (lake), Swi. 114/C5
Empalme, Mex. 200/C3
Empalme, SAfr. 165/E3
Empedrado, Arg. 215/E2
Empedrado, Chile 216/B2
Empoli, It. 117/D5
Emporia, Ks, US 187/H3
'Emrāni, Iran 147/G2
Ems (Eems) (riv.),
Ger.,Neth. 108/D2
Ems-Jade (canal),
Ger. 109/E2
Emsbüren, Ger. 109/E4
Emsdetten, Ger. 109/E4
Emskirchen, Ger. 112/D3
Emsland (reg.), Ger. 98/D2
Emstek, Ger. 109/F3
Emsworth, Eng, UK 91/F5
Emyvale, Ire. 92/B3
Ena, Japan 133/E3
Enbetsu, Japan 134/B1
Encantada, Cerro (peak),
Mex. 200/B3
Encantada, Cerro de la
(peak), Mex. 200/B2
Encarnación de Díaz,
Mex. 200/E4
Enchi, Gha. 160/E5
Encinitas, Ca, US 194/C4
Enciso, Col. 210/C3
Encontrados, Ven. 210/C2
Encounter (bay),
Austl. 173/A2
Encruzilhada do Sul,
Braz. 213/A4
Encs, Hun. 99/L4
Endau (marsh), Kenya 162/C3
Ende, Indo. 139/F5
Endeavour River NP,
Austl. 172/B1
Enderby, BC, Can. 184/D3
Enderby Land (phys. reg.),
Ant. 218/D
Enderlin, ND, US 185/J4
Endicott, NY, US 188/E3
Endingen, Ger. 114/D1
Ene (riv.), Peru 208/D6
Eneabba, Austl. 170/B4

Enebakk, Nor. 96/D2
Enewetak (isl.) 174/F3
Mrsh. 174/F3
Enez, Turk. 105/K2
Enfield (bor.),
Eng, UK 88/C2
Engaño (cape), Phil. 137/D4
Engaru, Japan 134/C1
Engelberg, Swi. 115/E4
Engelhartszell, Aus. 113/G5
Engel's, Rus. 121/H2
Engelskirchen, Ger. 111/G2
Engelsmanplaat (isl.),
Neth. 108/D2
Engen, Ger. 115/E2
Engenheiro Navarro,
Braz. 212/B5
Engenheiro Paulo de Frontin,
Braz. 213/K7
Enger, Ger. 109/F4
Engerwitzdorf, Aus. 113/H6
Enggano (isl.), Indo. 138/B5
Enghershatu, Erit. 146/C5
Enghien, Belg. 110/D2
Engi, Swi. 115/F4
England, UK 90/D2
Englefontaine, Fr. 110/C3
Englehart, On, Can. 188/E2
Englewood, Co, US 195/C3
Englewood, NJ, US 197/K8
Englewood Cliffs,
NJ, US 197/K8
English (riv.),
On, Can. 185/K3
English (chan.),
Fr.,UK 100/B2
English Bay, Ak, US 192/H4
English Bāzār,
India 143/G3
English Creek,
NJ, US 196/D5
Englishtown, NJ, US 196/D3
Enguera, Sp. 103/E3
Enguri (riv.), Geo. 121/G4
Enhlat, Mong. 128/J2
Enid, Ok, US 187/H3
Eniwa, Japan 134/B2
Enkenbach-Alsenborn,
Ger. 111/G5
Enkhuizen, Neth. 108/C3
Enkirch, Ger. 111/G4
Enköping, Swe. 96/G2
Enna, It. 104/D4
Ennedi (plat.), Chad 155/K4
Ennepe (riv.), Ger. 109/E6
Ennepetal, Ger. 109/E6
Ennery, Fr. 88/J4
Enningerloh, Ger. 109/F5
Ennis, Mt, US 184/F4
Ennis, Tx, US 187/J4
Ennis, Ire. 89/P10
Enniscorthy, Ire. 89/Q10
Enniskerry, Ire. 92/B5
Enniskillen, NI, UK 89/Q9
Ennistimon, Ire. 89/P10
Enns (riv.), Aus. 99/H5
Enogger (res.),
Austl. 172/E6
Enola, Pa, US 196/B3
Enontekiö, Fin. 95/G1
Enoree (riv.), SC, US 191/H3
Enping, China 141/K3
Enrick (riv.), Sc, UK 94/B2
Enrique Carbó,
Arg. 217/J10
Enriquillo, DRep. 203/J2
Enschede, Neth. 108/D4
Ensdorf, Ger. 113/E4
Ense, Ger. 109/E5
Enseleni, SAfr. 165/E3
Ensenada, Mex. 200/A2
Ensenada, Arg. 217/K11
Enshi, China 137/C1
Ensisheim, Fr. 114/D2
Entebbe (int'l arpt.),
Ugan. 162/B2
Entebbe, Ugan. 162/B2
Entenbühl (peak),
Ger. 113/F3
Enterprise, Al, US 191/G4
Enterprise, Ut, US 195/K11
Entlebuch, Swi. 114/E4
Entre Rios, Braz. 212/C3
Entre Rios (mts.),
Hon. 203/E3
Entroncamento, Port. 102/A3
Entzheim, Fr. 114/D1
Enugu, Nga. 161/G5
Enugu (state), Nga. 161/G5
Enumclaw, Wa, US 184/C4
Enushū (sea), Japan 135/M6
Envira, Braz. 214/D2
Enz (riv.), Ger. 101/H2
Enza (riv.), It. 116/C4
Épano Arkhánai,
Gre. 105/J5
Epanomí, Gre. 105/H2
Epe, Nga. 161/F5
Epe, Neth. 108/C4
Epéhy, Fr. 110/C3
Epernay, Fr. 100/E2
Epfig, Fr. 114/D1
Ephrata, Pa, US 196/B3
Epi (isl.), Van. 174/F6
Epiais-Rhus, Fr. 88/J4

Epídhavros (Epidaurus) (ruin), Gre. 105/H4
Épinal, Fr. 114/C1
Épinay-sur-Orge, Fr. 88/J6
Épinay-sur-Seine, Fr. 88/J5
Epira, Guy. 211/G3
Epirus (reg.), Gre. 105/G3
Épône, Fr. 110/A6
Eppelborn, Ger. 111/F5
Eppelheim, Ger. 112/B4
Eppenbrunn, Ger. 111/G5
Eppeville, Fr. 110/C4
Epping (for.), Eng, UK 88/D2
Epping, Eng, UK 88/D1
Epping Forest NP, Austl. 172/B3
Eppingen, Ger. 112/B4
Eppishausen, Ger. 115/G1
Epsom, Eng, UK 88/C3
Epsom and Ewell, Eng, UK 91/F4
Epte (riv.), Fr. 110/A4
Equator (fall), Ecu. 210/A4
Equatorial Guinea (ctry.) 154/G7
Équihen-Plage, Fr. 110/A2
Er (lake), China 141/H2
Er Rachidia, Mor. 156/D3
Er Reina, Isr. 149/G6
Er Rif (mts.), Mor. 154/D1
Era (riv.), It. 117/D6
Eraclea, It. 117/F1
Eraclea (ruin), It. 104/E2
Eraclea Minoa (ruin), It. 104/C4
Éragny, Fr. 88/J4
Erandique, Hon. 202/D3
Eravur, SrL. 140/D6
Erawan NP, Thai. 136/B3
Erba, It. 116/C1
Erbaa, Turk. 148/D1
Erbach, Ger. 112/B3
Erbendorf, Ger. 113/F3
Erbeskopf (peak), Ger. 111/G4
Ercan (int'l arpt.), Cyp. 149/C2
Erçek, Turk. 148/E2
Erçek (lake), Turk. 148/E2
Ercilla, Chile 216/B3
Erciş, Turk. 148/E2
Erciyes (peak), Turk. 148/C2
Erclin (riv.), Fr. 110/C3
Érd, Hun. 107/Q10
Erda, Ut, US 195/J12
Erdek (gulf), Turk. 107/H5
Erdek, Turk. 107/H5
Erdemli, Turk. 149/D1
Erdenet, Mong. 128/H2
Erdi-Ma (plat.), Chad 155/K4
Erding, Ger. 113/E6
Erdre (riv.), Fr. 100/C3
Erdweg, Ger. 112/E6
Erechim, Braz. 213/A3
Ereen Davaanï (mts.), Mong. 129/K2
Ereğli, Turk. 148/C2
Ereğli, Turk. 107/K5
Eremo di Camaldoli, It. 117/E5
Erenhaberga (mts.), China 128/D3
Erenhot, China 129/K3
Erenler, Turk. 107/K5
Erentepe, Turk. 148/E2
Erepecu, Lago do (lake), Braz. 209/G4
Eresma (riv.), Sp. 102/C2
Erétria, Gre. 105/H3
Ereymentaū, Kaz. 145/F2
Érezée, Belg. 111/E3
Erfa (riv.), Ger. 112/C3
Erfoud, Mor. 156/D3
Erft (riv.), Ger. 98/D3
Erftstadt, Ger. 111/F2
Erfurt, Ger. 98/F3
'Erg Chech (des.), Mali,Alg. 154/E3
'Erg Iguidi (des.), Alg.,Mrta. 156/D4
Ergene Nehri (riv.), Turk. 107/H5
Erguig (riv.), Chad 154/J5
Ergun Youqi, China 129/M1
Ergun Zuoqi, China 129/M1
Ericeira, Port. 103/P10
Ericht (lake), Sc, UK 94/B3
Ericht (riv.), Sc, UK 94/B3
Erickson, Mb, Can. 185/J3
Erickson, BC, Can. 184/D3
Erie (lake), Can.,US 188/D3
Erie, Co, US 195/B2
Erie (canal), NY, US 189/S9
Erie (co.), NY, US 189/S10
Erie, Pa, US 188/D3
Erie (int'l arpt.), Pa, US 188/D3
Eriksdale, Mb, Can. 185/J3
Eriksmalå, Swe. 96/F3
Erikub (isl.), Mrsh. 174/F4
Erímanthos (peak), Gre. 105/G4
Erimo, Japan 134/C2
Erimo-misaki (cape), Japan 134/C3
Erithraí, Gre. 105/H3
Eritrea (ctry.) 155/N5
Erkelenz, Ger. 111/F1
Erken (isl.), Swe. 97/H1
Erkheim, Ger. 115/G1
Erkner, Ger. 98/Q7
Erkrath, Ger. 108/D6
Erlach, Swi. 114/D3
Erlands Point-Kitsap Lake, Wa, US 193/B2
Erlangen, Ger. 112/E3
Erlau (riv.), Ger. 113/G5
Erlenbach (riv.), Ger. 112/B4
Erlenbach am Main, Ger. 112/C3
Erlenbach bei Marktheidenfeld, Ger. 112/C3
Erlenbach im Simmental, Swi. 114/D4
Erlinsbach, Swi. 114/E3
Erlongshan (res.), China 130/F2
Erme (riv.), Eng, UK 90/C6
Ermelo, SAfr. 165/E2
Ermelo, Neth. 108/C4
Ermenek (riv.), Turk. 149/C1
Ermenek, Turk. 149/C1
Ermenonville, Fr. 88/L4
Ermióni, Gre. 105/H4
Ermont, Fr. 88/J5
Ermoúpolis, Gre. 105/J4
Erms (riv.), Ger. 112/C6
Erndtebrück, Ger. 111/H2
Ernée (riv.), Fr. 100/C2
Ernée, Fr. 100/C2
Ernesto Cortissoz (int'l arpt.), Col. 210/C2
Ernsthofen, Aus. 113/H6
Erode, India 140/C5
Erolzheim, Ger. 115/G1
Erowal Bay, Austl. 173/D2
Erpel, Ger. 111/G2
Erquelinnes, Belg. 111/D3
Errigal (mtn.), Ire. 89/P9
Erris Head (pt.), Ire. 89/P9
Erro (riv.), It. 116/B4
Errochty (lake), Sc, UK 94/B3
Erromango (isl.), Van. 174/F6
Erse (riv.), Ger. 109/H4
Ersekë, Alb. 105/G2
Erstein, Fr. 114/D1
Erstfeld, Swi. 115/E4
Ertingen, Ger. 115/F1
Ertis (riv.), Kaz. 122/H4
Ertix (riv.), China 128/E2
Eruh, Turk. 148/E2
Eruwa, Nga. 161/F5
Erwin, Tn, US 188/D4
Erwitte, Ger. 109/F5
Eryuan, China 141/G2
Erzegebirge (Krušné Hory) (mts.), Czh.,Ger. 101/K1
Erzen (riv.), Alb. 105/F2
Erzhausen, Ger. 112/B3
Erzincan, Turk. 148/D2
Erzurum, Turk. 148/E2
Erzurum (prov.), Turk. 148/E1
Es Senia (int'l arpt.), Alg. 158/E5
Esan-misaki (cape), Japan 134/B3
Esashi, Japan 134/C1
Esashi, Japan 134/B3
Esashi, Japan 134/B4
Esbiye, Turk. 148/D1
Esbjerg, Den. 96/C4
Esbjerg (int'l arpt.), Den. 96/C4
Esbly, Fr. 88/L5
Esbo (Espoo), Fin. 97/L1
Escada, Braz. 212/D3
Escalante (riv.), Ut, US 186/E3
Escalón, Mex. 200/D3
Escalona, Sp. 102/C2
Escambia (riv.), Fl, US 191/G4
Escaudain, Fr. 110/C3
Escaut (riv.), Fr. 98/B3
Esch (riv.), Fr. 111/E6
Esch-sur-Alzette, Lux. 111/E4
Esch-sur-Sure, Lux. 111/E4
Eschach (riv.), Ger. 115/E1
Eschau, Fr. 114/D1
Eschborn, Ger. 112/B2
Eschede, Ger. 109/H3
Eschen, Licht. 115/F3
Eschenbach, Ger. 112/C5
Eschenbach in der Oberpfalz, Ger. 113/E3
Eschershausen, Ger. 109/G5
Esches (riv.), Fr. 110/B5
Escholzmatt, Swi. 114/D4
Eschwege, Ger. 109/H6
Eschweiler, Ger. 111/F2
Escobedo (int'l arpt.), Mex. 201/E3
Escoma, Bol. 214/D4
Escondido, Ca, US 194/C4
Escuinapa de Hidalgo, Mex. 200/D4
Escuintla, Guat. 202/D3
Esdraelon, Plain of (plain), Isr. 149/G6
Eséka, Camr. 154/H7
Esenboga (int'l arpt.), Turk. 148/C1
Esence (peak), Turk. 148/D2
Esens, Ger. 109/E1
Esera (riv.), Sp. 103/F1
Eşfahān, Iran 146/F2
Esfandak, Iran 147/H3
Esgair Ddu (peak), Wal, UK 90/C1
Esha Ness (cape), Sc, UK 89/W13
Esher, Eng, UK 88/B2
Eshowe, SAfr. 165/E3
Esil, Kaz. 145/E2
Esil (riv.), Kaz. 145/E2
Esine, It. 115/G6
Esino (riv.), It. 117/G6
Esk (riv.), Eng, UK 93/E2
Eskdale (valley), Sc, UK 94/C6
Eskifjördhur, Ice. 95/Q6
Eskil, Turk. 148/C2
Eskilstuna, Swe. 96/G2
Eskimalatya, Turk. 148/D2
Eskimo (lakes), NW, Can. 180/C2
Eskipazar, Turk. 148/C1
Eskişehir, Turk. 148/B2
Eskişehir (prov.), Turk. 148/B2
Esla (riv.), Sp. 102/C1
Eslāmābād, Iran 146/E2
Eslohe, Ger. 109/F6
Eslöv, Swe. 96/E4
Eşme, Turk. 148/B2
Esmeralda, Cuba 203/G1
Esmeraldas, Ecu. 210/B4
Esmeraldas (dept.), Ecu. 210/B4
Esneux, Belg. 111/E2
Espada (pt.), Col. 210/D1
Espalion, Fr. 100/E4
Española, NM, US 187/F4
Espanola, On, Can. 188/D2
Española (isl.), Ecu. 214/F7
Esparraguera, Sp. 103/K6
Esparta, Hon. 202/E3
Esparto, Ca, US 193/K9
Espejo, Sp. 102/C4
Espelkamp, Ger. 109/F4
Esperança, Braz. 212/D2
Esperance (bay), Austl. 170/D5
Esperance, Austl. 170/D5
Esperantina, Braz. 212/B1
Esperantinópolis, Braz. 212/A2
Esperanza, Arg., Ant. 218/W
Esperanza (inlet), BC, Can. 184/B3
Esperanza (mts.), Hon. 202/E3
Esperanza, Mex. 200/C3
Esperanza, Mex. 201/M8
Esperanza, Peru 214/D3
Espichel (cape), Port. 103/P11
Espinal, Mex. 201/M6
Espinal, Col. 210/C3
Espinar, Peru 214/D4
Espinhaço, Serra do (mts.), Braz. 209/K7
Espinho, Port. 102/A2
Espinillo (pt.), Uru. 217/F2
Espinosa, Braz. 212/B4
Espírito Santo (state), Braz. 213/D2
Espiritu Santo (isl.), Van. 174/F6
Espíritu Santo (bay), Mex. 202/E2
Espita, Mex. 202/D1
Esplanada, Braz. 212/C3
Espluga de Francolí, Sp. 103/E2
Espluges, Sp. 103/L7
Esposende, Port. 102/A2
Espungabera, Moz. 163/F5
Espy, Pa, US 196/B1
Esqueda, Mex. 200/C2
Esquel, Arg. 216/C4
Esquina, Arg. 215/E3
Essaouira, Mor. 156/C3
Esse (riv.), Ger. 109/G5
Essen, Belg. 108/B6
Essen, Ger. 108/E6
Essen, Ger. 109/E3
Essenbach, Ger. 113/F5
Essendon (mt.), Austl. 170/D3
Essenheim, Ger. 111/H4
Essequibo (riv.), Guy. 205/D2
Essequibo Island-West Demerara (pol. reg.), Guy. 211/G3
Essex, On, Can. 193/G7
Essex (co.), On, Can. 193/G7
Essex (co.), Eng, UK 88/E1
Essex, Md, US 196/B5
Essex (co.), NJ, US 196/D2
Essex Fells, NJ, US 197/H8
Esslingen, Ger. 112/C5
Essômes-sur-Marne, Fr. 110/C5
Essonne (riv.), Fr. 100/E2
Est, Canal de l' (canal), Fr. 111/E5
Estaca de Bares, Punta de la (cape), Sp. 102/B1
Estación Santa Engracia, Mex. 201/F3
Estados, Isla de los (isl.), Arg. 215/D7
Eşţahbān, Iran 146/F3
Estaires, Fr. 110/B2
Estância, Braz. 212/C3
Estats, Pico de (peak), Sp. 103/F1
Estavayer-le-Lac, Swi. 114/C4
Estcourt, SAfr. 165/E3
Este, It. 117/E2
Este, Punta del (pt.), Cuba 198/E3
Este Sudeste, Cayos del (isls.), Col. 203/F3
Esteio, Braz. 213/B4
Estelí, Nic. 202/E3
Estell Manor (Risley), NJ, US 196/D5
Estella, Sp. 102/D1
Estelle (mtn.), Ca, US 194/C3
Estelle, La, US 195/P17
Estepa, Sp. 102/C4
Estepona, Sp. 102/C4
Ester, Ak, US 192/J3
Esterhazy, Sk, Can. 185/H3
Esterias (cape), Gabon 154/G7
Esternay, Fr. 110/C6
Estero de Agiabampo (lag.), Mex. 200/C3
Estéron (riv.), Fr. 101/G5
Esterwegen, Ger. 109/E3
Estes Park, Co, US 195/A2
Estevan, Sk, Can. 185/H3
Estinnes-au-Mont, Belg. 111/D3
Eston, Sk, Can. 184/F3
Eston and South Bank, Eng, UK 93/G2
Estonia (ctry.) 97/L2
Estoril, Port. 103/P10
Estral Beach, Mi, US 193/F8
Estrées-Saint-Denis, Fr. 110/B5
Estrela, Serra da (mts.), Port. 102/A3
Estrela, Serra da (peak), Port. 102/B2
Estrella (pt.), Mex. 200/B2
Estrelto, Serra do (range), Braz. 212/B3
Estremoz, Port. 102/B3
Estrondo, Serra do (mts.), Braz. 209/J5
Esztergom, Hun. 106/D2
Et Taiyiba, Isr. 149/G7
Et Tira, Isr. 149/F7
Etah, India 142/B2
Étain, Fr. 111/E5
Etal (isl.), Micr. 174/E4
Étalle, Belg. 111/E4
Étaples, Fr. 110/A2
Etāwah, India 142/B2
Etāwah Branch (riv.), India 142/B2
Etchojoa, Mex. 200/C3
Ethelbert, Mb, Can. 185/H3
Ethiopia (ctry.) 155/N5
Ethiopian (plat.), Eth. 155/N6
Eti (riv.), Japan 135/K5
Etili, Turk. 107/H6
Étival-Clairefontaine, Fr. 114/C1
Etive, Loch (inlet), Sc, UK 94/A4
Etna (peak), It. 104/D4
Etna, Monte (Mount Etna) (vol.), It. 104/D4
Etne, Nor. 96/A2
Etobicoke, Can. 189/Q8
Etolin (str.), Ak, US 192/E3
Eton, Eng, UK 88/B2
Etorofu (isl.), Rus. 129/S2
Etosha (salt pan), Namb. 163/C4
Etosha NP, Namb. 163/C4
Etowah, Ok, US 195/N15
Étrépilly, Fr. 88/L4
Etropole, Bul. 105/J1
Etroubles, It. 114/D6
Ettadhamen Douarhicher, Tun. 158/M6
Ettelbruck, Lux. 111/F4
Etten-Leur, Neth. 108/B5
Ettenheim, Ger. 114/D1
Etterbeek, Belg. 111/D2
Etters (Goldsboro), Pa, US 196/B3
Ettlingen, Ger. 112/B5
Ettrick Pen (peak), Sc, UK 94/C6
Ettrick Water (riv.), Sc, UK 94/C5
Ettringen, Ger. 115/G1
Eu, Fr. 110/A3
'Eua (isl.), Tonga 175/H7
Eubenangee Swamp NP, Austl. 172/B2
Euclid, Oh, US 188/D3
Euclides da Cunha, Braz. 212/C3
Eudora, Ar, US 187/K4
Eudunda, Austl. 173/A2
Euerbach, Ger. 112/D2
Eufaula, Al, US 191/G4
Eufaula (lake), Ok, US 185/J4
Eugendorf, Aus. 113/G7
Eugene, Or, US 184/C4
Eugene O'Neill NHS, Ca, US 193/L11
Eugenia (pt.), Mex. 200/B3
Eugowra, Austl. 173/D2
Eume, Embalse de (res.), Sp. 102/B1
Eungella NP, Austl. 172/C3
Eunice, La, US 187/J5
Eunice, NM, US 187/G4
Eupen, Belg. 111/F2
Euphrates (riv.), Iraq,Syria 148/E3
Eura, Fin. 97/K1
Eurajoki, Fin. 97/J1
Eure (riv.), Fr. 100/D2
Eure (dept.), Fr. 110/A5
Eure-et-Loir (dept.), Fr. 110/A6
Eureka (sound), Nun., Can. 181/S7
Eureka, Ca, US 184/B5
Eureka, Mo, US 195/F9
Eureka, Mt, US 184/E3
Eureka, Nv, US 186/D3
Eureka, SD, US 185/J4
Euroa, Austl. 173/C3
Eurodisney, Fr. 88/L5
Euron (riv.), Fr. 114/C1
Europa (pt.), Gib. 102/C4
Europabrücke, Aus. 115/H3
Europe (cont.) 27
Europoort, Neth. 108/B5
Euskirchen, Ger. 111/F2
Eussenheim, Ger. 112/C3
Eustis, Fl, US 191/H4
Euston, Austl. 173/B2
Eutin, Ger. 96/D4
Eutini, Malw. 162/B5
Eutsuk (lake), BC, Can. 184/B2
Euville, Fr. 111/E6
Évain, Qu, Can. 188/E1
Evander, SAfr. 164/E2
Evans (mt.), Co, US 187/F3
Evans (lake), Qu, Can. 188/E1
Evans, Co, US 195/C2
Evans (str.), Nun., Can. 181/H2
Evans Head, Austl. 173/E1
Evanston, Wy, US 184/F5
Evansville, In, US 188/C4
Evansville, Wy, US 187/F2
Evaporation (basin), Ut, US 184/E5
Evart, Mi, US 188/C3
Evaton, SAfr. 164/D2
Evaz, Iran 146/F3
Eve, Fr. 88/L4
Even Yehuda, Isr. 149/F7
Evenlode (riv.), Eng, UK 91/E3
Evenkiyskiy Aut. Okrug, Rus. 122/K3
Everard (cape), Austl. 173/D3
Everard (lake), Austl. 167/C4
Everard (mt.), Austl. 171/G3
Everest (peak), China,Nepal 140/E2
Everest (Sagarmatha) (mtn.), China,Nepal 143/F2
Everett, Wa, US 184/C4
Evergem, Belg. 110/C1
Everglades (swamp), Fl, US 191/H5
Everglades NP, Fl, US 191/H5
Evergreen, Al, US 191/G4
Evergreen, Co, US 195/B3
Evergreen Park, Il, US 193/Q16
Everswinkel, Ger. 109/E5
Evesham, Eng, UK 91/E2
Evesham, Vale of (valley), Eng, UK 90/D2
Évian-les-Bains, Fr. 114/C5
Évinos (riv.), Gre. 105/G3
Evje, Nor. 96/B2
Evolène, Swi. 114/D5
Évora, Port. 102/B3
Évora (dist.), Port. 102/A3
Évreux, Fr. 100/D2
Évron, Fr. 100/C2
Evrótas (riv.), Gre. 105/H4
Évry, Fr. 88/K6
Évvoia (gulf), Gre. 105/H3
Évvoia (isl.), Gre. 105/H3
Evxinoúpolis, Gre. 105/H3
Ewa Beach, Hi, US 182/V13
Ewa Villages, Hi, US 182/V13
Ewan, NJ, US 196/C4
Ewarton, Jam. 203/G2
Ewaso Ng'iro (riv.), Kenya 162/C2
Ewell, Eng, UK 88/C3
Ewing, NJ, US 196/D3
Exaplátanos, Gre. 105/H2
Excelsior Springs, Mo, US 195/E5
Excursion Inlet, Ak, US 192/L4
Exe (riv.), Eng, UK 90/C4
Exeter, NH, US 189/G3
Exmoor (upland), Eng, UK 90/C4
Exmoor NP, Eng, UK 90/C4
Exmore, Va, US 191/K2
Exmouth, Austl. 170/B2
Exmouth (gulf), Austl. 170/B2
Exmouth (pen.), Chile 217/B6
Extrema, Braz. 213/G7
Extremadura (reg.), Sp. 102/B3
Exu, Braz. 212/C2
Exuma (sound), Bahm. 199/F3
Eyak, Ak, US 192/J3
Eyasi (lake), Tanz. 163/F1
Eyb (riv.), Ger. 112/C5
Eydehamn, Nor. 96/C2
Eyemouth, Sc, UK 94/D5
Eyguières, Fr. 100/F5
Eyn Hemed (ruin), Isr. 149/G8
Eyre (pen.), Austl. 167/C4
Eyre North (lake), Austl. 167/C3
Eyre South (lake), Austl. 167/C3
Ézanville, Fr. 88/K4
Ezequiel Ramos Mexía (res.), Arg. 216/C3
Ezhou, China 137/B1
Ezine, Turk. 105/K3
Ezzane (well), Alg. 154/H3

F

F.E. Walter (res.), Pa, US 196/C1
Fabbrico, It. 117/D3
Fabens, Tx, US 190/B4
Fabero, Sp. 102/B1
Fåborg, Den. 96/D4
Fabriano, It. 101/K5
Facatativá, Col. 208/D3
Faches-Thumesnil, Fr. 110/C2
Fada (lake), Sc, UK 94/A1
Fada-N'Gourma, Burk. 161/F3
Faenza, It. 117/E4
Fafa (riv.), CAfr. 155/J6
Fafe, Port. 102/A2
Fafen Shet' (riv.), Eth. 155/P6
Făgăraş, Rom. 107/G3
Fagersta, Swe. 96/F2
Faggiola (peak), It. 117/E4
Fagnano (lake), Arg. 217/D7
Fagnano Olona, It. 116/B1
Fagnières, Fr. 111/D6
Faguibine (lake), Mali 154/D4
Fahl (well), Alg. 157/F3
Fahrenzhausen, Ger. 113/E6
Faial (isl.), Azor., Port. 103/S12
Faido, Swi. 115/E5
Failsworth, Eng, UK 93/F4
Fains-Véel, Fr. 111/E6
Fair Haven, Mi, US 193/G6
Fair Haven, Vt, US 188/F3
Fair Hill, Md, US 196/C4
Fair Isle (isl.), Sc, UK 89/W14
Fair Lawn, NJ, US 197/J8
Fair Oaks, Ca, US 193/M9
Fairbanks, Ak, US 192/J3
Fairfax, Ca, US 193/J11
Fairfax, Va, US 196/A6
Fairfax (co.), Va, US 196/A6
Fairfield, Ca, US 186/B3
Fairfield, Ct, US 197/E1
Fairfield (co.), Ct, US 197/L7
Fairfield, Mt, US 184/F4
Fairfield, NJ, US 197/H8
Fairfield, Pa, US 196/A4
Fairfield, Tx, US 187/H5
Fairfield, Ut, US 195/J13
Fairland, Md, US 196/B5
Fairlee, Md, US 196/B5
Fairless Hills, Pa, US 196/D3
Fairlie, Sc, UK 94/B5
Fairmont, WV, US 188/D4
Fairmont City, Il, US 195/G8
Fairmount, Ks, US 195/D5
Fairplay, Co, US 190/B2
Fairton, NJ, US 196/C5
Fairview, NJ, US 197/K8
Fairview, Ok, US 187/H3
Fairview Heights, Il, US 195/G8
Fairway, Ks, US 195/D5
Fairweather (mt.), Ak, US 192/L4
Fairweather (cape), Ak, US 192/L4
Fairweather (mt.), BC, Can. 180/C3
Faisalābad, Pak. 144/B4
Faistós (ruin), Gre. 105/J5
Faizābād, India 142/D2
Fajardo, PR 199/M8
Fakahina (isl.), FrPol. 159/M6
Fakaofo (isl.), Tok. 159/H5
Fakarava (isl.), FrPol. 159/L6
Fako (peak), Camr. 154/G7
Fakse, Den. 96/E4
Fakse Ladeplads, Den. 96/E4
Faku, China 130/E2
Fal (riv.), Eng, UK 90/B6
Fālākāta, India 143/G2
Falāmah, WBnk. 149/G7
Fálanna, Gre. 105/H3
Falcon (res.), Mex.,US 190/D5
Falcon (cape), Alg. 158/D2
Falcón (state), Ven. 210/D2
Falconara Marittima, It. 117/G5
Falémé (riv.), Mali 154/C5
Falfurrias, Tx, US 190/D5
Falher, Ab, Can. 184/D2
Falkenberg, Swe. 96/E3
Falkensee, Ger. 98/Q6
Falkenstein, Ger. 113/F4
Falkenstein, Ger. 113/E3
Falkirk, Sc, UK 94/C5
Falkirk (pol. reg.), Sc, UK 94/C5
Falkland (isls.), UK 217/E7
Falkland, Sc, UK 94/C4
Falkland Sound (str.), UK 217/E7
Falköping, Swe. 96/E2
Fall City, Wa, US 193/D2
Fall River, Ma, US 189/G3
Fallbrook, Ca, US 194/C4
Fallere (peak), It. 114/D6
Falling Spring, Il, US 195/G8
Fallingbostel, Ger. 109/G3
Fallis, Ok, US 195/N14
Fallon, Nv, US 186/C3
Falls Church, Va, US 196/A6
Fallston, Md, US 196/B4
Falmouth, Anti. 199/N8
Falmouth, Eng, UK 90/A6
Falmouth (bay), Eng, UK 90/A6
False Pass, Ak, US 192/F5
Falshöft (pt.), Ger. 96/C4
Falso (cape), Hon. 203/F3
Falso, Cabo (cape), Mex. 200/C4
Falso Cabo de Hornos (cape), Chile 217/C7
Falster (isl.), Den. 95/E5
Falterona (peak), It. 117/E5
Fălticeni, Rom. 107/H2
Falun, Swe. 96/F1
Famagusta (bay), Cyp. 149/C2
Famagusta (dist.), Cyp. 149/C2
Famagusta, Cyp. 149/C2
Fameck, Fr. 111/F5
Famenne (reg.), Belg. 111/E3
Fammau, Moel (peak), Wal, UK 93/E5
Fan Si Pan (peak), Viet. 141/H3
Fana, Nor. 96/A1
Fanchang, China 130/D5
Fandriana, Madg. 165/H8
Fang Xian, China 130/B4
Fangatau (isl.), FrPol. 159/L6
Fangataufa (isl.), FrPol. 159/L7
Fangcheng, China 130/C4
Fangcheng Gezu Zizhixian, China 141/J3
Fangshan, China 130/B3
Fanjing (peak), China 141/J2
Fannich (lake), Sc, UK 94/A1
Fanning (Tabuaeran) (isl.), Kiri. 159/K4
Fano, It. 117/G5
Fanø (isl.), Den. 96/C4
Fanshi, China 130/C3
Fanwood, NJ, US 197/H9
Faqīrwāli, Pak. 144/B5
Fāqūs, Egypt 149/B4
Fara Novarese, It. 116/B1
Faradje, D.R. Congo 162/A2
Farafangana, Madg. 165/H8
Farāfirah, Wāḥāt al (oasis), Egypt 159/A3
Farāh, Afg. 147/H2
Farāh (riv.), Afg. 147/H2
Farallon (isls.), Ca, US 186/B3
Farallon de Medinilla (isl.), NMar. 174/D3
Farallon de Pajaros (isl.), NMar. 174/D2
Farallones de Cali, PN, Col. 208/C3
Faranah (pol. reg.), Gui. 160/C4
Faranah, Gui. 160/C4
Farángi Samariás NP, Gre. 105/H5
Faraony (riv.), Madg. 165/H8
Faraulep (isl.), Micr. 174/D4
Farciennes, Belg. 111/D3
Fareham, Eng, UK 91/E5
Faremoutiers, Fr. 110/C6
Farewell, Ak, US 192/H3
Farewell (cape), NZ 159/S11
Färgelanda, Swe. 96/D2
Farghona (pol. reg.), Uzb. 145/F4
Farghona, Uzb. 145/F4
Fargo, ND, US 185/J4
Faribault, Mn, US 185/K4
Farīdābād, India 144/D5
Farīdkot, India 144/C4
Farīdpur, Bang. 143/G4
Farīdpur (pol. reg.), Bang. 143/G4
Farīdpur, India 142/B1
Fāriskūr, Egypt 149/B4
Färjestaden, Swe. 96/G3
Farkadhón, Gre. 105/H3
Farkasgyepú, Hun. 106/C2
Farley, Mo, US 195/D5
Farmers, Co, US 195/C2
Farmingdale, NJ, US 196/D3
Farmingdale, NY, US 197/M9
Farmington, De, US 196/C6
Farmington, Me, US 189/G2
Farmington, Mi, US 193/F7
Farmington, Mo, US 187/K3
Farmington, NM, US 186/E3
Farmington, Ut, US 195/K12
Farmington Hills, Mi, US 193/E6
Farnborough, Eng, UK 91/F4
Farnham, Eng, UK 91/F4
Farnham Royal, Eng, UK 88/B2
Farnworth, Eng, UK 93/F4
Faro, Yk, Can. 192/M3
Faro (dist.), Port. 102/A4
Faro, Port. 102/B4
Faro (int'l arpt.), Port. 102/B4
Faro, PN du, Camr. 154/H6
Faroe (isls.), Den. 218/G
Fåron (isl.), Swe. 97/H3
Fårösund, Swe. 97/H3
Farquhar (cape), Austl. 170/B2
Farr West, Ut, US 195/J11
Farroupilha, Braz. 213/B4
Farrukhābād, India 142/B2
Fársala, Gre. 105/H3
Farsø, Den. 96/C3
Farson, Wy, US 184/F5
Farsund, Nor. 96/B2
Fartak, Ras (pt.), Yem. 146/F5
Farwell, Tx, US 187/G4
Fasā, Iran 146/F3
Fasano, It. 105/E2
Faşıkan (pass), Turk. 149/C1
Fassberg, Ger. 109/H3
Fast Castle (pt.), Sc, UK 94/D5
Fastiv, Ukr. 120/D2
Fatagar Tuting (cape), Indo. 139/H4
Fatahjang, Pak. 144/B3
Fatehābād, India 144/C5
Fatehpur, India 142/C3
Fatehpur, India 142/C2
Fatehpur, India 147/K3
Fatick (pol. reg.), Sen. 160/A3
Fatick, Sen. 160/A3
Fátima, Port. 102/A3
Fatsa, Turk. 148/D1
Fatu Hiva (isl.), FrPol. 159/M6
Faucille, Col de la (pass), Fr. 114/C5
Faucilles (mts.), Fr. 98/C4
Faughan (riv.), NI, UK 92/A2
Fauglia, It. 116/D5
Fauldhouse, Sc, UK 94/C5
Faulkton, SD, US 185/J4
Faulquemont, Fr. 111/F5
Faure (isl.), Austl. 170/B3
Făurei, Rom. 107/H3
Fauske, Nor. 95/E2
Faust, Ut, US 195/J13
Fauvillers, Belg. 111/E4
Faux, Tête de (peak), Fr. 114/D1
Favalto (peak), It. 117/F6
Favara, It. 104/C4
Fave (riv.), Fr. 114/C1
Faverges, Fr. 114/C6
Faverney, Fr. 114/C2
Faversham, Eng, UK 91/G4
Favières, Fr. 88/L5
Favignana, It. 104/C4
Favria, It. 116/A2
Favrieux, Fr. 88/G5
Fawn (riv.), On, Can. 185/L2
Fawn Grove, Pa, US 196/B4
Faxaflói (bay), Ice. 95/M7
Faxinal, Braz. 213/B2
Faya-Largeau, Chad 155/J4
Fayette, Al, US 191/G3
Fayette, Ms, US 187/K5
Fayetteville, Tn, US 191/G3
Fayetteville, Ga, US 191/G3
Fayetteville, NC, US 191/J3
Fayl-la-Forêt, Fr. 114/B2
Fazao, Monts du (mts.), Togo 161/F4
Fazao, PN du, Togo 161/F4
Fdérik, Mrta. 156/B5
Feale (riv.), Ire. 89/P10
Fear (cape), NC, US 191/J3
Feasterville-Trevose, Pa, US 196/D3
Feather (riv.), Ca, US 186/B3
Featherstone, Eng, UK 93/G4
Fécamp, Fr. 100/D2
Fecht (riv.), Fr. 114/D1
Federal Hall Nat'l Mem., NY, US 197/K9
Federal Heights, Co, US 195/B3
Federally Admin. Tribal Areas, Pak. 144/A2
Federsee (lake), Ger. 112/C6
Fedje, Nor. 96/A1
Feeny, NI, UK 92/A1
Fegersheim, Fr. 112/A6
Fehérgyarmat, Hun. 106/F2
Fehmarn (isl.), Den. 96/D4
Fehmarn Belt (str.), Den. 98/F1
Fei Huang (riv.), China 130/D4
Fei Xian, China 130/D4
Feia, Lagoa (lake), Braz. 213/D2
Feicheng, China 130/D3
Feidong, China 130/D5
Feignies, Fr. 110/C3
Feijó, Braz. 214/D3
Feillans, Fr. 114/A5
Feira, Port. 102/A2
Feira de Santana, Braz. 212/C4
Feistritz (riv.), Aus. 101/L3
Feixi, China 130/D5
Fejér (co.), Hun. 106/D2
Fejø (isl.), Ger. 96/D4
Feke, Turk. 148/C2
Feketić, Serb. 106/D3
Felanitx, Sp. 103/G3
Feldafing, Ger. 115/H2
Feldaist (riv.), Aus. 113/H6
Feldberg (peak), Ger. 114/E2
Feldkirch, Aus. 115/F3
Feldkirchen an der Donau, Aus. 113/H6
Feldkirchen bei Graz, Aus. 106/B2

Feldkirchen in Kärnten, Aus. 101/L3
Feletto, It. 116/A2
Feletto Umberto, It. 117/G1
Felino, It. 116/D3
Felipe Carillo Puerto, Mex. 202/D2
Felixdorf, Aus. 106/C2
Felixlândia, Braz. 213/C1
Felixstowe, Eng, UK 91/H3
Felizzano, It. 116/B3
Fell, Ger. 111/F4
Fellbach, Ger. 112/C5
Felling, Eng, UK 93/G2
Felsberg, Ger. 109/G6
Felsberg, Swi. 115/F4
Felton, Pa, US 196/B4
Felton, De, US 196/C5
Fema (peak), It. 101/K5
Femø (isl.), Den. 96/D4
Femundsmarka NP, Nor. 95/D3
Fénay, Fr. 114/B3
Fene, Sp. 102/A1
Fener (pt.), Turk. 149/D1
Fénérive, Madg. 163/K10
Feng Xian, China 130/D4
Fengári (peak), Gre. 105/J2
Fengcheng, China 129/L6
Fengcheng, China 131/C2
Fenghuang, China 141/J2
Fengle (riv.), China 130/D5
Fengnan, China 130/J7
Fengning, China 130/D2
Fengqing, China 141/G3
Fengqiu, China 130/C4
Fengrun, China 130/J7
Fengshan, Tai. 137/D3
Fengtai, China 130/H7
Fengxian, China 130/L9
Fengyang, China 130/D4
Fengyüan, Tai. 137/D3
Fengzhen, China 130/C2
Fenimore Pass (chan.), Ak, US 192/C5
Fenoarivo Atsinanana, Madg. 165/J7
Fens (phys. reg.), Eng, UK 91/G1
Fensmark, Den. 96/D4
Fensterbach (riv.), Ger. 113/F4
Fenton, Mi, US 188/D3
Fenton, Mo, US 195/G8
Fenton (lake), Mi, US 193/E7
Fenxi, China 130/B3
Feodosiya, Ukr. 120/E3
Fer, Cap de (cape), Alg. 158/K6
Ferbane, Ire. 89/Q10
Ferdinandshof, Ger. 99/G2
Fère-Champenoise, Fr. 110/C6
Fère-en-Tardenois, Fr. 110/C5
Ferentino, It. 104/C2
Ferento (ruin), It. 104/C1
Fergus Falls, Mn, US 185/J4
Ferguson, Mo, US 195/G8
Ferguson (lake), Nun., Can. 180/F2
Ferihegy (int'l arpt.), Hun. 106/D2
Ferkéssédougou, C.d'Iv. 160/D4
Ferlach, Aus. 101/L3
Fermanagh (dist.), NI, UK 92/A3
Fermi National Accelerator Laboratory, Il, US 193/P16
Fermignano, It. 117/F5
Fermin (pt.), Ca, US 194/F8
Fermo, It. 101/K5
Fermoselle, Sp. 102/B2
Fermoy, Ire. 89/P10
Fernán-Núñez, Sp. 102/C4
Fernandina (isl.), Ecu. 214/E7
Fernandina Beach, Fl, US 191/H4
Fernando de Noronha (isl.), Braz. 205/F3
Fernandópolis, Braz. 213/B2
Ferndale, Md, US 196/B5
Ferndale, Mi, US 193/F7
Ferney-Voltaire, Fr. 114/C5
Fernie, BC, Can. 184/E3
Fernpass (pass), Aus. 115/G3
Ferntree Gully NP, Austl. 173/G5
Ferrandina, It. 104/E2
Ferrara (prov.), It. 117/E3
Ferrara, It. 117/E3
Ferrat (cape), Alg. 158/E5
Ferreira do Alentejo, Port. 102/A3
Ferrelview, Mo, US 195/D5
Ferreñafe, Peru 214/B2
Ferret (cape), Fr. 100/C4
Ferrette, Fr. 114/D3
Ferriday, La, US 187/K5
Ferriere, It. 116/C3
Ferrière-la-Grande, Fr. 110/D3
Ferrières, Belg. 111/E3
Ferryden, Sc, UK 94/D3
Ferryfield (int'l arpt.), Eng, UK 91/G5
Ferryhill, Eng, UK 93/G2
Fertő (Neusiedler See) (lake), Aus. 101/M3
Ferté-Bernard, Fr. 100/D2
Fértil (valley), Arg. 215/C3
Ferwerd, Neth. 108/C2
Fès, Mor. 158/B2
Fès (prov.), Mor. 158/B3
Fesches-le-Châtel, Fr. 114/C2
Feshie (riv.), Sc, UK 94/C2
Fessenheim, Fr. 114/D2
Festival Centre, Austl. 171/M8
Feteşti, Rom. 107/H3
Fethaland (pt.), Sc, UK 89/W13
Fethiye, Turk. 148/B2
Feucherolles, Fr. 88/H5
Feucht, Ger. 112/E4
Feuchtwangen, Ger. 112/D4
Feuilles (lake), Qu, Can. 181/J3
Feuilles, Rivière aux (riv.), Qu, Can. 181/J3
Feuquières, Fr. 110/A4
Feuquières-en-Vimeu, Fr. 110/A3
Feurs, Fr. 100/F4
Fevzipaşa, Turk. 149/E1
Feyzābād, Afg. 147/K1
Fez (Saïss) (int'l arpt.), Mor. 158/B3
Fezzan (reg.), Libya 154/H2
Fferna, Moel (peak), Wal, UK 93/E6
Ffestiniog, Wal, UK 92/E6
Fianarantsoa (prov.), Madg. 165/H8
Fianarantsoa, Madg. 165/H8
Fianga, Chad 154/J6
Ficarolo, It. 117/E3
Fichtelberg (peak), Ger. 113/F2
Fichtelgebirge (mts.), Ger. 98/F3
Fichtelnaab (riv.), Ger. 113/E3
Ficksburg, SAfr. 164/D3
Fidenza, It. 116/D3
Fié (riv.), Gui. 160/C4
Field (riv.), Austl. 171/M9
Fieldon, Il, US 195/G7
Fieni, Rom. 107/G3
Fier (riv.), Fr. 114/B6
Fierzë (lake), Alb. 105/G1
Fiesch, Swi. 114/E5
Fiesole, It. 117/E5
Fiesso, It. 117/F2
Fiesso Umbertiano, It. 117/E3
Fiesta Texas, Tx, US 195/T20
Fife, Wa, US 193/C3
Fife (pol. reg.), Sc, UK 94/D4
Fife Ness (pt.), Sc, UK 94/D4
Fifth Cataract (falls), Sudan 159/C5
Figalo (cape), Alg. 158/D2
Figari, Fr. 104/A2
Figeac, Fr. 100/E4
Figline Valdarno, It. 117/E5
Figueira da Foz, Port. 102/A2
Figueres, Sp. 103/G1
Figuig, Mor. 157/E2
Figuig (prov.), Mor. 158/C3
Fiherenana (riv.), Madg. 165/G8
Fiji (ctry.) 174/G6
Filadelfia, Par. 215/D1
Filadélfia, Braz. 212/A2
Filattiera, It. 116/C4
Filchner Ice Shelf, Ant. 218/Y
Filey (bay), Eng, UK 93/H3
Filí, Gre. 105/N8
Filiaşi, Rom. 107/F3
Filiatai, Gre. 105/G3
Filiatrá, Gre. 105/G4
Filicudi (isl.), It. 104/D3
Filingué, Niger 161/F3
Filippiás, Gre. 105/G3
Filippoi (ruin), Gre. 105/J2
Filipstad, Swe. 96/F2
Filisur, Swi. 115/F4
Fillière (riv.), Fr. 114/C6
Fillmore, Ca, US 194/B2
Fillmore, Ut, US 186/D3
Filomeno Mata, Mex. 201/M6
Filótion, Gre. 105/J4
Filottrano, It. 117/G6
Fils (riv.), Ger. 112/C5
Filsum, Ger. 109/E2
Fimi (riv.), D.R. Congo 155/J8
Fina, Forêt Classée de, Mali 160/C3
Finale Emilia, It. 117/E3
Finale Ligure, It. 116/B4
Fiñana, Sp. 102/D4
Finch Hatton, Austl. 172/C3
Findel (int'l arpt.), Lux. 111/F4
Findhorn, Sc, UK 94/C1
Findhorn (riv.), Sc, UK 94/B2
Findlay, Oh, US 188/D3
Findochty, Sc, UK 94/D1
Finesville, NJ, US 196/C2
Fingal, Austl. 173/C4
Finger (lake), On, Can. 185/K2
Finhaut, Swi. 114/C5
Finike, Turk. 149/B1
Finisterre, Sp. 102/A1
Finisterre (cape), Sp. 102/A1
Finke (riv.), Austl. 171/G3
Finke Gorge NP, Austl. 171/G3
Finkenstein, Aus. 101/K3
Finksburg, Md, US 196/B5
Finland (ctry.) 95/H2
Finland (gulf), Eur. 95/H2
Finlay (riv.), BC, Can. 180/D3
Finlay (mts.), Tx, US 190/B4
Finley, Austl. 173/C2
Finn (riv.), Ire. 89/Q9
Finnentrop, Ger. 109/E6
Finnigan (mt.), Austl. 172/B1
Finnis (cape), Austl. 171/G5
Finnmark (co.), Nor. 95/G1
Fino Mornasco, It. 116/C1
Finsing, Ger. 113/E6
Finspång, Swe. 96/F2
Finsteraarhorn (peak), Swi. 114/E4
Finström, Fin. 97/H1
Fintel, Ger. 109/G2
Fintona, NI, UK 92/A3
Fionn Loch (lake), Sc, UK 94/A1
Fiora (riv.), It. 101/J5
Fiorano, It. 117/D3
Fiordland NP, NZ 159/R12
Fiorenzuola d'Arda, It. 116/C3
Fircrest, Wa, US 193/C3
Fire Island Nat'l Seashore, NY, US 197/E2
Firenze (prov.), It. 117/E5
Firenze (Florence), It. 117/E5
Firenzuola, It. 117/E4
Firestone, Co, US 195/C2
Firmat, Arg. 216/E2
Firmi, Fr. 100/E4
Firminy, Fr. 100/F4
Fīrozābād, India 142/B2
Firozpur, India 144/C4
First Cataract (falls), Egypt 159/C3
Fīrūz Kūh, Iran 146/F1
Fīrūzābād, Iran 146/F3
Fischa (riv.), Aus. 107/P7
Fischach, Ger. 115/G1
Fischamend Markt, Aus. 107/P7
Fischbacher Alpen (mts.), Aus. 101/L3
Fischen im Allgäu, Ger. 115/G3
Fischer, Tx, US 195/U20
Fish (riv.), Namb. 163/C5
Fisher (bay), Mb, Can. 185/J3
Fisher (str.), Nun., Can. 181/H2
Fisher Branch, Mb, Can. 185/J3
Fisherman (isl.), Austl. 172/F6
Fishers (isl.), NY, US 197/G1
Fishguard, Wal, UK 90/B3
Fisht (peak), Rus. 120/F4
Fismes, Fr. 110/C5
Fitful Head (pt.), Sc, UK 89/W14
Fitjar, Nor. 96/A2
Fitton (mt.), Yk, Can. 192/L2
Fitzgerald, Ga, US 191/H4
Fitzgerald River NP, Austl. 170/C5
Fitzroy (peak), Arg. 217/B6
Fitzroy (riv.), Austl. 167/B2
Fitzwilliam (str.), NW, Can. 181/R7
Fiume Veneto, It. 117/F1
Fiumicino, It. 104/C2
Five Sisters (peak), Sc, UK 94/A2
Fivemiletown, NI, UK 92/A3
Fivizzano, It. 116/D4
Fjell, Nor. 96/A1
Fjerritslev, Den. 96/C3
Fjugesta, Swe. 96/F2
Flå, Nor. 96/C1
Flachslanden, Ger. 112/D4
Fladungen, Ger. 112/D1
Flagler, Co, US 190/C2
Flagler Beach, Fl, US 191/H4
Flagstaff, Az, US 186/E4
Flambeau (riv.), Wi, US 185/L4
Flamborough, On, Can. 189/Q9
Flamborough Head (pt.), Eng, UK 93/H3
Fläming (hills), Ger. 98/G2
Flaming Gorge (res.), Ut,Wy, US 184/F5
Flaming Gorge Nat'l Rec. Area, Ut,Wy, US 186/E2
Flamingo Field (int'l arpt.), NAnt. 210/D1
Flanagan (riv.), On, Can. 185/K2
Flanders (reg.), Fr. 100/E1
Flanders, NY, US 197/F2
Flat Holm (isl.), Eng, UK 90/C4
Flat River, Mo, US 187/K3
Flathead (riv.), Mt, US 184/E4
Flathead (lake), Mt, US 184/E4
Flathead, South Fork (riv.), Mt, US 184/E3
Flattery (cape), Austl. 172/B1
Flattery (cape), Wa, US 184/B3
Flavio Alfaro, Ecu. 210/B5
Flawil, Swi. 115/F3
Flaxlanden, Fr. 114/D2
Fleet, Eng, UK 91/F4
Fleetwood, Pa, US 196/C3
Fleetwood, Eng, UK 93/E4
Flekkefjord, Nor. 96/B2
Flemington, NJ, US 196/D2
Flemington Racecourse, Austl. 173/F5
Flemish Brabant (prov.), Belg. 111/D2
Flen, Swe. 96/G2
Flensburg, Ger. 96/C4
Flero, It. 116/D2
Fleron, Belg. 111/E2
Flers, Fr. 100/C2
Flesland (int'l arpt.), Nor. 96/A1
Fletschhorn (peak), Swi. 114/D5
Fleurance, Fr. 100/D5
Fleurier, Swi. 114/C4
Fleurus, Belg. 111/D3
Fleury-les-Aubrais, Fr. 100/D3
Flevoland (prov.), Neth. 108/C4
Flevoland (isl.), Neth. 98/C2
Flexenpass (pass), Aus. 115/G3
Flieden, Ger. 112/C2
Flieden (riv.), Ger. 112/C2
Fliess, Aus. 115/G3
Flims, Swi. 115/F4
Flin Flon, Mb, Can. 185/H2
Flinders (bay), Austl. 170/B5
Flinders (ranges), Austl. 171/H5
Flinders (reef), Austl. 167/D2
Flinders (reefs), Austl. 167/D4
Flinders (riv.), Austl. 167/D2
Flinders Chase NP, Austl. 171/H5
Flinders Ranges NP, Austl. 171/H4
Flinders Reefs (isls.), Austl. 172/C2
Flines-lez-Raches, Fr. 110/C3
Flint (lake), Nun., Can. 181/J2
Flint (isl.), Kiri. 159/K6
Flint, Wal, UK 93/E5
Flint (hills), Ks, US 187/H3
Flint (riv.), Ga, US 191/G4
Flint, Mi, US 188/D3
Flint, South Branch (riv.), Mi, US 193/F5
Flintbek, Ger. 96/D4
Flintshire (co.), Wal, UK 93/E5
Flisa, Nor. 96/E1
Flix, Sp. 103/F2
Flixecourt, Fr. 110/B3
Flize, Fr. 111/D4
Floby, Swe. 96/E2
Floda, Swe. 96/E3
Flögelner See (riv.), Ger. 109/F1
Flöha (riv.), Ger. 99/G3
Floing, Fr. 111/D4
Flonheim, Ger. 112/B3
Flora (mt.), Austl. 170/C2
Flora, Nor. 95/C3
Flora, Il, US 187/K3
Floral Park, NY, US 197/L9
Florange, Fr. 111/F5
Florânia, Braz. 212/C2
Floraville, Il, US 195/G9
Floreffe, Belg. 111/D3
Florence, Al, US 191/G3
Florence, Az, US 186/E4
Florence, SC, US 191/J3
Florence (Firenze), It. 101/J5
Florence-Graham, Ca, US 194/F8
Florencia, Col. 210/C4
Florennes, Belg. 111/D3
Florenville, Belg. 111/E4
Flores (isl.), Indo. 139/F5
Flores (sea), Indo. 139/E5
Flores, Guat. 202/D2
Flores (dept.), Uru. 217/F2
Flores do Piauí, Braz. 212/B2
Floresta, Braz. 212/C3
Florham Park, NJ, US 197/H8
Floriano, Braz. 212/B2
Florianópolis, Braz. 213/B3
Florida, Col. 210/B4
Florida, Cuba 203/G1
Florida (str.), Cuba,US 183/K7
Florida, Hon. 202/D3
Florida, Peru 214/B2
Florida, Uru. 217/K11
Florida (dept.), Uru. 217/F2
Florida (state), US 191/H4
Florida (bay), Fl, US 191/H5
Florida, NY, US 196/D1
Florida Keys (isls.), Fl, US 191/H5
Floridablanca, Col. 210/C3
Floridia, It. 104/D4
Florin, Ca, US 193/M10
Flórina, Gre. 105/G2
Florissant, Mo, US 195/G8
Florissant Fossil Beds Nat'l Mon., Co, US 190/B2
Flörsbachtal, Ger. 112/C2
Flörsheim am Main, Ger. 112/B2
Flörsheim-Dalsheim, Ger. 112/B3
Florstadt, Ger. 112/B2
Flossenbürg, Ger. 113/F3
Floyd, Mo, US 195/E5
Floydada, Tx, US 187/G4
Flüchthorn (peak), Aus. 115/G4
Flüelapass (pass), Swi. 115/F4
Flüelen, Swi. 115/E4
Fluessen (lake), Neth. 108/C3
Flums, Swi. 115/F3
Flushing, Mi, US 188/D3
Fly (riv.), PNG 174/D5
Flying Fish (cape), Ant. 218/T
Fnjóská (riv.), Ice. 95/P6
Foam Lake, Sk, Can. 185/H3
Foča, Bosn. 106/D4
Fochabers, Sc, UK 94/C1
Fochville, SAfr. 164/P13
Fockbek, Ger. 96/C4
Focşani, Rom. 107/H3
Fogang, China 141/K3
Foggia, It. 104/D2
Foglia (riv.), It. 117/F5
Foglizzo, It. 116/A2
Föglö (isl.), Fin. 97/J3
Fogo (isl.), CpV. 151/J10
Fohnsdorf, Aus. 101/L3
Föhren, Ger. 111/F4
Foix, Fr. 100/D5
Folarskardnuten (peak), Nor. 96/B1
Folda (inlet), Nor. 95/E2
Földeák, Hun. 106/E2
Folégandros (isl.), Gre. 105/J4
Folembray, Fr. 110/C4
Foley (isl.), Nun., Can. 181/H2
Folgaria, It. 115/H6
Foligno, It. 101/K5
Folkestone, Eng, UK 91/H4
Folkston, Ga, US 191/H4
Follainville-Dennemont, Fr. 88/H4
Follonica, Golfo di (gulf), It. 101/J5
Folschviller, Fr. 111/F5
Folsom, NJ, US 196/D4
Fomboni, Com. 165/G6
Fond du Lac, Wi, US 185/L5
Fond du Lac, Sk, Can. 180/F3
Fond du Lac (riv.), Sk, Can. 180/F3
Fondi, It. 104/C2
Fondo, It. 115/H5
Fongen (peak), Nor. 95/D3
Fonni, It. 104/A2
Fonsagrada, Sp. 102/B1
Fonseca, Col. 210/C2
Fonseca (gulf), Nic. 182/D5
Font Sancte, Pic de la (peak), Fr. 101/G4
Fontaine, Fr. 100/F4
Fontaine-Châalis, Fr. 88/L4
Fontaine-lès-Dijon, Fr. 114/A3
Fontaine-lès-Luxeuil, Fr. 114/C2
Fontaine-L'Evêque, Belg. 111/D3
Fontainebleau, Fr. 100/E2
Fontana, Ca, US 194/C2
Fontanarossa (int'l arpt.), It. 104/D4
Fontanella, It. 116/C2
Fontanellato, It. 116/D3
Fontaniva, It. 117/E1
Fonte Boa, Braz. 211/E5
Fontenailles, Fr. 88/L6
Fontenais, Swi. 114/D3
Fontenay-en-Parisis, Fr. 88/K4
Fontenay-le-Comte, Fr. 100/C3
Fontenay-le-Fleury, Fr. 88/J5
Fontenay-les-Briis, Fr. 88/J6
Fontenay-Saint-Père, Fr. 88/H4
Fontenay-sous-Bois, Fr. 88/K5
Fontenay-Trésigny, Fr. 88/L5
Fontenelle (res.), Wy, US 184/F5
Fontoy, Fr. 111/F5
Fontur (pt.), Ice. 95/P6
Foping, China 128/J5
Foraker (mt.), Ak, US 192/H3
Forbach, Fr. 111/F5
Forbach, Ger. 112/B5
Forbes, Austl. 173/D2
Forbesganj, India 143/F2
Forcarey, Sp. 102/A1
Forchheim, Ger. 112/E3
Forclaz, Col de la (pass), Swi. 114/D5
Førde, Nor. 95/C3
Fords, NJ, US 197/H9
Foreland (pt.), Eng, UK 90/C4
Foreland, The (pt.), Eng, UK 91/E5
Foremost, Ab, Can. 184/F3
Foreness (pt.), Eng, UK 91/H4
Forest, Ms, US 191/F3
Forest Hill, Md, US 196/B4
Forest Park, Ok, US 195/N14
Forestier (pen.), Austl. 173/D4
Forestier (cape), Austl. 173/D4
Forestville, Qu, Can. 189/G1
Forestville, Md, US 196/B6
Forez, Monts du (mts.), Fr. 100/E4
Forfar, Sc, UK 94/D3
Forges-les-Bains, Fr. 88/J6
Forggensee (lake), Ger. 115/G2
Forillon NP, Qu, Can. 189/H1
Forked River, NJ, US 196/D4
Forkill, NI, UK 92/B3
Forks, Wa, US 184/B4
Forli, It. 117/F4
Forli-Cesena (prov.), It. 117/F4
Forlimpopoli, It. 117/F4
Formartine (reg.), Sc, UK 94/D2
Formby, Eng, UK 93/E4
Formby (pt.), Eng, UK 93/E4
Formentera, Isla de (isl.), Sp. 103/F3
Formentor (cape), Sp. 103/G3
Formerie, Fr. 110/A4
Formia, It. 104/C2
Formiga, Braz. 213/C2
Formigine, It. 117/D3
Formignana, It. 117/E3
Formosa, Arg. 215/E2
Formosa, Braz. 212/A4
Formosa (peak), SAfr. 164/C4
Formosa (isl.), GBis. 160/B4
Formosa do Rio Prêto, Braz. 212/A3
Formosa, Serra (mts.), Braz. 209/G6
Formoso (riv.), Braz. 209/J6
Fornacelle, It. 117/E5
Fornaci di Barga, It. 116/D4
Fornæs (cape), Den. 96/D3
Fornebu (int'l arpt.), Nor. 96/D2
Fornovo di Taro, It. 116/D3
Forres, Sc, UK 94/C1
Forrest City, Ar, US 187/K4
Forsand, Nor. 96/B2
Forshaga, Swe. 96/E2
Forssa, Fin. 97/K1
Forstern, Ger. 113/E6
Forstinning, Ger. 113/E6
Forsyth, Mt, US 184/G4
Forsyth, Ga, US 191/H3
Forsyth (range), Austl. 172/A3
Forsythe NWR, NJ, US 196/D5
Fort Abbās, Pak. 144/B5
Fort Augustus, Sc, UK 94/B2
Fort Beaufort, SAfr. 164/D4
Fort Belvoir, Va, US 196/A6
Fort Benton, Mt, US 184/F4
Fort Bragg, Ca, US 184/C6
Fort Chambly Nat'l Hist. Park, Qu, Can. 189/P7
Fort Chipewyan, Ab, Can. 180/E3
Fort Cobb (res.), Ok, US 187/H4
Fort Collins, Co, US 195/B1
Fort Collins Museum, Co, US 195/B1
Fort Davis, Tx, US 187/G5
Fort de Douaumont, Fr. 111/E5
Fort-de-France, Guad. 199/N9
Fort de Vaux, Fr. 111/E5
Fort Desaix Mil. Res., Mart., Fr. 199/N9
Fort Dodge, Ia, US 185/K5
Fort Erie, On, Can. 189/S10
Fort Frances, On, Can. 185/K3
Fort Frederica Nat'l Mon., Ga, US 191/H4
Fort George Nat'l Hist. Park, On, Can. 189/R9
Fort Gibson (lake), Ok, US 190/E3
Fort Good Hope, NW, Can. 180/D2
Fort Hancock, NJ, US 197/J10
Fort Howard, Md, US 196/B5
Fort Kent, Me, US 189/G2
Fort Lauderdale, Fl, US 191/H5
Fort Lauderdale-Hollywood (int'l arpt.), Fl, US 191/H5
Fort Lee, NJ, US 197/K8
Fort Lewis, Wa, US 193/B3
Fort Liard, NW, Can. 180/D2
Fort Liberté, Haiti 203/J2
Fort Lupton, Co, US 195/C2
Fort Macleod, Ab, Can. 184/E3
Fort Madison, Ia, US 185/L5
Fort-Mahon-Plage, Fr. 110/A3
Fort Malden Nat'l Hist. Park, On, Can. 193/F7
Fort-Mardyck, Fr. 110/B1
Fort Matanzas Nat'l Mon., Fl, US 191/H4
Fort McDowell Ind. Res., Az, US 195/S18
Fort McHenry Nat'l Mon., Md, US 196/B5
Fort McMurray, Ab, Can. 180/E3
Fort McPherson, NW, Can. 192/M2
Fort Meade, Md, US 196/B5
Fort Morgan, Co, US 187/G2
Fort Myers, Fl, US 191/H5
Fort Nelson, BC, Can. 180/D3
Fort Nelson (riv.), BC, Can. 180/D3
Fort Nottingham, SAfr. 165/E3
Fort Payne, Al, US 191/G3
Fort Peck (dam), Mt, US 185/G4
Fort Peck (lake), Mt, US 184/G4
Fort Pierce, Fl, US 191/H5
Fort Portal, Ugan. 162/A2
Fort Providence, NW, Can. 180/E2
Fort Qu'Appelle, Sk, Can. 185/H3
Fort Randall (dam), SD, US 185/J5
Fort Resolution, NW, Can. 180/E2
Fort Saint James, BC, Can. 184/B2
Fort Saint John, BC, Can. 180/D3
Fort Saskatchewan, Ab, Can. 184/E2
Fort Scott, Ks, US 187/J3
Fort-Shevchenko, Kaz. 121/J3
Fort Simpson, NW, Can. 180/D2
Fort Smith, Ar, US 187/J4
Fort Smith, NW, Can. 180/E2
Fort Stanwix Nat'l Mon., NY, US 188/F3
Fort Stockton, Tx, US 187/G5
Fort Sumner, NM, US 187/F4
Fort Sumter, SC, US 191/J3
Fort Tilden, NY, US 197/K9
Fort Totten, ND, US 185/J4
Fort Vasquez Museum, Co, US 195/C2
Fort Vermilion, Ab, Can. 180/E3
Fort Wadsworth, NY, US 197/J9
Fort Walton Beach, Fl, US 191/G4
Fort Wayne, In, US 188/C3
Fort Wellington Nat'l Hist. Park, Can. 188/F2
Fort William, Sc, UK 94/A3
Fort Yates, ND, US 185/H4
Fort Yukon, Ak, US 192/J2
Fortaleza, Braz. 212/C1
Fortaleza dos Nogueiras, Braz. 212/A2
Fortaleza Santa Teresa, Uru. 217/G2
Forte dei Marmi, It. 116/D5
Fortescue (riv.), Austl. 170/C2
Fortescue, NJ, US 196/C5
Forth, Sc, UK 94/C5
Forth (riv.), Sc, UK 94/B4
Forth, Firth of (inlet), Sc, UK 94/C4
Fortín, Mex. 201/N8
Fortore (riv.), It. 104/D2
Fortrose, Sc, UK 94/B1
Fortuna, Braz. 212/A2
Fortuna, Arg. 216/D2
Fortuna Ledge, Ak, US 192/F3
Fortune (bay), Nf, Can. 189/L2
Fortune, Nf, Can. 189/L2
Forty Fort, Pa, US 196/C1
Forty Mile Scrub NP, Austl. 172/B2
Foshan, China 141/K3
Fosheim (pen.), Nun., Can. 181/S7
Foss (riv.), Eng, UK 93/G3
Fossalta di Piave, It. 117/F1
Fossalta di Portogruaro, It. 117/F1
Fossano, It. 116/A3
Fosses, Fr. 88/K4
Fosses-la-Ville, Belg. 111/D3
Fossil, Or, US 184/C4
Fossil Creek (res.), Co, US 195/B2
Fossò, It. 117/F2
Fossombrone, It. 117/F5
Foster, Austl. 173/C3
Foster Pond, Il, US 195/G9
Fosterburg, Il, US 195/G8
Fostoria, Oh, US 188/D3
Fót, Hun. 107/R9
Foucarmont, Fr. 110/A4
Foucherans, Fr. 114/B3
Foug, Fr. 111/E6
Fougères, Fr. 100/C2
Fougerolles, Fr. 114/C2
Fouilloy, Fr. 110/B4
Foul (bay), Egypt, Sudan 155/N3
Foula (isl.), Sc, UK 89/V13
Foulness (pt.), Eng, UK 91/G3
Foulness (isl.), Eng, UK 91/G3
Foulness (riv.), Eng, UK 93/H4
Foum Zguid, Mor. 156/D3
Foumban, Camr. 154/H6
Foundiougne, Sen. 160/A3
Fountain, Il, US 195/G9
Fountain Hill, Pa, US 196/C2
Fountain Hills, Az, US 195/S18
Fountain Valley, Ca, US 194/G8
Fountains Abbey, Eng, UK 93/G3
Fourchambault, Fr. 100/E3
Fourche La Fave (riv.), Ar, US 187/J4
Fourges, Fr. 88/G4
Fourmies, Fr. 110/D4
Fourth Cataract (falls), Sudan 159/C5
Fouta Djallon (phys. reg.), Gui. 154/C5
Foveaux (str.), NZ 159/R12
Fowey (riv.), Eng, UK 90/B6
Fowman, Iran 146/E1
Fox (isls.), Ak, US 192/E5
Fox (mtn.), Yk, Can. 192/M3
Fox (riv.), Il,Wi, US 185/L5
Fox (isl.), Wa, US 193/B3
Fox Creek, Ab, Can. 184/D2
Fox Glacier, NZ 159/S11
Fox Lake, Il, US 193/P15
Fox River Grove, Il, US 193/P15
Fox Valley, Sk, Can. 184/F3
Foxe (pen.), Nun., Can. 181/J2
Foxe (chan.), Nun., Can. 181/H2
Foxe Basin (chan.), Nun., Can. 181/J2
Foxen (lake), Swe. 96/D2
Foyle (riv.), NI, UK 92/A2
Foz, Sp. 102/B1
Foz do Iguaçu, Braz. 215/F2
Frackville, Pa, US 196/B2
Fraga, Sp. 103/F2
Fragosa, Cayo (isl.), Cuba 203/G1
Fraiburgo, Braz. 213/B3
Frailes, Cordillera de los (mts.), Ven. 208/E7
Fraisans, Fr. 114/B3
Fraize, Fr. 114/D1
Frameries, Belg. 110/C3
Framlingham, Eng, UK 91/H2
Frammersbach, Ger. 112/C2
Franca, Braz. 213/C2
Francavilla al Mare, It. 104/D1
Francavilla Fontana, It. 105/E2
Francavilla in Sinni, It. 104/E2
France (ctry.) 100/D3
Frances (cape), Cuba 203/F1
Frances (lake), Yk, Can. 180/C2
Francés Viejo (cape), DRep. 199/H4
Franceville, Gabon 154/H8
Franche-Comté (pol. reg.), Fr. 114/B5
Franche-Comteé (pol. reg.), Fr. 101/G3
Francis Case (lake), SD, US 185/J5
Francisco de Orellana, Peru 214/C1
Francisco Escárcega, Mex. 202/D2
Francisco Javier Mina, Mex. 200/C3
Francisco Sá, Braz. 212/B5
Francisco Zarco, Mex. 200/A1
Francistown, Bots. 163/E5
Franco da Rocha, Braz. 213/G8
Francolino, It. 117/E3
Franconville, Fr. 88/J5
Franeker, Neth. 108/C2
Frangy, Fr. 114/B5
Frank Hahn NP, Austl. 170/C5
Franken Wald (for.), Ger. 113/E2
Frankenau, Ger. 109/F6
Frankenberg-Eder, Ger. 109/F6
Frankenburg am Hausruck, Aus. 113/G6
Frankenhöhe (mts.), Ger. 98/F4
Frankenmarkt, Aus. 113/G7
Frankenmuth, Mi, US 188/D3
Frankenthal, Ger. 112/B3
Frankfort (cap.), Ky, US 188/C4
Frankfort, SAfr. 164/E2
Frankfurt, Ger. 99/H2
Frankfurt (int'l arpt.), Ger. 112/B2
Frankfurt am Main, Ger. 112/B2
Fränkische Alb (mts.), Ger. 98/F4
Fränkische Rezat (riv.), Ger. 112/D4
Fränkische Saale (riv.), Ger. 98/E3
Fränkische Schweiz (reg.), Ger. 101/J2
Fränkische Schweiz (reg.), Ger. 98/F4
Frankland (cape), Austl. 173/C3
Franklin (pt.), Ak, US 192/G1
Franklin, NC, US 191/H3
Franklin, La, US 187/K5
Franklin, Ky, US 188/C4
Franklin, In, US 188/C4
Franklin, Tn, US 188/C5
Franklin, WV, US 188/E4
Franklin, NJ, US 196/D1
Franklin (mts.), NW, Can. 180/D2
Franklin (bay), NW, Can. 180/D2
Franklin, Mi, US 193/F6
Franklin D. Roosevelt (lake), Wa, US 184/D3
Franklin Lakes, NJ, US 197/J7
Franklin-Lower Gordon Wild Rivers NP, Austl. 173/C4
Franklin Mineral Museum, NJ, US 196/D1
Franklin Park, Il, US 193/Q16
Franklin Square, NY, US 197/L9
Franksville, Wi, US 193/Q14
Franois, Fr. 114/B3
Franschhoek, SAfr. 164/L10
Fransisco Beltrão, Braz. 215/F2
Fransisco Morato, Braz. 213/G8
Františkovy Lázně, Czh. 113/F2

Franz – Gener

Franz Josef Land (isls.), Rus. 218/C
Franz Joseph Strauss (int'l arpt.), Ger. 113/E6
Franzburg, Ger. 96/E4
Fraser (isl.), Austl. 167/E3
Fraser (mt.), Austl. 170/C3
Fraser (riv.), BC, Can. 184/C2
Fraser, Mi, US 193/G6
Fraser Lake, BC, Can. 184/B2
Fraser NP, Austl. 173/C3
Fraserburg, SAfr. 164/C3
Fraserburgh, Sc, UK 94/D1
Frasne, Fr. 114/C4
Frassine (riv.), It. 117/E2
Frassino, It. 117/D2
Frastanz, Aus. 115/F3
Frati, Monte dei (peak), It. 117/F5
Frauenfeld, Swi. 115/E2
Fraunberg, Ger. 113/F6
Fray Bentos, Uru. 217/J10
Fray Marcos, Uru. 217/L11
Frazier Park, Ca, US 186/C4
Frechen, Ger. 111/F2
Freckenfeld, Ger. 112/B4
Fred (mt.), Les. 164/E3
Frederica, De, US 196/C6
Fredericia, Den. 96/C4
Frederick (reef), Austl. 167/E3
Frederick, Co, US 195/C2
Frederick, Md, US 188/E4
Frederick (co.), Md, US 196/A5
Frederick, Ok, US 187/H4
Fredericksburg, Pa, US 196/B3
Fredericksburg, Tx, US 187/H5
Frederickton, Austl. 173/E1
Fredericton (cap.), NB, Can. 189/H2
Frederik Willem IV (falls), Sur. 211/G4
Frederiks, Den. 96/C3
Frederiksborg (co.), Den. 96/E4
Frederiksborg Slot (Frederiksborg Castle), Den. 96/E4
Frederikshavn, Den. 96/D3
Frederiksted, USVI 199/M8
Fredersdorf bei Berlin, Ger. 98/Q7
Fredonia, Az, US 186/D3
Fredonia, NY, US 188/E3
Fredriksberg, Swe. 96/F1
Fredrikstad, Nor. 96/D2
Free State (prov.), SAfr. 164/P13
Freeburg, Il, US 195/H9
Freeburg, Pa, US 196/B2
Freedom, Ok, US 190/D2
Freehold, NJ, US 196/D3
Freeland, Pa, US 196/C1
Freeland, Md, US 196/B4
Freeland, Wa, US 193/B1
Freeling (mt.), Austl. 171/G2
Freeling Heights (peak), Austl. 171/H4
Freemansburg, Pa, US 196/C2
Freeport, Bahm. 199/F2
Freeport, Il, US 185/L5
Freeport, NY, US 197/L9
Freeport, Tx, US 187/J5
Freer, Tx, US 190/D5
Freetown (cap.), SLeo. 160/B4
Fregenal de la Sierra, Sp. 102/B3
Fréhel (cape), Fr. 100/B2
Frei Inocêncio, Braz. 213/D1
Freib Mulde (riv.), Ger. 98/G3
Freiberg, Ger. 99/G3
Freiburg, Ger. 109/G1
Freiburg, Ger. 114/D2
Freienbach, Swi. 115/E3
Freihung, Ger. 113/E3
Freilassing, Ger. 113/F7
Freinsheim, Ger. 112/B3
Freire, Chile 216/B3
Freisen, Ger. 111/G4
Freising, Ger. 113/E6
Freistadt, Aus. 113/H5
Freital, Ger. 99/G3
Freixo de Espada à Cinta, Port. 102/B2
Frejorgues (int'l arpt.), Fr. 100/E5
Fréjus, Fr. 101/G5
Frekhaug, Nor. 96/A1
Frémainfille, Fr. 88/H4
Fremdingen, Ger. 112/D5
Frémécourt, Fr. 88/J4
Fremont (riv.), Ut, US 186/E3
Fremont, Oh, US 188/D3
Fremont, Mi, US 188/C3
Fremont, Ca, US 186/B3
Fremont (isl.), Ut, US 195/J11
French (riv.), On, Can. 188/D2
French Creek State Park, Pa, US 196/C3
French Frigate Shoals (bar), Hi, US 159/J2
French Guiana (dpcy.), Fr. 209/H3
French Polynesia (terr.), Fr. 159/L6
Frenchman (riv.), Can.,US 180/F4
Frenchman's (bay), On, Can. 189/R8
Frenchmans Cap (peak), Austl. 173/C4
Frenchtown, NJ, US 196/C2
Frenda, Alg. 158/F5
Frépillon, Fr. 88/J4
Freren, Ger. 109/E4
Fresco (riv.), Braz. 209/H5
Fresco, C.d'Iv. 160/D5
Fresia, Chile 216/B4
Fresnes, Fr. 88/J5
Fresnes-en-Woëvre, Fr. 111/E5
Fresnillo, Mex. 200/E4
Fresno, Ca, US 186/C3
Fresnoy-le-Grand, Fr. 110/C4
Fresse-sur-Moselle, Fr. 114/C2
Fressenneville, Fr. 110/A3
Fretin, Fr. 110/C2
Freuchie (lake), Sc, UK 94/C3
Freudenberg, Ger. 113/E4
Freudenberg, Ger. 111/G2
Freudenburg, Ger. 111/F4
Freudenstadt, Ger. 115/E1
Frévent, Fr. 110/B3
Freycinet (har.), Austl. 170/B3
Freycinet NP, Austl. 173/D4
Freyming-Merlebach, Fr. 111/F5
Freystadt, Ger. 113/E4
Freyung, Ger. 113/G5
Fria (cape), Namb. 163/B4
Frias, Arg. 215/C2
Frías, Peru 214/B2
Fribourg, Swi. 114/D4
Fribourg (canton), Swi. 114/D4
Frick, Swi. 114/E3
Frickenhausen am Main, Ger. 112/D3
Fridingen an der Donau, Ger. 115/E1
Fridolfing, Ger. 113/F6
Friedberg, Ger. 112/B2
Friedberg, Ger. 112/D6
Friedeburg, Ger. 109/E2
Friedrichsdorf, Ger. 112/B2
Friedrichshafen, Ger. 115/F2
Friedrichstadt, Ger. 96/C4
Friedrichsthal, Ger. 111/G5
Frielendorf, Ger. 109/G7
Friesenhagen, Ger. 111/G2
Friesenheim, Ger. 114/D1
Friesland (prov.), Neth. 108/C2
Friesoythe, Ger. 109/E2
Frignicourt, Fr. 111/D6
Frio (riv.), Tx, US 187/H5
Friockheim, Sc, UK 94/D3
Friol, Sp. 102/B1
Frisange, Lux. 111/F4
Fristad, Swe. 96/E3
Fritsla, Swe. 96/E3
Fritzlar, Ger. 109/G6
Friuli-Venezia Giula (prov.), It. 101/K3
Friville-Escarbotin, Fr. 110/A3
Frobisher (bay), Nun., Can. 181/K2
Frogmore, Eng, UK 88/A3
Frohavet (inlet), Nor. 95/D3
Frohnleiten, Aus. 101/L3
Froid-Chapelle, Belg. 111/D3
Froideconche, Fr. 114/C2
Froissy, Fr. 110/B4
Froland, Nor. 96/C2
Frolovo, Rus. 121/G2
Frome (lake), Austl. 167/D4
Frome (riv.), Austl. 171/H4
Frome, Eng, UK 90/D4
Frome (riv.), Eng, UK 90/D5
Froncles, Fr. 114/B1
Front (range), Co, US 187/F2
Fronteira, Port. 102/B3
Frontenhausen, Ger. 113/F5
Frontera, Mex. 202/C2
Frontera Comalapa, Mex. 202/C3
Frontier Army Museum, Ks, US 195/D5
Frontignan, Fr. 100/E5
Fronton, Fr. 100/D5
Frosinone, It. 104/C2
Frösö, Swe. 95/E3
Frotey-lès-Vesoul, Fr. 114/C2
Frouard, Fr. 111/F6
Frövi, Swe. 96/F2
Frøya (isl.), Nor. 95/D3
Frozen (str.), Nun., Can. 181/H2
Fruges, Fr. 110/B2
Fruit Heights, Ut, US 195/K11
Fruška Gora NP, Cro. 106/D3
Frutal, Braz. 213/B1
Frutigen, Swi. 114/D4
Frutillar, Chile 216/B4
Fryazino, Rus. 119/X9
Frýdek-Místek, Czh. 99/K4
Fu Xian, China 130/B4
Fu'an, China 137/C2
Fucecchio, It. 117/D5
Fucheng, China 130/D3
Fuchskaute (peak), Ger. 101/H1
Fuchū, Japan 132/C3
Fuchū, Japan 135/C3
Fuchuan, China 137/B3
Fuchun (riv.), China 130/D5
Fuding, China 137/D2
Fuengirola, Sp. 102/C4
Fuenlabrada, Sp. 103/N9
Fuensalida, Sp. 102/C2
Fuente, Sp. 103/N8
Fuente de Cantos, Sp. 102/B3
Fuente del Maestre, Sp. 102/B3
Fuente Obejuna, Sp. 102/C3
Fuentelapeña, Sp. 102/C2
Fuentes de Oñoro, Sp. 102/B2
Fuentesaúco, Sp. 102/C2
Fuerte (riv.), Mex. 200/C3
Fuerte Olimpo, Par. 208/G8
Fuerteventura (isl.) Canl., Sp. 156/B3
Fuga (isl.), Phil. 137/D4
Fuglebjerg, Den. 96/D4
Fugong, China 141/G2
Fugou, China 130/C4
Fuhai, China 128/E2
Fuhne (riv.), Ger. 98/F3
Fuhse (riv.), Ger. 109/H4
Fuji, Japan 133/F3
Fuji (riv.), Japan 133/F3
Fuji-san (peak), Japan 133/F3
Fuji-Hakone-Izu NP, Japan 133/F3
Fujian (prov.), China 129/L6
Fujieda, Japan 133/F3
Fujihashi, Japan 135/K4
Fujiidera, Japan 135/J6
Fujikawa, Japan 135/B3
Fujimi, Japan 135/D2
Fujino, Japan 135/C2
Fujinomiya, Japan 135/B3
Fujioka, Japan 133/F2
Fujioka, Japan 135/D1
Fujioka, Japan 133/F3
Fujisawa, Japan 133/F3
Fujishiro, Japan 135/E2
Fujiwara, Japan 135/K5
Fujiyoshida, Japan 133/F3
Fukagawa, Japan 134/C2
Fukang, China 128/E3
Fukaya, Japan 135/C1
Fukiage, Japan 135/C1
Fukuchiyama, Japan 135/H5
Fukue, Japan 132/A4
Fukui (pref.), Japan 132/E3
Fukui, Japan 132/E2
Fukuoka, Japan 132/B4
Fukuoka, Japan 135/M4
Fukuoka (int'l arpt.), Japan 132/B4
Fukuoka (pref.), Japan 132/B4
Fukuroi, Japan 133/E3
Fukushima, Japan 133/G2
Fukushima (pref.), Japan 133/F2
Fukushima, Japan 134/B3
Fukuyama, Japan 132/C3
Fūlādī (mtn.), Afg. 147/J2
Fulda (riv.), Ger. 98/E3
Fulda, Ger. 112/C1
Fullerton, Ca, US 194/G8
Fullerton (Whitehall), Pa, US 196/C2
Fully, Swi. 114/D5
Fulpmes, Aus. 115/H3
Fulton, Mo, US 187/K3
Fulton, NY, US 188/E3
Fulton, Ky, US 188/B4
Fulufjället (peak), Swe. 96/E1
Fumaiolo (peak), It. 117/F5
Fumay, Fr. 111/D4
Fumel, Fr. 100/D4
Fumin, China 141/H2
Funabashi, Japan 135/D2
Funafuti (cap.), Tuv. 174/G5
Funafuti (isl.), Tuv. 174/G5
Funan, China 130/C4
Funchal, Port. 156/A2
Funchal (int'l arpt.), Port. 156/A2
Fundación, Col. 210/C2
Fundão, Port. 102/B2
Fundy (bay), US,Can. 189/H2
Fundy NP, NB, Can. 189/H2
Funhalouro, Moz. 163/F5
Funing, China 141/J3
Funing, China 130/D4
Fuorn, Pass dal (Ofenpass) (pass), Swi. 115/G4
Fuping, China 130/C3
Fuqing, China 137/C2
Fuquan, China 141/J2
Fur (riv.), China 131/C2
Furan (riv.), Fr. 114/B6
Furano, Japan 134/C2
Fürfeld, Ger. 111/G4
Furmanov, Rus. 118/J4
Furnas (res.), Braz. 209/J8
Furneaux Group (isls.), Austl. 167/D4
Fürstenau, Ger. 109/E3
Fürstenfeld, Aus. 101/M3
Fürstenfeldbruck, Ger. 112/E6
Fürstenwalde, Ger. 99/H2
Fürth, Ger. 112/B3
Fürth, Ger. 112/D4
Furth im Wald, Ger. 113/F4
Furtwangen im Schwarzwald, Ger. 114/E1
Furudal, Swe. 96/F1
Furukawa, Japan 134/B4
Fury and Hecla (str.), Nun., Can. 181/H2
Fushan, China 130/B4
Fushan, China 130/E3
Fushun, China 131/B2
Fushun, China 141/J2
Fusignano, It. 117/E4
Fusio, Swi. 115/E5
Fuso, Japan 135/L5
Fussa, Japan 135/C2
Füssen, Ger. 115/G2
Fusui, China 136/D1
Futaba, Japan 135/A2
Futaleufú, Chile 216/C4
Futami, Japan 135/L7
Futog, Serb. 106/D3
Futrono, Chile 216/B4
Futtsu, Japan 133/F3
Futuna (isl.), Wall., Fr. 174/H6
Fuwah, Egypt 149/B4
Fuxian (lake), China 141/H3
Fuxin, China 130/E2
Fuxin Monggolzu Zizhixian, China 130/E2
Fuyang, China 130/C4
Fuyi (riv.), China 137/B2
Fuyu, China 129/M2
Fuyu, China 129/M2
Fuyuan, China 141/H2
Fuyun, China 128/E2
Füzesabony, Hun. 106/E2
Fuzhou, China 137/C2
Fyn (co.), Den. 96/D4
Fyn (isl.), Den. 95/D5
Fyne, Loch (inlet), Sc, UK 94/A5
Fyresdal, Nor. 96/C2

G

Ga Vache (isl.), Haiti 203/H2
Gaast, Neth. 108/C2
Gabas (riv.), Fr. 100/C5
Gabela, Ang. 163/B3
Gabes (gov.), Tun. 157/H2
Gabes (gulf), Tun. 157/H2
Gabicce Mare, It. 117/F5
Gablingen, Ger. 112/D6
Gablitz, Aus. 107/N7
Gabon (ctry.) 154/H7
Gaborone (cap.), Bots. 163/E5
Gabriel Leyva Solano, Mex. 200/C3
Gabrovo, Bul. 105/J1
Gaby, It. 116/A1
Gacko, Bosn. 105/F1
Gādarwāra, India 142/B4
Gaddy, Ok, US 195/N15
Gadmen, Swi. 115/E4
Gadsden, Al, US 191/G3
Găeşti, Rom. 107/G3
Gaeta, It. 104/C2
Gaeta, Golfo di (gulf), It. 104/C2
Gaferut (isl.), Micr. 174/D4
Gaffney, SC, US 191/H3
Gafsa, Tun. 157/H2
Gafsa (gov.), Tun. 157/H2
Gagarin, Rus. 118/G5
Gaggenau, Ger. 112/B5
Gaggio Montano, It. 117/D4
Gaglianico, It. 116/B1
Gagnoa, C.d'Iv. 160/D5
Gagny, Fr. 88/K5
Gagra, Geo. 120/G4
Gagret, India 144/D4
Gai Xian, China 131/B2
Gaichtpass (pass), Aus. 115/G3
Gail (riv.), Aus. 101/K3
Gaildorf, Ger. 112/C5
Gaillac, Fr. 100/D5
Gailtaler (mts.), Aus. 101/K3
Gaiman, Arg. 216/D4
Gaimersheim, Ger. 113/E5
Gainesville, Tx, US 187/H4
Gainesville, Ga, US 191/H3
Gainesville, Fl, US 191/H4
Gainsborough, Eng, UK 93/H5
Gairdner (lake), Austl. 167/C4
Gairn (riv.), Sc, UK 94/C2
Gais, Swi. 115/F3
Gaiserwald, Swi. 115/F3
Gaizina (peak), Lat. 97/L3
Gakarosa (peak), SAfr. 164/C2
Gakona, Ak, US 192/J3
Galana (riv.), Kenya 162/C3
Galand, Iran 147/G1
Galapagar, Sp. 103/M8
Galápagos (isls.), Ecu. 214/E6
Galápagos (dept.), Ecu. 214/E7
Galápagos, PN, Ecu. 214/E7
Galashiels, Sc, UK 94/D5
Galaţi (prov.), Rom. 107/H3
Galaţi, Rom. 107/J3
Galatina, It. 105/F2
Galatiní, Gre. 105/G2
Galátista, Gre. 105/H2
Galatone, It. 105/F2
Galb Azefal (hill), WSah. 156/B5
Galbiate, It. 116/C1
Galdácano, Sp. 102/D1
Gáldar, Canl., Sp. 156/B3
Galeana, Mex. 201/E3
Galela, Indo. 139/G3
Galena, Ak, US 192/G3
Galena, Md, US 196/C5
Galeota (pt.), Trin. 211/F2
Galera (pt.), Ecu. 210/A4
Galera (pt.), Trin. 211/F2
Galera (pt.), Chile 216/B3
Galesburg, Il, US 185/L5
Galey (riv.), Ire. 89/P10
Galga (riv.), Hun. 107/R9
Galgamácsa, Hun. 107/R9
Galgorm, NI, UK 92/B2
Galich, Rus. 118/J4
Galicia (aut. comm.), Sp. 102/A1
Galičica NP, FYROM 105/G2
Galiléia, Braz. 213/D1
Galileo Galilei (int'l arpt.), It. 116/D5
Galinakopf (peak), Aus. 115/F3
Galion, Oh, US 188/D3
Gallan Head (pt.), Sc, UK 89/Q7
Gallarate, It. 116/B1
Gallatin, Tn, US 188/C4
Galle, SrL. 140/D6
Gallegos (riv.), Arg. 215/B7
Galliate, It. 116/B2
Gallicano, It. 116/D4
Galliera Veneta, It. 117/E1
Gallinas (mts.), NM, US 190/B3
Gallinas (pt.), Col. 210/D1
Gallipoli, It. 105/E2
Gallipoli (pen.), Turk. 107/H5
Gällivare, Swe. 95/G2
Gallneukirchen, Aus. 113/H6
Gallo (cape), It. 104/C3
Gallo (lake), It. 115/G4
Gallspach, Aus. 113/G6
Galluis, Fr. 88/H5
Gallup, NM, US 186/E4
Gallur, Sp. 102/E2
Gally (riv.), Fr. 88/H5
Galston, Sc, UK 94/B5
Galten, Den. 96/C3
Galtymore (peak), Ire. 89/P10
Galva, La, US 195/P16
Galvarino, Chile 216/B3
Galveston, Tx, US 187/J5
Galveston (bay), Tx, US 187/J5
Galveston (isl.), Tx, US 187/J5
Gálvez, Sp. 102/C3
Galway, Ire. 89/P10
Galway (bay), Ire. 89/P10
Galzignano, It. 117/E2
Gam (riv.), Viet. 141/J3
Gamaches, Fr. 110/A4
Gamagara (riv.), SAfr. 164/C2
Gamagōri, Japan 135/M6
Gamarra, Col. 210/C2
Gamba, China 143/G1
Gambaga, Gha. 161/E4
Gambaga Scarp (cliff), Gha. 161/E4
Gambais, Fr. 88/H5
Gambara, It. 116/D2
Gambat, Pak. 140/A2
Gambela NP, Eth. 155/M6
Gambell, Ak, US 192/D3
Gambellara, It. 117/E2
Gamber, Md, US 196/B5
Gambettola, It. 117/F4
Gambia, The (ctry.) 160/B3
Gambia (riv.), Gam. 160/A3
Gambier (isls.), FrPol. 159/M7
Gámbita, Col. 210/C3
Gambo, Nf, Can. 189/L1
Gambolò, It. 116/B2
Gambsheim, Fr. 112/A5
Gaming, Aus. 101/L3
Gamka (riv.), SAfr. 164/C4
Gamkab (riv.), Namb. 164/B3
Gamleby, Swe. 96/G3
Gammelstad, Swe. 95/G2
Gammertingen, Ger. 115/F1
Gammon Ranges NP, Austl. 171/H4
Gamo, Japan 135/K5
Gampern, Aus. 113/G7
Gamud (peak), Eth. 162/C1
Gan (riv.), China 129/L6
Gan, Fr. 100/C5
Gananoque, On, Can. 188/E2
Găncă, Azer. 121/H4
Ganda, Ang. 163/B3
Gandajika, D.R. Congo 163/D2
Gandak (riv.), India 143/E2
Gandaki (zone), Nepal 142/D1
Gander (lake), Nf, Can. 189/L1
Gander, Nf, Can. 189/L1
Ganderkesee, Ger. 109/F2
Gandesa, Sp. 103/F2
Gāndhi Sāgar (res.), India 140/B3
Gāndhīdhām, India 147/K4
Gandhinagar, India 147/K4
Gandía, Sp. 103/E3
Gandino, It. 116/C1
Gandoca-Manzanillo NWR, CR 203/F4
Gandu, Braz. 212/C4
Ganeb (well), Mrta. 160/C2
Ganesh (mtn.), China 143/E1
Gangāpur, India 147/L4
Gangārāmpur, India 143/G3
Gangaw, Myan. 141/F3
Gangca, China 128/H4
Gangdisê (mts.), China 128/D5
Gangelt, Ger. 111/F2
Ganges, Fr. 100/E5
Ganges (riv.), Asia 128/E7
Ganges (Ganga) (riv.), India 142/B1
Ganges, Mouths of the (delta), Bang. 143/G5
Gangi, It. 104/D4
Gangkofen, Ger. 113/F6
Gangoh, India 144/D5
Gangtok, India 143/G2
Ganluo, China 141/H2
Gannat, Fr. 100/E3
Ganquan, China 130/B3
Gansbaai, SAfr. 164/L11
Gänserndorf, Aus. 107/P7
Gansu (prov.), China 128/H4
Gantrisch (peak), Swi. 114/D4
Ganyu, China 130/D4
Ganzhou, China 137/B2
Ganzlin, Ger. 98/G2
Ganzourgou (prov.), Burk. 161/E3
Gao (pol. reg.), Mali 161/F2
Gao, Mali 161/E2
Gao'an, China 137/C2
Gaocheng, China 130/C3
Gaochun, China 130/D5
Gaomi, China 130/D3
Gaoping, China 130/C4
Gaoqing, China 130/D3
Gaor Bheinn (Gulvain) (peak), Sc, UK 94/A3
Gaotai, China 128/G4
Gaotang, China 130/D3
Gaoua, Burk. 160/E4
Gaoyang, China 130/C3
Gaoyi, China 130/C3
Gaoyou, China 130/D4
Gaozhou, China 141/K3
Gap, Fr. 101/G4
Gap, Pa, US 196/B4
Gar, China 128/C5
Garabogazköl Aylagy (gulf), Trkm. 121/K4
Garachiné, Pan. 203/G4
Garachiné (pt.), Pan. 203/G4
Garai (riv.), Bang. 140/E3
Garajonay, PN de, Canl., Sp. 156/A3
Garamba, PN de la, D.R. Congo 155/L7
Garancières, Fr. 110/A6
Garanhuns, Braz. 212/C3
Garbsen, Ger. 109/G4
Garça, Braz. 213/B2
Garças (riv.), Braz. 209/H7
Garching an der Alz, Ger. 113/F6
Garcia de Sota, Embalse de (res.), Sp. 102/C3
Gard (riv.), Fr. 100/F4
Garda (lake), It. 101/J4
Garda, It. 117/D1
Garde, Cap de (cape), Alg. 158/K6
Gardelegen, Ger. 98/F2
Garden (isl.), Austl. 170/K7
Garden City, Ga, US 191/H3
Garden City, NY, US 197/L9
Garden City, Mi, US 193/F7
Garden City Park, NY, US 197/L9
Garden Grove, Ca, US 194/G8
Garden Ridge, Tx, US 195/U20
Garden View, Pa, US 196/A1
Gardena, Ca, US 194/F8
Gardenstown, Sc, UK 94/D1
Gardēz, Afg. 147/J2
Gardiner, Mt, US 184/F4
Gardiner, Me, US 189/G2
Gardiner, Wa, US 193/B1
Gardiners (isl.), NY, US 197/F1
Gardiners (bay), NY, US 197/F1
Gardner (lake), Ks, US 195/D6
Gardner, Ks, US 195/D6
Gardone Val Trompia, It. 116/D1
Gare Loch (inlet), Sc, UK 94/B4
Gareat el Tarf (salt pan), Alg. 158/K7
Garelochhead, Sc, UK 94/B4
Garessio, It. 116/B4
Garet el Djenoun (peak), Alg. 157/G4
Garfield (mtn.), Mt, US 184/E4
Garfield, Ut, US 195/J12
Garfield, NJ, US 197/J8
Garforth, Eng, UK 93/G4
Gargaliánoi, Gre. 105/G4
Gargan (peak), Fr. 100/D4
Gargenville, Fr. 110/A6
Garges-lès-Gonesse, Fr. 88/K5
Gargnano, It. 117/D1
Garh Mahārāja, Pak. 144/A4
Garhākota, India 142/B4
Garhbeta, India 143/F4
Garhmuktesar, India 142/B1
Garibaldi, Braz. 213/B4
Garies, SAfr. 164/B3
Garioch (reg.), Sc, UK 94/D2
Garissa, Kenya 162/C3
Garland, Tx, US 187/H4
Garlasco, It. 116/B2
Garmisch-Partenkirchen, Ger. 115/H3
Garmsār, Iran 146/F1
Garnpung (lake), Austl. 173/B2
Garonne (riv.), Fr. 100/D4
Garopaba, Braz. 213/B4
Garou (lake), Mali 161/E2
Garoua, Camr. 154/H6
Garphyttan, Swe. 96/F2
Garraf (mts.), Sp. 103/K7
Garrel, Ger. 109/F3
Garrison (dam), ND, US 185/H4
Garrison, ND, US 185/H4
Garron (pt.), NI, UK 92/C1
Garrovillas, Sp. 102/B3
Garry (bay), Nun., Can. 181/H2
Garry (lake), Nun., Can. 180/F2
Garry (lake), Sc, UK 94/B2
Garry (riv.), Sc, UK 94/A2
Garsten, Aus. 113/H6
Garte (riv.), Ger. 109/H6
Gartempe (riv.), Fr. 100/D3
Gärtringen, Ger. 112/B5
Garut, Indo. 138/C5
Garvagh, NI, UK 92/B2
Garwa, India 142/D3
Garwolin, Pol. 99/L3
Garwood, NJ, US 197/H9
Gary, In, US 188/C3
Garza García, Mex. 201/E3
Garzê, China 128/H5
Garzón, Col. 210/C4
Gas, Fr. 88/G6
Gas City, In, US 188/C3
Gas-san (peak), Japan 134/B4
Gæsafjöll (peak), Ice. 95/P6
Gaschurn, Aus. 115/G4
Gasconade (riv.), Mo, US 187/J3
Gascony (reg.), Fr. 100/C5
Gascoyne (riv.), Austl. 167/A3
Gascoyne (mt.), Austl. 170/C3
Gaspar (str.), Indo. 138/C4
Gaspar, Braz. 213/B3
Gaspé, Qu, Can. 189/H1
Gaspé (pen.), Qu, Can. 189/H1
Gaspé, Cap de (cape), Qu, Can. 189/H1
Gaspoltshofen, Aus. 113/G6
Gasport, NY, US 189/S9
Gassino Torinese, It. 116/A2
Gastins, Fr. 88/M6
Gaston (lake), NC, US 191/J2
Gastonia, NC, US 191/H3
Gastoúni, Gre. 105/G4
Gata (cape), Sp. 102/D4
Gata (cape), Cyp. 149/C2
Gata de Gorgos, Sp. 103/F3
Gata, Sierra de (mts.), Sp. 102/B2
Gatchina, Rus. 97/P2
Gatehouse-of-Fleet, Sc, UK 92/D2
Gates of the Arctic NP and Prsv., Ak, US 192/G2
Gateshead (isl.), Nun., Can. 180/F1
Gateshead, Eng, UK 93/G2
Gateshead (co.), Eng, UK 93/G2
Gatesville, Tx, US 190/D4
Gateway Arch (arch), Mo, US 195/G8
Gateway NRA, NJ,NY, US 197/K9
Gatineau, Qu, Can. 188/F2
Gatineau (riv.), Qu, Can. 181/J4
Gatow, Ger. 98/Q7
Gattaran, Phil. 137/D4
Gattendorf, Aus. 101/M2
Gattinara, It. 116/B1
Gatton, Austl. 172/D4
Gatún (dam), Pan. 203/G4
Gatún (lake), Pan. 203/G4
Gatwick (int'l arpt.), Eng, UK 88/C3
Gau Algesheim, Ger. 112/B3
Gau Bischofsheim, Ger. 112/B3
Gau Odernheim, Ger. 112/B3
Gaubickelheim, Ger. 111/H4
Gauchy, Fr. 110/C4
Gaucín, Sp. 102/C4
Gauja (riv.), Est.,Lat. 97/L3
Gauja NP, Lat. 97/L3
Gaukönigshofen, Ger. 112/C3
Gaunless (riv.), Eng, UK 93/G2
Gaupne, Nor. 95/C3
Gaur (riv.), Sc, UK 94/B3
Gauri Sankar (peak), Nepal 143/F2
Gauripur, India 143/G2
Gausta (peak), Nor. 96/C2
Gauting, Ger. 113/E6
Gavà, Sp. 103/L7
Gávdhos (isl.), Gre. 105/J5
Gavere, Belg. 110/C2
Gavi, It. 116/B3
Gavião, Port. 102/B3
Gavirate, It. 116/B1
Gävle, Swe. 96/G1
Gävleborg (co.), Swe. 95/E3
Gawler (ranges), Austl. 167/C4
Gawler, Austl. 171/H5
Gay (peak), WV, US 188/D4
Gay, Rus. 121/L2
Gaya, Niger 161/F4
Gayaza, Ugan. 162/A3
Gaylord, Mi, US 188/C2
Gayndah, Austl. 172/C4
Gaza Strip, Isr. 148/C4
Gazeran, Fr. 88/H6
Gaziantep (prov.), Turk. 148/D2
Gaziantep, Turk. 148/D2
Gaziköy, Turk. 107/H5
Gazipaşa, Turk. 149/C1
Gazon de Faing (peak), Fr. 114/D1
Gazzaniga, It. 116/C1
Gbadolite, D.R. Congo 155/K7
Gbarnga, Libr. 160/C5
Gbongan, Nga. 161/G5
Gdańsk (gulf), Pol. 99/K1
Gdańsk, Pol. 96/H4
Gdynia, Pol. 96/H4
Ge (lake), China 130/D5
Geal Charn (peak), Sc, UK 94/C2
Geal Charn (peak), Sc, UK 94/A3
Gebaberg (peak), Ger. 112/D1
Gebe (isl.), Indo. 139/G3
Gebhardshain, Ger. 111/G2
Gebiz, Turk. 149/B1
Gebze, Turk. 107/J5
Gede (peak), Indo. 138/C5
Gedern, Ger. 112/C2
Gedi Ruins Nat'l Mon., Kenya 162/D3
Gedikbulak, Turk. 148/E2
Gedinne, Belg. 111/D4
Gediz, Turk. 148/B2
Gediz (riv.), Turk. 148/A2
Gedser (cape), Den. 96/D4
Gedser, Den. 96/D4
Gedsted, Den. 96/C3
Geel, Belg. 111/E1
Geelong, Austl. 173/C3
Geelvink (chan.), Austl. 167/A3
Geertruidenberg, Neth. 108/B5
Geeste (riv.), Ger. 109/F1
Geeste, Ger. 109/E3
Geesthacht, Ger. 109/H2
Geeveston, Austl. 173/C4
Gefrees, Ger. 113/E2
Gē'gyai, China 128/D5
Gehrde, Ger. 109/F3
Gehrden, Ger. 109/G4
Geifas (peak), Wal, UK 90/C2
Geikie (riv.), Sk, Can. 180/F3
Geilenkirchen, Ger. 111/F2
Geilo, Nor. 96/C1
Geinō, Japan 135/K6
Geiselhöring, Ger. 113/F5
Geiselwind, Ger. 112/D3
Geisenfeld, Ger. 113/E5
Geisenhausen, Ger. 113/F6
Geisenheim, Ger. 111/G4
Geislingen, Ger. 115/E1
Geislingen an der Steige, Ger. 112/C5
Geita, Tanz. 162/B3
Gejiu, China 141/H3
Gela, It. 104/D4
Gela, Golfo di (gulf), It. 104/D4
Gelai (peak), Tanz. 162/C3
Gelderland (prov.), Neth. 108/C4
Geldermalsen, Neth. 108/C5
Geldern, Ger. 108/D5
Geldersheim, Ger. 112/D2
Geldrop, Neth. 108/C6
Geleen, Neth. 111/E2
Gelendost, Turk. 148/B2
Gelendzhik, Rus. 120/F3
Gelibolu (Gallipoli), Turk. 105/K2
Gelibolu Yarımadas NP, Turk. 105/K2
Gelincik (peak), Turk. 148/E2
Gelligaer, Wal, UK 90/C3
Gelnhausen, Ger. 112/C2
Gelsenkirchen, Ger. 108/E5
Geltendorf, Ger. 115/H1
Gelterkinden, Swi. 114/D3
Gelting, Ger. 96/C4
Gemas, Malay. 138/B3
Gembloux, Belg. 111/D2
Gemena, D.R. Congo 155/J7
Gemert, Neth. 108/C5
Gemlik (gulf), Turk. 107/J5
Gemlik, Turk. 107/J5
Gemona del Friuli, It. 101/K3
Gemsbok NP, Bots. 163/D6
Gemuk (mtn.), Ak, US 192/G3
Gemünden am Main, Ger. 112/C2
Genalē Wenz (riv.), Eth. 155/N6
Genappe, Belg. 111/D2
Genay, Fr. 114/A6
Genç, Turk. 148/E2
Gendringen, Neth. 108/D5
Gendt, Neth. 108/C5
Genemuiden, Neth. 108/D3
General Abelardo L. Rodriguez (int'l arpt.), Mex. 200/A1
General Acha, Arg. 216/D3
General Alfredo Vasquez Cobo (int'l arpt.), Col. 214/D2
General Alvear, Arg. 216/D2
General Alvear, Arg. 216/E3
General Arenales, Arg. 216/E2

General Belgrano, Arg. 216/F2
General Belgrano II, Arg., Ant. 218/X
General Cabrera, Arg. 216/E2
General Carrera (lake), Chile 215/B6
General Cepeda, Mex. 201/E3
General Conesa, Arg. 216/D4
General Deheza, Arg. 216/E2
General Edward Lawrence Logan (Logan Int'l) (int'l arpt.), Ma, US 189/G3
General Enrique Godoy, Arg. 216/D3
General Francisco Villa, Mex. 201/F3
General Galarza, Arg. 217/J10
General Grant Nat'l Mem., NY, US 197/K8
General Juan Álvarez, PN, Mex. 201/F5
General Juan José Ríos, Mex. 200/C3
General Juan Madariaga, Arg. 217/F3
General La Madrid, Arg. 216/E3
General Lagos, Chile 214/D5
General Las Heras, Arg. 217/J11
General Lavalle, Arg. 217/K12
General Martín Miguel de Güemes, Arg. 215/C1
General Pico, Arg. 216/E2
General Pinedo, Arg. 215/D2
General Pinto, Arg. 216/E2
General Roca, Arg. 216/D3
General San Martín, Arg. 216/E3
General San Martín, Arg. 217/J11
General San Martín, Arg., Ant. 218/V
General Santiago Marino (int'l arpt.),Ven. 211/F2
General Terán, Mex. 201/F3
General-Toshevo, Bul. 107/J4
General Viamonte, Arg. 216/E2
General Villalobas (int'l arpt.), Mex. 200/D2
General Villegas, Arg. 216/E2
General Zaragoza, Mex. 201/F4
Generoso (peak), Swi. 115/F6
Genesee (co.), Mi, US 193/E6
Genesee (riv.), NY, US 188/E3
Genesee, Wi, US 193/P14
Genesee Depot, Wi, US 193/P14
Geneseo, Il, US 185/L5
Geneseo, NY, US 188/E3
Geneva (Léman) (lake), Fr. 101/G3
Geneva (Genève), Swi. 101/G3
Geneva (int'l arpt.), Swi. 114/C5
Geneva, Al, US 191/G4
Geneva, Ne, US 187/H2
Geneva, NY, US 188/E3
Geneva, Ut, US 195/K13
Genève (canton), Swi. 114/C5
Genève, Swi. 114/C5
Gengenbach, Ger. 114/E1
Génicourt, Fr. 88/J4
Genk, Belg. 111/E2
Genlis, Fr. 114/B3
Gennach (riv.), Ger. 115/G2
Gennargentu (mts.), It. 104/A2
Gennep, Neth. 108/C5
Gennevilliers, Fr. 88/J5
Genoa (Genova), It. 101/H4
Genoa City, Wi, US 193/P14
Genova (prov.), It. 116/C4
Genova (Genoa), It. 116/B4
Genova, Golfo di (gulf), It. 101/H4
Genovesa (isl.), Ecu. 214/F6
Gensingen, Ger. 111/G4
Gent-Brugge Kanaal (canal), Belg. 110/C1
Gent (Ghent), Belg. 110/C1
Genteng (cape), Indo. 138/C5
Genteng, Indo. 138/D5
Geographe (bay), Austl. 170/B5
Geographe (chan.), Austl. 170/B3
Georg von Neumayer, Ger., Ant. 218/Z
George (lake), Austl. 171/D2
George (pt.), Austl. 172/C3
George (riv.), Qu, Can. 181/K3
George, SAfr. 164/C4
George (lake), Ugan. 162/A3
George (lake), Fl, US 191/H4
George Land (isl.), Rus. 122/E2
George Town, Austl. 173/C4
George Town (cap.), Cay. 203/F2
George Town, Malay. 138/B2
George V (coast), Ant. 218/L
George Washington Birthplace Nat'l Mon., Va, US 191/J2
George West, Tx, US 190/D4
Georgensmünd, Ger. 112/E4
Georges (riv.), Austl. 172/G9
Georgetown, Austl. 172/A2
Georgetown, Gam. 160/B3
Georgetown (cap.), Guy. 211/G3
Georgetown, StV. 199/N9
Georgetown, Ct, US 197/E1
Georgetown, Ga, US 191/H4
Georgetown, Ky, US 188/C4
Georgetown, SC, US 191/J3
Georgetown, Tx, US 187/H5
Georgi Traykov, Bul. 107/H4
Georgia (ctry.) 121/G4
Georgia, Strait of (str.), BC, Can. 184/B3
Georgia (state), US 191/G3
Georgian (bay), On, Can. 181/H4
Georgian Bay Islands NP, On, Can. 188/D2
Georgina (riv.), Austl. 167/C3
Georgsmarienhütte, Ger. 109/F4
Gepatsch (lake), Aus. 115/G4
Gera, Ger. 98/G3
Geraardsbergen, Belg. 110/C2
Geral de Goiás, Serra (mts.), Braz. 209/J6
Geral, Serra (mts.), Braz. 215/F2
Geraldine, NZ 159/S11
Geraldton, Austl. 170/B4
Gérardmer, Fr. 114/C1
Gerasdorf bei Wien, Aus. 107/N7
Gerbéviller, Fr. 114/C1
Gerbier de Jonc (peak), Fr. 100/F4
Gerbrunn, Ger. 112/C3
Gerdau (riv.), Ger. 109/H3
Gerdine (mt.), Ak, US 192/H3
Gerede, Turk. 107/L5
Geretsried, Ger. 115/H2
Gérgal, Sp. 102/D4
Gerger, Turk. 148/D2
Gerlach, Nv, US 184/D5
Gerlachovský Štít (peak), Slvk. 99/L4
Gerlafingen, Swi. 114/D3
Germantown, Tn, US 187/K4
Germantown, Md, US 196/A5
Germany (ctry.) 98/E3
Germering, Ger. 113/E6
Germersheim, Ger. 112/B4
Germigny-l'Evêque, Fr. 88/L5
Germinaga, It. 115/E6
Germiston, SAfr. 164/E2
Gernsbach, Ger. 112/B5
Geroldsgrün, Ger. 113/E2
Gerolsbach, Ger. 113/E5
Gerolstein, Ger. 111/F3
Gerolzhofen, Ger. 112/D3
Gerpinnes, Belg. 111/D3
Gerra (Verzasca), Swi. 115/E5
Gerringong, Austl. 173/D2
Gers (riv.), Fr. 100/D5
Gersau, Swi. 115/E4
Gersfeld, Ger. 112/C2
Gersheim, Ger. 111/G5
Gerspenz (riv.), Ger. 112/B3
Gerstetten, Ger. 112/E5
Gerstheim, Fr. 114/D1
Gersthofen, Ger. 112/D6
Gerstungen, Ger. 109/H7
Gêrzê, China 128/D5
Gerze, Turk. 120/E4
Gescher, Ger. 108/E5
Geseke, Ger. 109/F5
Gespunsart, Fr. 111/D4
Gessertshausen, Ger. 112/D6
Gestro Wenz (riv.), Eth. 155/P6
Gesves, Belg. 111/E3
Geta, Fin. 97/H1
Getafe, Sp. 103/N9
Gete (riv.), Belg. 111/E2
Getinge, Swe. 96/E3
Gettorf, Ger. 96/C4
Gettysburg, SD, US 185/J4
Gettysburg, Pa, US 188/E4
Gettysburg Nat'l Mil. Park, Pa, US 196/A4
Getúlio Vargas, Braz. 213/A3
Geul (riv.), Neth. 111/E2
Geureudong (peak), Indo. 138/A3
Geurie, Austl. 173/D2
Gevaş, Turk. 148/E2
Gevelsberg, Ger. 109/E6
Gevgelija, FYROM 105/H2
Gex, Fr. 114/C5
Geyer, Ger. 113/F1
Geyersberg (peak), Ger. 112/C3
Geyikli, Turk. 105/K3
Geyser (reef), Madg. 165/H6
Geyve, Turk. 107/K5
Gez (riv.), China 145/F5
Ghadāmis, Libya 157/H3
Ghaggar (riv.), India 144/C5
Ghaghara (riv.), India 142/C2
Ghakhar, Pak. 144/C3
Ghana (ctry.) 161/E4
Ghanzi, Bots. 163/D5
Gharaunda, India 144/D5
Ghardaïa, Alg. 157/F2
Ghardaïa (prov.), Alg. 157/F3
Ghardimaou, Tun. 158/L6
Gharghoda, India 142/D4
Gharyān, Libya 154/H1
Ghāt, Libya 157/H4
Ghātāl, India 143/F4
Ghātampur, India 142/C2
Ghātsīla, India 143/F4
Ghazal, Bahr el (riv.), Chad 154/J5
Ghazaouet, Alg. 158/D2
Ghāzīpur, India 142/D3
Ghaznī, Afg. 147/J2
Ghedi, It. 116/D2
Gheens, La, US 195/P17
Ghemme, It. 116/B1
Ghenghis Khan, Wall of, Mong. 129/K2
Gheorghe Gheorghiu-Dej, Rom. 107/H2
Gheorgheni, Rom. 107/G2
Gherla, Rom. 107/F2
Ghilarza, It. 104/A2
Ghinda (Gĭnda), Erit. 146/C5
Ghio (lake), Arg. 216/C5
Ghirārah (gulf), Tun. 157/H2
Ghisalba, It. 116/C1
Ghisonaccia, Fr. 104/A1
Ghotki, Pak. 140/A2
Ghugri (riv.), India 143/F3
Ghūriān, Afg. 147/H2
Ghuzayyil, Bi'r al (well), Libya 154/H2
Giannutri (isl.), It. 104/B1
Giant's Castle (peak), SAfr. 164/E3
Giant's Causeway, NI, UK 92/B1
Giant Sequoia Nat'l Mon., Ca, US 186/C4
Giarre, It. 104/D4
Gibbons, Ab, Can. 184/E2
Gibbstown, NJ, US 196/C4
Gibloux (peak), Swi. 114/D4
Gibraleón, Sp. 102/B4
Gibraltar (pt.), Eng, UK 93/J5
Gibraltar (cap.), Gib. 102/C4
Gibraltar (str.), Mor.,Sp. 102/B5
Gibraltar (res.), Ca, US 194/A1
Gibraltar, Mi, US 193/F7
Gibraltar, Ven. 199/G6
Gibraltar Range NP, Austl. 173/E1
Gibson (des.), Austl. 167/B3
Gibson Desert Nature Reserve, Austl. 170/E3
Giddarbāha, India 144/C4
Giddings, Tx, US 187/H5
Giddings, Co, US 195/B1
Gidi (pass), Egypt 149/C4
Giebelstadt, Ger. 112/C3
Gieboldehausen, Ger. 109/H5
Gien, Fr. 100/E3
Giengen an der Brenz, Ger. 112/D5
Gier (riv.), Fr. 100/F4
Giessbachfälle (falls), Swi. 114/E4
Giessen (riv.), Fr.,Ger. 114/D1
Giessen, Ger. 112/B1
Giessendam, Neth. 108/B5
Gieten, Neth. 108/D2
Gif-sur-Yvette, Fr. 88/J5
Gīfān, Iran 121/L5
Gifford, Fl, US 191/H5
Gifford (riv.), Nun., Can. 181/H1
Giffre (riv.), Fr. 114/C5
Gifhorn, Ger. 109/H4
Gifu, Japan 135/L5
Giganta, Sierra de la (mts.), Mex. 200/C3
Gigante, Col. 210/C4
Giglio (isl.), It. 104/B1
Gijón, Sp. 102/C1
Gil de Vilches, PN, Chile 216/C2
Gila (riv.), Az, US 186/D4
Gila Bend, Az, US 186/D4
Gila Cliff Dwellings Nat'l Mon., NM, US 186/E4
Gila River Ind. Res., Az, US 195/R19
Gilbert, Mn, US 188/A2
Gilbert (riv.), Austl. 167/D2
Gilbert, Az, US 195/S19
Gilbert (isls.), Kiri. 174/G5
Gilberts, Il, US 193/P15
Gilbués, Braz. 212/A3
Gilching, Ger. 112/E6
Gilcrest, Co, US 195/C2
Gilford, NI, UK 92/B3
Gilford Park, NJ, US 196/D4
Gilgandra, Austl. 173/D1
Gilgil, Kenya 162/C3
Gilgit (riv.), Pak. 145/F5
Gilles (lake), Austl. 171/H5
Gillette, Wy, US 185/G4
Gillies Bay, BC, Can. 184/B3
Gillingham, Eng, UK 91/G4
Gillot (int'l arpt.), Reun., Fr. 165/S15
Gilly, Swi. 114/C5
Gilman Hot Springs, Ca, US 194/D3
Gilmer, Tx, US 187/J4
Gilpin, Co, US 195/A3
Gilgit (riv.), Pak. 147/K1
Gilze, Neth. 108/B5
Gīmbī, Eth. 155/N6
Gimbsheim, Ger. 112/B3
Gimel, Swi. 114/C4
Gimie (mt.), StL. 199/N9
Gimli, Mb, Can. 185/J3
Gimo, Swe. 96/H1
Gin Gin, Austl. 172/C4
Ginan, Japan 135/L5
Gingelom, Belg. 111/E2
Gingin, Austl. 170/B4
Gingindlovu, SAfr. 165/E3
Gingoog, Phil. 137/E6
Gingst, Ger. 96/E4
Ginosa, It. 104/E2
Ginowan, Japan 133/J7
Gioia (gulf), It. 104/D3
Gioia del Colle, It. 104/E2
Gioia Tauro, It. 104/D3
Giornico, Swi. 115/E5
Gioŭra (isl.), Gre. 105/J3
Gioveretto (peak), It. 115/G5
Giovi (peak), It. 117/E5
Gipping (riv.), Eng, UK 91/G2
Girardot, Col. 208/D3
Girardville, Pa, US 196/B2
Giraumont, Fr. 111/E5
Girdle Ness (pt.), Sc, UK 94/D2
Giresun (prov.), Turk. 148/D1
Giresun, Turk. 148/D1
Girgnasco, It. 116/B1
Girīdīh, India 143/F3
Girifalco, It. 104/E3
Girling (res.), Eng, UK 88/C2
Giromagny, Fr. 114/C2
Girón, Ecu. 210/B5
Girón, Col. 210/C3
Girona, Sp. 103/G2
Gironcourt-sur-Vraine, Fr. 114/B1
Gironde (riv.), Fr. 100/C4
Gironella, Sp. 103/F1
Girraween NP, Austl. 173/D1
Giru, Austl. 172/B2
Girvan, Sc, UK 92/D1
Gisborne, NZ 159/T10
Gisenyi, Rwa. 162/A3
Gislaved, Swe. 96/E3
Gisors, Fr. 110/A5
Gistel, Belg. 110/B1
Gistrup, Den. 96/D3
Gitega, Buru. 162/A3
Gittsfjället (peak), Swe. 95/E2
Giubiasco, Swi. 115/F5
Giugliano in Campania, It. 106/B5
Giulianova, It. 101/K5
Giurgiu (prov.), Rom. 107/G3
Giurgiu, Rom. 107/G4
Giussano, It. 116/C1
Giv'at Brenner, Isr. 149/F8
Giv'at Hayyim, Isr. 149/F7
Giv'atayim, Isr. 149/F7
Give, Den. 96/C4
Givet, Fr. 111/D3
Givors, Fr. 100/F4
Givrine, Col de la (pass), Swi. 114/C5
Giyani, SAfr. 163/F5
Gizhiga (bay), Rus. 123/R3
Gizo, Sol. 174/E5
Giżycko, Pol. 97/J4
Gjerdrum, Nor. 96/D1
Gjerlev, Den. 96/D3
Gjerstad, Nor. 96/C2
Gjirokastër, Alb. 105/G2
Gjoa Haven, Nun., Can. 180/G2
Gjøvik, Nor. 96/D1
Glabbeek, Belg. 111/E2
Glace Bay, NS, Can. 189/K2
Glacier (peak), Wa, US 184/C3
Glacier Bay NP and Prsv., Ak, US 192/L4
Glacier NP, BC, Can. 184/D3
Gladbeck, Ger. 108/D5
Gladewater, Tx, US 187/J4
Gladstone, Mo, US 195/D5
Gladstone, Austl. 172/C3
Gladstone, Austl. 171/H5
Gladwin, Mi, US 188/C3
Glafsfjorden (lake), Swe. 96/D2
Glåma (riv.), Nor. 95/D3
Glamis, Sc, UK 94/D3
Glamsbjerg, Den. 96/D4
Glan, Phil. 137/E6
Glan (riv.), Ger. 98/D4
Glanamman, Wal, UK 90/C3
Gland, Swi. 114/C5
Gland (riv.), Fr. 111/D4
Glandorf, Ger. 109/F4
Glärnisch (range), Swi. 115/E3
Glarus, Swi. 115/E3
Glarus (canton), Swi. 115/E4
Glarus Alps (range), Swi. 101/H3
Glas Maol (peak), Sc, UK 94/C3
Glasgow, Mt, US 184/G3
Glasgow, Ky, US 188/C4
Glasgow, De, US 196/C4
Glasgow, Sc, UK 94/B5
Glashütten, Ger. 112/B2
Glaslyn (riv.), Wal, UK 92/D6
Glass (mts.), Ok, US 190/D2
Glass (lake), Sc, UK 94/B1
Glass (riv.), Sc, UK 94/B2
Glassboro, NJ, US 196/C4
Glastonbury, Eng, UK 90/D4
Glatt (riv.), Ger. 112/B6
Glattbach, Ger. 112/C3
Glattfelden, Swi. 115/E2
Glavinitsa, Bul. 107/H4
Glazoué, Ben. 161/F5
Glazov, Rus. 119/M4
Glems (riv.), Ger. 112/C5
Glen (riv.), Eng, UK 93/H6
Glen Burnie, Md, US 196/B5
Glen Canyon (dam), Az, US 186/E3
Glen Canyon Nat'l Rec. Area, US 186/E3
Glen Carbon, Il, US 195/H8
Glen Coe (pass), Sc, UK 94/B3
Glen Cove, NY, US 197/L8
Glen Gardner, NJ, US 196/D2
Glen Haven, Co, US 195/B2
Glen Innes, Austl. 173/D1
Glen Lyon, Pa, US 196/B1
Glen Mòr (valley), Sc, UK 94/B2
Glen Park, Mo, US 195/G9
Glen Ridge, NJ, US 197/J8
Glen Rock, Pa, US 196/B4
Glen Rock, NJ, US 197/J8
Glen Ullin, ND, US 185/H4
Glenaire, Mo, US 195/E5
Glenan, Iles de (isls.), Fr. 100/A3
Glenarm, NI, UK 92/C2
Glenarm (riv.), NI, UK 92/C2
Glenavy, NI, UK 92/B2
Glenbawn (dam), Austl. 173/D2
Glenboro, Mb, Can. 185/J3
Glencoe, SAfr. 165/E3
Glencoe, Mo, US 195/F8
Glencoe, Il, US 193/Q15
Glencoe, Sc, UK 94/A3
Glendale, Or, US 184/C5
Glendale, Az, US 195/R18
Glendale, Ca, US 194/F7
Glendale Heights, Il, US 193/P16
Glenden, Austl. 172/C3
Glendive, Mt, US 185/G4
Glendo (res.), Wy, US 185/G5
Glendora, Ca, US 194/C2
Glendun (riv.), NI, UK 92/B1
Glenealy, Ire. 92/B6
Glenelg (riv.), Austl. 173/B3
Glenelg, Md, US 196/B5
Glenelg, Sc, UK 89/R8
Glenelly (riv.), NI, UK 92/A2
Glengarry (range), Austl. 170/C3
Glenluce, Sc, UK 92/D2
Glenmere (lake), NY, US 196/D1
Glennallen, Ak, US 192/J3
Glenolden, Pa, US 196/C4
Glenorie, Austl. 172/H8
Glenpool, Ok, US 187/H4
Glenrothes, Sc, UK 94/C4
Glens Falls, NY, US 188/F3
Glenshane (pass), NI, UK 92/B2
Glenside, Pa, US 196/C3
Glenties, Ire. 89/P9
Glenveagh NP, Ire. 89/Q9
Glenview, Il, US 193/Q15
Glenwood, NJ, US 196/D1
Glenwood Springs, Co, US 186/F3
Gleouraich (peak), Sc, UK 94/A2
Glifádha, Gre. 105/N9
Glimåkra, Swe. 96/F3
Glina, Cro. 106/C3
Glinde, Ger. 109/H1
Glindow, Ger. 98/P7
Gliwice, Pol. 99/K3
Globe, Az, US 186/E4
Glockturm (peak), Aus. 115/G4
Gloggnitz, Aus. 99/H5
Głogów, Pol. 99/J3
Głogówek, Pol. 99/J3
Glonn (riv.), Ger. 112/E6
Gloria (bay), Cuba 203/G1
Glorieuses, Iles (isls.), Reun., Fr. 165/H5
Glorious (mt.), Austl. 172/E6
Glory of Russia (cape), Ak, US 192/D3
Glossop, Eng, UK 93/G5
Gloster, Ms, US 187/K5
Gloucester, Austl. 173/D1
Gloucester, On, Can. 188/F2
Gloucester, Eng, UK 90/D3
Gloucester (co.), NJ, US 196/C4
Gloucester City, NJ, US 196/C4
Gloucestershire (co.), Eng, UK 90/D3
Glovers (reef), Belz. 202/E2
Glovertown, Nf, Can. 189/L1
Głowno, Pol. 99/K3
Głubczyce, Pol. 99/J3
Głuchołazy, Pol. 99/J3
Glücksburg, Ger. 96/C4
Glückstadt, Ger. 109/G1
Glyndon, Md, US 196/B5
Glyngøre, Den. 96/C3
Glynn, NI, UK 92/C2
Gmünd, Aus. 99/H4
Gmunden, Aus. 113/G7
Gnagna (prov.), Burk. 161/E3
Gnarrenburg, Ger. 109/G2
Gniew, Pol. 97/H5
Gniezno, Pol. 99/J2
Gnjilane, Kos. 106/E4
Gnowangerup, Austl. 170/C5
Gō (riv.), Japan 132/C3
Go Cong, Viet. 136/D4
Goa (state), India 140/B4
Goālpāra, India 143/H2
Goat Fell (peak), Sc, UK 94/A5
Goba, Eth. 155/N6
Gobabis, Namb. 163/C5
Gobardānga, India 143/G4
Gobernador Castro, Arg. 216/F2
Gobernador Costa, Arg. 216/C5
Gobernador Gregores, Arg. 217/C6
Gobernador Mansilla, Arg. 217/J10
Gobi (des.), China,Mong. 128/H4
Göblberg (peak), Aus. 113/G6
Gobō, Japan 132/D4
Goch, Ger. 108/D5
Gochsheim, Ger. 112/D2
Godalming, Eng, UK 91/F4
Godāvari (riv.), India 140/C4
Goddā, India 143/F3
Godeanu (peak), Rom. 106/F3
Godech, Bul. 105/H1
Goderich, On, Can. 188/D3
Godfrey, Il, US 195/G8
Gōdo, Japan 135/L5
Gödöllő, Hun. 99/K5
Godoy Cruz, Arg. 216/C2
Gods (riv.), Mb, Can. 180/G3
Gods (lake), Mb, Can. 180/G3
Gods Mercy (bay), Nun., Can. 181/H2
Godthåb (Nuuk), Grld. 177/M3
Godwin Austen (K2) (peak), Pak. 144/D2
Goéland (lake), Qu, Can. 188/E1
Goeree (isl.), Neth. 108/A5
Goes, Neth. 108/A5
Gogebic (range), Mi, US 185/L4
Göggingen, Ger. 112/D6
Gogland (isl.), Rus. 97/M1
Gogōme, Japan 134/B4
Gogounou, Ben. 161/F4
Gogra (riv.), India 140/D2
Gohad, India 142/B2
Gohāna, India 144/D5
Gohbach (riv.), Ger. 109/G3
Goiana, Braz. 212/D2
Goiandira, Braz. 213/B1
Goiânia, Braz. 209/J7
Goianinha, Braz. 212/D2
Goiás, Braz. 209/H7
Goiás (state), Braz. 212/A5
Goiatuba, Braz. 213/B1
Goil (lake), Sc, UK 94/B4
Goirle, Neth. 108/C5
Góis, Port. 102/A2
Goito, It. 117/D2
Gojō, Japan 132/D3
Gojra, Pak. 144/B4
Gok (riv.), Turk. 120/E4
Goka, Japan 135/D1
Gokase (riv.), Japan 132/B4
Gokashō, Japan 135/K5
Gokasho (bay), Japan 135/L7
Gökçeada (isl.), Turk. 148/A1
Gökçebey, Turk. 107/L5
Gökçekaya (dam), Turk. 148/B1
Göksu (riv.), Turk. 148/D2
Göksun, Turk. 148/D2
Göktepe, Turk. 149/C1
Gol, Nor. 96/C1
Gola Gokarannāth, India 142/C1
Golan Hts. (reg.), Syria 149/D3
Golasecca, It. 116/B1
Gölbaşı, Turk. 148/D2
Golbey, Fr. 114/C1
Golborne, Eng, UK 93/F5
Gölcük, Turk. 107/J5
Gold (coast), Gha. 154/E7
Gold (mtn.), Wa, US 193/B2
Gold Bar, Wa, US 193/D2
Gold Beach, Or, US 184/B5
Gold Coast, Austl. 172/D5
Gold Hill, Co, US 195/B2
Gold River, BC, Can. 184/B3
Goldach, Swi. 115/F3
Gołdap, Pol. 97/K4
Goldbach, Ger. 112/C3
Goldberg, Ger. 96/E5
Golden, BC, Can. 184/D3
Golden, Co, US 195/B3
Golden Eagle, Il, US 195/F8
Golden Gate (chan.), Ca, US 193/J11
Golden Gate Highlands NP, SAfr. 164/D3
Golden Hinde (peak), BC, Can. 184/B3
Golden Temple, India 144/C4
Goldendale, Wa, US 184/C4
Goldene Aue (reg.), Ger. 98/F3
Goldenstedt, Ger. 109/F3
Goldkronach, Ger. 113/E2
Goldman, Mo, US 195/F9
Goldmine (mtn.), Az, US 195/S19
Goldsboro, NC, US 191/J3
Goldsboro, Md, US 196/C5
Goldsby, Ok, US 195/N15
Goldsworthy, Austl. 170/C2
Goldthwaite, Tx, US 190/D4
Göle, Turk. 148/E1
Goleniów, Pol. 96/F5
Golfito NWR, CR 203/F4
Golfo Aranci, It. 104/A2
Golfo de Santa Clara, Mex. 200/B2
Gölhisar, Turk. 149/A1
Goliad, Tx, US 187/H5
Gölköy, Turk. 148/D1
Gollach (riv.), Ger. 112/D3
Göllheim, Ger. 112/B3
Gölmarmara, Turk. 148/A2
Golmud, China 128/F4
Golovin, Ak, US 192/F3
Golovnina (peak), Rus. 134/D2
Golpāyegān, Iran 146/F2
Gölpazarı, Turk. 107/K5
Gols, Aus. 101/M3
Golts, Md, US 196/C5
Golub-Dobrzyń, Pol. 99/K2
Golubovci (int'l arpt.), Mont. 106/D4
Golyam Perelik (peak), Bul. 105/J2
Golyama Kamchiya (riv.), Bul. 107/H4
Golyama Syutkya (peak), Bul. 105/J2
Goma, D.R. Congo 162/A3
Goma (int'l arpt.), D.R. Congo 162/A3
Gomaringen, Ger. 112/C6
Gomati (riv.), India 142/C2
Gombe (state), Nga. 161/H4
Gombe (riv.), Tanz. 162/A4
Gombe NP, Tanz. 162/A4
Gomera (isl.), Canl., Sp. 156/A4
Gómez Farías, Mex. 200/D2
Gómez Palacio, Mex. 200/E3
Gomīshān, Iran 146/F1
Gommern, Ger. 98/F2
Gomoh, India 143/F4
Goms (valley), Swi. 114/E5
Gonābād, Iran 147/G2
Gonaïves, Haiti 203/H2
Gonarezhou NP, Zim. 163/F5
Gonâve (gulf), Haiti 199/G4
Gonâve (isl.), Haiti 203/H2
Gonbad-e Qābūs, Iran 147/G1
Gonbadlī, Iran 145/D5
Gönc, Hun. 99/L4
Gonçalves Dias, Braz. 212/A2
Gondelsheim, Ger. 112/B4
Gonder, Eth. 155/N5
Gondia, India 140/D3
Gondomar, Sp. 102/A1
Gondomar, Port. 102/A2
Gondrecourt-le-Château, Fr. 114/B1
Gondreville, Fr. 111/E6
Gondrexange (lake), Fr. 111/F6
Gönen, Turk. 107/H5
Gonesse, Fr. 88/K5
Gong Xian, China 141/H2
Gong Xian, China 130/C4
Gong'an, China 141/K3
Gongbo'gyamda, China 141/F2
Gongcheng, China 137/B3
Gongga (peak), China 141/H2
Gonggar, China 143/H1
Gonghe, China 128/H4
Gongliu, China 128/D3
Gongola (riv.), Nga. 154/H5
Gongshan Drungzu Nuzu Zizhixian, China 141/G2
Gongzhuling, China 130/F2
Goñi, Uru. 217/K10
Gonjo, China 128/G5
Gónnoi, Gre. 105/H3
Gonohe, Japan 134/B3
Gonubie, SAfr. 164/D4
Gönyű, Hun. 106/C2
Gonzaga, It. 117/D3
Gonzales, Tx, US 187/H5
González, Mex. 201/F4
Good Hope, La, US 195/P17
Good Hope, Cape of (cape), SAfr. 164/L11
Goodenough (cape), Ant. 218/J
Goodnews Bay, Ak, US 192/F4
Goodooga, Austl. 173/C1
Goodrich, Mi, US 193/F6
Goodwick, Wal, UK 90/B2
Goodwood, SAfr. 164/L10
Goodyear, Az, US 195/R19
Gooimeer (lake), Neth. 108/C4
Goole, Eng, UK 93/H4
Goolgowi, Austl. 173/C2
Gooloogong, Austl. 173/D2
Goolwa, Austl. 171/H5
Goomalling, Austl. 170/C4
Goombungee, Austl. 172/C4
Goondiwindi, Austl. 172/C5
Goongarrie NP, Austl. 170/D4
Goor, Neth. 108/D4
Goose (lake), Mb, Can. 185/H2
Goose (lake), Ca,Or, US 184/C5
Goose (pt.), De, US 196/C5
Goose (pt.), La, US 195/Q16
Gopālganj, India 143/E2
Gopālpur, Bang. 143/G3
Gopat (riv.), India 142/D3
Göppingen, Ger. 112/C5
Góra, Pol. 99/J3
Góra Kalwaria, Pol. 99/L3
Goražde, Bosn. 106/D4
Gorczański NP, Pol. 99/L4
Gorda (pt.), Cuba 203/F1
Gorda (pt.), Nic. 203/F3
Gorda (pt.), Nic. 203/F4
Gordevio, Swi. 115/E5
Gørding, Den. 96/C4
Gordola, Swi. 115/E5
Gordon, Austl. 173/C4
Gordon (lake), Austl. 167/D5
Gordonsbaai, SAfr. 164/L11
Gordonvale, Austl. 172/B2
Gore (pt.), Ak, US 192/H4
Goré, Chad 154/J6
Gorē, Eth. 155/N6
Gore, NZ 159/R12
Gorebridge, Sc, UK 94/C5
Görele, Turk. 148/D1
Goresbridge, Ire. 89/Q10
Gorey, Chl, UK 100/B2
Gorey, Ire. 89/Q10
Gorgān, Iran 147/F1
Gorge du Loup, Lux. 111/F4
Gorges du Ziz, Mor. 156/D2
Gorgol (pol. reg.), Mrta. 160/B3
Gorgol (riv.), Mrta. 160/B2
Gorgona, Isola di (isl.), It. 116/C6
Gorgonzola, It. 116/C1
Gori, Geo. 121/H4
Gorinchem, Neth. 108/B5
Gorizia, It. 117/G1
Gorizia (prov.), It. 117/G1
Gorj (prov.), Rom. 107/F3
Gorki, Bela. 120/D1
Gor'kiy (res.), Rus. 118/J4
Gorlice, Pol. 99/L4
Görlitz, Ger. 99/H3
Gorllwyn (peak), Wal, UK 90/C2
Gorman, Tx, US 187/H4
Gormanstown, Ire. 92/B4
Gormī, India 142/B2
Gorner (glacier), Swi. 114/D6
Gornji Milanovac, Serb. 106/E3
Gornji Vakuf, Bosn. 106/C4
Gorno-Altay Aut. Rep., Rus. 122/J4
Goro, It. 117/F3
Gorodets, Rus. 119/J4
Gorom Gorom, Burk. 161/E3
Gorong (isl.), Indo. 139/H4
Gorongoza, Moz. 163/F4
Gorontalo, Indo. 139/F3
Gorssel, Neth. 108/D4
Gorst, Wa, US 193/B2
Gortin, NI, UK 92/A2
Görwihl, Ger. 114/E2
Goryn' (riv.), Ukr. 120/C2
Gorzano (peak), It. 101/K5
Gorzów Wielkopolski, Pol. 99/H2
Gosainganj, India 142/D2
Göschenen, Swi. 115/E4
Gōse, Japan 135/J7
Gosen, Japan 133/F2
Gosford, Austl. 173/D2
Gosforth, Eng, UK 93/G2
Goshen, NJ, US 196/D5
Goshogawara, Japan 134/B3
Goslar, Ger. 109/H5
Gospić, Cro. 106/B3
Gosport, Eng, UK 91/E5
Gossas, Sen. 160/A3
Gossau, Swi. 115/F3
Gossersweiler-Stein, Ger. 111/G5
Gostivar, FYROM 105/G2
Gostyń, Pol. 99/J3
Gostynin, Pol. 99/K2
Göta (riv.), Swe. 96/G2

Götal – Guada

Götaland (reg.), Swe. 96/E3
Göteborg, Swe. 96/D3
Göteborg Och Bohus (co.), Swe. 95/D4
Gotel (mts.), Nga. 154/H6
Gotemba, Japan 133/F3
Götene, Swe. 96/E2
Gotha, Ger. 109/H7
Gotland (co.), Swe. 95/F4
Gotland (isl.), Swe. 95/F4
Gotse Delchev, Bul. 105/H2
Gotska Sandön (isl.), Swe. 97/H2
Gotska Sandön NP, Swe. 97/H2
Gōtsu, Japan 132/C3
Gottenheim, Ger. 114/D1
Göttingen, Ger. 109/G5
Gottmadingen, Ger. 115/E2
Gottolengo, It. 116/D2
Götzis, Aus. 115/F3
Gouda, Neth. 108/B4
Gouda, SAfr. 164/L10
Gough (isl.), StH 80/J7
Gouin (res.), Qu, Can. 181/J4
Goulais (riv.), On, Can. 188/C2
Goulburn (riv.), Austl. 173/D2
Goulburn, Austl. 173/D2
Goulburn (isls.), Austl. 167/C2
Gould, Ar, US 190/F3
Gould (mt.), Austl. 170/C3
Gouldsboro, Pa, US 196/C1
Goulimine, Mor. 156/C3
Goulmima, Mor. 156/D3
Goundam, Mali 160/E2
Goupillières, Fr. 88/H5
Gourdon, Fr. 100/D4
Gouré, Niger 161/H3
Gourin, Fr. 100/B2
Gourits (riv.), SAfr. 164/C4
Gourma (phys. reg.), Burk. 161/F3
Gourma (prov.), Burk. 161/F3
Gourma Rharous, Mali 161/E2
Gournay-en-Bray, Fr. 110/A5
Gourock, Sc, UK 94/B5
Goussainville, Fr. 88/K4
Gouvêa, Braz. 213/D1
Gouveia, Port. 102/B2
Gouvieux, Fr. 88/K4
Gouvy, Belg. 111/E3
Gouyave, Gren. 199/N9
Govardhan, India 142/A2
Goverla (peak), Ukr. 107/G1
Governador Archer, Braz. 212/A2
Governador Dix-Sept Rosado, Braz. 212/C2
Governador Eugênio Barros, Braz. 212/A2
Governador Valadares, Braz. 213/D1
Governor Generoso, Phil. 137/E6
Governors (isl.), NY, US 197/J9
Govi-Altay (prov.), Mong. 128/F2
Govĭ Altayn (mts.), Mong. 128/G3
Govind Sāgar (res.), India 144/D4
Govindgarh, India 142/C3
Gower (pen.), Wal, UK 90/B3
Goya, Arg. 215/E2
Goyllarisquizga, Peru 214/B3
Göynük, Turk. 107/K5
Goyt (riv.), Eng, UK 93/F5
Gozaisho-yama (peak), Japan 135/K5
Gözeli, Turk. 148/D2
Gozo (isl.), Malta 104/D4
Gozzano, It. 116/B1
Graaff-Reinet, SAfr. 164/D4
Graafschap (phys. reg.), Neth. 108/D4
Graben, Ger. 115/G1
Graberberg (peak), Namb. 164/B2
Grabouw, SAfr. 164/L11
Grabow, Ger. 98/F2
Graça Aranha, Braz. 212/A2
Gračac, Cro. 106/B3
Gračanica, Bosn. 106/D3
Gracemere, Austl. 172/C3
Graceville, Fl, US 191/G4
Grächen, Swi. 114/D5
Gracias, Hon. 202/D3
Gracias a Dios (cape), Hon. 203/F3
Graciosa (isl.), Azor., Port. 103/S12
Grad Sofiya (prov.), Bul. 105/H1
Gradačac, Bosn. 106/D3
Gradisca d'Isonzo, It. 117/G1
Grado, It. 117/G1
Grado, Sp. 102/B1
Grady (co.), Ok, US 195/M15
Gräfelfing, Ger. 113/E6
Grafenau, Ger. 113/G5
Gräfenberg, Ger. 112/E3
Grafenrheinfeld, Ger. 112/D3
Gräfentonna, Ger. 109/H6
Grafenwöhr, Ger. 113/E3
Graffignana, It. 116/C2
Grafing bei München, Ger. 113/E6
Gråfjell (peak), Nor. 96/C1
Grafrath, Ger. 115/H1
Grafton, Austl. 173/E1
Grafton, ND, US 185/J3
Grafton, WV, US 188/D4
Grafton, Il, US 195/G8
Grafton Passage, Austl. 172/B2
Graham, Tx, US 187/H4
Graham (isl.), Nun., Can. 181/S7
Graham (isl.), BC, Can. 180/C3
Graham Bell (isl.), Rus. 122/G1
Graham Land (phys. reg.), Ant. 218/V
Grahamstown, SAfr. 164/D4
Graian Alps (range), It. 101/G4
Grain (coast), Libr. 154/D6
Grain Valley, Mo, US 195/E5
Grainau, Ger. 115/H3
Grajaú (riv.), Braz. 209/J5
Grajaú, Braz. 212/A2
Grajewo, Pol. 97/K5
Gram, Den. 96/C4
Gramada, Bul. 106/F4
Gramastetten, Aus. 113/H6
Gramat, Fr. 100/D4
Gramat, Causse de (plat.), Fr. 100/D4
Gramatneusiedl, Aus. 107/N7
Grampian (pol. reg.), Sc, UK 94/C2
Grampian (mts.), Sc, UK 94/B3
Grampians NP, Austl. 173/B3
Grampians, The (phys. reg.), Austl. 173/B3
Gramsbergen, Neth. 108/D3
Gramsh, Alb. 105/G2
Gran, Nor. 96/D1
Gran Altiplanicie Central (plat.), Arg. 215/C6
Gran Bajo de San Julián (plain),Arg. 217/C6
Gran Bajo Oriental (plain), Arg. 215/C6
Gran Canaria (isl.), Canl., Sp. 156/B4
Gran Canaria (int'l arpt.), Canl., Sp. 156/B4
Gran Chaco (plain), SAm. 205/C5
Gran Isla del Maíz (isl.), Nic. 203/F3
Gran Laguna Salada (lag.), Arg. 216/D5
Gran Paradiso, PN del, It. 101/G4
Gran Piedra (hill), Cuba 203/H2
Gran Pilastro (peak), It. 101/J3
Gran Vilaya (ruin), Peru 214/B2
Granada, Col. 210/C4
Granada, Nic. 202/E4
Granada, Sp. 102/D4
Granadilla de Abona, Canl., Sp. 156/A3
Granados, Mex. 200/C2
Granard, Ire. 89/Q10
Granarolo dell'Emilia, It. 117/E3
Granbury, Tx, US 187/H4
Grand (lake), Nf, Can. 181/L4
Grand (canal), China 130/D4
Grand (falls), Kenya 162/C3
Grand (canal), Az, US 195/R18
Grand (isl.), NY, US 185/M4
Grand (isl.), Mi, US 188/C2
Grand (riv.), Mo, US 190/E2
Grand (riv.), SD, US 185/H4
Grand Bahama (isl.), Bahm. 199/F2
Grand Bank, Nf, Can. 189/L2
Grand Bassa (co.), Libr. 160/C5
Grand-Bassam, C.d'Iv. 160/E5
Grand Bay, NB, Can. 189/H2
Grand Canal d'Alsace (canal), Fr. 114/D2
Grand Canyon, Az, US 186/D3
Grand Canyon Nat'l Park, Az, US 186/D3
Grand Canyon-Parashant Nat'l Mon., Az, US 186/D3
Grand Cape Mount (co.), Libr. 160/C5
Grand Cayman (isl.), Cay. 182/E4
Grand Centre, Ab, Can. 184/F2
Grand-Charmont, Fr. 114/C2
Grand Colombier (peak), Fr. 114/B6
Grand Combine (peak), Swi. 114/D6
Grand Coulee, Wa, US 184/D4
Grand Coulee (dam), Wa, US 184/D4
Grand Drumont (peak), Fr. 114/C2
Grand Erg de Bilma (des.), Niger 154/H4
Grand Erg Occidental (des.), Alg. 157/E3
Grand Erg Oriental (des.), Alg. 157/G3
Grand Falls, NB, Can. 189/H2
Grand Falls, Nf, Can. 189/L1
Grand Forks, ND, US 185/J4
Grand Forks, BC, Can. 184/D3
Grand-Fort-Philippe, Fr. 110/B2
Grand Gabes, Tun. 157/H2
Grand Goâve, Haiti 203/H2
Grand Haven, Mi, US 188/C3
Grand Isle, La, US 191/F4
Grand Jide (co.), Libr. 160/D5
Grand Junction, Co, US 186/E3
Grand-Iahou, C.d'Iv. 160/D5
Grand Lake o' the Cherokees (lake), Ok, US 187/J3
Grand Manan (isl.), NB, Can. 189/H2
Grand-Mère, Qu, Can. 189/F2
Grand Mont Ruan (peak), Fr. 114/C5
Grand Muveran (peak), Swi. 114/D5
Grand-Popo, Ben. 161/F5
Grand Portage Nat'l Mon., Mn, US 185/L4
Grand Rapids, Mb, Can. 185/J2
Grand Rapids, Mi, US 188/C3
Grand Rhône (riv.), Fr. 100/F5
Grand Saint-Bernard, Col du (pass), Swi. 114/D6
Grand Staircase-Escalante Nat'l Mon., Ut, US 186/E3
Grand Taureau (peak), Fr. 114/C4
Grand Teton NP, Wy, US 186/E2
Grandcour, Swi. 114/C4
Grande (bay), Arg. 217/C6
Grande (isl.), Braz. 213/C2
Grande (lake), Braz. 211/H5
Grande (riv.), Braz. 208/J7
Grande (peak), It. 104/C1
Grande (peak), It. 104/C4
Grande (pt.), Pan. 203/G4
Grande Cache, Ab, Can. 184/D2
Grande Comore (isl.), Com. 165/G5
Grande de Gurupá, Ilha (isl.), Braz. 209/H4
Grande de Manacapuru, Lago (lake), Braz. 208/F4
Grande de Matagalpa (riv.), Nic. 182/D5
Grande de Santiago (riv.), Mex. 200/D4
Grande de Tierra del Fuego (isl.), Arg.,Chile 215/C7
Grande Dixence, Barrage de la (dam), Swi. 114/D5
Grande do Curuaí (lake), Braz. 211/H5
Grande Miquelon (isl.), StP., Fr. 189/K2
Grande Prairie, Ab, Can. 184/D2
Grande Saline, Haiti 203/H2
Grande, Serra (mts.), Braz. 211/F4
Grande-Synthe, Fr. 110/B1
Grande-Terre (isl.), Guad. 199/J4
Grandes Jorasses (peak), It. 114/D6
Grandfresnoy, Fr. 110/B5
Grândola, Port. 102/A3
Grandpuits-Bailly-Carrois, Fr. 88/L6
Grandson, Swi. 114/C4
Grandview, Wa, US 184/D4
Grandview, Mb, Can. 185/H3
Grandview, Tx, US 187/H4
Grandview, Mo, US 195/D6
Grandvillars, Fr. 114/C2
Grandvilliers, Fr. 110/A4
Graneros, Chile 216/N9
Granfjället (peak), Swe. 96/E1
Grange, Mont de (peak), Fr. 114/C5
Grangemouth, Sc, UK 94/C4
Granger (mt.), Yk, Can. 192/L3
Granges-sur-Vologne, Fr. 114/C1
Grängesberg, Swe. 96/F1
Grangeville, Id, US 184/D4
Granisle, BC, Can. 184/B2
Granite (peak), Mt, US 184/F4
Granite, Ut, US 195/K12
Granite City, Il, US 195/G8
Granite Reef Aqueduct, Az, US 195/S18
Granites, The (peak), Austl. 171/F2
Granja, Braz. 212/B1
Granollers, Sp. 103/L6
Grantham, Eng, UK 93/H6
Grantown-on-Spey, Sc, UK 94/C2
Grants, NM, US 186/F4
Grants Pass, Or, US 184/C5
Granville, Fr. 100/C2
Granville (lake), Mb, Can. 180/F3
Grão Mogol, Braz. 212/B5
Grapeview, Wa, US 193/B3
Gras-Ellenbach, Ger. 112/B3
Grasberg, Ger. 109/F2
Grasbrunn, Ger. 113/E6
Grasø (isl.), Swe. 96/H1
Grasonville, Md, US 196/B6
Grass (lake), Il, US 193/P15
Grasse, Fr. 101/G5
Grassie, On, Can. 189/Q9
Grasslands NP, Sk, Can. 184/G3
Grassy, Austl. 173/C4
Grassy Park, SAfr. 164/L11
Grästorp, Swe. 96/E2
Gratkorn, Aus. 101/L3
Gratz, Pa, US 196/B2
Graubünden (canton), Swi. 115/F4
Graulhet, Fr. 100/E5
Graus, Sp. 103/F1
Gravatá, Braz. 212/D3
Grave, Neth. 108/C5
Gravedona, It. 115/F5
Gravelbourg, Sk, Can. 184/G3
Gravelines, Fr. 110/B2
Gravellona Toce, It. 115/E6
Gravenhurst, On, Can. 188/E2
Grävenwiesbach, Ger. 112/B2
Gravesend, Eng, UK 88/E2
Gravina di Puglia, It. 104/E2
Gravois (pt.), Haiti 203/H2
Gray, Fr. 114/B3
Grayling, Ak, US 192/F3
Grayling, Mi, US 188/C2
Grays (har.), Wa, US 184/B4
Grays (lake), Id, US 184/F5
Grays, Eng, UK 88/E2
Grayslake, Il, US 193/P15
Grayson, Sk, Can. 185/H3
Graz, Aus. 101/L3
Grazalema, Sp. 102/C4
Great (lake), Austl. 173/C4
Great (plain), Can.,US 185/G3
Great (basin), Nv, US 182/C4
Great (falls), NJ, US 197/J8
Great Abaco (isl.), Bahm. 199/F2
Great Alfold (plain), Serb. 106/D2
Great America, Ca, US 193/L12
Great Australian Bight (bay), Austl. 167/B4
Great Barrier (reef), Austl. 167/D2
Great Barrier (isl.), NZ 159/T10
Great Basin NP, Nv, US 186/D3
Great Bear (lake), NW, Can. 180/D2
Great Bend, Ks, US 187/H3
Great Bitter (lake), Egypt 149/C4
Great Brak (riv.), SAfr. 164/C3
Great Britain (isl.), UK 89/T9
Great Cedar (swamp), NJ, US 196/D5
Great Coco (isl.), Myan. 141/F5
Great Cumbrae (isl.), Sc, UK 94/B5
Great Divide (basin), Wy, US 184/F5
Great Dividing (range), Austl. 167/D2
Great Egg (har.), NJ, US 196/D5
Great Egg Harbor (riv.), NJ, US 196/D4
Great Exuma (isl.), Bahm. 199/F3
Great Falls, Mt, US 184/F4
Great Fish (riv.), SAfr. 164/D4
Great Fish (pt.), SAfr. 164/D4
Great Guana Cay (isl.), Bahm. 199/F3
Great Harwood, Eng, UK 93/F4
Great Himalaya (range), Asia 128/D6
Great Inagua (isl.), Bahm. 199/G3
Great Indian (des.), India, Pak. 140/B2
Great Karoo (plat.), SAfr. 163/D7
Great Kei (riv.), SAfr. 164/D4
Great Mis Tor (hill), Eng, UK 90/B5
Great Missenden, Eng, UK 91/F3
Great Neck, NY, US 197/L8
Great Nicobar (isl.), India 141/F6
Great Ouse (riv.), Eng, UK 91/E2
Great Oyster (bay), Austl. 173/D4
Great Palace, Rus. 119/S7
Great Palace, Rus. 119/T7
Great Peconic (bay), NY, US 197/F2
Great Pee Dee (riv.), SC, US 191/J3
Great Piece Meadows (swamp), NJ, US 197/H8
Great Rift (valley), Afr. 163/F1
Great Ruaha (riv.), Tanz. 163/F2
Great Salt (lake), Ut, US 186/D2
Great Salt Lake (des.), Ut, US 186/D2
Great Sand Dunes Nat'l Park Co, US 187/F3
Great Sand Sea (des.), Egypt, Li 155/K2
Great Sandy (des.), Austl. 167/B2
Great Scarcies (riv.), SLeo. 160/B4
Great Shunner Fell (peak), Eng, UK 93/F3
Great Slave (lake), NW, Can. 180/E2
Great Smoky Mountains NP, NC,Tn, US 191/H3
Great South (bay), NY, US 197/E2
Great Stour (riv.), Eng, UK 91/G4
Great. Tenasserim (riv.), Myan. 136/B3
Great Victoria (des.), Austl. 167/B3
Great Victoria Desert Nature Rsv., Austl. 171/E4
Great Wall, China 128/J4
Great Western Tiers (mts.),Austl. 173/C4
Great Winterhoek (peak), SAfr. 164/L10
Great Yarmouth, Eng, UK 91/H1
Great Zab (riv.), Iraq 148/E2
Great Zimbabwe (ruin), Zim. 163/F5
Greater Accra (pol. reg.), Gha. 161/F5
Greater Antilles (isls.), NAm. 199/F3
Greater Buffalo (int'l arpt.), NY, US 189/S10
Greater Cincinnati (int'l arpt.), Ky, US 188/C4
Greater London (co.), Eng, UK 88/D2
Greater Manchester (co.), Eng, UK 93/F4
Greater Pittsburgh (int'l arpt.), Pa, US 188/D3
Greater Rochester (int'l arpt.), NY, US 188/E3
Greater Sunda (isls.), Indo. 138/C4
Grebenhain, Ger. 112/C2
Grebenstein, Ger. 109/G6
Grébon (peak), Niger 161/H2
Grecco, Uru. 217/K10
Greco (peak), It. 104/C2
Greco (cape), Cyp. 149/D2
Greding, Ger. 113/E4
Gredos, Sierra de (mts.), Sp. 102/C2
Greece (ctry.) 105/G3
Greeley, Co, US 195/C2
Greeley Number 2 (canal), Co, US 195/C2
Greely (fjord), Nun., Can. 181/S6
Green (cape), Austl. 173/D3
Green (riv.), Ky, US 188/C4
Green (bay), Mi,Wi, US 185/M4
Green (riv.), Ut,Wy, US 186/E3
Green (mts.), Vt, US 188/F3
Green Bay, Wi, US 185/M4
Green Cove Springs, Fl, US 191/H4
Green Creek, NJ, US 196/D5
Green Haven, Md, US 196/B5
Green Lane (res.), Pa, US 196/C3
Green Lowther (peak), Sc, UK 94/C6
Green Pond, NJ, US 196/D1
Green River, Wy, US 184/F5
Green Valley, Az, US 186/E5
Green Valley, Ca, US 194/B1
Green Valley Lake, Ca, US 194/C2
Green Village, NJ, US 197/H9
Greenbelt, Md, US 196/B6
Greenbushes, Austl. 170/C5
Greencastle, In, US 188/C4
Greencastle, Ire. 92/B1
Greendale, Wi, US 193/Q14
Greeneville, Tn, US 188/D4
Greenfield, In, US 188/C4
Greenfield, Ma, US 189/F3
Greenfield, Wi, US 193/P14
Greenfield Park, Qu, Can. 189/P7
Greenisland, NI, UK 92/C2
Greenland (sea) 177/R2
Greenmount, Md, US 196/B4
Greenock, Sc, UK 94/B5
Greenough (riv.), Austl. 170/B4
Greenough (mt.), Ak, US 192/K2
Greenport, NY, US 197/F1
Greensboro, Al, US 191/G3
Greensboro, NC, US 191/J2
Greensburg, In, US 188/C4
Greensburg, Pa, US 188/E3
Greenvale, Austl. 172/B2
Greenville, Libr. 160/C5
Greenville, Al, US 191/G4
Greenville, Ca, US 184/C5
Greenville, Mi, US 188/C3
Greenville, Ms, US 187/K4
Greenville, NC, US 191/J3
Greenville, Oh, US 188/C3
Greenville, SC, US 191/H3
Greenville, Tx, US 187/H4
Greenwater (riv.), Wa, US 193/D3
Greenwell Point, Austl. 173/D2
Greenwich, Ct, US 197/L7
Greenwich (bor.), Eng, UK 88/D2
Greenwich (pt.), Ct, US 197/L8
Greenwich Observatory, Eng, UK 88/D2
Greenwood (lake), SC, US 191/H3
Greenwood, SC, US 191/H3
Greenwood, Ms, US 187/K4
Greenwood, Mo, US 195/E6
Greenwood, De, US 196/C6
Greenwood Lake, NY, US 196/D1
Greers Ferry (lake), Ar, US 187/J4
Grefrath, Ger. 108/D6
Gregório (riv.), Braz. 208/D5
Gregory, SD, US 185/J5
Gregory (range), Austl. 167/D2
Gregory (lake), Austl. 167/B3
Greifswald, Ger. 96/E4
Greifswalder Bodden (bay), Ger. 99/G1
Greimberg (peak), Aus. 101/L3
Greiz, Ger. 101/K1
Gremyachinsk, Rus. 119/N4
Grenå, Den. 96/D3
Grenada, Ms, US 187/K4
Grenada (ctry.) 199/N10
Grenade, Fr. 100/D5
Grenay, Fr. 110/B3
Grenchen, Swi. 114/D3
Grenfell, Austl. 173/D2
Grenfell, Sk, Can. 185/H3
Grennach (riv.), Ger. 112/D6
Grenoble, Fr. 100/F4
Grenzach-Wyhlen, Ger. 114/D2
Gressåmoen NP, Nor. 95/E2
Greta (riv.), Eng, UK 93/E2
Gretna, Mb, Can. 185/J3
Gretna, La, US 195/P17
Gretna, Sc, UK 93/E2
Grettstadt, Ger. 112/D3
Gretz-Armainvilliers, Fr. 88/L5
Greve (riv.), It. 117/E5
Greve in Chianti, It. 117/E5
Grevelingendam (dam), Neth. 108/B5
Greven, Ger. 109/E4
Grevená, Gre. 105/G2
Grevenbroich, Ger. 111/F1
Grevenmacher (dist.), Lux. 111/F4
Grevenmacher, Lux. 111/F4
Grevesmühlen, Ger. 98/F2
Grevlingen (chan.), Neth. 108/A5
Grey (range), Austl. 167/D3
Grey (riv.), Nf, Can. 189/K2
Grey (pt.), NI, UK 92/C2
Grey Abbey, NI, UK 92/C2
Grey Hunter (peak), Yk, Can. 192/L3
Grey Peaks NP, Austl. 172/B2
Greybull, Wy, US 184/F4
Greylingstad, SAfr. 164/E2
Greymouth, NZ 159/S11
Greystones, Ire. 92/B5
Greytown, SAfr. 165/E3
Grez-Doiceau, Belg. 111/D2
Grezzana, It. 117/E1
Gribbin (pt.), Eng, UK 90/B6
Griefensee (lake), Swi. 115/E3
Griekwastad, SAfr. 164/C3
Griend (isl.), Neth. 108/C2
Gries am Brenner, Aus. 115/H3
Griesheim, Ger. 112/B3
Grieskirchen, Aus. 113/G6
Grieskogel (peak), Aus. 115/H3
Griesstätt, Ger. 113/F7
Griffin, Ga, US 191/G3
Griffith, Austl. 173/C2
Griffith, In, US 193/R16
Griffith Park, Ca, US 194/F7
Grigna (peak), It. 115/F6
Grignano Polesine, It. 117/E2
Grigny, Fr. 88/K6
Grijalva (riv.), Mex. 202/C2
Grijpskerk, Neth. 108/D2
Grim (cape), Austl. 173/C4
Grimbergen, Belg. 111/D2
Grimisuat, Swi. 114/D5
Grimmen, Ger. 96/E4
Grimsby, On, Can. 189/Q9
Grimsby, Eng, UK 93/H4
Grimselpass (pass), Swi. 115/E4
Grimsey (isl.), Ice. 95/N6
Grimstad, Nor. 96/C2
Grindavík, Ice. 95/M7
Grindelwald, Swi. 114/E4
Grindsted, Den. 96/C4
Grinnell (pen.), Nun., Can. 181/S7
Grintavec (peak), Slov. 101/L3
Griqualand East (reg.), SAfr. 164/E3
Griqualand West (reg.), SAfr. 164/C2
Gris-Nez (cape), Fr. 110/A2
Grise Fiord, Nun., Can. 181/S7
Grisslehamn, Swe. 97/H1
Grisy-les-Plâtres, Fr. 88/J4
Grisy-Suisnes, Fr. 88/L5
Grivette (riv.), Fr. 88/L4
Grizzly (bay), Ca, US 193/K10
Grmeč (mts.), Bosn. 106/C3
Groaíras, Braz. 212/B1
Grobbendonk, Belg. 108/B6
Gröbenzell, Ger. 113/E6
Groblershoop, SAfr. 164/C3
Grodków, Pol. 99/J3
Grodzisk Wielkopolski, Pol. 99/J2
Groenlo, Neth. 108/D4
Groesbeck, Tx, US 190/D4
Groesbeek, Neth. 108/C5
Groix (isl.), Fr. 100/B3
Grójec, Pol. 99/L3
Grombalia, Tun. 158/M6
Grömitz, Ger. 96/D4
Gromo, It. 115/F6
Gronau, Ger. 108/E4
Gronau, Ger. 109/G4
Groningen, Neth. 108/D2
Groningen (prov.), Neth. 108/D2
Gronlait (peak), It. 115/H5
Grono, Swi. 115/F5
Groot (riv.), SAfr. 163/D7
Groot-Marico (riv.), SAfr. 164/D2
Grootdraaidam (res.), SAfr. 164/Q13
Groote Eylandt (isl.), Austl. 167/C2
Grootegast, Neth. 108/D2
Grootfontein, Namb. 163/C4
Grootvloer (salt pan), SAfr. 164/C3
Gropello Cairoli, It. 116/B2
Gros Islet, StL. 199/N9
Gros Morne (peak), Nf, Can. 189/K1
Gros Morne NP, Nf, Can. 189/K1
Grosbliederstroff, Fr. 111/G5
Grosio, It. 115/G5
Grosne (riv.), Fr. 100/F3
Grosrouvre, Fr. 88/H5
Grosse Bieberau, Ger. 112/B3
Gross-Enzersdorf, Aus. 107/P7
Gross-Gerungs, Aus. 99/H4
Gross Oesingen, Ger. 109/H3
Gross Umstadt, Ger. 112/B3
Gross-Zimmern, Ger. 112/B3
Grossaitingen, Ger. 115/G1
Grossalmerode, Ger. 109/G6
Grossbeeren, Ger. 98/Q7
Grossbottwar, Ger. 112/C5
Grossbreitenbach, Ger. 112/D1
Grosse (isl.), Mi, US 193/F7
Grosse Aue (riv.), Ger. 109/F4
Grosse Ile, Mi, US 193/F7
Grosse Laber (riv.), Ger. 113/F5
Grosse Mühl (riv.), Aus. 113/G6
Grosse Münzenberg (peak), Namb. 164/A2
Grosse Nister (riv.), Ger. 111/G2
Grosse Pointe, Mi, US 193/G7
Grosse Pointe Farms, Mi, US 193/G7
Grosse Pointe Park, Mi, US 193/G7
Grosse Pointe Shores, Mi, US 193/G7
Grosse Pointe Woods, Mi, US 193/G7
Grosse Rodl (riv.), Aus. 113/H6
Grossengottern, Ger. 109/H6
Grossenkneten, Ger. 109/F3
Grossenlüder, Ger. 112/C1
Grossenwiehe, Ger. 96/C4
Grosser Ahrensberg (peak), Ger. 109/G5
Grosser Aletsch (glacier), Swi. 114/D5
Grosser Arber (peak), Ger. 113/G4
Grosser Beer-Berg (peak), Ger. 101/J1
Grosser Bösenstein (peak), Aus. 101/L3
Grosser Daumen (peak), Ger. 115/G3
Grosser Feldberg (peak), Ger. 112/B2
Grosser Gleichberg (peak), Ger. 112/D2
Grosser Heuberg (mts.), Ger. 112/B6
Grosser Knechtsand (isl.), Ger. 109/F1
Grosser Peilstein (peak), Aus. 99/H4
Grosser Plessower (lake), Ger. 98/P7
Grosser Priel (peak), Aus. 101/L3
Grosser Rachel (peak), Ger. 113/G5
Grosser Seddiner (lake), Ger. 98/P7
Grosser Selchower (lake), Ger. 98/Q7
Grosses Meer (lake), Ger. 109/E2
Grosses Moor (swamp), Ger. 109/H3
Grosseto, It. 101/J5
Grossgerau, Ger. 112/B3
Grossglienicke, Ger. 98/Q7
Grossglockner (peak), Aus. 101/K3
Grosshansdorf, Ger. 109/H1
Grossheubach, Ger. 112/C3
Grosskrotzenburg, Ger. 112/B2
Grossmaischeid, Ger. 111/G3
Grosso (cape), Fr. 101/H5
Grossrosseln, Ger. 111/F5
Grosssiegharts, Aus. 99/H4
Grosswallstadt, Ger. 112/C3
Grosswangen, Swi. 114/E3
Grosuplje, Slov. 101/L4
Grote Gete (riv.), Belg. 111/D2
Groton, SD, US 185/J4
Grotta Gigante, It. 117/G1
Grottaglie, It. 104/E2
Grottammare, It. 101/K5
Grouard Mission, Ab, Can. 184/D2
Groundhog (riv.), On, Can. 188/D1
Grouw, Neth. 108/C2
Grovdageaidnu-Kautokeino, Nor. 95/G1
Grove, Ok, US 187/J3
Grove (pt.), Md, US 196/B5
Grover, Mo, US 195/F8
Grover City, Ca, US 186/B4
Groves, Tx, US 187/J5
Groveton, Va, US 196/A6
Groznyy, Rus. 121/H4
Grudovo, Bul. 107/H4
Grudziądz, Pol. 99/K2
Grumeti (riv.), Tanz. 162/B3
Grums, Swe. 96/E2
Grünau im Almtal, Aus. 113/G7
Grünburg, Aus. 113/H7
Gründau, Ger. 112/C2
Grüne (pt.), Eng, UK 93/E2
Grünsfeld, Ger. 112/C3
Grünstadt, Ger. 112/B3
Grünwald, Ger. 113/E6
Gruyères, Swi. 114/D4
Gryazi, Rus. 120/F1
Grycksbo, Swe. 96/F1
Gryfice, Pol. 96/F5
Gryfino, Pol. 99/H2
Gryon, Swi. 114/D5
Gschwandt, Aus. 113/G7
Gschwend, Ger. 112/C5
Gsteig, Swi. 114/D5
Gua, India 143/E4
Guabún (pt.), Chile 216/B4
Guaca, Col. 210/C3
Guacanayabo (gulf), Cuba 199/F3
Guacarí, Col. 210/B4
Guachochi, Mex. 200/D3
Guácimo, CR 203/F4
Guaçuí, Braz. 213/D2
Guadalajara, Mex. 200/E4
Guadalajara, Sp. 102/D2
Guadalcanal, Sp. 102/C3
Guadalcanal (isl.), Sol. 174/E6
Guadalentín (riv.), Sp. 102/D4
Guadalimar (riv.), Sp. 102/D3
Guadalix (riv.), Sp. 103/N8
Guadalope (riv.), Sp. 103/E2
Guadalquivir (riv.), Sp. 102/D4
Guadalupe, Braz. 212/B2
Guadalupe, Col. 210/C4
Guadalupe, Mex. 200/E4
Guadalupe, Mex. 201/E3
Guadalupe (isl.), Mex. 177/E7
Guadalupe, Pan. 203/G4
Guadalupe, Peru 214/C4
Guadalupe, Peru 214/B2
Guadalupe, Sp. 102/C3
Guadalupe (mts.), NM,Tx, US 190/B3
Guadalupe (co.), Tx, US 195/U20
Guadalupe (peak), Tx, US 187/F5
Guadalupe (riv.), Tx, US 190/D4
Guadalupe Mountains NP, Tx, US 187/F5
Guadalupe, Sierra de (mts.), Sp. 102/C3
Guadalupe Victoria, Mex. 200/B1
Guadalupe Victoria, Mex. 200/D3
Guadalupe Victoria, Mex. 201/M7
Guadarrama (riv.), Sp. 102/C3
Guadarrama, Ven. 210/D2

Guadarrama, Sp. 103/M8
Guadarrama, Sierra de (mts.), Sp. 102/C2
Guadeloupe (isl.), Guad., Fr. 199/N8
Guadeloupe NP, Guad., Fr. 199/N8
Guadeloupe Passage (chan.), Guad., Fr. 199/J4
Guadiana (riv.), Port.,Sp. 102/B3
Guadiana Menor (riv.), Sp. 102/D4
Guadix, Sp. 102/D4
Guafo (isl.), Chile 216/B4
Guafo, Boca del (mouth), Chile 216/B4
Guagua Pichincha (peak), Ecu. 210/B5
Guaíba, Braz. 213/B4
Guaíba (riv.), Braz. 213/B4
Guáimaro, Cuba 203/G1
Guainía (riv.), Col. 208/E3
Guainía (dept.), Col. 210/D4
Guaiquinima (peak), Ven. 211/F3
Guaíra, Braz. 215/F1
Guaíra, Braz. 213/B2
Guaiteca (isl.), Chile 216/B4
Guajará-Mirim, Braz. 208/E6
Guajira (pen.), Col. 210/D1
Gualaceo, Ecu. 210/B5
Gualaco, Hon. 202/E3
Gualán, Guat. 202/D3
Gualaquiza, Ecu. 214/B1
Gualeguay, Arg. 217/J10
Gualeguaychú, Arg. 217/J10
Gualtieri, It. 116/D3
Guam (isl.), Pac., US 174/D3
Guamal, Col. 210/C2
Guamblin, Isla (isl.), Chile 216/A5
Guamote, Ecu. 214/B1
Guamúchil, Mex. 200/C3
Gu'an, China 130/H7
Guan Xian, China 128/H5
Guan Xian, China 130/C3
Guanabacoa, Cuba 203/F1
Guanabara (bay), Braz. 213/K7
Guanahacabibes (gulf), Cuba 203/E1
Guanahacabibes (pen.), Cuba 203/E1
Guanaja, Hon. 202/E2
Guanaja (isl.), Hon. 202/E2
Guanajay, Cuba 203/F1
Guanajuato, Mex. 201/E4
Guanajuato (state), Mex. 182/A3
Guanambi, Braz. 212/B4
Guanape, Ven. 211/E2
Guanare, Ven. 210/D2
Guanare (riv.), Ven. 208/E2
Guanarito, Ven. 210/D2
Guanay (peak), Ven. 211/E3
Guandi (mtn.), China 130/B3
Guane, Cuba 203/E1
Guangchang, China 137/C2
Guangde, China 130/D5
Guangdong (prov.), China 129/K7
Guangfeng, China 137/C2
Guangling, China 130/C3
Guanglu (isl.), China 131/B3
Guangnan, China 141/J3
Guangping, China 137/C2
Guangping, China 130/C3
Guangrao, China 130/D3
Guangshan, China 130/C4
Guangxi Zhuangzu (aut. reg.), China 128/J7
Guangyuan, China 128/J5
Guangze, China 137/C2
Guangzhou, China 141/K3
Guanhães, Braz. 213/D1
Guanipa (riv.), Ven. 208/F2
Guannan, China 130/D4
Guantánamo, Cuba 203/H1
Guantánamo Bay U.S. Naval Base, Cuba 203/H2
Guantao, China 130/C3
Guanting (res.), China 130/G6
Guanujo, Ecu. 210/B5
Guanyun, China 130/D4
Guapi, Col. 210/B4
Guaporé, Braz. 213/B4
Guaporé (riv.), Braz. 205/C4
Guaqui, Bol. 214/D5
Guarabira, Braz. 212/D2
Guaraci, Braz. 213/B2
Guaraciaba do Norte, Braz. 212/B2
Guaraí, Braz. 209/J5
Guaramirim, Braz. 213/B3
Guaranda, Ecu. 210/B5
Guarani, Braz. 213/K6
Guarapari, Braz. 213/D2
Guarapuava, Braz. 213/B3
Guarará, Braz. 213/K6
Guararapes (int'l arpt.), Braz. 212/D3
Guararapes, Braz. 213/B2
Guaratinga, Braz. 212/C5
Guaratinguetá, Braz. 213/H7
Guaratuba, Braz. 213/B3
Guarda (dist.), Port. 102/B2
Guarda, Port. 102/B2
Guardamar, Sp. 103/E3
Guardamiglio, It. 116/C2
Guardarrama (riv.), Sp. 103/N8
Guardia Alta (peak), It. 115/H4
Guardia Mitre, Arg. 216/E4
Guardia Sanframondi, It. 106/B5
Guardiagrele, It. 104/D1
Guareña, Sp. 102/B3
Guarico (pt.), Cuba 203/H1
Guárico (riv.), Ven. 211/E2
Guárico (state), Ven. 211/E2
Guárico, Embalse de (res.), Ven. 211/E2
Guarujá, Braz. 213/G9
Guarulhos, Braz. 213/G8
Guarulhos (int'l arpt.), Braz. 213/G8
Guarumal, Pan. 203/F5
Guasave, Mex. 200/C3
Guasdualito, Ven. 210/D3
Guasimal, Cuba 203/G1
Guasipati, Ven. 211/F3
Guastalla, It. 116/D3
Guatemala (ctry.) 202/D3
Guatemala (cap.), Guat. 202/D3
Guateque, Col. 210/C3
Guaviare (dept.), Col. 210/C4
Guaviare (riv.), Col. 208/E3
Guaxupé, Braz. 213/G6
Guayabero (riv.), Col. 210/C4
Guayabo, Cayo (isl.), Cuba 203/G1
Guayalejo (riv.), Mex. 201/F4
Guayama, PR 199/M8
Guayape (riv.), Hon. 202/E3
Guayaquil (gulf), Ecu.,Peru 205/A3
Guayaquil, Ecu. 210/B5
Guayaquil, Gulf of (gulf), Ecu.,Peru 214/A1
Guayaramerín, Bol. 208/E6
Guayas, Ecu. 210/B5
Guayas (prov.), Ecu. 210/A5
Guayas (riv.), Col. 210/C4
Guaymas, Mex. 200/C3
Gubakha, Rus. 119/N4
Gubbio, It. 117/F6
Guben, Ger. 99/H3
Gubin, Pol. 99/H3
Gubkin, Rus. 120/F2
Gucheng, China 130/B4
Gucheng, China 130/C3
Gúdar, Sierra de (range), Sp. 103/E2
Gudenå (riv.), Den. 96/D3
Gudensberg, Ger. 109/G6
Gudermes, Rus. 121/H4
Gudivāda, India 140/D4
Gudow, Ger. 109/H1
Güdül, Turk. 107/L5
Gūdūr, India 140/C5
Guebli (lake), Mrta. 156/B5
Guebwiller, Fr. 114/D2
Guecho, Sp. 102/D1
Guelb Azefal (hill), Mrta. 156/B5
Guelb er Rîchât (peak), Mrta. 156/C5
Guelma, Alg. 158/K6
Guelma (prov.), Alg. 158/K6
Guelph, On, Can. 188/D3
Guémené-Penfao, Fr. 100/C3
Guénange, Fr. 111/F5
Guérande, Fr. 100/B3
Guerara, Alg. 157/G2
Guérard, Fr. 88/L5
Guercif, Mor. 158/C2
Guéret, Fr. 100/D3
Guernes, Fr. 88/G4
Guernsey (int'l arpt.), Chl, UK 100/B2
Guernsey (isl.), Chl, UK 100/B2
Guerrero (state), Mex. 182/B4
Guerrero, Mex. 200/D2
Guerrero Negro, Mex. 200/B3
Guerville, Fr. 88/H5
Guesle (riv.), Fr. 88/H6
Gueugnon, Fr. 100/F3
Gueux, Fr. 110/C5
Gugē (peak), Eth. 155/N6
Guggisberg, Swi. 114/D4
Guglielmo Marconi (int'l arpt.), It. 117/E3
Güglingen, Ger. 112/B4
Guguan (isl.), NMar. 174/D3
Guguletu, SAfr. 164/L11
Gui (riv.), China 137/B3
Guiana Highlands (uplands), SAm. 205/C2
Guichen, Fr. 100/C3
Guichón, Uru. 217/K10
Guidder, Camr. 154/H6
Guidimaka (pol. reg.), Mrta. 160/B3
Guiding, China 141/J2
Guidizzolo, It. 116/D2
Guidong, China 141/K2
Guidonia, It. 104/C2
Guiglo, C.d'Iv. 160/D5
Guignes-Rabutin, Fr. 88/L6
Guihulngan, Phil. 139/F1
Guija, Moz. 163/F5
Guijuelo, Sp. 102/C2
Guilder (peak), Ut, US 195/L11
Guilderton, Austl. 170/B4
Guildford, Eng, UK 88/B3
Guilherand, Fr. 100/F4
Guilin (int'l arpt.), China 137/B2
Guilin, China 141/K2
Guillaume-Delisle (lake), Qu, Can. 181/J3
Guillena, Sp. 102/B4
Guimarães, Braz. 212/A1
Guimarães, Port. 102/A2
Guimba, Phil. 137/D4
Guimeng (mtn.), China 130/D4
Guinan, China 128/H4
Guinard (riv.), Sc, UK 94/A1
Guinea (ctry.) 160/C4
Guinea (gulf), Afr. 151/C4
Guinea-Bissau (ctry.) 160/B3
Guînes, Fr. 110/A2
Guingamp, Fr. 100/B2
Guinguinéo, Sen. 160/B3
Guiones (pt.), CR 202/E4
Guipavas, Fr. 100/A2
Guipavas (int'l arpt.), Fr. 100/A2
Guir, Oued (riv.), Alg. 156/E2
Guiratinga, Braz. 209/H7
Güiria, Ven. 211/F2
Guisborough, Eng, UK 93/G2
Guiscard, Fr. 110/C4
Guise, Fr. 110/C4
Guitiriz, Sp. 102/B1
Guitrancourt, Fr. 88/H4
Guiuan, Phil. 137/E5
Güiza (riv.), Col. 210/B4
Guizhou (prov.), China 128/J6
Gujan-Mestras, Fr. 100/C4
Gūjar Khān, Pak. 144/B3
Gujarāt (state), India 140/B3
Gujrānwāla, Pak. 144/C3
Gujrāt, Pak. 144/C3
Gukovo, Rus. 120/F2
Gulaothi, India 142/A1
Gulargambone, Austl. 173/D1
Gulbarga, India 140/C4
Guldenbach (riv.), Ger. 111/G3
Güldüzü, Turk. 149/E1
Gulen, Nor. 96/A1
Gulf Coastal (plain), Tx, US 190/D5
Gulf Islands Nat'l Seashore, US 191/F4
Gulf Shores, Al, US 191/G4
Gulfport, Ms, US 191/F4
Gulgong, Austl. 173/D2
Guliston, Uzb. 145/E4
Gulkana, Ak, US 192/J3
Gull Lake, Sk, Can. 184/F3
Gulladuff, NI, UK 92/B2
Gullane, Sc, UK 94/D4
Gullane (pt.), Sc, UK 94/D4
Gullspång, Swe. 96/F2
Güllükdağı (Termessos) NP, Turk. 149/B1
Gulmarg, India 144/C2
Gülnar, Turk. 149/C1
Gulpen, Neth. 111/E2
Gülpınar, Turk. 105/K3
Gulu, Ugan. 162/B2
Gulyantsi, Bul. 107/G4
Gumal (riv.), Pak. 144/A4
Gumare, Bots. 163/D4
Gumbrechtshoffen, Fr. 111/G6
Gumdag, Trkm. 121/K5
Gumeracha, Austl. 171/M8
Gumia, India 143/E4
Gumla, India 143/E4
Gumma (pref.), Japan 133/F2
Gummersbach, Ger. 111/G1
Gumpoldskirchen, Aus. 107/N7
Gumti (riv.), India 143/H4
Gümüşhacıköy, Turk. 120/E4
Gümüşhane, Turk. 148/D1
Gümüşhane (prov.), Turk. 148/D1
Guna (peak), Eth. 155/N5
Gunbower, Austl. 173/B2
Gundagai, Austl. 173/D2
Gundelfingen, Ger. 114/D1
Gundelfingen an der Donau, Ger. 112/D5
Gundelsheim, Ger. 112/C4
Gundersheim, Ger. 112/B3
Gundershoffen, Fr. 111/G6
Gündoğmuş, Turk. 149/C1
Güneydoğu Toroslar (mts.), Turk. 148/D2
Gunisao (riv.), Mb, Can. 185/J2
Gunisao (lake), Mb, Can. 185/J2
Gunja, Cro. 106/D3
Gunn City, Mo, US 195/E6
Gunnaur, India 142/B1
Gunnebo, Swe. 96/G3
Gunnedah, Austl. 173/D1
Gunning, Austl. 173/D2
Gunnison (riv.), Co, US 186/F3
Gunnison, Ut, US 186/E3
Gunpowder (riv.), Md, US 196/B5
Gunpowder Falls State Park, Md, US 196/B4
Gunskirchen, Aus. 113/G6
Guntersblum, Ger. 112/B3
Guntersville, Al, US 191/G3
Guntersville (lake), Al, US 191/G3
Guntramsdorf, Aus. 107/N7
Guntūr, India 140/D4
Günz (riv.), Ger. 98/F4
Günzburg, Ger. 112/D6
Gunzenhausen, Ger. 112/D4
Guoyang, China 130/D4
Gura Humorului, Rom. 107/G2
Gurāgē (peak), Eth. 155/N6
Gurbantünggut (des.), China 128/E2
Gurdāspur, India 144/C3
Gurgaon, India 144/D5
Gürgentepe, Turk. 148/D1
Gurguéia (riv.), Braz. 209/K6
Guri (dam), Ven. 211/F3
Guri (res.), Ven. 211/F3
Gurk (riv.), Aus. 101/L3
Gurkthaler Alpen (mts.), Aus. 101/K3
Gurnee, Il, US 193/Q15
Guro, Moz. 163/F4
Gürpınar, Turk. 148/E2
Gursarai, India 142/B3
Gürsu, Turk. 148/B1
Guru Sikhar (peak), India 147/K4
Gürün, Turk. 148/D2
Gurupi, Braz. 209/J6
Gurupi (riv.), Braz. 209/J4
Gurupi, Serra do (mts.), Braz. 209/J4
Gus'-Khrustal'nyy, Rus. 118/J5
Gusau, Nga. 161/G3
Gushi, China 130/C4
Gushikawa, Japan 133/J7
Gusinje, Serb. 106/D4
Guskhara, India 143/F4
Guspini, It. 104/A3
Gussola, It. 116/D3
Gustavo Díaz Ordaz, Mex. 200/C3
Gustavo Díaz Ordaz, Mex. 200/B3
Gusterath, Ger. 111/F4
Güstrow, Ger. 96/E5
Gusum, Swe. 96/G2
Gutau, Aus. 113/H6
Gütersloh, Ger. 109/F5
Guthrie, Tx, US 187/G4
Guthrie, Ok, US 195/N14
Gutiérrez Zamora, Mex. 201/M6
Guttannen, Swi. 115/E4
Guttenberg, NJ, US 197/K8
Güttingen, Swi. 115/F2
Gutulia NP, Nor. 95/E3
Guwāhati, India 141/F2
Guxhagen, Ger. 109/G6
Guxian, China 130/B3
Guy Fawkes River NP, Austl. 173/E1
Guyana (ctry.) 211/G3
Guyancourt, Fr. 88/J5
Guyandotte (riv.), WV, US 191/H2
Guyang, China 130/B2
Guyenne (reg.), Fr. 100/C4
Guymon, Ok, US 187/G3
Guyra, Austl. 173/D1
Guyuan, China 128/J4
Güzelbağ, Turk. 149/B1
Güzelsu, Turk. 149/B1
Guzhang, China 141/J2
Guzhen, China 130/D4
Guzmán (lake), Mex. 200/D2
Gwādar, Pak. 147/H3
Gwaii Haanas NP, BC, Can. 180/C3
Gwalior, India 142/B2
Gwanda, Zim. 163/E5
Gwandalan, Austl. 173/D2
Gwash (riv.), Eng, UK 91/F1
Gwaunceste (peak), Wal, UK 90/C2
Gwda (riv.), Pol. 99/J2
Gwersyllt, Wal, UK 93/E5
Gweru, Zim. 163/E4
Gwydir (riv.), Austl. 173/D1
Gwynedd (co.), Wal, UK 92/D5
Gwyrfai (riv.), Wal, UK 92/D5
Gy, Fr. 114/B3
Gya (pass), China 143/E1
Gyaca, China 141/F2
Gyál, Hun. 107/R10
Gyasikan, Gha. 161/F5
Gyda (pen.), Rus. 125/G2
Gyhum, Ger. 109/G2
Gyirong, China 143/E1
Gyldenløveshøj (peak), Den. 96/D4
Gympie, Austl. 172/D4
Gyōda, Japan 135/C1
Gyoma, Hun. 106/E2
Gyömrő, Hun. 107/R10
Győr, Hun. 106/C2
Győr-Moson-Sopron (co.), Hun. 99/J5
Győrújbarát, Hun. 106/C2
Gyumri, Arm. 121/G4
Gyzylarbat, Trkm. 121/L5
Gžira, Malta 104/L7

H

Hå, Nor. 96/A2
Ha Giang, Viet. 141/H3
Ha Noi (Hanoi) (cap.), Viet. 141/J3
Haacht, Belg. 111/D2
Haag, Aus. 113/H6
Haag am Hausruck, Aus. 113/G6
Haag an der Amper, Ger. 113/E6
Haag in Oberbayern, Ger. 113/F6
Haaksbergen, Neth. 108/D4
Haaltert, Belg. 110/D2
Haamstede, Neth. 108/A5
Haan, Ger. 108/E6
Ha'apai Group (isl.), Tonga 175/H7
Haapavesi, Fin. 95/H2
Haapsalu, Est. 97/K2
Haar, Ger. 113/E6
Haardt (mts.), Ger. 101/G2
Haarlem, Neth. 108/B4
Haast, NZ 175/R11
Haasts Bluff Abor. Land, Austl. 171/F2
Hab (riv.), Pak. 147/J3
Habahe, China 128/E2
Habartov, Czh. 113/F2
Habbānīyah, Iraq 148/E3
Habicht (peak), Aus. 115/H3
Habiganj, Bang. 143/H3
Habikino, Japan 135/J6
Habomai (isls.), Rus. 134/D2
HaBonim, Isr. 149/F6
Haboro, Japan 134/B1
Hābra, India 143/G4
Habsheim, Fr. 114/D2
Hacha (falls), Ven. 211/F3
Hache (riv.), Ger. 109/F3
Hachenburg, Ger. 111/G2
Hachijō, Japan 133/F4
Hachikai, Japan 135/L5
Hachimori, Japan 134/B3
Hachinohe, Japan 134/B3
Hachiōji, Japan 133/F3
Hacıbektaş, Turk. 148/C2
Hacienda Heights, Ca, US 194/G8
Hacılar, Turk. 148/C2
Hack (mt.), Austl. 171/H4
Hackensack, NJ, US 197/J8
Hackensack (riv.), NJ, US 197/J9
Hackettstown, NJ, US 196/D2
Hackney (bor.), Eng, UK 88/C2
Ḩadabat al Jilf al Kabīr (plat.), Egypt 159/A4
Hadāli, Pak. 144/B3
Hadamar, Ger. 112/B2
Hadano, Japan 133/F3
Hadarba (cape), Sudan 159/D4
Ḩadd, Ra's al (pt.), Ōman 147/G4
Haddenham, Eng, UK 91/F3
Haddington, Sc, UK 94/D5
Haddonfield, NJ, US 196/C4
Hadejia (riv.), Nga. 161/H3
Hadelner (canal), Ger. 109/F1
Hadera, Isr. 149/F7
Haderslev, Den. 96/C4
Hadhramaut (reg.), Yem. 146/E6
Hadım, Turk. 149/C1
Hadjout, Alg. 158/G4
Hadleigh, Eng, UK 88/E2
Hadley (bay), Nun., Can. 180/F1
Hadlow, Eng, UK 88/E3
Hadrian's Wall, Eng, UK 93/F1
Hadselfjorden (inlet), Nor. 95/E1
Hadsten, Den. 96/D3
Hadsund, Den. 96/D3
Haeju (bay), NKor. 131/C4
Haeju, NKor. 131/C3
Haena (pt.), Hi, US 182/S9
Haenam, SKor. 131/D5
Hafik, Turk. 148/D2
Hāfizābād, Pak. 144/B3
Hāflong, India 141/F2
Hafnarfjördhur, Ice. 95/N7
Hafnarhreppur, Ice. 95/P7
Haft Gel, Iran 146/E2
Hafun (pt.), Som. 155/R5
Hagåtña (cap.), Guam 174/D3
Hagelstadt, Ger. 113/F5
Hagemeister (isl.), Ak, US 192/F4
Hagen, Ger. 109/E6
Hagen am Teutoburger Wald, Ger. 109/E4
Hagen im Bremischen, Ger. 109/F2
Hagenow, Ger. 96/D5
Hagerman, NM, US 190/B3
Hagerstown, Md, US 188/E4
Hagetmau, Fr. 100/C5
Hagfors, Swe. 96/E1
Hagi, Japan 132/B3
Hagnau am Bodensee, Ger. 115/F2
Hags (pt.), Ire. 89/P10
Hague, Sk, Can. 185/G2
Hague, Cap de la (cape), Fr. 100/C2
Haguenau, Fr. 111/G6
Hahashima (isls.), Japan 174/D2
Hahaya (int'l arpt.), Com. 165/G5
Hahle (riv.), Ger. 109/H5
Hahndorf, Austl. 171/M9
Hahnenbach (riv.), Ger. 111/G4
Hahnstätten, Ger. 112/B2
Hahnville, La, US 195/P17
Ḩaḩrā Awbāri (des.), Libya 154/H2
Hai (riv.), China 130/D3
Hai Duong, Viet. 136/D1
Hai Phong, Viet. 141/J3
Hai Van (pass), Viet. 136/E2
Hai'an, China 130/E4
Haibach, Ger. 112/C3
Haibara, Japan 135/J6
Haicheng, China 131/B2
Haidenaab (riv.), Ger. 113/E3
Haidershofen, Aus. 113/H6
Haifa (dist.), Isr. 149/D3
Haifeng, China 137/C3
Haiger, Ger. 101/H1
Haigerloch, Ger. 112/B6
Haikou (int'l arpt.), China 137/B3
Haikou, China 141/K3
Haiku-Pauwela, Hi, US 182/T10
Ḩā'il, SAr. 146/D3
Hailākāndi, India 141/F3
Hailar, China 129/L2
Hailar (riv.), China 129/M2
Haileybury, On, Can. 188/E2
Hailsham, Eng, UK 91/G5
Hailun, China 129/N2
Haimen, China 130/E5
Haimhausen, Ger. 113/E6
Haiming, Aus. 115/G3
Haiming, Ger. 113/F6
Haina, Ger. 109/F6
Hainan (isl.), China 129/B4
Hainan (prov.), China 128/J8
Hainan (str.), China 129/B3
Hainaut (prov.), Belg. 110/B2
Hainburg, Ger. 112/C1
Haines, Ak, US 192/L3
Haines City, Fl, US 191/H4
Haines Junction, Yk, Can. 192/L3
Hainesville, NJ, US 196/D1
Hainesville, Il, US 193/P15
Hainich (mts.), Ger. 98/F3
Haining, China 130/L9
Haiti (ctry.) 203/H2
Haixia (str.), China 129/K7
Haixing, China 130/D3
Haiyan, China 137/B3
Haiyan, China 128/H4
Haiyang (isl.), China 131/B3
Haiyang, China 130/E3
Haiyuan, China 128/J4
Haizhou (bay), China 130/D4
Háj (peak), Czh. 113/F2
Hajdú-Bihar (co.), Hun. 106/E2
Hajdúböszörmény, Hun. 99/L5
Hajdúdorog, Hun. 99/L5
Hajdúhadház, Hun. 106/E2
Hajdúnánás, Hun. 99/L5
Hajdúszoboszló, Hun. 99/L5
Hajiki-zaki (pt.), Japan 133/F1
Hājīpur, India 143/E3
Ḩajjah, Yem. 146/D5
Hajnówka, Pol. 99/M2
Hājo, India 143/H2
Hajós, Hun. 106/D2
Haka, Myan. 141/F3
Hakee (mt.), Austl. 171/G3
Hakkari (prov.), Turk. 148/E2
Hakken-san (peak), Japan 132/D3
Hakkōda-san (peak), Japan 134/B3
Hakodate, Japan 134/B3
Hakone, Japan 135/C3
Hakone-yama (peak), Japan 135/C3
Haku-san (peak), Japan 133/E2
Hakui, Japan 133/E2
Hakusan, Japan 135/K6
Hakusan NP, Japan 133/E2
Hakushū, Japan 135/A2
Hāla, Pak. 147/J3
Ḩalab (prov.), Syria 148/D2
Ḩalab (Aleppo), Syria 149/E1
Ḩalabjah, Iraq 148/E3
Halachó, Mex. 201/M6
Halawa, Hi, US 182/T10
Halcon (mt.), Phil. 139/F1
Halden, Nor. 96/D2
Haldensleben, Ger. 98/F2
Haldenwang, Ger. 115/G2
Haldīa, India 143/G4
Haldībāri, India 143/G2
Haldimand, On, Can. 189/Q10
Haldimand-Norfolk (co.), On, Can. 189/Q10
Hale (riv.), Austl. 171/G3
Hale (mt.), Austl. 170/C3
Hale, Eng, UK 93/F5
Haleakala NP, Hi, US 182/T10
Haledon, NJ, US 197/J8
Haleiwa, Hi, US 182/V12
Halen, Belg. 111/E2
Hales Corners, Wi, US 193/P14
Halesowen, Eng, UK 90/D2
Haleyville, Al, US 191/G3
Half Assini, Gha. 160/E5
Half Falls (mtn.), Pa, US 196/A3
Half Moon Bay, Ca, US 193/K12
Half Tide Beach, Austl. 172/C3
Halfing, Ger. 113/F7
Halfweg, Neth. 108/B4
Ḩalḩūl, WBnk. 149/D4
Haliburton Highlands (uplands), On, Can. 188/E2
Halifax (cap.), NS, Can. 189/J2
Halifax (int'l arpt.), NS, Can. 189/J2
Halifax (bay), Austl. 167/D2
Halifax, Austl. 172/B2
Halifax, Pa, US 196/B3
Halifax, Eng, UK 93/G4
Halikko, Fin. 97/K1
Halīl (riv.), Iran 147/G3
Haliun, Mong. 128/G2
Halkett (cape), Ak, US 192/H1
Hall, Austl. 173/C2
Hall (pen.), Nun., Can. 181/K2
Hall (isls.), Micr. 174/E4
Hall (isl.), Ak, US 192/D3
Hall Beach, Nun., Can. 181/H2
Hall Park, Ok, US 195/N15
Halladale (riv.), Sc, UK 89/S7
Hallam (Hellam), Pa, US 196/B4
Halland (co.), Swe. 95/E4
Hällbybrunn, Swe. 96/G2
Halle, Ger. 109/F4
Halle, Ger. 99/G3
Halle, Belg. 111/D2
Halle-Neustadt, Ger. 98/F3
Hällefors, Swe. 96/F2
Hälleforsnäs, Swe. 96/G2
Hallein, Aus. 101/K3
Hallenberg, Ger. 109/F6
Hallertau (reg.), Ger. 113/E5
Hallettsville, Tx, US 187/H5
Halley, UK, Ant. 218/Y
Hallingdalselvi (riv.), Nor. 96/C1
Hallock, Mn, US 185/J3
Hallsberg, Swe. 96/F2
Hallstahammar, Swe. 96/G2
Hallstavik, Swe. 96/H1
Hallu (riv.), Fr. 98/B4
Halluin, Fr. 110/C2
Hallwang, Aus. 113/G7
Hallwilersee (lake), Swi. 114/E3
Hallyŏ Haesang NP, SKor. 131/E5
Halmahera (sea), Indo. 139/G4
Halmahera (isl.), Indo. 139/G3
Halmstad, Swe. 96/E3
Hals, Den. 96/D3
Hälsingborg (Helsingborg), Swe. 96/E3
Halsteren, Neth. 108/B5
Haltern, Ger. 109/E5
Halton (co.), On, Can. 189/Q8
Halton (co.), Eng, UK 93/F5
Halton Hills, On, Can. 189/Q8
Halver, Ger. 109/E6
Halverder Aa (riv.), Ger. 109/E4
Ham, Fr. 110/C4
Ham, Oued El (riv.), Alg. 158/G5
Ham-sous-Varsberg, Fr. 111/F5
Hamada, Japan 132/C3
Hamada de Tinrhert (plat.), Alg. 157/G4
Hamada du Drâa (plat.), Alg. 154/D2
Hamada du Tinrhert (plat.), Arg. 154/G2
Hamada Safia (plat.), Mali 156/D5
Hamadān, Iran 146/E2
Hamādat Marzūq (plat.), Libya 157/H4
Hamadat Tinghert (uplands),Libya 154/H2
Ḩamādat Tinghert (uplands),Libya 157/H3
Ḩamāh (prov.), Syria 149/E2
Hamajima, Japan 135/L7
Hamakita, Japan 133/E3
Hamam, Turk. 149/E1
Hamamatsu, Japan 133/E3
Hamami (reg.), Mrta. 156/C5
Hamanaka, Japan 134/D2
Hamar, Nor. 96/D1
Ḩamāṭah (peak), Egypt 159/C3
Hamath Tiberias NP, Isr. 149/D3
Hamatombetsu, Japan 134/C1
Hambantota, SrL. 140/D6
Hambergen, Ger. 109/F2
Hambleton (hills), Eng, UK 93/G3
Hambühren, Ger. 109/G3
Hamburg, NY, US 188/E3
Hamburg, Ger. 109/G1
Hamburg, NJ, US 196/D1
Hamburg, Pa, US 196/C2
Hamburg (state), Ger. 96/D5
Hamburg (Fuhlsbüttel) (int'l arpt.), Ger. 109/G1
Häme (prov.), Fin. 95/G3
Hämeenkyrö, Fin. 97/K1
Hämeenlinna, Fin. 97/L1
Hamel, Il, US 195/H8
Hamelin Pool (bay), Austl. 170/B3
Hameln, Ger. 109/G4
Hamersley (range), Austl. 167/A3
Hamersley Range NP, Austl. 170/C2
Hamford Water (inlet), Eng, UK 91/H3
Hamgyŏng-bukto (prov.), NKor. 131/E2
Hamgyŏng-namdo (prov.), NKor. 131/D2
Ḩamh, Syria 148/D3
Hamhŭng, NKor. 131/D3
Hamhŭng-si (prov.), NKor. 131/D3
Hami, China 128/F3
Hamilton, Austl. 173/B3
Hamilton, Mt, US 184/E4
Hamilton, Tx, US 187/H5
Hamilton, Al, US 191/G3
Hamilton (har.), On, Can. 189/Q9
Hamilton, NZ 175/T10
Hamilton, On, Can. 189/Q9
Hamilton (inlet), Nf, Can. 181/L3
Hamilton (mt.), Ca, US 193/L12
Hamilton, Sc, UK 94/B5
Hamilton Mil. Res., NY, US 197/J9
Hamilton-Wentworth (co.), On, Can. 189/Q9
Hamina, Fin. 97/M1
Hamīrpur, India 142/C3
Hamīrpur, India 144/D4
Hamlin, Tx, US 187/G4
Hamm, Ger. 109/E5
Hamm, Ger. 112/B3
Hamm, Ger. 111/G2
Hamma-Bouziane, Alg. 158/K6
Hammam Lif, Tun. 158/M6
Hammamat (gulf), Tun. 158/M6
Hammarland, Fin. 97/H1
Hammarön (isl.), Swe. 96/E2
Hammarstrand, Swe. 95/F3
Hamme (riv.), Ger. 109/F2
Hamme, Belg. 111/D1
Hammel, Den. 96/C3
Hammelburg, Ger. 112/C2
Hammerfest, Nor. 95/G1
Hammershus, Den. 96/F4
Hammersmith and Fulham (bor.), Eng, UK 88/A1
Hamminkeln, Ger. 108/D5
Hammonasset (pt.), Ct, US 197/F1
Hammond, In, US 188/C3
Hammond, La, US 191/F4
Hammonton, NJ, US 196/D4
Hamnvik, Nor. 95/F1
Hamois, Belg. 111/E3
Hamont-Achel, Belg. 108/C6
Hampshire Downs (hills), Eng, UK 91/E4
Hampstead, Md, US 196/B4
Hampton, Pa, US 196/A4
Hampton Bays, NY, US 197/F2
Hampton Court, Eng, UK 88/C2
Hampton Nat'l Hist. Site, Md, US 196/B5
Hamp'yŏng, SKor. 131/D5
Hamtramck, Mi, US 193/F7
Hamura, Japan 135/C2
Hamyang, SKor. 131/D5
Hamyŏl, SKor. 131/D4
Han (riv.), China 125/M6
Hana (riv.), India 142/C5
Hana, Hi, US 182/U10
Hanak, Turk. 148/E1
Hanamaki, Japan 134/B4
Hanamalo (pt.), Hi, US 182/U11
Hanang (peak), Tanz. 162/B4
Hanau, Ger. 112/B2
Hanazono, Japan 135/C1
Hancocks Bridge, NJ, US 196/C5
Handa, Japan 135/L6
Handawor, India 144/C2
Handeloh, Ger. 109/G2
Handiā, India 142/D3
Hanford, Ca, US 186/C3
Hanford Reach Nat'l Mon., Wa, US 184/D4
Hangayn (mts.), Mong. 128/G2
Hangingstone (hill), Eng, UK 90/C5
Hangklip (cape), SAfr. 164/L11
Hangu, Pak. 144/A3
Hangzhou (bay), China 130/L9
Hanhofen, Ger. 112/B4
Hanhöhiy (mts.), Mong. 128/F2
Hani, Turk. 148/E2
Haninge, Swe. 96/H2
Hankensbüttel, Ger. 109/H3
Hankey, SAfr. 164/D4
Hankinson, ND, US 185/J4
Hanko (Hangö), Fin. 97/K2
Hanley, Sk, Can. 185/G3
Hanna, Ab, Can. 184/F3
Hannan, Japan 135/H7
Hanningfield (res.), Eng, UK 88/E2
Hannō, Japan 135/C2
Hannover (int'l arpt.), Ger. 109/G4
Hannover, Ger. 109/G4
Hannut, Belg. 111/E2
Hanöbukten (bay), Swe. 95/E5
Hanover, NH, US 189/F3

Hanover, On, Can. 188/D2
Hanover, SAfr. 164/D3
Hanover, Pa, US 196/B4
Hanover (isl.), Chile 217/B6
Hanover Park, Il, US 193/P16
Hansen (dam), Ca, US 194/F7
Hanshan, China 130/D5
Hanshou, China 137/B2
Hänsi, India 144/C5
Hanstedt, Ger. 109/H2
Hanstholm, Den. 96/C3
Hansville, Wa, US 193/B2
Hantzsch (riv.), Nun., Can. 181/J2
Hanumängarh, India 144/C5
Hanwood, Austl. 173/C2
Hanyü, China 135/D1
Hanyuan, China 141/H2
Hanzhong, China 128/J5
Hao (isl.), FrPol. 175/L6
Haparanda, Swe. 95/G2
Hapch'ŏn, SKor. 131/E5
Happy Valley (res.), Austl. 171/M9
Happy Valley-Goose Bay, Nf, Can. 181/K3
Haptök, SKor. 131/D4
Häpur, India 142/A1
Haquira, Peru 214/C4
Har-Ayrag, Mong. 129/J2
Har Karmel (Mount Carmel) (peak), Isr. 149/G6
Har Meron (peak), Isr. 149/D3
Har Ramon (peak), Isr. 149/D4
Hara, Japan 135/A2
Harahan, La, US 195/P17
Haramachi, Japan 133/G2
Harappa (ruin), Pak. 144/B4
Harare (cap.), Zim. 163/F4
Harash, Bi'r al (well), Libya 155/K2
Haravilliers, Fr. 88/J4
Harbel, Libr. 160/C5
Harbeson, De, US 196/C6
Harbin, China 129/N2
Harbiye, Turk. 149/E1
Harbonnières, Fr. 110/B4
Harbour Breton, Nf, Can. 189/L2
Harbour Grace, Nf, Can. 189/L2
Hårby, Den. 96/D4
Hard, Aus. 115/F3
Hardä, India 147/L4
Hardangervidda NP, Nor. 96/B1
Hardau (riv.), Ger. 109/H3
Hardegsen, Ger. 109/G5
Hardenberg, Neth. 108/D3
Harderwijk, Neth. 108/C4
Hardheim, Ger. 112/C3
Hardin, Mt, US 184/G4
Harding, SAfr. 165/E3
Hardoi, India 142/C2
Hardoi Branch (riv.), India 142/C2
Hardricourt, Fr. 88/H4
Hardy (pen.), Chile 217/C7
Hare (bay), Nf, Can. 189/L1
Hare Dimona (peak), Isr. 149/G4
Harefield, Eng, UK 88/B2
Harelbeke, Belg. 110/C2
Haren, Ger. 109/E3
Haren, Neth. 108/D2
Härer, Eth. 155/P6
Harford (co.), Md, US 196/B4
Hargesheim, Ger. 111/G4
Hargeville, Fr. 88/H5
Hargeysa, Som. 155/P6
Harghita (prov.), Rom. 107/G2
Harghita (peak), Rom. 107/G2
Hari (riv.), Indo. 138/B4
Hari (str.), Est. 97/K2
Harihar, India 147/L6
Härim, Syria 149/E1
Harima (sea), Japan 132/D3
Harimä, Japan 149/D3
Harima, Japan 135/G6
Harima (bay), Japan 135/G6
Haringey (bor.), Eng, UK 88/C2
Haringhäta (riv.), Bang. 143/G4
Haringvliet (chan.), Neth. 108/B5
Haringvlietdam (dam), Neth. 108/B5
Haripur, Pak. 144/B3
Harirüd (riv.), Afg. 147/H2
Häris, WBnk. 149/G7
Harjavalta, Fin. 97/K1
Harlan, Ky, US 188/D4
Harlech, Wal, UK 92/D6
Harlingen, Tx, US 190/D5
Harlingen, Neth. 108/C2
Harlow, Eng, UK 88/D1
Harlowton, Mt, US 184/F4
Harmannsdorf, Aus. 107/N7
Harmelen, Neth. 108/B4
Harnes, Fr. 110/B3
Harney (lake), Or, US 184/D5
Harney (peak), SD, US 185/H5
Harney (valley), Or, US 184/D5
Harney, Md, US 196/A4
Harnoli, Pak. 144/A3
Haro (cape), Mex. 200/C3

Haro, Sp. 102/D1
Harold, Ca, US 194/B1
Harpenden, Eng, UK 91/F3
Harper (mt.), Yk, Can. 192/L3
Harper, Ks, US 187/H4
Harper, Libr. 160/D5
Harper, Wa, US 193/B2
Harper Woods, Mi, US 193/F7
Harpstedt, Ger. 109/F3
Harqin Zuoyi Monggolzu Zizhixian, China 130/D2
Harrah, Ok, US 195/N15
Harrai, India 142/B4
Harran, Turk. 148/D2
Harricana (riv.), Qu, Can. 181/J4
Harriman, Tn, US 188/C5
Harriman, NY, US 196/D1
Harrington, Austl. 173/E1
Harrington, De, US 196/C6
Harrington Park, NJ, US 197/K8
Harris (mt.), Austl. 171/F3
Harris (lake), Austl. 171/G4
Harris (isl.), Sc, UK 89/Q8
Harris Park, Co, US 195/B4
Hasselt, Neth. 108/D3
Harrisburg, Ne, US 185/H5
Harrisburg, Il, US 188/B4
Harrisburg (cap.), Pa, US 196/B3
Harrislee, Ger. 96/C4
Harrismith, SAfr. 164/E3
Harrison (bay), Ak, US 192/H1
Harrison, Ar, US 187/J3
Harrison, Mi, US 188/C2
Harrison, NY, US 197/L8
Harrison, NJ, US 197/J9
Harrison (cape), Nf, Can. 181/L3
Harrison (lake), BC, Can. 184/C3
Harrisonville, Il, US 195/G9
Harrisonville, Mo, US 195/E6
Harrisville, Ut, US 195/K11
Harrodsburg, Ky, US 188/C4
Harrogate, Eng, UK 93/G4
Harrow (bor.), Eng, UK 88/B2
Harry S Truman (res.), Mo, US 187/J3
Harseböl, Ger. 96/C4
Harsefeld, Ger. 109/G2
Harsewinkel, Ger. 109/F5
Harson's Island, Mi, US 193/G6
Hart (lake), Or, US 186/C2
Hart, Mi, US 188/C3
Hart (riv.), Yk, Can. 180/C2
Hart (riv.), Eng, UK 88/A3
Hart (isl.), NY, US 197/K8
Hart Fell (peak), Sc, UK 94/C6
Hartbeesrivier (riv.), SAfr. 164/C3
Härteigen (peak), Nor. 96/B1
Hatay (prov.), Turk. 148/C2
Hartelkanaal (riv.), Neth. 108/B5
Hatch (int'l arpt.), Arg. 217/B6
Hateg, Rom. 106/F3
Hartford (cap.), Ct, US 189/F3
Hartford, Il, US 195/G8
Hartford, NJ, US 196/D4
Hartford City, In, US 188/D3
Hartheim, Ger. 114/D2
Hartington, Ne, US 187/H2
Hartkirchen, Aus. 113/H6
Hartland (pt.), Eng, UK 90/B4
Hartland, Mi, US 193/E6
Hartlepool, Eng, UK 93/G2
Hartlepool (co.), Eng, UK 93/G2
Hartleton, Pa, US 196/A2
Hartley Wintney, Eng, UK 88/A3
Hartly, De, US 196/C5
Hartney, Mb, Can. 185/H3
Hartsdale, NY, US 197/K7
Hartselle, Al, US 191/G3
Hartshill, Eng, UK 91/E1
Hartstene (isl.), Wa, US 193/B3
Hartwell, Ga, US 191/H3
Hartwell (lake), Ga,Sc, US 191/H3
Hartz Mountain NP, Austl. 173/C4
Harun (peak), Indo. 139/E3
Härünäbäd, Pak. 144/B5
Härut (riv.), Afg. 147/H2
Harvard (mt.), Co, US 185/J4
Harvey, ND, US 185/J4
Harvey, Il, US 195/P17
Harvey, Austl. 170/B5
Harvey, Il, US 193/Q16
Harveys (lake), Pa, US 196/B1
Harwich, Eng, UK 91/H3
Haryana (state), India 140/C2
Harz (mts.), Ger. 98/F3
Hasan Abdäl, Pak. 144/B3
Hasan (peak), Turk. 148/C2
Hasanpur, India 142/B1
Hasbrouck Heights, NJ, US 197/J8
Hasdo (riv.), India 142/D4
Hase (riv.), Ger. 98/D2
Hasel (riv.), Ger. 112/D1
Haselünne, Ger. 109/E3

Hasenmatt (peak), Swi. 114/D3
Hashima, Japan 135/L5
Hashimoto, Japan 132/D3
Hasi el Farsia (well), WSah. 156/C4
Häsilpur, Pak. 144/B5
Haskell, Tx, US 187/H4
Haslach an der Mühl, Aus. 113/H5
Haslach im Kinzigtal, Ger. 114/E1
Hasle bei Burgdorf, Swi. 114/D3
Haslemere, Eng, UK 91/F4
Haslingden, Eng, UK 93/F4
Hasloh, Ger. 109/G1
Haspres, Fr. 110/C3
Hassa, Turk. 149/E1
Hassan, India 140/C5
Hassan (El Aaiún) (int'l arpt.), WSah. 156/C4
Hassberge (hills), Ger. 112/D2
Hassel, Ger. 109/G3
Hassel Sound (str.), Nun., Can. 181/S7
Hasselt, Neth. 108/D3
Hasselt, Belg. 111/E2
Hassfurt, Ger. 112/D2
Hassi Bahbah, Alg. 158/G5
Hassi bou Zid (well), Alg. 157/F3
Hassi el Hadjar (well), Alg. 157/G3
Hassi el Mislane (well), Alg. 157/H4
Hassi er Rebib (well), Alg. 157/H4
Hässleholm, Swe. 96/E3
Hasslo (int'l arpt.), Swe. 96/G2
Hassloch, Ger. 112/B4
Haste, Ger. 109/G4
Hastings, Austl. 173/C4
Hastings, Ne, US 187/H2
Hastings, Mi, US 188/C3
Hastings, NZ 175/T10
Hastings, Eng, UK 91/G5
Hastings Battlesite, Eng, UK 91/G5
Hastings-On-Hudson, NY, US 197/K7
Hasuda, Japan 135/D2
Hasunuma, Japan 135/E2
Hasvik, Nor. 95/G1
Hat Chao Mai NP, Thai. 136/B5
Hat Head, Austl. 173/E1
Hat Head NP, Austl. 173/E1
Hat Nai Yang NP, Thai. 136/B5
Hat Yai, Thai. 136/C5
Hat Yai (int'l arpt.), Thai. 136/C5
Hatashō, Japan 135/K5
Hatavch, Mong. 129/K2
Hatboro, Pa, US 196/C3
Hatch, NM, US 186/E4
Hatcher (peak), Arg. 217/B6
Hateg, Rom. 106/F3
Hatfield, Pa, US 196/C3
Hatfield, Eng, UK 88/C1
Hatfield Peverel, Eng, UK 88/E1
Hatgal, Mong. 128/H1
Hathras, India 142/B2
Häthras, India 142/B2
Hätia, North (isl.), Bang. 143/H4
Hätia, South (isl.), Bang. 143/H4
Hätjibah, Ras (pt.), SAr. 146/C4
Hato (int'l arpt.), NAnt. 210/D1
Hato Corozal, Col. 210/D3
Hato Mayor, DRep. 199/H4
Hatogaya, Japan 135/D2
Hatoyama, Japan 135/C2
Hatsu (isl.), Japan 135/L5
Hatta, India 142/B3
Hatta, Japan 135/A2
Hattah-Kulkyne NP, Austl. 171/J5
Hattem, Neth. 108/D4
Hatten, Ger. 109/F2
Hatteras, NC, US 191/K3
Hatteras (cape), NC, US 191/K3
Hattersheim am Mein, Ger. 112/B2
Hattiesburg, Ms, US 191/F4
Hattieville, Belz. 202/D2
Hattingen, Ger. 109/E6
Hattula, Fin. 97/L1
Hatzenbühl, Ger. 112/B4
Hatzfeld, Ger. 109/F6
Hau Giang (riv.), Viet. 136/D4
Haubourdin, Fr. 110/B2
Haud (reg.), Eth. 155/Q6
Hauge, Nor. 96/B2
Hayling (isl.), Eng, UK 91/F5
Haukipudas, Fin. 95/G2
Haukivesi (lake), Fin. 97/M1
Haune (riv.), Ger. 98/E3
Haunsberg (peak), Aus. 113/F7
Hauppauge, NY, US 197/E2
Hauraki (gulf), NZ 175/S10
Haus, Nor. 96/A1

Hausach, Ger. 114/E1
Hausjärvi, Fin. 97/L1
Hausleiten, Aus. 107/N7
Hausstock (peak), Swi. 115/F4
Haut Atlas (mts.), Mor. 154/D1
Haut-Rhin (dept.), Fr. 114/D2
Haute-Normandie (pol. reg.), Fr. 100/D2
Haute-Saône (dept.), Fr. 114/B2
Haute-Savoie (dept.), Fr. 114/C5
Hautefeuille, Fr. 88/L5
Hautes Fagnes (uplands), Belg. 111/E3
Hauteurs de Gâtine (uplands), Fr. 100/C3
Hauteville-Lompnes, Fr. 114/B6
Hautmont, Fr. 110/C3
Hauts (plat.), Alg.,Mor. 157/E2
Hauula, Hi, US 182/W12
Havant, Eng, UK 91/F5
Havasu (lake), Az,Ca, US 186/D4
Havdhem, Swe. 96/H3
Havel (canal), Ger. 98/P6
Havel (riv.), Ger. 99/G2
Havelange, Belg. 111/E3
Haveli, Pak. 144/B4
Haveli (riv.), ND, US 185/H4
Haveliän, Pak. 144/B2
Havelländischer Grosser Hauptkanal (canal), Ger. 98/P6
Havelock, NC, US 191/J3
Havelock NP, Austl. 172/G9
Havencore (isl.), Eng, UK 91/G3
Haverfordwest, Wal, UK 90/B3
Haverhill, Ma, US 189/G3
Haverhill, Eng, UK 91/G2
Havering (bor.), Eng, UK 88/D2
Haverstraw, NY, US 196/D1
Haviland, Ks, US 187/H4
Havířov, Czh. 99/K4
Havixbeck, Ger. 109/E5
Havre, Ne, US 187/H2
Havre, Il, US 193/P15
Havre, Mt, US 184/F3
Havre de Grace, Md, US 196/B4
Havre-Saint-Pierre, Qu, Can. 189/J1
Havsa, Turk. 105/K2
Havza, Turk. 148/C1
Haw (riv.), NC, US 191/J3
Hawaii (state), US 182/S10
Hawaii (isl.), Hi, US 182/U11
Hawaiian (isls.), Hi, US 175/H2
Hawaii Kai, Hi, US 182/W13
Hawaii Volcanoes NP, Hi, US 182/U11
Hawaiian Gardens, Ca, US 194/F8
Hawalli, Kuw. 146/E3
Hawarden, Wal, UK 93/E5
Hawera, NZ 175/S10
Haweswater (res.), Eng, UK 93/F2
Hawi, Hi, US 182/U10
Hawick, Sc, UK 94/D6
Hawke (cape), Austl. 173/E2
Hawke (bay), NZ 167/H6
Hawkesbury, On, Can. 188/F2
Hawkesbury (isl.), BC, Can. 184/A2
Hawkesbury (riv.), Austl. 172/G8
Hawks Nest, Austl. 173/E2
Haworth, NJ, US 197/K8
Haworth, Eng, UK 93/F4
Hawsh 'Isá, Egypt 149/B4
Hawthorn, SAfr. 164/L11
Hawthorn Woods, Il, US 193/P15
Hawthorne, Nv, US 186/C3
Hawthorne, Ca, US 194/F8
Hawthorne, Nv, US 197/J8
Hawthorne, NY, US 197/K8
Hawwärah, Jor. 149/D3
Haxby, Eng, UK 93/G3
Hay (pt.), Austl. 172/C3
Hay (riv.), Ab,BC, Can. 180/E3
Hay River, NW, Can. 180/E2
Hayachine-san (peak), Japan 134/B4
Hayakawa, Japan 135/A3
Hayama, Japan 135/C3
Hayange, Fr. 111/F4
Haybes, Fr. 111/D4
Haydock, Eng, UK 93/F5
Hayes (mt.), Ak, US 192/J3
Hayes (pen.), Grld. 181/T7
Hayes (riv.), Mb, Can. 185/K2
Hayingen, Ger. 115/F1
Haylaastay, Mong. 129/K2
Hayle, Eng, UK 90/A6
Hayling (isl.), Eng, UK 91/F5
Haymana, Turk. 148/C2
Haymarket, Va, US 196/A5
Haynesville, La, US 187/J4
Hayrabolu, Turk. 107/H5
Hays, Ks, US 187/H3
Hays (co.), Tx, US 195/U20
Haysyn, Ukr. 120/D2
Hayward, Wi, US 185/L4

Hazär (mtn.), Iran 147/G3
Hazard, Ky, US 188/D4
Hazäribag, India 143/E4
Hazebrouck, Fr. 110/B2
Hazel Park, Mi, US 193/F7
Hazelwood, Mo, US 195/G8
Hazen (bay), Ak, US 192/E3
Hazen (str.), NW,Nun., Can. 181/R7
Hazlehurst, Ms, US 187/K5
Hazlemere, Eng, UK 88/A2
Hazlet, NJ, US 197/J10
Hazleton (mts.), BC, Can. 184/A2
Hazleton, Pa, US 196/C2
Hazlett (lake), Austl. 171/F2
Hazratbal Mosque, India 144/C2
Hazu, Japan 135/M6
He (riv.), China 137/B3
He Xian, China 130/D5
Headcorn, Eng, UK 91/G4
Heads of Ayr (pt.), Sc, UK 94/B6
Healdsburg, Ca, US 186/B3
Healesville, Austl. 173/G5
Healy, Ak, US 192/J3
Heanor, Eng, UK 93/G6
Heard (isl.), Austl. 218/E
Hearst, On, Can. 188/D1
Heart (riv.), ND, US 185/H4
Heart Law (hill), Sc, UK 94/D5
Heath (pt.), Qu, Can. 189/J1
Heathcote, Austl. 173/C3
Heathcote NP, Austl. 172/G9
Heathrow (int'l arpt.), Eng, UK 88/B2
Hebbronville, Tx, US 190/D5
Hebei (prov.), China 129/K4
Hebertshausen, Ger. 113/E6
Hebrides (isls.), UK 89/Q8
Hebrides (sea), Sc, UK 89/Q8
Hebron, Ne, US 187/H2
Hebron, Il, US 193/P15
Heby, Swe. 96/G2
Hecate (str.), BC, Can. 180/C3
Hecelchakán, Mex. 202/D1
Hechi, China 141/J3
Hechingen, Ger. 112/B6
Hechtel, Belg. 111/E1
Hechthausen, Ger. 109/G1
Hecker, Il, US 195/H9
Hecla, SD, US 185/J4
Hecla and Griper (bay), NW,Nun., Can. 181/R7
Hector (mt.), Ab, Can. 184/D3
Heddal, Nor. 96/C2
Hedel, Neth. 108/C5
Hedemora, Swe. 96/F1
Hedensted, Den. 96/C4
Hedmark (co.), Nor. 95/D3
Hedo-misaki (cape), Japan 133/K7
Hédouville, Fr. 88/J4
Heede, Ger. 109/E3
Heek, Ger. 109/E4
Heemskerk, Neth. 108/B3
Heemstede, Neth. 108/B4
Heerde, Neth. 108/D4
Heerenveen, Neth. 108/C3
Heerhugowaard, Neth. 108/B3
Heerlen, Neth. 111/E2
Heers, Belg. 111/E2
Heesch, Neth. 108/C5
Heeslingen, Ger. 109/G2
Heeze, Neth. 108/C6
Hefa (Haifa), Isr. 149/F6
Hefei, China 130/D5
Hefeng Tujiazu Zizhixian, China 137/B2
Hefner (lake), Ok, US 195/M14
Hegang, China 129/P2
Hegau (mts.), Ger. 101/H3
Hegau (reg.), Ger. 98/E5
Heggenes, Nor. 96/C1
Hegins, Pa, US 196/B2
Hegura, Japan 135/L5
Hei (riv.), Japan 134/B4
Heide, Ger. 96/C4
Heideck, Ger. 112/E4
Heidelberg, SAfr. 164/C4
Heidelberg, SAfr. 164/E2
Heidelberg, Ger. 112/B4
Heiden, Ger. 108/D5
Heiden, Swi. 115/F3
Heidenheim, Ger. 112/D5
Heidenreichstein, Aus. 99/H4
Heiderscheid, Lux. 111/E4
Heigenbrücken, Ger. 112/C2
Heihe, China 129/N1
Heikendorf, Ger. 96/D4
Heilbron, SAfr. 164/D2
Heilbronn, Ger. 112/C4
Heiligenberg, Ger. 115/F2
Heiligenblut, Aus. 101/K3
Heiligenhafen, Ger. 96/D3
Heiligenhaus, Ger. 108/D6
Heiligenstadt, Ger. 109/H6
Heilong (Amur) (riv.), China, Rus. 123/N5
Heilongjiang (prov.), China 129/N2
Heiloo, Neth. 108/B3

Heimaey (isl.), Ice. 95/N7
Heimbach, Ger. 111/F2
Heimberg, Swi. 114/D4
Heimsheim, Ger. 112/B5
Heino, Neth. 108/D4
Heinola, Fin. 97/M1
Heinsberg, Ger. 111/F1
Heishan, China 131/B2
Heist-op-den-Berg, Belg. 111/D1
Heitersheim, Ger. 114/D2
Heiwa, Japan 135/L5
Hejian, China 130/D3
Hejin, China 130/B4
Hejing, China 128/E3
Hekimhan, Turk. 148/D2
Hekinan, Japan 135/L6
Hekla (vol.), Ice. 95/N7
Hekou, China 141/H3
Hel, Pol. 97/H4
Helan (mts.), China 128/J4
Helbe (riv.), Ger. 109/H6
Helden, Neth. 108/D6
Helena (cap.), Mt, US 184/E4
Helena, Austl. 170/L6
Helensburgh, Sc, UK 94/B4
Helgasjön (lake), Swe. 96/F3
Helgoland (isl.), Ger. 96/B4
Helgoländer (bay), Wa, US 193/B3
Helgoländer (bay), Ger. 96/C5
Heliodora, Braz. 213/H7
Heliport (int'l arpt.), Swe. 96/E3
Hellas (see Greece)
Helleh (riv.), Iran 146/F3
Hellendoorn, Neth. 108/D4
Hellenthal, Ger. 111/F2
Hellertown, Pa, US 196/C2
Hellevoetsluis, Neth. 108/B5
Hellin, Sp. 102/E3
Hells (canyon), Id, US 184/D4
Hells Canyon Nat'l Rec. Area, US 184/D4
Hell's Gate NP, Kenya 162/C3
Helmand (riv.), Afg. 147/H2
Helmbrechts, Ger. 113/E2
Helmet (mtn.), Ak, US 192/K2
Helmetta, NJ, US 197/H10
Helmond, Neth. 108/C6
Helmstadt, Ger. 112/C3
Helmstedt, Ger. 98/F2
Helong, China 129/N3
Helotes, Tx, US 195/T20
Helper, Ut, US 186/E3
Helsenhorn (peak), Swi. 114/E5
Helsingør, Den. 96/E3
Helsinki (Helsingfors) (cap.), Fin. 95/H3
Helsinki-Vantaa (int'l arpt.), Fin. 97/L1
Hem (riv.), Fr. 110/B2
Hemau, Ger. 113/E4
Heeia, Hi, US 182/W13
Hemel Hempstead, Eng, UK 88/B1
Hemer, Ger. 109/E6
Hemet, Ca, US 194/D3
Hemmingen, Ger. 109/G4
Hemmoor, Ger. 109/G1
Hemphill, Tx, US 190/E4
Hempstead, Tx, US 187/H5
Hempstead (har.), NY, US 197/L8
Hempstead, NY, US 197/L9
Hemse, Swe. 96/H3
Hemsedal, Nor. 96/C1
Hemsworth, Eng, UK 93/G4
Henan (prov.), China 129/K5
Henares (riv.), Sp. 102/D2
Henashi-zaki (pt.), Japan 134/A3
Hendaye, Fr. 100/C5
Hendek, Turk. 107/K5
Henderson, NC, US 188/E4
Henderson, Nv, US 186/D3
Henderson, Tn, US 188/B5
Henderson, Ky, US 188/C4
Henderson, Co, US 195/C3
Henderson, Arg. 216/E3
Henderson, Md, US 196/C5
Hendersonville, Tn, US 188/C4
Hendersonville, NC, US 191/H3
Hendrik-Ido-Ambacht, Neth. 108/B5
Hendrik Verwoerdam (res.), SAfr. 164/D3
Hendrina, SAfr. 164/E2
Henefer, Ut, US 195/L11
Heng (mtn.), China 130/C3
Heng (riv.), China 130/L8
Heng Xian, China 141/J3
Hengduan (mts.), China 128/G6
Hengelo, Neth. 108/D4
Hengersberg, Ger. 113/G5
Hengoed, Wal, UK 90/C3
Hengshan, China 137/B2
Hengshan, China 130/B3
Hengshui, China 130/C3
Hengyang, China 137/B2

Hénin-Beaumont, Fr. 110/B3
Henley-on-Thames, Eng, UK 91/F3
Henlopen (cape), De, US 196/C6
Henlopen Acres, De, US 196/C6
Henndorf am Wallersee, Aus. 113/G7
Henne, Den. 96/C4
Hennebont, Fr. 100/B3
Hennef, Ger. 111/G2
Hennenman, SAfr. 164/D2
Hennigsdorf, Ger. 98/Q6
Henrietta, Tx, US 187/H4
Henrietta Maria (cape), On, Can. 181/H3
Henry (cape), BC, Can. 192/M5
Henry (mts.), Ut, US 186/E3
Henry Ford Museum and Greenfield Village Historical Site, Mi, US 193/E7
Henryetta, Ok, US 187/J4
Henryville, Pa, US 196/C1
Henty, Austl. 173/C2
Henzada, Myan. 141/G4
Heping, China 137/B3
Heppenheim an der Bergstrasse, Ger. 112/B3
Hepu, China 141/J3
Heqing, China 141/H2
Heradhsvötn (riv.), Ice. 95/N6
Herät, Afg. 147/H2
Herbert, Sk, Can. 184/G3
Herbert River (falls), Austl. 172/B2
Herbert River Falls NP, Austl. 172/B2
Herberton, Austl. 172/B2
Herbeumont, Belg. 111/E4
Herbolzheim, Ger. 114/D1
Herbrechtingen, Ger. 112/D5
Herbstein, Ger. 112/C1
Hercegnovi, Mont. 106/D4
Hercílio Luz (int'l arpt.), Braz. 213/B3
Herculaneum, Mo, US 195/G9
Herculaneum (ruin), It. 104/D2
Hercules, Ca, US 193/K10
Herdecke, Ger. 109/E6
Herdorf, Ger. 111/G2
Hereford, Eng, UK 90/D2
Hereford, Md, US 196/B4
Hereford (inlet), NJ, US 196/D5
Hereford, Pa, US 196/C3
Hereford, Tx, US 187/G4
Herefordshire (co.), Eng, UK 90/D2
Hereheretue (isl.), FrPol. 175/L7
Herentals, Belg. 108/B6
Herford, Ger. 109/F4
Hergiswil, Swi. 115/E4
Héricourt, Fr. 114/C2
Hérimoncourt, Fr. 114/C3
Herington, Ks, US 187/H3
Herisau, Swi. 115/F3
Herk (riv.), Belg. 111/E2
Herk-de-Stad, Belg. 111/E2
Hèrlèn Gol (Kerulen) (riv.), Mong. 129/K2
Herleshausen, Ger. 109/H6
Herma Ness (cape), Sc, UK 89/W13
Hermann, Mo, US 187/K3
Hermannsburg, Ger. 109/H3
Hermannsburg, Austl. 171/G2
Hermannsverk, Nor. 96/B1
Hermanus, SAfr. 164/L11
Hermeray, Fr. 88/G6
Hermersberg, Ger. 111/F5
Hermes, Fr. 110/B5
Hermeskeil, Ger. 111/F4
Hermiston, Or, US 184/D4
Hermitage, Rus. 119/T7
Hermosa Beach, Ca, US 194/F8
Hermosillo, Mex. 200/C2
Hernández, Mex. 200/E4
Hernando, Ms, US 187/K4
Hernani, Sp. 102/E1
Herndon, Pa, US 196/B2
Herne, Ger. 109/E5
Herne, Belg. 110/D2
Herne Bay, Eng, UK 91/H4
Herning, Den. 96/C3
Heroes de la Independencia, Mex. 200/B3
Heroica Caborca, Mex. 200/B2
Heroica Ciudad de Tlaxiaco, Mex. 202/B2
Heroica Nogales, Mex. 200/C2
Heroldsberg, Ger. 112/E3
Hérouville, Fr. 88/J4
Hérouville-Saint-Clair, Fr. 100/C2
Heroy, Nor. 95/D1
Herpf (riv.), Ger. 112/D1
Herre, Nor. 96/C2
Herrenberg, Ger. 112/B5
Herrera, Sp. 102/C4
Herrera de Pisuerga, Sp. 102/C1
Herrera del Duque, Sp. 102/C3
Herrero (pt.), Mex. 202/E2
Herrestad, Swe. 96/D2
Herrieden, Ger. 112/D4
Herriman, Ut, US 195/J12
Herrljunga, Swe. 96/E2
Herrsching am Ammersee, Ger. 115/H2
Hersbruck, Ger. 113/E3
Herschbach, Ger. 111/G2
Herscheid, Ger. 109/E6
Herselt, Belg. 111/D1
Hershey, Pa, US 196/B3
Hersheypark, Pa, US 196/B3
Herstal, Belg. 111/E2
Herten, Ger. 109/E5
Herve, Belg. 111/E2
Herxheim bei Landau, Ger. 112/B4
Herzberg am Harz, Ger. 109/H5
Herzbrock-Clarholz, Ger. 109/F5
Herzele, Belg. 110/C2
Herzliyya, Isr. 149/F7
Herzogenaurach, Ger. 112/D3
Herzogenbuchsee, Swi. 114/D3
Herzogenburg, Aus. 106/B4
Herzogenrath, Ger. 111/F2
Hesbaye (plat.), Belg. 98/C3
Hesdin, Fr. 110/B3
Hesel, Ger. 109/E2
Heshui, China 128/J4
Heshun, China 130/C3
Hésingue, Fr. 114/D2
Hesperange, Lux. 111/F4
Hesperia, Ca, US 194/C2
Hess (riv.), Yk, Can. 180/C2
Hessel (riv.), Ger. 109/F5
Hesselø (isl.), Den. 96/D3
Hessen (state), Ger. 101/H1
Hessen, Ger. 98/F4
Hessisch Lichtenau, Ger. 109/G6
Hessisch Oldendorf, Ger. 109/G4
Heteauğä, Nepal 143/E2
Heteren, Neth. 108/C5
Hettenleidelheim, Ger. 112/B3
Hettinger, ND, US 185/H4
Hetton-le-Hole, Eng, UK 93/G2
Hettstadt, Ger. 112/C3
Hetzerath, Ger. 111/F4
Heubach (riv.), Ger. 109/E5
Heubach, Ger. 112/C5
Heuchelheim, Ger. 112/B1
Heukuppe (peak), Aus. 99/H5
Heusden, Neth. 108/C5
Heusden-Zolder, Belg. 111/E1
Heusenstamm, Ger. 112/B2
Heusweiler, Ger. 111/F5
Hève, Cap de la (cape), Fr. 100/D2
Heves, Hun. 106/E2
Heves (co.), Hun. 99/L5
Hewitt, NJ, US 197/H8
Hewlett (pt.), NY, US 197/L8
Hewlett, NY, US 197/L9
Hex River (mts.), SAfr. 164/L10
Hex River (pass), SAfr. 164/L10
Hexenkopf (peak), Aus. 115/G3
Heyerode, Ger. 109/H6
Heythuysen, Neth. 108/C6
Heywood, Austl. 173/B3
Heywood, Eng, UK 93/F4
Heze, China 130/C4
Hialeah, Fl, US 191/H5
Hiawatha, Ks, US 187/J3
Hibbing, Mn, US 185/K4
Hibbs (pt.), Austl. 173/C4
Hicacos (pt.), Cuba 199/F1
Hichisō, Japan 135/M4
Hickman (mt.), BC, Can. 192/M4
Hickory, NC, US 191/H3
Hickory, La, US 195/T4
Hickory Run State Park, Pa, US 196/C2
Hicksville, NY, US 197/L8
Hico, Tx, US 187/H5
Hida, Japan 135/L4
Hida (riv.), Japan 132/D4
Hidaka, Japan 135/A2
Hidaka (riv.), Japan 132/D4
Hidaka (mts.), Japan 134/C2
Hidaka, Japan 134/C2
Hidalgo, Mex. 201/F3
Hidalgo (state), Mex. 182/B3
Hidalgo del Parral, Mex. 200/D3
Hidden Hills, Ca, US 194/E7
Hiddenhausen, Ger. 109/F4
Hidrolândia, Braz. 212/B2
Hierapolis (ruin), Turk. 148/B2
Hieroglyphic (mts.), Az, US 195/R18
Hierro (isl.), Canl., Sp. 156/A4

Hieve (lake), Ger. 109/E2
Higashi-Chichibu, Japan 135/C1
Higashi-Matsuyama, Japan 135/C1
Higashi-Ōsaka, Japan 135/J6
Higashikurume, Japan 135/D2
Higashimurayama, Japan 135/C2
Higashine, Japan 134/B4
Higashiura, Japan 135/G6
Higashiura, Japan 135/L6
Higashiyoshino, Japan 135/J7
High (des.), Or, US 184/C5
High (hill), Pa, US 196/C1
High (isl.), China 129/V10
High Bridge, NJ, US 196/D2
High Island, Tx, US 190/E4
High Level, Ab, Can. 180/E3
High Point, NC, US 191/H3
High Ridge, Mo, US 195/F9
High River, Ab, Can. 184/E3
High Street (peak), Eng, UK 93/F3
High Willhays (hill), Eng, UK 90/B5
High Wycombe, Eng, UK 91/F3
Higham, Eng, UK 88/E2
Higham Ferrers, Eng, UK 91/F2
Highland, Ca, US 194/C2
Highland, Ut, US 195/K13
Highland, In, US 193/R16
Highland (pol. reg.), Sc, UK 94/A2
Highland Lakes, NJ, US 196/D1
Highland Park, Co, US 195/A4
Highland Park, Mi, US 193/F7
Highland Park, NJ, US 197/H10
Highlands, NJ, US 197/K10
Highrock (lake), Mb, Can. 185/H2
Highspire, Pa, US 196/B3
Hightstown, NJ, US 196/D3
Highwood, Il, US 193/Q15
Higley, Az, US 195/S19
Higuera de Zaragoza, Mex. 200/C3
Hihyā, Egypt 149/B4
Hiidenportin NP, Fin. 95/J3
Hiiumaa (isl.), Est. 97/K2
Híjar, Sp. 103/E2
Hijāz, Jabal al (mts.), SAr. 146/C3
Hiji, Japan 132/B4
Hijuelas de Conchalí, Chile 216/N8
Hikami, Japan 135/H5
Hikari, Japan 135/F2
Hikone, Japan 135/K5
Hikueru (isl.), FrPol. 175/L6
Hikurangi (peak), NZ 175/T10
Hildburghausen, Ger. 112/D2
Hilden, Ger. 111/F1
Hilders, Ger. 112/C1
Hildesheim, Ger. 109/G4
Hilgermissen, Ger. 109/G3
Hill (isl.), Pa, US 196/B3
Hill City, Ks, US 187/H3
Hill of Fare (hill), Sc, UK 94/D2
Hill of Stake (hill), Sc, UK 94/B5
Hillaby (mt.), Bar. 199/P9
Hillburn, NY, US 197/J7
Hillcrest, NY, US 197/J7
Hille, Ger. 109/F4
Hillegom, Neth. 108/B4
Hillerød, Den. 96/E4
Hillesheim, Ger. 111/F3
Hillingdon (bor.), Eng, UK 88/B2
Hillsboro, Md, US 196/C6
Hillsboro, ND, US 185/J4
Hillsboro, Oh, US 188/D4
Hillsboro, Or, US 184/C4
Hillsboro, Tx, US 187/H4
Hillsborough (chan.), Austl. 172/C3
Hillsborough, Ca, US 193/K11
Hillsborough, NJ, US 196/D3
Hillsdale, Mi, US 188/C3
Hillsdale, Ks, US 195/D6
Hillsdale (lake), Ks, US 195/D6
Hillsdale, NJ, US 197/J7
Hillside, NJ, US 197/J9
Hillside, Sc, UK 94/D3
Hillston, Austl. 173/C2
Hillswick, Sc, UK 89/W13
Hilltop, Co, US 195/C4
Hilltown, NI, UK 92/B3
Hilo, Hi, US 182/U11
Hilongos, Phil. 137/D5
Hilpoltstein, Ger. 112/E4
Hilpsford (pt.), Eng, UK 93/E3
Hilsa, India 143/E3
Hilterfingen, Swi. 114/D4
Hilton Head (isl.), SC, US 191/H3
Hilton Head Island, SC, US 191/H3
Hilvarenbeek, Neth. 108/C6
Hilversum, Neth. 108/C4
Hilzingen, Ger. 115/E2
Himāchal Pradesh (state), India 144/D3
Himalaya (range), Asia 125/G6
Himālchuli (peak), Nepal 143/E1
Himamaylan, Phil. 137/D5
Himanka, Fin. 95/G2
Himberg, Aus. 107/N7
Himeji, Japan 132/D3
Himeji Castle, Japan 132/D3
Himi, Japan 133/E2
Himmelpforten, Ger. 109/G1
Ḩimş (prov.), Syria 148/D3
Ḩimş, Syria 149/E2
Hinche, Haiti 203/H2
Hinchinbrook (isl.), Austl. 167/D2
Hinchinbrook Entrance (chan.), Ak., US 192/J3
Hinchinbrook Island NP, Austl. 172/B2
Hinckley, Eng, UK 91/E1
Hincks Conservation Park, Austl. 171/H5
Hindan (riv.), India 142/A1
Hindaun, India 142/A2
Hindelang, Ger. 115/G3
Hindeloopen, Neth. 108/C3
Hindley, Eng, UK 93/F4
Hindmarsh (lake), Austl. 173/B3
Hindu Kush (mts.), Asia 125/F6
Hindupur, India 140/C5
Hinesville, Ga, US 191/H4
Hinganghāt, India 140/C3
Hingol (riv.), Pak. 147/J3
Hingoli, India 140/C4
Hingorja, Pak. 147/J3
Hınıs, Turk. 148/E2
Hino, Japan 135/K5
Hino, Japan 135/C2
Hino (riv.), Japan 135/K5
Hino-misaki (cape), Japan 132/C3
Hinode, Japan 135/C2
Hinohara, Japan 135/C2
Hinojosa del Duque, Sp. 102/C3
Hinsdale, Il, US 193/Q16
Hinte, Ger. 109/E2
Hinterbrühl, Aus. 107/N7
Hinterrhein (riv.), Swi. 115/F4
Hinterrugg (peak), Swi. 115/F3
Hinterweidenthal, Ger. 111/G5
Hinton, Ab, Can. 184/D2
Hinton, WV, US 188/D4
Hinwil, Swi. 115/E3
Hipólito Bouchard, Arg. 216/E2
Hippolytushoef, Neth. 108/B3
Hipswell, Eng, UK 93/G3
Hira Highlands (uplands), Japan 135/J5
Hirado, Japan 132/A4
Hirakata, Japan 135/J6
Hirakud (res.), India 140/D3
Hiraman (riv.), Kenya 162/C3
Hiran (riv.), India 142/B4
Hiranai, Japan 134/B3
Hirara, Japan 133/H8
Hirata, Japan 132/C3
Hirata, Japan 135/L5
Hiratsuka, Japan 135/C3
Hirfanli (dam), Turk. 148/C2
Hirlău, Rom. 107/H2
Hiro'o, Japan 134/C2
Hirosaki, Japan 134/B3
Hiroshima, Japan 132/C3
Hiroshima (pref.), Japan 132/C3
Hirschaid, Ger. 112/D3
Hirschau, Ger. 113/E3
Hirschhorn, Ger. 112/B4
Hirson, Fr. 111/D4
Hîrşova, Rom. 107/H3
Hirtshals, Den. 96/C3
Hirukawa, Japan 135/M4
Hisai, Japan 135/K6
Hisarcık, Turk. 148/B2
Hisbān, Jor. 149/D4
Ḩişn al 'Abr, Yem. 146/E5
Hispaniola (isl.), DRep.,Haiti 199/G4
Historic Houses of Odessa, De, US 196/C5
Historic Towne of Smithville, NJ, US 196/D5
Hisua, India 143/E3
Hīt, Iraq 148/E3
Hitachi, Japan 133/G2
Hitachi-Ōta, Japan 133/G2
Hitchin, Eng, UK 91/F3
Hitoyoshi, Japan 132/B4
Hitra (isl.), Nor. 95/C3
Hittisau, Aus. 115/F3
Hitzacker, Ger. 98/F2
Hitzkirch, Swi. 115/E3
Hiyoshi, Japan 135/J5
Hizan, Turk. 148/E2
Hjälmaren (lake), Swe. 96/G2
Hjartfjellet (peak), Nor. 95/E2
Hjelmeland, Nor. 96/B2
Hjerm, Den. 96/C3
Hjo, Swe. 96/F2
Hjørring, Den. 96/C3
Hka (riv.), Myan. 136/B1
Hkakabo (peak), Myan. 141/G2
Hlabisa, SAfr. 165/E3
Hlohovec, Slvk. 106/C1
Hluboká nad Vltava, Czh. 113/H4
Hluhluwe, SAfr. 165/F3
Hlukhiv, Ukr. 120/E2
Hmawbi, Myan. 141/G4
Ho, Gha. 161/F5
Hoa Binh, Viet. 136/D1
Hoare (bay), Nun., Can. 181/K2
Hobara, Japan 133/G2
Hobart, Austl. 173/C4
Hobart (int'l arpt.), Austl. 173/C4
Hobart, Wa, US 193/D3
Hobbs, NM, US 187/G4
Hoboken, Belg. 108/B6
Hoboken, NJ, US 197/J9
Hoboksar Monggol Zizhixian, China 128/E2
Hobro, Den. 96/C3
Hochalmspitze (peak), Aus. 101/K3
Höchberg, Ger. 112/C3
Hochdorf, Ger. 115/F1
Hochfelden, Fr. 111/G6
Hochfinstler (peak), Swi. 115/F3
Hochgrat (peak), Ger. 115/G3
Hochheim am Main, Ger. 112/B2
Hochkönig (peak), Aus. 101/K3
Hŏch'ŏn (riv.), NKor. 131/D2
Hochschwab (peak), Aus. 101/L3
Hochsimmer (peak), Ger. 111/G3
Hochspeyer, Ger. 111/G5
Höchst, Aus. 115/F3
Höchst im Odenwald, Ger. 112/B3
Hochstadt am Main, Ger. 112/E2
Höchstadt an der Aisch, Ger. 112/D3
Hochstädt an der Donau, Ger. 112/D5
Hochstetten-Dhaun, Ger. 111/G4
Hochvogel (peak), Aus. 115/G3
Hochwang (peak), Swi. 115/F4
Hockenheim, Ger. 112/B4
Hockessin, De, US 196/C4
Hockley, Eng, UK 88/F2
Hod Hasharon, Isr. 149/F7
Hodal, India 142/A2
Hodder (riv.), Eng, UK 93/F4
Hoddesdon, Eng, UK 88/D1
Hodenhagen, Ger. 109/G3
Hodges (lake), Ca, US 194/C4
Hodgeville, Sk, Can. 184/G3
Hodh (phys. reg.), Mrta. 160/C2
Hodh El Gharbi (pol. reg.), Mrta. 160/C2
Hódmezővásárhely, Hun. 106/E2
Hodonín, Czh. 99/J4
Hoekse Waard (isl.), Neth. 108/B5
Hoensbroek, Neth. 111/E2
Hoeselt, Belg. 111/E2
Hoevelaken, Neth. 108/C4
Hoeven, Neth. 108/B5
Hoeybuktmoen (int'l arpt.), Nor. 95/J1
Hof, Ger. 113/E2
Hofbieber, Ger. 112/C1
Höfdhakaupstadhur, Ice. 95/N6
Hoffman Estates, Il, US 193/P15
Hofgeismar, Ger. 109/G6
Hofheim am Taunus, Ger. 112/B2
Hofheim in Unterfranken, Ger. 112/D2
Hofmeyr, SAfr. 164/D3
Hofong Qagan Salt (lake), China 130/B3
Hofors, Swe. 96/G1
Hofsá (riv.), Ice. 95/P6
Hofsjökull (glacier), Ice. 95/N7
Hōfu, Japan 132/B3
Hogarth (mt.), Austl. 171/H2
Hogyész, Hun. 106/D2
Hoh Xil (mts.), China 128/E4
Höhbürd, Mong. 128/H2
Hohe Acht (peak), Ger. 111/G3
Hohe Geige (peak), Aus. 115/G4
Hohe Tauern (mts.), Aus. 101/K3
Hohe Tauern NP, Aus. 101/K3
Hohegrass (peak), Ger. 109/G6
Hohen Neuendorf, Ger. 98/Q6
Hohenbrunn, Ger. 113/E6
Hohenems, Aus. 115/F3
Hohenhameln, Ger. 109/H4
Hohenlinden, Ger. 113/E6
Hohenlockstedt, Ger. 98/E2
Hohenloher Ebene (plain), Ger. 98/E4
Hohenpeissenberg, Ger. 115/G2
Hohenroth, Ger. 112/D2
Hoher Dachstein (peak), Aus. 101/K3
Hoher Ifen (peak), Ger. 115/G3
Hoher Randen (peak), Ger. 115/E2
Hohgant (peak), Swi. 114/D4
Hohhot, China 129/K3
Höhn, Ger. 111/G2
Hohneck (peak), Fr. 114/D1
Hohnstorf, Ger. 109/H2
Hohokam Pima Nat'l Mon., Az, US 186/E4
Höhr-Grenzhausen, Ger. 111/G3
Hoi An, Viet. 136/E3
Hoima, Ugan. 162/A2
Hoisington, Ks, US 187/H3
Højby, Den. 96/D4
Højer, Den. 96/C4
Hōjō, Japan 132/C4
Hokitika, NZ 175/S11
Hokkaidō (isl.), Japan 134/B2
Hokksund, Nor. 96/C2
Hokota, Japan 133/G2
Hokudan, Japan 135/G6
Hokusei, Japan 135/L5
Hol, Nor. 96/C1
Holbox, Mex. 202/E1
Holbrook, Austl. 173/C2
Holbrook, Az, US 186/E4
Holbrook, NY, US 197/E2
Holderness (pen.), Eng, UK 93/H4
Holdorf, Ger. 109/F3
Holdrege, Ne, US 187/H2
Holeby, Den. 96/D4
Holguín, Cuba 203/G1
Holiday Hills, Il, US 193/P15
Holitna (riv.), Ak, US 192/G3
Höljes, Swe. 96/E1
Holladay-Cottonwood, Ut, US 195/K12
Holland, Mi, US 188/C3
Holland (pt.), Md, US 196/B6
Hollandale, Ms, US 187/K4
Hollandse IJssel (riv.), Neth. 108/B5
Hollandstoun, Sc, UK 89/V14
Hollenstedt, Ger. 109/G2
Hollfeld, Ger. 112/E3
Holliday, Ks, US 195/D5
Hollis, Ok, US 187/H4
Hollis, Ak, US 192/M4
Hollister, Ca, US 186/B3
Hollister (mt.), Austl. 170/B2
Hollogne-aux-Pierres, Belg. 111/E2
Hollola, Fin. 97/L1
Höllviksnäs, Swe. 96/E4
Holly, Wa, US 193/B2
Holly Springs, Ms, US 191/F3
Hollywood, Fl, US 191/H5
Hollywood Bowl, Ca, US 194/F7
Hollywood Park, Tx, US 195/U20
Holm, Ger. 109/G1
Holman, NW, Can. 180/E1
Hólmavík, Ice. 95/N6
Holmdel, NJ, US 196/D3
Holmes (reefs), Austl. 167/D2
Holmesdale (valley), Eng, UK 88/C3
Holmestrand, Nor. 96/D2
Holmfirth, Eng, UK 93/G4
Holmsjön (lake), Swe. 95/F3
Holmsund, Swe. 95/G3
Holon, Isr. 149/F7
Holstebro, Den. 96/C3
Holston (riv.), Tn, US 191/H2
Holt, Mo, US 195/E5
Holt, Ca, US 193/M11
Holtålen, Nor. 95/D3
Holten, Neth. 108/D4
Holtland, Ger. 109/E2
Holton, Ks, US 187/J3
Holtsville, NY, US 197/E2
Holy (isl.), Sc, UK 94/A5
Holy Cross, Ak, US 192/G3
Holyhead, Wal, UK 92/D5
Holyoke, Co, US 187/G2
Holyoke, Ma, US 189/F3
Holywell, Wal, UK 93/E5
Holywood, NI, UK 92/C2
Holzkirchen, Ger. 101/J3
Holzminden, Ger. 109/G5
Holzwickede, Ger. 109/E5
Hom (riv.), Namb. 164/B3
Homberg, Ger. 109/G6
Homberg, Ger. 108/D6
Hombori Tondo (peak), Mali 161/E3
Hombourg-Haut, Fr. 111/F5
Homburg, Ger. 111/G5
Home (bay), Nun., Can. 181/K2
Home Hill, Austl. 172/B2
Homécourt, Fr. 111/E5
Homeland, Ca, US 194/C3
Homer, Ak, US 192/H4
Homer, La, US 187/J4
Homestead, Fl, US 191/H5
Homestead Nat'l Mon. of America, Ne, US 187/H2
Homewood, Al, US 191/G3
Homewood, Il, US 193/Q16
Homib (riv.), Erit. 146/C5
Hommersåk, Nor. 96/A2
Homochitto (riv.), Ms, US 190/F4
Homyel', Bela. 120/D1
Homyel'skaya Voblasts Bela. 120/D1
Hon Quan, Viet. 136/D4
Honaunau-Napoopoo, Hi, US 182/U11
Honbetsu, Japan 134/C2
Honddu (riv.), Wal, UK 90/C2
Hondeklipbaai, SAfr. 164/B3
Hondo (riv.), Belz. 202/D2
Hondo, Japan 132/B4
Hondo, Tx, US 187/H5
Hondschoote, Fr. 110/B2
Hondsrug (reg.), Neth. 108/D3
Hondsrug (hills), Neth. 98/D2
Honduras (gulf), NAm. 202/E2
Honduras (ctry.) 202/E3
Honey (lake), Ca, US 184/C5
Honey Brook, Pa, US 196/C3
Honey Creek, Wi, US 193/P14
Hong (isl.), SKor. 131/C5
Hong (lake), China 130/C5
Hong (riv.), China 130/C4
Hong Gai, Viet. 141/J3
Hong Kong (dpcy.), China 137/B3
Hong Kong (isl.), China 137/B3
Hong'an, China 130/C5
Hongch'ŏn, SKor. 131/D4
Hongdu (riv.), China 141/J2
Honghu, China 137/B2
Hongjiang, China 141/J2
Hongqiao (int'l arpt.), China 130/L8
Hongshui (riv.), China 128/J6
Hongsŏng, SKor. 131/D4
Hongtong, China 130/B3
Honguedo (passg.), Qu, Can. 189/H1
Hongwŏn, NKor. 131/D2
Hongze, China 130/D4
Hœnheim, Fr. 111/G6
Honiara (cap.), Sol. 174/E5
Honjō, Japan 134/B4
Honjō, Japan 135/C1
Honolulu (cap.), Hi, US 182/T10
Honolulu (co.), Hi, US 182/V13
Honolulu (int'l arpt.), Hi, US 182/W13
Honouliuli, Hi, US 182/V13
Hönow, Ger. 98/Q6
Honshū (isl.), Japan 129/Q5
Hood (pt.), Austl. 170/C5
Hood, Ca, US 193/L10
Hood (mt.), Ca, US 193/J10
Hood (mt.), Or, US 184/C4
Hood Canal (str.), Wa, US 184/C4
Hoofddorp, Neth. 108/B4
Hoogeloon, Neth. 108/C6
Hoogeveen, Neth. 108/D3
Hoogeveense Vaart (canal), Neth. 108/D3
Hoogezand, Neth. 108/D2
Hooghly (riv.), India 143/F5
Hooghly-Chinsura, India 143/G4
Hoogkarspel, Neth. 108/C3
Hooglede, Belg. 110/C2
Hoogstraten, Belg. 108/B6
Hook (pt.), Ire. 89/Q10
Hook (sound), Austl. 172/C3
Hookena, Hi, US 182/U11
Hoonah, Ak, US 192/L4
Hooper, Ut, US 195/J11
Hooper Bay, Ak, US 192/E3
Hoopeston, Il, US 188/C3
Hoopstad, SAfr. 164/D2
Höör, Swe. 96/E4
Hoorn, Neth. 108/C3
Hoornse Hop (bay), Neth. 108/C3
Hoover (dam), Az, US 186/D3
Hoover, Mo, US 195/D5
Hopa, Turk. 148/E1
Hopatcong, NJ, US 196/D2
Hopatcong (lake), NJ, US 196/D2
Hope (lake), Austl. 167/A4
Hope, BC, Can. 184/C3
Hope, Ak, US 192/J3
Hope, NJ, US 196/D2
Hope Vale Aboriginal Community, Austl. 172/B1
Hopedale, Nf, Can. 181/K3
Hopelchén, Mex. 202/D2
Hopeman, Sc, UK 94/C1
Hopes Advance (cape), Qu, Can. 181/K2
Hope's Nose (pt.), Eng, UK 90/C6
Hopetown, SAfr. 164/D3
Hopewell, NJ, US 196/D3
Hopewell Furnace NHS, Pa, US 196/C3
Hopkins (riv.), Austl. 173/B3
Hopkins (lake), Austl. 167/B3
Hopkinsville, Ky, US 188/C4
Hoppecke (riv.), Ger. 109/F6
Hoppegarten, Ger. 98/Q6
Hoppstädten-Weiersbach, Ger. 111/G4
Hopsten, Ger. 109/E4
Hoquiam, Wa, US 184/C4
Horace (mtn.), Ak, US 192/J2
Horado, Japan 135/L4
Hōrai-san (peak), Japan 135/J5
Horasan, Turk. 148/E1
Horažďovice, Czh. 113/G4
Horb am Neckar, Ger. 112/B6
Horbourg-Wihr, Fr. 114/D1
Hörbranz, Aus. 115/F2
Horche, Sp. 102/D2
Horconcitos, Pan. 203/F4
Hordaland (co.), Nor. 95/C3
Hördt, Ger. 112/B4
Hœrdt, Fr. 111/G6
Horezu, Rom. 107/G3
Horgau, Ger. 112/D6
Horgen, Swi. 115/E3
Horine, Mo, US 195/G9
Horinger, China 130/B2
Horley, Eng, UK 88/C3
Horlivka, Ukr. 120/F2
Hormigüeros, PR 199/M8
Hormuz (str.), Oman 147/G3
Horn, Aus. 101/L2
Horn (pt.), Ice. 218/H
Horn-Bad Meinberg, Ger. 109/F5
Hornachuelos, Sp. 102/C4
Hornád (riv.), Slvk. 99/L4
Hornavan (lake), Swe. 95/F2
Hornbach, Ger. 111/G5
Hornberg, Ger. 115/E1
Horndal, Swe. 96/G1
Horneburg, Ger. 109/G1
Hornell, NY, US 188/E3
Horní Bříza, Czh. 113/G3
Horní Slavkov, Czh. 113/F2
Hornisgrinde (peak), Ger. 112/B5
Hornos (cape), Chile 217/D7
Hornoy-le-Bourg, Fr. 110/A4
Hornslet, Den. 96/D3
Hörnum (cape), Ger. 96/C4
Horoshiri-dake (peak), Japan 134/C2
Hořovice, Czh. 113/G3
Horqin Zuoyi Houqi, China 130/E2
Horqin Zuoyi Zhongqi, China 130/E1
Hörsching, Aus. 113/H6
Horse Cave, Ky, US 188/C4
Horsefly (lake), BC, Can. 184/C2
Horsens, Den. 96/C4
Horseshoe (lake), Il, US 195/G8
Horseshoe (lake), Co, US 195/B2
Horsetooth (res.), Co, US 195/B1
Horsey (isl.), Eng, UK 91/H3
Horsforth, Eng, UK 93/G4
Horsham, Austl. 173/B3
Horsham, Eng, UK 91/F4
Horsham, Pa, US 196/C3
Horšovský Týn, Czh. 113/F3
Horst, Neth. 108/D6
Hörstel, Ger. 109/E4
Horstmar, Ger. 109/E4
Horta, Azor., Port. 103/S12
Horten, Nor. 96/D2
Hortes, Fr. 114/B2
Hortobágyi NP, Hun. 106/E2
Horton (pt.), NY, US 197/F1
Horton (riv.), NW, Can. 180/D2
Høruphav, Den. 96/C4
Horusický Rybník (lake), Czh. 113/H4
Hørve, Den. 96/D4
Horvot Dor, Isr. 149/F6
Horw, Swi. 115/E3
Horwich, Eng, UK 93/F4
Horwood (lake), On, Can. 188/D2
Hösbach, Ger. 112/C2
Hosenfeld, Ger. 112/C1
Hoshiārpur, India 144/C4
Hosingen, Lux. 111/F3
Hospental, Swi. 115/E4
Hosszúpereszteg, Hun. 106/C2
Hoste (isl.), Chile 217/C7
Hot Springs, SD, US 185/H5
Hot Springs NP, Ar, US 187/J4
Hotaka, Japan 133/E2
Hotaka-dake (peak), Japan 133/E2
Hotan, China 128/C4
Hotan (riv.), China 128/D4
Hotazel, SAfr. 164/C2
Hotont, Mong. 128/H2
Hottah (lake), NW, Can. 180/E2
Hottentot (bay), Namb. 164/A2
Hotton, Belg. 111/E3
Houari Boumedienne (int'l arpt.), Alg. 158/G4
Houdain, Fr. 110/B3
Houdan, Fr. 88/G5
Houet (prov.), Burk. 160/D4
Houffalize, Belg. 111/E3
Houghton Lake, Mi, US 188/C2
Houghton-le-Spring, Eng, UK 93/G2
Houilles, Fr. 88/J5
Houlton, Me, US 189/H2
Houma, China 130/B4
Houplines, Fr. 110/B2
Hourdel (pt.), Fr. 110/A3
Hourn, Loch (inlet), Sc, UK 94/A2
Hourtin, Fr. 100/C4
Housatonic (riv.), Ct, US 197/E1
House (range), Ut, US 186/D3
House Springs, Mo, US 195/F9
Housesteads Roman Fort, Eng, UK 93/F1
Houssen, Fr. 114/D1
Houston, BC, Can. 184/B2
Houston, Ak, US 192/J3
Houston, De, US 196/C6
Houston, Mo, US 187/K3
Houston, Ms, US 191/F3
Houston, Tx, US 187/J5
Houtbaai, SAfr. 164/L11
Houten, Neth. 108/C4
Houthulst, Belg. 110/B2
Houtman Abrolhos (isl.), Austl. 170/B4
Houtribdijk (dam), Neth. 108/C3
Houtskär (isl.), Fin. 97/J1
Houyet, Belg. 111/E3
Hov, Nor. 96/D1
Hova, Swe. 96/F2
Hovd, Mong. 128/F2
Hovd (prov.), Mong. 128/F2
Hövelhof, Ger. 109/F5
Hovenweep Nat'l Mon., Ut, US 186/E3
Hovfjället (peak), Swe. 96/E1
Hovmantorp, Swe. 96/F3
Hövsgöl (prov.), Mong. 128/G1
Hovsta, Swe. 96/F2
Howard, Austl. 172/D4
Howard (hill), Ak, US 192/H2
Howard (pass), Ak, US 192/G2
Howard (co.), Md, US 196/B5
Howard Hanson (res.), Wa, US 193/D3
Howard Hanson (dam), Wa, US 193/D3
Howe (cape), Austl. 173/D3
Howe of the Mearns (reg.), Sc, UK 94/D3
Howell, Mi, US 188/D3
Howell, NJ, US 196/D3
Howick, SAfr. 165/E3
Howland (isl.), Pac., US 175/H4
Höxter, Ger. 109/G5
Hoxud, China 128/E3
Hoy (isl.), Sc, UK 89/V14
Hoya, Ger. 109/G3
Hōya, Japan 135/D2
Høyanger, Nor. 96/B1
Hoyerswerda, Ger. 99/H3
Hoylake, Eng, UK 93/E5
Hoyland Nether, Eng, UK 93/G4
Hoyo de Manzanares, Sp. 103/N8
Hoyos, Sp. 102/B2
Hoyoux (riv.), Belg. 111/E3
Hozumi, Japan 135/L5
Hracholusky (res.), Czh. 113/F3
Hradec Králové, Czh. 99/H3
Hradiště (peak), Czh. 113/G2
Hrasnica, Bosn. 106/D4
Hrastnik, Slov. 101/L3
Hrazdan, Arm. 121/H4
Hrodna, Bela. 97/K5
Hrodzyenskaya Voblasts Bela. 118/E5
Hrolleifsborg (peak), Ice. 95/M6
Hron (riv.), Slvk. 99/K4
Hronov, Czh. 99/J3
Hrubieszów, Pol. 99/M3
Hrubý Jeseník (mts.), Czh.,Pol. 99/J3
Hrútafjöll (peak), Ice. 95/P6
Hsinchu, Tai. 137/D3
Hua (peak), China 130/B4
Hua Hin, Thai. 136/B3
Hua Xian, China 130/C4
Hua'an, China 137/C2
Huacaybamba, Peru 214/B3
Huachi, China 128/J4
Huacho, Peru 214/B3
Huachón, Peru 214/C3
Huachuca City, Az, US 186/E5
Huacrachuco, Peru 214/B3
Huade, China 129/K3
Huahine (isl.), FrPol. 175/K6
Huai (riv.), China 130/C4
Huai'an, China 130/C2
Huai'an, China 130/D4
Huaibei, China 129/L5
Huaibin, China 130/C4
Huaiji, China 141/K3
Huailai, China 130/G6
Huainan, China 130/C3
Huairou, China 130/H6
Huaiyang, China 130/C4
Huaiyin, China 130/D4
Huaiyin, China 130/D4
Huaiyuan, China 130/D4
Huajicori, Mex. 200/D4
Huajuapan de León, Mex. 202/B2
Hualahuises, Mex. 201/F3
Hualañé, Chile 216/C2
Hualgayoc, Peru 214/B2
Hualien, Tai. 137/D3
Hualla, Peru 214/C4
Huallaga (riv.), Peru 214/B3
Huallanca, Peru 214/B3
Huallanca, Peru 214/B3
Huamachuco, Peru 214/B3
Huamantanga, Peru 214/B3
Huamantla, Mex. 201/M7
Huambo, Ang. 163/C3
Huambos, Peru 214/B2
Huan (riv.), China 130/C5
Huan Xian, China 128/J4
Huancané, Peru 214/D4
Huancapi, Peru 214/C4
Huancaspata, Peru 214/B3
Huancavelica (dept.), Peru 214/C4
Huancavelica, Peru 214/C4
Huancayo, Peru 214/C4
Huanchaca (peak), Bol. 208/E8
Huang (riv.), China 125/L6
Huangchuan, China 130/C4
Huanggang (peak), China 137/C2
Huanghua, China 130/D3
Huangling, China 130/B4
Huanglong, China 130/B4
Huangping, China 141/J2
Huangqi (lake), China 130/C2
Huangshan, China 137/C2
Huangtang (lake), China 130/C5
Huangtu (plat.), China 130/B4
Huanguelén, Arg. 216/E3
Huangyan, China 137/D2
Huangzhong, China 128/H4
Huanren, China 131/C2
Huanta, Peru 214/C4
Huantai, China 130/D3
Huántar, Peru 214/B3
Huánuco (dept.), Peru 214/C3
Huánuco, Peru 214/B3
Huanuni, Bol. 208/E7
Huapi (mts.), Nic. 203/E3
Huaquechula, Mex. 201/L8
Huaquillas, Ecu. 214/A1
Huaral, Peru 214/B3
Huaraz, Peru 214/B3
Huari, Peru 214/B3
Huaricolca, Peru 214/C3
Huarina, Bol. 214/D5
Huarmey, Peru 214/B3
Huarochirí, Peru 214/B4
Huarocondo, Peru 214/C4
Huarong, China 137/B2
Huásabas, Mex. 200/C2
Huasahuasi, Peru 214/C3
Huascarán (peak), Peru 214/B3
Huatabampo, Mex. 200/C3
Huatunas (lake), Bol. 208/E6
Huatusco, Mex. 201/N7
Huauchinango, Mex. 201/L6
Huaura, Peru 214/B3
Huautla de Jiménez, Mex. 202/B2
Huayacocotla, Mex. 201/L6
Huaying, China 137/A1
Huaylas, Peru 214/B3
Huayllay, Peru 214/B3
Huayopata, Peru 214/C4
Huayuan, China 141/J2
Huazhou, China 141/K3
Hubbard (mt.), Ak, US 192/L3
Hubbard Creek (res.), Tx, US 187/H4
Hubei (prov.), China 129/K5
Hubei (pass), China 130/B4
Hubli-Dhārwār, India 147/L5
Huch'ang, NKor. 131/D2
Hückelhoven, Ger. 111/F1
Hückeswagen, Ger. 111/G1
Hucknall, Eng, UK 93/G5
Huddersfield, Eng, UK 93/G4
Huddinge, Swe. 96/G2
Hude, Ger. 109/F2
Hudiksvall, Swe. 96/G1
Hudson (cape), Ant. 218/L
Hudson (bay), Can. 181/H2
Hudson (str.), Nun.,Qu, Can. 181/J2
Hudson, Qu, Can. 189/M7
Hudson, Co, US 195/C2
Hudson (co.), NJ, US 197/J9
Hudson (riv.), NJ,NY, US 188/F3
Hudson, NY, US 188/F3
Hudson Bay, Sk, Can. 185/H2
Hudson's Hope, BC, Can. 180/D3
Hue, Viet. 136/D2
Huedin, Rom. 107/F2
Huehuetenango, Guat. 202/D3
Huehuetla, Mex. 201/L6
Huehuetlán, Mex. 201/L8
Huejotzingo, Mex. 201/L7
Huejuquilla el Alto, Mex. 200/E4
Huejutla de Reyes, Mex. 202/B1
Huelma, Sp. 102/D4
Huelva, Sp. 102/B4
Huelva (riv.), Sp. 102/B4
Huequi (vol.), Chile 216/B4
Huercal-Overa, Sp. 102/E4
Huerfano (riv.), Co, US 187/F3
Huesca, Sp. 103/E1
Huéscar, Sp. 102/D4
Huetamo de Nuñez, Mex. 201/E5
Huete, Sp. 102/D2
Huexoculco, Mex. 201/R10
Hüfingen, Ger. 115/E2
Hugh Town, Eng, UK 89/Q12
Hughenden, Austl. 172/B3
Hughenden Valley, Eng, UK 88/A2
Hughes, Ak, US 192/H2
Hughes, Arg. 216/E2
Hughesville, Pa, US 196/B1
Hugfing, Ger. 115/H2
Hugli (riv.), India 140/E3
Hugo, Ok, US 187/J4
Huguan, China 130/C3
Hui Xian, China 130/C4
Hui'an, China 137/C2
Huib-Hoch (plat.), Namb. 164/B2
Huichang, China 137/C2
Huichapan, Mex. 201/K6
Hŭich'ŏn, NKor. 131/D2
Huila (dept.), Col. 210/C4
Huila, Nevado del (peak), Col. 210/C4

Huilai, China 137/C3
Huilango, Mex. 201/Q9
Huili, China 141/H2
Huimanguillo, Mex. 202/C2
Huimin, China 130/D3
Huinca Renancó,
Arg. 216/D2
Huining, China 128/C4
Hüisaek-pong (peak),
NKor. 131/D2
Huishui, China 141/J2
Huisne (riv.), Fr. 100/D2
Huissen, Neth. 108/C4
Huitong, China 141/J2
Huittinen, Fin. 97/K1
Huitzilan, Mex. 201/M7
Huitzilan, Mex. 201/M7
Huitzuco, Mex. 201/K8
Huixcolotla, Mex. 201/M8
Huixquilucan, Mex. 201/Q10
Huixtla, Mex. 202/C3
Huize, China 141/H2
Huizen, Neth. 108/C4
Hujra, Pak. 144/B4
Hulan, China 129/N2
Hulett, Wy, US 185/G4
Hull (riv.), Eng, UK 93/H4
Hullbridge, Eng, UK 88/E2
Hüllhorst, Ger. 109/F4
Hulst, Neth. 108/B6
Hultsfred, Swe. 96/F3
Huma, China 129/N1
Huma (riv.), China 129/M1
Humahuaca, Arg. 215/C1
Humaitá, Braz. 208/F5
Humansdorp, SAfr. 164/D4
Humay, Peru 214/C4
Humber (riv.), Nf, Can. 189/K1
Humber (bay),
On, Can. 189/P7
Humber (riv.), Eng, UK 93/H4
Humberto de Campos,
Braz. 212/B1
Humble, Tx, US 187/J5
Humboldt, Sk, Can. 185/G2
Humboldt (bay), Col. 203/C5
Humboldt (range),
Nv, US 186/D2
Humboldt (riv.),
Nv, US 186/C2
Humboldt, Tn, US 188/B5
Hume (lake), Austl. 173/C2
Húmeda, Pampa (plain),
Arg. 216/E2
Humenné, Slvk. 99/L4
Humida, Pampa (plain),
Arg. 215/D4
Humlum, Den. 96/C3
Hummels Wharf,
Pa, US 196/B2
Hummelstown,
Pa, US 196/B3
Humphrey (pt.), Ak, US 192/K2
Humphreys (peak),
Az, US 186/E4
Hün, Libya 154/J2
Húnaflói (bay), Ice. 95/N6
Hunan (prov.), China 129/K6
Hundsangen, Ger. 111/G3
Hunedoara, Rom. 106/F3
Hunedoara (prov.),
Rom. 106/F3
Hünenberg, Swi. 115/E3
Hünfeld, Ger. 101/H1
Hung Yen, Viet. 136/D1
Hungarian, Hun. 107/H9
Hungary (ctry.) 106/D2
Hungen, Ger. 112/B2
Hüngnam, NKor. 131/D3
Hunjiang, China 131/D2
Hunnebostrand, Swe. 96/C2
Hunsel, Neth. 108/C6
Hunsrück (mts.), Ger. 98/D4
Hunte (riv.), Ger. 98/E2
Hunter (isl.), Austl. 167/D5
Hunter (riv.), Austl. 173/D2
Hunter (mt.), Ak, US 192/H3
Hunter, Tx, US 195/U20
Hunterdon (co.),
NJ, US 196/C2
Huntingburg, In, US 188/C4
Huntingdon, Eng, UK 91/F2
Huntington, In, US 188/C3
Huntington, NY, US 197/M8
Huntington (bay),
NY, US 197/M8
Huntington Bay,
NY, US 197/M8
Huntington Beach,
Ca, US 194/G8
Huntington Park,
Ca, US 194/F8
Huntington Station,
NY, US 197/M8
Huntington Woods,
Mi, US 193/F7
Huntley, Il, US 193/P15
Huntly, NZ 175/T10
Huntly, Sc, UK 94/D2
Hunts Inlet, BC, Can. 192/M4
Hunts Point, Wa, US 193/C2
Huntsville, Al, US 191/G3
Huntsville, On, Can. 188/E2
Huntsville, Ut, US 195/K11
Huntsville (res.),
Pa, US 196/B1
Hunucmá, Mex. 202/D1
Hünxe, Ger. 108/D5
Hunyuan, China 130/C3
Huo (mtn.), China 130/B3
Huo (mtn.), China 130/D5
Huocheng, China 128/D3
Huojia, China 130/C4
Huolin Gol, China 129/L2
Huoqiu, China 130/D4

Huoshan, China 130/D5
Huozhou, China 130/B3
Hurdal, Nor. 96/D1
Hure Qi, China 130/E2
Hurepoix (reg.), Fr. 88/H6
Hurley, NM, US 186/E4
Hurley, Eng, UK 88/A2
Hurley (riv.), Ire. 92/B4
Hurlford, Sc, UK 94/B5
Huron (lake), Can.,US 188/D2
Huron (mts.), Mi, US 188/B2
Huron (pt.), Mi, US 193/G6
Huron (riv.), Mi, US 193/E7
Hurricane, WV, US 188/D4
Hurtaut (riv.), Fr. 110/D4
Hürtgenwald (reg.),
Ger. 111/F2
Hürth, Ger. 111/F2
Hurup, Den. 96/C3
Husainābād, India 143/E3
Húsavík, Ice. 95/P6
Huscarán, PN, Peru 214/B3
Husher, Wi, US 193/Q14
Huşi, Rom. 107/J2
Huskisson, Austl. 173/D2
Huslia, Ak, US 192/G2
Husnes, Nor. 96/A2
Husum, Ger. 96/C4
Husum, Swe. 95/F3
Hutag, Mong. 128/H2
Hutchinson, Mn, US 185/K4
Hutchinson, Ks, US 187/H3
Hüttisheim, Ger. 115/F1
Hüttlingen, Ger. 112/D5
Hütton (mt.), Austl. 172/C4
Hutton, Eng, UK 88/E2
Huttwil, Swi. 114/D3
Hutuo (riv.), China 130/C3
Huwwārah, WBnk. 149/G7
Huy, Belg. 111/E2
Huyton-with-Roby,
Eng, UK 93/F5
Huzhou, China 130/L9
Hvammstangi, Ice. 95/N6
Hvannadalshnúkur
(peak), Ice. 95/P7
Hvar (isl.), Cro. 104/E1
Hvide Sande, Den. 96/C4
Hvítá (riv.), Ice. 95/N7
Hvolsvöllur, Ice. 95/N7
Hwange, Zim. 163/E4
Hwange (Wankie) NP,
Zim. 163/E4
Hwanghae-bukto (prov.),
NKor. 131/D3
Hwanghae-namdo (prov.),
NKor. 131/C3
Hwangju, NKor. 131/C3
Hwangju (riv.), NKor. 131/C3
Hwasun, SKor. 131/D5
Hyades (range), Chile 216/B5
Hyattstown, Md, US 196/A5
Hyattsville, Md, US 196/A6
Hydaburg, Ak, US 192/M4
Hyde, Eng, UK 93/F5
Hyder, Ak, US 192/M4
Hyderābād, India 140/C4
Hyderābād, Pak. 147/J3
Hyères, Fr. 100/F5
Hyères, Îles d' (isls.),
Fr 101/G5
Hyesan, NKor. 131/E2
Hygiene, Co, US 195/B2
Hyland (riv.), Yk, Can. 180/D2
Hyllestad, Nor. 96/A1
Hyltebruk, Swe. 96/E3
Hylton (hill), Ky, US 188/D4
Hyō-no-sen (peak),
Japan 132/D3
Hyōgo (pref.), Japan 132/D3
Hyöndüng-san (peak),
SKor. 131/G6
Hyrum, Ut, US 186/E2
Hythe, Eng, UK 91/H4
Hyūga, Japan 132/B4
Hyvinkää, Fin. 97/L1
Hywel, Moel (peak),
Wal, UK 90/C2

I

I-n-Amenas, Alg. 157/H3
I-n-Azaoua, Oued (riv.),
Niger 157/H5
I-n-Dagouber (well),
Mali 157/E5
I-n-Échaï (well), Mali 161/E1
I-n-Gall, Niger 161/G2
I-n-Guezzam, Alg. 161/G2
I-n-Milach (well),
Mali 161/E2
I-n-Sâkâne, 'Erg (des.),
Mali 161/E1
I-n-Salah, Alg. 157/F4
I-n-Tassik (well),
Mali 161/F2
Iacanga, Braz. 213/B2
Iaciara, Braz. 212/A4
Iaco (riv.), Braz. 208/E6
Iaçu, Braz. 212/B4
Iáf di Montasio (peak),
It. 101/K3
Iakora, Madg. 165/H8
Ialomiţa (prov.), Rom. 107/H3
Ialomiţa (riv.), Rom. 107/H3
Ianapera, Madg. 165/H8
Iapu, Braz. 213/D1
Iaşi, Rom. 107/H2
Iaşi (prov.), Rom. 107/H2
Iasmos, Gre. 105/J2
Iatan, Mo, US 195/D5

Iba, Phil. 137/C4
Ibadan, Nga. 161/F5
Ibagué, Col. 208/C3
Ibaiti, Braz. 213/B2
Ibajay, Phil. 137/D5
Ibanda, Ugan. 162/A3
Ibans (lake), Hon. 203/E3
Ibapaba, Serra da
(range), Braz. 212/B1
Ibar (riv.), Kos., Serb. 106/E4
Ibara, Japan 132/C3
Ibaraki (pref.), Japan 135/K6
Ibaraki, Japan 135/J6
Ibaraki, Japan 135/E1
Ibarra, Ecu. 210/B4
Ibarreta, Arg. 215/E2
Ibb, Yem. 146/D6
Ibba (riv.), Sudan 155/L6
Iğdır, Turk. 148/F2
Ibbenbüren, Ger. 109/E4
Igel, Ger. 111/F4
Iggesund, Swe. 96/G1
Ightham, Eng, UK 88/D3
Iganga, Ugan. 162/B2
Igaporã, Braz. 212/B4
Igara Paraná (riv.),
Col. 210/C5
Igarapava, Braz. 213/C2
Igarapé Grande, Braz. 212/B2
Igarapé-Miri, Braz. 209/J4
Igaratá, Braz. 213/G8
Igarka, Rus. 122/J3
Igatpuri, India 140/B4
Igdet (peak), Mor. 156/C3
Igdır, Turk. 148/F2
Igel, Ger. 111/F4
Igiugig, Ak, US 192/G4
Iglesias, It. 104/A3
Igli, Alg. 157/E3
Igling, Ger. 115/G1
Igloolik, Nun., Can. 181/H2
Ignace, On, Can. 185/L3
Ignacio, Co, US 193/J10
Ignacio de la Llave,
Mex. 201/P8
Ignacio Zaragoza,
Mex. 200/D2
Igneada Burnu (cape),
Turk. 107/J5
Igney, Fr. 114/C1
Ignon (riv.), Fr. 114/A2
Igny, Fr. 88/J5
Igombe (riv.), Tanz. 162/B4
Igoumenítsa, Gre. 105/G3
Igra, Rus. 119/M4
Igreja, Morro da
(peak), Braz. 213/B4
Iguaçu (riv.), Braz. 205/D5
Iguaçu, PN do, Braz. 215/F2
Iguala, Mex. 201/K8
Igualada, Sp. 103/F2
Iguape, Braz. 213/C3
Iguatu, Braz. 212/C2
Iguazú, PN del, Arg. 215/F2
Iguetti (lake), Mrta. 156/C4
Iheya (isl.), Japan 133/J7
Ihhayrhan, Mong. 128/J2
Ihosy, Madg. 165/H8
Ihtiman, Bul. 105/H2
Ii, Fin. 95/H2
Iida, Japan 135/E3
Iide-san (peak), Japan 133/F2
Iijoki (riv.), Fin. 95/J2
Iinan, Japan 135/K7
Iisalmi, Fin. 95/H2
Iitaka, Japan 135/K7
Iitti, Fin. 97/M1
Iiyama, Japan 133/F2
Iizuka, Japan 132/B4
Ijebu Ode, Nga. 161/F5
Ijill (peak), Mrta. 156/B5
Ijill (lake), Mrta. 156/B5
Ijira, Japan 135/L4
IJmeer (bay), Neth. 108/B4
IJmuiden, Neth. 108/B4
Ijnaoun (well), Mrta. 160/B2
Ijoki (riv.), Fin. 95/H2
Ijoubbane, 'Erg (des.),
Mali 156/D5
Ijzer (riv.), Belg. 110/B1
Ik (riv.), Rus. 119/M5
Ikahavo (isl.), Madg. 165/H8
Ikalamavony, Madg. 165/H8
Ikare, Nga. 161/G5
Ikaria (isl.), Gre. 105/J4
Ikaria, Gre. 148/A2
Ikaruga, Japan 135/J6
Ikeda, Japan 132/C3
Ikeda, Japan 134/C2
Ikeda, Japan 135/H6
Ikeja, Nga. 161/F5
Ikela, D.R. Congo 162/A3
Ikenokoya-yama (peak),
Japan 135/K7
Ikerre, Nga. 161/G5
Ikhtiman, Bul. 105/N9
Iki (isl.), Japan 132/A4
Iki (chan.), Japan 132/A4
Ikire, Nga. 161/G5
Ikirun, Nga. 161/G5
Ikizce, Turk. 148/C2
Ikizdere, Turk. 148/E1
Ikoma, Japan 135/J6
Ikongo, Madg. 165/H8
Ikopa (riv.), Madg. 165/H7
Ikorodu, Nga. 161/F5
Ikuno, Japan 135/J6
Ila Orangun, Nga. 161/G4
Ilabaya, Peru 214/D5
Ilagan, Phil. 137/D4
Ilam, Nepal 143/F2
Ilam, Iran 146/E2
Ilan, Tai. 137/D3
Ilanz, Swi. 116/B5
Ilaro, Nga. 161/F5
Ilave, Peru 214/D5
Iława, Pol. 99/K2

Ilawe-Ekiti, Nga. 161/G5
Ile (riv.), China.,Kaz. 128/C3
Ile-à-la-Crosse,
Sk, Can. 184/G2
Ile-à-la-Crosse (lake),
Sk, Can. 184/G2
Ile-de-France (pol. reg.),
Fr. 110/A6
Ilebo, D.R. Congo 163/D1
Ilek (riv.), Rus. 121/K2
Iles Ehotilés, PN des,
C.d'Iv. 160/E5
Iles Tristao, Îles (isls.),
Gui. 160/B4
Ilesha, Nga. 161/G5
Ilfis (riv.), Swi. 114/D4
Ilgaz, Turk. 120/E4
Ilgın, Turk. 148/B2
Ilha Grande (bay),
Braz. 213/J8
Ilha Grande, Baía de
(bay), Braz. 213/C2
Ilha Solteira, Represa
(res.), Braz. 209/H7
Ilhabela, Braz. 213/H8
Ilhavo, Port. 102/A2
Ilhéus, Braz. 212/C4
Iliamna, Ak, US 192/H4
Iliamna (lake),
Ak, US 192/G4
Iliamna (vol.), Ak, US 192/H3
Iliç, Turk. 148/D2
Ilica, Turk. 121/G5
Ilijaš, Bosn. 106/D4
Iliniza (peak), Ecu. 210/B5
Ilirska Bistrica, Slov. 101/L4
Ilisu (dam), Turk. 148/E2
Ilisu (res.), Turk. 148/E2
Ilium (Troy) (ruin), Turk. 105/K3
Ilkeston, Eng, UK 93/G6
Ilkley, Eng, UK 93/G4
Ill (riv.), Aus. 101/H3
Ill (riv.), Fr. 101/G3
Illana, Sp. 102/D2
Illapel, Chile 215/B3
Illasi (riv.), It. 117/E1
Illbillee (mt.), Austl. 171/G3
Illéla, Niger 161/G3
Iller (riv.), Ger. 101/J2
Illertissen, Ger. 115/G1
Illescas, Sp. 102/D2
Illiers-Combray, Fr. 100/D2
Illimani (peak), Bol. 208/E7
Illinois (riv.), Il, US 188/B3
Illinois (state), US 188/B4
Illizi, Alg. 157/H4
Illizi (prov.), Alg. 157/G4
Illkirch-Graffenstaden,
Fr. 114/D1
Illmensee, Ger. 115/F2
Illnau, Swi. 115/E3
Illora, Sp. 102/D4
Illovo, SAfr. 165/E3
Illzach, Fr. 114/D2
Ilm (riv.), Ger. 98/F4
Ilmajoki, Fin. 95/G3
Ilme (riv.), Ger. 109/G5
Il'men (lake), Rus. 122/D4
Ilmenau (riv.), Ger. 109/H2
Ilo, Peru 214/D5
Ilobu, Nga. 161/G5
Ilorin, Nga. 161/G4
Ilovlya (riv.), Rus. 121/H2
Ilpendam, Neth. 108/B4
Ilsede, Ger. 109/H4
Ilsenburg, Ger. 109/H5
Ilsfeld, Ger. 112/C4
Ilshofen, Ger. 112/C4
Ilyas Burnu (pt.), Turk. 107/H5
Ilych (riv.), Rus. 119/N3
Ilz (riv.), Ger. 99/G4
Iłża, Braz. 215/F2
Imaichi, Japan 133/F2
Imaloto (riv.), Madg. 165/H8
Imamoğlu, Turk. 148/C2
Imandra (lake), Rus. 95/J2
Imari, Japan 132/A4
Imatra, Fin. 97/N1
Imazu, Japan 135/K5
Imba (lake), Japan 135/E2
Imbabura (prov.),
Ecu. 210/B4
Imbituba, Braz. 213/B4
Imbituva, Braz. 213/B3
Imeni Moskvy (canal),
Rus. 119/W9
Imerimandroso, Madg. 165/J7
Imi n'tanout, Mor. 156/C3
Imişli, Azer. 121/J5
Imittós (peak), Gre. 105/N9
Imja (isl.), SKor. 131/C5
Imlay, Nv, US 184/D5
Immendingen, Ger. 115/E2
Immenhausen, Ger. 109/G6
Immenstaad am Bodensee,
Ger. 115/F2
Immenstadt im Allgäu,
Ger. 115/G2
Immingham, Eng, UK 93/H4
Immokalee, Fl, US 191/H5
Imnavait (mtn.),
Ak, US 192/J2
Imo (state), Nga. 161/G5
Imola, It. 117/E4
Imouzzèr-Kandar,
Mor. 158/B3
Imperatriz, Braz. 212/A2
Imperia, It. 116/B5
Imperia (prov.), It. 116/B5
Imperia, Sk, Can. 185/G3
Imperial, Peru 214/B4
Imperial (dam), Mex.
Imperial, Ne, US 187/G2

Imperial, Mo, US 195/G9
Imperial Beach,
Ca, US 194/C5
Imperial Palace,
Japan 135/D4
Impero (riv.), It. 116/B5
Impfondo, Congo 155/J7
Imphāl, India 141/F3
Imphy, Fr. 100/C3
Impruneta, It. 117/E5
Imrali (isl.), Turk. 107/J5
Imranlı, Turk. 148/D2
Imroz, Gre. 105/J2
Imshil, SKor. 131/D5
Imst, Aus. 115/G3
Imuris, Mex. 200/C2
Ina, Japan 133/E3
Ina, Japan 135/D2
Ina, Japan 135/D2
Ina (riv.), Pol. 96/F5
Inabe, Japan 135/L5
Inabu, Japan 135/M5
Inagawa, Japan 135/H6
Inagi, Japan 135/C2
Inajá, Braz. 212/C3
Inambari (riv.), Peru 214/D4
Inami, Japan 135/G6
Inaouene (riv.), Mor. 158/B2
Inapari, Peru 214/D3
Inarijärvi (lake), Fin. 95/H1
Inău (peak), Rom. 107/G2
Inawashiro (lake),
Japan 133/F2
Inazawa, Japan 135/L5
Inca, Sp. 103/G3
Incekum (pt.), Turk. 149/C1
Incheville, Fr. 110/A3
Inchinnan, Sc, UK 94/B5
Inchkeith (isl.),
Sc, UK 94/C4
Inchnadamph, Sc, UK 89/R7
Inch'ŏn, SKor. 131/F7
Inkster, Mi, US 193/F7
Inland (sea), Japan 132/D4
Inle (lake), Myan. 141/G3
Ina (riv.), Aus. 115/G3
Inn (riv.), Ger. 101/K2
Inn (riv.), Swi. 101/J3
Innbach (riv.), Aus. 113/H6
Innellan, Sc, UK 94/B5
Inner (chan.), Belz. 202/D2
Inner (sound), Sc, UK 89/R8
Inner Hebrides (isls.),
Sc, UK 89/Q8
Inner Mongolia (reg.),
China 125/L5
Innerdouny (hill),
Sc, UK 94/C4
Innerleithen, Sc, UK 94/C5
Innerste (riv.), Ger. 109/G4
Innertkirchen, Swi. 115/E4
Innes NP, Austl. 171/H5
Innisfail, Ab, Can. 184/E2
Innisfail, Austl. 172/B2
Innoko (riv.), Ak, US 192/G3
Innsbruck, Aus. 115/H3
Innviertel (reg.), Aus. 113/G6
Inny (riv.), Eng, UK 90/B5
Ino, Japan 132/C4
Inocência, Braz. 213/B1
Independência,
Braz. 212/B2
Independencia, Peru 214/B4
Index, Wa, US 193/D2
India (ctry.) 125/G7
Indian (ocean) 81/N6
Indian Echo Caverns,
Pa, US 196/B3
Indian Head, Sk, Can. 185/H3
Indian Hills, Co, US 195/B3
Indian Peaks Wilderness
Area, Co, US 195/A2
Indiana (state), US 188/C3
Indiana, Pa, US 188/E3
Indianapolis (int'l arpt.),
In, US 188/C4
Indianapolis (cap.),
In, US 188/C4
Indianola, Ms, US 187/K4
Indianola, Ia, US 193/B2
Indiantown, Fl, US 191/H5
Indiaporã, Braz. 213/B1
Indigirka (riv.), Rus. 123/P3
Indio, Ca, US 186/C4
Indira Gandhi (int'l arpt.),
India 125/G7
Indochina (reg.), Laos 141/H4
Indonesia (ctry.) 125/J7
Indore, India 147/L4
Indragiri (riv.), Indo. 138/B4
Indramayu (cape),
Indo. 138/C5
Indrāvati (riv.), India 140/D5
Indre (riv.), Fr. 100/D3
Indre Arna, Nor. 96/A1
Indrois (riv.), Fr. 100/D3
Induno Olona, It. 115/E6
Indus (riv.), Asia 140/D3
Industry, Ca, US 194/G7
Inebolu, Turk. 120/E4
Inece, Turk. 107/H5
Inecik, Turk. 107/H5
Inedbirenne (int'l arpt.),
Alg. 157/H4
Inegöl, Turk. 148/B1
Iner (riv.), Ger. 112/C3
Ineu, Rom. 106/E2
Inezgane, Mor. 156/C3
Inezgane (Agadir)
(int'l arpt.), Mor. 156/C3
Infanta (cape), SAfr. 164/C4
Infiernillo (res.),
Mex. 182/A4
Infiernillo, Presa del
(dam), Mex. 200/E5
Infiesto, Sp. 102/C1

Ingapirca (ruin), Ecu. 210/B5
Ingatestone, Eng, UK 88/E2
Ingelmunster, Belg. 110/C2
Ingeniero Jacobacci,
Arg. 216/C4
Ingeniero Luiggi,
Arg. 216/D2
Ingenio, Canl., Sp. 156/B4
Ingersheim, Fr. 114/D1
Ingettolgoy, Mong. 128/H2
Ingham, Austl. 172/B2
Ingleside, Md, US 196/C5
Inglewood, Austl. 173/B3
Inglewood, Ca, US 194/F8
Inglewood-Finn Hill,
Wa, US 193/C2
Inglis, Fl, US 191/H4
Ingoda (riv.), Rus. 123/M4
Ingolstadt, Ger. 113/E5
Ingrid Christianson
(coast), Ant. 218/F
Ingushetia, Resp.,
Rus. 121/H4
Ingwavuma, SAfr. 165/E2
Ingwiller, Fr. 111/G6
Inhambane, Moz. 163/G5
Inhambupe, Braz. 212/C4
Inharrime, Moz. 163/G5
Inhuma, Braz. 212/B2
Inhumas, Braz. 213/B1
Iniesta, Sp. 102/E3
Inifel (well), Alg. 157/F3
Inini (riv.), FrG. 211/H4
Inírida (riv.), Col. 208/D3
Inishbofin (isl.), Ire. 92/A1
Inishowen (pen.), Ire. 92/A1
Inishowen (pt.), Ire. 92/B1
Inje, SKor. 131/E3
Injune, Austl. 172/C4
Inkster, Mi, US 193/F7
Inland (sea), Japan 132/D4
Inle (lake), Myan. 141/G3
Inn (riv.), Aus. 115/G3
Inn (riv.), Ger. 101/K2
Inn (riv.), Swi. 101/J3
Innbach (riv.), Aus. 113/H6
Innellan, Sc, UK 94/B5
Inner (chan.), Belz. 202/D2
Inner (sound), Sc, UK 89/R8
Inner Hebrides (isls.),
Sc, UK 89/Q8
Inner Mongolia (reg.),
China 125/L5
Innerdouny (hill),
Sc, UK 94/C4
Innerleithen, Sc, UK 94/C5
Innerste (riv.), Ger. 109/G4
Innertkirchen, Swi. 115/E4
Innes NP, Austl. 171/H5
Innisfail, Ab, Can. 184/E2
Innisfail, Austl. 172/B2
Innoko (riv.), Ak, US 192/G3
Innsbruck, Aus. 115/H3
Innviertel (reg.), Aus. 113/G6
Inny (riv.), Eng, UK 90/B5
Ino, Japan 132/C4
Inocência, Braz. 213/B1
Inongo, D.R. Congo 155/J8
Inönü, Turk. 148/B2
Inowrocław, Pol. 99/K2
Insch, Sc, UK 94/D2
Inscription (cape),
Austl. 170/B3
Insein, Myan. 141/G4
Inside (passg.),
BC, Can. 184/A2
Insjön, Swe. 96/F1
Inta, Rus. 119/N2
Intendente Alvear,
Arg. 216/E2
Intepe, Turk. 105/K2
Intercourse, Pa, US 196/B3
Interior (plat.),
BC, Can. 184/B2
Interlaken, Swi. 114/D4
Internacional (int'l arpt.),
Braz. 214/D2
Internacional (int'l arpt.),
Mex. 201/C3
International Peace Garden,
ND, US 185/H3
Inthanon (peak), Thai. 141/G4
Intorsura Buzăului,
Rom. 107/H3
Intracoastal Waterway,
La, US 195/P17
Inuyama, Japan 135/L5
Inútil (bay), Chile 216/C7
Inubō-zaki (pt.), Japan 135/F2
Inukjuak, Qu, Can. 181/J3
Inuvik, NW, Can. 192/M2
Inuyama, Japan 135/L5
Inver (bay), Sc, UK 89/R8
Inverbervie, Sc, UK 94/D3
Invercargill, NZ 175/R12
Inverclyde (pol. reg.),
Sc, UK 94/B5
Inverell, Austl. 173/D1
Invergordon, Sc, UK 89/S8
Inverie, Sc, UK 89/R8
Inverigo, It. 116/C1
Inverkeithing, Sc, UK 94/C4
Inverloch, Austl. 173/G9
Invermay, Sk, Can. 185/H3
Inverness, Sc, UK 89/S8
Inverness, Al, US 193/J11
Inverness, Fl, US 191/H4
Inverness (co.),
NS, Can. 189/J2
Inveruno, It. 116/C2
Inverurie, Sc, UK 94/D2

Investigator (str.),
Austl. 167/C4
Invorio, It. 116/B1
Inwood, NY, US 197/L9
Inyanga, Zim. 163/F4
Inyangani (peak), Zim. 163/F4
Inymney (peak), Rus. 192/D2
Inza, Rus. 121/H1
Inzai, Japan 135/E2
Inzago, It. 116/C2
Inzigkofen, Ger. 115/F1
Iō-shima (isl.), Japan 132/B6
Ioánnina (int'l arpt.),
Gre. 105/G3
Ioánnina, Gre. 105/G3
Iona (isl.), Sc, UK 89/Q8
Iona PN da, Ang. 163/B4
Ione, Co, US 195/C2
Ione, Mi, US 188/C3
Ionia, It. 104/E3
Ionian (sea), Gre. 105/F3
Ionian (isls.), Gre. 105/F3
Ios (isl.), Gre. 105/J4
Iouîk (cape), Mrta. 160/A2
Iowa (state), US 187/J2
Iowa (riv.), Ia, US 185/K5
Iowa Falls, Ia, US 185/K5
Ipameri, Braz. 213/B1
Ipanema, Braz. 213/D1
Iparía, Peru 214/C3
Ipatinga, Braz. 213/D1
Ipel' (riv.), Slvk. 99/K4
Iphofen, Ger. 112/D3
Ipiales, Col. 210/B4
Ipiaú, Braz. 212/C4
Ipil, Phil. 137/D6
Ipirá, Braz. 212/C4
Ipiranga, Braz. 213/B3
Ipoh, Malay. 138/B3
Ipoly (riv.), Hun. 99/K4
Iporá, Braz. 209/H7
Ipsala, Turk. 105/K2
Ipsheim, Ger. 112/D3
Ipswich, SD, US 185/J4
Ipswich, Eng, UK 91/H2
Ipu, Braz. 212/B2
Ipuã, Braz. 213/B2
Ipubi, Braz. 212/B2
Ipueiras, Braz. 212/B2
Ipumba (hill), Tanz. 162/B4
Ipun, Isla (isl.), Chile 216/B5
Iqaluit (cap.), Nun,
Can. 181/K2
Iquique, Chile 208/D8
Iquitos, Peru 214/C1
Irago (chan.), Japan 135/L6
Irago-misaki (cape),
Japan 135/M6
Iráklia, Gre. 105/J4
Iráklia (isl.), Gre. 105/J4
Iráklion, Gre. 105/J5
Iráklion (int'l arpt.),
Gre. 105/J5
Iramaia, Braz. 212/B4
Iran (ctry.) 146/F2
Irapa, Ven. 211/F2
Irapuato, Mex. 201/E4
Iraq (ctry.) 146/D2
Irará, Braz. 212/C4
Irati, Braz. 213/B3
Iraucuba, Braz. 212/C1
Irbid (gov.), Jor. 149/D3
Irbid, Jor. 149/D3
Irbil, Iraq 148/F2
Irecê, Braz. 212/B3
Ireland (ctry.) 89/F/10
Ireland's Eye (isl.), Ire. 92/B5
Iremel' (peak), Rus. 119/N5
Iretama, Braz. 213/A3
Irfon (riv.), Wal, UK 90/C2
Irharhar, Oued (riv.),
Alg. 157/G4
Irhazer Oua-n-Agadez
(riv.), Niger 161/G2
Iri, SKor. 131/D5
Irian Jaya (reg.), Indo. 139/H4
Iricoume (mts.), Braz. 211/G4
Irig, Serb. 106/D3
Iriga, Tanz. 162/B4
Iriomote (isl.), Japan 137/D3
Iriri (riv.), Braz. 209/H4
Irish (sea), Ire. 87/C4
Irlam, Eng, UK 93/F5
Irõ-zaki (pt.), Japan 133/F3
Iroise (bay), Fr. 100/A2
Iron Baron, Austl. 171/H5
Iron Knob, Austl. 171/H5
Iron Mountain, Mi, US 185/L4
Irondale, Co, US 195/C3
Irondequoit, Oh, US 198/T7
Ironton, Mo, US 195/K13
Ironton, Ut, US 195/K11
Ironwood, Mi, US 185/L3
Ironwood Forest Nat'l Mon.,
Az, US 186/E4
Iroquois (riv.), Il, US 188/C3
Irpa (riv.), Rus. 119/W10
Irrawaddy (Ayeyarwady)
(riv.), Myan. 141/F4
Irrawaddy, Mouths of the
(delta), Myan. 141/F4
Irsch, Ger. 111/F4
Irsen (riv.), Ger. 111/F3
Irsina, It. 104/E2
Irt (riv.), Eng, UK 93/E3
Irthing (riv.), Eng, UK 93/F1
Irthlingborough,
Eng, UK 91/F2

Irtysh (riv.), Rus. 125/G4
Iruma, Japan 135/C2
Irumu, D.R. Congo 162/A2
Irún, Sp. 102/E1
Irvine, Ca, US 194/G8
Irvine, Sc, UK 94/B5
Irvine (bay), Sc, UK 94/B5
Irvine (riv.), Sc, UK 94/B5
Irving, Tx, US 190/D3
Irvington, NJ, US 197/J9
Irvington, NY, US 197/K7
Is (peak), Sudan 159/C4
Is-sur-Tille, Fr. 114/B2
Īsa Khel, Pak. 144/A3
Isaac (riv.), Austl. 167/D3
Isabela (isl.), Ecu. 214/E7
Isabela, Phil. 139/F2
Isabela, PR 199/M8
Isabelia (mts.), Nic. 202/E3
Isabella (bay), Nun., Can. 181/K2
Isaccea, Rom. 107/J3
Isachsen (cape), Nun., Can. 181/R7
Ísafjardhardjúp (inlet), Ice. 95/M6
Ísafjördhur, Ice. 95/M6
Isahaya, Japan 132/B4
Isalo, PN de l', Madg. 165/H8
Isalo Ruiniform (mass.), Madg. 165/H8
Isana (riv.), Col. 210/D4
Isandhlwana Battlesite, SAfr. 165/E3
Isangano NP, Zam. 162/A5
Isaouanne-n-Irarraren (des.), Alg. 157/G4
Isaouanne-n-Tifernine (des.), Alg. 157/G4
Isarco (riv.), It. 101/J3
Isarco (Eisack) (riv.), It. 115/H4
Isaszeg, Hun. 107/R9
Isawa, Japan 135/B2
Isbergues, Fr. 110/B2
Iscar, Sp. 102/C2
Ischgl, Aus. 115/G3
Ischia, It. 106/A5
Ise (bay), Japan 133/E3
Ise (riv.), Eng, UK 91/F2
Ise, Japan 135/L7
Ise-Shima NP, Japan 133/E3
Isehara, Japan 133/F3
Iselin, NJ, US 197/H9
Isen, Ger. 113/F6
Isen (riv.), Ger. 98/G4
Isenthal, Swi. 115/E4
Iseo (lake), It. 101/J4
Iseo, It. 116/D1
Iseo, Lago d' (lake), It. 116/C1
Isère (riv.), Fr. 100/F4
Isère (dept.), Fr. 114/B6
Iserlohn, Ger. 109/E6
Isernia, It. 104/D2
Isesaki, Japan 133/F2
Iset' (riv.), Rus. 145/D1
Iseyin, Nga. 161/F5
'Isfiyā, Isr. 149/G6
Ishi (riv.), Japan 135/J7
Ishibashi, Japan 133/F2
Ishibe, Japan 135/K5
Ishidoriya, Japan 134/B4
Ishigaki (isl.), Japan 137/D3
Ishige, Japan 133/F2
Ishikari, Japan 134/B2
Ishikari (bay), Japan 134/B2
Ishikari (mts.), Japan 134/C2
Ishikari (riv.), Japan 134/B2
Ishikawa (pref.), Japan 133/E2
Ishikawa, Japan 133/G2
Ishiki, Japan 135/M6
Ishim (riv.), Rus. 122/H4
Ishim, Rus. 119/R4
Ishimbay, Rus. 121/L1
Ishinomaki, Japan 134/B4
Ishioka, Japan 133/G2
Ishizuchi-san (peak), Japan 132/C4
Isiboro Sécure, PN, Bol. 208/E7
Isigny-sur-Mer, Fr. 100/C2
Isil'kul', Rus. 145/F2
Isiolo, Kenya 162/C2
Isiro, D.R. Congo 155/L7
Isisford, Austl. 172/B4
Iskenderun, Turk. 149/E1
Iskenderun, Gulf of (gulf), Turk. 149/D1
Iskilip, Turk. 148/C1
Iskŭr (riv.), Aus. 107/G4
Iskŭr (res.), Bul. 107/F4
Iskŭr (riv.), Bul. 105/H1
Isla, Mex. 202/C2
Isla (riv.), Sc, UK 94/C3
Isla Aguada, Mex. 202/D2
Isla Cabritos, PN, DRep. 203/J2
Isla Cedros, Mex. 200/B2
Isla Cristina, Sp. 102/B4
Isla de Maipo, Chile 216/N8
Isla de Salamanca, PN, Col. 210/C2
Isla de San Andrés (int'l arpt.), Col. 203/F3
Isla Gorge NP, Austl. 172/C4
Isla Guamblin, PN, Chile 216/B5
Isla Isabela, PN, Mex. 200/D4
Isla Magdalena, PN, Chile 215/B5
Isla Mujeres, Mex. 202/E1
Islâhiye, Turk. 149/E1
Islām Kot, Pak. 147/K4
Islāmābād (cap. terr.), Pak. 144/B3
Islāmābād (cap.), Pak. 144/B3
Islāmābād/Rāwalpindi (int'l arpt.), Pak. 144/B3
Islāmnagar, India 142/B1
Islamorada, Fl, US 191/H5
Islāmpur, India 143/G2
Islāmpur, India 143/E3
Island (lake), Mb, Can. 180/G3
Island (co.), Wa, US 193/B2
Island Beach State Park, NJ, US 196/D4
Island Lagoon (lake), Austl. 171/H4
Island Lake, Mb, Can. 185/K2
Island Lake, Il, US 193/P15
Island Park, NY, US 197/L9
Islands (bay), Nf, Can. 189/K1
Islay, Peru 214/C5
Islay (isl.), Sc, UK 89/Q9
Isle (riv.), Fr. 100/D4
Isle of Anglesey (co.), Wal, UK 92/D5
Isle of Ely (phys. reg.), Eng, UK 91/G2
Isle of Portland (pen.), Eng, UK 90/D5
Isle of Thanet (phys. reg.), Eng, UK 91/H4
Isle of Wight (co.), Eng, UK 91/E5
Isle Royale NP, Mi, US 188/B2
Isleton, Ca, US 193/L10
Islington (bor.), Eng, UK 88/A1
Islip, NY, US 197/E2
Ismailovo Park, Rus. 119/W9
Ismaning, Ger. 113/E6
Isny, Ger. 115/G2
Isoanala, Madg. 165/H8
Isobe, Japan 135/L7
Isojärven NP, Fin. 97/L1
Isojärvi (lake), Fin. 97/J1
Isoka, Zam. 162/B5
Isola del Liri, It. 104/C2
Isola della Scala, It. 117/D2
Isola di Capo Rizzuto, It. 104/E3
Isola Vicentina, It. 117/E1
Isonzo (riv.), It. 117/G1
Isorella, It. 116/D2
Isparta, Turk. 148/B2
Isparta (prov.), Turk. 148/B2
Isperikh, Bul. 107/H4
Ispir, Turk. 121/G4
Israel (ctry.) 149/C3
Issaquah, Wa, US 193/C2
Issel (riv.), Ger. 108/D5
Isselburg, Ger. 108/D5
Issenheim, Fr. 114/D2
Issia, C.d'Iv. 160/D5
Issoire, Fr. 100/E4
Issou, Fr. 88/H5
Issoudun, Fr. 100/E3
Issum, Ger. 108/D5
Issy-les-Moulineaux, Fr. 88/J5
Istállós-kó (peak), Hun. 106/E1
Istanbul (prov.), Turk. 107/J5
Istanbul, Turk. 107/J5
Istead Rise, Eng, UK 88/E2
Istiaía, Gre. 105/H3
Istmina, Col. 210/B3
Istok, Kos. 106/E4
Istra (riv.), Rus. 119/W9
Istrana, It. 117/F1
Istranca (mts.), Turk. 107/H5
Istres, Fr. 100/F5
Istria (pen.), Cro. 106/A3
Isulan, Phil. 139/F2
Isumi, Japan 135/E3
Itabaiana, Braz. 212/C3
Itabaiana, Braz. 212/D2
Itabaianinha, Braz. 212/C3
Itabapoana (riv.), Braz. 213/D2
Itaberaba, Braz. 212/B4
Itabira, Braz. 213/D1
Itabirito, Braz. 213/D2
Itaboraí, Braz. 213/L7
Itabuna, Braz. 212/C4
Itacaiunas (riv.), Braz. 209/H5
Itacarambi, Braz. 212/A4
Itacoatiara, Braz. 208/G4
Itacuaí (riv.), Braz. 208/D5
Itacuruba, Braz. 212/C3
Itaguaí, Braz. 213/K7
Itaguara, Braz. 213/C2
Itaguatins, Braz. 212/A2
Itagüí, Col. 208/C2
Itaí, Braz. 213/B2
Itaíba, Braz. 212/C3
Itaiçaba, Braz. 212/C2
Itainópolis, Braz. 212/B2
Itaiópolis, Braz. 213/B3
Itaipú (dam), Par. 215/F2
Itaipu (res.), Braz.,Par. 215/F1
Itaituba, Braz. 209/G4
Itajá, Braz. 213/B1
Itajaí, Braz. 213/B3
Itajaí (riv.), Braz. 213/B3
Itajubá, Braz. 213/H7
Itajuípe, Braz. 212/C4
Itako, Japan 133/G3
Itakura, Japan 135/D1
Italy (ctry.) 85/F4
Italy, Tx, US 187/H4
Itamaraju, Braz. 212/C5
Itamarandiba, Braz. 212/B5
Itambacuri, Braz. 212/B5
Itambé, Braz. 212/B4
Itambé, Pico de (peak), Braz. 212/B5
Itami, Japan 135/H6
Itamonte, Braz. 213/J7
Itampolo, Madg. 165/G9
Itanhaém, Braz. 213/G9
Itanhandu, Braz. 213/C2
Itanhém, Braz. 212/B5
Itanhém (riv.), Braz. 213/D1
Itanhomi, Braz. 213/D1
Itaobim, Braz. 212/B5
Itaocara, Braz. 213/D2
Itapagé, Braz. 212/C1
Itaparica (isl.), Braz. 212/C4
Itapé, Braz. 212/C4
Itapebi, Braz. 212/C4
Itapecerica, Braz. 213/C2
Itapecuru-Mirim, Braz. 212/A1
Itapemirim, Braz. 213/D2
Itaperuna, Braz. 213/D2
Itapetim, Braz. 212/C2
Itapetinga, Braz. 212/B4
Itapetininga, Braz. 213/B2
Itapeva, Braz. 213/B2
Itapevi, Braz. 213/G8
Itapicuri (riv.), Braz. 212/C3
Itapicuru (riv.), Braz. 209/K5
Itapipoca, Braz. 212/C1
Itapira, Braz. 213/G7
Itapitanga, Braz. 212/C4
Itaporanga, Braz. 213/B2
Itaquaquecetuba, Braz. 213/G8
Itarantim, Braz. 212/B4
Itararé, Braz. 213/B3
Itariri, Braz. 213/F9
Itārsi, India 142/A4
Itatiaia, PN de, Braz. 213/J7
Itatiba, Braz. 213/G7
Itaueira (riv.), Braz. 209/K5
Itaueira, Braz. 212/B2
Itaúna, Braz. 213/C2
Itayanagi, Japan 134/B3
Itbayat, Phil. 137/D3
Itbayat (isl.), Phil. 137/D3
Itchen (riv.), Eng, UK 91/E4
Itéa, Gre. 105/H3
Iténez (riv.), Bol. 205/C4
Itezhi-Tezhi (dam), Zam. 163/E4
Ith (hills), Ger. 109/G4
Ithaca, NY, US 188/E3
Ithaca, (Itháki) (isl.), Gre. 105/G3
Itháki, Gre. 105/G3
Ithon (riv.), Wal, UK 90/C2
Itimbiri (riv.), D.R. Congo 155/K7
Itinga, Braz. 212/B5
Itiruçu, Braz. 212/B4
Itō, Japan 133/F3
Itogon, Phil. 137/D4
Itoigawa, Japan 133/E2
Itoman, Japan 133/J7
Iton (riv.), Fr. 100/D2
Itonuki, Japan 135/L5
Itororó, Braz. 212/B4
Itsukaichi, Japan 135/C2
Itter (riv.), Ger. 109/F6
Itterbeck, Ger. 108/D3
Ittiri, It. 104/A2
Itu, Braz. 213/C2
Ituango, Col. 210/C3
Ituberá, Braz. 212/C4
Ituí (riv.), Braz. 208/D5
Ituiutaba, Braz. 213/B1
Itumbiara, Braz. 213/B1
Itumbiara, Barragem (res.), Braz. 213/B1
Itumirim, Braz. 213/J6
Ituna, Sk, Can. 185/H3
Itupiranga, Braz. 209/J5
Ituporanga, Braz. 213/B3
Iturama, Braz. 213/B1
Ituri (riv.), D.R. Congo 162/A2
Itutinga, Represa de (res.), Braz. 213/C2
Ituverava, Braz. 213/C2
Ituxi (riv.), Braz. 208/E5
Ituzaingó, Uru. 217/K11
Ityāy al Bārūd, Egypt 149/B4
Itz (riv.), Ger. 98/F3
Iul'tin (peak), Rus. 192/C2
Iúna, Braz. 213/D2
Ivaí (riv.), Braz. 213/B3
Ivaiporã, Braz. 213/B3
Ivalojoki (riv.), Fin. 95/H1
Ivančice, Czh. 101/M2
Ivanec, Cro. 101/M3
Ivanhoe, Austl. 173/C2
Ivanhoe (riv.), On, Can. 188/D1
Ivanjica, Serb. 106/E4
Ivanjska, Bosn. 106/C3
Ivankovo, Cro. 106/D3
Ivano-Frankivs'k, Ukr. 120/C2
Ivano-Frankivs'ka Oblasti, Ukr. 120/C2
Ivanof Bay, Ak, US 192/G4
Ivanovo, Rus. 118/J4
Ivanovovskaya Oblast, Rus. 118/J4
Ivato, Madg. 165/H8
Ivato (int'l arpt.), Madg. 165/H7
Ivaylovgrad (res.), Bul. 105/J2
Ivaylovgrad, Bul. 105/K2
Ivdel, Rus. 122/G3
Iveragh (pen.), Ire. 88/P11
Iverny, Fr. 88/L5
Ivindo (riv.), Gabon 154/H7
Ivohibe, Madg. 165/H8
Ivondro (riv.), Madg. 165/J7
Ivory (coast), C.d'Iv. 154/D7
Ivösjön (lake), Swe. 96/F3
Ivrea, It. 116/A2
Ivrindi, Turk. 148/A2
Ivry-sur-Seine, Fr. 88/K5
Ivujivik, Qu, Can. 181/J2
Ivvavik NP, Yk, Can. 180/B2
Iwafune, Japan 135/D1
Iwai, Japan 133/F2
Iwaizumi, Japan 134/B4
Iwaki, Japan 133/G2
Iwaki-san (peak), Japan 134/B3
Iwakuni, Japan 132/C3
Iwakura, Japan 135/L5
Iwama, Japan 135/E1
Iwami, Japan 132/D3
Iwamizawa, Japan 134/B2
Iwamura, Japan 135/M5
Iwanai, Japan 134/B2
Iwanuma, Japan 133/G1
Iwasaki, Japan 134/A3
Iwata, Japan 133/E3
Iwataki, Japan 135/H4
Iwate (pref.), Japan 134/B4
Iwate, Japan 134/B4
Iwate-san (peak), Japan 134/B4
Iwatsuki, Japan 135/D2
Iwere Ile, Nga. 161/F5
Iwo, Nga. 161/G5
Iwo Jima (isl.), Japan 174/D2
Iwŏn, NKor. 131/E2
Iwuy, Fr. 110/C3
Ixcán (riv.), Guat. 202/D3
Ixelles, Belg. 111/D2
Ixmiquilpan, Mex. 201/K6
Ixopo, SAfr. 165/E3
Ixtapaluca, Mex. 201/L7
Ixtapan de la Sal, Mex. 201/K8
Ixtlán del Río, Mex. 200/D4
Iyo (sea), Japan 132/B4
Iyo, Japan 132/C4
Izabal (lake), Guat. 198/D4
Īzad Khvāst, Iran 146/F2
Izamal, Mex. 202/D1
Izberbash, Rus. 121/H4
Izegem, Belg. 110/C2
Izhevsk, Rus. 119/M4
Izhma (riv.), Rus. 119/M2
Izhora (riv.), Rus. 119/T7
Izi (well), Alg. 157/F3
Izigan (cape), Ak, US 192/E5
Izkī, Oman 147/G4
Izmayil, Ukr. 107/J3
Izmir, Turk. 148/A2
Izmir (prov.), Turk. 148/A2
Izmit (gulf), Turk. 107/J5
Izmit, Turk. 107/J5
Iznájar, Sp. 102/C4
Iznik, Turk. 107/J5
Iznik (lake), Turk. 107/J5
Izola, Slov. 117/G1
Izra', Syria 149/E3
Izsák, Hun. 106/D2
Iztaccíhuatl-Popocatépetl, PN, Mex. 201/L7
Izu (pen.), Japan 133/F3
Izu (isls.), Japan 133/F4
Izúcar de Matamoros, Mex. 201/L8
Izuhara, Japan 132/A3
Izumi, Japan 132/B4
Izumi, Japan 134/B4
Izumi, Japan 135/H7
Izumi-Ōtsu, Japan 135/H7
Izumi-Sano, Japan 135/H7
Izumo, Japan 132/C3
Izunagaoka, Japan 135/B3
Izushi, Japan 135/G5
Izyum, Ukr. 120/F2

J

J. Paul Getty Museum, Ca, US 194/E7
Jääsjärvi (lake), Fin. 97/M1
Jaba', WBnk. 149/G7
Jabal 'Abd al 'Azāz (mts.), Syria 148/D2
Jabal Abu Rujmayn (mts.), Syria 148/D3
Jabal Abyad (plat.), Sudan 159/B5
Jabal al 'Arab (mts.), Syria 149/E3
Jabal an Nusayriyab (mts.), Syria 149/E2
Jabal ar Ruwaq (mts.), Syria 148/D3
Jabal as Sawdā' (hills), Libya 154/H2
Jabal ash Shaykh (peak), Leb. 149/D3
Jabāl Lubnān (gov.), Leb. 149/D2
Jabal Ramm (peak), Jor. 149/D5
Jabal 'Unāzah (peak), SAr. 148/D3
Jabalí (pt.), Pan. 203/F5
Jabalón (riv.), Sp. 102/D3
Jabalpur, India 142/B4
Jabālyah, Gaza 149/D4
Jabbeke, Belg. 110/C1
Jablah, Syria 149/D2
Jablanica (mts.), Alb. 105/G2
Jablonec nad Nisou, Czh. 99/H3
Jaboatão dos Guararapes, Braz. 212/D3
Jaboticabal, Braz. 213/B2
Jabuka, Serb. 106/E3
Jabung (cape), Indo. 138/B4
Jaca, Sp. 103/E1
Jacaré (riv.), Braz. 212/B3
Jacareí, Braz. 213/H8
Jaceel (riv.), Som. 155/Q5
Jáchymov, Czh. 113/F2
Jacinto, Braz. 212/B5
Jacinto Arauz, Arg. 216/E3
Jackman, Me, US 189/G2
Jackpot, Nv, US 184/E5
Jacks Mountain (ridge), Pa, US 196/A2
Jacksboro, Tx, US 187/H4
Jackson, Al, US 191/G4
Jackson, Ca, US 186/B3
Jackson, La, US 187/K5
Jackson, Mi, US 188/C3
Jackson, Mo, US 187/K3
Jackson (co.), Mo, US 195/E5
Jackson (cap.), Ms, US 187/K4
Jackson (mts.), Nv, US 184/D5
Jackson, Tn, US 188/B5
Jackson, Wy, US 184/F5
Jackson (lake), Wy, US 186/E2
Jacksonville, Al, US 191/G3
Jacksonville, Ar, US 187/J4
Jacksonville, Fl, US 191/H4
Jacksonville (int'l arpt.), Fl, US 191/H4
Jacksonville, Il, US 187/K3
Jacksonville, NC, US 191/J3
Jacksonville Beach, Fl, US 191/H4
Jacktown, Ok, US 195/N14
Jacmel, Haiti 203/H2
Jacobābād, Pak. 147/J3
Jacobina, Braz. 212/B3
Jacobsdal, SAfr. 164/D3
Jacobstown, NJ, US 196/D3
Jacobus, Pa, US 196/B4
Jacomo (lake), Mo, US 195/E6
Jacona de Plancarte, Mex. 200/E5
Jacques-Cartier (riv.), Qu, Can. 189/G2
Jacques Cartier (peak), Qu, Can. 189/H1
Jacuí (riv.), Braz. 215/F2
Jacuípe (riv.), Braz. 209/L6
Jacupiranga, Braz. 213/B3
Jacura, Ven. 210/D2
Jadacaquiva, Ven. 210/D2
Jaddi (pt.), Pak. 147/H3
Jade, Ger. 109/F2
Jade (riv.), Ger. 109/F1
Jade (bay), Ger. 98/E2
Jadebusen (bay), Ger. 109/F2
Jaén, Peru 214/B2
Jaén, Sp. 102/D4
Jaffa (cape), Austl. 173/A3
Jaffna, SrL. 140/C6
Jagādhri, India 144/D4
Jagdīspur, India 143/E3
Jagersfontein, SAfr. 164/D3
Jægerspris, Den. 96/D4
Jagna, Phil. 137/D6
Jagraon, India 144/C4
Jagst (riv.), Ger. 101/J2
Jagtiāl, India 140/C4
Jaguaquara, Braz. 212/C4
Jaguarão, Braz. 215/F3
Jaguarão (riv.), Braz. 217/G2
Jaguarari, Braz. 212/B3
Jaguaretama, Braz. 212/C2
Jaguariaíva, Braz. 213/B3
Jaguaribara, Braz. 212/C2
Jaguaribe (riv.), Braz. 209/L5
Jaguaribe, Braz. 212/C2
Jaguariúna, Braz. 213/G7
Jaguaruana, Braz. 212/C2
Jagungal (mt.), Austl. 173/D3
Jahānābād, India 143/E3
Jahāngīra, Pak. 144/B3
Jahāngīrābād, India 142/B1
Jahrom, Iran 146/F3
Jaicós, Braz. 212/B2
Jailolo, Indo. 139/G3
Jailu (riv.), China 130/C4
Jainca, China 128/H4
Jāis, India 142/C2
Jaisalmer, India 147/K3
Jaisinghnagar, India 142/C4
Jājapur, India 140/E3
Jājarm, Iran 147/G1
Jajce, Bosn. 106/C3
Jakarta (cap.), Indo. 138/C5
Jakobstad (Pietarsaari), Fin. 118/D3
Jal, NM, US 187/G4
Jala, Mex. 200/D4
Jalacingo, Mex. 201/M7
Jalaid Qi, China 129/M2
Jalal-Abad, Kyr. 145/F4
Jalal-Abad (obl.), Kyr. 145/F4
Jalālābād, Afg. 144/A2
Jalālābād, India 142/B2
Jalālābād, India 144/C4
Jalālābād, India 144/D5
Jalāli, India 142/B2
Jalālpur, India 142/D2
Jalālpur, Pak. 144/C3
Jalālpur Pīrwāla, Pak. 144/A5
Jalamah, WBnk. 149/G6
Jalangi (riv.), India 143/G3
Jalapa, Guat. 202/D3
Jalapa, Mex. 201/N7
Jalapa, Mex. 202/C2
Jalatlaco, Mex. 201/Q10
Jālaun, India 142/B2
Jaldhāka (riv.), India 143/G2
Jales, Braz. 213/B2
Jalesar, India 142/B2
Jalingo, Nga. 154/H6
Jalisco, Mex. 200/D4
Jallouvre, Pic de (peak), Fr . 114/C6
Jalon (riv.), Sp. 102/E2
Jalostotitlán, Mex. 200/E4
Jalpa, Mex. 200/E4
Jalpa de Méndez, Mex. 202/C2
Jalpan de Serra, Mex. 201/F4
Jaltenango de la Paz, Mex. 202/C3
Jaltepec (riv.), Mex. 202/C2
Jáltipan de Morelos, Mex. 202/C2
Jālūd, WBnk. 149/G7
Jaluit (isl.), Mrsh. 174/F4
Jalūlā', Iraq 148/F3
Jam, Iran 146/F3
Jamaame, Som. 155/P7
Jamaare (riv.), Nga. 154/H5
Jamaica (ctry.) 203/G2
Jamaica (chan.), Jam. 203/H2
Jamaica (bay), NY, US 196/K9
Jamālpur, Bang. 143/G3
Jamanxim (riv.), Braz. 209/G5
Jamapa, Mex. 201/N7
Jamari (riv.), Braz. 208/F5
Jambi, Indo. 138/B4
Jambuair (cape), Indo. 138/A2
James (pt.), Chile 216/B5
James (bay), Qu, Can. 181/H3
James (peak), Ut, US 195/K11
James (riv.), Va, US 185/J4
James Campbell NWR, Hi, US 182/V12
James M. Cox Dayton (int'l arpt.), Oh, US 188/C4
James Ross (str.), Nun., Can. 180/G1
Jamesburg, NJ, US 196/D3
Jamestown, Austl. 171/H5
Jamestown, Co, US 195/B2
Jamestown, ND, US 185/J4
Jamestown, NY, US 188/E3
Jamestown, Tn, US 188/C4
Jamīrāpāt (range), India 142/D4
Jāmke, Pak. 144/C3
Jammerbugt (bay), Den. 96/C3
Jammu and Kashmīr (state), India 144/C3
Jāmpur, Pak. 144/A5
Jāmtāra, India 143/F4
Jämtland (co.), Swe. 95/E3
Jamūi, India 143/F3
Jamuna (riv.), Bang. 143/G3
Jan (lake), Sk, Can. 185/H2
Jan Kempdorp, SAfr. 164/D2
Jan Mayen (isl.), Nor. 218/G
Jan Smuts (Johannesburg) (int'l arpt.), SAfr. 164/E2
Janakkala, Fin. 97/L1
Janakpur, Nepal 143/E2
Janakpur (zone), Nepal 143/E2
Janaúba, Braz. 212/B4
Janaucu, Ilha (isl.), Braz. 209/H3
Jandaia do Sul, Braz. 213/B2
Jandaq, Iran 147/F2
Jandowae, Austl. 172/C4
Jándula (riv.), Sp. 102/C4
Jangaon, India 140/C4
Jangipur, India 143/G3
Janikowo, Pol. 99/K2
Janīn, WBnk. 149/G7
Janja, Bosn. 106/D3
Janjevo, Kos. 106/E4
Janos, Mex. 200/C2
Jánoshalma, Hun. 106/D2
Jánosháza, Hun. 106/C2
Janów Lubelski, Pol. 99/M3
Jansenville, SAfr. 164/D4
Januária, Braz. 212/A4
Janvry, Fr. 88/J6
Janzé, Fr. 100/C3
Japan (ctry.) 129/Q4
Japan, Sea of (sea), Asia 129/P3
Japanese Alps NP, Japan 133/E2
Japurá (riv.), Braz. 205/C3
Jaqué, Pan. 203/G5
Jarābulus, Syria 148/D2
Jaraíz de la Vera, Sp. 102/C2
Jarama (riv.), Sp. 102/D2
Jaramānah, Syria 149/E3
Jarandilla de la Vera, Sp. 102/C2
Jarānwāla, Pak. 144/B4
Jarash, Jor. 149/D3
Järbo, Swe. 96/G1
Jarby (pt.), IM, UK 92/D3
Jardim, Braz. 212/C2
Jardín América, Arg. 215/E2
Jardines de la Reina (arch.), Cuba 203/G1
Jardinópolis, Braz. 213/C2
Jargalant, Mong. 128/G2
Jari (riv.), Braz. 205/D2
Jaridih, India 143/F4
Jarmen, Ger. 96/E5
Järna, Swe. 96/G2
Jarny, Fr. 111/E5
Jarocin, Pol. 99/J3
Jaroměř, Czh. 99/H3
Jarosław, Pol. 99/M3
Jarrettsville, Md, US 196/B4
Jarrow, Eng, UK 93/G2
Jars (plain), Laos 136/C2
Jarud Qi, China 130/E1
Järvenpää, Fin. 97/L1
Jarville-la-Malgrange, Fr. 111/F6
Jarvis (isl.), Pac., US 175/J5
Järvsö, Swe. 96/G1
Jáse-Nagykun-Szolnok (prov.), Hun. 106/E2
Jashpurnagar, India 143/E4
Jasidih, India 143/F3
Jāsk, Iran 147/G3
Jasło, Pol. 99/L4
Jason (isl.), Mald. 217/E6
Jasper, Ab, Can. 184/D2
Jasper, Al, US 191/G3
Jasper, Fl, US 191/H4
Jasper, Tx, US 187/J5
Jasper, Ga, US 191/G3
Jasper, In, US 188/C4
Jasper NP, Ab, Can. 184/D2
Jaspur, India 142/B1
Jastrebarsko, Cro. 106/B3
Jastrowie, Pol. 99/J2
Jastrzębie Zdroj, Pol. 99/K4
Jaswantnagar, India 142/B2
Jászapáti, Hun. 99/L5
Jászárokszállás, Hun. 106/D2
Jászberény, Hun. 99/K5
Jataí, Braz. 213/B1
Jatapu (riv.), Braz. 208/G3
Jatāra, India 142/B3
Jatate (riv.), Mex. 202/D2
Jāti, Pak. 147/J4
Jatibonico, Cuba 203/G1
Játiva, Sp. 103/E3
Jatoi Janūbi, Pak. 144/A5
Jaú (riv.), Braz. 208/F4
Jaú, Braz. 213/B2
Jaua Sarisarinama, PN, Ven. 208/F3
Jauaperi (riv.), Braz. 208/F3
Jauaperi (riv.), Braz. 211/F5
Jauaru, Serra (mts.), Braz. 209/H4
Jaudon, Mo, US 195/D6
Jauharābād, Pak. 144/B3
Jauja, Peru 214/C3
Jaumave, Mex. 201/F4
Jaun, Swi. 114/D4
Jaunay-Clan, Fr. 100/D3
Jaunpass (pass), Swi. 114/D4
Java (isl.), Indo. 138/C5
Java (sea), Indo. 138/D5
Javari (riv.), Braz. 208/D5
Jávea, Sp. 103/F3
Javier (isl.), Chile 217/B5
Javorie (peak), Slvk. 106/D1
Javornice (riv.), Czh. 113/G2
Javorník (peak), Czh. 113/G4
Javorová Skála (peak), Czh. 113/H3
Jawāla Mukhi, India 144/D4
Jawor, Pol. 99/J3
Jayanca, Peru 214/B2
Jayapura, Indo. 139/K4
Jaynagar, India 143/F2
Jaynagar, India 143/G4
Jayton, Tx, US 187/G4
Jbel Bani (mts.), Mor. 156/D3
Jean Lafitte, La, US 195/P17
Jeberos, Peru 214/B2
Jebjerg, Den. 96/C3
Jed Water (riv.), Sc, UK 94/D6
Jedburgh, Sc, UK 94/D6
Jedlicze, Pol. 99/L4
Jędrzejów, Pol. 99/L3
Jeetze (riv.), Ger. 98/F2
Jefferson (co.), Co, US 195/B3
Jefferson (parish), La, US 195/P17
Jefferson (riv.), La, US 195/P17
Jefferson (co.), Mo, US 195/F9
Jefferson (mt.), Or, US 184/C4
Jefferson, Tx, US 187/J4
Jefferson (co.), Wi, US 193/N14
Jefferson City (cap.), Mo, US 187/J3
Jeffersonville, In, US 188/C4
Jeffrey City, Wy, US 186/F2
Jeffreys Bay, SAfr. 164/D4
Jegenstorf, Swi. 114/D3
Jeinemeni (peak), Chile 216/B5
Jēkabpils, Lat. 97/L3
Jelcz-Laskowice, Pol. 99/J3
Jelenia Góra, Pol. 99/H3
Jelep (pass), China 140/E2
Jelgava, Lat. 97/K3
Jemaa Sahim, Mor. 156/C2
Jemappes, Belg. 110/C3
Jember, Indo. 138/D5
Jemez Pueblo, NM, US 186/F4
Jeminay, China 128/E2
Jemmal, Tun. 158/M7
Jempang (lake), Indo. 139/E4
Jena, La, US 187/J5
Jena, Ger. 98/F3
Jenaz, Swi. 115/F4
Jenbach, Aus. 101/J3
Jendouba, Tun. 158/L6
Jendouba (gov.), Tun. 158/L6
Jeneponto, Indo. 139/E5
Jengen, Ger. 115/G2
Jenkintown, Pa, US 196/C3
Jennings, La, US 187/J5
Jennings, Mo, US 195/G8
Jenny Lind (isl.), Nun., Can. 180/F2
Jens Muck (isl.), Nun., Can. 181/H2
Jeppener, Arg. 217/J11
Jequetepeque, Peru 214/B2
Jequié, Braz. 212/B4
Jequitaí, Braz. 212/A5
Jequitinhonha, Braz. 212/B5
Jequitinhonha (riv.), Braz. 205/E4
Jerada, Mor. 158/C2
Jerba (isl.), Tun. 155/H2
Jérémie, Haiti 203/H2
Jeremoabo, Braz. 212/C3
Jerez de García Salinas, Mex. 200/E4
Jerez de la Frontera, Sp. 102/B4
Jerez de los Caballeros, Sp. 102/B3
Jericho, Austl. 172/B3
Jericho, NY, US 197/L8
Jericho (Arīḩā), Isr. 149/D4
Jericó, Braz. 212/C2
Jerilderie, Austl. 173/C2
Jerissa, Tun. 158/L7
Jerramungup, Austl. 170/C5
Jersey (isl.), Chl, UK 100/B2
Jersey (co.), Il, US 195/G7
Jersey City, NJ, US 197/J9
Jersey City (res.), NJ, US 197/H8
Jersey Shore, Pa, US 196/A1
Jerumenha, Braz. 212/B2
Jerusalem (dist.), Isr. 149/D4
Jerusalem (Yerushalayim) (cap.), Isr. 149/G8
Jervis (inlet), BC, Can. 184/C3
Jervis Bay, Austl. 173/D2
Jerzu, It. 104/A3
Jesberg, Ger. 109/G6
Jesenice, Slov. 101/L3
Jesenice (res.), Czh. 113/F2
Jesi, It. 117/G5
Jessheim, Nor. 96/D1
Jessore (pol. reg.), Bang. 143/G4
Jesuânia, Braz. 213/H6
Jesup, Ga, US 191/H4
Jésus (isl.), Qu, Can. 189/N6
Jesús Carranza, Mex. 202/C2
Jesús de Machaca, Bol. 214/D5
Jesús María, Arg. 215/D3
Jesús Menéndez, Cuba 203/G1
Jeta, Ilha de (isl.), GBis. 160/A4
Jetmore, Ks, US 187/H3
Jetpur, India 147/K4
Jettingen-Scheppach, Ger. 112/D6
Jetzendorf, Ger. 113/E6
Jeumont, Fr. 111/D3
Jevenstedt, Ger. 98/E1
Jever, Ger. 109/E1
Jevnaker, Nor. 96/D1
Jewar, India 142/A1
Jewel Cave Nat'l Mon., SD, US 185/H5
Jezerce (peak), Alb. 105/F1
Jezerní Stěna (peak), Czh. 113/G4
Jeziorak (lake), Pol. 99/K2
Jhā Jhā, India 143/F3
Jhajjar, India 144/D5
Jhālawār, India 147/L4
Jhalida, India 143/E4
Jhālū, India 142/B1
Jhang Sadar, Pak. 144/B4
Jhanjhārpur, India 143/F2
Jhānsi, India 142/B3
Jhārgrām, India 143/F4
Jharia, India 143/F4
Jharkhand (state), India 143/E4
Jhārsuguda, India 143/E5
Jhawāriān, Pak. 144/B3
Jhelum, Pak. 144/B3
Jhelum (riv.), Pak. 147/K2
Jhenida, Bang. 143/G4
Jhumra, Pak. 144/B4
Ji-Paraná, Braz. 208/F6
Ji Xian, China 130/C4
Ji Xian, China 130/H6
Jia Xian, China 130/B3
Jiading, China 130/L8
Jiahe, China 141/K2
Jialing (riv.), China 125/K6
Jiamusi, China 129/P2
Jian (riv.), China 137/B3
Jianchang, China 130/D2
Jiang (riv.), China 136/E1
Jiang Xian, China 130/B4
Jiang'an, China 141/J2
Jiangcheng Hanizu Yizu Zizhixian, China 141/H3
Jiangchuan, China 141/H3
Jiangdu, China 130/D4
Jianghua Yaozu Zizhixian, China 141/K3
Jiangjin, China 141/J2
Jiangmen, China 141/K3
Jiangning, China 130/D5
Jiangsu (prov.), China 129/L5
Jiangxi (prov.), China 129/K6
Jiangyin, China 130/E5
Jiangyong, China 141/K2
Jiangyou, China 128/H5

Jianhe, China 141/J2
Jianhu, China 130/D4
Jianli, China 137/B2
Jian'ou, China 137/C2
Jianshi, China 129/J5
Jianshui, China 141/H3
Jianyang, China 137/C2
Jiaocheng, China 130/C3
Jiaohe, China 129/N3
Jiaojiang, China 137/D2
Jiaokou, China 130/C3
Jiaoling, China 137/C3
Jiaonan, China 130/D4
Jiaozuo, China 130/C4
Jiashan, China 130/D4
Jiashan, China 130/L9
Jiashi, China 145/G5
Jiaxiang, China 130/D4
Jiaxing, China 130/L9
Jiayin, China 129/P2
Jiayu, China 137/B2
Jiayuguan, China 128/G4
Jibou, Rom. 107/F2
Jibsh, Ra's (pt.), Oman 147/G4
Jicarón (isl.), Pan. 203/F5
Jičín, Czh. 99/H3
Jiddah, SAr. 146/C4
Jieshou, China 130/C4
Jiexiu, China 130/B3
Jieyang, China 137/C3
Jifnā, Isr. 149/G8
Jigalong Abor. Land, Austl. 170/D2
Jigawa (prov.), Nga. 161/H4
Jiguaní, Cuba 203/G1
Jigzhi, China 128/H5
Jihlava (riv.), Czh. 101/L2
Jihlava, Czh. 99/H4
Jihlavský (pol. reg.), Czh. 99/H4
Jijel, Alg. 158/H4
Jijel (prov.), Alg. 158/H4
Jijia (riv.), Rom. 107/H2
Jijiga, Eth. 155/P6
Jijona, Sp. 103/E3
Jilhã, Represa (res.), Braz. 213/B2
Jilhava (riv.), Czh. 99/H4
Jilib, Som. 155/P7
Jilin, China 129/N3
Jilin (prov.), China 129/N3
Jiloca (riv.), Sp. 102/E2
Jilotepec, Mex. 201/K7
Jílové u Prahy, Czh. 113/H3
Jim Thorpe, Pa, US 196/C2
Jīma, Eth. 155/N6
Jimaní, DRep. 203/J2
Jimbolia, Rom. 106/E3
Jimboomba, Austl. 172/D4
Jimena de la Frontera, Sp. 102/C4
Jiménez, Mex. 200/D3
Jiménez, Mex. 201/E2
Jimo, China 130/E3
Jimokuji, Japan 135/L5
Jimsar, China 128/E3
Jin (riv.), China 141/K2
Jin Xian, China 130/C3
Jinan, China 130/D3
Jinchang, China 128/H4
Jincheng, China 130/C4
Jinchuan, China 128/H5
Jinci Temple, China 130/C3
Jīnd, India 144/D5
Jindabyne (dam), Austl. 173/D3
Jindabyne, Austl. 173/D3
Jindřichuv Hradec, Czh. 99/H4
Jing Xian, China 129/L5
Jing Xian, China 141/J2
Jingbian, China 130/B3
Jingde, China 137/C1
Jingdezhen, China 137/C2
Jingdong, China 141/H3
Jinggangshan, China 141/K2
Jinghai, China 130/H7
Jinghe, China 128/D3
Jinghong, China 141/H3
Jingjiang, China 130/E4
Jingle, China 130/B3
Jingmen, China 130/C5
Jingshan, China 130/C5
Jingxi, China 141/J3
Jingyuan, China 128/H4
Jinhu, China 130/D4
Jinhua, China 137/C2
Jining, China 130/C2
Jining, China 130/D4
Jinja, Ugan. 162/B2
Jinkouhe, China 141/H2
Jinotega, Nic. 202/E3
Jinotepe, Nic. 202/E4
Jinping, China 141/J2
Jinsha, China 141/J2
Jinsha (riv.), China 125/J7
Jinshan, China 130/L9
Jinshi, China 141/K2
Jintan, China 130/D5
Jintotolo (chan.), Phil. 137/D5
Jintūr, India 147/L5
Jinxi, China 137/C2
Jinxi, China 130/E2
Jinxian, China 137/C2
Jinxiang, China 130/D4
Jinyun, China 137/D2
Jinzhai, China 130/C5
Jinzhou (bay), China 131/A3
Jinzhou, China 130/E2
Jiparana (riv.), Braz. 208/F5
Jipijapa, Ecu. 210/A5
Jiquilpan de Juárez, Mex. 200/E5
Jiquipilco, Mex. 201/Q9
Jiřkov, Czh. 113/G1
Jishan, China 130/B4
Jishou, China 141/J2
Jishui, China 137/C2
Jisr ash Shughūr, Syria 149/E2
Jiu (riv.), Rom. 107/F3
Jiujiang, China 137/C2
Jiujiang, China 137/C2
Jiulong, China 141/H2
Jiutai, China 129/N3
Jiutepec, Mex. 201/K8
Jiuwan (mts.), China 128/J6
Jixi, China 129/P2
Jixi, China 137/C1
Jiyang, China 130/D3
Jiyuan, China 130/C4
Jīzān, SAr. 146/D5
Jize, China 130/C3
Jizera (riv.), Czh. 99/H3
Jizō-zaki (pt.), Japan 132/C3
Jizzakh, Uzb. 145/E4
Jizzakh (pol. reg.), Uzb. 145/E4
Joaçaba, Braz. 213/B3
Joachín, Mex. 201/N8
Joaíma, Braz. 212/B5
João Câmara, Braz. 212/D2
João Lisboa, Braz. 212/A2
João Monlevade, Braz. 213/D1
João Pessoa, Braz. 212/D2
João Pinheiro, Braz. 212/A5
Joaquín V. González, Arg. 215/D2
Jobabo, Cuba 203/G1
Jockgrim, Ger. 112/B4
Jocón, Hon. 202/E3
Jódar, Sp. 102/D4
Jodhpur, India 147/K3
Jodoigne, Belg. 111/D2
Joensuu, Fin. 95/J3
Jōetsu, Japan 133/F2
Jogbani, India 143/F2
Johannesberg, Ger. 112/C2
Johannesburg, SAfr. 164/E2
Johanngeorgenstadt, Ger. 113/F2
Johilla (riv.), India 142/C4
John Day, Or, US 184/D4
John Day (riv.), Or, US 184/D4
John Day Fossil Beds Nat'l Mon., Or, US 184/C4
John Day, Middle Fork (riv.), Or, US 184/D4
John Day, North Fork (riv.), Or, US 184/D4
John F. Kennedy (int'l arpt.), NY, US 197/K9
John Forrest NP, Austl. 170/L6
John H. Kerr (res.), NC,Va, US 191/J2
John Martin (res.), Co, US 190/C2
John Wayne/Orange County (int'l arpt.), Ca, US 194/G8
Johnson (co.), Ks, US 195/D6
Johnson City, Tn, US 188/D4
Johnsonburg, NJ, US 196/D2
Johnsons Crossing, Yk, Can. 192/M3
Johnston (falls), Zam. 162/A5
Johnston (lake), Austl. 167/B4
Johnston Atoll (isl.), Pac., US 175/J3
Johnstone, Sc, UK 94/B5
Johnstown, Pa, US 188/E3
Johnstown, Co, US 195/C2
Johnsville, Md, US 196/A4
Johor Baharu, Malay. 138/B3
Jöhstadt, Ger. 113/G1
Joigny, Fr. 100/E3
Joinvile, Braz. 213/B3
Joinville, Fr. 114/B1
Jojutla, Mex. 201/K8
Jokioinen, Fin. 97/K1
Jokkmokk, Swe. 95/F2
Jökulsargljufur NP, Ice. 95/P6
Jolanda di Savoia, It. 117/E3
Joliette, Qu, Can. 188/F2
Jollyville, Tx, US 187/H5
Jolo (isl.), Phil. 139/F2
Jolo, Phil. 139/F2
Jomala, Fin. 97/H1
Jombang, Indo. 138/D5
Jomda, China 128/G5
Jomo Kenyatta (int'l arpt.), Kenya 162/C3
Jona, Swi. 115/E3
Jonacatepec, Mex. 201/L8
Jonava, Lith. 97/L4
Jonchery-sur-Vesle, Fr. 110/C5
Jones, Ok, US 195/N14
Jones (inlet), NY, US 197/L9
Jones (mtn.), Pa, US 196/A2
Jones (sound), Nun., Can. 181/S7
Jones Beach State Park, NY, US 197/L9
Jonesboro, Ar, US 187/K4
Jonesboro, La, US 187/J4
Jönköping, Swe. 96/F3
Jönköping (co.), Swe. 95/E4
Jonquière, Qu, Can. 189/G1
Jonuta, Mex. 198/C4
Joondalup (lake), Austl. 170/K6
Joplin, Mo, US 187/J3
Joppatowne (Joppa), Md, US 196/B5
Jora, India 142/A2
Jordan, Mt, US 184/G4
Jordan, On, Can. 189/R9
Jordan (riv.), Isr.,Jor. 149/D4
Jordan (ctry.) 146/C2
Jordan Valley, Or, US 184/D5
Jordânia, Braz. 212/B4
Jorge (cape), Chile 217/B6
Jorge Chavez (int'l arpt.), Peru 214/B4
Jork, Ger. 109/G1
Jornada del Muerto (valley), NM, US 190/B3
Jørpeland, Nor. 96/B2
Jos (plat.), Nga. 154/G6
Jos, Nga. 161/H4
Jose Abad Santos, Phil. 139/G2
José Batlle y Ordóñez, Uru. 217/G2
José Bonifácio, Braz. 213/B2
José Cardel, Mex. 201/N7
José de Freitas, Braz. 212/B2
José de San Martín, Arg. 215/B5
José Enrique Rodó, Uru. 217/K10
José María Morelos, Mex. 202/D2
Jose Marti (int'l arpt.), Cuba 203/F1
José Pedro Varela, Uru. 217/G2
José, South (dept.), Uru. 217/F2
Josefa Camejo (int'l arpt.), Ven. 210/D2
Joseph Bonaparte (gulf), Austl. 167/B2
Joshin-Etsu Kogen NP, Japan 133/F2
Joshua (pt.), Ct, US 197/F1
Joshua Tree NP, Ca, US 186/D4
Jossa (riv.), Ger. 112/C2
Jotunheimen NP, Nor. 96/C1
Jouanne (riv.), Fr. 100/C2
Jouarre, Fr. 88/M5
Joué-lès-Tours, Fr. 100/D3
Jœuf, Fr. 111/F5
Jourama Falls NP, Austl. 172/B2
Jourdanton, Tx, US 187/H5
Joure, Neth. 108/C3
Joutseno, Fin. 97/N1
Joux (lake), Swi. 114/C4
Jouy-en-Josas, Fr. 88/J5
Jouy-le-Châtel, Fr. 88/M6
Jouy-le-Moutier, Fr. 88/J4
Jouy-sur-Morin, Fr. 110/C6
Jovellanos, Cuba 203/F1
Joveyn (riv.), Iran 147/G1
Jowai, India 141/F2
Joy (mt.), Yk, Can. 192/M3
Jōyō, Japan 135/J6
Jozankei Spa, Japan 134/B2
Ju Xian, China 130/D4
Juan Aldama, Mex. 200/E3
Juan de Fuca, Strait of (str.), US,Can. 184/B3
Juan de Nova (isl.), Reun., Fr. 165/G7
Juan Fernández (isls.), Chile 205/A6
Juan José Paso, Arg. 216/E2
Juan L. Lacaze, Uru. 217/K11
Juan Santamaria (int'l arpt.), CR 203/E4
Juancheng, China 130/C4
Juangriego, Ven. 211/F2
Juanjuí, Peru 214/B2
Juárez, Arg. 216/F3
Juarez, Sierra de (mts.), Mex. 186/D4
Juatinga, Ponta de (pt.), Braz. 213/J8
Juazeirinho, Braz. 212/C2
Juazeiro, Braz. 212/B3
Juazeiro do Norte, Braz. 212/C2
Juba, Sudan 155/M7
Jubany, Arg., Ant. 218/W
Jubba (riv.), Som. 155/P7
Jübek, Ger. 98/E1
Jubones (riv.), Ecu. 214/B1
Juby (cape), Mor. 156/B4
Júcar (riv.), Sp. 102/D3
Jucás, Braz. 212/C2
Jüchen, Ger. 111/F1
Juchipila, Mex. 200/E4
Juchique de Ferrer, Mex. 201/N7
Juchitán de Zaragoza, Mex. 202/C2
Juchitepec, Mex. 201/R10
Jucurutu, Braz. 212/C2
Judaberg, Nor. 96/A2
Judenburg, Aus. 101/L3
Judith (riv.), Mt, US 184/F4
Juelsminde, Den. 96/D4
Juhaynah, Egypt 159/B3
Juigalpa, Nic. 203/E3
Juilly, Fr. 88/L4
Juine (riv.), Fr. 100/E2
Juist (isl.), Ger. 108/D1
Juist, Ger. 108/E1
Juiz de Fora, Braz. 213/K6
Jujurieux, Fr. 114/B5
Julbach, Ger. 113/F6
Julesburg, Co, US 185/H5
Juli, Peru 214/D5
Julia Creek, Austl. 172/A3
Juliaca, Peru 214/D4
Julian Alps (mts.), It. 101/K3
Juliana Top (peak), Sur. 209/G3
Jülich, Ger. 111/F2
Julio A. Mella, Cuba 203/H1
Juliustown, NJ, US 196/D3
Jullundur, India 144/C4
Julu, China 130/C3
Jumbilla, Peru 214/B2
Jumeauville, Fr. 88/H5
Jumilla, Sp. 102/E3
Juminda (pt.), Est. 97/L2
Jumla, Nepal 142/D1
Jümme (riv.), Ger. 109/E2
Jūmonji, Japan 134/B4
Junāgadh, India 147/K4
Junan, China 130/D4
Juncal (peak), Chile 216/N8
Junction, Ut, US 186/D3
Junction, Tx, US 187/H5
Junction City, Or, US 184/C4
Jundiaí, Braz. 213/G8
Jundu (mts.), China 130/H6
Juneda, Sp. 103/F2
Junee, Austl. 173/C2
Jungar Qi, China 130/B3
Jungfrau (peak), Swi. 114/D4
Jungfraujoch, Swi. 114/D4
Junglinster, Lux. 111/F4
Juniata (co.), Pa, US 196/A2
Juniata (riv.), Pa, US 188/E3
Junik, Kos. 106/E4
Junín, Peru 214/B3
Junín (dept.), Peru 214/C3
Junín, Ecu. 210/A5
Junín, Arg. 216/C2
Junín, Arg. 216/E2
Junín de los Andes, Arg. 216/C3
Juniper Hills, Ca, US 194/C2
Junji (pass), China 130/C3
Juno Beach, Fl, US 191/H5
Junqueirópolis, Braz. 213/B2
Junsele, Swe. 95/F3
Juparanã, Lagoa (lake), Braz. 213/D1
Jupiter (riv.), Qu, Can. 189/J1
Jupiter, Fl, US 191/H5
Jupiter (mt.), Wa, US 193/A2
Juquiá, Braz. 213/C3
Juquitiba, Braz. 213/F8
Jur (riv.), Sudan 155/L6
Jur pri Bratislave, Slvk. 106/C1
Jura (mts.), Fr. 100/F3
Jura (dept.), Fr. 114/B4
Jura (pen.), Sc, UK 89/B8
Jura (isl.), Sc, UK 89/Q9
Juradó, Col. 210/B3
Jurançon, Fr. 100/C5
Jurbise, Belg. 110/C2
Jurien, Austl. 170/B4
Jūrmala, Lat. 97/K3
Juruá (riv.), Braz. 205/C3
Juruena (riv.), Braz. 205/D4
Juruti, Braz. 209/G4
Jushiyama, Japan 135/L5
Juskatla, BC, Can. 192/M5
Jussey, Fr. 114/B2
Jussy, Swi. 114/C5
Jussy, Fr. 110/C4
Justo Daract, Arg. 216/D2
Jutaí, Braz. 208/E5
Jutaí (riv.), Braz. 208/E4
Jutiapa, Guat. 202/D3
Juticalpa, Hon. 202/E3
Jutland, NJ, US 196/D2
Jutland (pen.), Den. 95/D4
Juventud, La (isl.), Cuba 203/F1
Juye, China 130/D4
Juzhang (riv.), China 130/C5
Juziers, Fr. 88/H4
Južna Morava (riv.), Serb. 106/E4
Jyderup, Den. 96/D4

K

Ka (riv.), Nga. 154/F5
Ka (isl.), NKor. 131/C3
Ka Lae (cape), Hi, US 182/U11
Kaaawa, Hi, US 182/W12
Kaabong, Ugan. 162/B2
Kaala (peak), Hi, US 182/V12
Kaaualu, Hi, US 182/U11
Kaap Plato (plat.), SAfr. 164/C3
Kaarina, Fin. 97/K1
Kaarst, Ger. 108/D6
Kaba, Hun. 106/E2
Kabadak (riv.), Bang. 143/G4
Kabaena (isl.), Indo. 139/F5
Kabah (ruin), Mex. 202/D1
Kabale, SLeo. 160/C4
Kabale, Ugan. 162/A3
Kabalega (falls), Ugan. 162/A2
Kabalega NP, Ugan. 155/M7
Kabalo, D.R. Congo 163/E2
Kabamba, Lac (lake), D.R. Congo 163/E2
Kabankalan, Phil. 139/F2
Kabardino-Balkaria, Resp., Rus. 121/G4
Kabare, D.R. Congo 162/A3
Kaberamaido, Ugan. 162/B2
Kabinakagani (lake), On, Can. 188/C1
Kabinda, D.R. Congo 163/D2
Kabīr, Oued el (riv.), Alg. 158/H4
Kabīrwāla, Pak. 144/A4
Kableshkovo, Bul. 107/H4
Kābol (Kabul) (cap.), Afg. 147/J2
Kabompo (riv.), Zam. 163/D3
Kabongo, D.R. Congo 163/E2
Kabrai, India 142/C3
Kābul (riv.), Afg. 147/J2
Kabul (Kābol) (cap.), Afg. 147/J2
Kaburuang (isl.), Indo. 139/G3
Kabwe, Zam. 163/E3
Kačanik, Kos. 106/E4
Kachalola, Zam. 163/F3
Kachemak, Ak, US 192/H4
Kachemak (bay), Ak, US 192/H4
Kachin (div), Myan. 141/G2
Kaçkar Dai (peak), Turk. 148/E1
Kadaianallur, India 140/C6
Kadam (peak), Ugan. 162/B2
Kadam (isl.), Myan. 141/G5
Kadan (isl.), Myan. 136/B3
Kadaň, Czh. 113/G2
Kadavu (isl.), Fiji 174/G6
Kadéï (riv.), CAfr.,Camr. 154/J7
Kadina, Austl. 171/H5
Kadınhanı, Turk. 148/C2
Kadiogo (prov.), Burk. 161/E3
Kadiolo, Mali 160/D4
Kadiri, India 140/C5
Kadirli, Turk. 148/D2
Kadışehri, Turk. 148/C1
Kadoka, SD, US 185/H5
Kadoma, Zim. 163/E4
Kadoma, Japan 135/J6
Kaduna, Nga. 161/G4
Kaduna (riv.), Nga. 161/G4
Kaduna (state), Nga. 161/G4
Kāduqli, Sudan 155/L5
Kaech'ŏn, NKor. 131/C3
Kaédi, Mrta. 160/B2
Kaélé, Camr. 154/H5
Kaena (pt.), Hi, US 182/V12
Kaeng Krachan NP, Thai. 136/B3
Kaesŏng, NKor. 131/D3
Kaesŏng-si (prov.), NKor. 131/D4
Kafar Jar Ghar (mts.), Afg. 147/J2
Kaffraria (reg.), SAfr. 164/D4
Kaffrine, Sen. 160/B3
Kafirévs (cape), Gre. 105/J3
Kafr Ash Shaykh (gov.), Egypt 159/B1
Kafr ash Shaykh, Egypt 149/B4
Kafr az Zayyāt, Egypt 149/B4
Kafr Kannā, Isr. 149/G6
Kafr Mandā, Isr. 149/G6
Kafr Qari', Isr. 149/G6
Kafr Qāsim, Isr. 149/F7
Kafu (riv.), Ugan. 162/A2
Kafue (riv.), Zam. 163/E4
Kafue, Zam. 163/E4
Kafue NP, Zam. 163/E3
Kaga, Japan 132/E2
Kaga Bandoro, CAfr. 155/J6
Kagan, Uzb. 145/D5
Kāgān (valley), Pak. 144/B2
Kagawa (pref.), Japan 132/D3
Kagera (riv.), Tanz. 162/A3
Kağızman, Turk. 148/E1
Kagoshima (int'l arpt.), Japan 132/B5
Kagoshima, Japan 132/B5
Kagoshima (bay), Japan 132/B5
Kagoshima (dept.), Japan 133/L5
Kahaluu, Hi, US 182/W13
Kahama, Tanz. 162/B3
Kahayan (riv.), Indo. 138/D4
Kahiu (pt.), Hi, US 182/T10
Kahl am Main, Ger. 112/C2
Kāhna, Pak. 144/C4
Kahoka, Mo, US 185/L5
Kahoolawe (isl.), Hi, US 182/T10
Kahperusvaara (peak), Fin. 95/G1
Kahraman Maraş (prov.), Turk. 148/D2
Kahramanmaraş, Turk. 148/D2
Kahror Pakka, Pak. 144/A5
Kâhta, Turk. 148/D2
Kahuku, Hi, US 182/W12
Kahuku (pt.), Hi, US 182/W12
Kahului, Hi, US 182/T10
Kahuzi-Biega, PN de, D.R. Congo 163/E1
Kai (isls.), Indo. 139/H5
Kai Besar (isl.), Indo. 139/H5
Kai Kecil (isl.), Indo. 139/H5
Kaiapoi, NZ 175/S11
Kaibab (plat.), Az, US 186/D3
Kaibara, Japan 135/H5
Kaieteur (falls), Guy. 211/G3
Kaieteur NP, Guy. 211/G3
Kaifeng, China 129/K5
Kaifeng, China 130/C4
Kaihua, China 137/C2
Kaikohe, NZ 175/S10
Kaikoura, NZ 175/S11
Kaili, China 141/J2
Kailu, China 130/E2
Kailua, Hi, US 182/U11
Kailua, Hi, US 182/W13
Kaimganj, India 142/B2
Kaimur (range), India 142/C3
Kainab (riv.), Namb. 164/B2
Kainach (riv.), Aus. 106/B2
Kainan, Japan 132/D3
Kainji (dam), Nga. 161/G4
Kainji (lake), Nga. 161/G4
Kainji Lake NP, Nga. 161/F4
Kainoúryion, Gre. 105/G3
Kaipara (har.), NZ 175/S10
Kairāna, India 144/D5
Kairi, Austl. 172/B2
Kairouan, Tun. 158/L7
Kairouan (gov.), Tun. 158/L7
Kaisei, Japan 135/C3
Kaiseregg (peak), Swi. 114/D4
Kaisersesch, Ger. 111/G3
Kaiserslautern, Ger. 111/G5
Kaisheim, Ger. 112/D5
Kaitaia, NZ 175/S10
Kaithal, India 144/D5
Kaiwi (chan.), Hi, US 182/T10
Kaiyang, China 141/J2
Kaiyuan, China 141/H3
Kaiyuan, China 130/F2
Kaizu, Japan 135/L5
Kaizuka, Japan 135/H7
Kajaani, Fin. 95/H2
Kaji-san (peak), SKor. 131/E5
Kajiado, Kenya 162/C3
Kajikazawa, Japan 135/A2
Kakamas, SAfr. 164/C3
Kakamega, Kenya 162/B2
Kakamigahara, Japan 135/L5
Kakanj, Bosn. 106/D3
Kake, Ak, US 192/M4
Kaketsa (mtn.), BC, Can. 192/M4
Kakhovka, Ukr. 107/L2
Kakhovs'ke Vodoskhovyshche (res.), Ukr. 120/E3
Kākināda, India 140/D4
Kakiri, Ugan. 162/B2
Kako (riv.), Japan 135/G6
Kakogawa, Japan 135/G6
Kākori, India 142/C2
Kakrāla, India 142/B2
Kakrima (riv.), Gui. 160/B4
Kaktovik, Ak, US 192/K1
Kakuda, Japan 133/G2
Kakunodate, Japan 134/B4
Kalaa Kbira, Tun. 158/M7
Kalaat El Andalous, Tun. 158/M6
Kālābāgh, Pak. 144/A3
Kalabo, Zam. 163/D3
Kalach, Rus. 121/G2
Kalach-na-Donu, Rus. 121/G2
Kalachinsk, Rus. 145/F1
Kaladan (riv.), Myan. 141/F3
Kālāgarh, India 142/B1
Kalahari (des.), Namb. 164/C2
Kalahari-Gemsbok NP, SAfr. 163/C6
Kalaheo, Hi, US 182/S10
Kalaiya, Nepal 143/E2
Kalalé, Ben. 161/F4
Kalamákion, Gre. 105/N8
Kalamaloué, PN de, Camr. 154/H5
Kalamariá, Gre. 105/H2
Kalamáta, Gre. 105/H4
Kalamazoo, Mi, US 188/C3
Kalampáka, Gre. 105/G3
Kalandy, Madg. 165/J6
Kalaoa, Hi, US 182/U11
Kalasin, Thai. 136/C2
Kalāswāla, Pak. 144/C3
Kalāt, Pak. 147/J3
Kalaupapa, Hi, US 182/T10
Kalávrita, Gre. 105/H3
Kalbach, Ger. 112/C1
Kalbar, Austl. 172/D4
Kalbarri, Austl. 170/B3
Kalbarri NP, Austl. 170/B3
Kaldakvísl (riv.), Ice. 95/N7
Kale, Turk. 120/F4
Kale, Turk. 149/A1
Kalecik, Turk. 148/C1
Kalefeld, Ger. 109/H5
Kalemie (int'l arpt.), D.R. Congo 162/A4
Kalemie, D.R. Congo 162/A4
Kalemyo, Myan. 141/F3
Kalety, Pol. 99/K3
Kalewa, Myan. 141/F3
Kaleya, Zam. 163/E4
Kalgoorlie-Boulder, Austl. 170/D4
Kāli (riv.), India 142/B1
Kāli (riv.), India 142/B2
Kāli (riv.), Nepal 142/D2
Kalianda, Indo. 138/C5
Kalima, D.R. Congo 155/L8
Kalimantan (reg.), Indo. 138/D4
Kálimnos, Gre. 148/A2
Kálimnos (isl.), Gre. 148/A2
Kālimpong, India 143/G2
Kaliningrad, Rus. 119/W9
Kaliningrad, Rus. 97/J4
Kaliningradskaya Oblast, Rus. 118/D5
Kalininsk, Rus. 121/H2
Kalinkavichy, Bela. 120/D1
Kaliro, Ugan. 162/B2
Kalisizo, Ugan. 162/A3
Kalispell, Mt, US 184/E3
Kalisz, Pol. 99/K3
Kalix, Swe. 95/G2
Kalixälven (riv.), Swe. 95/G2
Kāliyāganj, India 143/G3
Kalkaska, Mi, US 188/C2
Kallham, Aus. 113/G6
Kallinge, Swe. 96/F3
Kallinge (int'l arpt.), Swe. 96/F3
Kallithéa, Gre. 105/N9
Kallsjön (lake), Swe. 95/E3
Kalmar, Swe. 96/G3
Kalmar (co.), Swe. 95/F4
Kalmar (int'l arpt.), Swe. 96/G3
Kalmarsund (sound), Swe. 96/G3
Kalmthout, Belg. 108/B6
Kalmykia, Resp., Rus. 122/E5
Kālna, India 143/G4
Kalni (riv.), Bang. 143/H3
Kalocsa, Hun. 106/D2
Kalofer, Bul. 105/J1
Kalohi (chan.), Hi, US 182/T10
Kalokhórion, Gre. 105/H2
Kālol, India 147/K4
Kalomo, Zam. 163/E4
Kalongo, Ugan. 162/B2
Kālpi, India 142/B2
Kalpin, China 128/C3
Kalsdorf bei Graz, Aus. 101/L3
Kaltag, Ak, US 192/G3
Kaltbrunn, Swi. 115/F3
Kaltenleutgeben, Aus. 107/N7
Kaltennordheim, Ger. 112/D1
Kaltern (Caldaro), It. 101/J3
Kalu (riv.), SrL. 140/D6
Kaluga, Rus. 118/H5
Kalundborg, Den. 96/D4
Kalungu, Ugan. 162/A3
Kalungwishi (riv.), Zam. 162/A5
Kalūr Kot, Pak. 144/A3
Kalush, Ukr. 120/C2
Kalutara, SrL. 140/C6
Kaluzhskaya Oblast, Rus. 118/G5
Kalyān, India 147/K5
Kama, D.R. Congo 163/E1
Kama (res.), Rus. 119/M4
Kama (riv.), Rus. 119/M4
Kamagaya, Japan 135/E2
Kamaishi, Japan 134/B4
Kamakou (peak), Hi, US 182/T10
Kamakura, Japan 135/D3
Kamālia, Pak. 144/B4
Kamalo, Hi, US 182/T10
Kāman, India 142/A2
Kaman, Turk. 148/C2
Kamango (lake), Mali 160/E2
Kamanjab, Namb. 163/B4
Kamarang, Guy. 211/F3
Kāmāreddi, India 140/C4
Kāmārhāti, India 143/G4
Kamaria (falls), Guy. 211/G3
Kambalda, Austl. 170/D4
Kambar, Pak. 140/A2
Kambara, Japan 135/B3
Kambia, SLeo. 160/B4
Kambove, D.R. Congo 163/E3
Kambuno (peak), Indo. 139/F4
Kamchatka (pen.), Rus. 125/Q4
Kamchatskaya Oblast, Rus. 123/R4
Kamchiya (riv.), Bul. 107/H4
Kamen, Ger. 109/E5
Kamen'-na-Obi, Rus. 145/H2
Kamenka, Rus. 121/H1
Kameno, Bul. 107/H4
Kamensk-Shakhtinskiy, Rus. 120/G2
Kamensk-Ural'skiy, Rus. 119/P4
Kameoka, Japan 135/J6
Kameyama, Japan 135/K6
Kami, Japan 135/G5
Kami (isl.), Japan 135/M6
Kami-koshiki (isl.), Japan 132/A5
Kamiah, Id, US 184/D4
Kamień Pomorski, Pol. 96/F5
Kamieskroon, SAfr. 164/B3
Kamifukuoka, Japan 135/D2
Kamiiso, Japan 134/B3
Kamiishizu, Japan 135/L5
Kamiizumi, Japan 135/C1
Kamikawa, Japan 134/C2
Kamikuishiki, Japan 135/B2
Kamilo (pt.), Hi, US 182/U11
Kamina, D.R. Congo 163/E2
Kaminaka, Japan 135/J5
Kaminoho, Japan 135/M4
Kaminoyama, Japan 133/G1
Kamisato, Japan 135/C1
Kamishak (bay), Ak, US 192/H4
Kamiyahagi, Japan 135/M5
Kamiyaku, Japan 133/L5
Kamla (riv.), India 143/F3
Kamloops, BC, Can. 184/C3
Kammaki, Japan 135/J7
Kamnik, Slov. 101/L3
Kamo, Japan 135/J6
Kamo, Japan 133/F2
Kamo (riv.), Japan 135/E3
Kamogawa, Japan 133/G3
Kamojima, Japan 132/D3
Kamoke, Pak. 144/C4
Kamp (riv.), Aus. 99/H4
Kamp-Bornhofen, Ger. 111/G3
Kamp-Lintfort, Ger. 108/D5
Kampala (cap.), Ugan. 162/B2
Kampar, Malay. 138/B3
Kampar (riv.), Indo. 138/B3
Kampen, Neth. 108/C3
Kampen, Ger. 96/C4
Kamphaeng Phet, Thai. 136/C5
Kamphaeng Phet (ruin), Thai. 136/B2
Kampinoski NP, Pol. 99/L2
Kamp'o, SKor. 131/E5
Kampong Kuala Besut, Malay. 138/B2
Kampong Saom (bay), Camb. 138/B1
Kampong Saom, Camb. 136/C4
Kampville, Mo, US 195/F8
Kamsack, Sk, Can. 185/H3
Kamsdorf, Ger. 113/E1
Kamuchawie (lake), Mb,Sk, Can. 185/H1
Kamui-misaki (cape), Japan 134/B2
Kámuk (mtn.), CR 203/F4
Kamuli, Ugan. 162/B2
Kam'yanets'-Podil's'kyy, Ukr. 120/C2
Kamyshin, Rus. 121/H2
Kanaaupscow (riv.), Qu, Can. 181/J3
Kanab, Ut, US 186/D3
Kanaga (vol.), Ak, US 192/C6
Kanairiktok (riv.), Nf, Can. 181/K3
Kanan, Japan 135/J7
Kananga, D.R. Congo 163/D2
Kanangra-Boyd NP, Austl. 173/D2
Kanash, Rus. 119/K5
Kanasin, Mex. 202/D1
Kanawake Ind. Res., Qu, Can. 189/N7
Kanawha (riv.), WV, US 191/H2
Kanazawa, Japan 133/E2
Kanchanaburi, Thai. 136/B3
Kānchenjunga (peak), Nepal 140/E2
Kānchīpuram, India 140/C5
Kandahār, Afg. 147/J2
Kandalaksha, Rus. 118/G2
Kandalaksha (gulf), Rus. 95/K2
Kándanos, Gre. 105/H5
Kandé, Togo 161/F4
Kandel (peak), Ger. 114/E1
Kandel, Ger. 112/B4
Kander (riv.), Swi. 114/D4
Kandern, Ger. 114/D2
Kandersteg, Swi. 114/D5
Kandhkot, Pak. 147/J3
Kāndhla, India 144/D5
Kandi, Ben. 161/F4
Kāndi, India 143/G4
Kandi (cape), Indo. 139/F3
Kandıra, Turk. 107/K5
Kandos, Austl. 173/D2
Kandukūr, India 140/C4
Kandy, SrL. 140/D6
Kane (basin), Grld. 181/T7
Kane (co.), Il, US 193/P16
Kanem (reg.), Chad 154/H5
Kaneohe, Hi, US 182/W13
Kaneohe (bay), Hi, US 182/W13
Kaneohe Marine Air Corps Station, Hi, US 182/W13
Kaneville, Il, US 193/N16
Kaneyama, Japan 134/B4
Kang, Bots. 163/D5
Kanga (riv.), Bang. 143/G5
Kangaba, Mali 160/C4
Kangal, Turk. 148/D2
Kangan, Iran 146/F3
Kangan Abor. Land, Austl. 170/C2
Kanganpur, Pak. 144/C4
Kangar, Malay. 136/C5
Kangaroo (isl.), Austl. 167/C4
Kangasala, Fin. 97/L1
Kangāvar, Iran 146/E2
Kangbao, China 129/K3
Kangding, China 128/H5
Kangean (isls.), Indo. 139/E5
Kanggye, NKor. 131/D2
Kanggyŏng, SKor. 131/D4
Kanghwa, SKor. 131/F6
Kangiqsualujjuaq, Qu, Can. 181/K3
Kangiqsujuaq, Qu, Can. 181/J2
Kangirsuk, Qu, Can. 181/J2
Kangjin, SKor. 131/D5
Kangmar, China 143/G1
Kangnam (mts.), NKor. 131/C2
Kangnŭng, SKor. 131/E4
Kangping, China 130/E2
Kāngra, India 144/D3
Kangrinboqê (peak), China 128/D5
Kangshan, Tai. 137/D3
Kangto (peak), China 141/F2
Kangwŏn-do (prov.), SKor. 131/E4
Kanha NP, India 142/C4
Kanhān (riv.), India 140/C3
Kani, Japan 135/M5
Kanie, Japan 135/L5
Kanin (pen.), Rus. 218/C
Kanin Nos (pt.), Rus. 122/E3
Kaniva, Austl. 173/B3
Kanjiža, Serb. 106/E2
Kankakee (riv.), Il,In, US 188/C3
Kankan (pol. reg.), Gui. 160/C4

Kankan, Gui. 160/C4
Kanmuri-yama (peak), Japan 132/C3
Kannami, Japan 135/B3
Kannapolis, NC, US 191/H3
Kannauj, India 142/B2
Kannon-zaki (pt.), Japan 135/D3
Kannus, Fin. 95/G3
Kano, Nga. 161/H4
Kano (state), Nga. 161/H4
Kan'onji, Japan 132/C3
Kanouse (mtn.), NJ, US 197/H7
Kanoya, Japan 132/B5
Kanra, Japan 135/B1
Kansai (int'l arpt.), Japan 135/H7
Kansai (isl.), Japan 135/H7
Kansas (state), US 187/H3
Kansas (riv.), Ks, US 187/H3
Kansas City (int'l arpt.), Mo, US 187/J3
Kansas City, Ks, US 195/D5
Kansas City, Mo, US 195/D5
Kansasville, Wi, US 193/P14
Kansk, Rus. 122/K4
Kansŏng, SKor. 131/E3
Kantābānji, India 140/D3
Kānth, India 142/B1
Kantō (prov.), Japan 133/F2
Kantunilkin, Mex. 202/E1
Kanuku (mts.), Guy. 208/G3
Kanuma, Japan 133/F2
Kanye, Bots. 163/E5
Kaohsiung, Tai. 137/D3
Kaohsiung (int'l arpt.), Tai. 137/D3
Kaokoveld (mts.), Namb. 163/B4
Kaolack, Sen. 160/A3
Kaolack (pol. reg.), Sen. 160/B3
Kaolinovo, Bul. 107/H4
Kaoma, Zam. 163/D3
Kapaa, Hi, US 182/S9
Kapaahu, Hi, US 182/U11
Kapaau, Hi, US 182/U10
Kapalong, Phil. 137/E6
Kapan, Arm. 121/H5
Kapchorwa, Ugan. 162/B2
Kapellen, Belg. 108/B6
Kapenguria, Kenya 162/B2
Kapidaği (pen.), Turk. 107/H5
Kapingamarangi (isl.), Micr. 174/E4
Kapiri Mposhi, Zam. 163/E3
Kapiskau (riv.), On, Can. 181/H3
Kaplice, Czh. 113/H5
Kapos (riv.), Hun. 106/C2
Kaposvár, Hun. 106/C2
Kappl, Aus. 115/G3
Kapsan, NKor. 131/E2
Kapuas (riv.), Indo. 138/C4
Kapuas Hulu (mts.), Indo.,Malay. 138/D3
Kapunda, Austl. 171/H5
Kapūrthala, India 144/C4
Kapuskasing, On, Can. 188/D1
Kapuskasing (riv.), On, Can. 188/D1
Kapuvár, Hun. 101/M3
Kapydzhik (peak), Azer. 121/H5
Kap'yŏng, SKor. 131/D4
Kara (riv.), Rus. 119/Q1
Kara (sea), Rus. 218/A
Kara, Togo 161/F4
Kara-saki (pt.), Japan 132/A3
Karaali, Turk. 148/C2
Karabiğa, Turk. 107/H5
Karabük, Turk. 148/C1
Karaburun, Turk. 107/J5
Karaca (peak), Turk. 148/D2
Karacabey, Turk. 148/B1
Karacaköy, Turk. 107/J5
Karaçal (peak), Turk. 149/C1
Karacaoğlan, Turk. 107/H5
Karachayevo-Cherkesiya, Resp., Rus. 121/G4
Karachev, Rus. 120/E1
Karāchi, Pak. 147/J4
Karadere, Turk. 107/K5
Karaginskiy (isl.), Rus. 125/R4
Karaj, Iran 146/F1
Karakax (riv.), China 147/L1
Karakaya (dam), Turk. 148/D2
Karakelong (isl.), Indo. 139/G3
Karakhoto (ruin), China 128/H3
Karakol, Kyr. 145/G4
Karakoram (range), India 128/C4
Karakoram (pass), India 144/D2
Karakoro (riv.), Mali 160/C3
Karakorum (ruin), Mong. 128/H2
Karakorum (ruin), Mong. 145/G5
Karakorum (pass), China 147/L1
Karaköse, Turk. 148/E2
Karaköy, Turk. 148/E2
Karakul' (lake), Taj. 145/F5
Karakumy (des.), Trkm. 122/F5
Karakyon (peak), Trkm. 145/B4
Karakyr (peak), Trkm. 147/H1
Karam (riv.), Indo. 139/E4
Karaman (prov.), Turk. 148/C2
Karaman, Turk. 148/C2
Karamay, China 128/D2
Karamea Bight (bay), NZ 175/S11
Karamoja (prov.), Ugan. 162/B2
Karamürsel, Turk. 107/J5
Karangasem, Indo. 139/E5
Karanginskiy (isl.), Rus. 123/S4
Karanginskiy (bay), Rus. 123/S4
Kāranja, India 140/C3
Karanpur, India 144/B5
Karapınar, Turk. 148/C2
Karasabai, Guy. 211/G3
Karaşar, Turk. 107/L5
Karasburg, Namb. 164/B3
Karasjohka-Karasjok, Nor. 95/H1
Karasu, Turk. 107/K5
Karasu, Japan 135/L6
Karasuk, Rus. 145/G2
Karatá (lag.), Nic. 203/F3
Karataş, Turk. 149/D1
Karatoya (riv.), Bang. 143/G3
Karatsu, Japan 132/A4
Karauli, India 142/A2
Karaurgan, Turk. 148/E1
Karáva (peak), Gre. 105/G3
Karawang, Indo. 138/C5
Karayaka, Turk. 120/F4
Karayazı, Turk. 148/E2
Karazhal, Kaz. 145/F3
Karbalā' (gov.), Iraq 148/E3
Karbalā', Iraq 148/F3
Karben, Ger. 112/B2
Karcag, Hun. 106/E2
Kardhámila, Gre. 105/K3
Kardhítsa, Gre. 105/G3
Kardhitsomagoúla, Gre. 105/G3
Kareha (riv.), India 143/E3
Karelī, India 142/B4
Karelia (reg.), Rus. 95/J2
Karelia, Resp., Rus. 122/D3
Karera, India 142/B3
Karesuando, Swe. 95/G1
Karēt (reg.), Mrta. 156/D4
Karf Ash Shaykh (gov.) 148/B4
Kargı, Turk. 148/C1
Kargil, India 144/D2
Karhal, India 142/B2
Karhijärvi (lake), Fin. 97/K1
Karhula, Fin. 97/M1
Kariá, Gre. 105/G3
Karia Ba Mohammed, Mor. 158/B2
Kariaí, Gre. 105/J2
Karianga, Madg. 165/H8
Kariba (dam), Zam. 163/E4
Kariba (lake), Zam.,Zim. 151/E6
Kariba, Zim. 163/E4
Kariba-yama (peak), Japan 134/A2
Karibib, Namb. 163/C5
Karimama, Ben. 161/F3
Karimata (isl.), Indo. 138/D4
Karimata (str.), Indo. 138/C4
Karīmnagar, India 140/C4
Karimunjawa (isls.), Indo. 138/D5
Kariótissa, Gre. 105/H2
Karise, Den. 96/E4
Karisimbi (vol.), D.R. Congo 162/A3
Karisimbi (vol.), Rwa. 163/E1
Káristos, Gre. 105/J3
Kariya, Japan 135/L6
Karkaar (mts.), Som. 155/Q6
Kārkal, India 140/B5
Karkar (isl.), PNG 174/D5
Karkinits'ka Zatoka (gulf), Ukr. 120/D3
Karkkila, Fin. 97/L1
Karkonski NP, Pol. 99/H3
Karla Marksa (peak), Taj. 147/K1
Karlholmsbruk, Swe. 96/G1
Karlino, Pol. 96/F4
Karlovac, Cro. 106/B3
Karlovarský (pol. reg.), Czh. 113/F2
Karlovo, Bul. 105/J1
Karlovy Vary, Czh. 113/F2
Karlsdorf-Neuthard, Ger. 112/B4
Karlsfeld, Ger. 113/E6
Karlshamn, Swe. 96/F3
Karlshuld, Ger. 112/E5
Karlskoga, Swe. 96/F2
Karlskron, Ger. 113/E5
Karlskrona, Swe. 96/F3
Karlsruhe, Ger. 112/B4
Karlstad, Swe. 96/E2
Karlstadt, Ger. 112/C3
Karlstein am Main, Ger. 112/C2
Karluk, Ak, US 192/H4
Karmāla, India 147/L5
Karnali (riv.), Nepal 142/C1
Karnali (zone), Nepal 142/C1
Karnaphuli (res.), Bang. 143/H4
Karnataka (state), India 140/C4
Karnes City, Tx, US 187/H5
Karnobat, Bul. 105/K1
Kärnten (prov.), Aus. 101/K3
Karonga, Malw. 162/B5
Karoo NP, SAfr. 164/D4
Karoo NP, SAfr. 164/C4
Karoonda, Austl. 173/A2
Karor, Pak. 144/A4
Karoso (cape), Indo. 139/E5
Kárpathos, Gre. 148/A3
Kárpathos (isl.), Gre. 148/A3
Karpatskiy NP, Ukr. 107/G1
Karpenísion, Gre. 105/G3
Karratha, Austl. 170/C2
Kars, Turk. 148/E1
Kars (prov.), Turk. 148/E1
Kars (riv.), Turk. 121/G4
Kärsämäki, Fin. 118/E3
Karsantı, Turk. 148/C2
Karshi (int'l arpt.), Uzb. 145/E5
Kartaly, Rus. 121/M1
Kartārpur, India 144/C4
Kartuzy, Pol. 96/H4
Karuah, Austl. 173/D2
Karuma (falls), Ugan. 162/B2
Karumba, Austl. 172/A2
Karūn (riv.), Iran 146/E2
Karup, Den. 96/C3
Karviná, Czh. 99/K4
Kaş, Turk. 149/A1
Kås, Den. 96/C3
Kasaan, Ak, US 192/M4
Kasabonika (lake), On, Can. 185/L2
Kasagi, Japan 135/J6
Kasahara, Japan 135/M5
Kāsai (riv.), India 143/F4
Kasai, Japan 132/D3
Kasai (riv.), D.R. Congo 163/C1
Kasama, Zam. 162/A5
Kasama, Japan 133/G2
Kasamatsu, Japan 135/L5
Kasane, Bots. 163/E4
Kasaoka, Japan 132/C3
Kasar (cape), Sudan 159/D5
Kāsaragod, India 140/C5
Kasartori-yama (peak), Japan 135/K6
Kasba (lake), NW,Nun., Can. 180/F2
Kasba Tadla, Mor. 156/D2
Kaseda, Japan 132/B5
Kasese, Ugan. 162/A2
Kashaf (riv.), Iran 147/H1
Kāshān, Iran 146/F2
Kashi, China 145/G5
Kashiba, Japan 135/J6
Kashihara, Japan 135/J6
Kashima, Japan 132/B4
Kashima, Japan 133/G3
Kashima (bay), Japan 135/F1
Kashin, Rus. 118/H4
Kāshīpur, India 142/B1
Kashiwa, Japan 135/D2
Kashiwara, Japan 135/J6
Kashiwazaki, Japan 133/F2
Kāshmar, Iran 147/G1
Kashmir (reg.), India,Pak. 145/G5
Kashmūnd Ghar (range), Afg. 144/A2
Kasigau (peak), Kenya 162/C3
Kasigluk, Ak, US 192/F3
Kasilof, Ak, US 192/H3
Kasimov, Rus. 118/J5
Kasiruta (isl.), Indo. 139/G4
Kasiui (isl.), Indo. 139/H4
Kaskaskia (riv.), Il, US 187/K3
Kaslo, BC, Can. 184/D3
Kasongo, D.R. Congo 163/E1
Kásos (isl.), Gre. 148/A3
Kaspichan, Bul. 107/H4
Kaspiysk, Rus. 121/H4
Kassala, Sudan 146/C5
Kassándria, Gre. 105/H2
Kassándra (pen.), Gre. 105/H3
Kassel, Ger. 109/G6
Kasserine, Tun. 158/L7
Kasserine (gov.), Tun. 158/L7
Kassikaityu (riv.), Guy. 211/G4
Kassler, Co, US 195/B4
Kasson, Mn, US 185/K4
Kastamonu, Turk. 148/C1
Kastamonu (prov.), Turk. 148/C1
Kastanéai, Gre. 105/K2
Kaštel Stari, Cro. 106/C4
Kaštel Sućurac, Cro. 106/C4
Kastellaun, Ger. 111/G3
Kastéllion, Gre. 105/J5
Kasterlee, Belg. 108/B6
Kastl, Ger. 113/E4
Kastoría, Gre. 105/G2
Kastrakíou (lake), Gre. 105/G3
Kasuga, Japan 135/H5
Kasuga, Japan 135/K5
Kasugai, Japan 135/B2
Kasugai, Japan 135/L5
Kasukabe, Japan 133/F3
Kasumiga (lake), Japan 133/G2
Kasungu, Malw. 163/F3
Kasūr, Pak. 144/C4
Kat O Chau (isl.), China 129/V9
Katahdin (mt.), Me, US 189/G2
Katákolon, Gre. 105/G4
Katanga (reg.), D.R. Congo 163/D2
Katanga (pol. reg.), D.R. Congo 162/A5
Katangi, India 142/B4
Katanning, Austl. 170/C5
Katano, Japan 135/J6
Katastárion, Gre. 105/G4
Katavi NP, Tanz. 162/A4
Katchall (isl.), India 141/F6
Kateríni, Gre. 105/H2
Kates Needle (peak), Ak, US 192/M4
Katete, Zam. 163/F3
Katghora, India 142/D4
Kāthgodām, India 142/B1
Kathiawar (pen.), India 147/K4
Kathleen (mt.), Austl. 171/G2
Kāthmāndu (cap.), Nepal 143/E2
Kathua, India 144/C3
Kati, Mali 160/C3
Katiola, C.d'Iv. 160/D4
Katlehong, SAfr. 164/E2
Katlenburg-Lindau, Ger. 109/H5
Katmai (vol.), Ak, US 192/H4
Katmai NP, Ak, US 192/G4
Káto Akhaïa, Gre. 105/G3
Katokhí, Gre. 105/G3
Katonah, NY, US 197/E1
Katonga (riv.), Ugan. 162/A2
Katoúna, Gre. 105/G3
Katowice, Pol. 99/K3
Katra, India 144/C3
Kātrās, India 143/F4
Katrine (lake), Sc, UK 94/B4
Katrineholm, Swe. 96/G2
Katsikás, Gre. 105/G3
Katsina (state), Nga. 161/G3
Katsina, Nga. 161/G3
Katsina Ala (riv.), Nga. 161/H5
Katsunuma, Japan 135/B2
Katsura (riv.), Japan 135/J5
Katsuragi, Japan 132/D3
Katsuragi-san (peak), Japan 135/H7
Katsuta, Japan 133/G2
Katsuura, Japan 133/G3
Katsuyama, Japan 132/E2
Katsuyama, Japan 135/B3
Kattakurgan, Uzb. 145/E5
Kattegat (str.), Den. 96/D3
Katumbi, Malw. 162/B5
Kātwa, India 143/G4
Katwe-Kabatooro, Ugan. 162/A3
Katwijk aan Zee, Neth. 108/B4
Katy, Tx, US 187/J5
Katzenbach (riv.), Ger. 112/B4
Katzenbuckel (peak), Ger. 112/C4
Katzenelnbogen, Ger. 111/G3
Katzhütte, Ger. 112/D1
Katzwinkel, Ger. 111/F3
Kau-ye (isl.), Myan. 136/B4
Kauai (chan.), Hi, US 182/S10
Kauai (isl.), Hi, US 182/S9
Kaufbeuren, Ger. 115/G2
Kaufering, Ger. 115/G1
Kaufungen, Ger. 109/G6
Kauhava, Fin. 118/D3
Kauhola (pt.), Hi, US 182/U10
Kauiki (pt.), Hi, US 182/U10
Kaukaveld (uplands), Namb. 163/C5
Kaukura (isl.), FrPol. 175/L6
Kaulakahi (chan.), Hi, US 182/R9
Kaulsdorf, Ger. 113/E1
Kaumalapau, Hi, US 182/T10
Kauna (pt.), Hi, US 182/U11
Kaunakakai, Hi, US 182/T10
Kaunas (int'l arpt.), Lith. 97/K4
Kaunas (res.), Lith. 97/L4
Kaunas, Lith. 97/K4
Kaupanger, Nor. 96/B1
Kauttua, Fin. 97/K1
Kavadarci, FYROM 105/H2
Kavajë, Alb. 105/F2
Kavála, Gre. 105/J2
Kavalerovo, Rus. 129/Q3
Kāvali, India 140/C5
Kavangel (isls.), Palau 174/C4
Kavaratti, India 140/B5
Kavarna, Bul. 107/J4
Kavgolovskoye (lake), Rus. 119/T6
Kavieng, PNG 174/E5
Kavīr-e Namak (dry lake), Iran 145/C6
Kävlinge, Swe. 96/E4
Kaw (lake), Ok, US 187/H3
Kawa (ruin), Sudan 159/B5
Kawabe, Japan 134/B4
Kawachi, Japan 135/E2
Kawachi-Nagano, Japan 135/J7
Kawage, Japan 135/L6
Kawagoe, Japan 133/F3
Kawagoe, Japan 135/L5
Kawaguchi, Japan 133/F3
Kawaguchiko, Japan 135/B3
Kawai, Japan 135/J6
Kawaihoa (pt.), Hi, US 182/R10
Kawaikini (peak), Hi, US 182/S9
Kawajima, Japan 135/C2
Kawakami, Japan 135/B2
Kawakami, Japan 135/J7
Kawamata, Japan 133/G2
Kawambwa, Zam. 162/A5
Kawamoto, Japan 135/C1
Kawanishi, Japan 135/H6
Kawanishi, Japan 135/J6
Kawardha, India 142/C4
Kawartha (lakes), On, Can. 188/E2
Kawasaki, Japan 133/F3
Kawasato, Japan 135/D1
Kawashima, Japan 135/L5
Kawaue, Japan 135/M4
Kawela (Kawela Bay), Hi, US 182/V12
Kawerau, NZ 175/T10
Kawlin, Myan. 141/G3
Kawthaung, Myan. 136/B4
Kax (riv.), China 128/D3
Kay (pt.), Yk, Can. 192/L2
Kaya, SKor. 131/E5
Kaya, Japan 135/H5
Kaya-san (peak), SKor. 131/D4
Kayadibi, Turk. 148/C2
Kayagangiri (peak), CAfr. 154/J6
Kayah (state), Myan. 141/G4
Kayan (riv.), Indo. 139/E3
Kayanga (riv.), Sen. 160/B3
Kaycee, Wy, US 184/G5
Kayenta, Az, US 186/E3
Kayes, Mali 160/C3
Kayes (pol. reg.), Mali 160/C3
Kayin (state), Myan. 141/G4
Kayl, Lux. 111/F5
Kaymaz, Turk. 107/K5
Kaynarca, Turk. 107/J5
Kaynaşlı, Turk. 107/K5
Kayoa (isl.), Indo. 139/G3
Kayser (mts.), Sur. 211/G4
Kayseri, Turk. 148/C2
Kayseri (prov.), Turk. 148/C2
Kaysersberg, Fr. 114/D1
Kaysville, Ut, US 195/K11
Kayuagung, Indo. 138/B4
Kazakhstan (ctry.) 122/G5
Kazan', Rus. 119/L5
Kazan (int'l arpt.), Rus. 119/L5
Kazan (riv.), Nun., Can. 180/F2
Kazancı, Turk. 149/C1
Kazanlı, Turk. 149/D1
Kazanlŭk, Bul. 105/J1
Kazbek (peak), Geo. 121/H4
Kāzerūn, Iran 146/F3
Kazgar (riv.), China 128/C4
Kazimierza Wielka, Pol. 99/L3
Kâzımkarabekir, Turk. 148/C2
Kazincbarcika, Hun. 99/L4
Kazo, Japan 135/D1
Kazuno, Japan 134/B3
Ke Ga (cape), Viet. 136/E3
Ké Macina, Mali 160/D3
Kéa (isl.), Gre. 105/J4
Kéa, Gre. 105/J4
Keaau, Hi, US 182/U11
Keady, NI, UK 92/B3
Keahole (pt.), Hi, US 182/T11
Keanapapa (pt.), Hi, US 182/T10
Keansburg, NJ, US 197/J10
Kearney, Ne, US 187/H2
Kearney, Mo, US 195/E5
Kearns, Ut, US 195/K12
Kearny, NJ, US 197/J8
Kearny (pt.), NI, UK 92/C3
Keawakapu, Hi, US 182/T10
Keawekaheka (pt.), Hi, US 182/U11
Keban (dam), Turk. 148/D2
Kebbi (state), Nga. 161/G4
Kébémer, Sen. 160/A3
Kebili, Tun. 158/M6
Kebnekaise (peak), Swe. 95/F2
Kebumen, Indo. 138/C5
Kecel, Hun. 106/D2
Keçiborlu, Turk. 148/B2
Kecskemét, Hun. 106/D2
Kedah (state), Malay. 136/C5
Kėdainiai, Lith. 97/K4
Kediri, Indo. 138/D5
Kédougou, Sen. 160/B3
Kędzierzyn-Koźle, Pol. 99/K3
Keego Harbor, Mi, US 193/F6
Keele (riv.), NW, Can. 180/D2
Keele (peak), Yk, Can. 180/C2
Keelung, Tai. 137/D2
Keelung, Japan 133/G8
Keen (mt.), Sc, UK 94/D3
Keene, NH, US 189/F3
Keepit (dam), Austl. 173/D1
Keer-Weer (cape), Austl. 172/A1
Keetmanshoop, Namb. 164/B2
Kefallinía (isl.), Gre. 105/G3
Kefar Sava, Isr. 149/F7
Kefar Vitkin, Isr. 149/F7
Keflavík, Ice. 95/M7
Keflavik (int'l arpt.), Ice. 95/M7
Kehl, Ger. 114/D1
Kehrsatz, Swi. 114/D4
Keighley, Eng, UK 93/G4
Keihoku, Japan 135/J5
Keimoes, SAfr. 164/C3
Kéita (riv.), Chad 155/J6
Keith, Austl. 173/B3
Keith, Sc, UK 94/D1
Kejimkujik NP, NS, Can. 189/H2
Kekaha, Hi, US 182/S10
Kékes (peak), Hun. 99/K5
Kelan, China 130/B3
Kelang (isl.), Indo. 139/G4
Kelang, Malay. 138/B3
Kelberg, Ger. 111/F3
Kelbia, Sebkhet (swamp), Tun. 158/M7
Keles, Turk. 120/D5
Kelheim, Ger. 113/E5
Kelkheim, Ger. 112/B2
Kelkıt, Turk. 120/F4
Kelkıt (riv.), Turk. 148/D1
Kell, Ger. 111/F4
Kellenhusen, Ger. 96/D4
Keller (peak), Ca, US 194/C2
Keller (lake), NW, Can. 180/D2
Kellerberrin, Austl. 170/C4
Kellogg, Id, US 184/D4
Kells, NI, UK 92/B2
Kélo, Chad 154/J6
Kelowna, BC, Can. 184/D3
Kelsey (pt.), Eng, UK 90/A6
Kelso, Wa, US 184/C4
Kelso, Sc, UK 94/D5
Kelsterbach, Ger. 112/B2
Keluang, Malay. 138/B3
Kelvington, Sk, Can. 185/H2
Kem', Rus. 118/G2
Kem' (riv.), Rus. 122/D3
Kemah, Turk. 120/F5
Kemaliye, Turk. 148/D2
Kemalpaşa, Turk. 148/E1
Kemasik, Malay. 138/B3
Kematen an der Ybbs, Aus. 113/H6
Kematen in Tirol, Aus. 115/H3
Kembs, Fr. 114/D2
Kemecse, Hun. 99/L4
Kemena (riv.), Malay. 138/D3
Kemence, Hun. 99/K4
Kemer, Turk. 149/B1
Kemer (dam), Turk. 148/B2
Kemerhisar, Turk. 148/C2
Kemerovo, Rus. 122/J4
Kemerovskaya Oblast, Rus. 122/J4
Kemi, Fin. 95/H2
Kemijärvi, Fin. 118/E2
Kemijoki (riv.), Fin. 95/H2
Kemmerer, Wy, US 184/F5
Kemnath, Ger. 113/E3
Kemnay, Sc, UK 94/D2
Kemp (lake), Tx, US 187/H4
Kempele, Fin. 118/E2
Kempen, Ger. 108/D6
Kempenich, Ger. 111/G3
Kempenland (phys. reg.), Belg. 108/C6
Kempisch Kanaal (canal), Belg. 111/E1
Kempsey, Austl. 173/E1
Kempston, Eng, UK 91/F2
Kempt (res.), Qu, Can. 188/F2
Kempten, Ger. 115/G2
Kempton, Austl. 173/C4
Kempton Park, SAfr. 164/Q13
Kemptown, Md, US 196/A5
Kemri, India 142/B1
Kemul (peak), Indo. 139/E3
Ken (riv.), India 142/C3
Ken (lake), Sc, UK 92/D1
Ken-zaki (pt.), Japan 135/D3
Kenadsa, Alg. 157/E3
Kenai, Ak, US 192/H3
Kenai Fjords NP, Ak, US 192/H4
Kendal, Eng, UK 93/F3
Kendalia, Tx, US 195/T20
Kendall, Austl. 173/E1
Kendall, Fl, US 191/H5
Kendall (co.), Il, US 193/P16
Kendall (co.), Tx, US 195/T20
Kendall Park, NJ, US 196/D3
Kendallville, In, US 188/C3
Kendari, Indo. 139/F4
Kéndavros, Gre. 105/J2
Kendel (riv.), Ger. 108/D5
Kendrāpāra, India 140/E3
Kénédougou (prov.), Burk. 160/D4
Kenema, SLeo. 160/C5
Kenge, D.R. Congo 163/C1
Kenhardt, SAfr. 164/C3
Kenhorst, Pa, US 196/C3
Kenié-Baoulé, Réserve de, Mali 160/C3
Kenilworth, Eng, UK 91/E2
Kenilworth, NJ, US 197/H9
Kénitra, Mor. 158/A2
Kénitra (prov.), Mor. 158/A2
Kenli, China 130/D3
Kenmare, ND, US 185/H3
Kenmare, Ire. 89/P11
Kenmore, NY, US 189/S10
Kenmore, Wa, US 193/C2
Kenn (reef), Austl. 167/E3
Kenn, Ger. 111/F4
Kennebec (riv.), Me, US 189/G2
Kennebunk, Me, US 189/G3
Kennedy (chan.), Grld.,Nun., Can. 181/T6
Kennedy (range), Austl. 170/B3
Kennedy Entrance (chan.) 192/H4
Kennedyville, Md, US 196/C5
Kennelbach, Aus. 115/F3
Kennemerduinen, NP de, Neth. 108/B4
Kenner, La, US 195/P17
Kennet (riv.), Eng, UK 91/E4
Kennet and Avon (canal), Eng, UK 90/D4
Kenneth, Ks, US 195/D6
Kennett, Mo, US 187/K3
Kennett Square, Pa, US 196/C4
Kennewick, Wa, US 184/D4
Keno Hill, Yk, Can. 192/L3
Kenogami (riv.), On, Can. 181/H3
Kenora, On, Can. 185/K3
Kenosha, Wi, US 193/Q14
Kenosha (co.), Wi, US 193/P14
Kensico (res.), NY, US 197/K7
Kensington and Chelsea (bor.), Eng, UK 88/A1
Kent (pen.), Nun., Can. 180/F2
Kent (co.), On, Can. 193/G6
Kent (riv.), Eng, UK 93/F3
Kent (isl.), Md, US 196/B6
Kent (pt.), Md, US 196/B6
Kent (lake), Mi, US 193/E7
Kent, Oh, US 188/D3
Kent, Wa, US 184/C4
Kent County (int'l arpt.), Mi, US 188/C3
Kent Group (isls.), Austl. 173/C3
Kentau, Kaz. 145/E4
Kenton, De, US 196/C5
Kenton, Oh, US 188/D3
Kentucky (state), US 191/G2
Kentucky (riv.), Ky, US 188/C4
Kentucky (lake), Ky, US 191/F2
Kentville, NS, Can. 189/H2
Kenya (ctry.) 162/C2
Kenzingen, Ger. 114/D1
Keonjhar, India 140/E3
Kep i Gjuhëzës (cape), Alb. 105/F2
Kep i Rodonit (cape), Alb. 105/F2
Kępno, Pol. 99/J3
Keppel Sands, Austl. 172/C3
Kerala (state), India 140/C5
Kéran, PN de la, Togo 161/F4
Kerang, Austl. 173/B2
Keratéa, Gre. 105/N9
Kerava, Fin. 97/L1
Kerch' (str.), Rus.,Ukr. 120/F3
Kerch, Ukr. 120/F3
Keremeos, BC, Can. 184/D3
Kerempe Burnu (cape), Turk. 148/C1
Keren, Erit. 146/C5
Kerepestarcsa, Hun. 107/R9
Keret' (lake), Rus. 95/K2
Kerguélen (isl.), Fr. 81/N8
Kericho, Kenya 162/B3
Kerikeri (cape), NZ 175/S9
Kerinci (peak), Indo. 138/B4
Kerio (riv.), Kenya 162/C2
Kerio Valley Nat'l Rsv., Kenya 162/B2
Kerkdriel, Neth. 108/C5
Kerken, Ger. 108/D6
Kerkenah (isl.), Tun. 157/H2
Kerki, Trkm. 145/E5
Kerkínis (lake), Gre. 105/H2
Kérkira, Gre. 105/F3
Kerkrade, Neth. 111/F2
Kerkwijk, Neth. 108/C5
Kermadec (isls.), NZ 174/G8
Kermān, Iran 147/G2
Kern (riv.), Ca, US 186/C4
Kern, South Kern (riv.), Ca, US 186/C4
Kerns, Swi. 115/E4
Kéros (isl.), Gre. 105/J4
Kérou, Ben. 161/F4
Kerr (lake), Ok, US 187/J4
Kerr (res.), NC,Va, US 191/J2
Kerrobert, Sk, Can. 184/F3
Kerrville, Tx, US 187/H5
Kert (riv.), Mor. 158/C2
Kerulen (riv.), Mong. 129/K3
Kerzaz, Alg. 157/E3
Kerzenheim, Ger. 111/H4
Kerzers, Swi. 114/D4
Kesagami (riv.), On, Can. 188/D1
Keşan, Turk. 105/K2
Kesch (peak), Swi. 115/F4
Kesen'numa, Japan 134/B4
Keshan, China 129/N2
Keshod, India 140/B3
Keski-Suomi (prov.), Fin. 95/H3
Keskin, Turk. 148/C2
Kesselbach (riv.), Ger. 112/D5
Kestel, Turk. 148/B1
Kesteren, Neth. 108/C5
Keszthely, Hun. 106/C2
Ket' (riv.), Rus. 122/J4
Keta, Gha. 161/F5
Keta (riv.), Rus. 122/K3
Ketchikan, Ak, US 192/M4
Kete Krachi, Gha. 161/E5
Ketelmeer (lake), Neth. 108/C3
Kétou, Ben. 161/F5
Kętrzyn, Pol. 97/J4
Ketsch, Ger. 112/B4
Kettering, Eng, UK 91/F2
Kettle (riv.), Mn, US 184/D3
Kettle Moraine State Forest, Wi, US 193/P14
Ketzin, Ger. 98/P7
Keukenhof, Neth. 108/B4
Kevelaer, Ger. 108/D5
Kewaunee, Wi, US 188/C2
Keweenaw (pen.), Mi, US 185/L4
Keweenaw (pt.), Mi, US 185/M4
Keweenaw (bay), Mi, US 185/L4
Key Largo, Fl, US 191/H5
Key West, Fl, US 191/H5
Keymar, Md, US 196/A4
Keyport, NJ, US 197/J10
Keyport, Wa, US 193/B2
Keystone (lake), Ok, US 187/H3
Kežmarok, Slvk. 99/L4
Khaanziir (cape), Som. 155/Q5
Khabarovsk, Rus. 129/Q2
Khabarovskiy Kray, Rus. 123/P4
Khagaria, India 143/F3
Khair, India 142/A2
Khairābād, India 142/C2
Khairpur, Pak. 144/B5
Khairpur, Pak. 147/J3
Khakasiya, Resp., Rus. 123/P6
Khalándrion, Gre. 105/N8
Khalīlābād, India 142/D2
Khalkhāl, Iran 146/E1
Khalkhidhikhi (pen.), Gre. 105/H2
Khalkidhón, Gre. 105/H2
Khalkís, Gre. 105/H3
Khamar-Daban (mts.), Rus. 128/H1
Khambhāliya, India 147/J4
Khambhat, India 147/K4
Khamīs Mushayţ, SAr. 146/D5
Khammam, India 140/D4
Khamr, Yem. 146/D5
Khān Yūnus, Gaza 149/D4
Khānābād, Afg. 147/J1
Khānaqīn, Iraq 148/F3
Khandwa, India 140/C3
Khanem (well), Alg. 157/F3
Khānewāl, Pak. 144/A4
Khangāh Dogrān, Pak. 144/B4
Khāngarh, Pak. 144/A5
Khaniá, Gre. 105/J5
Khanka (lake), China,Rus. 129/P3
Khanna, India 144/D4
Khānpur, Pak. 144/A5
Khanty-Mansiysk, Rus. 122/G3
Khanty-Mansiyskiy Aut. Okrug, Rus. 122/G3
Khao Chamao-Khao Wong NP, Thai. 136/C3
Khao Khitchakut NP, Thai. 136/C3
Khao Laem (res.), Thai. 141/G4
Khao Sam Roi Yot NP, Thai. 136/B3
Khao Yai NP, Thai. 136/C3
Kharagpur, India 143/F4
Kharagpur, India 143/F3
Kharak, Pak. 144/A3
Khārān, Pak. 147/J3
Kharar, India 143/F4
Kharar, India 144/D4
Kharbatā, Isr. 149/G8
Khargon, India 147/L4
Khāriān, Pak. 144/B3
Kharkiv, Ukr. 120/F2
Kharkiv (int'l arpt.), Ukr. 120/F2
Kharkivs'ka Oblasti, Ukr. 120/F2
Kharmanli, Bul. 105/J2
Kharovsk, Rus. 118/J4
Kharrouf (riv.), Mor. 158/B2
Kharsia, India 142/D5
Khartoum (Kharţūm) (cap.), Sudan 146/B5
Khasavyurt, Rus. 121/H4
Khāsh (riv.), Afg. 147/H2
Khashuri, Geo. 121/G4
Khasi (hills), India 143/H3
Khaskovo (pol. reg.), Bul. 105/J2
Khaskovo (prov.), Bul. 107/G5
Khatanga (riv.), Rus. 218/Z
Khatanga (gulf), Rus. 123/L2
Khatauli, India 144/D5
Khātegaon, India 142/A4
Khatīma, India 142/B1
Khatlon (obl.), Taj. 145/E5
Khatmia (pass), Egypt 149/C4

Khātra, India 143/F4
Khatt Atoui (riv.), Mrta. 154/B3
Khaur, Pak. 144/B3
Khaybar (pass), Afg. 144/A2
Khazzān Dūkān (res.), Iraq 148/F3
Khazzān Jabal Al Awliyā (dam), Sudan 155/M4
Khekra, India 144/D5
Khemis el Khechna, Alg. 158/G4
Khemis Miliana, Alg. 158/G4
Khémisset (prov.), Mor. 158/A3
Khémisset, Mor. 158/A3
Khenchela (prov.), Alg. 157/G2
Khenchela, Alg. 158/K7
Khénifra, Mor. 156/D2
Khepoyarvi (lake), Rus. 119/T6
Kheri, India 142/C2
Khersān (riv.), Iran 146/F2
Kherson, Ukr. 107/L2
Kherson (int'l arpt.), Ukr. 107/L2
Khersons'ka Oblasti, Ukr. 120/E3
Khilok, Rus. 129/K1
Khimki, Rus. 119/W9
Khíos, Gre. 105/K3
Khíos (isl.), Gre. 105/K3
Khirpai, India 143/F4
Khisarya, Bul. 105/J1
Khiva, Rus. 145/D4
Khlebarovo, Bul. 107/H4
Khmel'nyts'ka Oblasti, Ukr. 120/C2
Khmel'nytskyy, Ukr. 120/C2
Kho Sawai (plat.), Thai. 141/H4
Khodzheyli, Uzb. 145/C4
Khojak (pass), Pak. 147/J2
Kholm, Afg. 147/J1
Kholmsk, Rus. 129/R2
Khomeynīshahr, Iran 146/F2
Khon Kaen, Thai. 136/C2
Khopër (riv.), Rus. 122/E4
Khor (riv.), Rus. 123/P5
Khóra Sfakíon, Gre. 105/J5
Khorazm (pol. reg.), Uzb. 145/D4
Khoríon, Gre. 148/A2
Khorramābād, Iran 146/E2
Khorramshahr, Iran 146/E2
Khorugh, Taj. 147/K1
Khotol (mtn.), Ak, US 192/G3
Khouribga, Mor. 156/D2
Khowai, India 141/F3
Khrisoúpolis, Gre. 105/J2
Khromtaū, Kaz. 121/L2
Khrysí (riv.), Gre. 105/J5
Khuan Ubon Ratana (lake), Thai. 136/C2
Khudiān, Pak. 144/C4
Khuis, Bots. 164/C2
Khujand, Taj. 145/E4
Khulna (pol. div.), Bang. 143/G4
Khūnjeräb (pass), Pak. 147/L1
Khunjerab NP, Pak. 145/G5
Khunti, India 143/E4
Khurai, India 142/B3
Khurda, India 140/E3
Khurja, India 142/A1
Khushāb, Pak. 144/B3
Khust, Ukr. 99/M4
Khūtār, India 142/C1
Khuzdar, Pak. 147/J3
Khvalynka, Rus. 129/P3
Khvonsār, Iran 146/F2
Khvor, Iran 147/G2
Khvoy, Iran 146/E1
Khwaja Rawash (int'l arpt.), Afg. 145/E6
Khyber (pass), Pak. 144/A2
Kia, Sol. 174/E5
Kiama, Austl. 173/D2
Kiamichi (mts.), Ok, US 190/E3
Kiana, Ak, US 192/F2
Kibæk, Den. 96/C3
Kibali (riv.), D.R. Congo 162/A2
Kibergneset (pt.), Nor. 95/J1
Kibo (Kilimanjaro) (peak), Tanz. 162/C3
Kiboga, Ugan. 162/A3
Kibrısçık, Turk. 107/K5
Kibwezi, Kenya 162/C3
Kičevo, FYROM 105/G2
Kichha, India 142/B1
Kickapoo, Ks, US 187/F2
Kidal, Mali 161/F2
Kidal (pol. reg.), Mali 161/F2
Kidapawan, Phil. 139/G2
Kidderminster, Eng, UK 90/D2
Kidepo Valley NP, Ugan. 155/M7
Kidsgrove, Eng, UK 93/F5
Kiel (bay), Den. 95/D5
Kiel, Ger. 96/D4
Kielce, Pol. 99/L3
Kielder (res.), Eng, UK 94/C4
Kien An, Viet. 136/D1
Kierspe, Ger. 111/G2

Kiev (Kyyiv) (cap.), Ukr. 120/D2
Kiffa, Mrta. 160/C2
Kifisiá, Gre. 105/N8
Kigali (cap.), Rwa. 162/A3
Kigali (Gregoire Kayibanda) (int'l arpt.), Rwa. 162/A3
Kiği, Turk. 148/E2
Kigoma (pol. reg.), Tanz. 162/A4
Kigoma, Tanz. 162/A4
Kigye, SKor. 131/E4
Kihei, Hi, US 182/T10
Kihnu (isl.), Est. 97/L2
Kiholo, Hi, US 182/U11
Kihti (str.), Fin. 97/J1
Kii (chan.), Japan 132/D4
Kii (mts.), Japan 132/D4
Kijang, SKor. 131/E5
Kikai (isl.), Japan 133/L6
Kikepa (pt.), Hi, US 182/R9
Kikiktat (mtn.), Ak, US 192/M1
Kikinda, Serb. 106/E3
Kikuchi, D.R. Congo 163/C2
Kikwit, D.R. Congo 163/C2
Kil, Swe. 96/E2
Kilafors, Swe. 96/G1
Kilauea, Hi, US 182/S9
Kilbarchan, Sc, UK 94/B5
Kilberry, Ire. 89/Q10
Kilbirnie, Sc, UK 94/B5
Kilbrannan (sound), Sc, UK 94/A5
Kilchu, NKor. 131/E2
Kilcoole, Ire. 92/B5
Kilcormac, Ire. 89/Q10
Kilcoy, Austl. 172/D4
Kildare, Ire. 89/Q10
Kildeer, Il, US 193/P15
Kil'den (isl.), Rus. 118/G1
Kilembe Estates, Ugan. 162/A2
Kilgarvan, Ire. 89/P11
Kilgore, Tx, US 187/D4
Kilian (isl.), Nun., Can. 180/E1
Kilifi, Kenya 162/C3
Kilimanjaro (pol. reg.), Tanz. 162/C3
Kilimanjaro (int'l arpt.), Tanz. 162/C3
Kilimanjaro NP, Tanz. 162/C3
Kilimli, Turk. 107/K5
Kilinochchi, SrL. 140/D6
Kilis, Turk. 149/E1
Kiliya, Ukr. 107/J3
Kilkee, Ire. 89/P10
Kilkeel, NI, UK 92/B3
Kilkenny, Ire. 89/Q10
Kilkenny (co.), Ire. 92/A6
Kilkis, Gre. 105/H2
Kilkivan, Austl. 172/D4
Kill Van Kull (riv.), NJ,NY, US 197/J9
Killam, Ab, Can. 184/F2
Killarney, Austl. 173/E1
Killarney, Mb, Can. 185/J3
Killarney, Ire. 89/P10
Killarney NP, Ire. 89/P10
Killdeer, ND, US 185/H4
Killdeer, Tx, US 187/H5
Killeen, Tx, US 187/H5
Killenaule, Ire. 89/Q10
Killiecrankie, Pass of (pass), Sc, UK 94/C3
Killin, Sc, UK 94/B4
Killinchy, NI, UK 92/C3
Killinek (isl.), Nun., Can. 181/K2
Killíni (peak), Gre. 105/H4
Killíni, Gre. 105/G4
Killough, NI, UK 92/C3
Killybegs, Ire. 89/P9
Kilmacanogue, Ire. 92/B5
Kilmacolm, Sc, UK 94/B5
Kilmacow, Ire. 89/Q10
Kilmallock, Ire. 89/P10
Kilmar Tor (hill), Eng, UK 90/B5
Kilmarnock, Sc, UK 94/B5
Kilmaurs, Sc, UK 94/B5
Kilmichael (pt.), Ire. 92/B6
Kilmore, Austl. 173/C3
Kilmore Quay, Ire. 89/Q10
Kilombero (riv.), Tanz. 162/C5
Kilosa, Tanz. 162/C4
Kilraghts, NI, UK 92/B1
Kilrea, NI, UK 92/B2
Kilrush, Ire. 89/P10
Kilsyth, Sc, UK 94/C4
Kilwa Kivinje, Tanz. 162/C5
Kilwinning, Sc, UK 94/B5
Kimba, Austl. 171/H5
Kimball, SD, US 185/J5
Kimbe, PNG 174/E5
Kimberley (cape), Austl. 172/B2
Kimberley (plat.), Austl. 167/B2
Kimberley, BC, Can. 184/D3
Kimberley, SAfr. 164/D3
Kimch'aek, NKor. 131/E2
Kimch'ŏn, SKor. 131/E4
Kimhae, SKor. 131/E5
Kimhae (int'l arpt.), SKor. 131/E5
Kimi, Gre. 105/J3
Kímina, Gre. 105/H2

Kimitsu, Japan 133/F3
Kimje, SKor. 131/D5
Kimméria, Gre. 105/J2
Kimmirut, Nun., Can. 181/K2
Kimolos (isl.), Gre. 105/J4
Kimovsk, Rus. 120/F1
Kimp'o, SKor. 131/F6
Kimp'o (int'l arpt.), SKor. 131/F6
Kimpō-zan (peak), Japan 135/B2
Kimry, Rus. 118/H4
Kinabalu (peak), Malay. 139/E2
Kinabatangan (riv.), Malay. 139/E2
Kinango, Kenya 162/C4
Kinbasket (lake), BC, Can. 184/D2
Kincaid, Sk, Can. 184/G3
Kincardine, On, Can. 188/D2
Kincardine, Sc, UK 94/C4
Kinchega NP, Austl. 173/B2
Kinder Scout (peak), Eng, UK 93/G5
Kindersley, Sk, Can. 184/F3
Kindia, Gui. 160/B4
Kindia (pol. reg.), Gui. 160/B4
Kinding, Ger. 113/E5
Kindsbach, Ger. 111/G5
Kindu, D.R. Congo 163/E1
Kinel', Rus. 121/J1
Kineshma, Rus. 118/J4
King (lake), Austl. 170/C5
King (mt.), Austl. 172/B4
King (sound), Austl. 167/B2
Kinel' (riv.), Rus. 121/J1
Kinel', Rus. 121/J1
King (pt.), BC, Can. 184/B2
King (pt.), BC, Can. 192/N4
King (peak), Yk, Can. 192/K3
King (co.), Wa, US 193/D2
King Christian (isl.), Nun., Can. 181/R7
King Christian IX Land (reg.), Grld. 177/P3
King Christian X Land (reg.),Grld. 177/Q2
King City, Ca, US 186/B3
King Cove, Ak, US 192/F4
King Frederik VI Coast (reg.), Grld. 177/N3
King Frederik VIII Land (reg.), Grld. 177/Q2
King George (isls.), Qu, Can. 181/J3
King George Is. (isls.), FrPol. 175/L6
King George's (res.), Eng, UK 88/C2
King Leopold (ranges), Austl. 167/B2
King of Prussia, Pa, US 196/C3
King Salmon, Ak, US 192/G4
King William (isl.), Nun., Can. 180/G2
King William's Town, SAfr. 164/D4
Kingaroy, Austl. 172/C4
Kingfisher, Ok, US 187/H4
Kingfisher (co.), Ok, US 195/M14
Kinghorn, Sc, UK 94/C4
Kinglake NP, Austl. 173/G5
Kingman, Ks, US 187/H3
Kingman, Az, US 186/D4
Kingman (reef), Pac., US 175/J4
Kings (riv.), Ca, US 186/C3
Kings (co.), NY, US 197/K9
Kings (peak), Ut, US 186/E2
Kings Canyon NP, Ca, US 186/C3
Kings Langley, Eng, UK 88/B1
King's Lynn, Eng, UK 91/G1
Kings Park, Austl. 170/K6
Kings Point, NY, US 197/L8
King's Seat (hill), Sc, UK 94/C4
Kingsbridge, Eng, UK 90/C6
Kingscote, Austl. 171/H5
Kingscourt, Ire. 89/Q10
Kingsford, Mi, US 188/B2
Kingsport, Tn, US 188/D4
Kingston, Austl. 174/F7
Kingston, On, Can. 189/G2
Kingston, NY, US 188/F3
Kingston (cap.), Jam. 203/G2
Kingston, Pa, US 196/C1
Kingston, Austl. 196/D3
Kingston S.E., Austl. 173/A3
Kingston upon Hull, Eng, UK 93/H4
Kingston upon Hull (co.), Eng, UK 93/H4
Kingston upon Thames (bor.), Eng, UK 88/C2
Kingstown (cap.), StV. 199/N9
Kingstree, SC, US 191/J3
Kingsville, Tx, US 190/D5
Kingsville, Md, US 196/B5
Kingswood, Eng, UK 90/D4
Kingussie, Sc, UK 94/B2
Kınık, Turk. 148/A2

Kinkaid (mt.), Ak, US 192/L4
Kinkala, Congo 163/B1
Kinki (prov.), Japan 132/D3
Kinlochewe, Sc, UK 94/A1
Kinlochleven, Sc, UK 94/B3
Kinloss, Sc, UK 94/C1
Kinna, Swe. 96/E3
Kinnairds (pt.), Sc, UK 94/D1
Kinnelon, NJ, US 197/H8
Kinnelon (lake), NJ, US 197/H8
Kinnitty, Ire. 89/Q10
Kino (riv.), Japan 132/D3
Kinoje (riv.), On, Can. 188/D1
Kinomoto, Japan 135/K5
Kinrooi, Belg. 111/E1
Kinrweiler, Ger. 112/B4
Kintore, Sc, UK 94/D2
Kintyre (isl.), Sc, UK 89/R8
Kintzheim, Fr. 114/D1
Kinu (riv.), Japan 133/F2
Kinvarra, Ire. 89/P10
Kinyeti (peak), Sudan 155/M7
Kinzig (riv.), Ger. 98/E4
Kipahulu, Hi, US 182/T10
Kíparissía (gulf), Gre. 105/G4
Kíparissía, Gre. 105/G4
Kipawa (lake), Qu, Can. 188/E2
Kipkarren (riv.), Kenya 162/B2
Kipling, Sk, Can. 185/H3
Kipnuk, Ak, US 192/F4
Kippel, Swi. 114/D5
Kippen, Sc, UK 94/B4
Kippure (peak), Ire. 92/B5
Kipushi, D.R. Congo 163/E3
Kira, Japan 135/M6
Kira Panayía (isl.), Gre. 105/H3
Kirakira, Sol. 174/F6
Kiranomena, Madg. 165/H7
Kiratpur, India 142/B1
Kirazlı, Turk. 105/K2
Kirby, Tx, US 195/U21
Kircasalih, Turk. 105/K2
Kirchberg, Swi. 114/D3
Kirchberg, Swi. 115/F3
Kirchberg, Ger. 111/G5
Kirchberg, Ger. 113/F1
Kirchberg an der Iller, Ger. 115/G1
Kirchberg an der Jagst, Ger. 112/C4
Kirchdorf, Ger. 109/F3
Kirchdorf an der Krems, Aus. 113/H7
Kirchenlamitz, Ger. 113/E2
Kirchenthumbach, Ger. 113/E3
Kirchheim, Ger. 115/G1
Kirchheim bei München, Ger. 113/E6
Kirchheim unter Teck, Ger. 112/C5
Kirchheimbolanden, Ger. 112/B3
Kirchhundem, Ger. 109/F6
Kirchlengern, Ger. 109/F4
Kirchlinteln, Ger. 109/G3
Kirchsee (lake), Ger. 115/H2
Kirchseeon, Ger. 113/E6
Kirchweidach, Ger. 113/F6
Kirchzarten, Ger. 114/D5
Kirchzell, Ger. 112/C3
Kircudbright (bay), Sc, UK 92/D2
Kirkby, Eng, UK 93/F4
Kirkby in Ashfield, Eng, UK 93/H4
Kirkcaldy, Sc, UK 94/C4
Kirkconnel, Sc, UK 94/C5
Kirkcudbright, Sc, UK 92/D2
Kirkee, India 147/K5
Kirkenær, Nor. 96/E1
Kirkintilloch, Sc, UK 94/B5
Kirklees (co.), Eng, UK 93/G4
Kirkkonummi (Kyrkslätt), Fin. 97/L1
Kirkland, Qu, Can. 189/N7

Kirkland (hill), Sc, UK 94/C6
Kirkland Lake, On, Can. 188/D1
Kırklar (peak), Turk. 148/A2
Kırklareli, Turk. 107/H5
Kırklareli (prov.), Turk. 107/H5
Kirkliston, Sc, UK 94/C5
Kirkstone (pass), Eng, UK 93/F3
Kirkūk, Iraq 148/F3
Kirkwall, Sc, UK 89/V14
Kirkwood, SAfr. 164/D4
Kirkwood, De, US 196/C4
Kirn, Ger. 111/G4
Kirov, Rus. 120/F1
Kirov, Rus. 119/L4
Kirovskaya Oblast, Rus. 119/L3
Kirovo-Chepetsk, Rus. 119/L4
Kirovohrad, Ukr. 120/E2
Kirovohrads'ka Oblasti, Ukr. 120/D2
Kirovsk, Rus. 118/G2
Kirov, Rus. 119/L4
Kirriemuir, Sc, UK 94/D3
Kirsanov, Rus. 121/G1
Kirşehir (prov.), Turk. 148/C1
Kirşehir, Turk. 148/C1
Kirtachi, Niger 160/F3
Kirthar NP, Pak. 147/J4
Kirton, Eng, UK 93/H5
Kiruna, Swe. 95/G2
Kiryū, Japan 133/F2
Kisa, Swe. 96/F3
Kisai, Japan 135/D1
Kisakata, Japan 134/A4
Kisangani, D.R. Congo 155/L7
Kisarazu, Japan 133/F3
Kisber, Hun. 99/K5
Kiselëvsk, Rus. 122/J4
Kishangani, India 143/F2
Kishangarh, India 147/K3
Kishiwada, Japan 132/D3
Kishorganj, Bang. 143/H3
Kishtwar, India 144/C2
Kishwaukee (riv.), Il, US 193/N15
Kisii, Kenya 162/B3
Kisis (vol.), Ak, US 192/B5
Kiska (isl.), Ak, US 192/B6
Kiskatinaw (riv.), BC, Can. 184/C2
Kiskitto (lake), Mb, Can. 185/J2
Kiskőrös, Hun. 106/D2
Kiskunfélegyháza, Hun. 106/D2
Kiskunhalas, Hun. 106/D2
Kiskunmajsa, Hun. 106/D2
Kiskunsági Nemzeti NP, Hun. 106/D2
Kislovodsk, Rus. 121/G4
Kismaayo (Chisimayu), Som. 155/P8
Kiso (riv.), Japan 133/E3
Kisogawa, Japan 135/L5
Kisosaki, Japan 135/L5
Kissamos, Gre. 105/H5
Kissimmee (lake), Fl, US 191/H4
Kissimmee, Fl, US 191/H4
Kissing, Ger. 112/D6
Kississing (lake), Mb, Can. 185/H2
Kisslegg, Ger. 115/F2
Kist, Ger. 112/C3
Kisújszállás, Hun. 106/E2
Kisumu, Kenya 162/B3
Kisvárda, Hun. 99/M4
Kita, Mali 160/C3
Kita (lake), Japan 133/G2
Kita-Ibaraki, Japan 133/G2
Kitaaki, SAfr. 135/B1
Kitadaitō (isl.), Japan 133/L8
Kitagata, Japan 135/L5
Kitakami (mts.), Japan 134/B4
Kitakami (riv.), Japan 134/B4
Kitakami, Japan 134/B4
Kitami, Japan 134/B4
Kitakawabe, Japan 135/D1
Kitakyūshū, Japan 132/B5
Kitale, Kenya 162/B2
Kitami, Japan 134/C1
Kitamimaki, Japan 135/A1
Kitan (str.), Japan 135/G7
Kitangiri (lake), Tanz. 162/B4
Kitaura, Japan 135/F1
Kitchener, On, Can. 188/D3
Kitgum, Sudan 162/B2
Kithira, Gre. 105/H4
Kithira (isl.), Gre. 105/H4
Kithnos, Gre. 105/J4
Kithnos (isl.), Gre. 105/J4
Kitimat Arm (lake), BC, Can. 184/A2
Kitsap (co.), Wa, US 193/B3
Kittanning, Pa, US 196/C1
Kittatinny (mts.), NJ, US 196/C1
Kittery, Me, US 189/G3
Kittredge, Co, US 195/B3
Kitui, Kenya 162/C3

Kitumbeine (peak), Tanz. 162/C3
Kitwe, Zam. 163/E3
Kitzbühel, Aus. 101/K3
Kitzingen, Ger. 112/D3
Kiunga Marine Nat'l Rsv., Kenya 162/D3
Kiuruvesi, Fin. 118/E3
Kivalina, Ak, US 192/F2
Kivalo (mts.), Fin. 95/H2
Kivijärvi (lake), Fin. 97/M1
Kiviôli, Est. 97/M2
Kivu (lake), D.R. Congo 162/A3
Knížecí Stolec (peak), Czh. 113/H5
Kıyıköy, Turk. 107/J5
Kiyokawa, Japan 135/C3
Kiyosu, Japan 135/L5
Kizel, Rus. 119/N4
Kizil (riv.), China 122/H6
Kızılcadağ, Turk. 149/A1
Kızılcahamam, Turk. 148/C1
Kızıldag NP, Turk. 148/B2
Kızılhisar, Turk. 148/B2
Kızılırmak (riv.), Turk. 148/C1
Kızıltepe, Turk. 148/E2
Kızılyaka, Turk. 149/C1
Kizlyar, Rus. 121/H4
Kizu (riv.), Japan 132/E3
Kizu, Japan 135/J6
Kizukuri, Japan 134/B3
Kjerkestinden (peak), Nor. 95/F1
Kjevik (int'l arpt.), Nor. 96/C2
Kjølen (mts.), Nor. 95/F2
Klabava (riv.), Czh. 113/G3
Kladanj, Bosn. 106/D3
Kladno, Czh. 113/H2
Kladovo, Serb. 106/F3
Klagenfurt, Aus. 101/L3
Klaipėda, Lith. 97/J4
Klamath (mts.), Ca,Or, US 184/C5
Klamath (riv.), Ca,Or, US 184/C5
Klamath Falls, Or, US 184/C5
Klangenan, Indo. 138/C5
Klarälven (riv.), Swe. 95/E3
Klarup, Den. 96/D3
Klášterec nad Ohří, Czh. 113/G2
Klatovy, Czh. 113/G4
Klaus, Aus. 115/F4
Klausen (Chiusa), It. 115/H4
Klausenpass (pass), Swi. 115/E4
Klawock, Ak, US 192/M4
Klaza (mtn.), Yk, Can. 192/L3
Klazienaveen, Neth. 108/E3
Kleinblittersdorf, Ger. 111/G5
Kleine Elster (riv.), Ger. 99/G3
Kleine Emme (riv.), Swi. 114/E4
Kleine Gete (riv.), Belg. 111/D2
Kleine Laber (riv.), Ger. 113/F5
Kleine Nete (riv.), Belg. 111/D1
Kleinheubach, Ger. 112/C3
Kleinlützel, Swi. 114/D3
Kleinmachnow, Ger. 98/G2
Kleinmond, SAfr. 164/L11
Kleinolifants (riv.), SAfr. 164/Q12
Kleinrinderfeld, Ger. 112/C3
Kleinsee, SAfr. 164/B3
Kleinwallstadt, Ger. 112/C3
Kleinwinternheim, Ger. 112/B3
Kleppe, Nor. 96/A2
Kleppestø, Nor. 96/A1
Klerksdorp, SAfr. 164/D3
Klet' (peak), Czh. 113/H5
Kleve, Ger. 108/D5
Klina, Kos. 106/E4
Klingenberg am Main, Ger. 112/C3
Klingenmünster, Ger. 112/B4
Klingenthal, Ger. 113/F2
Klínovec (peak), Czh. 113/F2
Klintehamn, Swe. 96/H3
Klintsy, Rus. 120/E1
Klip (riv.), SAfr. 164/E2
Klippan, Swe. 96/E3
Klipplaat, SAfr. 164/D4
Klitmøller, Den. 96/C3
Kljajićevo, Serb. 106/D3
Ključ, Bosn. 106/C3
Kłodawa, Pol. 99/K2
Kłodzko, Pol. 99/J3
Klöntaler-See (lake), Swi. 115/E4
Klosterbach (riv.), Ger. 109/H2
Klosterlechfeld, Ger. 115/G1
Klosterneuburg, Aus. 107/N7
Klosters, Swi. 115/F4
Klosterwappen (peak), Aus. 99/H5
Klötze, Ger. 98/F2
Kloten, Swi. 115/E3
Klouto, Togo 160/E4
Kluane NP, Yk, Can. 192/K3
Kluczbork, Pol. 99/K3
Klukwan, Ak, US 192/L3
Klundert, Neth. 108/B5
Klyaz'ma (riv.), Rus. 118/J4
Klyuchevskaya (peak), Rus. 123/S4

Knäred, Swe. 96/E3
Knaresborough, Eng, UK 93/G3
Knee (lake), Mb, Can. 185/K2
Knetzgau, Ger. 112/D3
Knezha, Bul. 107/G4
Knight (inlet), BC, Can. 184/B3
Knighton, Wal, UK 90/C2
Knightsen, Ca, US 193/L11
Knin, Cro. 106/C3
Knittelfeld, Aus. 101/L3
Knittlingen, Ger. 112/B4
Knivsta, Swe. 96/G2
Knob (cape), Austl. 170/C5
Knob (peak), Phil. 139/F1
Knobby (pt.), Austl. 170/B4
Knoch (hill), Sc, UK 94/D1
Knockcloghrim, NI, UK 92/B2
Knøsen (pt.), Swe. 96/E4
Knøsen (peak), Den. 96/D3
Knosós (Knossos) (ruin), Gre. 105/J5
Knottingley, Eng, UK 93/G4
Knott's Berry Farm, Ca, US 194/G8
Knowsley (co.), Eng, UK 93/F5
Knox (coast), Ant. 218/G
Knox (cape), BC, Can. 192/M4
Knox City, Tx, US 187/H4
Knoxville, Tn, US 188/D5
Knutsford, Eng, UK 93/F5
Knysna, SAfr. 164/C4
Ko (riv.), Sen. 160/B3
Ko-saki (pt.), Japan 132/A3
Ko Samut NP, Thai. 136/C5
Koali, Hi, US 182/T10
Koani, Tanz. 162/C4
Koäth, India 143/E3
Kolkasrags (pt.), Lat. 97/K3
Köbe, Japan 135/H6
København (int'l arpt.), Den. 96/E4
Kōbern-Gondorf, Ger. 111/G3
Kobipato (peak), Indo. 139/G4
Koblach, Aus. 115/F3
Koblenz, Swi. 115/E2
Koblenz, Ger. 111/G3
Kobryn, Bela. 99/N2
Kobuchizawa, Japan 135/A2
Kobuk, Ak, US 192/G2
Kobuk (riv.), Ak, US 192/G2
Kobuk Valley NP, Ak, US 192/G2
Kobushi-ga-take (peak), Japan 133/F3
Kocába (riv.), Czh. 113/H3
Kocaeli (prov.), Turk. 107/J5
Koçalı, Turk. 148/D2
Koçani, FYROM 105/H2
Kocapınar, Turk. 148/E2
Koçevje, Slov. 101/L4
Koch (isl.), Nun., Can. 181/J2
Koch'ang, SKor. 131/D5
Koch'ang, SKor. 131/D5
Kochel am See, Ger. 115/H2
Kochelsee (lake), Ger. 115/H2
Kocher (riv.), Ger. 101/H2
Kochkorovo, Bul. 107/H4
Kōchi, Japan 132/C4
Kōchi (pref.), Japan 132/C4
Kodaira, Japan 135/C2
Kodala, India 140/E4
Kodarmā, India 143/E3
Kodiak, Ak, US 192/H4
Kodiak (isl.), Ak, US 192/H4
Kodinār, India 147/K4
Kodomari, Japan 134/B3
Kodry (hills), Mol. 107/J2
Koekelare, Belg. 110/B1
Koel (riv.), India 140/D3
Koes, Namb. 164/C2
Koesan, SKor. 131/D4
Koetari (riv.), Sur. 211/G4
Kofa (mts.), Az, US 186/D4
Kofarnihon (riv.), Taj. 145/E5
Kofçaz, Turk. 107/H5
Koffiefontein, SAfr. 164/D3
Kofiau (isl.), Indo. 139/G4
Koforidua, Gha. 161/E5
Kōfu, Japan 133/F3
Koganei, Japan 135/C2
Køge (bay), Den. 96/E4
Kogi, Nga. 161/G5
Kogon (riv.), Gui. 160/C3
Kōgushi, Japan 132/B4
Kohat, Pak. 144/A3
Kohima, India 141/K5
Kohku, Japan 135/K5
Kohmet, Den. 96/C3
Kohtla-Järve, Est. 97/M2
Kohŭng, SKor. 131/D5
Koimisis, Gre. 105/H2
Koito (riv.), Japan 135/D3
Koiva (riv.), Lat. 97/M3
Koji (isl.), SKor. 131/E5
Kojonup, Austl. 170/C5
Kojovská (peak), Slvk. 99/L4
Kok (riv.), Myan. 136/B1

Kōka, Japan 135/K6
Kokai (riv.), Japan 135/E2
Kōkar (isl.), Fin. 97/J3
Kokemäenjoki (riv.), Fin. 97/J1
Kokhonak, Ak, US 192/H4
Kokkola (Karleby), Fin. 118/D3
Koko Head (pt.), Hi, US 182/W13
Kokomo, In, US 188/C3
Kokrajhar, India 143/H2
Kokrines, Ak, US 192/G2
Koksan, NKor. 131/D3
Kökshetaū, Kaz. 145/E2
Kökshetaū (obl.), Kaz. 145/E2
Koksijde, Belg. 110/B1
Koksoak (riv.), Qu, Can. 181/K3
Kokstad, SAfr. 164/E3
Kokubu, Japan 132/B5
Kola (pen.), Rus. 218/D2
Kola (riv.), Rus. 118/G1
Kolaka, Indo. 139/F4
Kolār, India 140/C5
Kolāras, India 142/A3
Kolašin, Mont. 106/D4
Kolbäck, Swe. 96/G2
Kol'bay (cape), Kaz. 145/B4
Kolbermoor, Ger. 101/K3
Kolbuszowa, Pol. 99/L3
Kolda, Sen. 160/B3
Kolda (pol. reg.), Sen. 160/B3
Kolding, Den. 96/C4
Kölen (mts.), Swe. 95/E2
Kolgompya (cape), Rus. 97/N2
Kolguyev (isl.), Rus. 218/C
Kolhāpur, India 147/K5
Koliba (riv.), Gui. 160/B3
Koliganek, Ak, US 192/G4
Kolín, Czh. 99/H3
Kolka, Lat. 97/K3
Kolkata (Calcutta), India 143/G4
Kolkata (Calcutta) (int'l arpt.), India 143/G4
Kollbach (riv.), Ger. 113/F5
Kollnburg, Ger. 113/F4
Kollum, Neth. 108/D2
Köln (Cologne), Ger. 111/F2
Kolno, Pol. 99/L2
Koło, Pol. 120/A1
Koloa, Hi, US 182/S10
Kołobrzeg, Pol. 96/F4
Kolokani, Mali 160/C3
Kolomna, Rus. 118/H5
Kolomyya, Ukr. 107/G1
Kolondiéba, Mali 160/C4
Kolossa (riv.), Mali 160/D3
Kolpashevo, Rus. 122/J4
Kolpino, Rus. 118/F4
Kolsva, Swe. 96/F2
Kolubara (riv.), Serb. 106/D3
Koluszki, Pol. 99/K3
Kolva (riv.), Rus. 119/N2
Kolwezi, D.R. Congo 163/E3
Kolyma (range), Rus. 125/Q3
Kolyma (riv.), Rus. 123/R2
Kolyma Lowland (plain), Rus. 123/R2
Kom (peak), Bul. 105/H1
Komádi, Hun. 106/E2
Komadugu Gana (riv.), Niger,Nga. 154/H3
Komadugu Yobe (riv.), Nga. 161/H2
Komae, Japan 135/D2
Komaki, Japan 135/L5
Komandorskiye (isls.), Rus. 125/R4
Komárno, Slvk. 106/D2
Komárom, Hun. 106/D2
Komárom-Esztergom (prov.), Hun. 106/D2
Komatirivier (riv.), SAfr. 164/Q13
Komatke, Az, US 195/R19
Komatsu (int'l arpt.), Japan 132/E2
Komatsushima, Japan 132/D3
Kombissiri, Burk. 161/E3
Kombóti, Gre. 162/B3
Komga, SAfr. 164/D4
Komi, Resp., Rus. 119/M2
Komi-Permyatskiy Aut. Okrug, Rus. 119/M2
Komló, Hun. 106/D2
Kommetjie, SAfr. 164/L11
Kommunizma (peak), Taj. 145/F5
Komodo (isl.), Indo. 139/E5
Komodo Island NP, Indo. 139/E5
Komoé (riv.), C.d'Iv. 154/E6
Komono, Japan 135/L6
Komoran (isl.), Indo. 139/L5
Komoro, Japan 135/B1
Komotiní, Gre. 105/J2
Kompasberg (peak), SAfr. 164/D3
Komsomolets (isl.), Rus. 125/J1
Komsomol'skiy, Rus. 119/P2
Komūr (str.), SKor. 131/D5
Konakovo, Rus. 118/G4
Kōnan, Japan 135/C1
Kōnan, Japan 135/L5

Kōnan, Japan 135/K6
Konár (riv.), India 143/E4
Konar (res.), India 143/E4
Konar (riv.), Afg. 144/A2
Konaweha (riv.), Indo. 139/F4
Konda, Japan 135/H6
Kondagaon, India 140/D4
Kondinin, Austl. 170/C5
Kondoa, Tanz. 162/B4
Kondopoga, Rus. 118/G3
Kondūz, Afg. 145/E5
Kong, C.d'Iv. 160/D4
Kong (riv.), Laos 136/D3
Kong (isl.), Camb. 136/C4
Kong Miao, China 130/D4
Kongiganak, Ak, US 192/K4
Kongju, SKor. 131/D4
Kongō-zan (peak), Japan 135/J7
Kongolo, D.R. Congo 163/E2
Kongoussi, Burk. 161/E3
Kongsberg, Nor. 96/C2
Kongsvinger, Nor. 96/F1
Kongur (peak), China 145/G3
Koniecpol, Pol. 99/K3
Königs Wusterhausen, Ger. 98/Q7
Königsberg in Bayern, Ger. 112/D2
Königsberg-Stein, Ger. 112/B5
Königsbronn, Ger. 112/D5
Königsbrunn, Ger. 115/G1
Königsdorf, Ger. 115/H2
Königsfeld im Schwarzwald, Ger. 115/E1
Königslutter am Elm, Ger. 109/H4
Königstein im Taunus, Ger. 112/B2
Königswinter, Ger. 111/G2
Konin, Pol. 99/K2
Kónitsa, Gre. 105/G2
Köniz, Swi. 114/D4
Konjic, Bosn. 106/C4
Könkämäeno (riv.), Fin. 118/D1
Konkouré (riv.), Gui. 160/B4
Konnevesi, Fin. 118/E3
Konolfingen, Swi. 114/D4
Kōnosu, Japan 135/D1
Konotop, Ukr. 120/E2
Konqi (riv.), China 122/J5
Konsen (plat.), Japan 134/D2
Końskie, Pol. 99/L3
Konstancin-Jeziorna, Pol. 99/L2
Konstantynów Łódzki, Pol. 99/K3
Konstanz, Ger. 115/F2
Kontich, Belg. 111/D1
Kontiolahti, Fin. 118/F3
Konuralp, Turk. 107/K5
Kóny, Hun.
Konya, Turk. 148/C2
Konya (prov.), Turk. 148/C2
Konz, Ger. 111/F4
Koondrook, Austl. 173/D2
Koorawatha, Austl. 173/D2
Koorda, Austl. 170/C4
Kootenai (lake), Id, US 184/D3
Kootenay (lake), BC, Can. 180/E3
Kootenay NP, BC, Can. 184/D3
Kootingal, Austl. 173/D1
Kop-Geįdi (pass), Turk. 148/E2
Kopāganj, India 142/D2
Kopargaon, India 147/K5
Kópavogur, Ice. 95/N7
Kope (mts.), C.d'Iv. 160/D5
Köpenick, Ger. 98/Q7
Koper, Slov. 101/K4
Kopervik, Nor. 96/A2
Kopeysk, Rus. 119/P5
Kopfing im Innkreis, Aus. 113/G6
Köping, Swe. 96/G2
Kopondei (cape), Indo. 139/F5
Koporskiy (bay), Rus. 97/N2
Koppang, Nor. 96/D1
Kopparberg, Swe.
Kopparberg (co.), Swe. 95/E3
Koppies, SAfr. 164/D2
Koprivnica, Cro. 106/C2
Koprivshtitsa, Bul. 105/J1
Köprü, Turk. 149/B1
Köprülü, Turk. 149/C1
Köprülü Kanyon NP, Turk. 148/B2
Kor (riv.), Iran 146/F2
Kora, India 142/C2
Kōra, Japan 135/K5
Kora NP, Kenya 162/C3
Korab (peak), Alb. 105/G2
Koráb (peak), Czh. 113/G4
Korakuen Garden, Japan 132/C3
Koraluk (riv.), Nf, Can. 181/K3
Korana (riv.), Cro. 101/L4
Koraput, India 142/D4
Korba, India 142/D4
Korba, Tun. 158/M6
Korbach, Ger. 109/F2
Korçë, Alb. 105/G2
Korčula (isl.), Cro. 104/E1
Korčulanski Kanal (chan.), Cro. 104/E1
Kord Kūy, Iran 146/F1

Kordel, Ger. 111/F4
Korea (bay), China,NKor. 131/B3
Korea (str.), Japan,SKor. 132/A4
Korea, North (ctry.) 131/D2
Korea, South (ctry.) 131/D4
Korean Folk Village, SKor. 131/G7
Korenovsk, Rus. 120/F3
Korhogo, C.d'Iv. 160/D4
Korinós, Gre. 105/H2
Kórinthos (Corinth), Gre. 105/H4
Kőris-hegy (peak), Hun. 106/C2
Kōriyama, Japan 133/G2
Korizo, Passe de (pass), Chad 154/J3
Korkodon (riv.), Rus. 123/R3
Korkuteli, Turk. 149/B1
Korla, China 128/E3
Kormakiti (cape), Cyp. 149/C2
Körmend, Hun. 101/M3
Kornat (isl.), Cro. 106/B4
Körner, Ger. 109/H6
Korneuburg, Aus. 107/N7
Korntal-Münchingen, Ger. 112/C5
Kornwestheim, Ger. 112/C5
Koro (sea), Fiji 174/G6
Köroğlu (peak), Turk. 107/K5
Korogwe, Tanz. 162/C4
Koroit, Austl. 173/B3
Koronadal, Phil. 137/D6
Korónia (lake), Gre. 105/H2
Koropion, Gre. 105/N9
Koror (cap.), Palau 174/C4
Körös (riv.), Hun. 106/E2
Korosten', Ukr. 120/D2
Korostyshiv, Ukr. 120/D2
Korotaikha (riv.), Rus. 119/P1
Korovin (vol.), Ak, US 192/D5
Korpo (Korppoo), Fin. 97/J1
Korsakov, Rus. 129/R2
Korschenbroich, Ger. 108/D4
Korsør, Den. 96/D4
Korsze, Pol. 97/J4
Kortemark, Belg. 110/C1
Kortenaken, Belg. 111/E2
Kortenberg, Belg. 111/E2
Kortessem, Belg. 111/E2
Kortrijk, Belg. 110/C2
Koryak (range), Rus. 125/R3
Koryakskiy Aut. Okrug, Rus. 123/S3
Koryazhma, Rus. 119/K3
Kōryō, Japan 135/J6
Koryŏng, SKor. 131/E5
Kōshim (riv.), Kaz. 145/B3
Koshigaya, Japan 133/F2
Koshiki (isls.), Japan 133/K5
Kosi, India 142/A2
Kosi (zone), Nepal 143/F2
Kosi (riv.), India 143/F2
Košice, Slvk. 99/L4
Košický (pol. reg.), Slvk. 99/L4
Koskinoú, Gre. 148/B2
Kosoba (lake), Rus. 145/G3
Kosŏng, SKor. 131/E5
Kosŏng, NKor. 131/E3
Kosovo (ctry.) 106/E4
Kosovo Polje, Kos. 106/E4
Kosovska Kamenica, Kos. 106/E4
Kosovska Mitrovica, Kos. 106/E4
Kosový (riv.), Czh. 113/F3
Kosrae (isl.), Micr. 174/F4
Kossi (riv.), Burk. 160/D3
Kossou, Barrage de (dam), C.d'Iv. 160/D5
Kossou, Lac de (lake), C.d'Iv. 154/D6
Kosta, Swe.
Kostelec nad Černými Lesy, Czh. 113/H3
Koster, SAfr. 164/D2
Kostinbrod, Bul. 105/H1
Kostopil', Ukr. 120/C2
Kostroma (riv.), Rus. 118/J4
Kostrzenice, Pol. 99/H2
Kostroma, Rus. 118/J4
Kostromskaya Oblast, Rus. 118/J4
Kostrzyn, Pol. 99/H2
Kostrzyn, Pol. 99/J2
Kostyantynivka, Ukr. 120/F2
Kosuge, Japan 135/B2
Kos'va (riv.), Rus. 119/N4
Kos'yu (riv.), Rus. 119/N2
Koszalin, Pol. 96/C4
Kőszeg, Hun. 101/M3

Kot Kapūra, India 144/C4
Kot Mūmin, Pak. 144/B3
Kot Rādha Kishan, Pak. 144/C4
Kot Samāba, Pak. 144/A5
Kota, India 142/D4
Kota, Indo. 147/L3
Kōta, Japan 135/M6
Kota Baharu, Malay. 141/H6
Kota Kinabalu, Malay. 139/E2
Kotaagung, Indo. 138/B5
Kotabaru, Indo. 138/B4
Kotabumi, Indo. 138/D4
Kotapād, India 140/D4
Kotdwāra, India 142/B1
Kotel, Bul. 105/K1
Kotel'nich, Rus. 119/L4
Kotel'nikovo, Rus. 121/G3
Kotel'nyy (isl.), Rus. 123/P2
Kothagūdem, India 140/D4
Köthen, Ger. 98/F3
Kotido, Ugan. 162/B2
Kotka, Fin. 97/M1
Kotli Lohārān, Pak. 144/C3
Kotlik, Ak, US 192/F3
Kotlin (isl.), Rus. 119/S7
Kotō, Japan 135/K5
Kotoka (int'l arpt.), Gha. 161/E5
Kotor, Mont. 106/D4
Kotor Varoš, Bosn. 106/C3
Kotovo, Rus. 121/H2
Kotovsk, Rus. 121/G1
Kotri, Pak. 147/J3
Kottayam, India 140/C6
Kottūru, CAfr. 155/K6
Kotuy (riv.), Rus. 125/K3
Kotzebue, Ak, US 192/F2
Kotzebue (sound), Ak, US 192/E2
Kötzting, Ger. 113/F4
Kouchibouguac NP, NB, Can. 189/H2
Koudougou, Burk. 161/E3
Koufonision (isl.), Gre. 105/J5
Kougarok (mtn.), Ak, US 192/E2
Koukdjuak (riv.), Nun., Can. 181/J2
Koula-Moutou, Gabon 154/H8
Koulikoro, Mali 160/D3
Koulikoro (pol. reg.), Mali 160/C3
Koulountou (riv.), Sen. 160/B3
Koumbi Saleh (ruin), Mrta. 160/D3
Koumi, Japan 135/A1
Kouroussa, Chad 155/J6
Koundara, Gui. 160/B3
Kounradskiy, Kaz. 145/G3
Kountze, Tx, US 187/J5
Koupela, Burk. 161/E3
Kouritenga (prov.), Burk. 161/E3
Kourou, FrG. 209/H2
Koussi (peak), Chad 155/J4
Koutiala, Mali 160/D3
Kouvola, Fin. 97/M1
Kovačica, Serb. 106/E3
Kovada Gölü NP, Turk. 148/B2
Kovashi (riv.), Rus. 119/S7
Kovdozero (lake), Rus. 95/J2
Kovel', Ukr. 120/C2
Kovilj, Serb. 106/E3
Kovilpatti, India 140/C6
Kovrov, Rus. 118/J4
Kovur, India 140/C5
Kovylkino, Rus. 121/G1
Kowanyama Aboriginal Community, Austl. 172/H4
Kowkcheh (riv.), Afg. 147/J1
Kowl-e Namaksār (lake), Afg. 145/D6
Kowloon, China 137/B3
Kowt-e 'Ashrow, Afg. 147/J2
Kōyaguchi, Japan 135/J7
Kōyama, Japan 132/B5
Kōyanre, Bul. 107/G4
Koyuk (riv.), Ak, US 192/F3
Koyukuk, Ak, US 192/G3
Koyukuk, South Fork (riv.), Ak, US 192/G3
Kozaki, Japan 135/M6
Kozākī, Japan 135/E2
Kozan, Turk. 148/C2
Kozara NP, Aus. 106/C3
Kozhikode (Calicut), India 140/C5
Kozhozero (lake), Rus. 118/H3
Kozhva (riv.), Rus. 119/M2
Kozienice, Pol. 99/L3
Kozloduy, Bul. 107/G4
Kozlu, Turk. 148/E2
Koźmin, Pol. 99/J3
Koźnitsa (peak), Bul. 105/H2
Kożuchów, Pol. 99/H3
Kozyatyn, Ukr. 120/D2

Kraai (riv.), SAfr. 164/D3
Kraaifontein, SAfr. 164/L10
Krabi, Thai. 136/B4
Kragerø, Nor. 96/C2
Kraiburg am Inn, Ger. 113/F6
Kraichbach (riv.), Ger. 112/B4
Kraichgau (reg.), Ger. 101/H2
Krailling, Ger. 113/E6
Krakatau (vol.), Indo. 138/C5
Kraków, Pol. 99/K3
Kralendijk, NAnt. 210/D1
Kraljevo, Serb. 106/E4
Kralupy nad Vltavou, Czh. 113/H2
Kramators'k, Ukr. 120/F2
Kramfors, Swe. 95/F3
Krammer (chan.), Neth. 108/B5
Kranéa Elassónos, Gre. 105/G3
Kranenbitten (int'l arpt.), Aus. 115/H3
Kranenburg, Ger. 108/D5
Kranídhion, Gre. 105/H4
Kranj, Slov. 101/L3
Kranskop, SAfr. 165/E3
Krapkowice, Pol. 99/J3
Kraslice, Czh. 113/F2
Krásník, Pol. 99/M3
Krásnik Fabryczny, Pol. 99/M3
Krasnoarmeysk, Rus. 121/G1
Krasnodar, Rus. 120/F3
Krasnodar (int'l arpt.), Rus. 120/F3
Krasnodarskiy Kray, Rus. 122/D5
Krasnogorsk, Rus. 119/W9
Krasnohrad, Ukr. 120/F2
Krasnokamensk, Rus. 129/L1
Krasnokamsk, Rus. 119/M4
Krasnoslobodsk, Rus. 121/H2
Krasnotur'insk, Rus. 122/G4
Krasnoural'sk, Rus. 119/P4
Krasnovodsk (int'l arpt.), Trkm. 121/K5
Krasnovodsk (Trkmenbashi), Trkm. 121/K5
Krasnoyarsk, Rus. 122/J4
Krasnoyarskiy Kray, Rus. 122/J4
Krasnyy Kut, Rus. 121/H2
Krasnyy Luch, Ukr. 120/F2
Krasnyy Sulin, Rus. 120/G3
Kratovo, FYROM 105/H1
Krautheim, Ger. 112/D4
Kravanh (mts.), Camb. 141/H5
Kreb en Nâga (cliff), Mali 156/D5
Kreck (riv.), Ger. 112/D2
Krefeld, Ger. 108/D6
Kreiensen, Ger. 109/G5
Kremastón (lake), Gre. 105/G3
Křemelna (riv.), Czh. 113/G4
Kremenchuk, Ukr. 120/E2
Kremenchuts'ke Vodoskhovyshche (res.), Ukr. 120/E2
Kremlin, Rus. 119/W9
Kremmen, Ger. 98/Q6
Kremmling, Co, US 186/F2
Krempe, Ger. 109/G1
Krems an der Donau, Aus. 99/H4
Kremsmünster, Aus. 113/H6
Krenglbach, Aus. 113/G6
Kresgeville, Pa, US 196/C2
Kresna, Bul. 105/H2
Kressbronn am Bodensee, Ger. 115/F2
Kresta (gulf), Rus. 123/T3
Kréstena, Gre. 105/G4
Kretinga, Lith. 97/J4
Kreuzau, Ger. 111/F2
Kreuzberg (peak), Ger. 112/C2
Kreuzlingen, Swi. 115/F2
Kreuztal, Ger. 111/G2
Kreuzwertheim, Ger. 112/C4
Kría Vrísi, Gre. 105/H2
Kribi, Camr. 154/H7
Krieglach, Aus. 101/L3
Kriens, Swi. 115/E3
Kriftel, Ger. 112/B2
Kril'on (pen.), Rus. 134/B1
Kril'on (cape), Rus. 134/C1
Krimpen aan de IJssel, Neth. 108/B5
Krinídhes, Gre. 105/J2
Kríos (cape), Gre. 105/H5
Krishna (riv.), India 140/D3
Krishnagiri, India 140/C5
Krishnanagar, India 143/G4
Kristala, Swe. 96/G3
Kristianstad, Nor. 96/B2
Kristiansand, Swe. 96/F3
Kristianstad (co.), Swe. 95/E4
Kristianstad (int'l arpt.), Swe. 96/F3
Kristiansund, Nor. 95/C3
Kristinehamn, Swe. 96/F2

Kriva Palanka, FYROM 105/H1
Krk (isl.), Cro. 106/B3
Krka (riv.), Cro. 106/B3
Krokom, Swe. 95/E3
Krókos, Gre. 105/G2
Krolevets', Ukr. 120/E2
Kromach, Ger. 112/C2
Kroměříž, Czh. 99/J4
Kronach, Ger. 112/C2
Kronberg im Taunus, Ger. 112/B2
Kronoberg (co.), Swe. 95/E4
Kronshtadt, Rus. 119/S6
Kronstorf, Aus. 113/H6
Kroombit Tops NP, Austl. 172/C4
Kroonstad, SAfr. 164/D2
Kropotkin, Rus. 121/G3
Kropp, Ger. 96/C4
Krosno, Pol. 99/L4
Krosno Odrzańskie, Pol. 99/H2
Krotoszyn, Pol. 99/J3
Krottenkopf (peak), Ger. 115/G3
Krousón, Gre. 105/J5
Krŏv, Ger. 111/G4
Krško, Slov. 101/L4
Kruckau (riv.), Ger. 109/G1
Kruger NP, SAfr. 165/E2
Krugersdorp, SAfr. 164/P13
Kruglitsa (peak), Rus. 119/N5
Kruibeke, Belg. 108/B6
Kruisfontein, SAfr. 164/D4
Krujë, Alb. 105/G1
Krumbach, Ger. 115/G1
Krummenau, Swi. 115/F3
Krumvgrad, Bul. 105/J2
Krupina, Bul. 105/H1
Kruša, Den. 96/C4
Krusenstern (cape), Ak, US 192/F2
Kruševac, Serb. 106/E4
Kruševo, FYROM 105/G1
Krušné Hory (Erzgebirge) (mts.), Czh.,Ger. 101/N1
Kruszwica, Pol. 99/J2
Kruzof (isl.), Ak, US 192/L4
Krychaw, Bela. 120/D1
Krym, Aut. Rep., Ukr. 120/E3
Krynica, Pol. 99/L4
Kryvyy Rih, Ukr. 107/L2
Krzyż, Pol. 99/H2
Ksar el Kebir, Mor. 158/B2
Ksar Hellal, Tun. 158/N7
Ksel (peak), Alg. 157/F2
Ksour Essef, Tun. 158/N7
Ktima, Cyp. 149/C2
Ku-Ring-Gai NP, Austl. 172/H8
Ku Sathan (peak), Thai. 136/C2
Kuah, Malay. 136/B5
Kuala Belait, Bru. 138/D3
Kuala Dungun, Malay. 138/B3
Kuala Kerai, Malay. 141/H6
Kuala Lipis, Malay. 138/B3
Kuala Lumpur (cap.), Malay. 138/B3
Kuala Pilah, Malay. 138/B3
Kuala Selangor, Malay. 138/B3
Kuala Terengganu, Malay. 141/H6
Kualapu, Hi, US 182/T10
Kuancheng, China 130/D2
Kuandian, China 131/C2
Kuban' (riv.), Rus. 122/D5
Kubaysah, Iraq 148/E3
Kubenskoye (lake), Rus. 118/H4
Kubokawa, Japan 132/C4
Kubrat, Bul. 107/H4
Kučevo, Serb. 106/E3
Kuchen (peak), Aus. 115/G3
Kuchen, Ger. 112/D5
Kuching, Malay. 138/D3
Kuchino (isl.), Japan 133/K6
Kuchinoerabu (isl.), Japan 132/A5
Kuchl, Aus. 101/K3
Küçükbahçe, Turk. 105/H2
Küçükkuyu, Turk. 105/H2
Kudamatsu, Japan 133/B3
Kudat, Malay. 139/E2
Kudus, Indo. 138/D5
Kudymkar, Rus. 119/M4
Kufrah (oasis), Libya
Kufrinjah, Jor. 149/D3
Kufstein, Aus. 101/K3
Kuglugtuk, Nun., Can. 180/E2
Kuhardt, Ger. 112/B4
Kühbach, Ger. 115/H1
Kuhmo, Fin. 118/F2
Kühnhaide, Ger.
Kühpäyeh, Iran 146/F2
Kuinder of Tjonger (riv.), Neth. 108/C3
Kuito, Ang. 163/C4
Kuiu (isl.), Ak, US 180/L4
Kujawsko-Pomorskie (prov.), Pol. 99/K2
Kujawy (reg.), Pol. 99/K2

Kuji, Japan 134/B3
Kujū-san (peak), Japan 132/B4
Kujūkuri, Japan 135/G3
Kuki, Japan 133/F2
Kukizaki, Japan 135/C3
Kukkia (lake), Fin. 97/L1
Kül (riv.), Iran 146/F4
Kula, Bul. 106/F4
Kula, Serb. 106/D3
Kula Kangri (peak), Bhu. 143/H1
Kulachi, Pak. 144/A4
Kulai, Malay. 138/B4
Kulal (mt.), Kenya 162/C2
Kulaly (isl.), Kaz. 121/J3
Kulandag (mts.), Kaz. 145/B4
Kuldīga, Lat. 97/J3
Kulebaki, Rus. 118/J5
Kulgām, India 144/C3
Kulmbach, Ger. 113/E2
Kulob, Taj. 147/J1
Kuloy (riv.), Rus. 118/J2
Kulpahār, India 142/B3
Kulpmont, Pa, US 196/B2
Kulpsville, Pa, US 196/C3
Kul'sary, Kaz. 121/K3
Külsheim, Ger. 112/C3
Kulsi (riv.), India 143/H2
Kulti, India 143/F4
Kulu, China 145/G2
Kulunda (lake), Rus. 145/G2
Kulunda, Rus. 145/G2
Kum (riv.), SKor. 131/D4
Kuma (riv.), Rus. 122/E5
Kumagaya, Japan 133/F2
Kumaishi, Japan 134/A2
Kumamoto, Japan 132/B4
Kumamoto (int'l arpt.), Japan 132/B4
Kumamoto (pref.), Japan 135/K6
Kumano, Japan 132/B4
Kumano (riv.), Japan 132/D4
Kumanovo, FYROM 105/G1
Kumār (riv.), Bang. 143/G4
Kumasi, Gha. 161/E5
Kumatori, Japan 135/H7
Kumba, Camr. 154/G7
Kumbia, Austl. 172/C4
Kumbo, Camr. 154/H6
Kümch'on, SKor. 131/F6
Kumé (isl.), Japan 137/E2
Kumertau, Rus. 121/K1
Kumgang-san (peak), NKor. 131/E3
Kumho (riv.), SKor. 131/E5
Kumi, Ugan. 162/B2
Kumi, SKor. 131/E4
Kumihama, Japan 135/G4
Kumi-sunlu, Turk. 148/E2
Kumiyama, Japan 135/J6
Kumkale, Turk. 107/H6
Kumköy, Turk. 105/M6
Kumla, Swe. 96/F2
Kumluca, Turk. 149/B1
Kumo, Nga. 154/H5
Kumon (range), Myan. 141/G2
Kumsan, SKor. 131/D4
Kumta, India 147/K6
Kunashiri (isl.), Japan 123/Q5
Künch, India 142/B3
Kunda, India 142/C2
Kundarkhi, India 142/B1
Kundapura (Coondapoor), India 147/K6
Kundelungu, PN de, D.R. Congo 163/E3
Kundla, Pak. 144/A3
Kundli, India 144/C4
Kunduz, Pak. 144/A3
Kunene (riv.), NKor. 131/C3
Kungälv, Swe. 96/D3
Kungrad, Uzb.
Kungsangen (int'l arpt.), Swe. 96/G2
Kungsbacka, Swe. 96/G2
Kungshamn, Swe. 119/N4
Kungur, Rus. 119/N4
Kunhegyes, Hun. 106/E2
Kunigami, Japan 137/E4
Kuningan, Indo. 138/C5
Kunisaki, Japan 132/B4
Kunitachi, Japan 135/D1
Kunjāh, Pak. 144/B3
Kunlong, China 141/G3
Kunlun (mts.), China 128/D4
Kunmadaras, Hun. 99/L5
Kunming, China 130/D5
Kunsan, SKor. 131/D5
Kunshan, China 130/L8
Kunszentmárton, Hun. 106/E2
Kunu (riv.), India 147/L3
Kunwār (riv.), India 147/L3
Kunwi, SKor. 131/E4
Kunya (mtn.), China
Künzell, Ger. 112/C1
Künžvartské (pass), 113/G5
Kuohijärvi (lake), Fin. 97/M1
Kuolimo (lake), Fin. 97/M1
Kuopio, Fin. 95/H3
Kuopio (prov.), Fin. 95/H3
Kupa (riv.), Cro. 106/B3
Kupang, Indo. 139/G5
Kupino, Rus. 122/H4
Kupreanof (isl.), Ak, US 180/C3

Kup'yans'k, Ukr. 120/F2
Kuqa, China 129/L3
Kür (riv.), Azer. 121/J5
Kurashiki, Japan 133/F2
Kukalaya (riv.), Nic. 203/E3
Kurayoshi, Japan 132/C3
Kurdistan (reg.), 106/F4
Kürdzhali, Bul. 105/J2
Kürdzhali (res.), Bul. 105/J2
Küre (mts.), Turk. 148/C1
Kure, Turk. 148/C1
Kure (isl.), Hi, US 174/H2
Küressaare, Est. 97/K2
Kureyka (riv.), Rus. 122/K3
Kurgan, Rus. 119/Q5
Kurganskaya Oblast, Rus. 118/U5
Kuria (isl.), Kiri. 174/G4
Kuria Muria (isls.), Oman 147/G5
Kuri̇ğrām, Bang. 143/G3
Kurihashi, Japan 135/D1
Kurikoma-yama (peak), Japan 134/B4
Kuril (isls.), Rus. 125/Q5
Kurinwas (riv.), Nic. 203/E3
Kurisawa, Japan 134/B2
Kuriyama, Japan 134/B2
Kürkçü, Turk. 149/C1
Kurla, India 145/G2
Kurnool, India 140/C4
Kuro-shima (isl.), 131/D4
Kurodashō, Japan 135/G5
Kuroishi, Japan 134/B3
Kuroiso, Japan 133/G2
Kuroso-yama (peak), Japan 135/K6
Kurotaki, Japan 135/J7
Kurrajong, Austl. 172/G8
Kurram (riv.), 144/B2
Kurri Kurri, Austl.
Kurrimine Beach, Austl. 172/B2
Kuršėnai, Lith. 97/K3
Kurseong, India 143/G2
Kursiu Nerija NP, Lith. 97/J4
Kursk, Rus. 120/F2
Kurskaya Oblast, Rus. 120/F2
Kurskaya Spit (bar), Rus. 97/J4
Kurskiy (lag.), Lith.,Rus. 97/J4
Kuršumlija, Serb. 106/E4
Kuršunlu, Turk. 148/C1
Kurtalan, Turk. 148/E2
Kürten, Ger. 111/G1
Kuru (riv.), Sudan 155/L6
Kuruca (pass), Turk. 148/E2
Kuruçay, Turk. 148/D2
Kuruçay (riv.), Turk. 121/G4
Kuruktag (mts.), China 128/E3
Kuruman, SAfr. 164/C2
Kurumsirivier (riv.), SAfr. 164/C2
Kurume, Japan 132/B4
Kurunegala, SrL. 140/D6
Kurupukari, Guy. 211/G3
Kurur, Sudan
Kur'ye, SKor. 131/D5
Kuryong (riv.), NKor. 131/C3
Kuş Cenneti NP, Turk. 148/B1
Kuşadası, Turk. 148/A2
Kusatsu, Japan 133/J5
Kusel, Ger. 111/G4
Kushālgarh, India 147/K4
Kushida (riv.), Japan 135/K7
Kushigata, Japan 135/M5
Kushikino, Japan 132/B5
Kushima, Japan 132/B5
Kushimoto, Japan 132/D2
Kushiro, Japan 134/D2
Kushiro (riv.), Japan 134/D2
Kushiro-Shitsugen NP, Japan 134/D2
Kushtia, Bang. 143/G4
Kushva, Rus. 119/N4
Kuskokwim (bay), Ak, US 192/F4
Kuskokwim (mts.), Ak, US 192/G3
Kuskokwim, North Fork (riv.), Ak, US 192/H3
Kuskokwim, South Fork (riv.), Ak, US 192/H3
Küsnacht, Swi. 115/E3
Kusŏng, NKor. 131/C3
Kussharo (lake), Japan 134/D2
Küssnacht am Rigi, Swi. 115/E3
Küstenkanal (canal), Ger. 108/E3
Kusterdingen, Ger. 112/C5

Kusu, Japan 135/L6
Kut (isl.), Thai. 141/H5
Kütahya, Turk. 148/B2
K'ut'aisi (int'l arpt.), Geo. 121/G4
K'ut'aisi, Geo. 121/G4
Kutch (reg.), India 147/J4
Kutch, Gulf of (gulf), India 147/J4
Kutchan, Japan 134/B1
Kutcharo (lake), Japan 134/C1
Kuttenholz, Ger. 109/G2
Kutná Hora, Czh. 99/H4
Kutno, Pol. 99/K2
Kutsuki, Japan 135/J5
Kuttawa, Swi. 114/E3
Kutu, D.R. Congo 155/J8
Kutzenhausen, Ger. 112/D6
Kutztown, Pa, US 196/C2
Kuujjua (riv.), NW, Can. 180/E1
Kuujjuaq, Qu, Can. 181/K3
Kuusamo, Fin. 95/J2
Kuusankoski, Fin. 97/M1
Kuutse (hill), Est. 97/M2
Kuvandyk, Rus. 121/K2
Kuwait (ctry.) 146/E3
Kuwait (cap.), Kuw. 146/E3
Kuwānā (riv.), India 140/D2
Kuwana, Japan 135/L5
Kuznetsk, Rus. 121/H1
Kuzucubelen, Turk. 149/C1
Kuzitrin (riv.), Ak, US 192/E2
Kvaløy (isl.), Nor. 95/F1
Kvænndrup, Den. 96/D4
Kvarner (gulf), Cro. 106/B3
Kvarnerić (chan.), Cro. 106/B3
Kvigtinden (peak), Nor. 95/E2
Kvinesdal, Nor. 96/B2
Kvinnherad, Nor. 96/B2
Kviteseid, Nor. 96/C2
Kwa (riv.), D.R. Congo 163/C1
Kwach'ŏn, SKor. 131/F7
Kwajalein (isl.), Mrsh. 174/F4
Kwale, Nga. 161/G4
KwaMashu, SAfr. 165/E3
Kwanak-san (peak), SKor. 131/F7
Kwangch'ŏn, SKor. 131/D4
Kwangju, SKor. 131/D5
Kwangju, SKor. 131/G7
Kwangju-Gwangyŏksi (prov.), SKor. 131/D5
Kwangmyŏng, SKor. 131/F7
Kwango, D.R. Congo 163/C2
Kwangsang, SKor.
Kwania (lake), Ugan. 155/M7
Kwansan, SKor. 131/D5
Kwara (state), Nga. 161/G4
Kwaraha (peak), Tanz. 162/B4
Kwataboahegan (riv.), On, Can. 188/D1
Kwazulu Natal (prov.), SAfr. 165/E3
Kwekwe, Zim. 163/E4
Kwethluk, Ak, US 192/F3
Kwidzyn, Pol. 97/H5
Kwigillingok, Ak, US 192/F4
Kwili (riv.), D.R. Congo 163/C1
Kwilu, D.R. Congo 163/C1
Kwinana, Austl. 170/K7
Kyabé, Chad 155/J6
Kyabram, Austl. 173/C3
Kyaiktiyo Pagoda, Myan. 136/B2
Kyaikto, Myan. 141/G4
Kyakhta, Rus. 128/J1
Kyan-zaki (cape), Japan 133/J7
Kyangin, Myan. 141/G4
Kyaukpadaung, Myan. 141/G3
Kyaukpyu, Myan. 141/F4
Kyaukse, Myan. 141/G3
Kyenjojo, Ugan. 162/A2
Kyeryong-san NP, SKor. 131/D4
Kyiv, Ukr. 120/D2
Kyle, Sk, Can. 184/F3
Kyle (reg.), Sc, UK 94/B5
Kyll (riv.), Ger. 111/F3
Kym (riv.), Eng, UK 91/F2
Kymijoki (riv.), Fin. 97/M1
Kymore, India 142/C3
Kyneton, Austl. 173/C3
Kynšperk nad Ohří, Czh. 113/F2
Kyoga (lake), Ugan. 155/M7
Kyoga-misaki (cape), Japan 132/D3
Kyogle, Austl. 172/D5
Kyonan, Japan 133/F3
Kyŏngbok Palace, SKor. 131/F6
Kyŏnggi (bay), SKor. 131/C4
Kyŏnggi-do (prov.), SKor. 131/D4

Kyŏng – Laoan

Kyŏngju, SKor. 131/E5
Kyŏngju NP, SKor. 131/E5
Kyŏngsan, SKor. 131/E5
Kyŏngsang-bukto (prov.), SKor. 131/E4
Kyŏngsang-namdo (prov.), SKor. 131/E5
Kyōto (pref.), Japan 132/D3
Kyōto, Japan 135/J5
Kyōtō Imperial Palace, Japan 135/J6
Kyōwa, Japan 135/E1
Kyrenia (dist.), Cyp. 149/C2
Kyrenia, Cyp. 149/C2
Kyrgyzstan (ctry.) 145/F4
Kyritz, Ger. 98/G2
Kyrösjärvi (lake), Fin. 97/K1
Kythrea, Cyp. 149/C2
Kyūshū (isl.), Japan 132/B5
Kyūshū Highlands (uplands), Japan 132/B4
Kyustendil, Bul. 105/H1
Kywebwe, Myan. 141/F4
Kyyivs'ka Oblasti, Ukr. 120/D2
Kyyivs'ke Vodoskhovyshche (res.), Ukr. 120/D2
Kyzyl, Rus. 128/F1

L

La Algaba, Sp. 102/B4
La Almunia de Doña Godina, Sp. 102/E2
La Amistad Int'l Park, CR 198/E6
La Araucanía (pol. reg.), Chile 216/B3
La Ascensión, Mex. 201/F3
La Asunción, Ven. 211/F2
La Aurora (int'l arpt.), Guat. 202/D3
La Babia, Mex. 190/C4
La Baie, Qu, Can. 189/G1
La Banda, Arg. 215/D2
La Bañeza, Sp. 102/C1
La Bassée, Fr. 110/B2
La Baule-Escoublac, Fr. 100/B3
La Belle, Fl, US 191/H5
La Birse (riv.), Swi. 114/D3
La Blanquilla (isl.), Ven. 211/E2
La Bocana, Mex. 200/B3
La Bresse, Fr. 114/C2
La Broque, Fr. 114/D1
La Calera, Chile 216/N8
La Campana, Sp. 102/C4
La Cañada (peak), Cuba 203/F1
La Canada-Flintridge, Ca, US 194/F7
La Capelle, Fr. 110/C4
La Carlota, Sp. 102/C4
La Carlota, Arg. 216/E2
La Carolina, Sp. 102/D3
La Catedral (peak), Mex. 201/Q9
La Ceiba, Hon. 202/E3
La Ceiba (int'l arpt.), Hon. 202/E3
La Celle-les-Bordes, Fr. 88/H6
La Celle-Saint-Cloud, Fr. 88/J5
La Celle-sur-Morin, Fr. 88/L5
La Chapelle-de-Guinchay, Fr. 114/A5
La Chapelle-Saint-Luc, Fr. 100/F2
La Chaux-de-Bonds, Swi. 114/C3
La Chinita (int'l arpt.), Ven. 210/D2
La Chorrera, Pan. 203/G4
La Cienega, NM, US 187/F4
La Ciotat, Fr. 100/F5
La Clusaz, Fr. 114/C6
La Concepción, Nic. 202/E4
La Concepción, Pan. 203/F4
La Concepcíon, Ven. 210/D2
La Coronilla, Uru. 217/G2
La Coruña, Sp. 102/A1
La Couronne, Fr. 100/D4
La Crèche, Fr. 100/C3
La Crescenta-Montrose, Ca, US 194/F7
La Croix-en-Brie, Fr. 88/M6
La Croix, Lac (lake), On, Can. 185/L3
La Cruz, Chile 216/N8
La Cruz, Col. 210/B4
La Cruz, CR 202/E4
La Cruz, Mex. 200/D4
La Cruz, Uru. 217/K10
La Cumbre (vol.), Ecu. 214/E7
La Dôle (peak), Swi. 114/C5
La Dorada, Col. 208/D2
La Dormida, Arg. 216/D2
La Esperanza, Hon. 202/D3
La Estrada, Sp. 102/A1
La Estrella, Chile 216/N9
La Falda, Arg. 215/D3
La Fayette, Ga, US 191/G3
La Fère, Fr. 110/C4
La Ferté-Gaucher, Fr. 110/C6
La Ferté-Macé, Fr. 100/C2
La Ferté-Milon, Fr. 88/M7
La Ferté-Sous-Jouarre, Fr. 110/C6
La Flèche, Fr. 100/C3
La Fría, Ven. 210/C2
La Galite (isl.), Tun. 158/L6
La Garamba NP, D.R. Congo 162/A2
La Garita (mts.), Co, US 190/B2
La Garriga, Sp. 103/L6
La Gineta, Sp. 102/E3
La Gloria, Col. 210/C2
La Goulette, Tun. 158/M6
La Gran Sabana (plain), Ven. 208/F2
La Grande, Or, US 184/D4
La Grande (riv.), Qu, Can. 181/J3
La Grande Ruine (peak), Fr. 101/G4
La Grange, Ga, US 191/G3
La Grange, Tx, US 187/H5
La Grita, Ven. 203/J4
La Gruyère (lake), Swi. 114/D4
La Guajira (dept.), Col. 210/C2
La Guajira (pen.), Col. 210/D1
La Guardia, Sp. 102/A2
La Guardia (int'l arpt.), NY, US 197/K8
La Habana (Havana) (cap.), Cuba 198/E3
La Habra, Ca, US 194/G8
La Have (riv.), NS, Can. 189/H2
La Higuera, Chile 215/B2
La Honda, Ca, US 193/K12
La Houssaye-en-Brie, Fr. 88/L5
La Huaca, Peru 214/A2
La Huacana, Mex. 201/E5
La Huerta, Mex. 200/D5
La Isla, Mex. 201/Q10
La Jalca, Peru 214/B2
La Joya, Peru 214/D5
La Joya de los Sachas, Ecu. 210/B5
La Junta, Co, US 187/G3
La Junta, Mex. 200/D2
La Laguna, Canl., Sp. 156/A3
La Libertad, Ecu. 210/A5
La Libertad, Guat. 202/D2
La Libertad, Hon. 202/E3
La Libertad (dept.), Peru 214/B3
La Ligua, Chile 216/C2
La Línea de la Concepción, Sp. 102/C4
La Llagosta, Sp. 103/L6
La Loche, Sk, Can. 184/F1
La Loggia, It. 116/A3
La Louvière, Belg. 111/D3
La Luisiana, Sp. 102/C4
La Luz, NM, US 187/F4
La Machine, Fr. 100/E3
La Maddalena, It. 104/A2
La Madeleine, Fr. 110/C2
La Malbaie, Qu, Can. 189/G2
La Marsá, Tun. 158/M6
La Martre (lake), NW, Can. 180/E2
La Masica, Hon. 202/E3
La Mauricie NP, Qu, Can. 188/F2
La Mensura (peak), Col. 210/C4
La Merca, Sp. 102/B1
La Merced, Peru 214/C3
La Mesa, Ca, US 194/C5
La Mesa (int'l arpt.), Hon. 202/E3
La Mesa, Ven. 210/D2
La Mira, Mex. 200/E5
La Mirada, Ca, US 194/F8
La Moine (riv.), Il, US 188/B3
La Montaña (phys. reg.), Peru 214/C3
La Moure, ND, US 185/J4
La Neuveville, Swi. 114/D3
La Norville, Fr. 88/J6
La Orchila (isl.), Ven. 199/H5
La Orotava, Canl., Sp. 156/A3
La Oroya, Peru 214/C3
La Palma, Pan. 203/G4
La Palma (isl.), Sp. 156/A3
La Paloma, Uru. 217/G2
La Pampa (prov.), Arg. 216/D3
La Paz, Arg. 215/E3
La Paz, Arg. 216/D2
La Paz (cap.), Bol. 208/E7
La Paz (dept.), Bol. 214/D4
La Paz, Col. 210/C2
La Paz, Col. 210/C3
La Paz, Hon. 202/E3
La Paz, Mex. 200/C3
La Paz (bay), Mex. 200/C3
La Paz, Uru. 217/K11
La Pêche, Qu, Can. 188/F2
La Peña, Pan. 198/E6
La Perla, Mex. 200/D2
La Pérouse (str.), Japan,Rus 129/R2
La Pérouse (str.), Japan,Rus. 125/P5
La Petite-Raon, Fr. 114/C1
La Piedad Cavadas, Mex. 200/E4
La Plata, Md, US 188/E4
La Plata, Col. 210/C4
La Plata, Arg. 217/K11
La Pobla de Lillet, Sp. 103/F1
La Pocatière, Qu, Can. 189/G2
La Pola de Gordón, Sp. 102/C1
La Ponge (lake), Sk, Can. 184/G2
La Porte, In, US 188/C3
La Prairie, Qu, Can. 189/P7
La Pryor, Tx, US 187/H5
La Puebla, Sp. 103/G3
La Puebla de Almoradiel, Sp. 102/D3
La Puebla de Cazalla, Sp. 102/C4
La Puebla de Montalbán, Sp. 102/C3
La Puente, Ca, US 194/G7
La Puntilla (pt.), Ecu. 210/A5
La Quebrada, Ven. 210/D2
La Queue-les-Yvelines, Fr. 110/A6
La Quiaca, Arg. 208/E8
La Rambla, Sp. 102/C4
La Reforma, Mex. 200/C3
La Rinconada, Sp. 102/C4
La Rioja, Arg. 215/C2
La Rioja (aut. comm.), Sp. 102/D1
La Rioja (prov.), Sp. 102/D1
La Robla, Sp. 102/C1
La Roche (lake), Sk, Can. 184/F1
La Roche, Swi. 114/D4
La Roche-en-Ardenne, Belg. 111/E3
La Roche-sur-Foron, Fr. 114/C5
La Roche-sur-Yon, Fr. 100/C3
La Rochelle, Fr. 100/C3
La Roda, Sp. 102/D3
La Romana, DRep. 199/H4
La Ronge, Sk, Can. 185/G2
La Rúa, Sp. 102/B1
La Salle, Co, US 195/C2
La Sarraz, Swi. 114/C4
La Sarre, Qu, Can. 188/E1
La Sauvette (peak), Fr. 101/G5
La Scie, Nf, Can. 189/L1
La Serena, Chile 215/B2
La Seu d'Urgell, Sp. 103/F1
La Seyne-sur-Mer, Fr. 100/F5
La Sierpe, Cuba 203/G1
La Sila (mts.), It. 104/E3
La Silueta (peak), Chile 217/B7
La Solana, Sp. 102/D3
La Souterraine, Fr. 100/D3
La Spezia (prov.), It. 116/C4
La Spezia, It. 116/C4
La Tabatière, Qu, Can. 189/K1
La Teste, Fr. 100/C4
La Tête à l'Ane (peak), Fr. 114/C6
La Tigra, PN, Hon. 202/E3
La Toma, Arg. 216/D2
La Tortue (isl.), Haiti 203/H1
La Tortuga (isl.), Ven. 211/E2
La Tortuga, Isla (isl.), Ven. 208/E1
La Tour-de-Peilz, Swi. 114/C5
La Tour-de-Trême, Swi. 114/D4
La Tremblade, Fr. 100/C4
La Trinitaria, Mex. 202/C2
La Troncal, Ecu. 210/B5
La Tuque, Qu, Can. 189/F2
La Turbie, Fr. 116/H8
La Unión, Chile 216/B4
La Unión, Col. 210/B4
La Unión, ESal. 202/E3
La Unión, Mex. 201/E5
La Unión, Peru 214/A2
La Unión, Peru 214/B3
La Unión, Sp. 103/E4
La Unión, Ven. 210/E2
La Vecilla, Sp. 102/C1
La Verna, It. 117/E5
La Verne, Ca, US 194/C2
La Vernia, Tx, US 195/U21
La Verrière, Fr. 88/H5
La Víbora, Mex. 190/C5
La Victoria, Ven. 208/E1
La Victoria, Ven. 210/D3
La Wantzenau, Fr. 111/G6
Laa an der Thaya, Aus. 101/M2
Laaber, Ger. 113/E4
Laage, Ger. 96/E5
Laakirchen, Aus. 113/G7
Laarne, Belg. 110/C1
Laas Caanood, Som. 155/Q6
Laas Qoray, Som. 155/Q5
Laatzen, Ger. 109/G4
Laax, Swi. 115/F5
Labason, Phil. 137/D6
L'Abbaye, Swi. 114/C4
Labdah (Leptis Magna) (ruin), Libya 154/H1
Labé, Gui. 160/B4
Labé (pol. reg.), Gui. 160/B4
Labe (Elbe) (riv.), Czh. 101/L1
Laberweinting, Ger. 113/F5
Labian (cape), Malay. 139/E2
Labin, Cro. 106/B3
Labinsk, Rus. 121/G3
Labná (ruin), Mex. 202/D1
Laborde, Arg. 216/E2
Laborec (riv.), Slvk. 99/L4
Laboulaye, Arg. 216/E2
Labrador (reg.), Nf, Can. 181/K3
Labrador (sea), Can.,Grld. 177/M4
Labrador City, Nf, Can. 181/K3
Lábrea, Braz. 208/F5
Labruguière, Fr. 100/E5
Labry, Fr. 111/E5
Labuk (riv.), Malay. 139/E2
Labuk (bay), Malay. 139/E2
Labuništa, FYROM 105/G2
Labutta, Myan. 141/F4
Laç, Alb. 105/F2
Lac Afwein (riv.), Kenya 162/C2
Lac du Bonnet, Mb, Can. 185/J3
Lac La Biche, Ab, Can. 184/F2
Lac-Mégantic, Qu, Can. 189/G2
L'Acadie, Qu, Can. 189/P7
Lacantum (riv.), Mex. 202/D2
Lacaune, Fr. 100/E5
Laccadive (sea), India 140/B5
Lacchiarella, It. 116/C2
Lacepede (bay), Austl. 173/A3
Lach Dera (riv.), Som. 155/P7
Lacha (lake), Rus. 118/H3
Lachapelle-aux-Pots, Fr. 110/A5
Lachay (pt.), Peru 214/B3
Lachen, Swi. 115/E3
Lachenaie, Qu, Can. 189/N6
Lachendorf, Ger. 109/H3
Lāchi, Pak. 144/A3
L'Achigan (riv.), Qu, Can. 189/N6
Lachine, Qu, Can. 189/N7
Lachlan (riv.), Austl. 173/C2
Lachte (riv.), Ger. 109/H3
Lackawanna, NY, US 189/S10
Lackawanna (co.), Pa, US 196/C1
Läckö, Swe. 96/E2
Lacombe, Ab, Can. 184/E2
Lacombe, La, US 195/Q16
Laconia, NH, US 189/G3
Lacroix-Saint-Ouen, Fr. 110/B5
Ladainha, Braz. 212/B5
Ladakh (mts.), India 147/L2
Ladbergen, Ger. 109/E4
Ladder (hills), Sc, UK 94/C2
Lądek-Zdrój, Pol. 99/J3
Ladenburg, Ger. 112/B4
Ladera Heights, Ca, US 194/F8
Ladismith, SAfr. 164/C4
Ladispoli, It. 104/C2
Ladoga (lake), Rus. 218/D
Ladoix-Serrigny, Fr. 114/A3
Ladrillero (mtn.), Chile 217/B7
Ladue, Mo, US 195/G8
Lādwa, India 144/D5
Lady Isle (isl.), Sc, UK 94/B5
Ladybank, Sc, UK 94/C4
Ladybower (res.), Eng, UK 93/G5
Ladybrand, SAfr. 164/D3
Ladysmith, SAfr. 165/E3
Lae (isl.), Mrsh. 174/F4
Laer, Ger. 109/E4
Lafayette, Ca, US 193/K11
Lafayette, Co, US 195/B3
Lafayette, In, US 188/C3
Lafayette, La, US 187/J5
Lafayette, NJ, US 196/D1
Lafia, Nga. 161/H4
Lafitte, La, US 195/P17
Laflamme (riv.), Qu, Can. 188/E1
Lafnitz (riv.), Aus. 101/L3
Lafontaine, Qu, Can. 189/M6
Lafourche (parish), La, US 195/T17
Laga Balal (riv.), Kenya 162/C2
Laga Mado Gali (riv.), Kenya 162/C2
Laga Merille (riv.), Kenya 162/C2
Lagan, Swe. 96/E3
Lagan (riv.), Swe. 96/E3
Lagarto, Braz. 212/C3
Lagawe, Phil. 137/D4
Lagdo, Lac de (lake), Camr. 154/H6
Lage, Ger. 109/F5
Lage Vaart (canal), Neth. 108/C4
Lågen (riv.), Nor. 96/C1
Lages, Braz. 213/B3
Laggan (lake), Sc, UK 94/B3
Lagh Bogal (riv.), Kenya 162/C2
Lagh Bor (riv.), Kenya 155/N7
Lagh Kutulo (riv.), Kenya 162/D2
Laghouat (prov.), Alg. 157/F2
Laghouat, Alg. 157/F2
Lagnieu, Fr. 114/B6
Lagny-le-Sec, Fr. 88/L4
Lagny-sur-Marne, Fr. 88/L5
Lago da Pedra, Braz. 212/A2
Lago de Atitlán, PN, Guat. 202/D3
Lago Puelo, PN, Arg. 216/C4
Lago Verde, Chile 216/C5
Lagoa, Port. 102/A4
Lagoa da Prata, Braz. 213/C2
Lagoa Formosa, Braz. 213/C1
Lagoa Vermelha, Braz. 213/B4
Lagoda (lake), Rus. 95/J3
Lagonegro, It. 104/D2
Lagord, Fr. 100/C3
Lagos, Nga. 161/F5
Lagos (state), Nga. 161/F5
Lagos, Port. 102/A4
Lagos de Moreno, Mex. 200/E4
Lagosanto, It. 117/F3
Laguardia, Sp. 102/D1
Laguna, Braz. 213/B4
Laguna Beach, Ca, US 194/C3
Laguna Blanca, PN, Arg. 216/C3
Laguna de Duero, Sp. 102/C2
Laguna de la Restinga, PN, Ven. 211/E2
Laguna del Laja, PN, Chile 216/C3
Laguna del Rey, Mex. 200/E3
Laguna Hills, Ca, US 194/C3
Laguna San Rafael, PN, Chile 215/B6
Lagunas, Peru 214/C2
Lagunas, Peru 214/B2
Lagunas de Chacahua, PN, Mex. 202/B2
Lagunas de Montebello, Mex. 198/C4
Lagunas de Zempoala, PN, Mex. 201/Q10
Lagunillas, Ven. 210/D2
Laguntara (lag.), Hon. 203/E3
Lahad Datu, Malay. 139/E2
Lahār, India 142/B2
Lāharpur, India 142/C2
Lahat, Indo. 138/B4
Lāhījān, Iran 146/F1
Lahn (riv.), Ger. 98/E3
Lahnstein, Ger. 111/G3
Laholm, Swe. 96/E3
Laholms (bay), Den. 96/F3
Lahore, Pak. 144/C4
Lahore (int'l arpt.), Pak. 144/C4
Lahr, Ger. 114/D1
Lahti, Fin. 97/L1
Laï, Chad 154/J6
Lai Chau, Viet. 136/C1
Lai'an, China 130/D4
Laibin, China 137/A3
Laichingen, Ger. 112/C5
Laidon (lake), Sc, UK 94/B3
Laie, Hi, US 182/W12
Laifeng Tujiazu Zizhixian, China 137/A2
L'Aigle, Fr. 100/D2
Laigueglia, It. 116/B5
Laihia, Fin. 95/G3
Lainate, It. 116/C1
Laingsburg, SAfr. 164/C4
Lainioälven (riv.), Swe. 95/G1
Laishui, China 130/G7
Laisvall, Swe. 95/F2
Laitila, Fin. 97/J1
Laives (Leifers), It. 115/H5
Laiwu, China 130/D3
Laixi, China 130/E3
Laiyuan, China 130/C3
Laizhou (bay), China 130/D3
Laja (lake), Chile 216/C3
Lajas, Peru 214/B2
Laje, Braz. 212/B3
Lajeado, Braz. 213/B4
Lajedo, Braz. 212/C3
Lajes, Braz. 212/C2
Lajes, Azor., Port. 103/S12
Lajes (int'l arpt.), Azor., Port. 103/S12
Lajing (pass), Nepal 143/E1
Lajinha, Braz. 213/D2
Lajosmizse, Hun. 106/D2
L'Akagera, PN de, Rwa. 162/A3
Lakato, Madg. 165/J7
Lake (co.), Il, US 193/P15
Lake Aluma, Ok, US 195/N14
Lake Amadeus Abor. Land, Austl. 171/F3
Lake Arrowhead, Ca, US 194/C2
Lake Barrington, Il, US 193/P15
Lake Beulah, Wi, US 193/P14
Lake Bluff, Il, US 193/Q15
Lake Boga, Austl. 173/B2
Lake Bogoria Nat'l Rsv., Kenya 162/C2
Lake Bolac, Austl. 173/B3
Lake Cargelligo, Austl. 173/C2
Lake Catherine, Il, US 193/P15
Lake Chany (lake), Rus. 145/G2
Lake Charles, La, US 187/J5
Lake Chelan Nat'l Rec. Area, Wa, US 184/C3
Lake City, Fl, US 191/H4
Lake Clark NP and Prsv., Ak, US 192/G3
Lake District NP, Eng, UK 93/E2
Lake Elsinore, Ca, US 194/C3
Lake Forest, Il, US 193/Q15
Lake Forest Park, Wa, US 193/C2
Lake Fork (res.), Tx, US 190/E3
Lake Grace, Austl. 170/C5
Lake Havasu City, Az, US 186/D4
Lake Hiwassee, Ok, US 195/N14
Lake in the Hills, Il, US 193/P15
Lake Jackson, Tx, US 187/J5
Lake Lotawana, Mo, US 195/E6
Lake Louise, Ab, Can. 184/D3
Lake Malawi NP, Malw. 163/F3
Lake Manyara NP, Tanz. 162/B3
Lake Mburo NP, Ugan. 162/A3
Lake Mead Nat'l Rec. Area, US 186/D4
Lake Meredith Nat'l Rec. Area, Tx, US 190/C3
Lake Minchumina, Ak, US 192/H3
Lake Mohawk, NJ, US 196/D1
Lake Nakuru NP, Kenya 162/C3
Lake of the Woods (lake), US,Can. 185/K3
Lake Orion, Mi, US 193/F6
Lake Point Junction, Ut, US 195/J12
Lake Providence, La, US 187/K4
Lake Ronkonkoma, NY, US 197/E2
Lake Shore, Md, US 196/B5
Lake Station, In, US 193/R16
Lake Success, NY, US 197/L8
Lake Villa, Il, US 193/P15
Lake Wales, Fl, US 191/H5
Lake Winnebago, Mo, US 195/E6
Lake Worth, Fl, US 191/H5
Lake Zurich, Il, US 193/P15
Lakehurst, NJ, US 196/D3
Lakehurst Naval Air Eng. Ctr., NJ, US 196/D3
Lakeland, Fl, US 191/H4
Lakeland Village, Ca, US 194/C3
Lakemoor, Il, US 193/P15
Lakeport, Ca, US 186/B3
Lakes Entrance, Austl. 173/D3
Lakes NP, The, Austl. 173/C3
Lakesfjorden (inlet), Nor. 95/H1
Lakeside, Ca, US 194/D5
Lakeview, Or, US 184/C5
Lakeview, Ut, US 195/K13
Lakeview, Ca, US 194/C3
Lakeville (lake), Mi, US 193/F6
Lakeway, Tx, US 187/H5
Lakewood, Wa, US 184/C3
Lakewood, Co, US 195/B3
Lakewood, NJ, US 196/D3
Lakewood, Ca, US 194/F8
Lakewood, Il, US 193/P15
Lakhemaa NP, Est. 97/L2
Lakhīmpur, India 142/C2
Lakhnādon, India 142/B4
Laki (vol.), Ice. 95/N7
Lakki, Pak. 144/A3
Lakkíon, Gre. 148/A2
Lakonía (gulf), Gre. 105/H4
Lakshadweep (isls.), India 140/B5
Lakshadweep (terr.), India 140/B6
Lal Suhanra NP, Pak. 144/B5
Lāla Mūsa, Pak. 144/B3
Lalana (riv.), Madg. 165/H8
Lalang (riv.), Indo. 138/B4
Lālganj, India 143/E3
Lālgola, India 143/G3
Lāliān, Pak. 144/B4
Lalín, Sp. 102/A1
Lalinde, Fr. 100/D4
Lalitpur, India 142/B3
Lalitpur (Pāṭan), Nepal 143/E2
Lalla Rookh Abor. Land, Austl. 170/C2
Lamachan (peak), Sc, UK 92/D1
Lamadrid, Mex. 190/C5
Lamanai (ruin), Belz. 202/D2
Lamandau (riv.), Indo. 138/D4
Lamar, Co, US 187/G3
Lamarche, Fr. 114/B1
Lamarche-sur-Saône, Fr. 114/B3
Lamarque, Arg. 216/D3
Lamas, Peru 214/B2
Lambach, Aus. 113/G6
Lamballe, Fr. 100/B2
Lambaré, Par. 215/E2
Lambaréné, Gabon 154/H8
Lambari, Braz. 213/H6
Lambay (isl.), Ire. 89/Q10
Lambayeque (dept.), Peru 214/A2
Lambayeque, Peru 214/B2
Lambé Coba (riv.), Mali 160/C3
Lambert-St. Louis (int'l arpt.), Mo, US 187/K3
Lambert's Bay, SAfr. 164/B4
Lambertville, Mi, US 188/D3
Lambertville, NJ, US 196/D3
Lambesc, Fr. 100/F5
Lambeth (bor.), Eng, UK 88/C2
Lambrama, Peru 214/C4
Lambrecht, Ger. 112/B4
Lambro (riv.), It. 116/C2
Lambsheim, Ger. 112/B3
Lambton (co.), On, Can. 193/H6
Lambunao, Phil. 137/D5
Lamego, Port. 102/B2
Lamèque (isl.), NB, Can. 189/H2
Lameroo, Austl. 171/J5
Lamesa, Tx, US 187/G4
Lamía, Gre. 105/H3
Lamington (riv.), NJ, US 196/D2
Lamington NP, Austl. 172/D5
Lamitan, Phil. 137/D6
Lamlash, Sc, UK 94/A5
Lamma (isl.), China 129/U11
Lammermuir (hills), Sc, UK 94/D5
Lammhult, Swe. 96/F3
Lammi, Fin. 97/L1
Lamone (riv.), It. 101/J4
Lamont, Ca, US 186/C4
Lamorlaye, Fr. 88/K4
Lamotrek (isl.), Micr. 174/D4
Lampa, Chile 216/N8
Lampa, Peru 214/D4
Lampang, Thai. 136/B2
Lampasas, Tx, US 187/H5
Lampasas (riv.), Tx, US 190/D4
Lampazos de Naranjo, Mex. 201/E3
Lampedusa, It. 104/C5
Lampedusa (isl.), It. 104/C5
Lampertheim, Ger. 112/B3
Lampeter, Pa, US 196/B4
Lamphun, Thai. 136/B2
Lampman, Sk, Can. 185/H3
Lamporecchio, It. 117/D5
Lamstedt, Ger. 109/G1
Lamu, Kenya 162/D3
Lamud, Peru 214/B2
Lamwa (peak), Ugan. 162/B2
Lan Sang NP, Thai. 136/B2
Lana, It. 115/H4
Lana, Río de la (riv.), Mex. 202/C2
Lanai (isl.), Hi, US 182/T10
Lanaihale (peak), Hi, US 182/T10
Lanaken, Belg. 111/E2
Lanark, Sc, UK 94/C5
Lanbi (isl.), Myan. 141/G5
Lancang Lahuzu Zizhixian, China 141/G3
Lancashire (co.), Eng, UK 93/F4
Lancashire (plain), Eng, UK 93/E4
Lancaster (sound), Nun., Can. 181/H1
Lancaster, Eng, UK 93/F3
Lancaster, Ca, US 186/C4
Lancaster, NY, US 189/S10
Lancaster, Pa, US 196/B3
Lancaster (co.), Pa, US 196/B4
Lancaster, SC, US 191/H3
Lancelin, Austl. 170/B4
Lanciano, It. 104/D1
L'Ancienne-Lorette, Qu, Can. 189/G2
Lanco, Chile 216/B3
Lańcut, Pol. 99/M3
Lancy, Swi. 114/C5
Land Kehdingen (reg.), Ger. 109/G1
Landau an der Isar, Ger. 113/F5
Landau in der Pfalz, Ger. 112/B4
Landeck, Aus. 115/G3
Landen, Belg. 111/E2
Lander, Wy, US 184/F5
Landerneau, Fr. 100/A2
Landes (reg.), Fr. 100/C4
Landes de Lanvaux (mts.), Fr. 100/B3
Landesbergen, Ger. 109/G3
Landis, Sk, Can. 184/F2
Landis Valley Museum, Pa, US 196/B3
Landisburg, Pa, US 196/A3
Landivisiau, Fr. 100/A2
Landrecies, Fr. 110/C3
Landri Sales, Braz. 212/B2
Landriano, It. 116/C2
Land's End (pt.), Eng, UK 90/A6
Landsberg, Ger. 115/G1
Landser, Fr. 114/D2
Landshut, Ger. 113/F5
Landskrona, Swe. 96/E4
Landsmeer, Neth. 108/B4
Landstuhl, Ger. 111/G5
Landvetter (int'l arpt.), Swe. 96/E3
Lane End, Eng, UK 88/A2
Lanester, Fr. 100/B3
Lanett, Al, US 191/G3
Lang Craig (pt.), Sc, UK 94/D3
Lang Kha Tuk (peak), Thai. 136/B4
Lang Son, Viet. 141/J3
Lang Suan, Thai. 136/B4
Langadhás, Gre. 105/H2
Langdon, ND, US 185/J3
Langeac, Fr. 100/E4
Langebaanweg, SAfr. 164/L10
Langeberg (mts.), SAfr. 164/L10
Langeland (isl.), Ger. 96/D4
Langelsheim, Ger. 109/H5
Langen, Ger. 109/F1
Langen, Ger. 112/B3
Langenaltheim, Ger. 112/D5
Langenargen, Ger. 115/F2
Langenau, Ger. 112/D5
Langenbach, Ger. 113/E6
Langenberg, Ger. 109/E6
Langenburg, Sk, Can. 185/H3
Längenfeld, Aus. 115/G3
Langenfeld, Ger. 111/F1
Langenhagen, Ger. 109/G4
Langenhorn, Ger. 96/C4
Langenlois, Aus. 99/H4
Langenpreising, Ger. 113/E6
Langenselbold, Ger. 112/C2
Langenstein, Aus. 113/H6
Langenthal, Swi. 114/D3
Langenzenn, Ger. 112/D3
Langenzersdorf, Aus. 107/N7
Langeoog, Ger. 109/E1
Langeoog (isl.), Ger. 109/E1
Langerringen, Ger. 115/G1
Langeskov, Den. 96/D4
Langesund, Nor. 96/C2
Langeten (riv.), Swi. 114/D3
Langfang, China 130/H7
Langfurth, Ger. 112/D4
Langham, Sk, Can. 184/G2
Langhirano, It. 116/D3
Langholm, Sc, UK 93/F1
Langhorne, Pa, US 196/D3
Langjökull (glacier), Ice. 95/N7
Langkawi (isl.), Malay. 141/G6
Langley, Wa, US 193/C1
Langnau im Emmental, Swi. 114/D4
Langney (pt.), Eng, UK 91/G5
Langogne, Fr. 100/E4
Langon, Fr. 100/C4
Langøya (isl.), Nor. 95/E1
Langquaid, Ger. 113/F5
Langres, Fr. 114/B2
Langres, Plateau de (plat.), Fr. 100/F3
Langsa, Indo. 138/A3
Langshyttan, Swe. 96/G1
Langtang Lirung (peak), Nepal 143/E1
Langtang NP, Nepal 143/E1
Langtry, Tx, US 190/C4
Languedoc (reg.), Fr. 100/E5
Languedoc-Roussillon (pol. reg.), Fr. 100/E5
Langwedel, Ger. 109/G3
Langweid an Lech, Ger. 112/E6
Langwies, Swi. 115/F4
Langxi, China 130/D5
Lanham-Seabrook, Md, US 196/B6
Lanigan, Sk, Can. 185/G3
Laniloa (pt.), Hi, US 182/W12
Lanin (vol.), Arg. 216/C3
Lanin, PN, Arg. 215/B4
Länkäran, Azer. 121/J5
Lanlacuni Bajo, Peru 214/D4
Lannemezan (plat.), Fr. 100/D5
Lannion (bay), Fr. 100/B2
Lannion, Fr. 100/B2
Lansdale, Pa, US 196/C3
Lansdowne, India 142/B1
Lansdowne, Pa, US 196/C4
Lansdowne-Baltimore Highlands, Md, US 196/B5
Lansford, Pa, US 196/C2
Lanshan, China 141/K2
Lansing (cap.), Mi, US 188/C3
Lansing, Ks, US 195/D5
Lansing, Il, US 193/Q16
Lanta (isl.), Thai. 141/G6
Lantau (chan.), China 129/T11
Lantau (peak), China 129/T11
Lantau (isl.), China 129/T10
Lanterne (riv.), Fr. 114/C2
Lanús, Arg. 217/J11
Lanusei, It. 104/A3
Lanxi, China 137/C2
Lanzarote (int'l arpt.), Canl., Sp. 156/B3
Lanzarote (isl.), Canl., Sp. 156/B3
Lanžhot, Czh. 99/J4
Lanzhou, China 128/H4
Lao (mts.), China 131/D2
Lao (peak), China 130/E3
Lao Cai, Viet. 136/C1
Laoag, Phil. 137/D4
Laoang, Phil. 137/E5

Laohekou, China 130/B4
Laojun (mtn.), China 130/B4
Laon, Fr. 110/C4
Laos (ctry.) 136/C2
Laoshan, China 130/E3
Laotuding (peak), China 131/C2
Laou (riv.), Mor. 158/B2
Lapa, Braz. 213/B3
Lapeer, Mi, US 188/D3
Lapeer (co.), Mi, US 193/F6
Lapinlahti, Fin. 118/E3
Lapithos, Cyp. 149/C2
Lapland (reg.), Swe. 218/D
Laporte, Co, US 195/B1
Lappeenranta, Fin. 97/N1
Lappersdorf, Ger. 113/F4
Lappi (prov.), Fin. 95/H2
Laptev (sea), Rus. 125/M2
Lapua, Fin. 118/D3
Lapy, Pol. 99/M2
L'Aquila, It. 104/C1
Lär, Iran 147/F3
Lara, Austl. 173/C3
Lara (state), Ven. 210/D2
Laracha, Sp. 102/A1
Larache (prov.), Mor. 158/B2
Larache, Mor. 158/B2
Laragne-Montéglin, Fr. 100/F4
Laramie, Wy, US 185/G5
Laramie (riv.), Wy, US 185/G5
Laramie (mts.), Wy, US 185/G5
Laranjeiras do Sul, Braz. 213/A3
Larat (isl.), Indo. 139/H5
Larba, Alg. 158/G4
Larchmont, NY, US 197/K8
Lærdalsøyri, Nor. 96/B1
Laredo, Peru 214/B3
Laredo (int'l arpt.), Tx, US 190/D5
Laredo, Tx, US 190/D5
Laredo, Sp. 102/D1
Laren, Neth. 108/C4
Lares, Peru 214/C4
Largo, Fl, US 191/H5
Largo, Md, US 196/B6
Largo (bay), Sc, UK 94/D4
Largo, Cayo (isl.), Cuba 203/F1
Largs, Sc, UK 94/B5
Largue (riv.), Fr. 114/C2
Lariang (riv.), Indo. 139/E4
Larino, It. 104/D2
Lárisa, Gre. 105/H3
Lark (riv.), Eng, UK 91/G2
Lärkäna, Pak. 147/J3
Larkhall, Sc, UK 94/C5
Larkspur, Ca, US 193/J11
Larmor-Plage, Fr. 100/B3
Larnaca (int'l arpt.), Cyp. 149/C2
Larnaca (dist.), Cyp. 149/C2
Larnaca, Cyp. 149/C2
Larne, NI, UK 92/C2
Larne (dist.), NI, UK 92/C2
Larne Lough (inlet), NI, UK 92/C2
Larned, Ks, US 187/H3
Larochette, Lux. 111/F4
Laroque-d'Olmes, Fr. 100/D5
Larose, La, US 191/F4
Larreynaga, Nic. 202/E3
Larroque, Arg. 217/J10
Larsen Bay, Ak, US 192/H4
Larsen Ice Shelf, Ant. 218/V
Larsen Sound (bay), Nun., Can. 180/G1
L'Artois, Collines de (hills), Fr. 98/A3
Laruns, Fr. 100/C5
Larvik, Nor. 96/D2
Las Animas, Co, US 187/G3
Las Aves (isls.), Ven. 199/H5
Las Breñas, Arg. 215/D2
Las Cabezas de San Juan, Sp. 102/C4
Las Cabras, Chile 216/N9
Las Cruces, NM, US 186/E4
Las Delicias, Ven. 210/C3
Las Eutimias, Mex. 190/C4
Las Flores, Arg. 216/F3
Las Guacamayas, Mex. 200/E5
Las Hermosas, PN, Col. 210/C4
Las Higueras, Arg. 216/D2
Las Lajas, Arg. 216/C3
Las Lajas (peak), Arg. 216/C3
Las Lomas, Peru 214/A2
Las Lomitas, Arg. 215/D1
Las Margaritas, Mex. 202/D2
Las Martinas, Cuba 203/E1
Las Mercedes, Ven. 211/E2
Las Minas (peak), Hon. 202/D3
Las Nieves, Mex. 200/D3
Las Orquídeas, PN, Col. 210/C4
Las Palmas, Pan. 203/F4
Las Palmas de Cocalán, Chile 216/N9
Las Palmas de Gran Canaria, Canl., Sp. 156/B3
Las Pedroñeras, Sp. 102/D3
Las Perdices, Arg. 216/E2
Las Perlas (arch.), Pan. 203/G4

Las Piedras, Peru 214/D4
Las Piedras, Ven. 210/C2
Las Piedras, Uru. 217/K11
Las Pipinas, Arg. 217/D2
Las Rozas de Madrid, Sp. 103/N9
Las Tablas, Pan. 203/F5
Las Varas, Mex. 200/D4
Las Varillas, Arg. 215/D3
Las Vegas, NM, US 187/F4
Las Vegas, Nv, US 186/D3
Lasalle, Qu, Can. 189/N7
Lasberg, Aus. 113/H6
Lascano, Uru. 217/G2
Lashio, Myan. 141/G3
Lashkar Gāh, Afg. 147/H2
Lasne-Chapelle-Saint-Lambert, Belg. 111/D2
Læsø (isl.), Den. 96/D3
Lasolo (riv.), Indo. 139/F4
Lassen (peak), Ca, US 184/C3
Lassen Volcanic NP, Ca, US 186/B2
L'Assomption, Qu, Can. 189/N6
L'Assomption (co.), Qu, Can. 189/N6
L'Assomption (riv.), Qu, Can. 189/P6
Last Mountain (lake), Sk, Can. 185/G3
Lastovo (isl.), Cro. 104/E1
Lastovski (chan.), Cro. 106/C4
Lastovski Kanal (chan.), Cro. 104/E1
Lastra a Signa, It. 117/E5
Lastrup, Ger. 109/E3
Lata, Sol. 174/F6
Latacunga, Ecu. 210/B5
Latady (isl.), Ant. 218/U
L'Atakora (prov.), Ben. 161/F4
Lätehär, India 143/E4
Latemar (peak), It. 115/H5
Laterza, It. 104/E2
Lathan (riv.), Fr. 100/C3
Lathrop, Ca, US 193/M11
Latina, It. 104/C2
Latisana, It. 117/G1
Latorica (riv.), Slvk.,Ukr. 99/M4
Latrobe, Austl. 173/C4
Latrobe (mt.), Austl. 173/C3
Latrobe, Pa, US 192/B3
Latrobe (riv.), Austl. 173/C4
Lattes, Fr. 100/E5
Lattingtown, NY, US 197/L8
Lātūr, India 147/L5
Latvia (ctry.) 97/L3
Lau Group (isl.), Fiji 174/H6
Laubach, Ger. 112/B1
Lauca, PN, Chile 208/D7
Lauch (riv.), Fr. 101/G3
Lauchert (riv.), Ger. 112/C6
Lauchheim, Ger. 112/D5
Lauda-Königshofen, Ger. 112/C3
Lauder, Sc, UK 94/D5
Lauderdale (lakes), Wi, US 193/N14
Lauenbrück, Ger. 109/G2
Lauenburg, Ger. 109/G2
Lauenen, Swi. 114/D5
Lauenförde, Ger. 109/H5
Lauer (riv.), Ger. 112/D2
Lauf, Ger. 112/E3
Laufach, Ger. 112/C2
Laufen, Swi. 114/D3
Laufen, Ger. 113/F7
Laufenburg, Swi. 114/E2
Lauffen am Neckar, Ger. 112/C4
Laughlen (mt.), Austl. 171/G2
Lauhanvuoren NP, Fin. 118/D3
Lauingen, Ger. 112/D5
Laupahoehoe, Hi, US 182/U11
Laupen, Swi. 114/D3
Lauperswil, Swi. 114/D4
Laupheim, Ger. 115/F1
Laura, Austl. 171/H5
Laureana di Borrello, It. 104/E3
Laurel, Mt, US 184/F4
Laurel, Ms, US 191/F4
Laurel, NJ, US 196/B5
Laurel Springs, NJ, US 196/C4
Laureldale, Pa, US 196/A2
Laurelton, Pa, US 196/A2
Laurence Harbor, NJ, US 197/J10
Laurencekirk, Sc, UK 94/D4
Laurens, SC, US 191/H3
Laurentian (plat.), On, Can. 180/G3
Laurentides, Qu, Can. 189/N6
Laurinburg, NC, US 191/J3
Laurium, Mi, US 185/L4
Lausanne, Swi. 114/C4
Lauscha, Ger. 112/E2
Laut (isl.), Indo. 139/E4
Lautaro, Chile 216/B3
Lauter (riv.), Fr. 113/F1
Lauter, Ger. 112/E2
Lauterach (riv.), Ger. 113/E4
Lauterbach, Ger. 112/C1
Lauterbach (riv.), Ger. 112/C2

Lauterbach, Ger. 112/C1
Lauterbourg, Fr. 112/B5
Lauterbrunnen, Swi. 114/D4
Lauterecken, Ger. 111/G4
Lauve, Nor. 96/D2
Lauwers (chan.), Neth. 108/D1
Lauwersmeer (lake), Neth. 108/D2
Lava Beds Nat'l Mon., Ca, US 184/C5
Lavagna (riv.), It. 116/C3
Lavagna, It. 116/C4
Laval, Fr. 100/C2
Laval, Qu, Can. 189/N6
Lavalleja (dept.), Uru. 217/G2
Lavallette, NJ, US 196/D4
Lavans-lès-Saint-Claude, Fr. 114/B5
Lavant (riv.), Aus. 101/L3
Lavapié (pt.), Chile 216/B3
Lavaur, Fr. 100/D5
Laveen, Az, US 195/R19
Lavelanet, Fr. 100/D5
Laveno, It. 115/E6
Laverton, Austl. 170/D4
Lavezzola, It. 117/E3
Lavino (riv.), It. 117/E4
Lavis, It. 115/H5
Lavos, Port. 102/A2
Lavras, Braz. 213/C2
Lavras da Mangabeira, Braz. 212/C2
Lávrion, Gre. 105/J4
Lāwar Khās, India 142/A1
Lawarai (pass), Pak. 144/A2
Lawit (peak), Malay. 141/M6
Lawit (peak), Indo. 138/D3
Lawndale, Ca, US 194/F8
Lawnhill, BC, Can. 192/M5
Lawrence, Ks, US 187/J3
Lawrence, Ma, US 189/G3
Lawrence, NY, US 197/L9
Lawrenceburg, In, US 188/C4
Lawrenceburg, Ky, US 191/G2
Lawrenceburg, Tn, US 191/G3
Lawrencetown, NI, UK 92/B3
Lawrenceville, Ga, US 191/H3
Lawrenceville, NJ, US 196/D3
Lawson, Mo, US 195/E5
Lawu (peak), Indo. 138/D5
Laxey, IM, UK 92/D3
Laxou, Fr. 111/F6
Lay (riv.), Fr. 100/C3
Lay-Saint-Christophe, Fr. 111/F6
Laya (riv.), Rus. 119/N2
Layar (cape), Indo. 139/E4
Laylän, Iraq 148/F3
Layon (riv.), Fr. 100/C3
Laysan (isl.), Hi, US 175/U2
Layton, NJ, US 196/D1
Layton, Ut, US 195/K11
Lazarevac, Serb. 106/E3
Lázaro Cárdenas, Mex. 200/B2
Lázaro Cárdenas, Mex. 200/E5
Lazio (prov.), It. 101/J5
Łbriktepe, Turk. 105/K2
Le Ban-Saint-Martin, Fr. 111/F5
Le Blanc, Fr. 100/D3
Le Blanc-Mesnil, Fr. 88/K5
Le Breuil, Fr. 100/F3
Le Cannet, Fr. 101/G5
Le Cateau-Cambrésis, Fr. 110/C3
Le Chasseral (peak), Swi. 114/D3
Le Chasseron (peak), Swi. 114/C4
Le Chesnay, Fr. 88/J5
Le Chesne, Fr. 111/D4
Le Cheval Blanc (peak), Fr. 114/C5
Le Cheylard, Fr. 100/F4
Le Cornate (peak), It. 101/J5
Le Creusot, Fr. 100/F3
Le Crotoy, Fr. 110/A3
Le Gore, Md, US 196/A4
Le Grammont (peak), Swi. 114/C5
Le Grand (cape), Austl. 170/D5
Le Grand Ballon (peak), Fr. 101/G3
Le Grau-du-Roi, Fr. 100/F5
Le Grazie, It. 116/D3
Le Havre, Fr. 100/D2
Le Landeron, Swi. 114/D3
Le Lavandou, Fr. 101/G5
Le Locle, Swi. 114/C3
Le Luc, Fr. 101/G5
Le Mans, Fr. 100/D2
Le Mée-sur-Seine, Fr. 88/K4
Le Mesnil-Amelot, Fr. 88/K4
Le Mesnil-Aubry, Fr. 88/K4
Le Mesnil-Esnard, Fr. 88/K5
Le Mesnil-le-Roi, Fr. 88/J4

Le Mesnil-Saint-Denis, Fr. 88/H5
Le Mesnil-sur-Oger, Fr. 110/D6
Le Môle (peak), Fr. 114/C5
Le Morond (peak), Fr. 114/C4
Le Moure de la Gardille (peak), Fr. 100/E4
Le Murge (mts.), It. 104/E2
Le Noirmont (peak), Fr. 114/C4
Le Noirmont (peak), Swi. 114/C5
Le Noirmont, Swi. 114/C4
Le Nouvion-en-Thiérache, Fr. 110/C3
Le Palais, Fr. 100/B3
Le Palais-sur-Vienne, Fr. 100/D4
Le Passage, Fr. 100/D4
Le Perray-en-Yvelines, Fr. 88/H5
Le Petit Ballon (peak), Fr. 114/D2
Le Plessis-Belleville, Fr. 88/L4
Le Plessis-Feu-Aussoux, Fr. 88/M5
Le Plessis-Placy, Fr. 88/L4
Le Port, Reun., Fr. 165/S15
Le Portel, Fr. 110/A2
Le Puy-en-Velay, Fr. 100/E4
Le Quesnoy, Fr. 110/C3
Le Russey, Fr. 114/C3
Le Suchet (peak), Swi. 114/C4
Le Tampon, Reun., Fr. 165/S15
Le Teil, Fr. 100/F4
Le Tholy, Fr. 114/C1
Le Touquet-Paris-Plage, Fr. 110/A2
Le Tréport, Fr. 110/A3
Le Val-d'Ajol, Fr. 114/C2
Le Vésinet, Fr. 88/J5
Le Vigan, Fr. 100/E5
Lea (riv.), Eng, UK 91/F3
Lea, Gha. 160/E4
Leach (lake), Ca, US 185/K4
Leach (riv.), Eng, UK 91/E3
Leacock-Leola-Bareville, Pa, US 196/B3
Lead, SD, US 185/H4
Leader, Sk, Can. 184/F3
Leader Water (riv.), Sc, UK 94/D5
Leadon (riv.), Eng, UK 90/D3
Leadville, Co, US 190/B2
Leaf (riv.), Ms, US 191/F4
Leaghur (lake), Austl. 173/B2
League City, Tx, US 187/H5
Leakey, Tx, US 187/H5
Leam (riv.), Eng, UK 91/E2
Leamington, On, Can. 188/D3
Leander (pt.), Austl. 170/B4
Leaota (peak), Rom. 107/G3
Learmont, Austl. 170/B2
Leatherhead, Eng, UK 88/C3
Leavenworth, Ks, US 195/D5
Leavenworth (co.), Ks, US 195/D5
Leavenworth, Wa, US 184/C4
Leawood, Ks, US 195/D6
Leba, Pol. 96/G4
Lebach, Ger. 111/F5
Lebak, Phil. 137/D6
Lebane, Serb. 106/E4
Lebanon (ctry.) 149/D3
Lebanon (mts.), Leb. 149/D3
Lebanon, In, US 188/C3
Lebanon, Ky, US 188/C4
Lebanon, Mo, US 187/J4
Lebanon, NH, US 189/F3
Lebanon, NJ, US 196/D2
Lebanon, Or, US 184/C4
Lebanon, Pa, US 196/B3
Lebanon, Tn, US 188/C4
Lebbeke, Belg. 111/D2
Lebedyn, Ukr. 120/E2
Lebel-sur-Quévillon, Qu, Can. 188/E1
Lebene (mts.), Mor. 158/B2
Lébény, Hun. 106/C2
Lębork, Pol. 96/G4
Lebrija, Sp. 102/B4
Lebu, Chile 215/B4
Lebu, Chile 216/B3
Leça da Palmeira, Port. 102/A2
Lecce, It. 105/F2
Lecco, It. 116/C1
Lecco (prov.), It. 116/C1
Lecco, Lago di (lake), It. 116/C1
Lech, Aus. 115/G3
Lech (riv.), Ger. 101/K2
Lechang, China 141/K2
Lechbruck, Ger. 115/G2
Leche (lake), Cuba 203/G1
Lechtaler Alps (mts.), Aus. 115/G3
Leck, Ger. 96/C4
Lectoure, Fr. 100/D5
Łęczna, Pol. 99/M3
Leda (riv.), Ger. 109/E2
Ledang (peak), Malay. 138/B3
Lede, Belg. 110/C2
Ledegem, Belg. 110/C2
Ledesma, Sp. 102/B2
Ledge Point, Austl. 170/B4
Ledong, China 141/J4

Ledro (lake), It. 115/G6
Ledu (peak), It. 115/F5
Leduc, Ab, Can. 184/E2
Lee (riv.), Ire. 89/P11
Lee (mtn.), Pa, US 196/B1
Leech (lake), Mn, US 185/K4
Leeds, Eng, UK 93/G4
Leeds (co.), Eng, UK 93/G4
Leeds and Bradford (int'l arpt.), Eng, UK 93/G4
Leeds and Liverpool (canal), Eng, UK 93/G4
Leeds Point, NJ, US 196/D5
Leegebruch, Ger. 98/O6
Leek, Neth. 108/D2
Leek, Eng, UK 93/F5
Leeman, Austl. 170/B4
Leer, Ger. 109/E2
Leerdam, Neth. 108/C5
Leersum, Neth. 108/C4
Lees Summit, Mo, US 195/E6
Leesburg, Fl, US 191/H4
Leesburg, NJ, US 196/D5
Leese, Ger. 109/G3
Leesport, Pa, US 196/C3
Leesville, La, US 187/J5
Leeton, Austl. 173/C2
Leeu (riv.), SAfr. 164/L10
Leeudoringstad, SAfr. 164/D2
Leeuwarden, Neth. 108/C2
Leeuwin (cape), Austl. 170/B5
Leeuwin-Naturaliste NP, Austl. 170/B5
Leeward (isls.), NAm. 199/J4
Leff (riv.), Fr. 100/B2
Lefka, Cyp. 149/C2
Lefo (peak), Camr. 161/H5
Lefroy (lake), Austl. 170/D4
Legana, Austl. 173/C4
Leganés, Sp. 103/N9
Legaspi, Phil. 137/D5
Legau, Ger. 115/G2
Legazpia, Sp. 102/D1
Legges Tor (peak), Austl. 173/C4
Legionowo, Pol. 99/L2
Léglise, Fr. 111/E4
Legnago, It. 117/E2
Legnano, It. 101/H4
Legnaro, It. 117/E2
Legnica, Pol. 99/J3
Legnone (peak), It. 115/F5
Leh, India 144/D2
Leh Palace, India 144/D2
Lehi, Ut, US 195/K13
Lehigh (co.), Pa, US 196/C2
Lehigh Acres, Fl, US 191/H5
Lehighton, Pa, US 196/C2
Lehinch, Ire. 89/P10
Lehrberg, Ger. 112/D4
Lehrte, Ger. 109/G4
Lei (riv.), China 141/K2
Leiah, Pak. 144/A4
Leiblfing, Ger. 113/F5
Leibo, China 141/H2
Leicester, Eng, UK 91/E1
Leicester (co.), Eng, UK 91/E1
Leicestershire (co.), Eng, UK 93/H6
Leichhardt (dam), Austl. 171/H2
Leichhardt (riv.), Austl. 167/C2
Leichlingen, Ger. 111/G1
Leiden, Neth. 108/B4
Leiderdorp, Neth. 108/B4
Leidschendam, Neth. 108/B4
Leie (riv.), Belg. 100/E1
Leifers (Laives), It. 101/J3
Leigh, Eng, UK 93/F5
Leigh Creek, Austl. 171/H4
Leimebamba, Peru 214/B2
Leimen, Ger. 112/B4
Leimersheim, Ger. 112/B4
Leine (riv.), Ger. 98/D3
Leinefelde, Ger. 109/H6
Leinfelden-Echterdingen, Ger. 112/C5
Leinster (mt.), Ire. 89/Q10
Leinster, Austl. 170/D3
Leinster (reg.), Ire. 92/A5
Leipheim, Ger. 112/D6
Leipsic, De, US 196/C5
Leipsic (riv.), De, US 196/C5
Leipzig, Ger. 98/G3
Leiria, Port. 102/A3
Leiria (dist.), Port. 102/A3
Leisler (mt.), Austl. 170/F3
Leith (hill), Eng, UK 88/B3
Leitha (riv.), Aus. 101/K2
Leixlip, Ire. 92/B5
Leizhou (pen.), China 141/J3
Lek (riv.), Neth. 98/C3
Le Kef (gov.), Tun. 158/L6
Le Kef, Tun. 158/L6
Lekhainá, Gre. 105/G4
Lekki (lag.), Nga. 161/G5
Lekkerkerk, Neth. 108/B5
Leksands-Noret, Swe. 96/F1
Leksozero (lake), Rus. 95/M3
Lelai (cape), Indo. 139/G3
Leland, Ms, US 187/K4
Leláng (lake), Swe. 96/E2

Leling, China 130/D3
Lelystad, Neth. 108/C3
Lem, Den. 96/C3
Lema (peak), It. 115/E5
Léman (Geneva) (lake), Fr. 101/G3
Lemberg (peak), Ger. 115/E1
Lembu (peak), Indo. 138/A3
Leme, Braz. 213/B2
Lemenjoen NP, Fin. 95/H1
Lemgo, Ger. 109/F4
Lemland (isl.), Fin. 97/H2
Lemland, Fin. 97/J1
Lemmer, Neth. 108/C3
Lemmon, SD, US 185/H4
Lemon Grove, Ca, US 194/C5
Lempa (riv.), ESal. 202/D3
Lempäälä, Fin. 97/K1
Lempdes, Fr. 100/E4
Lemva (riv.), Rus. 119/P2
Lemvig, Den. 96/C3
Lemwerder, Ger. 109/F2
Lena (riv.), Rus. 125/M3
Lena, Nor. 96/D1
Lenape, Ks, US 195/D6
Lenape (lake), NJ, US 196/D5
Lençóis Maranhenses, PN dos, Braz. 209/K4
Lençóis Paulista, Braz. 213/B2
Lendinara, It. 117/E2
Lenexa, Ks, US 195/D6
Lenggries, Ger. 115/H2
Lengnau, Swi. 114/D3
Lengshuitan, China 141/K2
Lengua de Vaca (pt.), Chile 215/B3
Lenhartsville, Pa, US 196/C2
Lenina (peak), Taj. 145/F3
Leninabad (int'l arpt.), Taj. 145/E2
Leningradskaya Oblast, Rus. 118/G3
Leninobod (obl.), Taj. 145/E5
Leninogorsk, Rus. 119/M5
Leninsk-Kuznetskiy, Rus. 122/J4
Leninváros, Hun. 99/L5
Lenk, Swi. 114/D5
Lenne (riv.), Ger. 111/G1
Lennestadt, Ger. 109/F6
Lennox (isl.), Chile 217/D7
Lennox (hills), Sc, UK 94/B4
Lennoxtown, Sc, UK 94/B5
Leno, It. 116/D2
Lenoir, NC, US 191/H3
Lenoir City, Tn, US 191/G3
Lenola, It. 104/C2
Lens, Swi. 114/D5
Lens, Belg. 110/C2
Lensahn, Ger. 96/D4
Lensk, Rus. 123/M3
Lenting, Ger. 113/E5
Lenvik, Nor. 95/G2
Leny, Pass of (pass), Sc, UK 94/B4
Lenzburg, Swi. 114/E3
Lenzing, Aus. 113/G7
Lenzkirch, Ger. 115/E2
Léo, Burk. 161/E4
Leoben, Aus. 101/L3
Leográ (riv.), It. 117/E1
Leola, SD, US 185/J4
León (int'l arpt.), Mex. 200/E4
León, Nic. 202/E3
León, Sp. 102/C1
León (riv.), Tx, US 190/D4
León, Étang de (lake), Fr. 100/C4
Leon-Guanajuato (int'l arpt.), Mex. 201/E4
Leon Springs, Tx, US 195/T20
Leon Valley, Tx, US 195/T21
Leona Valley, Ca, US 194/B1
Leonard, Mi, US 193/F6
Leonardo, NJ, US 197/J10
Leonardo da Vinci (int'l arpt.), It. 104/C2
Leonberg, Ger. 112/C5
Leonding, Aus. 113/H6
Leone (peak), It. 114/E5
Leones, Arg. 216/E2
Leonforte, It. 104/D4
Leongatha, Austl. 173/C3
Leonia, NJ, US 197/K8
Leonídhion, Gre. 105/H4
Leonora, Austl. 170/D4
Leopoldina, Braz. 213/L6
Leopoldkanaal (canal), Belg. 110/C1
Leopoldsburg, Belg. 110/C1
Leopoldsdorf, Aus. 107/H5
Leopoldsdorf im Marchfelde, Aus. 107/H4
Leopoldshöhe, Ger. 109/F4
Leoville, Sk, Can. 184/G2
Lepaera, Hon. 202/D3

Lépanges-sur-Vologne, Fr. 114/C1
Lepe, Sp. 102/B4
Lepenoú, Gre. 105/G3
L'Epiphanie, Qu, Can. 189/P6
Lepontine Alps (mts.), Swi. 101/H3
Leptokariá, Gre. 105/H2
Léraba (riv.), Burk. 160/D4
Lercara Friddi, It. 104/C4
Lerdo de Tejada, Mex. 202/C2
Leribe, Les. 164/E3
Lerici, It. 116/D3
Lerín, Sp. 102/E1
Lerma, Mex. 201/Q10
Lerma (riv.), Mex. 200/D4
Lermoos, Aus. 115/G3
Lérouville, Fr. 111/E6
Lerum, Swe. 96/E3
Lerwick, Sc, UK 89/W13
Léry (lake), La, US 195/O17
Léry, Qu, Can. 189/N7
Les Alluets-le-Roi, Fr. 88/H5
Les Bois, Swi. 114/C3
Les Breuleux, Swi. 114/D3
Les Brévaires, Fr. 88/H5
Les Cayes, Haiti 203/H2
Les Cèdres, Qu, Can. 189/M7
Les Clayes-sous-Bois, Fr. 88/H5
Les Contamines-Montjoie, Fr. 114/C6
Les Diablerets (range), Swi. 114/D5
Les Essarts-le-Roi, Fr. 88/H5
Les Gets, Fr. 114/C5
Les Hautes-Rivières, Fr. 111/D4
Les Herbiers, Fr. 100/C3
Les Islettes, Fr. 111/E5
Les Mesnuls, Fr. 88/H5
Les Molières, Fr. 88/J6
Les Mureaux, Fr. 88/H4
Les Ponts-de-Martel, Swi. 114/C4
Les Rousses, Fr. 114/C5
Les Sables-d'Olonne, Fr. 100/C3
Les Salines (int'l arpt.), Alg. 158/K6
Les Ulis, Fr. 88/J5
Les Verrières, Swi. 114/C4
Lesa, It. 116/B1
Leshan, China 141/H2
Lésigny, Fr. 88/K5
Lesima (peak), It. 116/C3
Lesja, Nor. 95/D3
Lesjöfors, Swe. 96/F2
Lesko, Pol. 99/M4
Leskovac, Serb. 106/E4
Leslie, Sc, UK 94/C4
Lesmahagow, Sc, UK 94/C5
Lesneven, Fr. 100/A2
Lesnica, Serb. 106/D3
L'gov, Rus. 120/F2
Lesosibirsk, Rus. 122/J4
Lesotho (ctry.) 164/E6
Lesozavodsk, Rus. 129/P2
Lesparre-Médoc, Fr. 100/C4
Lesquin (int'l arpt.), Fr. 110/C2
Lesse (riv.), Belg. 98/C3
Lessebo, Swe. 96/F3
Lesser Antilles (isls.), NAm. 199/M8
Lesser Caucasus (mts.), Asia 121/G4
Lesser Slave (lake), Ab, Can. 180/E3
Lesser Sunda (isls.), Indo. 139/E5
Lessines, Belg. 110/C2
Lesung (peak), Indo. 138/D3
Lésvos (isl.), Gre. 105/J3
Leszno, Pol. 99/J3
Létavértes, Hun. 106/E2
Letchworth, Eng, UK 91/F3
Letham, Sc, UK 94/D4
Lethbridge, Ab, Can. 184/E3
Lethe (riv.), Ger. 109/F2
Lethem, Guy. 211/G4
Leti (isls.), Indo. 139/G5
Leticia, Col. 214/D2
Leting, China 130/D3
Letlhakane, Bots. 163/E6
Letlhakeng, Bots. 163/D5
Letnitsa, Bul. 107/G4
Letpadan, Myan. 141/G4
Letsôk-Aw (isl.), Myan. 138/A1
Letterkenny, Ire. 89/O9
Leucate, Fr. 100/E5
Leuchars, Sc, UK 94/D4
Leuk, Swi. 114/D5
Leukerbad, Swi. 114/D5
Leun, Ger. 112/B2
Leusden-Zuid, Neth. 108/C4
Leuser (peak), Indo. 138/A3
Leutenhausen, Ger. 115/G2
Leutkirch im Allgäu, Ger. 115/G2
Leuze-en-Hainaut, Belg. 110/C2
Levádhia, Gre. 105/H3
Levallois-Perret, Fr. 88/J5
Levanger, Nor. 95/D3
Levante, Riviera di (coast), It. 116/C4
Lévanto, It. 116/C4
Levasy, Mo, US 195/E6
Level (isl.), Chile 216/B5
Level, Md, US 196/B4

Levelland, Tx, US 187/G4
Levelock, Ak, US 192/G4
Leven (pt.), SAfr. 165/F2
Leven, Sc, UK 94/D4
Leven (riv.), Sc, UK 94/C4
Leven (lake), Sc, UK 94/A3
Leverburgh, Sc, UK 89/Q8
Leverkusen, Ger. 111/F1
Levice, Slvk. 106/D1
Levico Terme, It. 115/H5
Levier, Fr. 114/C3
Levin, NZ 175/T11
Lévis-Saint-Nom, Fr. 88/H5
Levittown, Pa, US 196/D3
Levittown, NY, US 197/L9
Levkás, Gre. 105/G3
Levkás (isl.), Gre. 105/G3
Levkímmi, Gre. 105/G3
Levoča, Slvk. 99/L4
Levrier (bay), Mrta. 156/A5
Levski, Bul. 107/G4
Lewes, Eng, UK 91/G5
Lewin Brzeski, Pol. 99/J3
Lewis (riv.), Wa, US 184/C4
Lewis (range), Mt, US 184/E3
Lewis (hills), Nf, Can. 189/K1
Lewis (pass), NZ 175/S11
Lewis (isl.), Sc, UK 89/O7
Lewis and Clark (lake), Ne,SD, US 185/J5
Lewis Smith (lake), Al, US 191/G3
Lewisburg, Tn, US 191/G3
Lewisburg, WV, US 188/D4
Lewisburg, Pa, US 196/B2
Lewisham (bor.), Eng, UK 88/C2
Lewisporte, Nf, Can. 189/L1
Lewiston, Id, US 184/D4
Lewiston, Me, US 189/G2
Lewiston, NY, US 189/R9
Lewistown, Mt, US 184/F4
Lewistown, Pa, US 188/E3
Lewotobi (peak), Indo. 139/F5
Lexington, Ky, US 188/C4
Lexington, NC, US 191/H3
Lexington, Ne, US 185/J5
Lexington, Tn, US 188/B5
Lexington Park, Md, US 188/E4
Leyburn, Eng, UK 93/G3
Leyden, Co, US 195/B3
Leye, China 141/J3
Leyland, Eng, UK 93/F4
Leysin, Swi. 114/D5
Leytron, Swi. 114/D5
Lez (riv.), Fr. 100/F4
Łężajsk, Pol. 99/M3
Lezhë, Alb. 105/F2
Lézignan-Corbières, Fr. 100/E5
Lezuza, Sp. 102/D3
Lhanbryd, Sc, UK 94/C1
Lhari, China 128/F5
Lhasa, China 140/F2
Lhazê, China 140/E2
L'Hongrin (lake), Swi. 114/D5
Lhorong, China 128/G5
L'Hospitalet de Llobregat, Sp. 103/L7
Lhozhag, China 143/H1
Lhünzê, China 141/G2
Li (riv.), China 137/B2
Li (riv.), China 141/K2
Li (mtn.), China 130/B4
Li (riv.), China 141/K2
Li Xian, China 137/B3
Lian (riv.), China 137/B3
Lian Xian, China 141/K3
Liancheng, China 137/C2
Liancourt, Fr. 110/B5
Liancourt Rocks (isl.), Asia 130/C2
Liangcheng, China 132/B2
Liangpran (peak), Indo. 138/D3
Liangzi (lake), China 130/C5
Lianhua, China 137/C2
Lianjiang, China 137/C2
Lianjiang, China 141/K3
Liannan Yaozu Zizhixian, China 137/B3
Lianshui, China 137/B2
Lianyuan, China 137/B2
Lianyungang, China 130/D4
Liao (riv.), China 125/M5
Liaocheng, China 130/C3
Liaodong (pen.), China 131/E3
Liaodong (isls.), China 130/E3
Liaodong, Gulf of (gulf), China 129/M3
Liaoning (prov.), China 129/M3
Liaoyang, China 129/N3
Liaoyuan, China 129/N3
Liaozhong, China 130/E3
Liard (riv.), NW, Can. 180/D2
Libenge, D.R. Congo 155/J7
Libercourt, Fr. 110/C2
Liberdade (riv.), Braz. 209/H6
Liberdade, Braz. 213/J7
Liberec, Czh. 99/H3
Liberecký (pol. reg.), Czh. 99/H3

Liber – Loppi

Liberia, CR 203/E4
Liberia (ctry.) 160/C5
Libertad, Belz. 202/D2
Libertad, Ven. 210/D2
Libertad, Uru. 217/K11
Libertador General San Martín, Arg. 215/D1
Liberty, Ky, US 188/C4
Liberty (res.), Md, US 196/B5
Liberty, Ms, US 187/K5
Liberty, Mo, US 195/E5
Liberty, Tx, US 187/J5
Liberty, Ut, US 195/K11
Liberty Grove, Md, US 196/B4
Libertyville, Il, US 193/P15
Libin, Belg. 111/E4
Libo, China 141/J2
Libobo (cape), Indo. 139/G4
Liboc (riv.), Czh. 99/G3
Libochovice, Czh. 113/H2
Libon, Phil. 137/D5
Librazhd, Alb. 105/G2
Libres, Mex. 201/M7
Libreville (cap.), Gabon 154/G7
Libya (ctry.) 154/J2
Libyan (plat.), Libya 155/K1
Libyan (des.), Egypt,Libya 155/K2
Licantén, Chile 216/B2
Licata, It. 104/C4
Lice, Turk. 148/E2
Lich, Ger. 112/B1
Licheng, China 130/C3
Licheng, China 130/D3
Lichfield, Eng, UK 91/E1
Lichinga, Moz. 163/G3
Lichtenau, Ger. 109/F5
Lichtenau, Ger. 112/D4
Lichtenau, Ger. 112/B5
Lichtenburg, SAfr. 164/D2
Lichtenfels, Ger. 112/D2
Lichtenrade, Ger. 98/Q7
Lichtensteig, Swi. 115/F3
Lichtenvoorde, Neth. 108/D5
Lichtervelde, Belg. 110/C1
Lichuan, China 137/A1
Licinio de Almeida, Braz. 212/B4
Lick Observatory, Ca, US 193/L12
Licking (riv.), Ky, US 188/C4
Licosa (cape), It. 104/D2
Licques, Fr. 110/A2
Lida, Bela. 97/L5
Liddell Water (riv.), Sc, UK 93/F1
Liddes, Swi. 114/D6
Liddon (gulf), NW, Can. 181/R7
Lidhorikíon, Gre. 105/H3
Lidingö, Swe. 96/H2
Lidköping, Swe. 96/E2
Lido, It. 117/F2
Lido di Iesolo, It. 117/F1
Lido di Ostia, It. 104/C2
Lidzbark, Pol. 99/K2
Lidzbark Warmiński, Pol. 97/J4
Liebenau, Aus. 113/H5
Liebenbergsvlei (riv.), SAfr. 164/E2
Liebig (mt.), Austl. 171/F2
Liechtenstein (ctry.) 115/F3
Liedekerke, Belg. 111/D2
Liège, Belg. 111/E2
Liège (prov.), Belg. 111/E3
Lieksa, Fin. 118/F3
Lienden, Neth. 108/C5
Lienen, Ger. 109/E4
Lienz, Aus. 101/K3
Liepāja, Lat. 97/J3
Lier, Belg. 111/D1
Lierneux, Belg. 111/E3
Lieser (riv.), Ger. 111/F3
Liesjärven NP, Fin. 97/K1
Liesse-Notre-Dame, Fr. 110/C4
Liestal, Swi. 114/D3
Lieto, Fin. 97/K1
Liévin, Fr. 110/B3
Lièvre (riv.), Qu, Can. 188/F2
Liez (lake), Fr. 114/B2
Liezen, Aus. 101/L3
Liffey (riv.), Ire. 92/B5
Liffol-le-Grand, Fr. 114/B1
Lifford, Ire. 89/Q9
Ligao, Phil. 139/F1
Lightning Ridge, Austl. 173/C1
Lightwater, Eng, UK 88/B3
Lignano Sabbiadoro, It. 117/G1
Ligny-en-Barrois, Fr. 111/E6
Ligoncio (peak), It. 115/F5
Ligoúrion, Gre. 105/H4
Liguori, Mo, US 195/G9
Liguria (pol. reg.), It. 116/B4
Liguria (prov), It. 101/H4
Ligurian (sea), Fr.,It. 101/H5
Lihou (reefs), Austl. 167/E2
Lihue, Hi, US 182/S10
Lijiang Naxizu Zizhixian, China 141/H2
Lijin, China 130/D3
Likasi, D.R. Congo 163/E3
Likely, BC, Can. 184/C2
Likoma (isl.), Malw. 163/F3
Likouala (riv.), Congo 154/H7
Likova (riv.), Rus. 119/W9
L'Île-Perrot, Qu, Can. 189/N7
L'Île-Rousse, Fr. 104/A1
Liliāni, Pak. 144/B3
Lilienthal, Ger. 109/F2
Liling, China 141/K2
Lilla Edet, Swe. 96/E2
Lille, Belg. 108/B6
Lille, Fr. 110/C2
Lille Bælt (chan.), Ger. 96/C4
Lillehammer, Nor. 96/D1
Lillers, Fr. 110/B2
Lillesand, Nor. 96/C2
Lillestrøm, Nor. 96/D2
Lilliwaup, Wa, US 193/A3
Lillo, Sp. 102/D3
Lillooet, BC, Can. 184/C3
Lillooet (riv.), BC, Can. 184/C3
Lilongwe (cap.), Malw. 163/F3
Liloy, Phil. 137/D6
Lim (riv.), Serb. 106/D4
Lima, Arg. 217/J11
Lima (riv.), It. 117/D4
Lima (cap.), Peru 214/B4
Lima (dept.), Peru 214/B3
Lima (riv.), Port. 103/A2
Lima, Oh, US 188/C3
Lima Duarte, Braz. 213/K6
Limache, Chile 216/N8
Limanowa, Pol. 99/L4
Limassol, Cyp. 149/C2
Limassol (dist.), Cyp. 149/C2
Limavady (dist.), NI, UK 92/A2
Limavady, NI, UK 92/B1
Limay (riv.), Arg. 216/C4
Limbach, Ger. 112/C4
Limbani, Peru 214/D4
Limbara (peak), It. 104/A2
Limbdi, India 147/K4
Limbé, Haiti 203/H2
Limbiate, It. 116/C1
Limbourg, Belg. 111/E2
Limburg (prov.), Belg. 111/E1
Limburg an der Lahn, Ger. 112/B2
Limburgerhof, Ger. 112/B4
Lime Village, Ak, US 192/G3
Limedsforsen, Swe. 96/E1
Limeira, Braz. 213/C2
Limekilns, Sc, UK 94/C4
Limena, It. 117/E2
Limenária, Gre. 105/J2
Limerick, Ire. 89/P10
Limfjorden (chan.), Den. 96/C3
Limidario (peak), It. 115/E5
Limite, It. 117/D5
Limmat (riv.), Swi. 115/E3
Limmen Bight (bay), Austl. 167/C2
Límni, Gre. 105/H3
Límnos (isl.), Gre. 105/J3
Limoeiro, Braz. 212/D2
Limoeiro do Norte, Braz. 212/C2
Limoges, Fr. 100/D4
Limogne, Causse de (plat.), Fr. 100/D4
Limón, CR 203/F4
Limón, Hon. 203/E3
Limours, Fr. 88/J6
Limousin (mts.), Fr. 100/D4
Limousin (pol. reg.), Fr. 100/D4
Limoux, Fr. 100/E5
Limpopo (riv.), Moz. 163/F5
Lin Xian, China 130/C3
Lin'an, China 137/C1
Linapacan (isl.), Phil. 137/C5
Linard (peak), Swi. 115/G4
Linares, Mex. 201/F3
Linares, Sp. 102/D3
Linares, Chile 216/C2
Linariá, Gre. 105/J3
Linate (int'l arpt.), It. 116/C2
Lincang, China 141/H3
Lincheng, China 130/C3
Linchuan, China 137/C2
Lincoln, Arg. 216/E2
Lincoln (sea), Can.,Grld. 177/L1
Lincoln, On, Can. 189/R9
Lincoln, Eng, UK 93/H5
Lincoln, De, US 196/C6
Lincoln, Il, US 185/L5
Lincoln, Me, US 189/G2
Lincoln (cap.), Ne, US 185/J5
Lincoln (co.), Ok, US 195/N14
Lincoln, Pa, US 196/B3
Lincoln Beach, Or, US 184/B4
Lincoln City, Or, US 184/B4
Lincoln Heath (woodld.), Eng, UK 93/H5
Lincoln NP, Austl. 171/G5
Lincoln Park, Mi, US 193/F7
Lincoln Park, NJ, US 197/H8
Lincolnshire (co.), Eng, UK 93/H5
Lincolnshire Wolds (grsld.), Eng, UK 93/H4
Lincroft, NJ, US 196/D3
Lind, Den. 96/C3
Lind NP, Austl. 173/D3
Lindau, Ger. 115/F2
Lindau, Swi. 115/E3
Linde (riv.), Neth. 108/D3
Lindeman (chan.), Austl. 172/C3
Linden, Ger. 112/B1
Linden, Guy. 211/G3
Linden, Al, US 191/G3
Linden, NJ, US 197/J9
Linden, Mi, US 193/E6
Linden, Tx, US 187/J4
Linden Beach, On, Can. 193/G7
Lindenberg im Allgäu, Ger. 115/F2
Lindenfels, Ger. 112/B3
Lindenhurst, NY, US 197/E2
Lindenhurst, Il, US 193/P15
Lindenwold, NJ, US 196/D4
Lindern, Ger. 109/E3
Lindesberg, Swe. 96/F2
Lindesnes (cape), Nor. 96/B3
Lindewitt, Ger. 96/C4
Lindhorst, Ger. 109/E5
Líndhos (ruin), Gre. 148/B2
Lindi (pol. reg.), Tanz. 162/C5
Lindi, Tanz. 162/C5
Lindlar, Ger. 111/G1
Lindley, SAfr. 164/D2
Lindome, Swe. 96/E3
Lindon, Ut, US 195/K13
Lindre (lake), Fr. 111/F6
Lindsay, Ca, US 186/C3
Lindsay, On, Can. 188/E2
Lindsay (mt.), Austl. 170/C5
Lindsay (mt.), Austl. 171/F3
Lindsdal, Swe. 96/G3
Line (isls.), Kiri. 175/J4
Line Mountain (mtn.), Pa, US 196/B2
Líneas de Nazca, Peru 214/C4
Lineboro, Md, US 196/B4
Linfen, China 130/B3
Ling (riv.), Sc, UK 94/A2
Ling Xian, China 141/K2
Ling Xian, China 130/D3
Lingbao, China 130/B4
Lingbi, China 130/D4
Lingchuan, China 141/K2
Lingchuan, China 130/C4
Linge (riv.), Neth. 108/C5
Lingen, Ger. 109/E3
Lingfield, Eng, UK 88/C3
Lingga (isls.), Indo. 138/B3
Linglestown, Pa, US 196/B3
Lingolsheim, Fr. 114/D1
Lingqiu, China 130/C3
Lingshan, China 141/J3
Lingshan, China 130/C3
Lingshi, China 130/B3
Lingshui, China 141/J4
Linguère, Sen. 160/B3
Lingyin Si, China 130/L9
Lingyuan, China 130/D2
Lingyun, China 141/J3
Linhai, China 137/D2
Linhares, Braz. 213/D1
Linhe, China 128/J3
Linköping, Swe. 96/F2
Linli, China 137/B2
Linlithgow, Sc, UK 94/C5
Linliu (mtn.), China 130/C3
Linney (pt.), Wal, UK 90/A3
Linnhe (lake), Sc, UK 94/A3
Linnich, Ger. 111/F2
Linntown, Pa, US 196/B2
Linosa (isl.), It. 158/N7
Linqing, China 130/C3
Linqu, China 130/D3
Linquan, China 130/C4
Linru, China 130/C4
Lins, Braz. 213/B2
Linschoten, Neth. 108/B4
Linshu, China 130/D4
Linta (riv.), Madg. 165/H9
Linth (riv.), Swi. 115/F3
Linthal, Swi. 115/F4
Linton, ND, US 185/H4
Linwood, Eng, UK 93/H5
Linwu, China 141/K2
Linxi, China 130/C3
Linyi, China 130/B4
Linyi, China 130/D3
Linyi, China 130/D4
Linying, China 130/C4
Linz (int'l arpt.), Aus. 113/H6
Linz, Aus. 113/H6
Linz am Rhein, Ger. 111/G2
Linzhang, China 130/C3
Lion (gulf), Fr.,Sp. 103/G1
Lipa, Phil. 137/D5
Lipari (isl.), It. 104/D3
Lipari (isls.), It. 104/D3
Lipari, It. 104/D3
Liperi, Fin. 118/F3
Lipetsk, Rus. 120/F1
Lipetsk (int'l arpt.), Rus. 120/F1
Lipetskaya Oblast, Rus. 120/F1
Lipez, Cordillera de (mts.), Bol. 208/E8
Liping, China 141/J2
Lipljan, Kos. 106/E4
Lipno (res.), Czh. 113/H5
Lipno, Pol. 99/K2
Lipno, Údolní nádrž (lake), Czh. 101/L2
Lipova, Rom. 106/E2
Lippe (riv.), Ger. 98/D3
Lippstadt, Ger. 109/F5
Liptovský Svätý Mikuláš, Slvk. 99/K4
Liptrap (cape), Austl. 173/C3
Lira, Ugan. 162/B2
Lircay, Peru 214/C4
Liri (riv.), It. 104/C2
Liria, Sp. 103/E3
Liro (riv.), It. 115/F5
Lisboa (dist.), Port. 102/A3
Lisboa (int'l arpt.), Port. 103/P10
Lisboa (Lisbon) (cap.), Port. 103/P10
Lisbon, ND, US 185/J4
Lisbon, Me, US 189/G2
Lisbon, Md, US 196/A5
Lisburn, NI, UK 92/B2
Lisburn (dist.), NI, UK 92/B3
Lisburne (cape), Ak, US 192/E2
Lisdoonvarna, Ire. 89/P10
Liseleje, Den. 96/D3
Lisha (riv.), China 141/H2
Lishu, China 130/F2
Lishui, China 137/C2
Lisianski (isl.), Hi, US 175/H2
Lisieux, Fr. 100/D2
Liski, Rus. 120/F2
Lisle, Il, US 193/P16
L'Isle-Adam, Fr. 88/J4
L'Isle-en-Dodon, Fr. 100/D5
L'Isle-sur-la-Sorgue, Fr. 100/F5
L'Isle-sur-le-Doubs, Fr. 114/C3
Lisle-sur-Tarn, Fr. 100/D5
Lismore, Austl. 173/E1
Lisnacree, NI, UK 92/B3
Lišov, Czh. 113/H4
Lispeszentadorján, Hun. 106/C2
Lisse, Neth. 108/B4
Lisses, Fr. 88/K6
List, Ger. 96/C4
Lister (riv.), Ger. 109/E6
Listowel, On, Can. 188/D3
Listowel, Ire. 89/P10
Lit. Scarcies (riv.), SLeo. 160/B4
Litang, China 128/H6
Litang (riv.), China 141/H2
Līṭānī (riv.), Leb. 149/D3
Litavka (riv.), Czh. 113/G3
Litchfield, Mn, US 185/K4
Litchfield, Il, US 187/K3
Litchfield Park, Az, US 195/R19
Lith, Neth. 108/C5
Litherland, Eng, UK 93/F5
Lithgow, Austl. 173/D2
Lithuania (ctry.) 97/K4
Litija, Slov. 101/L3
Litiz, Pa, US 196/B3
Litókhoron, Gre. 105/H2
Litoměřice, Czh. 113/H1
Littabella NP, Austl. 172/D4
Littau, Swi. 115/E3
Little (riv.), Ar, US 187/J4
Little (riv.), Ga, US 191/H4
Little (riv.), Tx, US 190/D4
Little (riv.), NC, US 191/J3
Little (riv.), Ok, US 195/N15
Little Abitibi (riv.), On, Can. 188/D1
Little Andaman (isl.), India 141/F5
Little Belt (mts.), Mt, US 184/F4
Little Bighorn Battlefield Nat'l Mon., Mt, US 184/G4
Little Bitter (lake), Egypt 149/C4
Little Blue (riv.), Ks,Ne, US 187/H2
Little Calumet (riv.), Il, US 193/Q16
Little Cayman (isl.), Cay. 199/E4
Little Colorado (riv.), Az, US 186/E4
Little Creek, De, US 196/C5
Little Cumbrae (isl.), Sc, UK 94/A5
Little Current (riv.), On, Can. 185/M3
Little Current, On, Can. 188/D2
Little Desert NP, Austl. 173/B3
Little Diomede (isl.), Ak, US 192/E2
Little Egg (har.), NJ, US 196/D4
Little Falls, Mn, US 185/K4
Little Falls, NJ, US 197/J8
Little Ferry, NJ, US 197/J8
Little Fork (riv.), Mn, US 185/K3
Little Inagua (isl.), Bahm. 199/G3
Little Karoo (valley), SAfr. 164/C4
Little Lehigh (riv.), Pa, US 196/C3
Little Minch (str.), Sc, UK 89/Q8
Little Missouri (riv.), Ar, US 187/J4
Little Neck (bay), NY, US 197/K8
Little Nicobar (isl.), India 141/F6
Little Para (res.), Austl. 171/M8
Little Para (riv.), Austl. 171/M8
Little Patuxent (riv.), Md, US 196/B5
Little Peconic (bay), NY, US 197/F2
Little Platte (riv.), Mo, US 195/D5
Little Prairie, Wi, US 193/N14
Little Red (riv.), Ar, US 187/J4
Little Rock (cap.), Ar, US 187/J4
Little Schuylkill (riv.), Pa, US 196/B2
Little Sioux (riv.), Ia, US 185/K5
Little Smoky (riv.), Ab, Can. 184/D2
Little Snake (riv.), Co, US 186/E2
Little Stour (riv.), Eng, UK 91/H4
Little Wabash (riv.), Il, US 187/K3
Little White (riv.), SD, US 187/G2
Little Wood (riv.), Id, US 184/E5
Little Zab (riv.), Iraq 148/E3
Littleborough, Eng, UK 93/F4
Littlefield, Tx, US 187/G4
Littlehampton, Eng, UK 91/F5
Littlerock, Ca, US 194/C1
Littlestown, Pa, US 196/A4
Littleton, NH, US 189/G2
Littleton, Co, US 195/B3
Litvínov, Czh. 113/G1
Liu (riv.), China 137/A3
Liu (riv.), China 130/E2
Liuba, China 128/J5
Liucheng, China 141/J3
Liulin, China 130/B3
Liuwa Plain NP, Zam. 163/D3
Liuyang, China 141/K2
Liuzhou, China 141/J3
Livádhion, Gre. 105/H2
Livanátai, Gre. 105/H3
Live Oak, Fl, US 191/H4
Live Oak, Tx, US 195/U20
Livengood, Ak, US 192/J2
Livenza (riv.), It. 117/F2
Liverdun, Fr. 111/F6
Livermore (mt.), Tx, US 187/F5
Liverpool (cape), Nun., Can. 181/J1
Liverpool, NS, Can. 189/H2
Liverpool (bay), NW, Can. 180/C1
Liverpool, Eng, UK 93/F5
Liverpool (co.), Eng, UK 93/F5
Liverpool (bay), Wal, UK 93/E5
Liverpool, Pa, US 196/B2
Livigno, It. 115/G4
Livilliers, Fr. 88/J4
Livingston, Guat. 202/D3
Livingston, Sc, UK 94/C5
Livingston (co.), Mi, US 193/E6
Livingston, Mt, US 184/F4
Livingston, NJ, US 197/H8
Livingston, Tx, US 187/J5
Livingston (lake), Tx, US 187/J5
Livingstone, Zam. 163/E4
Livingstone (falls), Congo 163/B2
Livingstone (range), Ab, Can. 184/E3
Livno, Bosn. 106/C4
Livny, Rus. 120/F1
Livojoki (riv.), Fin. 95/H2
Livonia, Mi, US 188/D3
Livorno (prov.), It. 116/D6
Livorno, It. 116/D5
Livorno Ferraris, It. 116/B2
Livramento do Brumado, Braz. 212/B4
Livron-sur-Drôme, Fr. 100/F4
Livry-Gargan, Fr. 88/K5
Lixin, China 130/D4
Lixnaw, Ire. 89/P10
Lixoúrion, Gre. 105/G3
Lixus (ruin), Mor. 158/A2
Liyang, China 130/D5
Lizard (pt.), Eng, UK 90/A7
Lizard, The (pen.), Eng, UK 90/A6
Lizy-sur-Ourcq, Fr. 110/C5
Ljubic, Serb. 106/E4
Ljubija, Bosn. 106/C3
Ljubinje, Bosn. 105/F1
Ljubljana (cap.), Slov. 101/L3
Ljubuški, Bosn. 105/E1
Ljungan (riv.), Swe. 95/F3
Ljungby, Swe. 96/E3
Ljungsbro, Swe. 96/F2
Ljungskile, Swe. 96/D2
Ljusnan (riv.), Swe. 95/E3
Ljusne, Swe. 96/G1
Ljusterø (isl.), Swe. 97/H2
Lkst (peak), Mor. 156/C3
Llabanere (int'l arpt.), Fr. 100/E5
Llaillay, Chile 216/N8
Llaima (vol.), Chile 216/C3
Llallagua, Bol. 208/E7
Llalli, Peru 214/D4
Llanberis, Pass of (pass), Wal, UK 92/D5
Llancañelo (lake), Arg. 216/C2
Llandovery, Wal, UK 90/C3
Llandrindod Wells, Wal, UK 90/C2
Llandudno, Wal, UK 92/E5
Llanes, Sp. 102/C1
Llanfairfechan, Wal, UK 92/E5
Llangollen, Wal, UK 93/E6
Llanidloes, Wal, UK 90/C2
Llano (riv.), Tx, US 187/H5
Llano, Tx, US 187/H5
Llano Estacado (plain), US 187/G4
Llanos (plain), Col.,Ven. 210/D3
Llanquihue (lake), Chile 216/B4
Llata, Peru 214/B3
Lleida, Sp. 103/F2
Llera de Canales, Mex. 201/F4
Llerena, Sp. 102/B3
Lleyn (pen.), Wal, UK 92/D6
Llivia, Sp. 103/F1
Llobregat (riv.), Sp. 103/F1
Llodio, Sp. 102/D1
Lloret de Mar, Sp. 103/G2
Llorona (pt.), CR 198/E6
Lloyd (pt.), NY, US 197/M8
Lloyd Harbor, NY, US 197/M8
Lloydminster, Sk, Can. 184/F2
Lloyds (riv.), Nf, Can. 189/K1
Lluchmayor, Sp. 103/G3
Llullaillaco (vol.), Arg.,Chile 215/C1
Llwchwr (riv.), Wal, UK 90/B3
Llynfi (riv.), Wal, UK 90/C3
Loa (riv.), Chile 208/E8
Loa, Ut, US 186/E3
Loanhead, Sc, UK 94/C5
Loano, It. 116/B4
Loaoya (canal), Sp. 103/N8
Lobbes, Belg. 111/D3
Lobería, Arg. 216/F3
Lobethal, Austl. 171/M8
Lobez, Pol. 99/H2
Lobito, Ang. 163/B3
Lobitos, Peru 214/A2
Lobo (riv.), C.d'Iv. 160/D5
Lobos, Arg. 217/J11
Lobos de Tierra, Isla (isl.), Peru 208/B5
Lobos, Punta de (pt.), Chile 216/M9
Locarno, Swi. 115/E5
Loch na Sealga (lake), Sc, UK 94/A1
Loch Raven (res.), Md, US 196/B5
Lochaber (reg.), Sc, UK 94/A3
Locharbriggs, Sc, UK 92/E1
Lochau, Aus. 115/F2
Lochboisdale, Sc, UK 89/Q8
Lochbuie, Co, US 195/C2
Lochem, Neth. 108/D4
Loches, Fr. 100/D3
Lochgelly, Sc, UK 94/C4
Lochgilphead, Sc, UK 94/A4
Lochindorb (lake), Sc, UK 94/C2
Lochmaben, Sc, UK 92/E1
Lochmaddy, Sc, UK 89/Q8
Łochów, Pol. 99/L2
Lochristi, Belg. 110/C1
Lochwinnoch, Sc, UK 94/B5
Lochy (lake), Sc, UK 94/B3
Lochy (riv.), Sc, UK 94/B3
Lock, Austl. 171/G5
Lock Haven, Pa, US 188/E3
Locke, Ca, US 193/L10
Lockerbie, Sc, UK 93/E1
Lockhart, Austl. 173/C2
Lockington, Austl. 173/C3
Locknitz (riv.), Ger. 98/F2
Lockport, NY, US 189/S9
Lockport, Il, US 193/P16
Lockwood (res.), Eng, UK 88/C2
Locon, Fr. 110/B2
Locri, It. 104/E3
Locumba, Peru 214/D5
Locust Fork (riv.), Al, US 191/G3
Lod, Isr. 149/F8
Loddon (riv.), Austl. 173/A1
Loddon (riv.), Eng, UK 91/E4
Lodenice (riv.), Czh. 113/H2
Lodève, Fr. 100/E5
Lodeynoye Pole, Rus. 118/G3
Lodhrān, Pak. 144/A5
Lodi, It. 116/C2
Lodi (prov.), It. 116/C2
Lodi, Ca, US 186/B3
Lodi, NJ, US 197/J8
Lodi Vecchio, It. 116/C2
Lodja, D.R. Congo 163/D1
Lodosa, Sp. 102/D1
Lodrino, Swi. 115/E5
Łódź, Pol. 99/K3
Łodzkie (prov.), Pol. 99/K3
Loei, Thai. 136/C2
Loenen, Neth. 108/C4
Loeriesfontein, SAfr. 164/B3
Lofa (co.), Libr. 160/C5
Lofa (riv.), Libr. 160/C5
Löffingen, Ger. 115/E2
Lofoten (isle.), Nor. 95/D2
Lofty (range), Austl. 170/C3
Lofty (mt.), Austl. 171/M8
Logan (mt.), Yk, Can. 192/K3
Logan, NM, US 190/C3
Logan, Oh, US 188/D4
Logan (co.), Ok, US 195/N14
Logan, Ut, US 184/F5
Logan, WV, US 188/D4
Logansport, In, US 188/C3
Loganton, Pa, US 196/A1
Loganville, Pa, US 196/B4
Logatec, Slov. 101/L4
Logone (riv.), Chad 154/J6
Lograto, It. 116/D2
Logroño, Sp. 102/D1
Logrosán, Sp. 102/C3
Løgstør, Den. 96/C3
Løgten, Den. 96/D3
Lohals, Den. 96/D4
Lohārdaga, India 143/E4
Lohfelden, Ger. 109/G6
Lohja, Fin. 97/L1
Lohjanjärvi (lake), Fin. 97/K1
Lohmar, Ger. 111/G2
Löhnberg, Ger. 112/B1
Lohne, Ger. 109/F3
Löhne, Ger. 109/F4
Lohr, Ger. 112/C3
Loi-kaw, Myan. 141/G4
Loi Lun (range), China,Myan. 128/G7
Loing (riv.), Fr. 98/B5
Loir (riv.), Fr. 100/D3
Loire (riv.), Fr. 100/C3
Loisin (riv.), Fr. 111/E5
Loita (hills), Kenya 155/N8
Loja (prov.), Ecu. 214/B2
Loja, Ecu. 214/B2
Loja, Sp. 102/C4
Løjt Kirkeby, Den. 96/C4
Lokeren, Belg. 110/D1
Lokitaung, Kenya 162/B1
Løkken, Den. 96/C3
Lokoja, Nga. 161/G5
Lokolo (riv.), D.R. Congo 155/K8
Lokomby, Madg. 165/H8
Lokoro (riv.), D.R. Congo 155/J8
Lökösháza, Hun. 106/E2
Lokossa, Ben. 161/F5
Loks (isl.), Nun., Can. 181/K2
Lol (riv.), Sudan 155/L6
Lolland (isl.), Den. 95/D5
Lollar, Ger. 112/B3
Lolo (peak), Mt, US 184/E4
Lolui (isl.), Ugan. 162/B3
Lom, Nor. 95/D3
Lom Sak, Thai. 136/C2
Loma (mts.), SLeo. 154/C6
Loma (pt.), Ca, US 194/C5
Loma Bonita, Mex. 202/C2
Loma Linda, Ca, US 194/C2
Loma Mansa (peak), SLeo. 160/C4
Loma Negra, Arg. 216/E3
Lomami (riv.), D.R. Congo 157/K8
Lomas de Zamora, Arg. 217/J11
Lomazzo, It. 116/C1
Lombard, Il, US 193/P16
Lombarda, Serra (mts.), Braz. 209/H3
Lombardia, Mex. 200/E5
Lombardia (pol. reg.), It. 101/H4
Lomblen (isl.), Indo. 139/F5
Lombok (isl.), Indo. 139/E5
Lomé (int'l arpt.), Togo 161/F5
Lomé (cap.), Togo 161/F5
Lomello, It. 116/B2
Lomita, Ca, US 194/F8
Lomma, Swe. 96/E4
Lomme, Fr. 110/B2
Lommel, Belg. 108/C6
Lomnice (riv.), Czh. 113/G4
Lomnice nad Lužnicí, Czh. 113/H4
Lomond (lake), Sc, UK 94/B4
Lomond (hills), Sc, UK 94/C4
Lomone (riv.), It. 117/E4
Lomonosov, Rus. 119/S7
Lompobatang (peak), Indo. 139/E5
Lompoc, Ca, US 186/B4
Łomża, Pol. 99/M2
Lonato, It. 116/D2
Lonāvale, India 147/K5
Loncoche, Chile 216/B3
Loncopué, Arg. 216/C3
Londerzeel, Belg. 111/D2
London, On, Can. 188/D3
London (reef), Nic. 203/F3
London (cap.), UK 88/C2
London, Ky, US 188/C4
London, City of (bor.), Eng, UK 88/A1
Londonderry (cape), Austl. 167/B2
Londonderry (isl.), Chile 217/C7
Londonderry (dist.), NI, UK 92/A2
Londonderry, NI, UK 92/A2
Londrina, Braz. 213/B2
Lone (riv.), Eng, UK 93/F3
Lone Grove, Ok, US 187/H4
Lone Jack, Mo, US 195/E6
Lone Pine Sanctuary, Austl. 172/E7
Lonesome NP, Austl. 172/C4
Long, Ak, US 192/G3
Long (lake), On, Can. 185/M3
Long (lake), Sc, UK 94/A2
Long (riv.), China 137/A3
Long (isl.), Bahm. 199/F3
Long (isl.), NY, US 189/F3
Long (mtn.), Wal, UK 90/C1
Long (str.), Rus. 123/T2
Long Beach, Wa, US 184/B4
Long Beach, On, Can. 189/R10
Long Beach (isl.), NJ, US 196/D4
Long Beach, Ca, US 194/F8
Long Beach, NY, US 197/L9
Long Branch, NJ, US 196/E3
Long Cay (isl.), India 203/H1
Long Crag (hill), Eng, UK 94/E6
Long Eaton, Eng, UK 93/G6
Long Grove, Il, US 193/P15
Long Hill, Ct, US 197/E1
Long, Loch (inlet), Sc, UK 94/B4
Long Mynd, The (hill), Eng, UK 90/D1
Long Neck (pt.), Ct, US 197/M7
Long Range (mts.), Nf, Can. 189/K2
Long Valley, NJ, US 196/D2
Long Xuyen, Viet. 136/D4
Longá (riv.), Braz. 212/B1
Longare, It. 117/E2
Longaví, Chile 216/C2
Longboat Key, Fl, US 191/H5
Longbranch, Wa, US 193/B3
Longchang, China 141/J2
Longchuan, China 137/C3
Longchuan, China 141/G3
Longde, China 128/J4
Longeau (riv.), Fr. 111/E5
Longeville-en-Barrois, Fr. 111/E6
Longeville-lès-Metz, Fr. 111/F5
Longeville-lès-Saint-Avold, Fr. 111/F5
Longfellow (mts.), Me, US 189/G2
Longfield, Eng, UK 88/D2
Longford, Austl. 173/C4
Longford, Ire. 89/Q10
Longhua, China 130/D2
Longhui, China 141/K2
Longjumeau, Fr. 88/J5
Longkou, China 130/E3
Longlac, On, Can. 185/M3
Longli, China 141/J2
Longmen, China 141/K3
Longmen Shiyao, China 130/C4
Longmont, Co, US 195/B2
Longnan, China 137/B3
Longniddry, Sc, UK 94/D5
Longonot (peak), Kenya 162/C3
Longperrier, Fr. 88/K4
Longpont-sur-Orge, Fr. 88/J6
Longport, NJ, US 196/D5
Longpré-les-Corps-Saints, Fr. 110/A3
Longquan, China 137/C2
Longreach, Austl. 172/B3
Longshan, China 137/A2
Longshou (mts.), China 128/H4
Longueau, Fr. 110/B4
Longueil-Annel, Fr. 110/B5
Longuenesse, Fr. 110/B2
Longuesse, Fr. 88/H4
Longueuil, Qu, Can. 189/P6
Longuyon, Fr. 111/E5
Longvic, Fr. 114/B3
Longview, Wa, US 184/C4
Longview, Tx, US 187/J4
Longwood Gardens, Pa, US 196/C4
Longwy, Fr. 111/E4
Longyan, China 137/C2
Longyearbyen, Nor. 122/B2
Longyou, China 137/C2
Longzhou, China 136/D1
Loni, India 144/D5
Lonigo, It. 117/E2
Löningen, Ger. 109/E3
Lonquimay, Arg. 216/E3
Lons, Fr. 100/C5
Lons-le-Saunier, Fr. 114/B4
Lönsboda, Swe. 96/F3
Lontzen, Belg. 111/F2
Lonza (riv.), Swi. 114/D5
Looe (isl.), Eng, UK 90/B6
Lookout (cape), NC, US 191/J3
Lookout (pt.), Austl. 172/B1
Loolmalasin (peak), Tanz. 162/B3
Loon Lake, Sk, Can. 184/F2
Loon op Zand, Neth. 108/C5
Loop Head (pt.), Ire. 88/P10
Loos, Fr. 110/C2
Lop Buri, Thai. 136/C3
Lopary, Madg. 165/H8
Lopez (cape), Gabon 154/G8
López Mateos, Mex. 201/Q9
Lopik, Neth. 108/B5
Lopori (riv.), D.R. Congo 155/K7
Lopphavet (bay), Nor. 95/G1
Loppi, Fin. 97/L1

Lora del Río, Sp. 102/C4
Lorain, Oh, US 188/D3
Loralai, Pak. 147/J2
Lorca, Sp. 102/E4
Lord Howe (isl.), Austl. 174/E8
Lordsburg, NM, US 186/E4
Lorelei, Ger. 111/G3
Lorena, Braz. 213/H7
Lorengau, PNG 174/D5
Lørenskog, Nor. 96/D2
Lorentz (riv.), Indo. 139/J5
Lorentzsluizen (dam), Neth. 108/C2
Loreo, It. 117/F2
Loreto, Braz. 212/A2
Loreto, It. 117/G6
Loreto, Mex. 200/C3
Loreto (int'l arpt.), Mex. 200/C3
Loreto, Mex. 200/E4
Loreto, Ecu. 210/B5
Loreto (state), Peru 210/C5
Lorette, Mb, Can. 185/J3
Lorgues, Fr. 101/G5
Lorian (swamp), Kenya 155/N7
Lorica, Col. 210/C2
Lorient, Fr. 100/B3
L'Oriental (pol. reg.), Mor. 157/E2
Lorillard (riv.), Nun., Can. 180/G2
Lorinci, Hun. 99/K5
Loring, Ks, US 195/D5
Loriol-sur-Drôme, Fr. 100/F4
Lorn, Firth of (inlet), Sc, UK 89/Q8
Lorne, Austl. 173/B3
Lorosuk (peak), Kenya 162/B2
Lorquin, Fr. 111/G6
Lörrach, Ger. 114/D2
Lorrain (plat.), Fr. 98/D4
Lorraine, Qu, Can. 189/N6
Lorraine (pol. reg.), Fr. 101/G2
Lorraine (reg.), Fr. 111/F5
Lorsch, Ger. 112/B3
Lorup, Ger. 109/E3
Los Alamitos, Ca, US 194/F8
Los Alamos, NM, US 187/F4
Los Alerces, PN, Arg. 215/B5
Los Altos, Ca, US 193/K12
Los Amates, Guat. 202/D3
Los Andes, Chile 216/N8
Los Andes, Col. 210/B4
Los Angeles, Chile 216/B3
Los Angeles, Ca, US 194/F7
Los Angeles (co.), Ca, US 194/B2
Los Angeles (int'l arpt.), Ca, US 194/F8
Los Angeles (riv.), Ca, US 194/B2
Los Angeles Outer (har.), Ca, US 194/F8
Los Aquijes, Peru 214/C4
Los Aztecas, Mex. 201/F4
Los Banos, Ca, US 186/B3
Los Barrios, Sp. 102/C5
Los Canareos (arch.), Cuba 203/F1
Los Cardales, Arg. 217/J11
Los Cerrillos, Arg. 217/K11
Los Chonos (arch.), Chile 216/B5
Los Corrales de Buelna, Sp. 102/C1
Los Glaciares, PN, Arg. 215/B6
Los Katios, PN, Col. 210/B3
Los Lagos, Chile 216/B3
Los Lagos (pol. reg.), Chile 216/B4
Los Llanos de Aridane, Canl., Sp. 156/A3
Los Lunas, NM, US 186/F4
Los Mármoles, PN, Mex. 202/B1
Los Menucos, Arg. 216/C4
Los Mochis, Mex. 200/C3
Los Mosquitos (gulf), Pan. 203/F4
Los Muermos, Chile 216/B4
Los Navalmorales, Sp. 102/C3
Los Navalucillos, Sp. 102/C3
Los Órganos, Peru 214/A2
Los Padres National Forest, Ca, US 194/A1
Los Palacios y Villafranca, Sp. 102/C4
Los Pingüinos, PN, Chile 217/C7
Los Planes, Mex. 200/C3
Los Reyes, Mex. 201/R10
Los Reyes de Salgado, Mex. 200/E5
Los Ríos (prov.), Ecu. 214/B1
Los Roques, Islas (isls.), Ven. 208/E1
Los Santos, Pan. 203/F5
Los Santos de Maimona, Sp. 102/B3
Los Sauces, Chile 216/B3
Los Taques, Ven. 210/D2
Los Teques, Ven. 208/E1
Los Testigos (isls.), Ven. 211/F2
Los Vilos, Chile 216/C1
Los Yébenes, Sp. 102/D3
Losai Nat'l Rsv., Kenya 162/C2
Losheim, Ger. 111/F4
Losice, Pol. 99/M2
Lošinj (isl.), Cro. 106/B3

Losne, Fr. 114/B3
Losone, Swi. 115/E5
Losoya, Tx, US 195/U21
Lossburg, Ger. 115/E1
Losser, Neth. 108/E4
Lossie (riv.), Sc, UK 94/C1
Lössnitz, Ger. 113/F1
Lossoganeu (hill), Tanz. 162/C4
Lost River (range), Id, US 186/D1
Lost River Caverns, Pa, US 196/C2
Lostallo, Swi. 115/F5
Lot (riv.), Fr. 100/D4
Lota, Chile 216/B3
Lotawana (lake), Mo, US 195/E6
Løten, Nor. 96/D1
Lotte, Ger. 109/E4
Lotuke (peak), Sudan 162/B1
Lotung, Tai. 137/D3
Lou (riv.), China 130/B5
Louang Namtha, Laos 141/H3
Louangphrabang, Laos 141/H4
Loubomo, Congo 163/B1
Loudéac, Fr. 100/B2
Loudi, China 141/K2
Loudun, Fr. 100/D3
Loue (riv.), Fr. 100/F3
Loufan, China 130/B3
Louga (pol. reg.), Sen. 160/B3
Louga, Sen. 160/A3
Lough Foyle (lake), UK 92/A1
Loughborough, Eng, UK 91/E1
Loughbrickland, NI, UK 92/B3
Lougheed (isl.), Nun., Can. 181/R7
Loughgall, NI, UK 92/B3
Loughrea, Ire. 89/P10
Loughton, Eng, UK 88/D2
Louhans, Fr. 114/B4
Louis Botha (Durban) (int'l arpt.), SAfr. 165/E3
Louisiade (arch.), PNG 174/E6
Louisiana (state), US 190/E4
Louisville, Co, US 195/B3
Louisville, Ky, US 188/C4
Louisville, Ms, US 191/F3
Loukkos (riv.), Mor. 158/A2
Loulé, Port. 102/A4
Louny, Czh. 113/G2
Loup (riv.), Ne, US 185/J5
Loup, Middle (riv.), Ne, US 185/H5
Loup, North (riv.), Ne, US 185/H5
Loup, South (riv.), Ne, US 185/J5
Lourches, Fr. 110/C3
Lourdes, Fr. 100/C5
Lourdes/Tarbes (int'l arpt.), Fr. 100/D5
Loures, Port. 103/P10
Louriçal, Port. 102/A2
Lourinhã, Port. 102/A3
Lousã, Port. 102/A2
Louth, Eng, UK 93/H5
Louth (co.), Ire. 92/B4
Louth, Ire. 92/B4
Loutrá Aidhipsoú, Gre. 105/H3
Loutrákion, Gre. 105/H4
Loútsa, Gre. 105/P9
Louvain (Leuven), Belg. 111/D2
Louveira, Braz. 213/G8
Louviers, Fr. 100/D2
Louviers, Co, US 195/B4
Louvigné-du-Désert, Fr. 100/C2
Louvres, Fr. 88/K4
Louvroil, Fr. 99/J2
Lovaart (riv.), Belg. 110/B1
Lovat' (riv.), Rus. 118/F4
Lovat' (riv.), Bela.,Rus. 97/P3
Lovćen NP, Mont. 106/D4
Love Point, Md, US 196/B5
Lovech (prov.), Bul. 105/J1
Loveland, Co, US 195/B2
Loveland (lake), Co, US 195/B2
Lovell, Wy, US 184/F4
Lovelock, Nv, US 186/C2
Lovere, It. 116/D1
Loving, NM, US 187/G4
Lovington, NM, US 187/G4
Lovios, Sp. 102/A2
Lövő, Hun. 101/M3
Lovosice, Czh. 113/H1
Lovozero (lake), Rus. 118/G2
Low (cape), Nun., Can. 181/H2
Lowa (riv.), D.R. Congo 157/L8
Lowell, Ma, US 189/G3
Löwen (riv.), Namb. 164/C4
Löwenstein, Ger. 112/C4
Lower (bay), NJ, US 196/D2
Lower (dam), Wa, US 193/D3
Lower Arrow (lake), BC, Can. 184/D3
Lower Engadine (valley), Swi. 115/G4
Lower Ganges (canal), India 142/B2

Lower Glenelg NP, Austl. 173/B3
Lower Hutt, NZ 175/S11
Lower Kalskag, Ak, US 192/F3
Lower Latham (res.), Co, US 195/C2
Lower Otay (lake), Ca, US 194/D5
Lower Red (lake), Mn, US 185/K4
Lower Rhine (riv.), Neth. 108/C5
Lower Rouge (riv.), Mi, US 193/E7
Lower Trajan's Wall, Mol.,Ukr. 120/D3
Lower Tunguska (riv.), Rus. 125/J3
Lower Zambezi NP, Zam. 98/F2
Lowestoft, Eng, UK 91/H2
Lowi (riv.), D.R. Congo 163/E1
Lowicz, Pol. 99/K2
Lowther (hills), Sc, UK 94/C6
Loxstedt, Ger. 109/F2
Loxton, SAfr. 164/C3
Loxton, Austl. 171/J5
Loyalton, Pa, US 196/A3
Loyalty (isls.), NCal., Fr. 174/F7
Loyettes, Fr. 114/B6
Loyne (lake), Sc, UK 94/A2
Loysville, Pa, US 196/A3
Loznica, Serb. 106/D3
Loznitsa, Bul. 107/H4
Lozova, Ukr. 120/F2
Lozovik, Serb. 106/E3
Luachimo (riv.), Ang. 163/C3
Lu (mtn.), China 130/D3
Lu (riv.), China 130/C5
Lu Xian, China 141/J2
Lualaba (riv.), D.R. Congo 163/E1
Luan, China 130/D3
Luan Xian, China 130/D3
Luanchuan, China 130/C4
Luanco, Sp. 102/C1
Luanda (cap.), Ang. 163/B2
Luang (peak), Thai. 136/B4
Luang Lagoon (lag.), Thai. 141/H6
Luangwa (riv.), Zam. 163/F2
Luangwe, Zam. 162/A5
Luanping, China 130/D2
Luanshya, Zam. 163/E3
Luapula (prov.), D.R. Congo 162/A5
Luarca, Sp. 102/B1
Luba, EqG. 154/G7
Lubaantun (ruin), Belz. 202/D2
Lubaczów, Pol. 99/M3
Lubango, Ang. 163/B3
Lubansenshi (riv.), Zam. 162/A5
Lubartów, Pol. 99/M3
Lubawa, Pol. 99/K2
Lübbecke, Ger. 109/F4
Lübbeek, Belg. 111/D2
Lübben, Belg. 111/D2
Lubero (riv.), D.R. Congo 162/A4
Lubero, D.R. Congo 162/A3
Lubień Kujawski, Pol. 99/K2
Lubin, Pol. 99/J3
Lublin, Pol. 99/M3
Lubliniec, Pol. 99/K3
Lubnaig (lake), Sc, UK 94/B4
Lubny, Ukr. 120/E2
Luboń, Pol. 99/J2
Lubrín, Sp. 102/D4
Lubudi, D.R. Congo 163/E2
Lubukkinggau, Indo. 138/B3
Lubuklinggau, Indo. 138/B3
Lubuksikaping, Indo. 138/B3
Lubumbashi, D.R. Congo 163/E3
Lubuskie (prov.), Pol. 99/H2
Lucan, Ire. 92/B5
Lucania (mt.), Yk, Can. 192/K3
Lucas González, Arg. 217/J10
Lucca (prov.), It. 116/D5
Lucca, It. 116/D1
Luce (bay), Sc, UK 92/D2
Lucedale, Ms, US 191/F4
Lucélia, Braz. 213/B2
Lucena, Phil. 137/D5
Lucena, Sp. 102/C4
Lucena del Cid, Sp. 102/E3
Lučenec, Slvk. 99/K4
Lucens, Swi. 114/C4
Lucerne (lake), Swi. 101/H3
Lucerne (Vierwaldstättersee) (lake), Swi. 115/E3
Lucheng, China 130/C3
Lüchow, Ger. 98/F2

Lucrecia (cape), Cuba 203/H1
Lucrezia, It. 117/F5
Luda Kamchiya (riv.), Bul. 105/K1
Lüdenscheid, Ger. 109/E6
Lüderitz, Namb. 164/A2
Ludhiâna, India 144/C4
Ludian, China 141/H2
Ludinghausen, Ger. 109/E5
Ludington, Mi, US 188/C3
Ludogorie (reg.), Bul. 107/H4
Ludvika, Swe. 96/F1
Ludwigs (canal), Ger. 113/E4
Ludwigsburg, Ger. 112/C5
Ludwigsfelde, Ger. 98/Q7
Ludwigshafen, Ger. 115/F2
Ludwigshafen, Ger. 112/B4
Ludwigslust, Ger. 98/F2
Ludwigsstadt, Ger. 113/E2
Luebo, D.R. Congo 163/D2
Luena, Ang. 163/C3
Lufeng, China 137/C3
Lufkin, Tx, US 187/J5
Luga (bay), Rus. 97/N2
Luga (riv.), Rus. 97/N2
Lugano, It. 117/D2
Lugagnano Val d'Arda, It. 116/C3
Lugano, Swi. 115/E6
Lugano (lake), It. 115/E6
Luganville, Van. 174/F6
Lugards (falls), Kenya 162/C3
Lugavčina, Serb. 106/E3
Lügde, Ger. 109/G5
Lugenda (riv.), Moz. 163/G3
Lugg (riv.), Eng, UK 90/C2
Lugg (riv.), Wal, UK 90/C2
Lugnaquillia (peak), Ire. 92/B6
Lugo, It. 117/E4
Lugo, Sp. 102/B1
Lugogo (riv.), Ugan. 162/B2
Lugoj, Rom. 106/E3
Lugrin, Fr. 114/C5
Lugunga (peak), Tanz. 162/C4
Luhan (int'l arpt.), Ukr. 120/F2
Luhans'k, Ukr. 120/F2
Luhans'ka Oblasti, Ukr. 120/F2
Lühe (riv.), Ger. 109/H2
Luhe, China 130/D4
Luhe (riv.), Ger. 113/F3
Luhe-Wildenau, Ger. 113/F3
Luhern, Swi. 114/D3
Luhombero (peak), Tanz. 162/C4
Lütjehorn (isl.), Ger. 108/D1
Lütjenburg, Ger. 96/D4
Luton, Eng, UK 91/F3
Luton (co.), Eng, UK 91/F3
Luton (int'l arpt.), Eng, UK 91/F3
Luino, It. 115/E6
Luis B. Sánchez, Mex. 200/B1
Luis Correia, Braz. 212/B1
Luján, Arg. 217/J11
Lujiang, China 130/D5
Lukácsháza, Hun. 101/M3
Lukang, Tai. 137/D3
Lukavac, Bosn. 106/D3
Luke (mt.), Austl. 170/C3
Lukenie (riv.), D.R. Congo 163/C1
Lukovit, Bul. 105/J1
Luków, Pol. 99/M3
Lukuga (riv.), D.R. Congo 162/A4
Lukulu, Zam. 163/D3
Lukunor (isl.), Micr. 174/E4
Luleå, Swe. 118/D2
Luleälven (riv.), Swe. 95/G2
Luliang, China 141/J3
Luling, La, US 195/P17
Luling (pass), China 130/B4
Luling, China 130/D3
Lulonga (riv.), D.R. Congo 151/E4
Lulsgate (int'l arpt.), Eng, UK 90/D4
Lulua (riv.), D.R. Congo 163/D2
Lumangwe (falls), Zam. 162/A5
Luz, Braz. 213/C1

Lünen, Ger. 109/E5
Lunenburg, NS, Can. 189/H2
Lunestedt, Ger. 109/F2
Lune (bay), Eng, UK 90/C3
Lung Kwu Chau (isl.), China 129/T10
Lunga (riv.), Zam. 163/E3
Lungern, Swi. 115/E4
Lungi, SLeo. 160/B4
Lungi (Freetown) (int'l arpt.), SLeo. 160/B4
Lunglei, India 141/F3
Lungue-Bungo (riv.), Ang. 163/C3
Luni (riv.), India 147/K3
Lünne, Ger. 109/E4
Luocheng, China 141/J3
Luodian, China 141/J2
Luoding, China 130/C4
Luohe, China 130/C4
Luoma (lake), China 130/D4
Luongo (riv.), Zam. 162/A5
Luoning, China 130/B4
Luotian, China 130/C4
Luoshuikan, China 137/A1
Luoyang, China 130/C4
Luoyuan, China 137/C2
Luozi, D.R. Congo 163/B1
Lupanshui, China 141/H2
Luqa (riv.), Malta 104/L7
Luqa (int'l arpt.), Malta 104/L7
Luqu, China 128/H5
Luquan, China 141/H2
Lürah (riv.), Afg. 147/J2
Lure, Fr. 114/C2
Lurgan, NI, UK 92/B3
Luri, Fr. 101/H5
Lurín, Peru 214/C5
Lúrio, Moz. 163/H3
Lúrio (riv.), Moz. 163/G3
Lurnfeld, Aus. 101/K3
Lurøy, Nor. 95/E2
Lusaka (cap.), Zam. 163/E3
Lusambo, D.R. Congo 163/D1
Lusen (peak), Ger. 113/G5
Lusenga NP, Zam. 162/A5
Lushan, China 130/C4
Lushi, China 130/B4
Lushnjë, Alb. 105/F2
Lushoto, Tanz. 162/C4
Lushui, China 141/G2
Lusignan, Fr. 100/D3
Lusk, Wy, US 185/G5
Lusk, Ire. 92/B4
Lustenau, Aus. 115/F3
Lutanga (riv.), D.R. Congo 155/J7
Luther, Ok, US 195/N14
Luthern, Swi. 114/D3
Lutherville, Md, US 196/B5
Lütjehorn (isl.), Ger. 108/D1
Lütjenburg, Ger. 96/D4
Luton, Eng, UK 91/F3
Luton (co.), Eng, UK 91/F3
Luton (int'l arpt.), Eng, UK 91/F3
Lutry, Swi. 114/C5
Lutselk'e, NW, Can. 180/E2
Luts'k, Ukr. 120/C2
Lutter (riv.), Ger. 109/F5
Lutterbach, Fr. 114/D2
Lutz (riv.), Aus. 115/F3
Lützow-Holm (bay), Ant. 218/C
Luumäki, Fin. 97/M1
Luverne, Mn, US 185/J5
Luvua (riv.), D.R. Congo 162/A4
Luwegu (riv.), Tanz. 163/G2
Luwero, Zam. 162/A5
Luwingu, Zam. 162/A5
Lux, Fr. 114/A4
Luxembourg (ctry.) 111/E4
Luxembourg (prov.), Belg. 111/E4
Luxembourg (cap.), Lux. 111/F4
Luxeuil-les-Bains, Fr. 114/C2
Luxi, China 141/H3
Luxi, China 141/K2
Luxor (int'l arpt.), Egypt 159/C3
Luyi, China 130/C4
Luz (coast), Port.,Sp. 102/B4
Luza (riv.), Rus. 119/L3
Luzarches, Fr. 88/K4
Luzein, Swi. 115/F3
Luzern, Swi. 115/E3
Luzern (canton), Swi. 114/E3
Luzerne (co.), Pa, US 196/A1
Luzhai, China 141/J3
Luzhi, China 141/J2
Luziânia, Braz. 212/A5
Luzilândia, Braz. 212/B1
Lužnice (riv.), Czh. 99/H4
Luzon (isl.), Phil. 137/D4
Luzon (str.), Phil. 137/D3
Lužuice (riv.), Czh. 101/L2
Luzzara, It. 117/D3
Luzzi, It. 104/E3
L'viv, Ukr. 120/C2
L'vivs'ka Oblasti, Ukr. 120/B2
Lwala (peak), Ugan. 162/B2
Lwi (riv.), Myan. 136/C1
Lyantonde, Ugan. 162/A3
Lyapin (riv.), Rus. 119/P2
Lyckeby, Swe. 96/F3
Lycksele, Swe. 95/F2
Lycoming (co.), Pa, US 196/A1
Lyell Brown (mt.), Austl. 171/F2

Lykens, Pa, US 196/B2
Lyman, Wy, US 184/F5
Lyme (bay), Eng, UK 90/C5
Lymington, Eng, UK 91/E5
Lymm, Eng, UK 93/F5
Lyna (riv.), Pol. 99/L1
Lynas (pt.), Wal, UK 92/D5
Lynbrook, NY, US 197/L9
Lynches (riv.), SC, US 191/H3
Lyndhurst, NJ, US 197/J8
Lyne (riv.), Eng, UK 93/F1
Lyngdal, Nor. 96/B2
Lyngen (inlet), Nor. 95/G1
Lynn, Ma, US 189/G3
Lynn Haven, Fl, US 191/G4
Lynn Lake, Mb, Can. 180/F3
Lynnwood, Ca, US 194/F8
Lynx (lake), NW, Can. 180/F2
Lyon, Fr. 114/B6
Lyon (riv.), Sc, UK 94/B3
Lyon Lake, Sc, UK 94/B3
Lyon (Satolas) (int'l arpt.), Fr. 114/B6
Lyons, Ks, US 187/H3
Lyons, Co, US 195/B2
Lyons (riv.), Austl. 170/C3
Lyons, Wi, US 193/P14
Lype (hill), Eng, UK 90/C4
Lyra (reef), PNG 174/E5
Lys (riv.), Fr. 116/A1
Lys (riv.), Fr. 100/E1
Lys-lez-Lannoy, Fr. 110/C2
Lysá (peak), Czh. 99/K4
Lysá nad Labem, Czh. 113/H1
Lysaker, Nor. 96/D2
Lysekil, Swe. 96/D2
Lysica (peak), Pol. 99/L3
Lysina (peak), Czh. 113/F2
Lyss, Swi. 114/D3
Lystrup, Den. 96/D3
Lys'va, Rus. 119/N4
Lysychans'k, Ukr. 120/F2
Lytham Saint Anne's, Eng, UK 93/F4
Lytle, Tx, US 187/H5
Lytle Creek, Ca, US 194/C2
Lytton, BC, Can. 184/C3
Lytton, NI, UK 92/B4
Lyuban', Rus. 118/G4
Lyubertsy, Rus. 119/W9
Lyubotyn, Ukr. 120/F2
Lyudinovo, Rus. 120/E1
Lywd (riv.), Wal, UK 90/C3

M

M. Aleman (res.), Mex. 198/B4
Ma-Ubin, Myan. 141/G4
Ma'alot-Tarshiha, Isr. 149/D3
Ma'an (gov.), Jor. 149/E4
Maanit, Mong. 128/H2
Maanit, Mong. 128/J2
Maanselkä (mts.), Fin. 95/H1
Ma'anshan, China 130/D5
Maarheeze, Neth. 108/C6
Maarianhamina (Mariehamn), Fin. 97/H1
Ma'arrat an Nu'mān, Syria 149/E2
Maarssen, Neth. 108/C4
Maartensdijk, Neth. 108/C4
Maas (riv.), Belg. 100/F1
Maasbracht, Neth. 111/E1
Maasbree, Neth. 108/D6
Maaseik, Belg. 111/E1
Maassluis, Neth. 108/B5
Maastricht, Neth. 111/E2
Maastricht (int'l arpt.), Neth. 111/E2
Mabalacad, Phil. 137/D4
Mabalane, Moz. 163/F5
Mabaruma, Guy. 211/G2
Mabian, China 141/H2
Mabinay, Phil. 137/D6
Mabopane, SAfr. 164/Q12
Mabote, Moz. 163/F5
Mabton, Wa, US 193/G6
Mac Robertson Land (phys. reg.), Ant. 218/D
Macá (peak), Chile 216/B5
Macachin, Arg. 216/E3
Macaé, Braz. 213/K7
Macael, Sp. 102/D4
Macaíba, Braz. 212/D2
Mação, Port. 102/A3
Macapá, Braz. 209/H3
Macará, Ecu. 214/B1
Macarani, Braz. 212/D4
Macaravita, Col. 210/D2
Macari, Peru 214/D4
Macas, Ecu. 210/B5
Macau, Braz. 212/D2
Macau, China 137/B3
Macau (dpcy.), China 137/B3
Macaúbas, Braz. 212/C4
Macauley (isl.), NZ 174/G7
Macauva, PN, Col. 210/D1
Macaya, Pic de (peak), Haiti 203/H2
Maccagno, It. 115/E5
Macclenny, Fl, US 191/H4
Macclesfield (canal), Eng, UK 93/F5
Macclesfield, Eng, UK 93/F5
Macdhui (peak), SAfr. 164/D3

Macdona, Tx, US 195/T21
MacDonald (lake), Austl. 171/F2
Macdonnell (ranges), Austl. 167/Q3
Macduff, Sc, UK 94/D1
Maceda, Sp. 102/B1
Macedonia (reg.), Gre. 105/G2
Macedonia (int'l arpt.), Gre. 105/H2
Macedonia (Former Yugoslav Republic of Macedonia) (ctry.) 105/G2
Maceió (pt.), Braz. 212/C2
Maceió, Braz. 212/D3
Macerata (prov.), It. 117/G6
Macerata, It. 101/K5
Macfarlane (lake), Austl. 171/H3
Machacalis, Braz. 212/B5
Machacamarca, Bol. 208/E7
Machache (peak), Les. 164/D3
Machachi, Ecu. 210/B5
Machado, Braz. 213/H6
Machado (swamp), Col. 210/C2
Machakos, Kenya 162/C3
Machala, Ecu. 214/B1
Machali, Chile 216/N9
Machalilla, PN, Ecu. 210/A5
Machanga, Moz. 163/F5
Machaquilá (riv.), Guat. 202/D2
Machars, The (pen.), Sc, UK 92/D2
Machattie (lake), Austl. 171/H3
Machaze, Moz. 163/F5
Machecoul, Fr. 100/C3
Machemma (ruin), SAfr. 163/E5
Machens, Mo, US 195/G8
Macheng, China 130/C5
Machias, Me, US 189/H2
Machichaco (cape), Sp. 102/D1
Machida, Japan 135/C2
Machilipatnam, India 140/D4
Machiques, Ven. 210/C2
Machovo Jezero (lake), Czh. 113/H1
Machu Picchu (ruin), Peru 214/C4
Machupo (riv.), Bol. 208/F6
Machynlleth, Wal, UK 90/C1
Măcin, Rom. 107/J3
Macina (phys. reg.), Mali 154/E4
Macintyre (riv.), Austl. 173/D1
Mackay, Austl. 172/C3
Mackay (lake), Austl. 171/F2
Mackenzie, BC, Can. 184/C2
Mackenzie, Austl. 172/C3
Mackenzie (bay), NW,Yk, Can. 180/C2
Mackenzie (mts.), NW, Can. 180/C2
Mackenzie (riv.), NW, Can. 180/E2
Mackenzie King (isl.), NW, Can. 181/R7
Mackinac Island, Mi, US 188/C2
Mackinaw City, Mi, US 188/C2
Macklin, Sk, Can. 184/F2
Macknade, Austl. 172/B2
Macksville, Austl. 173/E1
Maclean, Austl. 173/E1
Maclear, SAfr. 164/E3
Macleay (riv.), Austl. 172/F3
Macleod (lake), Austl. 170/B3
Macmillan (riv.), Yk, Can. 192/L3
Macomb, Il, US 185/L6
Macomb (co.), Mi, US 193/G6
Macomb, Ok, US 195/N15
Macomer, It. 104/A2
Mâcon, Fr. 100/F3
Macon, Ga, US 191/H3
Macon, Mo, US 187/J3
Macondes, Planalto dos (plat.), Moz. 162/C5
Macosquin, NI, UK 92/B1
Macotera, Sp. 102/C2
Macoupin (co.), Il, US 195/G7
Macquarie (har.), Austl. 173/C4
Macquarie (riv.), Austl. 81/S8
Macquarie (riv.), Austl. 173/C1
Macroom, Ire. 89/P11
Macuelizo, Hon. 202/D3
Macuim (riv.), Braz. 208/F5
Macuira, PN, Col. 210/D1
Macuma, Ecu. 214/B1
Macumba (riv.), Austl. 171/H3
Macungie, Pa, US 196/C2
Macusani, Peru 214/D4
Macuspana, Mex. 202/C2
Macuzari, Presa (dam), Mex. 200/C3
Mădaba, Jor. 149/D4
Madagascar (ctry.) 165/H8

Madan, Bul. 105/J2
Madanapalle, India 140/C5
Madaoua, Niger 161/G3
Madaras, Hun. 106/D2
Madauk, Myan. 141/G4
Madawaska, Me, US 189/G2
Madawaska (reg.), On, Can. 188/E2
Madden (dam), Pan. 210/B2
Madeira (aut. reg.), Port. 103/U14
Madeira (riv.), Braz. 208/F5
Mädelegabel (peak), Ger. 115/G3
Madeleine, Îles de la (isls.), Qu, Can. 189/J2
Madeline (isl.), Wi, US 185/L4
Maden, Turk. 148/D2
Mäder, Aus. 115/F3
Madera, Mex. 200/C2
Maderas (vol.), Nic. 203/E4
Madgaon (Margao), India 147/K5
Madhipura, India 143/F2
Madhubani, India 143/F3
Madhumati (riv.), Bang. 143/G4
Madhupur, India 143/F3
Madhya Pradesh (state), India 140/C3
Madidi (riv.), Bol. 208/E6
Madīnat ath Thawrah, Syria 148/D3
Madirovalo, Madg. 165/H7
Madison, Al, US 191/G3
Madison, Ca, US 193/K9
Madison, Ct, US 197/F1
Madison, Fl, US 191/H4
Madison, Il, US 195/G8
Madison, In, US 188/C4
Madison, Ms, US 191/F3
Madison (co.), Oh, US 195/G8
Madison, Ne, US 185/J5
Madison, NJ, US 197/H9
Madison (co.), Wi, US 193/F6
Madison, SD, US 185/J4
Madison Heights, Mi, US 193/F6
Madisonville, Tx, US 187/J5
Madisonville, Ky, US 188/C4
Madiun, Indo. 138/D5
Mado Gashi, Kenya 162/C2
Madoi, China 128/G5
Madon (riv.), Fr. 98/D4
Madrakah, Ra's al (pt.), Oman 147/G5
Madre (lag.), Mex. 201/F4
Madre (lag.), Tx, US 190/D5
Madre de Deus de Minas, Braz. 213/J6
Madre de Dios (riv.), Bol. 208/E6
Madre de Dios (isl.), Chile 217/A6
Madre de Dios (dept.), Peru 214/C4
Madre del Sur, Sierra (mts.), Mex. 198/A4
Madre Occidental, Sierra (mts.), Mex. 200/D3
Madre Oriental, Sierra (mts.), Mex. 201/F4
Madrid (aut. comm.), Sp. 102/C2
Madrid (cap.), Sp. 103/N9
Madridejos, Sp. 102/D3
Madrigal de las Altas Torres, Sp. 102/C2
Madrigalejo, Sp. 102/C3
Madrisahorn (peak), Swi. 115/F4
Madroñera, Sp. 102/C3
Madugula, India 140/D4
Madura (isl.), Indo. 138/D5
Madurai, India 140/C6
Mae Hong Son, Thai. 141/G2
Mae Ping NP, Thai. 136/B2
Mae Tho (peak), Thai. 136/B2
Mae Va (mtn.), Thai. 136/B2
Maebashi, Japan 133/F2
Maella, Sp. 102/E2
Maep'o, SKor. 131/E4
Maerne, It. 117/F1
Maestra, Sierra (mts.), Cuba 203/G2
Maevatanana-Ambanivohitra, Madg. 165/H7
Maewo (isl.), Van. 174/F6
Mafeteng, Les. 164/D3
Maffra, Austl. 173/C3
Mafia (chan.), Tanz. 162/C5
Mafia (isl.), Tanz. 162/C5
Mafikeng, SAfr. 164/D2
Mafou (riv.), Gui. 160/C3
Mafra, Braz. 213/B3
Mafra, Port. 103/P10
Magadan, Rus. 123/R4
Magadino, Swi. 115/E5
Magalies Berg (mts.), SAfr. 164/P12
Magaliesburg, SAfr. 164/P12
Magallanes y Antártica Chilena (prov.), Chile 217/C7

Magan – Maran

Magangué, Col. 210/C2
Mağara, Turk. 149/C1
Magaria, Niger 161/H3
Magat (riv.), Phil. 137/D4
Magazine (mtn.), Ar, US 187/J4
Magdalena, Arg. 217/K11
Magdalena, Bol. 208/F6
Magdalena (riv.), Col. 210/C3
Magdalena (dept.), Col. 210/C2
Magdalena (peak), Malay. 139/E3
Magdalena de Kino, Mex. 200/C2
Magdeburg, Ger. 98/F2
Magdelaine Cays (isls.), Austl. 167/E2
Magé, Braz. 213/K7
Mage-shima (isl.), Japan 132/B5
Magee, Ms, US 191/F4
Magee (isl.), NI, UK 92/C2
Magelang, Indo. 138/D5
Magellan (str.), Arg.,Chile 217/C7
Magenta, It. 116/B2
Magenta (lake), Austl. 170/C5
Magerøya (isl.), Nor. 95/H1
Maggia, Swi. 115/E5
Maggia (riv.), Swi. 115/E5
Maggio (peak), It. 117/E6
Maggiorasca (peak), It. 116/C3
Maggiore (peak), It. 117/E5
Maggiore (lake), It. 101/H4
Maghāghah, Egypt 159/B2
Maghar, India 142/D2
Maghera, NI, UK 92/B2
Magherafelt (co.), NI, UK 92/B2
Magherafelt, NI, UK 92/B2
Maghīla (peak), Tun. 158/L7
Maghnia, Alg. 158/D2
Magilligan (pt.), NI, UK 92/B1
Maglaj, Bosn. 106/D3
Maglić (peak), Mont. 106/D4
Maglie, It. 105/F2
Maglod, Hun. 107/R10
Magna, Ut, US 195/J12
Magnac-Laval, Fr. 100/D3
Magnetawan (riv.), On, Can. 188/D2
Magnetic Passage, Austl. 172/B2
Magnitogorsk, Rus. 119/N5
Magnitogorsk (int'l arpt.), Rus. 119/N5
Magnolia, Ar, US 187/J4
Magnolia, De, US 196/C5
Magny-en-Vexin, Fr. 110/A5
Magny-les-Hameaux, Fr. 88/J5
Mago NP, Eth. 155/N6
Mágoè, Moz. 163/F4
Magog, Qu, Can. 189/F2
Magpie (riv.), Qu, Can. 189/H1
Magpie (lake), Qu, Can. 189/H1
Magpie Ouest (riv.), Qu, Can. 189/H1
Magra (riv.), It. 116/C4
Magreta, It. 117/D3
Maguan, China 136/D1
Magude, Moz. 163/F6
Magugnano, It. 117/D1
Magway (Magwe), Myan. 141/F3
Magway (div.), Myan. 141/F3
Maha Sarakham, Thai. 136/C2
Mahābād, Iran 146/E1
Mahabe, Madg. 165/H8
Mahābhārat (range), Nepal 142/C1
Mahabo, Madg. 165/H8
Mahaboboka, Madg. 165/H7
Mahād, India 147/K5
Mahadeo (range), India 142/A4
Mahaica, Guy. 211/G3
Mahaica-Berbice (pol. reg.), Guy. 211/G3
Mahaicony Village, Guy. 211/G3
Mahajamba (riv.), Madg. 165/H7
Mahajamba (bay), Madg. 165/H6
Mahajanga (prov.), Madg. 165/H6
Mahajanga, Madg. 165/H6
Mahajilo (riv.), Madg. 165/H7
Mahakali (zone), Nepal 142/C1
Mahakam (riv.), Indo. 139/E3
Mahalapye, Bots. 163/E5
Mahale Mountains NP, Tanz. 162/A4
Maḩallāt, Iran 146/F2
Maham, India 144/D5
Māhān (riv.), India 142/D4
Māhān, Iran 147/G2
Mahānadī (riv.), India 140/D3
Mahananda (riv.), India 143/F3
Mahandiabani (riv.), C.d'Iv. 160/D4
Mahanoro, Madg. 165/J7
Mahanoy City, Pa, US 196/B2
Mahantango (mtn.), Pa, US 196/B2
Mahārājganj, India 143/E2
Mahārājganj, India 142/D2
Mahārajpur, India 140/C2
Mahārāshtra (state), India 140/B4
Mahāsamund, India 140/D3
Mahāshān (ruin), Bang. 143/G3
Mahasoabe, Madg. 165/H8
Mahavavy (riv.), Madg. 165/H7
Mahawa (riv.), India 142/B1
Mahazoarivo, Madg. 165/H8
Mahazoma, Madg. 165/H7
Mahbubnagar, India 140/C4
Mahdia, Guy. 211/G3
Mahdia, Tun. 158/M7
Mahdia (prov.), Tun. 158/M7
Mahébourg, Mrts. 165/T15
Mahendranagar, Nepal 142/C1
Mahesāna, India 147/K4
Mahgawān, India 142/B2
Mahia (pen.), NZ 175/T10
Mahilyow (int'l arpt.), Bela. 97/P5
Mahilyow, Bela. 97/P5
Mahilyowskaya Voblasts Bela. 118/F5
Mahīshādal, India 143/F4
Mahitsy, Madg. 165/H7
Mahlaing, Myan. 141/G3
Mahlberg, Ger. 114/D1
Mahleur (lake), Or, US 184/D5
Mahlow, Ger. 98/Q7
Mahmel (peak), Alg. 154/G1
Maḩmūd-e 'Erāqī, Afg. 147/J1
Mahmūdābād, India 142/C2
Mahón, Sp. 103/H3
Mahroni, India 142/B3
Mahukona, Hi, US 182/U10
Mahuva, India 147/K4
Mahwah, India 142/A2
Mahwah, NJ, US 197/J7
Mai-Ndombe (lake), D.R. Congo 155/J8
Maia, Port. 102/A2
Maiala NP, Austl. 172/E6
Maials, Sp. 103/F2
Maiana (isl.), Kiri. 174/G4
Maicao, Col. 210/C2
Maîche, Fr. 114/C3
Maicuru (riv.), Braz. 209/H3
Maidenhead, Eng, UK 91/F3
Maidens, Sc, UK 94/B6
Maidstone, Sk, Can. 184/F2
Maidstone, Eng, UK 91/G4
Maidstone, On, Can. 193/G7
Maiduguri, Nga. 154/H5
Maienfeld, Swi. 115/F4
Maigue (riv.), Ire. 89/P10
Maihar, India 142/C3
Maihara, Japan 135/K5
Maikala (range), India 142/C4
Maiko, PN de la, D.R. Congo 155/L8
Mailāni, India 142/C1
Maili, Hi, US 182/V13
Mailly-le-Camp, Fr. 111/D6
Mailsi, Pak. 144/B5
Main (riv.), NI, UK 92/B2
Main (riv.), Ger. 98/E4
Main-Donau (canal), Ger. 112/D3
Main Range NP, Austl. 172/C5
Maināguri, India 143/G2
Mainbernheim, Ger. 112/D3
Maincy, Fr. 88/L6
Maine (state), US 189/G2
Maine (riv.), Ire. 89/P10
Maine (reg.), Fr. 100/C2
Maine, Collines du (hills), Fr. 100/C2
Maine, Gulf of (gulf), Me, US 189/G3
Mainhardt, Ger. 112/C4
Mainhausen, Ger. 112/B2
Mainland (isl.), Sc, UK 89/V14
Mainling, China 141/F2
Mainpurī, India 142/B2
Mainstockheim, Ger. 112/D3
Maintirano, Madg. 165/H7
Mainz, Ger. 112/B3
Maio (isl.), CpV. 151/K10
Maipo (vol.), Chile 216/P9
Maipo (riv.), Chile 216/N8
Maipú, Arg. 216/F3
Maipú, Chile 216/N8
Maira (riv.), It. 101/G4
Maire (str.), Arg. 217/D7
Mairiporã, Braz. 213/G8
Mairwa, India 143/E2
Mais Gate (int'l arpt.), Haiti 203/H2
Maisach, Ger. 112/E6
Maisí (cape), Cuba 199/G3
Maisome (isl.), Tanz. 162/A3
Maison-Rouge, Fr. 88/M6
Maisons-Alfort, Fr. 88/K5
Maisons-Laffitte, Fr. 88/J5
Maithon (res.), India 143/F4
Maitland, Austl. 173/D2
Maitland (riv.), On, Can. 188/D3
Maitland, Austl. 171/H5
Maitri, India, Ant. 218/A
Maizhokunggar, China 141/F2
Maizières-lès-Metz, Fr. 111/F5
Maizuru, Japan 135/H5
Maizuru (bay), Japan 135/H4
Maja e Zezë (peak), Alb. 105/G2
Majadahonda, Sp. 103/N9
Majagual, Col. 210/C2
Majardah (mts.), Alg. 158/K6
Majāz Al Bāb, Tun. 158/L6
Majdanpek, Serb. 106/E3
Majene, Indo. 139/E4
Majia (riv.), China 130/D3
Majiang, China 137/A2
Majorca (isl.), Sp. 103/G3
Majur, Serb. 106/D3
Majuro (cap.), Mrsh. 174/G4
Makabe, Japan 135/E1
Makaha, Hi, US 182/V13
Makakilo City, Hi, US 182/V13
Makālu (peak), China 143/F2
Makālu (peak), Nepal 140/E2
Makarska, Cro. 105/E1
Makassar (str.), Indo. 139/E4
Makatea (isl.), FrPol. 175/L6
Makawao, Hi, US 182/T10
Makay (mass.), Madg. 165/H8
Makemo (isl.), FrPol. 175/L6
Makena, Hi, US 182/T10
Makeni, SLeo. 160/B4
Makgadikgadi (salt pans), Bots. 163/D5
Makhachkala, Rus. 121/H4
Makhdūmpur, Pak. 144/B4
Makhfar al Busayyah, Iraq 146/E2
Makhmūr, Iraq 148/E3
Makian (isl.), Indo. 139/G3
Makin (isl.), Kiri. 174/G4
Makino, Japan 135/K5
Makinsk, Kaz. 145/F2
Makioka, Japan 135/B2
Makiyivka, Ukr. 120/F2
Makkah, SAr. 146/C4
Makkovik, Nf, Can. 181/L3
Makó, Hun. 106/E2
Makokou, Gabon 154/H7
Makonde (plat.), Tanz. 162/C5
Maków Mazowiecki, Pol. 99/L2
Makrakómi, Gre. 105/H3
Makran (coast), Iran 147/G3
Makran (reg.), Iran 147/H3
Makrokhórion, Gre. 105/H2
Maksutlu, Turk. 105/K2
Makteir (reg.), Mrta. 156/C5
Makthar, Tun. 158/L7
Makurazaki, Japan 132/B5
Makurdi, Nga. 161/H5
Makushin (vol.), Ak, US 192/E5
Mal Abrigo, Uru. 217/K11
Mala (pt.), CR 202/E4
Mala (pt.), Pan. 203/G5
Mala, Peru 214/B4
Malabar (coast), India 140/B5
Malabata (pt.), Mor. 158/B2
Malabo (cap.), EqG. 154/G7
Malacacheta, Braz. 212/B5
Malacca (str.), Asia 138/A3
Malacky, Slvk. 99/J4
Maladers, Swi. 115/F4
Maladzyechna, Bela. 97/M4
Málaga (int'l arpt.), Sp. 102/C4
Málaga, Sp. 102/C4
Malaga, NJ, US 196/C4
Malaga Cove (bay), Ca, US 194/F8
Malagarasi (riv.), Tanz. 162/A4
Malagón, Sp. 102/D3
Malagueta (bay), Cuba 203/G1
Malahide, Ire. 92/B5
Malaimbandy, Madg. 165/H8
Malaita (isl.), Sol. 174/F5
Malakāl, Sudan 155/M6
Malakangiri, India 140/D4
Malakwāl, Pak. 144/B3
Malambo, Col. 210/C2
Malang, Indo. 138/D5
Malangawa, Nepal 143/E2
Malanje, Ang. 163/C2
Malans, Swi. 115/F4
Malanville, Ben. 161/F4
Malargüe, Arg. 216/C2
Malartic, Qu, Can. 188/E1
Malasoro (pt.), Indo. 139/E5
Malatya (prov.), Turk. 148/D2
Malatya, Turk. 148/D2
Malaut, India 144/C4
Malawi (ctry.) 163/F3
Malawi (Nyasa) (lake), Malw. 162/B5
Malay (pen.), Thai. 141/G6
Malaya (reg.), Malay. 138/B3
Malaya Vishera, Rus. 97/Q2
Malaybalay, Phil. 137/E6
Malāyer, Iran 146/E2
Malaysia (ctry.) 138/C2
Malazemel'skaya (tundra), Rus. 119/L2
Malazgirt, Turk. 148/E2
Malbaie (riv.), Qu, Can. 189/G1
Malbork, Pol. 97/H4
Malcesine, It. 117/D1
Malchin, Ger. 96/E5
Malcontenta, It. 117/F2
Maldegem, Belg. 110/C1
Malden, Mo, US 187/K3
Malden (isl.), Kiri. 175/K5
Maldive (isls.), Mald. 140/B6
Maldives (ctry.) 125/G9
Maldon, Austl. 173/C3
Maldon, Eng, UK 91/G3
Maldonado, Uru. 217/G2
Maldonado (dept.), Uru. 217/G2
Male (cap.), Mald. 125/G9
Maléa (cape), Gre. 105/H4
Mālegaon, India 147/K4
Malekula (isl.), Van. 174/F6
Malemort-sur-Corrèze, Fr. 100/D4
Malente, Ger. 96/D4
Maleny, Austl. 172/D4
Maleo, It. 116/C2
Malesína, Gre. 105/H3
Malfa, It. 104/D3
Malgobek, Rus. 121/H4
Malgrat de Mar, Sp. 103/G2
Malgrate, It. 116/C1
Malheur (lake), Or, US 186/C2
Malheur (riv.), Or, US 184/D5
Malheureux (cape), Mrts. 165/T14
Mali (riv.), Myan. 141/G2
Mali (isl.), Myan. 136/B3
Mali (ctry.) 154/E4
Mali Lošinj, Cro. 106/B3
Mália, Gre. 105/J5
Malibu, Ca, US 194/B2
Malīhābād, India 142/C2
Mälilla, Swe. 96/F3
Malin Head (pt.), Ire. 89/Q9
Malinau, Indo. 139/E3
Malindang (mt.), Phil. 139/F2
Malindi, Kenya 162/D3
Maling (pass), China 130/C3
Malio (riv.), Madg. 165/H8
Malipo, China 136/D1
Malīr Cantonment, Pak. 147/J4
Malka Mari NP, Kenya 155/P7
Malkara, Turk. 107/H5
Malko Tŭrnovo, Bul. 107/H5
Mallacoota, Austl. 173/D3
Mallaig, Sc, UK 89/R8
Mallānwān, India 142/C2
Mallasvesi (lake), Fin. 97/K1
Mallee Cliffs NP, Austl. 173/B2
Mallén, Sp. 102/E2
Malleray, Swi. 114/D3
Mallero (riv.), It. 115/F5
Mallersdorf-Pfaffenberg, Ger. 113/F5
Malles (Mals), It. 115/G4
Malloa, Chile 216/N9
Mallow, Ire. 89/P10
Malmberget, Swe. 95/G2
Malmédy, Belg. 111/F3
Malmesbury, SAfr. 164/L10
Malmköping, Swe. 96/G2
Malmö, Swe. 96/E4
Malmöhus (co.), Swe. 95/E5
Malmslätt, Swe. 96/F2
Malnate, It. 116/B1
Malo, It. 117/E1
Maloelap (isl.), Mrsh. 174/G4
Malone, NY, US 188/F2
Malong, China 141/H2
Malonje (peak), Tanz. 162/A5
Malonno, It. 115/G5
Małopolska (uplands), Pol. 99/K3
Małopolskie (prov.), Pol. 99/K4
Malpartida de Cáceres, Sp. 102/B3
Malpartida de Plasencia, Sp. 102/B3
Malpelo (isl.), Col. 208/B3
Malpensa (int'l arpt.), It. 116/B1
Malpica, Sp. 102/A1
Malsch (riv.), Aus. 113/H5
Malsch, Ger. 112/B5
Malše (riv.), Czh. 99/H4
Mälstek (peak), Czh. 113/G4
Malta, Mt, US 184/G3
Malta, Braz. 212/C2
Malta (chan.), Malta 104/C4
Malta (ctry.) 104/L7
Maltahöhe, Namb. 163/C5
Maltby, Eng, UK 93/G5
Malters, Swi. 114/E3
Maltorne (riv.), Fr. 88/G6
Malung, Swe. 96/E1
Malvaglia, Swi. 115/E5
Malvan, India 147/K5
Malveira, Port. 103/P10
Malvern, Pa, US 196/C3
Malverne, NY, US 197/L9
Malvinas (Falkland) (isls.), UK 218/W
Malvy Uzen' (riv.), Rus. 121/H2
Malyn, Ukr. 120/D2
Malyy Yenisey (riv.), Rus. 128/G1
Malzéville, Fr. 111/F6
Mamanguape, Braz. 212/D2
Mamaroneck, NY, US 197/L8
Mamba, Zam. 163/E4
Mamba, Japan 135/B1
Mambajao, Phil. 137/D6
Mambasa, D.R. Congo 162/A2
Mamberamo (riv.), Indo. 139/J4
Mambéré (riv.), CAfr. 154/J7
Mambij, Syria 148/D2
Mamburao, Phil. 137/D5
Mamer, Lux. 111/F4
Mamers, Fr. 100/D2
Mamfé, Camr. 161/H5
Mammendorf, Ger. 115/H1
Mamming, Ger. 113/F5
Mammoth, Az, US 186/E4
Mammoth Cave NP, Ky, US 191/G2
Mamoré (riv.), Braz. 208/E6
Mamou, La, US 187/J5
Mamoutzou, May. 165/H6
Mampikony, Madg. 165/H7
Mampong, Gha. 161/E5
Mamry (lake), Pol. 97/J4
Mamuju, Indo. 139/E4
Mamuru (riv.), Braz. 209/G4
Mamwera (peak), Tanz. 162/C4
Man, C.d'Iv. 160/D5
Man, Isle of (isl.), IM, UK 92/D3
Man Mia (peak), Thai. 136/B4
Mana (riv.), FrG. 211/H3
Manabl (prov.), Ecu. 210/A5
Manacapuru, Braz. 208/F4
Manacle (pt.), Eng, UK 90/A6
Manacor, Sp. 103/G3
Manado, Indo. 139/F3
Manage, Belg. 111/D3
Managua (cap.), Nic. 202/E3
Managua (lake), Nic. 202/E3
Manahawkin, NJ, US 196/D4
Manakambahiny, Madg. 165/J7
Manakara, Madg. 165/J8
Manalapan, NJ, US 196/D3
Manāli, India 144/D3
Manambaho (riv.), Madg. 165/H7
Manambolo (riv.), Madg. 165/H7
Mananantanana (riv.), Madg. 165/H8
Mananara, Madg. 165/J7
Mananara (riv.), Madg. 165/H8
Mananjary, Madg. 165/J8
Mananjary (riv.), Madg. 165/H8
Manara (pt.), It. 116/C4
Manaratsandry, Madg. 165/H7
Manas, China 128/E3
Manas (int'l arpt.), Kyr. 145/F4
Manas (peak), Kyr. 145/F4
Manās (riv.), India 143/H2
Manas (riv.), China 128/E2
Manāslu (peak), Nepal 143/E1
Manasquan, NJ, US 196/D3
Manasquan (riv.), NJ, US 196/D3
Manassa, Co, US 190/B2
Manastir Dečani, Kos. 105/G1
Manastir Gračanica, Kos. 106/E4
Manastir Sopoćani, Serb. 106/E4
Manatsuru, Japan 135/C3
Manaus, Braz. 208/F4
Manawatu (riv.), NZ 175/T11
Mañazo, Peru 214/D4
Manazuru-misaki (cape), Japan 135/C3
Mance (riv.), Fr. 114/B2
Mancha Real, Sp. 102/D4
Mancheng, China 130/G7
Mancherāl, India 140/C4
Manchester (lake), Austl. 172/E7
Manchester, Eng, UK 93/F5
Manchester (co.), Eng, UK 93/F5
Manchester (Ringway) (int'l arpt.), Eng, UK 93/F5
Manchester, Ky, US 188/D4
Manchester, Mo, US 195/F8
Manchester, Md, US 196/B4
Manchester, NH, US 189/G3
Manchester, Pa, US 196/B3
Manchester, Tn, US 191/G3
Manchester, Wa, US 193/B2
Manchuria (reg.), China 129/M3
Mancieulles, Fr. 111/E5
Máncora, Peru 214/A2
Mand (riv.), Iran 147/F3
Manda, PN de, Chad 155/J6
Mandabe, Madg. 165/H8
Mandaguari, Braz. 213/B2
Mandal, India 140/B3
Mandal, Nor. 96/B2
Mandal-Ovoo, Mong. 128/H3
Mandala (peak), Indo. 139/K4
Mandalay, Myan. 141/G3
Mandalay (div.), Myan. 141/G3
Mandalgovī, Mong. 128/J2
Mandalī, Iraq 146/E2
Mandan, ND, US 185/H4
Mandasavu (peak), Indo. 139/F5
Mandaue, Phil. 137/D5
Mandeb (str.), Afr.,Asia 151/G3
Mandello del Lario, It. 115/F6
Mandera, Kenya 155/P7
Mandeure, Fr. 114/C3
Mandeville, La, US 195/P16
Mandeville, Jam. 203/G2
Mandi Bahāuddīn, Pak. 144/B3
Mandi Dabwāli, India 144/C5
Mandi Sādiqganj, Pak. 144/B4
Mandié, Moz. 163/F4
Mandiola (isl.), Indo. 139/G4
Mandira (res.), India 143/E4
Mandla, India 142/C4
Mandø (isl.), Den. 96/C4
Mándok, Hun. 99/M4
Mandoto, Madg. 165/H7
Mandoúdhion, Gre. 105/H3
Mándra, Gre. 105/N8
Mandrare (riv.), Madg. 165/H9
Mandritsara, Madg. 165/J6
Mandsaur, India 147/L4
Mandurah, Austl. 170/B5
Manduria, It. 105/E2
Māndvi, India 147/J4
Mandya, India 140/C5
Mane (pass), Nepal 142/D1
Manéngouba, Massif du (peak), Camr. 161/H5
Maner, India 143/E3
Manerbio, It. 116/D2
Manfalūt, Egypt 146/B3
Manfredonia, It. 104/D2
Manfredonia, Golfo di (gulf), It. 104/D2
Mang (riv.), China 130/B4
Manga, Braz. 212/B4
Manga, Burk. 161/E4
Mangabeiras, Chapada das (hills), Braz. 209/J6
Mangai, D.R. Congo 163/C1
Mangaia (isl.), Cookls. 175/K7
Mangaldai, India 141/F2
Mangaldan, Phil. 137/D4
Mangalia, Rom. 107/J4
Mangalisa (peak), Tanz. 162/C4
Mangalore, India 140/B5
Mangaratiba, Braz. 213/J7
Mangareva (isl.), FrPol. 175/M7
Manger, Nor. 96/A1
Mangghystaū (obl.), Kaz. 122/F5
Mangghystaū Tübegi (pen.), Kaz. 121/J3
Mangghystaū Üstirti (plat.), Kaz. 121/K4
Mangkalihat (cape), Indo. 139/E3
Mangla (dam), Pak. 144/B3
Mangla, Pak. 144/B3
Mangla (res.), Pak. 144/B3
Manglaralto, Ecu. 214/A1
Manglares (pt.), Col. 210/B4
Manglaur, India 142/A1
Mangles (bay), Austl. 170/K7
Mango, Togo 161/F4
Mangoche, Malw. 163/G3
Mangoky (riv.), Madg. 163/J11
Mangole (isl.), Indo. 139/G4
Mangoro (riv.), Madg. 165/J7
Mangotsfield, Eng, UK 90/D4
Māngrol, India 147/K4
Mangualde, Port. 102/B2
Mangueira (lake), Braz. 217/G2
Mangum, Ok, US 187/H4
Manhasset, NY, US 197/L8
Manhasset (bay), NY, US 197/L8
Manhattan, Mt, US 184/F4
Manhattan (isl.), NY, US 197/K9
Manhattan Beach, Ca, US 194/F8
Manhay, Belg. 111/E3
Manheim, Pa, US 196/B3
Manhiça, Moz. 163/F6
Manhuaçu, Braz. 213/D2
Manhumirim, Braz. 213/D2
Mania (riv.), Madg. 165/H7
Maniamba, Moz. 163/G3
Maniāri (riv.), India 142/C4
Manicoré (riv.), Braz. 208/F5
Manicoré, Braz. 208/F5
Manicouagan (riv.), Qu, Can. 181/K3
Manicouagan (res.), Qu, Can. 189/G1
Manifold (cape), Austl. 172/C3
Manigotagan, Mb, Can. 185/J3
Manihāri, India 143/F3
Manihi (isl.), FrPol. 175/L6
Manihiki (isl.), Cookls. 175/J6
Manikarchar, India 143/G3
Manila (cap.), Phil. 137/D5
Manilla, Austl. 173/D1
Maningory (riv.), Madg. 165/J7
Manipa (str.), Indo. 139/G4
Manipat (hills), India 142/D4
Manipur (state), India 141/F3
Manisa (prov.), Turk. 148/B2
Manistee (riv.), Mi, US 188/C2
Manistee, Mi, US 188/C2
Manistique, Mi, US 188/C2
Manitoba (prov.), Can. 180/G3
Manitoba (lake), Mb, Can. 185/J3
Manitou (riv.), Qu, Can. 189/H1
Manitou Springs, Co, US 187/F3
Manitoulin (isl.), On, Can. 188/D2
Manitowoc, Wi, US 185/M4
Maniwaki, Qu, Can. 188/F2
Manizales, Col. 208/C2
Manja, Madg. 165/H8
Manjakandriana, Madg. 165/J7
Manjimup, Austl. 170/C5
Mankono, C.d'Iv. 160/D4
Manley Hot Springs, Ak, US 192/H2
Manlleu, Sp. 102/D1
Manlyutka, Rus. 119/R4
Manmād, India 147/K4
Mannar, SrL. 140/C6
Mannar (gulf), India,SrL. 140/C6
Männedorf, Swi. 115/E3
Mannetjiesberg (peak), SAfr. 164/C4
Mannheim, Ger. 112/B4
Manning, SC, US 191/H3
Manning (cape), NW, Can. 181/Q7
Manning, Ab, Can. 180/E3
Mannington Meadow (lake), NJ, US 196/C4
Männlifluh (peak), Swi. 114/D4
Mannum, Austl. 171/H5
Mano (riv.), Libr. 154/C6
Manokotak, Ak, US 192/G4
Manolo Fortich, Phil. 137/D6
Manombo, Madg. 165/G8
Manono, D.R. Congo 163/E2
Manorville, NY, US 197/F2
Manosque, Fr. 100/F5
Manouane (riv.), Qu, Can. 189/G1
Manouane (lake), Qu, Can. 189/G1
Manp'o, NKor. 131/D2
Manra (Sydney) (isl.), Kiri. 175/H5
Manresa, Sp. 103/K6
Mansa, Zam. 162/A5
Mānsa, India 144/C5
Mansa Konko, Gam. 160/B3
Mansalay, Phil. 139/F1
Mānsehra, Pak. 144/B2
Mansel (isl.), Nun., Can. 181/H2
Mansfield, Austl. 173/C3
Mansfield, Eng, UK 93/G5
Mansfield, La, US 187/J4
Mansfield, Oh, US 188/D3
Mansfield Woodhouse, Eng, UK 93/G5
Mansilla de las Mulas, Sp. 102/C1
Manta, Ecu. 210/A5
Mantalingajan (mt.), Phil. 139/E2
Mantaro (riv.), Peru 208/C6
Manteca, Ca, US 186/B3
Mantecal, Ven. 210/D3
Manteigas, Port. 102/B2
Mantena, Braz. 213/D1
Manthani, India 140/C4
Manti, Ut, US 186/E3
Mantiqueira, Serra da (mts.), Braz. 209/K8
Mantorp, Swe. 96/F2
Mantova (prov.), It. 116/D2
Mantova, It. 117/D2
Mäntsälä, Fin. 97/L1
Mantua, Cuba 203/E1
Mantua, NJ, US 196/C4
Mantua, Ut, US 195/K11
Manturovo, Rus. 119/K4
Mäntyharju, Fin. 97/M1
Manu (riv.), India 208/D6
Manú, Peru 214/D4
Manú, PN, Peru 208/D6
Manua (isls.), ASam. 175/J6
Manuae Atoll (atoll), Cookls. 175/K6
Manuel Alves da Natividade (riv.), Braz. 209/J6
Manuel Benavides, Mex. 190/C4
Manuel J. Cobo, Arg. 217/K11
Manui (isl.), Indo. 139/F4
Manuk (riv.), Indo. 138/C5
Manukau, NZ 175/S10
Manumuskin (riv.), NJ, US 196/D5
Manuripe (riv.), Bol. 208/E6
Manuripe Heath Amazonica, Reserva Nacional, Bol. 214/D4
Manus (isl.), PNG 174/D5
Manville, NJ, US 196/D2
Many, La, US 187/J5
Many Farms, Az, US 186/E3
Manyara (lake), Tanz. 162/B3
Manych (riv.), Rus. 122/E5
Manych-Gudilo (lake), Rus. 121/G3
Manzanares, Sp. 102/D3
Manzanares (riv.), Sp. 103/N8
Manzanares el Real, Sp. 103/N8
Manzanillo, Mex. 200/D5
Manzanillo (int'l arpt.), Mex. 200/D5
Manzanillo, Cuba 203/G1
Manzano (mts.), NM, US 190/B3
Manzano, It. 117/G1
Manzhouli, China 129/L2
Manzilah, Buḩayrat al (lake), Egypt 149/B4
Manzini, Swaz. 165/E2
Mao, Chad 154/J5
Maoke (mts.), Indo. 139/J4
Maoming, China 141/K3
Mapastepec, Mex. 202/C3
Mapi (riv.), Indo. 139/J5
Mapimí, Bolsón de (depr.), Mex. 200/D3
Mapire, Ven. 211/E3
Maple (riv.), ND, US 185/J4
Maple Creek, Sk, Can. 184/F3
Maple Grove, Qu, Can. 189/N7
Maple Park, Il, US 193/N16
Maple Shade, NJ, US 196/D4
Maple Valley, Wa, US 193/C3
Mapleton, Ut, US 195/K13
Maplewood, Mo, US 195/G8
Maplewood, NJ, US 197/H9
Maporal, Ven. 210/D3
Mapuera (riv.), Braz. 208/G3
Maputo (int'l arpt.), Moz. 165/F2
Maputo (cap.), Moz. 165/F2
Maqdam (cape), Sudan 159/D5
Maqên Gangri (peak), China 128/G5
Maquan (Damqog) (riv.), China 142/E1
Maquinchao, Arg. 216/C4
Maquoketa (riv.), Ia, US 187/K2
Mar (mts.), Braz. 205/E5
Mar (reg.), Sc, UK 94/D2
Mar Chiquita (lake), Arg. 215/D3
Mar de Ajó, Arg. 217/F3
Mar del Plata, Arg. 216/F3
Mar del Tuyú, Arg. 217/F3
Mara (pol. reg.), Tanz. 162/B3
Mara (riv.), Tanz. 162/B3
Marabá, Braz. 209/J5
Maracá, Ilha de (isl.), Braz. 209/H3
Maracaibo, Ven. 210/D2
Maracaibo (lake), Ven. 210/D2
Maracaju, Serra de (mts.), Braz. 209/G8
Maracás, Braz. 212/B4
Maracás, Chapada de (hills), Braz. 212/B4
Maracay, Ven. 208/E1
Maracena, Sp. 102/D4
Marādah, Libya 154/J2
Maradi, Niger 161/G3
Maradi (dept.), Niger 161/G3
Marāgheh, Iran 146/E1
Mārahra, India 142/B2
Marahuaca (peak), Ven. 211/E4
Marais de St-Gond (swamp), Fr. 110/C6
Marais des Cygnes (riv.), Ks,Mo, US 187/J3
Marajó (bay), Braz. 209/J4
Marajó, Ilha de (isl.), Braz. 209/H4
Maralal, Kenya 162/C2
Maralinga-Tjarutja Abor. Land, Austl. 171/F4
Maramag, Phil. 137/E6
Marambaia, Ilha (isl.), Braz. 213/K8
Maramureş (co.), Rom. 99/M5
Marana, Az, US 186/E4
Marana (lag.), Cro. 117/G1
Marand, Iran 121/H5
Marang, Malay. 138/B2
Marangani, Peru 214/D4
Maranguape, Braz. 212/C1
Maranhão (riv.), Braz. 209/J6
Maranhão (state), Braz. 212/A2
Marano Lagunare, It. 117/G1
Marano sul Panaro, It. 117/D4
Marano Vicentino, It. 117/E1
Maranoa (riv.), Austl. 167/D3
Marañón (riv.), Peru 214/B2
Marans, Fr. 100/C3

Maraoue, PN de la, C.d'Iv. 160/D5
Marapi (peak), Indo. 138/B4
Maras (peak), Indo. 138/C4
Mărăşeşti, Rom. 107/H3
Marathon, On, Can. 185/M3
Marathon, Fl, US 191/H5
Marathon, Tx, US 190/C4
Marathón, Gre. 105/N8
Marau, Braz. 213/A4
Marauliānwāla, Pak. 144/B3
Maravatío de Ocampo, Mex. 201/E5
Marawi, Phil. 137/D6
Marbach, Swi. 114/D4
Marbach am Neckar, Ger. 112/C5
Marbache, Fr. 111/F6
Marbella, Sp. 102/C4
Marble Bar, Austl. 170/C2
Marbleton, Wy, US 184/F5
Marburg, Ger. 101/H1
Marburg (lake), Pa, US 196/B4
Marca, Ponta da (pt.), Ang. 163/B4
Marcali, Hun. 106/C2
Marcallo, It. 116/B2
Marcapata, Peru 214/D4
March, Eng, UK 91/G1
Marche (prov.), It. 101/K5
Marche (mts.), Fr. 100/D3
Marche-en-Famenne, Belg. 111/E3
Marchémoret, Fr. 88/L4
Marchena, Sp. 102/C4
Marchena (isl.), Ecu. 214/E6
Marcheno, It. 116/D1
Marchiennes, Fr. 110/C3
Marchin, Belg. 111/E3
Marchtrenk, Aus. 113/H6
Marciana Marina, It. 104/B1
Marcilly, Fr. 88/L4
Marcilly-sur-Tille, Fr. 114/B2
Marck, Fr. 110/A2
Marckolsheim, Fr. 114/D1
Marco, Braz. 212/B1
Marco, Fl, US 191/H5
Marco Polo (int'l arpt.), It. 117/F2
Marcoing, Fr. 110/C3
Marcon, It. 117/F1
Marcona, Peru 214/C4
Marconi (mt.), BC, Can. 184/E3
Marcos Juárez, Arg. 216/E2
Marcoussis, Fr. 88/J6
Marcovia, Hon. 202/E3
Marcq-en-Barœul, Fr. 110/C2
Marcus Baker (mt.), Ak, US 192/J3
Marcy (mt.), NY, US 188/F2
Mardān, Pak. 144/B2
Marden, Eng, UK 88/E3
Mardeuil, Fr. 110/C5
Mardin (town), Turk. 148/E2
Marecchia (riv.), It. 117/F5
Maree (lake), Sc, UK 89/R8
Mareeba, Austl. 172/B2
Mareil-sur-Mauldre, Fr. 88/H5
Marengo, Il, US 193/N15
Marennes, Fr. 100/C4
Mareuil-sur-Ourcq, Fr. 88/M4
Marfa, Tx, US 187/F5
Margalla Hills NP, Pak. 144/B3
Marganets', Ukr. 120/E3
Margao (Madgaon), India 147/K5
Margaret (mt.), Austl. 170/C2
Margaret River, Austl. 170/B5
Margarita (peak), Ca, US 194/C4
Margarita, Isla de (isl.), Ven. 208/F1
Margarition, Gre. 105/G3
Margate, SAfr. 165/E3
Margate, Eng, UK 91/H4
Margate City, NJ, US 196/D5
Margeride, Monts de la (mts.), Fr. 100/E4
Margherita (peak), Ugan. 162/A2
Marghilon, Uzb. 145/F4
Marghita, Rom. 106/F2
Margny-lès-Compiègne, Fr. 110/B5
Margos, Peru 214/B3
Margosatubig, Phil. 137/D6
Margraten, Neth. 111/E2
Mari, Braz. 212/D2
Maria (mt.), Austl. 173/D4
María Cleófas (isl.), Mex. 200/D4
Maria da Fé, Braz. 213/H7
Maria Island NP, Austl. 173/D4
María Madre (isl.), Mex. 200/D4
María Magdalena (isl.), Mex. 200/D4
Maria van Diemen (cape), NZ 175/S9
Mariāhū, India 142/D3
Marian, Austl. 172/C3
Marianao, Cuba 203/F1
Marianna, Fl, US 191/G4
Marianna, Ar, US 187/K4
Mariano Comense, It. 116/C1
Mariano Marcos, Phil. 137/D6
Mariánské Lázně, Czh. 113/F3
Marias (riv.), Mt, US 184/F3
Mariato (pt.), Pan. 203/F5
Maribo, Den. 96/D4
Maribor, Slov. 101/L3
Maricá, Braz. 213/L7
Maricopa (co.), Az, US 195/R18
Marié (riv.), Braz. 208/E4
Marie Byrd Land (phys. reg.), Ant. 218/S
Marie-Galante (isl.), Dom. 199/J4
Mariehamn (int'l arpt.), Fin. 97/H1
Mariel, Cuba 203/F1
Marienhafe, Ger. 109/E1
Marienheide, Ger. 111/G1
Mariental, Namb. 163/C5
Mariestad, Swe. 96/E2
Marietta, Ok, US 187/H4
Marietta, Ga, US 191/G3
Marietta, Pa, US 196/B3
Marignane, Fr. 100/F5
Marigot, Dom. 199/N9
Marijampolė, Lith. 97/K4
Marília, Braz. 213/B2
Marín, Sp. 102/A1
Marin (co.), Ca, US 193/J10
Marin-Epagnier, Swi. 114/D3
Marina, It. 104/D3
Marina del Rey, Ca, US 194/F8
Marina del Rey (har.), Ca, US 194/F8
Marina di Andora, It. 116/B5
Marina di Montemarciano, It. 117/G5
Marina di Ravenna, It. 117/F4
Marine Nat'l Rsv., Kenya 162/D3
Marine World Africa USA, Ca, US 193/K10
Marineland, Austl. 171/M8
Marines, Fr. 88/H4
Marinette, Wi, US 185/M4
Maringá, Braz. 213/B2
Marinha Grande, Port. 102/A3
Marinhas, Port. 102/A2
Marion (reef), Austl. 167/E2
Marion, Al, US 191/G3
Marion, In, US 188/C3
Marion, Ky, US 188/B4
Marion, Mi, US 188/C2
Marion, Oh, US 188/D3
Marion (lake), SC, US 191/H3
Maripa, Ven. 211/E3
Mariposa, Ca, US 186/C3
Mariscal Estigarribia, Par. 208/F8
Mariscal Sucre (int'l arpt.), Ecu. 210/B5
Maritime Alps (mts.), Fr. 101/G4
Maritsa (riv.), Bul. 107/H5
Mariupol', Ukr. 120/F3
Mariupol' (int'l arpt.), Ukr. 120/F3
Mariy-El, Resp., Rus. 122/G6
Marj 'Uyūn, Leb. 149/D3
Mark (riv.), Belg. 108/B6
Mark Twain NWR, Il, US 195/F7
Mark Twain (lake), Mo, US 187/J3
Mark Twain NWR, Mo, US 195/G8
Marka (riv.), Ger. 109/E3
Marka (Merca), Som. 155/P7
Markam, China 141/G2
Markaryd, Swe. 96/E3
Markdorf, Ger. 115/F2
Markelsdorfer (pt.), Ger. 96/D4
Marken (isl.), Neth. 108/C4
Markerwaard (polder), Neth. 108/C3
Market Harborough, Eng, UK 91/F2
Markgroningen, Ger. 112/C5
Markham, On, Can. 189/R8
Markham (bay), Nun., Can. 181/J2
Marki, Pol. 99/L2
Markinch, Sc, UK 94/C4
Markit, China 145/G5
Markleeville, Ca, US 186/C3
Markneukirchen, Ger. 113/F2
Markópoulon, Gre. 105/N9
Markovac, Serb. 106/E3
Marks, Rus. 121/H2
Marksville, La, US 187/J5
Markt Bibart, Ger. 112/D3
Markt Erlbach, Ger. 112/D4
Markt Indersdorf, Ger. 113/E6
Markt Rettenbach, Ger. 115/G2
Markt Sankt Florian, Aus. 113/H6
Markt Schwaben, Ger. 113/E6
Marktbreit, Ger. 112/D3
Marktheidenfeld, Ger. 112/C3
Marktl, Ger. 113/F6
Marktoberdorf, Ger. 115/G2
Marktredwitz, Ger. 113/F3
Marl, Ger. 109/E5
Marla, Austl. 171/G3
Marlboro, NJ, US 196/D3
Marlboro (Upper Marlboro), Md, US 196/B6
Marle, Fr. 110/C4
Marlengo (Marling), It. 115/H4
Marlenheim, Fr. 111/G6
Marles-en-Brie, Fr. 88/L5
Marles-les-Mines, Fr. 110/B3
Marlow, Eng, UK 91/F3
Marlow, Ger. 96/E4
Marlton, NJ, US 196/D4
Marly, Fr. 111/F5
Marly, Fr. 110/C3
Marly-la-Ville, Fr. 88/K4
Marly-le-Roi, Fr. 88/J5
Marmagão, India 147/K5
Marmande, Fr. 100/D4
Marmara, Turk. 107/H5
Marmara (isl.), Turk. 107/H5
Marmara (sea), Turk. 107/J5
Marmaraereğlisi, Turk. 107/H5
Marmaris, Turk. 148/B2
Marmelos (riv.), Braz. 208/F5
Marmion (lake), Austl. 170/D4
Marmirolo, It. 117/D2
Marmolada (peak), It. 101/J3
Marmolejo, Sp. 102/C3
Marmontana (peak), It. 115/F5
Marmora, NJ, US 196/D5
Marmoutier, Fr. 111/G6
Marnay, Fr. 114/B3
Marnaz, Fr. 114/C5
Marne (riv.), Fr. 100/F2
Marne, Ger. 96/C5
Marne (dept.), Fr. 110/C6
Marne au Rhin, Canal de la (canal), Fr. 111/D6
Maro (reef), Hi, US 175/H2
Maroa, Ven. 211/E4
Maroantsetra, Madg. 165/J6
Marokau (isl.), FrPol. 175/L6
Marolambo, Madg. 165/J8
Maroldsweisach, Ger. 112/D2
Marolles-en-Brie, Fr. 88/M5
Marolles-en-Hurepoix, Fr. 88/J6
Maromokotro (peak), Madg. 165/J6
Marondera, Zim. 163/F4
Marone, It. 116/D1
Maroni (riv.), FrG.,Sur. 209/H3
Maroochydore-Mooloolaba, Austl. 172/D4
Maroon Town, Jam. 203/G2
Marostica, It. 117/E1
Marotandrano, Madg. 165/J7
Marotiri (Bass Is.) (isls.), FrPol. 175/L7
Marotta, It. 117/G5
Maroua, Camr. 154/H5
Marouini (riv.), FrG. 211/H4
Marovato, Madg. 165/J6
Marovoay, Madg. 165/H7
Marowijne (dist.), Sur. 211/H3
Marpingen, Ger. 111/G5
Marple, Eng, UK 93/F5
Marquan (riv.), China 140/E2
Marquard, SAfr. 164/D3
Marquarie (riv.), Austl. 173/C1
Marquesas (isls.), FrPol. 175/M5
Marquise, Fr. 110/A2
Marracuene, Moz. 165/F2
Marradi, It. 117/E4
Marrah (mts.), Sudan 155/K5
Marrah (peak), Sudan 155/K5
Marrakech, Mor. 156/D3
Marrero, La, US 195/P17
Marromeu, Moz. 163/G4
Marrupa, Moz. 163/G3
Mars (peak), It. 116/A1
Marsá al Burayqah, Libya 155/J1
Marsá Maṭrūḩ (cap.), Egypt 159/A2
Marsabit, Kenya 162/C2
Marsabit Nat'l Rsv., Kenya 162/C2
Marsala, It. 104/C4
Marsange (riv.), Fr. 88/L5
Marsannay, Fr. 114/A3
Marsberg, Ger. 109/F6
Marsciano, It. 101/K5
Marsdiep Texelstroom (chan.), Neth. 108/B3
Marseille, Fr. 100/F5
Marseille-en-Beauvaisis, Fr. 110/A4
Marsh (isl.), La, US 190/E4
Marshall (riv.), Austl. 171/H2
Marshall, Sk, Can. 184/F2
Marshall, Co, US 195/B3
Marshall, Mn, US 185/K4
Marshall, Mo, US 187/J3
Marshall, Tx, US 187/J4
Marshall, Ut, US 195/J12
Marshall Islands (ctry.) 174/G3
Marshallton, De, US 196/C4
Marshalltown, Ia, US 185/K5
Marshdale, Co, US 195/B3
Marshfield, Mo, US 187/J3
Märsta, Swe. 96/G2
Marston (lake), Co, US 195/B3
Marsyandi (riv.), Nepal 143/E1
Marta, It. 104/B1
Martaban, Myan. 136/B2
Martaban (gulf), Myan. 136/B2
Martapura, Indo. 138/D4
Marte R. Gomez, Mex. 200/C3
Martelange, Belg. 111/E4
Martellago, It. 117/F1
Martensville, Sk, Can. 184/G2
Martfeld, Ger. 109/G3
Martha's Vineyard (isl.), Ma, US 189/G3
Martignacco, It. 117/G1
Martigny, Swi. 114/D5
Martigny-les-Bains, Fr. 114/B1
Martigues, Fr. 100/F5
Martil, Mor. 158/B2
Martin, Tn, US 188/B4
Martin (lake), Al, US 191/G3
Martin Vaz (isls.), Braz. 209/N8
Martina Franca, It. 105/E2
Martinengo, It. 116/C1
Martinez, Ga, US 191/H3
Martínez de la Torre, Mex. 201/M6
Martinho Campos, Braz. 213/C1
Martinique (isl.), Fr. 199/N9
Martinique Passage (chan.), Dom.,Mart. 199/J4
Martínon, Gre. 105/H3
Martinópole, Braz. 212/B1
Martinópolis, Braz. 213/B2
Martins, Braz. 212/C2
Martins Creek, Pa, US 196/C2
Martinsburg, WV, US 188/E4
Martinsville, Va, US 188/E4
Martorell, Sp. 103/K7
Martos, Sp. 102/D4
Martre (riv.), Qu, Can. 188/F1
Martres-Tolosane, Fr. 100/D5
Marty, SD, US 185/J5
Marugame, Japan 132/C3
Maruim, Braz. 212/C3
Maruko, Japan 133/F2
Marum, Neth. 108/D2
Maruoka, Japan 132/E2
Marutea (isl.), FrPol. 175/M7
Marv Dasht, Iran 146/F3
Marxheim, Ger. 112/D5
Mary, Trkm. 147/H1
Mary Anne Passage, Austl. 170/B2
Mary Esther, Fl, US 191/G4
Mary-sur-Marne, Fr. 88/M4
Maryborough, Austl. 173/B3
Maryborough, Austl. 172/D4
Marydale, SAfr. 164/C3
Marydel, Md, US 196/C5
Maryfield, Sk, Can. 185/H3
Maryland (co.), Libr. 160/C5
Maryland (state), US 188/E4
Maryland City, Md, US 196/B5
Maryland Heights, Mo, US 195/G8
Maryland Line, Md, US 196/B4
Marystown, Nf, Can. 189/L2
Marysville, Ks, US 187/H3
Marysville, Pa, US 196/B3
Maryville, Tn, US 191/H3
Maryville, Il, US 195/H8
Marzabotto, It. 117/E4
Marzano (peak), It. 104/D2
Marzo (pt.), Col. 210/B3
Marzūq, Libya 154/H2
Masada (ruin), Isr. 149/D4
Masai Mara Nat'l Rsv., Kenya 163/F1
Masai Steppe (grsld.), Tanz. 162/C4
Masaka, Ugan. 162/A3
Masamagrell, Sp. 103/E3
Masamba, Indo. 139/F4
Masan, SKor. 131/E5
Masangwe (hill), Tanz. 162/A4
Masaya, Nic. 202/E4
Masbate (isl.), Phil. 137/D5
Mascara, Alg. 158/F5
Mascarene (isls.), Mrts 165/T15
Mascota, Mex. 200/D4
Mascouche, Qu, Can. 189/N6
Maselheim, Ger. 115/F1
Maserà di Padova, It. 117/E2
Maseru (cap.), Les. 164/D3
Masevaux, Fr. 114/D2
Masfjorden, Nor. 96/A1
Mashan, China 137/A3
Mashhad (int'l arpt.), Iran 145/C5
Mashike, Japan 134/B2
Māshkīd (riv.), Iran 147/H3
Mashtūl as Sūq, Egypt 149/B4
Mashū (lake), Japan 134/D2
Masiaca, Mex. 200/C3
Maside, Sp. 102/A1
Masim (peak), Rus. 121/L1
Masindi, Ugan. 162/A2
Maşīrah, Jazīrat (isl.), Oman 147/G4
Masisea, Peru 214/C3
Masjed-e Soleymān, Iran 146/E2
Mask (lake), Ire. 89/P10
Masker (peak), Mor. 156/D2
Masnou, Sp. 103/L7
Masoala (cape), Madg. 165/J6
Masoala (pen.), Madg. 163/L10
Masoarivo, Madg. 165/H7
Mason, Mi, US 188/C3
Mason, Tx, US 187/H5
Mason (co.), Wa, US 193/A3
Mason (lake), Wa, US 193/B3
Mason and Dixon Line, Pa, US 196/B4
Masone, It. 116/B4
Masonville, Co, US 195/B2
Masquefa, Sp. 103/K6
Massa, It. 116/D4
Massa-Carrara (prov.), It. 116/C4
Massa Finalese, It. 117/E3
Massa Fiscaglia, It. 117/F3
Massa Lombarda, It. 117/E4
Massa Marittima, It. 101/J5
Massa Martana, It. 101/K5
Massachusetts (state), US 189/F3
Massachusetts (bay), Ma, US 189/G3
Massaciuccoli, Lago di (lake), It. 116/D5
Massafra, It. 105/E2
Massangena, Moz. 163/F5
Massapê, Braz. 212/B1
Massapequa, NY, US 197/M9
Massapequa Park, NY, US 197/M9
Massarosa, It. 116/D5
Massbach, Ger. 112/D2
Massena, NY, US 188/F2
Masset, BC, Can. 192/M4
Massey (sound), Nun., Can. 181/S7
Massey, Md, US 196/C5
Massillon, Oh, US 188/D3
Massy, Fr. 88/J5
Masterton, NZ 175/T11
Mastgat (chan.), Neth. 108/B5
Mastic, NY, US 197/F2
Mastic Beach, NY, US 197/F2
Mastnik (riv.), Czh. 113/H3
Mastūj (riv.), Pak. 144/A2
Mastung, Pak. 147/J3
Masuda, Japan 132/B3
Masuho, Japan 135/A2
Masurai (peak), Indo. 138/B4
Masvingo, Zim. 163/F5
Maswa Game Rsv., Tanz. 162/B3
Maşyāf, Syria 149/E2
Mat (riv.), Alb. 105/F2
Mata Grande, Braz. 212/C3
Mata Utu, Fr. 175/H6
Mātābhānga, India 143/G2
Matadi, D.R. Congo 163/B2
Matador, Tx, US 187/G4
Matagalpa, Nic. 202/E3
Matagami (lake), Qu, Can. 188/E1
Matagorda (bay), Tx, US 190/D4
Matagorda (isl.), Tx, US 190/D4
Matale, SrL. 140/D6
Matam, Sen. 160/B3
Matamoras, Pa, US 196/D1
Matamoros, Mex. 200/E3
Ma'ţan as Sarra (well), Libya 155/K3
Matandu (riv.), Tanz. 162/C5
Matane (riv.), Qu, Can. 189/H1
Matane, Qu, Can. 189/H1
Matanga, Madg. 165/H8
Matanzas, Cuba 198/E3
Matão, Braz. 213/B2
Matape (riv.), Mex. 200/C2
Matapedia (riv.), Qu, Can. 189/H1
Mataquito (riv.), Chile 216/C2
Matara (ruin), Erit. 146/C6
Matara, SrL. 140/D6
Mataram, Indo. 139/E5
Mataránga, Gre. 105/G3
Mataró, Sp. 103/L6
Matatiele, SAfr. 164/E3
Mataura (riv.), NZ 175/R12
Matawan, NJ, US 197/J10
Matehuala, Mex. 201/E4
Matéri, Ben. 161/F4
Maternillos (pt.), Cuba 199/F3
Mátészalka, Hun. 99/M5
Mateur, Tun. 158/L6
Mathay, Fr. 114/C3
Matheniko Game Rsv., Ugan. 162/B2
Mathew's (peak), Kenya 162/C2
Mathews (lake), Ca, US 194/C3
Mathis, Tx, US 190/D4
Mathoura, Austl. 173/C2
Mathurā, India 142/A2
Mati, Phil. 137/E6
Matias Barbosa, Braz. 213/K6
Matias Olímpio, Braz. 212/B1
Matías Romero, Mex. 202/C2
Matiguas, Nic. 203/E3
Matilija (dam), Ca, US 194/A2
Matinha, Braz. 212/A2
Matinhos, Braz. 213/B3
Matinicock (pt.), NY, US 197/L8
Matiyuri (riv.), Ven. 210/D3
Mātla (riv.), India 143/G5
Matlock, Eng, UK 93/G5
Mato Grosso (plat.), Braz. 209/G6
Mato Grosso do Sul (state), Braz. 213/A1
Mato Grosso, Planalto do (plat.), Braz. 209/H6
Mato Verde, Braz. 212/B4
Matopos, Zim. 163/E5
Matosinhos, Port. 102/A2
Matoya (bay), Japan 135/L7
Maţraḩ, Oman 147/G4
Matrei am Brenner, Aus. 115/H3
Matrei in Osttirol, Aus. 101/K3
Matriz de Camaragibe, Braz. 212/D3
Matroosberg (peak), SAfr. 164/L10
Matsalu (gulf), Est. 97/K2
Matsapa (Manzini) (int'l arpt.), Swaz. 165/E2
Matsiatra (riv.), Madg. 165/H8
Matsoandakana, Madg. 165/J6
Matsubara, Japan 135/J6
Matsubushi, Japan 135/D2
Matsuda, Japan 135/C3
Matsudo, Japan 135/D2
Matsue, Japan 132/C3
Matsuida, Japan 135/B1
Matsumae, Japan 134/B3
Matsumoto, Japan 133/E2
Matsuo, Japan 135/E2
Matsusaka, Japan 135/L6
Matsushima, Japan 134/B4
Matsutō, Japan 132/E2
Matsuyama, Japan 132/C4
Matt, Swi. 115/F4
Mattagami (riv.), On, Can. 188/D1
Mattarello, It. 115/H6
Mattawa, On, Can. 188/E2
Matterhorn (peak), It.,Swi. 114/D6
Mattertal (valley), Swi. 114/D5
Mattese, Mo, US 195/G9
Matthews (mtn.), Ak, US 192/H2
Mattig (riv.), Aus. 113/G6
Mattighofen, Aus. 113/G6
Mattituck, NY, US 197/F2
Mattmarksee (lake), Swi. 114/D5
Mattō, Japan 132/E2
Mattock (riv.), Ire. 92/B4
Mattsee, Aus. 113/G7
Matucana, Peru 214/B3
Maturín, Ven. 211/F2
Matusadona NP, Zim. 163/E4
Matzen, Aus. 107/P7
Maú (riv.), Guy. 208/G3
Mau (peak), Kenya 162/B3
Mau Aimma, India 142/C3
Mau Rānīpur, India 142/B3
Mauá, Braz. 213/C2
Maubert-Fontaine, Fr. 111/D4
Maubeuge, Fr. 110/C3
Maubourguet, Fr. 100/D5
Mauchline, Sc, UK 94/B5
Maud (pt.), Austl. 170/B2
Maud, Sc, UK 94/D1
Maudaha, India 142/C3
Mauerbach, Aus. 107/N7
Mauerkirchen, Aus. 113/G6
Maués, Braz. 208/G4
Maués Açu (riv.), Braz. 208/G4
Maug (isls.), NMar. 174/D2
Mauganj, India 142/C3
Maughold, IM, UK 92/D3
Maughold (pt.), IM, UK 92/D3
Mauguio, Fr. 100/F5
Maui (isl.), Hi, US 182/T10
Mauke (isl.), CookIs. 175/K7
Maulbronn, Ger. 112/B5
Mauldre (riv.), Fr. 110/A6
Maule (pol. reg.), Chile 216/B2
Maule (riv.), Chile 216/C2
Maule, Fr. 88/H5
Mauléon, Fr. 100/C3
Maullín, Chile 216/B4
Maumee (riv.), In,Oh, US 188/C3
Maun, Bots. 163/D4
Mauna Kea (peak), Hi, US 182/U11
Mauna Loa (peak), Hi, US 182/U11
Maunath Bhanjan, India 142/D3
Maungdaw, Myan. 141/F3
Mauperthuis, Fr. 88/M5
Maupertus (int'l arpt.), Fr. 100/C2
Maupiti (isl.), FrPol. 175/K6
Maur, Swi. 115/E3
Maurāwān, India 142/C2
Maurecourt, Fr. 88/J5
Maurepas (lake), La, US 195/P16
Maurepas, Fr. 110/A6
Mauriac, Fr. 100/E4
Maurice (lake), Austl. 171/F4
Maurice (riv.), NJ, US 196/C5
Mauricetown, NJ, US 196/D5
Maurienne (valley), Fr. 101/G4
Maurilândia, Braz. 213/B1
Mauritania (ctry.) 154/C4
Mauriti, Braz. 212/C2
Mauritius (ctry.) 165/T15
Mauston, Wi, US 185/L5
Mauthausen, Aus. 113/H6
Mauvoisin, Barrage de (dam), Swi. 114/D6
Mavrommátion, Gre. 105/H3
Mavrovo NP, FYROM 105/G2
Maw Daung (pass), Thai. 136/B4
Mawāna, India 142/A1
Mawlaik, Myan. 141/F3
Mawlamyine (Moulmein), Myan. 136/B2
Mawson, Austl., Ant. 218/E
Maxaranguape, Braz. 212/D2
Maxcanú, Mex. 202/D1
Maxdorf, Ger. 112/B4
Maxéville, Fr. 111/F6
Maxhütte-Haidhof, Ger. 113/F4
May (cape), NJ, US 196/D5
May-en-Multien, Fr. 88/M4
May, Isle of (isl.), Sc, UK 94/D4
May Pen, Jam. 203/G2
Maya (isl.), Indo. 138/C4
Maya (riv.), Rus. 125/N4
Maya (mts.), Guat. 202/D2
Maya-san (peak), Japan 135/H6
Mayaguana (isl.), Bahm. 199/G3
Mayaguana Passage (chan.), Bahm. 203/H1
Mayagüez, PR 199/M8
Mayakovskogo (peak), Taj. 147/K1
Mayang, China 141/J2
Mayarí, Cuba 203/H1
Maybee, Mi, US 193/E8
Maybole, Sc, UK 94/B6
Maydān, Iraq 146/E2
Mayen, Ger. 111/G3
Mayenne, Fr. 100/C2
Mayenne (riv.), Fr. 100/C3
Mayerthorpe, Ab, Can. 184/E2
Mayfield, Ky, US 188/B4
Mayfield, Sc, UK 94/C5
Maykop, Rus. 120/G3
Maymyo, Myan. 141/G3
Maynooth, Ire. 89/Q10
Mayo (riv.), Arg. 215/B6
Mayo, Yk, Can. 192/L3
Mayo, Md, US 196/B6
Mayotte (isl.), May. 165/H6
Mays Landing, NJ, US 196/D5
Maysville, Ky, US 188/D4
Maythalūn, WBnk. 149/G7
Mayville, ND, US 185/J4
Maywood, NJ, US 197/J8
Maywood, Il, US 193/Q16
Maywood, Ca, US 194/F8
Mazabuka, Zam. 163/E4
Mazagão, Braz. 209/H4
Mazamet, Fr. 100/E5
Mazán, Peru 214/C1
Mazār-e Sharīf, Afg. 147/J1
Mazara del Vallo, It. 104/C4
Mazara, Val di (valley), It. 104/C4
Mazarrón, Sp. 102/E4
Mazaruni (riv.), Guy. 208/G2
Mazatán, Mex. 200/C2
Mazatenango, Guat. 202/D3
Mazatlán, Mex. 200/D4
Mažeikiai, Lith. 97/K3
Mazeppa NP, Austl. 172/B3
Mazgirt, Turk. 148/D2
Mazıkıran (pass), Turk. 148/D2
Mazingarbe, Fr. 110/B3
Mazocruz, Peru 214/D5
Mazong (peak), China 128/G3
Mazowieckie (prov.), Pol. 99/L2
Mazury (reg.), Pol. 99/L2
Mazyr, Bela. 120/D1
Mbabala (isl.), Zam. 162/A5
Mbabane (cap.), Swaz. 165/E2
Mbabo (peak), Camr. 154/H6
Mbacké, Sen. 160/B3
Mbaïki, CAfr. 155/J7
Mbakaou, Lac de (lake), Camr. 154/H6
Mbala, Zam. 162/A5
Mbale, Ugan. 162/B2
Mbalmayo, Camr. 154/H7
Mbandaka, D.R. Congo 155/J7
Mbarangandu (riv.), Tanz. 162/C5
Mbarara, Ugan. 162/A3
Mbata, CAfr. 155/J7
Mbeya (peak), Tanz. 162/B5
Mbeya (range), Tanz. 163/F2
Mbeya, Tanz. 162/B5
Mbeya (pol. reg.), Tanz. 162/B5
Mbini, EqG. 154/G7
Mbini (riv.), EqG.,Gabon 154/H7
Mbirizi, Ugan. 162/A3
Mbomou (riv.), CAfr. 155/L6
M'Bour, Sen. 160/A3
Mbuji-Mayi, D.R. Congo 163/D2
Mbwemburu (riv.), Tanz. 162/C5
McAdoo, Pa, US 196/C2
McAfee, NJ, US 196/D1
McAlester, Ok, US 187/J4
McAlisterville, Pa, US 196/A2
McAllen, Tx, US 190/D5
McBride, BC, Can. 184/C2
McCall, Id, US 184/D4
McCarran (int'l arpt.), Nv, US 186/D3
McCarthy, Ak, US 192/K3
McClain (co.), Ok, US 195/M15
McClure, Pa, US 196/A2
McClusky, Il, US 195/G7
McClusky, ND, US 185/H4
McComb, Ms, US 187/K5
McConaughy (lake), Ne, US 185/H5
McCook, Ne, US 187/G2
McCormick, SC, US 191/H3
McCreary, Mb, Can. 185/J3
McCullom Lake, Il, US 193/P15
McDaniel, Md, US 196/B6
McDermitt, Nv, US 184/D5
McDonald (mt.), Ak, US 192/F3
McDonald (isls.), Austl. 81/N8
McDonnell (mt.), Austl. 171/H5
McDougall (pass), NW,Yk, Can. 192/L2
McDowell (mts.), Az, US 195/S18
McElhattan, Pa, US 196/A1
McGhee Tyson (int'l arpt.), Tn, US 191/H3
McGrath, Ak, US 192/G3
McGregor (riv.), BC, Can. 184/C2
McGregor, On, Can. 193/G7
McHenry (co.), Il, US 193/N15
McKean (isl.), Kiri. 175/H5
McKeand (riv.), Nun., Can. 181/K2
McKee City, NJ, US 196/D5
McKeesport, Pa, US 188/E3
McKenzie, Tn, US 188/B4
McKinlay, Austl. 172/A3
McKinley (mt.), Ak, US 192/H3
McKinleyville, Ca, US 184/B5
McLaughlin, SD, US 185/H4
McLean, Va, US 196/A6
McLennan, Ab, Can. 184/D2
McLeod (lake), Austl. 170/B3
McLeod (riv.), BC, Can. 184/D2
McLeod (bay), NW, Can. 180/E2
McLeod Lake, BC, Can. 184/C2
M'Clintock (chan.), Nun., Can. 180/F1
McLoud, Ok, US 195/N15
M'Clure (str.), NW, Can. 181/Q7
McMinnville, Or, US 184/C4
McMinnville, Tn, US 188/C5
McMurdo, US, Ant. 218/M
McNeil (isl.), Wa, US 193/B3
McPherson, Ks, US 187/H3
McQueeney, Tx, US 195/U20
Mdantsane, SAfr. 164/D4
M'diq, Mor. 158/B2
Me-akan-dake (peak), Japan 134/C2
Mead, Co, US 195/C2
Mead (lake), Az,Nv, US 186/D3
Meade (riv.), Ak, US 192/G2
Meadow Lake, Sk, Can. 184/F2
Meadow Valley Wash (riv.), Nv, US 186/D3

Meadowbrook, Il, US 195/G8
Meadowlands Sports Complex, NJ, US 197/J8
Meadows, Md, US 196/B6
Meadville, Ms, US 191/F4
Meadville, Pa, US 188/D3
Mealhada, Port. 102/A2
Meall a' Bhuiridh (peak), Sc, UK 94/B3
Meall Buidhe (peak), Sc, UK 94/B3
Meall Dearg (peak), Sc, UK 94/C4
Meall Dubh (peak), Sc, UK 94/C4
Meall nam Fuaran (peak), Sc, UK 94/C4
Meall Tairneachan (peak), Sc, UK 94/C3
Mearim (riv.), Braz. 209/J5
Meat (mtn.), Ak, US 192/F2
Meath (co.), Ire. 92/B4
Meath Park, Sk, Can. 185/G2
Méaulte, Fr. 110/B4
Meaux, Fr. 88/L5
Mecapalapa, Mex. 201/M6
Mecatina,Rivière du Petit (riv.), Nf,Qu, Can. 181/K3
Mecca, Mo, US 195/D5
Mechanicsburg, Pa, US 196/B3
Mechanicsburg Naval Rsv., Pa, US 196/B3
Mechelen, Belg. 111/D1
Mecheria, Alg. 157/E2
Mechi (zone), Nepal 143/F2
Mechra-Bel-Ksiri, Mor. 158/B2
Mecidiye, Turk. 105/K2
Mecitözü, Turk. 148/C1
Meckenbeuren, Ger. 115/F2
Meckenheim, Ger. 111/G2
Mecklenburg-Vorpommern (state), Ger. 96/E5
Mecklenburger (bay), Ger. 98/F1
Mecuia (peak), Moz. 163/G3
Meda, It. 116/C1
Medak, India 140/C4
Medan, Indo. 138/A3
Médanos, Arg. 216/E3
Medanos de Coro, PN, Ven. 210/D2
Medanosa (pt.), Arg. 217/D6
Mede Lomellina, It. 116/B2
Médéa, Alg. 158/G4
Médéa (prov.), Alg. 158/G4
Medebach, Ger. 109/F6
Medeiros Neto, Braz. 212/B5
Medel (peak), Swi. 115/E4
Medellín, Col. 208/C2
Medemblik, Neth. 108/C3
Meden (riv.), Eng, UK 93/G5
Medenine, Tun. 157/H2
Medenine (gov.), Tun. 157/H2
Medesano, It. 116/D3
Medetsiz (peak), Turk. 148/C2
Medford, Or, US 184/C5
Medford, NY, US 197/E2
Medford Lakes, NJ, US 196/D4
Medgidia, Rom. 107/J3
Media, Pa, US 196/C4
Media Luna, La (isls.), Hon. 203/F3
Mediaş, Rom. 107/G2
Medical Lake, Wa, US 184/D4
Medicine Bow, Wy, US 185/G3
Medicine Bow (range), Wy, US 186/F2
Medicine Hat, Ab, Can. 184/F3
Medina (riv.), Tx, US 187/H5
Medina, Braz. 212/B5
Medina, Col. 210/C3
Medina, ND, US 185/J4
Medina, Oh, US 188/D3
Medina, Wa, US 193/C2
Medina de Pomar, Sp. 102/D1
Medina de Rioseco, Sp. 102/C2
Medina del Campo, Sp. 102/C2
Medina-Sidonia, Sp. 102/C4
Medinaceli, Sp. 102/D2
Medinipur, India 143/F4
Mediouna, Mor. 156/D2
Mediterranean (sea) section
Mednogorsk, Rus. 121/L2
Medole, It. 116/D2
Medolla, It. 117/E3
Meðugorje, Bosn. 106/C4
Medvditsa (riv.), Rus. 122/E5
Medvezh'i (isls.), Rus. 123/S2
Medvezh'yegorsk, Rus. 118/G3
Medvode, Slov. 101/L3
Medway (riv.), Eng, UK 91/G4
Meekatharra, Austl. 170/C3
Meeker, Co, US 186/F2
Meeker Park, Co, US 195/A2
Meerbusch, Ger. 108/D6
Meerhout, Belg. 111/E1
Meersburg, Ger. 115/F2
Meerssen, Neth. 111/E2

Meerut, India 142/A1
Meeteetse, Wy, US 184/F4
Megála Kalívia, Gre. 105/G3
Megáli Panayía, Gre. 105/H2
Megálon Khorion, Gre. 148/A2
Megalópolis, Gre. 105/H4
Megantic (peak), Qu, Can. 189/G3
Mégara, Gre. 105/H3
Megève, Fr. 114/C6
Meghālaya (state), India 141/F2
Meghna (riv.), Bang. 143/H4
Megiddo, Isr. 149/G6
Mégiscane (lake), Qu, Can. 188/E1
Mégiscane (riv.), Qu, Can. 188/E1
Megista (isl.), Greece 149/A1
Mehaigne (riv.), Belg. 111/E2
Mehamn, Nor. 95/H1
Meharry (mt.), Austl. 170/C2
Mehdia, Alg. 158/F5
Mehdiya-Plage, Mor. 158/A2
Mehe (riv.), Ger. 109/G1
Mehedinți (prov.), Rom. 106/F3
Mehlingen, Ger. 111/G4
Mehlville, Mo, US 195/G9
Mehndāwal, India 142/D2
Mehrān (riv.), Iran 147/F3
Mehring, Ger. 111/F4
Mehrnbach, Aus. 113/G6
Mehtar Lām, Afg. 144/A2
Meia Ponte (riv.), Braz. 213/B1
Meiganga, Camr. 154/H6
Meighen (isl.), Nun., Can. 181/R7
Meigu, China 141/H2
Meihekou, China 129/N3
Meikle Bin (peak), Sc, UK 94/B4
Meikle Black Law (hill), Sc, UK 94/D5
Meikle Says Law (peak), Sc, UK 94/D5
Meiktila, Myan. 141/G3
Meilen, Swi. 115/E3
Meine, Ger. 109/H4
Meiners Oaks, Ca, US 194/A2
Meinersen, Ger. 109/H4
Meinerzhagen, Ger. 111/G1
Meiningen, Ger. 112/D1
Meiringen, Swi. 114/E4
Meisenheim, Ger. 111/G4
Meishan (res.), China 130/C5
Meissen, Ger. 99/G3
Meissner (peak), Ger. 109/G6
Meitan, China 137/A2
Meitingen, Ger. 112/D5
Meiwa, Japan 135/L6
Meix-devant-Virton, Belg. 111/E4
Meizhou, China 137/C3
Mejaniga, It. 117/E2
Mejaouda (well), Mrta. 156/D5
Mejorada del Campo, Sp. 103/N9
Mek'elē, Eth. 155/N5
Meknès (prov.), Mor. 158/B3
Meknès, Mor. 158/B3
Mekong (riv.), Asia 128/G5
Mekongga (peak), Indo. 139/F4
Mekoryuk, Ak, US 192/E3
Melaka, Malay. 138/B3
Melanesia (reg.) 174/E5
Melappālaiyam, India 140/C6
Melawi (riv.), Indo. 138/D4
Melbeck, Ger. 109/H2
Melbourne, Fl, US 191/H4
Melbourne (isl.), Nun., Can. 180/F2
Melbourne, Austl. 173/G5
Melbu, Nor. 95/E1
Melchor (isl.), Chile 216/B5
Melchor Múzquiz, Mex. 190/C5
Melchor Ocampo, Mex. 201/Q9
Meldola, It. 117/F4
Mele (cape), It. 116/B5
Melegnano, It. 116/C2
Melenci, Serb. 106/E3
Melenki, Rus. 118/J4
Melesse, Fr. 100/C2
Meleuz, Rus. 121/K1
Mélèzes (riv.), Qu, Can. 181/J3
Melfi, It. 104/D2
Melfort, Sk, Can. 185/G2
Melgar de Fernamental, Sp. 102/C1
Melhus, Nor. 95/D3
Melibocus (peak), Ger. 111/H3
Melide, Swi. 115/E6
Meligalás, Gre. 105/G4
Meliki, Gre. 105/H2
Melili (peak), Kenya 162/C3
Melilla, Sp. 158/C2
Melimoyu (peak), Chile 216/B5

Melipilla, Chile 216/N8
Mélisey, Fr. 114/C2
Melissano, It. 105/F3
Melissa, Mb, Can. 185/H3
Melito di Porto Salvo, It. 104/D4
Melitopol', Ukr. 120/E3
Melitota, Md, US 196/B5
Melkbosstrand, SAfr. 164/L10
Melksham, Eng, UK 90/D4
Mella (riv.), It. 116/D2
Mellan Fryken (lake), Swe. 96/E2
Melle, Ger. 109/F4
Melle, Belg. 110/C2
Mellea (riv.), It. 116/A3
Mellègue, Oued (riv.), Alg. 158/K7
Mellerud, Swe. 96/E2
Mellid, Sp. 102/A1
Mellieña, Malta 104/L7
Mellingen, Swi. 115/E3
Mellizo Sur (peak), Chile 217/B6
Mellrichstadt, Ger. 112/D2
Mellum (isl.), Ger. 109/F1
Melmoth, SAfr. 165/E3
Melnik, Bul. 105/H2
Mělník, Czh. 113/H3
Melo, Uru. 215/F3
Melocheville, Qu, Can. 189/N7
Melrose, Md, US 196/B4
Melrose, Sc, UK 94/D5
Melrose Abbey, Sc, UK 94/D5
Melrose Park, Il, US 193/Q16
Mels, Swi. 115/F3
Melsungen, Ger. 109/G6
Meltham, Eng, UK 93/G4
Melton, Austl. 173/C3
Melton Mowbray, Eng, UK 91/F1
Melun, Fr. 88/K6
Melville (cape), Phil. 139/E2
Melville, Sk, Can. 185/H3
Melville (isl.), Austl. 167/C2
Melville (bay), Austl. 167/G2
Melville, Il, US 195/G8
Melville (cape), Austl. 172/B1
Melville (lake), Nf, Can. 181/L3
Melville (pen.), Nun., Can. 181/H2
Melville, NY, US 197/M8
Melvindale, Mi, US 193/F7
Mélykút, Hun. 106/D2
Melzo, It. 116/C2
Memāri, India 143/G4
Memmert (isl.), Ger. 108/D1
Memmingen, Ger. 115/G2
Memphis, Mo, US 185/K5
Memphis, Tx, US 187/H4
Memphis, Tn, US 187/K4
Memphis (ruin), Egypt 149/B5
Memphis, Mi, US 193/G6
Mena, Ar, US 187/J4
Menaggio, It. 115/F5
Menai (str.), Wal, UK 92/D5
Menai Bridge, Wal, UK 92/D5
Ménaka, Mali 161/F3
Menan, Neth. 108/C2
Menarandra (riv.), Madg. 165/H9
Menard, Tx, US 187/H5
Menasalbas, Sp. 102/C3
Menavava (riv.), Madg. 165/H7
Mendawai (riv.), Indo. 138/D4
Mende, Fr. 100/E4
Menden, Ger. 109/E6
Mendenhall (cape), Ak, US 192/E4
Mendes, Braz. 213/K7
Méndez, Mex. 201/F3
Mendham, NJ, US 196/D2
Mendig, Ger. 111/G3
Mendip (hills), Eng, UK 90/D4
Mendocino, Ca, US 186/B3
Mendocino (cape), Ca, US 140/A3
Mendooran, Austl. 173/D1
Mendoza, Arg. 216/C2
Mendoza (prov.), Arg. 216/C2
Mendoza, Cuba 203/E1
Mendoza, Peru 214/B2
Mendoza (El Plumerillo) (int'l arpt.), Arg. 216/C2
Mene Grande, Ven. 210/D2
Menegosa (peak), It. 116/C3
Menemen, Turk. 120/C5
Menen, Belg. 110/C2
Menengai Crater, Kenya 162/C3
Menengiyn (plain), Mong. 129/L2
Menfi, It. 104/C4
Meng Xian, China 130/C4
Mengcheng, China 130/D4
Mengen, Ger. 115/F1
Mengersgereuth-Hämmern, Ger. 112/D2
Mengeš, Slov. 101/L3
Menggala, Indo. 138/C4

Menghai, China 136/C1
Mengibar, Sp. 102/D4
Mengkofen, Ger. 113/F5
Mengla, China 136/C1
Menglian Daizu Lahuzu Vazu Zizhixian, China 141/G3
Mengyin, China 130/D4
Mengzi, China 141/H3
Menindee (dam), Austl. 173/B2
Menindee (lake), Austl. 173/B2
Meningie, Austl. 173/A2
Menlo Park, Ca, US 193/K12
Menlo Park, NJ, US 197/H9
Menlolat (peak), Chile 216/B5
Mennecy, Fr. 88/K5
Menomonee Falls, Wi, US 188/B3
Menomonie, Wi, US 185/L4
Menongue, Ang. 163/C3
Menorca (int'l arpt.), Sp. 103/H3
Menorca (Minorca) (isl.), Sp. 103/H3
Mentasta Lake, Ak, US 192/K3
Mentawai (isls.), Indo. 138/A4
Mentawai (str.), Indo. 138/A4
Menteroda, Ger. 109/H6
Menthon-Saint-Bernard, Fr. 114/C6
Mentone, It. 187/G5
Mentone, Ca, US 194/C2
Mentor, Oh, US 188/D3
Mentue (riv.), Swi. 114/C4
Menucourt, Fr. 88/H4
Menuma, Japan 135/C1
Menyapa (peak), Indo. 139/E3
Meon (riv.), Eng, UK 91/E5
Meoquí, Mex. 200/D2
Mepistskaro (peak), Geo. 121/G4
Meppel, Neth. 108/D3
Meppen, Ger. 109/E3
Meppen, Il, US 195/F8
Mequinenzo, Embalse de (res.), Sp. 103/F2
Mera (riv.), It. 115/F5
Meramec (riv.), Mo, US 187/K3
Merano, It. 115/H4
Meratus (mts.), Indo. 138/D4
Meraux, La, US 195/Q17
Merbein, Austl. 173/B2
Mercaderes, Col. 210/C3
Mercantour, PN du, Fr. 101/G4
Mercatello sul Metauro, It. 117/F5
Mercato Saraceno, It. 117/F5
Merced (riv.), Ca, US 186/B3
Merced, Ca, US 186/B3
Mercedario (peak), Arg. 215/B3
Mercedes, Arg. 215/E2
Mercedes, Arg. 216/D2
Mercedes, Uru. 217/J11
Mercedes, Col. 217/J10
Mercer (co.), NJ, US 196/D3
Mercer (isl.), Wa, US 193/C2
Mercer Island, Wa, US 193/C2
Mercerville-Hamilton Square, NJ, US 196/D3
Merchtem, Belg. 111/D2
Mercier, Qu, Can. 189/N7
Mercoal, Ab, Can. 184/D2
Mercy (cape), Nun., Can. 181/K2
Mercy-le-Bas, Fr. 111/E5
Méré, Fr. 88/H5
Meredith (lake), Tx, US 187/G4
Meredith (cape), UK 217/E7
Merefa, Ukr. 120/F2
Merelbeke, Belg. 110/C2
Merenberg, Ger. 112/B1
Mergozzo, It. 115/E5
Mergui (arch.), Myan. 141/G5
Mergui (Myeik), Myan. 136/B3
Meric, Turk. 107/H5
Méricourt, Fr. 89/C4
Méricourt, Fr. 110/B3
Mérida, Sp. 102/B3
Mérida, Mex. 202/D1
Mérida, La, US 195/P17
Mérida (state), Ven. 210/D2
Mérida, Cordillera de (mts.), Ven. 208/D2
Meridian, Ms, US 191/F3
Meridian, Ok, US 195/N14
Meridian, Id, US 184/F5
Merignac, Fr. 100/C4
Mérignac (int'l arpt.), Fr. 100/C4

Merimbula, Austl. 173/D3
Merinda, Austl. 172/C3
Mering, Ger. 112/D6
Merinos, Uru. 217/K10
Merja Zerga (lake), Mor. 158/A2
Mērk, Hun. 106/F2
Merkendorf, Ger. 112/D4
Merksem, Belg. 108/B6
Merksplas, Belg. 108/B6
Merlimont, Fr. 110/A3
Merlo, Arg. 217/J11
Meroe (ruin), Sudan 146/B5
Merone, It. 116/C1
Merredin, Austl. 170/C4
Merriam, Ks, US 195/D5
Merrick, NY, US 197/L9
Merrick (peak), Sc, UK 92/D1
Merrill, Wi, US 185/L4
Merrill Creek (res.), NJ, US 196/C2
Merrimack, NH, US 189/G3
Merritt, BC, Can. 184/C3
Merritt Island, Fl, US 191/H4
Merriwa, Austl. 173/D2
Mers-les-Bains, Fr. 110/A3
Mersch, Lux. 111/F4
Merse (reg.), Sc, UK 94/D5
Mersey (riv.), Eng, UK 93/F5
Merseyside (co.), Eng, UK 93/F5
Mersing, Malay. 138/B3
Mertert, Lux. 111/F4
Mertesdorf, Ger. 111/F4
Merthyr Tydfil, Wal, UK 90/C3
Merthyr Tydfil (co.), Wal, UK 90/C3
Mértola, Port. 102/B4
Merton (bor.), Eng, UK 88/C2
Mertzon, Tx, US 187/G5
Mertziger, Ger. 111/G6
Mertzwiller, Fr. 111/G6
Meru (mt.), Tanz. 162/C2
Meru, Kenya 162/C2
Meru, Fr. 110/B5
Meru NP, Kenya 162/C2
Merwedekanaal (riv.), Neth. 108/C5
Méry-sur-Oise, Fr. 88/J4
Merzen, Ger. 109/E4
Merzenich, Ger. 111/F2
Merzifon, Turk. 148/C1
Merzig, Ger. 111/F5
Mesa (mtn.), Ak, US 192/G3
Mesa, Az, US 195/S19
Mesa (peak), Arg. 217/C6
Mesa Verde NP, Co, US 186/E3
Mesabi (range), Mn, US 185/K4
Mesach Mellet (hills), Libya 157/H4
Mesagne, It. 105/E2
Mesarás (gulf), Gre. 105/J5
Mescalero (ridge), NM, US 190/C3
Meschede, Ger. 109/F6
Mesco, Punta de (pt.), It. 116/C4
Mescolino (peak), It. 117/F5
Meseta de Montemayor (plat.), Arg. 216/D5
Mesgouez (lake), Qu, Can. 188/F1
Mesola, It. 117/F3
Mesolóngion, Gre. 105/G3
Mesomeloka, Madg. 165/J8
Mesopotamia (reg.), Mex. 200/D4
Mesoraca, It. 104/E3
Mespelbrunn, Ger. 112/C3
Mesquita, Tx, US 187/H4
Mesquite, Nv, US 195/H5
Mesrouh (peak), Mor. 156/E2
Messaad, Alg. 154/F1
Messancy, Belg. 111/E4
Messel, Ger. 112/B3
Messina, SAfr. 163/F5
Messina (str.), It. 104/D4
Messina, It. 104/D3
Messina (gulf), Gre. 105/H4
Messíni, Gre. 105/H4
Messkirch, Ger. 115/F2
Messstetten, Ger. 115/E1
Messy, Fr. 88/L5
Mesta (riv.), Bul. 107/F5
Mestre, It. 117/F2
Mesudiye, Turk. 120/F4
Mesumba (peak), Tanz. 162/C4
Mesurado (cape), Libr. 160/C5
Meta (dept.), Col. 210/C4
Meta (riv.), Col./Ven. 210/D3
Meta Incognita (pen.), Nun., Can. 181/K2

Methven, Sc, UK 94/C4
Metica (riv.), Col. 210/C4
Metković, Cro. 105/E1
Metlakatla, Ak, US 192/M4
Metlatonoc, Mex. 202/B2
Metlili Chaamba, Alg. 157/F2
Metnitz, Aus. 101/L3
Metro Toronto Zoo, On, Can. 189/R8
Metropolis, Il, US 188/B4
Metropolitan Oakland (int'l arpt.), Ca, US 186/B3
Metropolitana de Santiago (pol. reg.), Chile 216/N8
Métsovon, Gre. 105/G3
Mettawa, Il, US 193/Q15
Mettenheim, Ger. 113/F6
Mettet, Belg. 111/D3
Mettingen, Ger. 109/E4
Mettlach, Ger. 111/F4
Mettmach, Aus. 113/G6
Mettmann, Ger. 108/D6
Metu, Eth. 155/N6
Metuchen, NJ, US 197/H9
Metula, Isr. 149/D3
Metz, Fr. 111/F5
Metz-Nancy-Lorraine (int'l arpt.), Fr. 111/F6
Metzingen, Ger. 112/C5
Metztitlán, Mex. 201/L6
Meudon, Fr. 88/J5
Meudt, Ger. 111/G3
Meulan, Fr. 88/H4
Meulebeke, Belg. 110/C2
Meurthe (riv.), Fr. 114/C1
Meurthe-et-Moselle (dept.), Fr. 111/E6
Meuse (dept.), Fr. 111/E6
Meuse (riv.), Fr. 111/E6
Meuzin (riv.), Fr. 114/A3
Mevasseret Ziyyon, Isr. 149/D3
Mexborough, Eng, UK 93/G5
Mexia, Tx, US 187/H5
Mexiana, Ilha (isl.), Braz. 209/J3
Mexicalcingo, Mex. 201/Q10
Mexicali, Mex. 200/B1
Mexico (ctry.) 177/G7
Mexico (cap.), Mex. 201/Q10
Mexico, Ok, US 195/M15
Mexico, Pa, US 196/A2
Mexico (state), Mex. 198/A5
Mexico (gulf), NAm. 177/J7
Mexico, Mo, US 187/K3
Meximieux, Fr. 114/B6
Meybod, Iran 146/F2
Meyers Chuck, Ak, US 192/M4
Meyerton, SAfr. 164/Q13
Meymaneh, Afg. 147/H1
Meyrin, Swi. 114/C6
Meythet, Fr. 114/C6
Meyzieu, Fr. 114/B6
Mezdra, Bul. 105/H1
Mèze, Fr. 100/E5
Mezen' (riv.), Rus. 122/E3
Mezen' (bay), Rus. 119/J2
Mezha (riv.), Bela. 97/P4
Mezhdurechensk, Rus. 122/J4
Mezhdusharskiy (isl.), Rus. 122/E2
Mézières-sur-Seine, Fr. 88/H5
Mezőberény, Hun. 106/E2
Mezőkovácsháza, Hun. 106/E2
Mezőkövesd, Hun. 90/L5
Mezőtúr, Hun. 106/E2
Mezquital (riv.), Mex. 200/D4
Mezzana (peak), It. 115/G5
Mezzocorona, It. 115/G5
Mezzogoro, It. 117/F3
Mezzolombardo, It. 115/H5
Mfangano (isl.), Kenya 162/B3
Mga (riv.), Rus. 119/U7
M'goun (peak), Mor. 156/D3
Mhamdia Fouchana, Tun. 158/M6
Mhòr (lake), Sc, UK 94/B2
Mhow, India 147/L4
Mi-shima (isl.), Japan 132/B3
Mi Xian, China 130/C4
Miahuatlán de Porfirio Díaz, Mex. 202/B2
Miajadas, Sp. 102/C3
Miami, Az, US 186/E4
Miami, Fl, US 191/H5
Miami (co.), In, US 195/D6
Miami, Ok, US 187/J3
Miami Beach, Fl, US 191/H5
Miami (int'l arpt.), Fl, US 191/H5
Mian Channūn, Pak. 144/B4
Mianchi, China 130/C4
Miāndoāb, Iran 146/E1
Miandrivazo, Madg. 165/H7
Mīāneh, Iran 146/E1
Miāni, Pak. 144/B3
Mianning, China 141/H2
Mianus (riv.), Ct, US 197/E1
Miānwāli, Pak. 144/B3
Mianyang, China 128/H5
Mianzhu, China 128/H5
Miao'er (peak), China 137/B2
Miariarivo, Madg. 165/H8
Miary, Madg. 165/G8
Migori (riv.), Kenya 162/B3

Miass (riv.), Rus. 119/P5
Miastko, Pol. 96/G4
Mica Creek, BC, Can. 184/D2
Michalovce, Slvk. 99/L4
Michelfeld, Ger. 113/E3
Michelson (mt.), Ak, US 192/K2
Michelstadt, Ger. 112/C3
Michendorf, Ger. 98/O7
Michigan (state), US 188/C2
Michigan (lake), US 188/C2
Michigan City, In, US 188/C3
Michipicoten, On, Can. 188/C2
Michoacán de Ocampo (state), Mex. 198/A4
Michurin, Bul. 107/H4
Michurinsk, Rus. 121/G1
Mickle Fell (peak), Eng, UK 93/F2
Mico (riv.), Nic. 198/E5
Micoud, StL. 199/N9
Micronesia (reg.) 174/E3
Micronesia, Federated States of (ctry.) 174/D4
Mid Yell, Sc, UK 89/W13
Midal (well), Niger 161/G2
Midale, Sk, Can. 185/H3
Midar, Mor. 158/C2
Middelburg, SAfr. 164/D3
Middelburg, Neth. 108/A5
Middelburg, SAfr. 165/E2
Middelharnis, Neth. 108/B5
Middelkerke, Belg. 110/B1
Middle (bay), NY, US 197/L9
Middle Alkali (lake), Ca, US 186/C2
Middle Andaman (isl.), India 141/F5
Middle Caicos (isl.), UK 203/J1
Middle Concho (riv.), Tx, US 190/C4
Middle Raccoon (riv.), Ia, US 187/J2
Middle River, Md, US 196/B5
Middle Sister (peak), Or, US 184/C4
Middleburg, Md, US 196/A4
Middleburg, Ok, US 195/M15
Middleburg, Pa, US 196/A2
Middlebury, Vt, US 188/F2
Middlemount, Austl. 172/C3
Middleport, Pa, US 196/B2
Middlesboro, Ky, US 188/D4
Middlesbrough, Eng, UK 93/G2
Middlesbrough (co.), Eng, UK 93/G2
Middlesex (co.), Eng, UK 91/F4
Middlesex, NJ, US 196/D2
Middleton, Eng, UK 93/F4
Middleton, De, US 196/C5
Middletown, NJ, US 197/J10
Middletown, Czh. 113/G1
Midelt, Mor. 156/D2
Midi (canal), Fr. 100/D5
Midi-Pyrénées (pol. reg.), Fr. 100/D4
Midland, On, Can. 188/E2
Midland, Mi, US 188/C3
Midland, Tx, US 187/G5
Midland, Wa, US 193/C3
Midland Park, NJ, US 197/J8
Midleton, Ire. 89/P11
Midlothian, Il, US 193/Q16
Midlothian (pol. reg.), Sc, UK 94/C5
Midongy Atsimo, Madg. 165/H8
Midou (riv.), Fr. 100/C5
Midsayap, Phil. 137/D6
Midu, China 141/H2
Midvale, Ut, US 195/K12
Midway (isls.), Pac., US 174/H2
Midway, De, US 196/C6
Midway, Il, US 195/H8
Midway, Ut, US 195/K11
Midway, Ut, US 195/L12
Midyan (reg.), SAr. 146/C3
Midyat, Turk. 148/E2
Mie, Japan 132/B4
Mie (pref.), Japan 135/K7
Miechów, Pol. 99/L3
Miedzychód, Pol. 99/H2
Międzylesie, Pol. 99/J3
Międzyrzec Podlaski, Pol. 99/M3
Międzyrzecz, Pol. 99/H2
Międzyzdroje, Pol. 99/H2
Miehlen, Ger. 111/G3
Mielec, Pol. 99/L3
Miercurea Cluc, Rom. 107/G2
Mieres, Sp. 102/C1
Miesbach, Ger. 101/J3
Mifflinburg, Pa, US 196/A2
Mifflin, Pa, US 196/A2

Migori, Kenya 162/B3
Miguel Alemán, Mex. 200/C2
Miguel Aleman, Presa (dam), Mex. 201/M8
Miguel Alves, Braz. 212/B2
Miguel Auza, Mex. 200/E3
Miguel Calmon, Braz. 212/B3
Miguel Hidalgo (int'l arpt.), Mex. 200/E4
Miguel Hidalgo (res.), Mex. 200/C3
Miguel Pereira, Braz. 213/K7
Miguel Riglos, Arg. 216/E3
Miguelelito, Uru. 217/K11
Miguelópolis, Braz. 213/B2
Miguelturra, Sp. 102/D3
Migŭm, SKor. 131/G6
Mihama, Japan 135/L6
Mihara, Japan 132/C3
Mihara, Japan 135/J6
Miharu, Japan 133/G2
Mihla, Ger. 109/H6
Miho, Japan 135/M6
Mihrābpur, Pak. 147/J3
Mijares (riv.), Sp. 103/E2
Mijas, Sp. 102/C4
Mijdrecht, Neth. 108/B4
Mikasa, Japan 134/B2
Mikata (lake), Japan 135/L4
Mikawa (bay), Japan 135/M6
Mikhaylovka, Rus. 121/G2
Mikhmoret, Isr. 149/F7
Miki, Japan 135/G6
Mikinai, Gre. 105/H4
Mikinai (Mycenae) (ruins), Gre. 105/H4
Mikkeli (prov.), Fin. 95/H3
Mikonos, Gre. 105/J4
Mikonos (isl.), Gre. 105/J4
Mikri Prespa (lake), Alb./Gre. 105/G2
Mikri Prespa NP, Gre. 105/G2
Mikumi NP, Tanz. 163/G3
Mikuni, Japan 132/G2
Mikuni-tōge (pass), Japan 133/F2
Mikura (isl.), Japan 133/F4
Mila (prov.), Alg. 158/M4
Milagro, Ecu. 210/B5
Milak, India 142/B1
Milan (Milano), It. 101/H4
Milang, Austl. 173/A2
Milano (prov.), It. 116/C2
Milano (Milan), It. 101/H4
Milas, Turk. 148/A2
Milazzo, It. 104/D3
Milbank, SD, US 185/J4
Mildura, Austl. 173/B2
Miles, Tx, US 190/C4
Miles, Austl. 172/C4
Miles City, Mt, US 185/G4
Mileševka (peak), 113/G1
Milestone, Sk, Can. 185/G3
Miletto (peak), It. 104/D2
Milevsko, Czh. 113/H4
Milford, Ct, US 197/E1
Milford, De, US 196/C6
Milford (lake), Ks, US 190/D2
Milford, Mi, US 193/F6
Milford, NJ, US 196/C2
Milford Haven, Wal, UK 90/A3
Milford Haven (inlet), Wal, UK 90/A3
Milgis (riv.), Kenya 162/C2
Mili (isl.), Mrsh. 174/G4
Miliana, Alg. 158/G4
Milicz, Pol. 99/J3
Mililani Town, Hi, US 182/V10
Milk (hill), Eng, UK 91/E4
Milk, On, Can. 180/F4
Milk River, Ab, Can. 184/E3
Mill (isl.), Nun., Can. 181/J2
Mill (riv.), Ct, US 197/E1
Mill Neck, NY, US 197/L8
Millaa Millaa, Austl. 172/B2
Millau, Fr. 100/E4
Millbrae, Ca, US 193/K11
Millbrook (res.), Austl. 171/M8
Millburn, NJ, US 197/H8
Millcreek, Ut, US 195/K12
Mille Iles (riv.), Qu, Can. 189/N6
Mille Lacs (lake), Mn, US 185/K4
Milledgeville, Ga, US 191/H3
Miller, SD, US 185/J4
Millerovo, Rus. 121/G2
Millers Ferry (dam), Al, US 191/G3
Millersburg, Pa, US 196/B2
Millerstown, Pa, US 196/A2
Millersville, Pa, US 196/B3
Milleur (pt.), Sc, UK 92/C1
Millevaches (plat.), Fr. 100/D4
Milliarino, It. 116/D5
Millicent, Austl. 173/B3
Milliken, Co, US 195/B2
Millingen aan de Rijn, Neth. 108/C5

Millington, Md, US 196/C5
Millinocket, Me, US 189/G2
Millisle, NI, UK 92/C2
Millmerran, Austl. 172/C4
Millmont, Pa, US 196/A2
Millport, Sc, UK 94/B5
Mills Junction, Ut, US 195/J12
Millstadt, Il, US 195/G9
Millstone (riv.), NJ, US 196/D3
Millstream-Chichester NP, Austl. 170/C2
Millthorpe, Austl. 173/D2
Milltown, NJ, US 197/H10
Milltown Malbay, Ire. 89/P10
Millville, Pa, US 196/B1
Millville, NJ, US 196/C5
Millwood (lake), Ar, US 190/E3
Milmay, NJ, US 196/D5
Milnathort, Wal, UK 93/E5
Milne (bay), PNG 174/E5
Milngavie, Sc, UK 94/B5
Milnrow, Eng, UK 93/F4
Milo, Me, US 189/G2
Milo (riv.), Gui. 160/C4
Mililii, Hi, US 182/U11
Mílos (isl.), Gre. 105/J4
Mílos, Gre. 105/J4
Milseburg (peak), Ger. 112/C1
Miltenberg, Ger. 112/C3
Milton, Austl. 173/D2
Milton, On, Can. 189/Q8
Milton, NZ 175/R12
Milton (res.), Co, US 195/C2
Milton, Fl, US 191/G4
Milton, NH, US 189/G3
Milton, Pa, US 196/B1
Milton, Ut, US 195/K11
Milton, Wa, US 193/C3
Milton-Freewater, Or, US 184/D4
Milton Keynes, Eng, UK 91/F2
Milton Keynes (co.), Eng, UK 91/F2
Milton Ness (pt.), Sc, UK 94/D3
Milton of Campsie, Sc, UK 94/B5
Milwaukee, Wi, US 185/M5
Milwaukee (co.), Wi, US 193/P14
Milz (riv.), Ger. 112/D2
Mimi (riv.), Japan 132/B4
Mimizan, Fr. 100/C4
Mimmaya, Japan 134/B3
Min (riv.), China 128/H5
Min Xian, China 128/H5
Mīna (riv.), Alg. 158/F5
Mīnāb, Iran 147/G3
Minahasa (pen), Indo. 139/F3
Minakuchi, Japan 135/K6
Minamata, Japan 132/B4
Minami Alps NP, Japan 133/F3
Minami-tori-shima (isl.), Japan 174/E2
Minamiaiki, Japan 135/B1
Minamiashigara, Japan 135/C3
Minamichita, Japan 135/L6
Minamidaitō (isl.), Japan 133/L8
Minamiiō (isl.), Japan 174/D2
Minamikawara, Japan 135/C1
Minamimaki, Japan 135/A2
Minamiyamashiro, Japan 135/J6
Minano, Japan 135/C1
Minas, Cuba 203/G1
Minas (peak), Ecu. 210/B5
Minas, Uru. 217/G2
Minas de Matahambre, Cuba 203/F1
Minas de Riotinto, Sp. 102/B4
Minas Gerais (state), Braz. 212/A5
Minas Novas, Braz. 212/B5
Minatitlán, Mex. 202/C2
Minbu, Myan. 141/F3
Minbya, Myan. 141/F3
Minch, The (North Minch) (str.), Sc, UK 89/Q8
Minchinābād, Pak. 144/B4
Minchinmávida (vol.), Chile 216/B4
Mincio (riv.), It. 117/D2
Mindanao (isl.), Phil. 137/D6
Mindanao (sea), Phil. 139/F2
Mindel (riv.), Ger. 98/F4
Mindelheim, Ger. 115/G1
Mindelo, CpV. 151/J10
Minden, Ger. 109/F4
Minden, La, US 187/J4
Minden, Ne, US 187/H2
Mindoro (isl.), Phil. 137/D5
Mindoro (str.), Phil. 137/C5
Mine (pt.), Ire. 89/Q10
Mineiros, Braz. 209/H7
Mineola, Tx, US 187/J4
Mineola, NY, US 197/L8
Mineral del Monte, Mex. 201/L6
Mineral Wells, Tx, US 187/H4
Mineral'nye Vody (int'l arpt.), Rus. 121/G3
Mineral'nye Vody, Rus. 121/G3
Minerbe, It. 117/E2
Minerbio, It. 117/E3
Minerbio (pt.), Fr. 101/H5
Minersville, Pa, US 196/B2
Minfeld, Ger. 112/B4
Minfeng, China 128/D4
Ming (riv.), China 141/J3
Mingäçevir, Azer. 121/H4
Mingäçevir Su Anbari (res.), Azer. 121/H4
Mingan (riv.), Qu, Can. 189/J1
Mingāora, Pak. 144/B2
Mingenew, Austl. 170/B4
Minglanilla, Sp. 102/E3
Mingshui, China 129/N2
Mingxi, China 137/C2
Minhe, China 128/H4
Minhla, Myan. 141/G4
Minho (riv.), Sp. 102/A1
Minidoka Internment Nat'l Mon., Id, US 184/E6
Minigwal (lake), Austl. 170/D4
Minitonas, Mb, Can. 185/H2
Minlaton, Austl. 171/H5
Minle, China 128/H4
Minna, Nga. 161/G4
Minneapolis, Mn, US 185/K4
Minneapolis-St. Paul (Wold-Chamberlain) (int'l arpt.), Mn, US 185/K4
Minnedosa, Mb, Can. 185/J3
Minnesota (state), US 185/K4
Minnesota (riv.), Mn, US 185/K4
Minnigaff, Sc, UK 92/D2
Minnis (lake), On, Can. 188/B1
Minnitaki (lake), On, Can. 185/K3
Miño (riv.), Port.,Sp. 102/A1
Mino, Japan 135/L4
Minobu, Japan 133/F3
Minokamo, Japan 135/M5
Mino'o, Japan 135/H6
Mino'o (riv.), Japan 135/H6
Minori, Japan 135/E1
Minot, ND, US 185/H3
Minqin, China 128/H4
Minqing, China 137/C2
Minquan, China 130/C4
Minsener Oog (isl.), Ger. 109/F1
Minsk (cap.), Bela. 97/M5
Minsk (int'l arpt.), Bela. 97/M5
Mińsk Mazowiecki, Pol. 99/L2
Minskaya Voblasts Bela. 120/C1
Mintaka (pass), China 147/K1
Mintaka (pass), Pak. 145/F5
Mintlaw, Sc, UK 94/E1
Minto, Ak, US 192/J2
Minto, NB, Can. 189/H2
Minto (inlet), NW, Can. 180/E1
Minūf, Egypt 149/B4
Minusinsk, Rus. 122/K4
Minusio, Swi. 115/E5
Minyā al Qamḩ, Egypt 149/B4
Minyip, Austl. 173/B3
Miquan, China 128/E3
Mira, Port. 102/A2
Mira (riv.), Col. 210/B4
Mira Loma, Ca, US 194/C2
Mira Monte, Ca, US 194/A2
Mira Taglio, It. 117/F2
Mirabel (int'l arpt.), Qu, Can. 189/M6
Mirabel, Qu, Can. 189/M6
Mirabela, Braz. 212/A5
Mirabello, It. 117/E3
Miracema, Braz. 213/D2
Miracema do Norte, Braz. 209/J5
Miradolo Terme, It. 116/C2
Mirador, Braz. 212/A2
Mirador (pass), Chile 216/C4
Miraflores, Col. 210/C4
Miraflores, Col. 210/C3
Miraflores, Mex. 200/C4
Miraflores, Peru 214/B3
Miragoâne, Haiti 203/H2
Miraj, India 147/K5
Miramar, Ca, US 194/C5
Miramar, Arg. 216/F3
Miramar Naval Air Station, Ca, US 194/C5
Mirambéllou (gulf), Gre. 105/J5
Miramichi, NB, Can. 189/H2
Miramont-de-Guyenne, Fr. 100/D4
Miranda (riv.), Braz. 209/G8
Miranda de Ebro, Sp. 102/D1
Miranda do Corvo, Port. 102/A2
Miranda do Douro, Port. 102/B2
Mirande, Fr. 100/D5
Mirandela, Port. 102/B2
Mirandola, It. 101/J4
Mirandópolis, Braz. 213/B2
Mirano, It. 117/F2
Mīrānpur, India 142/A1
Mirante do Paranapanema, Braz. 213/B2
Mirassol, Braz. 213/B2
Miravalles (peak), Sp. 102/B1
Miravalles (vol.), CR 203/E4
Mirebalais, Haiti 203/H2
Mirebeau, Fr. 114/B3
Mirecourt, Fr. 114/C1
Mirfield, Eng, UK 93/G4
Miri, Malay. 138/D3
Miriam Vale, Austl. 172/C4
Mirim (lake), Braz. 215/F3
Mirimire, Ven. 210/D2
Mirina, Gre. 105/J3
Miritiparaná (riv.), Col. 210/D5
Mirna (riv.), Cro. 117/G2
Mirnyy, Rus. 123/M3
Mirnyy, Rus., Ant. 218/G
Mirond (lake), Sk, Can. 185/H2
Mirow, Ger. 98/G2
Mirror (lake), NJ, US 196/D4
Mirtóön (sea), Gre. 105/H4
Miryang, SKor. 131/E5
Mirzāpur, India 142/D3
Misa (riv.), It. 117/G5
Misāha (well), Egypt 159/A4
Misaka, Japan 135/B2
Misaki, Japan 132/D3
Misaki, Japan 135/E3
Misano Adriatico, It. 117/F5
Misantla, Mex. 201/N7
Misato, Japan 135/C1
Misato, Japan 135/D2
Misato, Japan 135/K6
Misawa, Japan 134/B3
Mishan, China 129/P2
Mishawaka, In, US 188/C3
Misheguk (mtn.), Ak, US 192/F2
Mishima, Japan 133/F3
Misilmeri, It. 104/C3
Misiones, Sierra de (mts.), Arg. 215/E2
Miskitos, Cayos (isls.), Nic. 198/E5
Miskolc, Hun. 99/L4
Misono, Japan 135/L6
Misool (isl.), Indo. 139/H4
Misquah (hills), Mn, US 185/L4
Mişrātah, Libya 154/J1
Mişrātah (pt.), Libya 155/L1
Missinaibi (lake), On, Can. 188/D1
Missinaibi (riv.), On, Can. 181/H3
Mission, Tx, US 190/D5
Mission (bay), Ca, US 194/C5
Mission, Ks, US 195/D5
Mission Beach, Austl. 172/B2
Mission Hills, Ks, US 195/D5
Mission Ind. Res., Ca, US 194/C4
Mission San Buenaventura, Ca, US 194/A2
Mission San Jose, Ca, US 193/L12
Mission San Juan Capistrano, Ca, US 194/C3
Mission Viejo, Ca, US 194/C3
Missisa (lake), On, Can. 185/M2
Missisicabi (riv.), Qu, Can. 188/E1
Mississauga, On, Can. 189/Q8
Mississippi (pt.), Austl. 170/D5
Mississippi (riv.), US 183/H5
Mississippi (state), US 191/F3
Mississippi (delta), La, US 191/F4
Mississippi River Gulf Outlet (canal), La, US 195/Q17
Missoula, Mt, US 184/E4
Missouri (riv.), US 183/G3
Missouri (state), US 187/J3
Missouri City, Mo, US 195/E5
Missouri City, Tx, US 187/J5
Mistaken (pt.), Nf, Can. 189/L2
Mistassibi (riv.), Qu, Can. 189/F1
Mistassibi Nord-Est (riv.), Qu, Can. 189/F1
Mistassini, Qu, Can. 189/F1
Mistassini (riv.), Qu, Can. 189/F1
Mistassini (lake), Qu, Can. 181/J3
Mistelbach an der Zaya, Aus. 101/M2
Misti (vol.), Peru 214/D5
Mistissini, Qu, Can. 188/F1
Mistrás (ruin), Gre. 105/H4
Mistretta, It. 104/D4
Misty Fjords Nat'l Mon., Ak, US 192/M4
Misugi, Japan 135/K6
Mita, Punta de (pt.), Mex. 200/D4
Mitaka, Japan 135/D2
Mitake, Japan 135/M5
Mitama, Japan 135/B2
Mitare, Ven. 210/D2
Mitchell, Austl. 172/B4
Mitchell (riv.), Austl. 172/A1
Mitchell, Il, US 195/G8
Mitchell (mt.), NC, US 191/H3
Mitchell, SD, US 185/J5
Mitchell River NP, Austl. 173/C3
Mitha Tiwāna, Pak. 144/B3
Mithankot, Pak. 144/A5
Mithi, Pak. 147/J4
Mithimna, Gre. 105/K3
Mitiaro (isl.), CookIs. 175/K6
Mitilíni, Gre. 105/K3
Mitla (pass), Egypt 149/C4
Mitla (ruin), Mex. 202/B2
Mito, Japan 133/G2
Mito, Japan 135/M6
Mitomi, Japan 135/B2
Mitra (peak), EqG. 154/G7
Mitre (pen.), Arg. 215/C7
Mitry-Mory, Fr. 88/K5
Mitsamiouli, Com. 165/G5
Mitsinjo, Madg. 165/H7
Mitsio, Nosy (isl.), Madg. 165/J6
Mits'iwa, Erit. 155/N4
Mitsue, Japan 135/K7
Mitsukaidō, Japan 133/F2
Mitsuke, Japan 133/F2
Mittagong, Austl. 173/D2
Mittagspitze (peak), Aus. 115/F3
Mittainville, Fr. 88/G5
Mittelberg, Aus. 115/G3
Mittelland (canal), Ger. 109/F4
Mittelradde (riv.), Ger. 109/E3
Mittenwald, Ger. 115/H3
Mittersill, Aus. 101/K3
Mitterteich, Ger. 113/F3
Mittlere-Isar (canal), Ger. 113/E6
Mittweida, Ger. 98/G3
Mitú, Col. 210/D4
Mitumba, Monts (mts.), D.R. Congo 163/E1
Mitwitz, Ger. 112/E2
Miura (pen.), Japan 135/D3
Miura, Japan 135/D3
Miwa, Japan 135/H5
Miwa, Japan 135/L5
Mixco Viejo (ruin), Guat. 202/D3
Mixquiahuala, Mex. 201/K6
Mixteco (riv.), Mex. 202/B2
Miya (riv.), Japan 135/K7
Miyagawa, Japan 135/K7
Miyagi (pref.), Japan 134/B4
Miyake (isl.), Japan 133/F3
Miyako, Japan 134/B4
Miyako (isls.), Japan 133/H8
Miyakonojō, Japan 132/B5
Miyama, Japan 135/J5
Miyama, Japan 135/L4
Miyanojō, Japan 132/B5
Miyashiro, Japan 135/D2
Miyazaki (pref.), Japan 132/B4
Miyazaki, Japan 132/B5
Miyazu, Japan 135/H4
Miyazu (bay), Japan 135/H4
Miyi, China 141/H2
Miyoshi, Japan 132/C3
Miyoshi, Japan 135/D2
Miyoshi, Japan 135/D3
Miyoshi, Japan 135/M5
Miyota, Japan 135/B1
Miyun, China 130/H6
Miyun (res.), China 130/H6
Mizen (pt.), Ire. 92/B6
Miziya, Bul. 107/F4
Mizoram (state), India 141/F3
Mizpah, NJ, US 196/D5
Miẕpe Ramon, Isr. 149/D4
Mizuho, Japan 135/C2
Mizuho, Japan 135/H5
Mizunami, Japan 135/M5
Mizusawa, Japan 134/B4
Mjölby, Swe. 96/F2
Mjøndalen, Nor. 96/D2
Mjörn (lake), Swe. 96/E3
Mjøsa (lake), Nor. 95/D3
Mkata (plain), Tanz. 162/C4
Mkokotoni, Tanz. 162/C4
Mkomazi Game Rsv., Tanz. 162/C4
Mkombo (riv.), Tanz. 162/A4
Mkondoa (riv.), Tanz. 162/C4
Mkorn (peak), Mor. 156/D3
Mkumbi (pt.), Tanz. 162/C4
Mkushi, Zam. 163/E3
Mkuze (riv.), SAfr. 165/F2
Mladá Boleslav, Czh. 113/H2
Mladá Vožice, Czh. 113/H3
Mladenovac, Serb. 106/E3
Mlala (hills), Tanz. 162/A4
Mława, Pol. 99/L2
Mljet (isl.), Cro. 105/E1
Mljet NP, Cro. 105/E1
Mmabatho, SAfr. 164/D2
Mnyera (riv.), Tanz. 162/B5
Mo Duc, Viet. 136/E3
Moa, Cuba 203/H1
Moa (isl.), Indo. 139/G5
Moa (riv.), SLeo. 160/C5
Moab, Ut, US 186/E3
Moala Group (isl.), Fiji 174/G6
Moama, Austl. 173/C1
Moamba, Moz. 165/F2
Moaña, Sp. 102/A1
Moanda, Gabon 154/H8
Moate, Ire. 89/Q10
Mobara, Japan 135/E3
Mobaye, CAfr. 155/K7
Moberly, Mo, US 187/J3
Moberly Lake, BC, Can. 184/C2
Mobile, Al, US 191/F4
Mobridge, SD, US 185/H4
Moca (pass), Turk. 149/C1
Mocache, Ecu. 210/B5
Mocajuba, Braz. 209/J4
Moçambique, Moz. 163/H4
Mocanaqua, Pa, US 196/B1
Mocha (riv.), Rus. 119/W9
Moche (ruin), Peru 214/B3
Mochima, PN, Ven. 211/E2
Mochizuki, Japan 135/A1
Mochudi, Bots. 163/E5
Mochumí, Peru 214/B2
Mocímboa da Praia, Moz. 162/D5
Möckeln (lake), Swe. 96/E3
Mockfjärd, Swe. 96/F1
Möckmühl, Ger. 112/C4
Moclín, Sp. 102/D4
Mocoa, Col. 210/B4
Mococa, Braz. 213/F6
Mocorito, Mex. 200/D3
Moctezuma, Mex. 201/E4
Moctezuma, Mex. 200/C2
Mocuba, Moz. 163/G4
Modāsa, India 147/K4
Modderrivier (riv.), SAfr. 164/D3
Modena (prov.), It. 117/D3
Modena, It. 117/D3
Moder (riv.), Fr. 101/G2
Modesto, Ca, US 186/B3
Modica, It. 104/D4
Modigliana, It. 117/E4
Modjeska, Ca, US 194/C3
Modjigo (reg.), Niger 154/H4
Mödling, Aus. 107/N7
Modot, Mong. 129/J2
Modriča, Bosn. 106/D3
Modugno, It. 104/E2
Moe, Austl. 173/C3
Moeb (bay), Namb. 164/A2
Moel-y-Llyn (peak), Wal, UK 90/C2
Moëlan-sur-Mer, Fr. 100/B3
Moelfre (peak), Wal, UK 90/C1
Moen, Nor. 95/F1
Moenkopi (riv.), US 186/E3
Moerai (isl.), FrPol. 175/K7
Moerbeke, Belg. 110/C1
Moers, Ger. 108/D6
Moervaart (riv.), Belg. 110/C1
Moesa (riv.), Swi. 115/F5
Moffat, Sc, UK 94/C6
Moffett Field Naval Air Sta., Ca, US 193/K12
Moga, India 144/C4
Mogadouro, Port. 102/B2
Mogami (riv.), Japan 134/B4
Mogami, Japan 134/B4
Mogaung, Myan. 141/G2
Mogent (riv.), Sp. 103/L6
Mogglingen, Ger. 112/C5
Moghul Gardens, India 144/C3
Mogi das Cruzes, Braz. 213/G8
Mogi-Guaçu, Braz. 213/G7
Mogi-Guaçu (riv.), Braz. 213/G7
Mogi-Mirim, Braz. 213/G7
Mogilno, Pol. 99/J2
Moglia, It. 117/D3
Mogliano Veneto, It. 117/F1
Möglingen, Ger. 112/C5
Mogoro, It. 104/A3
Mogotes (pt.), Arg. 216/F3
Mogotón (peak), Nic. 202/E3
Moguer, Sp. 102/B4
Mohács, Hun. 106/D3
Mohéli (isl.), Com. 165/G6
Mohales Hoek, Les. 164/D3
Mohall, ND, US 185/H3
Mohamed V (dam), Mor. 158/C2
Mohamed V, Barrage (res.), Mor. 158/C2
Mohamed V (Casablanca) (int'l arpt.), Mor. 156/D2
Mohammadia, Alg. 158/F5
Mohammadia-Znata (prov.), Mor. 158/A2
Mohammedia, Mor. 158/A3
Mohawk (lake), NJ, US 196/D1
Moheda, Swe. 96/F3
Mohembo, Bots. 163/D4
Mohican (cape), Ak, US 192/E3
Möhlin, Swi. 114/D2
Möhne (riv.), Ger. 109/F6
Möhnestausee (lake), Ger. 109/F5
Mohnton, Pa, US 196/C3
Moho, Peru 214/D4
Mohrsville, Pa, US 196/C3
Mohyliv-Podil's'kyy, Ukr. 107/H1
Moi (int'l arpt.), Kenya 162/C4
Moi, Nor. 96/B2
Moie, It. 117/G5
Moineşti, Rom. 107/H2
Moinkum (des.), Kaz. 122/H5
Moinsi (hills), Gha. 161/E5
Moira (riv.), On, Can. 188/E2
Moirans, Fr. 100/F4
Moirans-en-Montagne, Fr. 114/B5
Moisie (riv.), Qu, Can. 181/K3
Moislains, Fr. 110/B4
Moissac, Fr. 100/D4
Moisselles, Fr. 88/K4
Moisson, Fr. 88/G4
Moita, Port. 103/Q10
Moitaco, Ven. 211/E3
Mojácar, Sp. 102/E4
Mojave (riv.), Ca, US 186/C4
Mojave (des.), Ca, US 186/C4
Mojiang Hanizu Zizhixian, China 141/H3
Mojikit (lake), On, Can. 185/L3
Mojkovac, Mont. 106/D4
Mojos, Llanos de (plain), Bol. 208/E6
Moju (riv.), Braz. 209/J4
Mōka, Japan 133/F2
Mokameh, India 143/E3
Mokapu (pt.), Hi, US 182/W13
Mokau (riv.), NZ 175/S10
Mokelumne (riv.), Ca, US 186/B3
Mokelumne (aqueduct), Ca, US 193/M11
Mokena, Il, US 193/Q16
Mokil (isl.), Micr. 174/E4
Moknine, Tun. 158/M7
Mokochu (peak), Thai. 136/B3
Mokokchūng, India 141/F2
Mokolo, Camr. 154/H5
Mokp'o, SKor. 131/D5
Mokrin, Serb. 106/E3
Moksha (riv.), Rus. 121/G1
Mokuleia, Hi, US 182/V12
Mol, Serb. 106/E3
Mol, Belg. 108/C6
Moláoi, Gre. 105/H4
Molare, It. 116/B3
Molas, Punta (pt.), Mex. 202/E1
Molat (isl.), Cro. 106/B3
Molatón (peak), Sp. 102/E3
Molbergen, Ger. 109/E3
Mold, Wal, UK 93/E5
Moldavia (reg.), Rom. 107/H2
Moldavian Carpathians (range), Rom. 107/G2
Molde, Nor. 95/C3
Moldova (ctry.) 107/H2
Moldova (riv.), Rom. 107/G2
Moldova Nouă, Rom. 106/E3
Moldoveanu (peak), Rom. 107/G3
Mole (riv.), Eng, UK 90/C5
Mole NP, Gha. 161/E4
Môle Saint-Nicolas, Haiti 203/H2
Molepolole, Bots. 163/E5
Molina, Sp. 102/E2
Molina, Chile 216/C2
Molina de Segura, Sp. 102/E3
Moline, Il, US 185/L5
Molinella, It. 117/E3
Molinicos, Sp. 102/D3
Molino de Flores, PN, Mex. 201/R9
Molins de Rei, Sp. 103/L7
Molise (reg.), It. 104/D2
Molkom, Swe. 96/E2
Möll (riv.), Aus. 101/K3
Møllebjerg (peak), Den. 95/D5
Mollendo, Peru 214/C5
Mollendruz, Col du (pass), Swi. 114/C4
Mollerussa, Sp. 103/F2
Molles (pt.), Chile 216/C2
Molles, Uru. 217/K10
Mollet del Vallès, Sp. 103/L6
Mollis, Swi. 115/F3
Mölndal, Swe. 96/E3
Mölnlycke, Swe. 96/E3
Molodezhnaya, Rus., Ant. 218/D
Mologa (riv.), Rus. 118/G4
Molokai (isl.), Hi, US 182/T10
Moloma (riv.), Rus. 119/L4
Molong, Austl. 173/D2
Molopo (riv.), Bots. 164/C5
Mólos, Gre. 105/H3
Molsheim, Fr. 114/D1
Molteno, SAfr. 164/D3
Molu (isl.), Indo. 139/H5
Molucca (sea), Asia 139/G4
Molucca Islands (arch.), Indo. 139/G3
Molveno (lake), It. 115/G5
Molveno, It. 115/G5
Mombaça, Braz. 212/C2
Mombasa, Kenya 162/C4
Mombetsu, Japan 134/C1
Mombetsu, Japan 134/C2
Mömbris, Ger. 112/C2
Momchilgrad, Bul. 107/G5
Momfafa (cape), Indo. 139/H4
Momignies, Belg. 111/D3
Mömlingen, Ger. 112/C3
Momo, It. 116/B1
Momoishi, Japan 134/B3
Mompós, Col. 210/C2
Mon (state), Myan. 141/G4
Mon (riv.), Myan. 141/F3
Møn (isl.), Den. 95/E5
Mona (isl.), PR 199/M8
Mona (passg.), NAm. 199/L8
Monaco (ctry.) 116/J8
Monaco (cap.), Mona. 116/J8
Monaco, Port of (har.), Mona. 116/J8
Monadhliath (mts.), Sc, UK 94/B2
Monagas (state), Ven. 211/F2
Monaghan (co.), Ire. 92/A3
Monagrillo, Pan. 203/F4
Monagrillo (riv.), Pan. 203/F4
Monar (lake), Sc, UK 94/A2
Monashee (mts.), BC, Can. 184/D3
Monastir, Tun. 158/M7
Moncada, Sp. 103/E3
Moncalieri, It. 101/G4
Moncalvo, It. 116/B2
Monção, Braz. 212/A1
Moncayo, Sierra del (range), Sp. 102/E2
Mönch (peak), Swi. 114/D4
Monchegorsk, Rus. 118/G2
Mönchengladbach, Ger. 108/D6
Monchique, Serra de (mts.), Port. 102/A4
Monchique, Port. 102/A4
Moncks Corner, SC, US 191/H3
Monclova, Mex. 201/E3
Moncton, NB, Can. 189/H2
Mondego (cape), Port. 102/A2
Mondego (riv.), Port. 102/A2
Mondéjar, Sp. 102/D2
Mondolfo, It. 117/G5
Mondoñedo, Sp. 102/B1
Mondorf-les- Bains, Lux. 111/F4
Mondovì, It. 116/A4
Mondragón, Sp. 102/D1
Mondragone, It. 104/C2
Mondsee (lake), Aus. 113/G7
Mondsee, Aus. 113/G7
Moneglia, It. 116/C4
Monemvasía, Gre. 105/H4
Mones Cazón, Arg. 216/E3
Monesterio, Sp. 102/B3
Money (pt.), Sc, UK 92/C2
Moneyreagh, NI, UK 92/C2
Monferrato (reg.), It. 101/H4
Monforte, Sp. 102/B1
Monforte, Port. 102/B3
Mongaguá, Braz. 213/G9
Mongers (lake), Austl. 170/C4
Monghidoro, It. 117/E4
Mongo, Chad 155/J5
Mongo (riv.), Gui. 160/C4
Mongolia (ctry.) 128/G2
Mongu, Zam. 163/D4
Mönh Hayrhan (peak), Mong. 128/F2
Mönh Sarĭdag (peak), Mong. 128/H1
Monheim, Ger. 112/D5
Monheim, Ger. 111/F1
Monifieth, Sc, UK 94/D4
Moniquirá, Col. 210/C3
Monistrol de Montserrat, Sp. 103/K6
Monistrol-sur-Loire, Fr. 100/F4
Monitor (range), Nv, US 186/C3
Monkayo, Phil. 137/E6
Monkey (pt.), Nic. 203/F4
Monkey River Town, Belz. 202/D2
Mońki, Pol. 99/M2
Monks (isl.), Md, US 196/B5
Monmouth, Il, US 185/L5
Monmouth, Or, US 184/C4
Monmouth Beach, NJ, US 196/E3
Monmouth Junction, NJ, US 196/D3
Monmouth Mil. Res., NJ, US 196/D3
Monmouthshire (co.), Wal, UK 90/D3
Monmow (riv.), Eng, UK 90/C2
Monnickendam, Neth. 108/C4
Mono (riv.), Togo 154/F6
Mono (lake), Ca, US 186/C3
Mono (prov.), Ben. 161/F5
Monocacy (riv.), Md, US 196/A4
Monor, Hun. 106/D2
Monóvar, Sp. 103/E3
Monreal del Campo, Sp. 102/E2
Monreale, It. 104/C3
Monroe, Ct, US 197/E1
Monroe (lake), Fl, US 191/G2
Monroe, Ga, US 191/H3
Monroe, La, US 187/J4
Monroe, Mi, US 188/D3
Monroe, NC, US 191/H3
Monroe, NY, US 196/D1
Monroe, Ut, US 186/D3
Monroe, Wa, US 193/C2
Monroe, Wi, US 185/L5
Monroe City, Il, US 195/G9
Monroeville, Al, US 191/G4
Monroeville, NJ, US 196/C4
Monrovia (cap.), Libr. 160/C5
Monrovia, Ca, US 194/G7
Mons, Belg. 110/C3
Monsanto, Port. 102/B2
Monschau, Ger. 111/F2
Monsefú, Peru 214/B2
Monselice, It. 101/J4
Monsenhor Tabosa, Braz. 212/B2
Monsey, NY, US 197/J7
Monsheim, Ger. 112/B3
Monster, Neth. 108/B4
Mönsteras, Swe. 96/G3
Monsummano Terme, It. 117/D5
Mont-de-Marsan, Fr. 100/C5
Mont-Joli, Qu, Can. 189/G1
Mont-Laurier, Qu, Can. 188/F2
Mont Peko, PN du, C.d'Iv. 160/D5
Mont-Royal, Qu, Can. 189/N6
Mont-Saint-Martin, Fr. 111/E4
Mont-Saint-Michel, Qu, Can. 188/F2
Mont Sangbé, PN du, C.d'Iv. 160/D4
Mont-Sous-Vaudrey, Fr. 114/B4
Montà, It. 116/A3
Monta Fon (mts.), Aus. 115/F3
Montabaur, Ger. 111/G3
Montagnana, It. 117/E2
Montagne d'Ambre NP, Madg. 165/J6
Montagny-Sainte-Félicité, Fr. 88/L4
Montagu, SAfr. 164/M10
Montague (str.), Ak, US 192/J4
Montague, Tx, US 187/H4
Montague, PE, Can. 189/J2
Montague, NJ, US 196/D1
Montague (isl.), Ak, US 192/J4
Montaigu, Fr. 110/C3
Montaione, It. 117/D5
Montalbán, Sp. 103/E2
Montalbano Jonico, It. 104/E2
Montale, It. 117/E5
Montale, It. 117/D3
Montalieu-Vercieu, Fr. 114/B6
Montalvão, Port. 102/B3
Montalvo, Ca, US 194/A2
Montana, Bul. 107/F4
Montana (prov.), Bul. 106/F4
Montana, Swi. 114/D5
Montana (state), US 184/F4
Montanaro, It. 116/A2
Montanha, Braz. 212/B5
Montara, Ca, US 193/J11
Montargis, Fr. 100/E2
Montataire, Fr. 110/B5
Montauban, Fr. 100/D4
Montauk, NY, US 197/G1
Montauk (pt.), NY, US 197/G1
Montbard, Fr. 100/F3
Montbéliard, Fr. 114/C2
Montblanc, Sp. 103/F2
Montcada i Reixac, Sp. 103/L7
Montceau-les-Mines, Fr. 100/F3
Montclair, Ca, US 194/C2
Montclair, NJ, US 197/J8
Montcornet, Fr. 110/D4
Montdidier, Fr. 110/B4
Monte Albán (ruin), Mex. 202/B2
Monte Alegre, Braz. 209/H4
Monte Alegre de Goiás, Braz. 212/A4
Monte Alegre de Minas, Braz. 213/B1
Monte Alegre do Piauí, Braz. 212/A3
Monte Alto, Braz. 213/B2
Monte Azul, Braz. 212/B4
Monte Carmelo, Braz. 213/C1
Monte Carmelo, Ven. 210/D2
Monte Caseros, Arg. 215/E3
Monte Comán, Arg. 216/D2
Monte Escobedo, Mex. 200/E4
Monte Maíz, Arg. 216/E2
Monte Pascoal, PN de, Braz. 209/L7
Monte Pascoal, PN de, Braz. 212/C5
Monte Rosa (mts.), It. 114/D6
Monte San Savino, It. 117/E6
Montealegre, Sp. 102/E3
Montebello (isls.), Austl. 170/B2
Montebello, Ca, US 194/F7

Monte – Muğla

Montebello Vincentino, It. 117/E2
Montebelluna, It. 117/F1
Montebruno, It. 116/C3
Montecarlo, Arg. 215/F2
Montecassiano, It. 117/G6
Montecatini Terme, It. 117/D5
Montecavolo, It. 116/D3
Montecchio, It. 117/F5
Montechiaro d'Asti, It. 116/B2
Montecito, Ca, US 194/A2
Montecristo (isl.), It. 104/B1
Montecristo, PN, ESal. 202/D3
Montefeltro (reg.), It. 117/F5
Monteforte d'Alpone, It. 117/E2
Montefrío, Sp. 102/C4
Montego Bay, Jam. 203/G2
Montegranaro, It. 101/K5
Montegrotto Terme, It. 117/E2
Montehermoso, Sp. 102/B2
Monteiro, Braz. 212/C2
Montelavar, Port. 103/P10
Montélimar, Fr. 100/F4
Montellano, Sp. 102/C4
Montello, Nv, US 184/E5
Montelupo Fiorentino, It. 117/E5
Montemagno, It. 116/B3
Montemarciano, It. 117/G5
Montemor-o-Novo, Port. 102/A3
Montemor-o-Velho, Port. 102/A2
Montemorelos, Mex. 201/F3
Montemuro (peak), Port. 102/A2
Montendre, Fr. 100/C4
Montenegro, Braz. 213/B4
Montenero di Bisaccia, It. 104/D2
Montepulciano, It. 101/J5
Montereau-Faut-Yonne, Fr. 100/E2
Montereau-sur-le-Jard, Fr. 88/L6
Monterey, Ca, US 186/B3
Monterey (bay), Ca, US 186/B3
Monterey Park, Ca, US 194/F7
Montería, Col. 210/C2
Montero, Bol. 208/F7
Monteros, Arg. 215/C2
Monterosso (peak), It. 115/G4
Monterosso al Mare, It. 116/C4
Monterotondo, It. 104/C1
Monterrey, Mex. 201/E3
Monterrey, Sp. 102/B2
Montes (pt.), Arg. 217/C6
Montes Altos, Braz. 212/A2
Montes Claros, Braz. 212/B5
Montescaglioso, It. 104/E2
Montese, It. 117/D4
Montespertoli, It. 117/E5
Montesson, Fr. 88/J5
Monteux, Fr. 100/F4
Montevarchi, It. 117/E5
Montevideo, Mn, US 185/K4
Montevideo (cap.), Uru. 217/K11
Montevideo (dept.), Uru. 217/K11
Montévrain, Fr. 88/L5
Montezuma (peak), Az, US 195/R19
Montezuma Castle Nat'l Mon., Az, US 186/E4
Montfermeil, Fr. 88/K5
Montferrand-le-Château, Fr. 114/B3
Montfoort, Neth. 108/B4
Montfort-L'Amaury, Fr. 110/A6
Montgeron, Fr. 88/K5
Montgomery, Wal, UK 90/C1
Montgomery (cap.), Al, US 191/G3
Montgomery, Il, US 193/P16
Montgomery (co.), Md, US 196/A5
Montgomery, Pa, US 196/B1
Montgomery, WV, US 188/D4
Montgomery Village, Md, US 196/A5
Montgomeryville, Pa, US 196/C3
Montgrand (peak), Fr. 100/E5
Monthermé, Fr. 111/D4
Monthey, Swi. 114/C5
Monthureux-sur-Saône, Fr. 114/B1
Monthyon, Fr. 88/L4
Monti Sabini (mts.), It. 104/C1
Monticelli d'Ongina, It. 116/C2
Monticelli Terme, It. 116/D3
Monticello, Mo, US 185/L5
Monticello, Ky, US 188/C4
Monticello, In, US 188/C3
Monticello, La, US 187/K4
Monticello, Fl, US 191/H4
Monticello, Va, US 191/J2
Monticello Conte Otto, It. 117/E1
Montichiari, It. 116/D2
Montier-en-Der, Fr. 114/A1
Montignies-le-Tilleul, Belg. 111/D3
Montigny-en-Gohelle, Fr. 52/B3
Montigny-le-Bretonneux, Fr. 30/J5
Montigny-le-Roi, Fr. 114/B2
Montijo, Sp. 102/B3
Montijo, Port. 103/Q10
Montilla, Sp. 102/C4
Montivilliers, Fr. 100/D2
Montlebon, Fr. 114/C3
Montlhéry, Fr. 88/J6
Montluçon, Fr. 100/E3
Montluel, Fr. 114/B6
Montmagny, Qu, Can. 189/G2
Montmédy, Fr. 111/E4
Montmerle-sur-Saône, Fr. 114/A5
Montmirail, Fr. 110/C6
Montmorency, Fr. 88/J5
Montmorillon, Fr. 100/D3
Montmorot, Fr. 114/B4
Monto, Austl. 172/C4
Montodine, It. 116/C2
Montoir-de-Bretagne, Fr. 42/B3
Montois-la-Montagne, Fr. 111/F5
Montone (riv.), It. 117/E4
Montopoli, It. 117/D5
Montorio Veronese, It. 117/E2
Montoro, Sp. 102/C3
Montour (ridge), Pa, US 196/B2
Montour, Pa, US 196/B1
Montoursville, Pa, US 196/B1
Montpelier (cap.), Vt, US 189/F2
Montpellier, Fr. 100/E5
Montreal (lake), Sk, Can. 185/G2
Montreal (riv.), On, Can. 188/C2
Montréal, Qu, Can. 189/N6
Montréal-Est, Qu, Can. 189/N6
Montréal-la-Cluse, Fr. 114/B5
Montréal-Nord, Qu, Can. 189/N6
Montréjeau, Fr. 100/D5
Montreuil, Fr. 88/K5
Montreuil, Fr. 110/A3
Montreuil-Bellay, Fr. 100/C3
Montreuil-sur-Epte, Fr. 88/G4
Montreux, Swi. 114/C5
Montreux-Château, Fr. 114/C2
Montrevel-en-Bresse, Fr. 114/B5
Montricher, Swi. 114/C4
Montrose, Co, US 186/F3
Montrose (basin), Sc, UK 94/D3
Montrose, Sc, UK 94/D3
Montrouge, Fr. 88/J5
Montry, Fr. 88/L5
Monts, Fr. 100/D3
Montseny, PN, Sp. 103/L6
Montserrado (co.), Libr. 160/C5
Montserrat (peak), Sp. 103/F2
Montserrat (dpcy.), UK 199/N8
Montsoult, Fr. 88/J4
Montvale, NJ, US 197/J7
Montville, NJ, US 197/H8
Monywa, Myan. 141/G3
Monza, It. 116/C1
Monze, Zam. 163/E4
Monzingen, Ger. 111/G4
Monzón, Peru 214/B3
Monzón, Sp. 103/F2
Mooirivier, SAfr. 165/E3
Mool (riv.), SAfr. 164/P13
Moonta, Austl. 171/H5
Moora, Austl. 170/C4
Moorcroft, Wy, US 185/G4
Moordrecht, Neth. 108/B5
Moore (lake), Austl. 170/C4
Moore, Ok, US 195/N15
Moore Haven, Fl, US 191/H5
Moore River NP, Austl. 170/B4
Moorea (isl.), FrPol. 175/K6
Moorenweis, Ger. 115/H1
Moorestown, NJ, US 196/D4
Mooresville, NC, US 191/H3
Mooretown, On, Can. 193/H6
Moorfoot (hills), Sc, UK 94/C5
Moorhead, Mn, US 185/J4
Moorook, Austl. 173/B2
Moorpark, Ca, US 194/B2
Moorreesburg, SAfr. 164/L10
Moorslede, Belg. 110/C2
Moosburg, Ger. 113/E6
Moose (mtn.), Sk, Can. 185/H3
Moose (riv.), On, Can. 188/D1
Moose Creek, Ak, US 192/J3
Moose Jaw, Sk, Can. 185/G3
Moose Pass, Ak, US 192/J3
Moosehead (lake), Me, US 189/G2
Mooseheart (mtn.), Ak, US 192/H3
Mooseheart, Il, US 193/P16
Moosinning, Ger. 113/E6
Moosomin, Sk, Can. 185/H3
Moosonee, On, Can. 188/D1
Moosseedorf, Swi. 114/D3
Moosthenning, Ger. 113/F5
Mopti (pol. reg.), Mali 160/E3
Mopti, Mali 160/D3
Moquegua (dept.), Peru 214/D5
Moquegua, Peru 214/D5
Moquehuá, Arg. 217/J11
Mor (riv.), India 143/F4
Mór, Hun. 106/D2
Mora, Camr. 154/H5
Mora (riv.), NM, US 187/F4
Mora, NM, US 187/F4
Mora, Sp. 102/D3
Mora, Port. 102/A3
Mora, Swe. 96/F1
Mora de Rubielos, Sp. 103/E2
Morača (riv.), Mont. 106/D4
Morada Nova, Braz. 212/C2
Morada Nova de Minas, Braz. 213/C1
Morādābād, India 142/B1
Morado, PN, Chile 216/P8
Morafenobe, Madg. 165/H7
Morąg, Pol. 97/H5
Moraga, Ca, US 193/K11
Mórahalom, Hun. 106/D2
Morainvilliers, Fr. 88/H5
Moral de Calatrava, Sp. 102/D3
Moraleja, Sp. 102/B2
Morales, Guat. 202/D3
Moramanga, Madg. 165/J7
Moranbah, Austl. 172/C3
Morane (isl.), FrPol. 175/M7
Morangis, Fr. 88/K5
Morano Calabro, It. 104/E3
Morant Bay, Jam. 203/G2
Morar (lake), Sc, UK 89/R8
Morarano Chrome, Madg. 165/J7
Morat (lake), Swi. 114/D4
Morata de Tajuña, Sp. 103/N9
Moratalla, Sp. 102/E3
Moratuwa, SrL. 140/C6
Morava (riv.), Czh. 99/J4
Moravia (reg.), Czh. 99/J4
Moravská Třebová, Czh. 99/J4
Moravské Budějovice, Czh. 99/H4
Morawa, Austl. 170/C4
Morawhanna, Guy. 208/G2
Moray (pol. reg.), Sc, UK 94/E2
Moray Firth (inlet), Sc, UK 94/B1
Morbach, Ger. 111/G4
Morbegno, It. 115/F5
Morbier, Fr. 114/C4
Morbio Inferiore, Swi. 115/F6
Morbras (riv.), Fr. 88/K5
Mörbylånga, Swe. 96/G3
Morcenx, Fr. 100/C4
Morciano di Romagna, It. 117/F5
Morclan, Pic de (peak), Fr. 114/C5
Morden, Mb, Can. 185/J3
Mordoviya, Resp., Rus. 122/G6
Møre Og Romsdal (co.), Nor. 95/C3
Moreau (riv.), SD, US 185/H4
Morecambe (bay), Eng, UK 93/E3
Moree, Austl. 173/D1
Morehead, Ky, US 188/D4
Morehead City, NC, US 191/J3
Mörel, Swi. 114/E5
Morelia, Mex. 201/E5
Morella, Sp. 103/E2
Morelos (state), Mex. 198/A5
Morena, Sierra (range), Sp. 102/C4
Moreni, Rom. 107/G3
Moreno Valley, Ca, US 194/C3
Moresby (isl.), BC, Can. 180/C3
Moreton (bay), Austl. 172/F6
Moreton (cape), Austl. 172/D4
Moreton (isl.), Austl. 172/D4
Moreton Island NP, Austl. 172/D4
Moreuil, Fr. 110/B4
Moreyu (riv.), Rus. 119/P2
Morez, Fr. 114/C4
Morgan, Austl. 171/H5
Morgan (pt.), Ct, US 197/F1
Morgan, Ut, US 195/K11
Morgan (co.), Ut, US 195/K11
Morgan City, La, US 187/K5
Morganfield, Ky, US 188/C4
Morgantina (ruin), It. 104/D4
Morganton, NC, US 191/H3
Morgantown, Ky, US 188/C4
Morgantown, Pa, US 196/C3
Morge (riv.), Fr. 100/E3
Morgenzon, SAfr. 165/E2
Morges, Swi. 114/C4
Morgex, It. 114/D6
Morghāb (riv.), Afg. 147/H1
Morgongåva, Swe. 96/G2
Morguilla (pt.), Chile 216/B3
Morhange, Fr. 111/F6
Morhar (riv.), India 143/E3
Mori, It. 101/J4
Mori, Japan 134/B2
Mori Kazak Zizhixian, China 128/F3
Morialta Conservation Park, Austl. 171/M8
Moriarty, NM, US 187/F4
Morice (lake), BC, Can. 184/B2
Morie (lake), Sc, UK 94/B1
Moriguchi, Japan 135/J6
Morin Dawa Daurzu Zizhiqi, China 129/M2
Moringen, Ger. 109/G5
Morinville, Ab, Can. 184/E2
Morioka, Japan 134/B4
Morisset, Austl. 173/D2
Moriston (riv.), Sc, UK 94/B2
Moriya, Japan 135/D2
Moriyama, Japan 135/J5
Morlaix, Fr. 100/B2
Morlanwelz, Belg. 111/D3
Mörlenbach, Ger. 112/B3
Morley, Eng, UK 93/G4
Mormant, Fr. 88/L6
Mormond (hill), Sc, UK 94/D1
Mornaguia, Tun. 46/B4
Mornington (isl.), Austl. 167/C2
Mörnsheim, Ger. 112/D5
Moro, Pak. 147/J3
Moro (gulf), Phil. 137/D6
Morocco (ctry.) 156/D2
Morocelí, Hon. 202/E3
Morococha, Peru 214/B3
Morogoro (pol. reg.), Tanz. 162/C4
Morogoro, Tanz. 162/C4
Morombe, Madg. 165/G8
Mörön, Mong. 128/H2
Morón, Ven. 210/D2
Morón, Cuba 203/G1
Morón, Arg. 217/J11
Morón de la Frontera, Sp. 102/C4
Morona (riv.), Peru 208/C4
Morona-Santiago (dept.), Ecu. 210/B5
Morondava (riv.), Madg. 165/H8
Morondava, Madg. 165/H8
Moroni (cap.), Com. 165/G5
Morotai (isl.), Indo. 139/G3
Morotai (str.), Indo. 139/G3
Moroto, Ugan. 162/B2
Moroto (mt.), Ugan. 162/B2
Moroyama, Japan 135/C2
Morpará, Braz. 212/B3
Morpeth, Eng, UK 93/G1
Morphou, Cyp. 149/C2
Morphou (bay), Cyp. 149/C2
Morra (lake), Neth. 108/C3
Morrinhos, Braz. 213/B1
Morris (mt.), Austl. 171/F3
Morris, Mb, Can. 185/J3
Morris (res.), Ca, US 194/C2
Morris, Mn, US 185/K4
Morris (co.), NJ, US 196/D2
Morris Jesup (cape), Grld 218/J
Morris Plains, NJ, US 197/H8
Morrison, Co, US 195/B3
Morristown, NJ, US 196/D2
Morristown NHP, NJ, US 196/D2
Morrisville, Pa, US 196/D3
Morro Bay, Ca, US 186/B4
Morro de Môco (peak), Ang. 163/C3
Morro de Puercos (pt.), Pan. 203/F5
Morro do Chapéu, Braz. 212/B3
Morro, Punta del (pt.), Mex. 201/N7
Morrocoy, PN, Ven. 210/D2
Mórrope, Peru 214/A2
Morropón, Peru 214/B2
Morros, Braz. 212/A1
Morrosquillo (gulf), Col. 203/G4
Mörrum, Swe. 96/F3
Mors (isl.), Den. 96/D3
Morsang-sur-Orge, Fr. 88/K6
Morsbach, Ger. 111/G2
Morsbach, Fr. 111/F5
Morschwiller-le-Bas, Fr. 114/D2
Morse, Ks, US 195/D6
Morse Mill, Mo, US 195/F9
Morshansk, Rus. 121/G1
Morskoy (isl.), Kaz. 121/J3
Morsum, Ger. 109/G3
Mortagne (riv.), Fr. 114/C1
Mortagne-sur-Sèvre, Fr. 100/C3
Mortara, It. 116/B2
Mortcerf, Fr. 88/L5
Morte (pt.), Eng, UK 90/B4
Morte (riv.), Fr. 114/B3
Morteau, Fr. 114/C3
Mortefontaine, Fr. 88/K4
Mortegliano, It. 117/G1
Mortes, Rio das (riv.), Braz. 209/H6
Mortlake, Austl. 173/B3
Morton, Wa, US 184/C4
Morton, Il, US 187/K2
Morton Grove, Il, US 193/Q15
Morton NP, Austl. 173/D2
Morton NWR, NY, US 197/F2
Mortsel, Belg. 108/B6
Morungaba, Braz. 213/G7
Moruya, Austl. 173/D2
Morvan (plat.), Fr. 100/E3
Morven, Austl. 172/B4
Morven (peak), Sc, UK 94/C2
Morvi, India 147/K4
Morvillars, Fr. 114/C2
Morwell, Austl. 173/C3
Morzine, Fr. 114/C5
Mos, Sp. 102/A1
Mosbach, Ger. 112/C4
Mosby, Mo, US 195/E5
Moscavide, Port. 103/P10
Moscow (Moskva) (cap.), Rus. 119/W9
Moscow (upland), Rus. 118/F5
Moscow, Id, US 184/D4
Moscow University Ice Shelf, Ant. 218/J
Moselle (riv.), Fr. 101/G2
Moselle (dept.), Fr. 111/F5
Moselotte (riv.), Fr. 114/C2
Moses Lake, Wa, US 184/D4
Mosfellsbær, Ice. 95/N7
Mosgiel, NZ 175/S12
Moshaweng (riv.), SAfr. 164/C2
Moshchnyy (isl.), Rus. 97/M2
Moshi, Tanz. 162/C3
Moshoeshoe (Maseru) (int'l arpt.), Les. 164/D3
Mosina, Pol. 99/J2
Moskovskaya Oblast, Rus. 118/H5
Moskva (riv.), Rus. 118/G5
Moskva (Moscow) (cap.), Rus. 120/F1
Mosonmagyaróvár, Hun. 106/C2
Mosquera, Col. 210/B4
Mosquero, NM, US 187/G4
Mosquitia (phys. reg.), Hon. 203/E3
Mosquito (pt.), Pan. 203/G4
Mosquitos, Golfo de los (gulf), Pan. 203/F4
Moss, Nor. 96/D2
Moss Beach, Ca, US 193/J11
Moss Bluff, La, US 187/J5
Moss Point, Ms, US 191/F4
Moss-Side, NI, UK 92/B1
Moss Vale, Austl. 173/D2
Mosselbaai, SAfr. 164/C4
Mosses, Col des (pass), Swi. 114/D5
Mossi Highlands (uplands), Burk. 160/E4
Mössingen, Ger. 112/C6
Mossman, Austl. 172/B2
Mossoró, Braz. 212/C2
Most, Czh. 113/G1
Mostaganem (prov.), Alg. 158/F4
Mostaganem, Alg. 158/F5
Mostar, Bosn. 105/E1
Mostardas, Braz. 213/B4
Móstoles, Sp. 103/N9
Mota del Cuervo, Sp. 102/D3
Motagua (riv.), Guat. 198/D4
Motala, Swe. 96/F2
Motherwell, Sc, UK 94/C5
Motian (mtn.), China 130/E2
Motīhāri, India 143/E2
Motilla del Palancar, Sp. 102/E3
Motobu, Japan 133/J7
Motomiya, Japan 133/G2
Motono, Japan 135/E2
Motosu (lake), Japan 135/B3
Motosu, Japan 135/L5
Motovskiy (gulf), Rus. 95/K1
Motoyoshi, Japan 134/B4
Motozintla de Mendoza, Mex. 202/C3
Motril, Sp. 102/D4
Motsuta-misaki (cape), Japan 134/A2
Mott, ND, US 185/H4
Motta di Livenza, It. 117/F1
Motta Visconti, It. 116/B2
Mottarone (peak), It. 116/B1
Motueka, NZ 175/S11
Motul de Carrillo Puerto, Mex. 202/D1
Motupe, Peru 214/B2
Motygino, Rus. 122/K4
Mouchard, Fr. 114/B4
Mouchoir Passage (chan.), UK 203/J1
Moúdhros, Gre. 105/J3
Moudon, Swi. 114/C4
Mougris (well), Mrta. 160/B2
Mouhoun (prov.), Burk. 160/E3
Mouila, Gabon 154/H8
Mouïna (well), Alg. 157/F3
Moul (well), Niger 154/H4
Moulamein (riv.), Austl. 173/C2
Moulamein, Austl. 173/C2
Moulay Idriss, Mor. 158/B2
Moulins, Fr. 100/E3
Moulouya (riv.), Mor. 158/C2
Moultrie, Ga, US 191/H4
Moultrie (lake), SC, US 191/J3
Moundou, Chad 154/J6
Moundsville, WV, US 188/D4
Mount Aberdeen NP, Austl. 172/B3
Mount Abu, India 147/K4
Mount Airy, NC, US 188/D4
Mount Airy, Md, US 196/A5
Mount Allan Abor. Land, Austl. 171/G2
Mount Aspiring NP, NZ 175/R11
Mount Baker-Snoqualmie, Wa, US 193/D1
Mount Baker-Snoqualmie Nat'l For., Wa, US 193/D3
Mount Baldy, Ca, US 194/C2
Mount Barker, Austl. 170/C5
Mount Barker, Austl. 171/M9
Mount Barkly Abor. Land, Austl. 171/G2
Mount Beauty, Austl. 173/C3
Mount Bold (res.), Austl. 171/M9
Mount Buffalo NP, Austl. 173/C3
Mount Carmel, Il, US 188/C4
Mount Carmel, Pa, US 196/B2
Mount Darwin, Zim. 163/F4
Mount Diablo State Park, Ca, US 193/L11
Mount Eccles NP, Austl. 173/B3
Mount Elgon NP, Ugan. 162/B2
Mount Elliot NP, Austl. 172/B2
Mount Everard, Guy. 211/G3
Mount Field NP, Austl. 173/C4
Mount Gambier, Austl. 173/B3
Mount Garnet, Austl. 172/B2
Mount Holly, NJ, US 196/D4
Mount Holly Springs, Pa, US 196/A3
Mount Imlay NP, Austl. 173/D3
Mount Isa, Austl. 171/H2
Mount Joy, Pa, US 196/B3
Mount Kaputar NP, Austl. 173/D1
Mount Kenya NP, Kenya 162/C3
Mount Kisco, NY, US 197/E1
Mount Larcom, Austl. 172/C3
Mount Laurel, NJ, US 196/D4
Mount Lofty (ranges), Austl. 171/M9
Mount Magnet, Austl. 170/C4
Mount Mistake NP, Austl. 172/D4
Mount Morgan, Austl. 172/C3
Mount Morris, Mi, US 188/D3
Mount Nebo, Austl. 172/E6
Mount Olive, NC, US 191/J3
Mount Pearl, Nf, Can. 189/L2
Mount Penn, Pa, US 196/C3
Mount Pleasant, Ia, US 185/L5
Mount Pleasant, Mi, US 188/C3
Mount Pleasant, Ut, US 186/E3
Mount Pleasant, De, US 196/C4
Mount Pleasant (int'l arpt.), UK 217/F6
Mount Pleasant, Austl. 171/N8
Mount Pocono, Pa, US 196/C1
Mount Prospect, Il, US 193/P15
Mount Rainier, Md, US 196/B6
Mount Rainier NP, Wa, US 184/C4
Mount Remarkable NP, Austl. 171/H5
Mount Revelstoke NP, BC, Can. 184/D3
Mount Richmond NP, Austl. 173/B3
Mount Rushmore Nat'l Mem., SD, US 187/G2
Mount Spec NP, Austl. 172/B2
Mount St. Helens Nat'l Volcanic Mon., Wa, US 184/C4
Mount Sterling, Ky, US 188/D4
Mount Torrens, Austl. 171/M8
Mount Vernon, Il, US 187/K3
Mount Vernon, NY, US 197/K8
Mount Vernon, Oh, US 188/D3
Mount Vernon, Tx, US 187/J4
Mount Vernon, Va, US 196/A6
Mount Vernon, Wa, US 184/C3
Mount Walsh NP, Austl. 172/C4
Mount Warning NP, Austl. 172/D5
Mount Welcome Abor. Land, Austl. 170/C2
Mount William NP, Austl. 173/D4
Mount Wolf, Pa, US 196/B3
Mountain (riv.), NW, Can. 180/D2
Mountain Ash, Wal, UK 90/C3
Mountain Green, Ut, US 195/K11
Mountain Grove, Mo, US 187/J3
Mountain Home, Id, US 184/E5
Mountain Lakes, NJ, US 197/H8
Mountain Point, Ak, US 192/M4
Mountain Top, Pa, US 196/C1
Mountain View, Ar, US 187/J4
Mountain View, Ca, US 193/K12
Mountain View, Hi, US 182/U11
Mountain Village, Ak, US 192/F3
Mountain Zebra NP, SAfr. 164/D4
Mountainhome, Pa, US 196/C1
Mountainside, NJ, US 197/H9
Mountlake Terrace, Wa, US 193/C2
Mountmellick, Ire. 89/Q10
Mountrath, Ire. 89/Q10
Mount's (bay), Eng, UK 90/A6
Mountville, Pa, US 196/B3
Moura, Port. 102/B3
Moura, Austl. 172/C4
Mourão, Port. 102/B3
Mourenx, Fr. 100/C5
Mourmelon-le-Grand, Fr. 111/D5
Mourmelon-le-Petit, Fr. 111/D5
Mourne (mts.), NI, UK 92/B3
Mourniaí, Gre. 105/J5
Mouroux, Fr. 88/M5
Mouscron, Belg. 110/C2
Mousseaux-sur-Seine, Fr. 88/G4
Moussoro, Chad 154/J5
Moussy-le-Neuf, Fr. 88/K4
Moussy-le-Vieux, Fr. 88/K4
Mouths of the Niger, Nga. 154/G6
Moutier, Swi. 114/D3
Mouvaux, Fr. 110/C2
Mouy, Fr. 110/B5
Mouydir (plat.), Alg. 157/G4
Mouzákion, Gre. 105/G3
Mouzon (riv.), Fr. 114/B1
Mouzon, Fr. 111/E4
Moville, Ire. 92/A1
Moxotó (riv.), Braz. 212/C3
Moy, NI, UK 92/B3
Moyamba, SLeo. 160/B4
Moye (isl.), China 131/B4
Moyen Atlas (mts.), Mor. 154/D1
Moyenmoutier, Fr. 114/C1
Moyeuvre-Grande, Fr. 111/F5
Moyle (dist.), NI, UK 92/B1
Moyo (isl.), Indo. 139/E5
Moyo, Ugan. 162/A2
Moyobamba, Peru 214/B2
Moyowosi (riv.), Tanz. 162/A3
Moyu, China 128/C4
Moyuta, Guat. 202/D3
Mozambique (ctry.) 163/G4
Mozambique (chan.), Afr. 163/G5
Mozhaysk, Rus. 118/H5
Mozhga, Rus. 119/M4
Mozzanica, It. 116/C2
Mozzecane, It. 117/D2
Mpanda, Tanz. 162/A4
Mpigi, Ugan. 162/B2
Mpika, Zam. 162/A5
Mporokoso, Zam. 162/A5
Mpraeso, Gha. 161/E5
Mpulungu, Zam. 162/A5
Mpumalanga (prov.), SAfr. 165/E2
Mpwapwa, Tanz. 162/C4
Mrągowo, Pol. 97/J5
Mrkonjić Grad, Bosn. 106/C3
Msaken, Tun. 158/M7
M'Sila (prov.), Alg. 157/F2
M'sila, Alg. 158/H5
M'sila (riv.), Alg. 158/H5
Msoun (riv.), Mor. 158/C2
Msta (riv.), Rus. 118/G4
Mszana Dolna, Pol. 99/L4
Mtorwi (peak), Tanz. 162/B5
Mtsensk, Rus. 120/F1
Mtubatuba, SAfr. 165/F3
Mtunzini, SAfr. 165/E3
Mtwara, Tanz. 162/D5
Mtwara (pol. reg.), Tanz. 162/C5
Mu-kawa (riv.), Japan 134/C2
Mu Ko Similan NP, Thai. 136/B4
Mu Ko Surin NP, Thai. 136/B4
Mualama, Moz. 163/G4
Muan, SKor. 131/D5
Muang Hinboun, Laos 136/D2
Muang Khammouan, Laos 136/D2
Muang Khong, Laos 136/D3
Muang Khongxedon, Laos 136/D3
Muang Pak-lay, Laos 136/C2
Muang Pakxan, Laos 136/C2
Muang Sing, Laos 141/H3
Muang Vangviang, Laos 136/C2
Muang Xaignabouri, Laos 136/C2
Muang Xay, Laos 141/H3
Muar, Malay. 138/B3
Muarabungo, Indo. 138/B4
Muāri (pt.), Pak. 147/J4
Mubārakpur, India 142/D2
Mubende, Ugan. 162/A2
Mucajaí (riv.), Braz. 208/F3
Much, Ger. 111/G2
Muchinga (mts.), Zam. 163/F3
Muck (isl.), Sc, UK 89/Q8
Muckleshoot Ind. Res., Wa, US 193/C3
Mucojo, Moz. 163/H3
Mucupina (mtn.), Hon. 202/E3
Mucur, Turk. 148/C2
Mucuri (riv.), Braz. 209/K7
Mud Mountain (dam), Wa, US 193/D3
Mud Mountain (lake), Wa, US 193/D3
Mudanjiang, China 129/N3
Mudanya, Turk. 107/J5
Mudau, Ger. 112/C3
Mudbach (riv.), Ger. 112/C3
Muddan (riv.), China 129/N2
Muddus NP, Swe. 95/G2
Muddy Run (res.), Pa, US 196/B4
Müden, Ger. 109/H3
Mudersbach, Ger. 111/G2
Mudgee, Austl. 173/D2
Mudjatik (riv.), Sk, Can. 180/F3
Mudon, Myan. 136/B2
Mudurnu, Turk. 107/K5
Muela (peak), Chile 217/B7
Muerte, Cerro de la (peak), CR 203/F4
Muff, Ire. 92/A1
Mufulira, Zam. 163/E3
Mugardos, Sp. 102/A1
Mugegawa, Japan 135/L4
Mughal Sarai, India 142/D3
Mugi, Japan 135/L4
Mugía, Sp. 102/A1
Muğla, Turk. 148/B2

Muğla (prov.), Turk. 148/B2
Mughalzhar Taüy (mts.), Kaz. 145/C3
Muhamdi, India 142/C2
Muhammad (pt.), Egypt 159/C3
Muhammadābād, India 142/D3
Muhavura (vol.), Rwa. 162/A3
Muhila, Monts (mts.), D.R. Congo 163/E3
Mühlacker, Ger. 112/B5
Mühlbach (riv.), Ger. 112/A2
Mühldorf, Ger. 113/F6
Mühleberg, Swi. 114/D4
Mühlenbeck, Ger. 98/O6
Mühlhausen, Ger. 113/E4
Mühlheim am Main, Ger. 112/B2
Mühlheim an der Donau, Ger. 115/E1
Mühltroff, Ger. 113/E1
Mühlviertel (reg.), Aus. 99/G4
Muhos, Fin. 118/E2
Muhu (isl.), Est. 97/K2
Muiden, Neth. 108/C4
Muir of Ord, Sc, UK 94/B1
Muir Woods Nat'l Mon., Ca, US 193/J11
Muirkirk, Sc, UK 94/B5
Muizon, Fr. 110/C5
Muju, SKor. 131/D4
Mukacheve, Ukr. 99/M4
Mukawa, Japan 134/B2
Mukawwar (isl.), Sudan 159/D4
Mukden, Bol. 214/D3
Mukeriān, India 144/C4
Mukhayyam al Yarmūk, Syria 149/E3
Mukhmās, Isr. 149/G8
Mukinbudin, Austl. 170/C4
Mukō, Japan 135/J6
Mukono, Ugan. 162/B2
Mukoshima (isls.), Japan 174/D2
Muktsar, India 144/C4
Mukwonago, Wi, US 193/P14
Mula, Sp. 102/E3
Mulanje, Malw. 163/G4
Mulchatna (riv.), Ak, US 192/G4
Mulchén, Chile 216/B3
Mulde (riv.), Ger. 98/G3
Mulegé, Mex. 200/C3
Muleshoe, Tx, US 187/G4
Mulhacén, Cerro de (peak), Sp. 102/D4
Mülhausen, Ger. 109/H6
Mülheim an der Ruhr, Ger. 108/D6
Mulhouse, Fr. 114/D2
Muli (riv.), Indo. 139/J3
Muli Zangzu Zizhixian, China 141/H2
Muling (pass), China 130/D3
Mull (isl.), Sc, UK 89/B4
Mull of Galloway (pt.), Sc, UK 92/D2
Mull of Kintyre (pt.), Sc, UK 92/C1
Mull of Logan (pt.), Sc, UK 92/C1
Mullach Coire Mhic Fhearchair (peak), Sc, UK 94/A1
Mullaghcleevaun (peak), Ire. 92/B5
Mullaghmore (peak), NI, UK 92/B2
Mullaittivu, SrL. 140/D6
Mullardoch (lake), Sc, UK 94/A2
Muller (mts.), Indo. 138/D4
Mullewa, Austl. 170/B4
Müllheim, Ger. 114/D2
Müllheim, Swi. 115/F2
Mullica (riv.), NJ, US 196/D4
Mullica Hill, NJ, US 196/C4
Mullins, SC, US 191/J3
Mullumbimby, Austl. 173/E1
Mulobezi, Zam. 163/E4
Multai, India 142/B3
Multan, Pak. 144/A4
Multnomah (falls), Or, US 184/C4
Mulu (peak), Malay. 138/D3
Mulwala, Austl. 173/C2
Mum Nauk (pt.), Thai. 136/B5
Mumbai (Bombay), India 147/K5
Mumbwa, Zam. 163/E3
Mümling (riv.), Ger. 112/B3
Mumoni, Kenya 162/C2
Mun (riv.), Thai. 141/H4
Muna (isl.), Indo. 139/F4
Muna, Mex. 202/D1
Munamägi (hill), Est. 97/M3
Muncar, Indo. 138/D5
Münchberg, Ger. 113/E2
München (Munich), Ger. 113/E6
Münchenstein, Swi. 114/D2

Munchique (peak), Col. 210/B4
Munchique, PN, Col. 210/B4
Muncie, In, US 188/C3
Muncy, Pa, US 196/B1
Mundaring, Austl. 170/L6
Munday, Tx, US 187/H4
Mundelein, Il, US 193/Q15
Mundemba, Camr. 161/H5
Münden, Ger. 109/G6
Munderfing, Aus. 113/G6
Munderkingen, Ger. 115/F1
Murphy, NC, US 191/G3
Murphy, Mo, US 195/G9
Murr (riv.), Ger. 112/C5
Murra, Nic. 202/E3
Murramarang NP, Austl. 173/D2
Murray (riv.), Austl. 173/B2
Murray, Ky, US 188/B4
Murray (lake), SC, US 191/H3
Murray, Ut, US 195/K12
Murray Bridge, Austl. 171/H5
Murraysburg, SAfr. 164/C3
Murrayville, Austl. 173/B2
Murree, Pak. 144/B3
Murrieta, Ca, US 194/C3
Murrieta Hot Springs, Ca, US 194/C3
Murrumbidgee (riv.), Austl. 173/C2
Murrumburrah, Austl. 173/D2
Murrurundi, Austl. 173/D1
Murshidābād, India 143/G3
Murtala Muhammed (int'l arpt.), Nga. 161/F5
Murtaröl (peak), Swi. 115/G4
Murten, Swi. 114/D4
Murtoa, Austl. 173/B3
Murud (peak), Malay. 138/D3
Murupara, NZ 175/T10
Mururoa (isl.), FrPol. 175/M7
Murwāra, India 142/C4
Murwillumbah, Austl. 173/E1
Mürz (riv.), Aus. 99/H5
Mürzzuschlag, Aus. 99/H5
Muş (prov.), Turk. 148/E2
Muş, Turk. 148/E2
Musabeyli, Turk. 149/E1
Musāfirkhāna, India 142/C2
Musala (peak), Bul. 107/F4
Musan, NKor. 131/E1
Musashino, Japan 135/D2
Musconetcong (riv.), NJ, US 196/C2
Muscoot (res.), NY, US 197/E1
Muscoy, Ca, US 194/C2
Musekwapoort (pass), SAfr. 163/E5
Museum of Flight, Wa, US 193/C2
Musgrave (ranges), Austl. 171/F3
Musgrave Harbour, Nf, Can. 189/L1
Mushābāni, India 143/F4
Mushie, D.R. Congo 154/J8
Mushin, Nga. 138/B4
Musi (riv.), Indo. 138/B4
Musile di Piave, It. 117/F1
Musinga (peak), Col. 210/B3
Muskego, Wi, US 193/P14
Muskegon, Mi, US 188/C3
Muskegon (riv.), Mi, US 188/C3
Muskingum (riv.), Oh, US 188/D4
Muskoka (lake), On, Can. 188/E2
Musoma, Tanz. 162/B2
Musone (riv.), It. 117/G6
Musquaro (riv.), Qu, Can. 189/J1
Mussau (isl.), PNG 174/D5
Musselburgh, Sc, UK 94/C5
Musselshell (riv.), Mt, US 184/F4
Mussomeli, It. 104/C4
Musson, Belg. 111/E4
Mustafābād, Pak. 144/B4
Mustafakemalpaşa, Turk. 148/B1
Müstair, Swi. 115/G4
Mustang, Ok, US 195/M15
Musters (lake), Arg. 216/C5
Musu-dan (pt.), NKor. 131/E2
Musún (mtn.), Nic. 202/E3
Mušutište, Kos. 106/E4
Muswellbrook, Austl. 173/D2
Müt, Egypt 159/B3
Mut, Turk. 149/C1
Mutá, Ponta do (pt.), Braz. 212/C4
Mutare, Zim. 163/F4
Muthill, Sc, UK 94/C4
Mutis (peak), Indo. 139/F5
Na'īn, Iran 146/F2
Mutsamudu, Com. 165/H6
Mutsu (bay), Japan 134/B3
Mutsu, Japan 134/B3

Murmanskaya Oblast, Rus. 95/J1
Murnau, Ger. 115/H2
Muro, Sp. 103/G3
Muro, Japan 135/K6
Muro Lucano, It. 104/D2
Murom, Rus. 118/J5
Muroran, Japan 134/B2
Muros, Sp. 102/A1
Muroto, Japan 132/D4
Muroto-zaki (pt.), Japan 132/D4
Murowana Goślina, Pol. 99/J2
Mutsuzawa, Japan 135/E3
Muttekopf (peak), Aus. 115/G3
Muttenz, Swi. 114/D2
Mutters, Aus. 115/H3
Mutterstadt, Ger. 112/B4
Muttonville, Mi, US 193/G6
Mutum, Braz. 213/D1
Mutzig, Fr. 114/D1
Müynoq, Uzb. 121/L4
Muzaffargarh, Pak. 144/A4
Muzaffarnagar, India 144/D5
Muzaffarpur, India 143/E2
Muzambinho, Braz. 213/G6
Muzon (cape), Ak, US 192/M4
Muztag (peak), China 128/D4
Muztagata (peak), China 145/G5
Muzzana del Turgnano, It. 117/G1
Mwadui, Tanz. 162/B3
Mwana (cape), Kenya 162/D3
Mwanza (pol. reg.), Tanz. 162/B3
Mwanza, Tanz. 162/B3
Mweelrea (peak), Ire. 89/P10
Mweka, D.R. Congo 163/D1
Mwene-Ditu, D.R. Congo 163/D2
Mwense, Zam. 162/A5
Mweru (lake), D.R. Congo 163/E2
Mweru-Wantipa NP, Zam. 162/A5
Mwesi (mtn.), Tanz. 162/A4
Mwinilunga, Zam. 163/D3
My Son Temples (ruin), Viet. 136/D4
My Tho, Viet. 136/D4
Myall Lakes NP, Austl. 173/E2
Myanaung, Myan. 141/G4
Myanmar (Burma) (ctry.) 141/G3
Myebon, Myan. 141/F3
Myerstown, Pa, US 196/B3
Myggenäs, Swe. 96/D2
Myingyan, Myan. 141/G3
Myitkyinā, Myan. 141/G2
Myjava, Slvk. 99/J4
Mykolayiv, Ukr. 107/L2
Mykolayiv (int'l arpt.), Ukr. 107/L2
Mykolayivs'ka Oblasti, Ukr. 120/D3
Mylau, Ger. 113/F1
Mymensingh (pol. reg.), Bang. 143/H3
Mynämäki, Fin. 97/J1
Mynydd Eppynt (mts.), Wal, UK 90/C2
Mynydd Pencarreg (peak), Wal, UK 90/B2
Mynydd Preseli (mtn.), Wal, UK 90/B3
Myōgi, Japan 135/B1
Myohaung, Myan. 141/F3
Myōkō-san (peak), Japan 133/F2
Myōngch'ŏn, NKor. 131/E2
Myrhorod, Ukr. 120/E2
Myrtle Beach, SC, US 191/J3
Myrtle Creek, Or, US 184/C5
Myrtleford, Austl. 173/C3
Mysen, Nor. 96/D2
Myślenice, Pol. 99/K4
Myślibórz, Pol. 99/H2
Myslivna (peak), Czh. 113/H5
Mysore, India 140/C5
Mystery Bay Rec. Area, Wa, US 193/B1
Mystic Island, NJ, US 196/D4
Myszków, Pol. 99/K3
Mytishchi, Rus. 119/W9
Mže (riv.), Czh. 98/G4
Mzimba, Malw. 162/B5
Mzuzu, Malw. 162/B5

Nacala, Moz. 163/H3
Nacaome, Hon. 202/E3
Nachi-Katsuura, Japan 132/D4
Nachingwea, Tanz. 162/C5
Nachod, Czh. 113/H3
Nachrodt-Wiblingwerde, Ger. 109/G6
Nacimiento, Chile 216/B3
Naco, Mex. 200/C2
Nacogdoches, Tx, US 187/J5
Najin, NKor. 129/P3
Naju, SKor. 131/D5
Naka, Japan 135/G5
Naka (riv.), Japan 132/D4
Nakadōri (isl.), Japan 132/A4
Nakai, Japan 135/C3
Nakajō, Japan 133/F1
Nakalele (pt.), Hi, US 182/T10
Nakamichi, Japan 135/B2
Nakaminato, Japan 133/G2
Nakamura, Japan 132/C4
Nakano, Japan 133/F2
Nakano (lag.), Japan 135/H2
Nakasato, Japan 134/B3
Nakashibetsu, Japan 134/D2
Nakasongola, Ugan. 162/B2
Nakatane, Japan 133/L5
Nakatomi, Japan 135/A3
Nakatsu, Japan 132/B4
Nakatsugawa, Japan 133/E3
Nakazato, Japan 135/B1
Nakhodka, Rus. 129/P3
Nakhon Nayok, Thai. 136/C3
Nakhon Pathom, Thai. 136/C3
Nakhon Phanom, Thai. 136/D2
Nakhon Ratchasima, Thai. 136/C3
Nakhon Sawan, Thai. 136/C3
Nakhon Si Thammarat, Thai. 136/B4
Nakkila, Fin. 97/J1
Naklo nad Notecią, Pol. 99/J2
Naknek, Ak, US 192/G4
Nakodar, India 144/C4
Nakonde, Zam. 162/B5
Naksan-sa, SKor. 131/E3
Nakskov, Den. 96/D4
Naktong, SKor. 131/E4
Naktong (riv.), SKor. 131/E4
Nakūr, India 144/D5
Nakuru, Kenya 162/C3
Nakusp, BC, Can. 184/D3
Nāl (riv.), Pak. 147/J3
Nalayh, Mong. 128/J2
Nalbach, Ger. 111/F5
Nalbāri, India 143/H2
Nalbaugh NP, Austl. 173/D3
Nal'chik (int'l arpt.), Rus. 121/G4
Nal'chik, Rus. 121/G4
Nalgonda, India 140/C3
Nalhāti, India 143/F3
Naliya, India 147/J4
Nallihan, Turk. 107/K5
Nalón (riv.), Sp. 102/B1
Nago-Torbole, It. 115/G6
Nagod, India 142/C3
Nagold, Ger. 112/B5
Nagold (riv.), Ger. 112/B5
Nam (riv.), NKor. 131/D3
Nam Dinh, Viet. 141/J3
Nam Nao NP, Thai. 136/C2
Nam Un (res.), Thai. 136/C2
Namakzār-e Shadād (salt pan), Iran 147/G2
Namangan (pol. reg.), Uzb. 145/F4
Namangan, Uzb. 145/F4
Namanuete (isl.), Tuv. 174/G5
Namao, Ab, Can. 184/E2
Namasagali, Ugan. 162/B2
Namatanai, PNG 174/E5
Namborn, Ger. 111/G4
Nambour, Austl. 173/E1
Nambour (riv.), India 142/B1
Nambucca Heads, Austl. 173/E1
Namdae (riv.), NKor. 131/E2
Namdaeseid, Nor. 95/D2
Namegawa, Japan 135/C1
Namekagon (riv.), Wi, US 185/L4
Namentenga (prov.), Burk. 161/E3
Namerikawa, Japan 133/E2
Nametil, Moz. 163/G4
Namhae (isl.), SKor. 131/D5
Namib (des.), Namb. 163/C5
Namibe, Ang. 163/C5
Namibia (ctry.) 163/C5
Namie, Japan 134/B3
Namioka, Japan 134/B3
Namjagbarwa (peak), China 141/E2
Namling, China 141/F2
Namloser Wetterspitze (peak), Aus. 115/G3
Nammoku, Japan 135/B1
Namnoi (peak), Myan. 135/B1
Namoi (riv.), Austl. 173/D1
Namonuito (isl.), Micr. 174/D4
Namorik (isl.), Mrsh. 174/F4
Nampa, Id, US 184/D4
Nampo, NKor. 131/C3
Nampula, Moz. 163/G4
Namsê (pass), China 140/D2
Namsen (riv.), Nor. 95/D2
Namso, Nor. 95/D2

Naintré, Fr. 100/D3
Nairn (riv.), Sc, UK 94/B2
Nairn, Sc, UK 94/C1
Nairne, Austl. 171/M9
Nairobi (cap.), Kenya 162/C3
Nairobi NP, Kenya 162/C3
Naivasha, Kenya 162/C3
Naives-Rosières, Fr. 111/E6
Najafābād, Iran 146/F2
Nájera, Sp. 102/D1
Namu (isl.), Mrsh. 174/F4
Namur (prov.), Belg. 111/D3
Namur, Belg. 111/D3
Napuka (isl.), FrPol. 175/L6
Naqil Sumārah (pass), Yem. 146/D6
Nara, Mali 160/D3
Nāra (riv.), Pak. 147/J4
Nara, Japan 135/J6
Naracoorte, Austl. 173/B3
Naraini, India 142/C3
Naranbulag, Mong. 128/F2
Naranjal, Ecu. 210/B5
Naranjito, Ecu. 214/B1
Naranjos, Mex. 202/B1
Naraq, Iran 146/F2
Narasannapeta, India 140/D4
Narashino, Japan 135/E2
Narathiwat, Thai. 136/C5
Nārāyanganj, Bang. 143/H4
Nārāyani (zone), Nepal 143/E2
Narayani (riv.), Nepal 143/E2
Nārāyanpet, India 140/C4
Narbonne, Fr. 100/E5
Narceo (riv.), Sp. 102/B1
Nardò, It. 105/F2
Nare (pt.), Eng, UK 90/B4
Narellan, Austl. 172/G9
Narembeen, Austl. 170/C5
Nares (str.), Can.,Grld. 181/T6
Narew (riv.), Pol. 118/D5
Nargaña, Pan. 203/G4
Narinda (bay), Madg. 165/H6
Nariño (dept.), Col. 210/B4
Narita (int'l arpt.), Japan 133/G3
Narita, Japan 135/E2
Nariz (peak), Chile 217/C7
Narkatiāganj, India 143/E2
Narmada (riv.), India 140/C3
Narman, Turk. 121/G4
Narni, It. 104/C2
Narodnaya (peak), Rus. 119/P2
Narok, Kenya 162/B3
Narón, Sp. 102/A1
Narooma, Austl. 173/D3
Nārowāl, Pak. 144/C3
Nærøy, Nor. 95/D2
Narra, Phil. 139/E2
Narrabri, Austl. 173/D1
Narrandera, Austl. 173/C2
Narrogin, Austl. 170/C5
Narromine, Austl. 173/D2
Narrows (riv.), NY, US 197/J9
Narsimhapur, India 142/B4
Narsingarh, India 147/L4
Narsinghdi, Bang. 143/H4
Narusawa, Japan 135/B3
Naruto, Japan 132/D3
Narutō, Japan 135/E2
Narva (res.), Rus. 118/F4
Narva, Est.,Rus. 118/E4
Narva (bay), Est.,Rus. 97/M2
Narva, Est. 97/N2
Narvacan, Phil. 137/D4
Narvik, Nor. 95/F1
Narwāna, India 144/D5
Nar'yan-Mar, Rus. 119/M2
Naryn, Kyr. 145/G4
Naryn (obl.), Kyr. 145/G4
Naryn (riv.), Kyr. 122/H5
Naryn Qum (plain), Kaz. 121/J2
Narzole, It. 116/A3
Năsăud, Rom. 107/G2
Naschel, Arg. 216/D2
Nashua, NH, US 189/G3
Nashville (int'l arpt.), Tn, US 188/C4
Nashville (cap.), Tn, US 188/C4
Našice, Cro. 106/D3
Nasielsk, Pol. 99/L2
Nasijärvi (lake), Fin. 97/K1
Nāsik, India 147/K5
Nasirābād, India 147/K3
Naso (pt.), Phil. 139/F1
Nāsriganj, India 143/E3
Nass (riv.), BC, Can. 192/N4
Nassach (riv.), Ger. 112/D2
Nassarawa (state), Nga. 161/G4
Náousa, Gre. 105/J4
Nassau (bay), Chile 217/D7
Nassau (isl.), Cookls. 175/J6
Nassau, Ger. 111/G3
Nassau, De, US 196/C6
Nassau (isl.), NY, US 197/N5
Nasser (lake), Egypt 159/C4
Nassereith, Aus. 115/G3
Nässjö, Swe. 96/F3
Nassogne, Belg. 111/E3
Nastapoka (isls.), Qu, Can. 181/J3
Nāsik, India 147/K5
Natá, Pan. 210/A2
Natá, Pan. 210/A2
Natagaima, Col. 210/C4

Natal, Braz. 212/D2
Naṭanz, Iran 146/F2
Natashō, Japan 135/J5
Natashquan (riv.), Qu, Can. 181/K3
Natchez, Ms, US 187/K5
Natchez Trace Nat'l Parkway, US 188/C5
Natchitoches, La, US 187/J5
Naters, Swi. 114/D5
Nāthdwāra, India 147/K4
Natimuk, Austl. 173/B3
Nation (riv.), BC, Can. 184/B2
National Agriculture Research Center, Md, US 196/B6
National Aquarium, Md, US 196/B5
National Archaeological Museum, Gre. 105/N8
National City, Ca, US 194/C5
National Cowboy Hall of Fame and Western Heritage Center, Ok, US 195/N14
National Exhibition Centre, Eng, UK 91/E2
National Institutes of Health, Md, US 196/A6
National Museum, Mona. 116/J8
National Security Agency, Md, US 196/B5
Natitingou, Ben. 161/F4
Natl, Jor. 149/D4
Natron (lake), Tanz. 162/B3
Natternbach, Aus. 113/G6
Nattheim, Ger. 112/D5
Nättraby, Swe. 96/F3
Natuna (isls.), Indo. 138/C3
Natural Bridge Caverns, Tx, US 195/U20
Natural Bridges Nat'l Mon., Ut, US 186/E3
Naturaliste (cape), Austl. 173/D4
Naturaliste (chan.), Austl. 170/B3
Naturaliste (cape), Austl. 170/B5
Naturno (Naturns), It. 115/G4
Naucalpan, Mex. 201/Q10
Naucelle, Fr. 100/E4
Nauders, Aus. 115/G4
Naudesnek (pass), SAfr. 164/E3
Nauen, Ger. 98/P6
Naugachhia, India 143/F3
Naugaon Sādāt, India 142/B1
Nauhcampatépetl (vol.), Mex. 201/M7
Nauheim, Ger. 112/B3
Naujan, Phil. 137/D5
Naujoji-Akmenė, Lith. 97/K3
Naumburg, Ger. 109/G6
Naumburg, Ger. 98/F3
Nauort, Ger. 111/G3
Nā'ūr, Jor. 149/D4
Nauru (ctry.) 174/F5
Naushahra, India 144/C3
Naushahra Virkhan, Pak. 144/B4
Nauta, Peru 214/C2
Nautla, Mex. 201/N6
Nauvo (Nagu), Fin. 97/J1
Nava, Mex. 201/E2
Nava, Colle di (pass), It. 116/A4
Nava del Rey, Sp. 102/C2
Navajo (res.), NM, US 186/F3
Navajo Nat'l Mon., Az, US 186/E3
Navalcarnero, Sp. 103/M9
Navalmoral de la Mata, Sp. 102/C3
Navalvillar de Pela, Sp. 102/C3
Navapolatsk, Bela. 97/N4
Navarin (cape), Rus. 123/T3
Navarino (isl.), Chile 215/C8
Navarra (aut. comm.), Sp. 102/D1
Navarro, Arg. 217/J11
Navàs, Sp. 103/F2
Navas de San Juan, Sp. 102/D3
Navasota (riv.), Tx, US 201/F2
Navassa (isl.), Myan. 203/H2
Navax (pt.), Eng, UK 90/A6
Nave, It. 116/D1
Navenne, Fr. 114/C2
Navia, Sp. 102/B1
Navia (riv.), Sp. 102/B1
Navidad, Chile 216/N8
Navina, Ok, US 195/M14
Naviraí, Braz. 215/F1
Năvodari, Rom. 107/J3
Navojoa, Mex. 200/C3
Navolato, Mex. 200/D3
Návpaktos, Gre. 105/G3
Návplion, Gre. 105/H4
Navsāri, India 147/K4
Navy Board (inlet), Nun., Can. 181/H1
Navy Yard City, Wa, US 193/B2
Nawābganj, India 142/B1
Nawābganj, India 142/C2
Nawābganj, Bang. 143/G3
Nawābshāh, Pak. 147/J3
Nawāda, India 143/E3
Nawān Jandānwāla, Pak. 144/A3
Nawāshahr, India 144/D4
Nawāshahr, Pak. 144/B2
Nawoiy, Uzb. 145/E4
Nawoiy (pol. reg.), Uzb. 145/D4
Nawş, Ra's (pt.), Oman 147/G5
Naxçıvan, Azer. 121/H5
Naxçıvan Aut. Rep., Azer. 121/H5
Naxi, China 141/J2
Náxos, Gre. 105/J4
Náxos (isl.), Gre. 105/J4
Nay Pyi Taw (cap.), Myan. 141/G4
Nayarit (state), Mex. 200/D4
Nayong, China 141/J2
Nayoro, Japan 134/C1
Nayramadlïn (peak), Mong. 128/E2
Nayzatash (pass), Taj. 145/F5
Nazaré, Braz. 212/C4
Nazaré, Port. 102/A3
Nazaré do Piauí, Braz. 212/B2
Nazaré Paulista, Braz. 213/G8
Nazareth, Pa, US 196/C2
Nazareth, Belg. 110/C2
Nazas (riv.), Mex. 200/D3
Nazas, Mex. 200/D3
Nazca, Peru 214/C4
Naze, Japan 133/K6
Naze, The (pt.), Eng, UK 91/H3
Nazerat (Nazareth), Isr. 149/G6
Nazilli, Turk. 148/B2
Nazrēt, Eth. 155/N6
Nazyvayevsk, Rus. 145/F1
Nchelenge, Zam. 162/A5
Ncheu, Malw. 163/F3
Ndalatando, Ang. 163/B2
Ndali, Ben. 161/F4
Ndele, CAfr. 155/K6
Ndende (isl.), Sol. 174/F6
N'Djamena (cap.), Chad 154/J5
Ndola, Zam. 163/E3
Ndrhamcha (lake), Mrta. 160/B2
Né (riv.), Fr. 100/C4
Néa Alikarnassós, Gre. 105/J5
Néa Ankhíalos, Gre. 105/H3
Néa Artáki, Gre. 105/H3
Néa Ionía, Gre. 105/H3
Néa Ionía, Gre. 105/N8
Néa Kallikrátia, Gre. 105/H2
Néa Kíos, Gre. 105/H4
Néa Mikhanióna, Gre. 105/H2
Néa Moudhaniá, Gre. 105/H2
Néa Potídhaia, Gre. 105/H2
Néa Triglia, Gre. 105/H2
Néa Zíkhni, Gre. 105/H2
Neagh (lake), NI, UK 92/B2
Neale (lake), Austl. 171/F3
Neales (riv.), Austl. 171/G3
Neamṭ (prov.), Rom. 107/H2
Neauphle-le-Château, Fr. 88/H5
Neápolis, Gre. 105/H4
Neápolis, Gre. 105/G2
Neápolis, Gre. 105/J5
Near (isls.), Ak, US 192/A5
Neath, Wal, UK 90/C3
Neath (riv.), Wal, UK 90/C3
Neath Port Talbot (co.), Wal, UK 90/C3
Neavitt, Md, US 196/B6
Nebbi, Ugan. 162/A2
Nebel-Horn (peak), Ger. 115/G3
Nebikon, Swi. 114/D3
Nebitdag, Trkm. 121/K5
Neblina (peak), Braz. 211/E4
Nebo (mt.), Austl. 172/E6
Nebraska (state), US 187/G2
Nebrodi (mts.), It. 104/C4
Nechako (riv.), BC, Can. 180/D3
Neches (riv.), Tx, US 190/E4
Nechisar NP, Eth. 155/N6
Nechranice (res.), Czh. 113/G2
Neckar (riv.), Ger. 98/D4
Neckarbischofsheim, Ger. 112/B4
Neckargemünd, Ger. 112/B4
Neckarsteinach, Ger. 112/B4
Neckarsulm, Ger. 112/C4
Necker (isl.), Hi, US 175/J2
Necochea, Arg. 216/F3
Necoclí, Col. 210/B2
Necropoli (ruin), It. 104/C1
Neda, Sp. 102/A1
Nedelino, Bul. 107/G5
Nedelišće, Cro. 101/M3
Nederland, Tx, US 187/J5
Nederland, Co, US 195/A3
Nederweert, Neth. 108/C6
Neede, Neth. 108/D4
Needles, Ca, US 186/D4
Needles, The, Eng, UK 91/E5
Needmore, Ok, US 195/N15
Neepawa, Mb, Can. 185/J3
Neerabup NP, Austl. 170/K6
Neerpelt, Belg. 108/C6
Neetze (riv.), Ger. 109/H2
Neetze, Ger. 109/H2
Neffelbach (riv.), Ger. 111/F2
Neftekamsk, Rus. 119/M4
Nefud (des.), SAr. 146/D3
Nefyn, Wal, UK 92/D6
Negēlē, Eth. 155/N6
Negev (reg.), Isr. 148/C4
Negoiu (peak), Rom. 107/G3
Negombo, SrL. 140/C6
Negotin, Serb. 106/F3
Negotino, FYROM 105/H2
Negra (pt.), Peru 214/A2
Negra (range), Braz. 212/A3
Negra (pt.), Belz. 202/D2
Negrais (cape), Myan. 141/F4
Negrar, It. 117/D1
Negreira, Sp. 102/A1
Negrești, Rom. 107/H2
Negritos, Peru 214/A2
Negro (riv.), Arg. 215/D5
Negro (peak), Arg. 216/C3
Negro (riv.), Uru. 215/E3
Negros (isl.), Phil. 137/D6
Nehbandān, Iran 147/H2
Nei Monggol (aut. reg.), China 129/K3
Nei Monggol (plat.), China 129/K3
Neiafu, Tonga 175/H6
Neiba, DRep. 199/G4
Neiba (mts.), DRep. 203/J2
Neiderösterreich (prov.), Aus. 101/L2
Neige, Crêt de la (peak), Fr. 114/B5
Neihuang, China 130/C4
Neijiang, China 128/J6
Neilston, Sc, UK 94/B5
Neiqiu, China 130/C3
Neisse (riv.), Ger. 99/H3
Neiva, Col. 210/C4
Neixiang, China 130/B4
Nejanilini (lake), Mb, Can. 180/G3
Nejdek, Czh. 113/F2
Nejrab (int'l arpt.), Syria 149/E1
Nek'emtē, Eth. 155/N6
Neksø, Den. 96/F4
Nelas, Port. 102/B2
Nelidovo, Rus. 118/G4
Nellingen, Ger. 112/C5
Nellore, India 140/C5
Nelson (cape), Austl. 173/B3
Nelson (isl.), Ak, US 192/E3
Nelson (str.), Chile 215/A7
Nelson, BC, Can. 184/D3
Nelson, NZ 175/S11
Nelson (riv.), Mb, Can. 180/G3
Nelson, Eng, UK 93/F4
Nelson-Atkins Museum of Fine Art, Mo, US 195/D5
Nelson Bay, Austl. 173/E2
Nelson Lagoon, Ak, US 192/F4
Nelson Lakes NP, NZ 175/S11
Nelspruit, SAfr. 163/F6
Néma, Mrta. 160/D2
Néma, Dhar (cliff), Mrta. 160/D2
Neman (riv.), Rus. 99/M1
Nembro, It. 116/C1
Neméa, Gre. 105/H4
Nemingha, Austl. 173/D1
Nemira (peak), Rom. 107/H2
Nemours, Fr. 100/E2
Nemunas (riv.), Lith. 97/K4
Nemuro, Japan 134/D2
Nemuro (pen.), Japan 134/D2
Nen (riv.), China 129/M2
Nenagh, Ire. 89/P10
Nenana, Ak, US 192/J3
Nendaz, Swi. 114/D5
Nene (riv.), Eng, UK 93/J6
Nenetskiy Aut. Okrug, Rus. 119/L2
Nenjiang, China 129/N2
Nentershausen, Ger. 109/G6
Nentershausen, Ger. 111/G3
Nenzing, Aus. 115/F3
Neo Volcanica, Cordillera (mts.), Mex. 201/Q10
Néon Petrítsion, Gre. 105/H2
Neoria Husainpur, India 142/B1
Néos Marmarás, Gre. 105/H2
Neosho (riv.), Ks,Ok, US 187/J3
Nepal (ctry.) 142/D1
Nepālganj, Nepal 142/C1
Nepanagar, India 147/L4
Nepean, On, Can. 188/F2
Nepean (riv.), Austl. 172/G8
Nepeña, Peru 214/B3
Nepessina (lake), Mi, US 193/F6
Nephi, Ut, US 186/E3
Nepisiguit (riv.), NB, Can. 189/H2
Nepomuk, Czh. 113/G4
Neptune City, NJ, US 196/D3
Nera (riv.), It. 101/K5
Nérac, Fr. 100/D4
Neratovice, Czh. 113/H2
Nerekhta, Rus. 118/J4
Neresheim, Ger. 112/D5
Neretva (riv.), Bosn. 106/D4
Neris (riv.), Lith. 97/L4
Nerja, Sp. 102/D4
Nermete (pt.), Peru 214/A2
Nerokoúros, Gre. 105/J5
Nerone (peak), It. 117/F5
Nerpio, Sp. 102/D3
Nersingen, Ger. 112/D6
Nerva, Sp. 102/B4
Nervesa della Battaglia, It. 117/F1
Nerviano, It. 116/B1
Nes, Neth. 108/C2
Nes, Nor. 96/D1
Nes Ziyyona, Isr. 149/F8
Nesbyen, Nor. 96/C1
Nesebŭr, Bul. 105/K1
Nesher, Isr. 149/G6
Neskaupstadhur, Ice. 95/Q6
Nesle, Fr. 110/B4
Nesles-la-Vallée, Fr. 88/J4
Nesquehoning, Pa, US 196/C2
Ness (lake), Sc, UK 94/B2
Ness (riv.), Sc, UK 94/B2
Nesselrode (mt.), Ak, US 192/M4
Nesselwang, Ger. 115/G2
Nesslau, Swi. 115/F3
Neston, Eng, UK 93/E5
Nestórion, Gre. 105/G2
Néstos (riv.), Gre. 107/G5
Netanya, Isr. 149/F7
Netarhāt, India 143/E4
Netcong, NJ, US 196/D2
Nethe (riv.), Ger. 109/G5
Netherlands (ctry.) 98/C3
Netherlands Antilles (dpcy.), Neth. 199/H5
Netolice, Czh. 113/H4
Netphen, Ger. 111/H2
Netstal, Swi. 115/F3
Nette (riv.), Ger. 108/D6
Nettebach (riv.), Ger. 111/G3
Nettersheim, Ger. 111/F3
Nettetal, Ger. 108/D6
Nettilling (lake), Nun., Can. 181/J2
Nettuno, It. 104/C2
Netzschkau, Ger. 113/F1
Neu Darchau, Ger. 109/H2
Neu-Isenburg, Ger. 112/B2
Neu-Ulm, Ger. 112/D6
Neu Zittau, Ger. 98/Q7
Neubiberg, Ger. 113/E6
Neubrandenburg, Ger. 99/G2
Neubulach, Ger. 112/B5
Neuburg, Ger. 112/B5
Neuburg an der Donau, Ger. 112/E5
Neuburg an der Kammel, Ger. 115/G1
Neuchâtel, Swi. 114/C4
Neuchâtel (canton), Swi. 114/C4
Neuchâtel, Lac de (lake), Swi. 101/G3
Neuenbürg, Ger. 112/B5
Neuenburg am Rhein, Ger. 114/D2
Neuendettelsau, Ger. 112/D4
Neuenhagen, Ger. 98/Q6
Neuenhaus, Ger. 108/D3
Neuenkirchen, Ger. 109/F3
Neuenkirchen, Ger. 109/F3
Neuenkirchen, Ger. 109/E4
Neuenrade, Ger. 109/E6
Neuenstadt am Kocher, Ger. 112/C4
Neuenstein, Ger. 112/C4
Neuerburg, Ger. 111/F3
Neuf-Brisach, Fr. 114/D1
Neufahrn bei Freising, Ger. 113/E6
Neufchâteau, Fr. 114/B1
Neufchâteau, Belg. 111/E4
Neufchâtel-en-Bray, Fr. 100/D2
Neufchâtel-Hardelot, Fr. 110/A2
Neufchelles, Fr. 88/M4
Neufmanil, Fr. 111/D4
Neufmoutiers-en-Brie, Fr. 88/L5
Neuhaus am Inn, Ger. 113/G6
Neuhaus am Rennweg, Ger. 112/E1
Neuhaus-Schierschnitz, Ger. 112/E2
Neuhäusel, Ger. 111/G3
Neuhausen am Rheinfall, Swi. 115/E2
Neuhof, Ger. 112/C2
Neuhof an der Zenn, Ger. 112/D4
Neuhofen, Ger. 112/B4
Neuhofen an der Krems, Aus. 113/H6
Neuilly-en-Thelle, Fr. 110/B5
Neuilly-l'Évêque, Fr. 114/B2
Neuilly-sur-Marne, Fr. 88/K5
Neuilly-sur-Seine, Fr. 88/J5
Neukirchen, Ger. 96/C4
Neukirchen an der Vöckla, Aus. 113/G6
Neukirchen vorm Wald, Ger. 113/G5
Neumarkt am Wallersee, Aus. 113/G7
Neumarkt (Enga), It. 115/H5
Neumarkt im Mühlkreis, Aus. 113/H6
Neumarkt in der Oberpfalz, Ger. 113/E4
Neumarkt-Sankt Veit, Ger. 113/F6
Neumünster, Ger. 96/C4
Neunkirch, Swi. 115/E2
Neunkirchen, Aus. 101/M3
Neunkirchen, Ger. 111/H2
Neunkirchen, Ger. 111/G5
Neunkirchen-Seelscheid, Ger. 111/G2
Neupotz, Ger. 112/B4
Neuquén (riv.), Arg. 215/C4
Neuquén (prov.), Arg. 216/C3
Neuquén, Arg. 216/C3
Neuruppin, Ger. 98/G2
Neusäss, Ger. 112/D6
Neuse (riv.), NC, US 191/J3
Neusiedl am See, Aus. 101/M3
Neusiedler (lake), Aus. 99/J5
Neusiedler See (lake), Aus. 106/C2
Neuss, Ger. 108/D6
Neustadt, Ger. 111/G2
Neustadt am Rübenberge, Ger. 109/G3
Neustadt an der Aisch, Ger. 112/D3
Neustadt an der Donau, Ger. 113/E5
Neustadt an der Waldnaab, Ger. 113/F3
Neustadt an der Weinstrasse, Ger. 112/B4
Neustadt bei Coburg, Ger. 112/E2
Neustadt in Holstein, Ger. 96/D4
Neustift im Stubaital, Aus. 115/H3
Neustrelitz, Ger. 98/G2
Neutraubling, Ger. 113/F5
Neuves-Maisons, Fr. 100/F2
Neuvic, Fr. 100/E4
Neuville-sur-Saône, Fr. 114/A6
Neuwied, Ger. 111/G3
Neuzelle, Ger. 99/H2
Neva (riv.), Rus. 97/P2
Nevada (state), US 186/C3
Nevada, Mo, US 187/J3
Nevada (mts.), Col. 210/C2
Nevada, Sierra (mts.), Sp. 102/D4
Nevado de Colima PN, Mex. 200/D5
Nevado de Toluca, PN, Mex. 201/K7
Nevado del Huila, PN, Col. 208/C3
Nevado, Sierra del (mts.), Arg. 216/C3
Nevel', Rus. 97/N3
Nevele, Belg. 110/C1
Nevel'sk, Rus. 129/R2
Nevers, Fr. 100/E3
Nevesinje, Bosn. 105/F1
Nevinnomyssk, Rus. 121/G3
Nevis (isl.), StK. 199/N8
Nevis (peak), StK. 199/N8
Nevola (riv.), It. 117/G5
Nevşehir (prov.), Turk. 148/C2
Nevşehir, Turk. 148/C2
New (riv.), Guy. 208/G3
New (riv.), WV, US 188/D4
New Albany, In, US 188/C4
New Albany, Ms, US 191/F3
New Amsterdam, Guy. 211/G3
New Ancholme (riv.), Eng, UK 93/H4
New Athens, Il, US 195/H9
New Baltimore, Mi, US 193/G6
New Bataan, Phil. 137/E6
New Bedford, Ma, US 189/G3
New Berlin, Tx, US 195/U21
New Berlin, Pa, US 196/B2
New Berlin, Wi, US 193/P14
New Berlinville, Pa, US 196/C3
New Bern, NC, US 191/J3
New Braunfels, Tx, US 195/U20
New Britain, Ct, US 189/F3
New Britain (isl.), PNG 174/D5
New Britain, Pa, US 196/C3
New Brunswick (prov.), Can. 189/H2
New Brunswick, NJ, US 197/H10
New Buffalo, Pa, US 196/B3
New Buildings, NI, UK 92/A2
New Caledonia (isl.), NCal., Fr. 174/F7
New Caledonia (terr.), NCal., Fr. 174/F6
New Canaan, Ct, US 197/M7
New Castle, De, US 196/C4
New Castle (co.), De, US 196/C5
New Castle, In, US 188/C4
New Castle, Pa, US 188/D3
New Chicago, In, US 193/R16
New City, NY, US 197/K7
New Columbia, Pa, US 196/B1
New Columbus, Pa, US 196/B1
New Cumberland, Pa, US 196/B3
New Cumnock, Sc, UK 94/B6
New Delhi (cap.), India 144/D5
New Denver, BC, Can. 184/D3
New Egypt, NJ, US 196/D3
New England NP, Austl. 173/E1
New Freedom, Pa, US 196/B4
New Galloway, Sc, UK 92/D1
New Georgia (isls.), Sol. 174/E5
New Georgia (sound), Sol. 174/E5
New Glasgow, NS, Can. 189/J2
New Glasgow, Qu, Can. 189/N6
New Gretna, NJ, US 196/D4
New Guinea (isl.), Indo.,PNG 174/C5
New Hampshire (state), US 189/G3
New Hanover, SAfr. 165/E3
New Hanover, Il, US 195/G9
New Hanover (isl.), PNG 174/D5
New Haven, Ct, US 189/F3
New Haven, Mi, US 193/G6
New Hebrides (isls.), Van. 174/F6
New Holland, Pa, US 196/B3
New Hope, Pa, US 196/D3
New Hyde Park, NY, US 197/L9
New Iberia, La, US 187/K5
New Ireland (isl.), PNG 174/E5
New Jersey (state), US 196/D3
New Kensington, Pa, US 188/E3
New Kowloon, China 129/U10
New Lenox, Il, US 193/Q16
New Lisbon, NJ, US 196/D4
New Liskeard, On, Can. 188/E2
New London, Ct, US 189/F3
New Madrid, Mo, US 187/K3
New Market, Md, US 196/A5
New Meadows, Id, US 184/D4
New Mexico (state), US 186/G4
New Milford, NJ, US 197/J8
New Mills, Eng, UK 93/F5
New Norfolk, Austl. 173/C4
New Orleans, La, US 195/P17
New Orleans (Moisant Field), La, US 195/P17
New Oxford, Pa, US 196/A4
New Philadelphia, Oh, US 188/D3
New Philadelphia, Pa, US 196/B2
New Pitsligo, Sc, UK 94/D1
New Plymouth, NZ 175/S10
New Port Richey, Fl, US 191/H4
New Providence (isl.), Bahm. 199/F3
New Providence, NJ, US 197/H9
New Richmond, Qu, Can. 189/H1
New River (mts.), Az, US 195/R18
New River, Az, US 195/R18
New Rochelle, NY, US 197/K8
New Rockford, ND, US 185/J4
New Romney, Eng, UK 91/G5
New Ross, Ire. 89/Q10
New Rossington, Eng, UK 93/G5
New Sarpy, La, US 195/P17
New Schwabenland (phys. reg.), Ant. 218/Z
New Scone, Sc, UK 94/C4
New Siberian (isls.), Rus. 125/N2
New Smyrna Beach, Fl, US 191/H4
New South Wales, Austl. 173/D1
New South Wales (state), Austl. 173/C2
New Stuyahok, Ak, US 192/G4
New Town, ND, US 185/H4
New Tripoli, Pa, US 196/C2
New Ulm, Mn, US 185/K4
New Waterford, NS, Can. 189/J2
New Westminster, BC, Can. 184/C3
New Windsor, Md, US 196/A4
New York (state), US 188/G3
New York, NY, US 197/K9
New Zealand (ctry.) 175/R10
Newark, Oh, US 188/D3
Newark, De, US 196/C4
Newark (int'l arpt.), NJ, US 197/J9
Newark, NJ, US 197/J9
Newark, Ca, US 193/K11
Newark (bay), NJ, US 197/J9
Newark-on-Trent, Eng, UK 93/H5
Newbern, Il, US 195/G8
Newberry, SC, US 191/H3
Newberry, Mi, US 188/C2
Newberry Nat'l Volcanic Mon., Or, US 184/C5
Newburgh, Sc, UK 94/C4
Newburgh, Eng, UK 93/G2
Newbury, Eng, UK 91/E4
Newcastle, Austl. 173/D2
Newcastle, SAfr. 165/E2
Newcastle, Ire. 89/P10
Newcastle, Ire. 92/B5
Newcastle, Ok, US 195/M15
Newcastle, NI, UK 92/C3
Newcastle (int'l arpt.), Eng, UK 93/G1
Newcastle, Wy, US 185/G5
Newcastle-under-Lyme, Eng, UK 93/F6
Newcastle upon Tyne, Eng, UK 93/G2
Newcastle upon Tyne (co.), Eng, UK 93/G1
Newcastleton, Sc, UK 93/F1
Newe Yam, Isr. 149/F6
Newel, Ger. 111/F4
Newell, Austl. 172/B2
Newellton, La, US 187/K4
Newenham (cape), Ak, US 192/F4
Newfane, NY, US 189/S9
Newfield, NJ, US 196/C4
Newfoundland (isl.), Can. 189/L1
Newfoundland, NJ, US 197/H7
Newfoundland, Pa, US 196/C1
Newfoundland and Labrador (prov.), Can. 181/K3
Newhalen, Ak, US 192/H4
Newham (bor.), Eng, UK 88/D2
Newhaven, Eng, UK 91/F5
Newington, Eng, UK 88/F3
Newkirk, Ok, US 187/H3
Newllano, La, US 187/J5
Newmains, Sc, UK 94/C5
Newman (mt.), Austl. 170/C2
Newman, Austl. 170/C2
Newmarket, On, Can. 188/E2
Newmarket, Eng, UK 91/G2
Newmill, Sc, UK 94/D1
Newnan, Ga, US 191/G3
Newport, Eng, UK 90/D1
Newport, Eng, UK 91/E5
Newport, Wal, UK 90/D3
Newport (co.), Wal, UK 90/C3
Newport, Ar, US 187/K4
Newport (bay), Ca, US 194/C3
Newport, De, US 196/C4
Newport, Ky, US 188/C4
Newport, NJ, US 196/C5
Newport, Or, US 184/B4
Newport, Pa, US 196/A3
Newport, RI, US 189/G3
Newport, Tn, US 188/D5
Newport, Vt, US 189/F2
Newport, Wa, US 184/D3
Newport Beach, Ca, US 194/G8
Newport Meadows (lake), NJ, US 196/C5
Newport-on-Tay, Sc, UK 94/D4
Newport Pagnell, Eng, UK 91/F2
Newquay, Eng, UK 90/A6
Newry, NI, UK 92/B3
Newry (dist.), NI, UK 92/B3
Newry (canal), NI, UK 92/B3
Newtok, Ak, US 192/F3
Newton, Tx, US 187/J5
Newton, Ma, US 189/G3
Newton, NJ, US 196/D1
Newton Abbot, Eng, UK 90/C5
Newton-le-Willows, Eng, UK 93/F5
Newton Mearns, Sc, UK 94/B5
Newton Stewart, Sc, UK 92/D2
Newton Tors (hill), Eng, UK 94/D5
Newtonmore, Sc, UK 94/B2
Newtonville, NJ, US 196/D4
Newtown, Austl. 173/B3
Newtown, Wal, UK 90/C1
Newtown, Pa, US 196/D3
Newtown Mount Kennedy, Ire. 92/B5
Newtown Saint Boswells, Sc, UK 94/D5
Newtown Square, Pa, US 196/C4
Newtownabbey, NI, UK 92/C2
Newtownards, NI, UK 92/C2
Newtownhamilton, NI, UK 92/B3
Newtownstewart, NI, UK 92/A2
Newtyle, Sc, UK 94/C3
Nextlalpan, Mex. 201/Q9
Neyagawa, Japan 135/J6
Neyrīz, Iran 147/F3
Neyshābūr, Iran 147/G1
Neyva (riv.), Rus. 119/P4
Neyveli, India 140/C5
Neyyāttinkara, India 140/C6
Nezahualcóyotl, Mex. 201/Q10
Neznayka (riv.), Rus. 119/W9
Nezperce, Id, US 184/D4
Ngabang, Indo. 138/C3
Ngabordamlu (cape), Indo. 139/H5
Ngabu, Malw. 163/F4
Ngai-Ndethya Nat'l Rsv., Kenya 162/C3
Ngamring, China 143/F1
Nganda (peak), Malw. 162/B5
Ngangerabeli (plain), Kenya 162/C3
Ngaoundéré, Camr. 154/H6
Ngarkat Conservation Park, Austl. 171/J5
Ngatik (isl.), Micr. 174/E4
Ngoan Muc (pass), Viet. 136/E4
Ngoc Linh (peak), Viet. 141/J4
Ngomeni (cape), Kenya 162/D3
Ngong, Kenya 162/C3
Ngonye (falls), Zam. 163/D4
Ngorongoro Consv. Area, Tanz. 162/B3
Ngounié (riv.), Gabon 154/H8
Nguigmi, Niger 154/H5
Ngulu (isl.), Micr. 174/C4
Ngumbe Sukani (pt.), Tanz. 162/C5
Nguru (mts.), Tanz. 162/C4
Ngwenya (peak), Swaz. 165/E2
Nha Trang, Viet. 136/E3
Nhamunda (riv.), Braz. 205/D3
Nhill, Austl. 173/B3
Nhlangano, Swaz. 165/E2
Niagara (falls), Can.,US 189/R9
Niagara (riv.), Can.,US 189/R9
Niagara (co.), On, Can. 189/R9
Niagara Falls, On, Can. 189/R9
Niagara Falls, NY, US 189/R9
Niagara-on-the-Lake, On, Can. 189/R9
Niamey (dept.), Niger 161/F3
Niamey (cap.), Niger 161/F3
Niamey (int'l arpt.), Niger 161/F3
Niamtougou, Togo 161/F4
Niandan (riv.), Afr. 161/G5
Niangara, D.R. Congo 155/L7
Niangay (lake), Mali 154/E4
Niangzi (pass), China 130/C3
Nias (isl.), Indo. 138/A3
Niassa (prov.), Moz. 162/B5
Nicaragua (ctry.) 203/E3
Nicaragua (lake), Nic. 203/E4
Nicastro-Sambiase, It. 104/E3
Nice, Fr. 101/G5
Niceville, Fl, US 191/G4
Nichinan, Japan 132/B5
Nichlaul, India 142/D2
Nicholas (chan.), Bang. 203/F1
Nichols Hills, Ok, US 195/M14
Nicholson (range), Austl. 170/C3
Nickerie (dist.), Sur. 211/G3
Nickerie (riv.), Sur. 211/G3
Nickol (bay), Austl. 170/C2
Nicobar (isls.), India 141/F6
Nicolás Bravo, Mex. 202/D2
Nicolás Romero, Mex. 201/Q9
Nicolet, Qu, Can. 189/F2
Nicolls (pt.), NY, US 197/E2

Nicoma Park, Ok, US 195/N15
Nicosia, It. 104/D4
Nicosia (cap.), Cyp. 149/C2
Nicosia (dist.), Cyp. 149/C2
Nicotera, It. 104/D3
Nicoya, CR 203/E4
Nicoya (gulf), CR 203/E4
Nicoya, Peninsula de (pen.), CR 203/E4
Nidau, Swi. 114/D3
Nidd (riv.), Eng, UK 93/G3
Nidda, Ger. 112/B2
Nidda (riv.), Ger. 98/E3
Niddatal, Ger. 112/B2
Nidder (riv.), Ger. 112/C2
Nideggen, Ger. 111/F2
Nidge (prov.), Turk. 148/C2
Nidwalden (canton), Swi. 115/E4
Nidzica, Pol. 99/L2
Niebüll, Ger. 96/C4
Nied (riv.), Fr. 101/G2
Niedenstein, Ger. 109/G6
Nieder-Olm, Ger. 111/H4
Niederanven, Lux. 111/F4
Niederbipp, Swi. 114/D3
Niederbronn-les-Bains, Fr. 111/G6
Niedere Tauern (mts.), Aus. 101/K3
Niederfischbach, Ger. 111/G2
Niederlausitz (reg.), Ger. 99/G3
Niedernhausen, Ger. 112/B2
Niederösterreich (prov.), Aus. 106/B2
Niedersachsen (state), Ger. 96/C5
Niedersächsisches Wattenmeer NP, Ger. 109/E1
Niedersachswerfen, Ger. 109/H5
Niederstetten, Ger. 112/C4
Niederstotzingen, Ger. 112/D5
Niederurnen, Swi. 115/F3
Niederwerrn, Ger. 112/D2
Niederwinkling, Ger. 113/F5
Niederzier, Ger. 111/F2
Niederzissen, Ger. 111/G3
Niefern-Öschelbronn, Ger. 112/B5
Niegocin (lake), Pol. 97/J5
Nieheim, Ger. 109/G5
Niemodlin, Pol. 99/J3
Nienburg, Ger. 109/G3
Nienhagen, Ger. 109/H3
Niénokoué (peak), C.d'Iv. 160/D5
Nieppe, Fr. 110/B2
Niéri (riv.), Sen. 160/B3
Niers (riv.), Ger. 111/F1
Nierstein, Ger. 112/B3
Niet Ban Tinh Xa, Viet. 136/D4
Nieuw-Amsterdam, Sur. 209/G2
Nieuw-Bergen, Neth. 108/D5
Nieuw-Loosdrecht, Neth. 108/C4
Nieuw-Nickerie, Sur. 211/G3
Nieuw-Schoonebeek, Neth. 108/D3
Nieuw-Vossemeer, Neth. 108/B5
Nieuwe Pekela, Neth. 108/D2
Nieuwegein, Neth. 108/C4
Nieuwerkerk aan de IJssel, Neth. 108/B5
Nieuweschans, Neth. 109/E2
Nieuwkoop, Neth. 108/B4
Nieuwleusen, Neth. 108/D3
Nieuwoudtville, SAfr. 164/B3
Nieuwpoort, Belg. 110/B1
Nieves, Mex. 200/E3
Niğde, Turk. 148/C2
Nigel, SAfr. 164/E2
Niger (ctry.) 154/G4
Niger (delta), Nga. 161/G5
Niger (riv.), Afr. 154/F5
Nigeria (ctry.) 154/G6
Nigg (bay), Sc, UK 94/B1
Nighthawk (lake), On, Can. 188/D1
Nightmute, Ak, US 192/F3
Nigrán, Sp. 102/A1
Nigríta, Gre. 105/H2
Nihoa (isl.), Hi, US 175/J2
Nihonmatsu, Japan 133/G2
Nihtaur, India 142/B1
Nii (isl.), Japan 133/F3
Niigata (int'l arpt.), Japan 133/F2
Niigata, Japan 133/F2
Niigata (pref.), Japan 134/A4
Niihama, Japan 132/C4
Niihari, Japan 135/E1
Niihau (isl.), Hi, US 182/R10
Niimi, Japan 132/C3
Niitsu, Japan 133/F2
Niiza, Japan 135/D2
Níjar, Sp. 102/D4
Nijkerk, Neth. 108/C4
Nijlen, Belg. 111/D1
Nijmegen, Neth. 108/C5
Níkaia, Gre. 105/H3
Nikel', Rus. 95/J1
Nikishka, Ak, US 192/H3
Nikísiani, Gre. 105/J2
Nikki, Ben. 161/F4
Nikkō, Japan 133/F2
Nikkō NP, Japan 133/F2
Niklasdorf, Aus. 101/L3
Nikolai, Ak, US 192/H3
Nikolayevsk-na-Amure, Rus. 123/Q4
Nikol'sk, Rus. 121/H1
Nikolski, Ak, US 192/E5
Nikonga (riv.), Tanz. 162/A3
Nikopol', Ukr. 120/E3
Nikopol, Bul. 107/G4
Niksar, Turk. 120/F4
Nīkshahr, Iran 147/H3
Nikšić, Mont. 106/D4
Nikumaroro (Gardner) (isl.), Kiri. 175/H5
Nikunau (isl.), Kiri. 174/G5
Nile (delta), Egypt 149/B4
Nile (riv.), Afr. 155/M2
Niles, Mi, US 188/C3
Niles, Oh, US 188/D3
Niles, Il, US 193/Q15
Ni'līn, Isr. 149/G8
Nilópolis, Braz. 213/K7
Nilsiä, Fin. 118/F3
Nilvange, Fr. 111/F5
Nīmāj, India 140/B2
Nimba (peak), C.d'Iv. 160/C5
Nimba (co.), Libr. 160/C5
Nîmes, Fr. 100/F5
Nimsbach (riv.), Ger. 111/F4
Nimule NP, Sudan 162/A2
Nin, Cro. 106/B3
Nīnawā (gov.), Iraq 148/E3
Nīnawá (Nineveh) (ruin), Iraq 148/E2
Ninepin Group (isls.), China 129/V11
Ninfas (pt.), Arg. 216/D4
Ning'an, China 129/N3
Ningbo, China 130/E5
Ningde, China 137/C2
Ningdu, China 137/C2
Ninggang, China 141/K2
Ninghua, China 137/C2
Ningjin, China 130/C3
Ningjin, China 130/D3
Ninglang Yizu Zizhixian, China 141/H2
Ningling, China 130/C4
Ningming, China 141/J3
Ningwu, China 130/C3
Ningxia Huizu (aut. reg.), China 128/J4
Ningxiang, China 137/B2
Ningyang, China 130/D4
Ningyuan, China 141/K2
Ninh Binh, Viet. 136/D1
Ninilchik, Ak, US 192/H3
Niningo (isls.), PNG 174/D5
Ninohe, Japan 134/B3
Ninomiya, Japan 135/C3
Ninove, Belg. 110/D2
Ninoy Aquino (int'l arpt.), Phil. 137/D5
Niobara (riv.), Ne, US 182/F3
Niobrara (riv.), Ne, US 185/H5
Niokolo-Koba, PN du, Sen. 160/B3
Niono, Mali 160/D3
Nioro-du-Rip, Sen. 160/B3
Nioro du Sahel, Mali 160/C3
Niort, Fr. 100/C3
Nipawin, Sk, Can. 185/H2
Nipe (bay), Cuba 203/H1
Nipigon, On, Can. 185/L3
Nipigon (lake), On, Can. 180/G3
Nipissing (lake), On, Can. 181/J4
Niquén, Chile 216/C3
Niquero, Cuba 203/G1
Nirasaki, Japan 133/F3
Nirayama, Japan 135/B3
Nirimba Army Afld., Austl. 172/G8
Nirmal, India 140/C4
Nirmāli, India 143/F2
Niš, Serb. 106/E4
Niš (int'l arpt.), Serb. 106/E4
Nišava (riv.), Serb. 105/H1
Niscemi, It. 104/D4
Nishiazai, Japan 135/K5
Nishibiwajima, Japan 135/L5
Nishiharu, Japan 135/L5
Nishikatsura, Japan 135/B2
Nishiki (riv.), Japan 132/B3
Nishiki, Japan 135/H5
Nishinomiya, Japan 135/H6
Nishino'omote, Japan 132/B5
Nishio, Japan 135/M6
Nishiwaki, Japan 135/G6
Nisko, Pol. 99/M3
Nisqually, Wa, US 193/B3
Nisqually (riv.), Wa, US 193/B3
Nisqually Ind. Res., Wa, US 193/B3
Nisqually Reach (str.), Wa, US 193/B3
Nissan (isl.), PNG 174/E5
Nisser (lake), Nor. 96/C2
Nisshin, Japan 135/M5
Nissum (bay), Den. 96/C3
Nisswa, Mn, US 185/K4
Nistru (riv.), Mol. 107/H1
Niterói, Braz. 213/K7
Nith (riv.), Sc, UK 94/C6
Nith (riv.), Sc, UK 92/E1
Nithsdale (valley), Sc, UK 92/E1
Nitra, Slvk. 106/D1
Nitra (riv.), Slvk. 99/K4
Nitrianský (pol. reg.), Slvk. 99/K4
Nitsa (riv.), Rus. 119/P4
Nitta, Japan 135/C1
Nittedal, Nor. 96/D1
Nittel, Ger. 111/F4
Nittenau, Ger. 113/F4
Niuafo'ou (isl.), Tonga 175/H6
Niuatoputapu Group (isls.), Tonga 175/H6
Niue (terr.), NZ 175/H7
Niue (isl.), Niue 175/J6
Niulakita (isl.), Tuv. 174/G6
Niulan (riv.), China 141/H2
Niut (peak), Indo. 138/C3
Niutao (isl.), Tuv. 174/G5
Nivelles, Belg. 111/D2
Nivernais, Collines de (hills), Fr. 100/E3
Niverville, Mb, Can. 185/J3
Niwot, Co, US 195/B2
Niyazov (int'l arpt.), Trkm. 145/C5
Niyodo (riv.), Japan 132/C4
Nizāmābād, India 140/C4
Nizhegorodskaya Oblast, Rus. 121/G1
Nizhnekama (res.), Rus. 119/M4
Nizhnekamsk, Rus. 119/L5
Nizhneudinsk, Rus. 123/K4
Nizhnevartovsk, Rus. 122/H3
Nizhniy Lomov, Rus. 121/G1
Nizhniy Novgorod, Rus. 119/K4
Nizhniy Tagil, Rus. 119/N4
Nizhyn, Ukr. 120/D2
Nizip, Turk. 148/D2
Nízke Tatry NP, Slvk. 120/A2
Nizza Monferrato, It. 116/B3
Nizzanim, Isr. 149/F8
Njardhvík, Ice. 95/M7
Njombe (riv.), Tanz. 162/B4
Nkandla, SAfr. 165/E3
Nkayi, Congo 163/B1
Nkhata Bay, Malw. 162/B5
N'kongsamba, Camr. 154/G7
Nkululu (riv.), Tanz. 162/B4
Nkusi (riv.), Ugan. 162/A2
Nmai (riv.), Myan. 141/G2
Noailles, Fr. 110/B5
Noākhāli (pol. reg.), Bang. 143/H4
Noale, It. 117/F1
Noāmundi, India 143/E4
Noank, Ct, US 197/F1
Noatak, Ak, US 192/F2
Noatak (riv.), Ak, US 192/F2
Noatak Nat'l Prsv., Ak, US 192/F2
Nobeoka, Japan 132/B4
Noble, Ok, US 195/N15
Noboa, Ecu. 210/A5
Noboribetsu, Japan 134/B2
Noce (riv.), It. 115/G5
Noceto, It. 116/D3
Noci, It. 105/E2
Nockamixon State Park, Pa, US 196/C3
Noda, Japan 135/D2
Nodagawa, Japan 135/H4
Noé (cape), Alg. 158/D2
Nogales, Az, US 186/E5
Nogales, Mex. 201/M8
Nogara, It. 117/E2
Nogaro, Fr. 100/C5
Nogat (riv.), Pol. 97/H4
Nogata, Japan 132/B4
Nogent, Fr. 114/B1
Nogent-l'Artaud, Fr. 110/C6
Nogent-le-Rotrou, Fr. 100/D2
Nogent-sur-Oise, Fr. 110/B5
Nogent-sur-Seine, Fr. 100/E2
Nogi, Japan 135/D1
Noginsk, Rus. 119/X9
Nogoa (riv.), Austl. 172/B4
Nogodan-san (peak), SKor. 131/D5
Nogoonnuur, Mong. 128/F2
Nogoyá, Arg. 215/E3
Nógrád (co.), Hun. 99/K5
Nogwak-san (peak), SKor. 131/E4
Nohar, India 144/C5
Noheji, Japan 134/B3
Nohfelden, Ger. 111/G4
Nohkú (pt.), Mex. 202/E2
Noi (riv.), Viet. 141/J5
Noidans-lès-Vesoul, Fr. 114/C2
Noire (riv.), Qu, Can. 188/E2
Noires, Montagnes (mts.), Fr. 100/B2
Noirmoutier, Île de (isl.), Fr. 100/B3
Noisiel, Fr. 110/B6
Noisy-le-Grand, Fr. 88/K5
Noisy-le-Mec, Fr. 88/K5
Noisy-le-Roi, Fr. 88/J5
Nojima-zaki (pt.), Japan 133/F3
Nokia, Fin. 97/K1
Nokilalaki (peak), Indo. 139/F4
Nola, CAfr. 154/J7
Noli, It. 116/B4
Noli, Capo di (cape), It. 116/B4
Nomadgi NP, Austl. 173/D2
Nombre de Dios, Mex. 200/D4
Nombre de Dios (mts.), Hon. 202/E3
Nome, Ak, US 192/E3
Nome (cape), Ak, US 192/F3
Nomény, Fr. 111/F6
Nomexy, Fr. 114/C1
Nomo-misaki (cape), Japan 132/B5
Nomo-zaki (pt.), Japan 132/A4
Nonacho (lake), NW, Can. 180/F2
Nonantola, It. 117/E3
Nondalton, Ak, US 192/H4
None, It. 101/G4
Nonette (riv.), Fr. 110/B5
Nong Han (res.), Thai. 136/D2
Nong Khai, Thai. 136/C2
Nong'an, China 129/N3
Nongoma, SAfr. 165/E2
Nongstoin, India 143/H3
Nonnweiler, Ger. 111/F4
Nonoava, Mex. 200/D3
Nonouti (isl.), Kiri. 174/G5
Nonri (isl.), China 130/E5
Nonsan, SKor. 131/D4
Nontron, Fr. 100/D4
Noord-Brabant (prov.), Neth. 108/C5
Noord Holland (prov.), Neth. 108/B3
Noordbeveland (isl.), Neth. 108/A5
Noorderhaaks (isl.), Neth. 108/B3
Noordhollandsch Kanaal (riv.), Neth. 108/B3
Noordostpolder (polder), Neth. 108/C3
Noordwijk aan Zee, Neth. 108/B4
Noordwijkerhout, Neth. 108/B4
Noordzeekanaal (canal), Neth. 108/B4
Noormarkku, Fin. 97/J1
Noorvik, Ak, US 192/F2
Nootka (isl.), BC, Can. 184/B3
Nora, Swe. 96/F2
Norala, Phil. 139/F2
Norberg, Swe. 96/F1
Norberto de la Riestra, Arg. 217/J11
Norchia (ruin), It. 104/B1
Norco, Ca, US 194/C3
Norco, La, US 195/P16
Nord (riv.), Qu, Can. 189/M6
Nord (canal), Fr. 110/B4
Nord (prov.), Fr. 110/C3
Nord-Kivu (pol. reg.), D.R. Congo 162/A3
Nord-Ostsee (Kiel) (canal), Ger. 109/G1
Nord-Ouest (prov.), Camr. 161/H5
Nord-Ouest (pol. reg.), Mor. 158/B2
Nord-Pas-de-Calais (pol. reg.), Fr. 100/D1
Nord-Radde (riv.), Ger. 109/E3
Nord-Sud Kanal (canal), Ger. 109/E3
Nord-Trøndelag (co.), Nor. 95/E2
Nordborg, Den. 96/C4
Nordby, Den. 96/D4
Norddeich, Ger. 109/E1
Nordela (int'l arpt.), Azor., Port. 103/T13
Norden, Ger. 109/E1
Nordenham, Ger. 109/F1
Nordenskjöld (arch.), Rus. 122/J2
Norderney, Ger. 109/E1
Norderney (isl.), Neth. 109/E1
Norderstedt, Ger. 109/G1
Nordhausen, Ger. 98/F3
Nordholz, Ger. 109/F1
Nordhorn, Ger. 109/E4
Nordhouse, Fr. 114/D1
Nordjylland (co.), Den. 96/C3
Nordkapp (cape), Nor. 95/H1
Nordkapp, Nor. 95/H1
Nordkinn (pt.), Nor. 95/H1
Nordkirchen, Ger. 109/E5
Nordland (co.), Nor. 95/E2
Nördlingen, Ger. 112/D5
Nordmaling, Swe. 95/F3
Nordreisa, Nor. 95/G1
Nordrhein-Westfalen (state), Ger. 98/E3
Nords Wharf, Austl. 173/D2
Nordwalde, Ger. 109/E4
Nore (riv.), Ire. 89/Q10
Noresund, Nor. 96/C1
Norfolk (mt.), Austl. 173/C4
Norfolk (lake), Ar,Mo, US 187/J3
Norfolk, Ne, US 185/J5
Norfolk (isl.), Austl. 174/F7
Norfolk Broads (swamp), Eng, UK 91/H1
Norg, Neth. 108/D2
Norheimsund, Nor. 96/B1
Norikura-dake (peak), Japan 133/E2
Noril'sk, Rus. 122/J3
Normal, Il, US 185/L5
Norman, Ok, US 195/N15
Norman Manley (int'l arpt.), Jam. 203/G2
Norman Wells, NW, Can. 180/D2
Normanby (isl.), PNG 174/E6
Normandie, Collines de (hills), Fr. 100/C2
Normandy (reg.), Fr. 100/C2
Normandy Beach, NJ, US 196/D4
Normandy Park, Wa, US 193/C3
Normanton, Austl. 172/A2
Normanton South, Eng, UK 93/G4
Norotshama (peak), Namb. 164/B3
Norquay, Sk, Can. 185/H3
Ñorquinco, Arg. 216/C4
Norrbotten (co.), Swe. 95/F2
Nørre Alslev, Den. 96/D4
Nørre Nebel, Den. 96/C4
Nørre Vorupør, Den. 96/C3
Norridge, Il, US 193/Q16
Norris (lake), Tn, US 191/G2
Norristown, Pa, US 196/C3
Norrköping, Swe. 96/G2
Norrland (reg.), Swe. 95/F2
Norrsundet, Swe. 96/G1
Norrtälje, Swe. 97/H2
Nors, Den. 96/C3
Norseman, Austl. 170/D5
Norsjö, Swe. 95/F2
Norte (pt.), Arg. 217/F3
Norte (pt.), Arg. 216/E4
Norte, Cabo do (cape), Braz. 209/J3
Norte de Santander (dept.), Col. 210/C2
Norte Los Rodeos (int'l arpt.), Sp. 156/A3
Norte, Serra do (mts.), Braz. 208/G6
Nortelândia, Braz. 209/G6
Nörten-Hardenberg, Ger. 109/G5
North (pt.), Austl. 173/C3
North (pt.), Austl. 173/C4
North (pt.), Austl. 170/B4
North (cape), PE, Can. 189/J2
North (sea), Eur. 94/D4
North (cape), NZ 175/S9
North (isl.), NZ 175/S10
North (sound), Sc, UK 89/V14
North (chan.), UK 92/C1
North (cape), Ak, US 192/D5
North (pt.), Md, US 196/B5
North Albanian Alps (mts.), Alb.,Mont. 106/D4
North America (cont.) 119
North Andaman (isl.), India 141/F5
North Arlington, NJ, US 197/J8
North Aulatsivik (isl.), Nf, Can. 181/K3
North Aurora, Il, US 193/P16
North Ayrshire (pol. reg.), Sc, UK 94/A5
North Battleford, Sk, Can. 184/F2
North Bay, On, Can. 188/E2
North Bay, Wi, US 193/Q14
North Beach, Md, US 196/B6
North Beach Haven, NJ, US 196/D4
North Bellmore, NY, US 197/L9
North Bend, Or, US 184/B5
North Bend, Wa, US 193/D3
North Bergen, NJ, US 197/J8
North Berwick, Sc, UK 94/D4
North Branch (riv.), Md, US 196/B5
North Branch, NJ, US 196/D2
North Branford, Ct, US 197/F1
North Brunswick, NJ, US 196/D3
North Buganda (prov.), Ugan. 162/B2
North Caicos (isl.), UK 203/J1
North Caldwell, NJ, US 197/J8
North Canadian (riv.), Ok, US 187/H3
North Cape May, NJ, US 196/D6
North Caribou (lake), On, Can. 185/L2
North Carolina (state), US 191/H3
North Cascades NP, Wa, US 184/C3
North Central (plain), Tx, US 201/F1
North Charleston, SC, US 191/J3
North Cowichan, BC, Can. 184/C3
North Dakota (state), US 185/H4
North Dorset Downs (uplands), Eng, UK 90/D5
North Down (dist.), NI, UK 92/C2
North East, Pa, US 188/E3
North East (pt.), Austl. 172/C3
North East, Md, US 196/C4
North Eastern (prov.), Kenya 162/C2
North Esk (riv.), Sc, UK 94/C5
North Foreland (pt.), Eng, UK 91/H4
North Fork Crow (riv.), Mn, US 185/K4
North Fort Myers, Fl, US 191/H5
North French (riv.), On, Can. 188/D1
North Frisian (isls.), Ger. 98/D1
North Front (int'l arpt.), UK 156/D1
North Gauhāti, India 143/H2
North Haledon, NJ, US 197/J8
North Hero, Vt, US 188/F2
North Highlands, Ca, US 193/L9
North Kansas City, Mo, US 195/D5
North Kitui Nat'l Rsv., Kenya 162/C3
North Korea (ctry.) 131/D2
North Lakhimpur, India 141/F2
North Lanarkshire (pol. reg.), Sc, UK 94/C5
North Las Vegas, Nv, US 186/D3
North Lincolnshire (co.), Eng, UK 93/H4
North Lindenhurst, NY, US 197/M9
North Little Rock, Ar, US 187/J4
North Luangwa NP, Zam. 163/F3
North Magnetic Pole 181/R7
North Minch (The Minch) (str.), Sc, UK 89/Q8
North Moose (lake), Mb, Can. 185/J2
North Mountain (mtn.), Pa, US 196/B1
North Myrtle Beach, SC, US 191/J3
North Ogden, Ut, US 195/K11
North Ossetian Aut. Rep., Rus. 121/G4
North Pacific (ocean) 80/A4
North Pine (riv.), Austl. 172/E6
North Plainfield, NJ, US 197/H9
North Platte, Ne, US 185/H5
North Platte (riv.), Ne,Wy, US 187/G2
North Pole, Ak, US 192/J3
North Pole 218/G
North Potomac, Md, US 196/A5
North Prairie, Wi, US 193/P14
North Puyallup, Wa, US 193/C3
North Raccoon (riv.), Ia, US 185/K5
North Ronaldsay (isl.), Sc, UK 89/V14
North Salt Lake, Ut, US 195/K12
North Saskatchewan (riv.), Ab,Sk, Can. 180/E3
North Shields, Eng, UK 93/G2
North Siberian Lowland (plain), Rus. 122/K2
North Skunk (riv.), Ia, US 187/J2
North Somerset (co.), Eng, UK 90/D4
North Stadbroke (isl.), Austl. 172/D4
North Taranaki Bight (bay), NZ 175/S10
North Thompson (riv.), BC, Can. 184/D3
North Tolsta, Sc, UK 89/Q7
North Tonawanda, NY, US 189/S9
North Tyne (riv.), Eng, UK 93/F1
North Tyneside (co.), Eng, UK 93/G1
North Uist (isl.), Sc, UK 89/Q8
North Umpqua (riv.), Or, US 186/B2
North Valley Stream, NY, US 197/L9
North Vancouver, BC, Can. 180/D4
North Wales, Pa, US 196/C3
North Weald Bassett, Eng, UK 88/D1
North West (cape), Austl. 170/B2
North-West Frontier (co.), India 144/A3
North West Highlands (uplands), Sc, UK 89/R8
North Wildwood, NJ, US 196/D6
North Wilton, Ct, US 197/E1
North York, Can. 189/Q8
North York Moors NP, Eng, UK 93/G3
North Yorkshire (co.), Eng, UK 93/G3
Northallerton, Eng, UK 93/G3
Northam, Austl. 170/C4
Northampton, Austl. 170/B4
Northampton, Eng, UK 91/F2
Northampton, Ma, US 189/F3
Northampton, Pa, US 196/C2
Northampton (co.), Pa, US 196/C2
Northampton Uplands (uplands), Eng, UK 91/E2
Northamptonshire (co.), Eng, UK 91/E2
Northbrook, Il, US 193/Q15
Northeast (cape), Ak, US 192/E3
Northeast (pt.), Bahm. 203/H1
Northeast (pt.), Jam. 203/G2
Northeast Land (isl.), Sval. 218/E
Northeast Lincolnshire (co.), Eng, UK 93/H4
Northeim, Ger. 109/G5
Northern (pol. reg.), Gha. 161/E4
Northern (dist.), Isr. 149/D3
Northern (pol. reg.), Malw. 162/B5
Northern (prov.), SLeo. 160/B4
Northern (prov.), Ugan. 162/B2
Northern Areas (terr.), Pak. 145/F5
Northern Cape (prov.), SAfr. 164/C3
Northern Cook (isls.), Cookls. 175/J6
Northern Dvina (riv.), Rus. 85/J2
Northern Light (lake), On, Can. 188/B1
Northern Mariana Islands (dpcy.), US 174/D3
Northern Province (prov.), SAfr. 164/E2
Northern Sporades (isls.), Gre. 105/J3
Northern Territory (terr.), Austl. 167/C2
Northern Ural (mts.), Rus. 119/N3
Northern Uvals (hills), Rus. 119/K4
Northfield, Mn, US 185/K4
Northfleet, Eng, UK 88/D2
Northglenn, Co, US 195/C3
Northport, Al, US 191/G3
Northport (Old Northport), NY, US 197/E2
Northumberland (str.), Can. 189/J2
Northumberland, Pa, US 196/B2
Northumberland NP, Eng, UK 94/D6
Northvale, NJ, US 197/K7
Northville, Mi, US 193/E7
Northway, Ak, US 192/K3
Northwest Gander (riv.), Nf, Can. 189/L1
Northwest Territories (terr.), Can. 180/D2
Northwich, Eng, UK 93/F5
Northwood, ND, US 185/J4
Norton (bay), Ak, US 192/F3
Norton (sound), Ak, US 192/E3
Norton Shores, Mi, US 188/C3
Nortorf, Ger. 96/C4
Norvegia (cape), Ant. 218/Y
Nörvenich, Ger. 111/F2
Norwalk, Oh, US 188/D3
Norwalk, Ca, US 194/F8
Norwalk, Ct, US 197/M7
Norwalk (riv.), Ct, US 197/M7
Norway (ctry.) 95/C3
Norwegian (bay), Nun., Can. 181/S7
Norwegian (sea), Eur. 85/D2
Norwich, NY, US 188/F3
Norwich, Eng, UK 91/H1
Norwich (int'l arpt.), Eng, UK 91/H1
Norwood, NJ, US 197/K8
Nos Emine (cape), Bul. 107/H4
Nos Kaliakra (pt.), Bul. 107/J4
Nos Maslen Nos (pt.), Bul. 107/H4
Nosappu-misaki (cape), Japan 134/D2
Nose, Japan 135/H6
Noshappu-misaki (cape), Japan 134/B1
Noshaq (peak), Afg. 147/K1
Noshiro, Japan 134/B3
Nosivka, Ukr. 120/D2
Nosong (cape), Malay. 139/E2
Noşratābād, Iran 147/G3
Noss Head (pt.), Sc, UK 89/S7
Nossa Senhora da Glória, Braz. 212/C3
Nossa Senhora das Dores, Braz. 212/C3
Nossebro, Swe. 96/E2
Nosy-Varika, Madg. 165/J8
Notch (cape), Chile 217/B6
Notec (riv.), Pol. 99/J2
Noto (pen.), Japan 133/E2
Noto, It. 104/D4
Noto Antica (ruin), It. 104/D4
Noto, Golfo di (gulf), It. 104/D4
Noto, Val di (valley), It. 104/D4
Notodden, Nor. 96/C2
Notogawa, Japan 135/K5
Notoro (lake), Japan 134/C1
Notre Dame (mts.), On, Can. 181/J4
Notre Dame (bay), Nf, Can. 181/L4
Notre Dame, Fr. 88/K5
Notre-Dame-de-l'Île-Perrot, Qu, Can. 189/N7
Notsé, Togo 161/F5
Nott (mt.), Austl. 171/G5
Nottaway (riv.), Qu, Can. 181/J3
Nøtterøy, Nor. 96/D2
Nottingham (isl.), Nun., Can. 181/H2
Nottingham, Eng, UK 93/G6
Nottingham (co.), Eng, UK 93/G6
Nottinghamshire (co.), Eng, UK 93/G5
Nottuln, Ger. 109/E5
Nouâdhibou, Mrta. 156/A5
Nouâdhibou (int'l arpt.), Mrta. 156/A5
Nouakchott (cap.), Mrta. 160/B2
Nouakchott (int'l arpt.), Mrta. 160/B2
Nouna, Burk. 160/E3
Noupoort, SAfr. 164/D3
Nouvion-sur-Meuse, Fr. 111/D4
Nœux-les-Mines, Fr. 110/B3
Nouzonville, Fr. 111/D4
Nova Andradina, Braz. 209/H8
Nova Cruz, Braz. 212/D2
Nová Dubnica, Slvk. 99/K4
Nova Friburgo, Braz. 213/D2
Nova Gorica, Slov. 117/G1
Nova Gradiška, Cro. 106/C3
Nova Iguaçu, Braz. 213/K7
Nova Kakhovka, Ukr. 107/L2
Nova Olinda, Braz. 212/C2
Nova Olinda do Norte, Braz. 208/G4
Nova Pazova, Serb. 106/E3
Nova Prata, Braz. 213/B4
Nova Russas, Braz. 212/B2
Nova Scotia (prov.), Can. 189/J2
Nova Sintra, CpV. 151/J11
Nova Soure, Braz. 212/C3
Nova Varoš, Serb. 106/D4
Nova Venécia, Braz. 213/D1
Nova Xavantina, Braz. 209/H6
Nova Zagora, Bul. 107/H4
Novaci, Rom. 107/F3
Novafeltria, It. 117/F5
Novara, It. 116/B2
Novate Mezzola, It. 115/F5
Novaya Sibir' (isl.), Rus. 123/R2
Novaya Zemlya (isl.), Rus. 218/C
Nove, It. 117/E1
Nové Hrady, Czh. 113/H5
Nové Město nad Váhom, Slvk. 99/J4
Nové Strašecí, Czh. 113/G2
Nové Zámky, Slvk. 106/D2
Novelda, Sp. 103/E3
Novellara, It. 117/D3
Noventa, It. 117/E2
Noventa di Piave, It. 117/F1
Noventa Vicentina, It. 117/E2
Novgorod, Rus. 97/P2
Novgorodskaya Oblast, Rus. 118/G4
Novi, Mi, US 193/E7
Novi Bečej, Serb. 106/E3
Novi di Modena, It. 117/D3
Novi Iskŭr, Bul. 107/F4
Novi Ligure, It. 101/H4
Novi Pazar, Serb. 106/E4
Novi Pazar, Bul. 107/H4
Novi Sad, Serb. 106/D3
Novi Vinodolski, Cro. 106/B3
Novillars, Fr. 114/C3
Nóvita, Col. 210/B3
Novo (riv.), Braz. 213/K6
Novo Alexeyevka (int'l arpt.), Geo. 121/H4

Novo A – Omolo

Novo Aripuanã, Braz. 208/F5
Novo Hamburgo, Braz. 213/B4
Novo Horizonte, Braz. 213/B2
Novo Miloševo, Serb. 106/E3
Novo Oriente, Braz. 212/B2
Novoanninskiy, Rus. 121/G2
Novocheboksarsk, Rus. 119/K4
Novocherkassk, Rus. 120/G3
Novogrudok, Bela. 97/L5
Novohrad-Volyns'kyy, Ukr. 120/C2
Novohradské Hory (mts.), Czh. 113/H5
Novokuybyshevsk, Rus. 121/J1
Novokuznetsk, Rus. 122/J4
Novolazarevskaya, Rus., Ant. 218/A
Novomoskovsk, Rus. 120/F1
Novorossiysk, Rus. 120/F3
Novoshakhtinsk, Rus. 120/F3
Novosibirsk (res.), Rus. 145/H2
Novosibirsk, Rus. 145/H1
Novosibirsk (Tolmachevo) (int'l arpt.), Rus. 145/H1
Novosibirskaya Oblast, Rus. 145/G1
Novotroitsk, Rus. 121/L2
Novoukrayinka, Ukr. 120/D2
Novovolyns'k, Ukr. 120/C2
Novovyatsk, Rus. 119/L4
Novozybkov, Rus. 120/D1
Novska, Cro. 106/C3
Nový Jičín, Czh. 99/K4
Nowa Dęba, Pol. 99/L3
Nowa Ruda, Pol. 99/J3
Nowa Sarzyna, Pol. 99/M3
Nowa Sól, Pol. 99/H3
Nowata, Ok, US 187/J3
Nowe, Pol. 99/K2
Nowe Miasto Lubawskie, Pol. 99/K2
Nowgong, India 142/B3
Nowitna (riv.), Ak, US 192/G3
Nowogard, Pol. 96/F5
Nowood (riv.), Wy, US 186/F1
Nowshāk (peak), Afg. 145/F5
Nowshera, Pak. 144/A2
Nowy Dwór Gdański, Pol. 97/H4
Nowy Sącz, Pol. 99/L4
Nowy Staw, Pol. 97/H4
Nowy Targ, Pol. 99/L4
Nowy Tomyśl, Pol. 99/J2
Noya, Sp. 102/A1
Noye (riv.), Fr. 110/B4
Noyon, Fr. 110/C4
Nsanje, Malw. 163/G4
Nsawam, Gha. 161/E5
Nsumbu NP, Zam. 162/A5
Nsuta, Gha. 161/E5
Ntoroko, Ugan. 162/A2
Ntungamo, Ugan. 162/A3
Ntusi, Ugan. 162/A2
Nu, Crêt du (peak), Fr. 114/B5
Nuangola, Pa, US 196/C1
Nūbah, Jibāl an (mts.), Sudan 155/M5
Nubian (des.), Sudan 159/C4
Nucet, Rom. 106/F2
Nucla, Co, US 190/A2
Nucourt, Fr. 88/H4
Nüdlingen, Ger. 112/D2
Nueces (riv.), Tx, US 190/D4
Nueltin (lake), Mb,Nun., Can. 180/G2
Nuenen, Neth. 108/C6
Nueva Alejandría, Peru 214/C2
Nueva Concepción, Guat. 202/D3
Nueva Esparta (state), Ven. 211/E2
Nueva Florida, Ven. 210/D2
Nueva Gerona, Cuba 203/F1
Nueva Helvecia, Uru. 217/K11
Nueva Imperial, Chile 216/B3
Nueva Italia de Ruiz, Mex. 200/E5
Nueva Loja, Ecu. 210/B4
Nueva Ocotepéque, Hon. 202/D3
Nueva Palmira, Uru. 217/J10
Nueva Rosita, Mex. 201/E3
Nueva Villa de Padilla, Mex. 201/F3
Nueve de Julio, Arg. 216/E2
Nuevitas, Cuba 203/G1
Nuevo, Ca, US 194/C3
Nuevo Balsas, Mex. 201/F5
Nuevo Berlín, Uru. 217/J10
Nuevo Casas Grandes, Mex. 200/D2
Nuevo Chagres, Pan. 203/F4
Nuevo, Gulfo (gulf), Arg. 215/D5
Nuevo Ideal, Mex. 200/D3
Nuevo Ixcatlán, Mex. 202/C2
Nuevo Laredo, Mex. 201/F3
Nuevo Leon (state), Mex. 198/A2
Nuevo Rocafuerte, Ecu. 210/C5
Nufenen, Swi. 115/F4
Nufenenpass (pass), Swi. 115/E5
Nuguria (isls.), PNG 174/E5
Nuhne (riv.), Ger. 109/F6
Nui (isl.), Tuv. 174/G5
Nuiqsut, Ak, US 192/H1
Nuits-Saint-Georges, Fr. 114/A3
Nukata, Japan 135/M6
Nuklunek (mtn.), Ak, US 192/F4
Nuku'alofa (cap.), Tonga 175/H7
Nukufetau (isl.), Tuv. 174/G5
Nukulaelae (isl.), Tuv. 174/H5
Nukumanu (atoll), PNG 174/E5
Nukunonu (isl.), Tok. 175/H5
Nukuoro (isl.), Micr. 174/E4
Nukus (int'l arpt.), Uzb. 145/C4
Nukus, Uzb. 145/C4
Nukutavake (isl.), FrPol. 175/M6
Nulato, Ak, US 192/G3
Nules, Sp. 103/E3
Nullarbor (plain), Austl. 170/E5
Nullarbor NP, Austl. 171/F4
Numana, It. 117/G5
Numansdorp, Neth. 108/B5
Numata, Japan 133/F2
Numazu, Japan 133/F3
Nümbrecht, Ger. 111/G2
Numfoor (isl.), Indo. 139/H4
Nummi, Fin. 97/K1
Numurkah, Austl. 173/C3
Nunapitchuk, Ak, US 192/F3
Nunchía, Col. 210/C3
Nundle, Austl. 173/D1
Nuneaton, Eng, UK 91/E1
Nungarin, Austl. 170/C4
Nungatta NP,Austl. 173/D3
Nunivak (isl.), Ak, US 192/E4
Nunningen, Swi. 114/D3
Nuñoa, Peru 214/D4
Nunspeet, Neth. 108/C4
Nuon (riv.), Libr. 160/C5
Nuoro, It. 104/A2
Nuquí, Col. 210/B3
Nur (mts.), Turk. 149/E1
Nura (riv.), Kaz. 145/F2
Nürburgring, Ger. 111/F3
Nure (riv.), It. 116/C3
Nuremberg, Pa, US 196/B2
Nurhak, Turk. 148/D2
Nuri (ruin), Sudan 159/B5
Nuriootpa, Austl. 171/H5
Nurmijärvi, Fin. 97/L1
Nürnberg (int'l arpt.), Ger. 112/E3
Nürnberg, Ger. 112/E4
Nürpur, Pak. 144/B3
Nurri (mt.), Austl. 173/C1
Nürtingen, Ger. 112/C5
Nushagak (riv.), Ak, US 192/G4
Nushki, Pak. 147/J3
Nutberry (hill), Sc, UK 94/C5
Nuth, Neth. 111/E2
Nuthe-Graben (riv.), Ger. 98/Q7
Nutley, NJ, US 197/J8
Nutwood, Il, US 195/F7
Nuuk (Godthåb), Grld. 177/M3
Nuvolento, It. 116/D1
Nuy (riv.), SAfr. 164/L10
Nüziders, Aus. 115/F3
Nxai Pan NP, Bots. 163/D4
Nyabisindu, Rwa. 162/A3
Nyack, NY, US 197/K7
Nyah, Austl. 173/B2
Nyah West, Austl. 173/B2
Nyainqêntanglha (peak), China 128/F5
Nyaki NP, Malw. 162/B5
Nyala, Sudan 155/K5
Nyalam, China 143/E1
Nyandoma, Rus. 118/J3
Nyanza (prov.), Kenya 162/B3
Nyasa (lake), Malw. 163/F3
Nybro, Swe. 96/F3
Nyêmo, China 143/H1
Nyeri, Kenya 162/C3
Nyima, China 128/E5
Nyírábrány, Hun. 106/F2
Nyíradony, Hun. 99/L5
Nyírbátor, Hun. 99/M5
Nyíregyháza, Hun. 99/L5
Nyírmada, Hun. 99/M4
Nyiru (mt.), Kenya 162/C2
Nykøbing, Den. 96/C3
Nykøbing, Den. 96/D4
Nyköping, Swe. 96/G2
Nylstroom, SAfr. 163/E5
Nynäshamn, Swe. 96/G2
Nyngan, Austl. 173/C1
Nyoman (riv.), Bela. 120/B1
Nyon, Swi. 114/C5
Nyons, Fr. 100/F4
Nýřany, Czh. 113/G3
Nýrsko, Czh. 113/G4
Nýrsko (res.), Czh. 113/G4
Nysa, Pol. 99/J3
Nyssa, Or, US 184/D5
Nysted, Den. 96/D4
Nyūdo-zaki (pt.), Japan 134/A4
Nyuk (lake), Rus. 118/F2
Nyúl, Hun. 106/C2
Nyunzu, D.R. Congo 163/E2
Nyūzen, Japan 133/E2
Nzega, Tanz. 162/B4
Nzérékoré (pol. reg.), Gui. 160/C4
Nzérékoré, Gui. 160/C5
Nzi (riv.), C.d'Iv. 154/E6

O

Ō-shima (isl.), Japan 134/A3
Oa, Mull of (pt.), Sc, UK 89/Q9
Oahe (dam), SD, US 185/H4
Oahe (lake), ND,SD, US 185/H4
Oahu (isl.), Hi, US 182/V13
Oak Forest, Il, US 193/Q16
Oak Grove, Mo, US 195/E6
Oak Hill, WV, US 188/D4
Oak Park, Il, US 193/Q16
Oak Park, Mi, US 193/F7
Oak Ridge, Tn, US 188/C4
Oak Ridge, NJ, US 196/D1
Oak View, Ca, US 194/A2
Oakbank, Mb, Can. 185/J3
Oakdale, La, US 187/J5
Oakes, ND, US 185/J4
Oakey, Austl. 172/C4
Oakham, Eng, UK 91/F1
Oakhurst, Ca, US 186/C3
Oakland, Ca, US 186/B3
Oakland, Md, US 196/B5
Oakland (co.), Mi, US 193/E6
Oakland (lake), Mi, US 193/F6
Oakland, NJ, US 197/J7
Oakland (bay), Wa, US 193/A3
Oaklands, Austl. 173/C2
Oakley, Ca, US 193/L10
Oakover (riv.), Austl. 170/D2
Oakridge, Or, US 184/C5
Oakville, La, US 195/P17
Oakville, Mo, US 195/G9
Oakville, On, Can. 189/Q9
Oakwood Hills, Il, US 193/P15
Oamaru, NZ 175/S12
Ōamishirasato, Japan 135/E2
Oat (mtn.), Ca, US 194/B2
Oatlands, Austl. 173/C4
Oaxaca (state), Mex. 198/B4
Oaxaca de Juárez, Mex. 202/B2
Ob' (gulf), Rus. 125/G3
Ob' (riv.), Rus. 125/F3
Ob Luang Gorge, Thai. 136/B2
Obama, Japan 135/J5
Obama (bay), Japan 135/J4
Oban (hills), Nga. 161/H5
Oban, Sc, UK 89/R8
Obanazawa, Japan 134/B4
Obara, Japan 135/M5
Obata, Japan 135/L7
Ober-Olm, Ger. 112/B3
Ober Ramstadt, Ger. 112/B3
Oberá, Arg. 215/E2
Oberalppass (pass), Swi. 115/E4
Oberalpstock (peak), Swi. 115/E4
Oberammergau, Ger. 115/H2
Oberasbach, Ger. 112/D4
Oberau, Ger. 115/H2
Oberburg, Swi. 114/D3
Oberderdingen, Ger. 112/B4
Oberdiessbach, Swi. 114/D4
Oberding, Ger. 113/E6
Oberdorf, Swi. 114/D3
Oberdorla, Ger. 109/H6
Oberelsbach, Ger. 112/D2
Oberentfelden, Swi. 114/E3
Oberglatt, Swi. 115/E3
Obergünzburg, Ger. 115/G2
Oberhaching, Ger. 113/E6
Oberhausen, Ger. 108/D6
Oberkirch, Ger. 114/E1
Oberkochen, Ger. 112/D5
Oberkotzau, Ger. 113/E2
Oberlausitz (reg.), Ger. 99/H3
Oberlin, Ks, US 187/G3
Obernai, Fr. 114/D1
Obernburg am Main, Ger. 112/C3
Oberndorf am Neckar, Ger. 115/E1
Oberndorf bei Salzburg, Aus. 113/F7
Oberneukirchen, Aus. 113/H6
Obernkirchen, Ger. 109/G4
Oberon, Austl. 173/D2
Oberösterreich (prov.), Aus. 99/G4
Oberpfälzer Wald (for.), Ger. 113/F3
Oberrieden, Swi. 115/E3
Oberriet, Swi. 115/F3
Obersaxen, Swi. 115/F4
Oberschleissheim, Ger. 113/E6
Oberschneiding, Ger. 113/F5
Obersiggenthal, Swi. 115/E3
Oberstammheim, Swi. 115/E2
Oberstaufen, Ger. 115/G2
Oberstdorf, Ger. 115/G3
Oberthal, Ger. 111/G4
Obertrum am See, Aus. 113/G7
Obertshausen, Ger. 112/B2
Oberursel, Ger. 112/B2
Oberuzwil, Swi. 115/F3
Oberviechtach, Ger. 113/F4
Oberwald, Swi. 115/E4
Oberwart, Aus. 106/C2
Oberwesel, Ger. 111/G3
Oberwil, Swi. 114/D4
Obfelden, Swi. 115/E3
Obi (str.), Indo. 139/G4
Obi (isls.), Indo. 139/G4
Óbidos, Braz. 209/G4
Óbidos, Port. 102/A3
Obihiro, Japan 134/C2
Obilić, Kos. 106/E4
Obing, Ger. 113/F6
Obira, Japan 134/B1
Obitsu (riv.), Japan 135/D3
Obluch'ye, Rus. 129/P2
Obninsk, Rus. 118/H5
Obo, CAfr. 155/L6
Oborniki, Pol. 99/J2
Oborniki Śląskie, Pol. 99/J3
Obra (riv.), Pol. 99/J2
Obrenovac, Serb. 106/E3
Obrež, Serb. 106/E4
Obrigheim, Ger. 112/C4
Obrigheim, Ger. 112/B3
Observatory, Austl. 173/G5
Obtrumer (lake), Aus. 113/F7
Ōbu, Japan 135/L6
Obuasi, Gha. 161/E5
Obw. (canton), Swi. 115/E4
Obzor, Bul. 107/H4
Ocala, Fl, US 191/H4
Ocampo, Mex. 200/E3
Ocaña, Sp. 102/D3
Ocaña, Col. 210/C2
Occhieppo Inferiore, It. 116/B1
Occhieppo Superiore, It. 116/A1
Occhiobello, It. 117/E3
Occidental, Cordillera (mts.), Ecu. 208/C3
Occimiano, It. 116/B2
Ocean (cape), Ak, US 192/L3
Ocean (co.), NJ, US 196/D4
Ocean Beach, NY, US 197/E2
Ocean City, Md, US 188/F4
Ocean City, NJ, US 196/D5
Ocean Falls, BC, Can. 184/B2
Ocean Gate, NJ, US 196/D4
Ocean Grove, NJ, US 196/D3
Ocean View, NJ, US 196/D5
Oceanographic Museum, Mona. 116/J8
Oceanside, Ca, US 194/C4
Oceanside, NY, US 197/L9
Oceanville, NJ, US 196/D5
Och'amch'ire, Geo. 121/G4
Ocheltree, Ks, US 195/D6
Ochiishi-misaki (cape), Japan 134/D2
Ochil (hills), Sc, UK 94/C4
Ocho Rios, Jam. 203/G2
Ochsenfurt, Ger. 112/D3
Ochsenhausen, Ger. 115/F1
Ochsenkopf (peak), Aus. 115/F3
Ochtendung, Ger. 111/G3
Ochtrup, Ger. 109/E4
Ochtum (riv.), Ger. 109/F2
Ockelbo, Swe. 96/G1
Ockenheim, Ger. 111/G4
Ocmulgee (riv.), Ga, US 191/H3
Ocmulgee Nat'l Mon., Ga, US 191/H3
Ocna Mureș, Rom. 107/F2
Ocna Sibiului, Rom. 107/G3
Ocoña (riv.), Peru 208/D6
Ocoña, Peru 214/C5
Oconee (lake), Ga, US 191/H3
Oconee (riv.), Ga, US 191/H3
Oconto, Wi, US 185/M4
Ocosingo, Mex. 202/C2
Ocotal, Nic. 202/E3
Ocotlán, Mex. 200/E4
Ocotlán de Morelos, Mex. 202/B2
Ocoyoacac, Mex. 201/Q10
Ocozocoautla de Espinosa, Mex. 202/C2
Ocracoke, NC, US 191/K3
Ocros, Peru 214/B3
Octeville, Fr. 100/C2
October Revolution (isl.), Rus. 125/H2
Oda (peak), Sudan 159/D4
Oda, Japan 132/C3
Oda, Gha. 161/E5
Odaesan NP, SKor. 131/E4
Ōdai, Japan 135/K7
Ōdaigahara-san (peak), Japan 132/E3
Ōdate, Japan 134/B3
Odawara, Japan 133/F3
Odda, Nor. 96/B1
Odder, Den. 96/D4
Odeborn (riv.), Ger. 109/F6
Odelzhausen, Ger. 112/E6
Odemira, Port. 102/A4
Ödemiş, Turk. 148/A2
Odendaalsrus, SAfr. 164/D2
Odense, Den. 96/D4
Odense (int'l arpt.), Den. 96/D4
Odenthal, Ger. 111/G1
Odenton, Md, US 196/B5
Odenwald (reg.), Ger. 112/B3
Oder (Odra) (riv.), Ger.,Pol. 99/H2
Oder-Spree Kanal (canal), Ger. 98/Q7
Oderen, Fr. 114/C2
Oderhaff (lag.), Ger. 99/H2
Oderzo, It. 117/F1
Odesa, Turk. 148/B1
Odesa, Ukr. 107/K2
Odes'ka Oblasti, Ukr. 120/D3
Odessa, De, US 196/C5
Odessa, Tx, US 187/G5
Odessa, Wa, US 184/D4
Odet (riv.), Fr. 100/B2
Odienné, C.d'Iv. 160/D4
Odintsovo, Rus. 119/W9
Odiongan, Phil. 137/D5
Odivelas, Port. 103/P10
Odobeşti, Rom. 107/H3
Odon (riv.), Fr. 100/C2
Odoorn, Neth. 108/D3
Odorheiu Secuiesc, Rom. 107/G2
Odžaci, Serb. 106/D3
Odzala, PN d', Congo 154/J7
Ōe, Japan 135/H5
Ōe-yama (peak), Japan 135/H5
Oegstgeest, Neth. 108/B4
Oeiras, Braz. 212/B2
Oelde, Ger. 109/F5
Oelsnitz, Ger. 113/F2
Oeno (isl.), Pitc. 175/M7
Oensingen, Swi. 114/D3
Oer-Erkenschwick, Ger. 109/E5
Oesling (mts.), Lux. 111/E4
Oesterdam (dam), Neth. 108/B6
Oestrich-Winkel, Ger. 112/B3
Oeta NP, Gre. 105/H3
Oetz, Aus. 115/G3
Oey'ŏn (isl.), SKor. 131/D3
Of, Turk. 148/E1
O'Fallon, Mo, US 195/F8
O'Fallon, Il, US 195/H8
Ofanto (riv.), It. 104/D2
Ofaqim, Isr. 149/D4
Ofenhorn (peak), Swi. 115/E5
Offa, Nga. 161/G4
Offaly (co.), Ire. 92/A5
Offanengo, It. 116/C2
Offement, Fr. 114/C2
Offenbach, Ger. 112/B2
Offenbach an der Queich, Ger. 112/B4
Offenburg, Ger. 114/D1
Offingen, Ger. 112/D6
Offstein, Ger. 112/B3
Oftersheim, Ger. 112/B4
Oftringen, Swi. 114/D3
Ōfunato, Japan 134/B4
Oga, Japan 134/A4
Oga (pen.), Japan 134/A4
Ogachi, Japan 134/B4
Ogadēn (reg.), Eth. 155/P6
Ōgaki, Japan 135/L5
Ogano, Japan 135/C2
Ogasawara, Japan 174/D2
Ogatsu, Japan 134/B4
Ogawa, Japan 135/E1
Ogawa, Japan 135/C1
Ogawara (lake), Japan 134/B3
Ogbomosho, Nga. 161/G4
Ogden, Ut, US 195/K11
Ogden Bay (bay), Ut, US 195/J11
Ogden, South Fork (riv.), Ut, US 195/K11
Ogdensburg, NY, US 188/F2
Ogdensburg, NJ, US 196/D1
Ogeechee (riv.), Ga, US 191/H3
Oggiono, It. 116/C1
Ogi, Japan 133/F2
Ogidaki (mtn.), On, Can. 188/D2
Ogies, SAfr. 164/E2
Ogilvie (mts.), Yk, Can. 180/C2
Ogilvie (riv.), Yk, Can. 180/C2
Ogles, Il, US 195/G8
Oglesby, Tx, US 201/F2
Oglio (riv.), It. 101/J4
Ognon (riv.), Fr. 98/C5
Ogoamas (peak), Indo. 139/F3
Ogoki (lake), On, Can. 185/M3
Ogoki (res.), On, Can. 185/L3
Ogoki (riv.), On, Can. 185/M3
Ogooué (riv.), Gabon 154/H8
Ogose, Japan 135/C2
Ogosta (riv.), Bul. 107/F4
Ogre, Lat. 97/L3
Oguchi, Japan 135/L5
Ogulin, Cro. 106/B3
Ogun (riv.), Nga. 154/F6
Ogun (state), Nga. 161/F5
Ogurjaly (isl.), Trkm. 145/B5
Oğuz, Turk. 148/D2
Oh Me Edge (hill), Eng, UK 94/D6
Ōhara, Japan 135/E3
Oharu, Japan 135/L5
Ōhata, Japan 134/B3
Ohey, Belg. 111/E3
O'Higgins (pol. reg.), Chile 216/B1
O'Higgins (lake), Chile 217/B6
Ohio (riv.), US 188/B4
Ohio (state), US 188/D3
Ōhira, Japan 135/D1
Ohlsdorf, Aus. 113/G7
Ohlstadt, Ger. 115/H2
Ohm (riv.), Ger. 112/C1
Ōho, Japan 135/E1
Ohoopee (riv.), Ga, US 191/H3
Ohře (riv.), Czh. 98/H3
Ohre (riv.), Ger. 98/F2
Ohrid, FYROM 105/G2
Ohrid (lake), Alb., Mac 105/G2
Oi (riv.), China 141/G2
Ōi, Japan 135/J5
Ōi, Japan 135/C3
Ōi, Japan 135/D2
Oiapoque (riv.), Braz. 209/H3
Oiapoque, Braz. 209/H3
Oich (lake), Sc, UK 94/B2
Oieras, Port. 103/P10
Oignies, Fr. 110/B3
Oignin (riv.), Fr. 114/B5
Oil City, Pa, US 188/E3
Oinófita, Gre. 105/H3
Oinoí, Gre. 105/N8
Oirschot, Neth. 108/C5
Oise (dept.), Fr. 110/B5
Oise (riv.), Fr. 98/B4
Oise à l'Aisne, Canal de l' (canal), Fr. 110/C4
Oiseaux du Djoudj, PN des, Sen. 160/A2
Ōiso, Japan 135/C3
Oissery, Fr. 88/L4
Oisterwijk, Neth. 108/C5
Ōita (riv.), Japan 132/B4
Ōita (pref.), Japan 132/B4
Ōita, Japan 132/B4
Ōizumi, Japan 135/C1
Ōizumi, Japan 135/A2
Ojai, Ca, US 194/A2
Ojcowski NP, Pol. 99/K3
Öjebyn, Swe. 95/G2
Ōji, Japan 135/J6
Ojima, Japan 135/C1
Ojinaga, Mex. 200/D2
Ojiya, Japan 133/F2
Ojo de Agua, Mex. 201/Q9
Ojo de Liebre (lag.), Mex. 200/B3
Ojocaliente, Mex. 200/E4
Ojos del Salado (peak), Chile 215/C2
Ojos Negros, Sp. 102/E2
Ojuelos de Jalisco, Mex. 201/E4
Oka, Qu, Can. 189/M7
Oka, Nga. 161/G5
Oka (riv.), Rus. 123/L4
Okabe, Japan 135/C1
Okahandja, Namb. 163/C5
Okak (isl.), Nf, Can. 181/K3
Okanagan (lake), BC, Can. 180/D4
Okanagan Falls, BC, Can. 184/D3
Okanda, PN de l', Gabon 163/B1
Okanogan, Wa, US 184/D3
Okanogan (riv.), Wa, US 184/D3
Okāra, Pak. 144/B4
Okavango (delta), Bots. 163/D4
Ōkawa, Japan 132/B4
Okaya, Japan 133/F2
Okayama (pref.), Japan 132/C3
Okayama, Japan 132/C3
Okazaki, Japan 135/M6
Okch'ŏn, SKor. 131/D4
Okęcie (int'l arpt.), Pol. 99/L2
Okeechobee, Fl, US 191/H5
Okeechobee (lake), Fl, US 191/H5
Okegawa, Japan 135/D2
Okement (riv.), Eng, UK 90/B5
Okha, Rus. 123/Q4
Ókhi Óros (peak), Gre. 105/J3
Okhotsk, Sea of (sea), Japan,Rus. 125/P4
Okhta (riv.), Rus. 119/T6
Okhtyrka, Ukr. 120/E2
Oki (isls.), Japan 132/C2
Okidaitō (isl.), Japan 133/L8
Okiep, SAfr. 164/B3
Okinawa (isl.), Japan 133/J7
Okinawa (pref.), Japan 133/J8
Okino-shima (isl.), Japan 132/C4
Okinoerabu (isl.), Japan 133/K7
Okitipupa, Nga. 161/G5
Okkan, Myan. 141/G4
Okku, SKor. 131/D5
Oklahoma (state), US 187/H4
Oklahoma City (cap.), Ok, US 195/M15
Okmulgee, Ok, US 187/J4
Oko, Nga. 161/G5
Okobaji (lakes), Ia, US 185/K5
Okok (riv.), Ugan. 162/B2
Okolona, Ms, US 191/F3
Okoppe, Japan 134/C1
Okotoks, Ab, Can. 184/E3
Okovango (riv.), Namb. 151/E6
Oksbøl, Den. 96/C4
Oksskolten (peak), Nor. 95/E2
Oktyabr'sk, Rus. 121/J1
Oktyabr'skiy, Rus. 119/M5
Ōkuchi, Japan 132/B4
Okulovka, Rus. 118/G4
Okushiri, Japan 134/A2
Okutama (lake), Japan 135/C2
Okutama, Japan 135/C2
Okwa (riv.), Bots. 163/D5
Ol Doinyo Sabuk NP, Kenya 162/C3
Ólafsfjördhur, Ice. 95/N6
Ólafsvík, Ice. 95/M7
Olalla, Wa, US 193/B3
Olan, Pic d' (peak), Fr. 101/G4
Olanchito, Hon. 202/E3
Öland (isl.), Swe. 95/F4
Ölands södra udde (pt.), Swe. 96/G3
Olathe, Ks, US 195/D6
Olavarría, Arg. 216/E3
Oława, Pol. 99/J3
Ölbach (riv.), Ger. 109/F5
Olberg, Az, US 195/S19
Olbia, It. 104/A2
Olching, Ger. 113/E6
Olcott, NY, US 189/S9
Old (riv.), Ca, US 193/L11
Old Bahama (chan.), Cuba 203/G1
Old Bar, Austl. 173/E1
Old Bedford (canal), Eng, UK 91/G2
Old Bethpage, NY, US 197/M9
Old Bridge, NJ, US 197/H10
Old City, Isr. 149/G8
Old Crow, Yk, Can. 192/L2
Old Faithful Geyser, Wy, US 184/F4
Old Field (pt.), NY, US 197/E2
Old Fort Niagara, NY, US 189/R9
Old Harbor, Ak, US 192/H4
Old Man of Hoy, Sc, UK 89/V14
Old Mill Creek, Il, US 193/Q15
Old Nene (riv.), Eng, UK 91/F2
Old Rhine (riv.), Neth. 108/B4
Old Saybrook, Ct, US 197/F1
Old Tappan, NJ, US 197/K8
Old Town, Me, US 189/G2
Old Windsor, Eng, UK 88/B2
Old Wives (lake), Sk, Can. 185/G3
Oldeani (peak), Tanz. 162/B3
Oldebroek, Neth. 108/C4
Oldemarkt, Neth. 108/C3
Oldenburg, Ger. 109/F2
Oldenburg, Ger. 96/D4
Oldenzaal, Neth. 108/D4
Oldham, Eng, UK 93/F4
Oldham (co.), Eng, UK 93/F4
Oldman (riv.), Ab, Can. 184/E3
Oldmeldrum, Sc, UK 94/D2
Oldoog (isl.), Ger. 109/E1
Olds, Ab, Can. 184/E3
Olduvai Gorge, Tanz. 162/B3
Oldwick, NJ, US 196/D2
Olean, NY, US 188/E3
Olecko, Pol. 97/K4
Oleggio, It. 116/B1
Oleiros, Port. 102/B3
Oleiros, Sp. 102/A1
Olekma (riv.), Rus. 123/N4
Oleksandriya, Ukr. 120/E2
Olele (pt.), Wa, US 193/B2
Olemari (riv.), Sur. 211/H4
Ølen, Nor. 96/A2
Olenegorsk, Rus. 118/G1
Olenëk (riv.), Rus. 123/L3
Olenek (bay), Rus. 123/M2
Oléron, Île (isl.), Fr. 100/C4
Olesa de Montserrat, Sp. 103/K6
Oleśnica, Pol. 99/J3
Olesno, Pol. 99/K3
Oley, Pa, US 196/C3
Olfen, Ger. 109/E5
Olga (mt.), Austl. 171/F3
Olginate, It. 116/C1
Ölgiy, Mong. 128/E2
Ølgod, Den. 96/C4
Olhão, Port. 102/B4
Öli Qoltyq Sory (swamp), Kaz. 145/B3
Oliena, It. 104/A2
Olifantshoek, SAfr. 164/P12
Olifantsrivier (riv.), SAfr. 163/E5
Olimarao (isl.), Micr. 174/D4
Olimbía (Olympia) (ruin), Gre. 105/G4
Ólimbos, Gre. 148/A3
Ólimbos NP (Olympos NP), Gre. 105/H2
Olímpia, Braz. 213/B2
Olimpos Beydağları NP, Turk. 149/B1
Olinalá, Mex. 202/B2
Olinda, Braz. 212/D3
Olindina, Braz. 212/C3
Oliva, Sp. 103/E3
Oliva de la Frontera, Sp. 102/B3
Olivais, Port. 102/A3
Oliveira, Braz. 213/C2
Olivenza, Sp. 102/B3
Oliver, BC, Can. 184/D3
Olivet, Fr. 100/D3
Olivone, Swi. 115/E4
Olla, La, US 187/J5
Ollachea, Peru 214/D4
Ollagüe (vol.) 208/E8
Ollainville, Fr. 88/J6
Ollería, Sp. 103/E3
Olleros, Peru 214/B3
Ollon, Swi. 114/D5
Ollūr, India 140/C5
Olmaliq, Uzb. 145/E4
Olmedo, Sp. 102/C2
Olmos, Peru 214/B2
Olmos Park, Tx, US 195/U21
Olmstead, Ut, US 195/K13
Olmué, Chile 216/N8
Olney, Tx, US 187/H4
Olney, Md, US 196/A5
Olofström, Swe. 96/F3
Olomane (riv.), Qu, Can. 189/J1
Olomouc, Czh. 99/J4
Olomoucký (pol. reg.), Czh. 99/J4
Olongapo, Phil. 137/D5
Olonne-sur-Mer, Fr. 100/C3
Olorgasailie Nat'l Mon., Kenya 162/C3
Oloron-Sainte-Marie, Fr. 100/C5
Olot, Sp. 103/G1
Oloy (range), Rus. 123/S3
Olpe (riv.), Ger. 109/F6
Olpe, Ger. 111/G1
Olsberg, Ger. 109/F6
Olst, Neth. 108/D4
Olsztyn, Pol. 97/J5
Olsztynek, Pol. 99/L2
Olt (prov.), Rom. 107/G3
Olt (riv.), Rom. 107/G3
Olte, Sierra de (hills), Arg. 216/C4
Olten, Swi. 114/D3
Oltenița, Rom. 107/H3
Olteț (riv.), Rom. 107/F3
Oltre il Colle, It. 115/F6
Oltu, Turk. 148/E1
Oltu (riv.), Turk. 148/E1
Olur, Turk. 148/E1
Olvera, Sp. 102/C4
Olympia (cap.), Wa, US 184/C4
Olympic (mts.), Wa, US 184/C4
Olympic Dam, Austl. 171/H4
Olympic Game Farm, Wa, US 193/A1
Olympic National Forest, Wa, US 193/A2
Olympic NP, Wa, US 184/B4
Olympic Park, SKor. 131/G6
Olympos (Mount Olympus) (peak), Gre. 105/H2
Olympus (mt.), Wa, US 184/C4
Olympus (peak), Cyp. 149/C2
Olyutorskiy (bay), Rus. 123/S3
Ōma, Japan 134/B3
Oma (riv.), Rus. 119/K2
Ōma-zaki (pt.), Japan 134/B3
Ōmachi, Japan 133/E2
Omae-zaki (pt.), Japan 133/F3
Ōmagari, Japan 134/B4
Omagh (dist.), NI, UK 92/A2
Omagh, NI, UK 92/A2
Omak, Wa, US 184/D3
Oman (ctry.) 147/G4
Oman (gulf), Asia 147/H4
Omar Torrijos Herrera (int'l arpt.), Pan. 203/G4
Omaruru, Namb. 163/C5
Omas, Peru 214/B4
Omatako (riv.), Namb. 163/C4
Omate, Peru 214/D5
Ombai (str.), Indo. 139/F5
Ombrone (riv.), It. 101/J5
Ombúes de Lavalle, Uru. 217/K10
Ōme, Japan 135/C2
Omeath, Ire. 92/B3
Omegna, It. 101/H4
Omeo, Austl. 173/C3
Ömerli, Turk. 148/E2
Ometepe (isl.), Nic. 202/E4
Ometepec, Mex. 202/B2
Ōmi, Japan 135/K5
Ōmihachiman, Japan 135/K5
Omiš, Cro. 104/E1
Omitlán (riv.), Mex. 202/B2
Ōmiya, Japan 133/G2
Ōmiya, Japan 135/H4
Ōmiya, Japan 135/K7
Ommaney (cape), Ak, US 192/M4
Ommen, Neth. 108/D3
Ömnögovĭ (prov.), Mong. 128/H3
Omo NP, Eth. 155/N6
Omo Wenz (riv.), Eth. 155/N6
Omodeo (lake), It. 104/A2
Omolon (riv.), Rus. 125/Q3

Omono (riv.), Japan 134/B4
Omsk, Rus. 145/F1
Omsk (int'l arpt.), Rus. 145/F2
Omskaya Oblast, Rus. 145/F1
Ōmu, Japan 134/C1
Omul (peak), Rom. 107/G3
Ōmura, Japan 132/A4
Omurtag, Bul. 107/H4
Ōmuta, Japan 132/B4
Omutninsk, Rus. 119/M4
Onagawa, Japan 134/B4
Onalaska, Tx, US 190/E4
Onaping (lake), On, Can. 188/D2
Oñate, Sp. 102/D1
Onaway, Mi, US 188/C2
Onchan, IM, UK 92/D3
Onda, Sp. 103/E3
Ondava (riv.), Slvk. 99/L4
Ondjiva, Ang. 163/C4
Ondo, Nga. 161/G5
Ondo (state), Nga. 161/G5
Öndörhaan, Mong. 129/K2
Onè, It. 117/E1
Onega, Rus. 118/H3
Onega (bay), Rus. 118/G2
Onega (lake), Rus. 218/D
Onega (pen.), Rus. 118/H2
Onega (riv.), Rus. 122/D3
Oneida, NY, US 188/F3
Oneida, Pa, US 196/B2
Oneonta, NY, US 188/F3
Onex, Swi. 114/C5
Ongjin, NKor. 131/C4
Ongole, India 140/D4
Ongtüstik Qazaqstan, Kaz. 122/G5
Onhaye, Belg. 111/D3
Onida, SD, US 185/H4
Onil, Sp. 103/E3
Onilahy (riv.), Ang. 165/G8
Onishi, Japan 135/C1
Onitsha, Nga. 161/G5
Onjuku, Japan 135/E3
Onkaparinga (riv.), Austl. 171/M8
Onnaing, Fr. 110/C3
Onny (riv.), Eng, UK 90/D2
Ōno, Japan 132/E3
Ono, Japan 132/D3
Ōno, Japan 135/L5
Onoda, Japan 132/B4
Onomichi, Japan 132/C3
Onon, Mong. 129/K2
Onon (riv.), Rus. 129/K1
Onoto, Ven. 211/E2
Onotoa (isl.), Kiri. 174/G5
Onrusrivier, SAfr. 164/L11
Onslow, Austl. 170/B2
Ontake-san (peak), Japan 133/E3
Ontario, Or, US 184/D4
Ontario, Ca, US 194/C2
Ontario (prov.), Can. 180/H3
Ontario (lake), Can.,US 188/E3
Ontelaunee (lake), Pa, US 196/C3
Onteniente, Sp. 103/E3
Ontonagon, Mi, US 185/L4
Ontong Java (isl.), Sol. 174/E5
Onyang, SKor. 131/D4
Onzaga, Col. 210/C3
Oologah (lake), Ok, US 190/D2
Oona River, BC, Can. 192/M5
Oost-Vlaanderen (prov.), Belg. 110/C2
Oost-Vlieland, Neth. 108/C2
Oostburg, Neth. 110/C1
Oostelijk Flevoland (polder), Neth. 108/C3
Oostende (Ostend), Belg. 110/B1
Oosterhout, Neth. 108/B5
Oosterscheidedam (dam),Neth. 108/A5
Oosterschelde (riv.), Neth. 98/B3
Oosterwolde, Neth. 108/D3
Oosterzele, Belg. 110/C2
Oostkamp, Belg. 110/C1
Oostvaarderplassen (lake),Neth. 108/C4
Oostzaan, Neth. 108/B4
Ootmarsum, Neth. 108/D4
Opaka, Bul. 107/H4
Opalenica, Pol. 99/J2
Opasatika (riv.), On, Can. 188/D1
Opatija, Cro. 106/B3
Opatów, Pol. 99/L3
Opava, Czh. 99/J4
Opelika, Al, US 191/G3
Opelousas, La, US 187/J5
Opera, It. 116/C2
Opfingen, Ger. 115/F1
Opglabbeek, Belg. 111/E1
Ophir, Ak, US 192/G3
Ophir, Ut, US 195/J13
Ophthalmia (range), Austl. 170/C2
Oploo, Neth. 108/C5
Opmeer, Neth. 108/B3
Opoczno, Pol. 99/L3
Opole, Pol. 99/J3
Opole Lubelskie, Pol. 99/L3
Opolskie (prov.), Pol. 99/J3
Opovo, Serb. 106/E3
Opp, Al, US 191/G4
Oppdal, Nor. 95/D3
Oppeano, It. 117/E2
Oppenau, Ger. 114/E1
Oppenheim, Ger. 112/B3
Oppland (co.), Nor. 95/D3
Opportunity, Wa, US 184/D4
Opwijk, Belg. 111/D2
Oquirrh (mts.), Ut, US 195/J12
Or 'Aqiva, Isr. 149/F6
Or, Mont d' (peak), Fr. 114/C4
Or Yehuda, Isr. 149/F7
Ora (riv.), Mex. 200/D3
Ōra, Japan 135/C1
Oradell, NJ, US 197/J8
Oradell (res.), NJ, US 197/J8
Orahovac, Kos. 106/E4
Orahovica, Cro. 106/C3
Orai, India 142/B3
Orain (riv.), Fr. 114/B4
Oral, Kaz. 121/J2
Oran, Alg. 158/E5
Orang (riv.), NKor. 131/E2
Orange, Austl. 173/D2
Orange (cape), Braz. 209/H3
Orange, Fr. 100/F4
Orange (riv.), Nam.,SAfr. 163/C6
Orange, Ca, US 194/G8
Orange, Ct, US 197/E1
Orange, NJ, US 197/J8
Orange (co.), NY, US 196/D1
Orange, Tx, US 187/J5
Orange, Va, US 188/E4
Orange Park, Fl, US 191/H4
Orange Walk, Belz. 202/D2
Orangeburg, NY, US 197/K7
Orangeburg, SC, US 191/H3
Orangeville, On, Can. 188/D3
Orangeville, Pa, US 196/B1
Orango (isl.), GBis. 160/A4
Oranienburg, Ger. 98/G6
Oranje (mts.), Sur. 211/H4
Oranjekanaal (riv.), Neth. 108/D3
Oranjemund, Namb. 164/B3
Oranjestad, Aruba. 210/D1
Oranmore, Ire. 89/P10
Orapa, Bots. 163/E5
Oras, Phil. 137/E5
Orăştie, Rom. 107/F3
Oravița, Rom. 106/E3
Orb (riv.), Fr. 100/E5
Orba (riv.), It. 116/B3
Orbe, Swi. 114/C4
Orbe (riv.), Swi. 114/C4
Orbey, Fr. 114/D1
Órbigo (riv.), Sp. 102/C1
Orbost, Austl. 173/D3
Örbyhus, Swe. 96/G1
Orcemont, Fr. 88/H6
Orcera, Sp. 102/D3
Orchamps, Fr. 114/B3
Orchamps-Vennes, Fr. 114/C3
Orchard (lake), Mi, US 193/F6
Orchard City, Co, US 186/F3
Orchard Farm, Mo, US 195/G8
Orchard Homes, Mt, US 184/E4
Orchard Lake Village, Mi, US 193/F6
Orchid (isl.), Tai. 137/D3
Orchies, Fr. 110/C3
Orchy (riv.), Sc, UK 94/B4
Orciano di Pesaro, It. 117/F5
Orco (riv.), It. 101/G4
Orcopampa, Peru 214/C4
Orcotuna, Peru 214/C3
Ord, Ne, US 185/J5
Ordaz (int'l arpt.), Mex. 200/D4
Ordes, Sp. 102/A1
Ordesa y Monte Perdido, PN de, Sp. 103/F1
Ordos (des.), China 128/J4
Ordos (Mu Us Shamo) (des.), China 128/J4
Ordu, Turk. 148/D1
Ordu (prov.), Turk. 148/D1
Ore, Nga. 161/G5
Orealla, Guy. 211/G3
Örebro, Swe. 96/F2
Örebro (prov.), Swe. 95/E4
Orebro (int'l arpt.), Swe. 96/F2
Oregon (state), US 184/C5
Oregon Caves Nat'l Mon., Or, US 184/C5
Oregon City, Or, US 184/C4
Öregrund, Swe. 96/H1
Orekhovo-Zuyevo, Rus. 118/H5
Orël, Rus. 120/F1
Orellana, Peru 214/C2
Orellana la Vieja, Sp. 102/C3
Orem, Ut, US 195/K13
Orenberg (int'l arpt.), Rus. 121/K2
Orenburg, Rus. 121/K2
Orenburgskaya Oblast, Rus. 145/B2
Orense, Sp. 102/B1
Orestiás, Gre. 105/K2
Øresund (sound), Swe. 96/E4
Oreti (riv.), NZ 175/R12
Orford, Austl. 173/C4
Orford (pt.), Eng, UK 91/H2
Organ Pipe Cactus Nat'l Mon., Az, US 186/D4
Órgãos, Serra dos (mts.), Braz. 213/K7
Orgaz, Sp. 102/D3
Orgelet, Fr. 114/B4
Orgeurs, Fr. 88/H5
Orgeval, Fr. 88/H5
Orgosolo, It. 104/A2
Orhaneli, Turk. 120/D5
Orhangazi, Turk. 107/J5
Orhei, Mol. 107/J2
Orhon (riv.), Mong. 128/J2
Oria, Sp. 102/D4
Orient (pt.), NY, US 197/F1
Oriental, Mex. 201/M7
Oriental, Cordillera (mts.), SAm. 208/C5
Orientale (prov.), D.R. Congo 162/A2
Oriente, Arg. 216/E3
Origny-Sainte-Benoîte, Fr. 110/C4
Orihuela, Sp. 103/E3
Orillia, On, Can. 188/E2
Orimattila, Fin. 97/L1
Orinda, Ca, US 193/K11
Orinoco (delta), Ven. 211/F2
Orinoco (riv.), Col.,Ven. 211/F2
Orio al Serio (int'l arpt.), It. 116/C1
Oriolo, It. 104/E2
Orion (lake), Mi, US 193/F6
Orissa (state), India 140/D3
Orissa Coast (canal), India 143/F5
Oristano, It. 104/A3
Oristano, Golfo di (gulf), It. 104/A3
Orivesi, Fin. 97/L1
Oriximiná, Braz. 209/G4
Orizaba, Mex. 201/M8
Orizona, Braz. 212/A5
Orjen (peak), Mont. 106/D4
Órjiva, Sp. 102/D4
Orke (riv.), Ger. 109/F6
Örkelljunga, Swe. 96/E3
Orkhomenós, Gre. 105/H3
Orkney, SAfr. 164/D2
Orkney (isls.), UK 218/G
Orla, Tx, US 190/C4
Orland Park, Il, US 193/Q16
Orlândia, Braz. 213/C2
Orlando (int'l arpt.), Fl, US 191/H4
Orlando, Fl, US 191/H4
Orlando, Capo d' (cape), It. 104/D3
Orléanais (reg.), Fr. 100/D2
Orleans, Ca, US 184/C5
Orleans (parish), La, US 195/P16
Orléans, Fr. 100/D3
Orlenbach, Ger. 112/D2
Orlik (res.), Czh. 113/H3
Orlová, Czh. 99/K4
Orlovskaya Oblast, Rus. 120/F1
Orly (int'l arpt.), Fr. 88/K5
Orly, Fr. 88/K5
Ormanlı, Turk. 107/K5
Ormea, It. 116/A4
Ormília, Gre. 105/H2
Ormiston, Sc, UK 94/D5
Ormoc, Phil. 137/D5
Ormond Beach, Fl, US 191/H4
Ormskirk, Eng, UK 93/F4
Ornain (riv.), Fr. 100/F2
Ornans, Fr. 114/C3
Ornavasso, It. 115/E6
Orne (riv.), Fr. 98/C4
Ørnes, Nor. 95/E2
Orneta, Pol. 97/J4
Örnsköldsvik, Swe. 95/F3
Oro (riv.), Mex. 212/C2
Oro Grande, Ca, US 194/C1
Oro, Monte d' (peak), Fr. 104/A1
Oro Valley, Az, US 186/E4
Orocó, Braz. 212/C3
Orocué, Col. 210/D3
Orodara, Burk. 160/E4
Orofino, Id, US 184/D4
Orolo (riv.), It. 117/E1
Oroluk (isl.), Micr. 174/E4
Oromocto, NB, Can. 189/H2
Oron-la-Ville, Swi. 114/C4
Orona (Hull) (isl.), Kiri. 175/H5
Orono, Me, US 189/G2
Orontes (riv.), Syria 148/D3
Oropesa, Sp. 102/C3
Oroqen Zizhiqi, China 129/M1
Orós, Braz. 212/C2
Orosei, It. 104/A2
Orosei, Golfo di (gulf), It. 104/A2
Orosháza, Hun. 106/E2
Oroszlány, Hun. 106/D2
Orovada, Nv, US 184/D5
Oroville, Wa, US 184/D3
Oroville, Ca, US 186/B3
Orphin, Fr. 88/H6
Orpund, Swi. 114/D3
Orrefors, Swe. 96/F3
Orrell, Eng, UK 93/F4
Orrick, Mo, US 195/E5
Orrin (riv.), Sc, UK 94/B2
Orrin (res.), Sc, UK 94/B2
Orroli, It. 104/A3
Orroroo, Austl. 171/H5
Orrtanna, Pa, US 196/A4
Orry-la-Ville, Fr. 88/K4
Orsa, Swe. 96/F1
Orsago, It. 117/F1
Orsay, Fr. 88/J5
Orsett, Eng, UK 88/E2
Orsha, Bela. 97/P4
Orsk, Rus. 121/L2
Orsonnens, Swi. 114/C4
Orşova, Rom. 106/F3
Ørsta, Nor. 95/C3
Orsundsbro, Swe. 96/G2
Orta (lake), It. 101/H4
Orta, Turk. 120/E4
Orta Nova, It. 104/D2
Ortaca, Turk. 148/B2
Ortaköy, Turk. 148/C1
Ortaköy, Turk. 148/C2
Ortega, Col. 210/C4
Ortegal (cape), Sp. 102/B1
Ortenberg, Ger. 112/C2
Orth an der Donau, Aus. 107/P7
Orthez, Fr. 100/C5
Ortigara (peak), It. 115/H5
Ortigueira, Sp. 102/B1
Orting, Wa, US 193/C3
Ortiz, Mex. 200/C2
Ortles (mts.), It. 101/J3
Ortles (peak), It. 115/G4
Ortón (riv.), Bol. 208/E6
Ortona, It. 104/D1
Ortonville, Mn, US 185/J4
Ortonville, Mi, US 193/F6
Örtze (riv.), Ger. 109/H3
Orūmīyeh, Iran 148/F2
Orurillo, Peru 214/D4
Oruro, Bol. 208/E7
Orust (isl.), Swe. 96/D2
Orvieto, It. 101/K5
Orvilliers, Fr. 88/G5
Orwell (riv.), Eng, UK 91/H2
Orwigsburg, Pa, US 196/B2
Oryakhovo, Bul. 107/F4
Orzinuovi, It. 116/C2
Orzysz, Pol. 97/J5
Os, Nor. 96/A1
Osa, Rus. 119/M4
Osa, Peninsula de (pen.), CR 208/B2
Osage (riv.), Mo, US 187/J3
Osage Beach, Mo, US 187/J3
Ōsaka (pref.), Japan 132/D3
Ōsaka (int'l arpt.), Japan 135/H6
Ōsaka, Japan 135/J6
Ōsaka Castle, Japan 135/H6
Osan, SKor. 131/D4
Osasco, Braz. 213/G8
Ōsato, Japan 135/C1
Osborn (mt.), Ak, US 192/E3
Osburg, Ger. 111/F4
Osby, Swe. 96/E3
Osceola, Ar, US 188/B5
Oschersleben, Ger. 98/F2
Oschiri, It. 104/A2
Oscura (mts.), NM, US 190/B3
Osdorf, Ger. 109/G1
Osh (obl.), Kyr. 145/F5
Osh, Kyr. 145/F4
Oshamambe, Japan 134/B2
Oshawa, On, Can. 189/S8
Oshika (pen.), Japan 134/B4
Oshino, Japan 135/B3
Oshkosh, Ne, US 185/H5
Oshnovīyeh, Iran 148/F2
Oshogbo, Nga. 161/G5
Osijek, Cro. 106/D3
Osio Sotto, It. 116/C1
Osipaonica, Serb. 106/E3
Oskarshamn, Swe. 96/G3
Oskarström, Swe. 96/E3
Oskol (riv.), Rus.,Ukr. 120/F2
Oslo (cap.), Nor. 96/D2
Osmānābād, India 147/L5
Osmancık, Turk. 148/C1
Osmaneli, Turk. 107/K5
Osmaniye, Turk. 149/E1
Osnabrück, Ger. 109/F4
Osnago, It. 116/C1
Osny, Fr. 88/J4
Oso (riv.), D.R. Congo 162/A3
Oso (mt.), Ca, US 193/M12
Osogna, Swi. 115/E5
Osório, Braz. 213/B4
Osorno, Sp. 102/C1
Osorno, Chile 216/B4
Osoyoos, BC, Can. 184/D3
Ospedaletti, It. 116/A5
Ospedaletto Euganeo, It. 117/E2
Ospitaletto, It. 116/D1
Osprey (reef), Austl. 167/D2
Oss, Neth. 108/C5
Ossa (mt.), Austl. 173/C4
Ossa, Sierra de (mts.), Port. 102/B3
Osse (riv.), Nga. 161/G5
Osséja, Fr. 100/D5
Ossett, Eng, UK 93/G4
Ossi, It. 104/A2
Ossining, NY, US 197/K7
Ostashkov, Rus. 118/G4
Ostbevern, Ger. 109/E4
Ostellato, It. 117/E3
Osten, Ger. 109/G1
Osterburg, Ger. 98/F2
Osterburken, Ger. 112/C4
Österbybruk, Swe. 96/G1
Österbymo, Swe. 96/F3
Ostercappeln, Ger. 109/F4
Osterdalälven (riv.), Swe. 96/F1
Osterems (chan.), Ger. 108/D1
Östergötland (co.), Swe. 95/E4
Osterhofen, Ger. 113/G5
Osterholz-Scharmbeck, Ger. 109/F2
Osteria Grande, It. 117/E4
Osterode am Harz, Ger. 109/H5
Östersund, Swe. 95/E3
Östervåla, Swe. 96/G1
Ostfildern, Ger. 112/C5
Østfold (co.), Nor. 95/D4
Ostfriesland (reg.), Ger. 109/E2
Östhammar, Swe. 96/H1
Ostheim vor der Rhön, Ger. 112/D2
Osthofen, Ger. 112/B3
Ostia Antica (ruin), It. 104/C2
Ostiano, It. 116/D2
Ostiglia, It. 117/E2
Ostional NWR, CR 202/E4
Ostra, It. 117/G5
Östra Silen (lake), Swe. 96/E2
Ostra Vetere, It. 117/G5
Ostrach (riv.), Ger. 112/C6
Ostrava, Czh. 99/K4
Ostravský (pol. reg.), Czh. 99/J4
Ostrhauderfehn, Ger. 109/E2
Oštri Rt (cape), Mont. 106/D4
Ostricourt, Fr. 110/C3
Ostróda, Pol. 97/H5
Ostrogozhsk, Rus. 120/F2
Ostrołęka, Pol. 99/L2
Ostrov, Czh. 113/F2
Ostrov, Rus. 97/N3
Ostrów Mazowiecka, Pol. 99/L2
Ostrów Wielkopolski, Pol. 99/J3
Ostrowiec Świętokrzyski, Pol. 99/L3
Ostrzeszów, Pol. 99/J3
Ostseebad Binz, Ger. 96/E4
Ostseebad Göhren, Ger. 96/E4
Ostseebad Prerow, Ger. 96/E4
Oststeinbek, Ger. 109/H1
Ostuni, It. 105/E2
Ostwald, Fr. 112/A5
Osŭm (riv.), Bul. 107/G4
Osum (riv.), Slvk. 106/E5
Ōsumi (isls.), Japan 132/B5
Ōsumi (pen.), Japan 132/B5
Osun (state), Nga. 161/G5
Osuna, Sp. 102/C4
Osvaldo Cruz, Braz. 213/B2
Oswaldtwistle, Eng, UK 93/F4
Oswego, NY, US 188/E3
Oswego, Il, US 193/P16
Oswestry, Eng, UK 93/E6
Oświęcim (Auschwitz), Pol. 99/K3
Ōta (riv.), Japan 132/C3
Ōta, Japan 133/F2
Ōtake, Japan 132/C3
Ōtaki, Japan 133/G3
Ōtaki, Japan 135/B2
Ōtakine-yama (peak), Japan 133/G2
Otava (riv.), Czh. 101/K2
Otavalo, Ecu. 210/B4
Otavi, Namb. 163/C4
Ōtawara, Japan 133/G2
Otay, Ca, US 194/C5
Oțelu Roşu, Rom. 106/F3
Otero de Rey, Sp. 102/B1
Oteros (riv.), Mex. 200/C3
Otgon Tenger (peak), Mong. 128/G2
Othello, Wa, US 184/D4
Othis, Fr. 88/L4
Othonoí (isl.), Gre. 105/F3
Oti (riv.), Gha. 161/F4
Otjiwarongo, Namb. 163/C5
Otley, Eng, UK 93/G4
Otočac, Cro. 106/B3
Otofuke, Japan 134/C2
Otog Qi, China 128/J4
Otok, Cro. 106/D3
Ōtone, Japan 135/D1
Otopeni (int'l arpt.), Rom. 107/H3
Otoskwin (riv.), On, Can. 185/L3
Otowa, Japan 135/M6
Otra (riv.), Nor. 96/B2
Otradnyy, Rus. 121/J1
Otranto, Strait of (str.), It. 105/F2
Otrokovice, Czh. 99/J4
Otse, Bots. 164/D2
Ōtsu, Japan 135/J5
Ōtsuchi, Japan 134/B4
Ōtsuki, Japan 135/B2
Otta, Nga. 161/F5
Ottawa (cap.), On, Can. 188/F2
Ottawa, Oh, US 188/C3
Ottawa, Ks, US 187/J3
Ottawa (int'l arpt.), On, Can. 188/F2
Ottawa (isls.), Nun., Can. 181/H3
Ottawa (riv.), On, Can. 188/E2
Ottensheim, Aus. 113/H6
Otter (riv.), Eng, UK 90/C5
Otterbach, Ger. 111/G5
Otterberg, Ger. 111/G4
Otterndorf, Ger. 109/F1
Ottersberg, Ger. 109/G2
Ottershaw, Eng, UK 88/B2
Otterville, Il, US 195/G7
Ottignies-Louvain-la-Neuve, Belg. 111/D2
Öttingen im Bayern, Ger. 112/D5
Ottmarsheim, Fr. 114/D2
Ottnang am Hausruck, Aus. 113/G6
Otto, Mo, US 195/F9
Ottobeuren, Ger. 115/G2
Ottobrunn, Ger. 113/E6
Ottone, It. 116/C3
Ottosdal, SAfr. 164/D2
Ottsville, Pa, US 196/C3
Ottumwa, Ia, US 185/K5
Ottweiler, Ger. 111/G5
Otumba de Gómez Farías, Mex. 201/L7
Otuzco, Peru 214/B2
Otway (cape), Austl. 173/B3
Otway (bay), Chile 217/C7
Otway NP, Austl. 173/B3
Otwock, Pol. 99/L2
Ötztal Alps (mts.), Aus. 101/J3
Ötztaler Ache (riv.), Aus. 115/G3
Ou (mts.), Japan 134/B4
Ouachita (mts.), Ok, US 187/J4
Ouachita (riv.), Ar,La, US 187/J4
Ouadda, CAfr. 155/K6
Ouaddaï (reg.), Chad 155/J5
Ouadi Haddad (riv.), Chad 155/J4
Ouadi Rimé (riv.), Chad 155/J5
Ouagadougou (int'l arpt.), Burk. 161/E3
Ouagadougou (cap.), Burk. 161/E3
Ouahigouya, Burk. 161/E3
Ouaka (riv.), CAfr. 155/K6
Oualâta, Dhar (cliff), Mrta. 160/D2
Ouallam, Niger 161/F3
Ouanda Djallé, CAfr. 155/K6
Ouanne (riv.), Fr. 100/E3
Ouarane (pol. reg.), Mrta. 154/C3
Ouarane (reg.), Mrta. 156/C5
Ouargla (prov.), Alg. 157/G3
Ouargla, Alg. 157/G3
Ouarkziz, Jebel (mts.), Mor. 156/C3
Ouarzazate (int'l arpt.), Mor. 156/D3
Ouarzazate, Mor. 156/D3
Ouasiemsca (riv.), Qu, Can. 188/F1
Oubangui (riv.), CAfr. 155/J7
Oubritenga (prov.), Burk. 161/E3
Ouche (riv.), Fr. 114/B3
Oud-Beijerland, Neth. 108/B5
Oud-Turnhout, Belg. 108/B6
Ouda, Japan 135/J7
Oudalan (prov.), Burk. 161/E3
Ouddorp, Neth. 108/A5
Oude IJssel (riv.), Neth. 108/D5
Oude Pekela, Neth. 108/E2
Oude Westereems (chan.), Neth. 108/D1
Oudenaarde, Belg. 110/C2
Oudenbosch, Neth. 108/B5
Oudenburg, Belg. 110/C1
Oudewater, Neth. 108/B4
Oudon (riv.), Fr. 100/C3
Oudtshoorn, SAfr. 164/C4
Oued el Hadjar (well), Mali 160/E2
Oued Moulouyadeu (riv.), Mor. 154/E1
Oued Sous (riv.), Mor. 154/D1
Oued Zem, Mor. 156/D2
Ouémé (riv.), Ben. 154/F6
Ouéme (prov.), Ben. 161/F5
Ouenza, Alg. 158/L7
Ouerrha (riv.), Mor. 158/B2
Ouessé, Ben. 161/F4
Ouesso, Congo 154/J7
Ouest (prov.), Camr. 161/H5
Ouest (pt.), Haiti 203/H1
Ouest (pt.), Haiti 203/H2
Ouezzane, Mor. 158/B2
Oughterard, Ire. 89/P10
Ouham (riv.), CAfr. 154/J6
Ouidah, Ben. 161/F5
Oujda, Mor. 158/D2
Oujda (prov.), Mor. 158/C2
Oujda (Angads) (int'l arpt.), Mor. 158/D2
Oulad Teïma, Mor. 156/C3
Oulangan NP, Fin. 118/F2
Ould Birni (well), Alg. 157/E4
Oulnina (peak), Austl. 171/H5
Oulu, Fin. 118/E2
Oulu (prov.), Fin. 95/H2
Oulujärvi (lake), Fin. 95/H2
Oum El Bouaghi, Alg. 158/K7
Oum er Rbia, Oued (riv.), Mor. 156/D2
Oum er Rhia (riv.), Mor. 154/D1
Ounasjoki (riv.), Fin. 95/H2
Oupeye, Belg. 111/E2
Our (riv.), Eur. 111/E4
Ource (riv.), Fr. 100/F3
Ourcq (riv.), Fr. 98/B4
Ourcq, Canal de l' (canal), Fr. 88/K5
Øure Anarjokka NP, Nor. 95/H1
Øure Dividal NP, Nor. 95/F1
Ouricuri, Braz. 212/B2
Ourinhos, Braz. 213/B2
Ourique, Port. 102/A4
Ouro Fino, Braz. 213/G7
Ouro, Ponta do (pt.), Moz. 165/F2
Ouro Preto, Braz. 213/D2
Ouroux-sur-Saône, Fr. 114/A4
Ourthe Occidentale (riv.), Belg. 111/E3
Ourthe Orientale (riv.), Belg. 111/E3
Ouse (riv.), Eng, UK 93/H4
Oust (riv.), Fr. 100/B3
Outaouais (riv.), Qu, Can. 188/E2
Outardes (riv.), Qu, Can. 189/G1
Outardes Quatre (lake), Qu, Can. 189/G1
Outeïd Arkas (well), Mali 160/D2
Outer Hebrides (isls.), Sc, UK 89/P8
Outes, Sp. 102/A1
Outjo, Namb. 163/C5
Outlook, Sk, Can. 184/G3
Outreau, Fr. 110/A2
Outremont, Qu, Can. 189/N6
Ouvèze (riv.), Fr. 100/F4
Ouyen, Austl. 173/B2
Ouzinkie, Ak, US 192/H4
Ovacık, Turk. 148/C2
Ovacık, Turk. 148/C1
Ovada, It. 116/B3
Ovalle, Chile 215/B3
Ovana (peak), Ven. 211/E3
Ovar, Port. 102/A2
Overath, Ger. 111/G2
Overflakkee (isl.), Neth. 108/B5
Overhalla, Nor. 95/D2
Overholser (lake), Ok, US 195/M14
Overijse, Belg. 111/D2
Overijssel (prov.), Neth. 108/D3
Overijssels (riv.), Neth. 108/D4
Överkalix, Swe. 95/G2
Overland, Mo, US 195/G8
Overland Park, Ks, US 195/D6
Overlea, Md, US 196/B5
Overo (peak), Arg. 216/C5
Overpelt, Belg. 108/C6
Overton, Nv, US 186/D3
Övertorneå, Swe. 118/D2
Överum, Swe. 96/G3
Oviedo, Sp. 102/C1
Ovoca, Ire. 92/B6
Övörhangay (prov.), Mong. 128/H2
Övre Fryken (lake), Swe. 96/E1
Øvre Pasvik NP, Nor. 95/J1
Ovriá, Gre. 105/G3
Owando, Congo 154/J8
Ōwani, Japan 134/B3
Owariasahi, Japan 135/M5
Owase, Japan 132/E3
Owassa (lake), NJ, US 196/D1
Owasso, Ok, US 187/J3
Owego, NY, US 188/E3
Owen (mt.), NZ 175/S11
Owen, Austl. 171/H5
Owen, Ger. 112/C5
Owen Falls (dam), Ugan. 162/B2
Owen Roberts (int'l arpt.), UK 203/F2
Owen Sound, On, Can. 188/D2
Owenkillew (riv.), NI, UK 92/A2
Owens (riv.), Ca, US 186/C3
Owensboro, Ky, US 188/C4
Owerri, Nga. 161/G5
Owingen, Ger. 115/F2
Owings, Md, US 196/B6
Owings Mills, Md, US 196/B5
Owl Creek (mts.), Wy, US 184/F4
Owo, Nga. 161/G5
Owosso, Mi, US 188/C3
Owyhee, Nv, US 184/D5
Owyhee (lake), Or, US 186/C2
Owyhee (mts.), Id, US 186/C2
Owyhee (riv.), Id,Or, US 184/D5
Owyhee, South Fork (riv.), Nv, US 184/D5
Oxapampa, Peru 214/C3
Oxbow, Sk, Can. 185/H3
Oxbow (lake), Mi, US 193/F6
Oxelösund, Swe. 96/G2
Oxford (lake), Mb, Can. 185/K2
Oxford, Eng, UK 91/E3
Oxford (canal), Eng, UK 91/E3
Oxford, Mi, US 193/F6
Oxford, Ms, US 191/F3
Oxford, Pa, US 196/C4
Oxfordshire (co.), Eng, UK 91/E3
Oxie, Swe. 96/E4
Oxkutzcab, Mex. 202/D1
Oxnard, Ca, US 194/A2
Oxnard Beach, Ca, US 194/A2
Oxon Hill (farm), Md, US 196/A6
Oxon Hill-Glassmanor, Md, US 196/B6
Oxted, Eng, UK 88/D3
Oyabe, Japan 133/E2
Oyama, Japan 133/F2
Oyama, Japan 135/B3
Ōyamada, Japan 135/K6
Ōyamazaki, Japan 135/J6
Oyapock (riv.), Fr. 209/H3
Oye-Plage, Fr. 110/B2
Oyem, Gabon 154/H7
Oyen, Ab, Can. 184/F3
Øyer, Nor. 96/D1
Oykell (riv.), Sc, UK 89/R8
Oyo (state), Nga. 161/F4
Oyo, Nga. 161/F5
Ōyodo (riv.), Japan 132/B5
Ōyodo, Japan 135/J7
Oyón, Peru 214/B3
Oyonnax, Fr. 114/B5
Oyster Bay, NY, US 197/L8
Oyster Bay (har.), NY, US 197/L8
Oyster Bay Cove, NY, US 197/L8
Oyster Bay NWR, NY, US 197/L8
Oyten, Ger. 109/G2
Oyyl (riv.), Kaz. 145/B3
Ozamiz, Phil. 137/D6
Ozanne (riv.), Fr. 100/D2
Ozark (plat.), Mo, US 187/J3
Ozark, Ar, US 187/J4
Ozark, Al, US 191/G4
Ozark (mts.), Ar,Mo, US 183/H4
Ozarks, Lake of the (lake), Mo, US 190/E2
Ózd, Hun. 99/L4
Ozernoy (cape), Rus. 123/S4
Ozette (lake), Wa, US 184/B3
Ozhiski (lake), On, Can. 185/L3
Ozieri, It. 104/A2
Ozimek, Pol. 99/K3
Özkonak, Turk. 148/C2
Ozoir-la-Ferrière, Fr. 88/L5
Ozona, Tx, US 187/G5
Ozora, Hun. 106/D2
Ozorków, Pol. 99/K3
Ozouer-le-Voulgis, Fr. 88/L6
Ōzu, Japan 132/C4
Ozuluama de Mascareñas, Mex. 202/B1
Ozzano dell'Emilia, It. 117/E4

P

P. K. Le Rouxdam (res.), SAfr. 164/D3
Pa-an, Myan. 136/B2
Pa Sak (riv.), Thai. 141/H4
Paar (riv.), Ger. 98/F4
Paarl, SAfr. 164/L10
Paauilo, Hi, US 182/U10
Pabbi, Pak. 144/A2
Pabellón de Arteaga, Mex. 200/E4
Pabianice, Pol. 99/K3
Pābna, Bang. 143/G3
Pābna (pol. reg.), Bang. 143/G3
Pacaás Novos, PN dos, Braz. 208/F6
Pacaás Novos, Serra dos (mts.), Braz. 208/F6
Pacajá (riv.), Braz. 209/H4
Pacajus, Braz. 212/C2
Pacaltsdorp, SAfr. 164/C4
Pacaraimã (mts.), Braz. 208/F3
Pacaya Samiria, Reserva Nacional, Peru 214/C2
Paccha, Peru 214/C3
Paceco, It. 104/C4
Pachacamac (ruin), Peru 214/B4
Pachaconas, Peru 214/C4
Pachamarca (riv.), Peru 214/C4
Pachino, It. 104/D4
Pachitea (riv.), Peru 214/C3
Pachiza, Peru 214/B2
Pachmarhi, India 142/B4
Pachuca, Mex. 201/L6
Pacific (ocean) 125/N8

Pacific (range), BC, Can. 184/B3
Pacific, Wa, US 193/C3
Pacific Palisades, Hi, US 182/W13
Pacifico (mtn.), Ca, US 194/B2
Pacinan (cape), Indo. 138/D5
Pacitan, Indo. 138/D5
Paço de Arcos, Port. 103/P10
Pad Īdan, Pak. 147/J3
Padampur, India 140/D3
Padang, Indo. 138/B4
Padangpanjang, Indo. 138/B4
Padangsidempuan, Indo. 138/A3
Paddock Lake, Wi, US 193/P14
Paddock Wood, Eng, UK 88/E3
Paderborn, Il, US 195/G9
Paderborn, Ger. 109/F5
Paderno, It. 117/F1
Padiham, Eng, UK 93/F4
Padilla, Bol. 208/F7
Padina, Serb. 106/E3
Padjelanta NP, Swe. 95/F2
Padova (prov.), It. 117/E2
Padova, It. 117/E2
Padrão, Ponta do (pt.), Ang. 163/B2
Padrauna, India 142/D2
Padre (isl.), Tx, US 190/D5
Padre Island Nat'l Seashore, Tx, US 190/D5
Padrón, Sp. 102/A1
Paducah, Ky, US 188/B4
Paducah, Tx, US 187/G4
Padul, Sp. 102/D4
Padula, It. 104/D2
Paektŏk-san (peak), SKor. 131/E4
Paektu-san (peak), NKor. 131/E2
Paese, It. 117/F1
Páez, Col. 210/C3
Páez, Col. 210/C4
Pafúri, Moz. 163/F5
Pag, Cro. 106/B3
Pag (isl.), Cro. 106/B3
Pagadian, Phil. 139/F2
Pagai Selatan (isl.), Indo. 138/B4
Pagai Utara (isl.), Indo. 138/B4
Pagan, Myan. 141/F3
Pagan (isl.), NMar. 174/D3
Paganica, It. 104/C1
Page, Az, US 186/E3
Pager (riv.), Ugan. 162/B2
Pagny-sur-Moselle, Fr. 111/F6
Pagosa Springs, Co, US 186/F3
Pagwachuan (riv.), On, Can. 188/C1
Pahala, Hi, US 182/U11
Pahang (riv.), Malay. 138/B3
Pahara (lag.), Nic. 203/F3
Pahārpur, Pak. 144/A3
Pahāsu, India 142/B1
Pahlgām, India 144/C2
Pahrump, Nv, US 186/D3
Pahuatlán, Mex. 201/L6
Pahute (mesa), Nv, US 186/C3
Pai (lake), China 130/C5
Paia, Hi, US 182/T10
Paignton, Eng, UK 90/C6
Paiján, Peru 214/B2
Päijänne (lake), Fin. 95/H3
Paikü (lake), China 143/E1
Pailolo (chan.), Hi, US 182/T10
Paimio, Fin. 97/K1
Paine (peak), Chile 217/B6
Paine, Chile 216/N8
Painesville, Oh, US 188/D3
Paint (lake), Mb, Can. 185/J2
Paint Rock, Tx, US 190/D4
Painted (des.), Az, US 186/E4
Paipa, Col. 210/C3
País Vasco (aut. comm.), Sp. 102/D1
Paisley, Sc, UK 94/B5
Paita, Peru 214/A2
Paithan, India 140/C4
Pajala, Swe. 95/G2
Paján, Ecu. 210/A5
Pajęczno, Pol. 99/K3
Pakanbaru, Indo. 138/B3
Pakch'ŏn, NKor. 131/C3
Pakenham, Austl. 173/G6
Pakenham (cape), Chile 217/B6
Pákhnes (peak), Gre. 105/J5
Pakhra (riv.), Rus. 119/W9
Pakistan (ctry.) 147/H3
Paklenica NP, Cro. 106/B3
Pakokku, Myan. 141/G3
Pakowki (lake), Ab, Can. 184/F3
Pākpattan, Pak. 144/B4
Pakrac, Cro. 106/C3
Paks, Hun. 106/D2
Pakwach, Ugan. 162/A2
Pakxe, Laos 136/D3
Pala, Chad 154/H6
Pala, Ca, US 194/C4
Pala Ind. Res., Ca, US 194/C4
Palace, Mona. 116/J8
Palafrugell, Sp. 103/G2
Palagonia, It. 104/D4
Palagruža (isls.), Cro. 104/E1
Pálairos, Gre. 105/G3
Palaiseau, Fr. 88/J5
Pālakollu, India 140/D4
Palamás, Gre. 105/H3
Palamós, Sp. 103/G2
Palana, Rus. 123/R4
Palangkaraya, Indo. 138/D4
Pālanpur, India 147/K4
Palaoa (pt.), Hi, US 182/T10
Palapye, Bots. 163/E5
Palar (riv.), India 140/C5
Palas de Rey, Sp. 102/B1
Palāsbāri, India 143/H2
Palatine, Il, US 193/P15
Palatka, Fl, US 191/H4
Palau (ctry.) 174/C4
Palau We (isl.), Indo. 138/A2
Palaw, Myan. 136/B3
Palawan (isl.), Phil. 137/C6
Palawan Passage (chan.), Phil. 137/C6
Pālayankottai, India 140/C6
Palazzolo Acreide, It. 104/D4
Palazzolo dello Stella, It. 117/G1
Palazzolo sull'Oglio, It. 116/C1
Palé, EqG. 154/G8
Pale, Bosn. 106/D4
Paleleh, Indo. 139/F3
Palembang, Indo. 138/B4
Palena (riv.), Chile 216/B4
Palena, Chile 216/C4
Palencia, Sp. 102/C1
Palenque, Mex. 202/D2
Palenque, PN, Mex. 202/C2
Palermo, It. 104/C3
Palermo, NJ, US 196/D5
Palese (int'l arpt.), It. 104/E2
Palestine (lake), Tx, US 190/E3
Palestro, It. 116/B2
Pālghar, India 147/K5
P'algong-san (peak), SKor. 131/D5
P'algong-san (peak), SKor. 131/E4
Palgrave (mt.), Austl. 170/B2
Palhano, Braz. 212/C2
Palhoça, Braz. 213/B3
Pāli, India 147/K3
Pali-Aike, PN, Chile 217/C7
Paliā Kalān, India 142/C1
Palić, Serb. 106/D2
Palikea (peak), Hi, US 182/V13
Palikir (cap.), Micr. 174/E4
Palioúrion (cape), Gre. 105/H3
Palisades (cliff), NJ,NY, US 197/K8
Palisades, NY, US 197/K8
Palisades Interstate Park, NJ, US 196/D1
Palisades Park, NJ, US 197/K8
Paliseul, Belg. 111/E4
Pālitāna, India 147/K4
Palizada, Mex. 198/C4
Paljenik (peak), Bosn. 106/C3
Palk (str.), India 140/C6
Pallamallawa, Austl. 173/D1
Pallarenda, Austl. 172/B2
Pallas-Ounastunturin NP, Fin. 95/H1
Pallasca, Peru 214/B3
Pallastunturi (peak), Fin. 95/H1
Palliser (cape), NZ 175/T11
Palm Bay, Fl, US 191/H4
Palm Beach (int'l arpt.), Fl, US 191/H5
Palm City, Ca, US 194/C5
Palm Harbor, Fl, US 191/H4
Palm Island Aboriginal Settlement, Austl. 172/B2
Palm Springs, Ca, US 186/C4
Palma, Moz. 162/D5
Palma (riv.), Braz. 209/J6
Palma, Sp. 103/G3
Palma del Río, Sp. 102/C4
Palma di Montechiaro, It. 104/C4
Palma Mallorca (int'l arpt.), Sp. 103/G3
Palma Soriano, Cuba 203/H1
Palmácia, Braz. 212/C2
Palmanova, It. 117/G1
Palmar (riv.), Ven. 203/H4
Palmares, Braz. 212/D3
Palmarito, Ven. 210/D3
Palmas, Braz. 213/A3
Palmas (cape), Libr. 160/D5
Palmdale, Ca, US 194/B1
Palmeira, Braz. 213/B3
Palmeira, CpV. 151/K10
Palmeira dos Índios, Braz. 212/C3
Palmeirais, Braz. 212/B2
Palmeiras (riv.), Braz. 212/A4
Palmeiras, Braz. 212/B4
Palmeirinhas, Ponta das (pt.), Ang. 163/B2
Palmela, Port. 103/Q10
Palmer, Ak, US 192/J3
Palmer, US, Ant. 218/V
Palmer, Wa, US 193/D3
Palmer Land (phys. reg.), Ant. 218/V
Palmerston, NZ 175/S12
Palmerston (cape), Austl. 172/C3
Palmerston Atoll (atoll), CookIs. 175/J6
Palmerston North, NZ 175/T11
Palmerston NP, Austl. 172/B2
Palmerton, Pa, US 196/C2
Palmetto, Fl, US 191/H5
Palmi, It. 104/D3
Palmilla, Chile 216/C2
Palmillas (pt.), Cuba 203/F1
Palmira, Col. 210/B4
Palmital, Braz. 213/B2
Palmitas, Uru. 217/K10
Palmyra, Ut, US 195/K13
Palmyra (isl.), PacUS 175/J4
Palmyra, Pa, US 196/B3
Palmyra (Tadmur) (ruin), Syria 148/D3
Palmyras (pt.), India 140/E3
Palni, India 140/C5
Palo, Phil. 137/D5
Palo Alto, Ca, US 186/B3
Palo Alto, Pa, US 196/B2
Palo Pinto, Tx, US 187/H4
Palo Verde, PN, CR 198/D5
Palomeu (riv.), Sur. 211/H4
Palon (peak), It. 117/E1
Palos (cape), Sp. 103/E4
Palos de la Frontera, Sp. 102/B4
Palos Hills, Il, US 193/Q16
Palos Verdes (hills), Ca, US 194/F8
Palos Verdes (pt.), Ca, US 194/F8
Palos Verdes Estates, Ca, US 194/F8
Palosco, It. 116/C1
Palpalá, Arg. 215/C1
Palpetu (cape), Indo. 139/G4
Paltamo, Fin. 118/E2
Palu, Indo. 139/E4
Palu, Turk. 148/D2
Paluan, Phil. 137/D5
Palwal, India 142/A1
Pamangkat, Indo. 138/C3
Pambula, Austl. 173/D3
Pamiers, Fr. 100/D5
Pamir (riv.), Afg.,Taj. 122/H6
Pamir (reg.), China,Taj. 122/H6
Pamlico (riv.), NC, US 191/J3
Pamlico (sound), NC, US 191/J3
Pampa, Tx, US 187/G4
Pampachiri, Peru 214/C4
Pampacolca, Peru 214/C4
Pampas (plain), Arg. 216/C3
Pampas, Peru 214/C4
Pampas, Peru 214/B3
Pampas (riv.), Peru 214/C4
Pampilhosa da Serra, Port. 102/B2
Pamplona, Sp. 102/E1
Pamplona, Col. 210/C3
Pampulha (int'l arpt.), Braz. 213/D1
Pāmpur, India 144/C2
Pamukova, Turk. 107/K5
Pan de Azúcar, PN, Chile 215/B2
Panaba, Mex. 202/D1
Panabo, Phil. 137/E6
Pānāgar, India 142/B4
Panagyurishte, Bul. 107/G4
Panaitan (isl.), Indo. 138/B5
Panaji, India 147/K5
Panama (ctry.) 203/F4
Panamá (bay), Pan. 203/G4
Panamá (cap.), Pan. 203/G4
Panama (canal), Pan. 203/F4
Panama (gulf), Pan. 203/G4
Panama City, Fl, US 191/G4
Panama, Isthmus of (isth.), Pan. 203/F4
Panamá Viejo (ruin), Pan. 210/B2
Panamint (range), Ca, US 186/C3
Panao, Peru 214/B3
Panaro (riv.), It. 101/J4
Panay (isl.), Phil. 137/D5
Pancake (range), Nv, US 186/C3
Pančevo, Serb. 106/E3
Pančicev vrh (peak), Serb. 106/E4
Pancilet (res.), India 143/F4
Panciu, Rom. 107/H3
Pandamatenga, Bots. 163/E4
Pandharpur, India 147/L5
Pandino, It. 116/C2
Pando, Uru. 217/L11
Pāndoh, India 144/D4
Pandrup, Den. 96/C3
Pandua, India 143/G4
Panevėžys, Lith. 97/L4
Panfilov, Kaz. 128/D3
Pangai, Tonga 175/H6
Pangaion (peak), Gre. 105/J2
Pangani, Tanz. 162/C4
Pangani (riv.), Tanz. 162/C3
Pangkalanberandan, Indo. 138/A3
Pangkalaseang (cape), Indo. 139/F4
Pangkalpinang, Indo. 138/C4
Pangnirtung, Nun., Can. 181/K2
Panguipulli, Chile 216/B3
Panguitch, Ut, US 186/D3
Pangutaran, Phil. 139/F2
Pangutaran (isl.), Phil. 137/C6
Paniai (lake), Indo. 139/J4
Paniau (peak), Hi, US 182/R10
Pānihāti, India 143/G4
Pānīpat, India 144/D5
Paniqui, Phil. 137/D4
Panj (riv.), Afg. 147/K1
Panjwīn, Iraq 146/E1
Panke (riv.), Ger. 98/Q6
P'anmunjŏm, NKor. 131/D4
Panna, India 142/C3
Pannawonica, Austl. 170/C2
Pannikin (isl.), Austl. 172/F7
Pano Lefkara, Cyp. 149/C2
Panorama, Braz. 213/B2
Pantanal (lowland), Braz. 209/G7
Pantanal Matogrossense, PN, Braz. 209/G7
Pantelleria, It. 104/B4
Pantelleria (isl.), It. 104/C4
Pantigliate, It. 116/C2
Pantin, Fr. 88/K5
Pantoja, Peru 210/C5
Pantón, Sp. 102/B1
Pantukan, Phil. 137/E6
Pánuco (riv.), Mex. 198/B3
Pánuco, Mex. 202/B1
Panzhihua, China 141/H2
Panzós, Guat. 202/D3
Pão de Açúcar, Braz. 212/C3
Paola, It. 104/E3
Paola, Malta 104/M7
Paoli, Pa, US 196/C3
Paonia, Co, US 186/F3
Paonta Sahib, India 144/D4
Paoua, CAfr. 154/J6
Pápa, Hun. 106/C2
Papa Westray (isl.), Sc, UK 89/V14
Papagayo (gulf), CR 198/D5
Papaikou, Hi, US 182/U11
Papanduva, Braz. 213/B3
Papantla, Mex. 201/M6
Papaplaya, Peru 214/C2
Papenburg, Ger. 109/E2
Papendrecht, Neth. 108/B5
Paphos, Cyp. 149/C2
Paphos (dist.), Cyp. 149/C2
Papingut (peak), Alb. 105/G2
Papisoi (cape), Indo. 139/H4
Pappenheim, Ger. 112/D5
Papua (gulf), PNG 174/D5
Papua New Guinea (ctry.) 174/D5
Papudo, Chile 216/C2
Papunya, Austl. 171/F2
Pará (riv.), Braz. 209/H4
Pará (state), Braz. 212/A1
Para (dist.), Sur. 211/H3
Pará (falls), Ven. 211/E3
Pará de Minas, Braz. 213/C1
Para, South (riv.), Austl. 171/M8
Para Wirra NP, Austl. 171/M8
Paraburdoo, Austl. 170/C2
Paracambi, Braz. 213/K7
Paracas (pen.), Peru 214/B4
Paracas, Reserva Nacional, Peru 214/B4
Paracatu, Braz. 212/A5
Paracatu (riv.), Braz. 212/A5
Paracel (isls.), China 141/K4
Paracho de Verduzco, Mex. 200/E5
Paraćin, Serb. 106/E4
Paracuru, Braz. 212/C1
Paradhision (int'l arpt.), Gre. 148/B2
Paradip, India 140/E3
Paradis, La, US 195/P17
Paradise (valley), Az, US 195/R18
Paradise, Mo, US 195/D5
Paradise, Pa, US 196/B4
Paradise Valley, Az, US 195/S18
Paragominas, Braz. 212/A1
Paraguá (riv.), Bol. 208/F6
Paragua (riv.), Ven. 208/F2
Paraguaçu, Braz. 213/H6
Paraguaçu (riv.), Braz. 205/E4
Paraguaçu Paulista, Braz. 213/B2
Paraguai (riv.), SAm. 205/D5
Paraguaipoa, Ven. 210/D2
Paraguaná, Peninsula de (pen.), Ven. 208/D1
Paraguarí, Par. 215/E2
Paraguay (ctry.) 205/C5
Paraguay (riv.), Par. 215/E1
Paraíba (state), Braz. 212/C2
Paraíba do Sul, Braz. 213/K7
Paraíba do Sul (riv.), Braz. 213/H8
Paraibano, Braz. 212/B2
Paraibuna (riv.), Braz. 213/H8
Paraim (riv.), Braz. 212/A3
Parainen (Pargas), Fin. 97/K1
Paraíso, Mex. 202/C2
Paraíso, CR 203/F4
Paraíso do Norte de Goiás, Braz. 209/J6
Paraisópolis, Braz. 213/H7
Parakou, Ben. 161/F4
Paramaribo (cap.), Sur. 209/G2
Paramaribo (dist.), Sur. 211/H3
Parambu, Braz. 212/B2
Paramillo (peak), Col. 210/C3
Paramillo, PN, Col. 208/C2
Paramirim (riv.), Braz. 209/K6
Paramirim, Braz. 212/B4
Paramithía, Gre. 105/G3
Paramount, Ca, US 194/F8
Paramus, NJ, US 197/J8
Paramushir (isl.), Rus. 125/Q5
Paraná, Arg. 215/D3
Paranã (riv.), Braz. 209/J6
Paraná (state), Braz. 213/B3
Paraná (riv.), SAm. 215/E3
Paraná Ibicuy (riv.), Arg. 217/J10
Paraná Urariá (riv.), Braz. 211/G5
Paranaguá, Braz. 213/B3
Paranaguá, Baía de (bay), Braz. 213/B3
Paranaíba (riv.), Braz. 209/J7
Paranaíba, Braz. 213/B1
Paranapanema (riv.), Braz. 215/F1
Paranapiacaba, Serra do (mts.), Braz. 215/G2
Paranatinga (riv.), Braz. 205/D4
Paranavaí, Braz. 215/F1
Parang, Phil. 139/F2
Paraopeba, Braz. 213/C1
Parapetí (riv.), Bol. 208/F7
Parati, Braz. 213/J8
Paratico, It. 116/C1
Paratinga, Braz. 212/B4
Paratinga (riv.), Braz. 213/H8
Paray-Vieille-Poste, Fr. 88/K5
Paràzinho, Braz. 212/D2
Pārbati (riv.), India 147/L4
Parbhani, India 147/L5
Parchim, Ger. 98/F2
Parczew, Pol. 99/M3
Pardes Ḩanna-Karkur, Isr. 149/F7
Pārdi, India 147/K4
Pardo (riv.), Braz. 209/J8
Pardone (cape), SAfr. 164/D4
Pardubice, Czh. 99/H3
Pardubický (pol. reg.), Czh. 99/J4
Pare, Indo. 138/D5
Pare (mts.), Tanz. 162/C3
Parece Vela (Okino-Tori-Shima) (isl.), Japan 125/N7
Parecis (mts.), Braz. 205/C4
Parede, Port. 103/P10
Paredes de Nava, Sp. 102/C1
Paredón, Mex. 202/C2
Paredones, Chile 216/C2
Parelhas, Braz. 212/C2
Parempuyre, Fr. 100/C4
Parenda, India 140/C4
Parent (lake), Qu, Can. 188/E1
Parentis-en-Born, Fr. 100/C4
Parepare, Indo. 139/E4
Parera, Arg. 216/D2
Parets del Vallès, Sp. 103/L6
Pargny-sur-Saulx, Fr. 111/D6
Paria (riv.), Ut, US 186/E3
Paria (gulf), Trin.,Ven. 211/F2
Paria, Peninsula de (pen.), Ven. 208/F1
Pariacoto, Peru 214/B3
Pariaguán, Ven. 211/E2
Pariaman, Indo. 138/B4
Parikkala, Fin. 95/J3
Parima (riv.), Braz. 211/F4
Parima, Serra (mts.), Braz. 208/F3
Parinacota (peak), Bol. 214/D5
Parinari, Peru 214/C2
Pariñas (pt.), Peru 214/A2
Paringa, Austl. 173/B2
Parîngu Mare (peak), Rom. 107/F3
Parintins, Braz. 209/G4
Paris, Ar, US 187/J4
Paris, Tx, US 187/J4
Paris (cap.), Fr. 88/K5
Paris (dept.), Fr. 110/B6
Parita (bay), Pan. 203/F4
Park (range), Co, US 186/F2
Park (pt.), Eng, UK 90/A5
Park City, Ut, US 195/L12
Park City, Il, US 193/Q15
Park Falls, Wi, US 185/L4
Park Rapids, Mn, US 185/K4
Park Ridge, Il, US 193/Q16
Park Ridge, NJ, US 197/J7
Park River, ND, US 185/J3
Parkano, Fin. 95/G3
Parker, Tx, US 187/H4
Parker, Az, US 186/D4
Parker, Co, US 195/C3
Parkersburg, WV, US 188/D4
Parkes, Austl. 173/D2
Parkesburg, Pa, US 196/C4
Parkgate, NI, UK 92/B2
Parksdale, Mo, US 195/F9
Parkside, Pa, US 196/C4
Parkstetten, Ger. 113/F5
Parkton, Md, US 196/B4
Parkville, Mo, US 195/D5
Parkville, Md, US 196/B5
Parkville, Pa, US 196/B4
Parkway-Sacramento, Ca, US 193/L9
Parla, Sp. 103/N9
Parlakhemundi, India 140/D4
Parli, India 147/L5
Parma, Oh, US 188/D3
Parma (prov.), It. 116/C3
Parma (riv.), It. 116/D3
Parma, It. 116/D3
Parmain, Fr. 88/J4
Parnaguá, Braz. 212/A3
Parnaíba, Braz. 212/B1
Parnaíba (riv.), Braz. 205/E3
Parnamirim, Braz. 212/C3
Parnamirim, Braz. 209/L5
Parnarama, Braz. 212/B2
Parnassós (peak), Gre. 105/H3
Parnassós NP, Gre. 105/H3
Párnis (peak), Gre. 105/N8
Párnis Óros NP, Gre. 105/N8
Párnon (mts.), Gre. 105/H4
Pärnu (bay), Est. 97/L2
Pärnu, Est. 97/L2
P'aro-ho (lake), SKor. 131/D3
Paron, Fr. 100/E2
Parona di Valpolicella, It. 117/D2
Paroo (riv.), Austl. 173/C1
Páros (isl.), Gre. 105/J4
Páros, Gre. 105/J4
Parow, SAfr. 164/L10
Parowan, Ut, US 186/D3
Parpan, Swi. 115/F4
Parral, Chile 216/C3
Parras de la Fuente, Mex. 200/E3
Parrett (riv.), Eng, UK 90/D4
Parrita, CR 203/E4
Parry (isls.), NW,Nun., Can. 181/R7
Parry (bay), Nun., Can. 181/H2
Parry (chan.), Nun., Can. 180/F1
Parry Sound, On, Can. 188/D2
Parsberg, Ger. 113/E4
Parseierspitze (peak), Aus. 115/G3
Parshall, ND, US 185/H4
Parsippany-Troy Hills, NJ, US 197/H8
Parsnip (riv.), BC, Can. 184/C2
Pårtefjället (peak), Swe. 95/F2
Partenstein, Ger. 112/C2
Parthenay, Fr. 100/C3
Partille, Swe. 96/E3
Partinico, It. 104/C3
Partizansk, Rus. 129/P3
Partizánske, Slvk. 99/K4
Partridge (riv.), On, Can. 188/D1
Partūr, India 147/L5
Paru (riv.), Braz. 209/H4
Paru de Oeste (riv.), Braz. 205/D2
Paruro, Peru 214/D4
Pārvathīpuram, India 140/D4
Parys, SAfr. 164/D2
Pas-de-Calais (dept.), Fr. 110/A3
Pas de Morgins (pass), Fr. 114/C5
Pasadena, Tx, US 187/J5
Pasadena, Nf, Can. 189/K1
Pasadena, Md, US 196/B5
Pasadena, Ca, US 194/F7
Pasado (cape), Ecu. 210/A5
Pasaje, Ecu. 214/B1
Pasaman (peak), Indo. 138/B3
Pasān, India 142/D4
Pascagoula, Ms, US 191/F4
Paşcani, Rom. 107/H2
Pasching, Aus. 113/H6
Pasco, Wa, US 184/D4
Pasco (dept.), Peru 214/C3
Pascua (riv.), Chile 217/B6
Pascua, Isla de (Easter) (isl.), Chile 175/Q7
Pascuales, Ecu. 214/B1
Pasewalk, Ger. 96/E5
Pasian di Prato, It. 117/G1
Pasiano, It. 117/F1
Pasig, Phil. 137/D5
Pasinler, Turk. 148/E2
Pasión, Río de la (riv.), Guat. 202/D2
Pasłęk, Pol. 97/H4
Pasłęka (riv.), Pol. 99/L2
Pasley (cape), Austl. 170/D5
Pašman (isl.), Cro. 106/B4
Pasni, Pak. 147/H3
Paso de Indios, Arg. 216/C4
Paso de los Libres, Arg. 215/E2
Paso de los Toros, Uru. 217/K10
Paso de Ovejas, Mex. 201/N7
Paso del Macho, Mex. 201/N8
Paso del Planchón (peak), Chile 216/C2
Paso Robles (El Paso de Robles), Ca, US 186/B4
Pasrūr, Pak. 144/C3
Pass (peak), Yk, Can. 192/M3
Passa Quatro, Braz. 213/J7
Passagem Franca, Braz. 212/B2
Passaic (riv.), NJ, US 196/D2
Passaic, NJ, US 197/J8
Passau, Ger. 113/G5
Passero (pt.), It. 104/D4
Passo Fundo, Braz. 213/A4
Passo Fundo, Barragem do (res.), Braz. 213/A3
Passons, It. 117/G1
Passoré (prov.), Burk. 161/E3
Passos, Braz. 213/C2
Passwang (peak), Swi. 114/D3
Passy, Fr. 114/C6
Pastavy, Bela. 97/M4
Pastaza (riv.), Ecu.,Peru 214/B2
Pastaza (dept.), Ecu. 210/B5
Pastek (riv.), Pol. 97/J5
Pasto, Col. 210/B4
Pastol (bay), Ak, US 192/F3
Pastoriza, Sp. 102/B1
Pastos Bons, Braz. 212/A2
Pasuruan, Indo. 138/D5
Pásztó, Hun. 99/K5
Pata, Bol. 214/D4
Patagonia (phys. reg.), Arg. 216/D4
Patah (peak), Indo. 138/B4
Pātan, India 147/K4
Pātan, India 147/K4
Pataná (peak), Braz. 213/B3
Patapsco (riv.), Md, US 196/A5
Patapsco, Md, US 196/B4
Pataudi, India 144/D5
Pataz, Peru 214/B2
Patchogue, NY, US 197/E2
Paterna, Sp. 103/E3
Paternò, It. 104/D4
Paterson, NJ, US 197/J8
Pathalgaon, India 142/D4
Pathānkot, India 144/C3
Pathein (Bassein), Myan. 141/F4
Pathfinder (res.), Wy, US 184/G5
Pati, Indo. 138/D5
Patía (riv.), Col. 208/C3
Patía, Col. 210/B4
Patiāla, India 144/D4
Patikul, Phil. 139/F2
Patna, India 143/E3
Patna, Sc, UK 94/B6
Patnongon, Phil. 139/F1
Patnos, Turk. 148/E2
Pato Branco, Braz. 213/A3
Patoka (riv.), In, US 191/G2
Patos, Braz. 212/C2
Patos, Alb. 105/F2
Patos de Minas, Braz. 213/C1
Patos, Lagoa dos (lake), Braz. 215/F3
Patrai (gulf), Gre. 105/G3
Pátrai, Gre. 105/G3
Pātrasāer, India 143/F4
Patrātu, India 143/E4
Patricia (mt.), Austl. 171/F2
Patricio Lynch (isl.), Chile 217/A6
Patrocínio, Braz. 213/C1
Patscherkofel (peak), Aus. 115/H3
Pattani, Thai. 136/C5
Pattensen, Ger. 109/G4
Patti, India 144/C4
Patti, It. 104/D3
Pattoki, Pak. 144/B4
Pattukkottai, India 140/C5
Pattullo (mt.), BC, Can. 192/N4
Patuākhāli (pol. reg.), Bang. 143/G4
Patuākhāli, Bang. 143/H4
Patuca (riv.), Hon. 198/D5
Patuca (mts.), Hon. 202/E3
Patuca (pt.), Hon. 203/E3
Patuxent (riv.), Md, US 196/B5
Patuxent NWR, Md, US 196/B5
Patuxent River State Park, Md, US 196/B5
Páty, Hun. 107/Q9
Pátzcuaro, Mex. 201/E5
Pau, Fr. 100/C5
Pau Brasil, Braz. 212/C4
Pau dos Ferros, Braz. 212/C2
Paucarbamba, Peru 214/C4
Paucartambo, Peru 214/C3
Paucartambo, Peru 214/D4
Pauillac, Fr. 100/C4
Pauini (riv.), Braz. 208/E5
Paulaya (riv.), Hon. 203/E3
Paulínia, Braz. 213/F7
Paulins Kill (riv.), NJ, US 196/D2
Paulistana, Braz. 212/B3
Paullo, It. 116/C2
Paulo Afonso, Braz. 212/C3
Paulo Afonso, PN de, Braz. 212/C3
Paulo Ramos, Braz. 212/A2
Paulpietersburg, SAfr. 165/E2
Pauls Valley, Ok, US 187/H4
Paulsboro, NJ, US 196/C4
Pauma Valley, Ca, US 194/D4
Paungde, Myan. 141/G4
Pavão, Braz. 212/B5
Pavel Banya, Bul. 105/J1
Pavia (prov.), It. 116/C2
Pavia, It. 116/C2
Pavie, Fr. 100/D5
Pavlikeni, Bul. 107/G4
Pavlodar (obl.), Kaz. 145/G2
Pavlodar, Kaz. 145/G2
Pavlof (vol.), Ak, US 192/F4
Pavlohrad, Ukr. 120/E2
Pavlovo, Rus. 118/J5
Pavone Canavese, It. 116/A2
Pavone del Mella, It. 116/D2
Pavullo nel Frignano, It. 117/D4
Paw Paw, Mi, US 188/C3
Pawan (riv.), Indo. 138/D4
Pawāyan, India 142/C1
Pawhuska, Ok, US 187/H3
Pawnee (riv.), Ks, US 187/G3
Pawtucket, RI, US 189/G3
Paxoí (isl.), Gre. 105/F3
Paxson, Ak, US 192/J3
Paxton, Austl. 173/D2
Pay-Khoy (mts.), Rus. 122/G3
Payakumbuh, Indo. 138/B4
Payerne, Swi. 114/C4
Payette (riv.), Id, US 184/D5
Payne (lake), Qu, Can. 181/J3
Paynesville, Austl. 173/C3
Pays de Caux (reg.), Fr. 100/D2
Pays de France (reg.), Fr. 88/K4
Pays de la Loire (reg.), Fr. 100/C3
Paysandú, Uru. 217/J10
Payson, Az, US 186/E4
Payson, Ut, US 186/E2
Payún (peak), Arg. 216/C3
Paz (riv.), Guat. 202/D3
Paz de Ariporo, Col. 210/D3
Paz de Río, Col. 210/C3
Pazar, Turk. 148/D1
Pazar, Turk. 121/G4
Pazarcık, Turk. 148/D2
Pazardzhik, Bul. 107/G4
Pazaryeri, Turk. 120/D5
Pazin, Cro. 106/A3
Peabiru, Braz. 213/A2
Peace (riv.), BC, Can. 180/D3
Peace Memorial Park, Japan 132/C3
Peaceful Valley, Co, US 195/B2
Peachland, BC, Can. 184/D3
Peachtree City, Ga, US 191/G3
Peak Charles NP, Austl. 170/D5
Peak District NP, Eng, UK 93/G5
Peak Hill, Austl. 170/C3
Peal de Becerro, Sp. 102/D4
Peapack-Gladstone, NJ, US 196/D2
Pearblossom, Ca, US 194/C1
Pearl (har.), Hi, US 182/W13
Pearl (riv.), La,Ms, US 191/F4
Pearl, Ms, US 191/F3
Pearl and Hermes (reef), Hi, US 175/H2
Pearl Beach, Mi, US 193/G6
Pearl City, Hi, US 182/W13
Pearl River (estu.), China 137/B3
Pearl River, La, US 195/Q16
Pearl River, NY, US 197/J7
Pearland, Ca, US 194/B1
Pearsall, Tx, US 187/H5
Pearson (int'l arpt.), On, Can. 189/Q8
Pearston, SAfr. 164/D4
Peary (chan.), Nun., Can. 181/R7
Pease (riv.), Tx, US 187/G4

Pebane, Moz. 163/G4
Pebas, Peru 214/D1
Pebble (isl.), Mald. 217/E6
Peć, Kos. 106/E4
Peccia, Swi. 115/E5
Peccioli, It. 117/D5
Pécel, Hun. 107/R10
Pech de Guillaument (peak), Fr. 100/E5
Pechanga Ind. Res., Ca, US 194/C4
Pechora, Rus. 119/N2
Pechora (bay), Rus. 119/M1
Pechora (riv.), Rus. 125/C3
Peckham, Co, US 195/C2
Peconic (riv.), NY, US 197/F2
Pecos, Tx, US 190/C4
Pecos (riv.), Tx, US 190/C4
Pecq, Belg. 110/C2
Pecquencourt, Fr. 110/C3
Pécs, Hun. 106/D2
Peculiar, Mo, US 195/E6
Pecy, Fr. 88/M6
Pedasí, Pan. 203/F5
Pedder (lake), Austl. 173/C4
Pedemonte, It. 117/D2
Pedernales (riv.), Tx, US 201/F2
Pederneiras, Braz. 213/B2
Pedley, Ca, US 194/C3
Pedra Azul, Braz. 212/D5
Pedra Lume, CpV. 151/K10
Pedralva, Braz. 213/H7
Pedregal, Ven. 210/D2
Pedreguer, Sp. 103/F3
Pedreira, Braz. 213/G7
Pedreiras, Braz. 212/A2
Pedricktown, NJ, US 196/C4
Pedro (pt.), SrL. 140/D6
Pedro Avelino, Braz. 212/C2
Pedro Bay, Ak, US 192/H4
Pedro Betancourt, Cuba 203/F1
Pedro Carbo, Ecu. 210/A5
Pedro Cays (isl.), Jam. 199/F4
Pedro Ii, Braz. 212/B2
Pedro IV (isl.), Braz. 211/E4
Pedro Juan Caballero, Par. 215/E1
Pedro Leopoldo, Braz. 213/C1
Pedro Luro, Arg. 216/E3
Pedro Osório, Braz. 213/A4
Peebles, Sc, UK 94/C5
Peedamulla Abor. Land, Austl. 170/B2
Peekskill, NY, US 196/E1
Peel (inlet), Austl. 172/F6
Peel (sound), Nun., Can. 180/G1
Peel (co.), On, Can. 189/D8
Peel (riv.), Yk, Can. 180/C2
Peel, IM, UK 92/D3
Peel Fell (peak), Eng, UK 94/D6
Peene (riv.), Ger. 98/F2
Peer, Belg. 111/E1
Pegasus (bay), NZ 175/S11
Pegnitz, Ger. 113/E3
Pegnitz (riv.), Ger. 98/F4
Pego, Sp. 103/F3
Pego do Altar, Barragem de (res.), Port. 102/A3
Pegognaga, It. 117/D3
Pegwell (bay), Eng, UK 91/H4
Pehlivanköy, Turk. 107/H5
Pehowa, India 144/D5
Pehuajó, Arg. 216/E2
Pehuenche (pass), Chile 216/C2
Pei Xian, China 130/D4
Peine, Ger. 109/H4
Peipus (lake), Est.,Rus. 97/M2
Peiting, Ger. 115/G2
Peixe (riv.), Braz. 213/C2
Peixoto, Reprêsa de (res.), Braz. 213/C2
Pekalongan, Indo. 138/C5
Pekan, Malay. 138/B3
Pekan Nanas, Malay. 138/B3
Pekhora (riv.), Rus. 119/W9
Pekin, Il, US 185/L5
Pelada, Pampa (plain), Arg. 216/C3
Pelado (vol.), Mex. 201/Q10
Pelagie (isl.), It. 104/C5
Peleaga (peak), Rom. 106/F3
Pelee (isl.), On, Can. 188/D3
Pelee (pt.), On, Can. 188/D3
Pelée (peak), Mart., Fr. 199/N9
Pelham, On, Can. 189/D9
Pelham, Al, US 191/G3
Pelham, NY, US 197/K8
Pelham Bay Park, NY, US 197/K8
Pelham Manor, NY, US 197/K8
Pelhřimov, Czh. 99/H4
Pelican (mts.), Ab, Can. 184/E2
Pelican (lake), Sk, Can. 185/H2
Pelican, Ak, US 192/L4
Pelican Narrows, Sk, Can. 185/H2
Pelindã, Ponta de (pt.), GBis. 160/A4
Pelister (peak), FYROM 105/G2

Pelister NP, FYROM 105/G2
Peljekaise NP, Swe. 95/F2
Peljesac (pen.), Cro. 105/E1
Peljesec (pen.), Cro. 106/C4
Pell Lake, Wi, US 193/P14
Pélla (ruin), Gre. 105/H2
Pélla, Gre. 105/H2
Pellegrini, Arg. 216/E3
Pellestrina, It. 117/F2
Pello, Fin. 118/E2
Penns Grove, NJ, US 196/C4
Penns Park, Pa, US 196/D3
Pennsauken, NJ, US 196/C3
Pennsburg, Pa, US 196/C3
Pennsville, NJ, US 196/C4
Pennsylvania (state), US 188/E3
Penny (str.), Nun., Can. 181/S7
Penobscot (riv.), Me, US 189/G2
Penola, Austl. 173/B3
Peñón Blanco, Mex. 200/D3
Penon de Al Hoceima (isl.), Sp. 158/C2
Penonomé, Pan. 203/F4
Penrhyn Mawr (pt.), Wal, UK 92/D6
Penrhyn Mawr (pt.), IM, UK 92/D5
Penrith, Eng, UK 93/F2
Pensacola, Fl, US 191/G4
Pensacola (mts.), Ant. 218/X
Pense, Sk, Can. 185/G3
Penshurst, Austl. 173/B3
Pentagon Fed. Govt. Res., Va, US 196/A6
Pentecost (isl.), Van. 174/F6
Pentecoste, Braz. 212/C1
Penteleu (peak), Rom. 107/H3
Penthalaz, Swi. 114/C4
Penticton, BC, Can. 184/D3
Pentire (pt.), Eng, UK 90/B5
Pentland, Austl. 172/B3
Pentland (hills), Sc, UK 94/C5
Pentland Firth (inlet), Sc, UK 89/V14
Peñuelas, PN, Chile 216/N8
Penwith (pen.), Eng, UK 90/A6
Penza, Rus. 121/H1
Penzance, Eng, UK 90/A6
Penzberg, Ger. 115/H2
Penzenskaya Oblast, Rus. 121/G1
Penzhina (riv.), Rus. 123/S3
Penzhina (bay), Rus. 123/S3
Penzing, Ger. 115/G1
Peoria, Az, US 195/R18
Pepe (cape), Cuba 203/F1
Pepeekeo, Hi, US 182/U11
Pepeekeo (pt.), Hi, US 182/U11
Pepinster, Belg. 111/E2
Pequannock, NJ, US 197/H8
Pequeña Isla del Maíz (isl.), Nic. 203/F3
Pequest (riv.), NJ, US 196/D2
Pench (riv.), India 142/B5
Perabumulih, Indo. 138/B4
Perales (riv.), Sp. 103/M9
Peralta, Sp. 102/E1
Pérama, Gre. 105/J5
Pérama, Gre. 105/N9
Percé, Qu, Can. 189/H1
Percée (peak), Fr. 114/C6
Perche, Collines du (hills), Fr. 100/D2
Percival (lakes), Austl. 170/E2
Pendleton, Or, US 184/D4
Percy Isles (chan.), Austl. 172/C3
Perdekop, SAfr. 165/E2
Pérdhika, Gre. 105/G3
Perdida (riv.), Braz. 212/A3
Perdido (mtn.), Sp. 103/F1
Peregian Beach, Austl. 172/D4
Pereira, Col. 208/C3
Pereira Barreto, Braz. 213/B2
Perelló, Sp. 103/F2
Perenjori, Austl. 170/B4
Peretola (int'l arpt.), It. 117/E5
Pergamino, Arg. 216/E2
Pergamum (ruin), Turk. 148/A2
Pergine Valsugana, It. 115/H5
Péribonca (riv.), Qu, Can. 189/G1
Perico, Cuba 203/F1
Pericos, Mex. 200/D3
Pericos, Mex. 200/D4
Périgueux, Fr. 100/D4
Périgny, Sierra de (mts.), Col. 208/D2
Peristéra (isl.), Gre. 105/H3
Peristéri, Gre. 105/N8
Perito Moreno, Arg. 216/C4
Perito Moreno, PN, Arg. 215/B6
Perkasie, Pa, US 196/C3

Pennine Alps (mts.), Swi. 101/G4
Pennine Chain (mts.), Eng, UK 93/F2
Pennington, NJ, US 196/D3
Pennino (peak), It. 101/K5
Penns Creek (mtn.), Pa, US 196/A2
Perl, Ger. 111/F5
Perlas (lag.), Nic. 198/E5
Perlas (pt.), Nic. 203/F3
Perleberg, Ger. 98/F2
Perlez, Serb. 106/E3
Perlis (state), Malay. 136/B5
Perm', Rus. 119/N4
Permskaya Oblast, Rus. 119/N4
Pérmet, Alb. 105/G2
Pernambuco (state), Braz. 212/C3
Pernate, It. 116/B2
Pernes-les-Fontaines, Fr. 100/F4
Pernik, Bul. 106/F4
Perniö, Fin. 97/K1
Peron (pen.), Austl. 170/B3
Péronne, Fr. 110/C3
Perote, Mex. 201/M7
Pérouges, Fr. 114/B6
Perpignan, Fr. 100/E5
Perray (riv.), Fr. 88/H6
Perrigny, Fr. 114/B4
Perris (res.), Ca, US 194/C3
Perris State Rec. Area, Ca, US 194/C3
Perros-Guirec, Fr. 100/B2
Perrot, Île (isl.), Qu, Can. 189/N7
Perry (riv.), Nun., Can. 180/F2
Perry, Fl, US 191/H4
Perry, Ga, US 191/H3
Perry, Ok, US 187/H3
Perry (co.), Pa, US 196/A3
Perry, Ut, US 195/J11
Perry Hall, Md, US 196/B5
Perryton, Tx, US 187/G3
Perryville, Ak, US 192/G4
Perryville, Md, US 196/B4
Persan, Fr. 88/J4
Persian (gulf), Asia 146/E3
Perstorp, Swe. 96/E3
Perth, Austl. 170/K6
Perth, Austl. 173/C4
Perth (int'l arpt.), Austl. 170/K6
Perth, On, Can. 188/E2
Perth, Sc, UK 94/C4
Perth Amboy, NJ, US 197/H9
Perth nd Kinross (pol. reg.), Sc, UK 94/C4
Perth Zoo, Austl. 170/K6
Pertuis, Fr. 100/F5
Pertuis Breton (inlet), Fr. 100/C3
Pertusato (cape), Fr. 104/A2
Peru (ctry.) 214/C3
Peru, Il, US 185/L5
Peru, In, US 188/C3
Perucáčko (lake), Bosn. 106/D4
Perugia, It. 101/K5
Peruíbe, Braz. 213/G9
Peruque, Mo, US 195/F8
Perushtitsa, Bul. 107/G4
Péruwelz, Belg. 110/C2
Pervari, Turk. 148/F2
Pervomays'k, Ukr. 107/K1
Pervomays'k, Rus. 119/J5
Pervomaysk, Rus. 119/J5
Pervoural'sk, Rus. 119/N4
Perwez, Belg. 111/D2
Péry, Swi. 114/D3
Pesa (riv.), It. 117/E5
Pesagi (peak), Indo. 138/B4
Pésaro, It. 117/F5
Pesaro e Urbino (prov.), It. 117/F5
Pescadores (Penghu) (isls.), China 137/C3
Pescantina, It. 117/D2
Pescara, It. 104/D1
Pescara (riv.), It. 104/C4
Peschanyy (cape), Kaz. 121/J4
Pesch (riv.), It. 117/D5
Pescia, It. 117/D5
Peseux, Swi. 114/C4
Pesha (riv.), Rus. 119/L2
Peshawar, Pak. 144/A2
Peshawar (int'l arpt.), Pak. 144/A2
Peshtera, Bul. 107/G4
Peshtigo, Wi, US 185/M4
Peshtigo (riv.), Wi, US 188/B2
Pesmes, Fr. 114/B3
Peso da Régua, Port. 102/B2
Pesqueira, Braz. 212/C3
Pessac, Fr. 100/C4
Pest (prov.), Hun. 106/D2
Pestovskoye (lake), Rus. 119/W9
Pestovo, Rus. 118/G4
Petah Tiqwa, Isr. 149/F7
Petal, Ms, US 191/F4
Petalión (gulf), Gre. 105/J4
Petaluma (riv.), Ca, US 193/J10
Pétange, Lux. 111/E4
Petare, Ven. 208/E1
Pétas, Gre. 105/G3
Petatlán (riv.), Mex. 200/D4
Petatlán, Mex. 201/E5
Petauke (riv.), Zam. 163/F3
Petawawa (riv.), On, Can. 188/E2
Petawawa, On, Can. 188/E2
Peten Itzá (lake), Guat. 202/D2
Petenwell (lake), Wi, US 185/L4
Peter (isl.), Nor. 218/U
Peterborough, Austl. 171/H5

Peterborough, On, Can. 188/E2
Peterborough, Eng, UK 91/F1
Peterborough (co.), Eng, UK 91/F1
Peterhead, Sc, UK 94/E1
Peterlee, Eng, UK 93/G2
Petermann Abor. Land, Austl. 171/F3
Peteroa (vol.), Chile 216/C2
Petersaurach, Ger. 112/D4
Petersberg, Ger. 112/C1
Petersburg, Ak, US 192/M4
Petersburg, Ger. 109/F4
Petershagen, Ger. 98/D6
Petershausen, Ger. 113/E6
Peterson, Ut, US 195/K11
Pétervására, Hun. 99/L4
Petilia Policastro, It. 104/E3
Pétionville, Haiti 203/H2
Petit Goâve, Haiti 203/H2
Petit Lac Manicouagan (lake), Qu, Can. 189/H1
Petit Loango, PN du, Gabon 162/A5
Petit-Noir, Fr. 114/B4
Petit Rosne (riv.), Fr. 88/J4
Petitcodiac, NB, Can. 189/H2
Petite Miquelon (isl.), StP., Fr. 189/K2
Petite Rivière de l'Artibonite, Haiti 203/H2
Petite Rivière Noire (peak), Mrts. 165/T15
Petite-Rosselle, Fr. 111/F5
Petitt Morin (riv.), Fr. 100/E2
Petketjärven NP, Fin. 118/F3
Petlåd, Rom. 107/H3
Petlalcingo, Mex. 202/B2
Peto, Mex. 202/D1
Petorca, Chile 216/C2
Petoskey, Mi, US 188/C2
Petra (Batrã') (ruin), Jor. 149/D4
Petra (isls.), Rus. 123/M2
Petrel, Sp. 103/E3
Petrella (peak), It. 104/C2
Petrella (peak), Kiri. 175/H5
Petrich, Bul. 107/F4
Petrified Forest NP, Az, US 195/S19
Petrila, Rom. 107/F3
Petrolândia, Braz. 212/C3
Petrolina, Braz. 212/B3
Petropavl, Kaz. 145/E2
Petropavlovsk-Kamchatskiy, Rus. 123/R4
Petrópolis, Braz. 213/K7
Petrovaradin, Serb. 106/D3
Petrovsk, Rus. 121/H1
Petrovsk-Zabaykal'skiy, Rus. 128/J1
Petrozavodsk, Rus. 118/G3
Petrus Steyn, SAfr. 164/E2
Petrusburg, SAfr. 164/D3
Petrusville, SAfr. 164/D3
Pettenbach, Aus. 113/H7
Petteril (riv.), Eng, UK 93/F2
Petzeck (peak), Aus. 101/K3
Peuerbach, Aus. 113/G6
Peulik (mt.), Ak, US 192/G4
Peumo, Chile 216/N9
Pevely, Mo, US 195/G9
Pewaukee (lake), Wi, US 193/X13
Pewaukee, Wi, US 193/P13
Peyrehorade, Fr. 100/C5
Peza (riv.), Rus. 119/K2
Pézenas, Fr. 100/E5
Pfaffenhausen, Ger. 115/G1
Pfaffenhofen an der Ilm, Ger. 112/D6
Pfaffenhofen an der Ilm, Ger. 113/E5
Pfaffenhofen, Ger. 113/E5
Pfäffikon, Swi. 115/E3
Pfaffing, Ger. 115/H1
Pfaffnau, Swi. 114/D3
Pfahl (ridge), Ger. 113/F4
Pfälzer Wald (mts.), Ger. 111/G5
Pfälzerwald (mts.), Ger. 112/A4
Pfarrhof Esternberg, Aus. 113/G5
Pfarrkirchen, Ger. 113/F5
Pfatter, Ger. 113/F5
Pfeffenhausen, Ger. 113/E5
Pfettrach (riv.), Ger. 113/E5
Pfieffe (riv.), Ger. 109/G6
Pfinztal, Ger. 112/B5
Pforzheim, Ger. 112/B5
Pfreimd (riv.), Ger. 113/F3
Pfronstetten, Ger. 115/F1
Pfronten, Ger. 115/G2
Pfullendorf, Ger. 115/F2
Pfullingen, Ger. 112/C6
Pfunds, Aus. 115/G3
Pfungstadt, Ger. 112/B4
Phagwāra, India 144/C4
Phalauda, India 144/D5
Phalempin, Fr. 110/C2
Phālia, Pak. 144/B3
Phalodi, India 147/K3

Phalsbourg, Fr. 111/G6
Phan Rang, Viet. 136/E4
Phan Thiet, Viet. 136/E4
Phanat Nikhom, Thai. 136/C3
Phang Hoei (range), Thai. 136/C3
Phangnga, Thai. 136/B4
Phanom Dongrak (mts.), Thai. 141/H5
Pharr, Tx, US 190/D5
Phatthalung, Thai. 136/C5
Phaya Fo (peak), Thai. 136/C3
Phayao, Thai. 136/B3
Phelan, Ca, US 194/C2
Phenix City, Al, US 191/G3
Phet Buri, Thai. 136/B3
Phetchabun, Thai. 136/C3
Phichit, Thai. 136/C3
Philadelphia, Ms, US 191/F3
Philadelphia, Pa, US 196/C4
Philadelphia (int'l arpt.), Pa, US 196/C4
Philip, SD, US 185/H4
Philip S.W. Goldson (int'l arpt.), Belz. 202/D2
Philippeville, Belg. 111/D3
Philippi, WV, US 188/D4
Philippines (ctry.) 137/D5
Philippsburg, Ger. 112/B4
Philipsburg, Mt, US 184/E4
Philipsdam (dam), Neth. 108/B5
Philipstown, SAfr. 164/D3
Phillaur, India 144/C4
Phillipsburg, NJ, US 196/C2
Phimai (ruin), Thai. 136/C3
Phitsanulok, Thai. 136/C3
Phnom Penh (Phnum Pénh) (cap.), Camb. 136/D4
Phnum Penh (int'l arpt.), Camb. 136/D4
Pho (pt.), Thai. 136/C5
Phoenix (cap.), Az, US 195/R19
Phoenix, La, US 195/Q17
Phoenix (isls.), Kiri. 175/H5
Phoenix Park, Ire. 92/B5
Phoenix Sky Harbor (int'l arpt.), Az, US 195/S19
Phoenixville, Pa, US 196/C3
Phongsali, Laos 141/H3
Phou Bia (peak), Laos 136/C2
Phou Huatt (peak), Viet. 141/H3
Phou Loi (peak), Laos 141/H3
Phou Xai Lai Leng (peak), Laos 136/D2
Phra Nakhon Si Ayutthaya, Thai. 136/C3
Phra Thong (isl.), Thai. 136/B4
Phrae, Thai. 136/C2
Phu Hin Rong Kla NP, Thai. 136/C2
Phu Kradung NP, Thai. 136/C2
Phu Luong (peak), Viet. 141/H3
Phu Phan NP, Thai. 136/D2
Phu Qua NP, Thai. 136/C2
Phu Quoc (isl.), Viet. 141/H5
Phu Tho, Viet. 141/J3
Phuket, Thai. 141/G6
Phuket (isl.), Thai. 136/B5
Phularwan, Pak. 144/B3
Phūlpur, India 142/D3
Piaçabuçu, Braz. 212/C3
Piacenza (prov.), It. 116/C2
Piacenza, It. 116/C2
Piadena, It. 116/D2
Pian di Serra (peak), It. 117/F6
Pian-Upe Game Rsv., Ugan. 162/B2
Piancó, Braz. 212/C2
Piancastagnaio, It. 104/B1
Pianella, It. 104/D2
Pianello val Tidone, It. 116/C3
Pianezza, It. 116/B2
Piangipane, It. 117/F4
Pianoro, It. 117/E4
Pianosa (isl.), It. 104/A1
Piarco (int'l arpt.), Trin. 211/F2
Piaseczno, Pol. 99/L2
Piatra Neamt, Rom. 107/H2
Piatra Ligure, It. 116/B4
Piauí (riv.), Braz. 212/B3
Piauí (state), Braz. 212/B2
Piave (riv.), It. 101/K3
Piazza, It. 116/D1
Piazza, It. 116/D1
Piazza al Sterchio, It. 116/D4
Piazza Armerina, It. 104/D4
Piazza Brembana, It. 115/F6
Piazzola sul Brenta, It. 117/E2
Pic (riv.), On, Can. 188/C1
Pic de Nore (peak), Fr. 100/E5
Pic d'Orhy (peak), Fr. 100/C5
Pic du Canigou (peak), Fr. 100/E5
Pica, Chile 208/E8
Picacho del Centinela (peak), Mex. 200/E2
Picachos, Cerro Dos (peak), Mex. 200/B2
Picardie (pol. reg.), Fr. 110/B4
Picardy (reg.), Fr. 110/B4
Picatinny Arsenal, NJ, US 196/D2
Picayune, Ms, US 191/F4
Piccolo (lag.), It. 105/E2

Pichacani, Peru 214/D5
Pichanal, Arg. 215/D1
Pichidegua, Chile 216/N9
Pichilemu, Chile 216/N9
Pichincha (dept.), Ecu. 210/B4
Pichincha, Ecu. 210/B5
Pichl bei Wels, Aus. 113/G6
Pichor, India 142/B3
Pichucalco, Mex. 202/C2
Pickens, Ms, US 187/K4
Pickering, On, Can. 189/R8
Pickering, Vale of (valley), Eng, UK 93/H3
Pickle Lake, On, Can. 185/L3
Picnic Bay, Austl. 172/B2
Pico (isl.), Azor., Port. 103/S12
Pico da Neblina, PN do, Braz. 208/F3
Pico de Orizaba, PN, Mex. 201/M7
Pico Rivera, Ca, US 194/F8
Pico Truncado, Arg. 216/D5
Picos, Braz. 212/B2
Picota, Peru 214/B2
Picsi, Peru 214/B2
Pili (peak), Phil. 137/D5
Pilibhit, India 142/B1
Pilica (riv.), Pol. 99/L3
Pilion (peak), Gre. 105/H3
Pilis, Hun. 106/D2
Pilis (peak), Hun. 107/R9
Pilis (mts.), Hun. 107/R9
Piliscsaba, Hun. 107/Q9
Pilisvörösvár, Hun. 107/Q9
Pilkhua, India 144/D5
Pillar (cape), Austl. 173/C4
Pillar (peak), SrL 140/D6
Pilligá, Austl. 173/C1
Pillon, Col du (pass), Swi. 114/D5
Pillow, Pa, US 196/B2
Pilões, Serra dos (mtn.), Braz. 212/A5
Pilos, Gre. 105/G4
Pilot (mtn.), Tn, US 188/C4
Pilot Point, Ak, US 192/G4
Pilot Station, Ak, US 192/F3
Pilsting, Ger. 113/F5
Pima, Az, US 186/E4
Pimpri-Chinchwad, India 147/K5
Piña (pt.), Pan. 203/G5
Pináculo (peak), Arg. 217/B6
Pinamar, Arg. 217/F3
Pinang (cape), Malay. 138/A2
Pinang (isl.), Malay. 138/A2
Pinar del Río, Cuba 203/F1
Pınarbaşı, Turk. 148/D2
Pınarhisar, Turk. 107/H5
Piñas, Ecu. 214/B1
Pinatubo (mt.), Phil. 137/D4
Pinawa, Mb, Can. 185/K3
Pincher Creek, Ab, Can. 184/E3
Pinckneyville, Il, US 185/L7
Pinconning, Mi, US 188/D3
Pincota, Rom. 106/E2
Pincourt, Qu, Can. 189/N7
Pińczów, Pol. 99/L3
Pind Dādan Khān, Pak. 144/B4
Pindamonhangaba, Braz. 213/H7
Pindaré (riv.), Braz. 209/J4
Pindaré-Mirim, Braz. 212/A1
Pindhos NP, Gre. 105/G3
Pindi Bhattiān, Pak. 144/B4
Pindi Gheb, Pak. 144/B3
Pindobaçu, Braz. 212/B3
Pindus (mts.), Gre. 105/G3
Pindwāra, India 147/K4
Pine Barrens (phys. reg.), NJ, US 196/D4
Pine Bluffs, Wy, US 185/G5
Pine Creek (pt.), Ct, US 197/E1
Pine Falls, Mb, Can. 185/J3
Pine Grove, It. 116/A5
Pine Hill, NJ, US 196/D4
Pine Island, Mn, US 188/A2
Pine Island Bay (flat), Ant. 218/S
Pine Lawn, Mo, US 195/G8
Pine Point, NW, Can. 180/E2
Pine Ridge, SD, US 185/H5
Pine, South Branch (riv.), Mi, US 193/G6
Pine, The (hills), Mi, US 185/G6
Pine Vergonte, It. 115/E6
Pinecliff (lake), NJ, US 197/H7
Pinecliffe, Co, US 195/B3
Pinedale, Wy, US 184/F5
Pinega (riv.), Rus. 122/E3
Pineimuta (riv.), On, Can. 185/L2

Pinelands, SAfr. 164/L10
Piñera, Uru. 217/K10
Pinerolo, It. 101/G4
Pinetown, SAfr. 165/E3
Pineuilh, Fr. 100/D4
Pineview (res.), Ut, US 195/K11
Pineville, La, US 187/J5
Pinewood Springs, Co, US 195/B2
Ping (riv.), Thai. 141/G4
Ping Chau (isl.), China 129/V9
Pingbian Miaozu Zizhixian, China 141/H3
Pingding, China 130/C3
Pingdingshan, China 130/C4
Pingdu, China 130/D3
Pingelap (riv.), Braz. 174/F4
Pingelly, Austl. 170/C5
Pinggu, China 130/H6
Pingguo, China 141/J3
Pinghe, China 137/C3
Pinghu, China 130/L9
Pingjiang, China 137/B2
Pingjing (pass), China 130/C5
Pingle, China 141/K3
Pinglu, China 130/B4
Pinglu, China 130/C3
Pingnan, China 137/B3
Pingquan, China 130/D2
Pingshan, China 130/C3
Pingshun, China 130/C3
Pingtan, China 137/C2
Pingtang, China 141/J2
P'ingtung, Tai. 137/D3
Pingxiang, China 141/K2
Pingxiang, China 141/J3
Pingxing Guan (pass), China 130/C3
Pingyao, China 130/C3
Pingyi, China 130/D4
Pingyin, China 130/D3
Pingyu, China 130/C4
Pingyuan, China 130/D3
Pinhal, Braz. 213/G7
Pinhal Novo, Port. 103/Q10
Pinhão, Braz. 213/B3
Pinheiro, Braz. 212/A1
Pinheiros, Braz. 212/B5
Pinhel, Port. 102/B2
Piniós (riv.), Gre. 105/G4
Pinjar (lake), Austl. 170/K6
Pinjarra, Austl. 170/B5
Pink, Ok, US 195/N15
Pinkafeld, Aus. 106/C2
Pinkawillinie Conservation Park, Austl. 171/G7
Pinkegat (chan.), Neth. 108/C2
Pinnacles Nat'l Mon., Ca, US 186/B3
Pinnaroo, Austl. 171/J5
Pinnau (riv.), Ger. 109/G1
Pinneberg, Ger. 109/G1
Pino Hachado (pass), Arg. 216/C3
Pino Torinese, It. 116/A2
Pinole, Ca, US 193/K10
Pinon Hills, Ca, US 194/C2
Pinos (mt.), Ca, US 186/C4
Pinos, Mex. 201/E4
Pinos, Isla de (Isla de la Juventud) (isl.), Cuba 198/E3
Pinos-Puente, Sp. 102/D4
Pinoso, Sp. 103/E3
Pins, Ile des (isl.), NCal. 174/F7
Pinsdorf, Aus. 113/G7
Pinsk, Bela. 120/C1
Pinta, Isla (isl.), Ecu. 214/E6
Pinto, Sp. 103/N9
Pinto, Chile 216/C3
Pinzolo, It. 115/G5
Pio Ix, Braz. 212/B2
Pio Xii, Braz. 212/A1
Piobbico, It. 117/F5
Pioche, Nv, US 186/D3
Piombino, It. 101/J5
Piombino Dese, It. 117/F1
Pioneer World, Austl. 170/L7
Pioner (isl.), Rus. 122/J2
Pionki, Pol. 99/L3
Piorini (riv.), Braz. 208/F4
Piorini (lake), Braz. 211/F5
Piota (riv.), It. 116/B3
Piotrków Trybunalski, Pol. 99/K3
Piove di Sacco, It. 117/E2
Piovene-Rocchette, It. 117/E1
Piparia, India 142/B4
Pipe Spring Nat'l Mon., Az, US 195/B2
Piper, Ks, US 195/D5
Pipersville, Pa, US 196/C3
Pipestone (riv.), On, Can. 180/G3
Piplan, Pak. 144/A3
Pipmuacan (res.), Qu, Can. 181/J1
Pippingarra Abor. Land, Austl. 170/C2
Pipra, India 142/D3
Pipraich, India 142/D2
Piqua, Oh, US 188/D3
Piquet Carneiro, Braz. 212/C2
Piquiri (riv.), Braz. 209/H7
Pir Mahal, Pak. 144/B4

Pir Panjal (range), India 144/C3
Piracanjuba, Braz. 213/B1
Piracicaba, Braz. 213/C2
Piracuruca, Braz. 212/B1
Pirae-bong (peak), NKor. 131/C2
Piraí, Braz. 213/K7
Piraí do Sul, Braz. 213/B3
Piraiévs, Gre. 105/N9
Piraju, Braz. 213/B2
Pirajuí, Braz. 213/B2
Pirámide (peak), Chile 217/B6
Piran, Slov. 117/G1
Pirané, Arg. 215/E2
Piranga (riv.), Braz. 213/D2
Piranhas (riv.), Braz. 209/L5
Piranji (riv.), Braz. 212/C2
Pirapemas, Braz. 212/A1
Pirapora, Braz. 212/A5
Pirapózinho, Braz. 213/B2
Pirarajá, Uru. 217/G2
Pirássununga, Braz. 213/C2
Pires do Rio, Braz. 213/B1
Pirgos, Gre. 105/G4
Pirgos, Gre. 105/J5
Piriápolis, Uru. 217/G2
Pirin (mts.), Bul. 107/F5
Pirin (peak), Bul. 107/F5
Pirin NP, Bul. 107/F5
Piripiri, Braz. 212/B2
Piritiba, Braz. 212/B3
Piritu, Ven. 210/D2
Pirkkala, Fin. 97/K1
Pirmasens, Ger. 111/G5
Pirna, Ger. 99/G3
Piro, India 143/E3
Pirot, Serb. 106/F4
Pirre (mtn.), Pan. 203/G5
Pirthipur, India 142/B3
Piru (lake), Ca, US 194/B1
Piru, Ca, US 194/B2
Piryíon, Gre. 105/J3
Pisa, It. 116/D5
Pisa (prov.), It. 117/D6
Pisac, Peru 214/D4
Pisanino (peak), It. 116/D4
Pisau (cape), Malay. 139/E2
Pisba, PN, Col. 210/C3
Piscataway, Md, US 196/B6
Piscataway, NJ, US 196/D2
Pisco (riv.), Peru 208/C6
Pisco, Peru 214/B4
Piscobamba, Peru 214/B3
Pisek (peak), Czh. 113/H3
Pisek, Czh. 113/H4
Pishan, China 128/C4
Pishin, Pak. 147/J2
Pishin, Iran 147/H3
Piskavica, Bosn. 106/C3
Pisoc (peak), Swi. 115/G4
Pisogne, It. 116/D1
Pissis (peak), Arg. 215/C2
Pistakee (lake), Il, US 193/P15
Pisticci, It. 104/E2
Pistoia (prov.), It. 117/D5
Pistoia, It. 117/D5
Pisuerga (riv.), Sp. 102/C1
Pisz, Pol. 99/L2
Pit (riv.), Ca, US 186/B2
Pitanga, Braz. 213/B3
Pitangui, Braz. 213/B2
Pitcairn (isl.), Pitc. 175/N7
Pitcairn Islands (dpcy.), UK 175/N7
Piteå, Swe. 95/G2
Piteälven (riv.), Swe. 95/F2
Pitești, Rom. 107/G3
Pithion, Gre. 105/K2
Pithoragarh, India 142/C1
Pitigliano, It. 104/B1
Pitiquito, Mex. 200/C2
Pitjantjatjara Abor. Lands, Austl. 171/F3
Pitkas Point, Ak, US 192/F3
Pitlochry, Sc, UK 94/C3
Pitman, NJ, US 196/C4
Pitmedden, Sc, UK 94/D2
Pitomača, Cro. 106/C3
Piton de la Fournaise (peak), Reun., Fr. 165/S15
Piton des Neiges (peak), Reun., Fr. 165/S15
Pitrufquén, Chile 216/B3
Pitt Water (bay), Austl. 172/H8
Pittenweem, Sc, UK 94/C3
Pittsburg, Ks, US 187/J3
Pittsburgh, Pa, US 188/E3
Pittsfield, Me, US 189/G2
Pittsfield, Ma, US 188/F3
Pittston, Pa, US 196/C3
Pittstown, NJ, US 196/C2
Pittsworth, Austl. 172/C4
Pitzbach (riv.), Aus. 115/G4
Piúí, Braz. 213/D2
Piui (riv.), It. 117/F3
Piumazzo, It. 117/E3
Piura, Peru 214/A2
Piura (dept.), Peru 214/A2
Pivdenny Buh (riv.), Ukr. 120/D2
Pivijay, Col. 210/C2
Pixoyal, Mex. 198/D4
Piz d'Err (peak), Swi. 115/F4
Pizacoma, Peru 214/D5
Pizarra, Sp. 102/C4
Pizhma (riv.), Rus. 119/K4
Pizol (peak), Swi. 115/F4

Pizzighettone, It. 116/C2
Pizzo, It. 104/E3
Pizzo dei Tre Signori (peak), It. 115/F6
Pizzo della Presolana (peak), It. 115/G5
Pizzo di Coca (peak), It. 115/G5
Pizzo di Vogorno (peak), Swi. 115/E5
Pizzuto (peak), It. 104/C1
Placentia, Nf, Can. 189/L2
Placentia (bay), Nf, Can. 189/L2
Placentia, Ca, US 194/G8
Placer, Phil. 137/E6
Placer (co.), Ca, US 193/M9
Placetas, Cuba 203/G1
Plachkovtsi, Bul. 107/G4
Plaffeien, Swi. 114/D4
Plai Mat (riv.), Thai. 136/C3
Plaidt, Ger. 111/G3
Plailly, Fr. 88/K4
Plain City, Ut, US 195/J11
Plain Dealing, La, US 187/J4
Plaine (riv.), Fr. 114/C1
Plainfield, NJ, US 197/H9
Plainfield, Il, US 193/P16
Plains, Tx, US 187/G4
Plains, Pa, US 196/C1
Plainsboro, NJ, US 196/D3
Plainview, Tx, US 187/G4
Plainview, Mn, US 188/A2
Plainview, NY, US 197/M8
Plaisir, Fr. 88/H5
Plan-les-Ouates, Swi. 114/C5
Planá, Czh. 113/F3
Plana Cays (isls.), Bahm. 203/H1
Planaltina, Braz. 212/A4
Plancher-Bas, Fr. 114/C2
Plancher-les-Mines, Fr. 114/C2
Plandište, Serb. 106/E3
Planeta Rica, Col. 210/C2
Planken, Lcht. 115/F3
Plant City, Fl, US 191/H4
Plantation, Fl, US 191/H5
Plaquemines (parish), La, US 195/Q17
Plasencia, Sp. 102/B2
Plasy, Czh. 113/G3
Plata (estu.), Arg.,Uru. 217/K11
Platani (riv.), It. 104/C4
Plate Taile, Barrage de la (dam), Belg. 111/D3
Plateau (state), Nga. 161/H4
Plati, Gre. 105/H2
Platinum, Ak, US 192/F4
Plato, Col. 210/C2
Platón Sánchez, Mex. 202/B1
Platte (riv.), Ne, US 187/H2
Platte City, Mo, US 195/D5
Platte, North (riv.), Ne,Wy, US 187/G2
Platte, South (riv.), Co, US 187/G2
Platteville, Co, US 195/C2
Plattling, Ger. 113/F5
Plattsburgh, NY, US 188/F2
Plauen, Ger. 113/F1
Plav, Serb. 106/D4
Plavna Dadaint (peak), Swi. 115/G4
Playa de los Muertos (ruin), Hon. 202/D3
Playa del Carmen, Mex. 202/E1
Playa Noriega (lake), Mex. 200/C2
Playa Vicente, Mex. 202/C2
Playas, Ecu. 210/A5
Playas (lake), NM, US 187/E5
Playas, Ecu. 210/A5
Playgreen (lake), Mb, Can. 185/J2
Pleasant (lake), Az, US 195/R18
Pleasant Grove, Ut, US 195/K13
Pleasant Hill, Ca, US 193/K11
Pleasant Hill, Mo, US 195/E6
Pleasant Hills, Md, US 196/B5
Pleasant Valley, Mo, US 195/E5
Pleasant View, Co, US 195/B3
Pleasant View, Ut, US 195/K11
Pleasanton, Ca, US 193/L11
Pleasanton, Tx, US 187/H5
Pleasantville, NJ, US 196/D5
Pleasantville, NY, US 197/K7
Pleaux, Fr. 100/E4
Pleinfeld, Ger. 112/D4
Pleiku, Viet. 136/E3
Plenty (riv.), Austl. 171/G3
Plenty (bay), NZ 175/T10
Plentywood, Mt, US 185/G3
Plérin, Fr. 100/B2
Plesná, Czh. 113/F2
Pleso (int'l arpt.), Cro. 106/C3
Pleszew, Pol. 99/J3
Plétipi (lake), Qu, Can. 189/G1
Plettenberg, Ger. 109/E6

Pleurtuit (int'l arpt.), Fr. 100/B2
Pleven, Bul. 107/G4
Pliska, Bul. 107/H4
Plitvice Lakes NP, Cro. 106/B3
Pljevlja, Mont. 106/D4
Plobsheim, Fr. 114/D1
Plöcckenstein (peak), Ger. 113/G5
Ploče, Cro. 105/E1
Plochingen, Ger. 112/C5
Plock, Pol. 99/K2
Pločno (peak), Bosn. 106/C4
Ploemeur, Fr. 100/B2
Ploiești, Rom. 107/H3
Plomárion, Gre. 105/K3
Plombières, Belg. 111/E2
Plombières-lès-Dijon, Fr. 114/A3
Plön, Ger. 96/D4
Płońsk, Pol. 99/L2
Plouay, Fr. 100/B3
Ploučnice (riv.), Czh. 99/H3
Ploufragan, Fr. 100/B2
Plougastel-Daoulas, Fr. 100/A2
Plouguernével, Fr. 100/B2
Plouzané, Fr. 100/A2
Plovdiv, Bul. 107/G4
Plovdiv (pol. reg.), Bul. 107/G4
Plover Cove (res.), China 129/U10
Pluguffan (int'l arpt.), Fr. 100/A3
Plum (isl.), NY, US 197/F1
Plumridge Lakes Nature Rsv., Austl. 170/E4
Plumsteadville, Pa, US 196/C3
Plunge, Lith. 97/J4
Plymouth (co.), Eng, UK 90/B6
Plymouth (sound), Eng, UK 90/B6
Plymouth (cap.), Monts. 199/N8
Plymouth, In, US 188/C3
Plymouth, NC, US 191/J3
Plymouth, NH, US 189/G3
Plymouth, Ct, US 196/C1
Plymouth, Wi, US 188/C3
Plynlimon (peak), Wal, UK 90/C2
Plzeň, Czh. 113/G3
Plzeňský (pol. reg.), Czh. 113/G4
PNC Bank Arts Center, NJ, US 197/J10
Pniel, SAfr. 164/L10
Po (riv.), It. 101/J4
Pô, Burk. 161/E4
Po di Venezia (riv.), It. 117/F2
Po di Volano (riv.), It. 117/E3
Po Klong Garai Cham Towers, Viet. 136/E4
Po, Mouths of the (delta), It. 101/K4
Po Toi Group (isls.), China 129/V11
Po, Valle del (valley), It. 101/J3
Poá, Braz. 213/G8
Poa (riv.), Ven. 211/E2
Poag, Il, US 195/G8
Pobé, Ben. 161/F5
Pobedy (peak), Kyr. 128/D3
Pobiedziska, Pol. 99/J2
Pobla de Segur, Sp. 103/F1
Pocahontas, Ar, US 187/K3
Poção de Pedra, Braz. 212/A2
Pochep, Rus. 120/E1
P'och'ŏn, SKor. 131/G6
Pocinhos, Braz. 212/C2
Pöcking, Ger. 115/H2
Pöcking, Ger. 113/G6
Pocklington (reef), PNG 174/E6
Poço Fundo, Braz. 213/H6
Pocões, Braz. 212/B4
Pocola, Ok, US 187/J4
Poconé, Braz. 209/G7
Pocono (riv.), Pa, US 196/C1
Pocono (lake), Pa, US 196/C1
Pocono Lake, Pa, US 196/C1
Pocono Pines, Pa, US 196/C1
Poços de Caldas, Braz. 213/G6
Pocrí, Pan. 203/F4
Poddbořany, Czh. 113/G2
Podenzano, It. 116/C2
Podgorica (cap.), Mont. 106/D4
Podkarpackie (prov.), Pol. 99/L4
Podlaskie (reg.), Pol. 99/M2
Podol'sk, Rus. 119/W9
Podor, Sen. 160/B2
Podporozh'ye, Rus. 118/G3
Podravska Slatina, Cro. 106/C3
Podujevo, Kos. 106/E4
Pofadder, SAfr. 164/B3

Poggibonsi, It. 117/E6
Poggio Renatico, It. 117/E3
Poggio Rusco, It. 117/E3
Poggiola, It. 117/E6
Pogromni (vol.), Ak, US 192/G5
P'ohang, SKor. 131/E4
Pohénégamook, Qu, Can. 189/G2
Pohja (Pojo), Fin. 97/K1
Pohjanmaa (reg.), Fin. 95/G3
Pohjois-Karjala (prov.), Fin. 118/F3
Pohnpei (isl.), Micr. 174/F4
Pohoiki, Hi, US 182/U11
Pohopoco Mtn. (mtn.), Pa, US 196/C2
Poigny-la-Forêt, Fr. 88/H5
Poing, Ger. 113/E6
Poinsett (cape), Ant. 218/H
Point (lake), NW, Can. 180/E2
Point au Fer (isl.), La, US 195/G8
Point Baker, Ak, US 192/M4
Point Fortin, Trin. 211/F2
Point Hope, Ak, US 192/E2
Point Lay, Ak, US 192/F2
Point Lookout (peak), Austl. 173/E1
Point Mugu Naval Air Sta., Ca, US 194/A2
Point Mugu State Park, Ca, US 194/A2
Point of Aire (pt.), Wal, UK 93/E5
Point of Ayre (pt.), IM, UK 92/D3
Point Pelee NP, On, Can. 188/D3
Point Pleasant, NJ, US 196/D3
Point Pleasant, Pa, US 196/C3
Point Pleasant, WV, US 188/D4
Point Pleasant Beach, NJ, US 196/D3
Point Salines (int'l arpt.), Gren. 211/F1
Point Salvation Abor. Rsv., Austl. 170/D4
Pointe-à-Pitre, Guad., Fr. 199/N8
Pointe à Raquette, Haiti 203/H2
Pointe-aux-Trembles, Qu, Can. 189/P6
Pointe-Calumet, Qu, Can. 189/N6
Pointe-Claire, Qu, Can. 189/N7
Pointe de Chassiron (pt.), Fr. 100/C3
Pointe de l'Arcouest (pt.), Fr. 100/B2
Pointe des Verres (peak), Fr. 114/C6
Pointe-du-Lac, Qu, Can. 189/F2
Pointe du Sablon (pt.), Fr. 100/F5
Pointe-Noire, Congo 163/B1
Poirino, It. 116/A3
Poissonier (pt.), Austl. 170/C1
Poissy, Fr. 88/J5
Poitiers, Fr. 100/D3
Poitou (reg.), Fr. 100/C3
Poitou-Charentes (reg.), Fr. 100/C3
Poix-de-Picardie, Fr. 110/A4
Poix-Terron, Fr. 111/D4
Pojuca, Braz. 212/C4
Pok Liu Chau (isl.), China 129/U11
Pokaran, India 147/K3
Pokharā, Nepal 142/D1
Pokhvistnevo, Rus. 121/K1
Pol-e Khomrī, Afg. 147/J1
Pola de Laviana, Sp. 102/C1
Pola de Siero, Sp. 102/C1
Polabská Nížina (phys. reg.), Czh. 101/L1
Pol'ana (peak), Slvk. 120/A2
Poland (ctry.), 99/K2
Polatlı, Turk. 132/C2
Polatsk, Bela. 97/N4
Polch, Ger. 111/G3
Połczyn-Zdrój, Pol. 96/G5
Pole of Inaccessibility, Ant. 218/E
Polesella, It. 117/E2
Polesine (reg.), It. 117/E2
Polgár, Hun. 106/E2
Pólgyo, SKor. 131/D5
Políaigos (isl.), Gre. 105/J4
Police, Pol. 96/F5
Policastro, Golfo di (gulf), It. 104/D3
Policoro, It. 104/E2
Poligny, Fr. 114/B4
Polikastron, Gre. 105/H2
Polikhni, Gre. 105/N6
Polikhnitos, Gre. 105/K3
Polillo (isls.), Phil. 137/D4
Polis, Cyp. 149/C2
Polístena, It. 104/E3
Políyiros, Gre. 105/H2
Polje, Slov. 101/L3

Polkowice, Pol. 99/J3
Polla, It. 104/D2
Pollença, Sp. 103/G3
Pollochic (riv.), Guat. 202/D3
Polomolok, Phil. 137/E6
Polonia (cape), Uru. 217/G2
Polonnaruwa, SrL. 140/D6
Polonne, Ukr. 120/C2
Polski Trŭmbesh, Bul. 107/G4
Polson, Mt, US 184/E4
Poltava, Ukr. 120/E2
Poltava'ka Oblasti, Ukr. 120/E2
Ponthévrard, Fr. 88/H6
Poluostrov Barsakel'mes (isl.), Kaz. 145/C3
Poluška (peak), Czh. 113/H5
Polvijärvi, Fin. 118/F3
Polyarnyy, Rus. 118/G1
Polynesia (reg.) 174/G6
Pomabamba, Peru 214/B3
Pomarance, It. 101/J5
Pomarico, It. 104/E2
Pomáz, Hun. 107/R9
Pomba (riv.), Som. 191/F3
Pombal, Braz. 212/C2
Pombal, Port. 102/A3
Pombas, CpV. 151/J9
Pomerania (reg.), Pol. 96/F4
Pomerania (bay), Ger.,Pol. 96/F4
Pomerode, Braz. 213/B3
Pomeroon-Supenaam (pol. reg.), Guy. 211/G3
Pomeroy, Wa, US 184/D4
Pomeroy, NI, UK 92/B2
Pommersfelden, Ger. 112/D3
Pomona, Ca, US 194/C2
Pomona, NJ, US 196/D5
Pomona, Md, US 196/B6
Pomorie, Bul. 107/H4
Pomorskie (prov.), Pol. 99/J1
Pomos (pt.), Cyp. 149/C2
Pompano Beach, Fl, US 191/H5
Pompei (ruin), It. 104/D2
Pompéu, Braz. 210/B4
Pompey, Fr. 111/F6
Pompeys Pillar Nat'l Mon., Mt, US 184/G4
Pompiano, It. 116/C2
Pompilta (lake), Austl. 171/J5
Pompton (riv.), NJ, US 197/H8
Pompton Lakes, NJ, US 197/H8
Poncarale, It. 116/D2
Ponce, PR, US 199/N8
Ponchatoula, La, US 195/P16
Poncheville (lake), Qu, Can. 188/E1
Pond, Mo, US 195/F8
Pond (pt.), Ct, US 197/E1
Pond Inlet, Nun., Can. 181/J1
Pondicherry, India 140/C5
Pondicherry (terr.), India 140/C5
Ponente, Riviera di (coast), It. 116/B5
Ponferrada, Sp. 102/B1
Pongdong, SKor. 131/D5
Ponghwa, SKor. 131/E4
Pongola (riv.), SAfr. 165/E2
Poni (prov.), Fr. 160/E4
Poniatowa, Pol. 99/M3
Ponnaiyar (riv.), India 140/C5
Ponoka, Ab, Can. 184/E2
Ponoy (riv.), Rus. 122/D3
Pons, Fr. 100/C4
Ponsacco, It. 116/D5
Pont-à-Celles, Belg. 111/D3
Pont-à-Marcq, Fr. 110/C2
Pont-D'Ain, Fr. 114/B5
Pont-de-Chéruy, Fr. 114/B6
Pont-de-Roide, Fr. 114/C3
Pont-de-Vaux, Fr. 114/A5
Pont-de-Veyle, Fr. 114/A5
Pont-du-Château, Fr. 100/A3
Pont-Remy, Fr. 110/A3
Pont-Saint-Esprit, Fr. 100/F4
Pont-Saint-Martin, It. 116/A1
Pont-Sainte-Maxence, Fr. 110/B5
Ponta Delgada, Azor., Port. 103/T13
Ponta do Pico (peak), Azor., Port. 103/S12
Ponta Grossa, Braz. 213/B3
Ponta Porã, Braz. 215/E1
Pontalina, Braz. 213/B1
Pontarlier, Fr. 114/C4
Pontassieve, It. 117/E5
Pontaumur, Fr. 100/E3
Pontault-Combault, Fr. 88/K5
Pontax (riv.), Qu, Can. 188/E1
Pontcarré, Fr. 88/L5
Pontchartrain (lake), La, US 191/H4
Pontchâteau, Fr. 100/B3
Ponte Alta do Bom Jesus, Braz. 212/A4
Ponte Alta do Tocantins, Braz. 212/A3
Ponte de Sor, Port. 102/A3
Ponte dell'Olio, It. 116/C2
Ponte di Legno, It. 115/G5
Ponte di Piave, It. 117/F1
Ponte do Lima, Port. 102/A2
Ponte Lambro, It. 116/C1
Ponte Nova, Braz. 213/D2
Ponte San Nicolò, It. 117/E2

Pontecagnano, It. 104/D2
Pontecorvo, It. 104/C2
Pontecurone, It. 116/B3
Pontedera, It. 116/D5
Pontefract, Eng, UK 93/G4
Ponteland, Eng, UK 93/G1
Pontelongo, It. 117/F2
Pontevedra, Sp. 102/A1
Pontevico, It. 116/D2
Ponthévrard, Fr. 88/H6
Ponthieu (reg.), Fr. 110/A3
Pontiac, Il, US 185/L5
Pontiac, Mi, US 188/D3
Pontiac (lake), Mi, US 193/E6
Pontianak, Indo. 138/C4
Pontivy, Fr. 100/B2
Pontoise, Fr. 88/J4
Pontoon Beach, Il, US 195/G8
Pontotoc, Ms, US 191/F3
Pontpoint, Fr. 110/B5
Pontremoli, It. 116/C4
Pontresina, Swi. 115/F5
Pontypool, Wal, UK 90/C3
Ponza, It. 104/C2
Ponziane, Isole (isls.), It. 104/C2
Poole, Eng, UK 90/E5
Poole (bay), Eng, UK 91/E5
Poole (co.), Eng, UK 91/E5
Poolewe, Sc, UK 89/R8
Poona (Pune), India 147/K5
Poondarrie (peak), Austl. 170/C3
Poondinna (mt.), Austl. 171/F3
Poopó (lake), Bol. 208/E7
Poortugaal, Neth. 108/B5
Pöösapää (pt.), Est. 97/K2
Poosepatuck Ind. Res., NY, US 197/F2
Popayán, Col. 210/B4
Poperinge, Belg. 110/B2
Popigochic (riv.), Mex. 200/C2
Popilta (lake), Austl. 171/J5
Popio (lake), Austl. 171/J5
Poplar (riv.), Mb,On, Can. 180/G3
Poplar (isl.), Md, US 196/B6
Poplar, Mt, US 185/G3
Poplar Bluff, Mo, US 187/K3
Poplarville, Ms, US 191/F4
Popocatépetl (vol.), Mex. 201/L7
Popoli, It. 104/C1
Popovo, Bul. 107/H4
Poppberg (peak), Ger. 113/E4
Poppenhausen, Ger. 112/D2
Poppenhausen, Ger. 112/D2
Poppi, It. 117/E5
Poprad, Slvk. 99/L4
Poprad (riv.), Slvk. 99/L4
Poranga, Braz. 212/B2
Porangatu, Braz. 209/J6
Porbandar, India 147/J4
Porcari, It. 116/D5
Porce (riv.), Col. 210/C3
Porcheville, Fr. 88/H5
Porcia, It. 117/F1
Porcuna, Sp. 102/C4
Porcupine (riv.), Can.,US 192/K2
Porcupine Gorge NP, Austl. 172/B3
Porcupine Plain, Sk, Can. 185/H2
Pordenone (prov.), It. 117/F2
Pordenone, It. 117/F1
Pordim, Bul. 107/G4
Pore, Col. 210/D3
Poreč, Cro. 117/G2
Poretta (int'l arpt.), Fr. 104/A1
Pori, Fin. 97/J1
Porirua, NZ 175/S11
Porlezza, It. 115/F5
Pornic, Fr. 100/B3
Porongurup NP, Austl. 170/C5
Póros, Gre. 105/H4
Porpoise (bay), Ant. 218/J
Porretta Terme, It. 117/D4
Porriño, Sp. 102/A1
Porsangen (inlet), Nor. 95/H1
Porsgrunn, Nor. 96/C2
Porsuk (riv.), Turk. 148/B2
Port (isl.), Japan 135/H6
Port Alberni, BC, Can. 184/B3
Port Albert, Austl. 173/C3
Port Alexander, Ak, US 192/M4
Port Alfred, SAfr. 164/D4
Port Alice, BC, Can. 184/B3
Port Angeles, Wa, US 184/C3
Port Antonio, Jam. 203/G2
Port Appin, Sc, UK 94/A3
Port Arthur, Tx, US 187/J5
Port au Choix, Nf, Can. 189/K1
Port-au-Prince (cap.), Haiti 203/H2
Port Augusta, Austl. 171/H5
Port Bannatyne, Sc, UK 94/A5
Port Blair, India 141/F5

Port Blakely, Wa, US 193/C2
Port Bolivar, Tx, US 190/E4
Port Bouët (Abidjan) (int'l arpt.), C.d'Iv. 160/E5
Port-Bouët, C.d'Iv. 160/E5
Port Broughton, Austl. 171/H5
Port Canning, India 143/G4
Port Carbon, Pa, US 196/B2
Port Charlotte, Fl, US 191/H5
Port Chester, NY, US 197/L8
Port Clements, BC, Can. 192/M5
Port Clinton, Oh, US 188/D3
Port Clinton, Pa, US 196/D2
Port Colborne, On, Can. 189/R10
Port Columbus (int'l arpt.), Oh, US 188/D4
Port Davey (har.), Austl. 173/C4
Port-de-Paix, Haiti 203/H2
Port Deposit, Md, US 196/B4
Port Dickson, Malay. 138/B3
Port Discovery (bay), Wa, US 193/B1
Port Douglas, Austl. 172/B2
Port Edward, BC, Can. 192/M4
Port Elgin, On, Can. 188/D2
Port Elizabeth, SAfr. 164/D4
Port Elizabeth, NJ, US 196/D5
Port Ellen, Sc, UK 89/Q9
Port Elliot, Austl. 171/H5
Port Erin, IM, UK 92/D3
Port-Eynon (pt.), Wal, UK 90/B3
Port Fairy, Austl. 173/B3
Port Gamble, Wa, US 193/B2
Port Gamble Ind. Res., Wa, US 193/B2
Port-Gentil, Gabon 154/G8
Port Gibson, Ms, US 187/K5
Port Glasgow, Sc, UK 94/A5
Port Graham, Ak, US 192/H4
Port Harcourt, Nga. 161/G5
Port Harcourt (int'l arpt.), Nga. 161/G5
Port Hardy, BC, Can. 184/B3
Port Hawkesbury, NS, Can. 189/J2
Port Hedland, Austl. 170/C2
Port Hedland (int'l arpt.), Austl. 170/C2
Port Heiden, Ak, US 192/G4
Port Hueneme, Ca, US 194/A2
Port Huron, Mi, US 188/D3

Port Hueneme, Ca, US 194/A2
Port Huron, Mi, US 188/D3
Port Isaac (bay), Eng, UK 90/B5
Port Jefferson, NY, US 197/E2
Port-la-Nouvelle, Fr. 100/E5
Port Lambton, On, Can. 193/H6
Port Lavaca, Tx, US 187/H5
Port Lincoln, Austl. 171/G5
Port Lions, Ak, US 192/H4
Port Loko, SLeo. 160/B4
Port-Louis, Guad., Fr. 199/N8
Port Louis (cap.), Mrts. 165/T15
Port Macdonnell, Austl. 173/B3
Port Macquarie, Austl. 173/E1
Port Madison Ind. Res., Wa, US 193/B2
Port Maria, Jam. 203/G2
Port McNeill, BC, Can. 184/B3
Port-Menier, Qu, Can. 189/H1
Port Monmouth, NJ, US 197/J10
Port Nolloth, SAfr. 164/B3
Port Norris, NJ, US 196/C5
Port of Ness, Sc, UK 89/Q7
Port-of-Spain (cap.), Trin. 211/F2
Port Orange, Fl, US 191/H4
Port Penn, De, US 196/C4
Port Phillip (bay), Austl. 173/C3
Port Pirie, Austl. 171/H5
Port Reading, NJ, US 197/J9
Port Republic, NJ, US 196/D4
Port Royal, Pa, US 196/A2
Port Saint Joe, Fl, US 191/G4
Port-Saint-Louis-du-Rhône, Fr. 100/F5
Port Saint Lucie, Fl, US 191/H5
Port Saint Mary, IM, UK 92/D3
Port Shepstone, SAfr. 165/E3
Port Stephens (bay), Austl. 173/E2
Port-sur-Saône, Fr. 114/C2
Port Townsend, Wa, US 184/C3
Port-Vendres, Fr. 100/E5
Port Victoria, Austl. 171/H5
Port-Vila (cap.), Van. 174/F6
Port Wakefield, Austl. 171/H5
Port Washington, NY, US 197/L8
Port Weld, Malay. 138/B3
Porta Westfalica (pass), Ger. 109/F4
Porta Westfalica, Ger. 109/F4
Portachuelo, Bol. 208/F7
Portadown, NI, UK 92/B3
Portaferry, NI, UK 92/C3
Portage, Mi, US 188/C3
Portage Des Sioux, Mo, US 195/G8
Portage la Prairie, Mb, Can. 185/J3
Portalegre (dist.), Port. 102/B3
Portalegre, Port. 102/B3
Portales, NM, US 187/G4
Portarlington, Ire. 89/Q10
Portbou, Sp. 103/G1
Porteirinha, Braz. 212/B4
Portel, Braz. 209/H4
Porters (lake), Pa, US 196/C1
Porterville, SAfr. 164/L10
Porterville, Ca, US 186/C3
Porterville, Ut, US 195/K12
Portes-lès-Valence, Fr. 100/F4
Portet-sur-Garonne, Fr. 100/D5
Portete (bay), Col. 203/J3
Portglenone, NI, UK 92/B2
Portimão, Port. 102/A4
Portishead, Eng, UK 90/D4
Portknockie, Sc, UK 94/D1
Portland, Austl. 173/D2
Portland, Austl. 173/B3
Portland (cape), Austl. 173/C4
Portland (pt.), Jam. 203/G2
Portland, In, US 188/C3
Portland, Me, US 189/G3
Portland, Or, US 184/C4
Portland (int'l arpt.), Or, US 184/C4
Portland, Tn, US 188/C4
Portland Canal (inlet), BC, Can. 192/M4
Portland Jetport (int'l arpt.), Me, US 189/G3
Portlaoise, Ire. 89/Q10
Portlaw, Ire. 89/Q10
Portlethen, Sc, UK 94/D2
Portmarnock, Ire. 92/B5
Portmore, Jam. 203/G2
Portneuf (riv.), Qu, Can. 189/G1
Porto (gulf), Fr. 104/A1
Porto, Port. 102/A2
Porto (dist.), Port. 102/A2
Porto (int'l arpt.), Port. 102/A2
Porto Azzurro, It. 101/J5
Porto Belo, Braz. 213/B3
Porto Calvo, Braz. 212/D3
Porto Ceresio, It. 115/E6
Pôrto da Fôlha, Braz. 212/C3
Porto de Mós, Port. 102/A3
Porto Empedocle, It. 104/C4
Porto Ercole, It. 104/B1
Porto Ferreira, Braz. 213/C2
Porto Franco, Braz. 212/A2
Porto Garibaldi, It. 117/F3
Porto Inglês, CpV. 151/K10
Porto Nacional, Braz. 209/J6
Porto-Novo (cap.), Ben. 161/F5
Porto Potenza Picena, It. 117/G6
Porto Recanati, It. 117/G6
Porto Sant'Elpidio, It. 101/K5
Porto Santo (isl.), Port. 156/A2
Porto Santo Stefano, It. 104/B1
Porto Seguro, Braz. 212/C5
Porto Tolle, It. 117/F3
Porto Torres, It. 104/A2
Porto União, Braz. 213/B3
Porto Valtravaglia, It. 115/E6
Porto-Vecchio, Fr. 104/A2
Porto Velho, Braz. 208/F5
Portobelo, PN, Pan. 203/G4
Portocannone, It. 104/D2
Portocivitanova, It. 101/K5
Portoferraio, It. 101/J5
Portofino, It. 116/C4
Portogruaro, It. 117/F1
Portomaggiore, It. 117/E3
Portovenere, It. 116/C4
Portoviejo, Ecu. 210/A5
Portpatrick, Sc, UK 92/C2
Portree, Sc, UK 89/Q8
Portrush, NI, UK 92/B1
Portsea (isl.), Eng, UK 91/E5
Portslade-by-Sea, Eng, UK 91/F5
Portsmouth, Dom. 199/N9
Portsmouth, Eng, UK 91/E5
Portsmouth (co.), Eng, UK 91/E5
Portsmouth, NH, US 189/G3
Portsoy, Sc, UK 94/D1
Portstewart, NI, UK 92/B1
Portugal (ctry.) 102/A3
Portugalete, Sp. 102/D1
Portuguesa (riv.), Ven. 210/D2
Portuguesa (state), Ven. 210/D2
Portumna, Ire. 89/P10
Porvenir, Chile 217/C7
Porvenir, Uru. 217/K10
Porzuna, Sp. 102/C3
Posada, It. 104/A2
Posadas, Arg. 215/E2
Posadas, Sp. 102/C4
Posavina (valley), Bosn. 106/C3
Poschiavo, Swi. 115/G5
Posio, Fin. 118/F2
Poso (lake), Indo. 139/F4
Posof, Turk. 148/E1
Posŏng, SKor. 131/D5
Posŏng (riv.), SKor. 131/D5
Posorja, Ecu. 210/A5
Posse, Braz. 212/A4
Possession (pt.), Wa, US 193/C2
Possession (sound), Wa, US 193/C2
Post, Tx, US 187/G4
Post Falls, Id, US 184/D4
Poste Maurice Cortier (ruin), Alg. 157/F5
Postmasburg, SAfr. 164/C3
Postojna, Slov. 101/L4
Postolprty, Czh. 113/G2
Potam, Mex. 200/C3
Potamós, Gre. 105/H5
Potaro-Siparuni (pol. reg.), Guy. 211/G3
Potchefstroom, SAfr. 164/D2
Poteau, Ok, US 187/J4
Potenza (riv.), It. 104/C1
Potenza, It. 104/D2
Potenza Picena, It. 117/G6
Potes, Sp. 102/C1
Potholes (res.), Wa, US 184/D4
Poti (riv.), Braz. 209/K5
P'ot'i, Geo. 121/G4
Potiraguá, Braz. 212/C4
Potomac (riv.), US 188/E4
Potomac, Md, US 196/A5
Potosí, Bol. 208/E7
Potosi, Mo, US 187/K3
Potrerillos, Chile 215/C2
Potsdam, NY, US 188/F2
Potsdam, Ger. 98/Q7
Pottawatomie (co.), Ok, US 195/N15
Pottendorf, Aus. 101/M3
Pottenstein, Ger. 113/E3
Potters Bar, Eng, UK 88/C1
Pöttmes, Ger. 112/E5
Pottstown, Pa, US 196/C3
Pottsville, Pa, US 196/B2
Pottuvil, SrL. 140/D6
Poudre d'Or, Mrts. 165/T15
Poughkeepsie, NY, US 188/F3
Pouilley-les-Vignes, Fr. 114/B3
Poulaphoucha (res.), Ire. 92/B5
Poulter (riv.), Eng, UK 93/G5
Poulton-le-Fylde, Eng, UK 93/F4
Poŭn, SKor. 131/D4
Pourri (peak), Fr. 101/G4
Pouru-Saint-Remy, Fr. 111/E4
Pouso Alegre, Braz. 213/H7
Pouthisat (riv.), Camb. 141/H5
Pouzauges, Fr. 100/C3
Považská Bystrica, Slvk. 99/K4
Povegliano Veronese, It. 117/D2
Poverty Point Nat'l Mon., La, US 187/K4
Poviglio, It. 116/D3
Póvoa de Varzim, Port. 102/A2
Povoação, Azor., Port. 103/T13
Povorino, Rus. 121/G2
Povungnituk (riv.), Qu, Can. 181/J2
Povungnituk, Qu, Can. 181/J2
Poway, Ca, US 194/C5
Powder (riv.), Mt,Wy, US 185/G4
Powell (lake), Az,Ut, US 186/E3
Powell, Wy, US 184/F4
Powell River, BC, Can. 184/B3
Power (res.), NY, US 189/R9
Powers (lake), Wi, US 193/P14
Powys (co.), Wal, UK 93/E6
Powys, Vale of (valley), Wal, UK 90/C1
Poxoreo, Braz. 209/H7
Poyang (lake), China 137/C2
Poynton, Eng, UK 93/F5
Poyo, Sp. 102/A1
Poysdorf, Aus. 99/J4
Poza Rica, Mex. 201/M6
Požarevac, Serb. 106/E3
Požega, Serb. 106/E4
Poznań, Pol. 99/J2
Pozo Alcón, Sp. 102/D4
Pozoblanco, Sp. 102/C3
Pozohondo, Sp. 102/E3
Pozuelo de Alarcón, Sp. 103/N9
Pozuelos, Ven. 211/E2
Pozuzo, Peru 214/C3
Pozza, It. 117/D3
Pozzallo, It. 104/D4
Pozzolo Formigaro, It. 116/B3
Pozzonovo, It. 117/E2
Ppa. de Salamanca (plain), Arg. 216/F1
Prabuty, Pol. 97/H5
Pracham Hiang (pt.), Thai. 136/B4
Prachatice, Czh. 113/H4
Prachin Buri (riv.), Thai. 136/C3
Prachin Buri, Thai. 136/C3
Prachuap Khiri Khan, Thai. 136/B4
Praděd (peak), Czh. 99/J3
Pradera, Col. 210/B4
Prades, Fr. 100/E5
Prado, Braz. 212/C5
Prado del Rey, Sp. 102/C4
Prado Flood Control (basin), Ca, US 194/C3
Pragelpass (pass), Swi. 115/E4
Praha (Prague) (cap.), Czh. 113/H2
Praha (peak), Czh. 113/G3
Praha (pol. reg.), Czh. 113/H2
Prahova (prov.), Rom. 107/G3
Praia (cap.), CpV. 151/K11
Praia (int'l arpt.), CpV. 151/K11
Praia da Vitória, Azor., Port. 103/S12
Praia Grande, Braz. 213/G9
Prairie Dog Town Fk. (riv.), Tx, US 187/G4
Prairie du Chien, Wi, US 185/L5
Prairie Grove, Il, US 193/P15
Prairie View, Tx, US 187/J5
Prairie Village, Ks, US 195/D6
Prairies (riv.), Qu, Can. 189/N6
Prairietown, Il, US 195/H8
Pralboino, It. 116/D2
Pralungo, It. 116/B1
Pram (riv.), Aus. 113/G6
Prambachkirchen, Aus. 113/G6
Pran Buri (res.), Thai. 141/G5
Prangins, Swi. 114/C5
Prānhita (riv.), India 140/C4
Prapat, Indo. 138/A3
Præstø, Den. 96/E4
Praszka, Pol. 99/K3
Prat, Chile, Ant. 218/W
Prata, Braz. 213/B1
Prata (riv.), Braz. 212/A5
Prata di Pordenone, It. 117/F1
Prathersville, Mo, US 195/E5
Prätlgau (valley), Swi. 115/F4
Prato, It. 117/E5
Prato (prov.), It. 117/E5
Prato allo Stelvio (Prad am Stilfserjoch), It. 115/G4
Prato (Leventina), Swi. 115/E5
Pratola Peligna, It. 104/C1
Pratomagno (mts.), It. 117/E5
Pratovecchio, It. 117/E5
Pratt (isl.), Chile 217/B6
Pratt, Ks, US 187/H3
Pratteln, Swi. 114/D2
Prattville, Al, US 191/G3
Prauthoy, Fr. 114/B2
Pravets, Bul. 105/H1
Pravia, Sp. 102/B1
Prawle (pt.), Eng, UK 90/C6
Praxedis G. Guerrero, Mex. 200/D2
Praya, Indo. 139/E5
Pré-Saint-Didier, It. 114/C6
Preah Vihear (ruin), Camb. 136/D3
Précy-sur-Oise, Fr. 110/B5
Predappio, It. 117/E4
Predazzo, It. 101/J3
Predeal, Rom. 107/G3
Predosa, It. 116/B3
Preeceville, Sk, Can. 185/H3
Preetz, Ger. 96/D4
Preganziol, It. 117/F1
Pregarten, Aus. 113/H6
Pregolya (riv.), Pol. 97/J4
Pregolya (riv.), Rus. 99/L1
Pregonero, Ven. 210/D2
Preissac (lake), Qu, Can. 188/E1
Premana, It. 115/F5
Prémery, Fr. 100/E3
Premià de Mar, Sp. 103/L7
Prenzlau, Ger. 99/G2
Přerov, Czh. 99/J4
Presanella (peak), It. 115/G5
Prescot, Eng, UK 93/F5
Prescott, Az, US 186/D4
Prescott, On, Can. 188/F2
Preševo, Serb. 106/E4
Presidencia Roque Sáenz Peña, Arg. 215/D2
Presidente Dutra, Braz. 212/A2
Presidente Epitácio, Braz. 213/A2
Presidente Olegário, Braz. 213/C1
Presidente Venceslau, Braz. 213/B2
Presidential Lake Estates, NJ, US 196/D4
Presidio, Tx, US 187/F5
Presidio (riv.), Mex. 200/D4
Preslav, Bul. 107/H4
Presles, Fr. 88/J4
Presles-en-Brie, Fr. 88/L5
Prešov, Slvk. 99/L4
Prešovský (pol. reg.), Slvk. 99/L4
Prespa (lake), Eur. 105/G2
Presque Isle, Me, US 189/G2
Pressath, Ger. 113/E3
Pressbaum, Aus. 107/N7
Prestatyn, Wal, UK 93/E5
Prestea, Gha. 161/E5
Prestfoss, Nor. 96/C1
Přeštice, Czh. 113/G3
Preston (cape), Austl. 170/C2
Preston, Md, US 196/C6
Preston, Wa, US 193/D2
Preston, Eng, UK 93/F4
Prestonpans, Sc, UK 94/D5
Prestonsburg, Ky, US 188/D4
Prestwich, Eng, UK 93/F4
Prestwick (int'l arpt.), Sc, UK 94/B5
Prestwick, Sc, UK 94/B6
Prêto (riv.), Braz. 209/J6
Pretoria (cap.), SAfr. 164/E2
Pretty Boy (res.), Md, US 196/B4
Preussisch Olendorf, Ger. 109/F4
Prevalje, Slov. 101/L3
Préveza, Gre. 105/G3
Prévost, Qu, Can. 189/M6
Prey Veng, Camb. 136/D4
Pribilof (isls.), Ak, US 192/D4
Priboj, Serb. 106/D4
Příbram, Czh. 113/H3
Price (riv.), Ut, US 186/E3
Price, Ut, US 186/E3
Price, Md, US 196/C5
Prichard, Al, US 191/F4
Prichsenstadt, Ger. 112/D3
Priego, Sp. 102/D2
Priego de Córdoba, Sp. 102/C4
Prien am Chiemsee, Ger. 113/F7
Prieska, SAfr. 164/C3
Priest (lake), Id, US 184/D3
Priest River, Id, US 184/D3
Prieta (mtn.), Sp. 102/C1
Prievidza, Slvk. 99/K4
Prignitz (reg.), Ger. 98/F2
Prijedor, Bosn. 106/C3
Prijepolje, Serb. 106/D4
Prikaspian (plain), Kaz.,Rus. 122/E5
Prikumsk, Rus. 121/H3
Prilep, FYROM 105/G2
Prilly, Swi. 114/C4
Prima Porta, It. 104/C1
Prima Tapia, Mex. 200/A1
Prime Hook NWR, De, US 196/C6
Primeira Cruz, Braz. 212/B1
Primero (cape), Chile 217/B6
Primorskiy Kray, Rus. 123/P5
Primorsko, Bul. 107/H4
Primorsko-Akhtarsk, Rus. 120/F3
Prims (riv.), Ger. 111/F4
Prince Albert, Sk, Can. 185/G2
Prince Albert (pen.), NW, Can. 180/E1
Prince Albert (sound), NW, Can. 180/E1
Prince Albert NP, Sk, Can. 180/F3
Prince Albert, SAfr. 164/C4
Prince Alfred (cape), NW, Can. 180/D1
Prince Charles (isl.), Nun., Can. 181/J2
Prince Edward (isl.), Can. 177/L5
Prince Edward Island (prov.), Can. 189/J2
Prince Edward Island NP, PE, Can. 189/J2
Prince Edward (isls.), SAfr. 81/L7
Prince George, BC, Can. 184/C2
Prince Georges (co.), Md, US 196/B6
Prince Gustav Adolf (sea), Nun., Can. 181/R7
Prince Leopold (isl.), Nun., Can. 180/G1
Prince of Wales (str.), NW, Can. 180/E1
Prince of Wales (isl.), Ak, US 180/C3
Prince Olav (coast), Ant. 218/D
Prince Patrick (isl.), NW, Can. 181/R7
Prince Regent (inlet), Nun., Can. 180/G1
Prince Rupert, BC, Can. 192/M4
Prince William (sound), Ak, US 180/B2
Princenhof (lake), Neth. 108/C2
Princes Risborough, Eng, UK 91/F3
Princes Town, Trin. 199/J5
Princesa Isabel, Braz. 212/C2
Princess Charlotte (bay), Austl. 172/A1
Princess Margaret (range), Nun., Can. 181/S6
Princess Royal (isl.), BC, Can. 180/C3
Princeton, Mn, US 185/K4
Princeton, BC, Can. 184/C3
Princeton, In, US 188/C4
Princeton, Ky, US 188/C4
Princeton, NJ, US 196/D3
Princeton Junction, NJ, US 196/D3
Princeville, Hi, US 182/S9
Príncipe (isl.), SaoT. 154/G7
Prindle (vol.), Ak, US 192/K3
Prineville, Or, US 184/C4
Pringsewu, Indo. 138/B5
Pringy, Fr. 114/C6
Prinsenbeek, Neth. 108/B5
Prinses Margriet (canal), Neth. 108/C3
Prinzapolka, Nic. 203/F3
Prinzapolka (riv.), Nic. 203/E3
Priolo di Gargallo, It. 104/D4
Prior (cape), Sp. 102/A1
Priore (peak), It. 101/K5
Priozersk, Rus. 97/P1
Pripet Marshes (swamp), Bela.,Ukr. 120/C1
Prlpyat' (riv.), Ukr. 120/C2
Prisdorf, Ger. 109/G1
Priština (cap.), Kos. 106/E4
Prittriching, Ger. 115/G1
Pritzwalk, Ger. 98/G2
Privas, Fr. 100/F4
Privolzhskiy, Rus. 121/H2
Priyutovo, Rus. 121/K1
Prizren, Kos. 106/E4
Prnjavor, Serb. 106/D3
Prnjavor, Bosn. 106/C3
Probištip, FYROM 105/H1
Probolinggo, Indo. 138/D5
Probstzella, Ger. 113/E1
Proctor (lake), Tx, US 190/D3
Proctor (pt.), La, US 195/Q17
Proddatūr, India 140/C5
Proença-a-Nova, Port. 102/B3
Profondeville, Belg. 111/D3
Progreso, Mex. 201/K6
Progreso, Mex. 202/D1
Progreso, Pan. 203/F4
Progreso, Uru. 217/K11
Progress, Rus. 129/N2
Progresso, It. 117/E3
Prokhladnyy, Rus. 121/G4
Prokuplje, Serb. 106/E4
Promised Land (lake), Pa, US 196/C1
Promissão, Braz. 213/B2
Promissão, Reprêsa (res.), Braz. 213/B2
Propriá, Braz. 212/C3
Propriano, Fr. 104/A2
Proserpine, Austl. 172/C3
Prosna (riv.), Pol. 99/J2
Prospect Park, NJ, US 197/J8
Prospector (mtn.), Yk, Can. 192/L3
Prosperidad, Phil. 137/E6
Prosperous, Ire. 89/Q10
Prostějov, Czh. 99/J4
Proston, Austl. 172/C4
Proszowice, Pol. 99/L3
Protivín, Czh. 113/H4
Provadiya, Bul. 107/H4
Provence (reg.), Fr. 100/F5
Provence (int'l arpt.), Fr. 100/F5
Provence-Alpes-Côte-d'Azur, Fr. 101/G4
Providence (cap.), RI, US 189/G3
Providencia, Isla de (isl.), Col. 198/E5
Providência, Serra de (mts.), Braz. 208/F6
Providenciales (isl.), Bahm. 203/H1
Provins, Fr. 100/E2
Provo, Ut, US 195/K13
Provo (riv.), Ut, US 195/K13
Provo (peak), Ut, US 195/K13
Provost, Ab, Can. 184/F2
Prozor, Bosn. 106/C4
Prudentópolis, Braz. 213/B3
Prudhoe (bay), Ak, US 192/J1
Prudhoe, Eng, UK 93/G2
Prudhoe Bay, Ak, US 192/J1
Prudnik, Pol. 99/J3
Prüm (riv.), Ger. 98/D4
Prüm, Ger. 111/F3
Prunay-en-Yvelines, Fr. 88/H6
Prunelli-di-Fiumorbo, Fr. 104/A1
Pruszcz Gdański, Pol. 96/H4
Pruszków, Pol. 99/L2
Prut (riv.), Eur. 107/J2
Prutz, Aus. 115/G3
Pryluky, Ukr. 120/E2
Pryor, Ok, US 187/J3
Prypyats' (riv.), Bela. 120/D2
Przasnysz, Pol. 99/L2
Przemków, Pol. 99/H3
Przemyśl, Pol. 99/M4
Przeworsk, Pol. 99/M3
Przylądek Rozewie (cape),Pol. 96/H4
Przysucha, Pol. 99/L3
Psakhná, Gre. 105/H3
Psará (isl.), Gre. 105/J3
Psárion, Gre. 105/G4
Psël (riv.), Rus.,Ukr. 120/E2
Pskov (lake), Rus. 118/E5
Pskov, Rus. 97/N3
Pskovskaya Oblast, Rus. 118/F4
Pšovka (riv.), Czh. 113/H2
Pszczyna, Pol. 99/K4
Ptolemaís, Gre. 105/G2
Ptuj, Slov. 101/L3
Pu Xian, China 130/B3
Puan, SKor. 131/D5
Pubei, China 137/A3
Pucacaca, Peru 214/B2
Pucallpa, Peru 214/C3
Pucará, Ecu. 214/B1
Pucará, Peru 214/B2
Pucará, Peru 214/D4
Pucarani, Bol. 214/D5
Pucaurco, Peru 210/D5
Puchenau, Aus. 113/H6
Pucheng, China 137/C2
Pucheng, China 130/B4
Puchheim, Ger. 113/E6
Puch'on, SKor. 131/F7
Puchuncaví, Chile 216/N8
Pucioasa, Rom. 107/G3
Puck, Pol. 96/H4
Pucking, Aus. 113/H6
Pucón, Chile 216/C3
Pucusana, Peru 214/B4
Pudasjärvi, Fin. 118/E2
Puderbach, Ger. 111/G2
Pudsey, Eng, UK 93/G4
Pudu (riv.), China 141/H2
Puebla (state), Mex. 198/B4
Puebla, Mex. 201/L7
Puebla de Alcocer, Sp. 102/C3
Puebla de Don Fadrique, Sp. 102/D4
Puebla de la Calzada, Sp. 102/B3
Puebla de Sanabria, Sp. 102/B1
Puebla de Trives, Sp. 102/B1
Puebla del Caramiñal, Sp. 102/A1
Pueblillo, Mex. 201/M6
Pueblito, Col. 210/C2
Pueblo, Co, US 187/F3
Pueblo Nuevo, Nic. 202/E3
Pueblo Nuevo, Ven. 210/D2
Pueblo Yaqui, Mex. 200/C3
Puente (hills), Ca, US 194/G8
Puente Alto, Chile 216/N8
Puente Caldelas, Sp. 102/A1
Puente-Ceso, Sp. 102/A1
Puente de Ixtla, Mex. 201/K8
Puente del Inca, Arg. 216/C2
Puente-Genil, Sp. 102/C4
Puente Nacional, Col. 210/C3
Puente Piedra, Peru 214/B3
Puenteareas, Sp. 102/A1
Puentedeume, Sp. 102/A1
Puentes de García Rodríguez, Sp. 102/B1
Pueo (pt.), Hi, US 182/R10
Puerco (riv.), NM, US 186/E4
Puerto Acosta, Bol. 214/D4
Puerto Aisén, Chile 216/B5
Puerto América, Peru 214/B2
Puerto Ángel, Mex. 202/B3
Puerto Armuelles, Pan. 203/F4
Puerto Asís, Col. 210/B4
Puerto Ayacucho, Ven. 211/E3
Puerto Ayora, Ecu. 214/E7
Puerto Baquerizo Moreno, Ecu. 214/F7
Puerto Barrios, Guat. 202/D3
Puerto Bermúdez, Peru 214/C3
Puerto Berrío, Col. 210/C3
Puerto Cabello, Ven. 210/D2
Puerto Cabezas, Nic. 203/F3
Puerto Carreño, Col. 211/E3
Puerto Cisnes, Chile 216/B5
Puerto Cortés, Mex. 200/C3
Puerto Cortés, Hon. 202/E3
Puerto Cumarebo, Ven. 210/D2
Puerto de la Cruz, Sp. 156/A3
Puerto de la Libertad, Mex. 200/B2
Puerto de Navacerrada (pass), Sp. 103/M8
Puerto del Rosario, Sp. 156/B3
Puerto del Son, Sp. 102/A1
Puerto Deseado, Arg. 217/D5
Puerto El Carmen, Ecu. 210/C4
Puerto Escondido, Col. 210/B2
Puerto Escondido, Mex. 202/B3
Puerto Heath, Bol. 214/D4
Puerto Iguazú, Arg. 215/F2
Puerto Inca, Peru 214/C3
Puerto Ingeniero Ibáñez, Chile 216/C5
Puerto Inírida, Col. 210/E4
Puerto La Cruz, Ven. 211/E2
Puerto Leguízamo, Col. 210/C5
Puerto Lempira, Hon. 203/F3
Puerto López, Col. 210/C3
Puerto Lumbreras, Sp. 102/E4
Puerto Madero, Mex. 202/C3
Puerto Madryn, Arg. 216/D4
Puerto Magdalena, Mex. 200/B3
Puerto Maldonado, Peru 214/D4
Puerto Montt, Chile 216/B4
Puerto Morazán, Nic. 202/E3
Puerto Morelos, Mex. 198/D3
Puerto Napo, Ecu. 210/B5
Puerto Natales, Chile 217/B6
Puerto Obaldía, Pan. 203/G4
Puerto Ocopa, Peru 214/C3
Puerto Padre, Cuba 203/G1
Puerto Páez, Ven. 211/E3
Puerto Peñasco, Mex. 200/B2
Puerto Píritu, Ven. 211/E2
Puerto Portillo, Peru 214/C3
Puerto Prado, Peru 214/C3
Puerto Princesa, Phil. 139/E2
Puerto Quellón, Chile 216/B4
Puerto Real, Sp. 102/B4
Puerto Rico, Col. 210/C4
Puerto Rico, Col. 210/C4
Puerto Rico (dpcy.), US 199/M8
Puerto Rondón, Col. 210/D3
Puerto San Carlos, Mex. 200/B3
Puerto San Julián, Arg. 217/D6
Puerto Santa Cruz, Arg. 217/C6
Puerto Serrano, Sp. 102/C4
Puerto Suárez, Bol. 208/G7
Puerto Supe, Peru 214/B3
Puerto Tejada, Col. 210/B4
Puerto Vallarta, Mex. 200/D4
Puerto Varas, Chile 216/B4
Puerto Viejo, CR 203/E4
Puerto Villamil, Ecu. 214/E7
Puerto Wilches, Col. 210/C3
Puerto Williams, Chile 217/D7
Puertollano, Sp. 102/C3
Pueyrredón (lake), Arg. 216/C5
Puffin (isl.), Wal, UK 92/D5
Pugachev, Rus. 121/J1
Puget (sound), Wa, US 193/C2
Puglia (prov.), It. 104/E2
Puigcerdà, Sp. 103/F1
Puiseux-en-France, Fr. 88/K4
Pujehun, SLeo. 160/C5
Pujiang, China 137/C2
Pujilí, Ecu. 210/B5
Pujŏn (lake), NKor. 131/D2
Pujut (cape), Indo. 138/C5
Pukalani, Hi, US 182/T10
Puk'an-san (peak), SKor. 131/F6
Puk'an-san NP, SKor. 131/D4
Pukapuka (isl.), Cookls. 175/J6
Pukarua (isl.), FrPol. 175/M6
Pukaskwa NP, On, Can. 188/C1
Pukch'ŏng, NKor. 131/E2
Pukdae (riv.), NKor. 131/E2
Pukhan (riv.), NKor.,SKor. 131/D3
Pukhrāyān, India 142/B2
Pukovac, Serb. 106/E4
Pukp'ot'ae-san (peak), NKor. 131/E2
Pula, Cro. 106/A3
Pulacayo, Bol. 208/E8
Pulandian (bay), China 131/A3
Pulanduta (pt.), Phil. 139/F1
Pulap (isl.), Micr. 174/D4
Pulaski, Va, US 188/D4
Pulaski, Tn, US 191/G3
Pulau (riv.), Indo. 139/J5
Puławy, Pol. 99/L3
Pulguk-sa, SKor. 131/E5
Pulheim, Ger. 111/F2
Pulisan (cape), Indo. 139/G3
Pulkovo (int'l arpt.), Rus. 119/T7
Pullach im Isartal, Ger. 115/H1
Pullman, Wa, US 184/D4
Pully, Swi. 114/C5
Pulsnitz (riv.), Ger. 99/G3
Pułtusk, Pol. 99/L2
Pülümür, Turk. 148/D2
Puluwat (isl.), Micr. 174/D4
Pulversheim, Fr. 114/D2
Pum (riv.), China 143/F1
Puma (lake), China 143/H1
Pumu (pass), China 143/H2
Puna de Atacama (plat.), Arg. 215/C2
Puná, Isla (isl.), Ecu. 208/B4
Punākha, Bhu. 143/G2
Punata, Bol. 208/E7
Pūnch, India 144/C3
Pūnch (riv.), India 144/C3
Pūndri, India 144/D5
Pune (Poona), India 147/K5
Punggai (cape), Malay. 138/B3
P'unggi, SKor. 131/E4
P'ungsan, NKor. 131/E2
Pungwe (falls), Zim. 163/F4
Punjab (plain), Pak. 147/K2
Punjab (state), Pak. 140/B2
Puno, Peru 214/D4
Puno (dept.), Peru 214/D4
Pūnpūn (riv.), India 143/E3
Punta, Ca, US 194/A2
Punta Alta, Arg. 216/E3
Punta Arena (pt.), Mex. 200/C4
Punta Arenas, Chile 217/C7
Punta Banda (cape), Mex. 200/A2
Punta Cardón, Ven. 210/D2
Punta Celarain (pt.), Mex. 202/E1
Punta Colnett (pt.), Mex. 200/A2
Punta Colonet, Mex. 200/A2
Punta de Bombón, Peru 214/D5
Punta de Mata, Ven. 211/F2
Punta del Este, Uru. 217/G2
Punta del Este (Capitán Curbelo) (int'l arpt.), Uru. 217/G2
Punta Gorda, Fl, US 191/H5
Punta Gorda (bay), Nic. 198/E5
Punta Gorda, Belz. 202/D2
Punta Marina, It. 117/F4
Punta Raisi (int'l arpt.), It. 104/C3
Punta Umbría, Sp. 102/B4
Puntarenas, CR 203/E4
Puolo (pt.), Hi, US 182/S10
Pupiales, Col. 210/B4
Pupuya (peak), Bol. 214/D4
Puquio, Peru 214/C4
Pur (riv.), Rus. 122/H3
Puracé (vol.), Col. 210/B4
Puracé, PN, Col. 208/C3
Pūranpur, India 142/C1
Purbeck (isl.), Eng, UK 90/D5
Purcell (mts.), BC, Can. 184/D3
Purcell, Ok, US 187/H4
Puré (riv.), Col. 210/D5
Purén, Chile 216/B3
Purgatoire (riv.), Co, US 187/G3
Pürgen, Ger. 115/G1
Purgstall an der Erlauf, Aus. 101/L2
Purī, India 140/D3
Purificación, Col. 210/C4
Purikari (pt.), Est. 97/L2
Purkersdorf, Aus. 107/N7
Purmerend, Neth. 108/B3
Pūrna, India 140/C4
Purnia, India 143/F3
Purranque, Chile 215/B5
Puruê (riv.), Braz. 210/D5
Purūlia, India 143/F4
Puruni (riv.), Guy. 211/G3
Purús (riv.), Braz. 205/C3

Purushottampur, India 140/D4
Pürvomay, Bul. 107/G4
Purwa, India 142/C2
Purwokerto, Indo. 138/C5
Pusad, India 140/C4
Pusan, SKor. 131/E5
Pusan-Gwangyŏksi (prov.), SKor. 131/E5
Pusat Gayo (mts.), Indo. 138/A3
Puschendorf, Ger. 112/D3
Pushkin, Rus. 119/T7
Püspökladány, Hun. 106/E2
Pusur (riv.), Bang. 143/G4
Putaendo, Chile 216/C2
Putian, China 137/C2
Putina, Peru 214/D4
Puting (cape), Indo. 138/D4
Putla de Guerrero, Mex. 202/B2
Putomayo (dept.), Col. 210/C4
Putorana (mts.), Rus. 122/K3
Putrachoique (peak), Arg. 216/C4
Putre, Chile 214/D5
Puttalam, SrL. 140/C6
Putte, Belg. 111/D1
Puttelange-aux-Lacs, Fr. 111/F5
Putten, Neth. 108/C4
Putten (isl.), Neth. 108/B5
Püttlach (riv.), Ger. 113/E3
Püttlingen, Ger. 111/F5
Putu (range), Libr. 160/C5
Putumayo (riv.), SAm. 210/C5
Putussibau, Indo. 138/D3
Puu Kukui (peak), Hi, US 182/T10
Puu Moaulanui (peak), Hi, US 182/T10
Puu o Mahuka Heiau State Mon., Hi, US 182/V12
Puuanahulu, Hi, US 182/U11
Puuiki, Hi, US 182/T10
Puula (lake), Fin. 97/M1
Puurs, Belg. 111/D1
Puuwai, Hi, US 182/R10
Puy de Sancy (peak), Fr. 100/E4
Puyallup, Wa, US 184/C4
Puyallup (riv.), Wa, US 193/C3
Puyallup Ind. Res., Wa, US 193/C3
Puyang, China 130/C4
Puyehue (lake), Chile 216/B4
Puyehue (vol.), Chile 216/B4
Puylaurens, Fr. 100/E5
Puymorens, Col de (pass), Fr. 100/D5
Puyŏ, SKor. 131/D4
Puyo, Ecu. 210/B5
Puzal, Sp. 103/E3
Pwani (pol. reg.), Tanz. 162/C4
Pwllheli, Wal, UK 92/D6
Pyandzh (riv.), Taj. 145/F5
Pyaozero (lake), Rus. 95/J2
Pyapon, Myan. 141/G4
Pyasina (riv.), Rus. 122/J2
Pyatigorsk, Rus. 121/G3
Pyfara (peak), Fr. 100/F4
Pyhä-Häkin NP, Fin. 118/E3
Pyhäjärvi, Fin. 118/E3
Pyhäjärvi (lake), Fin. 97/K1
Pyhäntä, Fin. 118/E2
Pyhätunturi (peak), Fin. 118/E2
Pyinmana, Myan. 141/G4
P'yŏngan-bukto (prov.), NKor. 131/C2
P'yŏngan-namdo (prov.), NKor. 131/C3
P'yŏngch'ang, SKor. 131/E4
P'yŏnggang, NKor. 131/D3
P'yŏnghae, SKor. 131/E4
P'yŏngsan, NKor. 131/D3
P'yŏngsong, NKor. 131/C3
P'yŏngt'aek, SKor. 131/D4
P'yŏngyang (int'l arpt.), NKor. 131/C3
P'yŏngyang (cap.), NKor. 131/C3
P'yŏngyang-si (prov.), NKor. 131/C3
Pyŏnsanbando NP, SKor. 131/D5
Pyramid (lake), Nv, US 186/B3
Pyramid (mtn.), BC, Can. 192/M4
Pyramids of Jīzah, Egypt 149/B5
Pyrenees (mts.), Fr.,Sp. 85/D4
Pyrénées Occidental, PN des, Fr. 100/C5
Pyryatyn, Ukr. 120/E2
Pyrzyce, Pol. 99/H2
Pyshma (riv.), Rus. 119/Q4
Pyu, Myan. 141/G4
Pyuthān, Nepal 142/D1

Q

Qā 'al Jafr (salt pan), Jor. 149/E4
Qabalān, WBnk. 149/G7
Qabāţiyah, WBnk. 149/G7
Qadima, Isr. 149/F7
Qādirpur Rān, Pak. 144/A4
Qā'en, Iran 147/G2
Qafa e Malit (pass), Alb. 105/G1
Qaffīn, WBnk. 149/G7
Qahar Youyi Qianqi, China 130/C2
Qahar Youyi Zhongqi, China 130/C2
Qaidam (basin), China 128/F4
Qalansuwa, Isr. 149/F7
Qal'at Dizah, Iraq 148/F2
Qal'eh-ye Now, Afg. 145/D6
Qalqīlyah, WBnk. 149/F7
Qalyūb, Egypt 149/B4
Qamdo, China 128/G5
Qamīnis, Libya 154/K1
Qapshagay Bögeni (res.), Kaz. 145/G4
Qapshaghay, Kaz. 145/G4
Qaraghandy, Kaz. 145/F3
Qaraghandy (obl.), Kaz. 145/F3
Qarataū, Kaz. 145/F4
Qarataū Zhotasy (mts.), Kaz. 145/E4
Qareh Chāy (riv.), Iran 146/E2
Qareh Sū (riv.), Iran 121/H5
Qarqan (riv.), China 128/E4
Qarrit (pass), Alb. 105/G2
Qarshi, Uzb. 145/E5
Qārūn (lake), Egypt 159/B2
Qashqadaryo (pol. reg.), Uzb. 145/D5
Qaşr-e Qand, Iran 147/H3
Qaşr-e-Shīrīn, Iran 146/E2
Qa'ţabah, Yem. 146/D6
Qatar (ctry.) 146/F3
Qattara (depr.), Egypt 148/A4
Qaţţīnah, Buḩayrat (lake), Syria 149/E2
Qaydaq Sory (swamp), Kaz. 121/K3
Qayyārah, Iraq 148/E3
Qazaqtyng Usaqshoqylyghy (uplands), Kaz. 122/H5
Qāzi Ahmad, Pak. 140/A2
Qazvīn, Iran 146/F1
Qedma, Isr. 149/F8
Qendrevica (peak), Alb. 105/F2
Qezel Owzan (riv.), Iran 146/E1
Qi Xian, China 130/C4
Qian (mts.), China 131/B2
Qian (riv.), China 130/D5
Qian'an, China 129/M3
Qianxi, China 130/J6
Qianyang, China 137/B2
Qiaojia, China 141/H2
Qibyā, Isr. 149/G8
Qidong, China 141/K2
Qidong, China 130/L8
Qiemo, China 128/E4
Qihe, China 130/D3
Qijiang, China 137/A2
Qikiqtarjuaq, Nun., Can. 181/K2
Qila Dīdār Singh, Pak. 144/C3
Qila Sobha Singh, Pak. 144/C3
Qilian (mts.), China 128/G4
Qilian (peak), China 128/G4
Qimantag (mts.), China 128/F4
Qimen, China 137/C2
Qin (mts.), China 130/B4
Qinā (gov.), Egypt 159/C3
Qing (riv.), China 137/B1
Qing'an, China 129/N2
Qingdao, China 130/E3
Qingfeng, China 130/C4
Qinghai (mts.), China 128/G4
Qinghai (prov.), China 128/G4
Qinghe, China 130/C3
Qinglong, China 130/D2
Qingpu, China 130/L8
Qingshui (riv.), China 137/A2
Qingshuihe, China 130/B3
Qingyuan, China 141/K3
Qingyun, China 130/D3
Qingzhou, China 130/D3
Qinhuangdao, China 130/D3
Qinshui, China 130/C4
Qinyang, China 130/C4
Qinyuan, China 130/C3
Qinzhou, China 141/J3
Qionghai, China 141/K4
Qionglai (mts.), China 128/H5
Qiongshan, China 141/K4
Qiongzhong, China 136/E2
Qiqihar, China 129/M2
Qira, China 128/D4
Qiryat Ata, Isr. 149/G6
Qiryat Bialik, Isr. 149/G6
Qiryat Gat, Isr. 149/D4
Qiryat Mal'akhi, Isr. 149/F8
Qiryat Motzkin, Isr. 149/G6
Qiryat Shemona, Isr. 149/D3
Qiryat Tiv'on, Isr. 149/G6
Qiryat Yam, Isr. 149/G6
Qitai, China 128/E3
Qitaihe, China 129/P2
Qixia, China 130/E3
Qixing (riv.), China 123/P5
Qizilqum (des.), Kaz. 122/G5
Qogir (peak), China 147/L1
Qom (riv.), Iran 146/F2
Qom, Iran 146/F2
Qomsheh, Iran 146/F2
Qondūz (riv.), Afg. 147/J1
Qonggyai, China 143/H1
Qoraqalpoghiston Aut. Rep., Uzb. 121/L3
Qormi, Malta 104/L7
Qorveh, Iran 146/E1
Qostanay (obl.), Kaz. 145/D2
Qostanay (int'l arpt.), Kaz. 119/P5
Qostanay, Kaz. 119/P5
Qoţūr, Iran 148/F2
Qu (riv.), China 129/L6
Quabbin (res.), Ma, US 189/F3
Quairading, Austl. 170/C5
Quakenbrück, Ger. 109/E3
Quakertown, Pa, US 196/C3
Quambatook, Austl. 173/B2
Quanah, Tx, US 187/H4
Quanbao (mtn.), China 130/B4
Quang Ngai, Viet. 136/E3
Quang Tri, Viet. 136/D2
Quanjiao, China 130/D4
Quannan, China 137/B3
Quantocks, The (hills), Eng, UK 90/C4
Quanzhou, China 137/C3
Qu'appelle (dam), Sk, Can. 185/G3
Qu'appelle (riv.), Sk, Can. 185/G3
Qu'appelle, Sk, Can. 185/H3
Quaqtaq, Qu, Can. 181/K2
Quaregnon, Belg. 110/C3
Quarles (mts.), Indo. 139/E4
Quarona, It. 116/B1
Quarrata, It. 117/D5
Quarryville, Pa, US 196/B4
Quarto d'Altino, It. 117/F1
Quartu Sant'Elena, It. 104/A3
Quartz Hill, Ca, US 194/B1
Quatre Bornes, Mrts. 165/T15
Quattervals (peak), Swi. 115/G4
Quba, Azer. 121/J4
Qūchān, Iran 147/G1
Queanbeyan, Austl. 173/D2
Québec (int'l arpt.), Qu, Can. 189/G2
Québec (cap.), Qu, Can. 189/G2
Québec (prov.), Can. 181/J3
Quebra-Cangalha, Serra (mts.), Braz. 213/H8
Quecholac, Mex. 201/M8
Quechutenango, Mex. 201/F5
Quedal (pt.), Chile 216/B4
Queen Alia (int'l arpt.), Jor. 149/E4
Queen Anne, Md, US 196/C6
Queen Annes (co.), Md, US 196/C5
Queen Charlotte, BC, Can. 192/M5
Queen Charlotte (isls.), BC, Can. 180/C3
Queen Charlotte (str.), BC, Can. 184/B3
Queen Charlotte (sound), BC, Can. 180/C3
Queen City, Tx, US 187/J4
Queen Creek, Az, US 195/S19
Queen Elizabeth (isls.), NW,Nun., Can. 181/Q7
Queen Mary (coast), Ant. 218/G
Queen Mary, Ca, US 194/F8
Queen Mary (res.), Eng, UK 88/B2
Queen Maud (mts.), Ant. 218/P
Queen Maud (gulf), Nun., Can. 180/F2
Queen Maud Land (phys. reg.), Ant. 218/Z
Queen Victoria Spring Nature Reserve, Austl. 170/D4
Queens (chan.), Nun., Can. 181/S7
Queens (co.), NY, US 197/E2
Queensberry (peak), Sc, UK 94/C6
Queensferry, Sc, UK 94/C5
Queensland, Austl. 173/B1
Queensland (state), Austl. 167/C3
Queenstown, Austl. 173/C4
Queenstown, SAfr. 164/D3
Queenstown, NZ 175/R12
Queenstown, Md, US 196/B6
Queich (riv.), Ger. 111/G5
Queidersbach, Ger. 111/G5
Queilén, Chile 216/B4
Queimada, Ilha (isl.), Braz. 209/H4
Queimadas, Braz. 212/D2
Queimadas, Braz. 212/C3
Quelimane, Moz. 163/G4
Queluz, Port. 103/P10
Quemado, Punta del (pt.), Cuba 203/H1
Quemú Quemú, Arg. 216/E3
Quepos, CR 203/E4
Quequén, Arg. 216/F3
Quequén Grande (riv.), Arg. 216/F3
Querecotillo, Peru 214/A2
Querétaro, Mex. 201/E4
Querétaro de Arteaga (state), Mex. 198/A5
Querimbas, Arquipélago das (arch.), Moz. 163/H3
Quero, It. 117/E1
Querobabi, Mex. 200/C2
Quesada, CR 203/E4
Quesada, Sp. 102/D4
Queshan, China 130/C4
Quesnel, BC, Can. 184/C2
Quesnel (lake), BC, Can. 180/D3
Quesnoy-sur-Deûle, Fr. 110/C2
Questa, NM, US 187/F3
Questembert, Fr. 100/B3
Quetigny, Fr. 114/B3
Quetta, Pak. 147/J2
Queulat, PN, Chile 216/B5
Quevedo, Ecu. 208/C4
Quevedo (riv.), Ecu. 210/B5
Quezaltenango, Guat. 202/D3
Quezon, Phil. 139/E2
Quezon City, Phil. 137/D5
Qufu, China 130/D4
Qui Nhon, Viet. 136/E3
Quibdó, Col. 210/B3
Quiberon, Fr. 100/B3
Quiberon (bay), Fr. 100/B3
Quíbor, Ven. 210/D2
Quicacha, Peru 214/C4
Quiçama, PN da, Ang. 163/B2
Quickborn, Ger. 109/G1
Quiers, Fr. 88/L6
Quierschied, Ger. 111/G5
Quila, Mex. 200/D3
Quilán (cape), Chile 216/B4
Quilca, Peru 214/C5
Quilcene, Wa, US 193/B2
Quiliano, It. 116/B4
Quilicura, Chile 216/N8
Quill (lakes), Sk, Can. 185/G2
Quillabamba, Peru 214/C4
Quillacollo, Bol. 208/E7
Quillagua (pt.), Chile 216/B4
Quillan, Fr. 100/E5
Quilleco, Chile 216/C3
Quillota, Chile 216/N8
Quilmaná, Peru 214/B4
Quilon, India 140/C6
Quilpie, Austl. 172/B4
Quilpué, Chile 216/N8
Quimilí, Arg. 215/D2
Quimper, Fr. 100/A2
Quimperlé, Fr. 100/B3
Quincey, Fr. 114/C2
Quincy, Wa, US 184/D4
Quincy, Fl, US 191/G4
Quincy, Ma, US 189/G3
Quincy-sous-Sénart, Fr. 88/K5
Quincy-Voisins, Fr. 88/L5
Quindío (dept.), Col. 210/A4
Quinhagak, Ak, US 192/F4
Quinn (riv.), Nv, US 186/C2
Quinns Rocks, Austl. 170/B4
Quintana de la Serena, Sp. 102/C3
Quintana Roo (state), Mex. 198/D4
Quintanar de la Orden, Sp. 102/D3
Quintanar del Rey, Sp. 102/E3
Quintero, Chile 216/N8
Quinto (riv.), Arg. 216/D2
Quinto, Sp. 103/E2
Quinto, Swi. 115/E4
Quinto di Treviso, It. 117/F1
Quinto di Valpantena, It. 117/E2
Quinton, NJ, US 196/C4
Quinzano d'Oglio, It. 116/C2
Quionga, Moz. 162/D5
Quipapá, Braz. 212/C3
Quirihue, Chile 216/B3
Quirindi, Austl. 173/D1
Quirinópolis, Braz. 213/B1
Quiriquire, Ven. 211/F2
Quiroga, Mex. 201/E5
Quiroga, Sp. 102/B1
Quiruvilca, Peru 214/B3
Quisiro, Ven. 210/D2
Quispamsis, NB, Can. 189/H2
Quissico, Moz. 163/F5
Quistello, It. 117/D3
Quitilipi, Arg. 215/D2
Quitman, Ga, US 191/H4
Quitman, Ms, US 191/F3
Quito (cap.), Ecu. 210/B5
Quixeramobim, Braz. 212/C2
Qujiang, China 141/K3
Qujing, China 141/H2
Quogue, NY, US 197/F2
Quoich (riv.), Nun., Can. 180/G2
Quoich (lake), Sc, UK 94/A2
Quoile (riv.), NI, UK 92/C3
Quoin (pt.), SAfr. 164/L11
Quorn, Austl. 171/H5
Qūqon, Uzb. 145/F4
Qŭrghonteppa, Taj. 147/J1
Qurnat as Sawdā' (peak), Leb. 149/E2
Qūş, Egypt 159/C3
Qusmuryn Köli (lake), Kaz. 145/D2
Qusum, China 128/F6
Quttinirpaaq NP, Nun., Can. 181/T6
Quwo, China 130/B4
Quwu (mts.), China 128/H4
Quyang, China 130/C3
Quzhou, China 137/C2
Quzhou, China 130/C3
Qyzylorda, Kaz. 145/E4
Qyzylorda (obl.), Kaz. 145/D4

R

Raab (riv.), Aus. 101/L3
Raab, Aus. 113/G6
Raabs an der Thaya, Aus. 99/H4
Raahe, Fin. 118/E2
Raalte, Neth. 108/D4
Raamsdonk, Neth. 108/B5
Ra'ananna, Isr. 149/F7
Raanes (pen.), Nun., Can. 181/S7
Rab (isl.), Cro. 106/B3
Rab, Cro. 106/B3
Rába (riv.), Hun. 106/C2
Rábahidvég, Hun. 101/M3
Rabat (cap.), Mor. 158/A2
Rabat, Malta 104/L7
Rabat (Sale) (int'l arpt.), Mor. 158/A2
Rabat (Victoria), Malta 104/L6
Rabbi (riv.), It. 101/K4
Rabgala (pass), China 143/F2
Rabil, CpV. 151/K10
Rabinal, Guat. 202/D3
Rabiusa (riv.), Swi. 115/F4
Rabka, Pol. 99/K4
Rabkavi-Banhatti, India 147/L5
Raby (pt.), On, Can. 189/S8
Racconigi, It. 101/G4
Raccoon (pt.), La, US 187/K5
Rach Gia (bay), Viet. 136/D4
Rach Gia, Viet. 136/D4
Racibórz, Pol. 99/K3
Racine (peak), Swi. 114/C3
Racine, Wi, US 185/M5
Racine (co.), Wi, US 193/P14
Rada Tilly, Arg. 216/D5
Radaur, India 144/D4
Rădăuţi, Rom. 107/G2
Radbuza (riv.), Czh. 98/G4
Radcliffe, Eng, UK 93/F4
Raddestorf, Ger. 109/F4
Rade de Caen (bay), Fr. 100/C2
Radeč (peak), Czh. 113/G3
Radevormwald, Ger. 109/E6
Radisson, Sk, Can. 184/G2
Radlett, Eng, UK 88/C2
Radnice, Czh. 113/G3
Radolfzell, Ger. 115/E2
Radom, Pol. 99/L3
Radomir, Bul. 106/F4
Radomsko, Pol. 99/K3
Radoviš, FYROM 105/H2
Radovljica, Slov. 101/L3
Radøy (isl.), Nor. 96/A1
Radstadt, Aus. 101/K3
Radviliškis, Lith. 97/K4
Radwá, Jabal (peak), SAr. 146/C4
Radziejów, Pol. 99/K2
Radzymin, Pol. 99/L2
Radzyń Podlaski, Pol. 99/M3
Rae (isth.), Nun., Can. 181/H2
Rae (riv.), Nun., Can. 180/E2
Rāe Bareli, India 142/C2
Rae-Edzo, NW, Can. 180/E2
Raeford, NC, US 191/J3
Raeren, Belg. 111/F2
Raesfeld, Ger. 108/D5
Raeside (lake), Austl. 170/D4
Rafael J. Garcia, Mex. 201/M7
Rafael Núñez (int'l arpt.), Col. 210/C2
Rafaela, Arg. 215/D3
Rafaḩ, Gaza 149/D4
Rafai, CAfr. 155/K7
Rafīdīyah, WBnk. 149/G7
Rafiganj, India 143/E3
Rafina, Gre. 105/P8
Rafsanjān, Iran 147/G2
Raft (riv.), Id, US 184/E5
Rafz, Swi. 115/E2
Ragang (mt.), Phil. 139/F2
Ragged (mt.), Austl. 170/D5
Ragged (pt.), Chile 217/B7
Rāghugarh, India 142/A3
Raghunāthpur, India 143/F4
Rago NP, Nor. 95/E2
Ragstone (range), Eng, UK 88/D3
Ragusa, It. 104/D4
Rāhatgarh, India 142/B4
Rahden, Ger. 109/F4
Rahīmyār Khān, Pak. 144/A5
Rahole Nat'l Rsv., Kenya 162/C2
Råholt, Nor. 96/D1
Rāhuri, India 140/B4
Rahway, NJ, US 197/H9
Raiatea (isl.), FrPol. 175/K6
Raichūr, India 140/C4
Raiganj, India 143/G3
Raigarh, India 142/D5
Raikot, India 144/C4
Railroad, Pa, US 196/B4
Railroad Canyon (res.), Ca, US 194/C3
Rainbach im Mühlkreis, Aus. 113/H5
Rainbow, Austl. 173/B2
Rainbow (valley), Az, US 195/R19
Rainbow, Ca, US 194/C4
Rainbow Beach, Austl. 172/D4
Rainbow Bridge Nat'l Mon., Ut, US 186/E3
Rainier (mt.), Wa, US 184/C4
Rainsville, Al, US 191/G3
Rainy (lake), On, Can. 180/G4
Rainy Lake (riv.), Can.,US 185/K3
Rainy River, On, Can. 185/K3
Raipur, India 140/D3
Rairoa (atoll), FrPol. 175/L6
Raisdorf, Ger. 96/D4
Raisen, India 142/A4
Rāisinghnagar, India 144/B5
Raisio, Fin. 97/K1
Raismes, Fr. 110/C3
Raivavae (isl.), FrPol. 175/L7
Rāiwind, Pak. 144/C4
Raizeux, Fr. 88/H6
Rāj Gāngpur, India 143/E4
Raja (pt.), Indo. 138/A3
Rāja Jang, Pak. 144/C4
Rājahmundry, India 140/D4
Rājampet, India 140/C5
Rajang (riv.), Malay. 138/D3
Rājanpur, Pak. 144/A5
Rājaori, India 144/C3
Rājapālaiyam, India 140/C6
Rājāpur, India 142/C3
Rājāpur, India 147/K5
Rājasthān (state), India 140/B2
Rājbirāj, Nepal 143/F2
Rājgarh, India 142/A2
Rājgarh, India 144/C5
Rājgarh, India 147/L4
Rājgir, India 143/E3
Rajka, Hun. 106/C1
Rājkot, India 147/K4
Rājmahal (hills), India 143/F3
Rājmahal, India 143/F3
Rājpur, India 143/G4
Rājpura, India 144/D4
Rājshāhi (pol. reg.), Bang. 143/G3
Rājshāhi (pol. div.), Bang. 143/G3
Rājshāhi, Bang. 143/G3
Rājula, India 147/K4
Raka (riv.), China 143/F1
Rakahanga (isl.), Cookls. 175/J5
Rakamaz, Hun. 106/E1
Rakaposhi (peak), Pak. 144/C1
Rakhine (state), Myan. 141/F4
Rakhshān (riv.), Pak. 147/H3
Rakkestad, Nor. 96/D2
Rakos-patak (riv.), Hun. 107/R9
Rakovnicky Potok (riv.), Czh. 113/G2
Rakovník, Czh. 113/G2
Rakovski, Bul. 107/G4
Rakushechnyy (cape), Kaz. 145/B4
Rakvere, Est. 97/M2
Raldon, It. 117/E2
Raleigh (cap.), NC, US 191/J3
Raleigh-Durham (int'l arpt.), NC, US 191/J3
Ralik Chain (isls.), Mrsh. 174/F4
Ralingen, Ger. 111/F4
Ralston, Ab, Can. 184/F3
Rām Allāh, Isr. 149/G8
Ramalho, Serra do (mts.), Braz. 209/K6
Ramapo (riv.), NJ, US 196/J7
Ramapo (mts.), NJ, US 197/H7
Ramat Gan, Isr. 149/F7
Ramat Hasharon, Isr. 149/F7
Rambervillers, Fr. 114/C1
Rame (pt.), Eng, UK 90/B6
Ramenskoye, Rus. 119/X9
Rāmeswaram, India 140/C6
Rāmgangā (riv.), India 142/B1
Rāmgarh, India 143/E4
Rāmhormoz, Iran 146/E2
Ramírez, Mex. 201/M7
Rāmjībanpur, India 143/F4
Ramla, Isr. 149/F8
Ramlu (peak), Erit. 146/D6
Ramme, Den. 96/C3
Rammūn, Isr. 149/G8
Rāmnagar, India 142/B1
Rāmnagar, India 142/D3
Rāmnagar, India 144/C3
Ramnäs, Swe. 96/G2
Ramonchamp, Fr. 114/C2
Ramor (lake), Ire. 92/A4
Ramos (riv.), Mex. 190/B5
Ramosch, Swi. 115/G4
Rampart, Ak, US 192/H2
Rampillon, Fr. 88/M6
Rāmpur, India 142/B1
Rāmpur, India 144/D4
Rāmpur Hāt, India 143/F3
Rāmpura Phūl, India 144/C4
Ramree (isl.), Myan. 141/F4
Rāmsanehīghāt, India 142/C2
Ramsbottom, Eng, UK 93/F4
Ramsden Heath, Eng, UK 88/E2
Ramsen, Swi. 115/E2
Ramsey (lake), On, Can. 188/D2
Ramsey (isl.), Wal, UK 90/A3
Ramsey, NJ, US 197/J7
Ramsey, IM, UK 92/D3
Ramsey (bay), IM, UK 92/D3
Ramsgate, Eng, UK 91/H4
Ramstein-Miesenbach, Ger. 111/G5
Ramu (riv.), PNG 174/D5
Rana, Nor. 95/E2
Rānāghāt, India 143/G4
Rancagua, Chile 216/N9
Rance (riv.), Fr. 100/E5
Rancharia, Braz. 213/B2
Rancheria (riv.), Col. 210/C2
Rānchī, India 143/E4
Rancho Palos Verdes, Ca, US 194/F8
Rancho Santa Fe, Ca, US 194/C4
Ranchos, Arg. 216/F2
Ranco (lake), Chile 216/B4
Rancocas, NJ, US 196/D4
Rancul, Arg. 216/D2
Randaberg, Nor. 96/A2
Randallstown, Md, US 196/B5
Randalstown, NI, UK 92/B2
Randazzo, It. 104/D4
Randburg, SAfr. 164/P13
Randers, Den. 96/D3
Randolph, NJ, US 196/D2
Randow (riv.), Ger. 99/H2
Randsfjorden (lake), Nor. 96/D1
Råneå, Swe. 118/D2
Rang (peak), Thai. 136/C2
Rang-du-Fliers, Fr. 110/A3
Rāngāmāti (pol. reg.), Bang. 143/H4
Rāngāmāti, Bang. 141/F3
Rangasa (cape), Indo. 139/E4
Rangely, Co, US 186/E2
Ranger, Tx, US 187/H4
Rangia, India 143/H2
Rangiora, NZ 175/S11
Rangiroa (isl.), FrPol. 175/L6
Rangoon (Yangon) (cap.), Myan. 141/G4
Rangpur, Bang. 143/G3
Rangpur (pol. reg.), Bang. 143/G3
Rangsdorf, Ger. 98/Q7
Rānībennur, India 147/L6
Rānīganj, India 143/F4
Rānīkhet, India 142/B1
Rānīpur, India 142/B3
Rankin, Tx, US 187/G5
Rankin Inlet, Nun., Can. 180/G2
Rankweil, Aus. 115/F3
Rannoch (lake), Sc, UK 94/B3
Ranohira, Madg. 165/H8
Ranomafana, Madg. 165/H8
Ranong, Thai. 136/B4
Ranotsara, Madg. 165/H8
Ransbach-Baumbach, Ger. 111/G3
Ransomville, NY, US 189/S9
Ranst, Belg. 108/B6
Ranstadt, Ger. 112/B2
Rantabe, Madg. 165/J6
Rantekombola (peak), Indo. 139/E4
Rantigny, Fr. 110/B5
Rantīs, WBnk. 149/G7
Rantoul, Il, US 185/L5
Rantsila, Fin. 118/E2
Ranzan, Japan 135/C1
Rao Co (peak), Laos 136/D2
Raon-l'Étape, Fr. 114/C1
Raoping, China 137/C3
Raoui, 'Erg er (des.), Alg. 156/E3
Raoul (isl.), NZ 174/H7
Raoyang (riv.), China 131/A2
Raoyang, China 130/C3
Rapa (isl.), FrPol. 175/L7
Rapallo, It. 116/C4
Rapel (lake), Chile 216/N9
Rapid City, SD, US 185/H4
Rappahannock (riv.), Va, US 188/E4
Rapper (cape), Chile 216/B5
Rāpti (zone), Nepal 142/D1
Rapti (riv.), India 140/D2
Rara NP, Nepal 142/D1
Raritan (bay), NJ, US 196/D3
Raritan (riv.), NJ, US 196/D2
Raritan, South Branch (riv.), NJ, US 196/D2
Raron, Swi. 114/D5
Rarotonga (isl.), Cookls. 175/J7
Ra's al 'Ayn, Syria 148/E2
Ra's al Basīt (pt.), Syria 149/D2
Ra's al Khaymah, UAE 147/G3
Ra's al Unūf, D.R.Congo 155/J7
Ra's An Naqb, Jor. 149/D5
Ra's aţ Ţīb (Cape Bon) (cape), Tun. 158/M6
Ras Dashen (peak), Eth. 155/N5
Râs el Ma, Alg. 158/D2
Râs el Oued, Alg. 158/H5
Ras il-Qammieħ (pt.), Malta 104/L7
Ras San Dimitri (pt.), Malta 104/L6
Ra's Şawqirah (pt.), Oman 147/G5
Rasa (pt.), Arg. 216/E4
Raschau, Ger. 113/F1
Rashaant, Mong. 128/F2
Rasharkin, NI, UK 92/B2
Rāshayyā, Leb. 149/D3
Rashīd, Egypt 149/B4
Rasht, Iran 146/E1
Raška, Serb. 106/E4
Rasmussen (basin), Nun., Can. 180/G2
Raso (cape), Port. 103/P10
Rason (lake), Austl. 170/E4
Rasrā, India 142/D3
Rassina, It. 117/E5
Rasskazovo, Rus. 121/G1
Rastatt, Ger. 112/B5
Rastede, Ger. 109/F2
Rasūlnagar, Pak. 144/B3
Rat Buri, Thai. 136/B3
Rata (cape), Indo. 138/B5
Ratak Chain (isls.), Mrsh. 174/F3
Ratangarh, India 147/K3
Ratanpur, India 142/D4
Rāth, India 142/B3
Rathbun (lake), Ia, US 185/K5
Rathcoole, Ire. 92/B5
Rathdowney, Ire. 89/Q10
Rathdrum, Ire. 92/B6
Rathedaung, Myan. 141/F3
Rathenow, Ger. 98/G2
Rathfriland, NI, UK 92/B3
Rathkeale, Ire. 89/P10
Rathlin (isl.), NI, UK 92/B1
Rathlin (sound), NI, UK 92/B1
Rathluirc, Ire. 89/P10
Rathmore, Ire. 89/P10
Rathnew, Ire. 92/B6
Ratia, India 144/C5
Ratingen, Ger. 108/D6
Ratlām, India 147/L4
Ratnāgiri, India 147/K5
Ratnapura, SrL. 140/D6
Ratoath, Ire. 92/B4
Raton, NM, US 187/F3
Rattray (pt.), Sc, UK 94/E1
Rättvik, Swe. 96/F1
Raub, Malay. 138/B3
Rauch, Arg. 216/F3
Raudales Malpaso, Mex. 202/C2
Raudhinúpur (pt.), Ice. 95/P6
Raufarhöfn, Ice. 95/P6
Raufoss, Nor. 96/D1
Rauhe Ebrach (riv.), Ger. 112/D3
Raul Soares, Braz. 213/D2
Rauma, Fin. 97/J1
Raunheim, Ger. 112/B2
Raurkela, India 143/E4
Rausu, Japan 134/D1
Rautjärvi, Fin. 97/N1
Ravanusa, It. 104/C4
Rāvar, Iran 147/G2
Ravarino, It. 117/E3
Ravels, Belg. 108/B6
Ravenna, It. 117/F4
Ravenna (prov.), It. 117/E4
Ravenna, Ca, US 194/B2
Ravensburg, Ger. 115/F2
Ravensdale, Wa, US 193/D3
Ravenshoe, Austl. 172/B2
Ravensthorpe, Austl. 170/D5
Ravenswood, WV, US 188/D4
Rāvi (riv.), Ind.,Pak. 147/K2
Ravne na Koroškem, Slov. 101/L3
Rawa Mazowiecka, Pol. 99/L3
Rāwah, Iraq 148/E3
Rawaki (Phoenix) (isl.), Kiri. 175/H5
Rāwalpindi, Pak. 144/B3
Rāwatsār, India 144/C5
Rawicz, Pol. 99/J3
Rawlins, Wy, US 184/G5
Rawlinson (mt.), Austl. 171/E3
Rawmarsh, Eng, UK 93/G5
Rawson, Arg. 216/D4
Rawtenstall, Eng, UK 93/F4
Raxaul Bazar, India 143/E2
Ray (cape), Nf, Can. 189/K2
Raya (peak), Indo. 138/D4
Rāyadrug, India 140/C5
Raychikhinsk, Rus. 129/N2
Rayleigh, Eng, UK 91/G3
Raymond, Ab, Can. 184/E3
Raymond, Wa, US 184/C4
Raymond, Co, US 195/B2
Raymond, Wi, US 193/P14
Raymondville, Tx, US 190/D5
Raymore, Sk, Can. 185/G3
Raymore, Mo, US 195/E6
Rayón, Mex. 201/F4
Rayón, Mex. 200/C2
Rayón, Mex. 201/Q10
Rayón, PN, Mex. 201/E5
Rayong, Thai. 136/C3
Raytown, Mo, US 195/E5
Rayville, La, US 187/K4
Raz, Pointe de (pt.),Fr. 100/A2
Razelm (lake), Rom. 107/J3
Razgrad, Bul. 107/H4
Razlog, Bul. 107/F5
Re di Castello (peak), It. 115/G5
Ré, Île de (isl.), Fr. 100/C3

Rea (riv.), Eng, UK 90/D1
Reading, Eng, UK 91/F4
Reading (co.), Eng, UK 91/F4
Reading, Pa, US 196/C3
Realicó, Arg. 216/D2
Realp, Swi. 115/E4
Reamstown, Pa, US 196/B3
Reao (isl.), FrPol. 175/M6
Réau, Fr. 88/K6
Rebais, Fr. 110/C6
Rebecca (lake),
Austl. 170/D4
Rębiechowo (int'l arpt.),
Pol. 96/H4
Rebouças, Braz. 213/B3
Rebstein, Swi. 115/F3
Rebun, Japan 134/B1
Recanati, It. 117/G6
Recco, It. 116/C4
Recherche (arch.),
Austl. 101/M3
Rechnitz, Aus. 101/M3
Rechthalten, Swi. 114/D4
Rechytsa, Bela. 120/D1
Recife (cape), SAfr. 164/D4
Recke, Ger. 109/E4
Reckingen, Swi. 115/E5
Recklinghausen,
Ger. 109/E5
Recknitz (riv.), Ger. 98/G2
Réclère, Swi. 114/C3
Recoaro Terme, It. 117/E1
Reconquista, Arg. 215/E2
Reconvilier, Swi. 114/D3
Recuay, Peru 214/B3
Red (sea), Afr.,Asia 146/C4
Red (riv.), Mb, Can. 185/J3
Red (riv.), China,Viet. 128/H7
Red (riv.), US 190/E4
Red (riv.), Mn, US 183/G2
Red (lakes), Mn, US 183/H2
Red (bay), NI, UK 92/B1
Red (riv.), Viet. 141/H3
Red Bank, NJ, US 196/D3
Red Bluff (lake),
Tx, US 187/G5
Red Bluff, Ca, US 186/B2
Red Cliffs, Austl. 173/B2
Red Cloud, Ne, US 187/H2
Red Deer, Ab, Can. 184/E2
Red Deer (riv.),
Sk, Can. 180/E3
Red Devil, Ak, US 192/G3
Red Hill (peak),
Hi, US 182/T10
Red Hill, Pa, US 196/C3
Red Indian (lake),
Nf, Can. 189/K1
Red Lake (riv.),
Mn, US 185/K3
Red Lake, On, Can. 185/K3
Red Lion, De, US 196/C4
Red Lion, Pa, US 196/B4
Red Lodge, Mt, US 184/F4
Red, North Fork (riv.),
US 187/G4
Red River of the North
(riv.), US,Can. 185/J3
Red Rock (lake),
Ia, US 185/K5
Red Rocks (pt.), Austl. 171/E5
Red Sea (hills), Sudan 159/D4
Red Volta (riv.), Burk. 161/E4
Red Wing, Mn, US 185/K4
Reda, Pol. 96/H4
Redange-sur-Attert,
Lux. 111/E4
Redbridge (bor.),
Eng, UK 88/D2
Redcar, Eng, UK 93/G2
Redcar and Cleveland (co.),
Eng, UK 93/G2
Redcliff, Ab, Can. 184/F3
Redcliffe (mt.),
Austl. 170/D4
Redden, De, US 196/C6
Reddersburg, SAfr. 164/D3
Redding, Ca, US 186/B2
Redding, Ct, US 197/E1
Redditch, Eng, UK 91/E2
Rede (riv.), Eng, UK 93/F1
Redenção do Gurguéia,
Braz. 212/A3
Redfield, SD, US 185/J4
Redford, Mi, US 193/F7
Redhill, Eng, UK 88/C3
Rédics, Hun. 106/C2
Redland, Md, US 196/A5
Redlands, Ca, US 194/C2
Redmond, Or, US 184/C4
Redmond, Wa, US 193/C3
Rednitz (riv.), Ger. 112/D4
Redon, Fr. 110/B4
Redondela, Sp. 102/A1
Redondo, Port. 102/B3
Redondo, Wa, US 193/C3
Redondo Beach,
Ca, US 194/F8
Redoubt (vol.),
Ak, US 192/H3
Redstone (riv.),
NW, Can. 180/D2
Redvers, Sk, Can. 185/H3
Redwater, Ab, Can. 184/E2
Redway, Ca, US 184/C5
Redwood Falls,
Mn, US 185/K4
Redwood NP,
Ca, US 186/A2
Ree, Lough (lake),
Ire. 89/P10
Reed City, Mi, US 188/C3
Reeding, Ok, US 195/M14
Reedley, Ca, US 186/C3
Reeds
(bay), NJ, US 196/D5

Reedsburg, Wi, US 185/L5
Reef (pt.), Belz. 201/J5
Reef (isls.), Sol. 174/F6
Reefton, NZ 175/S11
Rees, Ger. 108/D5
Reese (riv.), Nv, US 186/C3
Reesum, Ger. 109/G2
Reest (isl.), FrPol. 175/M6
Reeuwijk, Neth. 108/B4
Refahiye, Turk. 148/D2
Reforma, Mex. 202/C2
Refugio, Tx, US 190/D4
Rega (riv.), Pol. 96/F5
Regen, Ger. 113/G5
Regen (riv.), Ger. 113/F4
Regência, Pontal da (pt.),
Braz. 213/E1
Regeneração, Braz. 212/B2
Regensburg, Ger. 113/F4
Regensdorf, Swi. 115/E3
Regenstauf, Ger. 113/F4
Reggane, Alg. 157/F4
Regge (riv.), Neth. 108/D4
Reggello, It. 117/E5
Reggio di Calabria,
It. 104/D3
Reggio di Calabria
(prov.), It. 104/D3
Reggio Emilia
(prov.), It. 116/D3
Reggio nell'Emilia, It. 116/D3
Reggiolo, It. 117/D3
Reghin, Rom. 107/G2
Reghiolo, It. 117/D3
Regina (cap.),
Sk, Can. 185/G3
Regina, NM, US 190/B2
Regina Beach,
Sk, Can. 185/G3
Región Metropolitana
(pol. reg.), Chile 216/B1
Registro, Braz. 213/C3
Regnitz (riv.), Ger. 101/J2
Regoledo, It. 115/F5
Reguengos de Monsaraz,
Port. 102/B3
Rehau, Ger. 113/F2
Rehburg-Loccum,
Ger. 109/G4
Rehfelde, Ger. 98/Q6
Rehli, India 142/B4
Rehling, Ger. 112/D6
Rehlingen-Siersburg,
Ger. 111/F5
Rehoboth, Namb. 163/C5
Rěhovot, Isr. 149/F8
Rehrersburg,
Pa, US 196/B3
Reichelsheim, Ger. 112/B2
Reichelsheim, Ger. 112/B3
Reichenbach, Ger. 113/F1
Reichenbach im Kandertal,
Swi. 114/D4
Reichenberg-Steegen,
Ger. 111/G4
Reichenberg, Ger. 112/C3
Reichertshausen,
Ger. 113/E6
Reichshof, Ger. 111/G2
Reichshoffen, Fr. 111/G6
Reichstett, Fr. 111/G6
Reid (lake), Sk, Can. 184/F3
Reiden, Swi. 114/D3
Reigate, Eng, UK 88/C3
Reignier, Fr. 114/C5
Reims, Fr. 110/D5
Reina Adelaida (arch.),
Chile 215/A7
Reina Beatrix (int'l arpt.),
NAnt. 210/D1
Reinach, Swi. 114/D3
Reinach, Swi. 114/E3
Reinbek, Ger. 109/H1
Reindeer (isl.),
Mb, Can. 185/J2
Reindeer (lake),
Reston, Sk, Can. 180/F3
Reszel, Pol. 97/J4
Reston, Mb, Can. 185/H3
Reston, Va, US 196/A4
Reszel, Pol. 97/J4
Reinerton-Orwin-Muir,
Pa, US 196/B2
Reinheim, Ger. 112/B3
Reinosa, Sp. 102/C1
Reinsfeld, Ger. 111/F4
Reischach, Ger. 113/F6
Reisdorf, Lux. 111/F4
Reisduoddarhal'di (peak),
Nor. 95/G1
Reiskirchen, Ger. 112/B1
Reisterstown,
Md, US 196/B5
Reitdiep (riv.), Neth. 108/D2
Reitz, SAfr. 164/E2
Rejón (int'l arpt.),
Mex. 202/D1
Rekkam (plat.), Mor. 158/C2
Reliance, NW, Can. 180/F2
Relizane (prov.),
Alg. 158/F5
Relizane, Alg. 158/F5
Rellingen, Ger. 109/G1
Remagen, Ger. 111/G2
Remanso, Braz. 212/B3
Remanzacco, It. 117/F1
Remarde (riv.), Fr. 88/H6
Remarkable (mt.),
Austl. 171/H5
Rembang, Indo. 138/D5
Remchi, Alg. 158/D2
Remedios, Pan. 203/F4
Remich, Lux. 111/F4
Remicourt, Belg. 111/E2
Rémire, FrG. 209/H3
Remiremont, Fr. 114/C1

Remlingen, Ger. 109/H4
Rems (riv.), Ger. 101/H2
Remscheid, Ger. 109/E6
Remy, Fr. 110/B5
Rena, Nor. 96/D1
Renāla Khurd, Pak. 144/B4
Renan, Swi. 114/C3
Renarde (riv.), Fr. 88/J6
Renazzo, It. 117/E3
Renca, Chile 216/N8
Rench (riv.), Ger. 112/A5
Renchen, Ger. 114/E1
Rend (lake), Il, US 191/F2
Rendeux, Belg. 111/E3
Rendsburg, Ger. 96/C4
Renens, Swi. 114/C4
Renfrew, On, Can. 188/E2
Renfrew, Sc, UK 94/B5
Renfrewshire (pol. reg.),
Sc, UK 94/B5
Rengam, Malay. 138/B3
Rengo, Chile 216/N9
Renhua, China 141/K2
Reni, Ukr. 107/J3
Renish (pt.), Sc, UK 89/Q8
Renkum, Neth. 108/C5
Renmark, Austl. 171/J5
Rennell (isl.), Sol. 174/F6
Rennerod, Ger. 111/H2
Rennertshofen, Ger. 112/E5
Rennes, Fr. 100/C2
Renningen, Ger. 112/B5
Reno, Nv, US 186/C3
Reno (riv.), It. 101/J4
Renoster (riv.), SAfr. 164/D2
Renqiu, China 130/D3
Rensselaer, In, US 188/C3
Rentchler, Il, US 195/H9
Rentería, Sp. 102/E1
Renton, Wa, US 184/C4
Renton, Sc, UK 94/B5
Renwez, Fr. 111/D4
Réo, Burk. 161/E3
Reoti, India 143/E3
Răpcelak, Hun. 101/M3
Repelón, Col. 203/H4
Repentigny, Qu, Can. 189/P6
Replonges, Fr. 114/A5
Republic, Wa, US 184/D3
Republican (riv.),
Ks,Ne, US 187/H2
Repulse (bay), Austl. 172/C3
Repulse Bay (isl.),
Austl. 172/C3
Repulse Bay,
Nun., Can. 181/H2
Requena, Peru 214/C2
Requena, Sp. 103/E3
Requinoa, Chile 216/N9
Reriutaba, Braz. 212/B2
Reschensee (Resia)
(lake), It. 115/G4
Rescue (pt.), Chile 216/B5
Resegone (peak), It. 116/C1
Resen, FYROM 105/G2
Resende, Braz. 213/J7
Resende, Port. 102/B2
Reserve, NM, US 186/E4
Resia, Passo di (pass),
It. 115/G4
Resia (Reschensee)
(lake), It. 115/G4
Resistencia, Arg. 215/E2
Reşiţa, Rom. 106/E3
Res Jebel, Tun. 158/M6
Resolution (isl.),
Nun., Can. 181/K2
Resplendor, Braz. 213/D1
Restigouche (riv.),
NB, Can. 189/H2
Reston, Mb, Can. 185/H3
Reston, Va, US 196/A4
Reszel, Pol. 97/J4
Retalhuleu, Guat. 202/D3
Rethel, Fr. 111/D4
Rethem, Ger. 109/G3
Rethimnon, Gre. 105/J5
Retie, Belg. 108/C6
Retrazap NP, Rom. 106/F3
Rétság, Hun. 106/D2
Rettenberg, Ger. 115/G2
Rettenbach, Ger. 113/F6
Reus, Sp. 103/F2
Reusel, Neth. 108/C6
Reuss (riv.), Swi. 115/E4
Reuterstadt Stavenhagen,
Ger. 96/F1
Reutlingen, Ger. 112/C6
Reutov, Rus. 119/W9
Revadim, Isr. 149/F8
Réveillon (riv.), Fr. 88/K5
Revel, Fr. 100/D5
Revelstoke, BC, Can. 184/D3
Revere, It. 117/E2
Revfülöp, Hun. 106/C2
Revigny-sur-Ornain, Fr. 111/D6
Revillagigedo (isls.),
Mex. 200/B5
Revin, Fr. 111/D4
Revolyutsii (peak),
Taj. 145/K2
Revsbotn (inlet), Nor. 95/G1
Rewa, India 142/C3
Rewa (riv.), Guy. 211/G4
Rewari, India 142/A2
Rex (mtn.), Ak, US 192/J3
Rey, Isla del (isl.),
Pan. 203/G4
Reyes, Bol. 208/E6

Reyes (pt.), Ca, US 186/B3
Reyhanlı, Turk. 149/E1
Reykjanestá (cape),
Ice. 95/M7
Reykjavik (int'l arpt.),
Ice. 95/N7
Reykjavik (cap.),
Ice. 95/N7
Reynosa, Mex. 201/F3
Reyssouze (riv.), Fr. 114/B5
Rezé, Fr. 100/C3
Rēzekne, Lat. 97/M3
Rezzato, It. 116/D1
Rhaetian Alps (mts.),
Swi., Aus 101/H3
Rhallamane (reg.),
Mrta. 156/C5
Rhallamane (lake),
Mrta. 156/C4
Rhart (peak), Mor. 156/D3
Rhat (peak), Mor. 156/D3
Rhätikon (mts.),
Aus.,Swi. 115/F3
Rheda-Wiedenbrück,
Ger. 109/F5
Rhede, Ger. 108/D5
Rhede, Ger. 109/E2
Rheden, Neth. 108/D4
Rheidol (riv.), Wal, UK 90/C2
Rheinau, Swi. 115/E2
Rheinbach, Ger. 111/F2
Rheinberg, Ger. 108/D5
Rheinbreitbach, Ger. 111/G2
Rheinbrohl, Ger. 111/G3
Rheine, Ger. 109/E4
Rheinfall, Swi. 115/E2
Rheinfelden, Ger. 114/D2
Rheinland-Pfalz (state),
Ger. 112/A3
Rheinwaldhorn (peak),
Swi. 115/F5
Rheinzabern, Ger. 112/B4
Rhemiles (well), Alg. 156/D3
Rhenen, Neth. 108/C5
Rheris, Oued (riv.),
Mor. 156/D3
Rhinau, Fr. 114/D1
Rhine (riv.), Eur. 85/E4
Rhine-Herne (canal),
Ger. 109/E5
Rhinns (isl.), Sc, UK 89/Q9
Rhinns, The (pt.),
Sc, UK 92/C2
Rhino Camp, Ugan. 162/A2
Rhiou (riv.), Alg. 158/F5
Rhiou (riv.), Alg. 158/F5
Rhir (cape), Mor. 156/C3
Rhisnes, Belg. 111/D3
Rhiw (riv.), Wal, UK 90/C1
Rho, It. 116/C1
Rhode Island (state),
US 189/G3
Rhodes (isl.), Gre. 148/A3
Rhön (mts.), Ger. 112/D1
Rhondda, Wal, UK 90/C3
Rhondda Cynon Taff
(co.), Wal, UK 90/C3
Rhône (dept.), Fr. 114/A6
Rhône (riv.), Fr. 100/F4
Rhône (glacier), Swi. 115/E4
Rhône-Alpes (pol. reg.),
Fr. 114/B5
Rhône au Rhin (canal),
Fr. 114/B3
Rhonelle (riv.), Fr. 110/C3
Rhosllanerchrugog,
Wal, UK 93/E6
Rhum (isl.), Sc, UK 89/Q8
Rhume (riv.), Ger. 109/H5
Rhumel, Oued el (riv.),
Alg. 158/J4
Rhyddhywel (peak),
Wal, UK 90/C2
Rhyl, Wal, UK 92/E5
Riachão, Braz. 212/A2
Riachão das Neves,
Braz. 212/A3
Riachão do Jacuípe,
Braz. 212/C3
Riacho de Santana,
Braz. 212/B4
Riachuelo, Braz. 212/D2
Rialto, Ca, US 194/C2
Rianjo, Sp. 102/A1
Riaño, Sp. 102/C1
Riäsi, India 144/C3
Riau (isls.), Indo. 138/B3
Riaza, Sp. 102/D2
Ribadeo, Sp. 102/B1
Ribadesella, Sp. 102/C1
Riban'i Manamby (mts.),
Madg. 165/H9
Ribble (riv.), Eng, UK 93/F4
Ribblesdale (valley),
Eng, UK 93/F3
Ribe, Den. 96/C4
Ribe (co.), Den. 96/C4
Ribeauvillé, Fr. 114/D1
Ribécourt-Dreslincourt,
Fr. 110/B4
Ribeira (riv.), Braz. 213/C3
Ribeira Brava, CpV. 151/J10
Ribeira de Pena,
Port. 102/B2
Ribeira do Pombal,
Braz. 212/C3
Ribeira Grande,
Azor., Port. 103/T13
Ribeira Grande, CpV. 151/J9
Ribeirão, Braz. 212/D3
Ribeirão do Pinha,
Braz. 213/B2
Ribeiro Gonçalves,
Braz. 212/A2
Ribera, It. 104/C4

Riberalta, Bol. 208/E6
Ribniţa, Mol. 107/J2
Ribnitz-Damgarten,
Ger. 96/F4
Říčany u Prahy, Czh. 113/H3
Ricaurte, Col. 210/B4
Riccia, It. 104/D2
Riccione, It. 117/F5
Ricco'del Golfo, It. 116/C4
Rice (lake), On, Can. 188/E2
Richard Toll, Sen. 160/B2
Richards (isl.),
NW, Can. 180/C2
Richard's Bay, SAfr. 165/F3
Richardson (lakes),
Me, US 189/G2
Richboro, Pa, US 196/C3
Riche (cape), Austl. 170/C5
Richebourg, Fr. 88/G5
Richel (isl.), Neth. 108/C2
Richelieu, Qu, Can. 189/P7
Richfield, Ut, US 186/E3
Richfield, Pa, US 196/A2
Richhill, NI, UK 92/B3
Richland, NJ, US 196/D5
Richland, Ok, US 195/M14
Richland, Pa, US 196/B3
Richland Balsam (peak),
NC, US 191/H3
Richland Center,
Wi, US 185/L5
Richland Creek (res.),
Tx, US 187/H5
Richlandtown,
Pa, US 196/C3
Richmond, Austl. 172/A3
Richmond, BC, Can. 184/C3
Richmond, Qu, Can. 189/F2
Richmond, SAfr. 165/E3
Richmond, SAfr. 164/C3
Richmond, Il, US 193/P15
Richmond, Ky, US 188/C4
Richmond (co.),
NY, US 196/D2
Richmond Beach-Innis
Arden,
Wa, US 193/B2
Richmond Heights,
Mo, US 195/G8
Richmond Hill,
On, Can. 189/R8
Richmond Park (bor.),
Eng, UK 88/C2
Richmond Upon Thames
(bor.), Eng, UK 88/B2
Richmond-Windsor,
Austl. 172/G8
Richtersveld NP,
SAfr. 164/B3
Richterswil, Swi. 115/E3
Richwiller, Fr. 114/D2
Rickenbach, Ger. 114/D2
Ricketts Glen State Park,
Pa, US 196/B1
Rickmansworth,
Eng, UK 88/B2
Ricla, Sp. 102/E2
Ricse, Hun. 99/L4
Ridā', Yem. 146/D6
Ridderkerk, Neth. 108/B5
Rideau (lake), On, Can. 188/E2
Ridgecrest, Ca, US 186/C4
Ridgefield, Ct, US 197/E1
Ridgefield, NJ, US 197/K8
Ridgefield Park,
NJ, US 197/J8
Ridgeland, Ms, US 187/K4
Ridgely, Mo, US 195/D5
Ridgely, Md, US 196/C6
Ridgewood, NJ, US 197/J8
Ridgewood State Park,
NJ, US 196/D2
Riding Mountain NP,
Mb, Can. 185/H3
Ridlees Cairn (hill),
Eng, UK 94/D6
Riecito (riv.), Col. 210/D3
Ried im Innkreis,
Aus. 113/G6
Ried im Traunkreis,
Aus. 113/H6
Riede, Ger. 109/F3
Riedenburg, Ger. 113/E5
Riedesheim, Fr. 114/D2
Riedlingen, Ger. 112/F1
Riegelsberg, Ger. 111/F5
Riegelsville, Pa, US 196/C3
Riegsee (lake), Ger. 115/D2
Riehen, Swi. 114/D2
Riemst, Belg. 111/E2
Rieneck, Ger. 112/C2
Riesa, Ger. 99/G3
Riesco (isl.), Chile 215/B7
Riese Pio X, It. 117/E1
Riesi, It. 104/D4
Riet (riv.), SAfr. 164/D3
Rietberg, Ger. 109/F5
Rietbron, SAfr. 164/C4
Rieti, It. 104/C1
Rietschen, Ger. 99/H3
Rif (int'l arpt.), Ice. 95/N6
Riffe (lake), Wa, US 184/C4
Rifle, Co, US 186/F3
Rifsnes (pt.), Ice. 95/N6
Rift Valley (prov.),
Kenya 162/B2
Riga (gulf), Eur. 97/K2
Riga (Riga) (cap.),
Lat. 97/L3
Rigby, Id, US 184/F5
Rigestan (pol. reg.),
Afg. 147/H2
Riggins, Id, US 184/D4
Rigi (peak), Swi. 115/E4
Rignano sull'Arno, It. 117/E5

Rigolet, Nf, Can. 181/L3
Rihand (dam), India 142/D3
Rihand (riv.), India 142/D3
Rihand Săgar (res.),
India 140/D3
Riihimäki, Fin. 97/L1
Riiser-Larsen (pen.),
Ant. 218/C
Riiser-Larsen Ice Shelf,
Ant. 218/Y
Riisitunturin NP,
Fin. 118/F2
Rijeka, Cro. 106/B3
Rijksmuseum Kröller Müller,
Neth. 108/C4
Rijnsburg, Neth. 108/B4
Rijsbergen, Neth. 108/B5
Rijssen, Neth. 108/D4
Rijswijk, Neth. 108/B4
Rikers (isl.),
NY, US 197/K8
Rikitea, FrPol. 175/M7
Rikuchū-Kaigan NP,
Japan 134/C4
Rikuzentakata, Japan 134/B4
Rila, Bul. 107/F4
Rila (mts.), Bul. 107/F4
Ril'lieux-la-Pape, Fr. 114/A6
Rilski Manastir, Bul. 105/H1
Rimatara (isl.), FrPol. 175/K7
Rimavská Sobota,
Slvk. 99/L4
Rimbach, Ger. 112/B3
Rimbey, Ab, Can. 184/E2
Rimforsa, Swe. 96/F2
Rimini, It. 117/F4
Rîmnicu Sărat, Rom. 107/H3
Rîmnicu Vilcea, Rom. 107/G3
Rimogne, Fr. 111/D4
Rimouski, Qu, Can. 189/G1
Rimpar, Ger. 112/C3
Rinas (int'l arpt.), Alb. 105/F2
Rinbung, China 143/G1
Rinchnach, Ger. 113/G4
Rincón de la Vieja, PN,
CR 198/D5
Rincón de Romos,
Mex. 200/E4
Ringarooma, Austl. 173/C4
Ringboy (pt.), NI, UK 92/C3
Ringebu, Nor. 96/D1
Ringelspitz (peak),
Swi. 115/F4
Ringgold, La, US 187/J4
Ringkøbing (fjord),
Den. 96/B3
Ringkøbing, Den. 96/C3
Ringkøbing (co.), Den. 96/B3
Ringoes, NJ, US 196/D3
Ringsend, NI, UK 92/B1
Ringsted, Den. 96/D4
Ringtown, Pa, US 196/B2
Ringvaart (riv.), Neth. 108/B4
Ringvassøy (isl.),Nor. 95/F1
Ringwood, Eng, UK 91/E5
Ringwood, NJ, US 197/H7
Ringwood State Park,
NJ, US 196/D1
Rinia (isl.), Gre. 105/J4
Rinteln, Ger. 109/G4
Rinxent, Fr. 110/A2
Río Abiseo, PN,
Peru 208/C5
Rio Azul, Braz. 213/B3
Río Blanco, Mex. 201/M8
Rio Bonito, Braz. 213/L7
Río Branco, Braz. 208/E5
Rio Branco do Sul,
Braz. 213/B3
Río Bravo, Mex. 201/F3
Río Bueno, Chile 216/B4
Río Casca, Braz. 213/D2
Río Cauto, Cuba 203/G1
Rio Claro, Braz. 213/J7
Río Claro, Trin. 211/F2
Río Colorado, Arg. 216/D2
Río Cuarto, Arg. 216/D2
Rio de Janeiro, Braz. 213/K7
Rio de Janeiro (state),
Braz. 213/D2
Rio de Janeiro (int'l arpt.),
Braz. 213/K7
Rio Dell, Ca, US 184/B5
Río Gallegos, Arg. 217/C6
Rio Grande, Arg. 215/C7
Rio Grande, Braz. 213/A5
Rio Grande (riv.),
Mex.,US 187/F5
Rio Grande (plain),
Tx, US 198/B2
Rio Grande City,
Tx, US 190/D5
Río Grande da Serra,
Braz. 213/G8
Rio Grande Do Norte,
(state) Braz. 212/C2
Rio Grande do Piauí,
Braz. 212/B3
Rio Grande Valley,
Tx, US 190/D5
Río Lagartos, Mex. 202/D1
Río Largo, Braz. 212/D3
Río Mayo, Arg. 217/B5
Río Negrinho, Braz. 213/B3
Río Negro (prov.), Arg. 216/C3
Río Negro, Braz. 213/A3
Río Negro, Chile 216/B4

Río Negro, Embalse de
(res.), Uru. 215/E3
Riverton, Ut, US 195/K13
Río Paranaíba, Braz. 213/C1
Rio Pardo, Braz. 213/A4
Río Pilcomayo, PN,
Arg. 215/E2
Río Prêto (range),
Braz. 212/A5
Rio Rancho, NM, US 186/F4
Río Real, Braz. 212/C3
Río Saliceto, It. 117/D3
Río Simpson, PN,
Chile 216/B5
Río Tala, Arg. 217/J10
Río Tercero, Arg. 216/D2
Río Tigre, Ecu. 210/B5
Río Tinto, Braz. 212/D2
Rio Verde, Braz. 213/B1
Río Verde, Chile 217/C7
Río Verde, Mex. 201/F4
Río Verde de Mato Grosso,
Braz. 209/H7
Río Vista, Ca, US 193/L10
Riobamba, Ecu. 210/B5
Riohacha, Col. 210/C2
Rioja, Peru 214/B2
Riolândia, Braz. 213/B1
Riolo Terme, It. 117/E4
Riom, Fr. 100/E4
Riom-ès-Montagne,
Fr. 100/E4
Rion-des-Landes,
Fr. 100/C5
Riomaggiore, It. 116/C4
Road Town (cap.),
BVI 199/M8
Riondel, BC, Can. 184/D3
Rionegro, Col. 210/C3
Rionero in Vulture,
It. 104/D2
Riorges, Fr. 100/F3
Ríos, Sp. 102/B2
Ríos (lake), Chile 216/B5
Riosucio, Col. 210/B3
Riotán, Hon. 202/E2
Ripalti, Punta dei (pt.),
It. 104/B1
Ripanj, Serb. 106/E3
Riparbella, It. 116/D6
Ripley, Ms, US 191/F3
Ripley, Eng, UK 93/G5
Ripoll, Sp. 103/G1
Ripoll (riv.), Sp. 103/L6
Ripollet, Sp. 103/L6
Ripon, Wi, US 185/L5
Ripon, Eng, UK 93/G3
Riposto, It. 104/D4
Rippowam (riv.),
Ct, US 197/L7
Ripponden, Eng, UK 93/G4
Ris-Orangis, Fr. 88/K6
Risaralda (dept.), Col. 210/A4
Rishiri, Japan 134/B1
Rishiri-Rebun-Sarobetsu NP,
Japan 134/B1
Rishon Lez̧iyyon, Isr. 149/F8
Rising Sun,
Md, US 196/B4
Rising Sun-Lebanon,
De, US 196/C5
Risle (riv.), Fr. 100/C2
Risnjak (peak), Cro. 106/B3
Risnjak NP, Cro. 106/B3
Rišnov, Rom. 107/G3
Rison, Ar, US 187/J4
Risør, Nor. 96/C2
Riss (riv.), Ger. 115/F1
Ristiina, Fin. 97/M1
Ritacuba (peak), Col. 210/C3
Ritaiō (isl.), Japan 174/D2
Ritoio (peak), It. 117/E5
Ritterhude, Ger. 109/F2
Rittō, Japan 135/J5
Ritzville, Wa, US 184/D4
Riva, It. 115/G6
Riva Ligure, It. 116/A5
Riva Presso Chieri,
It. 116/A3
Riva San Vitale, Swi. 115/E6
Rivadavia, Arg. 215/C3
Rivadavia, Arg. 216/E2
Rivalta, It. 116/D2
Rivalta di Torino, It. 116/A3
Rivanazzano, It. 116/C2
Rivarolo Canavese,
It. 116/A2
Rivarolo Mantovano,
It. 116/D2
Rivas, Nic. 202/E4
Rive-de-Gier, Fr. 100/F4
River Cess, Libr. 160/C5
River Edge, NJ, US 197/J8
River Kwai Bridge,
Thai. 136/B3
River Rouge, Mi, US 193/F7
River Vale, NJ, US 197/J8
Rivera, Uru. 215/E3
Rivera, Swi. 115/E6
Rivera (isl.), Chile 216/B3
Rivera, Arg. 216/E3
Riverdale, NJ, US 197/H8
Riverdale, Ut, US 195/K11
Rivergaro, It. 116/C2
Riverhead, NY, US 197/F2
Riverside, NJ, US 196/D3
Riverside, Ca, US 194/C3
Riverside, Mo, US 195/D5
Riverside, NJ, US 196/D3
Riverside, Pa, US 196/B2
Riverton, Mb, Can. 185/J3

Riverton, NZ 175/R12
Riverton, Ut, US 195/K13
Riverton, Austl. 171/H5
Riverton, Austl. 173/C1
Riverview, NB, Can. 189/H2
Riverwoods,
Il, US 193/Q15
Riviera Beach,
Fl, US 191/H5
Riviera Beach,
Md, US 196/B5
Rivière-du-Loup,
Qu, Can. 189/G2
Riviersonderendreeks
(mts.), SAfr. 164/L11
Rivignano, It. 117/C1
Rivne, Ukr. 120/C2
Rivne'ska Oblasti,
Ukr. 120/C2
Rivoli, It. 101/G4
Rivolta d'Adda, It. 116/C1
Rixensart, Belg. 111/D2
Rixheim, Fr. 114/D2
Rīyāq, Leb. 149/D3
Rize, Turk. 148/E1
Rize (prov.), Turk. 148/E1
Rizhao, China 130/D4
Rizokarpasso, Cyp. 149/D2
Rizzuto (cape), It. 105/E3
Rjukan, Nor. 96/C2
Rkiz (lake), Mrta. 160/B2
Roa, Sp. 102/D2
Roa, Nor. 96/D1
Road Town (cap.),
BVI 199/M8
Roan (plat.), Co, US 186/E3
Roan Fell (hill), Sc, UK 93/F1
Roanne, Fr. 100/F3
Roanoke, Al, US 191/G3
Roanoke (riv.), Va, US 188/E4
Roanoke (isl.), NY, US 197/F2
Roatán (isl.), Hon. 198/D4
Roatán, Hon. 202/E2
Robāt Karīm, Iran 146/F1
Robbate, It. 116/C1
Robbins (isl.), Austl. 173/C4
Robbins, It. 116/B2
Robe, Austl. 173/A3
Robe (mt.), Austl. 173/B1
Robe, Eng, UK 89/P10
Robecchetto con Induno,
It. 116/B1
Röbel, Ger. 96/F4
Robert (peak), Fr. 114/B5
Robert Lee, Tx, US 187/G5
Roberts (mtn.),
Ak, US 192/E4
Roberts (Monrovia)
(int'l arpt.), Libr. 160/C5
Robertsfors, Swe. 95/G2
Robertsganj, India 142/D3
Robertson, SAfr. 164/L10
Robertsport, Libr. 160/C5
Robertstown, Ire. 89/Q10
Roberval, Qu, Can. 189/F1
Robesonia, Pa, US 196/B3
Robinson (ranges),
Austl. 170/C3
Robinson Crusoe (isl.),
Chile 205/B6
Robinson Gorge NP,
Austl. 172/C4
Robinvale, Austl. 173/B2
Roblin, Mb, Can. 185/H3
Roboré, Bol. 208/G7
Robson (mt.),
BC, Can. 184/D2
Robstown, Tx, US 190/D5
Roby, Tx, US 187/G4
Roc du Haut du Faite
(peak), Fr. 114/D1
Roca, Cabo da (cape),
Port. 103/P10
Roca Partida (isl.),
Mex. 200/B5
Roca Partida, Punta (pt.),
Mex. 202/C2
Rocafuerte, Ecu. 210/A5
Rocca San Casciano,
It. 117/E4
Roccabianca, It. 116/D2
Roccastrada, It. 101/J5
Rocciamelone (peak),
It. 101/G4
Rocha, Uru. 217/G2
Rocha (dept.), Uru. 217/G2
Rochdale, Eng, UK 93/F4
Rochdale (co.), Eng, UK 93/F4
Roche, Swi. 114/C5
Roche du Sapin Sec
(peak), Fr. 114/C1
Roche-lez-Beaupré,
Fr. 114/C3
Rochefort, Belg. 111/E3
Rochelle Park, NJ, US 197/J8
Rochers du Bourbet
(peak), Fr. 114/C2
Rochester, Austl. 173/C3
Rochester, Mn, US 185/K4
Rochester, NY, US 188/E3
Rochester, In, US 188/C3
Rochester, NH, US 189/G3
Rochester, Eng, UK 91/G4
Rochester, Mi, US 193/F7
Rochester, Wi, US 193/P14
Rochford, Eng, UK 88/F2
Rock (riv.), Ia,Mo, US 187/H2
Rock Creek, Yk, Can. 172/L3
Rock Forest, Qu, Can. 189/G2
Rock Glen, On, US 193/P14
Rock Hall, Md, US 196/B5
Rock Hill, SC, US 191/H3
Rock Island, Il, US 185/L5

Rock S – Sādri

Rock Springs, Wy, US 184/F5
Rockall (isl.), UK 85/C3
Rockaway, NJ, US 196/D2
Rockaway (riv.), NJ, US 196/D2
Rockaway (inlet), NY, US 197/K9
Rockaway (pt.), NY, US 197/K9
Rockdale, Il, US 193/P17
Rockefeller (plat.), Ant. 218/R
Rockenhausen, Ger. 111/G4
Rockford, Il, US 185/L5
Rockglen, Sk, Can. 185/G3
Rockhampton, Austl. 172/C3
Rockingham, NC, US 191/J3
Rockingham, Austl. 170/K7
Rockland, On, Can. 188/F2
Rockland, Me, US 189/G2
Rockland (co.), NY, US 196/D1
Rockland Lake, NY, US 197/K7
Rocklands (res.), Austl. 173/B3
Rockledge, Fl, US 191/H4
Rockledge, Pa, US 196/C3
Rockport, Tx, US 190/D4
Rocks, Md, US 196/B4
Rocksprings, Tx, US 187/G5
Rockstone, Guy. 211/G3
Rockville, Md, US 188/E4
Rockville Centre, NY, US 197/L9
Rockwall, Tx, US 187/H4
Rockwood, Tn, US 191/G3
Rocky (mtn.), Ky, US 188/D4
Rocky (mts.), Can.,US 177/E4
Rocky (pt.), NY, US 197/F1
Rocky Cape NP, Austl. 173/C4
Rocky Harbour, Nf, Can. 189/K1
Rocky Island (lake), On, Can. 188/D2
Rocky Mount, NC, US 191/J3
Rocky Mountain House, Ab, Can. 184/E2
Rocky Mountain NP, Co, US 186/F2
Rocroi, Fr. 111/D4
Rodach (riv.), Ger. 113/E2
Rodach bei Coburg, Ger. 112/D2
Rodalben, Ger. 111/G5
Rødberg, Nor. 96/C1
Rødbyhavn, Den. 96/D4
Roddickton, Nf, Can. 189/K1
Rødding, Den. 96/C4
Roden (riv.), Eng, UK 93/F6
Rodenbach, Ger. 112/C2
Rodeo, Mex. 200/D3
Rodeo, Ca, US 193/K10
Rödermark, Ger. 112/B3
Rodewisch, Ger. 113/F1
Rodez, Fr. 100/E4
Rodholívos, Gre. 105/H2
Ródhos (ruin), Gre. 148/B2
Ródhos (Rhodes), Gre. 148/B2
Rodigo, It. 116/D2
Roding (riv.), Eng, UK 88/D2
Roding, Ger. 113/F4
Rodinga (mt.), Austl. 171/G3
Rödinghausen, Ger. 109/F4
Rodoč, Bosn. 105/E1
Rodolfo Sánchez Toboada, Mex. 200/A2
Rodríguez, Uru. 217/K11
Roe (riv.), NI, UK 92/B2
Roebourne, Austl. 170/C2
Roebuck (bay), Austl. 167/B2
Roeland Park, Ks, US 195/D5
Roen (peak), It. 115/H5
Roer (riv.), Neth. 108/D6
Roermond, Neth. 108/C6
Roes Welcome Sound (str.), Nun., Can. 181/H2
Roeselare, Belg. 110/C2
Roesiger (lake), Wa, US 193/D2
Rogachev, Bela. 120/D1
Rogaland (co.), Nor. 95/C4
Rogaška Slatina, Slov. 101/L3
Rogatica, Bosn. 106/D4
Rogers (mt.), Va, US 188/D4
Rogers, Ar, US 187/J3
Rogers City, Mi, US 188/D2
Rogersville, Tn, US 188/D4
Roggwil, Swi. 114/D3
Rogliano, Fr. 101/H5
Roglio (riv.), It. 117/D5
Rognon (riv.), Fr. 100/F2
Rogoźno, Pol. 99/J2
Rogue (riv.), Or, US 186/B2
Rohl (riv.), Sudan 155/L6
Rohr, Ger. 113/E5
Rohrbach bei Mattersburg, Aus. 101/M3
Rohrbach in Oberösterreich, Aus. 113/G5
Rohrbach-lès-Bitche, Fr. 111/G5
Rohri, Pak. 147/J3
Röhrmoos, Ger. 113/E6
Rohtak, India 144/D5
Roi Et, Thai. 136/C2
Roine (lake), Fin. 97/L1
Roissy, Fr. 88/K5
Roissy-en-France, Fr. 88/K4
Rojas, Arg. 216/E2
Rojo (cape), PR 199/M8
Rojo, Cabo (cape), Mex. 202/B1
Rokan (riv.), Indo. 138/B3
Rokeby Croll Creek NP, Austl. 172/A1
Rokel (riv.), SLeo. 160/C4
Rokkasho, Japan 134/B3
Rokkō-san (peak), Japan 135/H6
Rokugō, Japan 135/A3
Rokycany, Czh. 113/G3
Rokytka (riv.), Czh. 113/H2
Rolampont, Fr. 114/B2
Rolândia, Braz. 213/B2
Rolava (riv.), Czh. 113/F2
Rolde, Neth. 108/D3
Rolla, ND, US 185/J3
Rolla, BC, Can. 184/C2
Rolla, Mo, US 187/K3
Rolle, Swi. 114/C5
Rolling Fork, Ms, US 187/K4
Rolling Hills Estates, Ca, US 194/F8
Rolling Meadows, Il, US 193/P15
Rollingbay, Wa, US 193/B2
Rollinsville, Co, US 195/A3
Rolo, It. 117/D3
Rom (peak), Ugan. 162/B2
Roma, Austl. 172/C4
Roma, Swe. 96/H3
Roma (Rome) (cap.), It. 104/C2
Romagnano Sesia, It. 116/B1
Romagnat, Fr. 100/E4
Romain (cape), SC, US 191/J3
Romaine (riv.), Qu, Can. 181/K3
Roman, Bul. 107/F4
Roman, Rom. 107/H2
Romang (str.), Indo. 139/G5
Romang (isl.), Indo. 139/G5
Romania (ctry.) 107/F3
Romano Canavese, It. 116/A2
Romano, Cayo (isl.), Cuba 203/G1
Romano d'Ezzelino, It. 117/E1
Romano di Lombardia, It. 116/C1
Romans d'Isonzo, It. 117/G1
Romans-sur-Isère, Fr. 100/F4
Romanshorn, Swi. 115/F2
Romanzof (cape), Ak, US 192/E3
Rombas, Fr. 111/F5
Romblon, Phil. 137/D5
Rome (cap.), It. 104/C2
Rome, Ga, US 191/G3
Rome, NY, US 188/F3
Rome, Wi, US 193/N14
Romenay, Fr. 114/B4
Romeoville, Il, US 193/P16
Römhild, Ger. 112/D2
Romilly-sur-Seine, Fr. 100/E2
Rommani, Mor. 156/D2
Rommerskirchen, Ger. 111/F1
Romney Marsh (phys. reg.), Eng, UK 91/G4
Romny, Ukr. 120/E2
Rømø (isl.), Den. 96/C4
Romoland, Ca, US 194/C3
Romont, Swi. 114/C4
Romorantin-Lanthenay, Fr. 100/D3
Romsey, Eng, UK 91/E5
Rømskog, Nor. 96/D2
Ronald Reagan Washington National (int'l arpt.), DC, US 196/A6
Ronan, Mt, US 184/E4
Roncade, It. 117/F1
Roncador Cay (isl.), Col. 203/G3
Roncador, Serra do (mts.), Braz. 209/H6
Ronchamp, Fr. 114/C2
Ronchi dei Legionari (int'l arpt.), It. 117/G1
Ronchi dei Legionari, It. 117/G1
Ronciglione, It. 104/C1
Ronco (riv.), It. 117/F5
Ronco All'Adige, It. 117/E2
Ronco Scrivia, It. 116/B3
Roncoferraro, It. 117/D2
Roncq, Fr. 110/C2
Ronda, Sp. 102/C4
Rondane NP, Nor. 95/D3
Ronde, Tête (peak), Swi. 114/D5
Rondonópolis, Braz. 209/H7
Rong (riv.), China 141/J2
Rong Xian, China 141/K3
Rongcheng, China 131/B4
Rongcheng, China 130/G7
Ronge (lake), Sk, Can. 180/F3
Rongelap (isl.), Mrsh. 174/F3
Rongerik (isl.), Mrsh. 174/F3
Ronkonkoma, NY, US 197/E2
Rønne, Den. 96/F4
Ronne Ice Shelf, Ant. 218/W
Ronneby, Swe. 96/F3
Ronnenberg, Ger. 109/G4
Ronquerolles, Fr. 88/J4
Ronsard (cape), Austl. 170/B3
Ronsberg, Ger. 115/G2
Ronse, Belg. 110/C2
Ronuro (riv.), Braz. 209/H6
Roodeport, SAfr. 164/P13
Rooiberg (peak), Namb. 164/B2
Roorkee, India 140/C2
Roosendaal, Neth. 108/B5
Roosevelt, Ut, US 186/E2
Roosevelt (canal), Az, US 195/S19
Roosevelt (riv.), Braz. 205/C4
Roosevelt (mt.), BC, Can. 180/D3
Roosevelt, NJ, US 196/D3
Roosevelt (isl.), Ant. 218/N
Roosevelt, NY, US 197/L9
Root (mt.), Ak, US 192/L4
Root (riv.), Wi, US 193/P14
Root, West Branch (riv.), Wi, US 193/P14
Roque Pérez, Arg. 217/J11
Roquetas de Mar, Sp. 102/D4
Roraima (peak), Braz. 208/F2
Roraima (peak), Ven. 211/F3
Roraima (state), Braz. 211/F4
Rorke's Drift, SAfr. 165/E3
Rorke's Drift Battlesite, SAfr. 165/E3
Rorketon, Mb, Can. 185/J3
Røros, Nor. 95/D3
Rorschach, Swi. 115/F3
Rosa (cape), Alg. 158/L6
Rosà, It. 117/E1
Rosa (lake), Bahm. 203/H1
Rosa Punta (pt.), Mex. 200/C3
Rosa Zárate, Ecu. 210/B4
Rosablanche (peak), Swi. 114/D5
Rosal, Sp. 102/A2
Rosales, Mex. 200/D2
Rosamorada, Mex. 200/D4
Rosanna (riv.), Aus. 115/G3
Rosario, Arg. 216/E2
Rosário, Braz. 212/A1
Rosario, Mex. 200/C3
Rosario, Mex. 200/D4
Rosario, Uru. 217/K11
Rosario de la Frontera, Arg. 215/D2
Rosario del Tala, Arg. 217/J10
Rosário do Sul, Braz. 215/F3
Rosarito, Mex. 200/A1
Rosarno, It. 104/D3
Rosas, Col. 210/B4
Rosas, Golfo di (gulf), Sp. 103/G1
Rosate, It. 116/C2
Rosay, Fr. 88/G5
Rosbach vor der Höhe, Ger. 112/B2
Rosche, Ger. 109/H3
Roscoff, Fr. 100/B2
Roscommon, Ire. 89/P10
Roscrea, Ire. 89/Q10
Rosdorf, Ger. 109/G5
Rose (isl.), ASam. 175/J6
Rose (pt.), BC, Can. 192/M4
Rose Belle, Mrts. 165/T15
Roseau, Mn, US 185/K3
Roseau (riv.), Mn, US 185/J3
Roseau (cap.), Dom. 199/N9
Roseaux, Haiti 203/H2
Rosebery, Austl. 173/C4
Roseburg, Or, US 184/C5
Rosedale, Ms, US 187/K4
Rosedale, Il, US 195/F7
Rosedale, Md, US 196/B5
Rosehearty, Sc, UK 94/D1
Roseira, Braz. 213/H7
Roseland, NJ, US 197/H8
Roselette, Aiguille de (peak), Fr. 114/C6
Roselle, NJ, US 197/H9
Roselle, Il, US 193/P16
Roselle Park, NJ, US 197/H9
Rosemead, Ca, US 194/F7
Rosemère, Qu, Can. 189/N6
Rosenberg, Tx, US 187/J5
Rosenberg, Ger. 112/D4
Rosenfeld, Ger. 115/E1
Rosenhayn, NJ, US 196/C5
Rosenheim, Ger. 101/K3
Roses, Sp. 103/G1
Roseto, Pa, US 196/C2
Roseto degli Abruzzi, It. 101/L5
Rosetown, Sk, Can. 184/G3
Rosetta (riv.), Egypt 149/B4
Roseville, Mi, US 193/G6
Rosewood Heights, Il, US 195/G8
Rosh Ha'ayin, Isr. 149/F7
Rosh Hakarmel (pt.), Isr. 149/F6
Rosh Haniqra (pt.), Isr. 149/D3
Rosheim, Fr. 114/D1
Rosières-en-Santerre, Fr. 110/B4
Rosignano Marittimo, It. 116/D6
Roşiori de Vede, Rom. 107/G3
Roskilde, Den. 96/E4
Roskilde (co.), Den. 96/D4
Roslavl', Rus. 120/E1
Roslev, Den. 96/C3
Rosmalen, Neth. 108/C5
Rosmaninhal, Port. 102/B3
Rosneath, Sc, UK 94/B4
Rosny-sous-Bois, Fr. 88/K5
Rosolina, It. 117/F2
Rosolini, It. 104/D4
Rosporden, Fr. 100/B3
Rösrath, Ger. 111/G2
Ross (isl.), Ant. 218/M
Ross (sea), Ant. 218/P
Ross, Austl. 173/C4
Ross (isl.), Mb, Can. 185/J2
Ross (pt.), On, Can. 189/S8
Ross (dist.), Sc, UK 94/C1
Ross Ice Shelf, Ant. 218/N
Rossa (peak), It. 101/K3
Rossa, Swi. 115/F5
Rossall (pt.), Eng, UK 93/E4
Rossano Stazione, It. 104/E3
Rossano Veneto, It. 117/E1
Rossbach, Ger. 113/F5
Rossberg (peak), Fr. 114/D2
Rossdorf, Ger. 112/B3
Rossel (isl.), PNG 174/E6
Rosselange, Fr. 111/F5
Rosshaupten, Ger. 115/G2
Rossiglione, It. 116/B3
Rossignol (lake), NS, Can. 189/H2
Rosskeeragh (pt.), Ire. 89/P9
Rossland, BC, Can. 184/D3
Rosso, Mrta. 160/B2
Rossosh', Rus. 120/F2
Rossstock (peak), Swi. 115/E4
Rosstal, Ger. 112/D4
Rossville, Ok, US 195/N14
Røst, Nor. 95/E2
Rosthern, Sk, Can. 185/G2
Rostock, Ger. 96/E4
Rostov, Rus. 120/F3
Rostov, Rus. 118/H4
Rostov (int'l arpt.), Rus. 120/F3
Rostovskaya Oblast, Rus. 121/G2
Rostrenen, Fr. 100/B2
Rostrevor, NI, UK 92/B3
Roswell, NM, US 187/F4
Rot (riv.), Ger. 98/E4
Rota, Sp. 102/B4
Rota (isl.), NMar. 174/D3
Rote Wand (peak), Aus. 115/F3
Rotenburg, Ger. 109/G2
Rotenburg an der Fulda, Ger. 109/G7
Roter Main (riv.), Ger. 98/F3
Rötgen, Ger. 111/F2
Roth (riv.), Ger. 115/G1
Roth bei Nürnberg, Ger. 112/E4
Rothaargebirge (mts.), Ger. 109/F6
Rothau, Fr. 114/D1
Röthenbach an der Pegnitz, Ger. 112/E4
Rothenberg, Ger. 112/B3
Rothenburg, Swi. 115/E3
Rothenburg ob der Tauber, Ger. 112/D4
Rothera, UK, Ant. 218/V
Rotherham, Eng, UK 93/G5
Rotherham (co.), Eng, UK 93/G5
Rothes, Sc, UK 94/C1
Rothesay, Sc, UK 94/A5
Rotheux-Rimière, Belg. 111/E2
Rothschild, Wi, US 185/L4
Rothwell, Eng, UK 91/F2
Rothwell, Eng, UK 93/G4
Roti (isl.), Indo. 139/F6
Rotorua, NZ 175/T10
Rotselaar, Belg. 111/D2
Rott (riv.), Ger. 98/G4
Rott am Inn, Ger. 113/F7
Rottach-Egern, Ger. 98/F5
Rotte (riv.), Fr. 111/F6
Rotten (riv.), Swi. 114/E5
Rottenacker, Ger. 115/F1
Röttenbach, Ger. 112/E4
Rottenberg, Ger. 112/C2
Rottenburg am Neckar, Ger. 112/B6
Rottenburg an der Laaber, Ger. 113/F5
Rotterdam (int'l arpt.), Neth. 108/B5
Rotterdam, Neth. 108/B5
Rotthalmünster, Ger. 113/G6
Röttingen, Ger. 112/C3
Rottne, Swe. 96/F3
Rottnest (isl.), Austl. 170/B5
Rottofreno, It. 116/C2
Rottum (riv.), Ger. 115/F1
Rottumeroog (isl.), Neth. 108/D1
Rottumerplaat (isl.), Neth. 108/D1
Rottweil, Ger. 115/E1
Rotuma (isl.), Fiji 174/G6
Rötz, Ger. 113/F4
Roubaix, Fr. 110/C2
Roubion (riv.), Fr. 100/F4
Roudnice nad Labem, Czh. 113/H2
Rouen, Fr. 100/D2
Rouffach, Fr. 114/D2
Rouge (riv.), Qu, Can. 181/J4
Rouge, Middle (riv.), Mi, US 193/F7
Rougemont, Fr. 114/C3
Rougemont-le-Château, Fr. 114/C2
Rough (riv.), Ky, US 191/G2
Roullet-Saint-Estèphe, Fr. 100/D4
Round (hill), Pa, US 196/B3
Round Hill (pt.), Austl. 172/C4
Round Lake, Il, US 193/P15
Round Lake Beach, Il, US 193/P15
Round Lake Park, Il, US 193/P15
Round Rock, Tx, US 187/H5
Round Valley (res.), NJ, US 196/D2
Roundup, Mt, US 184/F4
Roundway (hill), Eng, UK 90/E4
Rousay (isl.), Sc, UK 89/V14
Rousies, Fr. 110/D3
Rousínov, Czh. 99/J4
Roussillon, Fr. 100/F4
Rouvres, Fr. 88/M4
Rouvroy, Belg. 111/E4
Rouxville, SAfr. 164/D3
Rouyn-Noranda, Qu, Can. 188/E1
Rovaniemi, Fin. 118/E2
Rovaniemi (int'l arpt.), Fin. 118/E2
Rovasenda, It. 116/B1
Rovato, It. 116/C1
Roverbella, It. 117/D2
Rovereto, It. 117/D3
Rovereto, It. 115/H6
Rovigo (prov.), It. 117/E2
Rovigo, It. 117/E2
Rovinj, Cro. 117/G2
Rovuma (riv.), Moz. 162/B5
Rowley (isl.), Nun., Can. 139/J2
Rowley Shoals (isl.), Austl. 167/A2
Roxa (isl.), GBis. 160/B4
Roxana, Il, US 195/G8
Roxas, Phil. 137/C5
Roxas, Phil. 137/D4
Roxas, Phil. 137/D5
Roxboro, NC, US 188/E4
Roxen (lake), Swe. 96/F2
Roxo (cape), Sen. 160/A3
Roy, NM, US 190/B3
Roy, Ut, US 195/J11
Roy, Wa, US 193/B3
Roya (riv.), Fr. 101/G5
Royal (canal), Ire. 93/B3
Royal Botanical Garden, On, Can. 189/Q9
Royal Chitwan NP, Nepal 143/E2
Royal Lakes, Il, US 195/H7
Royal Natal NP, SAfr. 164/E3
Royal NP, Austl. 173/D2
Royal NP, The, Austl. 172/H9
Royal Oak, Mi, US 193/F7
Royal Paekje Tombs, SKor. 131/D4
Royal Tombs, Viet. 136/D2
Royal Tunbridge Wells, Eng, UK 91/G4
Royale, Isle (isl.), Mi, US 185/L4
Royalton, Pa, US 196/B3
Royan, Fr. 100/C4
Roye, Fr. 114/C2
Roye, Fr. 110/B4
Royersford, Pa, US 196/C3
Røyken, Nor. 96/D2
Royston, Eng, UK 91/F2
Royston, Eng, UK 93/G4
Royton, Eng, UK 93/F4
Rožaje, Mont. 106/E4
Rozay-en-Brie, Fr. 110/B6
Rozenburg, Neth. 108/B5
Rozhaya (riv.), Rus. 119/W9
Rožmberk (lake), Czh. 113/H4
Rožmital pod Třemšínem, Czh. 113/G3
Rožňava, Slvk. 99/L4
Roztoczański PN, Pol. 99/M3
Roztoky, Czh. 113/H2
Rozzano, It. 116/C2
Rrëshen, Alb. 105/F2
Rt Kamenjak (cape), Cro. 106/A3
Rt Ploča (pt.), Cro. 106/B4
Rtishchevo, Rus. 121/G1
Ruacana (falls), Ang. 163/B4
Ruaha NP, Tanz. 162/B4
Ruapehu (vol.), NZ 175/T10
Rub' al Khali (des.), SAr. 146/E5
Rubelles, Fr. 88/L6
Rubeshibe, Japan 134/C2
Rubí, Sp. 103/L7
Rubidoux, Ca, US 194/C3
Rubiera, It. 117/D3
Rubigen, Swi. 114/D4
Rubim, Braz. 212/B5
Rubizhne, Ukr. 120/F2
Rubondo NP, Tanz. 162/A3
Řubřina (riv.), Czh. 113/G4
Ruby, Ak, US 192/G3
Ruby (lake), Nv, US 186/D2
Ruby (mts.), Nv, US 186/D2
Rubyvale, Austl. 172/B3
Rucheng, China 137/B2
Rucphen, Neth. 108/B5
Ruda Woda (lake), Pol. 99/K2
Rudall River NP, Austl. 170/D2
Rūdarpur, India 142/D2
Rudauli, India 142/C2
Rüdersdorf, Ger. 98/Q7
Rüdesheim, Ger. 111/G4
Rudiano, It. 116/C2
Rudkøbing, Den. 96/D4
Rudnik, Pol. 99/M3
Rūdnyy, Kaz. 119/P5
Rudolf (isl.), Rus. 122/F1
Rudolstadt, Ger. 101/J1
Rudong, China 130/E4
Rūdsar, Iran 146/F1
Rue, Swi. 114/C4
Rue (pt.), NI, UK 92/B1
Rue, Fr. 110/A3
Rueda, Sp. 102/C2
Rueil-Malmaison, Fr. 88/J5
Ruell (riv.), Sc, UK 94/A4
Ruelle-sur-Touvre, Fr. 100/D4
Ruen (peak), Bul. 106/F4
Ruetzbach (riv.), Aus. 115/H3
Ruffano, It. 105/F3
Ruffec, Fr. 100/D3
Rufiji (riv.), Tanz. 162/C4
Rufina, It. 117/E5
Rufino, Arg. 216/E2
Rufisque, Sen. 160/A3
Rugao, China 130/E4
Rugby, ND, US 185/J3
Rugby, Eng, UK 91/E2
Rugeley, Eng, UK 91/E1
Rügen (isl.), Ger. 96/E4
Ruggell, Lcht. 115/F3
Ruhmannsfelden, Ger. 113/F5
Ruhnu saar (isl.), Lat. 97/K3
Ruhr (riv.), Ger. 98/D3
Ruhr (reg.), Ger. 98/E3
Ruhrgebiet (phys. reg.), Ger. 108/D6
Ruhstorf an der Rott, Ger. 113/F5
Rui'an, China 137/D2
Ruicheng, China 130/B4
Ruidoso, NM, US 187/F4
Ruinen, Neth. 108/D3
Ruiselede, Belg. 110/C1
Ruiz, Mex. 200/D4
Rujen (peak), FYROM 105/H1
Ruki (riv.), D.R. Congo 155/J8
Rukwa (lake), Tanz. 162/B4
Rukwa (pol. reg.), Tanz. 162/B4
Rulles (riv.), Belg. 111/E4
Rülzheim, Ger. 112/B4
Rum, Aus. 115/H3
Rum Cay (isl.), Bahm. 199/G3
Ruma, Serb. 106/D3
Ruma NP, Kenya 162/B3
Rumbek, Sudan 155/L6
Rumes, Belg. 110/C2
Rumford, Me, US 189/G2
Rumia, Pol. 96/H4
Rumilly, Fr. 114/B6
Rümlang, Swi. 115/E3
Rumoi, Japan 134/B2
Rumphi, Malw. 162/B5
Rumson, NJ, US 196/E3
Rumst, Belg. 111/D1
Rumuruti, Kenya 162/C2
Runabay (pt.), NI, UK 92/B1
Runan, China 130/C4
Runcorn, Eng, UK 93/F5
Runding, Ger. 113/F4
Rundu, Namb. 163/C4
Rungwa (riv.), Tanz. 162/B4
Rungwa Game Rsv., Tanz. 162/B4
Rungwe (peak), Tanz. 162/B5
Runkel, Ger. 112/B2
Runn (lake), Swe. 96/F1
Runnemede, NJ, US 196/C4
Running Springs, Ca, US 194/C2
Ruo (riv.), China 123/K5
Ruokolahti, Fin. 97/N1
Ruoqiang, China 128/E4
Rupat (isl.), Indo. 138/B3
Rupea, Rom. 107/G2
Rupel (riv.), Belg. 111/D1
Rupert (riv.), Qu, Can. 139/J3
Rūpnagar, India 144/D4
Ruppichteroth, Ger. 111/G2
Rupt-sur-Moselle, Fr. 114/C2
Rupununi (riv.), Guy. 211/G4
Rur (riv.), Ger. 98/D3
Rur-Strasse (lake), Ger. 111/F2
Rurrenabaque, Bol. 208/E6
Rurutu (isl.), FrPol. 175/K7
Rusape, Zim. 163/F4
Rüschegg, Swi. 114/D4
Rüschlikon, Swi. 115/E3
Ruscom (riv.), On, Can. 193/G7
Ruse, Bul. 107/G4
Ruse (pol. reg.), Bul. 107/G4
Rusera, India 143/F3
Rush (lake), Ut, US 195/J13
Rush, Ire. 92/B4
Rushan, China 130/E3
Rushden, Eng, UK 91/F2
Rushville, In, US 188/C4
Rusk, Tx, US 187/J5
Russ, Fr. 114/D1
Russ Lake Nat'l Rec. Area, Wa, US 184/C3
Russbach (riv.), Aus. 107/N7
Russell (isls.), Austl. 172/F7
Russell, Mb, Can. 185/H3
Russell (lake), Mb, Can. 185/H1
Russell (isl.), Nun., Can. 180/F1
Russell (lake), Ga,SC, US 191/H3
Russell Gulch, Co, US 195/A3
Russellville, Al, US 191/G3
Russellville, Ar, US 187/J4
Russellville, Ky, US 188/C4
Rüsselsheim, Ger. 112/B3
Russi, It. 117/F4
Russia (ctry.) 122/H3
Russian (riv.), Ca, US 186/B3
Russian Mission, Ak, US 192/F3
Russkaya, Rus., Ant. 218/Q
Rust'avi, Geo. 121/H4
Rustenburg, SAfr. 163/E6
Ruston, La, US 187/J4
Ruston, Wa, US 193/C3
Rute, Sp. 102/C4
Ruteng, Indo. 139/F5
Rüthen, Ger. 109/F6
Rutherford, NJ, US 197/J8
Rutherglen, Sc, UK 94/B5
Rüthi, Swi. 115/F3
Ruthin, Wal, UK 93/E5
Ruthven, On, Can. 193/G7
Rüti, Swi. 115/E3
Rüti, Swi. 115/F4
Rutland (co.), Eng, UK 91/F1
Rutland, Vt, US 188/F3
Rutland Water (res.), Eng, UK 91/F1
Rutog, China 128/C5
Rutshuru (riv.), D.R. Congo 162/A3
Ruukki, Fin. 118/E2
Ruurlo, Neth. 108/D4
Ruvo di Puglia, It. 104/E2
Ruvu (riv.), Tanz. 162/C4
Ruvubu (riv.), Buru. 162/A3
Ruvuma (pol. reg.), Tanz. 162/C5
Ruvuma (riv.), Moz.,Tanz. 162/B5
Ruwāndūz, Iraq 148/F2
Ruwenzori (range), Ugan. 162/A2
Ruwenzori NP, Ugan. 162/A3
Ruy Barbosa, Braz. 212/B4
Ruyang, China 130/C4
Ruzayevka, Rus. 121/H1
Ruzizi (riv.), D.R. Congo 162/A3
Ružomberok, Slvk. 99/K4
Ruzyně (int'l arpt.), Czh. 113/H2
Rwanda (ctry.) 162/A3
Ryan (mt.), Austl. 173/D2
Ryan (mt.), Austl. 172/A1
Ryan (inlet), Sc, UK 92/C2
Ryazan', Rus. 121/G1
Ryazanskaya Oblast, Rus. 121/G1
Ryazhsk, Rus. 120/G1
Rybachiy (pen.), Rus. 95/K1
Rybinsk, Rus. 118/H4
Rybinsk (res.), Rus. 118/H4
Rybnik, Pol. 99/K3
Rycroft, Ab, Can. 184/D2
Ryd, Swe. 96/F3
Rydaholm, Swe. 96/F3
Ryde, Eng, UK 91/E5
Ryde, Ca, US 193/L10
Rydet, Swe. 96/D3
Rye (bay), Eng, UK 91/G5
Rye, Eng, UK 91/G5
Rye, NY, US 197/L8
Rye (riv.), Eng, UK 93/H3
Rye Brook, NY, US 197/L7
Rye Patch (res.), Nv, US 186/C2
Rygge, Nor. 96/D2
Ryki, Pol. 99/L3
Rylstone, Austl. 173/D2
Ryōkami, Japan 135/B2
Ryōtsu, Japan 133/F1
Ryōzen-yama (peak), Japan 135/K5
Rypin, Pol. 99/K2
Rysy (peak), Pol. 99/L4
Ryton, Eng, UK 93/G2
Rytterknægten (peak), Den. 96/F4
Ryūgasaki, Japan 133/G3
Ryukyu (isls.), Japan 133/H7
Ryūō, Japan 135/B2
Ryūō, Japan 135/K5
Rzeszów, Pol. 99/M3
Rzhev, Rus. 118/G4

S

's-Graveland, Neth. 108/C4
's Gravendeel, Neth. 108/B5
's Heerenberg, Neth. 108/D5
's Hertogenbosch, Neth. 108/C5
Sa Dec, Viet. 136/D4
Saab (int'l arpt.), Swe. 96/F2
Sääksjärvi (lake), Fin. 97/K1
Saal an der Donau, Ger. 113/E5
Saalbach (riv.), Ger. 112/B4
Saaldorf, Ger. 113/E2
Saale (riv.), Ger. 98/F3
Saales, Col de (pass), Fr. 114/D1
Saalfeld, Ger. 101/J1
Saalfelden am Steinernen Meer, Aus. 101/K3
Saane (riv.), Swi. 114/D5
Saanen, Swi. 114/D5
Saanta (peak), Kenya 162/C2
Saar (riv.), Ger. 111/F5
Saarbrücken, Ger. 111/F5
Saarburg, Ger. 111/F4
Saaremaa (isl.), Est. 97/K2
Saarland (state), Ger. 101/G2
Saarlouis, Ger. 111/F5
Saas, Swi. 115/F4
Saas Fee, Swi. 114/D5
Saastal (valley), Swi. 114/D5
Sab (riv.), Camb. 136/D3
Saba (isl.), NAnt. 199/N8
Šabac, Serb. 106/D3
Sabadell, Sp. 103/L6
Sabae, Japan 132/E3
Sabah (reg.), Malay. 139/E2
Sabalgarh, India 142/A2
Sabana (arch.), Bang. 203/F1
Sabana de Uchire, Ven. 211/E2
Sabanalarga, Col. 210/C3
Sabanalarga, Col. 210/C2
Sabancuy, Mex. 202/D2
Sabaneta, Ven. 210/D2
Sabang, Indo. 138/A2
Sabanita, Pan. 203/G4
Sabasţīyah, WBnk. 149/G7
Sabat (riv.), Sudan 155/L6
Sabbio Chiese, It. 116/D1
Sabbioneta, It. 116/D3
Sabhā, Libya 154/H2
Sabie (riv.), Moz. 165/F2
Sabinal, Cayo (isl.), Cuba 203/G1
Sabiñánigo, Sp. 103/E1
Sabinas, Mex. 201/F5
Sabinas (riv.), Mex. 201/F5
Sabinas Hidalgo, Mex. 201/E5
Sabine (lake), La,Tx, US 187/J5
Sabine (riv.), La,Tx, US 187/J5
Sabinópolis, Braz. 213/D1
Sabkhat al Bardawīl (lag.), Egypt 149/C4
Sabkhat al Jabbūl (lake), Syria 148/D3
Sabkhat al Mūḩ (lake), Syria 148/D3
Sablayan, Phil. 137/D5
Sable (isl.), NS, Can. 189/K3
Sable (cape), NS, Can. 189/H3
Sablé-sur-Sarthe, Fr. 100/C3
Saboeiro, Braz. 212/C2
Sabor (riv.), Port. 102/B2
Sabra (cape), Indo. 139/H4
Sabrina (coast), Ant. 218/J
Sabugal, Port. 102/B2
Sabzevār, Iran 147/G1
Sacajawea (peak), Or, US 184/D4
Sácama, Col. 210/C3
Sacaton, Az, US 195/S19
Sacavém, Port. 103/P10
Saccarello (peak), It. 116/A4
Sacco (riv.), It. 104/C2
Sacedón, Sp. 102/D2
Săcele, Rom. 107/G3
Sachigo (lake), On, Can. 185/K2
Sachigo (riv.), On, Can. 180/G3
Sachs Harbour, NW, Can. 180/D1
Sachseln, Swi. 115/E4
Sachsen (state), Ger. 98/G3
Sachsen-Anhalt (state), Ger. 98/F3
Sachsenbrunn, Ger. 112/D2
Sachsenhagen, Ger. 109/G4
Sacile, It. 117/F1
Säckingen, Ger. 114/D2
Sackville, NB, Can. 189/H2
Saclay, Fr. 88/J5
Saco, Me, US 189/G3
Sacramento (cap.), Ca, US 186/B3
Sacramento, Braz. 213/C1
Sacramento (co.), Ca, US 193/M10
Sacramento (riv.), Ca, US 186/B2
Sacramento (valley), Ca, US 186/B3
Sacramento (mts.), NM, US 182/E5
Sacramento, Pampa del (plain), Peru 214/C2
Sacramento River Deep Water Ship Canal, Ca, US 193/L10
Sacratif (cape), Sp. 102/D4
Sacred (falls), Hi, US 182/W12
Sacro (peak), It. 104/E2
Sacro Monte, It. 116/B1
Sada, SAfr. 164/D4
Sádaba, Sp. 102/E1
Sadābād, India 142/B2
Sa'dah, Yem. 146/D5
Saddam (int'l arpt.), Iraq 148/F3
Saddle (hills), Ab,BC, Can. 184/C2
Saddle (riv.), NJ, US 197/J8
Saddle Brook, NJ, US 197/J8
Saddle River, NJ, US 197/J7
Saddle Rock, NY, US 197/K8
Saddle, The (peak), Sc, UK 94/A2
Saddleworth, Austl. 171/H5
Sādhaura, India 144/D4
Sādiqābād, Pak. 147/K3
Sado (isl.), Japan 129/Q4
Sado (riv.), Port. 102/A3
Sadovo, Bul. 107/G4
Sadowara, Japan 132/B4
Sādri, India 147/K3

Sadulshahar, India 144/C5
Saerbeck, Ger. 109/E4
Saeul, Lux. 111/E4
Safājah (well), Egypt 159/C3
Safed Koh (range), Pak. 144/A3
Saffānīyah, Ra's as (pt.), SAr. 146/E3
Saffig, Ger. 111/G3
Säffle, Swe. 96/E2
Safford, Az, US 186/E4
Saffron Walden, Eng, UK 91/G2
Safi (cape), Mor. 156/C2
Safi, Mor. 156/C2
Safīd (riv.), Afg. 147/J1
Safid Khers (mts.), Afg. 147/K1
Safid Kūh (mts.), Afg. 147/H2
Safidon, India 144/D5
Safien, Swi. 115/F4
Safīpur, India 142/C2
Şāfītā, Syria 149/E2
Safonovo, Rus. 118/G5
Safranbolu, Turk. 148/C1
Sag Harbor, NY, US 197/F2
Saga (pref.), Japan 132/A4
Saga, China 143/E1
Saga, Japan 132/B4
Sagae, Japan 134/B4
Sagaing, Myan. 141/G3
Sagaing (div.), Myan. 141/F3
Sagami (sea), Japan 133/F3
Sagami (riv.), Japan 135/C2
Sagami (lake), Japan 135/C2
Sagami (bay), Japan 135/C3
Sagamihara, Japan 133/F3
Sagamiko, Japan 135/C2
Sagamore Hill Nat'l Hist. Site, NY, US 197/M8
Sāgar, India 142/B4
Sagard, Ger. 96/E4
Sagarmatha (zone), Nepal 143/F2
Sagarmatha (Everest) (mtn.), China,Nepal 143/F2
Sagarmatha NP, Nepal 143/F2
Sagauli, India 143/E2
Sagavanirktok (riv.), Ak, US 192/J2
Sagay, Phil. 139/F1
Saggart, Ire. 92/B5
Saghyz (riv.), Kaz. 121/K2
Saginaw, Mi, US 188/D3
Saginaw (bay), Mi, US 188/D3
Saglek (bay), Nf, Can. 139/K3
Sagone, Golfe de (gulf), Fr. 104/A1
Sagter Ems (riv.), Ger. 109/E2
Sagua de Tánamo, Cuba 203/H1
Sagua la Grande, Cuba 203/F1
Saguaro NP, Az, US 186/E4
Saguenay (riv.), Qu, Can. 189/G1
Saguia el Hamra (riv.), WSah. 154/C2
Sagunto, Sp. 103/E3
Sagy, Fr. 88/H4
Sa'gya, China 143/G1
Saḩāb, Jor. 149/D4
Sahagún, Sp. 102/C1
Sahagún, Col. 210/C2
Sahagún, Mex. 201/L7
Saḩam, Jor. 149/D3
Sahand (mtn.), Iran 146/E1
Sahara (des.), Afr. 151/B2
Sahāranpur, India 144/D5
Saharsa, India 143/F3
Sahaspur, India 142/B1
Sahaswān, India 142/B1
Sahavato, Madg. 165/J8
Sahāwar, India 142/B2
Sahel (riv.), Alg. 158/H4
Sāhibganj, India 143/F3
Şahinli, Turk. 107/H5
Sāhīwāl, Pak. 144/B4
Sahiwal, Pak. 144/B4
Şaḩrā Marzūq (des.), Libya 154/H3
Şaḩrā' Rabyānah (des.), Libya 155/K3
Sahrho, Jebel (mts.), Mor. 156/D3
Sahuaripa, Mex. 200/C2
Sahuayo de Morelos, Mex. 200/E4
Šahy, Slvk. 99/K4
Sai (canal), India 140/D2
Sai Yok NP, Thai. 136/B3
Saïda, Alg. 158/F5
Saidpur, Bang. 143/G3
Saidpur, India 142/D3
Saignelégier, Swi. 114/D3
Saigō, Japan 132/C2
Saigon, Viet. 136/D4
Saijō, Japan 132/C4
Saikai NP, Japan 132/A4
Saiki, Japan 132/B4
Sailly, Fr. 88/H4
Sailly-sur-la-Lys, Fr. 110/B2
Sailu, India 147/L5
Saimaa (lake), Fin. 95/J3
Sain Alto, Mex. 200/E4
Sainghin-en-Weppes, Fr. 110/B2
Sains-du-Nord, Fr. 110/D3
Saint Abb's (pt.), Sc, UK 94/D5
Saint-Affrique, Fr. 100/E5
Saint Agnes (pt.), Eng, UK 90/A6
Saint Albans, WV, US 188/D4
Saint Alban's, Nf, Can. 189/L2
Saint Albans, Vt, US 188/F2
Saint Albans, Eng, UK 88/C1
Saint Albert, Ab, Can. 184/E2
Saint-Amable, Qu, Can. 189/P6
Saint-Amand-les-Eaux, Fr. 110/C3
Saint-Amand-Montrond, Fr. 100/E3
Saint-Amarin, Fr. 114/D2
Saint-Ambroise, Qu, Can. 189/G1
Saint-Amé, Fr. 114/C1
Saint-André, Reun., Fr. 165/S15
Saint-André, Fr. 110/C2
Saint-André-de-Cubzac, Fr. 100/C4
Saint-André-les-Vergers, Fr. 100/F2
Saint Andrew's (bay), Sc, UK 94/D4
Saint Andrews, Sc, UK 94/D4
Saint Ann (cape), SLeo. 160/B5
Saint Anns, On, Can. 189/Q9
Saint Ann's (pt.), Wal, UK 90/A3
Saint Ann's Bay, Jam. 199/F4
Saint Anthony, Nf, Can. 189/L1
Saint-Antoine, Qu, Can. 189/N6
Saint Arnaud, Austl. 173/B3
Saint-Arnoult-en-Yvelines, Fr. 88/H6
Saint Aubin, Chl, UK 100/B2
Saint-Aubin, Swi. 114/C4
Saint-Aubin, Fr. 114/B3
Saint-Augustin, Fr. 88/M5
Saint Augustine, Fl, US 191/H4
Saint Augustine Beach, Fl, US 191/H4
Saint Austell (bay), Eng, UK 90/B6
Saint Austell, Eng, UK 90/B6
Saint-Avé, Fr. 100/B3
Saint-Avold, Fr. 111/F5
Saint-Barthélemy (isl.), Fr. 199/N8
Saint-Barthélemy-d'Anjou, Fr. 100/C3
Saint-Barthélemy, Pic de (peak), Fr. 100/D5
Saint Bees (pt.), Eng, UK 92/E2
Saint-Benoît, Qu, Can. 189/M6
Saint-Benoît, Fr. 100/D3
Saint-Benoît, Reun., Fr. 165/S15
Saint Bernard, La, US 195/Q17
Saint Bernard (parish), La, US 195/Q17
Saint-Berthevin, Fr. 100/C2
Saint-Blaise, Swi. 114/C3
Saint-Blaise, Qu, Can. 189/P7
Saint Blaize (cape), SAfr. 164/C4
Saint Boswells, Sc, UK 94/D5
Saint-Brice-Courcelles, Fr. 110/C5
Saint-Brice-sous-Forêt, Fr. 88/K5
Saint Bride's (bay), Wal, UK 90/A3
Saint-Brieuc, Fr. 100/B2
Saint-Brieuc (bay), Fr. 100/B2
Saint-Bruno-de-Montarville, Qu, Can. 189/P6
Saint-Calais, Fr. 100/D3
Saint-Canut, Qu, Can. 189/M6
Saint Catharines, On, Can. 189/R9
Saint Catherine (mt.), Gren. 211/F1
Saint Catherine's (pt.), Eng, UK 91/E5
Saint Catherine's (hill), Eng, UK 91/E5
Saint-Céré, Fr. 100/D4
Saint-Cergue, Swi. 114/C5
Saint-Cergues, Fr. 114/C5
Saint-Chamond, Fr. 100/F4
Saint Charles, Il, US 193/P16
Saint Charles (parish), La, US 195/P17
Saint Charles, Md, US 188/E4
Saint Charles, Mo, US 195/G8
Saint Charles (co.), Mo, US 195/F8
Saint-Chély-d'Apcher, Fr. 100/E4
Saint-Chéron, Fr. 88/J6
Saint Christoffel (peak), NAnt. 210/D1
Saint Clair (lake), Can.,US 193/G7
Saint Clair (peak), Az, US 195/S18
Saint Clair (co.), Il, US 195/G9
Saint Clair (co.), Mi, US 193/G6
Saint Clair, Mi, US 188/D3
Saint Clair, Pa, US 196/B2
Saint Clair Beach, On, Can. 193/G7
Saint Clair Shores, Mi, US 193/G6
Saint-Claude, Fr. 114/B5
Saint Cloud, Mn, US 185/K4
Saint-Cloud, Fr. 88/J5
Saint-Constant, Qu, Can. 189/N7
Saint Croix (riv.), US 188/A2
Saint Croix (isl.), USVI 199/M8
Saint Cyr (mt.), Yk, Can. 192/M3
Saint-Cyr-l'École, Fr. 88/J5
Saint-Cyr-sous-Dourdan, Fr. 88/J6
Saint-Cyr-sur-Morin, Fr. 88/M5
Saint David's (pt.), Wal, UK 90/A3
Saint David's, Wal, UK 90/A3
Saint-Denis, Fr. 88/K5
Saint-Denis, Reun., Fr. 165/S15
Saint-Denis-en-Bugey, Fr. 114/B6
Saint-Dié, Fr. 114/C1
Saint-Dizier, Fr. 111/D6
Saint-Doulchard, Fr. 100/E3
Saint-Édouard, Qu, Can. 189/N7
Saint Eleanors, PE, Can. 189/J2
Saint Elias (cape), Ak, US 192/K4
Saint Elias (mt.), Ak, US 192/K3
Saint Elias (mts.), Ak, US 180/B2
Saint-Éloy-les-Mines, Fr. 100/E3
Saint-Esprit, Qu, Can. 189/N6
Saint-Estève, Fr. 100/E5
Saint-Étienne, Fr. 100/F4
Saint-Étienne-au-Mont, Fr. 110/A2
Saint-Étienne-de-Baïgorry, Fr. 100/C5
Saint-Étienne-de-Tinée, Fr. 101/G4
Saint-Étienne-du-Rouvray, Fr. 100/D2
Saint-Étienne-lès-Remiremont, Fr. 114/C1
Saint-Eustache, Qu, Can. 189/N6
Saint Eustatius (isl.), NAnt. 199/N8
Saint-Fargeau-Ponthierry, Fr. 88/K6
Saint-Félicien, Qu, Can. 189/F1
Saint-Félix, Fr. 114/B6
Saint-Florent-sur-Cher, Fr. 100/E3
Saint-Florentin Fr. 100/E2
Saint-Floris, PN de, CAfr. 155/K6
Saint-Four, Fr. 100/E4
Saint Francis (riv.), Ar, US 187/K4
Saint Francis (riv.), Mo, US 191/F2
Saint Francis, Ks, US 187/G3
Saint Francis (cape), SAfr. 164/D4
Saint Francis, Wi, US 193/Q14
Saint Francisville, La, US 187/K5
Saint Francois (mts.), Mo, US 191/F2
Saint Gallen (canton), Swi. 115/F3
Saint-Gaudens, Fr. 100/D5
Saint-Genis-Pouilly, Fr. 114/C5
Saint George, Austl. 172/C5
Saint George, NB, Can. 189/H2
Saint George (cape), Nf, Can. 189/K1
Saint George (isl.), Ak, US 192/E4
Saint George, Ak, US 192/E4
Saint George (pt.), Ca, US 184/B5
Saint George, SC, US 191/H3
Saint George, Ut, US 186/D3
Saint George's, Nf, Can. 189/K1
Saint George's (bay), Nf, Can. 189/J2
Saint-Georges, Qu, Can. 189/G2
Saint George's (cap.), Gren. 211/F1
Saint George's (chan.), Ire.,UK 89/Q11
Saint Georges, De, US 196/C4
Saint-Germain, Fr. 114/C2
Saint-Germain-de-la-Grange, Fr. 88/H5
Saint-Germain-du-Bois, Fr. 114/B4
Saint-Germain-du-Corbéis, Fr. 100/D2
Saint-Germain-du-Plain, Fr. 114/A4
Saint-Germain-en-Laye, Fr. 88/J5
Saint-Germain-lès-Corbeil, Fr. 88/K6
Saint-Germain-sous Doue, Fr. 88/M5
Saint-Germain-sur-Morin, Fr. 88/L5
Saint-Germer-de-Fly, Fr. 110/A5
Saint-Gervais, Fr. 88/H4
Saint-Gervais-les-Bains, Fr. 114/C6
Saint-Ghislain, Belg. 110/C3
Saint-Gilles, Fr. 100/F5
Saint-Gilles-Croix-de-Vie, Fr. 100/C3
Saint-Gingolph, Swi. 114/C5
Saint-Girons, Fr. 100/D5
Saint-Gobain, Fr. 110/C4
Saint Govan's (pt.), Wal, UK 90/B3
Saint-Gratien, Fr. 88/J5
Saint Hedwig, Tx, US 195/U21
Saint Helena (bay), SAfr. 163/C7
Saint Helena (isl.), Austl. 172/F6
Saint Helens, Austl. 173/D4
Saint Helens (pt.), Austl. 173/D4
Saint Helens, Eng, UK 93/F5
Saint Helens (co.), Eng, UK 93/F5
Saint Helens, Or, US 184/C4
Saint Helens (mt.), Wa, US 184/C4
Saint Helier (cap.), Chl, UK 100/B2
Saint-Herblain, Fr. 100/C3
Saint-Hilarion, Fr. 88/H6
Saint-Hippolyte, Fr. 114/C3
Saint-Honoré, Qu, Can. 189/G1
Saint-Hubert, Qu, Can. 189/P6
Saint-Hubert, Belg. 111/E3
Saint-Hyacinthe, Qu, Can. 188/F2
Saint Ignace (isl.), On, Can. 185/L3
Saint Ignace, Mi, US 188/C2
Saint-Imier, Swi. 114/D3
Saint-Isidore-de-Laprairie, Qu, Can. 189/N7
Saint Ives (bay), Eng, UK 90/A6
Saint Ives, Eng, UK 91/F2
Saint Ives, Eng, UK 90/A6
Saint Jacques (int'l arpt.), Fr. 100/C2
Saint-Jacques-le-Mineur, Qu, Can. 189/P7
Saint James, NY, US 197/E2
Saint James (cape), BC, Can. 180/C3
Saint-Jean (riv.), Qu, Can. 189/H1
Saint-Jean (lake), Qu, Can. 139/J4
Saint-Jean-d'Angély, Fr. 100/C4
Saint-Jean-de-la-Ruelle, Fr. 100/D3
Saint-Jean-de-Losne, Fr. 114/B3
Saint-Jean-Port-Joli, Qu, Can. 189/G2
Saint-Jean-sur-Richelieu, Qu, Can. 188/F2
Saint-Jeoire, Fr. 114/C5
Saint-Jérôme, Qu, Can. 189/N6
Saint Joe, La, US 195/Q16
Saint Joe (riv.), Id,Wa, US 186/E4
Saint John, NB, Can. 189/H2
Saint John (isl.), USVI 199/M8
Saint John (riv.), Me, US 189/G2
Saint John The Baptist (parish), La, US 195/P16
Saint Johns, Az, US 186/E4
Saint Johns (riv.), Fl, US 191/H4
Saint John's (cap.), Anti. 199/N8
Saint John's (pt.), NI, UK 92/C3
Saint Johnsbury, Vt, US 189/F2
Saint Jones (riv.), De, US 196/C5
Saint Joseph (riv.), In,Mi, US 188/C3
Saint Joseph (isl.), On, Can. 188/C2
Saint Joseph, La, US 187/K5
Saint Joseph, Mo, US 187/J3
Saint Joseph (lake), On, Can. 180/G3
Saint-Joseph, Reun., Fr. 165/S15
Saint-Juéry, Fr. 100/E5
Saint-Julien, Fr. 114/B3
Saint-Julien-en-Genevois, Fr. 114/C5
Saint-Julien-les-Villas, Fr. 100/F2
Saint-Junien, Fr. 100/D4
Saint-Just-en-Chaussée, Fr. 110/B4
Saint Kilda (isl.), UK 89/P8
Saint Kitts (isl.), StK. 199/J4
Saint Kitts and Nevis (ctry.) 199/N8
Saint-Lambert, Qu, Can. 189/P6
Saint Laurent, Mb, Can. 185/J3
Saint-Laurent (riv.), Qu, Can. 189/G1
Saint-Laurent, Qu, Can. 189/N6
Saint-Laurent-Blangy, Fr. 110/B3
Saint-Laurent-de-Cerdans, Fr. 100/E5
Saint-Laurent du Maroni, FrG. 209/H2
Saint-Laurent-en-Grandvaux, Fr. 114/B4
Saint-Laurent-sur-Saône, Fr. 114/A5
Saint Lawrence, Nf, Can. 189/L2
Saint Lawrence (riv.), Can.,US 188/F2
Saint Lawrence, Pa, US 196/C3
Saint Lawrence (isl.), Ak, US 192/D3
Saint Lawrence (gulf), Can. 189/J1
Saint Lawrence Islands NP, On, Can. 188/E2
Saint-Lazare, Qu, Can. 189/M7
Saint-Léger, Belg. 111/E4
Saint-Léger-en-Yvelines, Fr. 88/H5
Saint-Léger-lès-Domart, Fr. 110/B3
Saint Leonard (mt.), Austl. 173/G5
Saint-Léonard, Qu, Can. 189/N6
Saint-Léonard, Fr. 110/A2
Saint-Leu, Reun., Fr. 165/S15
Saint-Leu-d'Esserent, Fr. 110/B5
Saint-Leu-la-Forêt, Fr. 88/J4
Saint Llorenc del Munt, PN, Sp. 103/K6
Saint-Lô, Fr. 100/C2
Saint Louis, Sk, Can. 185/G2
Saint Louis (riv.), Mn, US 188/A2
Saint-Louis, Sen. 160/A2
Saint-Louis (pol. reg.), Sen. 160/B3
Saint Louis, Mo, US 195/G8
Saint Louis (co.), Mo, US 195/F8
Saint-Louis, Fr. 114/D2
Saint Louis (lake), Qu, Can. 189/N7
Saint-Louis, Reun., Fr. 165/S15
Saint-Louis-de-Gonzague, Qu, Can. 189/N7
Saint-Louis-de-Kent, NB, Can. 189/H2
Saint-Louis du Nord, Haiti 203/H2
Saint-Loup-sur-Semouse, Fr. 114/C2
Saint-Lubin-des-Joncherets, Fr. 100/D2
Saint-Luc, Qu, Can. 189/P7
Saint Lucia (ctry.) 199/N9
Saint Lucia (lake), SAfr. 165/F3
Saint Lucia (cape), SAfr. 165/F3
Saint Lucia (chan.), Mart.,StL. 199/N9
Saint Lucia Estuary, SAfr. 165/F3
Saint-Lucien, Fr. 88/G6
Saint Maarten (isl.), NAnt. 199/N8
Saint Magnus (bay), Sc, UK 89/W13
Saint-Maixent l'École, Fr. 100/C3
Saint Malo, Mb, Can. 185/J3
Saint-Malo, Fr. 100/B2
Saint-Malo, Golfe de (gulf), Fr. 100/B2
Saint-Mandrier-sur-Mer, Fr. 100/F5
Saint-Marc, Haiti 203/H2
Saint-Marc-sur-Richelieu, Qu, Can. 189/P6
Saint-Marcel, Fr. 114/A4
Saint-Mard, Fr. 88/L4
Saint Maries, Id, US 184/D4
Saint Martin (lake), Mb, Can. 185/J3
Saint-Martin (isl.), Guad., Fr. 199/N8
Saint-Martin, Swi. 114/D5
Saint-Martin-Boulogne, Fr. 110/A2
Saint-Martin-d'Ablois, Fr. 110/C6
Saint-Martin-d'Hères, Fr. 100/F4
Saint-Martin-du-Tertre, Fr. 88/K4
Saint-Martin-la-Garenne, Fr. 88/H4
Saint Martinville, La, US 187/K5
Saint Mary (cape), Gam. 160/A3
Saint Mary (peak), Austl. 171/H4
Saint Mary's, Ak, US 192/F3
Saint Marys, Austl. 173/D4
Saint Marys, Ga, US 191/H4
Saint Marys, Pa, US 188/E3
Saint Mary's, On, Can. 188/D3
Saint Mary's (riv.), NS, Can. 189/J2
Saint-Mathieu-de-Beloeil, Qu, Can. 189/N7
Saint Matthew (isl.), Ak, US 192/D3
Saint Matthews, SC, US 191/H3
Saint Matthias Group (isls.), PNG 174/E5
Saint-Maur-des-Fossés, Fr. 88/K5
Saint-Maurice, Swi. 114/D5
Saint-Maurice (riv.), Qu, Can. 139/J4
Saint-Max, Fr. 111/F6
Saint-Maximin-la-Sainte-Baume, Fr. 100/F5
Saint-Memmie, Fr. 111/D6
Saint-Méry, Fr. 88/L6
Saint Michael, Ak, US 192/F3
Saint Michaels, Md, US 196/B6
Saint-Michel (bay), Fr. 100/C2
Saint-Michel, Fr. 111/D4
Saint-Michel-sur-Meurthe, Fr. 114/C1
Saint-Michel-sur-Orge, Fr. 88/J6
Saint-Mihiel, Fr. 111/E6
Saint Monance, Sc, UK 94/D4
Saint-Nabord, Fr. 114/C1
Saint-Nazaire, Fr. 100/B3
Saint Neots, Eng, UK 91/F2
Saint-Nicolas, Belg. 111/E2
Saint-Nicolas-d'Aliermont, Fr. 100/D2
Saint Niklaus, Swi. 114/D5
Saint-Nom-la-Bretèche, Fr. 88/J5
Saint-Omer, Fr. 110/B2
Saint-Omer-en-Chaussée, Fr. 110/A4
Saint-Ouen, Fr. 110/B3
Saint-Ouen-en-Brie, Fr. 88/L6
Saint-Ouen-L'Aumône, Fr. 88/J4
Saint-Pamphile, Qu, Can. 189/G2
Saint-Pascal, Qu, Can. 189/G2
Saint-Pathus, Fr. 88/L4
Saint Paul, Ab, Can. 184/F2
Saint Paul (cape), Gha. 161/F5
Saint Paul (riv.), Libr. 154/C6
Saint Paul, Reun., Fr. 165/S15
Saint Paul, Ak, US 192/D4
Saint Paul (isl.), Ak, US 192/W23
Saint Paul, Ks, US 190/E2
Saint Paul (cap.), Mn, US 185/K4
Saint-Paul-lès-Dax, Fr. 100/C5
Saint Paul Rocks (isl.), Braz. 80/H5
Saint Paul's Church Nat'l Hist. Site, NY, US 197/K8
Saint-Pé-de-Bigorre, Fr. 100/C5
Saint Peter, Mn, US 185/K4
Saint Peter (isl.), Austl. 171/G5
Saint Peter Port (cap.), Chl, UK 100/B2
Saint Peters, Mo, US 195/F8
Saint Petersburg, Fl, US 191/H5
Saint Petersburg, Rus. 119/T7
Saint-Philippe-de-Laprairie, Qu, Can. 189/P7
Saint-Pierre (isl.), StP., Fr. 189/K2
Saint-Pierre, StP., Fr. 189/K2
Saint-Pierre, Mart., Fr. 199/N9
Saint-Pierre, Reun., Fr. 165/S15
Saint Pierre and Miquelon (dpcy.), Fr. 189/K2
Saint Pierre-des-Corps, Fr. 100/D3
Saint-Pierre-du-Mont, Fr. 100/C5
Saint-Pierre-du-Perray, Fr. 88/K6
Saint-Pierre-en-Faucigny, Fr. 114/C5
Saint Pierre-Jolys, Mb, Can. 185/J3
Saint-Pierre-sur-Dives, Fr. 100/C2
Saint-Point (lake), Fr. 114/C4
Saint-Pol-de-Léon, Fr. 100/B2
Saint-Pol-sur-Mer, Fr. 110/B1
Saint-Pol-sur-Ternoise, Fr. 110/B3
Saint-Pourçain-sur-Sioule, Fr. 100/E3
Saint-Prex, Swi. 114/C5
Saint-Prix, Fr. 88/J4
Saint-Quentin, Fr. 110/C4
Saint-Quentin, Canal de (canal), Fr. 110/C4
Saint-Rambert-en-Bugey, Fr. 114/B6
Saint-Raphaël, Fr. 101/G5
Saint-Rémi, Qu, Can. 189/N7
Saint-Rémy-de-Provence, Fr. 100/F5
Saint-Rémy-lès-Chevreuse, Fr. 88/J5
Saint-Rémy-l'Honoré, Fr. 88/H5
Saint-Roch-de-l'Achigan, Qu, Can. 189/N6
Saint Rose, La, US 195/P17
Saint Sampson's, Chl, UK 100/B2
Saint-Saulve, Fr. 110/C3
Saint-Sauveur, Fr. 114/C2
Saint-Sauveur-des-Monts, Qu, Can. 189/M6
Saint-Sever, Fr. 100/C5
Saint Simons (isl.), Ga, US 191/H4
Saint Simons Island, Ga, US 191/H4
Saint-Soupplets, Fr. 88/L4
Saint Stephen, NB, Can. 189/H2
Saint-Sulpice, Fr. 100/D5
Saint Tammany, La, US 195/Q16
Saint Tammany (parish), La, US 195/P16
Saint Thomas, On, Can. 188/D3
Saint Thomas (isl.), USVI 199/H4
Saint-Timothée, Qu, Can. 189/M7
Saint-Trivier-de-Courtes, Fr. 114/B5
Saint-Tropez, Fr. 101/G5
Saint-Urbain-Premier, Qu, Can. 189/N7
Saint-Ursanne, Swi. 114/D3
Saint-Valery-en-Caux, Fr. 100/D2
Saint-Valery-sur-Somme, Fr. 110/A3
Saint-Vallier, Fr. 100/F3
Saint-Vaury, Fr. 100/D3
Saint Vincent (pt.), Austl. 173/C4
Saint Vincent (isl.), StV. 199/N9
Saint Vincent, It. 116/A1
Saint Vincent and the Grenadines (ctry.) 199/N9
Saint-Vincent-de-Tyrosse, Fr. 100/C5
Saint Vincent Passage (chan.), StL.,StV. 199/N9
Saint-Vit, Fr. 114/B3
Saint-Vith, Belg. 111/F3
Saint-Vrain, Fr. 88/K6
Saint Walburg, Sk, Can. 184/F2
Saint-Witz, Fr. 88/K4
Saint-Yrieix-la-Perche, Fr. 100/D4
Sainte-Agathe-des-Monts, Qu, Can. 188/F2
Sainte-Anne-des-Monts, Qu, Can. 189/H1
Sainte-Anne-des-Plaines, Qu, Can. 189/N6
Sainte-Aulde, Fr. 88/M5
Sainte-Croix, Swi. 114/C4
Sainte-Croix-aux-Mines, Fr. 114/D1
Sainte-Geneviève-des-Bois, Fr. 88/K6
Sainte-Julie, Qu, Can. 189/P6
Sainte-Marie, Qu, Can. 189/G2
Sainte-Marie, Mart., Fr. 199/N9
Sainte-Marie-aux-Chênes, Fr. 111/F5
Sainte Marie, Nosy (isl.), Madg. 165/J7
Sainte-Martine, Qu, Can. 189/N7
Sainte-Maxime, Fr. 101/G5
Sainte-Mesme, Fr. 88/H6
Sainte Rose du Lac, Mb, Can. 185/J3
Sainte-Sigolène, Fr. 100/F4
Sainte-Thérèse, Qu, Can. 189/N6
Sainte-Tulle, Fr. 100/F5
Saintes, Fr. 100/C4
Sainthia, India 143/F4
Sāipal (peak), Nepal 140/D2
Saipan (isl.), NMar. 174/D3
Saitama (pref.), Japan 133/F2
Saito, Japan 132/B4
Saiwa Swamp NP, Kenya 162/B2
Sajama, Bol. 214/D5
Sajama, PN, Bol. 214/D5
Sajószentpéter, Hun. 99/L4
Sak (riv.), SAfr. 164/C3
Sakado, Japan 135/C2
Sakae, Japan 135/E2
Sakahogi, Japan 135/L5
Sakai, Japan 132/E2
Sakai, Japan 133/F2
Sakai (riv.), Japan 135/C3
Sakai, Japan 135/C1
Sakaide, Japan 132/C3
Sakaigawa, Japan 135/B2
Sakaiminato, Japan 132/C3
Sakakawea (lake), ND, US 185/H3
Sakami (lake), Qu, Can. 139/J3
Sakaraha, Madg. 165/H8
Sakarya (riv.), Turk. 148/B1
Sakarya (prov.), Turk. 107/K5
Sakauchi, Japan 135/K4
Sakawa, Japan 132/C4
Sakay (riv.), Madg. 165/H7
Sakçagöze, Turk. 148/D2
Sakeny (riv.), Madg. 165/H7
Sakété, Ben. 161/F5
Sakha (Yakutiya), Resp., Rus. 123/Q4
Sakhalin (gulf), Rus. 123/Q4
Sakhalin (isl.), Rus. 123/Q4
Sakhalinskaya Oblast, Rus. 123/Q4
Sakhnīn, Isr. 149/G6
Sakht Sar, Iran 146/F1
Şäki, Azer. 121/H4
Sakishima (isl.), Japan 133/G8
Sakmara (riv.), Rus. 145/C2
Sakon Nakhon, Thai. 136/D2
Sakrand, Pak. 147/J3
Sakti, India 142/D4
Saku, Japan 133/F2
Saku, Japan 135/A1
Sakura, Japan 135/E1
Sakura, Japan 135/E2
Sakuragawa, Japan 135/E2
Sakurai, Japan 135/J6
Saky, Ukr. 120/E3
Sakya Monastery, China 143/G1
Säkylä, Fin. 97/K1
Sal (isl.), CpV. 151/K10
Sal (pt.), Hon. 202/E3
Sal (riv.), Rus. 121/G3
Sal Rei, CpV. 151/K10
Šal'a, Slvk. 106/C1
Sala, Swe. 96/G2
Sala Baganza, It. 116/D3
Sala Consilina, It. 104/D2
Salada (lake), Mex. 200/B1
Saladas, Arg. 215/E2
Saladillo, Arg. 216/F2
Saladilio (riv.), Arg. 217/J11
Salado (riv.), Arg. 216/D3
Salado (riv.), Mex. 201/E3
Salado del Norte (riv.), Arg. 205/C5
Salaga, Gha. 161/E4
Şalaḩ Ad Din (gov.), Iraq 148/E3
Sălaj (prov.), Rom. 107/F2
Salālah, Oman 146/F5
Salamá, Guat. 202/D3
Salamajärven NP, Fin. 118/E3
Salamanca, Mex. 201/E4
Salamanca, Sp. 102/C2
Salamanca, NY, US 188/E3
Salamat (riv.), Chad 155/J6
Salamatof, Ak, US 192/H3
Salamina, Col. 210/C2
Salamís, Gre. 105/H3
Salamís (isl.), Gre. 105/N9
Salamīyah, Syria 149/E2
Salangen, Nor. 95/F1
Salas, Peru 214/B2
Salas, Sp. 102/B1
Salas de los Infantes, Sp. 102/D1
Salavat, Rus. 121/K1
Salaverry, Peru 214/B3
Salayar (isl.), Indo. 139/F5
Salbris, Fr. 100/E3
Salcantay (peak), Peru 214/C4
Saldaña, Sp. 102/C1
Saldanhabaai (bay), Safr. 164/K10
Saldus, Lat. 97/K3
Sale, Austl. 173/C3
Sale, It. 116/B3
Salé, Mor. 158/A2
Salé (prov.), Mor. 158/A3
Sale, Eng, UK 93/F5
Sale Marasino, It. 116/D1
Salebabu (isl.), Indo. 139/G3
Salekhard, Rus. 122/G3
Salem, Ger. 115/F2
Salem, India 140/C5
Salem, In, US 188/C4
Salem, Mi, US 193/E7
Salem, NH, US 189/G3
Salem, NJ, US 196/C4
Salem (co.), NJ, US 196/C4
Salem (cap.), Or, US 184/C4
Salemi, It. 104/C4
Salentina (pen.), It. 105/F2
Salerno, It. 104/D2
Salerno, Golfo di (gulf), It. 104/D2
Sales (pt.), Eng, UK 91/G3

Saleux, Fr. 110/B4
Salfīt, WBnk. 149/G7
Salford, Eng, UK 93/F5
Salford (co.), Eng, UK 93/F5
Salgado Filho (int'l arpt.), Braz. 213/B4
Salgar, Col. 210/C3
Salgesch, Swi. 114/D5
Salgótarján, Hun. 99/K4
Salgueiro, Braz. 212/C3
Salhus, Nor. 96/A1
Salies-de-Béarn, Fr. 100/C5
Salies-du-Salat, Fr. 100/D5
Şalīf, Yem. 146/D5
Salihli, Turk. 148/B2
Salihorsk, Bela. 120/C1
Salima, Malw. 163/F3
Salīmah (oasis), Sudan 159/B4
Salina, Ut, US 186/E3
Salina (isl.), It. 104/D3
Salina (pt.), Bahm. 203/H1
Salina Cruz, Mex. 202/C2
Salinas (riv.), Ca, US 186/B3
Salinas, Braz. 212/B5
Salinas, Ca, US 186/B3
Salinas (cape), Sp. 103/G3
Salinas, Ecu. 210/A5
Salinas de Hidalgo, Mex. 201/E4
Salinas Pueblo Missions Nat'l Mon., NM, US 187/F4
Salinas Y Aguada Blanca, Reserva Nacional, Peru 214/D4
Saline (riv.), Ks, US 190/D2
Saline, It. 117/D6
Saline, Sc, UK 94/C4
Salinópolis, Braz. 209/J4
Salins-les-Bains, Fr. 114/B4
Salisbury, NC, US 191/H3
Salisbury (plain), Eng, UK 90/D4
Salisbury, Eng, UK 91/E4
Salisbury (isl.), Nun., Can. 139/J2
Salisbury, NY, US 197/L9
Salitre (riv.), Braz. 212/B3
Salitre, Ecu. 210/B5
Salla, Fin. 118/F2
Salladasburg, Pa, US 196/A1
Sallanches, Fr. 114/C6
Salland (phys. reg.), Neth. 108/D4
Sallatouk (pt.), Gui. 160/B4
Sallaumines, Fr. 110/B3
Sallent, Sp. 103/F2
Salliqueló, Arg. 216/E3
Sallisaw, Ok, US 187/J4
Sally (pass), Ire. 92/B5
Salm (riv.), Ger. 111/F3
Salmān Pāk, Iraq 148/F3
Salmās, Iran 148/F2
Salmon (riv.), BC, Can. 184/C2
Salmon, Id, US 184/E4
Salmon (riv.), Id, US 184/E4
Salmon Arm, BC, Can. 184/D3
Salmon Falls (riv.), Id,Nv, US 186/D2
Salmon River (mts.), Id, US 184/E4
Salmon, South Fork (riv.), US 186/C2
Salmtal, Ger. 111/F4
Salò, It. 116/D1
Salo, Fin. 97/K1
Salon, India 142/C2
Salon (riv.), Fr. 98/C5
Salon-de-Provence, Fr. 100/F5
Salonga, PN de la, D.R. Congo 155/K8
Salonta, Rom. 106/E2
Salouël, Fr. 110/B4
Salpausselkä (mts.), Fin. 97/M1
Salpo, Peru 214/B3
Salses-le-Château, Fr. 100/E5
Sal'sk, Rus. 121/G3
Salso (riv.), It. 104/C4
Salsomaggiore Terme, It. 116/C3
Salt (riv.), SAfr. 164/C4
Salt (riv.), Az, US 195/R19
Salt (range), Pak. 144/B3
Salt Cay (isl.), UK 203/J1
Salt Draw (riv.), Tx, US 200/D2
Salt Fork Arkansas (riv.), Ks,Ok, US 187/H3
Salt Fork Red (riv.), Ok,Tx, US 187/G4
Salt Lake (co.), Ut, US 195/J12
Salt Lake City (cap.), Ut, US 195/K12
Salt Meadow NWR, Ct, US 197/F1
Salt, North Fork (riv.), Mo, US 187/J2
Salt River Ind. Res., Az, US 195/S18
Salta, Arg. 215/C1
Saltaire, NY, US 197/E2
Saltash, Eng, UK 90/B6
Saltcoats, Sc, UK 94/B5
Saltdal, Nor. 95/E2
Saltee (isls.), Ire. 89/Q10
Saltfjorden (inlet), Nor. 95/E2
Saltillo, Mex. 201/E3
Salto, Uru. 215/E3
Salto, Braz. 213/C2
Salto, Arg. 216/E2
Salto da Divisa, Braz. 212/C5
Salto del Guairá, Par. 215/F1
Salto Grande (res.), Arg. 215/E3
Salto Santiago, Represa de (res.), Braz. 213/A3
Salton Sea (lake), Ca, US 186/C4
Saltvik, Fin. 97/J1
Saluda (riv.), SC, US 191/H3
Salug, Phil. 137/D6
Saluggia, It. 116/B2
Salunga-Landisville, Pa, US 196/B3
Sālūr, India 140/D4
Salurn (Salorno), It. 115/H5
Salut, Îles du (isls.), FrG. 209/H2
Saluzzo, It. 101/G4
Salvación (bay), Chile 217/B6
Salvador (lake), La, US 195/P17
Salvaleón de Higüey, DRep. 199/H4
Salvaterra de Magos, Port. 102/A3
Salvatierra, Mex. 201/E4
Salvatierra de Miño, Sp. 102/A1
Salween (riv.), Asia 141/G4
Salyan, Azer. 121/J5
Salyersville, Ky, US 188/D4
Salza (riv.), Aus. 99/H5
Salzach (riv.), Ger. 98/G5
Salzano, It. 117/F1
Salzbergen, Ger. 109/E4
Salzburg, Aus. 101/K3
Salzburg (int'l arpt.), Aus. 101/K3
Salzburg (prov.), Aus. 99/G5
Salzgitter, Ger. 109/H4
Salzhausen, Ger. 109/H2
Salzhemmendorf, Ger. 109/G4
Salzkotten, Ger. 109/F5
Salzwedel, Ger. 98/F2
Sam Rayburn (res.), Tx, US 190/E4
Sam Sao (mts.), Laos,Viet. 136/C1
Sam Son, Viet. 136/D2
Sama, Sp. 102/C1
Samak (cape), Indo. 138/C4
Samales Group (isls.), Phil. 139/F2
Samālkha, India 144/D5
Sāmalkot, India 140/D4
Samāna, India 144/D4
Samaná (cape), DRep. 199/H4
Samana (isl.), Bahm. 203/H1
Samandağı, Turk. 149/D1
Samani, Japan 134/C2
Samaniego, Col. 210/B4
Samannūd, Egypt 149/B4
Samaqua (riv.), Qu, Can. 189/F1
Samar, Jor. 149/D3
Samar (isl.), Phil. 137/E5
Samara (riv.), Rus. 145/B2
Samara (int'l arpt.), Rus. 121/J1
Samara, Rus. 121/J1
Samarskaya Oblast, Rus. 145/A2
Samarai, PNG 174/E6
Samarate, It. 116/B1
Samaria (reg.), WBnk. 149/G7
Samarinda, Indo. 139/E4
Samarqand, Uzb. 145/E5
Samarqand (pol. reg.), Uzb. 145/E5
Sāmarrā', Iraq 148/E3
Samasata, Pak. 144/A5
Samāstipur, India 143/E3
Şamaxı, Azer. 121/J4
Sāmba, India 144/C3
Sambalpur, India 140/D3
Sambao (riv.), Madg. 165/H7
Sambar (cape), Indo. 138/D4
Sambas, Indo. 138/C3
Sambava, Madg. 165/J6
Sambhal, India 142/B1
Sambir, Ukr. 99/M4
Sambor Prei Kuk (ruin), Camb. 136/D3
Samborombón (riv.), Arg. 217/K11
Samborombón (bay), Arg. 217/F2
Sambre (riv.), Fr. 98/C3
Sambre à l'Oise, Canal de (canal), Fr. 110/C4
Sambriāl, Pak. 144/C3
Sambu, Japan 135/E2
Samburu Nat'l Rsv., Kenya 162/C2
Samch'ŏk, SKor. 131/E4
Samch'ŏnp'o, SKor. 131/E5
Samedan, Swi. 115/F4
Samer, Fr. 110/A2
Samfya Mission, Zam. 162/A5
Sámi, Gre. 105/G3
Samiria (riv.), Peru 214/C2
Samit (cape), Camb. 136/C4
Samkos (peak), Camb. 136/C3
Sammamish (lake), Wa, US 193/C2
Sammeron, Fr. 88/M5
Samnangjin, SKor. 131/E5
Samnaun, Swi. 115/G4
Samoa (ctry.) 175/H6
Samobor, Cro. 106/B3
Samoëns, Fr. 114/C5
Samoggia (riv.), It. 117/E4
Samokov, Bul. 107/F4
Samora (riv.), Port. 103/Q10
Samora Correia, Port. 103/Q10
Sámos (isl.), Gre. 148/A2
Sámos, Gre. 148/A2
Samothráki, Gre. 105/J2
Sampacho, Arg. 216/D2
Samper de Calanda, Sp. 103/E2
Sampit (riv.), Indo. 138/D4
Sampit, Indo. 138/D4
Samsø (isl.), Den. 96/D4
Samsø Bælt (chan.), Den. 96/D4
Samson (mt.), Austl. 172/E6
Samsonvale (lake), Austl. 172/E6
Samsun, Turk. 148/D1
Samsun (prov.), Turk. 148/C1
Samthar, India 142/B3
Samugheo, It. 104/A3
Samui (isl.), Thai. 141/H6
Samukawa, Japan 135/C3
Samundri, Pak. 144/B4
Samur (riv.), Azer.,Rus. 122/E5
Samut Prakan, Thai. 136/C3
Samut Sakhon, Thai. 136/C3
Samut Songkhram, Thai. 136/B3
Samye Monastery, China 143/H1
San (riv.), Camb. 136/D3
San, Mali 160/D3
San (riv.), Pol. 99/M3
San Adrián, Cabo de (cape), Sp. 102/A1
San Agustin (cape), Phil. 137/E6
San Agustín, Col. 210/B4
San Agustin de Guadalix, Sp. 103/N8
San Agustín, Parque Arqeológico, Col. 210/B4
San Ambrosio (isl.), Chile 205/B5
San Andreas (lake), Ca, US 193/J11
San Andres (mts.), NM, US 186/F4
San Andrés (lake), Mex. 202/B1
San Andrés, Col. 210/C3
San Andrés, Col. 203/F3
San Andrés Cuexcontitlán, Mex. 201/Q10
San Andrés de Giles, Arg. 217/J11
San Andrés de Machaca, Bol. 214/D5
San Andrés del Rabanedo, Sp. 102/C1
San Andrés, Isla de (isl.), Col. 198/E5
San Andrés Tuxtla, Mex. 202/C2
San Angelo, Tx, US 190/C4
San Anselmo, Ca, US 193/J11
San Antonio (cape), Arg. 217/F3
San Antonio, Chile 216/N8
San Antonio, Ecu. 210/B4
San Antonio, Mex. 200/C4
San Antonio, Peru 214/B4
San Antonio, Uru. 217/K11
San Antonio, Ven. 211/F2
San Antonio (mt.), Ca, US 194/C2
San Antonio, Tx, US 187/H5
San Antonio (int'l arpt.), Tx, US 187/H5
San Antonio (riv.), Tx, US 190/D4
San Antonio Abad, Sp. 103/F3
San Antonio de Areco, Arg. 217/J11
San Antonio de Caparo, Ven. 210/D3
San Antonio del Golfo, Ven. 211/F2
San Antonio del Táchira, Ven. 210/C3
San Antonio Oeste, Arg. 216/D4
San Antonio, Punta (pt.), Mex. 200/B2
San Augustine, Tx, US 190/E4
San Bartolo, Peru 214/B4
San Bartolomé de Tirajana, Canl. 103/X17
San Bartolome Tlaltelulco, Mex. 201/Q10
San Bartolomeo in Bosco, It. 117/E3
San Bartolomeo in Galdo, It. 104/D2
San Bautista, Uru. 217/L11
San Benedetto (range), It. 117/E5
San Benedetto del Tronto, It. 101/K5
San Benedetto in Alpe, It. 117/E5
San Benedetto Po, It. 117/D2
San Benedicto (isl.), Mex. 200/C5
San Bernardo, Chile 216/N8
San Bernardo (pt.), Col. 210/C2
San Bernardino, Ca, US 194/C2
San Bernardino (co.), Ca, US 194/C2
San Bernardino (mts.), Ca, US 194/C2
San Bernardino Nat'l Forest, Ca, US 194/C2
San Blas, Mex. 200/D4
San Blas, Mex. 200/C3
San Blas (cape), Fl, US 191/G4
San Bonifacio, It. 117/E2
San Borja, Bol. 208/E6
San Bruno, Mex. 200/B3
San Bruno, Ca, US 193/K11
San Buenaventura, Mex. 201/E3
San Buenaventura (Ventura), Ca, US 194/A2
San Candido (Innichen), It. 101/K3
San Carlos, Chile 216/C3
San Carlos, Mex. 201/E2
San Carlos, Mex. 201/F3
San Carlos, Nic. 203/E4
San Carlos, Pan. 210/B2
San Carlos, Phil. 137/D4
San Carlos, Uru. 217/G2
San Carlos, Ven. 210/D2
San Carlos (lake), Az, US 186/E4
San Carlos, Ca, US 193/K11
San Carlos de Bariloche, Arg. 216/C4
San Carlos de Bariloche (int'l arpt.), Arg. 216/C4
San Carlos de Río Negro, Ven. 211/E4
San Carlos del Zulia, Ven. 210/D2
San Casciano in Val di Pesa, It. 117/E5
San Cataldo, It. 105/F2
San Cayetano, Arg. 216/F3
San Cesario sul Panaro, It. 117/E3
San Ciro de Acosta, Mex. 201/F4
San Clemente (isl.), Ca, US 186/C4
San Clemente, Ca, US 194/C4
San Clemente, Sp. 102/D3
San Clemente, Chile 216/C2
San Clemente del Tuyú, Arg. 217/F3
San Colombano al Lambro, It. 116/C2
San Cristóbal, Arg. 215/D3
San Cristobal (isl.), Sol. 174/F6
San Cristóbal (vol.), Nic. 202/E3
San Cristóbal, Cuba 203/F1
San Cristóbal (isl.), Ecu. 214/F7
San Cristóbal, Ven. 210/C3
San Cristóbal de las Casas, Mex. 202/C2
San Cristobal Wash (riv.), Az, US 200/B1
San Damiano d'Asti, It. 116/B3
San Diego (cape), Arg. 217/D7
San Diego, Ca, US 194/C5
San Diego (aqueduct), Ca, US 194/C4
San Diego (bay), Ca, US 194/C5
San Diego (co.), Ca, US 194/C4
San Diego, Tx, US 190/D5
San Diego International-Lindbergh Field (int'l arpt.), Ca, US 194/C5
San Diego Naval Station, Ca, US 194/C5
San Diego Wild Animal Park, Ca, US 194/C4
San Diego Zoo, Ca, US 194/C5
San Diequito (riv.), Ca, US 194/C5
San Dimas, Ca, US 194/C2
San Donà di Piave, It. 117/F1
San Donnino, It. 117/E5
San Dorligo della Valle, It. 117/G1
San Esteban de Gormaz, Sp. 102/D2
San Felice Circeo, It. 104/C2
San Felice del Benaco, It. 116/D1
San Felice sul Panaro, It. 117/E3
San Felipe, Mex. 200/B2
San Felipe, Ven. 210/D2
San Felipe, Chile 216/N8
San Felipe de Puerto Plata, DRep. 199/G4
San Felipe de Vichayal, Peru 214/A2
San Felipe Jalapa de Díaz, Mex. 201/F5
San Felipe Torres Mochas, Mex. 201/E4
San Felix (isl.), Chile 205/A5
San Fernando, Arg. 217/J11
San Fernando, Chile 216/C2
San Fernando (riv.), Mex. 190/D5
San Fernando, Phil. 137/D4
San Fernando, Phil. 137/D4
San Fernando, Sp. 102/B4
San Fernando, Trin. 211/F2
San Fernando, Ca, US 194/F7
San Fernando (valley), Ca, US 194/B2
San Fernando de Apure, Ven. 211/E3
San Fernando de Atabapo, Ven. 210/E3
San Fernando de Henares, Sp. 103/N9
San Fernando de Presas, Mex. 201/F3
San Fior di Sopra, It. 117/F1
San Francesco al Campo, It. 116/A2
San Francisco, Arg. 215/D3
San Francisco, Col. 210/B4
San Francisco, ESal. 202/D3
San Francisco, Phil. 137/E6
San Francisco, Ven. 210/D2
San Francisco (riv.), Az,NM, US 186/E4
San Francisco, Ca, US 186/B3
San Francisco (co.), Ca, US 193/K11
San Francisco (int'l arpt.), Ca, US 186/B3
San Francisco Acuautla, Mex. 201/R10
San Francisco Bay NWR, Ca, US 193/K11
San Francisco, Cabo de (cape), Ecu. 210/A4
San Francisco Chimalpa, Mex. 201/Q10
San Francisco de la Paz, Hon. 202/E3
San Francisco de Macorís, DRep. 199/G4
San Francisco de Mostazal, Chile 216/N8
San Francisco del Mezquital, Mex. 200/D4
San Francisco del Monte de Oro, Arg. 216/D2
San Francisco del Oro, Mex. 200/D3
San Francisco del Rincón, Mex. 201/E4
San Francisco Telixtlahuaca, Mex. 198/B4
San Fratello, It. 104/D3
San Gabriel (riv.), Ca, US 194/C2
San Gabriel (pt.), Mex. 200/B2
San Gabriel (res.), Ca, US 194/C2
San Gabriel, Ecu. 210/B4
San Gabriel, Ca, US 194/F7
San Gavino Monreale, It. 104/A3
San Germán, Cuba 203/G1
San Germano Vercellese, It. 116/B2
San Gil, Col. 210/C3
San Gimignano, It. 117/E6
San Giorgio delle Pertiche, It. 117/E1
San Giorgio di Piano, It. 117/E3
San Giorgio Ionico, It. 105/E2
San Giorgio Piacentino, It. 116/C3
San Giovanni al Natisone, It. 117/G1
San Giovanni Bianco, It. 116/C1
San Giovanni Gemini, It. 104/C4
San Giovanni in Croce, It. 116/D2
San Giovanni in Fiore, It. 104/E3
San Giovanni in Marignano, It. 117/F5
San Giovanni in Persiceto, It. 117/E3
San Giovanni Lupatoto, It. 117/E2
San Giovanni Valdarno, It. 117/E5
San Giuliano, It. 116/B3
San Giuliano Terme, It. 116/D5
San Giustino, It. 117/F5
San Giusto Canavese, It. 116/A2
San Gorgonio (mtn.), Ca, US 186/C4
San Gottardo, Passo del (pass), Swi. 115/E4
San Gregorio, Arg. 216/E2
San Gregorio, Uru. 217/L10
San Gregorio, Ca, US 193/K12
San Guiliano Milanese, It. 116/C2
San Hipólito Punta (pt.), Mex. 200/B3
San Ignacio, Belz. 202/D2
San Ignacio, Bol. 208/E6
San Ignacio, Bol. 208/F7
San Ignacio, Chile 216/B3
San Ignacio, Mex. 200/B3
San Ignacio, Mex. 200/D3
San Ignacio, Peru 214/B2
San Ildefonso, Sp. 102/D2
San Isidro, Nic. 202/E3
San Isidro, CR 203/F4
San Jacinto, Col. 210/C2
San Jacinto, Uru. 217/L11
San Javier, Chile 216/C2
San Javier, Sp. 103/E4
San Javier, Uru. 217/J10
San Jerónimo, Mex. 200/E3
San Joaquín, Bol. 208/F6
San Joaquin (riv.), Ca, US 186/C3
San Joaquín, Col. 210/C3
San Joaquin (hills), Ca, US 194/G8
San Joaquin (co.), Ca, US 193/L11
San Joaquín (peak), Ecu. 214/F7
San Jorge (cape), Arg. 216/D5
San Jorge (gulf), Arg. 216/D5
San Jorge (riv.), Col. 210/C3
San Jorge (bay), Mex. 200/B2
San Jorge, Golfo di (gulf), Sp. 103/F2
San José (gulf), Arg. 216/D4
San José, Col. 210/B4
San José (cap.), CR 203/E4
San José (isl.), Mex. 200/C3
San José, Peru 214/D4
San José, Peru 214/B2
San Jose, Phil. 137/D4
San Jose, Phil. 137/D5
San José, Sp. 103/F3
San Jose (riv.), Uru. 217/K10
San José (dept.), Uru. 217/K11
San Jose, Ca, US 186/B3
San Jose (hills), Ca, US 194/G7
San Jose (int'l arpt.), Ca, US 186/B3
San Jose de Buenavista, Phil. 137/D5
San José de Chiquitos, Bol. 208/F7
San José de Guanipa, Ven. 211/E2
San José de Guaribe, Ven. 211/E2
San José de Jáchal, Arg. 215/C3
San José de la Esquina, Arg. 216/E2
San José de Los Molinos, Peru 214/C4
San José de los Remates, Nic. 202/E3
San José de Maipo, Chile 216/N8
San José de Mayo, Uru. 217/K11
San José de Raíces, Mex. 201/E3
San José de Seque, Ven. 210/D2
San José del Cabo, Mex. 200/C4
San José del Guaviare, Col. 210/C4
San José Iturbide, Mex. 201/E4
San José Viejo, Mex. 200/C4
San Juan, Arg. 215/C3
San Juan (riv.), Arg. 215/C3
San Juan, Peru 214/C4
San Juan (basin), NM, US 190/A2
San Juan (riv.), NM, US 190/B2
San Juan, Phil. 137/D5
San Juan, PR 199/M8
San Juan (riv.), Nic. 198/E5
San Juan (pt.), ESal. 202/D3
San Juan (mts.), Co, US 186/F3
San Juan (cape), Arg. 217/E7
San Juan Abajo, Mex. 200/D4
San Juan Bautista, Par. 215/E2
San Juan Bautista Coixtlahuaca, Mex. 202/B2
San Juan Bautista Tuxtepec, Mex. 202/B2
San Juan Bautista Valle Nacional, Mex. 202/B2
San Juan Capistrano, Ca, US 194/C3
San Juan de Alicante, Sp. 103/E3
San Juan de Aznalfarache, Sp. 102/B4
San Juan de la Costa, Mex. 200/C3
San Juan de Lima (pt.), Mex. 200/E5
San Juan de los Cayos, Ven. 210/D2
San Juan de los Lagos, Mex. 200/E4
San Juan de los Morros, Ven. 206/E2
San Juan del Norte, Nic. 203/F4
San Juan del Río, Mex. 201/F4
San Juan Guichicovi, Mex. 198/B4
San Juan Hot Springs, Ca, US 194/C3
San Juan Ixcaquixtla, Mex. 201/M8
San Juan Juquila Mixes, Mex. 202/C2
San Juan Nepomuceno, Col. 210/C2
San Juanico, Mex. 200/B3
San Juanico Punta (pt.), Mex. 200/B3
San Juanito, Mex. 200/D2
San Justo, Arg. 215/D3
San Lázaro (cape), Mex. 200/B3
San Lazzaro, It. 117/E4
San Leandro, Ca, US 193/K11
San Leandro (res.), Ca, US 193/K11
San Lorenzo (cape), Ecu. 208/B4
San Lorenzo, Bol. 208/E6
San Lorenzo (peak), Chile 217/B5
San Lorenzo, Ecu. 210/B4
San Lorenzo, Hon. 202/E3
San Lorenzo (cape), It. 104/A3
San Lorenzo (riv.), Mex. 200/D3
San Lorenzo, Nic. 202/E3
San Lorenzo, Peru 214/D3
San Lorenzo, Ca, US 193/K11
San Lorenzo al Mare, It. 116/A5
San Lorenzo de El Escorial, Sp. 103/M8
San Lorenzo in Campo, It. 117/F5
San Lucas, Nic. 202/E3
San Lucas, Cabo (cape), Mex. 200/C4
San Luis, Arg. 216/D2
San Luis, Cuba 203/H1
San Luis, Guat. 202/D2
San Luis, Peru 214/B4
San Luis, Ven. 210/D2
San Luis (valley), Co, US 190/B2
San Luis Acatlán, Mex. 202/B2
San Luis al Medio, Uru. 217/G2
San Luis de la Paz, Mex. 201/E4
San Luis Obispo, Ca, US 186/B4
San Luis Potosí (state), Mex. 198/A3
San Luis Potosí, Mex. 201/E4
San Luis Rey (riv.), Ca, US 194/C4
San Luis Rey, Ca, US 194/C4
San Luis Río Colorado, Mex. 200/B1
San Luis, Sierra de (mts.), Arg. 216/D2
San Manuel, Az, US 186/E4
San Marcello Pistoiese, It. 117/D4
San Marcos, Peru 214/B3
San Marcos, Peru 214/B2
San Marcos, Tx, US 187/H5
San Marcos, Ca, US 194/C4
San Marcos, Mex. 198/B4
San Marcos, Guat. 202/D3
San Marcos, CR 203/E4
San Marcos, Col. 210/C2
San Maria di Porto Novo, It. 117/G5
San Mariano, Phil. 137/D4
San Marino (ctry.) 117/F5
San Marino (cap.), SMar. 117/F5
San Marino, Ca, US 194/F7
San Martín (riv.), Bol. 208/F6
San Martín (dept.), Peru 214/B2
San Martín, Mex. 201/R9
San Martín, Col. 210/C4
San Martín (lake), Arg. 217/B6
San Martín, Arg. 216/C2
San Martín Cuautlalpan, Mex. 201/R10
San Martín de los Andes, Arg. 216/C4
San Martín de Valdeiglesias, Sp. 102/C2
San Martino Buon Albergo, It. 117/E2
San Martino-di-Lota, Fr. 104/A1
San Martino di Lupari, It. 117/E1
San Martino di Venezze, It. 117/E2
San Martino in Passiria (Sankt Martin in Passeier), It. 115/H4
San Martino in Rio, It. 117/D3
San Martino in Strada, It. 116/C2
San Martino Siccomario, It. 116/C2
San Mateo, Peru 214/B3
San Mateo, Sp. 103/F2
San Mateo, Ven. 211/E2
San Mateo, Ca, US 186/B3
San Mateo (co.), Ca, US 193/K12
San Mateo (mts.), NM, US 190/B3
San Mateo Atarasquillo, Mex. 201/Q10
San Mateo Xoloc, Mex. 201/Q9
San Matías, Bol. 208/G7
San Matías, Golfo (gulf), Arg. 216/D4
San Maurizio d'Opaglio, It. 116/B1
San Mauro Pascoli, It. 117/F4
San Mauro Torinese, It. 116/A2
San Michele al Tagliamento, It. 117/F1
San Miguel (riv.), Bol. 208/F6
San Miguel, Peru 214/B2
San Miguel, Peru 214/C4
San Miguel, Mex. 200/E2
San Miguel, ESal. 202/D3
San Miguel (gulf), Pan. 203/G4
San Miguel (riv.), Col. 210/B4
San Miguel Coatlincham, Mex. 201/R10
San Miguel de Allende, Mex. 201/E4
San Miguel de los Bancos, Ecu. 210/B4
San Miguel de Tucumán, Arg. 215/C2
San Miguel del Monte, Arg. 217/J11
San Miguel Tlaixpan, Mex. 201/R9
San Miguel Totolapan, Mex. 198/A4
San Miniato, It. 117/D5
San Nicolas (isl.), Ca, US 186/B4
San Nicolás de los Arroyos, Arg. 216/E2
San Nicolò, It. 116/C2
San Onofre (mtn.), Ca, US 194/C4
San Onofre, Ca, US 194/C4
San Onofre, Col. 210/C2
San Pablo, Chile 216/B4
San Pablo, Col. 210/B4
San Pablo, Peru 214/B2
San Pablo, Phil. 137/D5
San Pablo (int'l arpt.), Sp. 102/C4
San Pablo, Ven. 211/E2
San Pablo, Ca, US 193/K11
San Pablo (res.), Ca, US 193/K11
San Pablo Bay NWR, Ca, US 193/K10
San Pablo de las Salinas, Mex. 201/Q9
San Pablo Huixtepec, Mex. 202/B2
San Paolo, It. 116/D2
San Pawl il-Baħar, Malta 104/L7
San Pedro, Arg. 217/J10
San Pedro, Arg. 215/D1
San Pedro, Belz. 202/E2
San Pedro, Chile 216/N8
San Pedro (vol.), Chile 215/C1
San Pédro, C.d'Iv. 160/D5
San Pedro (riv.), Guat. 202/D2
San Pedro, Mex. 200/E3
San Pedro (riv.), Mex. 200/D3
San Pedro, Par. 215/E1
San Pedro Arriba, Mex. 201/Q10
San Pedro Carchá, Guat. 202/D3
San Pedro de Cajas, Peru 214/C3
San Pedro de la Cueva, Mex. 200/C2
San Pedro de Lloc, Peru 214/B2
San Pedro de Lóvago, Nic. 203/E3
San Pedro de Macorís, DRep. 199/H4
San Pedro del Pinatar, Sp. 103/E4
San Pedro Huamelula, Mex. 202/C2
San Pedro Pochutla, Mex. 202/B3
San Pedro, Sierra de (mts.), Sp. 102/B3
San Pedro Sula, Hon. 202/D3
San Pedro Tapanatepec, Mex. 202/C2
San Pedro Totoltepec, Mex. 201/Q10
San Pellegrino Terme, It. 116/C1
San Piero a Sieve, It. 117/E5
San Piero in Bagno, It. 117/E5
San Pietro (isl.), It. 104/A3
San Pietro in Casale, It. 117/E3
San Pietro in Gù, It. 117/E1
San Pietro in Vincoli, It. 117/F4
San Pietro in Volta, It. 117/F2
San Polo d'Enza, It. 116/D3
San Polo di Piave, It. 117/F1
San Possidonio, It. 117/D3
San Quentin, Ca, US 193/K11
San Quintín (cape), Mex. 200/B2
San Quintín, Mex. 200/B2
San Rafael (riv.), Ut, US 186/E3
San Rafael, Arg. 216/C2
San Rafael, Mex. 201/N6
San Rafael, Peru 214/B3
San Rafael, Peru 214/B2

San Rafael (hills), Ca, US 194/F7
San Rafael del Moján, Ven. 210/D2
San Ramón, CR 203/E4
San Ramón, Peru 214/C3
San Ramón, Uru. 217/L11
San Ramon, Ca, US 193/L11
San Ramón de la Nueva Orán, Arg. 215/D1
San Remo, It. 116/A5
San Rocco al Porto, It. 116/C2
San Romano, It. 117/D5
San Roque, Sp. 102/C4
San Rosendo, Chile 216/B3
San Saba (riv.), Tx, US 187/H5
San Salvador (cap.), ESal. 202/D3
San Salvador (riv.), Uru. 217/J10
San Salvador de Jujuy, Arg. 215/C1
San Salvador el Seco, Mex. 201/M7
San Salvador, Isla (isl.), Bahm. 199/G3
San Salvador (Watling) (isl.), Bahm. 199/G3
San Salvatore Monferrato, It. 116/B3
San Salvo, It. 104/D1
San Sebastián, Sp. 102/E1
San Sebastián de los Reyes, Sp. 103/N8
San Sebastián de Yalí, Nic. 202/E3
San Sebastiano, It. 116/D1
San Secondo Parmense, It. 116/D3
San Severo, It. 104/D2
San Telmo (pt.), Mex. 200/E5
San Timoteo, Ven. 210/D2
San Valentín (peak), Chile 216/B5
San Valentino, It. 117/G1
San Vicente (res.), Ca, US 194/D5
San Vicente, Mex. 200/A2
San Vicente, ESal. 202/D3
San Vicente, Chile 216/C2
San Vicente de Alcántara, Sp. 102/B3
San Vicente de Cañete, Peru 214/B4
San Vicente del Caguán, Col. 210/C4
San Vicente del Raspeig, Sp. 103/E3
San Vicino (peak), It. 101/K5
San Vincenzo, It. 101/J5
San Vito (cape), It. 104/C3
San Vito, CR 203/F4
San Vito al Tagliamento, It. 117/F1
San Ysidro, Ca, US 194/C5
Saña, Peru 214/B2
Sana (riv.), Bosn. 106/C3
Şan'ā (Sanaa) (cap.), Yem. 146/D5
Sanae IV, SAfr., Ant. 218/Z
Sanaga (riv.), Camr. 151/C4
Sanak (isl.), Ak, US 192/F5
Sanana (isl.), Indo. 139/G4
Sanandaj, Iran 146/E1
Sananduva, Braz. 213/B3
Sanaur, India 144/D4
Sanāwad, India 147/L4
Sanborn, NY, US 189/S9
Sanch'ŏng, SKor. 131/D5
Sancti Spiritu, Arg. 216/E2
Sancti Spíritus, Cuba 203/G1
Sand (riv.), Ab, Can. 184/F2
Sand (riv.), SAfr. 164/D3
Sand (pt.), Eng, UK 90/D4
Sand (hills), Ne, US 187/G2
Sand, Nor. 96/B2
Sand am Main, Ger. 112/D3
Sand Point, Ak, US 192/F4
Sanda, Japan 135/H6
Sanda (isl.), Sc, UK 92/C1
Sandakan, Malay. 139/E2
Sandane, Nor. 95/C3
Sandanski, Bul. 107/F5
Sandarne, Swe. 96/G1
Sanday (isl.), Sc, UK 89/V14
Sandbach, Eng, UK 93/F5
Sandberg, Ger. 112/C2
Sande, Ger. 109/F1
Sandefjord, Nor. 96/D2
Sandersville, Ga, US 191/H3
Sandhurst, Eng, UK 91/F4
Sandia, Peru 214/D4
Sandıklı, Turk. 148/B2
Sandīla, India 142/C2
Sandino, Cuba 198/E3
Sandnes, Nor. 96/A2
Sandomierz, Pol. 99/L3
Sandoná, Col. 210/B4
Sándorfalva, Hun. 106/E2
Sandougou (riv.), Sen. 160/B3
Sandover (riv.), Austl. 171/G2
Sandoway, Myan. 141/F4
Sandpoint, Id, US 184/D3
Sandrakatsy, Madg. 165/J7
Sandrigo, It. 117/E1
Sands (pt.), NY, US 197/L8
Sands Point, NY, US 197/L8
Sandspit, BC, Can. 192/M5
Sandstedt, Ger. 109/F2
Sandstone, Austl. 170/C3
Sandu Shuizu Zizhixian, China 141/J2
Sandusky, Mi, US 188/D3
Sandusky, Oh, US 188/D3
Sandvika, Nor. 96/D2
Sandviken, Swe. 96/G1
Sandweiler, Lux. 111/F4
Sandwell (co.), Eng, UK 90/D2
Sandwich (cape), Austl. 172/B2
Sandwich, Eng, UK 91/H4
Sandwīp (isl.), Bang. 143/H4
Sandy, Ut, US 195/K12
Sandy (cape), Austl. 172/D4
Sandy (lake), On, Can. 180/G3
Sandy (pt.), RI, US 197/G1
Sandy Bay, Sk, Can. 185/H2
Sandy Hook (bay), NJ, US 196/D3
Sandy Hook (bar), NJ, US 197/J10
Sandy Hook Lighthouse, NJ, US 197/J10
Sandy Springs, Ga, US 191/G3
Sanem, Lux. 111/E4
Sånfjällets NP, Swe. 95/E3
Sanford (mt.), Ak, US 192/K3
Sanford, Me, US 189/G3
Sanford, NC, US 191/J3
Sanford, Fl, US 191/H4
Sangamner, India 147/K5
Sangamon (riv.), Il, US 187/K3
Sangān (mtn.), Afg. 147/H2
Sangaria, India 144/C5
Sangatte, Fr. 110/A2
Sangay (vol.), Ecu. 210/B5
Sangay, PN, Ecu. 208/C4
Sangenjo, Sp. 102/A1
Sanggan (riv.), China 130/C2
Sanggau, Indo. 138/D3
Sanggou (bay), China 131/B4
Sangha (riv.), Congo 154/J7
Sangihe (isl.), Indo. 139/G3
Sangihe (isl.), Phil. 125/M9
Sangju, SKor. 131/E4
Sangkulirang, Indo. 139/E3
Sāngla, Pak. 144/B4
Sāngli, India 147/K5
Sangmélima, Camr. 154/H7
Sangō, Japan 135/J6
Sangre de Cristo (mts.), US 187/F3
Sangre Grande, Trin. 211/F2
Sangri, China 143/J1
Sangro (riv.), It. 104/D2
Sangrūr, India 144/C4
Sangster (int'l arpt.), Jam. 203/G2
Sangue, Rio do (riv.), Braz. 208/G6
Sangüesa, Sp. 102/E1
Sanguié (prov.), Burk. 161/E4
Sanguinetto, It. 117/E2
Sangzhi, China 137/B2
Sanhe, China 130/H7
Sani (pass), Les. 164/E3
Sāni Bheri (riv.), Nepal 142/D1
San'in Kaigin NP, Japan 132/D3
Saniquellie, Libr. 160/C5
Sanjō, Japan 133/F2
Sankanbiriwa (peak), SLeo. 160/C4
Sankh (riv.), India 143/E4
Sankoroni (riv.), Gui. 160/C4
Sankosh (riv.), India 143/G2
Sankt Aegyd am Neuwalde, Aus. 101/L3
Sankt Agatha, Aus. 113/G6
Sankt Andrä, Aus. 101/L3
Sankt Andrä-Wördern, Aus. 107/N7
Sankt Andreasberg, Ger. 109/H5
Sankt Anton am Arlberg, Aus. 115/G3
Sankt Augustin, Ger. 111/G2
Sankt Blasien, Ger. 114/E2
Sankt Florian am Inn, Aus. 113/G6
Sankt Gallen, Swi. 115/F3
Sankt Gallenkirch, Aus. 115/F3
Sankt Georgen bei Salzburg, Aus. 113/F7
Sankt Georgen im Attergau, Aus. 113/G7
Sankt Georgen im Schwarzwald, Ger. 115/E1
Sankt Goar, Ger. 111/G3
Sankt Goarshausen, Ger. 111/G3
Sankt Ingbert, Ger. 111/G5
Sankt Johann im Pongau, Aus. 101/K3
Sankt Johann in Tirol, Aus. 101/K3
Sankt Leonhard im Pitztal, Aus. 115/G3
Sankt Leonhard in Passeier (San Leonardo in Passiria), It. 115/H4
Sankt Marien, Aus. 113/H6
Sankt Martin im Mühlkreis, Aus. 113/H6
Sankt Michael in Obersteiermark, Aus. 101/L3
Sankt Moritz, Swi. 115/F5
Sankt Oswald bei Freistadt, Aus. 113/H5
Sankt Pantaleon, Aus. 113/F6
Sankt Peter am Hart, Aus. 113/G6
Sankt Peter in der Au, Aus. 113/H6
Sankt Peter-Ording, Ger. 96/C4
Sankt Pölten, Aus. 99/H4
Sankt Stephan, Swi. 114/D4
Sankt Ulrich bei Steyr, Aus. 113/H6
Sankt Valentin, Aus. 113/H6
Sankt Veit, Aus. 106/B1
Sankt Veit an der Glan, Aus. 101/L3
Sankt Wendel, Ger. 111/G5
Sankt Wolfgang, Ger. 113/F6
Sanlúcar de Barrameda, Sp. 102/B4
Sanmatenga (prov.), Burk. 161/E3
Sanmen, China 137/D2
Sanmenxia, China 130/B4
Sanming, China 137/C2
Sannan, Japan 135/H5
Sannazzaro de'Burgondi, It. 116/B2
Sannicandro Garganico, It. 104/D2
Sannikova (str.), Rus. 123/P2
San'nohe, Japan 134/B3
Sannois, Fr. 88/J5
Sano, Japan 133/F2
Sanok, Pol. 99/M4
Sanquhar, Sc, UK 94/C6
Sanquianga, PN, Col. 208/C3
Sans Bois (mts.), Ok, US 190/E3
Sansepolcro, It. 117/F5
Sanshui, China 137/B3
Sant Adrià de Besòs, Sp. 103/L7
Sant Boi de Llobregat, Sp. 103/L7
Sant Carles de la Ràpita, Sp. 103/F2
Sant Celoni, Sp. 103/L6
Sant Cugat del Vallès, Sp. 103/L7
Sant Feliu de Guíxols, Sp. 103/G2
Sant Feliu de Llobregat, Sp. 103/L7
Sant Julia, And. 100/D5
Sant Pere de Ribes, Sp. 103/K7
Sant Sadurní d'Anoia, Sp. 103/K7
Sant Vicenç de Castellet, Sp. 103/K6
Sant Vicenç dels Horts, Sp. 103/L7
Santa (riv.), Peru 214/B3
Santa, Peru 214/B3
Santa Ana, Bol. 208/E6
Santa Ana, Ecu. 210/A5
Santa Ana, ESal. 202/D3
Santa Ana, Hon. 202/E3
Santa Ana (vol.), ESal. 202/D3
Santa Ana, Mex. 200/C2
Santa Ana, Ca, US 194/G8
Santa Ana (riv.), Ca, US 194/C3
Santa Ana (mts.), Ca, US 194/C3
Santa Ana, Ven. 210/C3
Santa Ana, Ven. 210/D2
Santa Ana del Alto Beni, Bol. 208/E7
Santa Anna, Tx, US 187/H5
Santa Bárbara, Braz. 213/D1
Santa Bárbara, Chile 216/B3
Santa Bárbara, Hon. 202/D3
Santa Bárbara, Mex. 200/D3
Santa Barbara, Ca, US 194/A2
Santa Barbara (co.), Ca, US 194/A1
Santa Bárbara, Ven. 210/D3
Santa Bárbara, Ven. 210/D2
Santa Bárbara d'Oeste, Braz. 213/C2
Santa Barbara Mountains Nat'l Rec. Area, Ca, US 194/E7
Santa Catalina, Phil. 137/D6
Santa Catalina, Ven. 210/D3
Santa Catalina, Pan. 203/F4
Santa Catalina (isl.), CA, US 186/C4
Santa Catalina, Gulf of (gulf), Ca, US 186/C4
Santa Catarina (state), Braz. 213/B3
Santa Catarina, Mex. 201/E3
Santa Catarina, Ilha de (isl.), Braz. 215/G2
Santa Cecília, Braz. 213/B3
Santa Clara, Cuba 203/G1
Santa Clara, Mex. 200/E2
Santa Clara, Ven. 211/E2
Santa Clara, Ca, US 193/L12
Santa Clara (co.), Ca, US 193/L12
Santa Clara, Barragem de (res.), Port. 102/A4
Santa Clara de Olimar, Uru. 217/G2
Santa Clarita, Ca, US 194/B2
Santa Clotilde, Peru 210/C5
Santa Coloma de Farners, Sp. 103/G2
Santa Coloma de Gramanet, Sp. 103/L7
Santa Comba, Sp. 102/A1
Santa Croce di Magliano, It. 104/D2
Santa Croce sull'Arno, It. 117/D5
Santa Cruz (riv.), Az, US 187/E5
Santa Cruz, Braz. 212/C2
Santa Cruz, Peru 214/C2
Santa Cruz, Mex. 200/C2
Santa Cruz, Phil. 137/E6
Santa Cruz, Phil. 137/D5
Santa Cruz, Ca, US 186/B3
Santa Cruz, Phil. 137/D5
Santa Cruz (isls.), Sol. 174/F6
Santa Cruz (riv.), Arg. 217/C6
Santa Cruz (mts.), Guat. 202/D3
Santa Cruz, CR 202/E4
Santa Cruz, Chile 216/C2
Santa Cruz (prov.), Arg. 216/C5
Santa Cruz (isl.), Ecu. 214/E7
Santa Cruz da Graciosa, Azor., Port. 103/S12
Santa Cruz da Vitória, Braz. 212/C4
Santa Cruz das Flores, Azor., Port. 103/R12
Santa Cruz de Bucaral, Ven. 210/D2
Santa Cruz de El Seibo, DRep. 199/H4
Santa Cruz de la Palma, Sp. 156/A3
Santa Cruz de la Sierra, Bol. 208/F7
Santa Cruz de la Zarza, Sp. 102/D3
Santa Cruz de Mudela, Sp. 102/D3
Santa Cruz de Orinoco, Ven. 211/E2
Santa Cruz de Tenerife, Sp. 156/A3
Santa Cruz del Quiché, Guat. 202/D3
Santa Cruz del Sur, Cuba 203/G1
Santa Cruz do Capibaribe, Braz. 212/C2
Santa Cruz do Piauí, Braz. 212/B2
Santa Cruz do Rio Pardo, Braz. 213/B2
Santa Cruz do Sul, Braz. 213/A4
Santa Cruz Island (isl.), Ca, US 186/C4
Santa Elena, Peru 214/C2
Santa Elena (bay), CR 202/E4
Santa Elena, Hon. 202/E2
Santa Elena (cape), CR 202/E4
Santa Elena, Ecu. 210/A5
Santa Elena (peak), Arg. 216/D5
Santa Elena de Uairén, Ven. 211/F3
Santa Eugenia de Ribeira, Sp. 102/A1
Santa Eulalia del Río, Sp. 103/F3
Santa Fe, Arg. 215/D3
Santa Fe (cap.), NM, US 187/F4
Santa Fe (riv.), Fl, US 191/H4
Santa Fé, Sp. 102/D4
Santa Fe, Cuba 203/F1
Santa Fé do Sul, Braz. 213/B2
Santa Fe Springs, Ca, US 194/F8
Santa Felicia (dam), Ca, US 194/B2
Santa Filomena, Braz. 212/A3
Santa Giustina (lake), It. 115/H5
Santa Helena, Braz. 212/A1
Santa Helena de Goiás, Braz. 213/B1
Santa Inés (isl.), Chile 215/B7
Santa Inês, Braz. 212/C4
Santa Inês, Braz. 212/A1
Santa Isabel, Braz. 213/G8
Santa Isabel, Ecu. 214/B1
Santa Isabel (isl.), Sol. 174/E5
Santa Isabel (riv.), Guat. 202/D2
Santa Isabel, Arg. 216/D3
Santa Isabel, Arg. 216/E2
Santa Isabel de Sihuas, Peru 214/C5
Santa Isabel, Pico de (peak), EqG. 154/G7
Santa Juliana, Braz. 213/C1
Santa Lucía, Canl. 103/X17
Santa Lucía, Ecu. 210/B5
Santa Lucía, Peru 214/D4
Santa Lucía, Uru. 217/K11
Santa Lucía, Ven. 210/D2
Santa Lucia di Piave, It. 117/F1
Santa Luz, Braz. 212/C3
Santa Luzia, Braz. 212/A1
Santa Luzia, Braz. 213/D1
Santa Luzia, Braz. 212/C2
Santa Luzia (isl.), CpV. 151/J10
Santa Magdalena (isl.), Mex. 200/B3
Santa Magdalena, Arg. 216/E2
Santa Margarita (isl.), Mex. 200/B3
Santa Margarita (riv.), Ca, US 194/C4
Santa Margherita Ligure, It. 116/C4
Santa Maria, Braz. 215/F2
Santa Maria, Ca, US 186/B4
Santa Maria (riv.), Mex. 190/B4
Santa María (riv.), Mex. 200/D2
Santa Maria (bay), Mex. 200/C3
Santa Maria (cape), Port. 102/B4
Santa Maria (isl.), Azor., Port. 103/T13
Santa María (isl.), Chile 216/B3
Santa Maria, CpV. 151/K10
Santa María, Chile 216/N8
Santa María, Ecu. 214/E7
Santa María (isl.), Ecu. 214/E7
Santa Maria a Monte, It. 117/D5
Santa Maria, Cabo de (cape), Moz. 165/F2
Santa Maria Capua Vetere, It. 104/D2
Santa Maria, Chapadão de (hills), Braz. 212/A4
Santa Maria da Boa Vista, Braz. 212/C3
Santa Maria da Vitória, Braz. 212/A4
Santa María de Cayón, Sp. 102/D1
Santa María de Ipire, Ven. 211/E2
Santa María de Nanay, Peru 214/C1
Santa María del Oro, Mex. 200/D3
Santa Maria della Versa, It. 116/C3
Santa Maria di Leuca, Capo (cape), It. 105/F3
Santa Maria do Suaçui, Braz. 212/B5
Santa Maria Maddalena, It. 117/E3
Santa Maria Maggiore, It. 115/E5
Santa Maria Nuova, It. 117/G6
Santa María Xadani, Mex. 198/B4
Santa Marta, Col. 210/C2
Santa Marta Grande (cape), Braz. 213/B4
Santa Marta, Sierra Nevada de (mts.), Col. 210/C2
Santa Monica (bay), Ca, US 194/B3
Santa Monica (mts.), Ca, US 194/B2
Santa Monica, Ca, US 194/F7
Santa Monica Mountains Nat'l Rec. Area, Ca, US 194/B2
Santa Olalla del Cala, Sp. 102/B4
Santa Paula (peak), Ca, US 194/A2
Santa Paula, Ca, US 194/A2
Santa Pola, Sp. 103/E3
Santa Pola, Cabo de (cape), Sp. 103/E3
Santa Quitéria, Braz. 212/B2
Santa Quitéria do Maranhão, Braz. 212/B1
Santa Rita, Braz. 212/A1
Santa Rita, Braz. 212/D2
Santa Rita, Ven. 210/D2
Santa Rita de Cássia, Braz. 212/A3
Santa Rita do Sapucaí, Braz. 213/H7
Santa Rosa, Arg. 208/F8
Santa Rosa, Arg. 216/D3
Santa Rosa, Arg. 215/C3
Santa Rosa, Braz. 215/F2
Santa Rosa, PN, CR 202/E4
Santa Rosa, Peru 214/B1
Santa Rosa, Peru 214/D4
Santa Rosa, Uru. 217/K11
Santa Rosa, Ven. 210/D2
Santa Rosa, Ca, US 186/B3
Santa Rosa, NM, US 187/F4
Santa Rosa (range), Nv, US 186/C2
Santa Rosa and San Jacinto Mountains Nat'l Mon., Ca, US 186/C4
Santa Rosa, Bajo de (plain), Arg. 216/D4
Santa Rosa de Aguán, Hon. 202/E3
Santa Rosa de Copán, Hon. 202/D3
Santa Rosa de Osos, Col. 210/C3
Santa Rosa de Viterbo, Braz. 213/C2
Santa Rosa Island (isl.), Ca, US 186/B4
Santa Rosalía (pt.), Mex. 200/B2
Santa Rosalía, Mex. 200/B3
Santa Rosalía, Ven. 210/D2
Santa Rosalía, Ven. 211/E3
Santa Sofia, It. 117/E5
Santa Susana (mts.), Ca, US 194/B2
Santa Teresa (riv.), Braz. 209/J6
Santa Teresa, Austl. 171/G3
Santa Teresa Abor. Land, Austl. 171/G2
Santa Teresa, PN, Uru. 217/G2
Santa Teresinha, Braz. 209/H6
Santa Teresita, Arg. 217/F3
Santa Vitória, Braz. 213/B1
Santa Vitória do Palmar, Braz. 217/G2
Santa Ynez (mts.), Ca, US 194/A2
SantAantioco (isl.), It. 104/A3
Santaella, Sp. 102/C4
Sant'Agata Bolognese, It. 117/E3
Sant'Agata di Militello, It. 104/D3
Sant'Agata Feltria, It. 117/F5
Sant'Agostino, It. 117/E3
Sant'Alberto, It. 117/F3
Santan (canal), Az, US 195/S19
Santana, Braz. 212/A4
Santana (isl.), Braz. 212/B1
Santana do Acaraú, Braz. 212/B1
Santana do Ipanema, Braz. 212/C3
Santana do Livramento, Braz. 215/E3
Santander, Sp. 102/D1
Santander (dept.), Col. 210/C3
Santander de Quilichao, Col. 210/B4
Santander Jiménez, Mex. 201/F3
Sant'Angelo in Vado, It. 117/F5
Sant'Angelo Lodigiano, It. 116/C2
Sant'Antioco, It. 104/A3
Sant'Antonio, It. 117/D2
Santañy, Sp. 103/G3
Sant'Apollinare in Classe, It. 117/F4
Santarcángelo, It. 117/F4
Santarém, Braz. 209/H4
Santarém (dist.), Port. 102/A3
Santarém, Port. 102/A3
Sant'arsenio, It. 104/D2
Santee (riv.), SC, US 191/J3
Santee, Ca, US 194/D5
Sant'Eeufemia (gulf), It. 104/D3
Santena, It. 116/A3
Santerno (riv.), It. 101/J4
Santeuil, Fr. 88/H4
Santhia, It. 116/B2
Santiago, Braz. 215/F2
Santiago, Peru 214/C4
Santiago, Phil. 137/D4
Santiago (res.), Ca, US 194/C3
Santiago (peak), Ca, US 194/C3
Santiago (int'l arpt.), Sp. 102/A1
Santiago, Pan. 203/F4
Santiago (mtn.), Pan. 203/F4
Santiago (riv.), Peru 210/B5
Santiago (mts.), Tx, US 190/C4
Santiago (cap.), Chile 216/N8
Santiago (cape), Chile 217/B6
Santiago Cuautlalpan, Mex. 201/R10
Santiago Cuautlalpan, Mex. 201/Q9
Santiago de Cao, Peru 214/B2
Santiago de Chocorvos, Peru 214/C4
Santiago de Chuco, Peru 214/B3
Santiago de Compostela, Sp. 102/A1
Santiago de Cuba, Cuba 203/H1
Santiago de los Caballeros, DRep. 199/G4
Santiago de Machaca, Bol. 214/D5
Santiago del Estero, Arg. 215/D2
Santiago do Cacém, Port. 102/A3
Santiago Ixcuintla, Mex. 200/D4
Santiago Jamiltepec, Mex. 202/B2
Santiago Juxtlahuaca, Mex. 202/B2
Santiago Miahuatlán, Mex. 201/M8
Santiago Papasquiaro, Mex. 200/D3
Santiago Pinotepa Nacional, Mex. 202/B2
Santiago Tilapa, Mex. 201/Q10
Santiago Tolman, Mex. 201/R9
Santiago Vázquez, Uru. 217/K11
Santiago Zacatepec, Mex. 202/C2
Sant'Ilario d'Enza, It. 116/D3
Sāntipur, India 143/G4
Säntis (peak), Swi. 115/F3
Santisteban del Puerto, Sp. 102/D3
Santō, Japan 135/G5
Santō, Japan 135/K5
Santo Amaro, Braz. 212/C4
Santo Amaro, Ilha de (isl.), Braz. 213/G8
Santo Anastácio, Braz. 213/B2
Santo André, Braz. 213/G8
Santo Ângelo, Braz. 215/F2
Santo Antão (isl.), CpV. 151/J9
Santo António, SaoT. 154/G7
Santo Antônio de Jesus, Braz. 212/C4
Santo Antônio de Pádua, Braz. 213/D2
Santo Antônio do Içá, Braz. 210/E5
Santo Antônio do Jacinto, Braz. 212/B5
Santo Antônio dos Lopes, Braz. 212/A2
Santo Domingo (cap.), DRep. 199/H4
Santo Domingo, Mex. 201/E4
Santo Domingo (pt.), Mex. 200/B3
Santo Domingo, Cuba 203/F1
Santo Domingo, Chile 216/N8
Santo Domingo de la Calzada, Sp. 102/D1
Santo Domingo de los Colorados, Ecu. 210/B5
Santo Domingo Petapa, Mex. 202/C2
Santo Domingo Tehuantepec, Mex. 202/C2
Santo Domingo Zanatepec, Mex. 202/C2
Santo Estêvão, Braz. 212/C4
Santo Onofre (riv.), Braz. 212/B4
Santo Stefano Belbo, It. 116/B3
Santo Stefano d'Aveto, It. 116/C3
Santo Stefano di Magra, It. 116/C4
Santo Stino di Livenza, It. 117/F1
Santo Tomás, Peru 214/C4
Santo Tomás, Peru 214/B2
Santo Tomás, Mex. 200/A2
Santo Tomás (pt.), Mex. 200/A2
Santo Tomás (vol.), Ecu. 214/E7
Santo Tomé, Arg. 215/E2
Santo Tomé, Arg. 215/D3
Santoña, Sp. 102/D1
Santorso, It. 117/E1
Santos, Braz. 213/G8
Santos Dumont (int'l arpt.), Braz. 213/K7
Santos Dumont, Braz. 213/K6
Santos Reyes Nopala, Mex. 202/B2
Santuario di Crea, It. 116/B2
Santuario di Oropa, It. 116/A1
Sānūr, WBnk. 149/G7
Sanwa, Japan 135/D1
São Benedito, Braz. 212/B2
São Benedito do Rio Prêto, Braz. 212/B1
São Bento, Braz. 212/C2
São Bento, Braz. 212/A1
São Bento do Sapucaí, Braz. 213/H7
São Bento do Sul, Braz. 213/B3
São Bento do Una, Braz. 212/C3
São Bernardo do Campo, Braz. 213/G8
São Borja, Braz. 215/E2
São Carlos, Braz. 213/C2
São Cristóvão, Braz. 212/C3
São Desidério, Braz. 212/A4
São Domingos (riv.), Braz. 212/A4
São Domingos, Braz. 212/A4
São Domingos do Maranhão, Braz. 212/A2
São Félix do Xingu, Braz. 209/H5
São Fidélis, Braz. 213/D2
São Filipe, CpV. 151/J11
São Francisco, Braz. 212/A4
São Francisco (riv.), Braz. 205/F3
São Francisco do Sul, Braz. 213/B3
São Francisco, Ilha de (isl.), Braz. 215/G2
São Fransisco de Paula, Braz. 213/B4
São Gabriel, Braz. 215/F3
São Gabriel da Palha, Braz. 213/D1
São Gonçalo, Braz. 213/K7
São Gonçalo do Abaeté, Braz. 212/A5
São Gonçalo do Sapucaí, Braz. 213/H6
São Gotardo, Braz. 213/C1
São Joachim da Barra, Braz. 213/C2
São João Batista, Braz. 212/A1
São João Batista, Braz. 213/B3
São João da Aliança, Braz. 212/A4
São João da Barra, Braz. 213/D2
São João da Boa Vista, Braz. 213/G6
São João da Madeira, Port. 102/A2
São João da Pesqueira, Port. 102/B2
São João da Ponte, Braz. 212/A4
São João das Lampas, Port. 103/P10
São João de Meriti, Braz. 213/K7
São João del Rei, Braz. 213/C2
São João do Paraíso, Braz. 212/B4
São João do Piauí, Braz. 212/B3
São João dos Patos, Braz. 212/B2
São João Evangelista, Braz. 213/D1
São João, Ilhas de (isl.), Braz. 209/K4
São João Nepomuceno, Braz. 213/K6
São João, Serra de (mts.), Braz. 208/F5
São Joaquim, Braz. 213/B4
São Joaquim, PN de, Braz. 213/B4
São Jorge (isl.), Azor., Port. 103/S12
São José, Braz. 213/B3
São José da Laje, Braz. 212/C3
São José de Mipibu, Braz. 212/D2
São José de Piranhas, Braz. 212/C2
São José de Ribamar, Braz. 212/A1
São José do Belmonte, Braz. 212/C2
São José do Egito, Braz. 212/C2
São José do Norte, Braz. 213/A5
São José do Peixe, Braz. 212/B2
São José do Rio Pardo, Braz. 213/G6
São José do Rio Prêto, Braz. 213/B2
São José dos Campos, Braz. 213/H8
São José dos Pinhais, Braz. 213/B3
São Julião, Braz. 212/B2
São Leopoldo, Braz. 213/B4
São Lourenço (riv.), Braz. 209/G7
São Lourenço, Braz. 213/H7
São Lourenço, Port. 103/P11
São Lourenço do Sul, Braz. 213/B4
São Luís, Braz. 212/A1
São Luís do Curu, Braz. 212/C1
São Luís do Quitunde, Braz. 212/D3
São Manoel, Braz. 213/B2
São Marcos (riv.), Braz. 212/A5
São Marcos (bay), Braz. 205/E3
São Martinho do Porto, Port. 102/A3
São Mateus, Braz. 213/E1
São Mateus (riv.), Braz. 213/D1
São Mateus do Maranhão, Braz. 212/A2
São Mateus do Sul, Braz. 213/B3
São Miguel, Braz. 212/C2
São Miguel (isl.), Azor., Port. 103/T13
São Miguel Arcanjo, Braz. 213/B3
São Miguel do Tapuio, Braz. 212/B2
São Miguel dos Campos, Braz. 212/C3
São Nicolau (isl.), CpV. 151/J10
São Paulo (state), Braz. 213/B2
São Paulo, Braz. 213/G8
São Paulo de Olivença, Braz. 208/E4
São Paulo do Potengi, Braz. 212/D2
São Pedro da Aldeia, Braz. 213/D2
São Pedro do Piauí, Braz. 212/B2
São Pedro do Sul, Port. 102/A2
São Raimundo das Mangabeiras, Braz. 212/A2
São Raimundo Nonato, Braz. 212/B3
São Romão, Braz. 212/A5

São Roque, Cabo de (cape), Braz. 212/D2
São Roque do Pico, Azor., Port. 103/S12
São Sebastião (pt.), Moz. 163/G5
São Sebastião, Braz. 213/H8
São Sebastião do Paraíso, Braz. 213/C2
São Sebastião, Ilha de (isl.), Braz. 213/C2
São Simão, Barragem de (res.), Braz. 213/B1
São Teotónio, Port. 102/A4
São Tiago, Braz. 213/C2
São Tiago (isl.), CpV. 151/K10
São Tomé (cap.), SaoT. 154/G7
São Tomé (isl.), SaoT. 154/G7
São Tomé and Príncipe (ctry.) 154/F7
São Tomé, Cabo de (cape), Braz. 213/D2
São Vicente, Braz. 213/G8
São Vicente (cape), Port. 102/A4
São Vicente (isl.), CpV. 151/J10
Saône (riv.), Fr. 100/F3
Saône-et-Loire (dept.), Fr. 114/B4
Saori, Japan 135/L5
Saouru (riv.), Alg. 154/E1
Sápai, Gre. 105/J2
Sapallanga, Peru 214/C4
Sapanca, Turk. 107/K5
Sapatgrām, India 143/H2
Sapé, Braz. 212/D2
Sapele, Nga. 161/G5
Sapelo (isl.), Ga, US 191/H4
Şaphane, Turk. 120/D5
Sapiéndza (isl.), Gre. 105/G4
Sapkyo, SKor. 131/D4
Sapo (mts.), Pan. 203/G5
Sapo NP, Libr. 160/C5
Saposoa, Peru 214/B2
Sappemeer, Neth. 108/D2
Sapphire, Austl. 172/B3
Sappington, Mo, US 195/G8
Sapporo, Japan 134/B2
Sapri, It. 104/D2
Sapsi (isl.), SKor. 131/D5
Sapt Kosi (riv.), Nepal 143/F2
Sapucaí (riv.), Braz. 213/H7
Sapucaia, Braz. 213/L6
Saqqez, Iran 146/E1
Saquena, Peru 214/C2
Saquisilí, Ecu. 210/B5
Šar (mts.), Kos. 104/E3
Sar Dasht, Iran 148/F2
Sar-e Pol, Afg. 145/E5
Sara Buri, Thai. 136/C3
Sarāb, Iran 146/E1
Saraguro, Ecu. 214/B1
Sarāi Alamgir, Pak. 144/B3
Sarāi Sidhu, Pak. 144/A4
Sarajevo (cap.), Bosn. 106/D4
Saraland, Al, US 191/F4
Saramacca (dist.), Sur. 211/H3
Saran (peak), Indo. 138/D4
Saran', Kaz. 145/F3
Saranac Lake, NY, US 188/F2
Sarandapótamos (riv.), Gre. 105/N8
Sarandë, Alb. 105/G3
Sarandí de Navarro, Uru. 217/K10
Sarandí del Yi, Uru. 217/K10
Sarandí Grande, Uru. 217/K10
Sarangani (isls.), Phil. 139/G2
Sārangpur, India 147/L4
Saransk, Rus. 121/H1
Sarapul, Rus. 119/M4
Sarare (riv.), Ven. 210/D3
Sarasota, Fl, US 191/H5
Saratoga, Wy, US 184/G5
Saratoga, Ca, US 193/K12
Saratoga Springs, NY, US 188/F3
Saratov (res.), Rus. 121/J1
Saratov, Rus. 121/H2
Saratovskaya Oblast, Rus. 145/A2
Saravan, Laos 136/D3
Sarawak (reg.), Malay. 138/D3
Saray, Turk. 107/H5
Sarayacu, Ecu. 210/B5
Sarāyan (riv.), India 142/C2
Sarayköy, Turk. 148/B2
Sarayönü, Turk. 148/C2
Sárbogárd, Hun. 106/D2
Sarcelles, Fr. 88/K5
Sārda (riv.), India 142/C1
Sārda (canal), India 142/C2
Sarda (riv.), India 140/D2
Sardara, It. 104/A3
Sardārshahar, India 144/C5
Sardegna (prov.), It. 104/A2
Sardhana, India 144/D5
Sardinata, Col. 210/C2
Sardinaux, Cap des (cape), Fr. 101/G5
Sardinia (isl.), It. 104/A2
Sardis (lake), Ms, US 187/K4
Sardis (lake), Ok, US 187/J4
Sareks NP, Swe. 95/F2
Sarektjåkko (peak), Swe. 95/F2
Sarempaka (peak), Indo. 139/E4
Sarentino, It. 115/H4
Sarezzo, It. 116/D1
Sargans, Swi. 115/F3
Sargodha, Pak. 144/B3
Sarh, Chad 155/J6
Sārī, Iran 146/F1
Sari-Solenzara, Fr. 104/A2
Sariaya, Phil. 137/D5
Saribi (cape), Indo. 139/J4
Sarigan (isl.), NMar. 174/D3
Sarıgöl, Turk. 148/B2
Sarıkamış, Turk. 148/E1
Sarıkaya, Turk. 120/E5
Sarikaya (prov.), Turk. 148/C2
Sarikei, Malay. 138/D3
Sarina, Austl. 172/C3
Sarine (riv.), Swi. 101/G3
Sariñena, Sp. 103/E2
Sarīr Kalanshiyū (des.), Libya 154/K2
Sarīr Tibasti (des.), Libya 154/J3
Sarita, Tx, US 190/D5
Sariwŏn, NKor. 131/C3
Sarju (riv.), India 142/C1
Sark (isl.), Chl, UK 100/B2
Sarkad, Hun. 106/E2
Sarkant, Kaz. 128/C2
Şarkîkaraağaç, Turk. 148/B2
Şarkışla, Turk. 148/D2
Şarköy, Turk. 107/H5
Sarlat-la-Canéda, Fr. 100/D4
Sarleinsbach, Aus. 113/G5
Sarmato, It. 116/C2
Sarmeola, It. 117/E2
Sarmiento, Arg. 216/C5
Sarmiento (peak), Chile 217/C7
Särna, Swe. 96/E1
Sarnano, It. 101/K5
Sarnen, Swi. 115/E4
Sarnia, On, Can. 188/D3
Sarnico, It. 116/C1
Sarny, Ukr. 120/C2
Saroma (lake), Japan 134/C1
Saronic (gulf), Gre. 105/H4
Saronno, It. 116/C1
Saros (gulf), Turk. 107/H5
Sárospatak, Hun. 99/L4
Sarpsborg, Nor. 96/D2
Sarralbe, Fr. 111/G6
Sarre (riv.), Fr. 110/F6
Sarre-Union, Fr. 111/G6
Sarrebourg, Fr. 111/G6
Sarria, Sp. 102/B1
Sarroch, It. 104/A3
Sarry, Fr. 111/D6
Sarsāwa, India 144/D4
Sarsina, It. 117/F5
Sarstedt, Ger. 109/G4
Sarstún (riv.), Guat. 202/D3
Sartang (riv.), Rus. 123/P3
Sarteano, It. 104/B1
Sartène, Fr. 104/A2
Sarthe (riv.), Fr. 100/C3
Sartrouville, Fr. 88/J5
Sarufutsu, Japan 134/C1
Saruhanlı, Turk. 148/A2
Sárvár, Hun. 101/M3
Sárvíz (riv.), Hun. 106/D2
Saryesik Atyraū Qumy (des.), Kaz. 128/C2
Saryshaghan, Kaz. 145/F3
Sarysu (riv.), Kaz. 122/G5
Sarzana, It. 116/C4
Sas Van Gent, Neth. 110/C1
Sasaginnigak (lake), Mb, Can. 185/K3
Sasarām, India 143/E3
Sasayama, Japan 135/H5
Sasayama (riv.), Japan 135/H5
Sásd, Hun. 106/D2
Sasebo, Japan 132/A4
Sashima, Japan 135/D1
Saskatchewan (prov.), Can. 180/F3
Saskatchewan (riv.), Can. 180/E3
Saskatoon, Sk, Can. 184/G2
Saslaya (mtn.), Nic. 203/E3
Saslaya, PN, Nic. 203/E3
Sāsni, India 142/B2
Sasolburg, SAfr. 164/D2
Sasovo, Rus. 118/G5
Saspamco, Tx, US 195/U21
Sassafras, Md, US 196/C5
Sassafras (riv.), Md, US 196/B5
Sassandra (riv.), C.d'Iv. 154/D6
Sassandra, C.d'Iv. 160/D5
Sassari, It. 104/A2
Sassello, It. 116/B4
Sassenberg, Ger. 109/F4
Sassenheim, Neth. 108/B4
Sassnitz, Ger. 96/E4
Sasso Marconi, It. 117/E4
Sassocorvaro, It. 117/F5
Sassoferrato, It. 117/F6
Sassuolo, It. 117/D3
Sástago, Sp. 103/E2
Sasyk (lake), Ukr. 107/J3
Sata-misaki (cape), Japan 132/B5
Sātāra, India 147/K5
Satawan (isl.), Micr. 174/E4
Säter, Swe. 96/F1
Saticoy, Ca, US 194/A2
Satilla (riv.), Ga, US 191/H4
Satipo, Peru 214/C3
Sātkhira, Bang. 143/G4
Sátoraljaújhely, Hun. 99/L4
Satpayev, Kaz. 145/E3
Satpura (range), India 147/K4
Satte, Japan 135/D1
Satteins, Aus. 115/F3
Satteldorf, Ger. 112/D4
Sattler, Tx, US 195/U20
Satu Mare, Rom. 99/M5
Satu Mare (co.), Rom. 99/M5
Satun, Thai. 136/C5
Sauce, Peru 214/B2
Sauce Grande (riv.), Arg. 216/E3
Saucillo, Mex. 200/D2
Sauda, Nor. 96/B2
Saúde, Braz. 212/B3
Saudhárkrókur, Ice. 95/N6
Saudi Arabia (ctry.) 146/D4
Sauer (riv.), Ger. 109/F5
Sauerlach, Ger. 115/H2
Sauerland (reg.), Ger. 98/D3
Sauêruiná (riv.), Braz. 208/G6
Saugatuck (riv.), Ct, US 197/E1
Saujon, Fr. 100/C4
Sauk (riv.), Mn, US 185/K4
Sauk Centre, Mn, US 185/K4
Sauk Rapids, Mn, US 185/K4
Saül, FrG. 209/H3
Sauland, Nor. 96/C2
Sauldre (riv.), Fr. 100/D3
Saulgau, Ger. 115/F1
Saulheim, Ger. 112/B3
Saulieu, Fr. 100/F3
Sault-lès-Rethel, Fr. 111/D5
Sault Sainte Marie, On, Can. 188/C2
Sault Ste. Marie, Mi, US 188/C2
Saulx, Fr. 114/C2
Saulx (riv.), Fr. 98/C4
Saulxures-sur-Moselotte, Fr. 114/C2
Saumur, Fr. 100/C3
Saunders (peak), Austl. 170/E3
Saura (riv.), India 143/F3
Saurimo, Ang. 163/D2
Sausalito, Ca, US 193/J11
Sausseron (riv.), Fr. 88/J4
Sauteurs, Gren. 211/F1
Sava, It. 105/E2
Sava (riv.), Slov. 101/L3
Savá, Hon. 202/E3
Savage (dam), Ca, US 194/D5
Savage River, Austl. 173/C4
Savai'i (isl.), Sam. 175/H6
Savalou, Ben. 161/F5
Savane (riv.), Qu, Can. 189/G1
Savanna-la-Mar, Jam. 203/G2
Savannah, Ga, US 191/H3
Savannah, Tn, US 191/F3
Savannah (riv.), US 191/H3
Savannakhet, Laos 136/D2
Savant (lake), On, Can. 185/L3
Sāvantvādi, India 140/B4
Sävar, Swe. 95/G3
Savaştepe, Turk. 148/A2
Save (riv.), Moz. 163/F5
Sāveh, Iran 146/F1
Savena (riv.), It. 117/E4
Săveni, Rom. 107/H2
Saverdun, Fr. 100/D5
Saverne, Fr. 111/G6
Savièse, Swi. 114/D5
Savigliano, It. 101/G4
Savignano sul Panaro, It. 117/E4
Savignano sul Rubicone, It. 117/F4
Savigny-le-Temple, Fr. 88/K6
Savigny-sur-Orge, Fr. 88/K5
Savio (riv.), It. 101/K5
Sävja, Swe. 96/G2
Savognin, Swi. 115/F4
Savoie (dept.), Fr. 114/C6
Savona, BC, Can. 184/C3
Savona (prov.), It. 116/B4
Savona, It. 116/B4
Savoonga, Ak, US 192/D3
Savoy (reg.), Fr. 100/F4
Savoy Alps (mts.), Fr. 114/C6
Şavşat, Turk. 148/E1
Sävsjö, Swe. 96/F3
Savu (sea), Indo. 139/F5
Sawahlunto, Indo. 138/B4
Sawankhalok, Thai. 136/B2
Sawara, Japan 133/G3
Sawasaki-bana (pt.), Japan 133/F2
Sawatch (range), Co, US 186/F3
Sawdā', Jabal (peak), SAr. 146/D5
Saweba (cape), Indo. 139/H4
Sawel (mtn.), NI, UK 92/A2
Sawtell, Austl. 173/E1
Sawtooth (range), Id, US 184/E4
Sawtooth Nat'l Rec. Area, Id, US 184/E5
Sawu (isls.), Indo. 139/F6
Sax, Sp. 103/E3
Saxman, Ak, US 192/M4
Saxon, Swi. 114/D5
Say, Niger 161/F3
Saya, Japan 135/L5
Sayama, Japan 133/F3
Sayama, Japan 135/J6
Sayán, Peru 214/B3
Şaydā, Leb. 149/D3
Sayil (ruin), Mex. 202/D1
Saynbach (riv.), Ger. 111/G2
Sayreville, NJ, US 197/H10
Sayula, Mex. 200/E5
Sayville, NY, US 197/E2
Saywūn, Yem. 146/E5
Sazan (isl.), Alb. 105/F2
Sázava (riv.), Czh. 101/L2
Sbaa, Alg. 157/E3
Scafell Pikes (peak), Eng, UK 93/E3
Scalasaig, Sc, UK 89/Q8
Scald Law (peak), Sc, UK 94/C5
Scalea, It. 104/D3
Scalino (peak), It. 115/F5
Scalloway, Sc, UK 89/W13
Scammon Bay, Ak, US 192/E3
Scandia, Wa, US 193/B2
Scandiano, It. 117/D3
Scandicci, It. 117/E5
Scapa Flow (chan.), Sc, UK 89/V14
Scar Water (riv.), Sc, UK 92/E1
Scarborough, Can. 189/R8
Scarborough, Eng, UK 93/H3
Scarborough Shoal (isl.), Phil. 137/C4
Scardovari, It. 117/F3
Scarpe (riv.), Fr. 98/B3
Scarperia, It. 117/E5
Scarriff, Ire. 89/P10
Scarsdale, La, US 195/Q17
Scarsdale, NY, US 197/K7
Sceaux, Fr. 88/J5
Scenic Oaks, Tx, US 195/T20
Scey-sur-Saône-et-St-Albin, Fr. 114/B2
Schaefferstown, Pa, US 196/B3
Schaerbeek, Belg. 111/D2
Schaffhausen (canton), Swi. 115/E2
Schaffhausen, Swi. 115/E2
Schäftlarn, Ger. 115/H2
Schagen, Neth. 108/B3
Schaijk, Neth. 108/C5
Schalchen, Aus. 113/G6
Schalkau, Ger. 112/E2
Schalksmühle, Ger. 109/E6
Schanck (cape), Austl. 173/C3
Schangnau, Swi. 114/D4
Scharans, Swi. 115/F4
Schardenberg, Aus. 113/G5
Schärding, Aus. 113/G6
Scharfreiter (peak), Aus. 115/H3
Scharhorn (isl.), Ger. 109/F1
Scharnebeck, Ger. 109/H2
Scharnitz (pass), Ger. 115/H3
Scharnstein, Aus. 113/G7
Schashagen, Ger. 98/F1
Schattdorf, Swi. 115/E4
Schauenstein, Ger. 113/E2
Schaumburg, Il, US 193/P15
Scheemda, Neth. 108/D2
Scheer, Ger. 115/F1
Scheessel, Ger. 109/G2
Schefferville, Qu, Can. 139/K3
Scheibbs, Aus. 99/H4
Scheidegg, Ger. 115/F2
Scheinfeld, Ger. 112/D3
Schelde (riv.), Belg. 100/E1
Schelklingen, Ger. 112/C6
Schell Creek (range), Nv, US 186/D3
Schellerten, Ger. 109/H4
Schellville, Ca, US 193/K10
Schenectady, NY, US 188/F3
Schenefeld, Ger. 109/G1
Schermbeck, Ger. 108/D5
Scherpenzeel, Neth. 108/C3
Schertz, Tx, US 195/U20
Schesaplana (peak), Aus. 115/F3
Schesslitz, Ger. 112/E3
Scheyern, Ger. 113/E5
Schiedam, Neth. 108/B5
Schieder-Schwalenberg, Ger. 109/G5
Schiehallion (peak), Sc, UK 94/B3
Schier Monnikoog (isl.), Neth. 98/D2
Schierling, Ger. 113/F5
Schiermonnikoog (isl.), Neth. 108/D1
Schiermonnikoog, Neth. 108/D2
Schiers, Swi. 115/F4
Schifferstadt, Ger. 112/B4
Schiffweiler, Ger. 111/G5
Schijndel, Neth. 108/C5
Schilde, Belg. 108/B6
Schildmeer (lake), Neth. 108/D2
Schillighörn (cape), Ger. 109/F1
Schillingsfürst, Ger. 112/D4
Schiltach, Ger. 115/E1
Schiltigheim, Fr. 114/D1
Schinnen, Neth. 111/E2
Schinznach-Dorf, Swi. 114/E3
Schio, It. 117/E1
Schipbeek (riv.), Neth. 108/D4
Schirmeck, Fr. 114/D1
Schkumbin (riv.), Alb. 105/G2
Schladen, Ger. 109/H4
Schladming, Aus. 101/K3
Schlanders (Silandro), It. 101/J3
Schlangen, Ger. 109/F5
Schlangenbad, Ger. 112/B2
Schleiden, Ger. 111/F2
Schleitheim, Swi. 115/E2
Schleiz, Ger. 113/E1
Schlema, Ger. 113/F1
Schleswig, Ger. 96/C4
Schleswig-Holstein (state), Ger. 96/B4
Schleswig-Holsteinisches Wattenmeer NP, Ger. 96/C4
Schleuse (riv.), Ger. 112/D2
Schleusingen, Ger. 112/D1
Schliengen, Ger. 114/D2
Schlierbach, Aus. 113/H7
Schlieren, Swi. 115/E3
Schloss Herrenchiemsee, Ger. 113/F7
Schloss Holte-Stukenbrock, Ger. 109/F5
Schloss Sansoucci, Ger. 98/Q7
Schloss Wilhelmstein, Ger. 109/G4
Schlotheim, Ger. 109/H6
Schluchsee, Ger. 114/E2
Schlüchtern, Ger. 112/C2
Schlüsselfeld, Ger. 112/D3
Schlüsslberg, Aus. 113/G6
Schmalkalden, Ger. 101/J1
Schmallenberg, Ger. 109/F6
Schmeich (riv.), Ger. 112/C6
Schmelz, Ger. 111/F5
Schmiech (riv.), Ger. 115/F1
Schmitten, Swi. 114/D4
Schmitten, Ger. 112/B2
Schmutter (riv.), Ger. 112/D5
Schnaitsee, Ger. 113/F6
Schnaittach, Ger. 113/E3
Schnaittenbach, Ger. 113/F3
Schnarrtanne, Ger. 113/F1
Schnecksville, Pa, US 196/C2
Schneeberg (peak), Ger. 113/E2
Schneeberg, Ger. 113/F1
Schneeberg, Ger. 112/C3
Schneifel (upland), Ger. 98/D3
Schneverdingen, Ger. 109/G2
Schofield Barracks, Hi, US 182/V12
Schollene, Ger. 98/G2
Schöllkrippen, Ger. 112/C2
Schömberg, Ger. 115/E1
Schömberg, Ger. 112/B5
Schönaich, Ger. 112/C5
Schönau im Schwarzwald, Ger. 114/D2
Schönberg, Ger. 96/D4
Schönberg, Ger. 113/G5
Schondorf am Ammersee, Ger. 115/H1
Schondra (riv.), Ger. 112/C2
Schönebeck, Ger. 98/F2
Schöneck, Ger. 112/B2
Schönecken, Ger. 111/F3
Schönefeld (int'l arpt.), Ger. 98/Q7
Schongau, Ger. 115/G2
Schöningen, Ger. 98/F2
Schönsee, Ger. 113/F3
Schonungen, Ger. 112/D2
Schönwald, Ger. 113/E2
Schoonebeek, Neth. 108/D3
Schoonhoven, Neth. 108/B5
Schoorl, Neth. 108/B3
Schopfheim, Ger. 111/G4
Schopfloch, Ger. 112/D4
Schöppenstedt, Ger. 109/H4
Schörfling, Aus. 113/G7
Schorndorf, Ger. 112/C5
Schortens, Ger. 109/E1
Schoten, Belg. 108/B6
Schotten, Ger. 112/C1
Schouten (isl.), Austl. 173/D4
Schouten (isls.), Indo. 174/C5
Schouwen (isl.), Neth. 108/A5
Schramberg, Ger. 115/E1
Schrankogel (peak), Aus. 115/H3
Schreckhorn (peak), Swi. 114/E4
Schriesheim, Ger. 112/B4
Schrobenhausen, Ger. 112/E5
Schroffenstein (peak), Namb. 164/B2
Schrozberg, Ger. 112/C4
Schruns, Aus. 115/F3
Schübelbach, Swi. 115/E3
Schuby, Ger. 96/C4
Schulenburg, Tx, US 187/H5
Schulzendorf, Ger. 98/Q7
Schunter (riv.), Ger. 109/H4
Schüpfheim, Swi. 114/E4
Schussen (riv.), Ger. 115/F2
Schussenried, Ger. 115/F1
Schutter (riv.), Ger. 112/A6
Schutterwald, Ger. 114/D1
Schüttorf, Ger. 109/E4
Schuylkill (riv.), Pa, US 196/C3
Schuylkill Haven, Pa, US 196/B2
Schwabach, Ger. 112/D4
Schwabhausen bei Dachau, Ger. 113/E6
Schwäbisch Gmünd, Ger. 112/C5
Schwäbisch Hall, Ger. 112/C4
Schwäbische Alb (range), Ger. 98/E4
Schwabmünchen, Ger. 115/G1
Schwaig bei Nürnberg, Ger. 112/E4
Schwaigern, Ger. 112/C4
Schwalbach, Ger. 111/F5
Schwalbach am Taunus, Ger. 112/B2
Schwalm (riv.), Ger. 98/E3
Schwalmtal, Ger. 108/D6
Schwanden, Swi. 115/F4
Schwandorf im Bayern, Ger. 113/F4
Schwanebeck, Ger. 98/Q6
Schwanenstadt, Aus. 113/G6
Schwaner (mts.), Indo. 138/D4
Schwanewede, Ger. 109/F2
Schwanfeld, Ger. 112/D3
Schwangau, Ger. 115/G2
Schwarmstedt, Ger. 109/G3
Schwartz Elster (riv.), Ger. 99/G3
Schwartzerberg (peak), Namb. 164/B2
Schwarza (riv.), Ger. 112/E1
Schwarzach, Ger. 113/F5
Schwarzach (riv.), Ger. 113/E4
Schwarzach im Pongau, Aus. 101/K3
Schwarze Laber (riv.), Ger. 113/E4
Schwarzenbach am Wald, Ger. 113/E2
Schwarzenbek, Ger. 109/H1
Schwarzenberg, Ger. 113/F1
Schwarzenbruck, Ger. 112/E4
Schwarzenburg, Swi. 114/D4
Schwarzenfeld, Ger. 113/F4
Schwarzer Mann (peak), Ger. 111/F3
Schwarzhorn (peak), Aus. 115/H3
Schwarzwald (Black Forest) (for.), Ger. 112/B6
Schwaz, Aus. 101/J3
Schwebheim, Ger. 112/D3
Schwechat, Aus. 107/N7
Schwechat (int'l arpt.), Aus. 107/P7
Schwedt, Ger. 99/H2
Schwegenheim, Ger. 112/B4
Schweich, Ger. 111/F4
Schweighouse-sur-Moder, Fr. 111/G6
Schweinfurt, Ger. 112/D2
Schweitenkirchen, Ger. 113/E5
Schweizer-Reneke, SAfr. 164/D2
Schwelm, Ger. 109/E6
Schwendi, Ger. 115/F1
Schwenksville, Pa, US 196/C3
Schwerin, Ger. 96/D5
Schweriner (lake), Ger. 98/F2
Schwertberg, Aus. 113/H6
Schwerte, Ger. 109/E6
Schwetzingen, Ger. 112/B4
Schwinge (riv.), Ger. 109/G1
Schwörstadt, Ger. 114/D2
Schwülme (riv.), Ger. 109/G5
Schwülper, Ger. 109/H4
Schwyz (canton), Swi. 115/E3
Schwyz, Swi. 115/E3
Sciacca, It. 104/C4
Scicli, It. 104/D4
Scilly (isls.), Eng, UK 89/Q11
Ścinawa, Pol. 99/J3
Scionzier, Fr. 114/C5
Sciota, Pa, US 196/C2
Scioto (riv.), Oh, US 188/D4
Scobey, Mt, US 185/G3
Scolt (pt.), Eng, UK 91/G1
Scone, Austl. 173/D2
Scopello, It. 116/B1
Scordia, It. 104/D4
Scorzè, It. 117/F2
Scotch Corner, Eng, UK 93/G3
Scotch Plains, NJ, US 197/H9
Scotia (sea) 218/W
Scotland, UK 92/D1
Scott (cape), BC, Can. 180/D3
Scott (cape), NW, Can. 139/R7
Scott (lake), NW,Sk, Can. 180/F2
Scott, NZ, Ant. 218/M
Scott City, Ks, US 187/G3
Scott NP, Austl. 170/B5
Scott (reef), Austl. 167/B2
Scottburgh, SAfr. 165/E3
Scotts (cr.), Austl. 171/M9
Scottish Borders (pol. reg.), Sc, UK 94/C5
Scotts Bluff Nat'l Mon., Ne, US 187/F2
Scottsbluff, Ne, US 187/G2
Scottsboro, Al, US 191/G3
Scottsburg, In, US 188/C4
Scottsdale, Austl. 173/C4
Scottsdale, Az, US 186/E4
Scottsville, Ky, US 191/G2
Scottville, Mi, US 188/C2
Scourie, Sc, UK 89/R7
Scranton, Pa, US 188/F3
Scrivia (riv.), It. 116/B3
Scunthorpe, Eng, UK 93/H4
Scuol, Swi. 115/G4
Scuppernong (riv.), Wi, US 193/N14
Scurdie Ness (pt.), Sc, UK 94/D3
Scutari (lake), Alb., Mont. 106/D4
Sea Cliff, Ca, US 194/A2
Sea Cliff, NY, US 197/L8
Sea Girt, NJ, US 196/D3
Sea Isle City, NJ, US 196/D5
Sea Lake, Austl. 173/B2
Sea-Tac, Wa, US 193/C3
Seabeck, Wa, US 193/B2
Seabold, Wa, US 193/B2
Seabra, Braz. 212/B4
Seabrook, NJ, US 196/C5
Seaford, Eng, UK 91/G5
Seaford, NY, US 197/M9
Seaforde, NI, UK 92/C3
Seaforth, Austl. 172/C3
Seagraves, Tx, US 187/G4
Seaham, Eng, UK 93/G2
Seahorse (pt.), Nun, Can. 139/J2
Seahurst, Wa, US 193/C3
Seal, Eng, UK 88/D3
Seal (riv.), MB, Can. 180/G3
Seal (pt.), Chile 216/B5
Seal (cape), SAfr. 164/C4
Seal Beach, Ca, US 194/F8
Seale, Eng, UK 88/A3
Seamer, Eng, UK 93/H3
Seano, It. 117/E6
Searcy, Ar, US 187/K4
Seascale, Eng, UK 92/E3
Seaside, Or, US 184/B4
Seaside Heights, NJ, US 196/D4
Seaside Park, NJ, US 196/D4
Seaton, Eng, UK 90/C5
Seaton (riv.), Eng, UK 90/B6
Seaton Carew, Eng, UK 93/G2
Seattle, Wa, US 184/C4
Sébaco, Nic. 202/E3
Sebaou (riv.), Alg. 158/H4
Sebastian, Fl, US 191/H5
Sebastián Vizcaíno (bay), Mex. 200/B2
Sebayan (peak), Indo. 138/D4
Sebdou, Alg. 158/D2
Sébékoro, Mali 160/C3
Seben, Turk. 107/K5
Sebeş, Rom. 107/F3
Sebezh, Rus. 97/N3
Şebinkarahisar, Turk. 148/D1
Sebiş, Rom. 106/F2
Sebkhet al Kalīyah (drylake), Alg. 158/M7
Sebnitz, Ger. 99/H3
Seboruco, Ven. 210/C2
Sebou (riv.), Mor. 158/B2
Sebou, Oued (riv.), Mor. 156/D2
Sebring, Fl, US 191/H5
Sebuku (isl.), Indo. 139/E4
Secaucus, NJ, US 197/J8
Secchia (riv.), It. 101/J4
Sechura, Peru 214/A2
Sechura (bay), Peru 214/A2
Sechura, Desierto de (des.), Peru 214/A2
Seclin, Fr. 110/C2
Seco (riv.), Arg. 217/D6
Seco (riv.), Mex.,US 200/C2
Second Mountain (mtn.), Pa, US 196/B3
Second Watchung (mtn.), NJ, US 197/H9
Secunda, SAfr. 164/E2
Secure (riv.), Bol. 208/E7
Seda, Lith. 97/K3
Sedalia, Mo, US 187/J3
Sedan, Fr. 111/D4
Sedano, Sp. 102/D1
Sedaung (mtn.), Myan. 136/B3
Sedbergh, Eng, UK 93/F3
Seddülbahir, Turk. 105/K2
Sedeh, Iran 147/G2
Sederot, Isr. 149/D4
Sedgefield, Eng, UK 93/G2
Sedhiou, Sen. 160/B3
Sedlčany, Czh. 113/H3
Sedlo (peak), Czh. 113/H1
Sedona, Az, US 186/E4
Sedrata, Alg. 158/K6
Sędziszów, Pol. 99/L3
Sée (riv.), Fr. 100/C2
Seeb (int'l arpt.), Oman 147/G4
Seeboden, Aus. 101/K3
Seefeld in Tirol, Aus. 115/H3
Seeg, Ger. 115/G2
Seehausen, Ger. 98/F2
Seeheim, Namb. 164/B2
Seeheim-Jugenheim, Ger. 112/B3
Seekirchen Markt, Aus. 113/G7
Seekooi (riv.), SAfr. 164/D3
Seelow, Ger. 99/H2
Seeon-Seebruck, Ger. 113/F7
Seer Green, Eng, UK 88/B2
Sées, Fr. 100/D2
Seesen, Ger. 109/H5
Seeshaupt, Ger. 115/H2
Seeve (riv.), Ger. 109/G2
Seewalchen, Aus. 113/G7
Seewis im Prättigau, Swi. 115/F4
Şefaatlı, Turk. 148/C2
Sefrou, Mor. 158/B3
Sefton (co.), Eng, UK 93/E4
Segamat, Malay. 138/B3
Segarcea, Rom. 107/F3
Ségbana, Ben. 161/F4
Ségélo-Koro, C.d'Iv. 160/D4
Segelstad Bru, Nor. 96/D1
Seget, Indo. 139/H4
Segezha, Rus. 118/G3
Segorbe, Sp. 103/E3
Ségou, Mali 160/D3
Ségou (pol. reg.), Mali 160/D3
Segovia, Col. 210/C3
Segovia, Sp. 102/C2
Segozero (lake), Rus. 118/G3
Segrate, It. 116/C3
Segré, Fr. 100/C3
Segre (riv.), Sp. 103/F2
Seguam (isl.), Ak, US 192/D5
Séguédine, Niger 154/H3
Séguéla, C.d'Iv. 160/D5
Séguénéga, Burk. 161/E3
Seguin, Tx, US 190/D4
Segura (riv.), Sp. 102/D3
Segusino, It. 117/E2
Sehithwa, Bots. 163/D5
Sehnde, Ger. 109/G4
Sehonghong, Les. 164/E3
Sehore, India 140/C3
Sehwān, Pak. 147/J3
Seibersbach, Ger. 111/G4
Seiersberg, Aus. 106/B2
Seika, Japan 135/J6
Seiling, Ok, US 187/H3
Seille (riv.), Fr. 98/C5
Seinäjoki, Fin. 118/D3
Seine (riv.), On, Can. 185/L3
Seine (bay), Fr. 100/C2
Seine (riv.), Fr. 100/D2
Seine-et-Marne (dept.), Fr. 110/B5
Seine-Maritime (dept.), Fr. 110/A4
Seine-st-Denis (dept.), Fr. 110/B6
Seitenstetten, Aus. 113/H6
Seiwa, Japan 135/K7
Seix, Fr. 100/D5
Seixal, Port. 103/P10
Sejaka, Indo. 139/E4
Sejerø (isl.), Den. 96/D4
Sejny, Pol. 97/K4
Sekayu, Indo. 138/B4
Seke, Tanz. 162/A2
Sekenke, Tanz. 162/A3
Seki (riv.), Turk. 149/A1
Seki, Japan 135/L5
Seki, Japan 135/K6
Sekigahara, Japan 135/K5
Sekijo, Japan 135/D1
Sekiyado, Japan 135/D1
Sekondi, Gha. 161/E5
Sel, Nor. 95/D3
Selah, Wa, US 184/C4
Selaphum, Thai. 136/C2
Selargius, It. 104/A3
Selaru (isl.), Indo. 139/H5
Selatan (cape), Indo. 138/D4
Selawik (lake), Ak, US 192/F2
Selayar (isl.), Indo. 139/F5
Selb, Ger. 113/F2
Selbitz, Ger. 113/E2
Selbitz (riv.), Ger. 113/E2
Selbu, Nor. 95/D3
Selby, SD, US 185/H4
Selby, Eng, UK 93/G4
Selby-on-the-Bay, Md, US 196/B6
Selci, It. 117/F6
Selçuk, Turk. 148/A2
Selden, NY, US 197/E2
Sele (riv.), It. 104/D2
Selebi-Phikwe, Bots. 163/E5
Seleli (hill), Tanz. 162/B5
Selemdzha (riv.), Rus. 123/N4
Selenča, Serb. 106/D3
Selenge (prov.), Mong. 128/J2
Selenge (riv.), Mong. 128/J2
Selenginsk, Rus. 123/L4
Selenicë, Alb. 105/F2
Sélestat, Fr. 114/D1
Selety (riv.), Kaz. 145/F2
Seleznëvo, Rus. 97/N1
Selfoss, Ice. 95/N7
Sélibabi, Mrta. 160/B3
Seligenstadt, Ger. 112/B2
Seliger (lake), Rus. 118/G4
Selimbau, Indo. 138/D3
Selimiye, Turk. 148/A2
Selinsgrove, Pa, US 196/B2
Seljord, Nor. 96/C2
Selkan (tun.), Japan 134/B3
Selkirk, Sc, UK 94/D5
Selkirk, Mb, Can. 180/G3
Selkirk (mts.), BC, Can. 184/D3
Selleck, Wa, US 193/D3
Sellersville, Pa, US 196/C3
Sellières, Fr. 114/B4
Sells, Az, US 186/E5
Selly Oak, Eng, UK 90/E2
Selye, Hun. 106/C3
Selm, Ger. 109/E5
Selma, Al, US 191/G3
Selmer, Tn, US 191/F3
Selongey, Fr. 114/B2
Selouma, Gui. 160/C4
Selous Game Reserve, Tanz. 162/B4
Selsey, Eng, UK 91/F5
Selsey Bill (pt.), Eng, UK 91/F5
Selsingen, Ger. 109/G2
Sel'tso, Rus. 120/E1
Seltz, Fr. 112/B5
Sélune (riv.), Fr. 100/C2

Selvas (for.), Braz. 205/C3
Selvik, Nor. 95/R9
Selwyn, Austl. 172/A3
Selwyn (range), Austl. 172/A3
Selz (riv.), Ger. 101/H2
Semara, WSah. 154/C2
Semarang, Indo. 138/D5
Semarsot, India 142/D4
Sembehun, SLeo. 160/B5
Sembera (riv.), Czh. 113/H2
Semberong (riv.), Malay. 138/B3
Şemdinli, Turk. 148/F2
Séméac, Fr. 100/D5
Semenivka, Ukr. 120/E1
Semenivka, Ukr. 120/E2
Semenov, Rus. 119/K4
Semeru (peak), Indo. 138/D5
Semey, Kaz. 145/H2
Semikarakorsk, Rus. 121/G3
Semilovo, Rus. 121/G1
Semiluki, Rus. 120/F2
Seminole (lake), Ga, US 191/G4
Seminole, Tx, US 190/C3
Seminoe (res.), Wy, US 186/F2
Semitau, Indo. 138/D4
Semliki (riv.), D.R. Congo 162/A2
Semnān, Iran 146/F1
Semnon (riv.), Fr. 100/C3
Semois (riv.), Belg. 100/F2
Semporna, Malay. 139/E3
Semsales, Swi. 114/C4
Semskefjellet (peak), Nor. 95/E2
Sen (riv.), Camb. 141/H5
Sen-san (peak), Japan 135/G7
Sena, Thai. 141/H5
Senador Pompeu, Braz. 212/C2
Senaja, Malay. 139/E2
Senaki, Geo. 121/G4
Senanga, Zam. 163/D4
Sénas, Fr. 148/B5
Senatobia, Ms, US 191/F3
Sence (riv.), Eng, UK 91/E1
Send, Eng, UK 88/B3
Sendai (riv.), Japan 132/D3
Sendai, Japan 133/G1
Sendai, Japan 132/B5
Sendai (int'l arpt.), Japan 133/G1
Sendai (bay), Japan 134/B4
Sendai (riv.), Japan 132/B5
Senden, Ger. 112/D6
Senden, Ger. 109/E5
Sendenhorst, Ger. 109/E5
Senec, Slvk. 99/J4
Seneca Creek State Park, Md, US 196/A5
Seneffe, Belg. 111/D2
Senegal (ctry.) 160/B3
Sénégal (riv.), Afr. 160/B2
Senekal, SAfr. 164/D3
Seney NWR, Mi, US 188/C2
Senezhskoye (lake), Rus. 119/W8
Senfi, Gha. 161/E5
Senftenberg, Ger. 99/H3
Sengenthal, Ger. 113/E4
Sengilev, Rus. 121/J1
Sengor, Bhu. 143/H2
Senguer (riv.), Arg. 216/D3
Senhor do Bonfim, Braz. 212/B3
Senica, Slvk. 99/J4
Senirkent, Turk. 148/B2
Senise, It. 104/E2
Senj, Cro. 101/L4
Senja (isl.), Nor. 95/F1
Senkaku-Shotō (isl.), Japan 133/G8
Şenkaya, Turk. 148/E1
Şenköy, Turk. 149/E1
Senlis, Fr. 110/B5
Senmonoron, Camb. 136/D3
Sennan, Japan 135/H7
Sennar (dam), Sudan 155/M5
Senne (riv.), Belg. 111/D2
Sennecy-le-Grand, Fr. 114/A4
Sennfeld, Ger. 112/D2
Senno, Bela. 97/N4
Sennoy, Rus. 121/G2
Sennoy, Rus. 121/H1
Sennwald, Swi. 115/F3
Sennybridge, Wal, UK 90/C3
Séno (prov.), Burk. 161/F3
Senones, Fr. 114/C1
Senorbì, It. 104/A3
Senou (Bamako) (int'l arpt.), Mali 160/D3
Senovo, Bul. 107/H4
Sens, Fr. 100/E2
Sensuntepeque, ESal. 202/D3
Senta, Serb. 106/E3
Sentani, Indo. 139/K4
Sentery, D.R. Congo 163/E2
Senya Beraku, Gha. 161/E5
Senyavin (isls.), Micr. 174/E4
Senzig, Ger. 98/Q7
Seohāra, India 142/B1
Seon, Swi. 114/E3
Seondha, India 142/B2
Seoni, India 142/B4
Seonī Mālwā, India 142/A4
Seoul (Sŏul) (cap.), SKor. 131/D4
Seoul Grand Park, SKor. 131/G7
Seoul Jikhalsi (prov.), SKor. 131/D4
Sepetiba (bay), Braz. 213/J8
Sepik (riv.), PNG 174/D5
Sep'o, NKor. 131/D3
Sepo, Indo. 139/G3
Sępólno Krajeńskie, Pol. 99/J2
Sept-Îles, Qu, Can. 189/H2
Septemvri, Bul. 49/G4
Septeuil, Fr. 88/H5
Sepulveda (dam), Ca, US 194/F7
Sequeros, Sp. 102/B2
Sequoia NP, Ca, US 186/C3
Serafimovich, Rus. 121/G2
Seraincourt, Fr. 88/H4
Seraing, Belg. 111/E2
Serampore, India 143/G4
Séran (riv.), Fr. 114/D3
Serasan (str.), Indo.,Malay. 138/C3
Serasan, Indo. 138/C3
Seravezza, It. 116/D6
Serbia and Montenegro (ctry.) 106/D3
Serbia (reg.), Serb. 106/E4
Serchio (riv.), It. 116/D4
Serdobsk, Rus. 121/H1
Serebryansk, Kaz. 122/J5
Serednikovo, Rus. 118/H5
Seregno, It. 116/C2
Serein (riv.), Fr. 98/D4
Serémange-Erzange, Fr. 111/F5
Seremban, Malay. 138/B3
Serengeti NP, Tanz. 155/M8
Serenje, Zam. 163/F3
Serere, Ugan. 162/A1
Sergach, Rus. 119/K5
Sergeantsville, NJ, US 196/D3
Sergen, Turk. 107/H5
Sergeya Kirova (isls.), Rus. 122/J2
Sergeyevka, Kaz. 119/Q5
Sergipe (state), Braz. 212/C3
Sergiyev Posad, Rus. 118/H4
Sergnano, It. 116/C3
Seria, Bru. 138/D3
Seriate, It. 116/C2
Sérifontaine, Fr. 110/A5
Sérifos, Gre. 105/J4
Sérifos (isl.), Gre. 105/J4
Sérignan, Fr. 100/E5
Serik, Turk. 148/B2
Seringa, Serra da (mts.), Braz. 209/h5
Serio (riv.), It. 116/C2
Serkout (peak), Alg. 157/G5
Sermaize-les-Bains, Fr. 111/D6
Sermide, It. 117/E4
Sernovodsk, Rus. 121/J1
Sernur, Rus. 119/L4
Serón, Sp. 102/D4
Serós, Sp. 103/F2
Serottini (peak), It. 115/G5
Serov, Rus. 122/G4
Serowe, Bots. 163/E5
Serpa, Port. 102/B4
Serpeddi (peak), It. 104/A3
Serpent's Mouth (str.), Trin.,Ven. 211/F2
Serpentine (dam), Austl. 173/C4
Serpentine Lakes, Austl. 171/F4
Serpukhov, Rus. 118/H5
Serra (peak), It. 116/D6
Serra, Braz. 213/D2
Serra Branca, Braz. 212/C2
Serra da Bocaína, PN da, Braz. 213/J7
Serra da Canastra, PN da, Braz. 213/C2
Serra da Capivara, PN da, Braz. 212/B3
Serra da Estrela (peak), Port. 102/B2
Serra da Estrela (mts.), Port. 102/A3
Serra do Cipó, PN da, Braz. 213/D1
Serra dos Órgãos, PN da, Braz. 213/K7
Serra San Bruno, It. 104/E3
Serra San Quirico, It. 117/G7
Serra Talhada, Braz. 212/C2
Sérrai, Gre. 105/H2
Serralta di San Vito (peak), It. 104/E3
Serramanna, It. 104/A3
Serramazzoni, It. 117/D5
Serrana Bank (isl.), Col. 203/G3
Serranía de la Cerbatana (mts.), Ven. 211/E3
Serranía de la Neblina, PN, Ven. 211/E4
Serranías del Burro (mts.), Mex. 200/E2
Serranilla Bank (isl.), Col. 203/G3
Serrano, Arg. 216/E2
Serranópolis, Braz. 213/B1
Serrat (cape), Tun. 158/L6
Serravalle, It. 117/F4
Serravalle, SMar. 117/F6
Serravalle Scrivia, It. 116/B4
Serravalle Sesia, It. 116/B2
Serre (riv.), Fr. 98/B4
Serrenti, It. 104/A3
Serrinha, Braz. 212/C3
Serris, Fr. 88/L5
Sersale, It. 104/E3
Sertã, Port. 102/A3
Sertânia, Braz. 212/C3
Sertãozinho, Braz. 213/H2
Sertavul (pass), Turk. 148/C2
Serteng (mts.), China 128/F4
Serui, Indo. 139/J4
Seruyan (riv.), Indo. 138/D4
Servance, Fr. 114/C2
Servi, Turk. 148/E2
Sérvia, Gre. 105/G2
Serviceton, Austl. 173/B3
Sese (isls.), Ugan. 162/A3
Sesebi (ruin), Sudan 159/B4
Sesepe, Indo. 139/G4
Sesheke, Zam. 163/D4
Sesia (riv.), It. 101/H4
Sesimbra, Port. 102/A3
Sesimbra, Port. 103/P11
Seskar (isl.), Rus. 97/N1
Sespe, Ca, US 194/B2
Sespe (cr.), Ca, US 194/A1
Sespe Condor Sanctuary, Ca, US 194/C3
Sesslach, Ger. 112/D2
Sesto Calende, It. 116/B2
Sesto Fiorentino, It. 117/E6
Sesto San Giovanni, It. 116/C2
Sesto Ulteriano, It. 116/C3
Sestola, It. 117/D5
Sestra (riv.), Rus. 118/W9
Sestri Levante, It. 116/C5
Sestroretsk, Rus. 119/S6
Sestroretskiy (lake), Rus. 119/T6
Sestu, It. 104/A3
Sesvenna (peak), It. 115/G4
Sesvete, Cro. 106/C3
Šeta, Lith. 97/L4
Setana, Japan 134/A2
Sète, Fr. 100/E5
Sete Lagoas, Braz. 213/C1
Sethārja, Pak. 147/J3
Seti (riv.), Nepal 142/C1
Seti (zone), Nepal 142/C1
Sétif, Alg. 158/H4
Sétif (wilaya), Alg. 158/H4
Seto, Japan 135/M5
Seto-Naikai NP, Japan 132/C4
Setouchi, Japan 133/K6
Settat, Mor. 156/D2
Settepani (peak), It. 116/B5
Settimo Torinese, It. 116/A2
Settimo Vittone, It. 116/A1
Settle, Eng, UK 93/F3
Settsu, Japan 135/J6
Setúbal (dist.), Port. 102/A3
Setúbal (bay), Port. 102/A3
Setúbal, Port. 103/Q10
Seubersdorf, Ger. 113/E4
Seudre (riv.), Fr. 100/C4
Seugne (riv.), Fr. 100/C4
Seuil-d'Argonne, Fr. 111/E6
Seul (lake), On, Can. 180/G3
Seulimeum, Indo. 138/A2
Seurre, Fr. 114/B4
Seuzach, Swi. 115/E2
Sevan, Arm. 121/H4
Sevana (lake), Arm. 121/H4
Sevastopol', Ukr. 120/E3
Sevelen, Swi. 115/F3
Seven (riv.), Eng, UK 93/H3
Seven Heads (pt.), Ire. 89/P11
Seven Valleys, Pa, US 196/B4
Sevenoaks, Eng, UK 88/D3
Sevenoaks Weald, Eng, UK 88/D3
Severn (riv.), Wal, UK 93/F6
Severn (riv.), On, Can. 180/G3
Severn (riv.), Md, US 196/B5
Severn, Md, US 196/B5
Severna Park, Md, US 196/B5
Severnaya Osetiya-Alaniya, Resp., Rus. 121/G4
Severnaya Sos'va (riv.), Rus. 119/N3
Severnaya Zemlya (isls.), Rus. 122/J2
Severnyy, Rus. 119/P2
Severo-Kuril'sk, Rus. 123/R4
Severo-Yeniseyskiy, Rus. 122/K3
Severobaykal'sk, Rus. 123/L4
Severodvinsk, Rus. 118/H2
Severomorsk, Rus. 118/G1
Severomuysk, Rus. 123/M4
Severoural'sk, Rus. 119/N3
Severskaya, Rus. 120/F3
Severukha, Rus. 119/P4
Seveso, It. 116/C2
Sevier (des.), Ut, US 186/D3
Sevierville, Tn, US 191/H3
Sevilla, Col. 210/C3
Seville, Sp. 102/C4
Seville, Austl. 173/G5
Sevlievo, Bul. 107/G4
Sevnica, Slov. 106/B2
Sevojno, Serb. 106/D4
Sevran, Fr. 88/K5
Sevsk, Rus. 120/E1
Sewa (riv.), SLeo. 160/C5
Seward (pen.), Ak, US 192/E3
Seward, Ak, US 192/J3
Seward, Ne, US 187/H2
Sewaren, NJ, US 197/J9
Sewell, Chile 216/N9
Seyah Cheshmeh, Iran 121/H5
Seybaplaya, Mex. 202/D2
Seybouse, Oued (riv.), Alg. 158/K6
Seychelles (ctry.) 81/M6
Seydhisfjördhur, Ice. 95/Q6
Seydişehir, Turk. 148/B2
Seyhan (dam), Turk. 148/C2
Seyhan (riv.), Turk. 149/D1
Seyitgazi, Turk. 148/B2
Seym (riv.), Rus. 120/E2
Seymour, Austl. 173/C3
Seymour, Tx, US 187/H4
Seynod, Fr. 114/C6
Seyssel, Fr. 114/B6
Sežana, Slov. 101/K4
Sézanne, Fr. 110/C6
Sezimovo Ústí, Czh. 113/H4
Sezze, It. 104/C2
Sfax, Tun. 157/H2
Sfax (gov.), Tun. 157/H2
Sfîntu Gheorghe, Rom. 107/J3
Sfîntu Gheorghe, Rom. 107/G3
Sfîntu Gheorghe Branch (riv.), Rom. 107/J3
Sfizef, Alg. 158/E5
Sgurr na Lapaich (peak), Sc, UK 94/A2
Sha (riv.), China 130/C4
Sha Tin, China 129/U10
Shaanxi (prov.), China 128/J5
Shaba Nat'l Rsv., Kenya 162/C2
Shābāzpur (riv.), Bang. 143/H4
Shabeelle (riv.), Som. 155/P7
Shabla, Bul. 107/J4
Shabqadar, Pak. 144/A2
Shabunda, D.R. Congo 155/L8
Shache, China 145/G5
Shade (mtn.), Pa, US 196/A2
Shadrinsk, Rus. 119/P4
Shafter, Tx, US 190/B4
Shagamu, Nga. 161/F5
Shagany (lake), Ukr. 107/J3
Shageluk, Ak, US 192/G3
Shah Alam, Malay. 138/B3
Shāh Kot, Pak. 144/B4
Shāhābād, India 142/B2
Shāhābād, India 142/B1
Shāhābād, India 144/D4
Shahdād, Iran 147/G2
Shāhdādkot, Pak. 147/J3
Shahdol, India 142/C4
Shāhganj, India 142/D2
Shaḥḥāt, Libya 155/K1
Shāhjahānpur, India 142/B2
Shāhpur, Pak. 144/B3
Shāhpur Chākar, Pak. 140/A2
Shāhpura, India 142/C4
Shahr-e Kord, Iran 146/F2
Shāhrūd (Emāmshahr), Iran 147/F1
Shā'ib al Banāt (peak), Egypt 159/C3
Shaikhpura, India 143/E3
Shājāpur, India 147/L4
Shakargarh, Pak. 144/C3
Shakaskraal, SAfr. 165/E3
Shakawe, Bots. 163/D4
Shakhrisabz, Uzb. 145/E5
Shakhtinsk, Kaz. 145/F3
Shakhty, Rus. 120/G3
Shakhun'ya, Rus. 119/K4
Shaki, Nga. 161/F4
Shakotan (pen.), Japan 134/B2
Shaktoolik, Ak, US 192/F3
Shalbuzdag (peak), Rus. 121/H4
Shallow Reach (inlet), Austl. 171/M8
Shalqar, Kaz. 121/L3
Shaluli (mts.), China 128/G5
Shām, Jabal ash (peak), Oman 147/G4
Shama (riv.), Tanz. 163/F2
Shamattawa (riv.), On, Can. 139/H3
Shāmgarh, India 147/L4
Shāmīl, Iran 147/G3
Shāmli, India 144/D5
Shammar, Jabal (mts.), SAr. 146/D3
Shamokin, Pa, US 196/B2
Shamokin Dam, Pa, US 196/B2
Shamrock (mtn.), Yk, Can. 192/L3
Shamrock, Tx, US 187/G4
Shamsābād, India 142/B2
Shamva, Zim. 163/F4
Shan (plat.), Myan. 128/G7
Shan (state), Myan. 141/G3
Sha'nabī, Jabal ash (peak), Tun. 158/L7
Shandong (prov.), China 129/L4
Shandong (isl.), China 130/E3
Shangcai, China 130/C4
Shangcheng, China 130/C5
Shangdu, China 129/K3
Shanghai (prov.), China 129/M5
Shanghai, China 130/L8
Shanghang, China 137/C2
Shanghe, China 130/D3
Shangqiu, China 130/C4
Shangshui, China 130/C4
Shangyi, China 130/C2
Shangyou, China 137/B2
Shannon (riv.), Ire. 89/P10
Shanshan, China 128/F3
Shantar (isls.), Rus. 123/P4
Shantar (isl.), Rus. 125/N4
Shantou, China 137/C3
Shanxi (prov.), China 129/K4
Shanyin, China 130/C3
Shaoguan, China 141/K3
Shaowu, China 137/C2
Shaoxing, China 137/D2
Shaoyang, China 137/B2
Shaoyang, China 141/K2
Shapkina (riv.), Rus. 119/M2
Shaqlāwah, Iraq 148/F2
Sharafkhāneh, Iran 148/F2
Sharbatāt, Ra's ash (pt.), Oman 147/G5
Sharga, Mong. 128/G2
Shari, Japan 134/D2
Sharīngol, Mong. 128/J2
Shark (bay), Austl. 170/B3
Shark River (inlet), NJ, US 196/D3
Sharon, Pa, US 188/D3
Sharp (mtn.), Ut, US 195/K11
Sharpe (lake), SD, US 185/J4
Sharqpur, Pak. 144/C4
Shar'ya, Rus. 119/K4
Shashi, China 137/B1
Shasta (lake), Ca, US 184/C5
Shasta (mt.), Ca, US 184/C5
Shatskiy NP, Ukr. 99/M3
Shatt al Arab (riv.), Iraq 146/E2
Shaṭṭ al Jarīd (dry lake), Gabon 154/G1
Shattuck, Ok, US 187/H3
Shaunavon, Sk, Can. 184/F3
Shavano Park, Tx, US 195/T20
Shaw, Eng, UK 91/E4
Shawano, Wi, US 185/L4
Shawinigan, Qu, Can. 189/F2
Shawnee, Ok, US 187/H4
Shawnee (res.), Ok, US 195/N15
Shawnee, Ks, US 195/D5
Shay Gap, Austl. 170/D2
Shaykhān, Iraq 148/E2
Shchara (riv.), Bela. 120/C1
Shchekino, Rus. 120/F1
Shchelkovo, Rus. 119/W9
Shchigry, Rus. 120/F2
Shchūchīnsk, Kaz. 145/F2
She Xian, China 137/C2
Shea Stadium, NY, US 197/K9
Shebelē Wenz (riv.), Eth. 155/P6
Sheberghān, Afg. 147/J1
Sheboygan, Wi, US 185/M5
Shediac, NB, Can. 189/H2
Shee (riv.), Sc, UK 94/C3
Sheelin (lake), Ire. 92/A4
Sheep (mtn.), Ak, US 192/F2
Shefar'am, Isr. 149/G6
Shefayim, Isr. 149/F7
Sheffield, Austl. 173/C4
Sheffield, Eng, UK 93/G5
Sheffield (co.), Eng, UK 93/G5
Sheffield, Al, US 191/G3
Sheffield (lake), Ct, US 197/M7
Shehuén (riv.), Arg. 215/B6
Shek Uk (peak), China 129/V10
Shekak (riv.), On, Can. 188/C1
Shekhūpura, Pak. 144/B4
Shelagskiy (cape), Rus. 123/S2
Shelburne, NS, Can. 189/H3
Shelby, Mt, US 184/F3
Shelby, Ms, US 187/K4
Shelby, Mi, US 188/C3
Shelby, NC, US 191/H3
Shelbyville (lake), Il, US 191/F2
Shelbyville, Tn, US 191/G3
Shelbyville, In, US 188/C4
Sheldon Point, Ak, US 192/F3
Shelekhov (gulf), Rus. 125/Q3
Shelikof (str.), Ak, US 192/H4
Shell (pt.), Eng, UK 91/G4
Shell Lake, Wi, US 185/L4
Shell Rock (riv.), Ia, US 185/K5
Shellbrook, Sk, Can. 185/G2
Shelley (isl.), Pa, US 196/B3
Shelter (isl.), NY, US 197/F1
Shelter Island (sound), NY, US 197/F1
Shelton, Wa, US 184/C4
Shelton, Ct, US 197/E1
Shen Xian, China 130/C3
Shenandoah, Pa, US 196/B2
Shenandoah NP, Va, US 188/E4
Shenchi, China 130/C3
Sheng Xian, China 137/D2
Shenge (pt.), SLeo. 160/B5
Shengena (peak), Tanz. 162/C4
Shennongjia, China 130/B5
Shenqiu, China 130/C4
Shenyang, China 131/B2
Shenzhen, China 141/K3
Shepetivka, Ukr. 120/C2
Shepherd (isls.), Van. 174/F6
Sheppey, Isle of (isl.), Eng, UK 91/G4
Shepshed, Eng, UK 91/E1
Sheqi, China 130/C4
Sherbro (isl.), SLeo. 160/B5
Sherbrooke, Qu, Can. 189/G2
Shere (hill), Nga. 161/H4
Sheremetyevo (int'l arpt.), Rus. 119/W9
Sherghāti, India 143/E3
Sheridan, Wy, US 184/G4
Sheridan, Co, US 195/B3
Sherman, Tx, US 187/H4
Sherpur, Bang. 143/H3
Sherwood (pt.), Ct, US 197/E1
Shetland (isls.), UK 218/G
Sheung Shui-Fanling, China 129/U10
Shevchenko (int'l arpt.), Kaz. 121/J4
Sheyang (riv.), China 130/D4
Sheyang, China 130/E4
Sheyenne (riv.), ND, US 185/J4
Shi (riv.), China 130/C4
Shi San Ling, China 130/H6
Shibakawa, Japan 135/B3
Shibata, Japan 133/F2
Shibayama, Japan 135/E2
Shibecha, Japan 134/D2
Shibetsu, Japan 134/C1
Shibetsu, Japan 134/D2
Shibīn al Kaum, Egypt 149/B4
Shibīn al Qanāṭir, Egypt 149/B4
Shibogama (lake), On, Can. 185/L2
Shibotsu (isl.), Rus. 134/E2
Shibushi (bay), Japan 132/B5
Shicheng, China 137/C2
Shicheng (isl.), China 131/B3
Shickshinny, Pa, US 196/B1
Shiderty (riv.), Kaz. 145/F2
Shido, Japan 132/D3
Shiga, Japan 135/J5
Shigaraki, Japan 135/K6
Shihezi, China 128/E3
Shijak, Alb. 105/F2
Shijiazhuang, China 130/C3
Shijōnawate, Japan 135/J6
Shikabe, Japan 134/B2
Shikārpur, India 142/B1
Shikārpur, Pak. 147/J3
Shikata, Japan 135/G6
Shikatsu, Japan 135/L5
Shikishima, Japan 135/B2
Shikohābād, India 142/B2
Shikoku (isl.), Japan 132/C4
Shikoku (mts.), Japan 132/C4
Shikotsu (lake), Japan 134/B2
Shikotsu-Tōya NP, Japan 134/B2
Shildon, Eng, UK 93/G2
Shilka (riv.), Rus. 125/L4
Shilla (peak), India 144/D3
Shillington, Pa, US 196/C3
Shillong, India 141/F2
Shiloh, Il, US 195/H8
Shiloh, NJ, US 196/C5
Shilou, China 130/B3
Shimabara, Japan 132/B4
Shimagahara, Japan 135/K6
Shimamamoto, Japan 135/J6
Shimane (pref.), Japan 132/C3
Shimasahi, Japan 135/K5
Shimba Hills Nat'l Rsv., Kenya 162/C4
Shimbara (bay), Japan 132/B4
Shimber Berris (peak), Som. 155/Q5
Shimizu, Japan 134/C2
Shimizu, Japan 135/B3
Shimo-Koshiki (isl.), Japan 132/A5
Shimobe, Japan 135/A3
Shimoda, Japan 133/F3
Shimodate, Japan 133/F2
Shimofusa, Japan 135/E2
Shimoichi, Japan 135/J7
Shimokita (pen.), Japan 134/B3
Shimonita, Japan 135/B1
Shimonoseki, Japan 132/B4
Shimotsuma, Japan 135/D1
Shimoyama, Japan 135/M5
Shimukappu, Japan 134/C2
Shin, Japan 135/C1
Shin (lake), Sc, UK 89/R7
Shindo, SKor. 131/F6
Shingū, Japan 132/D4
Shinhyŏn, SKor. 132/A3
Shinji (lake), Japan 132/C3
Shinjō, Japan 133/G1
Shinjō, Japan 135/J7
Shinkawa, Japan 135/L5
Shinminato, Japan 133/E2
Shinnecock (bay), NY, US 197/F2
Shinnecock Ind. Res., NY, US 197/F2
Shinsei, Japan 135/L5
Shintoku, Japan 134/C2
Shintone, Japan 135/E2
Shinyanga, Tanz. 162/B3
Shinyanga (pol. reg.), Tanz. 162/B3
Shio-no-misaki (cape), Japan 132/D4
Shiogama, Japan 133/G1
Shioya-saki (pt.), Japan 133/G2
Ship Bottom, NJ, US 196/D4
Shipley, Eng, UK 93/G4
Shippan (pt.), Ct, US 197/L7
Shippegan, NB, Can. 189/H2
Shippo, Japan 135/L5
Shiprock, NM, US 186/E3
Shīr (mtn.), Iran 146/F2
Shirakami-misaki (cape), Japan 134/B3
Shirakawa, Japan 133/G2
Shirakawa, Japan 135/M4
Shirakawa-tōge (pass), Japan 132/E3
Shirako, Japan 135/E3
Shirane, Japan 135/A2
Shirane-san (peak), Japan 133/F3
Shirane-san (peak), Japan 133/F2
Shiranuka, Japan 134/D2
Shiraoi, Japan 134/B2
Shiraoka, Japan 135/D1
Shīrāz, Iran 146/F3
Shirbīn, Egypt 149/B4
Shiretoko-misaki (cape), Japan 134/D1
Shiretoko NP, Japan 134/D1
Shiriya-zaki (pt.), Japan 134/B3
Shirjiu (lake), China 130/D5
Shirley, NY, US 197/F2
Shiroi, Japan 135/E2
Shiroishi, Japan 133/G1
Shirone, Japan 133/F2
Shiroyama, Japan 135/C2
Shīrvān, Iran 147/G1
Shishaldin (vol.), Ak, US 192/F5
Shīshgarh, India 142/B1
Shishi, China 137/C3
Shishmaref, Ak, US 192/E2
Shishou, China 137/B2
Shisui, Japan 135/E2
Shithātha, Iraq 148/E3
Shivpurī, India 142/A3
Shivpuri NP, India 142/A3
Shixing, China 141/K3
Shiyan, China 130/B4
Shizhu, China 137/A2
Shizugawa, Japan 134/B4
Shizuishan, China 128/J4
Shizukuishi, Japan 134/B4
Shizunai, Japan 134/C2
Shizuoka (pref.), Japan 133/E3
Shkumbin (riv.), Alb. 106/E5
Shmidta (cape), Rus. 192/C2
Shoal (pt.), Austl. 170/B4
Shoal Lake, Mb, Can. 185/H3
Shoalhaven (riv.), Austl. 173/D2
Shōbara, Japan 132/C3
Shōbu, Japan 135/D1
Shōdo (isl.), Japan 132/D3
Shoemakersville, Pa, US 196/C3
Shokanbetsu-dake (peak), Japan 134/B2
Sholāpur, India 147/L5
Sholl (peak), Arg. 217/D6
Shomron (ruin), WBnk. 149/G7
Shōnan, Japan 135/E2
Shorāpur, India 140/C4
Shoreham-by-Sea, Eng, UK 91/F5
Shorewood, Wi, US 193/Q13
Shorewood, Il, US 193/P16
Shorkot, Pak. 144/B4
Short (mtn.), Tn, US 191/G3
Shortland (isls.), Sol. 174/E5
Shoshone (riv.), Wy, US 184/F4
Shoshone (mts.), Nv, US 186/C3
Shoshoni, Wy, US 184/F5
Shostka, Ukr. 120/E2
Shotts, Sc, UK 94/C5
Shou Xian, China 130/D4
Shouguang, China 130/D3
Shouyang, China 130/C3
Show Low, Az, US 186/E4
Shōwa, Japan 135/B3
Shōwa, Japan 135/D2
Shpanberga (chan.), Rus. 134/E2
Shpola, Ukr. 120/D2
Shreveport, La, US 187/J4
Shrewsbury, Mo, US 195/G8
Shrewsbury, Eng, UK 90/D1
Shrewsbury, Pa, US 196/B4
Shriner (mtn.), Pa, US 196/A2
Shropshire (co.), Eng, UK 93/E6
Shropshire Union (canal), Eng, UK 93/F6
Shū (riv.), Kaz. 123/H5
Shu (riv.), China 130/D5
Shuangbai, China 141/H3
Shuangcheng, China 129/N2
Shuangliao, China 130/E2
Shuangpai, China 141/K2
Shuangyashan, China 129/P2
Shu'ayb, Jabal an (peak), Yem. 146/D5
Shubrā al Khaymah, Egypt 149/B4
Shubrā Khīt, Egypt 149/B4
Shucheng, China 130/D5
Shu'fāṭ, Isr. 149/G8
Shufu, China 145/G5
Shuiyang (riv.), China 130/D5
Shujāābād, Pak. 144/A5
Shulan, China 129/N3
Shule, China 145/G5
Shule (riv.), China 122/K6
Shumagin (isls.), Ak, US 192/G4
Shumen, Bul. 107/H4
Shumerlya, Rus. 119/K5
Shuna (isl.), Sc, UK 94/A3
Shunak (peak), Kaz. 145/F3
Shungnak, Ak, US 192/G2
Shunyi, China 130/H6
Shuo Xian, China 130/C3
Shupīyan, India 144/C3
Shūr (riv.), Iran 147/G2
Shurugwi, Zim. 163/E4
Shūshtar, Iran 146/E2
Shuswap (lake), BC, Can. 184/D3
Shuwaykah, WBnk. 149/G7
Shuya, Rus. 118/J4
Shuyang, China 130/D4
Shwebo, Myan. 141/G3
Shwegyin, Myan. 141/G4
Shyghys Qazaqstan (obl.), Kaz. 122/J5
Shymkent, Kaz. 145/E4
Shyok (riv.), India 147/L2
Si Satchanalai (ruin), Thai. 136/B2
Si Xian, China 130/D4
Siāh Kūh (mts.), Afg. 147/H2
Siak (riv.), Indo. 138/B3
Siālkot, Pak. 144/C3
Sianów, Pol. 96/G4
Siapa (riv.), Ven. 211/E4
Siargao (isl.), Phil. 137/E6
Siasi, Phil. 139/F2
Siaton (pt.), Phil. 139/F2
Siaton, Phil. 137/D6
Siau (isl.), Indo. 139/G3
Šiauliai, Lith. 97/K4
Sibalom, Phil. 137/D5
Sibay, Rus. 121/L1
Sibbo (Sipoo), Fin. 97/L1
Šibenik, Cro. 106/B4
Siberia (reg.), Rus. 125/H3
Siberut (isl.), Indo. 138/A4
Sibi, Pak. 147/J3
Sibiloi NP, Kenya 155/N7
Sibiti, Congo 163/B1
Sibiu, Rom. 107/G3
Sibiu (prov.), Rom. 107/G2
Sibley, Mo, US 195/E5
Sibolga, Indo. 138/A3
Sibu, Malay. 138/D3
Sibuco, Phil. 139/F2
Sibut, CAfr. 155/J6
Sibuyan (isl.), Phil. 139/F1
Sibuyan (sea), Phil. 139/F1
Sicamous, BC, Can. 184/D3
Sichuan (prov.), China 128/H5
Sicilia (pol. reg.), It. 104/C4
Sicily (isl.), It. 104/C3
Sicily, Strait of (str.), It. 104/B3
Sico (riv.), Hon. 198/D4
Sicuani, Peru 214/D4
Šid, Serb. 106/D3
Siddipet, India 140/C4
Siderno Marina, It. 104/E3
Sideropólis, Braz. 213/B4
Sidewinder (mtn.), Ca, US 194/C1
Sidhaulī, India 142/C2
Sidhi, India 142/C3
Sidhirókastron, Gre. 105/H2
Sidhpur, India 147/K4
Sidi Aïssa, Alg. 158/G5
Sīdī Barrānī, Egypt 159/A2
Sidi Bel-Abbes, Alg. 158/E5
Sidi Bennour, Mor. 156/C2
Sidi Bouzid, Tun. 158/L7
Sidi Bou Zid (gov.), Tun. 158/L7
Sidi Ifni, Mor. 156/C3
Sidi Kacem, Mor. 158/B2
Sidi Kacem (prov.), Mor. 158/B2
Sīdī Sālim, Egypt 149/B4
Sidi Slimane, Mor. 158/B2
Sidi Yahya du Rharb, Mor. 158/A2
Sidlaw (hills), Sc, UK 94/C3
Sidmouth, Eng, UK 90/C5
Sidney, BC, Can. 184/C3
Sidney, Mt, US 185/G4
Sidney, Oh, US 188/C3
Sidney Lanier (lake), Ga, US 191/H3
Sidra (gulf), Libya 154/J1
Sieci, It. 117/E5
Siedlce, Pol. 99/M2
Sieg (riv.), Ger. 101/G1
Siegburg, Ger. 111/G2
Siegen, Ger. 111/H2
Siegenburg, Ger. 113/E5
Siegendorf im Burgenland, Aus. 101/M3
Siemianówka (lake), Pol. 99/M2
Siemiatycze, Pol. 99/M2
Siemreab, Camb. 136/C3
Siena (prov.), It. 117/E6
Siena, It. 101/J5
Sienne (riv.), Fr. 100/C2
Sieradz, Pol. 99/K3
Sieraków, Pol. 99/J2
Sierning, Aus. 113/H6
Sierpc, Pol. 99/K2
Sierra (peak), Ca, US 194/C3
Sierra Blanca, Tx, US 187/F5
Sierra de la Macarena, PN, Col. 208/D3
Sierra de San Pedro Mártir, Mex. 200/B2
Sierra Estrella (mts.), Az, US 195/R19
Sierra Grande, Arg. 216/D4
Sierra Leone (ctry.) 160/B4
Sierra Leone (cape), SLeo. 160/B4
Sierra Madre, Ca, US 194/F7
Sierra Mojada, Mex. 200/E3
Sierra Nevada (mts.), US 186/B3
Sierra Nevada de Santa Marta, PN, Col. 210/C2
Sierra Nevada, PN, Ven. 210/D2
Sierra Vieja (mts.), Mex.,US 190/B4
Sierra Vista, Az, US 186/E5
Sierras Bayas, Arg. 216/E3
Sierre, Swi. 114/D5
Siete Picos (peak), Sp. 103/M8

Siete – Somer

Siete Tazas, PN, Chile 216/C2
Sieve (riv.), It. 117/E5
Sif Fatima, Alg. 157/H3
Sífnos (isl.), Gre. 105/J4
Sig, Alg. 158/E5
Siga Hills (hills), Tanz. 162/B3
Sigean, Fr. 100/E5
Siġġiewi, Malta 104/L7
Sighetu Marmaţiei, Rom. 107/F2
Sighişoara, Rom. 107/G2
Sighty Crag (hill), Eng, UK 93/F1
Sigillo, It. 117/F6
Sigli, Indo. 138/A2
Sigli (cape), Alg. 158/H4
Siglufjördhur, Ice. 95/N6
Sigmaringen, Ger. 115/F1
Sigmarszell, Ger. 115/F2
Signa, It. 117/E5
Signal de la Mère Boitier (peak), Fr. 100/F3
Signal de Toussaines (peak), Fr. 100/B2
Signal d'Écouves (peak), Fr. 100/D2
Signal Hill, Ca, US 194/F8
Signau, Swi. 114/D4
Signy-L'Abbaye, Fr. 111/D4
Signy-le-Petit, Fr. 111/D4
Signy-Signets, Fr. 88/M5
Sigriswil, Swi. 114/D4
Sigtuna, Swe. 96/G2
Siguatepeque, Hon. 202/E3
Sigüenza, Sp. 102/D2
Sihl (riv.), Swi. 115/E3
Sihlsee (lake), Swi. 115/E3
Sihochac, Mex. 202/D2
Sihong, China 130/D4
Sihorā, India 142/C4
Sihuas, Peru 214/B3
Siilinjärvi, Fin. 118/E3
Siirt (prov.), Turk. 148/E2
Siirt, Turk. 148/E2
Sikandarābād, India 142/A1
Sikandarpur, India 143/E2
Sikandra Rao, India 142/B2
Sikanni Chief (riv.), BC, Can. 180/D3
Sīkar, India 147/L3
Sikasso, Mali 160/D4
Sikasso (pol. reg.), Mali 160/D4
Sikeston, Mo, US 187/K3
Sikhote-Alin' (mts.), Rus. 123/P5
Síkinos, Gre. 105/J4
Síkinos (isl.), Gre. 105/J4
Sikkim (state), India 143/G2
Siklós, Hun. 106/D3
Sikoúrion, Gre. 105/H3
Sil (riv.), Sp. 102/B1
Silai (riv.), India 143/F4
Silandro (Schlanders), It. 115/G4
Silao, India 143/E3
Silao, Mex. 201/E4
Sīlat Az Zahr, WBnk. 149/G7
Silay, Phil. 137/D5
Silchar, India 141/F3
Şile, Turk. 107/J5
Silea, It. 117/F1
Silenen, Swi. 115/E4
Silesia (reg.), Pol. 99/H3
Siletitengiz (lake), Kaz. 145/F2
Silgadhī, Nepal 142/C1
Siliana, Tun. 158/L6
Siliana (gov.), Tun. 158/L6
Silifke, Turk. 149/C1
Siliguri, India 143/G2
Silistra, Bul. 107/H3
Silivri, Turk. 107/J5
Siljan (lake), Swe. 96/F1
Siljansnäs, Swe. 96/F1
Silkeborg, Den. 96/C3
Sill (riv.), Aus. 115/H3
Silla, Sp. 103/E3
Silla Tombs, SKor. 131/E5
Sillamäe, Est. 97/M2
Sillānwāli, Pak. 144/B4
Sillaro (riv.), It. 117/E4
Silleda, Sp. 102/A1
Sillian, Aus. 101/K3
Sillustani (ruin), Peru 214/D4
Silly-le-Long, Fr. 88/L4
Siloam Springs, Ar, US 187/J3
Silopi, Turk. 148/E2
Silsbee, Tx, US 187/J5
Silsden, Eng, UK 93/G4
Silsersee (lake), Swi. 115/F5
Siltou (well), Chad 154/J4
Šilutė, Lith. 97/J4
Silvan (dam), Turk. 148/E2
Silvaplana, Swi. 115/F5
Silvassa, India 140/B3
Silver (lake), Or, US 186/B2
Silver (riv.), Or, US 186/C2
Silver (mtn.), Ca, US 194/C1
Silver Bay, Mn, US 185/L4
Silver City, NM, US 186/E4
Silver Lake, Wi, US 193/P14
Silver Lake-Fircrest, Wa, US 193/C2
Silver Meadow (lake), NJ, US 196/C5
Silver Run, Md, US 196/A4
Silver Spring, Md, US 196/A6
Silverado, Ca, US 194/C3
Silverton, Or, US 184/C4
Silverton, Co, US 186/F3
Silverton, NJ, US 196/D3
Silverwood (lake), Ca, US 194/C2
Silves, Port. 102/A4
Silvi, It. 104/D1
Silvia, Col. 210/B4
Silvies (riv.), Or, US 186/C2
Silvretta (mts.), Aus. 115/G4
Silz, Aus. 115/G3
Sim (cape), Mor. 156/C3
Simão Dias, Braz. 212/C3
Simard (lake), Qu, Can. 188/E2
Simav, Turk. 148/B2
Simbach am Inn, Ger. 113/G6
Simcoe, On, Can. 188/D3
Simcoe (lake), Qu, Can. 139/J4
Simdega, India 143/E4
Simēn (mts.), Eth. 155/N5
Simeria, Rom. 106/F3
Simeulue (isl.), Indo. 138/A3
Simferopol', Ukr. 120/E3
Simi (hills), Ca, US 194/B2
Simi Valley, Ca, US 194/B2
Similaun (peak), It. 101/J3
Similaun (peak), Aus.,It. 115/G4
Simiti, Col. 210/C3
Simitli, Bul. 107/F5
Simiyu (riv.), Tanz. 162/B3
Simla, India 144/D4
Simleu Silvaniei, Rom. 107/F2
Simme (riv.), Swi. 101/G3
Simmelsdorf, Ger. 113/E3
Simmerath, Ger. 111/F2
Simmerbach (riv.), Ger. 111/G4
Simmern, Ger. 111/G4
Simmertal, Ger. 111/G4
Simmszand (isl.), Neth. 108/D2
Simni (isl.), NKor. 131/C3
Simo, Fin. 118/E2
Simões, Braz. 212/B2
Simões Filho, Braz. 212/C4
Simojovel de Allende, Mex. 202/C2
Simón Bolívar (int'l arpt.), Ecu. 210/B5
Simoncello (peak), It. 117/F5
Simonstown, SAfr. 164/L11
Simpang-Kiri (riv.), Indo. 138/A3
Simpelveld, Neth. 111/E2
Simplicio Mendes, Braz. 212/B2
Simplon, Swi. 114/E5
Simplonpass (pass), Swi. 114/E5
Simpson (des.), Austl. 171/H3
Simpson (pen.), Nun., Can. 180/G2
Simpson (riv.), Nun., Can. 180/G2
Simpson Desert Conservation Park, Austl. 171/H3
Simpson Desert NP, Austl. 171/H3
Simpsons Gap NP, Austl. 171/G2
Simrishamn, Swe. 96/F4
Simunul, Phil. 139/E3
Sin-le-Noble, Fr. 110/C3
Sinai (pen.), Egypt 155/M1
Sinaia, Rom. 107/G3
Sinaloa (state), Mex. 200/D3
Sinaloa de Leyva, Mex. 200/C3
Sinalunga, It. 101/J5
Sinan, China 137/A2
Sīnāwin, Libya 157/H3
Sincé, Col. 210/C2
Sincelejo, Col. 210/C2
Sinceny, Fr. 110/C4
Sinch'ŏn, NKor. 131/C3
Sinclair, Wy, US 184/G5
Sinclair (lake), Ga, US 191/H3
Sinclair (pt.), Austl. 171/G5
Sincorá, Serra do (range), Braz. 212/B4
Sind (riv.), India 140/C2
Sindal, Den. 96/D3
Sindañgan, Phil. 137/D6
Sindangbarang, Indo. 138/C5
Sindelfingen, Ger. 112/C5
Sindh (prov.), Pak. 140/A2
Sindhulimādi, Nepal 143/E2
Sındırgı, Turk. 148/B2
Sinekçi, Turk. 107/H5
Sinendé, Ben. 161/F4
Sines, Port. 102/A4
Sines (cape), Port. 102/A4
Sinfra, C.d'Iv. 160/D5
Sing Buri, Thai. 136/C3
Singapore (ctry.) 138/B3
Singapore (cap.), Sing. 138/B3
Singen, Ger. 115/E2
Singeorz-Băi, Rom. 107/G2
Singida (pol. reg.), Tanz. 162/B4
Singida, Tanz. 162/B4
Singitic (gulf), Gre. 105/H2
Singkawang, Indo. 138/C3
Singkep (isl.), Indo. 138/B4
Singleton, Austl. 173/D2
Singleton (mt.), Austl. 170/C4
Singleton (mt.), Austl. 171/F2
Singou, Réserve Totale de Faune du, Burk. 161/F4
Sinincay, Ecu. 210/B5
Siniscola, It. 104/A2
Sinjār, Iraq 148/E2
Sinjil, WBnk. 149/G7
Sinn (riv.), Ger. 98/E3
Sinnam-dok-san (peak), NKor. 131/D2
Sinnamary, FrG. 209/H2
Sinnard, Co, US 195/C1
Sînnicolau Mare, Rom. 106/E2
Sinnūris, Egypt 149/B5
Sinnyŏng, SKor. 131/E4
Sino (co.), Libr. 160/C5
Sinoe (lake), Rom. 107/J3
Sinop, Braz. 209/G6
Sinop, Turk. 148/C1
Sinop (prov.), Turk. 148/C1
Sinop (pt.), Turk. 148/C1
Sinp'o, NKor. 131/E2
Sint-Genesius-Rode, Belg. 111/D2
Sint-Gillis-Waas, Belg. 108/B6
Sint-Katelijne-Waver, Belg. 111/D1
Sint-Laureins, Belg. 110/C1
Sint-Martens-Voeren, Belg. 111/E2
Sint-Michielsgestel, Neth. 108/C5
Sint-Niklaas, Belg. 108/B6
Sint-Oedenrode, Neth. 108/C5
Sint-Pieters-Leeuw, Belg. 111/D2
Sint-Truiden, Belg. 111/E2
Sint'aein, SKor. 131/D5
Sintang, Indo. 138/D3
Sinton, Tx, US 190/D4
Sintra, Port. 103/P10
Sintra (range), Port. 103/P10
Sinú (riv.), Col. 208/C2
Sinŭiju, NKor. 131/C2
Sinzheim, Ger. 112/B5
Sinzig, Ger. 111/G2
Sió (riv.), Hun. 106/D2
Siocon, Phil. 139/F2
Siófok, Hun. 106/D2
Sioma Ngwezi NP, Zam. 163/D4
Sion, Swi. 114/D5
Sion Mills, NI, UK 89/Q9
Sioule (riv.), Fr. 100/E4
Sioux City, Ia, US 185/J5
Sioux Lookout, On, Can. 185/L3
Sipalay, Phil. 137/D6
Sipaliwini (dist.), Sur. 211/H4
Sipaliwini (riv.), Sur. 211/G4
Sipanok (chan.), Mb,Sk, Can. 185/H2
Siparia, Trin. 211/F2
Sipí, Col. 210/B3
Siping, China 130/F2
Sipiwesk (lake), Mb, Can. 180/G3
Siple (isl.), Ant. 218/R
Siponto (ruin), It. 104/D2
Sipsey (riv.), Al, US 191/G3
Sipura (isl.), Indo. 138/A4
Siqueira Campos, Braz. 213/B2
Siquia (riv.), Nic. 198/E5
Siquisique, Ven. 210/D2
Sir Alexander (mt.), BC, Can. 184/C2
Sir Edward Pellew Group (isls.), Austl. 167/C2
Sir James Macbrien (mt.), NW, Can. 180/D2
Sir James Mitchell NP, Austl. 170/C5
Sir John (cape), Austl. 173/D4
Sir Seewoosagur Ramgoolam (int'l arpt.), Mrts. 165/T15
Sir Thomas (mt.), Austl. 171/F3
Sira (riv.), Nor. 95/C4
Siracusa (Syracuse), It. 104/D4
Sirājganj, Bang. 143/G3
Şiran, Turk. 148/D1
Sirdaryo (pol. reg.), Uzb. 145/E4
Siret, Rom. 107/H2
Siret (riv.), Rom. 107/H2
Sirha, Nepal 143/F2
Sirhind, India 144/D4
Sirik (cape), Malay. 138/D3
Sīrīk, Iran 147/G3
Sirikit (res.), Thai. 141/H4
Sirinhaém, Braz. 212/D3
Sīrīs, WBnk. 149/G7
Sirius (pt.), Ak, US 192/B5
Sirmilik Nat'l Park, Nun., Can. 139/J1
Sirmione, It. 116/D2
Sirnach, Swi. 115/F3
Şırnak, Turk. 148/E2
Širolo, It. 117/G5
Sironj, India 142/A3
Siros (isl.), Gre. 105/J4
Siroua (peak), Mor. 156/D3
Sirsa, India 144/C5
Sirsāganj, India 142/B2
Sirsi, India 142/B1
Sirsi, India 147/K6
Sisak, Cro. 106/C3
Sisaket, Thai. 136/D3
Sishui, China 130/D4
Sisikon, Swi. 115/E4
Sisipuk (lake), Mb,Sk, Can. 185/H2
Sissach, Swi. 114/D3
Sisseton, SD, US 185/J4
Sissili (prov.), Burk. 161/E4
Sissonne, Fr. 110/C4
Sissonville, WV, US 188/D4
Sisterdale, Tx, US 195/T20
Sisteron, Fr. 100/F4
Siswā Bāzār, India 142/D2
Sitacocha, Peru 214/B2
Sitākund, Bang. 143/H4
Sītāmarhi, India 143/E2
Sītāpur, India 142/C2
Sītārganj, India 142/B1
Siteki, Swaz. 165/E2
Site of World Trade Center, NY, US 197/J9
Sitges, Sp. 103/K7
Sithoniá (pen.), Gre. 105/J2
Sitía, Gre. 105/K5
Sitidgi (lake), NW, Can. 192/M2
Sítio Novo do Grajaú, Braz. 212/A2
Sitka, Ak, US 192/L4
Sitno (peak), Slvk. 106/D1
Sittard, Neth. 111/E2
Sittensen, Ger. 109/G2
Sitter (riv.), Swi. 115/F3
Sittingbourne, Eng, UK 91/G4
Sitton (peak), Ca, US 194/C3
Sittwe (Akyab), Myan. 141/F3
Sivac, Serb. 106/D3
Sivakāsi, India 140/C6
Sīvand, Iran 146/F2
Sivas, Turk. 148/D2
Sivas (prov.), Turk. 148/D2
Siverek, Turk. 148/D2
Siviriez, Swi. 114/C4
Sivrihisar, Turk. 148/B2
Sivry-Courtry, Fr. 88/L6
Siwa Oasis (oasis), Egypt 159/A2
Sīwah, Egypt 155/L2
Siwalik (range), Nepal 140/B1
Siwān, India 143/E2
Siwāni, India 144/C5
Six Flags Great Adventure, NJ, US 196/D3
Six Flags Great America, Il, US 193/Q15
Six Flags Magic Mountain, Ca, US 194/B2
Sixmilecross, NI, UK 92/A2
Sixth (falls), Sudan 155/M4
Siyabuswa, SAfr. 163/E6
Siyāna, India 142/B1
Siyang, China 130/D4
Siziano, It. 116/C2
Siziwang, China 129/K3
Sjælland (isl.), Den. 95/D5
Sjenica, Serb. 106/E4
Sjöbo, Swe. 96/E4
Sjónfridh (peak), Ice. 95/M6
Sjuntorp, Swe. 96/E2
Skaftafell NP, Ice. 95/P7
Skagen, Den. 96/D3
Skagens (The Skaw) (cape), Den. 96/D3
Skagern (lake), Swe. 96/F2
Skagerrak (str.), Den.,Nor. 96/C3
Skaget (peak), Nor. 96/C1
Skagway, Ak, US 192/L3
Skála, Gre. 105/H4
Skälderviken (bay), Swe. 96/E3
Skálfandafljót (riv.), Ice. 95/P7
Skalica, Slvk. 99/J4
Skalice (riv.), Czh. 101/K2
Skalka (res.), Czh. 113/F2
Skælskør, Den. 96/D4
Skanderborg, Den. 96/C3
Skåne (reg.), Swe. 96/E4
Skanes (int'l arpt.), Tun. 158/M7
Skånland, Nor. 95/F1
Skänninge, Swe. 96/F2
Skanör, Swe. 96/E4
Skantzoura (isl.), Gre. 105/J3
Skara, Swe. 96/E2
Skaraborg (co.), Swe. 95/E4
Skärblacka, Swe. 96/F2
Skåre, Swe. 96/E2
Skarszewy, Pol. 96/H4
Skarżysko-Kamienna, Pol. 99/L3
Skateraw, Sc, UK 94/D5
Skattkärr, Swe. 96/E2
Skawina, Pol. 99/K4
Skeena (riv.), BC, Can. 180/D3
Skeena (mts.), BC, Can. 180/D3
Skegness, Eng, UK 93/J5
Skellefteå, Swe. 95/G2
Skellefteälven (riv.), Swe. 95/F2
Skelleftehamn, Swe. 95/G2
Skelmersdale, Eng, UK 93/F4
Skelmorlie, Sc, UK 94/B5
Skerne (riv.), Eng, UK 93/G2
Skerries, Ire. 92/B4
Skhimatárion, Gre. 105/H3
Skhirat, Mor. 158/A3
Skhirat Temara (prov.), Mor. 158/A3
Skhiza (isl.), Gre. 105/G4
Skhodnya (riv.), Rus. 119/W9
Ski, Nor. 96/D2
Skiathos, Gre. 105/H3
Skiatook, Ok, US 187/H3
Skibbereen, Ire. 89/P11
Skidegate, BC, Can. 192/M5
Skídhra, Gre. 105/H2
Skien, Nor. 96/C2
Skierniewice, Pol. 99/L3
Skikda, Alg. 158/K6
Skinári (cape), Gre. 105/G4
Skinnskatteberg, Swe. 96/F2
Skipton, Eng, UK 93/F4
Skirfare (riv.), Eng, UK 93/F3
Skíros, Gre. 105/J3
Skive, Den. 96/C3
Skjærhollen, Nor. 96/D2
Skjeberg, Nor. 96/D2
Skjelåtinden (peak), Nor. 95/E2
Skjern, Den. 96/C4
Skjern (riv.), Den. 96/C4
Škofja Loka, Slov. 101/L3
Skoghall, Swe. 96/E2
Skogstorp, Swe. 96/G2
Skokholm (isl.), Wal, UK 90/A3
Skokie (riv.), Il, US 193/Q15
Skokloster, Swe. 96/G2
Sköllersta, Swe. 96/F2
Skolniki Park, Rus. 119/W9
Skomer (isl.), Wal, UK 90/A3
Skópelos (isl.), Gre. 105/H3
Skópelos, Gre. 105/H3
Skopin, Rus. 120/F1
Skopje (cap.), FYROM 105/G1
Skopje (int'l arpt.), FYROM 106/E5
Skotterud, Nor. 96/E2
Skoútari, Gre. 105/H2
Skövde, Swe. 96/E2
Skowhegan, Me, US 189/G2
Skukum (mt.), Yk, Can. 192/L3
Skull, Ire. 89/P11
Skultorp, Swe. 96/E2
Skultuna, Swe. 96/G2
Skunk (riv.), Ia, US 188/A3
Skurup, Swe. 99/G1
Skutskär, Swe. 96/G1
Skwentna, Ak, US 192/H3
Skwierzyna, Pol. 99/H2
Skye (isl.), Sc, UK 89/Q8
Skyring (sound), Chile 217/B7
Skytop, Pa, US 196/C1
Slagelse, Den. 96/D4
Slakovský Les (for.), Czh. 113/F2
Slamannan, Sc, UK 94/C5
Slana, Ak, US 192/K3
Slaná (riv.), Slvk. 99/L4
Slane, Ire. 92/B4
Slaney (riv.), Ire. 89/Q10
Slănic, Rom. 107/G3
Slănic-Moldova, Rom. 107/H2
Slantsy, Rus. 97/N2
Slaný, Czh. 113/H2
Slapy (res.), Czh. 113/H3
Śląskie (prov.), Pol. 99/K3
Slatedale, Pa, US 196/C2
Slatina, Rom. 107/G3
Slatington, Pa, US 196/C2
Slaton, Tx, US 187/G4
Slattum, Nor. 96/D1
Slaughter Beach, De, US 196/C6
Slaughterville, Ok, US 195/N15
Slave (coast), Afr. 161/F5
Slave (riv.), NW, Can. 180/E2
Slave Lake, Ab, Can. 184/E2
Slavgorod, Rus. 145/G2
Slavkov u Brna, Czh. 101/M2
Slavonia (reg.), Cro. 106/C3
Slavonska Požega, Cro. 106/C3
Slavonski Brod, Cro. 106/D3
Slavuta, Ukr. 120/C2
Slavyanovo, Bul. 107/G4
Slavyansk-na-Kubani, Rus. 120/F3
Sławno, Pol. 96/G4
Sleen, Neth. 108/D3
Sleeper (isls.), On, Can. 139/H3
Sleeping Bear Dunes Nat'l Lakeshore, US 188/C2
Sleepy Hollow, NY, US 197/K7
Sleepy Hollow, Il, US 193/P15
Sleetmute, Ak, US 192/G3
Slidell, La, US 195/Q16
Sliedrecht, Neth. 108/B5
Sliema, Malta 104/M7
Slieve Binnian (peak), NI, UK 92/C3
Slieve Croob (peak), NI, UK 92/C3
Slieve Donard (peak), NI, UK 92/C3
Slieve Gullion (peak), NI, UK 92/B3
Slieve Snaght (peak), Ire. 92/A1
Slioch (peak), Sc, UK 94/A1
Slite, Swe. 97/H3
Sliven, Bul. 107/H4
Slivnitsa, Bul. 106/F4
Sloan, NY, US 189/S10
Sloatsburg, NY, US 197/J7
Slobodskoy, Rus. 119/L4
Slobozia, Rom. 107/H3
Slochteren, Neth. 108/D2
Slonim, Bela. 120/C1
Sloten, Neth. 108/C3
Slotermeer (lake), Neth. 108/C3
Slough, Eng, UK 88/B2
Slough (co.), Eng, UK 88/B2
Slovakia (ctry.) 99/K4
Slovenia (ctry.) 106/B3
Slovenj Gradec, Slov. 101/L3
Slovenska Bistrica, Slov. 101/L3
Slovenská Ľupča, Slvk. 99/K4
Slovenske Konjice, Slov. 101/L3
Slovenské Rudohorie (mts.), Slvk. 99/L4
Slov'yans'k, Ukr. 120/F2
Słowiński PN, Pol. 96/G4
Słubice, Pol. 99/H2
Sluch' (riv.), Ukr. 120/C2
Sluderno (Schluderns), It. 115/G4
Sluis, Neth. 110/C1
Słupca, Pol. 99/J2
Słupia (riv.), Pol. 96/G4
Słupsk, Pol. 96/G4
Slutsk, Bela. 120/C1
Slyne Head (pt.), Ire. 88/F10
Smålandsstenar, Swe. 96/E3
Smallwood (res.), Nf, Can. 139/K3
Smeaton, Sk, Can. 185/G2
Smederevo, Serb. 106/E3
Smederevska Palanka, Serb. 106/E3
Smedjebacken, Swe. 96/F1
Smendou (riv.), Alg. 158/J4
Śmigiel, Pol. 99/J2
Smila, Ukr. 120/D2
Smilde, Neth. 108/D3
Smith (riv.), Mt, US 184/F4
Smith (inlet), BC, Can. 184/B3
Smith (isl.), Qu, Can. 139/J2
Smith Mountain (lake), Va, US 188/E4
Smith Village, Ok, US 195/N15
Smithburg, NJ, US 196/D3
Smithers, BC, Can. 184/B2
Smithfield, Ut, US 184/F5
Smithfield, NC, US 191/J3
Smiths Creek, Mi, US 193/G6
Smiths Falls, On, Can. 188/E2
Smithton, Austl. 173/C4
Smithton, Il, US 195/H9
Smithtown (bay), NY, US 197/E2
Smithtown, NY, US 197/E2
Smithville, Ok, US 190/E3
Smithville (lake), Mo, US 195/D5
Smithville, Mo, US 195/D5
Smoky (cape), Austl. 173/E1
Smoky (hills), Ks, US 187/H3
Smoky (riv.), Ab, Can. 180/E3
Smoky Hill (riv.), Ks, US 187/G3
Smoky Lake, Ab, Can. 184/E2
Smøla (isl.), Nor. 95/C3
Smolensk, Rus. 118/G5
Smolenskaya Oblast, Rus. 118/F5
Smólikas (peak), Gre. 105/G2
Smolyan, Bul. 107/G5
Smooth Rock Falls, On, Can. 188/D1
Smrčina (peak), Czh. 113/G5
Smutná (riv.), Czh. 113/H4
Smyadovo, Bul. 107/H4
Smyrna, Ga, US 191/G3
Smyrna (riv.), De, US 196/C5
Smyrna, De, US 196/C5
Snaefell (peak), IM, UK 92/D3
Snake (riv.), US 184/D4
Snake River (plain), Id, US 184/E5
Snares (isls.), NZ 175/R12
Snåsa, Nor. 95/E2
Snedsted, Den. 96/C3
Sneek, Neth. 108/C2
Sneekermeer (lake), Neth. 108/C2
Sneeuberg (peak), SAfr. 164/B4
Sneeuberg (mts.), SAfr. 164/D3
Sneeuwkop (peak), SAfr. 164/L11
Snejbjerg, Den. 96/C3
Sněžka (peak), Czh. 99/H3
Snežnik (peak), Slov. 101/L4
Sni Mills, Mo, US 195/E6
Śniardwy (lake), Pol. 99/L2
Snodland, Eng, UK 91/G4
Snøhetta (peak), Nor. 95/D3
Snohomish, Wa, US 193/C2
Snohomish (co.), Wa, US 193/C2
Snohomish (riv.), Wa, US 193/C2
Snoqualmie (riv.), Wa, US 193/D2
Snoqualmie (falls), Wa, US 193/D2
Snoqualmie, Wa, US 193/D2
Snoqualmie Falls, Wa, US 193/D2
Snoqualmie, Middle Fk. (riv.), Wa, US 193/D2
Snoqualmie, North Fork (riv.), Wa, US 193/D2
Snoqualmie, South Fork (riv.), Wa, US 193/D3
Snøtind (peak), Nor. 95/E2
Snowdon (peak), IM, UK 92/D5
Snowdonia NP, Wal, UK 92/D6
Snowflake, Az, US 186/E4
Snowtown, Austl. 171/H5
Snowy (peak), Ak, US 192/K2
Snowy (riv.), Austl. 173/D3
Snowy River NP, Austl. 173/D3
Snyder (co.), Pa, US 196/A2
Snydertown, Pa, US 196/B2
Snyderville, Ut, US 195/K12
Soalala, Madg. 165/H7
Soanierana-Ivongo, Madg. 165/J7
Soanindrariny, Madg. 165/H7
Soar (riv.), Eng, UK 93/G6
Soavina, Madg. 165/H8
Soavinandriana, Madg. 165/H7
Sobaek (mts.), SKor. 131/D5
Soběslav, Czh. 113/H4
Sobger (riv.), Indo. 139/K4
Sobhādero, Pak. 147/J3
Sobradinho, Represa (res.), Braz. 205/E3
Sobral, Braz. 212/B1
Sobretta (peak), It. 115/G5
Sobue, Japan 135/L5
Soc Trang, Viet. 136/D4
Soča (riv.), Slov. 101/K3
Socabaya, Peru 214/D5
Sochaczew, Pol. 99/L2
Sochi, Rus. 120/F4
Söch'ŏn, SKor. 131/D4
Söchtenau, Ger. 113/F7
Soci, It. 117/E5
Society (isls.), FrPol. 175/K6
Socorro, Braz. 213/G7
Socorro, Col. 210/C3
Socorro, NM, US 186/F4
Socorro (isl.), NM, Mex. 200/C5
Socorro, Tx, US 187/F5
Socota, Peru 214/B2
Socotá, Col. 210/C3
Socotra (isl.), Yem. 125/E8
Socuéllamos, Sp. 102/D3
Soda Springs, Id, US 184/F5
Sodankylä, Fin. 118/E2
Sodegaura, Japan 135/D3
Söderbärke, Swe. 96/F1
Söderfors, Swe. 96/G1
Söderhamn, Swe. 96/G1
Söderköping, Swe. 96/G2
Södermanland (co.), Swe. 95/E4
Södertälje, Swe. 96/G2
Sodo, Eth. 155/N6
Södu (riv.), NKor. 131/E2
Sodwana Bay NP, SAfr. 165/F2
Soest, Ger. 109/F5
Soest, Neth. 108/C4
Soeste (riv.), Ger. 98/D2
Sofádhes, Gre. 105/H3
Sofia (Sofiya) (cap.), Bul. 49/F4
Sofia (int'l arpt.), Bul. 107/F4
Sofiya (prov.), Bul. 49/F4
Sogamoso (riv.), Col. 210/C3
Sogamoso, Col. 210/C3
Sögel, Ger. 109/E3
Sogn Og Fjordane (co.), Nor. 95/C3
Sognafjorden (inlet), Nor. 95/C3
Sogndal, Nor. 96/B1
Søgne, Nor. 96/B2
Sogollé (well), Chad 154/J4
Soğuksu NP, Turk. 148/C1
Söğüt, Turk. 148/B1
Söğütlü, Turk. 107/K5
Sogwass (peak), Ugan. 162/B2
Sohāgpur, India 142/B4
Sohren, Ger. 111/G4
Sŏhŭng, NKor. 131/D3
Soignies, Belg. 111/D2
Soignolles-en-Brie, Fr. 88/L6
Soissons, Fr. 110/C5
Sōja, Japan 132/C3
Sojat, India 147/K3
Sŏjosŏn (bay), NKor. 131/C3
Sok (riv.), Rus. 121/J1
Sok (pt.), Thai. 136/C3
Sōka, Japan 135/D2
Sokch'o, SKor. 131/E3
Söke, Turk. 148/A2
Sokhós, Gre. 105/H2
Sokhumi, Geo. 121/G4
Sokna, Nor. 96/C1
Soko (isls.), China 129/T11
Soko Banja, Serb. 106/E4
Sokodé, Togo 161/F4
Sokol, Rus. 118/J4
Sokol (peak), Czh. 113/G4
Sokółka, Pol. 99/M2
Sokolov, Czh. 113/F2
Sokołów Podlaski, Pol. 99/M2
Sokoto (plain), Nga. 154/F5
Sokoto (riv.), Nga. 154/F5
Sokoto, Nga. 161/G3
Sokoto (state), Nga. 161/G3
Sol, Costa del (coast), Sp. 102/C4
Sol'-Iletsk, Rus. 121/K2
Sola, Nor. 96/A2
Sola (int'l arpt.), Nor. 96/A2
Solana, Phil. 137/D4
Solana Beach, Ca, US 194/C5
Solânea, Braz. 212/D2
Solano (pt.), Col. 210/B3
Solano, Phil. 137/D4
Solano (co.), Ca, US 193/L10
Solarolo, It. 117/E4
Solca, Rom. 107/G2
Sölden, Aus. 115/H4
Soldier (riv.), Ia, US 187/J2
Soldotna, Ak, US 192/H3
Soledad, Col. 210/C2
Soledad, Ven. 211/F2
Soledad Canyon (canyon), Ca, US 194/B2
Soledad de Doblado, Mex. 201/N7
Soledad de Graciano, Mex. 201/E4
Soledade, Braz. 213/A4
Solent, The (chan.), Eng, UK 91/E5
Solesino, It. 117/E2
Solesmes, Fr. 110/C3
Soleuvre (peak), Lux. 111/E4
Solferino, It. 116/D2
Solhan, Turk. 148/E2
Soliera, It. 117/D3
Soligo, It. 117/F1
Solihull, Eng, UK 91/E2
Solihull (co.), Eng, UK 91/E2
Solimões (riv.), Braz. 211/E5
Solingen, Ger. 108/E6
Sollefteå, Swe. 95/F3
Sollentuna, Swe. 96/G2
Sóller, Sp. 103/G3
Sollerön, Swe. 96/F1
Solling (mts.), Ger. 98/E3
Solmsbach (riv.), Ger. 112/B2
Søln (peak), Nor. 95/D3
Solnan (riv.), Fr. 100/F3
Solntsevo, Rus. 119/W9
Solo (riv.), Indo. 138/D5
Solok, Indo. 138/B4
Sololá, Guat. 202/D3
Solomon, Ak, US 192/F3
Solomon (riv.), Ks, US 187/H3
Solomon (sea), PNG,Sol. 174/D5
Solomon Islands (ctry.) 174/E6
Solomon, North Fork (riv.), US 187/G3
Solonchak Goklenkui (swamp), Trkm. 145/C4
Solonópole, Braz. 212/C2
Solothurn, Swi. 114/D3
Solothurn (canton), Swi. 114/D3
Solovetskiy (isls.), Rus. 118/G2
Solre-le-Château, Fr. 111/D3
Solsona, Sp. 103/F2
Solt, Hun. 106/D2
Šolta (isl.), Cro. 104/E1
Soltau, Ger. 109/G3
Soltustik Qazaqstan (obl.), Kaz. 122/G4
Soltvadkert, Hun. 106/D2
Solunska (peak), FYROM 105/G2
Solva (riv.), Wal, UK 90/A3
Solvang, Ca, US 186/B4
Sölvesborg, Swe. 96/F3
Solway Firth (inlet), Eng.,Sc, UK 92/E2
Solwezi, Zam. 163/E3
Solymár, Hun. 107/Q9
Sōma, Japan 133/G2
Soma, Turk. 148/A2
Somain, Fr. 110/C3
Somalia (ctry.) 155/Q6
Sombor, Serb. 106/D3
Sombra, On, Can. 193/H6
Sombreffe, Belg. 111/D2
Sombrerete, Mex. 200/E4
Sombrio, Braz. 213/B4
Someren, Neth. 108/C6
Somero, Fin. 97/K1
Somers, Mt, US 184/E3
Somers, Wi, US 193/Q14
Somers Point, NJ, US 196/D5
Somerset (isl.), Nun., Can. 180/G1
Somerset (co.), Eng, UK 90/D4
Somerset, Ky, US 188/C4
Somerset, NY, US 189/S9
Somerset, Pa, US 196/D3
Somerset, Tx, US 195/T21

Somerset East, SAfr. 164/D4
Somerset West, SAfr. 164/L11
Somersworth, NH, US 189/G3
Somerton, Az, US 186/D4
Somerville (lake), Tx, US 187/H5
Somerville, NJ, US 196/D2
Someş (riv.), Rom. 107/F2
Someşul Mare (riv.), Serb. 107/G2
Someswar (range), India 143/E2
Somis, Ca, US 194/B2
Sŏmjin (riv.), SKor. 131/D5
Somma Lombardo, It. 116/B1
Sommacampagna, It. 117/D2
Sommam (riv.), Alg. 158/H4
Sommariva del Bosco, It. 116/A3
Somme (bay), Fr. 100/D1
Somme (dept.), Fr. 110/B4
Somme (riv.), Fr. 98/B3
Somme, Canal de la (canal), Fr. 110/B4
Somme-Leuze, Belg. 111/E3
Somme-Soude (riv.), Fr. 111/D6
Sommedieue, Fr. 111/E5
Sommen (lake), Swe. 96/F2
Sommet de Finiels (peak), Fr. 100/E4
Sommevoire, Fr. 114/A1
Somogy (prov.), Hun. 106/C2
Somoto, Nic. 202/E3
Son (riv.), India 140/D3
Son Servera, Sp. 103/G3
Sona, It. 117/D2
Sonāmukhi, India 143/F4
Sonāmura, India 143/H4
Sonār (riv.), India 142/B4
Sonchamp, Fr. 88/H6
Sŏnch'ŏn, NKor. 131/C3
Soncino, It. 116/C2
Sondalo, It. 115/G5
Sønder Nissum, Den. 96/C3
Sonderborg (int'l arpt.), Den. 96/C4
Sønderborg, Den. 96/C4
Sonderend (riv.), SAfr. 164/L11
Sønderjylland (co.), Den. 96/C4
Sondica (int'l arpt.), Sp. 102/D1
Sondrio, It. 115/F5
Sondrio (dept.), It. 115/F5
Sonepur, India 140/D3
Song (peak), China 130/C4
Song Xian, China 130/C4
Songea, Tanz. 162/B5
Songeons, Fr. 110/A4
Songhua (riv.), China 129/P2
Sŏnghwan, SKor. 131/D4
Songi (isl.), SKor. 131/C5
Songino, Mong. 128/G2
Songjiang, China 130/L8
Sŏngju, SKor. 131/E5
Songkhla, Thai. 136/C5
Songkhram (riv.), Thai. 141/H4
Songling, China 129/M2
Songming, China 141/H2
Sŏngnam, SKor. 131/G7
Songnim, NKor. 131/C3
Songololo, D.R. Congo 163/B2
Songt'an, SKor. 131/D4
Songtao Miaozu Zizhixian, China 137/A2
Songxi, China 137/C2
Songzi, China 137/B1
Songzi (pass), China 130/C5
Soni, Japan 135/K6
Sonid Youqi, China 129/K3
Sonid Zuoqi, China 129/K3
Sonīpat, India 144/D5
Sonneberg, Ger. 112/E2
Sonnefeld, Ger. 112/E2
Sonnjoch (peak), Aus. 115/H3
Sonntagshorn (peak), Ger. 101/K3
Sonobe, Japan 135/H5
Sonoma (co.), Ca, US 193/J10
Sonoma (mts.), Ca, US 193/J10
Sonora (state), Mex. 200/C2
Sonora, Ca, US 186/B3
Sonora, Tx, US 187/G5
Sonoran Desert Nat'l Mon., Az, US 186/D4
Sonoyta, Mex. 200/B2
Sonoyta (riv.), Mex. 200/B2
Sonpur, India 143/E3
Sonqor, Iran 146/E2
Sŏnsan, SKor. 131/E4
Sonsbeck, Ger. 108/D5
Sonseca, Sp. 102/D3
Sonsonate, ESal. 202/D3
Sonsorol (isls.), Palau 174/C4
Sonta, Serb. 106/D3
Sontheim, Ger. 115/G2
Sontheim an der Brenz, Ger. 112/D5
Sonthofen, Ger. 115/G2
Sontra, Ger. 109/G6
Sonvico, Swi. 115/E5
Sopetrán, Col. 210/C3
Sopi (cape), Indo. 139/G3
Sopor, India 144/C2
Sopot, Bul. 107/G4
Sopot, Pol. 96/H4
Sopron, Hun. 101/M3
Sôr (riv.), Wal, UK 90/D3
Sor Karatuley (salt pan), Kaz. 145/C4
Sør-Trøndelag (co.), Nor. 95/D3
Sør-Varanger, Nor. 95/J1
Sora, It. 104/C2
Soragna, It. 116/D3
Sŏrak-san (peak), SKor. 131/E3
Sŏraksan NP, SKor. 131/E3
Sorata, Bol. 208/E7
Sorbas, Sp. 102/D4
Sorbolo, It. 116/D3
Sorcy-Saint-Martin, Fr. 111/E6
Sorel, Qu, Can. 188/F2
Sorell-Midway Point, Austl. 173/C4
Soresina, It. 116/C2
Sörforsa, Swe. 96/G1
Sorgues, Fr. 100/F5
Sorgun, Turk. 148/C2
Sori, It. 116/C4
Soria, Sp. 102/D2
Soriano (dept.), Uru. 216/J10
Soriano, Uru. 217/J10
Sorikmerapi (peak), Indo. 138/A3
Soritor, Peru 214/B2
Sormonne (riv.), Fr. 111/D4
Sorø, Den. 96/D4
Soro, Rio do (riv.), Braz. 209/J5
Soroca, Mol. 107/J1
Sorocaba, Braz. 213/C2
Sorochinsk, Rus. 121/K1
Sorol (isl.), Micr. 174/D4
Soron, India 142/B2
Sorong, Indo. 139/H4
Soroti, Ugan. 162/B2
Sørøya (isl.), Nor. 95/G1
Sørøysundet (chan.), Nor. 95/G1
Sorpestausee (lake), Ger. 109/E6
Sorraia (riv.), Port. 102/A3
Sorrento, It. 104/D2
Sorsele, Swe. 95/F2
Sorso, It. 104/A2
Sorsogon, Phil. 137/D5
Sort, Sp. 103/F1
Sörve (pt.), Est. 97/K3
Sos del Rey Católico, Sp. 102/E1
Sŏsan, SKor. 131/D4
Sŏsan Haean NP, SKor. 131/C4
Sösdala, Swe. 96/E3
Söse (riv.), Ger. 109/H5
Soshanguve, SAfr. 163/E6
Sosna (riv.), Rus. 120/F1
Sosneado (peak), Arg. 216/C2
Sosnogorsk, Rus. 119/M3
Sosnovka, Rus. 119/L4
Sosnowiec, Pol. 99/K3
Sospiro, It. 116/D2
Sosúa, DRep. 199/G4
Sos'va (riv.), Rus. 122/G3
Sot (riv.), India 142/B1
Soto del Real, Sp. 103/N8
Soto la Marina, Mex. 201/F4
Sotouboua, Togo 161/F4
Sottrum, Ger. 109/G2
Sotuta, Mex. 202/D1
Soude (riv.), Fr. 111/D6
Souderton, Pa, US 196/C3
Soúdha, Gre. 105/J5
Souffelweyersheim, Fr. 111/G6
Soufflenheim, Fr. 111/G6
Souflion, Gre. 105/K2
Soufrière (peak), StV. 199/N9
Soufrière (peak), Guad., Fr. 199/N8
Souillac, Fr. 100/D4
Souillac, Mrts. 165/T15
Souk Ahras, Alg. 158/K6
Souk Ahras (prov.), Alg. 158/K6
Souk el Arba du Rharb, Mor. 158/A2
Sŏul (Seoul) (cap.), SKor. 129/N4
Soultz-Haut-Rhin, Fr. 114/D2
Soultz-sous-Forêts, Fr. 112/A5
Soum (prov.), Burk. 161/E3
Soumagne, Belg. 111/E2
Sound, The (chan.), Den. 95/E5
Souppes-sur-Loing, Fr. 100/E2
Sour El Ghozlane, Alg. 158/G4
Sources, Mont aux (peak), Les. 164/E3
Soure, Braz. 209/J4
Soure, Port. 102/A2
Souris, Mb, Can. 185/H3
Souris, PE, Can. 189/J2
Souris (riv.), Can.,US 185/H3
Sourou (prov.), Burk. 160/E3
Sous le Vent, Iles (isls.), FrPol. 175/K6
Sousa, Braz. 212/C2
Sousse, Tun. 158/M7
Sousse (gov.), Tun. 158/M7
Sout (riv.), SAfr. 164/C3
South (mts.), NS, Can. 189/H2
South (bay), Nun., Can. 181/H2
South (cape), NZ 175/R12
South (isl.), NZ 175/S11
South (mtn.), Pa, US 196/A3
South Africa (ctry.) 163/D6
South Amboy, NJ, US 197/H10
South America (cont.) 147
South Andaman (isl.), India 141/F5
South Anna (riv.), Va, US 191/J2
South Augusta, Ga, US 191/H3
South Aulatsivik (isl.), Nf, Can. 181/K3
South Australia (state), Austl. 167/C3
South Ayrshire (pol. reg.), Sc, UK 94/B6
South Bend, In, US 188/C3
South Bend, Wa, US 184/C4
South Benfleet, Eng, UK 91/G3
South Buganda (prov.), Ugan. 162/A3
South Burlington, Vt, US 188/F2
South Caicos (isl.), UK 203/J1
South Carolina (state), US 191/H3
South China (sea), Asia 125/L8
South Colby, Wa, US 193/B2
South Dakota (state), US 185/H4
South Dorset Downs (uplands), Eng, UK 90/D5
South Downs (hills), Eng, UK 91/F5
South Dum Dum, India 143/G4
South East (pt.), Austl. 173/C3
South East (cape), Austl. 173/C4
South Elgin, Il, US 193/P16
South Esk (riv.), Austl. 173/C4
South Esk (riv.), Sc, UK 94/C3
South Farmingdale, NY, US 197/M9
South Fork, Co, US 190/B2
South Fulton, Tn, US 188/B4
South Gate, Md, US 196/B5
South Gate, Ca, US 194/F8
South Georgia (isl.), UK 80/H8
South Gloucestershire (co.), Eng, UK 90/D3
South Hams (plain), Eng, UK 90/C6
South Holland, Il, US 193/Q16
South Island NP, Kenya 162/C2
South Jordan, Ut, US 195/K12
South Koel (riv.), India 143/E4
South Korea (ctry.) 131/D4
South Lake Tahoe, Ca, US 186/C3
South Lanarkshire (pol. reg.), Sc, UK 94/E5
South Loup (riv.), Ne, US 185/J5
South Luangwa NP, Zam. 163/F3
South Lyon, Mi, US 193/E7
South Magnetic Pole, Ant. 218/K
South Moose (lake), Mb, Can. 185/J2
South Moresby NP and Prsv., BC, Can. 192/M5
South Naknek, Ak, US 192/G4
South Normanton, Eng, UK 93/G5
South Nyack, NY, US 197/K7
South Ockenden, Eng, UK 88/D2
South Ogden, Ut, US 195/K11
South Orange, NJ, US 197/J9
South Orkney (isls.), UK 218/X
South Ossetia (reg.), Geo. 121/G4
South Oxhey, Eng, UK 88/B2
South Oyster (bay), NY, US 197/M9
South Pacific (ocean) 80/B7
South Para (res.), Austl. 171/M8
South Pasadena, Ca, US 194/F7
South Pine (riv.), Austl. 172/E6
South Plainfield, NJ, US 197/H9
South Platte (riv.), Co, US 195/C2
South Polar (plat.), Ant. 218/Y
South Pole, Ant. 218/A
South Prairie, Wa, US 193/C3
South River, NJ, US 197/H10
South Rockwood, Mi, US 193/F7
South Ronaldsay (isl.), Sc, UK 89/V14
South Roxana, Il, US 195/G8
South Salt Lake, Ut, US 195/K12
South San Francisco, Ca, US 193/K11
South Sandwich (isls.), UK 80/H8
South Saskatchewan (riv.), Sk, Can. 180/E3
South Seaville, NJ, US 196/D5
South Shetland (isls.), UK 218/W
South Shields, Eng, UK 93/G2
South Sioux City, Ne, US 185/J5
South Skunk (riv.), Ia, US 187/J2
South Taranaki Bight (bay), NZ 175/S10
South Turkana Nat'l Rsv., Kenya 162/B2
South Tyne (riv.), Eng, UK 93/F2
South Tyneside (co.), Eng, UK 93/G2
South Ubian, Phil. 139/F2
South Uist (isl.), Sc, UK 89/Q8
South Umpqua (riv.), Or, US 186/B2
South Valley Stream, NY, US 197/L9
South Weber, Ut, US 195/K11
South West (cape), Austl. 173/C4
South West NP, Austl. 173/C4
South West Rocks, Austl. 173/E1
South Whittier, Ca, US 194/F8
South Williamsport, Pa, US 196/B1
South Woodham Ferrers, Eng, UK 88/E2
South Yorkshire (co.), Eng, UK 93/G5
Southampton (cape), Nun., Can. 181/H2
Southampton (isl.), Nun., Can. 181/H2
Southampton, On, Can. 188/D2
Southampton, Eng, UK 91/E5
Southampton (co.), Eng, UK 91/E5
Southampton, NY, US 197/F2
Southampton Water (inlet), Eng, UK 91/E5
Southaven, Ms, US 187/K4
Southeast (cape), Ak, US 192/E3
Southeast (pt.), Bahm. 203/H1
Southeast (pt.), Jam. 203/G2
Southend (int'l arpt.), Eng, UK 91/G3
Southend-on-Sea, Eng, UK 91/G3
Southend-on-Sea (co.), Eng, UK 91/G3
Southern (prov.), Ugan. 162/A3
Southern (dist.), Isr. 149/D4
Southern (riv.), Austl. 170/K7
Southern Alps (mts.), NZ 175/R11
Southern Cook (isls.), CookIs. 175/J6
Southern Cross, Austl. 170/C4
Southern Indian (lake), Mb, Can. 180/G3
Southern NP, Sudan 155/L6
Southern Pines, NC, US 191/J3
Southern Uplands (hills), Sc, UK 93/D1
Southern Ural (mts.), Rus. 119/N5
Southesk Tablelands (plat.), Austl. 167/B2
Southold, NY, US 197/F1
Southport, NC, US 191/J3
Southport, Eng, UK 93/E4
Southton, Tx, US 195/U21
Southwark (bor.), Eng, UK 88/A1
Southwood NP, Austl. 172/C4
Southworth, Wa, US 193/C3
Sovata, Rom. 107/G2
Soverato Marina, It. 104/E3
Sovere, It. 116/D1
Sovetsk, Rus. 97/J4
Sōwa, Japan 135/D1
Sowerby Bridge, Eng, UK 93/G4
Soweto, SAfr. 164/D2
Sōya-misaki (cape), Japan 134/B1
Soyana (riv.), Rus. 118/J2
Soyang (lake), SKor. 131/D4
Soyaux, Fr. 100/D4
Soyen, Ger. 113/F6
Soyhières, Swi. 114/D3
Sozh (riv.), Bela. 120/D1
Sozopol, Bul. 107/H4
Spa, Belg. 111/E3
Spada (lake), Wa, US 193/D2
Spain (ctry.) 102/C2
Spalding, Austl. 171/H5
Spalding, Eng, UK 93/H6
Spalt, Ger. 112/D4
Spanish Lake, Mo, US 195/G8
Spanish Town, Jam. 203/G2
Spannort (peak), Swi. 115/E4
Sparanise, It. 104/D2
Sparks, Nv, US 186/C3
Sparlingville, Mi, US 193/G6
Sparreholm, Swe. 96/G2
Sparta, NC, US 188/D4
Sparta, NJ, US 196/D1
Sparta, Tn, US 188/C5
Sparta, Wi, US 185/L5
Spartanburg, SC, US 191/H3
Spartel (cape), Mor. 158/B2
Spárti (Sparta), Gre. 105/H4
Spartivento (cape), It. 104/E4
Sparwood, BC, Can. 184/E3
Spassk-Dal'niy, Rus. 129/P3
Spáta, Gre. 105/N9
Spátha (cape), Gre. 105/H5
Spean (riv.), Sc, UK 94/B3
Speer (peak), Swi. 115/F3
Speer Canal (canal), Co, US 195/C2
Speicher, Swi. 115/F3
Speicher, Ger. 111/F4
Speichersdorf, Ger. 113/E3
Speke (gulf), Tanz. 162/B3
Speke (int'l arpt.), Eng, UK 93/F5
Spelle, Ger. 109/E4
Spencer (cape), Austl. 171/H5
Spencer (gulf), Austl. 171/H5
Spencer (pt.), Ak, US 192/E2
Spencer, Ia, US 185/K5
Spencer, Ok, US 195/N14
Spenge, Ger. 109/F4
Spennymoor, Eng, UK 93/G2
Spentrup, Den. 96/D3
Sperkhiás, Gre. 105/H3
Sperkhíos (riv.), Gre. 105/H3
Sperrin (mts.), NI, UK 92/A2
Spessart (range), Ger. 112/C3
Spétsai, Gre. 105/H4
Spey (riv.), Sc, UK 94/B2
Spey (bay), Sc, UK 94/C1
Speyer, Ger. 112/B4
Speyerbach (riv.), Ger. 112/B4
Spezzano Albanese, It. 104/E3
Špičák (peak), Czh. 113/F2
Spicer (isls.), Nun., Can. 181/H2
Spiekeroog (isl.), Ger. 109/E1
Spiez, Swi. 114/D4
Spigno Monferrato, It. 116/B3
Spijkenisse, Neth. 108/B5
Spike (mtn.), Ak, US 192/K2
Spilamberto, It. 117/E3
Spílion, Gre. 105/J5
Spilve (int'l arpt.), Lat. 97/L3
Spina (peak), It. 104/A2
Spinetta Marengo, It. 116/B3
Spino d'Adda, It. 116/C2
Spirano, It. 116/C1
Spirit River, Ab, Can. 184/D2
Spiritwood, Sk, Can. 184/G2
Spišská Nová Ves, Slvk. 99/L4
Spiti (riv.), India 144/D3
Spitsbergen (isl.), Sval. 218/E
Split, Cro. 106/C4
Split (int'l arpt.), Cro. 106/C4
Split (lake), Mb, Can. 180/G3
Splitrock (res.), NJ, US 197/H8
Spluga, Passo dello (pass), Swi. 115/F5
Splügen, Swi. 115/F4
Spokane, Wa, US 184/D4
Spokane (riv.), Wa, US 184/D4
Spöl (riv.), It. 115/G5
Spoleto, It. 101/K5
Spoon (riv.), Il, US 188/B3
Spooner, Wi, US 185/L4
Spotorno, It. 116/B4
Spotswood, NJ, US 197/H10
Sprague, Mb, Can. 185/K3
Sprang, Neth. 108/C5
Spratly (isls.) 138/D2
Spree (riv.), Ger. 99/H2
Sprendlingen, Ger. 111/G4
Spresiano, It. 117/F1
Sprimont, Belg. 111/E3
Spring, Tx, US 187/J5
Spring City, Pa, US 196/C3
Spring Grove, Pa, US 196/B4
Spring Grove, Il, US 193/P15
Spring Hill, Ks, US 195/D6
Spring Lake, NJ, US 196/D3
Spring Valley, Ca, US 194/D5
Spring Valley, NY, US 197/J7
Springbok, SAfr. 164/B3
Springdale, Nf, Can. 189/K1
Springdale, Ar, US 187/J3
Springe, Ger. 109/G4
Springer, NM, US 187/F3
Springerville, Az, US 186/E4
Springfield, Ma, US 189/F3
Springfield, Mo, US 187/J3
Springfield, NJ, US 197/H9
Springfield, Or, US 184/C4
Springfield, Tn, US 188/C4
Springfield, Vt, US 189/F3
Springfield, Va, US 196/A6
Springfontein, SAfr. 164/D3
Springhill, La, US 187/J4
Springhill, NS, Can. 189/H2
Springs, SAfr. 164/E2
Springs, NY, US 197/F1
Springside, Sk, Can. 185/H3
Springsure, Austl. 172/C4
Springville, Ut, US 195/K13
Sprockhövel, Ger. 109/E6
Spruce (peak), WV, US 188/E4
Spruce Run (res.), NJ, US 196/C2
Spui (riv.), Neth. 108/B5
Spurn (pt.), Eng, UK 93/J4
Squamish, BC, Can. 184/C3
Squaw Harbor, Ak, US 192/F4
Squaxin Island Ind. Res., Wa, US 193/A3
Squillace, Golfo di (gulf), It. 104/E3
Squinzano, It. 105/F2
Squires (mt.), Austl. 171/E3
Srbobran, Serb. 106/D3
Srebrenica, Bosn. 106/D3
Sredna (mts.), Bul. 107/G4
Srednogorie, Bul. 107/G4
Śrem, Pol. 99/J2
Sremčica, Serb. 106/E3
Sremska Mitrovica, Serb. 106/D3
Sreng (riv.), Camb. 136/C3
Srepok (riv.), Camb. 136/D3
Sri Dungargarh, India 147/K3
Sri Gangānagar, India 144/B5
Sri Jayewardenepura Kotte, (cap.), SrL. 140/C6
Sri Lanka (ctry.) 140/D6
Srīkākulam, India 140/D4
Srīnagar, India 144/C2
Srīvardhan, India 147/K5
Środa Śląska, Pol. 99/J3
Środa Wielkopolska, Pol. 99/J2
St. Albans, Vale of (valley), Eng, UK 88/B1
St. John's (cap.), Nf, Can. 189/L2
Stabbursdalen NP, Nor. 95/H1
Staberhuk (pt.), Ger. 96/D4
Stabroek, Belg. 108/B6
Stade, Ger. 109/G1
Staden, Belg. 110/C2
Stadl-Paura, Aus. 113/G6
Stadskanaal, Neth. 108/D3
Stadtbergen, Ger. 112/D6
Stadthagen, Ger. 109/G4
Stadtlauringen, Ger. 112/D2
Stadtlohn, Ger. 108/D5
Stadtoldendorf, Ger. 109/G5
Stadtsteinach, Ger. 113/E2
Stäfa, Swi. 115/E3
Staffanstorp, Swe. 96/E4
Staffelberg (peak), Ger. 112/E2
Staffelegg (pass), Swi. 114/E3
Staffelsee (lake), Ger. 115/H2
Staffhorst, Ger. 109/F3
Staffora (riv.), It. 116/C3
Stafford, Eng, UK 93/F6
Stagno, It. 116/D5
Stagnone Isole Della (isl.), It. 104/B4
Stahnsdorf, Ger. 98/Q7
Staines, Eng, UK 88/B2
Stains, Fr. 88/K5
Stakes (mt.), Ca, US 193/M12
Stakhanov, Ukr. 120/F2
Stalden, Swi. 114/D5
Stalingrad (Volgograd), Rus. 121/H2
Stallings, Il, US 195/G8
Stallworthy (cape), Nun., Can. 181/S6
Stalowa Wola, Pol. 99/M3
Stalybridge, Eng, UK 93/F5
Stamboliyski, Bul. 107/G4
Stamford, Eng, UK 91/F1
Stamford, Ct, US 197/L7
Stamford, Tx, US 187/H4
Stampa, Swi. 115/F5
Stampriet, Namb. 163/C5
Stamullen, Ire. 92/B4
Standerton, SAfr. 164/E2
Standish-with-Langtree, Eng, UK 93/F4
Standley (lake), Co, US 195/B3
Stanford-le-Hope, Eng, UK 91/G3
Stange, Nor. 96/D1
Stanger, SAfr. 165/E3
Stanghella, It. 117/E2
Stanhope, NJ, US 196/D2
Stanišić, Serb. 106/D3
Stanislaus (co.), Ca, US 193/M12
Stanislaus (riv.), Ca, US 186/B3
Stanley, Austl. 173/C4
Stanley (mt.), Austl. 173/C4
Stanley (mt.), Austl. 171/F2
Stanley, NB, Can. 189/H2
Stanley (falls), D.R. Congo 155/L8
Stanley (cap.), Falk. 217/F6
Stanley, Eng, UK 93/G2
Stanley, Sc, UK 94/C4
Stanley, ND, US 185/H3
Stanley, Ks, US 195/D6
Stanley (res.), India 140/C5
Stanley Draper (lake), Ok, US 195/N15
Stanovo, Serb. 106/E4
Stanovoy (range), Rus. 125/M4
Stans, Swi. 115/E4
Stansted (int'l arpt.), Eng, UK 91/G3
Stanthorpe, Austl. 172/C5
Stanton, Ky, US 188/D4
Stanton, Tx, US 187/G4
Stanton, De, US 196/C4
Stanton, NJ, US 196/D2
Stanton, Ca, US 194/G8
Staphorst, Neth. 108/D3
Staplehurst, Eng, UK 91/G4
Staples, On, Can. 193/G7
Stąporków, Pol. 99/L3
Stara Pazova, Serb. 106/E3
Stara Planina (mts.), Serb. 106/F3
Stara Zagora, Bul. 107/G4
Starachowice, Pol. 99/L3
Staranzano, It. 117/G1
Staraya Russa, Rus. 97/P2
Starbuck (isl.), Kiri. 175/K5
Starcke NP, Austl. 172/B1
Stargard Szczeciński, Pol. 96/F5
Starke, Fl, US 191/H4
Starkville, Ms, US 191/F3
Starnbergersee (lake), Ger. 115/H2
Starodub, Rus. 120/E1
Starogard Gdański, Pol. 96/H5
Start (bay), Eng, UK 90/C6
Start (pt.), Eng, UK 90/C6
Start (pt.), Sc, UK 89/V14
Startup, Wa, US 193/D2
Staryy Oskol', Rus. 120/F2
Staszów, Pol. 99/L3
State College, Pa, US 188/E3
State Fairgrounds, De, US 196/C6
State Park Place, Il, US 195/G8
Staten (isl.), NY, US 196/D2
States (int'l arpt.), Chl, UK 100/B2
Statesboro, Ga, US 191/H3
Statesville, NC, US 191/H3
Statue of Liberty Nat'l Mon., NY, US 197/J9
Staufen im Breisgau, Ger. 114/D2
Staufenberg, Ger. 98/E3
Stavanger, Nor. 96/A2
Staveley, Eng, UK 93/G5
Stavelot, Belg. 111/E3
Staveren, Neth. 108/C3
Stavern, Nor. 96/D2
Stavropol', Rus. 121/G3
Stavropol'skiy Kray, Rus. 122/E5
Stavrós, Gre. 105/H2
Stawell, Austl. 173/B3
Stayton, Or, US 184/C4
Ste-Marguerite (riv.), Qu, Can. 189/H1
Steamboat Slough (riv.), Ca, US 193/L10
Steamboat Springs, Co, US 186/F2
Stebbins, Ak, US 192/F3
Steckborn, Swi. 115/E2
Stederau (riv.), Ger. 109/H3
Steeg, Aus. 115/G3
Steele, ND, US 185/J4
Steele's Knowe (hill), Sc, UK 94/C4
Steelpoortrivier (riv.), SAfr. 165/E2
Steelton, Pa, US 196/B3
Steenbergen, Neth. 108/B5
Steens (mtn.), Or, US 186/C2
Steensby (inlet), Nun., Can. 181/J1
Steenvoorde, Fr. 110/B2
Steenwijk, Neth. 108/D3
Steep (pt.), Austl. 170/B3
Steep Holm (isl.), Eng, UK 90/C4
Steephill (lake), Sk, Can. 185/G1
Steeping (riv.), Eng, UK 93/J5
Steese Nat'l Conservation Area, Ak, US 192/J2
Stefansson (isl.), Nun., Can. 180/F1
Steffen (peak), Chile 216/C5
Steffisburg, Swi. 114/D4
Steg, Swi. 114/D5
Stege, Den. 96/E4
Steiermark (prov.), Aus. 99/H5
Steigerwald (for.), Ger. 101/J2
Steilacoom, Wa, US 193/B3
Steimbke, Ger. 109/G3
Stein, Neth. 111/E2
Stein am Rhein, Swi. 115/E2
Stein bei Nünnberg, Ger. 112/E4
Steina (riv.), Ger. 115/E2
Steinach, Ger. 113/F5
Steinach (riv.), Ger. 112/E2
Steinach am Brenner, Aus. 115/H3
Steinbach, Mb, Can. 185/J3
Steinbach an der Steyr, Aus. 113/H7
Steinbourg, Fr. 111/G6
Steinen, Ger. 114/D2
Steinerkirchen an der Traun, Aus. 113/G6
Steinfeld, Ger. 109/F3
Steinfeld, Ger. 112/B4
Steinfeld, Ger. 112/C3
Steinfort, Lux. 111/E4
Steingaden, Ger. 115/G2
Steinhagen, Ger. 109/F4
Steinhausen, Swi. 115/E3
Steinhausen an der Rottum, Ger. 115/F1
Steinheim, Ger. 109/G5
Steinheim am Albuch, Ger. 112/D5
Steinheim an der Murr, Ger. 112/C5
Steinhorst, Ger. 109/H3
Steinhuder (lake), Ger. 109/G4
Steinkjer, Nor. 95/D2
Steinsland, Nor. 96/A1
Steinweiler, Ger. 112/B4
Stekene, Belg. 108/B6
Stella, SAfr. 164/D2
Stella (peak), It. 115/F5
Stellarton, NS, Can. 189/J2
Stelle, Ger. 109/H2
Stellenbosch, SAfr. 164/L10
Stello (peak), Fr. 101/H5
Stelvio, Passo di (pass), It. 115/G4
Stelvio, PN Dello, It. 101/J3
Stenay, Fr. 111/E5
Stendal, Ger. 98/F2
Steneto NP, Bul. 107/G4
Stenhousemuir, Sc, UK 94/C4
Stenungsund, Swe. 96/D2
Stephansposching, Ger. 113/F5
Stephenville, Nf, Can. 189/K1
Stephenville, Tx, US 187/H4
Sterkstroom, SAfr. 164/D3
Sterling, Ak, US 192/H3
Sterling, Co, US 187/G2
Sterlitamak, Rus. 121/K1
Sternstein (peak), Aus. 113/H5
Sterzing (Vipiteno), It. 115/H4
Stęszew, Pol. 99/J2
Štěti, Czh. 113/H2
Stettler, Ab, Can. 184/E2
Steubenville, Oh, US 188/D3
Stevenage, Eng, UK 91/F3
Stevens Village, Ak, US 192/J2
Stevenson (lake), Mb, Can. 185/J2
Stevenson Entrance (str.), Ak, US 192/H4
Stevenston, Sc, UK 94/B5
Stevensville, Mt, US 184/E4
Stevensville, Md, US 196/B6
Stevinsluizen (dam), Neth. 108/C3
Stevzing (Vipiteno), It. 101/J3
Stewart, BC, Can. 192/N4
Stewart (riv.), Yk, Can. 180/C2
Stewart (isl.), NZ 175/R12
Stewart Crossing, Yk, Can. 192/L3
Stewarton, Sc, UK 94/B5
Stewartstown, Pa, US 196/B4
Stewartstown, NI, UK 92/B2
Stewartville, Mn, US 185/K5
Steynrus, SAfr. 164/D2
Steynsburg, SAfr. 164/D3
Steyr, Aus. 113/H6
Steyr (riv.), Aus. 99/H5
Steyregg, Aus. 113/H6
Steytlerville, SAfr. 164/D4
Stia, It. 117/E5
Stiava, It. 116/D5
Stickney (mt.), Wa, US 193/D2
Stiens, Neth. 108/C2
Stigler, Ok, US 187/J4
Stigtomta, Swe. 96/G2
Stikine (riv.), Can.,US 192/M4
Stilbaai, SAfr. 164/C4
Stilfontein, SAfr. 164/D2
Stilís, Gre. 105/H3
Still Creek (res.), Pa, US 196/C2
Still Pond, Md, US 196/B5
Stilling, Den. 96/D3
Stillings, Mo, US 195/D5
Stillwater (range), Nv, US 186/C3
Stillwater, Ok, US 187/H3
Stillwater, Pa, US 196/B1
Stillwater (lake), Pa, US 196/C1
Stilo (cape), It. 104/E3
Stilwell, Ok, US 187/J4
Stilwell, Ks, US 195/D6
Štimlje, Kos. 106/E4
Stimpfach, Ger. 112/D4
Stinchar (riv.), Sc, UK 92/D1
Stinnett, Tx, US 187/G4
Štip, FYROM 105/H2
Stiring-Wendel, Fr. 111/F5

Stírka (peak), Czh. 113/G4
Stirling (mt.), Austl. 170/C4
Stirling, Sc, UK 94/C4
Stirling (pol. reg.),
Sc, UK 94/B4
Stirling Range NP,
Austl. 170/C5
Stirone (riv.), It. 116/C3
Stjørdal, Nor. 95/D3
Stob a' Choin (peak),
Sc, UK 94/B4
Stob Choire Claurigh
(peak), Sc, UK 94/B4
Stochov, Czh. 113/G2
Stock, Eng, UK 88/E2
Stock (lake), Fr. 111/F6
Stockach, Ger. 115/F2
Stockerau, Aus. 107/N7
Stockertown,
Pa, US 196/C2
Stockholm (cap.),
Swe. 95/F4
Stockholm (co.),
Swe. 96/G2
Stockhorn (peak),
Swi. 114/D4
Stockport, Eng, UK 93/F5
Stockport (co.), Eng, UK 93/F5
Stocks (res.),
Eng, UK 93/F4
Stocksbridge,
Eng, UK 93/G5
Stockstadt am Rhein,
Ger. 112/B3
Stockton, Ca, US 186/B3
Stockton (lake),
Mo, US 187/G3
Stockton, NJ, US 196/D3
Stockton (plat.),
Tx, US 190/C4
Stockton, Ut, US 195/J13
Stockton-on-Tees,
Eng, UK 93/G2
Stockton-on-Tees (co.),
Eng, UK 93/G2
Stod, Czh. 113/G3
Stoddard, Ut, US 195/K11
Stoke (pt.), Eng, UK 90/B6
Stoke-on-Trent,
Eng, UK 93/F5
Stoke-on-Trent (co.),
Eng, UK 93/F5
Stoke Poges,
Eng, UK 88/B2
Stokenchurch,
Eng, UK 88/A2
Stokes (pt.), Austl. 173/B4
Stokes NP, Austl. 170/D5
Stolac, Bosn. 105/E1
Stolberg, Ger. 111/F2
Stolbovoy (isl.), Rus. 123/P2
Stöllet, Swe. 96/E1
Stolzenau, Ger. 109/G3
Stompneuspunt (pt.),
SAfr. 164/K10
Ston, Cro. 105/E1
Stone, Eng, UK 93/F6
Stone Harbor,
NJ, US 196/D5
Stonehaven, Sc, UK 94/D3
Stonehenge (ruin),
Eng, UK 91/E4
Stonehouse, Sc, UK 94/C5
Stonewall,
Mb, Can. 185/J3
Stoney Creek,
On, Can. 189/Q9
Stoney Point,
On, Can. 193/G7
Stoneyburn, Sc, UK 94/C5
Stonington, Ct, US 197/G1
Stony (pt.), Mb, Can. 185/J2
Stony Brook, NY, US 197/E2
Stony Creek (lake),
Mi, US 193/E7
Stony Mountain,
Mb, Can. 185/J3
Stony Point, NY, US 196/E1
Stony River, Ak, US 192/G3
Stony Tunguska (riv.),
Rus. 125/J3
Stonybrook-Wilshire,
Pa, US 196/B4
Stooping (riv.),
Co, US 188/D1
Stor (isl.), Nun., Can. 181/S7
Stör (riv.), Ger. 109/G1
Stor-Elvdal, Nor. 96/D1
Storå, Swe. 96/F2
Stora Le (lake), Swe. 96/D2
Stora Sjöfallets NP,
Swe. 95/F2
Storavan (lake), Swe. 95/F2
Stord (isl.), Nor. 96/A2
Store Bælt (chan.),
Den. 96/D4
Storebø, Nor. 96/A1
Støren, Nor. 95/D3
Storfors, Swe. 96/F2
Storm (bay), Austl. 175/C4
Stormberg (mtn.),
SAfr. 164/D3
Stormont, NI, UK 92/C2
Stornoway, Sc, UK 89/D7
Storo, It. 116/D1
Storr, The (peak),
Sc, UK 89/Q8
Storsjön (lake), Swe. 95/E3
Storsteinsfjellet (peak),
Nor. 95/F1
Storstrøm (co.), Den. 96/D4
Storvik, Swe. 96/G1
Storvreta, Swe. 96/G2
Story, Wy, US 184/G4
Stosch (isl.), Chile 217/A6

Stötten am Auerberg,
Ger. 115/G2
Stoughton, Sk, Can. 185/H3
Stoumont, Belg. 111/E3
Stour (riv.), Eng, UK 90/D5
Stourbridge,
Eng, UK 90/D2
Stourport-on-Severn,
Eng, UK 90/D2
Stovring, Den. 96/C3
Stowe, Pa, US 196/C3
Stowmarket, Eng, UK 91/G2
Stra, It. 117/F2
Strabane (dist.), NI 92/A2
Strabane, NI, UK 89/Q9
Stradella, It. 116/C2
Straelen, Ger. 108/D6
Strahan, Austl. 173/C4
Strakonice, Czh. 113/G4
Straldzha, Bul. 107/H4
Stralsund, Ger. 96/E4
Strambino, It. 116/A2
Strand, SAfr. 164/L11
Strangford, NI, UK 92/C3
Strangford (lake),
NI, UK 92/C3
Strängnäs, Swe. 96/G2
Strangways (mt.),
Austl. 171/G2
Stranocum, NI, UK 92/B1
Stranraer, Sc, UK 92/C2
Strasbourg, Fr. 114/D1
Strasbourg (Entzheim)
(int'l arpt.), Fr. 114/D1
Strasburg, Mo, US 195/E6
Strasburg, Pa, US 196/B4
Strassen, Lux. 111/F4
Strasshof an der Nordbahn,
Aus. 107/P7
Strasswalchen, Aus. 113/G7
Stratford, Tx, US 187/G3
Stratford, On, Can. 193/G3
Stratford, NZ 175/S10
Stratford, Ct, US 197/E1
Stratford, NJ, US 196/C4
Stratford (pt.), Ct, US 197/E1
Stratford (har.),
Ct, US 197/L8
Stratford and Worcester
(canal), Eng, UK 90/D2
Stratford-upon-Avon,
Eng, UK 91/E2
Strathalbyn, Austl. 171/H5
Strathaven, Sc, UK 94/B5
Strathbeg (bay),
Sc, UK 94/E1
Strathblane,
Sc, UK 94/B5
Strathearn (valley),
Sc, UK 94/C4
Strathmore,
Ab, Can. 184/E3
Strathmore (valley),
Sc, UK 94/C3
Strathpeffer,
Sc, UK 94/B1
Strathspey (valley),
Sc, UK 94/C2
Straubing, Ger. 113/F5
Straumnes Horn (pt.),
Ice. 95/M6
Strausberg, Ger. 98/Q6
Strausstown,
Pa, US 196/B3
Strawberry (peak),
Ca, US 194/B2
Strazhitsa, Bul. 107/G4
Streaky (bay), Austl. 171/G5
Streaky Bay, Austl. 171/G5
Streamwood, Il, US 193/P15
Streator, Il, US 185/L5
Středočeská Žulová
Vrchovina (mts.), Czh. 99/H4
Středočeský (pol. reg.),
Czh. 101/L2
Street, Md, US 196/B4
Strehaia, Rom. 107/F3
Streich (peak),
Rom. 107/G2
Strel'a (riv.), Czh. 99/G3
Suches, Bol. 214/D4
Suck (riv.), Ire. 89/P10
Sucre (cap.), Bol. 208/E7
Sucre, Qu, Can. 188/E1
Sucre (dept.), Col. 210/C2
Sucre, Ecu. 210/A5
Sucre (state), Ven. 211/F2
Sucúa, Ecu. 210/B5
Sucumbíos (prov.),
Ecu. 210/B4
Sucunduri (riv.),
Braz. 208/G5
Sucupira do Norte,
Braz. 212/A2
Sucuriú (riv.), Braz. 209/H7
Sud-Ouest (prov.),
Camr. 161/H5
Suda (riv.), Rus. 118/H4
Sudama, Japan 135/A2
Sudan (ctry.) 155/L5
Sudbury, On, Can. 188/D2
Sudbury, Eng, UK 91/G2
Suddie, Guy. 211/G3
Sude (riv.), Ger. 98/F2
Süderbrarup, Ger. 96/C4
Sudeten (mts.),
Czh.,Pol. 99/H3
Sudislerville, Md, US 196/C5
Südlohn, Ger. 108/D5
Sue (riv.), Sudan 155/L6
Sueca, Sp. 103/E3
Süedinenie, Bul. 107/G4
Suez (canal), Egypt 159/C2
Suez (gulf), Egypt 159/C2
Süf, Jor. 149/D3

Stronsay Firth (inlet),
Sc, UK 89/V14
Strood, Eng, UK 88/E2
Stropnice (riv.), Czh. 113/H5
Stroppiana, It. 116/B2
Stroud, Eng, UK 90/D3
Stroudsburg,
Pa, US 196/C2
Struan, Sc, UK 89/Q8
Struer, Den. 96/C3
Struga, FYROM 105/G2
Struisbaai (bay),
SAfr. 164/C4
Strule (riv.), NI, UK 92/A2
Struma (riv.), Bul. 120/B4
Strumble (pt.),
Wal, UK 90/A2
Strumica, FYROM 105/H2
Strydenburg, SAfr. 164/C3
Stryn, Nor. 95/C3
Strzegom, Pol. 99/J3
Strzelce Krajeńskie,
Pol. 99/H2
Strzelce Opolskie,
Pol. 120/A2
Strzelecki (mt.),
Austl. 173/D4
Strzelecki (mt.),
Austl. 171/G2
Strzelin, Pol. 99/J3
Strzelno, Pol. 99/K2
Strzyżów, Pol. 99/L4
Stuart (lake),
BC, Can. 184/B2
Stuart (riv.), BC, Can. 184/B2
Stuart, Fl, US 191/H5
Stuarts Draft,
Va, US 188/E4
Stubbekøbing, Den. 96/E4
Stubbenkammer (pt.),
Ger. 96/E4
Stühlingen, Ger. 115/E2
Stupava, Slvk. 101/M2
Stupino, Rus. 118/H5
Stura di Lanzo (riv.), It. 116/A2
Sturgeon (lake),
On, Can. 185/L3
Sturgeon (bay),
Mb, Can. 185/J3
Sturgeon (riv.),
On, Can. 188/D2
Sturgeon Falls,
On, Can. 188/E2
Sturgis, Mi, US 188/C3
Štúrovo, Slvk. 99/K5
Sturt (des.), Austl. 173/B1
Sturt (riv.), Austl. 173/B1
Sturt (mt.), Austl. 171/M8
Sturt NP, Austl. 173/B1
Sturup (int'l arpt.),
Swe. 96/E4
Stutterheim, SAfr. 164/D4
Stuttgart, Ger. 112/C5
Stykkishólmur, Ice. 95/M6
Styr (riv.), Ukr. 120/C2
Suaçui Grande (riv.),
Braz. 213/D1
Suakin (arch.), Sudan 155/N4
Suam (riv.), Kenya 162/B2
Suaqui Grande, Mex. 200/C2
Suār, India 142/B1
Suárez (riv.), Col. 210/C3
Subang, Indo. 138/C5
Subarnarekhā (riv.),
India 143/E4
Sūbāt (riv.), Sudan 155/M6
Subaytilah, Tun. 158/L7
Subei Monggolzu Zizhixian,
China 128/C4
Subi (isl.), Indo. 138/C3
Subotica, Serb. 106/D2
Succasunna-Kenvil,
NJ, US 196/D2
Succiso, Alpe di
(peak), It. 116/D4
Suceava, Rom. 107/H2
Suceava (prov.),
Rom. 107/G2
Suchedniów, Pol. 99/L3
Sullana, Peru 214/A2
Sully-sur-Loire, Fr. 100/E4
Sulmona, It. 104/C1
Sulphur (riv.),
Tx, US 187/J4
Sulphur, Ok, US 187/H4
Sulphur Springs,
Tx, US 187/J4
Sulphur Springs,
Ca, US 194/A2
Sultan, Wa, US 193/D2
Sultan-y-en-Brie, Fr. 88/K5
Sultan Kudarat, Phil. 137/D6
Sultānpur, India 142/D2
Sulu (arch.), Phil. 137/D6
Sulu (sea), Asia 137/D6
Sülüklü, Turk. 148/C2
Suluova, Turk. 120/E4
Suluq, Libya 155/K1
Sülysáp, Hun. 107/R10
Suma (riv.), Rus. 118/H2
Sumas, Wa, US 184/C2
Sumatra (isl.), Indo. 138/B4
Sumba (str.), Indo. 139/E5
Sumba (isl.), Indo. 139/E5
Sumbar (riv.), Trkm. 145/C5
Sumbawa (isl.),
Indo. 139/E5
Sumbawa Besar,
Indo. 139/E5
Sumbawanga, Tanz. 162/A4
Sumbe, Ang. 163/B3
Sumburgh Head (pt.),
Sc, UK 89/W14
Sumdum (mt.),
Ak, US 192/M4
Sümeg, Hun. 106/C2
Sumenep, Indo. 138/D5
Sumiswald, Swi. 114/D3
Summerland,
BC, Can. 184/D3
Summerland,
Ca, US 194/A2
Summerside,
PE, Can. 189/J2
Summerville,
SC, US 191/H3
Summerville,
Ga, US 191/G3
Summit, NJ, US 197/H9
Summit (co.),
Ut, US 195/K12
Summit Bridge,
De, US 196/C4
Summit Hill, Pa, US 196/C2
Summner, Wa, US 193/C3
Sumoto, Japan 132/D3
Sumperk, Czh. 99/J4
Sumqayit, Azer. 121/J4
Sums'ka Oblast, Ukr. 120/E2
Sumter, SC, US 191/H3
Sumy, Ukr. 120/E2
Sun (riv.), Mt, US 184/E4
Sun City, Az, US 195/R18
Sun City, Ca, US 194/C3
Sun City West,
Az, US 195/R18
Sun Kosi (riv.),
Nepal 143/F2
Sun Lakes, Az, US 195/S19
Sunagawa, Japan 134/B2
Sunām, India 144/C4
Sunami, Japan 135/L5
Sunbury, Pa, US 196/B2
Sunbury, Austl. 173/F5
Sunbury-on-Thames,
Eng, UK 88/B2
Sunch'ang, SKor. 131/D5
Sunch'ŏn, NKor. 131/C3
Sunch'ŏn, SKor. 131/D5
Suncook, NH, US 189/G3
Sunda (isls.), Indo. 138/D4
Sunda (str.), Indo. 138/B5
Sundance, Wy, US 185/G4
Sundarbans (phys. reg.),
India 143/G5
Sundargarh, India 143/E4
Sundarnagar, India 144/D4
Sundays (riv.),
SAfr. 164/D4
Sunderland, Eng, UK 93/G2
Sunderland
(co.), Eng, UK 93/G2
Sundern, Ger. 109/F6
Sundhouse, Fr. 114/D1
Sundown, Tx, US 187/G4
Sundown NP, Austl. 173/D1
Sundre, Ab, Can. 184/E3
Sunds, Den. 96/C3
Sungai Petani,
Malay. 141/H6
Sungaipenuh, Indo. 138/B4
Süngju, SKor. 131/D5
Sungurlare, Bul. 107/H4
Sungurlu, Turk. 148/C1
Suning, China 130/C3
Sunndal, Nor. 95/D3
Sunne, Swe. 96/E2
Sunningdale,
Eng, UK 91/F4
Sunnyside, Ca, US 194/C5
Sunnyside, Il, US 193/P15
Sunnyvale, Ca, US 186/B3
Sunol, Ca, US 193/L11
Sunomata, Japan 135/L5
Sunrise (riv.),
NJ, US 196/D1
Sunset, Ut, US 195/J11
Sunset Beach,
Hi, US 182/V12
Sunset Beach, Ca, US 194/F8
Sunset Country (reg.),
Austl. 173/B2
Sunset Crater Volcano
Nat'l Mon., Az, US 186/E4
Suntar-Khayata (mts.),
Rus. 123/P3
Süntel (mts.), Ger. 109/G4
Sunwi (isl.), NKor. 131/C4
Sunwu, China 129/N2
Sunyani, Gha. 161/E5
Sunzu (peak), Zam. 162/A4
Suo (sea), Japan 132/B4
Suomenlinna, Fin. 97/L1
Suomenselkä (reg.),
Fin. 95/H3
Suong, Camb. 136/D4
Supaul, India 143/F2
Supawna Meadows NWR,
NJ, US 196/C4
Supe, Peru 214/B3
Superior, Mt, US 184/E4

Sufers, Swi. 115/F4
Suffern, NY, US 197/J7
Suffolk (co.), NY, US 197/F2
Suffolk (co.), Eng, UK 91/G2
Suga (isl.), Japan 135/L2
Sugar Creek,
Mo, US 195/E5
Sugar Grove, Il, US 193/P16
Sugar Land, Tx, US 190/E4
Sugar Loaf (peak),
Wal, UK 90/C3
Sugar Notch,
Pa, US 196/C1
Sugenheim, Ger. 112/D3
Sugito, Japan 135/D1
Sugla (lake), Turk. 148/C2
Suhāj, Egypt 159/B3
Suhāj (gov.), Egypt 159/B3
Suhl, Ger. 112/D1
Suhlendorf, Ger. 109/H3
Suhut, Turk. 148/B2
Sui (riv.), China 137/B3
Sui (pt.), Thai. 136/B4
Sui Xian, China 130/C4
Suia-Missu (riv.),
Braz. 209/H6
Suichang, China 137/C2
Suichuan, China 141/K2
Suifenhe, China 129/P3
Suihua, China 129/N2
Suijiang, China 141/H2
Suileng, China 129/N2
Suilven (peak), Sc, UK 94/B1
Suining, China 130/D4
Suipacha, Arg. 217/J11
Suiping, China 130/C4
Suippe (riv.), Fr. 98/C4
Suippes, Fr. 111/D5
Suir (riv.), Ire. 89/Q10
Suis (well), Libya 157/H4
Suishō (isl.), Rus. 134/D2
Suitland-Silver Hill,
Md, US 196/B6
Suixi, China 141/K3
Suixi, China 130/D4
Suiyang, China 137/A2
Suize (riv.), Fr. 114/B2
Suizhong, China 130/E2
Suizhou, China 129/K5
Sukabumi, Indo. 138/C5
Sukadana (bay),
Indo. 138/C4
Sukadana, Indo. 138/C4
Sukagawa, Japan 133/G2
Sukheke, Pak. 144/B4
Sukhindol, Bul. 107/G4
Sukhinichi, Rus. 120/E1
Sukhodol'skoye (lake),
Rus. 97/N1
Sukhona (riv.), Rus. 122/E4
Sukhothai (ruin),
Thai. 136/B2
Sukhothai, Thai. 136/B2
Sukkur, Pak. 147/J3
Sukösd, Hun. 106/D2
Sukumo, Japan 132/C4
Sula (isls.), Indo. 139/G4
Sula (riv.), Rus. 119/L2
Sulaimān (range),
Pak. 147/J3
Sulakyurt, Turk. 148/C1
Sulawesi (Celebes) (isl.),
Indo. 139/F4
Sulb Temple (ruin),
Sudan 159/B4
Sulby (riv.), IM, UK 92/D3
Sulechów, Pol. 99/H2
Sulęcin, Pol. 99/H2
Sulejów, Pol. 99/K3
Sulejówek, Pol. 99/L2
Sulina, Rom. 107/J3
Sulina Branch (riv.),
Rom. 107/J3
Sulingen, Ger. 109/F3
Sulitjelma (peak),
Nor. 95/F2

Sulzberger (bay), Ant. 218/Q
Sulzburg, Ger. 114/D2
Sulzfluh (peak), Aus. 115/F3
Sulzheim, Ger. 112/D3
Šumadija (reg.), Serb. 106/E3
Sumapaz, PN, Col. 210/C4
Sumatra (isl.), Indo. 138/B4
Šür, Leb. 149/D3
Sur (pt.), Arg. 217/F3
Sur Reina Sofía
(int'l arpt.), Sp. 156/A3
Sura (riv.), Rus. 119/K5
Surabaya, Indo. 138/D5
Surada, India 140/D4
Surahammar, Swe. 96/G2
Sürajgarh, India 144/C5
Surak-san (peak),
SKor. 131/G6
Surakarta, Indo. 138/D5
Surallah, Phil. 139/F2
Suran (riv.), Fr. 114/B3
Šurany, Slvk. 106/D1
Surat, India 144/B5
Surat, Austl. 172/C4
Surat Thani, Thai. 136/B5
Suratgarh, India 144/B5
Surčin, Serb. 106/E3
Surdulica, Serb. 106/F4
Sure (riv.), Kenya 162/D2
Süre (riv.), Lux. 98/C4
Surendranagar, India 147/K4
Surf City, NJ, US 196/D4
Surgères, Fr. 100/C3
Surgut, Rus. 122/H3
Süri, India 143/F4
Surigao, Phil. 137/E6
Surin, Thai. 136/C3
Suriname (ctry.),
Rus. 123/Q2
Surma (riv.), Bang. 143/H3
Surprise, Az, US 195/R18
Surrey, BC, Can. 184/C3
Surrey (co.), Eng, UK 91/F4
Sürsee, Swi. 114/E3
Surt, Libya 154/J1
Surte, Swe. 96/D3
Surtsey (isl.), Ice. 95/N7
Surubim, Braz. 212/D2
Suruga (bay), Japan 133/F3
Surumu (riv.), Braz. 211/F4
Surveyor General's Corner,
Austl. 171/F3
Survilliers, Fr. 88/K4
Surwakwima (falls),
Guy. 211/F3
Surwold, Ger. 109/E3
Susaki, Japan 132/C4
Susanville, Ca, US 184/C5
Susegana, It. 117/F1
Suşehri, Turk. 148/D1
Sushan (isl.), China 131/B4
Susong, Japan 133/F3
Susquehanna (riv.),
Md,Pa, US 188/E3
Susquehanna NWR,
Md, US 196/B5
Sussex, NB, Can. 189/H2
Sussex (co.),
De, US 196/C6
Sussex Inlet, Austl. 173/D2
Sussex, Vale of (valley),
Eng, UK 91/F4
Sustenhorn
(peak), Swi. 115/E4
Sustenpass
(pass), Swi. 115/E4
Susteren, Neth. 111/E1
Susuman, Rus. 123/Q3
Susurluk, Turk. 148/B2
Süttöler, Turk. 148/B2
Sutherland, SAfr. 164/C4
Sutherland Springs,
Tx, US 195/U21
Sutherlin, Or, US 184/C5
Sutlej (riv.), India 144/D4
Sutjeska NP, Bosn. 105/F1
Sütlücc, Turk. 105/K2
Sutton, Ak, US 192/J3
Sutton (bor.), Eng, UK 88/C2
Sutton Coldfield,
Eng, UK 91/E1
Sutton in Ashfield,
Eng, UK 93/G5
Suttsu, Japan 134/D2
Süttler, Turk. 148/B2
Sütçüler, Turk. 148/B2
Suur (str.), Est. 97/K2
Suurberge (mts.),
SAfr. 164/D4
Suvorov (isl.),
Cookls. 175/J6
Suwaliyüh, Jor. 149/D3
Suwannee (riv.),
Fl, US 191/H4
Suwanose (isl.),
Japan 133/K6
Suwarrow (isl.),
Cookls. 175/J6
Suwŏn, SKor. 131/G7
Suyo, Peru 214/A2
Superior, Az, US 186/E4
Superior (upland),
Wi, US 188/C1
Superior, Co, US 195/B3
Superior (lake),
Can.,US 188/B2
Suphan Buri, Thai. 136/C3
Supiori (isl.), Indo. 139/J4
Sup'ung (res.),
China 131/C2
Sup'ung (dam),
NKor. 131/C2
Süq ash Shuyükh,
Iraq 146/E2
Suqaylabiyah, Syria 149/E2
Suqian, China 130/D4
Suquamish, Wa, US 193/B2
Suqutra (isl.), Yem. 145/H6
Šür, Leb. 149/D3
Suzhou, China 130/D4
Suzhou, China 130/L8
Suzi (riv.), China 131/C2
Suzu, Japan 133/E2
Suzu-misaki (cape),
Japan 133/E2
Suzuka (riv.), Japan 135/L6
Suzuka (range),
Japan 135/K6
Suzzara, It. 117/D3
Svalbard (isls.), Nor. 218/E
Svaneke, Den. 96/F4
Svängsta, Swe. 96/F3
Svanstein, Swe. 118/D2
Svatava (riv.), Czh. 113/F2
Svealand (reg.), Swe. 95/E4
Svedala, Swe. 96/A2
Sveio, Nor. 96/A2
Svelvik, Nor. 96/D2
Svendborg, Den. 96/D4
Svendsen (pen.),
Nun., Can. 181/S7
Svenljunga, Swe. 96/E3
Svenstrup, Den. 96/C3
Sverdlovskaya Oblast,
Rus. 122/G4
Sverdrup (chan.),
Nun., Can. 181/S7
Sverdrup (isls.),
Nun., Can. 181/S7
Svetlogorsk, Bela. 120/D1
Svetlograd, Rus. 121/G3
Svetlyy, Rus. 121/M2
Svetozarevo, Serb. 106/E4
Svilajnac, Serb. 106/E3
Svilengrad, Bul. 107/H5
Svishtov, Bul. 107/G4
Šitavyy, Czh. 99/J4
Svoboda, Rus. 106/E3
Svobodnyy, Rus. 129/N1
Svoge, Bul. 107/F4
Svratka (riv.), Czh. 101/M2
Svyatyy Nos (cape),
Rus. 123/Q2
Swābi, Pak. 144/B2
Swadlincote,
Eng, UK 91/E1
Swain (reefs), Austl. 172/D3
Swain (isls.), ASam. 175/H6
Swainsboro, Ga, US 191/H3
Swakopmund, Namb. 163/B5
Swale, The (riv.),
Eng, UK 91/G4
Swalmen, Neth. 108/D6
Swan (mt.), Austl. 171/G2
Swan (hills), Ab, Can. 180/E3
Swan (isls.), Hon. 198/E4
Swan Hill, Austl. 173/B2
Swan Hills,
Ab, Can. 184/E2
Swan Reach, Austl. 171/H5
Swan River,
Mb, Can. 185/H2
Swanscombe,
Eng, UK 88/D2
Swansea, Austl. 173/D4
Swansea (bay),
Eng, UK 90/C3
Swansea, Wal, UK 90/B3
Swansea (co.),
Wal, UK 90/B3
Swansea, Il, US 195/H8
Swart Kei (riv.), SAfr. 164/D3
Swarthmore, Pa, US 196/C4
Swartswood (lake),
NJ, US 196/D1
Swarzędz, Pol. 99/J2

T

Ta Khmau, Camb. 136/D4
Taabo, Barrage de
(dam), C.d'Iv. 160/D3
Tabaco, Phil. 137/D5
Tabaquite, Trin. 211/F2
Tabarqah, Tun. 158/L6
Tabas, Iran 147/G2
Tabasará (mts.), Pan. 203/F4
Tabasco (state), Mex. 198/C4
Tabatinga, Serra da
(mts.), Braz. 209/K6
Tabayama, Japan 135/B2
Tabelbala, Alg. 156/E3
Tabelbalet (well),
Alg. 157/G4
Ta'benghisa, Ponta (pt.),
Malta 104/L7
Taber, Ab, Can. 184/E3
Tabernes de Valldigna,
Sp. 103/E3
Tabiang, Kiri. 174/F5
Tabira, Braz. 212/D2
Tabiteuea (isl.), Kiri. 174/G5
Tablas (isl.), Phil. 137/D5
Tablas de Daimiel NP,
Sp. 102/D3
Table (bay), SAfr. 164/L10
Table (mtn.), SAfr. 164/L10
Table Rock (lake),
Mo, US 187/J3
Tabligbo, Togo 161/F5
Tábor, Czh. 113/H4
Tabora (pol. reg.),
Tanz. 162/B4
Tabora, Tanz. 162/B4
Tabou, C.d'Iv. 160/D5
Tabuk, Phil. 137/D3
Tabūk, SAfr. 146/C3

Tabuleiro do Norte, Braz. 212/C2
Tabwemasana (peak), Van. 174/F6
Tacabamba, Peru 214/B2
Tacámbaro de Codallos, Mex. 201/E5
Tacaná (vol.), Mex. 202/C3
Tacarcuna (mtn.), Pan. 203/G4
Tacheng, China 128/D2
Tachibana (bay), Japan 132/A4
Tachikawa, Japan 133/F3
Tachinger (lake), Ger. 113/F7
Táchira (state), Ven. 210/C3
Tachov, Czh. 113/F3
Tacloban, Phil. 137/E5
Tacna, Peru 214/D5
Tacna (dept.), Peru 214/D5
Tacoma, Wa, US 184/C4
Tacora (vol.), Chile 214/D5
Tacotalpa, Mex. 202/C2
Tacuarembó, Uru. 215/E3
Tacuarembó (dept.), Uru. 217/G2
Tacutu (riv.), Braz. 211/F4
Tadaoka, Japan 135/H7
Ta'Delimara (pt.), Malta 104/M7
Tademaït, Plateau du (plat.), Alg. 154/F2
Tādepallegūdem, India 140/D4
Tadley, Eng, UK 91/E4
Tadmur, Syria 148/D3
Tadó, Col. 210/B3
Tado, Japan 135/L5
Tadohae Hasang NP, SKor. 131/C5
Tadotsu, Japan 132/C3
Tādpatri, India 140/C5
Tadrart (mts.), Alg.,Libya 154/H2
Tadworth, Eng, UK 88/C3
T'aean, SKor. 131/D4
T'aebaek, SKor. 131/E4
Taebudo (isl.), SKor. 131/F7
Taech'ŏn, SKor. 131/D4
Taech'ŏng (isl.), SKor. 131/C4
Taedŏk, SKor. 131/D5
Taedong (riv.), NKor. 131/D3
Taegang-got (pt.), NKor. 131/D3
Taegu, SKor. 131/E5
Taegu Gwangyŏksi (prov.), SKor. 131/E5
Taehŭksan (isl.), SKor. 131/C5
Taehwa (isl.), NKor. 131/C3
T'aein, SKor. 131/D5
Taejŏn, SKor. 131/D4
Taejŏn Gwangyŏksi (prov.), SKor. 131/D4
Taeryŏng (riv.), NKor. 131/C2
Tafalla, Sp. 102/E1
Tafassasset, Oued (riv.), Alg. 157/H4
Taff (riv.), Wal, UK 90/C3
Tafí Viejo, Arg. 215/C2
Tafraout, Mor. 156/C3
Taft, La, US 195/P17
Taft, Iran 146/F2
Taftān (mtn.), Iran 147/H3
Taga, Japan 135/K5
Taganrog, Rus. 120/F3
Tagant (pol. reg.), Mrta. 160/C2
Tagarav (peak), Trkm. 121/L5
Tagawa, Japan 132/B4
Taggia, It. 116/A5
Taghit, Alg. 157/E3
Tagish, Yk, Can. 192/M3
Tagliamento (riv.), It. 101/K3
Taglio di Po, It. 117/F3
Tagolo (pt.), Phil. 139/F2
Taguasco, Cuba 203/G1
Taguatinga, Braz. 209/J7
Tagula (isl.), PNG 174/E6
Tagum, Phil. 137/E6
Tagun (riv.), Rus. 119/P4
Tagus (riv.), Port. 102/B3
Tagus Rio Tejo (lake), Port. 103/P10
Tagus (Tajo) (riv.), Sp. 102/C3
Tahan (peak), Malay. 138/B3
Tahanea (isl.), FrPol. 175/L6
Tahanroz'ka Zatoka (gulf), Rus.,Ukr. 120/F3
Tahara, Japan 135/M6
Tahat (peak), Alg. 157/G5
Tahat, Oued et (riv.), Alg. 158/F5
Tahe, China 129/M1
Tahilt, Mong. 128/G2
Tahir (pass), Turk. 148/E2
Tahiti (isl.), FrPol. 175/L6
Tahkuna (pt.), Est. 97/K2
Tahlequah, Ok, US 187/J4
Tahmoor, Austl. 173/D2
Tahneta (pass), Ak, US 192/J3
Tahoe (lake), Ca,Nv, US 186/C3
Tahoka, Tx, US 187/G4
Tahoua (dept.), Niger 161/G3
Tahoua, Niger 161/G3
Tahsis, BC, Can. 184/B3
Tahuamanu (riv.), Peru 214/D3
Tahuamanú, Peru 214/D3
Tahuata (isl.), FrPol. 175/L6
Tahulandang (isl.), Indo. 139/G3
Tahuya, Wa, US 193/A3
Tahuya (riv.), Wa, US 193/B3
Tai Long Wan (bay), China 129/V10
Tai Mo Shan (peak), China 129/U10
Taï, PN de, C.d'Iv. 154/D6
Tai Po, China 129/U10
Tai Xian, China 130/E4
Tai'an, China 131/B2
Tai'an, China 130/D3
Taiaret (well), Mor. 156/B5
Taibus, China 129/L3
Taicang, China 130/L8
T'aichung, Tai. 137/D3
Taiei, Japan 135/E2
Taieri (riv.), NZ 175/S12
Taigu, China 130/C3
Taihang (mts.), China 130/C3
Taihe, China 137/B2
Taihe, China 130/C4
Taikang, China 130/C4
Taiki, Japan 134/C2
Tailem Bend, Austl. 171/H5
Taima, Japan 135/J6
Tain, Sc, UK 94/B1
T'ainan, Tai. 137/D3
Taínaron (cape), Gre. 105/H4
Taingainony, Madg. 165/H8
Taino, It. 116/B1
Taiobeiras, Braz. 212/B4
T'aipei (cap.), Tai. 137/D2
Taiping, Malay. 138/B3
Taiping, China 137/C1
Taisha, Japan 132/C3
Taishan, China 137/B3
Taishi, Japan 135/J6
Taishun, China 137/C2
Taiskirchen im Innkreis, Aus. 113/G6
Taissy, Fr. 111/D5
Taitao (pen.), Chile 216/B5
Taiti (peak), Kenya 162/B2
T'aitung, Tai. 137/D3
Taiwan (ctry.) 137/D3
Taiwan (str.), China,Tai. 137/C3
Taixing, China 130/E4
Taïyetos (mts.), Gre. 105/H4
Taiyuan, China 130/C3
Taizhou, China 130/D4
Taizi (riv.), China 130/F2
Ta'izz, Yem. 146/D6
Tāj Mahal, India 142/B2
Tajikistan (ctry.) 145/E5
Tajima, Japan 133/F2
Tajimi, Japan 135/M5
Tajiri, Japan 135/H7
Tājpur, India 142/B1
Tajrish, Iran 146/F1
Tajumulco (vol.), Guat. 202/D3
Tajuña (riv.), Sp. 102/D2
Tak, Thai. 136/B2
Takahagi, Japan 133/G2
Takahama, Japan 135/J5
Takahama, Japan 135/L6
Takahashi (riv.), Japan 132/C3
Takahashi, Japan 132/C3
Takahata, Japan 133/G1
Takaishi, Japan 135/H6
Takamatsu, Japan 132/D3
Takami-yama (peak), Japan 135/K7
Takanabe, Japan 132/B4
Takane, Japan 135/A2
Takanosu, Japan 134/B3
Takanosu-yama (peak), Japan 135/C2
Takaoka, Japan 133/E2
Takapuna, NZ 175/S10
Takarazuka, Japan 135/H6
Takaroa (isl.), FrPol. 175/L6
Takasaki, Japan 133/F2
Takashima, Japan 135/K5
Takatomi, Japan 135/L5
Takatori, Japan 135/J7
Takatsuki, Japan 135/K5
Takatsuki, Japan 135/J6
Takayama, Japan 133/E2
Takefu, Japan 133/E3
Takehara, Japan 132/C3
Takestān, Iran 146/E1
Taketa, Japan 132/B4
Taketoyo, Japan 135/L6
Takhatgarh, India 140/B2
Takhatpur, India 142/C4
Takht-e Jamshīd (ruin), Iran 146/F3
Takht-i-Bhāi, Pak. 144/A2
Taki, Japan 135/L7
Takijuq (lake), Nun., Can. 180/E2
Takikawa, Japan 134/B2
Takino, Japan 135/G6
Takla (lake), BC, Can. 184/B2
Takla Makan (des.), China 128/D4
Tako, Japan 135/D2
Takoradi, Gha. 161/E5
Takouch (cape), Alg. 158/K6
Taksony, Hun. 107/R10
Tala, Mex. 200/E4
Talā, Egypt 149/B4
Tala, Uru. 217/L11
Talagang, Pak. 144/B3
Talagante, Chile 216/N8
Talāja, India 147/K4
Talak (phys. reg.), Niger 154/G4
Talamanca (mts.), CR 203/F4
Talamba, Pak. 144/B4
Talamona, It. 115/F5
Talang (peak), Indo. 138/B4
Talanga, Hon. 202/E3
Talange, Fr. 111/F5
Talant, Fr. 114/A3
Talara, Peru 214/A2
Talas (obl.), Kyr. 145/F4
Talas, Turk. 148/C2
Talas, Kyr. 145/F4
Talas (riv.), Kaz. 145/F4
Talaud (isl.), Phil. 139/G3
Talavera de la Reina, Sp. 102/C3
Talawakele, SrL. 140/D6
Talayuela, Sp. 102/C3
Talbingo, Austl. 173/D2
Talbot (mt.), Austl. 170/E3
Talbot (co.), Md, US 196/B6
Talca, Chile 216/C2
Talcahuano, Chile 216/B3
Tālcher, India 140/E3
Taldyqorghan (obl.), Kaz. 145/G3
Taldyqorghan, Kaz. 145/G3
Talence, Fr. 100/C4
Talent (riv.), Swi. 114/C4
Talfer (Talvera) (riv.), It. 115/H4
Talgar, Kaz. 145/G4
Taliabu (isl.), Indo. 139/F4
Taliouine, Mor. 156/D3
Talkeetna, Ak, US 192/H3
Talkhā, Egypt 149/B4
Tall 'Afar, Iraq 148/E2
Tall al Muqayyar (ruin), Iraq 146/E2
Tall 'Āsūr (peak), Isr. 149/G8
Tall Kayf, Iraq 148/E2
Talladega, Al, US 191/G3
Tallahassee (cap.), Fl, US 191/G4
Tallahatchie (riv.), Ms, US 187/K4
Tallangatta, Austl. 173/C3
Tallanstown, Ire. 92/B4
Tallering (peak), Austl. 170/B4
Talleyville, De, US 196/C4
Tallinn (cap.), Est. 97/L2
Tallman Mountain State Park, NY, US 197/K7
Talloires, Fr. 114/C6
Tallow, Ire. 89/Q10
Tallulah, La, US 187/K4
Tallulah (falls), Ga, US 191/H3
Talmassons, It. 117/G1
Talo (peak), Eth. 155/N5
Taloda, India 147/K4
Tāloqān, Afg. 147/J1
Taloyoak, Nun., Can. 180/G2
Talpa de Allende, Mex. 200/D4
Talsperre Pöhl (res.), Ger. 113/F1
Taltal, Chile 215/B2
Taltson (riv.), NW, Can. 180/E2
Talumphuk (pt.), Thai. 136/C4
Talvera (Talfer) (riv.), It. 115/H4
Talwāra, India 144/C4
Tam Ky, Viet. 136/E3
Tama, Japan 135/C2
Tama (riv.), Japan 135/D2
Tamagawa, Japan 135/C2
Tamaho, Japan 135/B2
Tamaki, Japan 135/L7
Tamalameque, Col. 210/C2
Tamale, Gha. 161/E4
Tamamura, Japan 135/C1
Taman, Indo. 138/D5
Taman-Rasset, Oued (riv.), Alg. 157/F5
Tamaná (peak), Col. 210/B3
Tamana (isl.), Kiri. 174/G5
Tamanar, Mor. 156/C3
Tamanghasset (prov.), Alg. 161/F1
Tamanghasset, Oued (riv.), Alg. 157/F5
Tamanrasset, Alg. 157/G5
Tamanrasset (prov.), Alg. 157/F4
Tamaqua, Pa, US 196/C2
Tamar (riv.), Eng, UK 90/B5
Tamara (isl.), Japan 133/H8
Tamari, Japan 135/E1
Tamarindo NWR, CR 202/E4
Tamarite de Litera, Sp. 103/F2
Tamaro (peak), Swi. 115/E5
Tamási, Hun. 106/D2
Tamatsukuri, Japan 135/E1
Tamaulipas (state), Mex. 198/B3
Tamazula de Gordiano, Mex. 200/E5
Tamazunchale, Mex. 202/B1
Tamba, Japan 135/H5
Tamba (uplands), Japan 135/H5
Tambacounda (pol. reg.), Sen. 160/B3
Tambacounda, Sen. 160/B3
Tambaoura, Falaise de (cliff), Mali 160/C3
Tambelan (isls.), Indo. 138/C3
Tambellup, Austl. 170/C5
Tambo (riv.), Peru 214/C3
Tambo (peak), Swi. 115/F5
Tambo, Austl. 172/B4
Tambo Colorado (ruin), Peru 214/C4
Tambo de Mora, Peru 214/B4
Tambo Grande, Peru 214/A2
Tambobamba, Peru 214/C4
Tambohorano, Madg. 165/G7
Tambopata (riv.), Peru 214/D4
Tambora (peak), Indo. 139/E5
Tamboril, Braz. 212/B2
Tamboritha (mt.), Austl. 173/C3
Tambov, Rus. 121/G1
Tambovskaya Oblast, Rus. 121/G1
Tambre (riv.), Sp. 102/A1
Tame (riv.), Eng, UK 91/E1
Tame, Col. 210/D3
Tâmega (riv.), Port. 102/B2
Tamentit, Alg. 157/E4
Tameside (co.), Eng, UK 93/F5
Tamgak (peak), Niger 161/H2
Tamgue (mass.), Gui. 160/B3
Tamiahua, Mex. 202/B1
Tamiahua (lag.), Mex. 202/B1
Tamil Nādu (state), India 140/C5
Taminango, Col. 210/B4
Tāmiyah, Egypt 149/B5
Tamlūk, India 143/F4
Tammany (mt.), NJ, US 196/C2
Tammela, Fin. 97/K1
Tammūn, WBnk. 149/D3
Tampa, Fl, US 191/H5
Tampa (int'l arpt.), Fl, US 191/H5
Tampere, Fin. 97/K1
Tampere-Pirkkala (int'l arpt.), Fin. 97/K1
Tampico, Mex. 202/B1
Tampoc (riv.), FrG. 211/H4
Tampon Ambohitra (peak), Madg. 165/J6
Tampulonanjing (peak), Indo. 138/A3
Tamra, Isr. 149/G6
Tamshiyacu, Peru 214/C2
Tamuín (riv.), Mex. 202/B1
Tamuín, Mex. 202/B1
Tamur (riv.), Nepal 143/F2
Tamworth, Austl. 173/D1
Tamworth, Eng, UK 91/E1
Tamyang, SKor. 131/D5
Tan (riv.), China 141/K3
Tan An, Viet. 136/D4
Tan-Tan, Mor. 156/C3
Tana (lake), Eth. 155/N5
Tana (riv.), Kenya 162/D3
Tana River Primate Nat'l Rsv., Kenya 162/D3
Tanabe, Japan 132/D4
Tanabe, Japan 135/J6
Tanabi, Braz. 213/B2
Tanacross, Ak, US 192/K3
Tanafjorden (estu.), Nor. 95/J1
Tanaga (vol.), Ak, US 192/C6
Tanaga (isl.), Ak, US 192/C6
Tanagura, Japan 133/G2
Tanah Merah, Malay. 141/H6
Tanahbala (isl.), Indo. 138/A4
Tanakpur, India 142/C1
Tanambe, Madg. 165/J6
Tanami (des.), Austl. 167/C2
Tanana, Ak, US 192/H2
Tanana (riv.), Ak, US 192/J3
Tanandava, Madg. 165/G8
Tanaro (riv.), It. 101/G4
Tancheng, China 130/D4
Tanch'ŏn, NKor. 131/E2
Tancítaro, Pico de (peak), Mex. 200/E5
Tancitaro, PN de, Mex. 198/A4
Tanda (lake), Mali 160/D3
Tānda, India 142/D2
Tānda, India 142/B1
Tăndărei, Rom. 107/H3
Tandil, Arg. 216/F3
Tāndliānwāla, Pak. 144/B4
Tando Ādam, Pak. 147/J3
Tando Allāhyār, Pak. 147/J3
Tando Muhammad Khān, Pak. 147/J3
Tandou (lake), Austl. 173/B2
Tandragee, NI, UK 92/B3
Tanem Taunggyi (range), Thai. 141/G4
Tanezrouft (des.), Alg. 157/E5
Tanezrouft-n-Ahenet (des), Alg. 157/F5
Tang (riv.), China 130/C4
Tanga, Tanz. 162/C4
Tanga (pol. reg.), Tanz. 162/C4
Tangail, Bang. 143/G3
Tangail (pol. reg.), Bang. 143/G3
Tanganyika (lake), D.R. Congo,Tanz. 162/A4
Tangará da Serra, Braz. 208/G6
Tangent (pt.), Ak, US 192/G1
Tanger, Mor. 158/B2
Tanger (prov.), Mor. 158/A2
Tangerhütte, Ger. 98/F2
Tangermünde, Ger. 98/F2
Tanggula (mts.), China 128/E5
Tanghe, China 130/C4
Tangi, Pak. 144/A2
Tangipahoa (riv.), La, US 195/P16
Tangipahoa (parish), La, US 195/P16
Tangjin, SKor. 131/D4
Tanglewilde-Thompson Place, Wa, US 193/B3
Tangshan, China 130/J7
Tangub, Phil. 137/D6
Tangyin, China 130/C4
Tangyuan, China 129/N2
Tanhaçu, Braz. 212/B4
Tanigumi, Japan 135/L4
Tanimbar (isl.), Indo. 139/H5
Taninges, Fr. 114/C5
Tanintharyi (div.), Myan. 141/G5
Tanjay, Phil. 137/D6
Tanjungbalai, Indo. 138/A3
Tanjungkarang-Telukbetung, Indo. 138/C5
Tanjungpandan, Indo. 138/C4
Tanjungpinang, Indo. 138/B3
Tanjungpura, Indo. 138/A3
Tānk, Pak. 144/A3
Tankwa Karoo NP, SAfr. 164/B4
Tann, Ger. 113/F6
Tanna (isl.), Van. 174/F6
Tannan, Japan 135/H5
Tannersville, Pa, US 196/C1
Tannheim, Aus. 115/G3
Tannu-Ola (mts.), Mong.,Rus. 128/F1
Tano (riv.), Gha. 154/E6
Tânout, Niger 161/H3
Tanquián de Escobedo, Mex. 202/B1
Tansen, Nepal 142/D2
Ṭanṭā, Egypt 149/B4
Tantallon, Md, US 196/A6
Tantō, Japan 135/G5
Tantoyuca, Mex. 202/B1
Tanuku, India 140/D4
Tanumshede, Swe. 96/D2
Tanunda, Austl. 173/A2
Tanyang, SKor. 131/E4
Tanzania (ctry.) 162/B4
Tanzawa-yama (peak), Japan 135/C3
Tao (isl.), Myan. 136/B4
Taolañaro, Madg. 165/H9
Taormina, It. 104/D4
Tāoru, India 144/D5
Taos, NM, US 187/F3
Taounate (town), Mor. 158/B2
Taounate, Mor. 158/B2
Taourirt, Alg. 157/F4
Taourirt, Mor. 158/C2
T'aoyüan, Tai. 137/D2
Taoyuan, China 141/K2
Tap Mun Chau (isl.), China 129/V10
Tap O'Noth (hill), Sc, UK 94/D2
Tapa, Est. 97/L2
Tapachula, Mex. 202/C3
Tapajós (riv.), Braz. 205/D3
Tapanahoni (riv.), Sur. 209/G3
Tapanti Nat'l Wild. Ref., CR 203/F4
Tapauá (riv.), Braz. 208/E5
Tapauá, Braz. 208/F5
Tapaz, Phil. 137/D5
Tapejara, Braz. 213/A4
Tapes, Braz. 213/B4
Tapeta, Libr. 160/C5
Tapia de Casariego, Sp. 102/B1
Tapiche (riv.), Peru 214/C2
Tapilula, Mex. 202/C2
Tapis (peak), Malay. 138/B3
Tapo, Peru 214/C3
Tapoa (prov.), Burk. 161/F3
Tapolca, Hun. 106/C2
Tappahannock, Va, US 188/E4
Tappan, NY, US 197/K7
Tappan Zee (lake), NY, US 197/E1
Tappan Zee (riv.), NY, US 197/K7
Tappi-zaki (pt.), Japan 134/B3
Tapps (lake), Wa, US 193/C3
Tāpti (riv.), India 147/J4
Ṭāq Kisrá (Ctesiphon) (ruin), Iraq 148/F3
Taquara, Braz. 213/B4
Taquari (riv.), Braz. 209/G7
Taquari, Braz. 213/B4
Taquaritinga, Braz. 213/B2
Taquarituba, Braz. 213/B2
Taquil, Ecu. 214/B1
Tar (riv.), Kyr. 145/G4
Tara, Rus. 145/F1
Tara (riv.), Bosn.,Mont. 106/D4
Tara, Austl. 172/C4
Taraba (state), Nga. 161/H5
Taraba (riv.), Nga. 161/H4
Tarābulus, Leb. 149/D2
Tarābulus (Tripoli) (cap.), Libya 154/H1
Tarakan, Indo. 139/E3
Taraklı, Turk. 107/K5
Taraku (isl.), Rus. 134/E2
Taralga, Austl. 173/D2
Taranagar, India 144/C5
Tarancón, Sp. 102/D2
Tarangire NP, Tanz. 163/G1
Taranto, It. 105/E2
Taranto, Golfo di (gulf), It. 104/E2
Tarapoto, Peru 214/B2
Tarare, Fr. 100/F4
Tarariras, Uru. 217/K11
Tarascon, Fr. 100/F5
Tarascon-sur-Ariège, Fr. 100/D5
Tarata, Peru 214/D5
Tarauacá, Braz. 214/D3
Tarauacá (riv.), Braz. 214/D2
Taravai (isl.), FrPol. 175/M7
Tarawa (cap.), Kiri. 174/G4
Tarawa (isl.), Kiri. 174/G4
Tarazona, Sp. 102/E3
Tarazona, Sp. 102/E2
Tarbagatay (mts.), Kaz. 128/D2
Tarbat Ness (pt.), Sc, UK 94/C1
Tarbela (dam), Pak. 144/B2
Tarbela (res.), Pak. 144/B2
Tarbes, Fr. 100/D5
Tarbolton, Sc, UK 94/B5
Tarboro, NC, US 191/J3
Tarcento, It. 101/K3
Tarcutta, Austl. 173/C2
Tardes (riv.), Fr. 100/E3
Tardienta, Sp. 103/E2
Tardoire (riv.), Fr. 100/D4
Taree, Austl. 173/E1
Tarf Water (riv.), Sc, UK 92/D2
Tarfâwi (well), Egypt 159/B4
Tarfaya, Mor. 156/B4
Target Rock NWR, NY, US 197/M8
Targuist, Mor. 158/B2
Tarhūnah, Libya 154/H1
Tarifa, Ecu. 214/B1
Tarifa, Sp. 102/C4
Tarija, Bol. 208/F8
Tariku (riv.), Indo. 139/J4
Tariku-Taritatu (plain), Indo. 139/J4
Tarim (basin), China 128/D4
Tarim (riv.), China 128/D3
Tarin (riv.), Afg. 147/J2
Tarin (Torino), It. 101/G4
Taritatu (riv.), Indo. 139/J4
Tarkastad, SAfr. 164/D4
Tarkhankut (cape), Ukr. 107/L3
Tarkwa, Gha. 161/E5
Tarlac, Phil. 137/D4
Tarma, Peru 214/C3
Tarmstedt, Ger. 109/G2
Tarn (riv.), Fr. 100/D5
Tarn Tāran, India 144/C4
Tarnak (riv.), Afg. 147/J2
Tarnobrzeg, Pol. 99/L3
Tarnów, Pol. 99/L3
Tärnsjö, Swe. 96/G1
Taro (riv.), It. 101/J4
Tarō, Japan 134/B4
Tārom, Iran 147/G3
Taroom, Austl. 172/C4
Tarouca, Port. 102/B2
Taroudannt, Mor. 156/C3
Tarp, Ger. 96/C4
Tarpa, Hun. 106/F1
Tarpon Springs, Fl, US 191/H4
Tarquinia, It. 104/B1
Tarqūmiyah, WBnk. 149/D4
Tarrafal, CpV. 151/K10
Tarragona, Sp. 103/F2
Tarraleah, Austl. 173/C4
Tàrrega, Sp. 103/F2
Tarrenz, Aus. 115/G3
Tarrytown, NY, US 197/K7
Tarsney Lakes, Mo, US 195/E6
Tarsus, Turk. 149/D1
Tarsus (riv.), Turk. 149/D1
Tartagal, Arg. 215/D1
Tartaro (riv.), It. 117/E2
Tartas, Fr. 100/C5
Tartu, Est. 97/M2
Ṭarṭūs (prov.), Syria 148/C3
Ṭarṭūs, Syria 149/D2
Tarui, Japan 135/L5
Tarumizu, Japan 132/B5
Tarutao NP, Thai. 136/B5
Tarvagatay (mts.), Mong. 128/G2
Taşağıl, Turk. 149/B1
Täsch, Swi. 114/D5
Taşçı, Turk. 148/C2
Tashkent (cap.), Uzb. 145/E4
Tashkent (int'l arpt.), Uzb. 145/E4
Tasikmalaya, Indo. 138/C5
Taşkent, Turk. 149/C1
Taşköprü, Turk. 120/E4
Taşlıçay, Turk. 148/E2
Tasman (pen.), Austl. 173/C4
Tasman (sea), Austl.,NZ 174/E8
Tasman (bay), NZ 175/S11
Tasman Head (cape), Austl. 173/C4
Tasmania, Austl. 173/C3
Tasmania (state), Austl. 173/C4
Tăşnad, Rom. 106/F2
Taşova, Turk. 148/D1
Tasquillo, Mex. 201/K6
Tassili-n-Ajjer (mts.), Alg. 157/G4
Tassili Oua-n Ahaggar (mts.), Alg. 157/G5
Tasu, BC, Can. 192/M5
Taşucu, Turk. 149/C1
Tata, Mor. 156/D3
Tata, Hun. 106/D2
Tatabánya, Hun. 106/D2
Tatachikapika (riv.), On, Can. 188/D2
Tatakoto (isl.), FrPol. 175/L6
Tatamy, Pa, US 196/C2
Tataouine, Tun. 157/H2
Tataouine (gov.), Tun. 157/H2
Tatar (str.), Rus. 125/P5
Tatarlar, Turk. 105/K2
Tatarsk, Rus. 145/G1
Tatarstan, Resp., Rus. 122/G6
Tate-yama (peak), Japan 133/E2
Tatebayashi, Japan 135/D1
Tateshina, Japan 135/A1
Tateyama, Japan 133/F3
Tathlina (lake), NW, Can. 180/E2
Tathra, Austl. 173/D3
Tatilt (well), Mrta. 160/B2
Tatitlek, Ak, US 192/J3
Tatnam (cape), Mb, Can. 180/G3
Tatomi, Japan 135/B2
Tatranský NP, Slvk. 99/K4
Tatsuno, Japan 133/E3
Tatsuta, Japan 135/L5
Tatura, Austl. 173/C3
Tatvan, Turk. 148/E2
Tauá, Braz. 212/B2
Taubaté, Braz. 213/H8
Tauber (riv.), Ger. 98/E4
Tauberbischofsheim, Ger. 112/C3
Tauca, Peru 214/B3
Taufkirchen, Ger. 113/F6
Taufkirchen an der Pram, Aus. 113/G6
Taufstein (peak), Ger. 112/C1
Taulihawa, Nepal 142/D2
Taung, SAfr. 164/D2
Taungdwingyi, Myan. 141/G3
Taunggyi, Myan. 141/G3
Taungup, Myan. 141/F4
Taunsa, Pak. 144/A4
Taunton, Ma, US 189/G3
Taunton, Eng, UK 90/C4
Taunus (range), Ger. 112/A2
Taunusstein, Ger. 112/B2
Taupo, NZ 175/T10
Taupo (lake), NZ 175/T10
Tauragė, Lith. 97/K4
Tauranga, NZ 175/T10
Taurion (riv.), Fr. 100/D3
Taurisano, It. 105/F3
Taurus (mts.), Turk. 148/C2
Tauste, Sp. 102/E2
Taute (riv.), Fr. 100/C2
Tauu (isls.), PNG 174/E5
Tavanbulag, Mong. 128/H2
Tavannes, Swi. 114/D3
Tavaputs (plat.), Ut, US 186/E3
Tavarnelle, It. 117/E5
Tavarnuzze, It. 117/E5
Tavas, Turk. 148/B2
Tavaux, Fr. 114/B3
Tavazzano, It. 116/C2
Tavda (riv.), Rus. 122/G4
Tavernerio, It. 116/C1
Taverny, Fr. 88/J4
Taviano, It. 105/F3
Tavira, Port. 102/B4
Tavoy (pt.), Myan. 136/B3
Tavoy (Dawei), Myan. 136/B3
Tavşanlı, Turk. 148/D2
Taw (riv.), Eng, UK 90/B6
Taw (riv.), Eng, UK 90/C5
Tawaramoto, Japan 135/J6
Tawas City, Mi, US 188/D2
Tawau, Malay. 139/E3
Tawe (riv.), Wal, UK 90/C3
Tawern, Ger. 111/F4
Tāwi (riv.), India 144/C3
Tawi-Tawi (isl.), Phil. 137/C6
Ṭāwūq, Iraq 148/F3
Taxco, Mex. 201/K8
Taxila (ruin), Pak. 144/B3
Taxila, Pak. 144/B3
Taxkorgan Tajik Zizhixian, China 147/L1
Tay (lake), Sc, UK 94/B3
Tay (riv.), Sc, UK 94/C3
Tay, Firth of (inlet), Sc, UK 94/C4
Tay Ninh, Viet. 136/D4
Tayabamba, Peru 214/B3
Taylor, Mi, US 193/F7
Taylorsville-Bennion, Ut, US 195/K12
Taymyr (riv.), Rus. 122/K2
Taymyr (isl.), Rus. 123/L2
Taymyr (pen.), Rus. 122/K2
Taymyrskiy Aut. Okrug, Rus. 122/J2
Tayoltita, Mex. 200/D3
Tayport, Sc, UK 94/D4
Tayrona, PN, Col. 210/C2
Tayshet, Rus. 123/K4
Taytay, Phil. 139/E1
Taz (riv.), Rus. 125/H3
Taza (prov.), Mor. 158/C2
Taza, Mor. 158/B2
Tazawako, Japan 134/B4
Tazekka (peak), Mor. 158/B2
Tazenakht, Mor. 156/D3
Tazewell, Tn, US 188/D4
Tāzirbū (oasis), Libya 155/K2
Tazumal (ruin), ESal. 202/D3
T'bilisi (cap.), Geo. 121/H4
T'boli, Phil. 137/D6
Tchamba, Togo 161/F4
Tchaourou, Ben. 161/F4
Tchefuncta (riv.), La, US 195/P16
Tchibanga, Gabon 154/H8
Tcholliré, Camr. 154/H6
Tczew, Pol. 97/H4
Te Anau, NZ 175/R12
Te Araroa, NZ 175/T10
Te Aroha, NZ 175/T10
Te Awamutu, NZ 175/T10
Te Kao, NZ 175/S9
Te Kuiti, NZ 175/T10
Tea (riv.), Braz. 208/E4
Teacapán, Mex. 200/D4
Teague, Tx, US 187/H5
Teaneck, NJ, US 197/J8
Teano, It. 104/D2
Teapa, Mex. 202/C2
Tearce, FYROM 105/G1
Tebak (peak), Indo. 138/B4
Tébessa (prov.), Alg. 157/G2
Tebessa (mts.), Alg. 158/L7
Tébessa, Alg. 158/L7
Tebesselamane (well), Mali 161/F2
Tebicuary (riv.), Par. 215/E2
Tebingtinggi, Indo. 138/A3
Tebourba, Tun. 104/A4
Tebulos-mta (peak), Rus. 121/H4
Tecalitlán, Mex. 200/E5
Tecamac, Mex. 201/R9
Tecamachalco, Mex. 201/M8
Tecate, Mex. 200/A1
Tech (riv.), Ger. 100/E5
Techirghiol, Rom. 107/J3
Tecirli, Turk. 148/D2
Tecka, Arg. 216/C4
Tecka (riv.), Arg. 216/C4
Tecklenberg, Ger. 109/E4
Tecolutla, Mex. 201/M6
Tecomán, Mex. 200/E5
Tecozautla, Mex. 201/K6
Tecpan de Galeana, Mex. 201/E5
Tecuala, Mex. 200/D4
Tecuci, Rom. 107/H3
Tecumseh, Mi, US 188/D3
Tecumseh, Ne, US 187/H2
Tecumseh, On, Can. 193/G7
Tedjert (well), Alg. 157/H1
Tedzhen (riv.), Trkm. 122/G6
Tees (bay), Eng, UK 93/G2
Tees (riv.), Eng, UK 93/G3
Teesside (int'l arpt.), Eng, UK 93/G3
Tefé (riv.), Braz. 208/E4
Tefé, Braz. 208/F4
Teferič, Serb. 106/E4
Tega (lake), Japan 135/E2
Tegal, Indo. 138/C5
Tegel (int'l arpt.), Ger. 98/Q6
Tegelen, Neth. 108/D6
Tegeler (lake), Ger. 98/Q6
Tegheri (well), Libya 157/H4
Teghra, India 143/E3
Tegid, Llyn (lake), Wal, UK 92/E6
Teglio, It. 115/G5
Tégouma (riv.), Niger 161/H3
Tegsh, Mong. 128/G2
Tegucigalpa (cap.), Hon. 202/E3
Tehek (lake), Nun., Can. 180/G2
Tehrān (cap.), Iran 146/F1
Tehuacán, Mex. 201/M8
Tehuantepec (isth.), Mex. 201/G5
Tehuantepec (riv.), Mex. 202/C2
Tehuantepec (gulf), Mex. 202/C3
Teide, Pico de (peak), Sp. 156/A3
Teifi (riv.), Wal, UK 90/B2
Teifiside (valley), Wal, UK 90/B2
Teiga (plat.), Sudan 155/L4
Teign (riv.), Eng, UK 90/C5
Teignmouth, Eng, UK 90/C5
Teisendorf, Ger. 113/F7
Teith (riv.), Sc, UK 94/B4
Tejen, Trkm. 147/H1
Tejn, Den. 96/F4
Tejupilco de Hidalgo, Mex. 201/E5
Tekamah, Ne, US 185/J5
Tekāri, India 143/E3
Tekax de Álvaro Obregón, Mex. 202/D1
Teke, Turk. 107/J5
Tekeli, Kaz. 145/G4

Tekes – Tlapa

Tekes (riv.), China 122/J5
Tekezē Wenz (riv.), Eth. 155/N5
Tekiliktag (peak), China 128/D4
Tekirdağ, Turk. 107/H5
Tekirdağ (prov.), Turk. 107/H5
Tekit, Mex. 202/D1
Tekkali, India 140/D4
Tekke, Turk. 148/D1
Tekkeköy, Turk. 148/D1
Tekman, Turk. 148/E2
Tel Aviv (dist.), Isr. 149/D3
Tel Aviv-Yafo, Isr. 149/F7
Tel Megiddo (ruin), Isr. 149/G6
Tela, Hon. 202/E3
Télagh, Alg. 158/D2
T'elavi, Geo. 121/H4
Telde, Sp. 156/B3
Télé (lake), Mali 160/D2
Telêmaco Borba, Braz. 213/B3
Telemark (co.), Nor. 95/D4
Telen (riv.), Indo. 139/E3
Teleorman (prov.), Rom. 107/G4
Telertheba (peak), Alg. 157/G4
Teles Pires (riv.), Braz. 205/D3
Telford, Pa, US 196/C3
Telford Dawley, Eng, UK 90/D1
Telfs, Aus. 115/H3
Telgate, It. 116/C1
Telgte, Ger. 109/E5
Telica, Nic. 202/E3
Télig (well), Mali 156/E5
Télimélé, Gui. 160/B4
Telkwa, BC, Can. 184/B2
Tell City, In, US 188/C4
Teller, Ak, US 192/E2
Telli (lake), Mrta. 156/C4
Tellicherry, India 140/C5
Tellin, Belg. 111/E3
Telluride, Co, US 186/F3
Telok Anson, Malay. 138/B3
Teloloapan, Mex. 201/F5
Telšiai, Lith. 97/K4
Teltow, Ger. 98/Q7
Teltow (reg.), Ger. 99/G2
Tema, Gha. 161/E5
Temagami (lake), On, Can. 188/D2
Temax, Mex. 202/D1
Tembilahan, Indo. 138/B4
Tembisa, SAfr. 164/E2
Temblador, Ven. 211/F2
Teme (riv.), Eng, UK 90/C2
Temecula, Ca, US 194/C4
Temelkovo, Bul. 106/F4
Temerin, Serb. 106/D3
Temerloh, Malay. 138/B3
Temirtaū, Kaz. 145/F2
Témiscamie (riv.), Qu, Can. 189/F1
Témiscaming, Qu, Can. 188/E2
Temoaya, Mex. 201/Q10
Temoe (isl.), FrPol. 175/M7
Temora, Austl. 173/C2
Tempe, Az, US 195/S19
Tempio Pausania, It. 104/A2
Temple, Pa, US 196/C3
Temple City, Ca, US 194/F7
Temple of Lady Chua Xu, Viet. 136/D4
Templemore, Ire. 89/Q10
Templepatrick, NI, UK 92/B2
Templeuve, Fr. 110/C2
Templeville, Md, US 196/C5
Templin, Ger. 99/G2
Templiner (lake), Ger. 98/Q7
Tempoal de Sánchez, Mex. 202/B1
Temryuk, Rus. 120/F3
Temse, Belg. 111/D1
Temuco, Chile 216/B3
Temuka, NZ 175/S11
Ten Boer, Neth. 108/D2
Tena, Ecu. 210/B5
Tena Kourou (peak), Mali 154/D5
Tenabo, Mex. 202/D1
Tenafly, NJ, US 197/K8
Tenakee Springs, Ak, US 192/L4
Tenancingo, Mex. 201/K8
Tenango, Mex. 201/R10
Tenango de Arista, Mex. 201/Q10
Tenasserim (range), Myan. 136/B3
Tenasserim, Myan. 136/B3
Tenay, Fr. 114/B6
Tenby, Wal, UK 90/B3
Tende, Fr. 101/G4
Tende, Col de (pass), Fr. 116/A4
Tenderovsk (bay), Ukr. 107/K2
Tenderovsk Spit (isl.), Ukr. 107/K2
Tendō, Japan 134/B4
Tendre (peak), Swi. 114/C4
Ténenkou, Mali 160/D3
Ténéré (des.), Niger 154/G4
Ténéré du Tafassasset (des.), Niger 154/G3
Tenerife, Col. 210/C2
Tenerife (isl.), Sp. 156/A3
Ténès, Alg. 158/F4
Tenes (riv.), Sp. 103/L6
Teng (riv.), Myan. 141/G3
Teng Xian, China 130/D4
Tenggarong, Indo. 139/E4
Tengger (des.), China 128/H4
Tengiz Köli (lake), Kaz. 122/G4
Tenguel, Ecu. 210/B5
Tenibres (peak), It. 101/G4
Teniente Enciso, PN, Par. 215/D1
Teningen, Ger. 114/D1
Tenja, Cro. 106/D3
Tenkodogo, Burk. 161/E4
Tenmile (riv.), Az, US 186/D4
Tennessee (state), US 191/G3
Tennessee (riv.), US 191/F3
Tenneville, Belg. 111/E3
Tennuaca (well), Mor. 156/B5
Teno, Chile 216/C2
Tenojoki (riv.), Fin. 95/H1
Tenosique de Pino Suárez, Mex. 202/D2
Tenri, Japan 135/J6
Tenryū, Japan 133/E3
Tenryū (riv.), Japan 133/E3
Tensift (pol. reg.), Mor. 156/C3
Tensift, Oued (riv.), Mor. 156/C3
Tenterfield, Austl. 173/E1
Tentolomatinan (peak), Indo. 139/F3
Tenus (peak), Kenya 162/B2
Teo, Sp. 102/A1
Teocaltiche, Mex. 198/A3
Teocelo, Mex. 201/N7
Teodelina, Arg. 216/E2
Teodoro Sampaio, Braz. 213/A2
Teófilo Otoni, Braz. 212/B5
Teopisca, Mex. 202/C2
Teotihuacán (ruin), Mex. 201/R9
Teotihuacán, Mex. 201/R9
Teotitlán del Camino, Mex. 202/B2
Tepache, Mex. 200/C2
Tepalcatepec, Mex. 200/E5
Tepalcingo, Mex. 201/L8
Tepatitlán de Morelos, Mex. 198/A3
Tepatlaxco, Mex. 201/M7
Tepeapulco, Mex. 201/L7
Tepebaşı, Turk. 149/C1
Tepehuaje, Mex. 201/F4
Tepehuanes, Mex. 200/D3
Tepeji del Río de Ocampo, Mex. 201/K7
Tepelenë, Alb. 105/G2
Tepelská Plošina (mts.), Czh. 113/F2
Tepetlaoxtoc, Mex. 201/R9
Tepexi, Mex. 201/M8
Tepexpan, Mex. 201/R9
Tepic, Mex. 200/D4
Teplá (riv.), Czh. 98/G3
Teplá Vltava (riv.), Czh. 113/G5
Teplice, Czh. 99/G3
Tepoca (cape), Mex. 200/B2
Tepoca, Cabo (cape), Mex. 200/B2
Tepoto (isl.), FrPol. 175/L6
Tepotzotlán, Mex. 201/Q9
Tepoztlán, Mex. 201/K8
Tequila, Mex. 200/E4
Tequisquiapan, Mex. 201/F4
Tequixquiac, Mex. 201/K7
Ter (riv.), Sp. 103/G1
Ter Aar, Neth. 108/B4
Téra, Niger 161/F3
Tera (riv.), Sp. 102/B1
Teraina (Washington) (isl.), Kiri. 175/J4
Teramo, It. 101/K5
Terang, Austl. 173/B3
Tercan, Turk. 148/E2
Terceira (isl.), Azor., Port. 103/S12
Terek (riv.), Rus. 121/H4
Terepaima, PN, Ven. 210/D2
Teresina, Braz. 212/B2
Teresópolis, Braz. 213/L7
Terespol, Pol. 99/M2
Tergnier, Fr. 110/C4
Tergun Daba (mts.), China 128/F4
Terheijden, Neth. 108/B5
Teriberskiy (pt.), Rus. 118/G1
Terkaplesterpoelen (lake), Neth. 108/C2
Terlan (Terlano), It. 115/H4
Termas de Río Hondo, Arg. 215/D2
Termini Imerese, It. 104/C4
Términos (lag.), Mex. 202/D2
Termiz, Uzb. 147/J1
Termo, Ca, US 184/C5
Termoli, It. 104/D1
Termonfeckin, Ire. 92/B4
Termunten, Neth. 108/E2
Ternate, Indo. 139/G3
Ternberg, Aus. 113/H7
Terneuzen, Neth. 108/A6
Terni, It. 104/C1
Ternin (riv.), Fr. 100/F3
Ternoise (riv.), Fr. 110/B3
Ternopil', Ukr. 120/C2
Ternopil's'ka Oblasti, Ukr. 120/C2
Terpeniya (bay), Rus. 123/Q5
Terpní, Gre. 105/H2
Terra Nova, Braz. 212/B4
Terra Nova, Braz. 212/C3
Terra Nova NP, Nf, Can. 189/L1
Terrace, BC, Can. 184/A2
Terrace Bay, On, Can. 185/M3
Terracina, It. 104/C2
Terråk, Nor. 95/E2
Terralba, It. 104/A3
Terranuova Bracciolini, It. 117/E5
Terrassa, Sp. 103/L6
Terrasson-la-Villedieu, Fr. 100/D4
Terre Hill, Pa, US 196/B3
Terrebonne, Qu, Can. 189/N6
Terrell Hills, Tx, US 195/U21
Terri (peak), Swi. 115/F4
Terry, Mt, US 185/G4
Terry (lake), Co, US 195/B2
Terrytown, La, US 195/P17
Terschelling (isl.), Neth. 108/C2
Tertenia, It. 104/A3
Teruel, Sp. 103/E2
Terutao (isl.), Thai. 141/G6
Tervel, Bul. 107/H4
Terza Grande (peak), It. 101/K3
Terzo d'Aquileia, It. 117/G1
Tešanj, Bosn. 106/C3
Tescou (riv.), Fr. 100/D5
Tesero, It. 115/H5
Teshekpuk (lake), Ak, US 192/G1
Teshikaga, Japan 134/D2
Teshio (riv.), Japan 134/C1
Teshio, Japan 134/B1
Teshio-dake (peak), Japan 134/C2
Teslić, Bosn. 106/C3
Teslin (riv.), Yk, Can. 180/C2
Teslin (lake), BC, Can. 180/C3
Tessaoua, Niger 161/G3
Tessenderlo, Belg. 111/E1
Tessenie (Teseney), Erit. 146/C5
Test (riv.), Eng, UK 91/E4
Testa del Gargano (pt.), It. 104/E2
Tét, Hun. 106/C2
Tete, Moz. 163/F4
Tête de l'Estrop (peak), Fr. 101/G4
Tetela, Mex. 201/M7
Teterow, Ger. 96/E5
Teteven, Bul. 107/G4
Tetiaroa (isl.), FrPol. 175/L6
Tetlin, Ak, US 192/K3
Teton (riv.), Mt, US 184/F4
Tétouan (prov.), Mor. 158/B2
Tétouan, Mor. 158/B2
Tetovo, FYROM 105/G1
Tettnang, Ger. 115/F2
Tetulia (riv.), Bang. 143/H4
Teublitz, Ger. 113/F4
Teuco (riv.), Arg. 215/D1
Teufen, Swi. 115/F3
Teúl de González Ortega, Mex. 200/E4
Teulada (cape), It. 104/A3
Teulon, Mb, Can. 185/J3
Teupasenti, Hon. 202/E3
Teuri (isl.), Japan 134/B1
Teuschnitz, Ger. 113/E2
Teutoburger Wald (for.), Ger. 109/F4
Tevere (Tiber) (riv.), It. 101/K5
Teverya, Isr. 149/D3
Teviot (riv.), Sc, UK 94/D6
Teviotdale (valley), Sc, UK 94/D6
Tewantin-Noosa, Austl. 172/D4
Tewkesbury, Eng, UK 90/D3
Texarkana, Tx, US 187/J4
Texas, Austl. 173/D1
Texas (state), US 190/C4
Texas City, Tx, US 187/J5
Texcoco, Mex. 201/R9
Texel (isl.), Neth. 98/C2
Texhoma, Ok, US 190/C2
Texmelucan, Mex. 201/L7
Texoma (lake), Ok,Tx, US 187/H4
Teyateyaneng, Les. 164/D3
Teykovo, Rus. 118/J4
Tezio (peak), It. 117/F6
Teziutlán, Mex. 201/M7
Tezonapa, Mex. 201/N8
Tezontepec, Mex. 201/L7
Tezontepec de Aldama, Mex. 201/K6
Tezoyuca, Mex. 201/R9
Tezpur, India 128/F6
Tezu, India 141/G2
Tezze, It. 117/E1
Tha-Anne (riv.), Nun., Can. 180/G2
Tha Chin (riv.), Thai. 136/B3
Thabana-Ntlenyana (peak), Les. 164/E3
Thabankulu (peak), SAfr. 165/E2
Thaen (pt.), Thai. 136/B4
Thai Binh, Viet. 141/J3
Thai Nguyen, Viet. 141/J3
Thailand (gulf), Asia 136/C4
Thailand (ctry.) 136/C3
Thākurdwāra, India 142/B1
Thal, Pak. 144/A3
Thal (des.), Pak. 144/A4
Thaleban NP, Thai. 136/C5
Thaleischweiler-Fröschen, Ger. 111/G5
Thalerhof (int'l arpt.), Aus. 101/L3
Thalgau, Aus. 113/G7
Thalheim bei Wels, Aus. 113/H6
Thalmässing, Ger. 112/E4
Thalwil, Swi. 115/E3
Thamar, Jabal (peak), Yem. 146/E6
Thame (riv.), Eng, UK 91/F3
Thames (riv.), On, Can. 188/D3
Thames, NZ 175/T10
Thames (riv), Eng., UK 91/G4
Thames Barrier, Eng, UK 88/D2
Thāna, India 147/K5
Thāna Bhawan, India 144/D5
Thānesar, India 144/D5
Thangool, Austl. 172/C4
Thanh Hoa, Viet. 141/J4
Thanjavur, India 140/C5
Thann, Fr. 114/D2
Thannhausen, Ger. 115/G1
Thaon-les-Vosges, Fr. 114/C1
Thar (des.), Pak. 144/A5
Tharād, India 147/K4
Thargomindah, Austl. 172/A5
Tharrawaddy, Myan. 141/G4
Thásos, Gre. 105/J2
Thásos (isl.), Gre. 105/J2
Thatcham, Eng, UK 91/E4
Thatcher, Az, US 186/E4
Thaton, Myan. 136/B2
Thaur, Aus. 115/H3
Thaya (riv.), Aus. 99/H4
Thayetmyo, Myan. 141/G4
Thayngen, Swi. 115/E2
Thazi, Myan. 141/G3
The Alamo, Tx, US 195/U21
The Dalles, Or, US 184/C4
The Hague ('s-Gravenhage) (cap.), Neth. 108/B4
The Oaks, Ca, US 194/B1
The Pas, Mb, Can. 185/H2
The Rock, Austl. 173/C2
The Valley (cap.), Angu. 199/N8
The Village, Ok, US 195/M14
The Woodlands, Tx, US 187/J5
The Wrekin (co.), Eng, UK 93/F6
Thebes (ruin), Egypt 159/C3
Theilheim, Ger. 112/D3
Thelma, Tx, US 195/T21
Thelon (riv.), NW,Nun., Can. 180/F2
Thémericourt, Fr. 88/H4
Theo (mt.), Austl. 171/F2
Theodore, Sk, Can. 185/H3
Theodore, Austl. 172/C4
Theodore Roosevelt (lake), Az, US 186/E4
Theodore Roosevelt NP, ND, US 185/G4
Thérain (riv.), Fr. 100/D2
Thermaic (gulf), Gre. 105/H2
Thérmi, Gre. 105/H2
Thermopílai (Thermopylae) (pass), Gre. 105/H3
Thermopolis, Wy, US 184/F5
Thérouanne (riv.), Fr. 88/L4
Thesprotikón, Gre. 105/G3
Thessalon, On, Can. 188/D2
Thessaloníki, Gre. 105/H2
Thessaly (reg.), Gre. 105/H3
Thet (riv.), Eng, UK 91/G2
Thetford, Eng, UK 91/G2
Thetford Mines, Qu, Can. 189/G2
Theunissen, SAfr. 164/D3
Theux, Belg. 111/E2
Thève (riv.), Fr. 88/K4
Theydon Bois, Eng, UK 88/D2
Thiais, Fr. 88/K5
Thiamis (riv.), Gre. 105/G3
Thiant, Fr. 110/C3
Thiaucourt-Regniéville, Fr. 111/E6
Thief River Falls, Mn, US 185/J3
Thielle (riv.), Swi. 114/C4
Thielsen (mt.), Or, US 184/C5
Thiene, It. 117/E1
Thiérache (reg.), Fr. 110/C4
Thierhaupten, Ger. 112/D5
Thiers, Fr. 100/E4
Thiers-sur-Thève, Fr. 88/K4
Thierville-sur-Meuse, Fr. 111/E5
Thiès (pol. reg.), Sen. 160/A3
Thiès, Sen. 160/A3
Thika, Kenya 162/C3
Thingvellir NP, Ice. 95/N7
Thionville, Fr. 111/F5
Thíra, Gre. 105/J4
Thíra (isl.), Gre. 105/J4
Third Cataract (falls), Sudan 159/B5
Third Lake, Il, US 193/Q15
Thirlmere (lake), Eng, UK 93/E2
Thirsty (mt.), Austl. 170/D5
Thirtymile (pt.), NY, US 189/V9
Thise, Fr. 114/C3
Thisted, Den. 96/C3
Thistilfjördhur (estu.), Ice. 95/P6
Thistle (isl.), Austl. 171/H5
Thistle (mtn.), Yk, Can. 192/L3
Thitu (isl.) 137/E5
Thívai, Gre. 105/H3
Thiverval-Grignon, Fr. 88/H5
Thjósa (riv.), Ice. 95/N7
Thlewiaza (riv.), Nun., Can. 180/G2
Thoiry, Fr. 88/H5
Tholen (isl.), Neth. 108/B5
Tholen, Neth. 108/B5
Tholey, Ger. 111/G5
Thomaston, Ga, US 191/G3
Thomastown, Ire. 89/Q10
Thomasville, Al, US 191/G4
Thomasville, Ga, US 191/H4
Thomasville, NC, US 191/H3
Thomasville, Pa, US 196/B4
Thompson, Mb, Can. 185/J2
Thompson (riv.), BC, Can. 184/C3
Thompson (lake), Austl. 170/K7
Thompson Falls, Mt, US 184/E4
Thomsen (riv.), NW, Can. 180/E1
Thomson (riv.), Austl. 172/A4
Thomson, Ga, US 191/H3
Thongwa, Myan. 136/B2
Thonnance-lès-Joinville, Fr. 114/B1
Thonon-les-Bains, Fr. 114/C5
Thoreau, NM, US 186/E4
Thorens-Glières, Fr. 114/C6
Thorhild, Ab, Can. 184/E2
Thorigny-sur-Marne, Fr. 88/L5
Thorlákshöfn, Ice. 95/N7
Thornaby-on-Tees, Eng, UK 93/G2
Thornbury, Eng, UK 90/D3
Thorndale, Pa, US 196/C4
Thorne, Eng, UK 93/H4
Thorne Bay, Ak, US 192/M4
Thornhill, Sc, UK 94/B4
Thornhill, Sc, UK 92/E1
Thornhurst, Pa, US 196/C1
Thornton, Co, US 195/C3
Thornton, Ca, US 193/M10
Thornton Cleveleys, Eng, UK 93/E4
Thorold, On, Can. 189/R9
Thórshöfn, Ice. 95/P6
Thouars, Fr. 100/C3
Thouet (riv.), Fr. 100/C3
Thourotte, Fr. 110/B5
Thousand Oaks, Ca, US 194/B2
Thowa (riv.), Kenya 162/C3
Thrace (reg.), Gre.,Turk. 105/J2
Thracian (sea), Gre. 105/J2
Thredbo Village, Austl. 173/D3
Three Bridges, NJ, US 196/D2
Three Forks, Mt, US 184/F4
Three Guardsmen (mtn.), BC, Can. 192/L4
Three Hills, Ab, Can. 184/E3
Three Hummock (isl.), Austl. 173/C4
Three Kings (isls.), NZ 175/S9
Three Mile (isl.), Pa, US 196/B3
Three Pagodas (pass), Myan. 136/B3
Three Points (cape), Gha. 161/E5
Three Rivers, Mi, US 188/C3
Three Rivers, Austl. 170/C3
Three Springs, Austl. 170/B4
Thriuvananthapuram, India 140/C6
Throssell (lake), Austl. 172/E3
Thrushel (riv.), Eng, UK 90/B5
Thu Dau Mot, Viet. 136/D4
Thuin, Belg. 111/D3
Thuir, Fr. 100/E5
Thulba (riv.), Ger. 112/C2
Thule Air Base, Den. 181/T2
Thun, Swi. 114/D4
Thunderbird (lake), Ok, US 195/N15
Thuner See (lake), Swi. 101/G3
Thung Salaeng Luang NP, Thai. 136/C2
Thüngersheim, Ger. 112/C3
Thur (riv.), Swi. 101/H3
Thurgau (canton), Swi. 115/E2
Thüringen (state), Ger. 101/J1
Thüringen, Aus. 115/F3
Thüringer Schiefergebirge (mts.), Ger. 112/E2
Thüringer Wald (for.), Ger. 101/J1
Thurles, Ire. 89/Q10
Thurnau, Ger. 113/E2
Thurø By, Den. 96/D4
Thurrock (co.), Eng, UK 91/G3
Thurso, Sc, UK 89/V14
Thurston (isl.), Ant. 218/T
Thurston (co.), Wa, US 193/A3
Thury-en-Valois, Fr. 88/M4
Thusis, Swi. 115/F4
Thyez, Fr. 114/C5
Thyolo, Malw. 163/G4
Ti-m-Merhsoï (riv.), Niger 161/G2
Ti-n-Jedane, Oued (riv.), Alg. 157/G4
Ti-n-Zaouâten, Alg. 154/F4
Ti-Tree Abor. Land, Austl. 171/G2
Tiahuanco (ruin), Bol. 214/D5
Tian (pt.), BC, Can. 192/M5
Tian Shan (mts.), China 128/C3
Tianchang, China 130/D4
Tianguá, Braz. 212/B1
Tianguistenco, Mex. 201/Q10
Tianjin (mun.), China 129/L4
Tianjin, China 130/H7
Tianlin, China 141/J3
Tianmen, China 137/B1
Tianmu (mts.), China 130/K9
Tianshui, China 128/J5
Tianyang, China 137/A3
Tianzhen, China 130/C2
Tianzhu, China 141/J2
Tiaret, Alg. 158/F5
Tibagi, Braz. 213/B3
Tibaji (riv.), Braz. 213/B3
Tibaná, Col. 210/C3
Tibati, Camr. 154/H6
Tibba, Pak. 144/A5
Tibé, Pic de (peak), Gui. 160/C4
Tiber (Tevere) (riv.), It. 101/J5
Tiberias (lake), Isr. 149/D3
Tibesti (mts.), Chad 154/J3
Tibet (reg.), China 125/H6
Tibet (Xizang) (aut. reg.), China 128/D5
Tibro, Swe. 96/F2
Tiburon (cape), Haiti 199/G4
Tiburon, Ca, US 193/K11
Tiburón, Isla (isl.), Mex. 200/B2
Ticaco, Peru 214/D5
Tichigan (lake), Wi, US 193/P14
Tichît, Dhar (cliff), Mrta. 160/C2
Ticino (canton), Swi. 115/E5
Ticleni, Rom. 107/F3
Ticllos, Peru 214/B3
Ticonderoga, NY, US 188/F3
Ticul, Mex. 202/D1
Tidaholm, Swe. 96/E2
Tidikelt (plain), Alg. 154/F2
Tidjikdja, Mrta. 160/C2
Tidone (riv.), It. 116/C3
Tidore (isl.), Indo. 139/G3
Tidra, Île (isl.), Mrta. 160/A2
Tidsit (lake), WSah. 156/B5
Tiede, PN del, Sp. 156/A3
Tiefencastel, Swi. 115/F4
Tiel, Neth. 108/C5
Tieling, China 130/E2
Tielt, Belg. 110/C2
Tielt-Winge, Belg. 111/D2
Tiemba (riv.), C.d'Iv. 160/D4
Tienen, Belg. 111/D2
Tieri, Austl. 172/C3
Tieroko (peak), Chad 155/J3
Tierp, Swe. 96/G1
Tierra Amarilla, NM, US 186/F3
Tierra Blanca, Mex. 201/N8
Tierra Colorada, Mex. 201/F5
Tierra del Fuego (isl.), Arg. 217/D7
Tierra del Fuego, Antártida e Islas del Atlántico Sur, Arg. 217/C7
Tierra del Fuego, PN, Arg. 217/C7
Tierradentro, Col. 210/B4
Tierranueva, Mex. 201/E4
Tiétar (riv.), Sp. 102/C2
Tietê (riv.), Braz. 205/D5
Tiffin, Oh, US 188/D3
Tiflet, Mor. 158/A3
Tifton, Ga, US 191/H4
Tigeaux, Fr. 88/L5
Tighina (Bendery), Mol. 107/J2
Tighvein (hill), Sc, UK 94/A6
Tignère, Camr. 154/H6
Tignieu-Jameyzieu, Fr. 114/B6
Tigre (riv.), Ven. 208/C4
Tigre (riv.), Ven. 211/F2
Tigre, Arg. 217/J11
Tigris (riv.), Iraq 146/E2
Tigui (well), Chad 155/J4
Tiguidit, Falaise de (cliff), Niger 161/G2
Tigzirt, Alg. 158/H4
Tihosuco, Mex. 202/D1
Tihuatlán, Mex. 202/B1
Tiilikkajärven NP, Fin. 118/F3
Tijāra, India 142/A2
Tijuana, Mex. 194/C5
Tijuca, PN da, Braz. 213/K7
Tijucas, Braz. 213/B3
Tijuco (riv.), Braz. 213/B1
Tikal (ruin), Guat. 202/D2
Tikamgarh, India 142/B3
Tikchik (lakes), Ak, US 192/G3
Tikehau (isl.), FrPol. 175/L6
Tikhoretsk, Rus. 120/G3
Tikhvin, Rus. 118/G4
Tikrīt, Iraq 148/E3
Tikveš (lake), FYROM 105/H2
Tila, Mex. 202/C2
Tilburg, Neth. 108/C5
Tilbury, Eng, UK 88/E2
Tilden, Tx, US 190/D4
Tilghman, Md, US 196/B6
Tilghman (isl.), Md, US 196/B6
Tilhar, India 142/B2
Tilin, Myan. 141/F3
Tilisarao, Arg. 216/D2
Till (riv.), Eng, UK 94/D5
Tillabéri (dept.), Niger 161/F3
Tillabéry, Niger 161/F3
Tillamook, Or, US 184/C4
Tille (riv.), Fr. 98/C5
Tillicoultry, Sc, UK 94/C4
Tilst, Den. 96/D3
Tilt (riv.), Sc, UK 94/C3
Tiltil, Chile 216/N8
Tim, Den. 96/C3
Timan (ridge), Rus. 122/F3
Timaná, Col. 210/C4
Timanfaya, PN de, Sp. 156/B3
Timaru, NZ 175/S11
Timashevsk, Rus. 120/F3
Timbákion, Gre. 105/J5
Timbaúba, Braz. 212/D2
Timbédra, Mrta. 160/C2
Timber Lake, SD, US 185/H4
Timberlane, La, US 195/Q17
Timberwood Park, Tx, US 195/U20
Timbiquí, Col. 210/B4
Timbiras, Braz. 212/B2
Timbó, Braz. 213/B3
Timboon, Austl. 173/B3
Timehri (int'l arpt.), Guy. 211/G3
Timelkam, Aus. 113/G6
Timfristós (peak), Gre. 105/G3
Timimoun, Alg. 157/F3
Timiris (cape), Mrta. 160/A2
Timiş (prov.), Rom. 106/E3
Timiş (riv.), Rom. 106/E3
Timişoara (int'l arpt.), Rom. 106/E3
Timişoara, Rom. 106/E3
Timmins, On, Can. 188/D1
Timms (hill), Wi, US 185/L4
Timnath, Co, US 195/C1
Timon, Braz. 212/B2
Timonium, Md, US 196/B5
Timor (isl.), ETim.,Indo. 139/F5
Timor (sea), Asia,Austl. 139/G5
Timóteo, Braz. 213/D1
Timpanogos Cave Nat'l Mon., Ut, US 186/E2
Timpanogos Nat'l Mon., Ut, US 195/K13
Timpson, Tx, US 187/J5
Timpton (riv.), Rus. 123/N4
Tims Ford (lake), Tn, US 191/G3
Timurnī, India 142/A4
Tin Can Bay, Austl. 172/D4
Tin Shui Wai, China 129/T10
Tina (riv.), SAfr. 164/B1
Tinaca (pt.), Phil. 137/E6
Tinaco, Ven. 210/D2
Tindivanam, India 140/C5
Tindouf, Alg. 156/C4
Tindouf (prov.), Alg. 156/D4
Tineo, Sp. 102/B1
Tingalpa (res.), Austl. 172/F7
Tingaringy NP, Austl. 173/D3
Tingha, Austl. 173/D1
Tingi (mts.), SLeo. 160/C4
Tingmerkpuk (mtn.), Ak, US 192/F2
Tingo María, Peru 214/C3
Tingsryd, Swe. 96/F3
Tinguiririca (vol.), Chile 216/C2
Tinharé, Ilha de (isl.), Braz. 209/L6
Tinian (isl.), NMar. 174/D3
Tinicum Nat'l Consv. Area, Pa, US 196/C4
Tinkisso (riv.), Gui. 160/C4
Tinley Park, Il, US 193/Q16
Tinogasta, Arg. 215/C2
Tinos, Gre. 105/J4
Tinos (isl.), Gre. 105/J4
Tinqueux, Fr. 110/C5
Tinrhir, Mor. 156/D3
Tinta, Peru 214/D4
Tintagel (pt.), Eng, UK 90/B5
Tintern Abbey, Eng, UK 90/D3
Tintigny, Belg. 111/E4
Tintinara, Austl. 173/B2
Tinto (riv.), Sp. 102/B4
Tinto (peak), Sc, UK 94/C5
Tinton Falls (New Shrewsbury), NJ, US 196/D3
Tinyahuarco, Peru 214/B3
Tioga, ND, US 185/H3
Tioman (isl.), Malay. 138/B3
Tione di Trento, It. 115/G5
Tipasa (prov.), Alg. 158/F4
Tipasa, Alg. 158/G4
Tipperary, Ire. 89/P10
Tiptūr, India 140/C5
Tir Rhiwiog (peak), Wal, UK 90/C1
Tiracambu, Serra do (mts.), Braz. 209/J4
Tiran (str.), Egypt, SA 159/C3
Tiran (isl.), Egypt,SAr 159/C3
Tirān (isl.), Egypt 155/M2
Tirano, It. 115/G5
Tirari (des.), Austl. 171/H4
Tiraspol, Mol. 107/J2
Tirat Karmel, Isr. 149/F6
Tire, Turk. 148/A2
Tirebolu, Turk. 120/F4
Tiree (isl.), Sc, UK 89/Q8
Tirest (well), Mali 161/F1
Tirgovişte, Rom. 107/G3
Tirgu Bujor, Rom. 107/H3
Tirgu Cărbuneşti, Rom. 107/F3
Tirgu Frumos, Rom. 107/H2
Tirgu Jiu, Rom. 107/F3
Tirgu Lăpuş, Rom. 107/F2
Tirgu Mureş, Rom. 107/G2
Tirgu Neamţ, Rom. 107/H2
Tirgu Ocna, Rom. 107/H2
Tirgu Secuiesc, Rom. 107/H2
Tirich Mīr (peak), Pak. 147/K1
Tiris (reg.), WSah. 156/B5
Tiris Zemmour (pol. reg.), Mrta. 156/C4
Tîrnava Mare (riv.), Rom. 107/G2
Tîrnava Mică (riv.), Rom. 107/F2
Tîrnăveni, Rom. 107/G2
Tírnavos, Gre. 105/H3
Tiros, Braz. 213/C1
Tirschenreuth, Ger. 113/F3
Tirstrup (int'l arpt.), Den. 96/D3
Tiruchchirāppalli, India 140/C5
Tiruchendūr, India 140/C6
Tiruchengodu, India 140/C5
Tirunelveli, India 140/C6
Tiruntán, Peru 214/C2
Tirupati, India 140/C5
Tiruppattūr, India 140/C5
Tiruppūr, India 140/C5
Tiruvannāmalai, India 140/C5
Tisa (riv.), Ukr. 107/G1
Tisdale, Sk, Can. 185/G2
Tishomingo, Ok, US 187/H4
Tissa, Mor. 158/B2
Tissemsilt (prov.), Alg. 158/F5
Tissemsilt, Alg. 158/F5
Tista (riv.), Bang. 143/G2
Tisza (riv.), Hun. 120/B3
Tiszaföldvár, Hun. 106/E2
Tiszafüred, Hun. 106/E2
Tiszakécske, Hun. 106/E2
Tiszalök, Hun. 106/E1
Tiszavasvári, Hun. 99/L5
Titano (peak), SMar. 117/F5
Titel, Serb. 106/E3
Titicaca (lake), Bol.,Peru 214/D4
Titisee-Neustadt, Ger. 114/E2
Titlagarh, India 140/D3
Titlis (peak), Swi. 115/E4
Tito, It. 104/D2
Titov Veles, FYROM 105/G2
Titov vrh (peak), FYROM 105/G2
Titting, Ger. 112/E5
Tittmoning, Ger. 113/F6
Titu, Rom. 107/G3
Titusville, Fl, US 191/H4
Titusville, NJ, US 196/D3
Tiva (riv.), Kenya 162/C3
Tivaouane, Sen. 160/A3
Tivat, Mont. 106/D4
Tiverton, Eng, UK 90/C5
Tiwanacu, Bol. 214/D5
Tixán, Ecu. 214/B1
Tixtla de Guerrero, Mex. 201/F5
Tizayuca, Mex. 201/L7
Tizi Ouzou (prov.), Alg. 158/H4
Tizi Ouzou, Alg. 158/H4
Tizimín, Mex. 202/D1
Tiznap (riv.), China 147/L1
Tiznit, Mor. 156/C3
Tjæreborg, Den. 96/C4
Tjeldstø, Nor. 96/A1
Tjeukemeer (lake), Neth. 108/C3
Tjøme, Nor. 96/D2
Tjorn (isl.), Den. 96/D3
Tlachichuca, Mex. 201/M7
Tlacolula de Matamoros, Mex. 202/B2
Tlacotalpan, Mex. 201/P8
Tlacotepec, Mex. 201/F5
Tlahualilo de Zaragoza, Mex. 200/E3
Tlalixcoyan, Mex. 201/N8
Tlalmanalco, Mex. 201/Q10
Tlalnepantla, Mex. 201/Q9
Tlaloc (vol.), Mex. 201/Q10
Tlaltenango de Sánchez Román, Mex. 200/E4
Tlaltizapan, Mex. 201/K8
Tlapa de Comonfort, Mex. 202/B2

Place	Ref
Tlapacoya (ruin), Mex.	201/Q10
Tlapacoyan, Mex.	201/M7
Tlapehuala, Mex.	201/E5
Tlaquepaque, Mex.	200/E4
Tlaquiltenango, Mex.	201/K8
Tlatlauquitepec, Mex.	201/M7
Tlaxcala (state), Mex.	198/A5
Tlaxcala, Mex.	201/L7
Tlaxco, Mex.	201/L7
Tlaxcoapan, Mex.	201/K6
Tlell, BC, Can.	192/M5
Tlemcen, Alg.	158/D2
Toabré, Pan.	203/F4
Toaca (peak), Rom.	107/G2
Toachi (riv.), Ecu.	210/B4
Toamasina, Madg.	165/J7
Toamasina (prov.), Madg.	165/J7
Toandos (pen.), Wa, US	193/B2
Toau (isl.), FrPol.	175/L6
Toay, Arg.	216/D3
Toba (lake), Indo.	138/A3
Toba (inlet), BC, Can.	184/B3
Toba, China	128/G5
Toba, Japan	135/L7
Toba Käkar (range), Pak.	147/J2
Toba Tek Singh, Pak.	144/B4
Tobago (isl.), Trin.	208/F1
Tobarra, Sp.	102/E3
Tobbio (peak), It.	116/B3
Tobermore, NI, UK	92/B2
Tobetsu, Japan	134/B2
Tobias Barreto, Braz.	212/C3
Tobin (lake), Austl.	170/E2
Tobique (riv.), NB, Can.	189/H2
Tobishima, Japan	135/L5
Tobol (riv.), Rus.	119/Q5
Tobu, Japan	135/A1
Tobyhanna (lake), Pa, US	196/C1
Tobyhanna (riv.), Pa, US	196/C1
Tobyhanna, Pa, US	196/C1
Tobyhanna St. Park, Pa, US	196/C1
Tobyl (riv.), Kaz.	121/M1
Tobysh (riv.), Rus.	119/L2
Tocache, Peru	214/B3
Tocantinópolis, Braz.	212/A2
Tocantins (riv.), Braz.	205/E4
Tocantins (state), Braz.	212/A3
Toccoa, Ga, US	191/H3
Toce (riv.), It.	101/H3
Tochigi (pref.), Japan	133/F2
Tochigi, Japan	133/F2
Tochimilco, Mex.	201/L8
Tochio, Japan	133/F2
Tocina, Sp.	102/C4
Töcksfors, Swe.	96/D2
Toco, Trin.	211/F2
Tocopilla, Chile	215/B1
Tocumen, Pan.	203/G4
Tocumwal, Austl.	173/C2
Tocuyito, Ven.	210/D2
Tocuyo (riv.), Ven.	208/E1
Toda, Japan	135/D2
Toda Bhim, India	140/C2
Todi, It.	104/C1
Tödi (peak), Swi.	115/E4
Todmorden, Eng, UK	93/F4
Todos os Santos, Baía de (bay), Braz.	212/C4
Todos Santos, Mex.	200/C4
Todtmoos, Ger.	114/D2
Todtnau, Ger.	114/D2
Toffal (hill), Mrta.	156/C5
Toffo, Ben.	161/F5
Tofield, Ab, Can.	184/E2
Tofua (isl.), Tonga	175/H6
Tōgane, Japan	135/E2
Togba (well), Mrta.	160/C2
Toggenburg (valley), Swi.	115/F3
Togher, Ire.	92/B5
Togiak, Ak, US	192/F4
Togo (ctry.)	161/F4
Tōgō, Japan	135/M5
Tögrög, Mong.	128/F2
Togtoh, China	130/B2
Tōgyu-san NP, SKor.	131/D5
Tohana, India	144/C5
Tohatchi, NM, US	190/A3
Tōhoku (prov.), Japan	133/F1
Toi, Japan	135/L5
Tōin, Japan	135/H6
Toiyabe (range), Nv, US	186/C3
Tojō, Japan	135/C2
Tojō, Japan	135/H6
Tok, Ak, US	192/K3
Tokachi (riv.), Japan	134/C2
Tōkai, Japan	135/L5
Tokaj, Hun.	99/L4
Tōkamachi, Japan	133/E2
Tokar Nat'l Rsv., Sudan	159/B4
Tokara (isls.), Japan	133/K6
Tokat, Turk.	148/D1
Tokat (prov.), Turk.	148/D1
Tŏkchŏk (isl.), NKor.	131/C4
Tŏkchŏk (arch.), NKor.	131/C4
Tokeen, Ak, US	192/M4
Tokelau (terr.), NZ	175/H5
Toki, Japan	135/M5
Toki (riv.), Japan	135/M5
Tokigawa, Japan	135/C2
Tokoname, Japan	135/L6
Tokoro (riv.), Japan	134/C2
Tokoro, Japan	134/D1
Tokoroa, NZ	175/T10
Tokorozawa, Japan	133/F3
Toksook Bay, Ak, US	192/E3
Toksun, China	128/E3
Tokuno (isl.), Japan	133/K7
Tokunoshima, Japan	133/K7
Tokushima (pref.), Japan	132/C4
Tokushima, Japan	132/C4
Tokuyama, Japan	132/B3
Tōkyō (cap.), Japan	133/F3
Tōkyō (pref.), Japan	133/F3
Tōkyō (bay), Japan	135/D2
Tōkyō Disneyland, Japan	135/D2
Tola, Nic.	202/E4
Tolbo, Mong.	128/F2
Toledo, Braz.	215/F1
Toledo, Phil.	137/D5
Toledo, Oh, US	188/D3
Toledo, Sp.	102/C3
Toledo, Uru.	217/K11
Toledo Bend (dam), La,Tx, US	187/J5
Toledo Bend (res.), La,Tx, US	187/J5
Toledo, Montes de (mts.), Sp.	102/C3
Tolentino, It.	101/K5
Tolfa, It.	104/B1
Tolhuaca, PN, Chile	216/C3
Toli, China	128/D2
Toliara (prov.), Madg.	165/H8
Toliara, Madg.	165/G8
Tolima (dept.), Col.	210/C4
Tolitoli, Indo.	139/F3
Tolka (riv.), Ire.	92/B5
Tolleson, Az, US	195/R19
Tolmezzo, It.	101/K3
Tolna (prov.), Hun.	106/D2
Tolna, Hun.	106/D2
Tolo (chan.), China	129/U10
Tolo, Gulf of (gulf), Indo.	139/F4
Tolosa, Sp.	102/D1
Tolsan (isl.), SKor.	131/D5
Tolt (riv.), Wa, US	193/D2
Tolt (res.), Wa, US	193/D2
Tolt, North Fork (riv.), Wa, US	193/D2
Tolt, South Fork (riv.), Wa, US	193/D2
Toltén, Chile	216/B3
Toltén (riv.), Chile	216/B3
Tolú, Col.	210/C2
Toluca, Mex.	201/Q10
Tolúviejo, Col.	210/C2
Tol'yatti, Rus.	121/J1
Tom' (riv.), Rus.	122/J4
Tom Price, Austl.	170/C2
Tom White (mt.), Ak, US	192/K3
Tomakomai, Japan	134/B2
Tomamae, Japan	134/B1
Tomar, Port.	102/A3
Tómaros (peak), Gre.	105/G3
Tomarza, Turk.	148/C2
Tomás, Peru	214/C4
Tomás de Berlanga, Ecu.	214/E7
Tomaszów Lubelski, Pol.	99/M3
Tomaszów Mazowiecki, Pol.	99/L3
Tomatlán, Mex.	200/D5
Tomb of Qinshihuang, China	130/B4
Tombador, Serra do (mts.), Braz.	208/G6
Tombigbee (riv.), Al,Ms, US	191/F3
Tombolo, It.	117/E1
Tombouctou, Mali	160/E2
Tombouctou (pol. reg.), Mali	156/D5
Tombstone, Az, US	186/E5
Tombua, Ang.	163/B4
Tomé, Chile	216/B3
Tomé, Île (isl.), Fr.	100/B2
Tomelilla, Swe.	96/E4
Tomelloso, Sp.	102/D3
Tomika, Japan	135/L5
Tominian, Mali	160/E3
Tomini (gulf), Indo.	139/F4
Tomiño, Sp.	102/A2
Tomioka, Japan	135/B1
Tomisato, Japan	135/D2
Tomiura, Japan	135/D3
Tomiya, Japan	133/F3
Tomizawa, Japan	135/A3
Tommot, Rus.	123/N4
Tomo (riv.), Rus.	208/E2
Tompa, Hun.	106/D2
Tompkinsville, Ky, US	188/C4
Toms (riv.), NJ, US	196/D3
Toms River, NJ, US	196/D4
Tomsk, Rus.	122/J4
Tomskaya Oblast, Rus.	122/H4
Tōmük, Turk.	149/D1
Tonalá, Mex.	202/C2
Tonale, Passo del (pass), It.	115/G5
Tonasket, Wa, US	184/D1
Tonawanda, NY, US	189/S9
Tonawanda Ind. Res., NY, US	189/S9
Tonbridge, Eng, UK	88/D3
Toncontín (int'l arpt.), Hon.	202/E3
Tondabayashi, Japan	135/J7
Tondano, Indo.	139/F3
Tondou, Massif du (plat.), CAfr.,Sudan	155/K6
Tondu (peak), Fr.	114/C6
Tone (riv.), Japan	133/G3
Tone (riv.), Japan	132/B3
Tonekābon, Iran	146/F1
Tonelagee (peak), Ire.	92/B5
Tonga (ctry.)	175/H7
Tongaat, SAfr.	165/H7
Tongareva (Penrhyn) (isl.), Cooks.	175/J5
Tongatapu (isl.), Tonga	175/H7
Tongbai, China	130/C4
Tongbu, SKor.	131/G6
Tongcheng, China	137/B2
Tongcheng, China	130/D5
Tongcheng, China	137/B2
T'ongch'ŏn, NKor.	131/D3
Tongde, China	130/G3
Tongdao Dongzu Zizhixian, China	141/J2
T'ongduch'ŏn, SKor.	131/G6
Tongeren, Belg.	111/E2
Tonggu, China	141/K2
Tonggu, China	141/K2
Tonghae, SKor.	131/E4
Tonghua, China	131/C2
Tonghua, China	131/C2
Tongliao, China	130/E2
Tongling, China	129/L5
Tongnae (riv.), NKor.	131/D2
Tongo (peak), Indo.	139/E5
Tongobory, Madg.	165/H8
Tongoma, China	141/J2
Tongsa (riv.), Bhu.	143/H2
Tongsa Dzong, Bhu.	143/H2
Tongshan, China	137/B2
Tongue (riv.), Mt, US	184/G4
Tongue, Sc, UK	89/K7
Tongwei, China	130/C4
Tongyu, China	129/M3
Tongyu, China	130/E2
Tonino-Anivskiy (pen.), Rus.	134/C1
Tönisvorst, Ger.	108/D6
Tonk, India	147/L3
Tonkawa, Ok, US	187/H4
Tonkin (gulf), China,Viet.	128/J7
Tonkoui (peak), C.d'Iv.	160/D5
Tonle Sap (lake), Camb.	141/H5
Tonneins, Fr.	100/D4
Tonnerre, Fr.	100/E3
Tönning, Ger.	96/C4
Tōno, Japan	134/B4
Tonopah, Nv, US	186/C3
Tonoshō, Japan	132/D3
Tonosí, Pan.	203/F5
Tons (riv.), India	142/C3
Tønsberg, Nor.	96/D2
Tonsina, Ak, US	192/J3
Tonstad, Nor.	96/B2
Tonto Nat'l For., Az, US	195/S18
Tonto Nat'l Mon., Az, US	186/E4
Tonya, Turk.	148/D1
Ton-y-Pandy, Wal, UK	90/C3
Toodyay, Austl.	170/C4
Tooele, Ut, US	195/J12
Tooele (co.), Ut, US	195/J13
Tooradin, Austl.	173/C3
Toowoomba, Austl.	172/C4
Topanaga State Park, Ca, US	194/B2
Topanga, Ca, US	194/B2
Topanga Beach, Ca, US	194/A2
Tope de Coroa (mtn.), Capv.	151/J10
Topia, Mex.	200/D3
Topolobampo, Mex.	200/C3
Topoľčany, Rom.	107/H4
Topolovgrad, Bul.	107/H4
Topozero (lake), Rus.	95/J2
Toppenish, Wa, US	184/C4
Toprakkale, Turk.	149/E1
Topton, Pa, US	196/C3
Tor (bay), Eng, UK	90/C4
Torahime, Japan	135/K5
Torata, Peru	214/D5
Torawitan (cape), Indo.	139/G3
Torbalı, Turk.	148/A2
Torbat-e Ḩeydarīyeh, Iran	147/G1
Torbat-e Jām, Iran	145/D2
Torbay, Nf, Can.	189/L2
Torbay (co.), Eng, UK	90/C4
Torbeck, Haiti	203/H2
Torbert (mt.), Ak, US	192/H3
Torcy, Fr.	88/K5
Tordera (riv.), Sp.	103/L6
Tordesillas, Sp.	102/C2
Töreboda, Swe.	96/F2
Torelló, Sp.	103/G1
Tory (isl.), Ire.	89/P9
Torfaen (co.), Wal, UK	90/C3
Torgelow, Ger.	96/E5
Torghay, Kaz.	145/D2
Torghay (riv.), Kaz.	145/D3
Torghay Ustirti (plat.), Kaz.	145/D2
Torhamnsudde (pt.), Swe.	96/F3
Torhout, Belg.	110/C1
Tori-shima (isl.), Japan	174/D1
Toride, Japan	135/E2
Torigni-sur-Vire, Fr.	100/C2
Torii-tōge (pass), Japan	133/E3
Toriñana (cape), Sp.	102/A1
Torino (prov.), It.	116/A2
Torino (Turin), It.	101/G4
Torkestān (mts.), Afg.	147/H1
Tormes (riv.), Sp.	102/C2
Torndirrup NP, Austl.	170/C6
Torneälven (riv.), Swe.	118/D2
Tornesch, Ger.	109/G2
Tornik (peak), Serb.	106/D4
Tornio, Fin.	95/H2
Tornionjoki (riv.), Fin.	95/G2
Toro, Sp.	102/C2
Toro, Cerro del (peak), Arg.,Chile	215/C2
Toro Nat'l Rsv., Ugan.	162/A2
Toro, PN, Ven.	210/D2
Törökbálint, Hun.	107/Q10
Törökszentmiklós, Hun.	106/E2
Toronaic (gulf), Gre.	105/H4
Torondoy, Ven.	210/D2
Toronto (cap.), On, Can.	189/R8
Toronto (isl.), On, Can.	189/R8
Toropets, Rus.	97/P3
Tororo, Ugan.	162/B2
Torote (riv.), Sp.	103/N8
Torp (int'l arpt.), Nor.	96/D2
Torpa, Swe.	96/E3
Torquay, Austl.	173/C3
Torquay, Eng, UK	90/C4
Torquemada, Sp.	102/C1
Torr (pt.), NI, UK	92/B1
Torrance, Ca, US	194/F8
Torraz, Tête du (peak), Fr.	114/C6
Torrazza Piemonte, It.	116/A2
Torre de Moncorvo, Port.	102/B2
Torre dè Passeri, It.	104/C1
Torre del Campo, Sp.	102/D4
Torre del Greco, It.	104/D2
Torre del Lago Puccini, It.	116/D5
Torre-Pacheco, Sp.	103/E4
Torrebelvicino, It.	117/E1
Torreblanca, Sp.	103/F2
Torredonjimeno, Sp.	102/D4
Torreglia, It.	117/E2
Torrejón de Ardoz, Sp.	103/N9
Torrejoncillo, Sp.	102/B3
Torrelaguna, Sp.	102/D2
Torrelavega, Sp.	102/C1
Torrelodones, Sp.	103/N8
Torremaggiore, It.	104/D2
Torremolinos, Sp.	102/C4
Torrens (isl.), Austl.	171/M8
Torrens (lake), Austl.	171/H4
Torrens (riv.), Austl.	171/M8
Torrente, Sp.	103/E3
Torreón, Mex.	200/D3
Torreperogil, Sp.	102/D3
Tôrres, Braz.	213/B4
Torres (str.), Austl.,PNG	172/B1
Torres (isls.), Van.	174/D6
Torres del Paine, PN, Chile	217/B6
Torres Novas, Port.	102/A3
Torres Vedras, Port.	102/A3
Torrevieja, Sp.	103/E4
Torri di Quartesolo, It.	117/E1
Torridge (riv.), Eng, UK	90/B5
Torrijos, Sp.	102/C3
Torrington, Wy, US	185/G5
Torrita di Siena, It.	101/J5
Torroella de Montgrí, Sp.	103/G1
Torrone Alto (peak), Swi.	115/F5
Torrox, Sp.	102/D4
Tórshavn, Den.	218/G
Tortola (isl.), UK	199/J4
Tortoli, It.	104/A3
Tortona, It.	116/B3
Tortosa, Sp.	103/F2
Tortosa (cape), Sp.	103/F2
Tortuga (isl.), Haiti	203/H2
Tortuguero, PN, CR	203/F4
Tortum, Turk.	121/G4
Torūd, Iran	147/F1
Torugart (pass), Kyr.	145/G4
Torul, Turk.	148/D1
Toruń, Pol.	99/K2
Torup, Swe.	96/E3
Torysa (riv.), Slvk.	99/L4
Tosa, Japan	132/C4
Tosa (bay), Japan	132/C4
Tosashimizu, Japan	132/C4
Tosagua, Ecu.	210/A5
Toscana (reg.), It.	116/C4
Toscana (reg.), It.	101/J5
Toscanella, It.	117/E4
Toscolano-Maderno, It.	116/D1
Toshi (isl.), Japan	135/L6
Toshibetsu (riv.), Japan	134/A2
Toshkent (pol. reg.), Uzb.	145/G4
Tosna (riv.), Rus.	119/T7
Tosno, Rus.	97/P2
Tosontsengel, Mong.	128/G2
Tostado, Arg.	216/D2
Tostedt, Ger.	109/G2
Tosu, Japan	132/B4
Tosya, Turk.	148/C1
Totana, Sp.	102/E4
Totness, Sur.	211/G3
Totowa, NJ, US	197/J8
Totten (inlet), Wa, US	193/A3
Tottenham, Austl.	173/C2
Tottington, Eng, UK	93/F4
Tottori, Japan	132/D3
Tottori (pref.), Japan	132/C3
Touat (reg.), Alg.	157/E4
Touba, C.d'Iv.	160/D4
Toubkal (peak), Mor.	156/D3
Toubkal, PN du, Mor.	156/D3
Touchwood (hills), Sk, Can.	185/G3
Toucy, Fr.	100/E3
Toudao (riv.), China	131/D1
Tougan, Burk.	160/E3
Touggourt, Alg.	157/G2
Toughkenamon, Pa, US	196/C4
Touil (riv.), Alg.	158/G5
Toul, Fr.	111/E6
Toulnustouc (riv.), Qu, Can.	189/H1
Toulon, Fr.	100/F5
Toulouse, Fr.	100/D5
Toumo (well), Niger	154/H3
Toumodi, C.d'Iv.	160/D5
Toungoo, Myan.	141/G4
Touquin, Fr.	88/M5
Toura, Monts du (mts.), C.d'Iv.	160/D5
Tourcoing, Fr.	110/C2
Tourfourine (well), Mali	156/D4
Tourlaville, Fr.	100/C2
Tournai, Belg.	110/C2
Tournan-en-Brie, Fr.	88/L5
Tournus, Fr.	114/A4
Touros, Braz.	212/D2
Tous, Embalse de (res.), Sp.	103/E3
Toussidé (peak), Chad	154/J3
Toussoro (peak), CAfr.	155/K6
Touws (riv.), SAfr.	164/M10
Touwsrivier, SAfr.	164/C4
Toužim, Czh.	113/G2
Tōv (prov.), Mong.	128/J2
Tovar, Ven.	210/D2
Tove (riv.), Eng, UK	91/E2
Towaco, NJ, US	197/H8
Towada, Japan	133/G2
Towada (lake), Japan	134/B3
Towada-Hachimantai NP, Japan	134/B3
Tower City, Pa, US	196/B2
Tower Hamlets (bor.), Eng, UK	88/A1
Tower of London, Eng, UK	88/C2
Towner, ND, US	185/H3
Townsend, Mt, US	184/F4
Townsend, De, US	196/C5
Townsend (mt.), Wa, US	193/A2
Townsends (inlet), NJ, US	196/D5
Townshend (cape), Austl.	172/C3
Townsville, Austl.	172/B2
Towson, Md, US	196/B5
Towuti (lake), Indo.	139/F4
Toya (lake), Japan	134/B2
Toyah, Tx, US	190/C4
Toyahvale, Tx, US	190/C4
Toyama (pref.), Japan	133/E2
Toyama, Japan	133/E2
Toyama (bay), Japan	133/E2
Toyo, Japan	132/C4
Toyoake, Japan	135/M5
Toyohashi, Japan	133/E3
Toyokawa, Japan	133/E3
Toyonaka, Japan	135/H6
Toyono, Japan	135/H6
Toyo'oka, Japan	132/D3
Toyosato, Japan	135/E1
Toyosato, Japan	135/K5
Toyoshina, Japan	133/E2
Toyota, Japan	135/M5
Toyotomi, Japan	134/B1
Toyoyama, Japan	135/L5
Tozeur, Tun.	157/H2
Tozeur (gov.), Tun.	157/G2
Tozi (mt.), Ak, US	192/H2
Trafalgar (cape), Sp.	102/B4
Trabuco Canyon, Ca, US	194/C3
Trabzon, Turk.	148/D1
Trabzon (prov.), Turk.	148/D1
Tracadie, NB, Can.	189/H2
Trachselwald, Swi.	114/D3
Tracy, Qu, Can.	188/F2
Tracy, Mo, US	195/Q5
Tracyton, Wa, US	193/B2
Tradate, It.	116/B1
Traben-Trarbach, Ger.	111/F3
Trafford (co.), Eng, UK	93/F5
Tragwein, Aus.	113/H6
Traiguén, Chile	216/B3
Trail, BC, Can.	184/D3
Traipu, Braz.	212/D3
Trairi, Braz.	212/C1
Traisen (riv.), Aus.	99/H5
Traiskirchen, Aus.	107/N7
Traismauer, Aus.	99/H4
Trakai NP, Lith.	97/L4
Traki, Lith.	97/L4
Tralee, Ire.	89/P10
Tralee (bay), Ire.	89/P10
Tramandaí, Braz.	213/B4
Tramelan, Swi.	114/D3
Tramin (Termeno), It.	115/H5
Tranås, Swe.	96/F2
Tranbjerg, Den.	96/D4
Trancoso, Port.	102/B2
Tranebjerg, Den.	96/D4
Tranemo, Swe.	96/E3
Tranent, Sc, UK	94/D5
Trang, Thai.	136/B5
Trangan (isl.), Indo.	139/H5
Trangie, Austl.	173/C2
Trängsletsjön (lake), Swe.	96/E1
Trani, It.	104/E2
Tranoroa, Madg.	165/H9
Transantarctic (mts.), Ant.	218/W
Transylvania (reg.), Rom.	106/F3
Transylvanian Alps (mts.), Rom.	106/F2
Trapani, It.	104/C3
Trapper (peak), Mt, US	184/E4
Trappes, Fr.	88/J5
Traralgon, Austl.	173/C3
Trasacco, It.	104/C2
Trasimeno (lake), It.	101/K5
Träslövsläge, Swe.	96/E3
Trat, Thai.	136/C4
Traun, Aus.	98/H4
Traun, Aus.	113/H6
Traunreut, Ger.	113/F7
Traunsee (lake), Aus.	113/K3
Traunstein, Ger.	113/F7
Trautmannsdorf an der Leitha, Aus.	107/P7
Travagliato, It.	116/D1
Trave (riv.), Ger.	98/F2
Travedona Monate, It.	116/B1
Travellers (lake), Austl.	173/B2
Travemünde, Ger.	98/F2
Traverse (peak), Ak, US	192/G2
Traverse (lake), Mn, SD, US	185/J4
Traverse City, Mi, US	188/C2
Travis (lake), Tx, US	190/D4
Travis AFB, Ca, US	193/L10
Travnik, Bosn.	106/C3
Trawsalt (peak), Wal, UK	90/C2
Trawsfynydd, Llyn (lake), Wal, UK	92/B3
Trbovlje, Slov.	101/L3
Tré-la-Tête (peak), Fr.	114/C6
Treachery (mt.), Austl.	171/G2
Trebaseleghe, It.	117/F1
Trebbia (riv.), It.	101/H4
Trebel (riv.), Ger.	98/G1
Třebíč, Czh.	99/H4
Trebinje, Bosn.	105/B1
Trebisacce, It.	104/E3
Třeboň, Czh.	113/H5
Trebonne, Austl.	172/B2
Trebujena, Sp.	102/B4
Trebur, Ger.	112/B3
Trecate, It.	116/B2
Tregnago, It.	117/E1
Treia, Ger.	96/C4
Treia, It.	101/K5
Treig (lake), Sc, UK	94/B3
Treinta de Agosto, Arg.	216/D3
Treinta y Tres (dept.), Uru.	217/G2
Treinta y Tres, Uru.	217/G2
Trélazé, Fr.	100/C3
Trelew, Arg.	216/D4
Trélissac, Fr.	100/D4
Trelleborg, Swe.	96/E4
Tremadoc (bay), Wal, UK	92/D6
Tremblestown (riv.), Ire.	92/B4
Trembleur (lake), BC, Can.	184/B2
Tremelo, Belg.	111/D2
Tremiti (isl.), It.	104/D1
Tremont, Pa, US	196/B2
Tremošná, Czh.	113/G3
Tremp, Sp.	103/F1
Tremšín (peak), Czh.	113/G3
Trenche (riv.), Qu, Can.	188/F1
Trenčiansky (pol. reg.), Slvk.	99/J4
Trenčín, Slvk.	99/K4
Trenel, Arg.	216/D2
Trenque Lauquen, Arg.	216/E2
Trent (riv.), Eng, UK	93/F6
Trent and Mersey (canal), Eng, UK	93/F6
Trentino-Alto Adige (pol. reg.), It.	101/J3
Trento, It.	115/H5
Trento (prov.), It.	115/G5
Trenton, On, Can.	188/E2
Trenton, Ga, US	191/G3
Trenton, Fl, US	191/H4
Trenton, Tn, US	188/B5
Trenton, Mo, US	187/J2
Trenton (cap.), NJ, US	196/D3
Trenzano, It.	116/D2
Tres Algarrobos, Arg.	216/E2
Tres Arroyos, Arg.	216/E3
Três Corações, Braz.	213/H6
Tres Irmãos, Represa (res.), Braz.	213/B2
Tres Isletas, Arg.	215/D2
Três Lagoas, Braz.	213/B2
Tres Lomas, Arg.	216/E3
Tres Marias, Braz.	212/A5
Tres Marías (isls.), Mex.	200/C4
Tres Marías, Mex.	201/Q10
Três Marias, Represa (res.), Braz.	209/J7
Tres Montes (cape), Chile	217/B5
Tres Morros, Alto de (peak), Col.	210/B3
Tres Picos, Arg.	216/C3
Tres Picos (peak), Mrta.	154/B4
Tres Picos, Arg.	216/C4
Tres Pontas, Braz.	213/H6
Tres Puntas (cape), Arg.	215/C4
Três Rios, Braz.	213/K7
Tres Valles, Mex.	202/B2
Tresa (riv.), Swi.	115/F5
Trescore Balneario, It.	116/C1
Trescore Cremasco, It.	116/C2
Tresigallo, It.	117/E3
Tresinaro (riv.), It.	116/D4
Trestina, It.	117/F6
Treuchtlingen, Ger.	112/E5
Treungen, Nor.	96/C2
Treuen, Ger.	113/F1
Treuenbrietzen, Ger.	98/G2
Treviglio, It.	116/C1
Trevignano, It.	117/F1
Treviso (int'l arpt.), It.	117/F1
Treviso (prov.), It.	117/F1
Treviso, It.	117/F1
Trevorton, Pa, US	196/B2
Trevose (pt.), Eng, UK	90/A5
Trezzano sul Naviglio, It.	116/C2
Trezzo sull'Adda, It.	116/C1
Trhové Sviny, Czh.	113/H5
Triabunna, Austl.	173/C4
Triadelphia (res.), Md, US	196/A5
Triângulos (reef), Mex.	202/C1
Tribbey, Ok, US	195/N16
Triberg, Ger.	115/E1
Tribhuvan (int'l arpt.), Nepal	143/E2
Tribugá (bay), Col.	210/B3
Tribulation (cape), Austl.	172/B2
Tribulaun (peak), Aus.	115/H4
Tricase, It.	105/F3
Trichūr, India	140/C5
Tricora (peak), Indo.	139/J4
Tricot, Fr.	88/K4
Tri-Château, Fr.	110/A5
Trier, Ger.	111/F4
Trierweiler, Ger.	111/F4
Triesen, Lcht.	115/F3
Trieste (int'l arpt.), It.	117/G1
Trieste (prov.), It.	117/G1
Trieste, It.	101/K4
Trieux, Fr.	111/E5
Triftern, Ger.	113/G6
Triggiano, It.	106/C5
Trigla NP, Slov.	101/K3
Triglav (peak), Slov.	101/K3
Trigolo, It.	116/C2
Trikala, Gre.	105/G3
Trikhonis (lake), Gre.	105/G3
Trilport, Fr.	110/B6
Trimbach, Swi.	114/D3
Trimble, Mo, US	195/D5
Trimmis, Swi.	115/F4
Trin, Swi.	115/F4
Trincomalee, SrL.	140/D6
Trindade, Braz.	209/J7
Trindade, Ilha da (isl.), Braz.	209/N8
Třinec, Czh.	99/K4
Tring, Eng, UK	91/F3
Trinidad (isl.), Arg.	215/D4
Trinidad, Bol.	208/F6
Trinidad (chan.), Chile	217/B6
Trinidad (gulf), Chile	217/A6
Trinidad, Col.	210/D3
Trinidad (isl.), Trin.	211/F2
Trinidad, Uru.	217/K10
Trinidad, Co, US	187/F3
Trinidad and Tobago (ctry.)	199/N10
Trinity (bay), Nf, Can.	189/L2
Trinity (isls.), Ak, US	192/H4
Trinity (riv.), Tx, US	190/D4
Trinity (range), Nv, US	186/C2
Trinity (riv.), Tx, US	190/E4
Trinity, West Fork (riv.), Tx, US	187/H4
Trino, It.	116/B2
Triolet, Mrts.	165/T15
Tripolis, Gre.	105/H4
Tripolitania (reg.), Libya	154/H1
Trippstadt, Ger.	111/G5
Tripunittura, India	140/C6
Tripura (state), India	141/F3
Trisanna (riv.), Aus.	115/G4
Trissino, It.	117/E1
Tristan da Cunha (isl.), StH.	80/J7
Triste (peak), Arg.	216/D4
Trisuli (riv.), Nepal	143/E2
Trittau, Ger.	109/H1
Trivero, It.	116/B1
Trnava, Slvk.	99/J4
Trnavský (pol. reg.), Slvk.	99/J4
Trobriand (isls.), PNG	174/E5
Trochtelfingen, Ger.	115/F1
Troesnes (riv.), It.	110/A5
Trofaiach, Aus.	101/L3
Trofarello, It.	116/A3
Trøgstad, Nor.	96/D2
Troia, It.	104/D2
Trois Fourches, Cap des (cape), Mor.	158/C2
Trois-Pistoles, Qu, Can.	189/G1
Trois-Ponts, Belg.	111/E3
Trois-Rivières, Qu, Can.	189/F2
Troisdorf, Ger.	111/G2
Troistorrents, Swi.	114/C5
Troisvierges, Lux.	111/F3
Troitsk, Rus.	119/P5
Trollhättan, Swe.	96/E2
Trombetas (riv.), Braz.	209/G3
Tromello, It.	116/B2
Tromie (riv.), Sc, UK	94/B3
Troms (co.), Nor.	95/F1
Tromsø, Nor.	95/F1
Tronador (peak), Arg.	216/C4
Trondheim, Nor.	95/D3
Trondheims-Fjorden (estu.), Nor.	95/D3
Tronville-en-Barrois, Fr.	111/E6
Tronzano Vercellese, It.	116/B2
Troodos (mts.), Cyp.	149/C2
Trool (lake), Sc, UK	92/D1
Troon, Sc, UK	94/B5
Trooper, Pa, US	196/C3
Tropea, It.	104/D3
Trosa, Swe.	96/G2
Trosly-Breuil, Fr.	110/B5
Trossingen, Ger.	115/E1
Trostan (peak), NI, UK	92/B1
Trostberg an der Alz, Ger.	113/F6
Trou du Nord, Haiti	203/H2
Troup (pt.), Sc, UK	94/D1
Trout Lake, NW, Can.	180/D2
Trout Lake, Ab, Can.	184/E1
Trowbridge, Eng, UK	90/D4
Troxelville, Pa, US	196/A2
Troy, Al, US	191/G4
Troy, Mo, US	188/B3
Troy, NY, US	188/F3
Troy, Oh, US	191/G1
Troy, Il, US	195/H8

Troy C – Urdor

Troy Center, Wi, US 193/N14
Troyan, Bul. 107/G4
Troyanski Prokhod (pass), Bul. 107/G4
Troyes, Fr. 100/F2
Trstenik, Serb. 106/E4
Trub, Swi. 114/D4
Truitt (peak), Yk, Can. 192/M3
Trujillo, Peru 214/B3
Trujillo, Sp. 102/C3
Trujillo, Ven. 210/D2
Trujillo (state), Ven. 210/D2
Trujillo, Hon. 202/E3
Truk (isls.), Micr. 174/E4
Trulben, Ger. 111/G5
Truman Library and Museum, Mo, US 195/E5
Trumau, Aus. 107/N8
Trumbauersville, Pa, US 196/C3
Trumbull, Ct, US 197/E1
Trümmelbachfälle (falls), Swi. 114/D4
Trün, Bul. 106/F4
Trundle, Austl. 173/C2
Truro, NS, Can. 189/J2
Truro, Eng, UK 90/A6
Truskmore (peak), Ire. 89/P9
Trüstenik, Bul. 107/G4
Truth or Consequences, NM, US 186/F4
Trutnov, Czh. 99/H3
Truyère (riv.), Fr. 100/E4
Trwyn Cilan (pt.), Wal, UK 92/D6
Tryavna, Bul. 107/G4
Trysil, Nor. 96/E1
Trysilelva (riv.), Nor. 96/D1
Trzcianka, Pol. 99/J2
Trzebiatów, Pol. 96/F4
Trzebnica, Pol. 99/J3
Trzemeszno, Pol. 99/J2
Tsabong, Bots. 164/C2
Tsagaan Bogd (peak), Mong. 128/G3
Tsakane, SAfr. 164/Q13
Tsalgar, Mong. 128/F2
Tsant, Mong. 128/J2
Tsao, Bots. 163/D5
Tsarahonenana, Madg. 165/J6
Tsaramandroso, Madg. 165/H7
Tsaratanana, Madg. 165/H7
Tsaratanana (mass.), Madg. 165/J6
Tsast (peak), Mong. 128/F2
Tsatsana (peak), Les. 164/E3
Tsavo East NP, Kenya 163/G1
Tsavo West NP, Kenya 163/G1
Tschagguns, Aus. 115/F3
Tschierv, Swi. 115/G4
Tschlin, Swi. 115/G4
Tselfat (peak), Mor. 158/B2
Tsetserleg, Mong. 128/F2
Tsetserleg, Mong. 128/H2
Tseung Kwan O, China 129/U10
Tsévié, Togo 161/F5
Tshane, Bots. 163/D5
Tshela, D.R. Congo 163/B1
Tshikapa, D.R. Congo 163/D2
Tshuapa (riv.), D.R. Congo 155/K8
Tsiafajavona (peak), Madg. 165/H7
Tsil'ma (riv.), Rus. 119/L2
Tsimlyansk (res.), Rus. 122/E5
Tsing Yi (isl.), China 129/U10
Tsiombe, Madg. 165/H9
Tsiribihina (riv.), Madg. 165/H7
Tsiroanomandidy, Madg. 165/H7
Tsitsikamma Forest and Coastal NP, SAfr. 164/C4
Tsivory, Madg. 165/H9
Ts'khinvali, Geo. 121/G4
Tsna (riv.), Rus. 118/G4
Tsomo (riv.), SAfr. 164/D3
Tsomog, Mong. 129/J2
Tsu, Japan 135/L6
Tsu (isl.), Japan 132/A3
Tsubame, Japan 133/F2
Tsubata, Japan 133/E2
Tsuchiura, Japan 133/G2
Tsuchiyama, Japan 135/K6
Tsuen Wan, China 129/U10
Tsugaru (pen.), Japan 134/B3
Tsuge, Japan 135/J6
Tsukidate, Japan 134/B4
Tsukigase, Japan 135/K6
Tsukuba, Japan 135/E1
Tsukude, Japan 135/M6
Tsukui, Japan 135/C2
Tsukumi, Japan 132/B4
Tsumeb, Namb. 163/C4
Tsuna, Japan 135/G7
Tsuru, Japan 133/F3
Tsuruga, Japan 132/E3
Tsurugashima, Japan 135/C2
Tsurugi, Japan 132/E2
Tsurugi-san (peak), Japan 132/D4
Tsuruoka, Japan 134/A4
Tsushima, Japan 135/L5
Tsuyama, Japan 132/D3
Tua (cape), Indo. 138/C5
Tua (riv.), Port.,Sp. 102/B2
Tuam, Ire. 89/P10
Tuamapu (chan.), Chile 216/B4
Tuamotu (arch.), FrPol. 175/L6
Tuan (pt.), Indo. 138/A3
Tuan (riv.), China 130/B4
Tuangku (isl.), Indo. 138/A3
Tuao, Phil. 137/D4
Tuapse, Rus. 120/F3
Tuba City, Az, US 186/E3
Tuban, Indo. 138/D5
Tuban (riv.), Yem. 146/D6
Tubarão, Braz. 213/B4
Tubbergen, Neth. 108/D4
Tübingen, Ger. 112/C5
Tubize, Belg. 111/D2
Tubmanburg, Libr. 160/C5
Ţubruq (Tobruk), Libya 155/K1
Tubuaï (isl.), FrPol. 175/K7
Tubualá, Pan. 203/G4
Tucacas, Ven. 210/D2
Tucano, Braz. 212/C3
Tuchola, Pol. 99/J2
Tuchów, Pol. 99/L4
Tuckahoe, NJ, US 196/D5
Tuckahoe (riv.), NJ, US 196/D5
Tuckahoe, NY, US 197/K8
Tuckerton, NJ, US 196/D4
Tucquegnieux, Fr. 111/E5
Tucson, Az, US 186/E4
Tucumcari, NM, US 187/G4
Tucupido, Ven. 211/E2
Tucupita, Ven. 211/F2
Tucuruí, Braz. 209/J4
Tucuruí (res.), Braz. 209/J4
Tudela, Sp. 102/E1
Tudela de Duero, Sp. 102/C2
Tuen Mun, China 129/T10
Tuenno, It. 115/H5
Tufanbeyli, Turk. 148/D2
Tug Fork (riv.), Ky,WV, US 191/H2
Tugela, SAfr. 165/E3
Tugela (falls), SAfr. 164/E3
Tugela (riv.), SAfr. 165/E3
Tughlakabad (ruin), India 144/D5
Tuguegarao, Phil. 137/D4
Tukangbesi (isls.), Indo. 139/F5
Ţūkh, Egypt 149/B4
Tuktoyaktuk, NW, Can. 192/M2
Tukums, Lat. 97/K3
Tukung (peak), Indo. 138/D4
Tukuyu, Tanz. 162/B5
Tukwila, Wa, US 193/C3
Tula (riv.), Kenya 162/C3
Tula, Mex. 201/F4
Tula, Rus. 120/F1
Tula (riv.), Mex. 201/K6
Tula, Mex. 201/K6
Tula, PN, Mex. 201/K6
Tulancingo, Mex. 201/L6
Tulare, Ca, US 186/C3
Tularosa (valley), NM, US 187/F4
Tularosa, NM, US 187/F4
Tulcán, Ecu. 210/B4
Tulcea, Rom. 107/J3
Tulcea (prov.), Rom. 107/J3
Tule (canal), Ca, US 193/L9
Tüledi (isls.), Rus. 145/B3
Tulia, Tx, US 187/G4
Tulik (vol.), Ak, US 192/E5
Tulin (isls.), PNG 174/E5
Tulita, NW, Can. 180/D2
Ţülkarm, WBnk. 149/G7
Tulla (lake), Sc, UK 94/B3
Tullahoma, Tn, US 191/G3
Tullamarine (int'l arpt.), Austl. 173/F5
Tullamore, Austl. 173/C2
Tullamore, Ire. 89/Q10
Tulle, Fr. 100/D4
Tullibody, Sc, UK 94/C4
Tullnerbach, Aus. 107/N7
Tullow, Ire. 89/Q10
Tully, Austl. 172/B2
Tullytown, Pa, US 196/D3
Tuloma (riv.), Rus. 122/D3
Tulsa, Ok, US 187/J3
Tulsipur, Nepal 142/D1
Tulsipur, India 142/D2
Tul'skaya Oblast, Rus. 120/F1
Tultitlán, Mex. 201/Q9
Tuluá, Col. 210/B3
Tuluksak, Ak, US 192/F3
Tulum, Mex. 202/E1
Tulum (ruin), Mex. 202/E1
Tulun, Rus. 123/L4
Tumacacori Nat'l Hist. Park, Az, US 186/E5
Tumaco, Col. 210/B4
Tumatumari, Guy. 211/G3
Tumauini, Phil. 137/D4
Tumba (lake), D.R. Congo 155/J8
Tumba, Swe. 96/G2
Tumbarumba, Austl. 173/D2
Tumbes (dept.), Peru 214/A1
Tumbes, Peru 214/A1
Tumbot (peak), Camb. 136/C3
Tumby Bay, Austl. 171/H5
Tumd Youqi, China 130/B2
Tumd Zuoqi, China 130/B2
Tumen, China 129/N3
Tumen (riv.), China 131/E1
Tumeremo, Ven. 211/F3
Tumereng, Guy. 211/F3
Tumkūr, India 140/C5
Tummel (riv.), Sc, UK 94/C3
Tumpat, Malay. 141/H6
Tumpu (peak), Indo. 139/F4
Tumu, Gha. 161/E4
Tumuc-Humac (mts.), Braz. 209/G3
Tumut, Austl. 173/D2
Tunadal, Swe. 118/C3
Tunceli (prov.), Turk. 148/D2
Tunceli, Turk. 148/D2
Tunchang, China 141/K4
Tundla, India 142/B2
Tundyk (riv.), Kaz. 145/G2
Tundzha (riv.), Bul. 107/H4
Tung Chung, China 129/T10
Tung Lung (riv.), China 129/V11
Tungabhadra (res.), India 140/C4
Tungabhadra (riv.), India 140/C4
Tungamah, Austl. 173/C3
Tungsan-got (pt.), NKor. 131/C4
Tungsten, NW, Can. 180/D2
Tungurahua (prov.), Ecu. 210/B5
Tünhel, Mong. 128/J2
Tūnis (cap.), Tun. 158/M6
Tūnis (gov.), Tun. 158/M6
Tunis, Gulf of (gulf), Tun. 158/M6
Tunisia (ctry.) 157/H2
Tunjá, Col. 210/C3
Tunliu, China 130/C3
Tunnels of Vinh Moc, Viet. 136/D2
Tuntum, Braz. 212/A2
Tuntutuliak, Ak, US 192/F3
Tunungayualuk (isl.), Nf, Can. 181/K3
Tunuyán (riv.), Arg. 216/C2
Tunuyán, Arg. 216/C2
Tuolumne (riv.), Ca, US 186/B3
Tuoniang (riv.), China 141/J3
Tupã, Braz. 213/B2
Tupaciguara, Braz. 213/B1
Tupai (isl.), FrPol. 175/K6
Tupambaé, Uru. 217/G2
Tuparro (riv.), Col. 210/D3
Tupelo, Ms, US 191/F3
Tupi Paulista, Braz. 213/B2
Tupiza, Bol. 208/E8
Tupper Lake, NY, US 188/F2
Tupungato, Arg. 216/C2
Tupungato (peak), Arg. 216/P8
Tura, India 143/H3
Tura (riv.), Rus. 122/G4
Tura, Rus. 123/L3
Turaiçu (riv.), Braz. 212/A1
Turan Lowland (plain), Uzb. 122/G5
Turangi, NZ 175/T10
Turbaco, Col. 210/C2
Turbat, Pak. 147/H3
Turbenthal, Swi. 115/E3
Turbo, Col. 210/B2
Turbotville, Pa, US 196/B1
Turčiansky Svätý Martin, Slvk. 120/A2
Turckheim, Fr. 114/D1
Turda, Rom. 107/F2
Tureia (isl.), FrPol. 175/M7
Turek, Pol. 99/K2
Turgeon (riv.), Qu, Can. 188/E1
Türgovishte, Bul. 107/H4
Turgutlu, Turk. 148/A2
Turhal, Turk. 148/D1
Turia (riv.), Sp. 103/E3
Turiaçu, Braz. 209/J4
Turkana (Rudolf) (lake), Kenya 162/C2
Türkeli, Turk. 120/E4
Túrkeve, Hun. 106/E2
Turkey (ctry.) 148/C2
Turkey (riv.), Ia, US 187/K2
Türkheim, Ger. 115/G1
Türkistan, Kaz. 145/E4
Türkmenbashi (Krasnowodsk), Trkm. 121/K5
Turkmenistan (ctry.) 145/C5
Türkoğlu, Turk. 148/D2
Turks (isls.), Haiti 199/G3
Turks and Caicos (isls.), UK 199/G3
Turks Island Passage (chan.), UK 203/J1
Turku (int'l arpt.), Fin. 97/K1
Turku Ja Pori (prov.), Fin. 95/G3
Turkwel (riv.), Kenya 162/B2
Turlock, Ca, US 186/B3
Turmalina, Braz. 212/B4
Turneffe (isls.), Belz. 198/D4
Turner (mt.), Austl. 170/C2
Turnersville, NJ, US 196/C4
Turnhouse (int'l arpt.), Sc, UK 94/C5
Turnhout, Belg. 108/B6
Turnor Lake, Sk, Can. 184/F1
Turnov, Czh. 99/H3
Turnu Măgurele, Rom. 107/G4
Tuross Head, Austl. 173/D3
Tuross Head, Austl. 173/D3
Turpan, China 128/E3
Turpan (depr.), China 128/E3
Turquino (peak), Cuba 203/G2
Turriaco, It. 117/G1
Turriff, Sc, UK 94/D1
Turt, Mong. 128/H1
Turtle (isls.), SLeo. 160/B5
Turtleford, Sk, Can. 184/F2
Turugart (pass), China 145/G4
Turukhansk, Rus. 122/J3
Tuscaloosa, Al, US 191/G3
Tuscano (arch.), It. 104/B1
Tuscarora, Nv, US 184/D5
Tuscarora (mtn.), Pa, US 196/A3
Tuscarora Ind. Res., US 189/S9
Tuskegee, Al, US 191/G3
Tustin, Ca, US 194/G8
Tuszyn, Pol. 99/K3
Tutak, Turk. 148/E2
Tutayev, Rus. 118/H4
Tuticorin, India 140/C6
Tutin, Serb. 106/E4
Tutóia, Braz. 212/B1
Tutong, Bru. 138/D3
Tutrakan, Bul. 107/H3
Tuttle Creek (lake), Ks, US 187/H3
Tuttlingen, Ger. 115/E2
Tutuila (isl.), ASam. 175/H6
Tutupaca (vol.), Peru 214/D5
Tututalak (mtn.), Ak, US 192/F2
Tutzing, Ger. 115/H2
Tuusula, Fin. 97/L1
Tuvalu (ctry.) 174/G5
Ţuwayq, Jabal (mts.), SAr. 146/E3
Tuxpan, Mex. 200/E5
Tuxpan, Mex. 200/D4
Tuxpan de Rodríguez Cano, Mex. 202/B1
Tuxtla Gutiérrez, Mex. 202/C2
Túy, Sp. 102/A1
Tuy Hoa, Viet. 136/E3
Tuyen Quang, Viet. 136/D1
Tuymazy, Rus. 119/M5
Tūysarkān, Iran 146/E2
Tuz (lake), It. 148/C2
Ţūz Khurmātū, Iraq 148/F3
Tuzigoot Nat'l Mon., Az, US 186/D4
Tuzla, Bosn. 106/D3
Tuzla, Turk. 149/D1
Tuzluca, Turk. 148/E1
Tuzlukçu, Turk. 148/B2
Tvååker, Swe. 96/E3
Tvedestrand, Nor. 96/C2
Tver', Rus. 118/G4
Tverskaya Oblast, Rus. 97/P3
Tvertsa (riv.), Rus. 118/G4
Tvŭrditsa, Bul. 107/G4
Twardogóra, Pol. 99/J3
Tweed (riv.), Sc, UK 94/C5
Tweed Heads, Austl. 172/D5
Twello, Neth. 108/D4
Twente (canal), Neth. 108/D4
Twente (pol. reg.), Neth. 108/D4
Twin Buttes (res.), Tx, US 187/G5
Twin Hills, Ak, US 192/F4
Twin Lakes, Wi, US 193/P14
Twin Rivers, NJ, US 196/D3
Twiste (riv.), Ger. 109/G6
Twistringen, Ger. 109/F3
Twizel, NZ 175/S11
Two Hills, Ab, Can. 184/F2
Two Rivers, Wi, US 185/M4
Twofold (bay), Austl. 173/D3
Twyford, Eng, UK 91/F4
Twymyn (riv.), Wal, UK 90/C1
Tyatya (vol.), Rus. 134/E1
Tychy, Pol. 99/K3
Tyendinaga, On, Can. 188/E2
Tyger (riv.), SC, US 191/H3
Tyldesley, Eng, UK 93/F4
Tylersville, Pa, US 196/A2
Tyn, Czh. 99/H4
Tyne (riv.), Sc, UK 94/D5
Tyne and Wear (co.), Eng, UK 93/G2
Tynemouth, Eng, UK 93/G1
Tynset, Nor. 95/C3
Tyonek, Ak, US 192/H3
Tyrifjorden (lake), Nor. 96/C1
Tyringe, Swe. 96/E3
Tyrnyauz, Rus. 121/G4
Tyrrell (lake), Austl. 173/B2
Tyrrhenian (sea), It. 104/B2
Tysnes, Nor. 96/A1
Tysnesøy (isl.), Nor. 96/A2
Tysons Corner, Va, US 196/A6
Tysse, Nor. 96/A1
Tystberga, Swe. 96/G2
Tyub-Karagan (pt.), Kaz. 121/J3
Tyuleniy (isl.), Rus. 121/H3
Tyumen (int'l arpt.), Rus. 119/Q4
Tyumen', Rus. 119/Q4
Tyumenskaya Oblast, Rus. 145/E1
Tyva, Resp., Rus. 122/K4
Tywi (riv.), Wal, UK 90/B3
Tzaneen, SAfr. 163/F5
Tzucacab, Mex. 202/D1

U

U.C.-Irvine, Ca, US 194/G8
U.K. Sovereign Base Area (gov.), Cyp. 149/C2
U.S. Naval Weapons Station, Ca, US 194/F8
U.S.S. Arizona Nat'l Mem., Hi, US 182/W13
Uad Assag (riv.), WSah. 156/B4
Uad Atui (riv.), WSah. 156/B5
Uad el Jat (riv.), WSah. 156/B4
Uad Tenuaiur (riv.), WSah. 156/A5
Uamh Bheag (peak), Sc, UK 94/B4
Uatumã (riv.), Braz. 208/G4
Uauá, Braz. 212/C3
Uaupés (riv.), Braz. 208/E3
Uaxactún (ruin), Guat. 202/D2
Ub, Serb. 106/E3
Ubá, Braz. 213/D2
Übach-Palenberg, Ger. 111/F2
Ubagan (riv.), Kaz. 119/Q5
Ubaira, Braz. 212/C4
Ubaitaba, Braz. 212/C4
Ubajara, Braz. 212/B1
Ubajara, PN de, Braz. 212/B1
Ubangi (riv.), D.R. Congo 151/D4
Ubatã, Braz. 212/C4
Ubatuba, Braz. 213/H8
Ubay, Phil. 137/D5
Ubaye (riv.), Fr. 101/G4
Ubbergen, Neth. 108/C5
Ube, Japan 132/B4
Úbeda, Sp. 102/D3
Uberaba (lake), Braz. 208/G7
Uberaba, Braz. 213/C1
Überherrn, Ger. 111/F5
Uberlândia, Braz. 213/B1
Überlingen, Ger. 115/F2
Überlingersee (lake), Ger. 115/E2
Ubia (peak), Indo. 139/J4
Ubinas, Peru 214/D5
Ubombo, SAfr. 165/F2
Ubon Ratchathani, Thai. 136/D3
Ubrique, Sp. 102/C4
Ubundu, D.R. Congo 155/L8
Ucayali (dept.), Peru 214/C3
Ucayali (riv.), Peru 214/C3
Uccle, Belg. 111/D2
Ucha (riv.), Rus. 119/W9
Uchaly, Rus. 119/N5
Uchāna, India 144/D5
Uchinskoye (res.), Rus. 119/W9
Uchiza, Peru 214/B3
Uchte, Ger. 109/F3
Uchte (riv.), Ger. 98/F2
Uchumarca, Peru 214/B2
Uchumayo, Peru 214/D5
Uchur (riv.), Rus. 123/P4
Ücker (riv.), Ger. 96/E5
Uckermark (reg.), Ger. 99/G2
Uckfield, Eng, UK 91/G5
Ucluelet, BC, Can. 184/B3
Uda (riv.), Rus. 123/M4
Udagamandalam, India 140/C5
Udaipur, India 147/K4
Udaipura, India 142/B4
Uddevalla, Swe. 96/D2
Uddingston, Sc, UK 94/B5
Uddjaure (lake), Swe. 95/F2
Üdem, Ger. 108/D5
Uden, Neth. 108/C5
Udenhout, Neth. 108/C5
Udgīr, India 140/C4
Udhampur, India 144/C3
Udine (prov.), It. 117/G1
Udine, It. 101/K3
Udipi, India 140/B5
Udmurtia, Resp., Rus. 122/Q6
Udon Thani, Thai. 136/C2
Ueckermünde, Ger. 96/F5
Ueda, Japan 133/F2
Uele (riv.), D.R. Congo 155/K7
Uelsen, Ger. 108/D3
Uelzen, Ger. 109/H3
Ueno, Japan 135/B1
Ueno, Japan 135/K6
Uenohara, Japan 133/F3
Uetendorf, Swi. 114/D4
Uetersen, Ger. 109/G1
Uetze, Ger. 109/H4
Ufa (riv.), Rus. 145/C1
Ufa, Rus. 119/M5
Uffenheim, Ger. 112/D3
Uffing, Ger. 115/H2
Ugalla (riv.), Tanz. 162/A4
Ugalla River Game Rsv., Tanz. 162/A4
Uganda (ctry.) 162/B2
Ugento, It. 105/F3
Ugie (riv.), Sc, UK 94/E1
Ugine, Fr. 114/C6
Uglich, Rus. 118/H4
Ugod, Hun. 106/C2
Ugra (riv.), Rus. 118/G5
Ugŭrchin, Bul. 107/G4
Uherské Hradiště, Czh. 99/J4
Uhingen, Ger. 112/C5
Úhlava (riv.), Czh. 99/G4
Úhlavka (riv.), Czh. 113/F3
Uibaí, Braz. 212/B3
Uíge, Ang. 163/C2
Ŭihŭng, SKor. 131/E4
Ŭijŏngbu, SKor. 131/G6
Ŭiju, NKor. 131/C2
Uilkraal (riv.), SAfr. 164/L11
Uilpata (peak), Rus. 121/G4
Uinta (mts.), Ut, US 186/E2
Uintah, Ut, US 195/K11
Uiraúna, Braz. 212/C2
Ŭiryŏng, SKor. 131/E5
Ŭisŏng, SKor. 131/E4
Uitenhage, SAfr. 164/D4
Uitgeest, Neth. 108/B3
Uithoorn, Neth. 108/B4
Uithuizen, Neth. 108/D2
Ujae (isl.), Mrsh. 174/F4
Ujelang (isl.), Mrsh. 174/F4
Újfehértó, Hun. 99/L5
Ujhāni, India 142/B1
Uji, Japan 135/J6
Uji (riv.), Japan 132/D3
Ujitawara, Japan 135/J6
Ujjain, India 147/L4
Ujung Pandang, Indo. 139/E5
Ukara (isl.), Tanz. 162/B3
Ukerewe (isl.), Tanz. 162/B3
Ukhta, Rus. 119/M3
Ukiah, Ca, US 186/B3
Uklāna, India 144/C5
Ukmergė, Lith. 97/L4
Ukraine (ctry.) 120/D2
Ulaanbaatar (cap.), Mong. 128/J2
Ulaangom, Mong. 128/F2
Ulaanjirem, Mong. 128/J2
Ulanhot, China 129/M2
Ulchin, SKor. 131/E4
Ulcumayo, Peru 214/C3
Ulefoss, Nor. 96/C2
Ulemiste (int'l arpt.), Est. 97/L2
Ulhāsnagar, India 147/K5
Uliastay, Mong. 128/G2
Ulindi (riv.), D.R. Congo 155/L8
Ulithi (isl.), Micr. 174/C3
Uljma, Serb. 106/E3
Ülken Borsyq Qumy (des.), Kaz. 145/C3
Ülken-Qobda (riv.), Kaz. 121/K2
Ulla (riv.), Sp. 102/A1
Ulla Ulla, Bol. 214/D4
Ulla Ulla, Reserva Nacional, Bol. 214/D4
Ulladulla, Austl. 173/D2
Ullapool, Sc, UK 89/R8
Ullared, Swe. 96/E3
Ulldecona, Sp. 103/F2
Ullensvang, Nor. 96/B1
Üllő, Hun. 107/R10
Ullsfjorden (estu.), Nor. 95/F1
Ullswater (lake), Eng, UK 93/F2
Ulm, Ger. 112/C6
Ulmarra, Austl. 173/E1
Ulmen, Ger. 111/F3
Ulricehamn, Swe. 96/E3
Ulrichen, Swi. 115/E5
Ulrichsberg, Aus. 113/G5
Ulrichstein, Ger. 112/C1
Ulrum, Neth. 108/D2
Ulsan, SKor. 131/E5
Ulstein, Nor. 95/C3
Ulster (reg.), Ire. 92/A3
Ulster (riv.), Ger. 112/C1
Ulster American Folk Park, NI, UK 92/A2
Ulúa (riv.), Hon. 202/E3
Uluçınar, Turk. 149/D1
Uludağ (peak), Turk. 148/B1
Uludoruk (peak), Turk. 146/D1
Uluguru (mts.), Tanz. 162/C4
Ulukışla, Turk. 148/C2
Ulundi, SAfr. 165/E3
Uluru NP, Austl. 171/F3
Ulverston, Eng, UK 93/E3
Ulverstone, Austl. 173/C4
Ulvik, Nor. 96/B1
Ulvila, Fin. 97/J1
Ul'yanovka, Rus. 97/P2
Ul'yanovsk, Rus. 119/L5
Ul'yanovskaya Oblast, Rus. 121/H1
Ulytaū (mts.),Kaz. 145/E3
Ulytau (peak), Kaz. 145/E3
Umag, Cro. 106/A3
Uman', Ukr. 120/D2
Umán, Mex. 202/D1
Umarizal, Braz. 212/C2
Umarkot, India 140/D4
Umāsi La (pass), India 144/D3
Umbertide, It. 101/K5
Umbogintwini, SAfr. 165/E3
Umboi (isl.), PNG 174/D5
Umbrail (peak), Swi. 115/G4
Umbrailpass (pass), Swi. 115/G4
Umbria (prov.), It. 101/K5
Umeå, Swe. 95/G3
Umeälven (riv.), Swe. 95/F2
Umfolozi (riv.), SAfr. 165/E3
Umgeni (riv.), SAfr. 165/E3
Umhausen, Aus. 115/G3
Umiat, Ak, US 192/H2
Umkirch, Ger. 114/D1
Umkomaas, SAfr. 165/E3
Umm Durmān, Sudan 155/M4
Umm el Faḥm, Isr. 149/G6
Umm Hibal (well), Egypt 159/C4
Ummendorf, Ger. 115/F1
Umnak (isl.), Ak, US 192/E5
Umnak Pass (chan.), Ak, US 192/E5
Umpqua (riv.), Or, US 184/C5
Umraniye, Turk. 148/B2
Ŭmsŏng, SKor. 131/D4
Umtata, SAfr. 164/E3
Umuahia, Nga. 161/G5
Umuarama, Braz. 215/F1
Umurbey, Turk. 105/K2
Umzimvubu (riv.), SAfr. 164/E3
Umzinto, SAfr. 165/E3
Una, Braz. 212/C4
Una, India 144/D4
Una (mt.), NZ 175/S11
Una (riv.), Bosn.,Cro. 101/L4
Unaí, Braz. 212/A5
Unalakleet, Ak, US 192/F3
Unalaska, Ak, US 192/E5
Unalaska (isl.), Ak, US 192/E5
Uncastillo, Sp. 103/E1
Unchahra, India 142/C3
Uncompahgre (plat.), Co, US 186/E3
Unden (lake), Swe. 96/F2
Undenheim, Ger. 112/B3
Underberg, SAfr. 164/E3
Underbool, Austl. 173/B2
Underwood, ND, US 185/H4
Unecha, Rus. 120/E1
Unga (isl.), Ak, US 192/F4
Ungama (bay), Kenya 163/H1
Ungarie, Austl. 173/C2
Ungava (pen.), Qu, Can. 181/J2
Ungava (bay), Qu, Can. 181/K3
Ungheni, Mol. 107/H2
Unhošť, Czh. 113/H2
União, Braz. 212/B2
União da Vitória, Braz. 213/B3
União dos Palmares, Braz. 212/C3
Unimak (isl.), Ak, US 192/E4
Unimak Pass (str.), Ak, US 192/E5
Unini (riv.), Braz. 208/F4
Union, Or, US 184/D4
Union, Mo, US 187/K3
Union, SC, US 191/H3
Union (lake), NJ, US 196/C5
Unión, Arg. 216/D2
Union, NJ, US 197/H9
Union (canal), Sc, UK 94/C5
Union Beach, NJ, US 197/J10
Union Bridge, Md, US 196/A4
Union City, Tn, US 188/B4
Union City, Ca, US 193/K11
Union City, NJ, US 197/J8
Unión de Reyes, Cuba 203/F1
Unión de Tula, Mex. 200/D5
Unión Hidalgo, Mex. 202/C2
Union Mills, Md, US 196/A4
Union Springs, Al, US 191/G3
Uniondale, SAfr. 164/C4
Uniondale, NY, US 197/L9
Uniontown, Pa, US 188/E4
Uniontown, Md, US 196/A4
Unionville, Mo, US 185/K5
United Arab Emirates (ctry.) 146/F4
United Kingdom (ctry.) 89/R9
United Nations, NY, US 197/K9
United Nations Mem. Cemetery, SKor. 131/E5
United States (range), Nun., Can. 181/T6
United States (ctry.) 124
United States Coast Guard Receiving Center, NJ, US 196/D6
United States Department of Energy, Md, US 196/A5
United States Naval Academy, Md, US 196/B6
United States Naval Reservation Mil. Res., PR 199/M8
Unity, Sk, Can. 184/F2
University City, Mo, US 195/G8
University Place, Wa, US 193/B3
Unjha, India 147/K4
Unkel, Ger. 111/G2
Unna, Ger. 109/E5
Unnão, India 142/C2
Ŭnsan-ŭp, NKor. 131/D3
Unst (isl.), Sc, UK 89/W13
Unter Pleichfeld, Ger. 112/D3
Unterägeri, Swi. 115/E3
Unterargen (riv.), Ger. 115/F2
Untergriesbach, Ger. 113/G5
Unterhaching, Ger. 113/E6
Unteriberg, Swi. 115/E3
Unterkulm, Swi. 114/E3
Unterlüss, Ger. 109/H3
Unterschleissheim, Ger. 113/E6
Untersee (lake), Swi. 115/E2
Unterseen, Swi. 114/D4
Untersiggenthal, Swi. 115/E3
Unterthingau, Ger. 115/G2
Untervaz, Swi. 115/F4
Unterweissenbach, Aus. 113/H6
Ünye, Turk. 148/D1
Unzen-Amakusa NP, Japan 132/A4
Unzen-dake (peak), Japan 132/B4
Unzha (riv.), Rus. 122/E4
Uozu, Japan 133/E2
Upala, CR 203/E4
Upanema, Braz. 212/C2
Upata, Ven. 211/F2
Upemba, Lac (lake), D.R. Congo 163/E2
Upemba, PN de l', D.R. Congo 163/E2
Uphall, Sc, UK 94/C5
Upington, SAfr. 164/C3
Upland, Pa, US 196/C4
Upleta, India 147/K4
Upolu (pt.), Hi, US 182/U10
Upolu (isl.), Sam. 175/H6
Upper (lake), Ca, US 186/B2
Upper (pen.), Mi, US 188/C2
Upper (bay), NY, US 196/D2
Upper Arrow (lake), BC, Can. 184/D3
Upper Darby, Pa, US 196/C4
Upper Demerara-Berbice (pol. reg.), Guy. 211/G3
Upper East (pol. reg.), Gha. 161/E4
Upper Engadine (valley), Swi. 115/F5
Upper Falls, Md, US 196/B5
Upper Ganges (canal), India 142/A1
Upper Hutt, NZ 175/T11
Upper Iowa (riv.), Ia, US 187/J2
Upper Klamath (lake), Or, US 184/C5
Upper Lough Erne (lake), NI, UK 89/Q9
Upper Missouri River Breaks Nat'l Mon., Mt, US 184/F4
Upper Peoria (lake), Il, US 185/L5
Upper Red (lake), Mn, US 185/K3
Upper Rouge (riv.), Mi, US 193/F7
Upper Saddle River, NJ, US 197/J7
Upper Takutu-Upper Essequibo (pol. reg.), Guy. 211/G4
Upper Thames (valley), Eng, UK 91/E3
Upper Trajan's Wall, Mol. 120/D3
Upper West (pol. reg.), Gha. 161/E4
Upperlands, NI, UK 92/B2
Upplands-Väsby, Swe. 96/G2
Uppsala, Swe. 96/G2
Uppsala (co.), Swe. 95/F3
Upright (cape), Ak, US 192/D3
Upstart (cape), Austl. 172/B2
Upton, Wy, US 185/G4
Urabá (gulf), Col. 210/B2
Uracoa, Ven. 211/F2
Urad Qianqi, China 130/B2
Uraga (chan.), Japan 135/D3
Urahoro, Japan 134/C2
Uraim (riv.), Braz. 212/A1
Urakawa, Japan 134/C2
Ural (mts.), Rus. 85/L2
Uralla, Austl. 173/D1
Urana, Austl. 173/C2
Urandi, Braz. 212/B4
Uraricoera (riv.), Braz. 208/F3
Urasoe, Japan 133/J7
Urawa, Japan 133/F3
Uray, Rus. 122/G3
Urayasu, Japan 135/D2
Urbach, Ger. 112/C5
Urbana, Md, US 196/A5
Urbania, It. 117/F5
Urbano Santos, Braz. 212/B1
Urbenville, Austl. 172/D5
Urbino, It. 117/F5
Urcos, Peru 214/D4
Urda, Sp. 102/D3
Urdinarrain, Arg. 217/J10
Urdorf, Swi. 115/E3

Ure (riv.), Eng, UK 93/G3
Ures, Mex. 200/C2
Ureshino, Japan 135/K6
Urewera NP, NZ 175/T10
Urfa (prov.), Turk. 148/D2
Urfa, Turk. 148/D2
Urft (riv.), Ger. 109/G6
Urft (lake), Ger. 111/F2
Urganch, Uzb. 145/D4
Urgnano, It. 116/C1
Urho Kekkosen NP, Fin. 95/H1
Uri, India 144/C2
Uri-Rotstock (peak), Swi. 115/E4
Uriangato, Mex. 201/E4
Uribante (riv.), Ven. 210/D3
Uribia, Col. 210/C2
Urie (riv.), Sc, UK 94/D2
Uriménil, Fr. 114/C1
Urique (riv.), Mex. 200/D3
Urjala, Fin. 97/K1
Urk, Neth. 108/C3
Urla, Turk. 148/A2
Urlaţi, Rom. 107/H3
Urmar, India 144/C4
Urmia (lake), Iran 148/F2
Urmitz, Ger. 111/G3
Urmston, Eng, UK 93/F5
Urnäsch, Swi. 115/F3
Urnersee (lake), Swi. 115/E4
Uroševac, Kos. 106/E4
Urr Water (riv.), Sc, UK 92/E1
Ursensollen, Ger. 113/E4
Ursulo Galván, Mex. 201/N7
Uruaçu, Braz. 209/J6
Uruapan, Mex. 200/E5
Urubamba (riv.), Peru 208/D6
Urubamba, Peru 214/C4
Urubu (riv.), Braz. 208/G4
Uruburetama, Braz. 212/C1
Uruçuca, Braz. 212/C4
Uruçuí, Braz. 212/A2
Uruçuí Preto (riv.), Braz. 212/A3
Uruçuí, Serra do (mts.), Braz. 209/K5
Urucuia (riv.), Braz. 209/J7
Uruguaiana, Braz. 215/E2
Uruguay (ctry.) 215/E3
Uruguay (riv.), SAm. 215/E2
Urumaco, Ven. 210/D2
Ürümqi, China 128/E3
Urunga, Austl. 173/E1
Uruoca, Braz. 212/B1
Urup (isl.), Rus. 125/Q5
Ururi, It. 104/D2
Urussanga, Braz. 213/B4
Uryupinsk, Rus. 121/G2
Urziceni, Rom. 107/H3
Us, Fr. 88/H4
Usa, Japan 132/B4
Usa (riv.), Rus. 122/F3
Uşak, Turk. 148/B2
Uşak (prov.), Turk. 148/B2
Usakos, Namb. 163/C5
Usborne (mt.), UK 217/F6
Uscio, It. 116/C4
Usedom (isl.), Ger. 96/E4
Useldange, Lux. 111/E4
Useless Loop, Austl. 170/B3
Ushibori, Japan 135/F2
Ushibuka, Japan 132/B4
Ushiku, Japan 135/E2
Ushtobe, Kaz. 145/G3
Ushuaia, Arg. 217/C7
Usibelli, Ak, US 192/J3
Usicayos, Peru 214/D4
Usilampatti, India 140/C6
Usingen, Ger. 112/B2
Üsküp, Turk. 107/H5
Uslar, Ger. 109/G5
Usman', Rus. 120/F1
Uspallata, Arg. 216/C2
Uspallata, Paso de (pass), Chile 216/N8
Usquil, Peru 214/B2
Ussel, Fr. 100/E4
Ussel (riv.), Ger. 112/D5
Usses (riv.), Fr. 114/C5
Ussuri (riv.), China,Rus. 123/P5
Ussuriysk, Rus. 129/P3
Ussy-sur-Marne, Fr. 88/M5
Ust'-Ilimsk, Rus. 123/L4
Ust'-Kamchatsk, Rus. 123/S4
Ust'-Kut, Rus. 123/L4
Ust'-Ordynskiy Buryatskiy Aut. Okrug, Rus. 123/Q7
Úštěk, Czh. 113/H1
Uster, Swi. 115/E3
Ústí nad Labem, Czh. 101/L1
Ustica (isl.), It. 104/C3
Ustica, It. 104/C3
Ustka, Pol. 96/G4
Ustrzyki Dolne, Pol. 99/M4
Ust'ya (riv.), Rus. 119/K3
Ustyurt (plat.), Kaz. 125/D5
Usu, China 128/D3
Usuda, Japan 135/A1
Usuki, Japan 132/B4
Usulután, ESal. 202/D3
Usumacinta (riv.), Mex. 198/C4
Utah (state), US 186/E3
Utah (co.), Ut, US 195/K13
Utah (lake), Ut, US 186/D2
Utangan (riv.), India 142/A2
Utano, Japan 135/J7
Utashinai, Japan 134/C2
Utena, Lith. 97/L4
Uterský (riv.), Czh. 113/G3
Uthai Thani, Thai. 136/C3
Utica, NY, US 188/F3
Utica, Mi, US 193/F6
Utiel, Sp. 102/E3
Utik (lake), Mb, Can. 185/J2
Utila (isl.), Hon. 202/E2
Utinga, Braz. 212/B4
Utirik (isl.), Mrsh. 174/G3
Utiroa, Kiri. 174/G5
Utmānzai, Pak. 144/A2
Utopia Abor. Land, Austl. 171/G2
Utraulā, India 142/D2
Utrecht, SAfr. 165/E2
Utrecht, Neth. 108/C4
Utrecht (prov.), Neth. 108/C4
Utrera, Sp. 102/C4
Utsunomiya, Japan 133/F2
Uttar Pradesh (state), India 140/C2
Uttaradit, Thai. 136/C2
Uttarranchal (state), India 142/B1
Uttenweiler, Ger. 115/F1
Uttoxeter, Eng, UK 93/G6
Utuado, PR 199/M8
Utupua (isl.), Sol. 174/F6
Uturoa, FrPol. 175/K6
Utzenstorf, Swi. 114/D3
Uusikaupunki, Fin. 97/J1
Uusimaa (prov.), Fin. 95/H3
Uva (riv.), Col. 208/E3
Uvalde, Tx, US 187/H5
Uvarovo, Rus. 121/G2
Uverito, Ven. 211/E2
Uvira, D.R. Congo 162/A3
Uvongo, SAfr. 165/E3
Uvs (prov.), Mong. 128/F2
Uwajima, Japan 132/C4
Uwimmerah (riv.), Indo. 139/K5
Uxin Qi, China 130/B3
Uxmal (ruin), Mex. 202/D1
Üydzin, Mong. 128/J3
Uyo, Nga. 161/G5
Üyönch, Mong. 128/F2
Uyuni, Bol. 208/E8
Uzbekistan (ctry.) 145/D4
Uzbekistan Nat'l Park, Uzb. 145/E5
Uzein (int'l arpt.), Fr. 100/C5
Uzerche, Fr. 100/D4
Uzès, Fr. 100/F4
Uzhhorod, Ukr. 99/M4
Uzhok (pass), Ukr. 99/M4
Užice, Serb. 106/D4
Uzlovaya, Rus. 120/F1
Uznach, Swi. 115/E3
Üzümlü, Turk. 148/D2
Uzunköprü, Turk. 105/K2
Uzwil, Swi. 115/F3

V

V.P. Rosales, PN, Chile 216/B4
Vaal (riv.), SAfr. 164/D2
Vaala, Fin. 95/H2
Vaalbos NP, SAfr. 164/D3
Vaaldam (res.), SAfr. 164/D2
Vaals, Neth. 111/F2
Vaalserberg (hill), Neth. 111/E2
Vaasa (prov.), Fin. 95/G3
Vaasa (int'l arpt.), Fin. 95/G3
Vaasa (Vasa), Fin. 95/G3
Vaassen, Neth. 108/C4
Vác, Hun. 106/D2
Vaca (mt.), Ca, US 193/K10
Vaca (mts.), Ca, US 193/K10
Vacaria, Braz. 213/B4
Vacaville, Ca, US 186/B3
Vachon (riv.), Qu, Can. 181/J2
Vada, It. 116/D6
Vado Ligure, It. 116/B4
Vadret (peak), Swi. 115/F4
Vadsø, Nor. 95/J1
Vadstena, Swe. 96/F2
Vaduz (cap.), Lcht. 115/F3
Vaernes (int'l arpt.), Nor. 95/D3
Vaga (riv.), Rus. 118/J3
Vågå, Nor. 95/D3
Vågan, Nor. 95/E1
Vaganski vrh (peak), Cro. 106/B3
Vagay (riv.), Rus. 119/R4
Vaggeryd, Swe. 96/F3
Vagney, Fr. 114/C1
Vagos, Port. 102/A2
Vågsøy, Nor. 95/C3
Vah (riv.), Slvk. 99/J4
Vahitahi (isl.), FrPol. 175/M6
Vaiano, It. 117/E5
Vaiano Cremasco, It. 116/C2
Vaich (lake), Sc, UK 94/B1
Vaihingen an der Enz, Ger. 112/B5
Vaijāpur, India 147/K5
Vail, Co, US 187/F3
Vailate, It. 116/C2
Vair (riv.), Fr. 114/B1
Vaisali (riv.), India 142/B2
Vaitupu (isl.), Tuv. 174/G5
Vaivre-et-Montoille, Fr. 114/C2
Vakfıkebir, Turk. 120/F4
Vakh (riv.), Rus. 122/J3
Vākhān (mts.), Afg. 147/K1
Vakhsh (riv.), Taj. 147/J1
Vál, Hun. 106/D2
Val-de-Marne (dept.), Fr. 110/B6
Val-d'Or, Qu, Can. 188/E1
Val Lagarina (valley), It. 117/D1
Val Marie, Sk, Can. 184/G3
Val Venosta (valley), It. 115/G4
Val Verda, Ut, US 195/K12
Val Verde, Ca, US 194/B2
Valais (canton), Swi. 114/D5
Valbo, Swe. 96/G1
Valburg, Neth. 108/C5
Valcheta, Arg. 216/D4
Valdagno, It. 117/E1
Valdahon, Fr. 114/C3
Valdai (hills), Rus. 118/G4
Valdarno (valley), It. 117/E5
Valdecañas, Embalse de (res.), Sp. 102/C3
Valdemarsvik, Swe. 96/G2
Valdemorillo, Sp. 103/M8
Valdense, Uru. 217/K11
Valdepeñas, Sp. 102/D3
Valderas, Sp. 102/C1
Valderrobres, Sp. 103/F2
Valdés (pen.), Arg. 216/E4
Valdeverdeja, Sp. 102/C3
Valdez, Ak, US 192/J3
Valdez, Ecu. 210/B4
Valdivia, Col. 210/C3
Valdivia, Chile 216/B3
Valdobbiadene, It. 117/F1
Valdoie, Fr. 114/C2
Valdosta, Ga, US 191/H4
Valdoviño, Sp. 102/A1
Vale, Or, US 184/D5
Vale of Glamorgan (co.), Wal, UK 90/C4
Valeggio sul Mincio, It. 117/D2
Valemount, BC, Can. 184/D2
Valença, Braz. 212/C4
Valença, Braz. 213/K7
Valença, Port. 102/A1
Valença do Piauí, Braz. 212/B2
Valence, Fr. 100/D4
Valence, Fr. 100/F4
Valence-sur-Baïse, Fr. 100/D5
Valencia, Ven. 208/E1
Valencia (int'l arpt.), Sp. 103/E3
Valencia, Sp. 103/E3
Valencia (aut. comm.), Sp. 102/E2
Valencia, Ecu. 210/B5
Valencia (isl.), Ire. 88/P11
Valencia de Alcántara, Sp. 102/B3
Valencia de Don Juan, Sp. 102/C1
Valencia, Golfo de (gulf), Sp. 103/F3
Valenciennes, Fr. 110/C3
Valendas, Swi. 115/F4
Vălenii de Munte, Rom. 107/H3
Valente, Braz. 212/C3
Valentigney, Fr. 114/C3
Valentim (range), Braz. 212/B2
Valentine, Tx, US 190/B4
Valentines, Uru. 217/G2
Valenton, Fr. 88/K5
Valenza, It. 116/B2
Våler, Nor. 96/D1
Våler, Nor. 96/D2
Valera, Ven. 210/D2
Valff, Fr. 114/D1
Valga, Est. 97/M3
Valhalla, NY, US 197/K7
Valinco, Golfe de (gulf), Fr. 104/A2
Valinhos, Braz. 213/F7
Valjevo, Serb. 106/D3
Valkeakoski, Fin. 97/K1
Valkeala, Fin. 97/M1
Valkenburg, Neth. 111/E2
Valkenswaard, Neth. 108/C6
Vall de Uxó, Sp. 103/E3
Valladolid, Sp. 102/C2
Valladolid (int'l arpt.), Sp. 102/C2
Valladolid, Mex. 202/D1
Vallangoujard, Fr. 88/J4
Valle, Ecu. 210/B5
Valle, Nor. 96/B2
Valle d'Aosta (pol. reg.), It. 101/G4
Valle de Bravo, Mex. 201/E5
Valle de Cauca (dept.), Col. 210/B4
Valle de Guanape, Ven. 211/E2
Valle de La Pascua, Ven. 208/E2
Valle de Santiago, Mex. 201/E4
Valle de Zaragoza, Mex. 190/B5
Valle Hermoso, Mex. 201/F3
Valle Lomellina, It. 116/B2
Valle Mosso, It. 116/B1
Vallecitos de Zaragoza, Mex. 201/E5
Vallecrosia, It. 101/G5
Valledupar, Col. 210/C2
Valleé de l'Azaouak (riv.), Mali 161/G2
Vallée du Ferlo (riv.), Sen. 160/B3
Valleé du Mboune (riv.), Sen. 160/B3
Valleé du Saloum (riv.), Sen. 160/B3
Valleé du Serpent (riv.), Mali 160/C3
Vallegrande, Bol. 208/F7
Vallehermoso, Sp. 156/A3
Vallejo, Ca, US 186/B3
Vallenar, Chile 215/B2
Vallendar, Ger. 111/G3
Valleroy, Fr. 111/E5
Valletta (cap.), Malta 104/M7
Valley Brook, Ok, US 195/N15
Valley Center, Ca, US 194/C4
Valley City, ND, US 185/J4
Valley Cottage, NY, US 197/K7
Valley East, On, Can. 188/D2
Valley Forge Nat'l Hist. Park, Pa, US 196/C3
Valley of Desolation, SAfr. 164/D4
Valley of the Kings, Egypt 159/C3
Valley Park, Mo, US 195/G8
Valley Spring, Tx, US 187/H5
Valley Stream, NY, US 197/L9
Vallière (riv.), Fr. 114/B4
Vallorbe, Swi. 114/C4
Valls, Sp. 103/F2
Valluga (peak), Aus. 115/G3
Valmayor (res.), Sp. 103/M8
Valme (riv.), Ger. 109/F6
Valmeyer, Il, US 195/G9
Valmiera, Lat. 97/L3
Valmondois, Fr. 88/J4
Valognes, Fr. 100/C2
Valois (reg.), Fr. 110/B5
Valona, Bay of (bay), Alb. 105/F2
Valpaços, Port. 102/B2
Vālpārai, India 140/C5
Valparaiso, Fl, US 191/G4
Valparaiso, In, US 188/C3
Valparaíso, Mex. 200/E4
Valparaíso (pol. reg.), Chile 216/C2
Valparaíso, Chile 216/N8
Valpovo, Cro. 106/D3
Valréas, Fr. 100/F4
Vals (riv.), SAfr. 164/D2
Vals, Swi. 115/F4
Vals-les-Bains, Fr. 100/F4
Valsād, India 147/K4
Valsaquillo (res.), Mex. 201/L8
Valsbaai (bay), SAfr. 163/C7
Valserine (riv.), Fr. 114/B5
Valserrhein (riv.), Swi. 115/F4
Valsura (riv.), It. 115/G4
Valtellina (valley), It. 115/F5
Valtice, Czh. 101/M2
Valuyki, Rus. 120/F2
Valverde, Sp. 156/A4
Valverde del Camino, Sp. 102/B4
Valyermo, Ca, US 194/C2
Våmhus, Swe. 96/F1
Vammala, Fin. 97/K1
Vámos, Gre. 105/J5
Vámosmikola, Hun. 106/D2
Vámospércs, Hun. 106/E2
Van, Turk. 148/E2
Van (lake), Turk. 148/E2
Van Buren, Me, US 189/H2
Van Buren, Ar, US 187/J4
Van Cortlandt Park, NY, US 197/K8
Van Diemen (cape), Austl. 167/C2
Van Diemen (gulf), Austl. 167/C2
Van Harinxmakanaal (riv.), Neth. 108/C2
Van Horn, Tx, US 187/F5
Van Norman Lakes, Ca, US 194/B2
Van Rees (mts.), Indo. 139/J4
Van Wert, Oh, US 188/C3
Vana-Javesi (lake), Fin. 97/K1
Vanadzor, Arm. 121/H4
Vanavaro (isl.), FrPol. 175/L7
Vancouver (mt.), Yk, Can. 192/L3
Vancouver, Wa, US 184/C4
Vancouver, BC, Can. 184/C3
Vancouver (int'l arpt.), BC, Can. 184/C3
Vancouver (cape), Austl. 170/C5
Vancouver (isl.), BC, Can. 180/D4
Vandalia, Mo, US 187/K3
Vandans, Aus. 115/F3
Vanderbijlpark, SAfr. 164/D2
Vanderbilt Museum, NY, US 197/E2
Vanderhoof, BC, Can. 184/B2
Vandœuvre-lès-Nancy, Fr. 111/F6
Vanegas, Mex. 201/E4
Vänern (lake), Swe. 96/E2
Vänersborg, Swe. 96/E2
Vangaindrano, Madg. 165/H8
Vanier (isl.), Nun., Can. 181/R7
Vanikolo (isl.), Sol. 174/F6
Vanil Noir (peak), Swi. 114/D4
Vanimo, PNG 174/D5
Vännäs, Swe. 95/F3
Vanne (riv.), Fr. 100/E2
Vannes, Fr. 100/B3
Vanoise, PN de la, Fr. 101/G4
Vanreenenpas (pass), SAfr. 164/E3
Vanrhynsdorp, SAfr. 164/B3
Vansbro, Swe. 96/F1
Vanse, Nor. 96/B2
Vansittart (isl.), Nun., Can. 181/H2
Vantaa, Fin. 97/L1
Vanua Levu (isl.), Fiji 174/G6
Vanuatu (ctry.) 174/F6
Vanwyksvlei, SAfr. 164/C3
Var (riv.), Fr. 101/G5
Vara (riv.), It. 116/C4
Vara, Swe. 96/E2
Varadero, Cuba 203/F1
Varaita (riv.), It. 116/A3
Varallo, It. 116/B1
Varāmīn, Iran 146/F1
Vārānāsi, India 142/D3
Varanger-Halvøya (pen.), Nor. 95/J1
Varangerfjorden (estu.), Nor. 95/J1
Varangéville, Fr. 111/F6
Varano (lake), It. 104/D2
Varano Borghi, It. 116/B1
Varaždin, Cro. 101/M3
Varazze, It. 116/B4
Varberg, Swe. 96/E3
Vardar (riv.), FYROM 105/G2
Varde, Den. 96/C4
Várdha, Gre. 105/G3
Vardø, Nor. 95/J1
Varel, Ger. 109/F2
Varenne (riv.), Fr. 100/C2
Varennes, Qu, Can. 189/P6
Varennes-Jarcy, Fr. 88/K5
Varennes-Vauzelles, Fr. 100/E3
Vareš, Bosn. 106/D3
Varese, It. 116/B1
Varese (prov.), It. 115/E6
Varese Ligure, It. 116/C4
Vårgårda, Swe. 96/E2
Vargem Grande, Braz. 212/B1
Vargem do Sul, Braz. 213/G6
Varginha, Braz. 213/H6
Vári, Gre. 105/H4
Varilhes, Fr. 100/D5
Värmeln (lake), Swe. 96/E2
Värmland (co.), Swe. 95/E3
Varna, Bul. 107/H4
Varna (pol. reg.), Bul. 107/H4
Värnamo, Swe. 96/F3
Varois-et-Chaignot, Fr. 114/B3
Varoška Rijeka, Bosn. 106/C3
Várpalota, Hun. 106/D2
Varraddes, Fr. 88/L5
Varsi, It. 116/C3
Vårsta, Swe. 96/G2
Vartholomión, Gre. 105/G4
Varto, Turk. 148/E2
Vartry (res.), Ire. 92/B5
Vartry (riv.), Ire. 92/B5
Várzea Alegre, Braz. 212/C2
Várzea da Palma, Braz. 212/A5
Várzea Grande, Braz. 212/B2
Várzea Grande, Braz. 209/G7
Varzelândia, Braz. 212/A4
Varzi, It. 116/C3
Varzo, It. 115/E5
Varzuga (riv.), Rus. 118/H2
Vas (prov.), Hun. 106/C2
Vasa Barris (riv.), Braz. 209/L5
Vásárosnamény, Hun. 99/M4
Vaşcău, Rom. 106/F2
Vashka (riv.), Rus. 119/K2
Vashon, Wa, US 193/C3
Vashon (isl.), Wa, US 193/C3
Vasiliká, Gre. 105/H2
Vasil'yevskiy (isl.), Rus. 119/S7
Vaslui (prov.), Rom. 107/H2
Vaslui, Rom. 107/H2
Vassar, Mi, US 188/D3
Vassdalsegga (peak), Nor. 96/B2
Vassouras, Braz. 213/K7
Västerås, Swe. 96/G2
Västerbotten (co.), Swe. 95/F2
Västerdalälven (riv.), Swe. 96/E1
Västernorrland (co.), Swe. 95/F3
Västervik, Swe. 96/G3
Västmanland (co.), Swe. 95/E3
Vasto, It. 104/D1
Västra Silen (lake), Swe. 96/E2
Vasvár, Hun. 106/C2
Vasyl'kiv, Ukr. 120/D2
Vaterstetten, Ger. 113/E6
Vatican City (ctry.) 104/C2
Vatnajökull (glacier), Ice. 95/P7
Vatomandry, Madg. 165/J7
Vatra Dornei, Rom. 107/G2
Vättern (lake), Swe. 95/E4
Vaucouleurs (riv.), Fr. 88/H5
Vaud (canton), Swi. 114/C4
Vaudoy-en-Brie, Fr. 88/M5
Vaudreuil-Dorion, Qu, Can. 189/M7
Vaughan, On, Can. 189/Q8
Vaughn, NM, US 187/F4
Vaughn, Wa, US 193/B3
Vaulruz, Swi. 114/C4
Vaulx-en-Velin, Fr. 114/A6
Vaupés (dept.), Col. 210/D4
Vaupés (riv.), Col. 210/D4
Vauréal, Fr. 88/J4
Vauvert, Fr. 100/F5
Vauvillers, Fr. 114/C2
Vaux (riv.), Fr. 98/C4
Vaux-sur-Seine, Fr. 88/H4
Vaux-sur-Sûre, Belg. 111/E4
Vauxhall, Ab, Can. 184/E3
Vavatenina, Madg. 165/J7
Vava'u Group (isls.), Tonga 175/H6
Vavuniya, SrL. 140/D6
Vawkavysk, Bela. 99/N2
Vaxjo (int'l arpt.), Swe. 96/F3
Växjö, Swe. 96/F3
Vaygach (isl.), Rus. 218/B
Vazante, Braz. 212/A5
Vázea Paulista, Braz. 213/G8
Vazuza (res.), Rus. 118/G5
Vazzola, It. 117/F1
Vecchiano, It. 116/D5
Vechigen, Swi. 114/D4
Vecht (riv.), Neth. 108/D3
Vechta, Ger. 109/F3
Vechte (riv.), Ger. 108/D3
Vecsés, Hun. 106/D2
Vedano Olona, It. 116/B1
Veddige, Swe. 96/E3
Vedea (riv.), Rom. 107/G3
Vedelago, It. 117/F1
Vedia, Arg. 216/E2
Vedra, Sp. 102/A1
Veendam, Neth. 108/D2
Veenendaal, Neth. 108/C4
Veere, Neth. 108/A5
Veerse Meer (res.), Neth. 108/A5
Vefsn, Nor. 95/E2
Vega, Tx, US 187/G4
Vega (pt.), Ak, US 192/B6
Vega (isl.), Nor. 95/D2
Vega de Alatorre, Mex. 201/N6
Vegafjorden (estu.), Nor. 95/D2
Veghel, Neth. 108/C5
Vègreville, Ab, Can. 184/E2
Végueta, Peru 214/B3
Vehkalahti, Fin. 97/M1
Vehne (riv.), Ger. 109/F2
Veigné, Fr. 100/D3
Veinticinco de Mayo, Arg. 216/E2
Veinticinco de Mayo, Arg. 216/D3
Veinticinco de Mayo, Uru. 217/K11
Veintiocho de Mayo, Ecu. 214/B1
Veintiocho de Noviembre, Arg. 217/B6
Veitsch, Aus. 106/B2
Veitshöchheim, Ger. 112/C3
Vejen, Den. 96/C4
Vejer de la Frontera, Sp. 102/C4
Vejle, Den. 96/C4
Vejle (co.), Den. 96/C4
Vejprty, Czh. 113/G2
Vela, Cabo de la (pt.), Col. 210/C1
Vela Luka, Cro. 104/E1
Velaines, Fr. 111/E6
Vélan (peak), Swi. 114/D6
Velardeña, Mex. 200/E3
Velas, Azor., Port. 103/S12
Velasco Ibarra, Ecu. 210/B5
Velázquez, Uru. 217/G2
Velbert, Ger. 108/E6
Velburg, Ger. 113/E4
Velddrif, SAfr. 164/L10
Velden, Ger. 113/F6
Velden am Wörthersee, Aus. 101/L3
Veldhoven, Neth. 108/C6
Velen, Ger. 108/D5
Velešta, FYROM 105/G2
Velestínon, Gre. 105/H3
Vélez, Col. 210/C3
Vélez-Blanco, Sp. 102/D4
Vélez-Málaga, Sp. 102/C4
Vélez-Rubio, Sp. 102/D4
Velhas, Rio das (riv.), Braz. 209/K7
Velika Gorica, Cro. 106/C3
Velika Kladuša, Bosn. 101/L4
Velika Plana, Serb. 106/E3
Velikaya (riv.), Rus. 118/F4
Velikiy Ustyug, Rus. 119/K3
Velikiye Luki, Rus. 97/P3
Veliko Tŭrnovo, Bul. 107/G4
Velille, Peru 214/D4
Vélingara, Sen. 160/B3
Vélizy-Villacoublay, Fr. 88/J5
Vel'ké Kapušany, Slvk. 106/F1
Vel'ký Krtíš, Slvk. 99/K4
Velký Zvon (peak), Czh. 113/F3
Vellberg, Ger. 112/C4
Velletri, It. 104/C2
Vellinge, Swe. 96/E4
Vellmar, Ger. 109/G6
Vellón (res.), Sp. 103/N8
Vellore, India 140/C5
Vélon, Gre. 105/H4
Vel'sk, Rus. 118/J3
Veluwe (phys. reg.), Neth. 108/C4
Veluwemeer (lake), Neth. 108/C4
Veluwezoom, NP, Neth. 108/C4
Velva, ND, US 185/H3
Velvary, Czh. 113/H2
Velvendós, Gre. 105/H2
Vémars, Fr. 88/K4
Vemb, Den. 96/C3
Véménd, Hun. 106/D2
Venachar (lake), Sc, UK 94/B4
Venado Tuerto, Arg. 216/E2
Venafro, It. 104/D2
Venamo (peak), Ven. 211/F3
Venâncio Aires, Braz. 213/A4
Venaria, It. 101/G4
Vence, Fr. 101/G5
Venceslau Brás, Braz. 213/B2
Vendas Novas, Port. 102/A3
Vendôme, Fr. 100/D3
Vendrell, Sp. 103/F2
Vendrest, Fr. 88/M4
Veneta, Laguna (lake), It. 117/F2
Venetie, Ak, US 192/J2
Veneto (pol. reg.), It. 101/J4
Venezia (prov.), It. 117/F1
Venezia, Golfo di (gulf), Eur. 117/F2
Venezia (Venice), It. 117/F2
Venezuela (gulf), Col.,Ven. 211/D2
Venezuela (ctry.) 211/E3
Vengurla, India 147/K5
Veniaminof (vol.), Ak, US 192/G4
Venice, Fl, US 191/H5
Venice, Il, US 195/G8
Venice (Venezia), It. 101/K4
Vénissieux, Fr. 100/F4
Venjan, Swe. 96/E1
Venjansjön (lake), Swe. 96/E1
Venkatagiri, India 140/C5
Venlo, Neth. 108/D6
Vennesla, Nor. 96/B2
Veno (bay), Den. 96/C3
Venoge (riv.), Swi. 114/C4
Venosa, It. 104/D2
Venray, Neth. 108/C5
Vent, Iles du (isls.), FrPol. 175/L6
Venta (riv.), Lat. 97/J3
Venta de Baños, Sp. 102/C2
Ventauri (riv.), Ven. 208/E3
Ventersburg, SAfr. 164/D3
Ventersdorp, SAfr. 164/D2
Venterstad, SAfr. 164/D3
Ventiseri, Fr. 104/A2
Ventnor, Eng, UK 91/E5
Ventnor City, NJ, US 196/D5
Ventspils, Lat. 97/J3
Ventuari (riv.), Ven. 211/E3
Ventura, Ca, US 194/A2
Ventura (co.), Ca, US 194/A2
Ventura (riv.), Ca, US 194/A2
Venturina, It. 101/J5
Venturosa, Braz. 212/C3
Venustiano Carranza, Mex. 198/C4
Venustiano Carranza (res.), Mex. 201/E3
Vép, Hun. 101/M3
Ver-sur-Launette, Fr. 88/L4
Vera, Arg. 215/D2
Vera, Sp. 102/E4
Vera Cruz, Pan. 210/B2
Veracruz, Mex. 201/N7
Veracruz-Llave (state), Mex. 198/B3
Veranópolis, Braz. 213/B4
Verāval, India 147/K4
Verbania, It. 115/E6
Verberie, Fr. 110/B5
Verbicaro, It. 104/D3
Vercelli, It. 116/B2
Vercelli (prov.), It. 114/E6
Verdal, Nor. 95/D3
Verde (riv.), Par. 215/D1
Verde (cape), Sen. 154/B5
Verde (riv.), Braz. 209/G6
Verde (riv.), Mex. 201/F4
Verde (coast), Sp. 102/B1
Verde (cape), It. 116/A5
Verde (bay), Arg. 216/E3
Verde Grande (riv.), Braz. 209/K7
Verden, Ger. 109/G3
Verdhikoússa, Gre. 105/G3
Verdigris (riv.), Ks, US 187/J3
Verdinho (riv.), Braz. 213/B1
Verdon (riv.), Fr. 100/F5
Verdugo (mts.), Ca, US 194/F7
Verdun, Qu, Can. 189/N7
Vereeniging, SAfr. 164/D2
Verena (peak), It. 115/H6
Vereshchagino, Rus. 119/M4
Veretskiy (pass), Ukr. 99/M4
Verga (cape), Gui. 160/B4
Vergara, Uru. 217/G2
Vergato, It. 117/E4
Vergennes, Vt, US 188/F2
Vergiate, It. 116/B1
Vergína (ruin), Gre. 105/H2
Verigenstadt, Ger. 115/F1
Verín, Sp. 102/B2
Veríssimo, Braz. 213/B1
Verkhnetulomskiy (res.), Rus. 118/F1
Verkhoyansk (range), Rus. 125/M2
Verkhoyansk, Rus. 123/P3
Verl, Ger. 109/F5
Vermenagna (riv.), It. 116/A4
Vermilion, Ab, Can. 184/F2
Vermilion (riv.), Ab, Can. 184/F2
Vermilion (range), Mn, US 185/K4
Vermilion Cliffs Nat'l Mon., Az, US 184/E3
Vermillion, SD, US 185/J5
Vermont (state), US 189/F2
Vernal, Ut, US 186/E2
Vernayaz, Swi. 114/D5
Vernazza, It. 116/C4
Verneuil-sur-Avre, Fr. 100/D2
Verneuil-sur-Seine, Fr. 88/H5
Verneukpan (salt pan), SAfr. 164/C3
Vernier, Swi. 114/C5
Vernon, BC, Can. 184/D3
Vernon, Fr. 100/D2
Vernon Hills, Il, US 193/Q15
Vernon Valley, NJ, US 196/D1
Vernouillet, Fr. 88/H5
Vero Beach, Fl, US 191/H5
Véroia, Gre. 105/H2
Verolanuova, It. 116/D2
Verolavecchia, It. 116/D2
Verolengo, It. 116/A2
Verona (prov.), It. 117/D1
Verona (int'l arpt.), It. 117/D2
Verona, It. 117/D2
Verona, NJ, US 197/J8
Verónica, Arg. 217/K11
Verrès, It. 116/A1
Verret, La, US 195/Q17
Verrières-le-Buisson, Fr . 88/J5
Versa (riv.), It. 116/B3
Versailles, Ky, US 188/C4
Versailles, Fr. 88/J5
Versigny, Fr. 88/L4
Verskla (riv.), Rus.,Ukr. 122/D4
Versmold, Ger. 109/F4
Versoix, Swi. 114/C5
Vert-le-Grand, Fr. 88/K6
Vert-le-Petit, Fr. 88/K6
Vert-Saint-Denis, Fr. 88/K6
Vertana (peak), It. 115/G4
Verte (peak), Fr. 114/C6
Vertemate, It. 116/C1
Vertientes, Cuba 203/G1
Vertou, Fr. 100/C3
Vertova, It. 116/C1
Vertus, Fr. 110/D6
Verviers, Belg. 111/E2
Vervins, Fr. 110/C4
Verwoerdburg, SAfr. 164/Q12
Veryan (bay), Eng, UK 90/B6
Verzasca (riv.), Swi. 115/E5
Verzasca (Gerra), Swi. 115/E5
Verzenay, Fr. 111/D5
Verzuolo, It. 101/G4
Verzy, Fr. 111/D5
Vescovato, Fr. 104/A1
Vescovato, It. 116/D2
Vesdre (riv.), Belg. 100/F1
Veselí nad Lužnicí, Czh. 113/H4
Veselyy (res.), Rus. 121/G3
Vesgre (riv.), Fr. 110/A6
Vesijärvi (lake), Fin. 97/L1
Vesle (riv.), Fr. 98/C4
Vesoul, Fr. 114/C2
Vespolate, It. 116/B2
Vest-Agder (co.), Nor. 95/C4
Vest-Sjælland (prov.), Den. 96/D4
Vest-Vlaanderen (prov.), Belg. 110/B2
Vestbjerg, Den. 96/C3
Vestby, Nor. 96/D2
Vesterålen (isls.), Nor. 95/E1
Vestfjorden (inlet), Nor. 95/E2
Vestfold (co.), Nor. 95/D4

Vestm – Wabu

Vestmannaeyjar, Ice. 95/N7
Vestone, It. 116/D1
Vestvågøy, Nor. 95/E1
Vestvågøya (isl.), Nor. 95/E1
Vesuvio (Vesuvius) (vol.), It. 104/D2
Veszprém (prov.), Hun. 106/C2
Veszprém, Hun. 106/C2
Vészto, Hun. 106/E2
Vet (riv.), SAfr. 164/D3
Vétheuil, Fr. 88/H4
Vetlanda, Swe. 96/F3
Vetluga (riv.), Rus. 122/E4
Vetralla, It. 104/C1
Vétraz, Fr. 114/C5
Větřni, Czh. 113/H5
Vettore (peak), It. 101/K5
Veude (riv.), Fr. 100/D3
Veurne, Belg. 110/B1
Vevey, Swi. 114/C5
Vex, Swi. 114/D5
Veybach (riv.), Ger. 111/F2
Veyle (riv.), Fr. 114/B5
Veyrier-du-Lac, Fr. 114/C6
Vézelise, Fr. 114/C1
Vézère (riv.), Fr. 100/D4
Vezirköprü, Turk. 148/C2
Vezza d'Oglio, It. 115/G5
Vezzano Ligure, It. 116/C4
Viacha, Bol. 208/E7
Viadana, It. 116/D3
Viana, Braz. 212/A1
Viana del Bollo, Sp. 102/B1
Viana do Alentejo, Port. 102/A3
Viana do Castelo, Port. 102/A2
Viana do Castelo (dist.), Port. 102/A2
Vianden, Lux. 111/F4
Vianen, Neth. 108/C4
Viangchan (Vientiane) (cap.), Laos 136/C2
Viar (riv.), Sp. 102/C4
Viareggio, It. 116/D5
Viarmes, Fr. 88/K4
Viaur (riv.), Fr. 100/E4
Vibbard, Mo, US 195/E5
Vibo Valentia, It. 104/E3
Viborg, Den. 96/C3
Viborg (co.), Den. 96/C3
Vic, Sp. 103/G2
Vic-en-Bigorre, Fr. 100/D5
Vic-Fezensac, Fr. 100/D5
Vicam, Mex. 200/C3
Vícar, Sp. 102/D4
Vicarello, It. 116/D5
Vicchio, It. 117/E6
Vice, Peru 214/A2
Vicente (pt.), Ca, US 194/F8
Vicente Guerrero, Mex. 200/E4
Vicente Guerrero, Mex. 200/A2
Vicente López, Arg. 217/J11
Vicenza, It. 117/E1
Vicenza (prov.), It. 115/H6
Vichada (riv.), Col. 208/E3
Vichada (dept.), Col. 210/D3
Vichaya, Bol. 214/D5
Vichuga, Rus. 118/J4
Vichy, Fr. 100/E3
Vickham (cape), Austl. 173/B3
Vicksburg, Ms, US 187/K4
Vicksburg Nat'l Mil. Park, Ms, US 187/K4
Vico, Fr. 104/A1
Vico (lake), It. 104/C1
Vico del Gargano, It. 106/B5
Vicopisano, It. 116/D5
Viçosa, Braz. 212/C3
Viçosa, Braz. 213/D2
Viçosa do Ceará, Braz. 212/B1
Vicosoprano, Swi. 115/F5
Vicou Gorge NP, Gre. 105/G3
Vicq, Fr. 88/H5
Victor Harbor, Austl. 171/H5
Victor Rosales, Mex. 200/E4
Victoria, Malay. 138/E2
Victoria (peak), Phil. 139/E2
Victoria, Austl. 173/B2
Victoria (falls), Zim. 163/E4
Victoria, Arg. 215/D3
Victoria (cap.), BC, Can. 184/C3
Victoria (riv.), Austl. 167/C2
Victoria (state), Austl. 173/C3
Victoria, China 141/K3
Victoria (mt.), Myan. 141/F3
Victoria, Rom. 107/G3
Victoria, Hon. 202/E3
Victoria, Chile 216/B3
Victoria (peak), Belz. 202/D2
Victoria, Gren. 211/F1
Victoria (isl.), NW,Nun., Can. 180/E1
Victoria (str.), Nun., Can. 180/F2
Victoria (lake), Afr. 162/B3
Victoria de las Tunas, Cuba 203/G1
Victoria Land (pol. reg.), Ant. 218/M
Victoria Nile (riv.), Ugan. 155/M7
Victoria West, SAfr. 164/C3
Victorias, Phil. 137/D5
Victoriaville, Qu, Can. 189/G2
Victorica, Arg. 216/D3
Victorville, Ca, US 194/C1
Victory Junction, Ks, US 195/D5
Vicuña Mackenna, Arg. 216/D2
Vidal (cape), SAfr. 165/F3
Vidalia, La, US 187/K5
Vidalia, Ga, US 191/H3
Videira, Braz. 213/B3
Videle, Rom. 107/G3
Vidhošt (peak), Czh. 113/G4
Vidigueira, Port. 102/B3
Vidigulfo, It. 116/C2
Vidin, Bul. 107/F4
Vidisha, India 142/A4
Vidnoye, Rus. 119/W9
Vidor, Tx, US 187/J5
Vidor, It. 117/F1
Vidöstern (lake), Swe. 96/F3
Vidourle (riv.), Fr. 100/E5
Vie (riv.), Fr. 100/D2
Viechtach, Ger. 113/F4
Viedma, Arg. 216/E4
Viedma (lake), Arg. 217/B6
Viehberg (peak), Aus. 113/H5
Vieille-Eglise-en-Yvelines, Fr. 88/H6
Viejo (peak), Peru 214/B2
Viella, Sp. 103/F1
Vielsalm, Belg. 111/E3
Vienenburg, Ger. 109/H5
Vienna, WV, US 188/D4
Vienna, Va, US 196/A6
Vienne, Fr. 100/F4
Vienne (riv.), Fr. 100/D3
Vientiane (int'l arpt.), Laos 136/C2
Vientiane (Viangchan) (cap.), Laos 136/C2
Vieques (isl.), PR 199/M8
Viére (riv.), Fr. 111/D6
Vierlingsbeek, Neth. 108/D5
Viernheim, Ger. 112/B3
Vierre (riv.), Belg. 111/E4
Viersen, Ger. 108/D6
Vierzon, Fr. 100/E3
Viesca, Mex. 200/E3
Vieste, It. 104/E2
Viet Tri, Viet. 141/J3
Vietnam (ctry.) 136/D2
Vieux-Boucau-les-Bains, Fr. 100/C5
Vieux Carré, La, US 195/P17
Vieux-Charmont, Fr. 114/C2
Vieux-Condé, Fr. 110/C3
Vieux Fort, StL. 199/N9
Vieux-Thann, Fr. 114/D2
Vieze (riv.), Swi. 114/C5
Viga, Phil. 137/D5
Vigan, Phil. 137/D4
Vigarano Mainarda, It. 117/E3
Vigasio, It. 117/D2
Vigevano, It. 116/B2
Viggiù, It. 115/E6
Vigia, Braz. 209/J4
Vigliano Biellese, It. 116/B1
Viglio (peak), It. 104/C2
Vignacourt, Fr. 110/B3
Vignanello, It. 104/C1
Vignemale (peak), Fr. 100/C5
Vigneulles-lès-Hattonchâtel, Fr. 111/E6
Vigneux-sur-Seine, Fr. 88/K5
Vignola, It. 117/D4
Vignot, Fr. 111/E6
Vigo, Sp. 102/A1
Vigodarzere, It. 117/E2
Vigonovo, It. 117/F2
Vigonza, It. 117/E2
Vigrestad, Nor. 96/A2
Viguzzolo, It. 116/B3
Vihanti, Fin. 118/E2
Vihāri, Pak. 144/B4
Vihti, Fin. 97/L1
Viitasaari, Fin. 118/E3
Vijayawada, India 140/D4
Vik, Ice. 95/N7
Vik, Nor. 96/B1
Vikersund, Nor. 96/C2
Vikeså, Nor. 96/B2
Vikhren (peak), Bul. 107/F5
Viking, Ab, Can. 184/F2
Vikmanshyttan, Swe. 96/F1
Vila Bittencourt, Braz. 210/D5
Vila de Sena, Moz. 163/G4
Vila do Bispo, Port. 102/A4
Vila do Conde, Port. 102/A2
Vila do Porto, Azor., Port. 103/T13
Vila Franca de Xira, Port. 103/P10
Vila Franca do Campo, Azor., Port. 103/T13
Vila Nova de Fozcoa, Port. 102/B2
Vila Nova de Gaia, Port. 102/A2
Vila Nova de Milfontes, Port. 102/A4
Vila Pouca de Aguiar, Port. 102/B2
Vila Real, Port. 102/B2
Vila Real (dist.), Port. 102/B2
Vila Velha Argolas, Braz. 213/D2
Vila Velha de Ródão, Port. 102/B3
Vila Verde, Port. 102/A2
Vila Viçosa, Port. 102/B3
Viladecans, Sp. 103/K7
Vilafranca del Penedès, Sp. 103/K7
Vilaine (riv.), Fr. 100/B3
Vilanandro (cape), Madg. 165/H7
Vilanculos, Moz. 163/G5
Vilanova i la Geltrù, Sp. 103/K7
Vilar Formoso, Port. 102/B2
Vilcabamba, Peru 214/B3
Vilcea (prov.), Rom. 107/F3
Vilches, Sp. 102/D3
Vilhelmina, Swe. 95/F2
Vilhena, Braz. 208/F6
Viliya (riv.), Bela. 118/E5
Viljandi, Est. 97/L2
Viljoenskroon, SAfr. 164/D2
Vil'kitsogo (str.), Rus. 123/K2
Villa Alemana, Chile 216/N8
Villa Alhué, Chile 216/N9
Villa Ángela, Arg. 215/D2
Villa Atuel, Arg. 216/D2
Villa Bartolomea, It. 117/E2
Villa Bruzual, Ven. 210/D2
Villa Cañás, Arg. 216/E2
Villa Carcina, It. 116/D1
Villa Carlos Paz, Arg. 215/D3
Villa Chañar Ladeado, Arg. 216/E2
Villa Constitución, Arg. 216/E2
Villa Corzo, Mex. 202/C2
Villa Cuauhtemoc, Mex. 201/Q10
Villa d'Almè, It. 116/C1
Villa de Arista, Mex. 201/E4
Villa de Cos, Mex. 200/E4
Villa de Costa Rica, Mex. 200/D3
Villa de La Paz, Mex. 201/E4
Villa de Reyes, Mex. 201/E4
Villa del Carbón, Mex. 201/Q9
Villa del Carmen, Uru. 217/K10
Villa del Río, Sp. 102/C4
Villa di Serio, It. 116/C1
Villa Dolores, Arg. 215/C3
Villa Dolores, Arg. 216/D1
Villa Flores, Mex. 202/C2
Villa Gesell, Arg. 217/F3
Villa Guardia, It. 116/C1
Villa Hidalgo, Mex. 200/D4
Villa Hidalgo, Mex. 200/C2
Villa Huidobro, Arg. 216/D2
Villa Iris, Arg. 216/D3
Villa Isabela, DRep. 203/J2
Villa Jaragua, DRep. 203/J2
Villa Juárez, Mex. 200/C3
Villa Juárez, Mex. 200/D3
Villa La Angostura, Arg. 216/C4
Villa Lázaro Cárdenas, Mex. 201/M6
Villa López, Mex. 200/D3
Villa Mantero, Arg. 217/J10
Villa María, Arg. 215/D3
Villa Minozzo, It. 116/D4
Villa Montes, Bol. 208/F8
Villa Nueva, Arg. 216/C2
Villa Nueva, Guat. 202/D3
Villa Nueva, Nic. 202/E3
Villa Opicina, It. 117/G1
Villa Park, Il, US 193/Q16
Villa Park, Ca, US 194/G8
Villa Regina, Arg. 216/D3
Villa Rica, Peru 214/C3
Villa Rosario, Col. 210/C3
Villa Sandino, Nic. 203/E3
Villa Sarmiento, Arg. 216/D2
Villa Serrano, Bol. 208/F7
Villa Unión, Arg. 215/C2
Villa Unión, Mex. 200/D4
Villa Valeria, Arg. 216/D2
Villa Verucchio, It. 117/F5
Villaba, Sp. 102/C1
Villablino, Sp. 102/B1
Villacañas, Sp. 102/D3
Villacarrillo, Sp. 102/D3
Villada, Sp. 102/C1
Villadiego, Sp. 102/C1
Villadose, It. 117/E2
Villadossola, It. 115/E5
Villafamés, Sp. 103/E2
Villafranca, Sp. 102/E1
Villafranca d'Asti, It. 116/B3
Villafranca de los Barros, Sp. 102/B3
Villafranca del Bierzo, Sp. 102/B1
Villafranca del Cid, Sp. 103/E2
Villafranca di Verona, It. 117/D2
Villafranca in Lunigiana, It. 116/C4
Villagarcía, Sp. 102/A1
Villagrán, Mex. 201/F3
Villaguay, Arg. 215/E3
Villahermosa, Sp. 102/D3
Villahermosa, Mex. 202/C2
Villajoyosa, Sp. 103/E3
Villalba, Sp. 102/B1
Villalcampo, Embalse de (res.), Sp. 102/B2
Villaldama, Mex. 190/C5
Villalón de Campos, Sp. 102/C1
Villalonga, Arg. 216/E3
Villalpando, Sp. 102/C2
Villamartín, Sp. 102/C4
Villandro (peak), It. 115/H4
Villanova, It. 117/F4
Villanova, It. 117/E4
Villanova d'Asti, It. 116/A3
Villanova Mondovì, It. 116/A4
Villanterio, It. 116/C2
Villanueva, Mex. 200/E4
Villanueva, Col. 210/C2
Villanueva, Hon. 202/E3
Villanueva de Arosa, Sp. 102/A1
Villanueva de Córdoba, Sp. 102/C3
Villanueva de la Serena, Sp. 102/C3
Villanueva de los Infantes, Sp. 102/D3
Villanueva de Oscos, Sp. 102/B1
Villanueva del Arzobispo, Sp. 102/D3
Villanueva sul Clisi, It. 116/D1
Villány, Hun. 106/D3
Villar del Arzobispo, Sp. 103/E3
Villarcayo, Sp. 102/D1
Villardevós, Sp. 102/B2
Villarreal de los Infantes, Sp. 103/E3
Villarrica, Par. 215/E2
Villarrica, Chile 216/B3
Villarrica (vol.), Chile 216/C3
Villarrica (lake), Chile 216/B3
Villarrica, PN, Chile 216/C3
Villarrobledo, Sp. 102/D3
Villarrubia de los Ojos, Sp. 102/D3
Villars-les-Dombes, Fr. 114/B6
Villars-sur-Glâne, Swi. 114/D4
Villas, NJ, US 196/D5
Villasana de Mena, Sp. 102/D1
Villasanta, It. 116/C1
Villastellone, It. 116/A3
Villaverde del Río, Sp. 102/C4
Villaverla, It. 117/E1
Villavicencio, Col. 210/C3
Villaviciosa, Sp. 102/C1
Villaviciosa de Odón, Sp. 103/N9
Villazón, Bol. 215/C1
Villecresnes, Fr. 88/K5
Villefranche-de-Rouergue, Fr. 100/E4
Villefranche-sur-Saône, Fr. 100/F4
Villejuif, Fr. 88/K5
Villemur-sur-Tarn, Fr. 100/D5
Villena, Sp. 103/E3
Villeneuve, Swi. 114/C5
Villeneuve-d'Ascq, Fr. 110/C2
Villeneuve-le-Comte, Fr. 88/L5
Villeneuve-le-Roi, Fr. 88/K5
Villeneuve-lès-Avignon, Fr. 100/F5
Villeneuve-Saint-Denis, Fr. 88/L5
Villeneuve-Saint-Georges, Fr. 88/K5
Villeneuve-Saint-Germain, Fr. 110/C5
Villeneuve-sur-Lot, Fr. 100/D4
Villeneuve-sur-Yonne, Fr. 100/E2
Villeneuve-Tolosane, Fr. 100/D5
Villennes-sur-Seine, Fr. 88/H5
Villeparisis, Fr. 88/K5
Villepinte, Fr. 88/K5
Villepreux, Fr. 88/J5
Villeroy, Fr. 88/L4
Villers-Bretonneux, Fr. 110/B4
Villers-Cotterêts, Fr. 110/C5
Villers-en-Arthies, Fr. 88/H4
Villers-le-Bouillet, Belg. 111/E2
Villers-le-Lac, Fr. 114/C3
Villers-lès-Nancy, Fr. 111/F6
Villers-Saint-Genest, Fr. 88/L4
Villers-Saint-Paul, Fr. 110/B5
Villers-Semeuse, Fr. 111/D4
Villersexel, Fr. 114/C2
Villerupt, Fr. 111/E5
Villette, Fr. 88/H5
Villeurbanne, Fr. 114/A6
Villevaudé, Fr. 88/K5
Villiers, SAfr. 164/E2
Villiers-en-Lieu, Fr. 111/D6
Villiers-le-Bel, Fr. 88/K4
Villiers-Saint-Georges, Fr. 110/C6
Villiers-sur-Marne, Fr. 88/K5
Villiers-sur-Morin, Fr. 88/L5
Villiersdorp, SAfr. 164/L10
Villieu-Loyes-Mollon, Fr. 114/B6
Villingen-Schwenningen, Ger. 115/E1
Villmar, Ger. 112/B2
Villongo, It. 116/C1
Villorba, It. 117/F1
Vilnius (int'l arpt.), Lith. 97/L4
Vilnius (cap.), Lith. 97/L4
Vils, Aus. 115/G2
Vils (riv.), Ger. 98/F4
Vilsbiburg, Ger. 113/F6
Vilseck, Ger. 113/E3
Vilshofen, Ger. 113/G5
Vilters, Swi. 115/F3
Vilvoorde, Belg. 111/D2
Vilyuy (riv.), Rus. 125/L3
Vilyuy (range), Rus. 123/M3
Vimercate, It. 116/C1
Vimeu (reg.), Fr. 110/A3
Vimmerby, Swe. 96/F3
Vimodrone, It. 116/C2
Vimperk, Czh. 113/G4
Vina (riv.), Camr. 154/H6
Viña del Mar, Chile 216/N8
Vinanivao, Madg. 165/J6
Vinaroz, Sp. 103/F2
Vincennes, In, US 188/C4
Vincennes (lake), Fr. 88/L5
Vincennes (bay), Ant. 218/H
Vincennes, Fr. 88/K5
Vincent, Ca, US 194/B1
Vincentown, NJ, US 196/D4
Vinces, Ecu. 210/B5
Vincey, Fr. 114/C1
Vinchos, Peru 214/C4
Vinci, It. 117/D5
Vindeby, Den. 96/D4
Vindeln, Swe. 95/F2
Vindhya (range), India 142/A4
Vineland, NJ, US 196/C5
Vineland Station, On, Can. 189/R9
Vineuil, Fr. 100/D3
Vingåker, Swe. 96/F2
Vinh, Viet. 136/D2
Vinh An, Viet. 137/A4
Vinh Long, Viet. 136/D4
Vinh Yen, Viet. 136/D1
Vinhais, Port. 102/B2
Vinhedo, Braz. 213/G8
Vinica, FYROM 105/H2
Vinita, Ok, US 187/J3
Vinju Mare, Rom. 106/F3
Vinkovci, Cro. 106/D3
Vinningen, Ger. 111/G5
Vinnyts'ka Oblasti, Ukr. 120/D2
Vinnytsya, Ukr. 120/D2
Vinon-sur-Verdon, Fr. 100/F5
Vinson Massif (peak), Ant. 218/U
Viola, De, US 196/C5
Viola, NY, US 197/J7
Violet, La, US 195/Q17
Violet Town, Austl. 173/C3
Viosne (riv.), Fr. 110/A5
Virac, Phil. 137/D5
Viracopos (int'l arpt.), Braz. 213/F7
Viranşehir, Turk. 148/D2
Virār, India 147/K5
Virden, Mb, Can. 185/H3
Vire, Fr. 100/C2
Vire (riv.), Fr. 100/C2
Viren (lake), Swe. 96/F2
Vireux-Wallerand, Fr. 111/D3
Virgem da Lapa, Braz. 212/B5
Virgin (riv.), US 186/D3
Virgin (isls.), UK,US 199/M8
Virgin Gorda (isl.), UK 199/M8
Virgin Islands NP, USVI 199/M8
Virginia, SAfr. 164/D3
Virginia (state), US 188/E4
Virginia City, Nv, US 186/C3
Virginia Water, Eng, UK 88/B2
Viriat, Fr. 114/B5
Virieu-le-Grand, Fr. 114/B6
Viroflay, Fr. 88/J5
Viroin (riv.), Belg. 111/D3
Viroqua, Wi, US 187/K2
Virovitica, Cro. 106/C3
Virserum, Swe. 96/F3
Virton, Belg. 111/E4
Virú, Peru 214/B3
Virudunagar, India 140/C6
Virunga, D.R. Congo 162/A3
Virunga NP, D.R. Congo 162/A3
Viry-Châtillon, Fr. 88/K6
Vis (isl.), Cro. 106/C4
Visaginas, Lith. 97/M4
Visalia, Ca, US 186/C3
Visandre (riv.), Fr. 88/M5
Visayan (sea), Phil. 137/D5
Visbek, Ger. 109/F3
Visby, Swe. 96/H3
Visconde do Rio Branco, Braz. 213/D2
Viscount Melville (sound), NW,Nun., Can. 181/R7
Visé, Belg. 111/E2
Višegrad, Bosn. 106/D4
Viseu, Port. 102/B2
Viseu (dist.), Port. 102/B2
Vişeu de Sus, Rom. 107/G2
Vishākhapatnam, India 140/D4
Vishera (riv.), Rus. 119/L3
Vishoek, SAfr. 164/L11
Viskafors, Swe. 96/E3
Vislanda, Swe. 96/F3
Visnagar, India 147/K4
Višnjevac, Cro. 106/D3
Visoko, Bosn. 106/D4
Visp, Swi. 114/D5
Visperterminen, Swi. 114/D5
Visselhövede, Ger. 109/G3
Vissenbjerg, Den. 96/D4
Vissoie, Swi. 114/D5
Vista, Ca, US 194/C4
Vistonís (lake), Gre. 105/J2
Vistula (riv.), Pol. 99/K2
Vit (riv.), Bul. 107/G4
Vita, Mb, Can. 185/J3
Viterbo, It. 104/C1
Vitez, Bosn. 106/C3
Viti Levu (isl.), Fiji 174/G6
Vitigudino, Sp. 102/B2
Vitim (plat.), Rus. 123/M4
Vitim (riv.), Rus. 125/L4
Vítkuv Kamen (peak), Czh. 113/H5
Vitomirica, Kos. 106/E4
Vitor, Peru 214/D5
Vitória, Braz. 213/D2
Vitoria, Sp. 102/D1
Vitória da Conquista, Braz. 212/B4
Vitória de Santo Antão, Braz. 212/D3
Vitória do Mearim, Braz. 212/A1
Vitorino Freire, Braz. 212/A2
Vitosha NP, Bul. 107/F4
Vitré, Fr. 100/C2
Vitrey-sur-Mance, Fr. 114/B2
Vitrolles, Fr. 100/F5
Vitry-en-Artois, Fr. 110/B3
Vitry-le-François, Fr. 111/D6
Vitry-sur-Seine, Fr. 88/K5
Vitsyebsk, Bela. 97/P4
Vitsyebskaya Voblasts, Bela. 118/E5
Vittangi, Swe. 95/G2
Vittel, Fr. 114/B1
Vittoria, It. 104/D4
Vittorio Veneto, It. 101/K4
Vivarais, Monts du (mts.), Fr. 100/F4
Viveiro, Sp. 102/B1
Viverone (lake), It. 116/B2
Viverone, It. 116/B2
Vivian, La, US 187/J4
Vivonne, Fr. 100/D3
Vizcaíno, Sierra (mts.), Mex. 200/B3
Vize, Turk. 107/H5
Vizhas (riv.), Rus. 119/K2
Vizianagaram, India 140/D4
Vlaardingen, Neth. 108/B5
Vlădeasa (peak), Rom. 107/F2
Vladikavkaz, Rus. 121/H4
Vladimir, Rus. 118/J4
Vladimirskaya Oblast, Rus. 118/J5
Vladivostok, Rus. 129/P3
Vlagtwedde, Neth. 109/E2
Vlăhiţa, Rom. 107/G2
Vlajna (peak), Serb. 106/E4
Vlasenica, Bosn. 106/D3
Vlašim, Czh. 101/L2
Vlasotince, Serb. 106/E4
Vlieland (isl.), Neth. 98/C2
Vliestroom (chan.), Neth. 108/C2
Vlijmen, Neth. 108/C5
Vlissingen, Neth. 108/A6
Vlotho, Ger. 109/F4
Vltava (riv.), Czh. 99/H4
Vnukovo (int'l arpt.), Rus. 119/W9
Vobarno, It. 116/D1
Vöcklabruck, Aus. 113/G6
Vöcklamarkt, Aus. 113/G6
Vodice, Cro. 106/B3
Vodlozero (lake), Rus. 118/H3
Vodňany, Czh. 113/H4
Vodskov, Den. 96/D3
Voerde, Ger. 108/D5
Vogan, Togo 161/F5
Vogelsberg (mts.), Ger. 101/H1
Voghera, It. 116/C3
Vogogna, It. 115/E6
Vogorno (lake), Swi. 115/E5
Vogtareuth, Ger. 113/F7
Vogtland (reg.), Ger. 98/F3
Vohenstrauss, Ger. 113/F3
Vohilava, Madg. 165/H8
Vohimena (cape), Madg. 165/H9
Vohipeno, Madg. 165/H8
Vohiposa, Madg. 165/H8
Voi, Kenya 162/C3
Void-Vacon, Fr. 111/E6
Voil (lake), Sc, UK 94/B4
Voinjama, Libr. 160/C4
Voinsles, Fr. 88/M5
Voiron, Fr. 100/F4
Voise (riv.), Fr. 100/D2
Voisey (bay), Nf, Can. 181/K3
Voiteur, Fr. 114/B4
Vojosë (riv.), Alb. 106/D5
Vojvodina (prov.), Serb. 106/D3
Völklingen, Ger. 111/F5
Volano, It. 115/H6
Volary, Czh. 113/G5
Volcán Barú, PN, Pan. 203/F4
Volcán Poás, PN, CR 203/E4
Volcano, Hi, US 182/U11
Volcano (isls.), Japan 174/C2
Volcans NP, Rwa. 162/A3
Volchiy Nos (cape), Rus. 97/Q1
Volda, Nor. 95/C3
Volendam, Neth. 108/C3
Volga (riv.), Rus. 85/J3
Volga-Baltic Waterway (canal), Rus. 118/H3
Volgelsheim, Fr. 114/D1
Volgodonsk, Rus. 121/G3
Volgograd (int'l arpt.), Rus. 121/H2
Volgograd (res.), Rus. 121/H2
Volgogradskaya Oblast, Rus. 121/G2
Volkach (riv.), Ger. 112/D3
Volkach, Ger. 112/D3
Volkeradam (dam), Neth. 108/B5
Völkermarkt, Aus. 101/L3
Volketswil, Swi. 115/E3
Volkhov, Rus. 97/Q2
Volkhov (riv.), Rus. 118/F4
Volkmarsen, Ger. 109/G6
Volksrust, SAfr. 165/E2
Volodymyr-Volyns'kyy, Ukr. 120/C2
Vologda, Rus. 118/H4
Vologdskaya Oblast, Rus. 118/J3
Vologne (riv.), Fr. 98/D4
Volos (gulf), Gre. 105/H3
Vólos, Gre. 105/H3
Volpago del Montello, It. 117/F1
Volpiano, It. 116/A2
Völs, Aus. 115/H3
Vol'sk, Rus. 121/H1
Volta (riv.), Gha. 154/F6
Volta (pol. reg.), Gha. 161/F5
Volta (lake), Gha. 161/E4
Volta Mantovana, It. 116/D2
Volta Redonda, Braz. 213/J7
Voltana, It. 117/E4
Volterra, It. 117/D6
Voltlage, Ger. 109/E4
Volturino (peak), It. 104/D2
Volturno (riv.), It. 104/D2
Volubilis (ruin), Mor. 158/B2
Vólvi (lake), Gre. 105/H2
Volyně, Czh. 113/G4
Volyňka (riv.), Czh. 113/G4
Volyns'ka Oblasti, Ukr. 120/C2
Volzhsk, Rus. 119/L5
Volzhskiy, Rus. 121/H2
Von Frank (mtn.), Ak, US 192/H3
Von Ormy, Tx, US 195/T21
Vondrozo, Madg. 165/H8
Vónitsa, Gre. 105/G3
Vonne (riv.), Fr. 100/D3
Voorburg, Neth. 108/B5
Voorne (isl.), Neth. 108/B5
Voorschoten, Neth. 108/B4
Voorst, Neth. 108/D4
Vopnafjördhur, Ice. 95/P6
Vorab (peak), Swi. 115/F4
Vorarlberg (prov.), Aus. 98/E5
Vorbach (riv.), Ger. 112/C4
Vorchdorf, Aus. 113/G6
Vorden, Neth. 108/D4
Vorderrhein (riv.), Swi. 101/H3
Vorderweissenbach, Aus. 113/H5
Vordingborg, Den. 96/D4
Voreppe, Fr. 100/F4
Vorkuta, Rus. 119/P2
Vorkuta (int'l arpt.), Rus. 119/Q2
Vormsi (isl.), Est. 97/K2
Vóroi, Gre. 105/J5
Vorona (riv.), Rus. 121/G1
Voronezh (int'l arpt.), Rus. 120/F2
Voronezh (riv.), Rus. 120/F1
Voronezh, Rus. 120/F2
Voronezhskaya Oblast, Rus. 121/G2
Voron'ya (riv.), Rus. 118/G1
Vorskla (riv.), Ukr. 120/E2
Vorst, Belg. 111/E1
Vörts (lake), Est. 97/L2
Võru, Est. 97/M3
Vorya (riv.), Rus. 119/X8
Vosburg, SAfr. 164/C3
Vösendorf, Aus. 107/N7
Vosges (dept.), Fr. 114/C1
Vosges (mts.), Fr. 98/D5
Voskresensk, Rus. 118/H5
Voss, Nor. 96/B1
Vostok (isl.), Kiri. 175/K6
Vostok (cape), Ant. 218/V
Vostok, Rus., Ant. 218/H
Votice, Czh. 113/H4
Votkinsk, Rus. 119/M4
Votkinsk (res.), Rus. 119/M4
Votorantim, Braz. 213/C2
Votuporanga, Braz. 213/B2
Vouga (riv.), Port. 102/A2
Vouglans (lake), Fr. 114/B5
Vouglans, Barrage de (dam), Fr. 114/B5
Voujeaucourt, Fr. 114/C3
Voúla, Gre. 105/N9
Voulangis, Fr. 88/L5
Vouvry, Swi. 114/C5
Voúxa (cape), Gre. 105/H5
Vouziers, Fr. 111/D5
Voy-Vozh, Rus. 119/M3
Voyageurs NP, Mn, US 188/A1
Voyeykov Ice Shelf, Ant. 218/J
Voytolovka (riv.), Rus. 119/T7
Vozhe (lake), Rus. 118/H3
Voznesens'k, Ukr. 107/K2
Vozrozhdeniya (isl.), Uzb. 145/C4
Vrå, Den. 96/C3
Vraine (riv.), Fr. 114/B1
Vrancea (prov.), Rom. 107/H3
Vrangelya (isl.), Rus. 123/T2
Vranjska Banja, Serb. 106/E4
Vranov nad Teplou, Slvk. 99/L4
Vrapčište, FYROM 105/G2
Vratsa, Bul. 107/F4
Vrbas, Serb. 106/D3
Vrbas (riv.), Bosn. 106/C3
Vrchy (peak), Czh. 113/H4
Vrede, SAfr. 164/E2
Vredefort, SAfr. 164/D2
Vreden, Ger. 108/D4
Vredenburg-Saldanha, SAfr. 164/K10
Vredendal, SAfr. 164/B3
Vresse-sur-Semois, Belg. 111/D4
Vrhnika, Slov. 101/L4
Vries, Neth. 108/D2
Vriezenveen, Neth. 108/D4
Vrigstad, Swe. 96/F3
Vrin (riv.), Fr. 98/B5
Vrindāban, India 142/A2
Vrnjačka Banja, Serb. 106/E4
Vrondádhos, Gre. 105/K3
Vršac, Serb. 106/E3
Vryburg, SAfr. 164/D2
Vryheid, SAfr. 165/E2
Vsetín, Czh. 99/K4
Vsevidof (mt.), Ak, US 192/E5
Vsevolozhsk, Rus. 119/T6
Vtáčnik (peak), Slvk. 99/K4
Vučitrn, Kos. 106/E4
Vught, Neth. 108/C5
Vukovar, Cro. 106/D3
Vulcan, Ab, Can. 184/E3
Vulcan, Rom. 107/F3
Vulcano (isl.), It. 104/D3
Vŭlchedrŭm, Bul. 107/F4
Vŭlchi Dol, Bul. 107/H4
Vulci (ruin), It. 104/B1
Vung Tau, Viet. 136/D4
Vuohijärvi (lake), Fin. 97/M1
Vuollerim, Swe. 95/G2
Vuoska (lake), Rus. 97/N1
Vuotso, Fin. 118/E1
Vŭrbitsa, Bul. 107/H4
Vuria (peak), Kenya 162/C3
Vŭrshets, Bul. 107/F4
Vyāra, India 147/K4
Vyatka (riv.), Rus. 122/E4
Vyatskiye Polyany, Rus. 119/L4
Vyazemskiy, Rus. 129/P2
Vyaz'ma, Rus. 118/G5
Vyborg, Rus. 97/N1
Vyborg (bay), Rus. 97/N1
Vychegda (riv.), Rus. 122/F3
Vygozero (lake), Rus. 118/G3
Vyhorlat (peak), Slvk. 99/M4
Vyksa, Rus. 118/J5
Vym' (riv.), Rus. 119/L3
Vynohradiv, Ukr. 99/M4
Vyrnwy (riv.), Wal, UK 90/C1
Vyshniy Volochek, Rus. 118/G4
Vyškov, Czh. 99/J4

W

W du Benin, PN du, Ben. 161/F4
W du Burkino Faso, PN du, Burk. 161/F4
W du Niger, PN du, Ben. 154/F5
W du Niger, PN du, Niger 161/F3
W. J. van Blommestein (lake), Sur. 209/G2
Wa, Gha. 161/E4
Waal, Ger. 115/G2
Waal (riv.), Neth. 108/C5
Waalre, Neth. 108/C6
Waalwijk, Neth. 108/C5
Waarschoot, Belg. 110/C1
Wabasca, Ab, Can. 184/E2
Wabasca (riv.), Ab, Can. 180/E3
Wabash, In, US 188/C3
Wabash (riv.), Il,In, US 188/C4
Wabē Shebelē Wenz (riv.), Eth. 155/P6
Wabern, Ger. 109/G6
Wabigoon (lake), On, Can. 185/K3
Wabowden, Mb, Can. 185/J2
Wąbrzeźno, Pol. 99/K2
Wabu (lake), China 130/D4

Wabu, SKor. 131/G6
Wachenheim an der Weinstrasse, Ger. 112/B4
Wachi, Japan 135/H5
Wachtebeke, Belg. 110/C1
Wachtendonk, Ger. 108/D6
Wächtersbach, Ger. 112/C2
Wackernheim, Ger. 112/B3
Wackersdorf, Ger. 113/F4
Waco, Tx, US 187/H5
Waconda (lake), Ks, US 187/H3
Waconia, Mn, US 185/K4
Wad Medanī, Sudan 155/M5
Wada, Japan 135/E3
Wadayama, Japan 135/G5
Wadbilliga NP, Austl. 173/D3
Waddān, Libya 154/J2
Waddell, Az, US 195/R18
Waddell (dam), Az, US 195/R18
Waddenzee (sound), Neth. 98/C2
Waddington (mt.), BC, Can. 184/B3
Waddinxveen, Neth. 108/B4
Waddy (pt.), Austl. 172/D4
Wadena, Sk, Can. 185/H3
Wadena, Mn, US 185/K4
Wädenswil, Swi. 115/E3
Wadern, Ger. 111/F4
Wadersloh, Ger. 109/F5
Wadgassen, Ger. 111/F5
Wādī al Layl, Tun. 158/M6
Wādī As Sīr, Jor. 149/D4
Wādī Majardah (riv.), Tun. 158/L6
Wādī Mūsá, Jor. 149/D4
Wading (riv.), NJ, US 196/D4
Wading River, NY, US 197/F2
Wadowice, Pol. 99/K4
Wadsworth, Il, US 193/Q15
Waegwan, SKor. 131/E5
Wafangdian, China 131/A3
Wagenfeld-Hasslingen, Ger. 109/F3
Wageningen, Neth. 108/C5
Wager (bay), NW, Can. 180/G2
Wagga Wagga, Austl. 173/C2
Waggaman, La, US 195/P17
Waghäusel, Ger. 112/B4
Wagin, Austl. 170/C5
Waging am See, Ger. 113/F7
Waginger (lake), Ger. 113/F7
Wägitaler-see (lake), Swi. 115/E3
Wagna, Aus. 101/L3
Wagner, Braz. 212/B4
Wągrowiec, Pol. 99/J2
Wagstaff, Ks, US 195/D6
Wāh, Pak. 144/B3
Wah Wah (range), Ut, US 186/D3
Wahiawa, Hi, US 182/V12
Wahlern, Swi. 114/D4
Wahpeton, ND, US 185/J4
Wahrenholz, Ger. 109/H3
Wai, India 140/B4
Waialee, Hi, US 182/V12
Waialua, Hi, US 182/V12
Waianae, Hi, US 182/V13
Waiau (riv.), NZ 175/S11
Waibamiao, China 130/D2
Waiblingen, Ger. 112/C5
Waidhaus, Ger. 113/F3
Waidhofen an der Thaya, Aus. 101/L2
Waidhofen an der Ybbs, Aus. 113/H7
Waigeo (isl.), Indo. 139/H3
Waigolshausen, Ger. 112/D3
Waihou (riv.), NZ 175/T10
Waikane, Hi, US 182/W12
Waikari, NZ 175/S11
Waikato (riv.), NZ 175/T10
Waikerie, Austl. 171/H5
Waikiki, Hi, US 182/W13
Waikoloa Village, Hi, US 182/U11
Wailuku, Hi, US 182/T10
Waimanalo, Hi, US 182/W13
Waimanalo Beach, Hi, US 182/W13
Waimate, NZ 175/S11
Waimea, Hi, US 182/S10
Waimea (falls), Hi, US 182/V12
Waimes, Belg. 111/F3
Wainfleet, On, Can. 189/R10
Waingangā (riv.), India 140/C3
Waini (riv.), Guy. 211/G2
Wainwright, Ak, US 192/F1
Wainwright, Ab, Can. 184/F2
Waipahu, Hi, US 182/V13
Waipio, Hi, US 182/U10
Waipio Acres, Hi, US 182/V13
Waipukurau, NZ 175/T10
Wairau (riv.), NZ 175/S11
Wairoa, NZ 175/T10
Waischenfeld, Ger. 113/E3
Waitaki (riv.), NZ 175/S11
Waitara, NZ 175/S10
Waizenkirchen, Aus. 113/G6
Wajima, Japan 133/E2
Waka (cape), Indo. 139/G4
Wakakusa, Japan 135/A2
Wakasa, Japan 132/D3
Wakasa (bay), Japan 135/H4
Wakaw, Sk, Can. 185/G2
Wakayama, Japan 132/D3
Wakayama (pref.), Japan 132/D4
Wake (isl.), Pac., US 174/F3
Wakefield, Eng, UK 93/G4
Wakefield (co.), Eng, UK 93/G4
Wakefield, Mi, US 188/B2
Wakema, Myan. 141/G4
Waki, Japan 132/D3
Wakkanai, Japan 134/B1
Wakool, Austl. 173/C2
Wakuya, Japan 134/B4
Wakwayowkastic (riv.), On, Can. 188/D1
Wala (riv.), Tanz. 162/B4
Walachia (reg.), Rom. 107/G3
Walagunya Abor. Land, Austl. 170/D2
Wałbrzych, Pol. 99/J3
Walbury (hill), Eng, UK 91/E4
Walcha, Austl. 173/D1
Walcheren (isl.), Neth. 108/A5
Walcourt, Belg. 111/D3
Wałcz, Pol. 99/J2
Wald, Swi. 115/E3
Wald, Ger. 113/F4
Waldbillig, Lux. 111/F4
Waldbreitbach, Ger. 111/G2
Waldbröl, Ger. 111/G2
Waldbronn, Ger. 112/B5
Waldbrunn, Ger. 112/C3
Waldburg, Ger. 115/F2
Walden, Co, US 187/F2
Waldenbuch, Ger. 112/C5
Waldenburg, Swi. 114/D3
Waldenburg, Ger. 112/C4
Waldershof, Ger. 113/F3
Waldesch, Ger. 111/G3
Waldheim, Sk, Can. 184/G2
Waldighofen, Fr. 114/D2
Walding, Aus. 113/H6
Waldkirch, Ger. 114/D1
Waldmünchen, Ger. 113/F4
Waldnaab (riv.), Ger. 113/F3
Waldrach, Ger. 111/F4
Waldron, Mo, US 195/D5
Waldsassen, Ger. 113/F3
Waldshut-Tiengen, Ger. 115/E2
Waldstetten, Ger. 112/C5
Waldviertel (reg.), Aus. 99/H4
Waldwick, NJ, US 197/J8
Walea (str.), Indo. 139/F4
Waleabahi (isl.), Indo. 139/F4
Walensee (lake), Swi. 115/F3
Walenstadt, Swi. 115/F3
Wales, Ak, US 192/E2
Wales, UK 90/B3
Wales (isl.), Nun., Can. 181/H2
Wales, Wi, US 193/P14
Walferdange, Lux. 111/F4
Walgett, Austl. 173/D1
Walhalla, ND, US 185/J3
Walhalla, SC, US 191/H3
Walhalla, Ger. 113/F4
Walker (riv.), Nv, US 186/C3
Walker (lake), Nv, US 186/C3
Walker (bay), SAfr. 164/L11
Walkerston, Austl. 172/C3
Walkerton, On, Can. 188/D2
Walkill (riv.), NY, US 196/D1
Walla Walla, Austl. 173/C2
Walla Walla, Wa, US 184/D4
Wallace, Id, US 184/E4
Wallaceburg, On, Can. 188/D3
Wallaroo, Austl. 171/H5
Wallasey, Eng, UK 93/E5
Walldorf, Ger. 112/B4
Walldürn, Ger. 112/C3
Walled (lake), Mi, US 193/F6
Walled City Hist. Site, SKor. 131/G7
Walled Lake, Mi, US 193/F6
Wallenhorst, Ger. 109/F4
Wallern im Burgenland, Aus. 101/M3
Wallers, Fr. 110/C3
Wallersee (lake), Aus. 113/G7
Wallerstein, Ger. 112/D5
Wallington, NJ, US 197/J8
Wallis (isls.), Wall., Fr. 175/H6
Wallis and Futuna (dpcy.), Fr. 174/G6
Wallisellen, Swi. 115/E3
Walloon Brabant (prov.), Belg. 111/D2
Wallowa (mts.), Or, US 184/D4
Wallsend, Eng, UK 93/G2
Wallumbilla, Austl. 172/C4
Walney, Isle of (isl.), Eng, UK 93/E3
Walnut, Ca, US 194/G7
Walnut Canyon Nat'l Mon., Az, US 186/E4
Walnut Creek, Ca, US 193/K11
Walnut Grove, Ca, US 193/L10
Walnut Park, Ca, US 194/F8
Walnut Ridge, Ar, US 187/K3
Walnutport, Pa, US 196/C2
Walpole, Austl. 170/C5
Walpole-Nornalup NP, Austl. 170/C5
Walrus (isls.), Ak, US 192/F4
Walsall, Eng, UK 91/E1
Walsall (co.), Eng, UK 91/E1
Walsenburg, Co, US 187/F3
Walsingham (cape), Nun., Can. 181/K2
Walsrode, Ger. 109/G3
Waltenhofen, Ger. 115/G2
Walter F. George (res.), Al,Ga, US 191/G4
Walterboro, SC, US 191/H3
Walter's Ash, Eng, UK 88/A2
Waltham Abbey, Eng, UK 88/D1
Waltham Forest (bor.), Eng, UK 88/A1
Walton-on-Thames, Eng, UK 88/B2
Waltrop, Ger. 109/E5
Walvis Bay, Namb. 163/B5
Walworth, Wi, US 193/N14
Walworth (co.), Wi, US 193/N14
Walyahmoning (peak), Austl. 170/C4
Walyunga NP, Austl. 170/L6
Walzenhausen, Swi. 115/F3
Wamba, Kenya 162/C2
Wamba, D.R. Congo 155/L7
Wamel, Neth. 108/C5
Wami (riv.), Tanz. 162/C4
Wampool (riv.), Eng, UK 93/E2
Wamsutter, Wy, US 184/G5
Wanaka, NZ 175/R11
Wanamassa, NJ, US 196/D3
Wanaque (res.), NJ, US 196/D1
Wanaque, NJ, US 197/H7
Wanda (mts.), China 129/P2
Wanda, Il, US 195/G8
Wandering, Austl. 170/C5
Wanding, China 141/G3
Wando, SKor. 131/D5
Wandoan, Austl. 172/C4
Wandsworth (bor.), Eng, UK 88/C2
Wanfried, Ger. 109/H6
Wang (riv.), Thai. 141/G4
Wang Hip (peak), Thai. 136/B4
Wanganui, NZ 175/T10
Wangaratta, Austl. 173/C3
Wangdu, China 130/C3
Wangen, Ger. 115/F2
Wangen an der Aare, Swi. 114/D3
Wangen bei Olten, Swi. 114/D3
Wangerooge (isl.), Ger. 109/E1
Wanggamet (peak), Indo. 139/F6
Wanghai Shan (peak), China 131/A2
Wängi, Swi. 115/E3
Wangjiang, China 137/C1
Wangpan (bay), China 130/E5
Wani (peak), Indo. 139/F4
Wanica (dist.), Sur. 211/H3
Wank (peak), Ger. 115/H2
Wanning, China 141/K4
Wanouchi, Japan 135/L5
Wanquan, China 130/C2
Wanrong, China 130/B4
Wansbeck (riv.), Eng, UK 93/G1
Wantagh, NY, US 197/M9
Wanxian, China 128/J5
Wanze, Belg. 111/E2
Wapakoneta, Oh, US 188/C3
Wapawekka (lake), Sk, Can. 185/G2
Wapiti (riv.), Ab,BC, Can. 184/D2
Wapoga (riv.), Indo. 139/J4
Wappapello (lake), Mo, US 187/K3
Wapsipinicon (riv.), Ia, US 185/K5
Wapwallopen, Pa, US 196/B1
Warabi, Japan 135/D2
Warangal, India 140/C4
Waratah, Austl. 173/C4
Warburg, Ger. 109/G6
Warburton, Pak. 144/B4
Warburton, Austl. 170/E3
Warburton Range Abor. Rsv., Austl. 170/E3
Warche (riv.), Belg. 111/F3
Ward, Co, US 195/A2
Ward, NZ 175/S11
Ward Cove, Ak, US 192/M4
Warden, SAfr. 164/E2
Warden (pt.), Eng, UK 91/G4
Wardenburg, Ger. 109/F2
Wardha, India 140/C3
Ward's Stone (peak), Eng, UK 93/F3
Ware, Eng, UK 91/F3
Waregem, Belg. 110/C2
Waremme, Belg. 111/E2
Waren, Ger. 96/E5
Warendorf, Ger. 109/E5
Waretown, NJ, US 196/D4
Warffum, Neth. 108/D2
Wargrave, Eng, UK 91/F4
Warialda, Austl. 173/D1
Warin Chamrap, Thai. 136/D3
Waringstown, NI, UK 92/B3
Warka, Pol. 99/L3
Warkworth, NZ 175/S10
Warlingham, Eng, UK 88/C3
Warmbad, Namb. 164/B3
Warme Bode (riv.), Ger. 109/H5
Warmebach (riv.), Ger. 109/G6
Warmenhuizen, Neth. 108/B3
Warmeriville, Fr. 111/D5
Warmia (reg.), Pol. 99/K1
Warmińsko-Mazurskie (prov.), Pol. 99/L2
Warminster, Eng, UK 90/D4
Warminster, Pa, US 196/C3
Warner (mts.), Ca, US 184/C5
Warner Robins, Ga, US 191/H3
Warnow (riv.), Ger. 96/D5
Warnsveld, Neth. 108/D4
Waroona, Austl. 170/B5
Warr Acres, Ok, US 195/M14
Warrabri, Austl. 171/G2
Warrandirinna (lake), Austl. 171/H3
Warrego (range), Austl. 172/B4
Warrego (riv.), Austl. 172/B4
Warren (pt.), NW, Can. 192/M2
Warren, Austl. 173/C1
Warren, Mn, US 185/J3
Warren, Oh, US 188/D3
Warren, Pa, US 188/E3
Warren, Ar, US 187/J4
Warren, Mi, US 188/D3
Warren, Ut, US 195/J11
Warren (riv.), Austl. 170/C5
Warren, NJ, US 196/D2
Warren (co.), NJ, US 196/C2
Warrenpoint, NI, UK 92/B3
Warrensburg, Mo, US 187/J3
Warrenton, SAfr. 164/D3
Warrenville, Il, US 193/P16
Warri, Nga. 161/G5
Warrington, Fl, US 191/G4
Warrington, Eng, UK 93/F5
Warrington (co.), Eng, UK 93/F5
Warrnambool, Austl. 173/B3
Warroad, Mn, US 185/K3
Warrumbungle NP, Austl. 173/D1
Warsaw, In, US 188/C3
Warsaw (Warszawa) (cap.), Pol. 99/L2
Warscheneck (peak), Aus. 106/B2
Warsop, Eng, UK 93/G5
Warstein, Ger. 109/F6
Warta (riv.), Pol. 99/H2
Wartberg an der Krems, Aus. 113/H7
Wartberg ob der Aist, Aus. 113/H6
Wartburg, Il, US 195/G9
Warwick, Austl. 172/D5
Warwick, Eng, UK 91/E2
Warwick, Md, US 196/C5
Warwick, NY, US 196/D1
Warwick, Ok, US 195/N14
Warwick, RI, US 189/G3
Warwickshire (co.), Eng, UK 91/E2
Wasatch (co.), Ut, US 195/K12
Wasatch (range), Ut, US 186/E2
Wasbank, SAfr. 165/E3
Wasburn (riv.), Eng, UK 93/G4
Wasco, Ca, US 186/C4
Waseca, Mn, US 185/K4
Wash, The (bay), Eng, UK 93/J6
Washburn (lake), Nun., Can. 180/F1
Washimiya, Japan 135/D1
Washington, Eng, UK 93/G2
Washington (cap.), US 196/A6
Washington (state), US 184/C4
Washington, Il, US 185/L5
Washington, NC, US 191/J3
Washington (mt.), NH, US 189/G2
Washington, NJ, US 196/D2
Washington, Pa, US 188/D3
Washington (lake), Wa, US 193/C2
Washington (isl.), Wi, US 185/M4
Washington Dulles (int'l arpt.), Va, US 188/E4
Washington Park, Il, US 195/G8
Washington Terrace, Ut, US 195/K11
Washingtonville, Pa, US 196/B1
Washita (riv.), Ok, US 187/H4
Washtenaw (co.), Mi, US 193/E7
Wasilków, Pol. 99/M2
Wasilla, Ak, US 192/J3
Waskaganish (Rupert House), Qu, Can. 188/E1
Waskasa (bay), Japan 132/D3
Waskey (mt.), Ak, US 192/G4
Waspán, Nic. 203/F3
Wasselonne, Fr. 111/G6
Wassen, Swi. 115/E4
Wassenaar, Neth. 108/B4
Wassenberg, Ger. 111/F1
Wasserbillig, Lux. 111/F4
Wasserburg, Ger. 112/D6
Wasserburg am Inn, Ger. 113/F6
Wasserkuppe (peak), Ger. 112/C2
Wassuk (range), Nv, US 182/C4
Wassy, Fr. 114/A1
Wast Water (lake), Eng, UK 93/E3
Wasur-Rawa Biru NP, Indo. 139/K5
Waswanipi (lake), Qu, Can. 188/E1
Wat Phu, Laos 136/D3
Watampone, Indo. 139/F4
Watarai, Japan 135/L7
Watarase (riv.), Japan 133/F2
Watari, Japan 133/G1
Watch Hill (pt.), RI, US 197/G1
Watchung, NJ, US 197/H9
Watchung (mts.), NJ, US 197/H9
Water of Ae (riv.), Sc, UK 92/E1
Water of Girvan (riv.), Sc, UK 94/B6
Water of Ken (riv.), Sc, UK 92/D1
Waterbury, Ct, US 188/F3
Wateree (lake), SC, US 191/H3
Wateree (riv.), SC, US 191/H3
Waterford, Mi, US 188/D3
Waterford, Ire. 89/Q10
Waterford, Ct, US 197/F1
Waterford Works, NJ, US 196/D4
Watergate (bay), Eng, UK 90/A6
Waterhen (riv.), Sk, Can. 184/F2
Waterhen (lake), Mb, Can. 185/J2
Waterloo, On, Can. 188/D3
Waterloo, Il, US 195/G9
Waterloo, Ok, US 195/N14
Waterloo, Belg. 111/D2
Waterloo Battlesite, Belg. 111/D2
Waterloo Village, NJ, US 196/D2
Watermael-Boitsfort, Belg. 110/D2
Waterton Lakes Nat'l Pk., Ab, Can. 184/E3
Watertown, NY, US 188/F3
Watertown, SD, US 185/J4
Waterville, Ire. 88/N11
Waterville, Me, US 189/G2
Waterville, Wa, US 184/C4
Waterway, La, US 195/P17
Watford, Eng, UK 88/B1
Watford City, ND, US 185/H4
Wath-upon-Dearne, Eng, UK 93/G4
Watheroo NP, Austl. 170/B4
Watkins, Co, US 195/C3
Watonwan (riv.), Mn, US 187/J1
Watowato (peak), Indo. 139/G3
Watrous, Sk, Can. 185/G3
Watsa, D.R. Congo 162/A2
Watseka, Il, US 188/C3
Watson Lake, Yk, Can. 180/D2
Watsontown, Pa, US 196/B1
Watsonville, Ca, US 186/B3
Watten, Fr. 110/B2
Wattenberg, Co, US 195/C2
Wattenheim, Ger. 112/B3
Wattens, Aus. 115/H3
Wattignies, Fr. 110/C2
Wattrelos, Fr. 110/C2
Wattwil, Swi. 115/F3
Wauchope, Austl. 173/E1
Wauchula, Fl, US 191/H5
Wauconda, Il, US 193/P15
Waukarlycarly (lake), Austl. 170/D2
Waukesha, Wi, US 187/K2
Waukesha (co.), Wi, US 193/P14
Waun Fâch (peak), Wal, UK 90/C3
Waun-Oer (peak), Wal, UK 90/C1
Wauna, Wa, US 193/B3
Waupun, Wi, US 185/L5
Waurika, Ok, US 187/H4
Wauseon, Oh, US 188/C3
Waveney (riv.), Eng, UK 91/H2
Waver (riv.), Eng, UK 93/E2
Wavre, Belg. 111/D2
Wavrin, Fr. 110/B2
Wāw, Sudan 155/L6
Wawa (riv.), Nic. 203/E3
Wawagosic (riv.), Qu, Can. 188/E1
Wawasang (peak), Nic. 203/E3
Wawayanda State Park, NJ, US 196/D1
Waxahachie, Tx, US 187/H4
Waycross, Ga, US 191/H4
Wayne, Ne, US 185/J5
Wayne (co.), Pa, US 196/C3
Wayne, Pa, US 196/C3
Wayne, NJ, US 197/J8
Wayne, Mi, US 193/F7
Wayne, Il, US 193/P16
Waynesboro, Pa, US 188/E4
Waynesboro, Ms, US 191/F4
Waynesboro, Ga, US 191/H3
Waynesville, NC, US 191/H3
Waynesville, Mo, US 187/J3
Waziers, Fr. 110/C3
Wazīrābād, Pak. 144/C3
Wazuka, Japan 135/J6
Wda (riv.), Pol. 99/K2
Weald, The (grsld.), Eng, UK 91/F4
Wear (riv.), Eng, UK 93/F2
Weatherby Lake, Mo, US 195/D5
Weatherford, Tx, US 190/D3
Weatherly, Pa, US 196/C2
Weaver (riv.), Eng, UK 93/F5
Weaverville, Ca, US 186/B2
Weber (co.), Ut, US 195/J11
Weber (riv.), Ut, US 195/J11
Weber Hill, Mo, US 195/F9
Webi Jubba (riv.), Som. 155/P7
Webster, SD, US 185/J4
Webster City, Ia, US 185/K5
Webster Groves, Mo, US 195/G8
Weddell (isl.), Mald. 217/E6
Weddell (sea) 218/X
Wedderburn, Austl. 173/B3
Weddin Mountains NP, Austl. 173/C2
Wedel, Ger. 109/G1
Wedemark, Ger. 109/G3
Wee Waa, Austl. 173/D1
Weed, Ca, US 186/B2
Weehawken, NJ, US 197/J8
Weekapaug, RI, US 197/G1
Weenen, SAfr. 165/E3
Weerselo, Neth. 108/D4
Weert, Neth. 108/C6
Weesen, Swi. 115/F3
Weesp, Neth. 108/C4
Wegberg, Ger. 111/F1
Weggis, Swi. 115/E3
Węgorzewo, Pol. 97/J4
Węgrów, Pol. 99/M2
Wegscheid, Ger. 113/G5
Wehingen, Ger. 115/E1
Wehr, Ger. 114/D2
Wehra (riv.), Ger. 114/D2
Wehre (riv.), Ger. 109/G6
Wehrheim, Ger. 112/B2
Wei Xian, China 130/C3
Wei Xian, China 130/C3
Weibersbrunn, Ger. 112/C3
Weichang, China 129/L3
Weida, Ger. 101/K1
Weiden, Ger. 113/F3
Weidenthal, Ger. 112/A4
Weifang, China 130/D3
Weihai, China 131/B4
Weihenzell, Ger. 112/D4
Weikersheim, Ger. 112/C4
Weil (riv.), Ger. 112/B2
Weil der Stadt, Ger. 112/B5
Weilburg, Ger. 112/B2
Weiler-Simmerberg, Ger. 115/F2
Weilerswist, Ger. 111/F2
Weilheim, Ger. 115/H2
Weilheim an der Teck, Ger. 112/C5
Weilmünster, Ger. 112/B2
Weimar, Ger. 98/F3
Weinan, China 130/B4
Weinfelden, Swi. 115/F2
Weingarten, Ger. 115/F2
Weingarten, Ger. 112/B4
Weinheim, Ger. 112/B3
Weinsberg, Ger. 112/C4
Weinstadt, Ger. 112/C5
Weinviertel (reg.), Aus. 101/M2
Weirton, WV, US 188/D3
Weisendorf, Ger. 112/D3
Weisenheim am Berg, Ger. 112/B3
Weiser (riv.), Id, US 184/D4
Weishan, China 130/D4
Weishi, China 130/C4
Weiskirchen, Ger. 111/F4
Weismain, Ger. 112/E2
Weiss (lake), Al, US 191/G3
Weissach, Ger. 112/B5
Weisse Elster (riv.), Ger. 98/G3
Weisse Laber (riv.), Ger. 113/E4
Weissenbach am Lech, Aus. 115/G3
Weissenburg im Bayern, Ger. 112/D4
Weissenfels, Ger. 98/F3
Weissenhorn, Ger. 115/G1
Weissenstadt, Ger. 113/E2
Weissenthurm, Ger. 111/G3
Weisser (peak), Ger. 111/F3
Weisser Main (riv.), Ger. 113/E2
Weisshorn (peak), Swi. 114/D5
Weissmies (peak), Swi. 114/D5
Weisswasser, Ger. 99/H3
Weistrach, Aus. 113/H6
Weitefeld, Ger. 111/G2
Weiterstadt, Ger. 112/B3
Weitra, Aus. 99/H4
Weixi, China 141/G2
Weiyuan, China 128/H4
Weiz, Aus. 101/L3
Weizhou (isl.), China 141/J3
Wejherowo, Pol. 96/H4
Welby, Co, US 195/C3
Welch, WV, US 188/D4
Welch (hill), Pa, US 196/A3
Weld (co.), Co, US 195/C2
Welden, Ger. 112/D6
Weldiya, Eth. 155/N5
Weldon Spring, Mo, US 195/F8
Welel (peak), Eth. 155/M6
Weligama, SrL. 140/D6
Welkenraedt, Belg. 111/E2
Welkom, SAfr. 164/D3
Welland (canal), On, Can. 189/R10
Welland, On, Can. 189/R10
Welland (riv.), Eng, UK 93/H6
Wellandport, On, Can. 189/R9
Wellen, Belg. 111/E2
Wellesley (isls.), Austl. 167/C2
Wellin, Belg. 111/E3
Wellingborough, Eng, UK 91/F2
Wellington (lake), Austl. 173/C3
Wellington, Austl. 173/D2
Wellington (chan.), Nun., Can. 181/S7
Wellington (isl.), Chile 217/B6
Wellington (cap.), NZ 175/S11
Wellington (int'l arpt.), NZ 175/S11
Wellington, SAfr. 164/L10
Wellington, Eng, UK 90/C5
Wellington, Tx, US 187/G4
Wells (lake), Austl. 170/D3
Wells, BC, Can. 184/C2
Wells, Eng, UK 90/D4
Wells, Nv, US 184/E5
Wellston, Oh, US 188/D4
Wellston, Ok, US 195/N14
Wellsville, Pa, US 196/B3
Wellton, Az, US 186/D4
Wels, Aus. 113/H6
Welschbillig, Ger. 111/F4
Welshnofen (Nova Levante), It. 115/H5
Welshpool, Wal, UK 90/C1
Welty, Co, US 195/B2
Welver, Ger. 109/E5
Welzheim, Ger. 112/C5
Wembere (riv.), Tanz. 163/F1
Wembley, Ab, Can. 184/D2
Wembley Stadium, Eng, UK 88/C2
Wemding, Ger. 112/D5
Wemmel, Belg. 111/D2
Wemyss Bay, Sc, UK 94/B5
Wen Xian, China 130/C4
Wenatchee, Wa, US 184/C4
Wenchang, China 141/K4
Wencheng, China 137/D2
Wenchi, Gha. 161/E5
Wendeburg, Ger. 109/H4
Wenden, Ger. 111/G2
Wendeng, China 131/B4
Wendover, Nv, US 184/E5
Wendover, Eng, UK 91/F3
Wengyuan, China 141/K3
Wenling, China 137/D2
Wenlock Edge (ridge), Eng, UK 90/D2
Wenne (riv.), Ger. 109/F6
Wennigsen, Ger. 109/G4
Wenonah, NJ, US 196/C4
Wenshan, China 141/H3
Wenshang, China 130/D4
Wenshui, China 130/C3
Wensleydale (valley), Eng, UK 93/F3
Went (riv.), Eng, UK 93/G4
Wentworth, Austl. 173/B2
Wenxi, China 130/B4
Wenzhou, China 137/D2
Wepener, SAfr. 164/D3
Wer, India 142/A2
Werdau, Ger. 101/K1
Werdohl, Ger. 109/E6
Werkendam, Neth. 108/B5
Werl, Ger. 109/E5
Werlte, Ger. 109/E3
Wermelskirchen, Ger. 111/G1
Wern (riv.), Ger. 112/C3
Wernberg-Köblitz, Ger. 113/F3
Werne an der Lippe, Ger. 109/E5
Werneck, Ger. 112/D3
Wernigerode, Ger. 109/H5
Werong (mt.), Austl. 173/D2
Werra (riv.), Ger. 98/E3
Werre (riv.), Ger. 98/E2
Werrikimbe NP, Austl. 173/E1
Werris Creek, Austl. 173/D1
Werse (riv.), Ger. 109/E5
Wertach (riv.), Ger. 112/D6
Wertheim, Ger. 112/C3
Wertheim NWR, NY, US 197/F2
Werther, Ger. 109/F4
Wertingen, Ger. 112/D5
Wervershoof, Neth. 108/C3
Wervik, Belg. 110/C2
Weschnitz (riv.), Ger. 112/B3
Wesergebirge (mts.), Ger. 109/F4
Wesel, Ger. 108/D5
Wesel-Datteln (canal), Ger. 109/E5
Weser (riv.), Ger. 98/E2
Weslaco, Tx, US 190/D5
Wesley Hills, NY, US 197/J7
Wessel (isls.), Austl. 167/C2
Wesselburen, Ger. 96/C4
Wesselsbron, SAfr. 164/D2
Wessex (reg.), Eng, UK 90/D4
Wessington Springs, SD, US 185/J4
West (pt.), Austl. 173/C4
West, Tx, US 187/H5
West (cape), NZ 175/R12
West (pt.), Wa, US 193/C2
West Allis, Wi, US 187/K2
West Alton, Mo, US 195/G8
West Babylon, NY, US 197/E2
West Bank (occ. zone), Isr. 149/D3
West Bend, Wi, US 185/L5
West Bengal (state), India 143/F4
West Berkshire (co.), Eng, UK 91/E4
West Bountiful, Ut, US 195/K12
West Branch, Mi, US 188/C2
West Bridgford, Eng, UK 93/G6
West Bromwich, Eng, UK 90/E1
West Caicos (isl.), UK 203/H1
West Calder, Sc, UK 94/C5
West Caldwell, NJ, US 197/H8
West Cape Howe NP, Austl. 170/C5
West Chester, Pa, US 196/C4
West Chicago, Il, US 193/P16
West Chyulu Game Consv. Area, Kenya 162/C3
West Coast NP, SAfr. 164/L10
West Columbia, SC, US 191/H3
West Covina, Ca, US 194/G7

West C – Woods

West Creek, NJ, US 196/D4
West Dunbartonshire (pol. reg.), Sc, UK 94/B5
West Elk (mts.), Co, US 190/B2
West End, Eng, UK 88/B3
West Falkland (isl.), Falk. 215/D7
West Fargo, ND, US 185/J4
West Fayu (isl.), Micr. 174/D4
West Frisian (isls.), Neth. 98/C2
West Glen (riv.), Eng, UK 93/H6
West Grove, Pa, US 196/C4
West Haven, Ct, US 197/F1
West Haverstraw, NY, US 196/E1
West Helena, Ar, US 187/K4
West Hempstead, NY, US 197/L9
West Hills, NY, US 197/M8
West Hollywood, Ca, US 194/F7
West Humber (riv.), On, Can. 189/Q8
West Ice Shelf, Ant. 218/F
West Indies (isls.), NAm. 203/F2
West Islet (isl.), Austl. 167/E3
West Islip, NY, US 197/E2
West Jordan, Ut, US 195/K12
West Kilbride, Sc, UK 94/B5
West Kingsdown, Eng, UK 88/D3
West Knock (peak), Sc, UK 94/D3
West Lamma (chan.), China 129/U11
West Lincoln, Ne, US 187/H2
West Lothian (pol. reg.), Sc, UK 187/H2
West Lunga NP, Zam. 163/D3
West Memphis, Ar, US 187/K4
West Midlands (co.), Eng, UK 91/E1
West Milford, NJ, US 197/H7
West Milton, Pa, US 196/B1
West Monroe, La, US 187/J4
West New York, NJ, US 197/J8
West Nyack, NY, US 197/K7
West Orange, NJ, US 197/J8
West Palm Beach, Fl, US 191/H5
West Paterson, NJ, US 197/J8
West Pensacola, Fl, US 191/G4
West Plains, Mo, US 187/K3
West Point, Ne, US 185/J5
West Point (lake), Al,Ga, US 191/G3
West Point, Ms, US 191/F3
West Point (mil. res.), NY, US 197/D1
West Point, Ut, US 195/J11
West Reading, Pa, US 196/C3
West Redding, Ct, US 197/E1
West Road (riv.), BC, Can. 184/B2
West Sacramento, Ca, US 193/L9
West Sayville, NY, US 197/E2
West Seneca, NY, US 189/S10
West Siberian (plain), Rus. 122/H3
West Sussex (co.), Eng, UK 91/F4
West-Terschelling, Neth. 108/C2
West Valley City, Ut, US 195/K12
West Vancouver, BC, Can. 184/C3
West Virginia (state), US 188/D4
West Warren, Ut, US 195/J11
West Water (riv.), Sc, UK 94/D3
West Weber, Ut, US 195/J11
West Wyalong, Austl. 173/C2
West York, Pa, US 196/B4
Westall (pt.), Austl. 171/G5
Westbrook, Ct, US 197/F1
Westbury, NY, US 197/L9
Westchester (co.), NY, US 197/E1
Westcott, Eng, UK 88/B3
Westerbork, Neth. 108/D3
Westerburg, Ger. 111/G2
Westerham, Eng, UK 88/D3
Westerheim, Ger. 115/G1
Westerholt, Ger. 109/E1
Westerkappeln, Ger. 109/E4
Westerland, Ger. 96/C4
Westerlo, Belg. 111/D1
Western (prov.), Kenya 162/B2
Western (des.), Egypt 155/L2
Western (prov.), Ugan. 162/A2
Western (pol. reg.), Gha. 161/E5
Western (chan.), SKor. 131/E5
Western Area (prov.), SLeo. 160/B4
Western Australia (state), Austl. 167/B3
Western Cape (prov.), SAfr. 164/C4
Western Ghats (mts.), India 147/K5
Western Run (riv.), Md, US 196/B4
Western Sahara (reg.) 154/B3
Western Sayans (mts.), Rus. 122/J4
Westerschelde (chan.), Belg. 108/A6
Westerstede, Ger. 109/E2
Westerville, Oh, US 188/D3
Westervoort, Neth. 108/C5
Westerwald (mts.), Ger. 98/D3
Westfield, NJ, US 197/H9
Westgat (chan.), Neth. 108/D2
Westhampton, NY, US 197/F2
Westhampton Beach, NY, US 197/F2
Westhausen, Ger. 112/D5
Westheim, Ger. 112/B4
Westhill, Sc, UK 94/D2
Westhofen, Ger. 112/B3
Westhoughton, Eng, UK 93/F4
Westkapelle, Neth. 108/A5
Westlake Village, Ca, US 194/B2
Westland, Mi, US 193/F7
Westland NP, NZ 175/R11
Westminster, Co, US 195/B3
Westminster, Md, US 196/B4
Westminster, Ca, US 194/F8
Westminster, City of (bor.), Eng, UK 88/A1
Westmont, Il, US 193/P16
Westmont (Haddon), NJ, US 196/C4
Westmorland (reg.), Eng, UK 93/F3
Westmount, Qu, Can. 189/N7
Weston, Mo, US 195/D5
Weston, Ct, US 197/E1
Weston-super-Mare, Eng, UK 90/D4
Westonaria, SAfr. 164/P13
Westport, Ire. 89/P10
Westport, NZ 175/S11
Westport, Ct, US 197/E1
Westray (isl.), Sc, UK 89/V14
Westview, Il, US 195/G8
Westwego, La, US 195/P17
Westwood, Ks, US 195/D5
Westwood, NJ, US 197/J8
Wet (mts.), Co, US 190/B2
Wetar (isl.), Indo. 139/G5
Wetar (str.), Indo. 139/G5
Wetaskiwin, Ab, Can. 184/E2
Wete, Tanz. 162/C4
Wététnagami (riv.), Qu, Can. 188/E1
Wetherell (lake), Austl. 173/B2
Wetter, Ger. 109/E6
Wetter (riv.), Ger. 112/B2
Wetterau (reg.), Ger. 112/C2
Wetteren, Belg. 110/C2
Wetterhorn (peak), Swi. 114/E4
Wettingen, Swi. 115/E3
Wettringen, Ger. 109/E4
Wetzikon, Swi. 115/E3
Wetzlar, Ger. 112/B1
Wetzstein (peak), Ger. 113/E2
Wevelgem, Belg. 110/C2
Wewak, PNG 174/D5
Wewoka, Ok, US 187/H4
Wexford, Ire. 89/Q10
Wey (riv.), Eng, UK 88/A3
Weybridge, Eng, UK 88/B2
Weyburn, Sk, Can. 185/H3
Weygand (ruin), Alg. 157/F4
Weyhausen, Ger. 109/H4
Weyland (pt.), Austl. 171/G5
Weymouth, Eng, UK 90/D5
Weymouth (bay), Eng, UK 90/D5
Wha Ti, NW, Can. 180/E2
Whakatane, NZ 175/T10
Whale Cove, Nun., Can. 180/G2
Whalsey (isl.), Sc, UK 89/W13
Whangarei, NZ 175/S10
Wharfe (riv.), Eng, UK 93/G3
Wheat Ridge, Co, US 195/B3
Wheatland, Wy, US 185/G5
Wheaton, Il, US 188/B3
Wheaton-Glenmont, Md, US 196/A5
Wheaton Village, NJ, US 196/C5
Wheeler (peak), Nv, US 186/D3
Wheeler (peak), NM, US 187/F3
Wheeler (lake), Al, US 191/G3
Wheeler Springs, Ca, US 194/A1
Wheeling, WV, US 188/D3
Wheeling, Il, US 193/Q15
Wheelwright, Arg. 216/E2
Whernside (peak), Eng, UK 93/F3
Whickham, Eng, UK 93/G2
Whidbey (pt.), Austl. 171/G5
Whinham (mt.), Austl. 171/F3
Whitburn, Sc, UK 94/C5
Whitby, On, Can. 189/S8
Whitby, Eng, UK 93/H3
White (lake), La, US 187/J5
White (riv.), Ar, US 187/J4
White (riv.), SD, US 185/H5
White (riv.), Tx, US 187/K2
White (lake), Austl. 171/F2
White (lake), On, Can. 188/C1
White (riv.), In, US 188/C4
White (pass), Ak, US 192/L3
White (sea), Rus. 118/H2
White (bay), Nf, Can. 181/L3
White Bear (riv.), Nf, Can. 189/K1
White City, Sk, Can. 185/G3
White Cliffs, Austl. 173/B1
White Coomb (peak), Sc, UK 94/C6
White Esk (riv.), Sc, UK 94/C6
White Fox, Sk, Can. 185/G2
White Hall, Md, US 196/B4
White Haven, Pa, US 196/C1
White Marsh, Md, US 196/B5
White Mountain, Ak, US 192/F3
White Mountains Nat'l Rec. Area, Ak, US 192/J2
White Nile (riv.), Sudan 155/M7
White Oak, Md, US 196/B5
White Otter (lake), On, Can. 185/K3
White Plains, NY, US 197/K7
White River, On, Can. 188/C1
White Rock, NM, US 190/B3
White Sands, NM, US 186/F4
White Sands Nat'l Mon., NM, US 186/F4
White Sulphur Springs, Mt, US 184/F4
White Volta (riv.), Gha. 161/E4
White, West Fork (riv.), In, US 188/C4
Whiteadder Water (riv.), Sc, UK 94/D5
Whitecourt, Ab, Can. 184/E2
Whiteface (riv.), Mn, US 185/K4
Whitefield, Eng, UK 93/F4
Whitefish, Mt, US 184/E3
Whitefish (bay), US,Can. 188/C2
Whiteford (pt.), Wal, UK 90/B3
Whiteford, Md, US 196/B4
Whitehall, Mt, US 184/E4
Whitehall, Mi, US 188/C3
Whitehaven, Eng, UK 92/E2
Whitehead, NI, UK 92/C2
Whitehills, Sc, UK 94/D1
Whitehorse (cap.), Yk, Can. 192/L3
Whitehorse (hill), Eng, UK 91/E3
Whitehouse, Tx, US 187/J4
Whitemouth (riv.), Mb, Can. 185/K3
Whiteriver, Az, US 186/E4
Whiteside (chan.), Chile 217/C7
Whitesville, NJ, US 196/D3
Whiteville, NC, US 191/J3
Whitewater (lake), On, Can. 185/L3
Whitewood, Sk, Can. 185/H3
Whithorn, Sc, UK 92/D2
Whiting, In, US 193/R16
Whitley Bay, Eng, UK 93/G1
Whitmore Village, Hi, US 182/V12
Whitney (lake), Tx, US 187/H4
Whitney, Tx, US 187/H5
Whitsand (bay), Eng, UK 90/B6
Whitstable, Eng, UK 91/H4
Whitsunday (isl.), Austl. 167/D3
Whittaker, Mi, US 193/E7
Whittier, Ak, US 192/J3
Whittier, Ca, US 194/F8
Whittlesea, Austl. 173/G5
Whitton, Austl. 173/C2
Whitworth, Eng, UK 93/F4
Wholdaia (lake), NW, Can. 180/F2
Whyalla, Austl. 171/H5
Wi (isl.), SKor. 131/D5
Wiang Kosai NP, Thai. 136/B2
Wiarton, On, Can. 188/D2
Wiawso, Gha. 161/E5
Wichabai, Guy. 211/G4
Wichelen, Belg. 110/C2
Wichita (riv.), Tx, US 187/H4
Wichita (mts.), Ok, US 187/H4
Wichita Falls, Tx, US 187/H4
Wick, Sc, UK 89/S7
Wickenburg, Az, US 186/D4
Wickepin, Austl. 170/C5
Wickford, Eng, UK 88/E2
Wickham, Austl. 170/C2
Wicklow (mts.), Ire. 89/Q10
Wicklow (pass), Ire. 92/B5
Wicklow, Ire. 92/B6
Wicklow (pt.), Ire. 92/B6
Wickriede (riv.), Ger. 109/F4
Wid (riv.), Eng, UK 88/E2
Widnau, Swi. 115/F3
Widnes, Eng, UK 93/F5
Więcbork, Pol. 99/J2
Wied (riv.), Ger. 101/G1
Wiedau (riv.), Ger. 109/G2
Wiefelstede, Ger. 109/F2
Wiehengebirge (ridge), Ger. 109/F4
Wiehl, Ger. 111/G2
Wielenbach, Ger. 115/H2
Wieliczka, Pol. 99/L4
Wielkopolski NP, Pol. 99/J2
Wielkopolskie (prov.), Pol. 99/J2
Wielsbeke, Belg. 110/C2
Wieluń, Pol. 99/K3
Wien (riv.), Aus. 107/N7
Wien (prov.), Aus. 99/J4
Wien (Vienna) (cap.), Aus. 107/N7
Wiener Neudorf, Aus. 107/N7
Wiener Neustadt, Aus. 101/M3
Wienerwald (reg.), Aus. 107/N7
Wienwald (reg.), Aus. 101/L2
Wieprz (riv.), Pol. 99/M3
Wierden, Neth. 108/D4
Wieringermeerpolder (polder), Neth. 108/B3
Wieringerwerf, Neth. 108/C3
Wieruszów, Pol. 99/K3
Wiesbaden, Ger. 112/B2
Wiese (riv.), Ger. 101/G3
Wiese (isl.), Rus. 218/A
Wieseck (riv.), Ger. 112/B1
Wiesendangen, Swi. 115/E2
Wiesensteig, Ger. 112/C5
Wiesent (riv.), Ger. 112/E4
Wiesentheid, Ger. 112/D3
Wiesloch, Ger. 112/B4
Wiesmoor, Ger. 109/E2
Wietmarschen, Ger. 109/D4
Wietze, Ger. 109/G3
Wietze (riv.), Ger. 109/G3
Wietzendorf, Ger. 109/G3
Wiezyca (peak), Pol. 96/H4
Wigan, Eng, UK 93/F4
Wigan (co.), Eng, UK 93/F4
Wiggins, Ms, US 191/F4
Wight (isl.), UK 91/E5
Wigierski NP, Pol. 99/M1
Wignehies, Fr. 110/D3
Wigry (lake), Pol. 97/K5
Wigston, Eng, UK 91/E1
Wigtown, Sc, UK 92/D2
Wigtown (bay), Sc, UK 92/D2
Wijchen, Neth. 108/C5
Wijhe, Neth. 108/D4
Wijk bij Duurstede, Neth. 108/C5
Wil, Swi. 115/F3
Wilber, Ne, US 187/H2
Wilberforce, Austl. 172/G8
Wilbur, Wa, US 184/D4
Wilburton, Ok, US 187/J4
Wilcannia, Austl. 173/B1
Wilchingen, Swi. 115/E2
Wilczek (isl.), Rus. 122/G1
Wild (coast), SAfr. 164/E4
Wild Creek (res.), Pa, US 196/C2
Wild Rice (riv.), Mn, US 185/J4
Wild World, Md, US 196/B6
Wildau, Ger. 98/Q7
Wildbad im Schwarzwald, Ger. 112/B5
Wildberg, Ger. 112/B5
Wilder, Ks, US 195/D5
Wilderswil, Swi. 114/D4
Wildeshausen, Ger. 109/F3
Wildflecken, Ger. 112/C2
Wildgrat (peak), Aus. 115/G3
Wildhaus, Swi. 115/F3
Wildhorn (peak), Swi. 114/D5
Wildomar, Ca, US 194/C3
Wildspitze (peak), Aus. 115/G4
Wildstrubel (peak), Swi. 114/D5
Wildwood, NJ, US 196/D6
Wildwood Crest, NJ, US 196/D6
Wilge (riv.), SAfr. 164/E2
Wilhelm II (coast), Ant. 218/F
Wilhelmina (mts.), Sur. 208/G3
Wilhelminakanaal (canal), Neth. 108/C5
Wilhelmshaven, Ger. 109/F1
Wilhering, Aus. 113/H6
Wilkes-Barre, Pa, US 196/C1
Wilkes Land (phys. reg.), Ant. 218/J
Wilkesboro, NC, US 188/D4
Wilkeson, Wa, US 193/C3
Wilkie, Sk, Can. 184/F2
Wilkins (sound), Ant. 218/U
Will (mt.), BC, Can. 192/N4
Will (co.), Il, US 193/P16
Willamette (riv.), Or, US 184/C4
Willandra NP, Austl. 173/C2
Willapa (bay), Wa, US 184/B4
Willard (bay), Ut, US 195/J11
Willard (res.), Ut, US 195/J11
Willard, Ut, US 195/J11
Willaura, Austl. 173/B3
Willcox, Az, US 186/E4
Willebadessen, Ger. 109/G5
Willebroek, Belg. 111/D1
Willemstad, Neth. 108/B5
Willemstad (cap.), NAnt. 210/D1
William (mt.), Austl. 173/B3
William B. Hartsfield Atlanta (int'l arpt.), Ga, US 191/G3
William Bay NP, Austl. 170/C5
Williams, Az, US 186/D4
Williams, Austl. 170/C5
Williams Lake, BC, Can. 184/C2
Williamsburg, Ky, US 188/C4
Williamsport, Pa, US 196/A1
Williamston, NC, US 191/J3
Williamstown, Pa, US 196/B2
Williamstown, NJ, US 196/D4
Williamsville, NY, US 189/S10
Willich, Ger. 108/D6
Willingboro, NJ, US 196/D3
Willingen, Ger. 109/F6
Willis, Tx, US 187/J5
Willis Islets (isls.), Austl. 167/E2
Willisau, Swi. 114/D3
Williston, ND, US 185/H3
Williston, Fl, US 191/H4
Williston, SAfr. 164/C3
Williston (lake), BC, Can. 180/D3
Williston Park, NY, US 197/L9
Willits, Ca, US 186/B3
Willmar, Mn, US 185/K4
Willow, Ak, US 192/H3
Willow (riv.), BC, Can. 184/C2
Willow Bunch, Sk, Can. 185/G3
Willow Grove, Pa, US 196/C3
Willow Grove, De, US 196/C5
Willow Grove Naval Air Sta., Pa, US 196/C3
Willow River, BC, Can. 184/C2
Willow Street, Pa, US 196/B4
Willow Tree, Austl. 173/D1
Willowbrook, Ca, US 194/F8
Willowbrook, Il, US 193/P16
Willowmore, SAfr. 164/C4
Willows, Ca, US 186/B3
Wills (lake), Austl. 167/B3
Wills Point, La, US 195/Q17
Willstätt, Ger. 114/D1
Willunga, Austl. 171/H5
Wilmette, Il, US 193/Q15
Wilmington, NC, US 191/J3
Wilmington, Austl. 171/H5
Wilmington, De, US 196/C4
Wilmington Island, Ga, US 191/H4
Wilmslow, Eng, UK 93/F5
Wilnsdorf, Ger. 111/H2
Wilrijk, Belg. 108/B6
Wilseder (peak), Ger. 109/G2
Wilson, NC, US 191/J3
Wilson (co.), Tx, US 195/U21
Wilson, NY, US 189/S9
Wilson (mt.), Ca, US 194/B2
Wilson, Pa, US 196/C2
Wilson (cape), Nun., Can. 181/H2
Wilsons Promontory (pen.), Austl. 167/D4
Wilsons Promontory NP, Austl. 173/C3
Wilsonville, Il, US 195/H7
Wilstedt, Ger. 109/G2
Wilster, Ger. 109/G1
Wilsum, Ger. 108/D3
Wilton, Eng, UK 91/E4
Wilton, Ct, US 197/E1
Wiltshire (co.), Eng, UK 91/E4
Wiltz, Lux. 111/E4
Wiltz (riv.), Lux. 111/E4
Wiluna, Austl. 170/D3
Wimborne Minster, Eng, UK 90/E5
Wimereux, Fr. 110/A2
Wimmis, Swi. 114/D4
Winam (gulf), Kenya 162/B3
Winburg, SAfr. 164/D3
Winchester, Ky, US 188/C4
Winchester, Tn, US 191/G3
Winchester, Ca, US 194/C3
Winchester, Eng, UK 91/E4
Winchester Mystery House, Ca, US 193/L12
Wind (riv.), Wy, US 184/F5
Wind (lake), Wi, US 193/P14
Wind Cave NP, SD, US 187/G2
Wind Gap, Pa, US 196/C2
Wind Lake, Wi, US 193/P14
Wind Point, Wi, US 193/Q14
Wind River (range), Wy, US 186/E2
Windach (riv.), Ger. 115/G2
Windach, Ger. 112/E6
Winder, Ga, US 191/H3
Windermere (lake), Eng, UK 93/F3
Windermere, Eng, UK 93/F3
Windesheim, Ger. 111/G4
Windhoek (cap.), Namb. 163/C5
Windlesham, Eng, UK 88/B2
Window Rock, Az, US 186/E4
Windrush (riv.), Eng, UK 91/E3
Windsbach, Ger. 112/D4
Windsor, Nf, Can. 189/L1
Windsor, NS, Can. 189/H2
Windsor, Qu, Can. 189/G2
Windsor, On, Can. 188/D3
Windsor, Eng, UK 91/F4
Windsor, Co, US 195/C2
Windsor (res.), Co, US 195/C1
Windsor, Pa, US 196/B4
Windsor and Maidenhead (co.), Eng, UK 91/F3
Windward (isls.), StV. 199/J5
Windward Passage (passg.), Cuba,Haiti 203/H2
Winfield, BC, Can. 184/D3
Winfield, Ks, US 187/H3
Winfield, Pa, US 196/B2
Winfield, Md, US 196/A5
Wingene, Belg. 110/C1
Winger, On, Can. 189/R10
Wingham, Austl. 173/E1
Winifred (lake), Austl. 170/D2
Winifreda, Arg. 216/D3
Winisk (riv.), On, Can. 181/H3
Winkler, Mb, Can. 185/J3
Winneba, Gha. 161/E5
Winnebago (lake), Wi, US 185/L5
Winnenden, Ger. 112/C5
Winner, SD, US 185/J5
Winnetka, Il, US 193/Q15
Winnett, Mt, US 184/F4
Winnfield, La, US 187/J5
Winningen, Ger. 111/G3
Winnipeg (cap.), Mb, Can. 185/J3
Winnipeg (int'l arpt.), Mb, Can. 185/J3
Winnipeg (riv.), Mb,On, Can. 185/K3
Winnipeg (lake), Mb, Can. 185/J3
Winnipeg Beach, Mb, Can. 185/J3
Winnipegosis, Mb, Can. 185/J3
Winnipegosis (lake), Mb, Can. 185/H2
Winnsboro, La, US 187/K4
Winnsboro, SC, US 191/H3
Winnweiler, Ger. 111/G4
Winschoten, Neth. 108/E2
Winsford, Eng, UK 93/F5
Winslow, Az, US 186/E4
Winslow, NJ, US 196/D4
Winslow, Wa, US 193/B2
Winston-Salem, NC, US 191/H2
Winsum, Neth. 108/D2
Winter Haven, Fl, US 191/H4
Winter Park, Fl, US 191/H4
Winterberg, Ger. 109/F6
Winterberge (mts.), SAfr. 164/D4
Winterlingen, Ger. 115/F1
Winters, Tx, US 187/H5
Winters, Ca, US 193/K9
Winters Run (riv.), Md, US 196/B4
Winterstaude (peak), Aus. 115/F3
Winterswijk, Neth. 108/D5
Winterthur, Swi. 115/E3
Winterthur Museum and Gardens, De, US 196/C4
Winthrop, Me, US 189/G2
Winton, Austl. 172/A3
Wintzenheim, Fr. 114/D1
Wipper (riv.), Ger. 98/F3
Wipperau (riv.), Ger. 109/H2
Wipperfürth, Ger. 111/G1
Wirges, Ger. 111/G3
Wirrabara, Austl. 171/H5
Wirral (co.), Eng, UK 93/E5
Wirral (pen.), Eng, UK 93/E5
Wisbech, Eng, UK 91/G1
Wisch, Neth. 108/D5
Wischhafen, Ger. 109/G1
Wisconsin (riv.), Wi, US 185/L5
Wisconsin (state), US 185/L4
Wiseman, Ak, US 192/H2
Wisenta (riv.), Ger. 113/E1
Wishaw, Sc, UK 94/C5
Wishek, ND, US 185/J4
Wisła, Pol. 99/K4
Wiślany (lag.), Pol. 97/H4
Wisłoka (riv.), Pol. 99/L4
Wismar, Ger. 96/D5
Wisner, La, US 187/K5
Wissant, Fr. 110/A2
Wissembourg, Fr. 111/G5
Wissen, Ger. 111/G2
Wissey (riv.), Eng, UK 91/G1
Wit Kei (riv.), SAfr. 164/D3
Witbank, SAfr. 164/E2
Witham, Eng, UK 91/G3
Witham (riv.), Eng, UK 93/H5
Witherspoon (mt.), Ak, US 192/J3
Withlacoochee (riv.), Fl,Ga, US 191/H4
Withnell, Eng, UK 93/F4
Witjira NP, Austl. 171/G3
Witkowo, Pol. 99/J2
Witney, Eng, UK 91/E3
Witnica, Pol. 99/H2
Witry-lès-Reims, Fr. 111/D5
Wittelsheim, Fr. 114/D2
Wittem, Neth. 111/E2
Witten, Ger. 109/E6
Wittenbach, Swi. 115/F3
Wittenberg, Ger. 98/G3
Wittenberge, Ger. 98/F2
Wittenburg, Ger. 96/D5
Wittenheim, Fr. 114/D2
Wittenoom, Austl. 170/C2
Wittingen, Ger. 109/H3
Wittislingen, Ger. 112/D5
Wittlich, Ger. 111/F4
Wittman, Md, US 196/B6
Wittmund, Ger. 109/E1
Wittmunder (riv.), Ger. 109/E1
Witton (pen.), Ger. 99/G1
Wittstock, Ger. 98/G2
Witu, Kenya 162/D3
Witwatersrand (reg.), SAfr. 164/P12
Witzenhausen, Ger. 109/G6
Wivenhoe (lake), Austl. 167/E3
Wixom, Mi, US 193/E6
Wkra (riv.), Pol. 99/L2
Władysławowo, Pol. 96/H4
Włocławek, Pol. 99/K2
Włocławskie (lake), Pol. 99/K2
Włodawa, Pol. 99/M3
Włoszczowa, Pol. 99/K3
Wobulenzi, Ugan. 162/B2
Wodonga, Austl. 173/C3
Wodzisław Śląski, Pol. 99/K4
Woensdrecht, Neth. 108/B6
Woerden, Neth. 108/B4
Wognum, Neth. 108/C3
Wohlen, Swi. 115/E3
Wohlen bei Bern, Swi. 114/D4
Wohlford (lake), Ca, US 194/C4
Woippy, Fr. 111/F5
Wokam (isl.), Indo. 139/H5
Woking, Eng, UK 88/B3
Wokingham, Eng, UK 91/F4
Wokingham (co.), Eng, UK 91/F4
Wŏlch'ul-san NP, SKor. 131/D5
Wolcott, Ks, US 195/D5
Wolcottsville, NY, US 189/S9
Wołczyn, Pol. 99/K3
Woleai (isl.), Micr. 174/D4
Wolf (mtn.), Ak, US 192/H2
Wolf (riv.), Wi, US 188/B2
Wolf (vol.), Ecu. 214/E7
Wolf (isl.), Ecu. 214/E6
Wolf (lake), In, US 193/Q16
Wolf Creek (mtn.), Ak, US 192/F3
Wolf Creek, Mt, US 184/E4
Wolf Point, Mt, US 185/G3
Wolfach, Ger. 115/E1
Wolfach (riv.), Ger. 112/B6
Wolfegg, Ger. 115/F2
Wolfen, Ger. 98/G3
Wolfenbüttel, Ger. 109/H4
Wolfern, Aus. 113/H6
Wölfersheim, Ger. 112/B2
Wolfhagen, Ger. 109/G6
Wolframs-Eschenbach, Ger. 112/D4
Wolfsburg, Ger. 109/H4
Wolfsegg am Hausruck, Aus. 113/G6
Wolfurt, Aus. 115/F3
Wolgast, Ger. 96/E4
Wolhusen, Swi. 114/E3
Wolin, Pol. 96/F5
Woliński PN, Pol. 99/H2
Wolkersdorf, Aus. 107/P7
Wollaston (isl.), Chile 215/C8
Wollaston (lake), Sk, Can. 180/F3
Wollaston (pen.), NW,Nun., Can. 180/E2
Wollemi NP, Austl. 173/D2
Wollerau, Swi. 115/E3
Wollongong, Austl. 173/D2
Wöllstadt, Ger. 112/B2
Wöllstein, Ger. 111/G4
Wolmaransstad, SAfr. 164/D2
Wolnzach, Ger. 113/E5
Wologizi (range), Libr. 154/C6
Wołomin, Pol. 99/L2
Wołów, Pol. 99/J3
Wolseley, SAfr. 164/L10
Wolsztyn, Pol. 99/J2
Woluwé-Saint-Lambert, Belg. 111/D2
Wolvega, Neth. 108/D3
Wolverhampton, Eng, UK 90/D1
Wolverhampton (co.), Eng, UK 90/D1
Wolverine Lake, Mi, US 193/F6
Wolziger (lake), Ger. 98/Q7
Woman (riv.), On, Can. 188/D2
Wombourne, Eng, UK 90/D1
Wombwell, Eng, UK 93/G4
Womelsdorf, Pa, US 196/B3
Wondai, Austl. 172/C4
Wonder (lake), Il, US 193/P16
Wondervu, Co, US 195/B3
Wondreb (riv.), Ger. 113/F3
Wong Chu (riv.), Bhu. 143/G2
Wongan Hills, Austl. 170/C4
Wŏnju, SKor. 131/D4
Wonnangatta-Moroka NP, Austl. 173/C3
Wŏnsan, NKor. 131/D3
Wonthaggi, Austl. 173/C3
Wonyulgunna (peak), Austl. 170/C3
Wood (mt.), Yk, Can. 192/K3
Wood (riv.), Sk, Can. 185/H2
Wood (mtn.), Sk, Can. 184/G3
Wood (riv.), Il, US 195/G8
Wood Buffalo NP, NW,Ab, Can. 180/E2
Wood Dale, Il, US 193/P16
Wood-Ridge, NJ, US 197/J8
Wood River, Il, US 195/G8
Woodbine, NJ, US 196/D5
Woodbine, Md, US 196/A5
Woodbridge, Ct, US 197/E1
Woodbridge, Ca, US 193/M10
Woodbridge, NJ, US 197/H9
Woodburn, Austl. 173/E1
Woodburn, Or, US 184/C4
Woodburn, Il, US 195/G7
Woodburn, On, Can. 189/Q9
Woodbury, NJ, US 196/C4
Woodcliff Lake, NJ, US 197/J7
Woodenbong, Austl. 173/E1
Woodenbridge, Ire. 92/B6
Woodend, Austl. 173/C3
Woodgate, Austl. 172/D4
Woodgate NP, Austl. 172/D4
Woodinville, Wa, US 193/C2
Woodland, Ca, US 186/B3
Woodlark (isl.), Sol. 174/E5
Woodlawn, Md, US 196/B5
Woodlawn Park, Ok, US 195/M14
Woodmere, NY, US 197/L9
Woodmont, Ct, US 197/F1
Woodridge, Il, US 193/P16
Woodroffe (mt.), Austl. 171/F3
Woods, Ok, US 195/N15
Woods (lake), On, Can. 180/G4
Woods Cross, Ut, US 195/K12

Woods Heights, Mo, US 195/E5
Woodsboro, Md, US 196/A4
Woodside, De, US 196/C5
Woodside, Austl. 171/M8
Woodside, Ca, US 193/K12
Woodside-Drifton, Pa, US 196/C2
Woodstock, Austl. 173/D2
Woodstock, NB, Can. 189/H2
Woodstock, Il, US 187/K2
Woodstock, Eng, UK 91/E3
Woodstock, Md, US 196/B5
Woodstown, NJ, US 196/C4
Woodville, Ms, US 187/K5
Woodway, Wa, US 193/C2
Woolgoolga, Austl. 173/E1
Wooli, Austl. 173/E1
Woolrich, Pa, US 196/A1
Woomera, Austl. 171/H4
Woomera Prohibited Area, Austl. 171/G4
Woonsocket, SD, US 187/H1
Woorabinda Aboriginal Community, Austl. 172/C4
Wooramel (riv.), Austl. 170/B3
Wooster, Oh, US 188/D3
Worb, Swi. 114/D4
Worcester, Ma, US 189/G3
Worcester, Eng, UK 90/D2
Worcester, SAfr. 164/L10
Worcestershire (co.), Eng, UK 90/D2
Worcester and Birmingham (canal), Eng, UK 90/D2
Worden, Il, US 195/H8
Wörgl, Aus. 101/K3
Workington, Eng, UK 92/E2
Worksop, Eng, UK 93/G5
Workum, Neth. 108/C3
Worland, Wy, US 184/G4
World 22
Wormer, Neth. 108/B3
Wormhoudt, Fr. 110/B2
Worms (pt.), Wal, UK 90/B3
Worms, Ger. 112/B3
Wörnitz (riv.), Ger. 101/J2
Worpswede, Ger. 109/F2
Wörrstadt, Ger. 112/B3
Wórsbach (riv.), Ger. 112/B2
Worsbrough, Eng, UK 93/G4
Worth, Il, US 193/Q16
Wörth am Rhein, Ger. 112/B4
Wörth an der Donau, Ger. 113/F4
Wörth an der Isar, Ger. 113/F5
Wortham, Tx, US 187/H5
Worthing, Eng, UK 91/F5
Wörthsee (lake), Ger. 112/E6
Worton, Md, US 196/B5
Wotho (isl.), Mrsh. 174/F3
Wotje (isl.), Mrsh. 174/G4
Woudenberg, Neth. 108/C4
Woudrichem, Neth. 108/B5
Wounta (lake), Nic. 203/F3
Wouw, Neth. 108/B5
Wowoni (isl.), Indo. 139/F4
Wrangel (isl.), Rus. 218/U
Wrangell, Ak, US 192/M4
Wrangell (mts.), Ak, US 180/B2
Wrangell-St. Elias NP and Prsv., Ak, US 192/K3
Wrath (cape), Sc, UK 89/R7
Wray, Co, US 187/G2
Wraysbury, Eng, UK 88/B2
Wraysbury (res.), Eng, UK 88/B2
Wreck (reef), Austl. 167/E3
Wreck (pt.), SAfr. 164/B3
Wrekin, The (hill), Eng, UK 90/D1
Wremen, Ger. 109/E2
Wrexham, Wal, UK 93/F5
Wrexham (co.), Wal, UK 93/E5
Wright, Wy, US 185/G5
Wrightstown, NJ, US 196/D3
Wrightwood, Ca, US 194/C2
Wrigley, NW, Can. 180/D2
Writtle, Eng, UK 91/G3
Wrocław, Pol. 99/J3
Września, Pol. 99/J2
Wschowa, Pol. 99/J3
Wu (riv.), China 137/A2
Wu'an, China 130/C3
Wuchang, China 129/N3
Wuchang (lake), China 130/D5
Wucheng, China 130/D3
Wuchuan, China 137/A2
Wuchuan, China 137/B3
Wuchuan, China 130/B2
Wudang (mtn.), China 130/B4
Wudi, China 130/D3
Wuding (riv.), China 130/B3
Wudinna, Austl. 171/G5
Wufeng, China 137/B1
Wugang, China 137/B2
Wuhai, China 128/J4
Wuhan, China 137/B1
Wuhe, China 130/D4
Wuhle (riv.), Ger. 98/Q6
Wuhu, China 130/D5
Wuhu, China 130/D5
Wuhua, China 137/C3
Wujal Wujal Aboriginal Community, Austl. 172/B1
Wujiang, China 130/L8
Wular (lake), India 144/C2
Wülfrath, Ger. 108/E6
Wulften, Ger. 109/H5
Wulian, China 130/D4
Wuling (mts.), China 137/B2
Wulong, China 141/J2
Wum, Camr. 161/H5
Wumang (isl.), China 131/B3
Wümme (riv.), Ger. 109/F2
Wūn, India 140/C3
Wungong (res.), Austl. 170/L7
Wuning, China 137/C2
Wünnenberg, Ger. 109/F5
Wünnewil, Swi. 114/D4
Wunsiedel, Ger. 113/F2
Wunstorf, Ger. 109/G4
Wupatki Nat'l Mon., Az, US 186/E4
Wuppertal, Ger. 109/E6
Wuqi, China 130/B3
Wuqia, China 145/G5
Wuqiang, China 130/C3
Wuqiao, China 130/D3
Würm (riv.), Ger. 111/H6
Würm K. (canal), Ger. 115/H1
Würselen, Ger. 111/F2
Würzburg, Ger. 112/C3
Wusheng (pass), China 130/C5
Wushi, China 128/C3
Wüstegarten (peak), Ger. 109/G6
Wüstenrot, Ger. 112/C4
Wusuli (riv.), China 129/P2
Wutach (riv.), Ger. 115/E2
Wutai (peak), China 130/C3
Wutai, China 130/C3
Wuteve (mt.), Libr. 160/C4
Wutha-Farnroda, Ger. 112/D1
Wutöschingen, Ger. 115/E2
Wuustwezel, Belg. 108/B6
Wuwei, China 128/H4
Wuwei, China 130/D5
Wuxi, China 130/L8
Wuxiang, China 130/C3
Wuyang, China 130/C4
Wuyi (mts.), China 137/C2
Wuyi, China 130/C3
Wuyuan, China 128/J3
Wuyuan, China 137/C2
Wuzhai, China 130/B3
Wuzhi (peak), China 141/J4
Wuzhi, China 130/C4
Wuzhi (peak), China 130/J6
Wuzhou, China 141/K3
Wyalkatchem, Austl. 170/C4
Wyandanch, NY, US 197/M8
Wyandotte (co.), Ks, US 195/D5
Wyandotte County (lake), Ks, US 195/D5
Wyandotte NWR, Mi, US 193/F7
Wyangala (dam), Austl. 173/D2
Wycheproof, Austl. 173/B3
Wyckoff, NJ, US 197/J8
Wye (riv.), Eng, UK 90/C2
Wye Mills, Md, US 196/B6
Wyee, Austl. 173/D2
Wyk, Ger. 96/C4
Wynigen, Swi. 114/D3
Wynne, Ar, US 187/K4
Wynyard, Austl. 173/C4
Wynyard, Sk, Can. 185/G3
Wyoming (state), US 184/F5
Wyoming, De, US 196/C5
Wyoming, Mi, US 188/C3
Wyoming, Pa, US 196/C1
Wyoming (range), Wy, US 186/E2
Wyomissing, Pa, US 196/C3
Wyperfeld NP, Austl. 173/B2
Wyralinu (peak), Austl. 170/D5
Wyre (riv.), Eng, UK 93/F4
Wyrzysk, Pol. 99/J2
Wysokie Mazowieckie, Pol. 99/M2
Wyszków, Pol. 99/L2

X

X-Can, Mex. 202/E1
Xa Binh Long, Viet. 136/D4
Xaçmaz, Azer. 121/J4
Xagħra, Malta 104/L6
Xai-Xai, Moz. 163/F6
Xainza, China 128/E5
Xaitongmoin, China 143/G1
Xaltianguis, Mex. 201/F5
Xan (riv.), Viet. 136/D3
Xankändı, Azer. 121/H5
Xanten, Ger. 108/D5
Xánthi, Gre. 105/J2
Xanxerê, Braz. 213/A3
Xar Moron (riv.), China 129/L3
Xarba (pass), China 143/E1
Xavantes, Represa de (res.), Braz. 213/B2
Xavantes, Serra dos (mts.), Braz. 209/J6
Xayar, China 128/D3
Xenia, Oh, US 188/D4
Xerta, Sp. 103/F2
Xertigny, Fr. 114/C1
Xi (lake), China 130/E2
Xi (riv.), China 129/K7
Xiaguan, China 141/H2
Xiajin, China 130/C3
Xiamen, China 137/C3
Xiamen (int'l arpt.), China 137/C3
Xi'an, China 130/B4
Xiang (riv.), China 129/K6
Xiangcheng, China 141/G2
Xiangcheng, China 130/C4
Xiangcheng, China 130/C4
Xiangfan, China 130/C4
Xiangfen, China 130/B4
Xianghe, China 130/H7
Xiangkhoang, Laos 136/C2
Xiangkhoang (plat.), Laos 136/C2
Xiangning, China 130/B4
Xiangshan, China 137/D2
Xiangshui, China 130/D4
Xiangtan, China 141/K2
Xiangxiang, China 137/B2
Xiangyuan, China 130/C3
Xiangyun, China 141/H2
Xianju, China 137/D2
Xianning, China 137/B2
Xiantao, China 137/B1
Xianyang, China 128/J5
Xiao Hinggan (mts.), China 129/N2
Xiao Xian, China 130/D4
Xiaogan, China 129/K5
Xiaoqing (riv.), China 130/D3
Xiaoshan, China 130/L9
Xiaowutai (peak), China 130/C3
Xiaoyi, China 130/B3
Xiapu, China 137/C2
Xiayi, China 130/D4
Xichang, China 141/H2
Xichou, China 141/H3
Xico, Mex. 201/N7
Xicohténcatl, Mex. 201/F4
Xicotepec, Mex. 201/M6
Xifei (riv.), China 130/C4
Xifeng, China 128/J4
Xifeng, China 141/J2
Xifeng, China 130/F2
Xigazê, China 143/G1
Xihua, China 130/C4
Xilin, China 141/J3
Xilitla, Mex. 202/B1
Xilókastron, Gre. 105/H3
Ximeng Vazu Zizhixian, China 141/G3
Xin (riv.), China 137/C2
Xin Barag Zuoqi, China 129/L2
Xin'an, China 130/C4
Xin'an (riv.), China 130/D5
Xin'anjiang (res.), China 137/C2
Xin'anjiang (res.), China 130/D5
Xinbin, China 131/C2
Xincai, China 130/C4
Xinchang, China 137/D2
Xincheng, China 137/A3
Xincheng, China 130/G7
Xinfeng, China 137/B2
Xinfeng, China 141/K3
Xinfengjiang (res.), China 137/B3
Xing'an, China 137/B2
Xingcheng, China 130/E2
Xinghua, China 130/D4
Xinglong, China 130/H6
Xingshan, China 130/B5
Xingtai, China 130/C3
Xingu (riv.), Braz. 209/H4
Xingu, PN do, Braz. 209/H6
Xingyang, China 130/C4
Xingzi, China 137/C2
Xinhe, China 128/D3
Xinhe, China 130/C3
Xinhua, China 137/B2
Xinhuang Dongzu Zizhixian, China 137/A2
Xining, China 128/H4
Xinji, China 130/C3
Xinjiang, China 130/B4
Xinjiang Uygur (reg.), China 125/H5
Xinjin, China 131/A3
Xinle, China 130/C3
Xinmin, China 131/B1
Xintai, China 130/D4
Xinxiang, China 130/C4
Xinyang, China 129/K5
Xinyang, China 130/C4
Xinye, China 130/C4
Xinyi, China 141/K3
Xinyi, China 130/D4
Xinyu, China 137/B2
Xinyuan, China 128/D3
Xinzheng, China 130/C4
Xinzo de Limia, Sp. 102/B1
Xiong Xian, China 130/H7
Xiping, China 130/C4
Xiqing (mts.), China 128/H5
Xique-Xique, Braz. 212/B3
Xitang, China 130/L9
Xitiao (riv.), China 130/K9
Xiu (riv.), China 137/B2
Xiuning, China 137/C2
Xiuwen, China 141/J2
Xiuwu, China 130/C4
Xiuyan, China 131/B2
Xixabangma (peak), China 143/E1
Xixia, China 130/B4
Xiyang (riv.), China 141/J3
Xizang (Tibet) (aut. reg.), China 128/D5
Xochicalco (ruin), Mex. 201/K8
Xonacatlán, Mex. 201/Q10
Xpujil, Mex. 202/D2
Xu (riv.), China 137/C2
Xuan'en, China 137/A2
Xuanhua, China 130/G6
Xuchang, China 130/C4
Xun (riv.), China 137/B3
Xun Xian, China 130/C4
Xunke, China 129/N2
Xunwu, China 137/C3
Xunyang, China 130/B4
Xupu, China 137/B2
Xuwen, China 141/K3
Xuyi, China 130/D4
Xuzhou, China 130/D4

Y

Y Llethr (peak), Wal, UK 92/E6
Ya'an, China 128/H6
Ya'bad, Isr. 149/G7
Yabassi, Camr. 154/G7
Yablanitsa, Bul. 107/G4
Yablonovyy (range), Rus. 125/L4
Yabrūd, Isr. 149/G8
Yabucoa, PR 199/M8
Yabuki, Japan 133/G2
Yabuzukahon, Japan 135/C1
Yachi (riv.), China 128/J6
Yachiho, Japan 135/A1
Yachimata, Japan 135/E2
Yachiyo, Japan 135/D1
Yachiyo, Japan 135/G5
Yachiyo, Japan 135/E2
Yacimiento Río Turbio, Arg. 217/B6
Yacuiba, Bol. 208/F8
Yacuma (riv.), Bol. 208/E6
Yacumbu, PN, Ven. 210/D2
Yādgīr, India 140/C4
Yadkin (riv.), NC, US 191/H2
Yaeyama (isls.), Japan 133/G8
Yāfā, Isr. 149/G6
Yağcılar, Turk. 148/B2
Yagi, Japan 135/J5
Yagorlytsk (gulf), Ukr. 107/K2
Yagoua, Camr. 154/J5
Yagradagzê (peak), China 128/G4
Yaguale (riv.), Hon. 202/E3
Yaguarón (riv.), Uru. 217/G2
Yaguas (riv.), Peru 210/D5
Yague del Sur (riv.), DRep. 203/J2
Yagur, Isr. 149/G6
Yahagi (riv.), Japan 135/M6
Yahualica de Gonzalez Gallo, Mex. 200/E4
Yahyalı, Turk. 148/C2
Yáios (Paxoí), Gre. 105/G3
Yaita, Japan 133/F2
Yaizu, Japan 133/F3
Yajalón, Mex. 202/C2
Yakacık, Turk. 149/E1
Yakapınar, Turk. 149/D1
Yakima (riv.), Wa, US 184/C4
Yakima, Wa, US 184/C4
Yakishiri (isl.), Japan 134/B1
Yako, Burk. 161/E3
Yakoruda, Bul. 107/F4
Yakumo, Japan 134/B2
Yakuno, Japan 135/G5
Yakutat (bay), Ak, US 180/B3
Yakutsk, Rus. 123/N3
Yala, Thai. 136/C5
Yalahua (lag.), Mex. 202/E1
Yalangoz, Turk. 149/E1
Yalata Abor. Land, Austl. 171/F4
Yalbac (hills), Belz. 202/D2
Yalgoo, Austl. 170/C4
Yalgorup NP, Austl. 170/B5
Yalnızçam, Turk. 148/E1
Yaloké, CAfr. 155/J6
Yalong (riv.), China 128/H5
Yalova, Turk. 107/J5
Yalova, Turk. 107/H5
Yalpuh (lake), Ukr. 107/J3
Yalta, Ukr. 120/E3
Yalu (riv.), China,NKor. 131/C2
Yalutorovsk, Rus. 145/E1
Yalvaç, Turk. 148/B2
Yamada, Japan 134/B4
Yamaga, Japan 132/B4
Yamagata, Japan 129/Q4
Yamagata, Japan 133/G1
Yamagata (pref.), Japan 134/A4
Yamaguchi (pref.), Japan 132/B3
Yamaguchi, Japan 132/B3
Yamakita, Japan 135/C3
Yamal (pen.), Rus. 122/G2
Yamalo-Nenetskiy Aut. Okrug, Rus. 122/H3
Yamanaka (lake), Japan 135/B3
Yamanashi, Japan 135/B2
Yamanie (falls), Austl. 172/B2
Yamanie Falls NP, Austl. 172/B2
Yamantau (peak), Rus. 119/N5
Yamaoka, Japan 135/M5
Yamarna Abor. Rsv., Austl. 170/D4
Yamashiro, Japan 135/J6
Yamato, Japan 135/B2
Yamato, Japan 135/E1
Yamato, Japan 135/C3
Yamato (riv.), Japan 135/J6
Yamato-Kōriyama, Japan 135/J6
Yamatotakada, Japan 135/J6
Yamazoe, Japan 135/K6
Yamba, Austl. 173/E1
Yambio, Sudan 155/L7
Yambol, Bul. 107/H4
Yambrasbamba, Peru 214/B2
Yamdena (isl.), Indo. 139/H5
Yamethin, Myan. 141/G3
Yamin (peak), Indo. 139/K4
Yamma Yamma (lake), Austl. 172/A4
Yamoto, Japan 134/B4
Yamoussoukro (cap.), C.d'Iv. 160/D5
Yampa (riv.), Co, US 186/F2
Yamuna (riv.), India 140/D2
Yamunānagar, India 144/D4
Yamzho Yumco (lake), China 140/F2
Yan (riv.), SrL. 140/D6
Yan Yean (res.), Austl. 173/G5
Yana (riv.), Rus. 125/N3
Yanagawa, Japan 132/B4
Yanahuanca, Peru 214/B3
Yanai, Japan 132/C4
Yanaizu, Japan 135/L5
Yan'an, China 130/B3
Yanaoca, Peru 214/D4
Yanaul, Rus. 119/M4
Yanbian, China 141/H2
Yancheng, China 130/C4
Yancheng, China 130/E4
Yanchep NP, Austl. 170/B4
Yanco, Austl. 173/C2
Yandeearra Abor. Rsv., Austl. 170/C2
Yandoon, Myan. 141/G4
Yanfolila, Mali 160/C4
Yangambi, D.R. Congo 155/K7
Yangbi (riv.), China 141/G2
Yangcheng, China 130/C4
Yangcheng (lake), China 130/L8
Yangchun, China 137/B3
Yangdang (mts.), China 137/C2
Yangdŏk, NKor. 131/D3
Yanggang-do (prov.), NKor. 131/D2
Yanggao, China 130/C2
Yanggu, SKor. 131/D3
Yanggu, China 130/C3
Yangiyul', Uzb. 145/E4
Yangjiang, China 141/K3
Yangma (isl.), China 131/A4
Yangon (div.), Myan. 141/G4
Yangp'yŏng, SKor. 131/D4
Yangqu, China 130/C3
Yangquan, China 130/C3
Yangsan, SKor. 131/E5
Yangshan, China 141/K3
Yangtze (Chang) (riv.), China 137/C1
Yangudi Rassa NP, Eth. 155/P5
Yangxin, China 137/C2
Yangxin, China 130/D3
Yangyang, SKor. 131/E3
Yangyuan, China 130/C2
Yangzhong, China 130/D4
Yangzhou, China 130/D4
Yanhe, China 137/A2
Yanji, China 129/N3
Yanjin, China 141/H2
Yanjin, China 130/C4
Yankari Game Reserve, Nga. 155/H6
Yankee Stadium, NY, US 197/K8
Yanling, China 130/C4
Yanmen (pass), China 130/C3
Yanshan, China 137/C2
Yanshan, China 141/H3
Yanshan, China 130/D3
Yanshi, China 130/C4
Yanshou, China 129/N2
Yantai, China 130/E3
Yanyuan, China 141/H2
Yanzhou, China 130/D4
Yao, Japan 135/J6
Yao'an, China 141/H2
Yaotsu, Japan 135/M5
Yaoundé (cap.), Camr. 154/H7
Yap (isls.), Micr. 174/C4
Yapacana, PN, Ven. 208/E3
Yapei, Gha. 161/E4
Yapen (isl.), Indo. 139/J4
Yapen (str.), Indo. 139/J4
Yapraklı, Turk. 148/C1
Yaqui (riv.), Mex. 200/C2
Yara, Cuba 203/G1
Yaracuy (state), Ven. 210/D2
Yaralıgöz (peak), Turk. 148/C1
Yaransk, Rus. 119/K4
Yardımcı (pt.), Turk. 149/B1
Yardley, Pa, US 196/D3
Yardville-Groveville, NJ, US 196/D3
Yare (riv.), Eng, UK 91/H1
Yarí (riv.), Col. 208/D3
Yari-ga-take (peak), Japan 133/E2
Yarımca, Turk. 107/J5
Yaritagua, Ven. 210/D2
Yarkant (riv.), China 128/C4
Yarloop, Austl. 170/B5
Yarlung Zangbo (Brahmaputra) (riv.), China 143/G1
Yarmouth, NS, Can. 189/H3
Yaroslavl', Rus. 118/H4
Yaroslavskaya Oblast, Rus. 118/H4
Yarpuz, Turk. 149/E1
Yarra (riv.), Austl. 173/G5
Yarra Glen, Austl. 173/G5
Yarram, Austl. 173/C3
Yarraman, Austl. 172/D4
Yarrawonga, Austl. 173/C3
Yarrow Point, Wa, US 193/C2
Yartsevo, Rus. 122/K3
Yarumal, Col. 210/C3
Yasato, Japan 135/E1
Yasawa Group (isls.), Fiji 174/G6
Yasel'da (riv.), Bela. 120/C1
Yashima, Japan 134/B4
Yashio, Japan 135/D2
Yashiro, Japan 135/G6
Yasnyy, Rus. 121/L2
Yasothon, Thai. 136/D3
Yass, Austl. 173/D2
Yasu (riv.), Japan 135/K6
Yasu, Japan 135/K5
Yasugi, Japan 132/C3
Yāsūj, Iran 146/F2
Yasun Burnu (pt.), Turk. 148/D1
Yasuni, PN, Ecu. 208/C4
Yatabe, Japan 133/G2
Yatağan, Turk. 148/B2
Yateley, Eng, UK 91/F4
Yatenga (prov.), Burk. 161/E3
Yathkyed (lake), Nun., Can. 180/G2
Yatomi, Japan 135/L5
Yatsu-ga-take (peak), Japan 135/A2
Yatsuo, Japan 133/E2
Yatsushiro, Japan 132/B4
Yatsushiro, Japan 135/B2
Yaṭṭah, WBnk. 149/D4
Yauca (riv.), Peru 214/C4
Yauca, Peru 214/C4
Yauco, PR 199/M8
Yauli, Peru 214/B3
Yaupi, Ecu. 210/B5
Yaután, Peru 214/B3
Yauyos, Peru 214/C4
Yauza (riv.), Rus. 119/W9
Yavarí (riv.), Braz.,Peru 214/C2
Yavarí Mirim (riv.), Peru 214/C2
Yavaros, Mex. 200/C3
Yavay (pen.), Rus. 122/H2
Yaviza, Pan. 203/G4
Yavne, Isr. 149/F8
Yavuzeli, Turk. 148/D2
Yawahara, Japan 135/E2
Yawata, Japan 135/J6
Yawatahama, Japan 132/C4
Yaxchilán (ruin), Guat. 202/D2
Yaygın, Turk. 148/E2
Yayladağı, Turk. 149/E2
Yayladere, Turk. 148/E2
Yazd, Iran 147/F2
Yazmān, Pak. 144/A5
Yazoo (riv.), Ms, US 187/K4
Yazoo City, Ms, US 187/K4
Ybbs (riv.), Aus. 99/H4
Ybbsitz, Aus. 101/L3
Yding Skovhøj (peak), Den. 96/C3
Ye, Myan. 136/B3
Ye Xian, China 130/D3
Yeay Sen (cape), Camb. 136/C4
Yecheng, China 145/G5
Yech'ŏn, SKor. 131/E4
Yecla, Sp. 103/E3
Yécora, Mex. 200/C2
Yecuatla, Mex. 201/N7
Yedigöller Nat'l Park, Turk. 107/K5
Yeditepe, Turk. 149/E2
Yéfira, Gre. 105/H2
Yefremov, Rus. 120/F1
Yegizkara (peak), Kaz. 145/D3
Yegorlak (riv.), Rus. 121/G3
Yehualtepec, Mex. 201/M8
Yehud, Isr. 149/F7
Yejmiadzin, Arm. 121/H4
Yekaterinburg (Sverdlovsk), Rus. 119/P4
Yekateriny (chan.), Rus. 134/E1
Yelabuga, Rus. 119/M5
Yelan', Rus. 121/G2
Yelarbon, Austl. 172/C5
Yelets, Rus. 120/F1
Yélimané, Mali 160/C3
Yelizovo, Rus. 123/R4
Yell (isl.), Sc, UK 89/W13
Yellel, Alg. 158/F5
Yellow (riv.), Fl, US 191/G4
Yellow (sea), Asia 129/M5
Yellow Grass, Sk, Can. 185/G3
Yellowknife (riv.), NW, Can. 180/E2
Yellowknife (cap.), NW, Can. 180/E2
Yellowstone (lake), Wy, US 184/F4
Yellowstone (riv.), Mt, US 185/G4
Yellowstone NP, US 186/E1
Yellville, Ar, US 187/J3
Yemen (ctry.) 146/E5
Yenakiyeve, Ukr. 120/F2
Yenangyaung, Myan. 141/F3
Yenda, Austl. 173/C2
Yendi, Gha. 161/E4
Yengisar, China 145/G5
Yeniçağa, Turk. 107/L5
Yenice, Turk. 149/D1
Yenice, Turk. 107/L5
Yenice, Turk. 107/H6
Yenice (riv.), Turk. 120/E4
Yeniceoba, Turk. 148/C2
Yeniköy, Turk. 107/H5
Yenişehir, Turk. 107/J5
Yenisey (riv.), Rus. 125/H3
Yeniseysk, Rus. 122/K4
Yeo (lake), Austl. 170/E3
Yeo Lake Nature Rsv., Austl. 170/E3
Yeoval, Austl. 173/D2
Yeovil, Eng, UK 90/D5
Yeppoon, Austl. 172/C3
Yeraifia (well), WSah. 156/B4
Yerakovoúni (peak), Gre. 105/H3
Yères (riv.), Fr. 110/A4
Yerevan (cap.), Arm. 121/H4
Yerevan (int'l arpt.), Arm. 121/H4
Yerington, Nv, US 186/C3
Yerköy, Turk. 148/C2
Yerlisu, Turk. 105/K2
Yermak, Kaz. 145/G2
Yeroḥam, Isr. 149/D4
Yerolimín, Gre. 105/H4
Yerre (riv.), Fr. 100/D2
Yerres, Fr. 88/K5
Yerupaja (peak), Peru 214/B3
Yesagyo, Myan. 141/G3
Yesan, SKor. 131/D4
Yeşilhisar, Turk. 148/C2
Yeşilırmak (riv.), Turk. 120/F4
Yeşilkent, Turk. 149/E1
Yeşilova, Turk. 148/B2
Yesodot, Isr. 149/F8
Yesŏng (riv.), NKor. 131/D3
Yessentuki, Rus. 121/G3
Yeste, Sp. 102/D3
Yetti (reg.), Mrta. 156/D4
Yeu, Île d' (isl.), Fr. 100/B3
Yevla, India 140/B3
Yevlax, Azer. 121/H4
Yevpatoriya, Ukr. 120/E3
Yèvre (riv.), Fr. 111/D5
Yeya (riv.), Rus. 120/G3
Yeysk, Rus. 120/F3
Ygos-Saint-Saturnin, Fr. 100/C5
Yi (riv.), Uru. 217/F2
Yialousa, Cyp. 149/D2
Yiannitsá, Gre. 105/H2
Yiánnouli, Gre. 105/H3
Yíaros (isl.), Gre. 105/J4
Yibin, China 128/H6
Yichang, China 129/K5
Yicheng, China 130/C5
Yicheng, China 130/B4
Yichuan, China 130/C4
Yichun, China 129/N2
Yichun, China 141/K2
Yifeng, China 141/K2
Yığılca, Turk. 107/K5
Yihuang, China 137/C2
Yıldız (peak), Turk. 148/D1
Yıldızeli, Turk. 148/D2
Yilehuli (mts.), China 129/M1
Yiliang, China 141/H2
Yima, China 130/B4
Yimen, China 141/H3
Yin (mts.), China 128/J3
Yinan, China 130/D4
Yinchuan, China 128/J4
Yindarlgooda (lake), Austl. 170/D4
Yingcheng, China 129/K5
Yingde, China 137/B3
Yingkou, China 131/B2
Yingshan, China 130/C5
Yingshang, China 130/D4
Yingtan, China 137/C2
Yining, China 128/D3
Yishan, China 137/A3
Yishui, China 130/D4
Yíthion, Gre. 105/H4
Yitong (riv.), SKor. 130/C5
Yiwu, China 128/F3
Yixing, China 130/K8
Yiyang, China 141/K2
Yiyang, China 130/C4
Yiyuan, China 130/D3
Yizhang, China 141/K2
Yizheng, China 130/D4
Ylöjärvi, Fin. 97/K1
Ynder (lake), Kaz. 121/K2
Yngaren (lake), Swe. 96/G2
Yobe (state), Nga. 161/H3
Yŏch'ŏn, SKor. 131/D5
Yodo (riv.), Japan 135/J6
Yoduma (riv.), Rus. 123/P4
Yoff (Dakar) (int'l arpt.), Sen. 160/A3
Yogo, Japan 135/K4
Yogoum (well), Chad 155/J4
Yoğuntaş, Turk. 107/H5
Yogyakarta, Indo. 138/D5
Yoho NP, BC, Can. 184/D3
Yoichi, Japan 134/B2
Yojoa (lake), Hon. 202/D3
Yŏju, SKor. 131/D4
Yokadouma, Camr. 154/J7
Yōkaichi, Japan 135/K5
Yokawa, Japan 135/H6
Yokkaichi, Japan 135/L6
Yokohama, Japan 133/F3
Yokoshiba, Japan 135/E2
Yokosuka, Japan 133/F3
Yokote, Japan 134/B4
Yokoze, Japan 135/C2
Yola, Nga. 154/H6
Yolaina (mts.), Nic. 203/E4
Yolboyu, Turk. 148/D2
Yolo, Ca, US 193/L9
Yolo (co.), Ca, US 193/L9
Yom (riv.), Thai. 141/H4
Yon (riv.), China 137/A3
Yon (riv.), Fr. 100/C3
Yonago, Japan 132/C3
Yonaguni (isl.), Japan 133/G8
Yonaha-dake (peak), Japan 133/K7
Yoneshiro (riv.), Japan 134/B3
Yonezawa, Japan 133/G2
Yŏng-yang, SKor. 131/E4
Yŏngam, SKor. 131/D5
Yongamp'o, NKor. 131/C3
Yong'an, China 137/C2
Yongchang, China 128/H4
Yongcheng, China 130/D4
Yŏngch'ŏn, SKor. 131/E5
Yongchun, China 137/C2
Yongde, China 141/G3
Yongding, China 137/C3
Yongding (riv.), China 130/G6
Yŏngdŏk, SKor. 131/E4
Yŏngdong, SKor. 131/D4
Yŏnggwang, SKor. 131/D5
Yŏnghae, SKor. 131/E4
Yonghe, China 130/B3
Yŏnghŭng (riv.), NKor. 131/D3
Yŏnghŭng, NKor. 131/D3
Yongji, China 130/B4
Yŏngjong (isl.), SKor. 131/F6
Yŏngju, SKor. 131/E4
Yongkang, China 137/D2
Yongmun-san (peak), SKor. 131/D4
Yongnian, China 130/C3
Yongqing, China 130/H7
Yongren, China 141/H2
Yŏngsan (riv.), SKor. 131/D5
Yongsheng, China 141/H2
Yongshun, China 141/J2
Yongtai, China 137/C2
Yŏngwŏl, SKor. 131/E4
Yongxing, China 137/B2
Yongxiu, China 137/C2
Yonkers, NY, US 197/K8
Yonne (riv.), Fr. 98/B5
Yono, Japan 135/D2
Yopal, Col. 210/C3
Yopurga, China 145/G5
Yoqne'am 'Illit, Isr. 149/G6
Yorba Linda, Ca, US 194/G8
Yorii, Japan 135/C1
York, Austl. 170/C4
York (cape), Austl. 167/D2
York (sound), Austl. 167/B2
York (riv.), Qu, Can. 189/H1
York, Eng, UK 93/G4
York (co.), Eng, UK 93/G4
York, Al, US 191/F3
York, Ne, US 185/J5
York, Pa, US 196/B4
York (co.), Pa, US 196/B4
York, SC, US 191/H3
York (riv.), Va, US 188/E4
York Haven, Pa, US 196/B3
York Landing, Mb, Can. 185/J1
York Minster, Eng, UK 93/G4
York Springs, Pa, US 196/A4
York, Vale of (valley), Eng, UK 93/G3
Yorke (pen.), Austl. 171/H5
Yorketown, Austl. 171/H5
Yorkshire Dales NP, Eng, UK 93/F3
Yorkshire Wolds (hills), Eng, UK 93/H3
Yorkton, Sk, Can. 185/H3
Yorktown, Tx, US 187/H5
Yorktown Heights, NY, US 197/E1
Yoro, Hon. 202/E3
Yōrō (riv.), Japan 135/E3

Yorō, Japan 135/L5
Yoroi-zaki (pt.), Japan 135/L2
Yoron (isl.), Japan 133/K7
Yorosso, Mali 160/D3
Yorubaland (plat.), Nga. 154/F6
Yos Sudarso (isl.), Indo. 139/J5
Yosemite NP, Ca, US 186/C3
Yoshida, Japan 135/C1
Yoshida, Japan 135/C1
Yoshii (riv.), Japan 141/J4
Yoshii, Japan 135/B1
Yoshikawa, Japan 135/D2
Yoshima (riv.), Japan 132/D3
Yoshimi, Japan 135/C1
Yoshino (riv.), Japan 132/C4
Yoshino, Japan 135/J7
Yoshino-Kumano NP, Japan 135/J7
Yoshkar-Ola, Rus. 119/L4
Yōsu, SKor. 131/D5
Yōtei-san (peak), Japan 134/B2
Yotsukaidō, Japan 135/E2
You (riv.), China 137/A3
Young, Austl. 173/D2
Young, Uru. 217/K10
Youngs (lake), Wa, US 193/C3
Youngstown, Oh, US 188/D3
Youngstown, NY, US 189/R9
Youngtown, Az, US 195/R18
Yountville, Ca, US 193/K10
Youssoufia, Mor. 156/C2
Youyang, China 141/J2
Yovi (peak), Ven. 211/E3
Yozgat, Turk. 148/C2
Ypsilanti, Mi, US 193/E7
Yr Eifl (peak), Wal, UK 92/D6
Yreka, Ca, US 186/B2
Yser (riv.), Fr. 98/B3
Ysieux (riv.), Fr. 88/K4
Ystad, Swe. 96/E4
Ysyk-Köl (lake), Kyr. 128/C3
Ysyk-Köl (obl.), Kyr. 145/G4
Ythan (riv.), Sc, UK 94/D2
Ytrac, Fr. 100/E4
Ytre Sula (isl.), Nor. 96/A1
Ytterby, Swe. 96/D3
Ytterbyn, Swe. 95/G2
Yü (peak), Tai. 137/D3
Yu (riv.), China 141/J3
Yu Xian, China 130/C3
Yu Xian, China 130/C4
Yuan (riv.), China 129/K6
Yuan (lake), China 130/C5
Yuan'an, China 130/B5
Yüanlin, Tai. 137/D3
Yuanping, China 130/C3
Yuanqu, China 130/B4
Yuanshi, China 130/C4
Yuanyang, China 130/C4
Yuba City, Ca, US 186/B3
Yūbari, Japan 134/B2
Yūbetsu, Japan 134/C1
Yūbetsu (riv.), Japan 134/C2
Yucaipa, Ca, US 194/C2
Yucatán (state), Mex. 202/D1
Yucatan (pen.), Mex. 202/D2
Yucatan (chan.), NAm. 200/E3
Yucca House Nat'l Mon., Co, US 186/E3
Yucheng, China 130/D3
Yucheng, China 130/C4
Yuci, China 130/C3
Yuen Long, China 129/U10
Yuendumu, Austl. 171/F2
Yuendumu Abor. Land, Austl. 171/F2
Yueqing, China 137/D2
Yueyang, China 137/B2
Yug (riv.), Rus. 122/E4
Yugan, China 137/C2
Yugawara, Japan 135/C3
Yugorskiy (pen.), Rus. 119/P1
Yuhang, China 137/L9
Yuhuan, China 137/D2
Yui, Japan 135/B3

Yujiang, China 137/C2
Yūki, Japan 133/F2
Yukon, Ok, US 195/M14
Yukon (riv.), Can.,US 192/L3
Yukon-Charley Rivers Nat'l Prsv., Ak, US 192/K2
Yukon Territory (terr.), Can. 192/L2
Yüksekova, Turk. 148/F2
Yukuhashi, Japan 132/B4
Yulara, Austl. 171/F3
Yuleba, Austl. 172/C4
Yulin, China 141/K3
Yulin, China 141/J4
Yulin, China 130/B3
Yuma, Az, US 186/D4
Yuma, Co, US 187/G2
Yumbarra Consv. Park, Austl. 171/G4
Yumbel, Chile 216/B3
Yumbo, Col. 210/B4
Yumen, China 128/G4
Yumin, China 128/D2
Yun (riv.), China 130/C5
Yun Xian, China 141/H3
Yun Xian, China 130/B4
Yunak, Turk. 148/B2
Yuncheng, China 130/C4
Yuncheng, China 130/B4
Yundum (Banjul) (int'l arpt.), Gam. 160/A3
Yungang Caves, China 130/C2
Yungas (phys. reg.), Bol. 208/E7
Yungay, Chile 216/B3
Yungk'ang, Tai. 137/D3
Yunguyo, Peru 214/D5
Yunkanjini Abor. Land, Austl. 171/F2
Yunlong, China 141/G2
Yunnan (prov.), China 128/H7
Yuntai (prefec.), China 130/D4
Yunxi, China 130/B4
Yunxiao, China 137/C3
Yunyan (riv.), China 130/D4
Yunzhong (mtn.), China 130/C3
Yuping, China 141/J2
Yupukarri, Guy. 211/G4
Yuqiao (res.), China 130/H7
Yuracyacu, Peru 214/B2
Yurga, Rus. 122/J4
Yuri (isl.), Rus. 134/E2
Yurimaguas, Peru 214/B2
Yuruari (riv.), Ven. 211/F3
Yürük, Turk. 107/H5
Yur'yevets, Rus. 118/J4
Yuryuzan' (riv.), Rus. 119/N5
Yuscarán, Hon. 202/E3
Yushan, China 137/C2
Yushe, China 130/C3
Yushu, China 129/N3
Yusŏng, SKor. 131/D4
Yusufeli, Turk. 148/E1
Yutai, China 130/D4
Yutian, China 128/D4
Yutian, China 130/H7
Yutz, Fr. 111/F5
Yuza, Japan 134/A4
Yuzawa, Japan 134/B4
Yuzhno-Sakhalinsk, Rus. 129/R2
Yverdon, Swi. 114/C4
Yvette (riv.), Fr. 110/B6
Yvoir, Belg. 111/D3
Yvonand, Swi. 114/C4
Yvron (riv.), Fr. 88/L6
Yzeure, Fr. 100/E3

Z

Za (riv.), Mor. 158/C2
Zaachila, Mex. 202/B2
Zaandam, Neth. 98/C2
Zaanstad, Neth. 108/B4
Zabbar, Malta 104/M7
Zaber (riv.), Ger. 112/C4
Ząbki, Pol. 99/L2
Ząbkowice Śląskie, Pol. 99/J3
Zabljak, Mont. 106/D4
Zábřeh, Czh. 99/J4
Zabrze, Pol. 99/K3

Zacapa, Guat. 202/D3
Zacapoaxtla, Mex. 201/M7
Zacapu, Mex. 201/E5
Zacatecas (state), Mex. 198/A3
Zacatecas, Mex. 200/E4
Zacatecoluca, ESal. 202/D3
Zacatelco, Mex. 201/L7
Zacatepec, Mex. 201/K8
Zacatlán, Mex. 201/M7
Zachary, La, US 191/F4
Zachodniopomorskie (prov.), Pol. 99/H2
Zacoalco de Torres, Mex. 200/E4
Zacualtipán, Mex. 202/B1
Zadar, Cro. 101/L4
Zadetkyi (isl.), Myan. 138/A2
Zafarwāl, Pak. 144/C3
Zafra, Sp. 102/B3
Żagań, Pol. 99/H3
Zaghouan, Tun. 158/M6
Zaghouan (gov.), Tun. 158/M6
Zagora, Mor. 156/D3
Zagorá, Gre. 105/H3
Zagorje ob Savi, Slov. 101/L3
Zagreb (cap.), Cro. 106/B3
Zagros (mts.), Iran 146/E1
Zāhedān, Iran 147/H3
Zahirābād, India 140/C4
Zahlah, Leb. 149/D3
Záhony, Hun. 99/M4
Zahrez Chergui (dry lake), Alg. 158/G5
Zaidín, Sp. 103/F2
Zaidpur, India 142/C2
Zaïo, Mor. 158/C2
Zaire (see Congo, Democratic Republic of the)
Zakamensk, Rus. 128/H1
Zakarpats'ka Oblasti, Ukr. 106/G4
Zakháro, Gre. 105/G4
Zakhodnyaya Dzvina (riv.), Bela. 118/E5
Zākhū, Iraq 148/E2
Zákinthos (isl.), Gre. 105/G4
Zákinthos, Gre. 105/G4
Zakopane, Pol. 99/K4
Zakouma, PN de, Chad 155/J5
Zala (riv.), Hun. 106/C2
Zala (prov.), Hun. 106/C2
Zalaapáti, Hun. 106/C2
Zalaegerszeg, Hun. 106/C2
Zalamea de la Serena, Sp. 102/C3
Zalamea la Real, Sp. 102/B4
Zalaszentgrót, Hun. 106/C2
Zalău, Rom. 107/F2
Žalec, Slov. 101/L3
Zaltan (well), Libya 155/J2
Zaltbommel, Neth. 108/C5
Zalun, Myan. 141/G4
Zamami (riv.), Myan. 136/B3
Zamania, India 142/D3
Zambezi (riv.), Zam. 163/E3
Zambezi (riv.), Afr. 163/F4
Zambia (ctry.) 163/E3
Zamboanga, Phil. 139/F2
Zambrów, Pol. 99/M2
Zamfora (riv.), Nga. 161/G3
Zami (riv.), Myan. 136/B3
Zamora (riv.), Ecu. 208/C4
Zamora, Ecu. 214/B2
Zamora, Sp. 102/C2
Zamora-Chinchipe (prov.), Ecu. 214/B2
Zamora de Hidalgo, Mex. 200/E5
Zamość, Pol. 99/M3
Zams, Aus. 115/G3
Záncara (riv.), Sp. 102/D3
Zanda, Chile 128/C5
Zandkreekdam (dam), Neth. 108/A5
Zandvoort, Neth. 108/A5
Zanè, It. 117/E1
Zanhuang, China 130/C3
Zanjān, Iran 146/E1
Zanjón (riv.), Arg. 186/E5
Zánka, Hun. 106/C2
Zanzibar, Tanz. 162/C4
Zanzibar (isl.), Tanz. 162/C4
Zanzibar (Kisauni) (int'l arpt.), Tanz. 162/C4

Zanzibar Central/South (res.), Pol. 162/C4
Zanzibar North (prov.), Tanz. 162/C4
Zanzibar Urban/West (pol. reg.), Tanz. 162/C4
Zanzuzi (hill), Tanz. 162/B3
Zaō-san (peak), Japan 133/G1
Zaoqiang, China 130/C3
Zaouiet Kounta, Alg. 157/E4
Zaoyang, China 130/C4
Zaozhuang, China 130/D4
Zapala, Arg. 216/C3
Zapaleri (peak), SA 215/C1
Zapallar, Chile 216/C2
Zapata, Tx, US 190/D5
Zapata (pen.), Cuba 203/F1
Zapatoca, Col. 210/C2
Zapatosa (lake), Col. 210/C2
Záplatský Rybník (lake), Czh. 113/H4
Zapolyarnyy, Rus. 118/F1
Zapopan, Mex. 200/E4
Zaporizhzhya, Ukr. 120/E3
Zaporizhzhya (int'l arpt.), Ukr. 120/E3
Zaporiz'ka Oblasti, Ukr. 120/E3
Zapotal, Ecu. 210/B5
Zapotillo, Ecu. 214/A2
Zaprešić, Cro. 106/B3
Zaqponeta, It. 117/F4
Zara, Turk. 148/D2
Zaragoza, Mex. 201/E2
Zaragoza (int'l arpt.), Sp. 103/F2
Zaragoza, Mex. 201/M7
Zaragoza (Saragossa), Sp. 103/F2
Zarah, Ks, US 195/D6
Zarand, Iran 147/G2
Zaranda (hill), Nga. 161/H4
Zárate, Arg. 217/J11
Zarauz, Sp. 102/D1
Zaraza, Ven. 211/E2
Zard (mtn.), Iran 146/F2
Zareh Sharan, Afg. 147/J2
Zargān, Iran 146/F3
Zaria, Nga. 161/G4
Zarmast (pass), Afg. 147/H2
Zărneşti, Rom. 107/G3
Zarnovica, Slvk. 106/D1
Zaros, Gre. 105/J5
Záruby (peak), Slvk. 106/C1
Zaruma, Ecu. 214/B1
Zarumilla, Peru 214/A1
Zary, Pol. 99/H3
Zarza la Mayor, Sp. 102/B3
Zarzal, Col. 210/B3
Zäskär (range), India 144/D3
Zäskär (riv.), India 144/D3
Zastron, SAfr. 164/D3
Zatec, Czh. 113/G2
Zauche (reg.), Ger. 98/P7
Zavalla, Arg. 216/E2
Zavdi'el, Isr. 149/F8
Zevenbergen, Neth. 108/B5
Zaventem, Belg. 111/D2
Zavet, Bul. 107/H4
Zavidovići, Bosn. 106/D3
Zavitinsk, Rus. 129/N1
Zawadzkie, Pol. 99/K3
Zawiercie, Pol. 99/K3
Zaysan, Kaz. 128/D2
Zaysan (lake), Kaz. 128/D2
Zayü (riv.), China 141/G2
Zaza (riv.), Cuba 203/G1
Zazáirda, Iran 147/H3
Zbaszyń, Pol. 99/H2
Žd'ár nad Sázavou, Czh. 99/H4
Zdice, Czh. 113/G3
Zduńska Wola, Pol. 99/K3
Zeballos (peak), Arg. 217/C5
Zebbug, Malta 104/L7
Zeddine (riv.), Alg. 158/F5
Zedelgem, Belg. 110/C1
Zeehan, Austl. 173/C4
Zeeland, Mi, US 188/C3
Zeeland (prov.), Neth. 108/A5
Zeerust, SAfr. 163/E6
Zeewolde, Neth. 108/C3
Zefat, Isr. 149/D3

Zegrzyńskie (res.), Pol. 99/L2
Zehdenick, Ger. 99/G2
Zeil (mt.), Austl. 171/G2
Zeil, Ger. 112/D2
Zeiselmauer, Aus. 107/N7
Zeist, Neth. 108/C4
Zeitz, Ger. 98/G3
Zejtun, Malta 104/M7
Zekharya, Isr. 149/F8
Zele, Belg. 110/D1
Zelenodol'sk, Rus. 119/L3
Zelenogorsk, Rus. 119/S6
Zelenokumsk, Rus. 121/G3
Zelhem, Neth. 108/D4
Zell, Swi. 115/E3
Zell, Swi. 114/D3
Zell, Ger. 111/G3
Zell am Harmersbach, Ger. 114/C1
Zell am Main, Ger. 112/C3
Zell am Moos, Aus. 113/G7
Zell an der Pram, Aus. 113/G6
Zell in Wiesental, Ger. 114/C2
Zellersee (lake), Aus. 112/C7
Zeltingen, Ger. 111/G3
Zelów, Pol. 99/K3
Zeltingen-Rachtig, Ger. 111/G3
Zeltweg, Aus. 101/L3
Zelzate, Belg. 110/C1
Zemaitija NP, Lith. 97/J3
Zembra (isls.), Tun. 158/M6
Zemen, Bul. 106/F4
Zemio, CAfr. 155/L6
Zemmer, Ger. 111/F4
Zemmora, Alg. 158/F5
Zempoala, Mex. 201/N7
Zempoala (peak), Mex. 201/Q10
Zempoaltepec, Cerro (peak), Mex. 202/C2
Zemst, Belg. 111/D2
Zenica, Bosn. 106/C3
Zenith, Wa, US 193/C3
Zenn (riv.), Ger. 112/D3
Zenne (riv.), Belg. 111/D1
Zenon Park, Sk, Can. 185/H2
Zentsūji, Japan 132/C3
Zepče, Bosn. 106/D3
Zepu, China 145/G5
Zeralda, Alg. 158/G4
Zerbst, Ger. 98/G3
Zeravshan (riv.), Taj.,Uzb. 145/G5
Zerengana, China 130/B3
Zernez, Swi. 115/G4
Zernien, Ger. 109/H2
Zernograd, Rus. 120/G3
Zero Branco, It. 117/F1
Zeta (lake), Nun., Can. 180/F1
Zetel, Ger. 109/E2
Zeuthen, Ger. 98/O7
Zeven, Ger. 109/G2
Zevenaar, Neth. 108/D5
Zevenbergen, Neth. 108/B5
Zevio, It. 117/E2
Zeya (res.), Rus. 125/M4
Zeya (riv.), Rus. 123/N4
Zeya-Bureya (plain), Rus. 123/N4
Zeytindağ, Turk. 148/A2
Zêzere (riv.), Port. 102/A3
Zghartā, Leb. 149/D2
Zgierz, Pol. 99/K3
Zhambyl (obl.), Kaz. 145/F4
Zhambyl, Kaz. 145/F4
Zhangaözen, Kaz. 121/K4
Zhangaqazaly, Kaz. 145/D3
Zhangatas, Kaz. 145/E4
Zhanghei, China 130/C2
Zhangjiakou, China 130/C2
Zhangping, China 137/C2
Zhangpu, China 137/C2
Zhangqiu, China 130/D3
Zhangshu, China 137/C2
Zhangwei (riv.), China 130/D3
Zhangzhou, China 137/C2
Zhangzi (isl.), China 131/B3
Zhangzi, China 130/C3
Zhanhua, China 130/D3

Zhanjiang, China 141/K3
Zhao Xian, China 130/C3
Zhao'an, China 137/C3
Zhaojue, China 141/H2
Zhaoqing, China 141/K3
Zhaotong, China 141/H2
Zhaoyuan, China 130/E3
Zhaozhou, China 129/N2
Zhāyang (Ural) (riv.), Kaz.,Rus. 122/F5
Zhayyq (riv.), Kaz. 122/F5
Zhecheng, China 130/C4
Zhejiang (prov.), China 130/G6
Zhelaniya (cape), Rus. 122/G2
Zheleznodorozhnyy, Rus. 119/L3
Zheleznogorsk, Rus. 120/E1
Zheleznogorsk-Ilimskiy, Rus. 123/L4
Zhenfeng Bouyeizu Miaozu Zizhixian, China 137/C2
Zhengding, China 130/C3
Zhenglan, China 130/C3
Zhengning, China 130/B4
Zhengyang, China 130/C4
Zhengzhou, China 130/C4
Zhenhai, China 137/D2
Zhenjiang, China 130/D4
Zhenkang, China 141/G3
Zhenning Bouyeizu Miaozu Zizhixian, China 141/J2
Zhenping, China 130/C4
Zhentou (riv.), China 130/C4
Zhenwu (mtn.), China 130/B3
Zhenxiong, China 141/H2
Zhenyba (riv.), China 130/D3
Zhenyuan, China 141/H3
Zhetiqara, Kaz. 121/M1
Zhezqazghan, Kaz. 145/E3
Zhezqazghan (obl.), Kaz. 145/E3
Zhicheng, China 137/B1
Zhigulevsk, Rus. 121/J1
Zhijiang, China 137/B1
Zhijin, China 141/J2
Zhiloy (isl.), Azer. 121/J4
Zhlobin, Bela. 120/D1
Zhmerynka, Ukr. 120/D2
Zhob, Pak. 147/J2
Zhob (riv.), Pak. 147/J2
Zhodino, Bela. 97/N4
Zhokhov (isl.), Rus. 123/R2
Zhongba, China 137/C3
Zhongshan, China 141/K3
Zhongxiang, China 130/C5
Zhongyang, China 130/B3
Zhoukou, China 130/C4
Zhoushan (isls.), China 137/D2
Zhouzhou, China 130/G7
Zhuanghe, China 131/B3
Zhucheng, China 130/D4
Zhuhai, China 141/K3
Zhuji, China 137/D2
Zhujiang Kou (bay), China 129/T10
Zhukovka, Rus. 120/E1
Zhukovskiy, Rus. 119/X9
Zhumadian, China 130/C4
Zhuolu, China 130/G6
Zhuozi, China 130/C2
Zhushan, China 130/B4
Zhuxi, China 130/B4
Zhuzhou, China 141/K2
Zhuzhou, China 141/K2
Zhytomyr, Ukr. 120/D2
Zhytomyrs'ka Oblasti, Ukr. 120/D2
Zi (riv.), China 137/B2
Zia (int'l arpt.), Bang. 143/H4
Zibo, China 130/D3
Ziębice, Pol. 99/J3
Zielona Góra, Pol. 99/H3
Zierenberg, Ger. 109/G6
Zierikzee, Neth. 108/A5
Ziftá, Egypt 149/B4
Zigong, China 141/H2
Zigui, China 130/B5
Ziguinchor (int'l arpt.), Sen. 160/A3
Ziguinchor, Sen. 160/A3
Ziguinchor (pol. reg.), Sen. 160/A3
Zihuatanejo, Mex. 201/E5
Zijing (mtn.), China 130/D3
Zikhron Ya'aqov, Isr. 149/F6

Zile, Turk. 148/C1
Zilina, Slvk. 99/K4
Zilinský (pol. reg.), Slvk. 99/K4
Zillah, Libya 154/J2
Ziller (riv.), Aus. 101/J3
Zillisheim, Fr. 114/D2
Zimapán, Mex. 201/F4
Zimba, Zam. 163/E4
Zimbabwe (ctry.) 163/E4
Zimla (well), Alg. 156/E4
Zimnicea, Rom. 107/G4
Zinapécuaro de Figueroa, Mex. 201/E5
Zinave, PN de, Moz. 163/F5
Zinder, Niger 161/H3
Zinder (dept.), Niger 161/H3
Ziniaré, Burk. 160/E3
Zinjin, China 137/C3
Zion, Md, US 196/C4
Zion NP, Ut, US 186/D3
Zippori, Isr. 149/G6
Zirc, Hun. 106/C2
Zirje (isl.), Cro. 106/B4
Zirl, Aus. 115/H3
Ziro, India 141/F2
Zitácuaro, Mex. 201/E5
Zítava (riv.), Slvk. 99/K5
Zittau, Ger. 99/H3
Živinice, Bosn. 106/D3
Ziwa Magharibi (pol. reg.), Tanz. 162/A3
Zixi, China 137/C2
Zixing, China 141/K2
Ziya (riv.), China 130/D3
Ziyyon, Isr. 149/G8
Ziz, Oued (riv.), Mor. 156/D2
Zlatna, Rom. 107/F2
Zlatograd, Bul. 107/G5
Zlatoust, Rus. 119/N5
Zlín, Czh. 99/J4
Zliv, Czh. 113/H4
Złocieniec, Pol. 99/J2
Zlot, Serb. 106/E3
Złotoryja, Pol. 99/H3
Złotów, Pol. 99/J2
Žlutice, Czh. 113/G2
Żmigród, Pol. 99/J3
Znam'yanka, Ukr. 120/E2
Žnin, Pol. 99/J2
Znojmo, Czh. 99/J4
Zocca, It. 117/D4
Zoersel, Belg. 108/B6
Zoetermeer, Neth. 108/B4
Zoeterwoude, Neth. 108/B4
Zofingen, Swi. 114/D3
Zogang, China 141/G2
Zográfos, Gre. 105/N9
Zohreh (riv.), Iran 146/F2
Zola, It. 117/E4
Zollikon, Swi. 115/E3
Zolotonosha, Ukr. 120/E2
Zomba, Malw. 163/G4
Zone (pt.), Eng, UK 90/A6
Zongolica, Mex. 201/N8
Zonguldak, Turk. 107/K5
Zonguldak (prov.), Turk. 107/K5
Zonhoven, Belg. 111/E2
Zonnebeke, Belg. 110/B2
Zörbig, Ger. 98/G3
Zottegem, Belg. 110/C2
Zou (prov.), Ben. 161/F5
Zou Xian, China 130/D4
Zouar, Mrta. 156/B5
Zound-Wéogo (prov.), Burk.
Zouping, China 130/D3
Zousfana, Oued (riv.), Alg. 157/E3
Zrenjanin, Serb. 106/E3
Zschopau (riv.), Ger. 113/F1
Zuata, Ven. 211/E2
Zubia, Sp. 102/D4
Zubūbā, Isr. 149/G6

Zucchero (peak), Swi. 115/E5
Zuckerhütl (peak), Aus. 115/H4
Zuehl, Tx, US 195/U21
Zug, Swi. 115/E3
Zugdidi, Geo. 121/G4
Zugersee (lake), Swi. 101/H3
Zughrār (well), Libya 157/H3
Zugspitze (peak), Ger. 115/G3
Zuid Holland (prov.), Neth. 108/A5
Zuid-Willemsvaart (canal), Belg.,Neth. 108/C6
Zuidbeveland (isl.), Neth. 108/A6
Zuidelijk Flevoland (polder), Neth. 108/C4
Zuidhorn, Neth. 108/D2
Zuidlaren, Neth. 108/D2
Zuidwolde, Neth. 108/D3
Zuienkerke, Belg. 110/C1
Zújar (riv.), Sp. 102/C3
Zújar, Embalse (res.), Sp. 102/C3
Zulia, (riv.), Ven. 208/D2
Zulia (state), Ven. 210/C2
Zülpich, Ger. 111/F2
Zulte, Belg. 110/C2
Zululand (reg.), SAfr. 165/E2
Zumárraga, Sp. 102/D1
Zumba, Ecu. 214/B2
Zumbo, Moz. 163/F4
Zumpango de Ocampo, Mex. 201/K7
Zumpango del Río, Mex. 201/F5
Zundert, Neth. 108/B6
Zunhua, China 130/H6
Zuni (riv.), Az,NM, US 186/E4
Zuni, NM, US 186/E4
Zuni (mts.), NM, US 190/A3
Zunyi, China 141/J2
Zuo (riv.), China 137/A3
Zuo Jiang (riv.), China 136/D1
Zuoquan, China 130/C3
Zuoyun, China 130/C2
Zuoz, Swi. 115/F4
Županja, Cro. 106/D3
Zur, Kos. 106/E4
Zurbāţīyah, Iraq 146/E2
Zürich (canton), Swi. 115/E2
Zürich, Swi. 115/E3
Zürich (int'l arpt.), Swi. 115/E3
Zürichsee (lake), Swi. 101/H3
Żurrieq, Malta 104/L7
Zuromin, Pol. 99/K2
Zurzach, Swi. 115/E2
Zusam (riv.), Ger. 101/J2
Zushi, Japan 135/D3
Zusmarshausen, Ger. 112/D6
Zutiua (riv.), Braz. 212/A2
Zutphen, Neth. 108/D4
Zuurberg NP, SAfr. 164/D4
Zuwārah, Libya 154/H1
Zuyevka, Rus. 119/L4
Zvishavane, Zim. 163/F5
Zvolen, Slvk. 120/A2
Zvornik, Bosn. 106/D3
Zvorničko (lake), Bosn. 106/D3
Zwarte Meer (lake), Neth. 108/D3
Zwartsluis, Neth. 108/D3
Zwedru, Libr. 160/D5
Zweibrücken, Ger. 111/G5
Zweisimmen, Swi. 114/D4
Zwevegem, Belg. 110/C2
Zwickau, Ger. 101/K1
Zwickauer Mulde (riv.), Ger. 98/G3
Zwijndrecht, Belg. 111/D1
Zwischenahner Meer (lake), Ger. 109/F2
Zwischenwasser, Aus. 115/F3
Zwoleń, Pol. 99/L3
Żychlin, Pol. 99/K2
Żyrardów, Pol. 99/L2
Żywiec, Pol. 99/K3

Acknowledgements

Publisher — Hammond World Atlas Corporation

Chairman Andreas Langenscheidt
President Marc Jennings
Vice President of Cartography Jennie Nichols
Director Database Resources Theophrastos E. Giouvanos

Cartography Walter H. Jones Jr., Sharon Lightner, Harry E. Morin
James Padykula, Thomas R. Rubino, Thomas J. Scheffer
Layout and Composition John A. DiGiorgio, Maribel Lopez
Cover Design Karen Prince

World Almanac Section
Content Development Consultant Richard W. Eiger
Editor Richard Hondula
Design and Page Layout Lee Goldstein

Photo Credits

Portraits on pages 10, 22, 36, 51, 55, 74 – APA Publication GMBH & Co. Verlag KG

Photos on pages 23, 27, 28, 33(L), 39, 40 – Vera Lorenz

Portraits on page 67 – Yang Zhao

Other photos, PhotoDisc™

Satellite images: NASA – Greece, Peloponnesus Peninsula – p.84

Pakistan, Indus River Delta – p.124; Egypt, Sinai Peninsula – p.150

Australia, Lake Eyre – p.166; United States, Grand Canyon – p.176

Argentina/Chile, Andes Mountains – p.204